Introducing

the
Penguin
Literature Library

Share your passion for reading!

Choose from hundreds of classic and contemporary favorites — from *Beowulf* to *Black Hawk Down*.

Visit us online to browse the entire list
PHSchool.com/language_arts

Teaching **Support Available** for every title!

D1256980

TEACHER'S EDITION

PRENTICE HALL
LITERATURE

Timeless Voices, Timeless Themes

THE AMERICAN EXPERIENCE

VOLUME I

Copyright © 2005 by Pearson Education, Inc., publishing as Pearson Prentice Hall, Upper Saddle River, New Jersey 07458. All rights reserved. Printed in the United States of America. This publication is protected by copyright, and permission should be obtained from the publisher prior to any prohibited reproduction, storage in a retrieval system, or transmission in any form or by any means, electronic, mechanical, photocopying, recording, or likewise. For information regarding permission(s), write to: Rights and Permissions Department.

(Acknowledgments appear on page R58, which constitutes an extension of this copyright page.)

Pearson Prentice Hall™ is a trademark of Pearson Education, Inc.
Pearson® is a registered trademark of Pearson plc.
Prentice Hall® is a registered trademark of Pearson Education, Inc.

PEARSON

Prentice
Hall

Upper Saddle River, New Jersey

Needham, Massachusetts

ISBN 0-13-180443-X

3 4 5 6 7 8 9 10   08 07 06 05 04

Get results with Prentice

The nation's leading language arts program

Prentice Hall Literature:

- Features a powerful combination of great literature and superior instruction.

- Ensures student success with a proven, research-based reading approach.

- Provides meaningful, logical, and systematic language skills instruction.

- Helps you monitor student progress with a rich array of assessment tools.

- Allows you to share the same great literature with all your students.

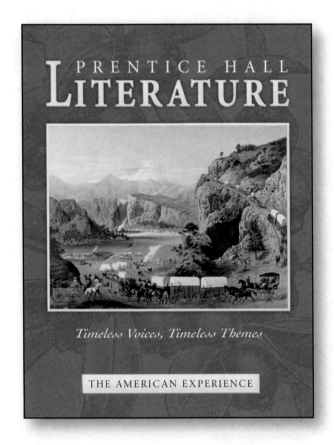

PRENTICE HALL
LITERATURE

Timeless Voices, Timeless Themes

THE AMERICAN EXPERIENCE

What educators think about Prentice Hall Literature

Increases student achievement

"Our teachers are extremely pleased with the series and feel it has contributed to <u>improved student performance</u>."
—*Dr. Karen Gibson, Program Leader, Appleton School District, Appleton, WI*

"I stay in touch with quite a number of teachers in the district who report that <u>scores have increased</u> on high-stakes performance tests for students using the *Prentice Hall Literature* program."
—*Audrey Hawkins, Language Arts Supervisor, Washington, D.C.*

Connects to students' lives

"<u>The pre-reading activities are extremely helpful</u>. The importance of making connections with literature is immeasurable— it makes education 'real' for students."
—*Matthew Scanlon, Language Arts Teacher, Chester, NJ*

"The entire program is '<u>student-friendly</u>' and yet does not 'talk down' to them with simplistic comments. The layout is easy to read and the selections inviting!"
—*Niki Locklear, Language Arts Teacher, Independence, KY*

"All around the buildings, you see students reading the literature book on their own time. You hear about them discussing the literature with other kids or asking their teachers about it. There's just a lot of talk about the book."
—*Patty Foster, Curriculum Consultant, Edmond Public School District, Edmond, OK*

Delivers the most comprehensive support

"The best features of the program are the vocabulary instruction and supporting lessons, literary analysis and connecting elements, use of Bloom's taxonomy in the Review and Assess sections, and the quality of literary selections."
—*Gail Hacker, Language Arts Teacher, North Charleston, SC*

"I like having the <u>Literary Analysis</u> feature to help explain theme, plot, characterization, etc.—many textbooks do not have this."
—*Sheila Colson, Language Arts Teacher, Philadelphia, PA*

"My teachers have <u>enthusiastically praised the *Reader's Companions*</u>. These tools allow everyone in the class to participate in the discussion so that no one, especially the struggling reader, feels left out."
—*Paulette Kirkwood, Communication Arts Supervisor, St. Louis, MO*

"Overall, I give the *Prentice Hall Literature* program a grade of 'A'!"
—*Kathy Litherland, Language Arts Teacher, Lincoln, IL*

The Prentice Hall difference

The truth about the single-column format

It's about reading.

The ability to read and understand text is the most vital and crucial lifelong skill students will possess. Teachers recognize that, through a variety of systematic instructional features and nondistracting point-of-use reading tools in the Student Edition, *Prentice Hall Literature* offers students more reading support in the Student Edition than any other program—thanks to the single-column format.

How is the single-column format more reader-friendly than the dual-column format?

While there are many reasons why the single column can be regarded as more readable than the dual-column format, its greatest virtue is the way the single-column format allows for embedded, nondistracting reading support. This support appears in the form of point-of-use annotations with comprehension checks, vocabulary support, literary analysis, and critical thinking and reading strategies throughout each selection, acting as a kind of "personal reading tutor."

Why don't all publishers use the single-column format?

Actually, all educational publishers use the single-column format in one way or another, usually in texts in other reading-intensive content areas such as social studies or science. Some publishers even use the single-column format in the ancillary reading support of their literature programs, precisely for the unique benefits that the single-column format conveys. *Prentice Hall Literature*, however, is the only program that provides the benefits of the single-column format consistently for every selection throughout the student text, providing a greater degree of reading support than any other reading program.

For more information, ask your representative for the brochure, *It's About Reading: Why* Prentice Hall Literature *Is the Nation's Leading Literature Program.*

Our unique Comparing Literary Works feature helps students dig deeper!

Meaningful content, meaningful connections

Successful critical thinkers need ample practice comparing works of literature. This feature, unique to *Prentice Hall Literature*, traces common themes, elements, styles, and forms to help students gain a deeper insight into their reading.

Setting the stage

Beginning with the Prepare to Read page, *Prentice Hall Literature* presents an element or concept for comparative study. Through the use of examples and modeling, students know what to look for in their reading as they compare selections.

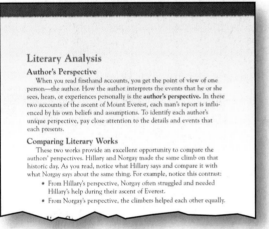

Literary Analysis

Author's Perspective

When you read firsthand accounts, you get the point of view of one person—the author. How the author interprets the events that he or she sees, hears, or experiences personally is the **author's perspective**. In these two accounts of the ascent of Mount Everest, each man's report is influenced by his own beliefs and assumptions. To identify each author's unique perspective, pay close attention to the details and events that each presents.

Comparing Literary Works

These two works provide an excellent opportunity to compare the authors' perspectives. Hillary and Norgay made the same climb on that historic day. As you read, notice what Hillary says and compare it with what Norgay says about the same thing. For example, notice this contrast:

- From Hillary's perspective, Norgay often struggled and needed Hillary's help during their ascent of Everest.
- From Norgay's perspective, the climbers helped each other equally.

Putting it all together

Students demonstrate and apply critical thinking skills following the selection groups through scaffolded questioning strategies. A variety of instructional tools like graphic organizers assist students in collecting and analyzing their observations.

Especially for grades 11 and 12

The Writing About Literature feature, designed especially for grades 11 and 12, takes Comparing Literary Works to the next level as students employ the writing process to demonstrate their proficiency in literary analysis.

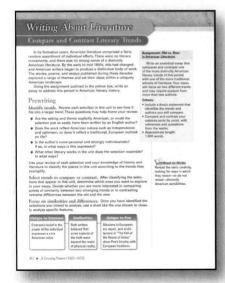

Share the same selection

Unique, appropriately leveled reading support that meets the needs of all your students.

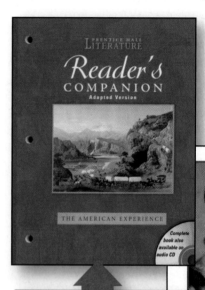

THE AMERICAN EXPERIENCE

Complete book also available on audio CD

Note: Each of the skills presented here match those that are introduced in the Student Edition of *Prentice Hall Literature* for seamless lesson integration.

PRENTICE HALL
LITERATURE

Timeless Voices, Timeless

THE AMER

Each selection begins with a summary that lets students know what the selection is about before they read.

A visual summary shows students the important ideas or details graphically.

Students interact directly with the text to activate prior knowledge, practice reading strategies, engage in literary analysis, and check their reading comprehension.

PREVIEW

Letter to Her Daughter From the New White House
Abigail Adams

Summary

In this selection, Abigail Adams describes her journey to Washington as First Lady. Washington is a new city, with just a few public buildings. The White House is huge, but there are no bells to ring for the thirty servants and there is very little firewood. Adams tells her daughter to tell others that she finds the house and city beautiful. She closes by saying that Mrs. Washington has just invited her to visit Mount Vernon.

Visual Summary

Topic
Life in the new city of Washington

Details						
woods until you reach city	river can be seen from window	grand house but no bells for servants	not enough firewood	six comfortable rooms	oval room very hand-some	invitat from N Washi

Main Idea Sentence
It is a beautiful spot, capable of every improvement, and, the more I view it, the more I am delighted with it.

Reader's Companion   © Pearson

Letter to Her Daughter From the New White House
Abigail Adams

Abigail Adams, like Barbara Bush, had the unusual experience of being the wife of one president, John Adams, and the mother of a later president, John Quincy Adams. Her husband spent years away from home during and after the American Revolution, and her letters to him and to her family provide unique insights into the period in which she lived.

Washington, 21 November, 1800

My Dear Child:

I arrived here on Sunday last, and without meeting with any accident worth noticing, except losing ourselves when we left Baltimore and going eight or nine miles on the Frederick road, by which means we were obliged to go the other eight through woods, where we wandered two hours without finding a guide or the path. Fortunately, a straggling black came up with us, and we engaged him as a guide to <u>extricate</u> us out of our difficulty; but woods are all you see from Baltimore until you reach the city, which is only so in name. Here and there is a small cot, without a glass window, interspersed amongst the forests, through which you travel miles without seeing any human being. In the city there are buildings enough, if they were compact and finished, to accommodate Congress and those attached to it; but as they are, and scattered as they are, I see no great comfort for them. The river, which runs up to Alexandria,[1] is in full view of my window, and I see the vessels as they pass and repass. The house is upon a grand and superb scale, requiring about thirty servants to attend and keep the apartments in proper order, and perform the ordinary business of the house and stables; an establishment very well proportioned to the President's salary. The lighting of the apartments, from the kitchen to parlors and chambers, is a tax indeed; and the fires we are obliged to keep to secure us from daily

Vocabulary Development: extricate (eks' tra kāt') *v.* set free

1. **Alexandria** city in northeastern Virginia.

© Pearson Education, Inc.   Letter to Her Daughter From the New White House **41**

♦ Activate Prior Knowledge

Think about what it must be like to move to a new home, especially if it is not quite finished. You can be excited about the new home and miss the previous home at the same time—and it is really difficult to avoid comparing the two. Notice how Abigail Adams struggles to stay positive in spite of the challenges of her new home.

♦ Reading Strategy

As you read nonfiction, it is important to know the difference between **facts**—statements that can be proven—and **opinions**—personal beliefs that cannot be proven. Reread the bracketed sentences. Write the section that is an opinion below.

_____

_____

_____

_____

♦ Literary Analysis

This selection is a **private letter** written by a mother to her daughter. Private letters are written in a conversational style and are intended to be read only by the person to whom they are addressed. Circle two phrases on this page that Adams may not have used if she had thought her letter would become public.

---

with all your students!

Choose the version that's right for your students

Reader's Companion

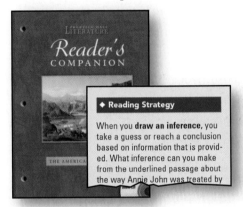

Basic reading support
- Full-length selections with interactive reading support
- Critical thinking questions
- Vocabulary and pronunciation guides

Adapted Version

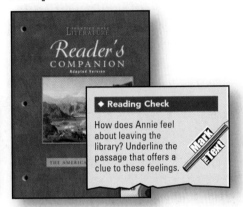

Enhanced reading support
- Selection adaptations and authentic text
- Enhanced design for easier readability
- Frequent Reading Checks and customized comprehension strategies

English Learner's Version

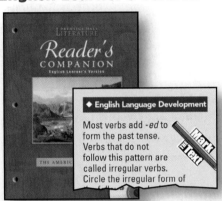

English learner's support
- Enhanced reading support
- Specialized vocabulary and pronunciation support
- Focus on idioms, colloquialisms, and cultural information

Need more reading support?

The Prentice Hall Reading Achievement System has the answer!

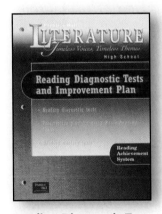

Reading Diagnostic Test and Improvement Plan
- Diagnostic tests determine what reading skills remediation is needed
- Individualized improvement plans guide teachers to specific skills lessons

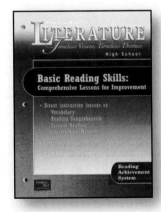

Basic Reading Skills: Comprehensive Lessons for Improvement
- Lesson plans for direct instruction
- Teaching transparencies for lesson modeling
- Blackline masters for student application and practice

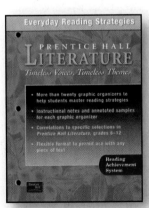

Everyday Reading Strategies
- More than 20 graphic organizers to help students master lifelong reading strategies
- Correlated to specific selections in *Prentice Hall Literature*

Prentice Hall Literature meets all your needs

Reading
Customize comprehensive reading instruction to ensure No Child Is Left Behind.

- Everyday Reading Strategies
- Teacher's Guidebook for Universal Access
- Reading Diagnostic and Improvement Plan
- Basic Reading Skills: Comprehensive Lessons for Improvement
- Basic Reading Skills: Teaching Transparencies
- Reader's Companion
- Reader's Companion, Adapted Version
- Reader's Companion, English Learner's Version

Assessment
Monitor and maintain Adequate Yearly Progress.

- Standardized Test Preparation: Diagnostic Tests
- Formal Assessment
- Open Book Tests
- Portfolio Assessment and Performance Management
- Review and Remediation Skillbook
- Skills Practice: Answers and Explanations Transparencies

Student Workbooks
Provide ample opportunities for skills practice and success on standardized tests.

- Selection Support: Skills Development Workbook
- Vocabulary and Spelling Practice Book
- Standardized Test Preparation Workbook
- Literary Analysis for Enrichment

Language Skills
Guarantee student success through consistent, systematic instruction in all language arts skills.

- Writing and Grammar Handbook Edition
- Integrated Lesson Planning Assistant
- Daily Language Practice Transparencies
- Vocabulary and Spelling Practice
- Writing Models and Graphic Organizers on Transparencies
- Fine Art Transparencies
- Extension Activities

Spanish Support
Meet the evolving needs of your Spanish speakers.

- *Literatura* Spanish Anthology (grades 6–8)
- *Literatura en español* Interactive Reader
- Spanish Readings Audio Program
- Spanish/English Summaries Audio Program

Technology
Plan, teach, and assess with a comprehensive, multimedia program for every grade level.

- Interactive Textbook Student Edition Online and on CD-ROM
- Standardized Test Preparation CD-ROM
- Reader's Companions Audio Program
- Listening to Literature Audio Program
- Listening to Music Audio Program
- Interest Grabber Video Program
- Got It! Assessment Video Program
- Literature in Performance Video Library

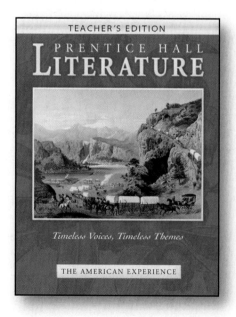

Prentice Hall Literature has the only Teacher's Edition that:

- provides a **Time and Resource Manager** for **EVERY** selection.
- encourages extensive planning support via direct instruction while helping set pace and priorities.
- gives all learners access to literature through ample customization notes.

ACADEMIC ACHIEVEMENT HANDBOOK

Research, Standards, and Planning Tools

PRENTICE HALL LITERATURE IS RESEARCH-BASED AND PROVEN TO WORK

The stakes for language arts educators are high. The plain fact is, you are expected to raise student achievement. Prentice Hall understands your dedicated efforts and gives you the confidence to meet this challenge. In developing Prentice Hall programs, the use of research studies is a central, guiding construct. Research on *Prentice Hall Literature* indicated that the key elements of a literature program that ensure student success are considerate text, consistent skills instruction, and an ongoing assessment strand. This research was conducted in three phases:

Phase 1: Exploratory Needs Assessment

Phase 2: Formative Research, Prototype Development, and Field Testing

Phase 3: Summative Research, Validation Research

1 EXPLORATORY NEEDS ASSESSMENT

In conjunction with Prentice Hall authors, research was done to explore educational research about reading. This research was incorporated into our instructional strategy and pedagogy to create a more effective literature program.

Along with periodic surveys concerning curriculum issues and challenges, we conducted specific product development research, which included discussions with teachers and advisory panels, focus groups, and quantitative surveys. We explored the specific needs of teachers, students, and other educators regarding each book we developed in *Prentice Hall Literature*.

2 FORMATIVE RESEARCH, PROTOTYPE DEVELOPMENT, AND FIELD TESTING

During this phase of research, we developed prototype materials for each feature in *Prentice Hall Literature*. Then we tested the materials, including field-testing with students and teachers using qualitative and quantitative evaluations. We received solid feedback in our early prototype testing. Results were channeled back into the program development for improvement. For example, teachers commented positively on the easy navigation of instructional pages.

3 SUMMATIVE RESEARCH, VALIDATION RESEARCH

Finally, we conducted and continue to conduct long-term research under actual classroom conditions. This research identifies what works and what can be improved in the next revision of *Prentice Hall Literature*. We also continue to monitor the program in the marketplace. We talk to our users about what works, and then we begin the cycle over again. Highlights of this research follow in the next section.

PRENTICE HALL RESEARCH TIMELINE

Exploratory needs assessment
(Quantitative & qualitative)

- Reading research
- Teacher interviews
- Classroom observations
- Mail surveys
- Conference participation

Formative research
(Quantitative & qualitative)

- Field testing of prototypes
- Classroom observations
- Teacher reviews
- Supervisor reviews
- Educator advisory panels
- Prentice Hall sales force input

Summative research
(Experimental and quasi-experimental study designs & qualitative research)

- Prepublication learner verification research
- Postpublication validation studies
- Classroom observations
- Evaluation of in-market results on standardized tests

PRENTICE HALL LITERATURE
RESEARCH-BASED AND CLASSROOM-TESTED FOR PROVEN RESULTS

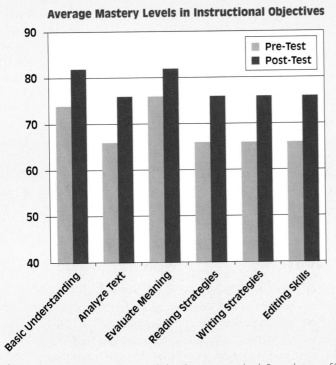

Average Mastery Levels in Instructional Objectives

† Scores between 0 and 49 are regarded as the nonmastery level. Scores between 50 and 74 are regarded as indications of partial mastery. Scores of 75 and above are regarded as the mastery level.

All tests were scored by CTB/McGraw Hill, the publisher of TerraNova™. Statistical analyses and conclusions were performed by an independent firm, Pulse Analytics, Inc., Ridgewood, New Jersey.

In a yearlong learner verification study, students using the *Prentice Hall Literature: Timeless Voices, Timeless Themes* program increased their mastery levels in several diagnostic skill areas for reading/language arts.

All students were tested at the start of the year with a nationally normed standardized test, the TerraNova™ Complete Battery Plus exam. At the end of the treatment period, students were retested with the same standardized test. Only students who completed both the pre- and post-tests were included in this analysis. All tests were scored by CTB/McGraw Hill, publisher of the TerraNova™.

In the study, students progressed from the partial mastery level to the mastery level (as defined by CTB/McGraw Hill)† in identifying reading strategies, analyzing text, writing strategies, and editing skills. In the other two reading objectives, Basic Understanding and Evaluate/Extend Meaning, the treatment group maintained mastery from the pre-test to the post-test.

PUTTING RESEARCH INTO PRACTICE

What Research Indicates

To aid comprehension, critical vocabulary words should be explained with meanings and background information before students read selections. To further improve reading fluency and comprehension, common prefixes and suffixes should be systematically introduced and explained (Carnine).

Studies indicate the efficacy of direct instruction of vocabulary, as well as programs that emphasize context. For a comprehensive approach, researchers advocate teaching decoding skills, introducing sight words, emphasizing context clues to determine if constructed meanings make sense, teaching vocabulary meanings explicitly, and extensively using comprehension strategies and modeling (Pressley, "What Should").

Integrate Language Skills

Vocabulary Development Lesson

Word Analysis: Latin Prefix *pre-*
The Latin prefix *pre-*, as found in *precluded*, means "before" or "in advance." Identify the word from the list below that best fits each definition.

preview   precaution   prejudice

1. To see in advance
2. Judgment without sufficient facts
3. Care taken in advance

Spelling Strategy
When you add an ending that begins with a vowel to a word that ends in a silent *e*, the *e* is usually dropped. For example, when adding *-ing* to the word *subside*, drop the silent *e* to form *subsiding*. Write the word formed b_____ the

Concept Development: Antonyms
Identify the antonym, or opposite, of the first word.

1. precluded: (a) prevented, (b) aided, (c) started
2. retribution: (a) reward, (b) disaster, (c) assignment
3. accosted: (a) sought, (b) retreated, (c) discovered
4. subsided: (a) increased, (b) created, (c) challenged
5. afflicted: (a) weary, (b) skeptical, (c) blessed
6. explicit: (a) unnecessary, (b) vague, (c) impatient

Prentice Hall's Response

Vocabulary instruction in *Prentice Hall Literature* utilizes a combination of direct instruction and context-based approaches. Vocabulary words and their definitions are introduced before the selection, then again at point-of-use in the minor column of the selection. Reading strategies model the use of context-based approaches before the selection, then students are encouraged to use these approaches to answer questions after the selection. Also, students are given opportunities to assimilate new vocabulary words by applying them in exercises that follow the selection.

Literature
in context History Connection

♦ **Cossack**
Zaroff was a Cossack, a member of a special Russian military unit that enjoyed an elite and privileged status. As a result, these soldiers were fiercely independent. When the czar—the ruler of Russia—was overthrown in the Russian Revolution of 1917, Cossacks like Zaroff were banished, executed, or forced into exile. As a Cossack, Zaroff is unwilling to acknowledge that the rules of ordinary people apply to him.

What Research Indicates

Schools that "beat the odds" in teaching middle- and high-school students to read and write well use materials that make overt connections among knowledge, skills, and ideas across lessons, classes, and grades, and across in-school and out-of-school applications (Langer).

Prentice Hall's Response

Prentice Hall Literature provides overt connections at the selection level with the Literature in Context features and at the unit level with the Connection to Literature features. The Teacher's Edition contains background information about each selection, author, and genre. Furthermore, students are encouraged to make connections between the literature selections and the fine art that illustrates the textbook. Extension Activities at the end of each selection and Reading Instructional Materials selections foster connections between students' reading and the world outside the classroom.

What Research Indicates

To enhance reading comprehension and retention, students must master reading strategies such as scanning, predicting, using background knowledge, summarizing main ideas, and asking questions (Every Child Reading).

Teaching a combination of reading comprehension techniques is the most effective way to increase students' understanding. When students use them appropriately, these techniques assist in recall, question answering, question generation, and summarization of texts. When used in combination, these techniques can improve results in standardized comprehension tests (National Reading Panel).

Prentice Hall's Response

Prentice Hall Literature provides extensive instruction in reading strategies with introduction, development, and conclusion of each reading skill. Reading strategies include predicting, questioning, rereading, scanning, drawing inferences, determining word meaning from context, using prior knowledge, identifying the main idea, and summarizing. Each reading skill is introduced in the Prepare to Read section of each selection. The skill is then practiced throughout the selection. Assessment of the skill occurs in the postselection material. Additionally, the Teacher's Edition provides direct instruction for the skills being taught at point-of-use in the selection.

Reading Strategy

Predicting

Predicting, or making guesses about what will happen before a story ends, can often help you check your understanding of a story.

- To make a prediction, start by looking for small but unusual details. These details might be minor events that catch your attention but that the characters in the story seem to ignore.
- Ask yourself what would happen if the detail were to become more important. In "The Birds," for example, think about what would happen if a disturbing detail were multiplied many times.
- Note your predictions, but be prepared to revise your guesses as the story develops.

Use a chart to help you record your predictions. The chart shown here presents a small but unusual detail from "The Birds."

Unusual Detail
Nat enjoys working alone.

Magnified Detail
When trouble comes, Nat will have to stand against it alone.

Prediction

What Research Indicates

In order to be effective, comprehension skills should be taught using a consistent format and sequence, with examples, practice, and review (Carnine).

Prentice Hall's Response

Comprehension skills are taught before the selection on the Prepare to Read page, along with appropriate examples. Students apply these skills by answering questions within the selection and directly afterward. In Reading Informational Material selections, reading skills are introduced before the selection, then tested immediately after.

STEP-BY-STEP TEACHING GUIDE	PACING GUIDE
PRETEACH	
Motivate Students and Provide Background	
Use the Motivation activity (ATE p. 4)	5 min.
Read and discuss the Preview material and Background information (SE/ATE p. 4) [A]	5 min.
Introduce the Concepts	
Introduce the Literary Analysis and Reading Strategy (SE/ATE p. 5) [A]	15 min.
Pronounce the vocabulary words and read their definitions (SE p. 5)	5 min.
TEACH	
Monitor Comprehension	
Informally monitor comprehension by circulating while students read independently or in groups [A]	30 min.
Monitor students' comprehension with the Reading Check notes (SE/ATE pp. 7, 9, 11)	as students read
Develop vocabulary with Vocabulary notes (SE pp. 7, 9, 10, 11; ATE p. 7)	as students read
Develop Understanding	
Develop students' understanding of mood with the Literary Analysis annotations (SE p. 8; ATE pp. 7, 8, 9, 11) [A]	10 min.
Develop students' ability to break down confusing sentences with the Reading Strategy annotations (SE p. 10; ATE pp. 8, 10)	10 min.
ASSESS	
Assess Mastery	
Assess students' mastery of the Reading Strategy and Literary Analysis by having them answer the Review and Assess questions (SE/ATE p. 13)	20 min.
Use one or more of the print and media Assessment Resources (ATE p. 15) [A]	up to 45 min.
EXTEND	
Apply Understanding	
Have students complete the Vocabulary Development Lesson and the Grammar Lesson (SE p. 14) [A]	20 min.
Apply students' ability to select precise details using the Writing Lesson (SE/ATE p. 15) [A]	45 min.
Apply students' understanding using one or more of the Extension Activities (SE p. 15)	20–90 min.

[A] **ACCELERATED INSTRUCTION:** Use the strategies and activities identified with an [A].

UNIVERSAL ACCESS
● = Below Level Students
▲ = On-Level Students
■ = Above Level Students

What Research Indicates

Text structure is vital to both comprehension and retention of information. "Signaling," through the use of headings, different typefaces, and pointer words, can aid significantly in comprehension. When text structure is "considerate," i.e. consistent and logically ordered, students are more likely to remember information (Armbruster).

Readers use structural cues to construct meaning from written texts. Headings, linguistic cues, and parallel structure aid comprehension and assist with key skills such as identifying the main idea in a passage (Goldman).

Prentice Hall's Response

The design of *Prentice Hall Literature* uses headings to identify particular skills or strategies, and uses graphic organizers to demonstrate skills such as identifying the main idea or making inferences. The structure and order of these various components is consistent throughout the program to maximize retention of information. Additionally, Reading Informational Materials selections explicitly identify the structure of informational materials such as brochures, contracts, and feature articles so that students will be familiar with the common features of these materials.

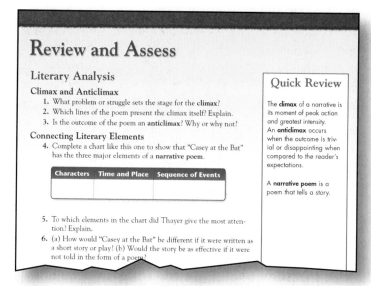

What Research Indicates

Because most real-world reading is nonfiction, students must gain fluency in reading informational texts. Necessary skills for reading nonfiction include activating prior knowledge, noting important headings and subheadings, skimming, determining a purpose for reading, finding main ideas and supporting details, using graphics and illustrations, and analyzing text structure (Harvey).

Prentice Hall's Response

In addition to the Nonfiction unit in each grade level of *Prentice Hall Literature*, every unit in each book includes at least one Reading Informational Materials selection. These selections consist of real-world nonfiction materials such as newspaper articles, product warranties, operating instructions, business letters, meeting agendas, and brochures. Skills taught with these informational materials include analyzing information, evaluating a text, using information to make a decision, questioning, recognizing different types of appeals, following steps in sequence, and following technical directions.

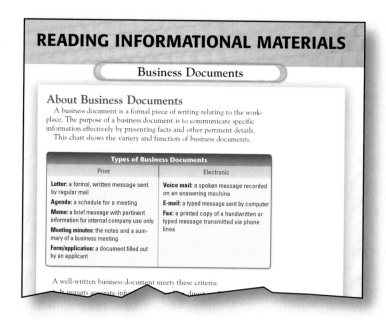

What Research Indicates

Research shows that engaged readers have higher achievement scores. Instructional techniques that can positively affect motivation include using reading strategies, linking to prior knowledge, introducing real-world interactions and related activities, promoting student choice in reading matter, having students ask their own questions, promoting collaboration between students, using scaffolding, assigning a variety of informational and literary texts, linking reading, writing, and knowledge through coherent instruction, and having students conduct self-evaluations of their work (Guthrie).

Prentice Hall's Response

Prentice Hall Literature incorporates multiple strategies to engage and motivate readers. Each selection is introduced with a section that connects to students' prior knowledge and demonstrates the reading strategy for the selection. These strategies motivate students to ask questions of the text and are specially designed to help foster reader autonomy. At each grade level, the literature selections include a diverse mixture of different genres, classic and contemporary works, and informational texts. The postselection section includes both response questions and scaffolded analytical questions that utilize the skills taught before the selection. Extension activities such as role plays and readers' panels promote collaboration among students. Writing Workshops and Listening and Speaking Workshops include rubrics and criteria charts that allow students to evaluate their work and that of their peers.

What Research Indicates

Schools that "beat the odds" in teaching middle- and high-school students to read and write well use test preparation that is integrated into ongoing goals, curriculum, and regular lessons (Langer).

Prentice Hall's Response

Prentice Hall Literature provides test preparation as a separate activity with Assessment Workshops at the end of each unit and with a Test Preparation workbook. The Test Preparation workbook is selection specific, allowing for integration of the assessment into regular lessons.

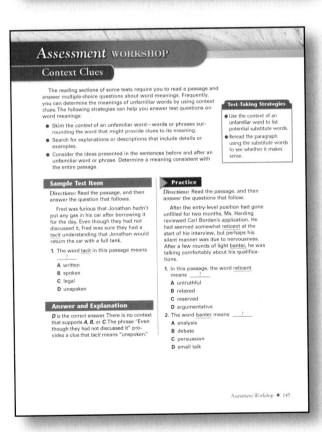

Incorporating Classroom Teacher Input

Market Needs Assessment

Prentice Hall conducted the following research to measure teacher responses to the literature textbooks in use in classrooms in 1999:

- **User Survey, September 9, 1999** Prentice Hall interviewed, by phone, 30 high-school teachers who used the previous edition of *Prentice Hall Literature*.

- **Focus Testing of Existing Programs, September 1999** Six focus groups of Grades 6–12 Language Arts teachers were conducted in three different cities. Participants reviewed then-current editions of *Prentice Hall Literature* and other literature programs.

- **Interviews with Department of Education Officials** Interviews were conducted in various key states in September and October 1999 and were ongoing through product development, December 2000.

Key Findings:

- The main reasons the program was adopted were:
    - Close fit with the curriculum
    - Selections offered
    - Amount and variety of the supplementary materials
    - Skill support
    - Thematic connections
    - Block scheduling resources
    - Test support

- Teachers liked the use of fine art.

- Teachers liked cross-curricular and real-world connections they perceived as solid and meaningful.

- Teachers preferred a streamlined design that was easy to work with; they considered the two-column design with call-out instructional boxes busy.

- Teachers wanted depth of information and instruction in Writing Workshops.

- Compared with other Language Arts textbooks, Prentice Hall was consistently cited by teachers as having strong instructional strategies.

- Commissioners and state and federal Department of Education officials asked that textbooks address the following elements:
    - Program pedagogy must include direct instruction in the Student Edition and Teacher's Edition.
    - Product must be research-based.
    - Reading skills such as decoding and phonics must be included.
    - Diagnostic testing and interventions need to be ongoing.
    - Program must be standards-based.

End Result:

In the new edition of *Prentice Hall Literature*, we've:

- retained the features that teachers love.

- developed a design that maintains a strong instructional focus through cleaner presentation. Selections appear in a single-column format, allowing instruction to be presented in a minor column.

- increased the length of Writing Workshops from two to four pages and included a full student model, a rubric, and more strategies for each stage of the writing process.

- developed the Student Edition and Teacher's Edition following the rules of direct instruction, defining terms at point-of-use and providing clear direction for students and teachers.

- consulted program authors and current research to confirm the direction and pedagogy of the series.

- developed Monitor Progress and Reteach notes in the Teacher's Edition for ongoing intervention opportunities.

- reviewed academic standards while instruction was developed.

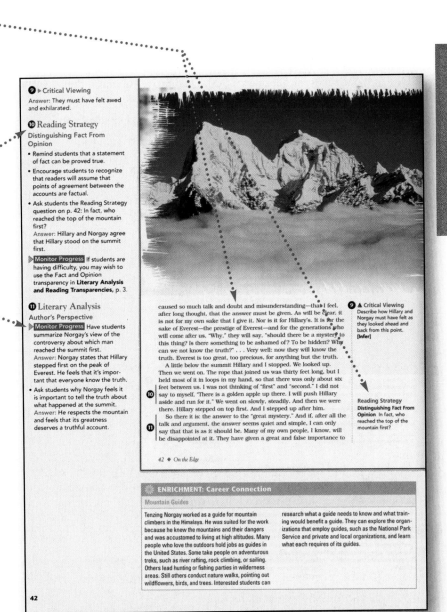

Formative Research

Prentice Hall conducted the following research to prototype and test new features, elements, and designs with teachers:

- **Prototype Testing: Focus Groups, December 1999** Focus groups were conducted among Grades 6–12 Language Arts teachers in New Jersey, Indiana, and California. Teachers reviewed several prototype versions of one literature selection.
- **Design Confirmation, February 2000, Quantitative Research** Using one-on-one interviews, Prentice Hall solicited reactions to prototype pages.
- **Design Confirmation, February 2000, Qualitative Research** Prentice Hall conducted two focus groups in New York for reactions to prototype pages.
- **Design Confirmation, April 2000** Prentice Hall conducted four focus groups in New Jersey and Oklahoma.

Ongoing Informal Research:

- In-school interviews
- Teacher advisory boards
- Adoption committee members

Key Findings:

- Most teachers agreed that the Student Edition should cover fewer elements in a more meaningful way.
- Teachers wanted vocabulary definitions to appear before selections; vocabulary words should be underlined at point-of-use within selections.
- Teachers wanted a visually engaging design that appealed to students.
- Teachers needed ancillary support for lower-level students.
- Teachers preferred Prentice Hall's ancillary package to that of the competitors, especially the following products:
    - Literature audiocassettes
    - Materials for high-level readers
    - Reader's Companions
- Teachers wanted a program that focused on the student by providing ways to engage and methods to teach important skills, and by offering accessibility for all ability levels. They also wanted a program that focused on the teacher by functioning as an aid or resource, rather than a way to train or "manage" teachers.

End Result:

In the new edition of *Prentice Hall Literature,* we've:

- developed the program according to the tenets of *considerate text.* These include:
    - a clear, consistent system of headings
    - chunked text to avoid paragraphs that are too dense
    - bulleted text when appropriate
    - boldfaced terms defined at point-of-use
- developed the Reading Achievement System to support lower-level students. Components include:
    - three levels of *Reader's Companions* to support struggling readers
    - *Basic Reading Skills: Comprehensive Lessons for Improvement*
    - *Teaching Guidebook for Universal Access*
- included panoramic images and large visuals to engage student interest.

Summary of Key Needs

Based on the collected research and classroom teacher input, Prentice Hall developed a literature program that meets these needs.

Strong skills instruction for successful test performance:

- Improved students' reading skills
- Strong instruction in communication skills
- Standardized test preparation

Strong teaching support and materials:

- Easy-to-follow materials for both students and teachers
- Instructional pathways to help all student populations—core, English-language learners, struggling readers, advanced students
- Companion Web site offering additional student activities, teacher resources, and professional development links

Standards-driven program with specific support/instruction for teachers:

- Strong skills activities and instruction with depth-based and standards-based outcomes
- Simple, direct lesson plans that clearly satisfy specific standards, including:
  – Daily lesson plans for special-education instruction
  – Daily lesson plans for English learners
  – Direct instruction in teaching reading and phonics

BIBLIOGRAPHY OF RESEARCH ARTICLES

Alexander, Patricia A., and Tamara Jetton. "Learning from Text: A Multidimensional and Developmental Perspective." In *Handbook of Reading Research*, vol. 3, ed. M. L. Kamil, P. B. Mosenthal, P. D. Pearson, and R. Barr, 285–310. Mahwah, N.J.: Lawrence Erlbaum Associates, 2000.

Armbruster, Bonnie, and Thomas H. Anderson. "On Selecting 'Considerate' Content Area Textbooks." *Remedial and Special Education*, vol. 9 (1): 47–52.

Blachowicz, Camille, and Peter Fisher. *Teaching Vocabulary in All Classrooms*. Upper Saddle River, N.J.: Prentice Hall, 1996.

Carnine, Douglas, Jerry Silbert, and Edward J. Kameenui. *Direct Instruction Reading. 3rd ed.* Upper Saddle River, N.J.: Prentice Hall, 1997.

Goldman, Susan R., and John A. Rakestraw, Jr. "Structural Aspects of Constructing Meaning From Text." In *Handbook of Reading Research*, vol. 3, ed. M. L. Kamil, P. B. Mosenthal, P. D. Pearson, and R. Barr, 311–335. Mahwah, N.J.: Lawrence Erlbaum Associates, 2000.

Guthrie, John T. and Allan Wigfield. "Engagement and Motivation in Reading." In *Handbook of Reading Research*, vol. 3, ed. M. L. Kamil, P. B. Mosenthal, P. D. Pearson, and R. Barr, 403–422. Mahwah, N.J.: Lawrence Erlbaum Associates, 2000.

Harvey, Stephanie, and Anne Goudvis. "Determining Importance in Text: The Nonfiction Connection." In *Strategies That Work: Teaching Comprehension to Enhance Understanding*. Portland, Me.: Stenhouse Publishers, 2000.

Langer, Judith. "Beating the Odds: Teaching Middle and High School Students to Read and Write Well," 1999. Center on English Learning and Achievement. May 2003. <http://cela.albany.edu/eie2/main.html>

Learning First Alliance. *Every Child Reading: An Action Plan*. Washington, D.C.: Learning First Alliance, 1998.

Morrow, Lesley Mandel. "Story Retelling: A Discussion Strategy to Develop and Assess Comprehension." In *Lively Discussions! Fostering Engaged Reading*, ed. Linda B. Gambrell and Janice F. Almasi, 265–285. Newark, Del.: International Reading Association, 1996.

National Reading Panel. *Teaching Children to Read: An Evidence-Based Assessment of the Scientific Research on Reading and Its Implications for Reading Instruction*. NIH Publication 00-4769. Bethesda, Md.: U.S. Department of Health and Human Services, 2000.

Pressley, Michael. "What Should Comprehension Instruction Be the Instruction Of?" In *Handbook of Reading Research*, vol. 3, ed. M. L. Kamil, P. B. Mosenthal, P. D. Pearson, and R. Barr, 545–562. Mahwah, N.J.: Lawrence Erlbaum Associates, 2000.

Pressley, Michael, Vera Woloshyn, et al. *Cognitive Strategy Instruction That REALLY Improves Children's Academic Performance*. Cambridge, Mass.: Brookline Books, 1995.

Powerful Research-Based Solutions to Guarantee Teacher and Student Success!

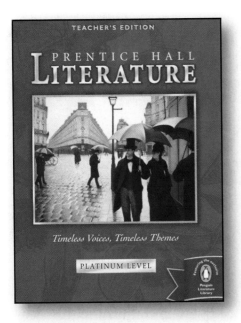

The Resource Teachers Use Most

The strategic instructional approach to teaching reading, grounded in reading research, is at the core of *Prentice Hall Literature*. This research is translated into direct program instruction to help teachers close the achievement gap in literacy.

Not only are teachers supported through research-based teaching techniques, but direct instruction within the Teacher's Edition offers customization ideas to reach students of all ability levels *before*, *during*, and *after* literary selections.

Anytime, Anywhere Professional Development

To enhance the powerful teacher support in *Prentice Hall Literature*, Prentice Hall offers the Online Literacy Series, powered by LessonLab. The *Prentice Hall Literature* authors lend their expertise to guide users of the Online Literacy Series toward exemplary practices and instructional methods. Five courses have been designed specifically to help teachers become even more proficient with their classroom materials, while mastering the skills they need to deliver the research-based strategy instruction.

Online Courses:

- Foundations of Coaching and Mentoring
- Active Learning: Structures to Engage All Students
- Vocabulary Development
- Comprehension of Literary and Informational Materials
- Literary Response and Analysis

The Online Literacy Series empowers administrators and teachers with the ability to:

- Observe a standards-based lesson
- Access resources, lesson plans, and student work
- Engage in ongoing dialogue with colleagues
- Apply best practices in your classroom
- Increase your content knowledge while building proficiency with your instructional materials

For more information, visit PHSchool.com/professional_development

NCTE/IRA STANDARDS CORRELATION

The National Council of Teachers of English (NCTE) and the International Reading Association (IRA), two professional organizations dedicated to improving the teaching and learning of English, have drafted a set of twelve comprehensive standards for the Language Arts. These standards are meant to provide a general framework for programs that encourage the development of language skills. The following pages show how *Prentice Hall Literature* meets these standards.

NCTE/IRA STANDARD	PRENTICE HALL LITERATURE
1. Students read a wide range of print and nonprint texts to build an understanding of texts, of themselves, and of the cultures of the United States and the world; to acquire new information; to respond to the needs and demands of society and the workplace; and for personal fulfillment. Among these texts are fiction and nonfiction, both classic and contemporary works.	• *Prentice Hall Literature* brings together the finest quality literature from around the world in a carefully balanced mix of classic and contemporary selections. • The Reading Informational Materials selections in each unit introduce students to real-world nonfiction texts and give them the tools to analyze informational materials, including editorials, warranties, business documents, critical reviews, and Web sites. • Each unit focuses on a particular era in American history. Introductory essays, timelines, and features provide historical background for the selections.
2. Students read a wide range of literature from many periods in many genres to build an understanding of the many dimensions (e.g., philosophical, ethical, aesthetic) of human experience.	*PH Literature: The American Experience* presents a survey of writing from pre-Columbian times to the present, including: • **Fiction** "The Far and the Near," Thomas Wolfe; "The Rockpile," James Baldwin; "The Life You Save May Be Your Own," Flannery O'Connor; "The Fall of the House of Usher," Edgar Allan Poe • **Poetry** "From the Dark Tower," Countee Cullen; "Chicago," Carl Sandburg; "Mending Wall," Robert Frost; "The Explorer," Gwendolyn Brooks; "Mirror," Sylvia Plath • **Nonfiction** "The Iroquois Constitution"; from *The Interesting Narrative of Olaudah Equiano;* "Speech in the Virginia Convention," Patrick Henry; from *The Autobiography,* Benjamin Franklin; "Crossing the Great Divide," Meriwether Lewis • **Drama** *The Crucible,* Arthur Miller The instructional material with each selection, coupled with full author biographies, places the literature in its appropriate context for students. In addition, unit introductions give an overview of the historical events and literary trends in each period.
3. Students apply a wide range of strategies to comprehend, interpret, evaluate, and appreciate texts. They draw on their prior experience, their interactions with other readers and writers, their knowledge of word meaning and of other texts, their word identification strategies, and their understanding of textual features (e.g., sound-letter correspondence, sentence structure, context, graphics).	• Reading skills and strategies are taught before, during, and after each selection. • The *Selection Support Skills Development Workbook* includes practice pages that reinforce the skills taught with every selection in the Student Edition, including vocabulary, grammar, reading strategies, and literary analysis.

NCTE/IRA STANDARD	PRENTICE HALL LITERATURE
4. Students adjust their use of spoken, written, and visual language (e.g., conventions, style, vocabulary) to communicate effectively with a variety of audiences and for different purposes.	• Vocabulary skills and strategies are taught before, during, and after each selection. • Writing lessons offered at both the selection level and the unit level provide instruction in the writing process. Each writing lesson contains links to *Prentice Hall Writing and Grammar* to further strengthen the program's support. • Listening and Speaking activities are among the Extension Activities that follow each selection. In addition, each unit ends with a Listening and Speaking Workshop.
5. Students employ a wide range of strategies as they write and use different writing process elements appropriately to communicate with different audiences for a variety of purposes.	• In the selection-level Writing Lessons, students are given consistent instruction in prewriting, drafting, and revising, as well as in developing the appropriate voice and tone for a specific audience. • Unit-level Writing Workshops provide in-depth instruction on prewriting strategies, such as note taking, outlining, and collecting source material; drafting strategies, such as point-by-point organization and pacing; and revising strategies, such as adding vivid language, adjusting tone, and varying sentence structure. • The Writing About Literature feature guides students in crafting literary criticism. Focusing on a particular literary period or common theme, this feature provides students with techniques to help them focus essays around a thesis, develop coherent drafts, and revise their writing into a final, polished form.
6. Students apply knowledge of language structure, language conventions (e.g., spelling and punctuation), media techniques, figurative language, and genre to create, critique, and discuss print and nonprint texts.	• Language arts skills development is thoroughly integrated in *Prentice Hall Literature.* Each selection includes applied grammar, usage, mechanics, writing, and word-study activities related to the reading. • Grammar and Style Lesson topics are taken from the context of the story so that authentic application comes naturally. • Listening and speaking instruction ranges from Extension Activities, such as evaluating advertisements and analyzing media messages, to Listening and Speaking Workshops.

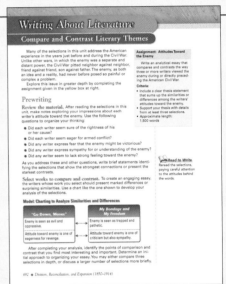

NCTE/IRA STANDARD	PRENTICE HALL LITERATURE
7. Students conduct research on issues and interests by generating ideas and questions, as well as by posing problems. They gather, evaluate, and synthesize data from a variety of sources (e.g., print and nonprint texts, artifacts, people) to communicate their discoveries in ways that suit their purpose and audience.	• Extension Activities encourage students to explore additional dimensions of the selections through collaborative research, panel presentations, and discussions. • Each grade level includes unit-level workshops on writing and delivering a research paper. • Students practice research skills, such as asking questions and evaluating data, at the selection level and in the Reading Informational Materials features.
8. Students use a variety of technological and information resources (e.g., libraries, databases, computer networks, video) to gather and synthesize information and to create and communicate knowledge.	• Students practice research skills, such as searching the Internet and summarizing primary research articles, at the selection level in the Research and Technology Extension Activities and in the Reading Informational Materials features.
9. Students develop an understanding of and respect for diversity in language use, patterns, and dialects across cultures, ethnic groups, geographic regions, and social roles.	Following is a representative sampling of selections that support this standard: "The Notorious Jumping Frog of Calaveras County," Mark Twain; "We Wear the Mask," Paul Laurence Dunbar; "An Account of the Battle of Bull Run," Stonewall Jackson; "The Love Song of J. Alfred Prufrock," T. S. Eliot; "old age sticks," E. E. Cummings; "A Worn Path," Eudora Welty • The Connections feature includes literary works from around the world, which are connected to individual selections in the Student Edition. • In the feature "The Development of American English," eminent word specialist Richard Lederer describes evolution in word usage in an engaging, high-interest format.

10. Students whose first language is not English make use of their first language to develop competency in the English language arts and to develop understanding of content across the curriculum.

- *Literatura en español* provides translations of one selection from each unit of the student textbook, along with summaries in English and Spanish of all textbook selections or groupings.

- The *Spanish/English Summaries Audio CDs* include summaries of every selection in both English and Spanish. These summaries provide help for struggling readers, special-education students, and English learners prior to having them read.

- The *Spanish Readings on Audio CDs* contain Spanish-language recordings of every selection in *Literatura en español*.

- The *Teaching Guidebook for Universal Access* gives proven strategies for adapting instruction for English-language learners. In addition, the *Reader's Companion English Learner's Version* provides language support for students who are ready to work in English.

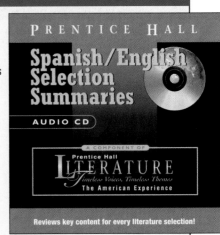

11. Students participate as knowledgeable, reflective, creative, and critical members of a variety of literacy communities.

- After each selection, the Extend Understanding question on the Review and Assess page and the Extension Activities invite students to go beyond the text to explore many connected areas.

- The Writing Workshop in each unit includes several publishing and presenting opportunities that allow students to share their writing with classmates or with a larger audience.

- Three levels of interactive readers—*Reader's Companion, Reader's Companion Adapted Version,* and *Reader's Companion English Learner's Version*—enable students at all ability levels to enjoy the same work of literature.

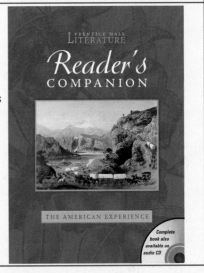

12. Students use spoken, written, and visual language to accomplish their own purposes (e.g., for learning, enjoyment, persuasion, and the exchange of information).

- Establishing a Purpose for Reading is one of the many Reading Strategies that are taught at each grade level.

- Students learn to read for information in the Reading Informational Materials selections. The instruction that accompanies these selections teaches students to understand and utilize a vast array of real-world nonfiction texts.

- Extension Activities at the selection level and Writing Lessons at the unit level often encourage students to choose their own topics for exploration.

READING INFORMATIONAL MATERIALS

NCTE/IRA STANDARDS

Program Planner

Selection	Reading	Literary Analysis	Vocabulary	Grammar
"The Earth on Turtle's Back," SE p. 16; **"When Grizzlies Walked Upright,"** SE p. 19; from **The Navajo Origin Legend,** SE p. 22; from **The Iroquois Constitution,** SE p. 24 Reading Level: Easy, Easy, Easy, Average	• Recognizing Cultural Details, SE p. 15; TR Selection Support, p. 3; TR Literary Analysis and Reading Transparencies, p. 1	• Origin Myths, SE p. 15; TR Selection Support, p. 4; TR Literary Analysis and Reading Transparencies, p. 2	• Vocabulary Development, SE p. 15: ablutions, protruded, confederate, disposition, deliberation • Latin Suffix -tion, SE p. 28; TR Selection Support, p. 1	• Compound Sentences, SE p. 28; TR Selection Support, p. 2; WG Writing and Grammar, pp. 466–467
"A Journey Through Texas," Alvar Núñez Cabeza de Vaca, SE p. 32; **"Boulders Taller Than the Great Tower of Seville,"** García López de Cárdenas, SE p. 37 Reading Level: Average, Average	• Signal Words, SE p. 31; TR Selection Support, p. 7; TR Literary Analysis and Reading Transparencies, p. 3	• Exploration Narratives, SE p. 31; TR Selection Support, p. 8; TR Literary Analysis and Reading Transparencies, p. 3	• Vocabulary Development, SE p. 31: entreated, feigned, mortality, subsided, traversed, dispatched • Latin Root -mort-, SE p. 40; TR Selection Support, p. 5	• Past and Perfect Verb Tenses, SE p. 40; TR Selection Support, p. 6; WG Writing and Grammar, pp. 532–545
from **The Interesting Narrative of the Life of Olaudah Equiano,** Olaudah Equiano, SE p. 44 Reading Level: Average	• Summarizing SE p. 43; TR Selection Support, p. 11; TR Literary Analysis and Reading Transparencies, p. 5	• Slave Narratives, SE p. 43; TR Selection Support, p. 12; TR Literary Analysis and Reading Transparencies, p. 6	• Vocabulary Development, SE p. 43: loathsome, pestilential, copious, improvident, avarice, pacify • Latin Root -vid-, SE p. 50; TR Selection Support, p. 9	• Active and Passive Voice, SE p. 50; TR Selection Support, p. 10; WG Writing and Grammar, pp. 552–554
from **Journal of the First Voyage to America,** Christopher Columbus, SE p. 62 Reading Level: Average	• Recognizing Author's Purpose, SE p. 61; TR Selection Support, p. 17; TR Literary Analysis and Reading Transparencies, p. 7	• Journal, SE p. 61; TR Selection Support, p. 18; TR Literary Analysis and Reading Transparencies, p. 8	• Vocabulary Development, SE p. 61: exquisite, affliction, indications, abundance • Latin Root -flict-, SE p. 66; TR Selection Support, p. 15	• Action and Linking Verbs, SE p. 66; TR Selection Support, p. 16; WG Writing and Grammar, p. 374
from **The General History of Virginia,** John Smith, SE p. 72; from **Of Plymouth Plantation,** William Bradford, SE p. 78 Reading Level: Challenging, Challenging	• Breaking Down Sentences, SE p. 71; TR Selection Support, p. 21; TR Literary Analysis and Reading Transparencies, p. 9	• Narrative Accounts, SE p. 71; TR Selection Support, p. 22; TR Literary Analysis and Reading Transparencies, p. 10	• Vocabulary Development, SE p. 71: pilfer, palisades, conceits, mollified, peril, loath, sundry, recompense • Related Forms of peril, SE p. 86; TR Selection Support, p. 19	• Singular and Plural Possessive Nouns, SE p. 86; TR Selection Support, p. 20; WG Writing and Grammar, p. 756
"Huswifery," Edward Taylor, SE p. 100; **"To My Dear and Loving Husband,"** Anne Bradstreet, SE p. 102 Reading Level: Challenging, Average	• Paraphrasing, SE p. 99; TR Selection Support, p. 27; TR Literary Analysis and Reading Transparencies, p. 11	• The Puritan Plain Style, SE p. 99; TR Selection Support, p. 28; TR Literary Analysis and Reading Transparencies, p. 12	• Vocabulary Development, SE p. 99: recompense, manifold, persevere • Anglo-Saxon suffix -fold, SE p. 104; TR Selection Support, p. 25	• Direct Address, SE p. 104; TR Selection Support, p. 26; WG Writing and Grammar, p. 696
from **Sinners in the Hands of an Angry God,** Jonathan Edwards, SE p. 108 Reading Level: Challenging	• Using Context Clues, SE p. 107; TR Selection Support, p. 31; TR Literary Analysis and Reading Transparencies, p. 13	• Sermon, SE p. 107; TR Selection Support, p. 32; TR Literary Analysis and Reading Transparencies, p. 14	• Vocabulary Development, SE p. 107: omnipotent, ineffable, dolorous • Latin Prefix omni-, SE p. 114; TR Selection Support, p. 29	• Forms of Adjectives and Adverbs, SE p. 114; TR Selection Support, p. 30; WG Writing and Grammar, p. 620

Program Planner

Selection	Reading	Literary Analysis	Vocabulary	Grammar
from **The Autobiography,** Benjamin Franklin, SE p. 140; from **Poor Richard's Almanack,** Benjamin Franklin, SE p. 146 Reading Level: Challenging, Challenging	• Drawing Conclusions, SE p. 139; TR Selection Support, p. 35; TR Literary Analysis and Reading Transparencies, p. 15	• Autobiography, SE p. 139; TR Selection Support, p. 36; TR Literary Analysis and Reading Transparencies, p. 16	• Vocabulary Development, SE p. 139: arduous, avarice, vigilance, disposition, foppery, felicity, squander, fasting • Word Root -vigil-, SE p. 150; TR Selection Support, p. 33	• Pronoun Case, SE p. 150; TR Selection Support, p. 34; WG Writing and Grammar, p. 562

Key to Program References: SE: Student Edition **TR:** Teaching Resources **WG:** Writing and Grammar

Unit 1 *Beginnings to 1750*

Writing	Extension Activities	Assessment	Technology
• Writing Lesson: Retelling of a Story, SE p. 29; WG Writing and Grammar, p. 80	• Listening and Speaking: Dramatic Reenactment, SE p. 29 • Research and Technology: Logo, SE p. 29 • TR Extension Activities, p. 1	• Selection Test, TR Formal Assessment, pp. 1–3 • TR Open Book Test, pp. 1–3 • Rubric [for Writing Lesson], TR Performance Assess. and Portfolio Mgmt., p. 15	• Interest Grabber Video, Tape 1 • Listening to Literature, Audio-cassettes, Side 1; Audio CDs, CD 1 • Got It! Assessment Videotapes, Tape 1 • WG Writing and Grammar iText
• Writing Lesson: Explorer's Journal, SE p. 41; WG Writing and Grammar, p. 105	• Listening and Speaking: Speech, SE p. 41 • Research and Technology: Exploration Booklet, SE p. 41 • TR Extension Activities, p. 2	• Selection Test, TR Formal Assessment, pp. 4–6 • TR Open Book Test, pp. 4–6 • Rubric [for Listening and Speaking activity], TR Performance Assess. and Portfolio Mgmt., p. 30	• Interest Grabber Video, Tape 1 • Listening to Literature, Audio-cassettes, Sides 1 and 2; Audio CDs, CD 1 • Got It! Assessment Videotapes, Tape 1 • WG Writing and Grammar iText
• Writing Lesson: Museum Placard SE p. 51; WG Writing and Grammar, p. 202	• Listening and Speaking: Debate, SE p. 51 • Research and Technology: Research Presentation, SE p. 51 • TR Extension Activities, p. 3	• Selection Test, TR Formal Assessment, pp. 7–9 • TR Open Book Test, pp. 7–9 • Rubric [for Listening and Speaking activity], TR Performance Assess. and Portfolio Mgmt., p. 26	• Interest Grabber Video, Tape 1 • Listening to Literature, Audio-cassettes, Side 2; Audio CDs, CD 1 • Got It! Assessment Videotapes, Tape 1 • WG Writing and Grammar iText
• Writing Lesson: Oral Report on the Voyage, SE p. 67; WG Writing and Grammar, p. 788	• Listening and Speaking: Humanities Presentation, SE p. 67 • Research and Technology: Chart, SE p. 67 • TR Extension Activities, p. 4	• Selection Test, TR Formal Assessment, pp. 16–18 • TR Open Book Test, pp. 10–12 • Rubric [for Listening and Speaking activity], TR Performance Assess. and Portfolio Mgmt., p. 30	• Interest Grabber Video, Tape 1 • Listening to Literature, Audio-cassettes, Side 1; Audio CDs, CD 1 • Got It! Assessment Videotapes, Tape 1 • WG Writing and Grammar iText
• Writing Lesson: Comparison of Narratives, SE p. 87; WG Writing and Grammar, p. 166	• Listening and Speaking: Persuasive Speech, SE p. 87 • Research and Technology: Menu, SE p. 87 • TR Extension Activities, p. 5	• Selection Test, TR Formal Assessment, pp. 19–21 • TR Open Book Test, pp. 13–15	• Interest Grabber Video, Tape 1 • Listening to Literature, Audio-cassettes, Sides 2 and 3; Audio CDs, CDs 1 and 2 • Got It! Assessment Videotapes, Tape 1 • WG Writing and Grammar iText
• Writing Lesson: Reflective Essay, SE p. 105; WG Writing and Grammar, p. 100	• Listening and Speaking: Informal Debate, SE p. 105 • Research and Technology: Graphic Display, SE p. 105 • TR Extension Activities, p. 6	• Selection Test, TR Formal Assessment, pp. 27–29 • TR Open Book Test, pp. 16–18 • Rubric [for Writing Lesson], TR Performance Assess. and Portfolio Mgmt., p. 11	• Interest Grabber Video, Tape 1 • Listening to Literature, Audio-cassettes, Side 3; Audio CDs, CD 2 • Got It! Assessment Videotapes, Tape 1 • WG Writing and Grammar iText
• Writing Lesson: Evaluation of Persuasion, SE p. 115; WG Writing and Grammar, p. 309	• Listening and Speaking: Oral Report, SE p. 115 • Research and Technology: Handbook, SE p. 115 • TR Extension Activities, p. 7	• Selection Test, TR Formal Assessment, pp. 30–32 • TR Open Book Test, pp. 19–21 • Rubric [for Listening and Speaking activity], TR Performance Assess. and Portfolio Mgmt., p. 17	• Interest Grabber Video, Tape 1 • Listening to Literature, Audio-cassettes, Side 3; Audio CDs, CD 2 • Got It! Assessment Videotapes, Tape 1 • WG Writing and Grammar iText

Unit 2 *A Nation is Born (1750–1800)*

Writing	Extension Activities	Assessment	Technology
• Writing Lesson: Autobiographical Account, SE p. 151; WG Writing and Grammar, p. 58	• Listening and Speaking: Class Improvement Plan, SE p. 151 • Research and Technology: Travel Brochure, SE p. 151 • TR Extension Activities, p. 8	• Selection Test, TR Formal Assessment, pp. 38–40 • TR Open Book Test, pp. 22–24 • Rubric [for Writing Lesson], TR Performance Assess. and Portfolio Mgmt., p. 9	• Interest Grabber Video, Tape 2 • Listening to Literature, Audio-cassettes, Side 4; Audio CDs, CD 2 • Got It! Assessment Videotapes, Tape 1 • WG Writing and Grammar iText

Program Planner

Selection	Reading	Literary Analysis	Vocabulary	Grammar
The Declaration of Independence, Thomas Jefferson, SE p. 156; from ***The Crisis,*** Thomas Paine, SE p. 160 Reading Level: Challenging, Average	• Recognizing Charged Words, SE p. 155; TR Selection Support, p. 39; TR Literary Analysis and Reading Transparencies, p. 17	• Persuasion, SE p. 155; TR Selection Support, p. 40; TR Literary Analysis and Reading Transparencies, p. 18	• Vocabulary Development, SE p. 155: unalienable, usurpations, perfidy, redress, magnanimity, acquiesce, consanguinity, impious, infidel • Latin Root -fid-, SE p. 164; TR Selection Support, p. 37	• Parallelism, SE p. 164; TR Selection Support, p. 38; WG Writing and Grammar, p. 504
"An Hymn to the Evening," Phillis Wheatley, SE p. 172; **"To His Excellency, General Washington,"** Phillis Wheatley, SE p. 174 Reading Level: Challenging, Average	• Clarifying Meaning, SE p. 171; TR Selection Support, p. 43; TR Literary Analysis and Reading Transparencies, p. 19	• Personification, SE p. 171; TR Selection Support, p. 44; TR Literary Analysis and Reading Transparencies, p. 20	• Vocabulary Development, SE p. 171: placid, scepter, celestial, refulgent, propitious, refluent, pensive • Latin Prefix re-, SE p. 178; TR Selection Support, p. 41	• Subject and Verb Agreement, SE p. 178; TR Selection Support, p. 42; WG Writing and Grammar, p. 584
"Speech in the Virginia Convention," Patrick Henry, SE p. 186; **"Speech in the Convention,"** Benjamin Franklin, SE p. 191 Reading Level: Challenging, Challenging	• Evaluating Persuasive Appeals, SE p. 185; TR Selection Support, p. 49; TR Literary Analysis and Reading Transparencies, p. 21	• Speeches, SE p. 185; TR Selection Support, p. 50; TR Literary Analysis and Reading Transparencies, p. 22	• Vocabulary Development, SE p. 185: arduous, infallibility, despotism, salutary, unanimity, posterity, manifest, insidious, subjugation, vigilant • Latin Suffixes -ity, SE p. 194; TR Selection Support, p. 47	• Double Negatives, SE p. 194; TR Selection Support, p. 48; WG Writing and Grammar, p. 642
"Letter to Her Daughter From the New White House," Abigail Adams, SE p. 204; from ***Letters From an American Farmer,*** Michel-Guillaume Jean de Crèvecoeur, SE p. 208 Reading Level: Average, Challenging	• Distinguishing Between Fact and Opinion, SE p. 203; TR Selection Support, p. 55; TR Literary Analysis and Reading Transparencies, p. 23	• Private and Public Letters (Epistles), SE p. 203; TR Selection Support, p. 56; TR Literary Analysis and Reading Transparencies, p. 24	• Vocabulary Development, SE p. 203: extricate, agues, asylum, penury, despotic, subsistence • Etymologies, SE p. 212; TR Selection Support, p. 53	• Semicolons, SE p. 212; TR Selection Support, p. 54; WG Writing and Grammar, p. 716

Program Planner

Selection	Reading	Literary Analysis	Vocabulary	Grammar
"The Devil and Tom Walker," Washington Irving, SE p. 242 Reading Level: Average	• Inferring Cultural Attitudes, SE p. 241; TR Selection Support, p. 61; TR Literary Analysis and Reading Transparencies, p. 25	• Third-Person Omniscient Point of View, SE p. 241; TR Selection Support, p. 62; TR Literary Analysis and Reading Transparencies, p. 26	• Vocabulary Development, SE p. 241: avarice, usurers, extort, ostentation, parsimony • Latin Prefix ex-, SE p. 254; TR Selection Support, p. 59	• Adjective Clauses, SE p. 254; TR Selection Support, p. 60; WG Writing and Grammar, p. 454
"A Psalm of Life," Henry Wadsworth Longfellow, SE p. 258; **"The Tide Rises, the Tide Falls,"** Henry Wadsworth Longfellow, SE p. 260 Reading Level: Average, Easy	• Associating Images With Life, SE p. 257; TR Selection Support, p. 65; TR Literary Analysis and Reading Transparencies, p. 27	• Stanza Form, SE p. 257; TR Selection Support, p. 66; TR Literary Analysis and Reading Transparencies, p. 28	• Vocabulary Development, SE p. 257: bivouac, sublime, efface • Latin Root -face-, SE p. 262; TR Selection Support, p. 63	• Inverted Word Order, SE p. 262; TR Selection Support, p. 64; WG Writing and Grammar, p. 490
"Thanatopsis," William Cullen Bryant, SE p. 267; **"Old Ironsides,"** Oliver Wendell Holmes, SE p. 270; **"The First Snowfall,"** James Russell Lowell, SE p. 272; from ***Snowbound,*** John Greenleaf Whittier, SE p. 275 Reading Level: Challenging, Average, Easy, Average	• Summarizing SE p. 266; TR Selection Support, p. 69; TR Literary Analysis and Reading Transparencies, p. 29	• Meter, SE p. 266; TR Selection Support, p. 70; TR Literary Analysis and Reading Transparencies, p. 30	• Vocabulary Development, SE p. 266: sepulcher, pensive, venerable, gloaming, ominous, querulous, patriarch • Latin Root -patr-, SE p. 282; TR Selection Support, p. 67	• Participles as Adjectives, SE p. 282; TR Selection Support, p. 68; WG Writing and Grammar, p. 442
"Crossing the Great Divide," Meriwether Lewis, SE p. 286; **"The Most Sublime Spectacle on Earth,"** John Wesley Powell, SE p. 289 Reading Level: Average, Average	• Noting Spatial Relationships, SE p. 285; TR Selection Support, p. 73; TR Literary Analysis and Reading Transparencies, p. 31	• Description, SE p. 285; TR Selection Support, p. 74; TR Literary Analysis and Reading Transparencies, p. 32	• Vocabulary Development, SE p. 285: conspicuous, sublime, labyrinth, excavated, demarcation, multifarious, multitudinous • Latin Prefix multi-, SE p. 294; TR Selection Support, p. 71	• Participial Phrases, SE p. 294; TR Selection Support, p. 72; WG Writing and Grammar, p. 442

Key to Program References: SE: Student Edition **TR:** Teaching Resources **WG:** Writing and Grammar

Unit 2 *A Nation is Born (1750–1800)*

Writing	Extension Activities	Assessment	Technology
• Writing Lesson: A Proposal to the Principal, SE p. 165; WG Writing and Grammar, p. 118	• Listening and Speaking: News Reports, SE p. 165 • Research and Technology: Précis, SE p. 165 • TR Extension Activities, p. 9	• Selection Test, TR Formal Assessment, pp. 39–40 • TR Open Book Test, pp. 25–27 • Rubric [for Writing Lesson], TR Performance Assess. and Portfolio Mgmt., p. 17	• Interest Grabber Video, Tape 2 • Listening to Literature, Audio-cassettes, Side 5; Audio CDs, CD 3 • Got It! Assessment Videotapes, Tape 1 • WG Writing and Grammar iText
• Writing Lesson: Inscription for a Monument, SE p. 179; WG Writing and Grammar, p. 131	• Listening and Speaking: Dramatic Reading, SE p. 179 • Research and Technology: Graphic Display, SE p. 179 • TR Extension Activities, p. 10	• Selection Test, TR Formal Assessment, pp. 42–44 • TR Open Book Test, pp. 28–30	• Interest Grabber Video, Tape 2 • Listening to Literature, Audio-cassettes, Side 5; Audio CDs, CD 3 • Got It! Assessment Videotapes, Tape 1 • WG Writing and Grammar iText
• Writing Lesson: Commentary on a Speech, SE p. 195; WG Writing and Grammar, p. 310	• Listening and Speaking: Debate, SE p. 195 • Research and Technology: Display, SE p. 195 • TR Extension Activities, p. 11	• Selection Test, TR Formal Assessment, pp. 51–53 • TR Open Book Test, pp. 31–33	• Interest Grabber Video, Tape 2 • Listening to Literature, Audio-cassettes, Sides 5 and 6; Audio CDs, CDs 3 and 4 • Got It! Assessment Videotapes, Tape 1 • WG Writing and Grammar iText
• Writing Lesson: Personal Letter, SE p. 213; WG Writing and Grammar, p. 153	• Listening and Speaking: Interview, SE p. 213 • Research and Technology: Advertisements, SE p. 213 • TR Extension Activities, p. 12	• Selection Test, TR Formal Assessment, pp. 59–63 • TR Open Book Test, pp. 34–36 • Rubric [for Writing Lesson], TR Performance Assess. and Portfolio Mgmt., p. 9	• Interest Grabber Video, Tape 2 • Listening to Literature, Audio-cassettes, Side 6; Audio CDs, CD 4 • Got It! Assessment Videotapes, Tape 1 • WG Writing and Grammar iText

Unit 3 *A Growing Nation (1800–1870)*

Writing	Extension Activities	Assessment	Technology
• Writing Lesson: Modern Retelling of a Story, SE p. 255; WG Writing and Grammar, p. 76	• Listening and Speaking: Enactment, SE p. 255 • Research and Technology: Essay, SE p. 255 • TR Extension Activities, p. 13	• Selection Test, TR Formal Assessment, pp. 67–69 • TR Open Book Test, pp. 37–39	• Interest Grabber Video, Tape 3 • Listening to Literature, Audio-cassettes, Side 7; Audio CDs, CD 5 • Got It! Assessment Videotapes, Tape 2 • WG Writing and Grammar iText
• Writing Lesson: Analytical Essay, SE p. 263; WG Writing and Grammar, p. 177	• Listening and Speaking: Recording, SE p. 263 • Research and Technology: Research Essay, SE p. 263 • TR Extension Activities, p. 14	• Selection Test, TR Formal Assessment, pp. 70–72 • TR Open Book Test, pp. 40–42	• Interest Grabber Video, Tape 3 • Listening to Literature, Audio-cassettes, Side 7; Audio CDs, CD 5 • Got It! Assessment Videotapes, Tape 2 • WG Writing and Grammar iText
• Writing Lesson: Précis, SE p. 283; WG Writing and Grammar, p. 857	• Listening and Speaking: Dramatic Reading, SE p. 283 • Research and Technology: Oral Presentation, SE p. 283 • TR Extension Activities, p. 15	• Selection Test, TR Formal Assessment, pp. 78–80 • TR Open Book Test, pp. 43–45	• Interest Grabber Video, Tape 3 • Listening to Literature, Audio-cassettes, Side 7; Audio CDs, CD 5 • Got It! Assessment Videotapes, Tape 2 • WG Writing and Grammar iText
• Writing Lesson: Description of a Natural Wonder, SE p. 295; WG Writing and Grammar, p. 100	• Listening and Speaking: Tourism Presentation, SE p. 295 • Research and Technology: Expedition Map, SE p. 295 • TR Extension Activities, p. 16	• Selection Test, TR Formal Assessment, pp. 78–80 • TR Open Book Test, pp. 46–48	• Interest Grabber Video, Tape 3 • Listening to Literature, Audio-cassettes, Side 8; Audio CDs, CD 5 • Got It! Assessment Videotapes, Tape 2 • WG Writing and Grammar iText

Program Planner

Selection	Reading	Literary Analysis	Vocabulary	Grammar
"The Fall of the House of Usher," Edgar Allan Poe, SE p. 308; **"The Raven,"** Poe, SE p. 326 Reading Level: Challenging, Average	• Breaking Down Long Sentences, SE p. 307; TR Selection Support, p. 79; TR Literary Analysis and Reading Transparencies, p. 33	• Single Effect, SE p. 307; TR Selection Support, p. 80; TR Literary Analysis and Reading Transparencies, p. 34	• Vocabulary Development, SE p. 307: importunate, munificent, equivocal, appellation, specious, anomalous, sentience, obeisance, craven • Latin Root -voc-, SE p. 332; TR Selection Support, p. 77	• Coordinate Adjectives, SE p. 332; TR Selection Support, p. 78; WG Writing and Grammar, p. 304
"The Minister's Black Veil," Nathaniel Hawthorne, SE p. 336 Reading Level: Challenging	• Drawing Inferences About Meaning, SE p. 335; TR Selection Support, p. 83; TR Literary Analysis and Reading Transparencies, p. 35	• Parable, SE p. 335; TR Selection Support, p. 84; TR Literary Analysis and Reading Transparencies, p. 36	• Vocabulary Development, SE p. 335: venerable, iniquity, indecorous, ostentatious, sagacious, vagary, tremulous, waggery, impertinent, obstinacy • Latin Root -equi-, SE p. 350; TR Selection Support, p. 81	• Varying Sentence Openers, SE p. 350; TR Selection Support, p. 82; WG Writing and Grammar, p. 489
from **Moby-Dick,** Herman Melville, SE p. 354 Reading Level: Challenging	• Recognizing Symbols, SE p. 353; TR Selection Support, p. 87; TR Literary Analysis and Reading Transparencies, p. 37	• Symbol, SE p. 353; TR Selection Support, p. 88; TR Literary Analysis and Reading Transparencies, p. 38	• Vocabulary Development, SE p. 353: inscrutable, maledictions, prescient, pertinaciously • Latin Prefix mal-, SE p. 372; TR Selection Support, p. 85	• Agreement With Collective Nouns, SE p. 372; TR Selection Support, p. 86; WG Writing and Grammar, p. 584
from **Nature,** Ralph Waldo Emerson, SE p. 388; from **Self-Reliance,** Emerson, SE p. 391; **"Concord Hymn,"** Emerson, SE p. 393; **"The Snowstorm,"** Emerson, SE p. 394 Reading Level: Average, Average, Average, Average	• Challenging the Text, SE p. 387; TR Selection Support, p. 93; TR Literary Analysis and Reading Transparencies, p. 39	• Transcendentalism, SE p. 387; TR Selection Support, p. 94; TR Literary Analysis and Reading Transparencies, p. 40	• Vocabulary Development, SE p. 387: blithe, connate, chaos, aversion, suffrage, divines, radiant, tumultuous, bastions • Latin Root -radi-, SE p. 398; TR Selection Support, p. 91	• Varying Sentence Length, SE p. 398; TR Selection Support, p. 92; WG Writing and Grammar, p. 487
from **Walden,** Henry David Thoreau, SE p. 402; from **Civil Disobedience,** Thoreau, SE p. 412 Reading Level: Challenging, Average	• Evaluating the Writer's Statement of Philosophy, SE p. 401; TR Selection Support, p. 97; TR Literary Analysis and Reading Transparencies, p. 41	• Style, SE p. 401; TR Selection Support, p. 98; TR Literary Analysis and Reading Transparencies, p. 42	• Vocabulary Development, SE p. 401: dilapidated, sublime, superfluous, evitable, magnanimity, expedient, posterity, alacrity • Latin Root -flu-, SE p. 415; TR Selection Support, p. 95	• Infinitives and Infinitive Phrases, SE p. 415; TR Selection Support, p. 96; WG Writing and Grammar, p. 442
Emily Dickinson's Poetry, Emily Dickinson, SE p. 420 Reading Level: Challenging, Average, Challenging, Challenging, Challenging, Average, Average	• Analyzing Images, SE p. 419; TR Selection Support, p. 101; TR Literary Analysis and Reading Transparencies, p. 43	• Slant Rhyme, SE p. 419; TR Selection Support, p. 102; TR Literary Analysis and Reading Transparencies, p. 44	• Vocabulary Development, SE p. 419: cornice, surmised, oppresses, finite, infinity • Latin Root -finis-, SE p. 430; TR Selection Support, p. 103	• Gerunds, SE p. 430; TR Selection Support, p. 104; WG Writing and Grammar, p. 442
Walt Whitman's Poetry, Walt Whitman, SE p. 434 Reading Level: Challenging, Average, Easy, Average, Average, Easy	• Inferring the Poet's Attitude, SE p. 433; TR Selection Support, p. 105; TR Literary Analysis and Reading Transparencies, p. 45	• Free Verse, SE p. 433; TR Selection Support, p. 106; TR Literary Analysis and Reading Transparencies, p. 46	• Vocabulary Development, SE p. 433: abeyance, effuse • Latin Root -fus-, SE p. 446; TR Selection Support, p. 103	• Pronoun and Antecedent Agreement, SE p. 446; TR Selection Support, p. 104; WG Writing and Grammar, p. 596

Program Planner

Selection	Reading	Literary Analysis	Vocabulary	Grammar
"An Episode of War," Stephen Crane, SE p. 476; **"Willie Has Gone to the War,"** Stephen Foster, SE p. 481 Reading Level: Average, Easy	• Recognizing Historical Details, SE p. 475; TR Selection Support, p. 110; TR Literary Analysis and Reading Transparencies, p. 47	• Realism and Naturalism, SE p. 475; TR Selection Support, p. 111; TR Literary Analysis and Reading Transparencies, p. 48	• Vocabulary Development, SE p. 475: precipitate, aggregation, inscrutable, disdainfully, glade • Latin Root -greg-, SE p. 484; TR Selection Support, p. 108	• Usage: like and as, SE p. 484; TR Selection Support, p. 109; WG Writing and Grammar, p. 648

Key to Program References: SE: Student Edition **TR:** Teaching Resources **WG:** Writing and Grammar

Unit 3 *A Growing Nation (1800–1870)*

Writing	Extension Activities	Assessment	Technology
• Writing Lesson: Literary Criticism, SE p. 333; WG Writing and Grammar, p. 16	• Listening and Speaking: Dramatic Reading, SE p. 333 • Research and Technology: Discussion, SE p. 333 • TR Extension Activities, p. 17	• Selection Test, TR Formal Assessment, pp. 85–87 • TR Open Book Test, pp. 49–51 • Rubric [for Writing Lesson], TR Performance Assess. and Portfolio Mgmt., p. 23	• Interest Grabber Video, Tape 3 • Listening to Literature, Audio-cassettes, Sides 9 and 10; Audio CDs, CD 6 • Got It! Assessment Videotapes, Tape 2 • WG Writing and Grammar iText
• Writing Lesson: Response to a Short Story, SE p. 351; WG Writing and Grammar, p. 304	• Listening and Speaking: Monologue, SE p. 351 • Research and Technology: Oral Presentation, SE p. 351 • TR Extension Activities, p. 18	• Selection Test, TR Formal Assessment, pp. 88–90 • TR Open Book Test, pp. 52–54 • Rubric [for Listening and Speaking activity], TR Performance Assess. and Portfolio Mgmt., p. 17	• Interest Grabber Video, Tape 3 • Listening to Literature, Audio-cassettes, Side 11; Audio CDs, CD 7 • Got It! Assessment Videotapes, Tape 2 • WG Writing and Grammar iText
• Writing Lesson: Character Study, SE p. 373; WG Writing and Grammar, p. 304	• Listening and Speaking: Monologue, SE p. 373 • Research and Technology: Report, SE p. 373 • TR Extension Activities, p. 19	• Selection Test, TR Formal Assessment, pp. 91–93 • TR Open Book Test, pp. 55–57 • Rubric [for Listening and Speaking activity], TR Performance Assess. and Portfolio Mgmt., p. 30	• Interest Grabber Video, Tape 3 • Listening to Literature, Audio-cassettes, Side 12; Audio CDs, CD 8 • Got It! Assessment Videotapes, Tape 2 • WG Writing and Grammar iText
• Writing Lesson: Critical Evaluation of a Philosophical Essay, SE p. 399; WG Writing and Grammar, p. 309	• Listening and Speaking: Public Service Announcement, SE p. 399 • Research and Technology: Profile, SE p. 399 • TR Extension Activities, p. 20	• Selection Test, TR Formal Assessment, pp. 99–101 • TR Open Book Test, pp. 58–60 • Rubric [for Writing Lesson], TR Performance Assess. and Portfolio Mgmt., p. 23	• Interest Grabber Video, Tape 3 • Listening to Literature, Audio-cassettes, Side 13; Audio CDs, CD 9 • Got It! Assessment Videotapes, Tape 2 • WG Writing and Grammar iText
• Writing Lesson: Editorial, SE p. 416; WG Writing and Grammar, p. 198	• Listening and Speaking: Debate, SE p. 416 • Research and Technology: Oral Presentation, SE p. 416 • TR Extension Activities, p. 21	• Selection Test, TR Formal Assessment, pp. 102–104 • TR Open Book Test, pp. 58–60	• Interest Grabber Video, Tape 2 • Listening to Literature, Audio-cassettes, Side 14; Audio CDs, CD 9 • Got It! Assessment Videotapes, Tape 2 • WG Writing and Grammar iText
• Writing Lesson: Letter to an Author, SE p. 431; WG Writing and Grammar, p. 309	• Listening and Speaking: Poetry Reading, SE p. 431 • Research and Technology: Report, SE p. 431 • TR Extension Activities, p. 22	• Selection Test, TR Formal Assessment, pp. 108–110 • TR Open Book Test, pp. 64–66 • Rubric [for Writing Lesson], TR Performance Assess. and Portfolio Mgmt., p. 12	• Interest Grabber Video, Tape 3 • Listening to Literature, Audio-cassettes, Sides 14 and 15; Audio CDs, CDs 9 and 10 • Got It! Assessment Videotapes, Tape 2 • WG Writing and Grammar iText
• Writing Lesson: Imitation of an Author's Style, SE p. 447; WG Writing and Grammar, p. 42	• Listening and Speaking: Collage, SE p. 447 • Research and Technology: Report, SE p. 447 • TR Extension Activities, p. 23	• Selection Test, TR Formal Assessment, pp. 111–113 • TR Open Book Test, pp. 67–69 • Rubric [for Listening and Speaking activity], TR Performance Assess. and Portfolio Mgmt., p. 30	• Interest Grabber Video, Tape 3 • Listening to Literature, Audio-cassettes, Side 15 and 16; Audio CDs, CD 10 • Got It! Assessment Videotapes, Tape 2 • WG Writing and Grammar iText

Unit 4 *Division, Reconciliation, and Expansion (1850–1914)*

Writing	Extension Activities	Assessment	Technology
• Writing Lesson: Field Report on Hospital Conditions, SE p. 485; WG Writing and Grammar, p. 104	• Listening and Speaking: Musical Presentation, SE p. 485 • Research and Technology: Definition Essay, SE p. 485 • TR Extension Activities, p. 24	• Selection Test, TR Formal Assessment, pp. 119–121 • TR Open Book Test, pp. 70–72	• Interest Grabber Video, Tape 4 • Listening to Literature, Audio-cassettes, Side 16; Audio CDs, CD 10 • Got It! Assessment Videotapes, Tape 3 • WG Writing and Grammar iText

Program Planner

Selection	Reading	Literary Analysis	Vocabulary	Grammar
"Swing Low, Sweet Chariot," SE p. 488; **"Go Down, Moses,"** SE p. 490 Reading Level: Easy, Average	• Listening, SE p. 487; TR Selection Support, p. 114; TR Literary Analysis and Reading Transparencies, p. 49	• Refrain, SE p. 487; TR Selection Support, p. 115; TR Literary Analysis and Reading Transparencies, p. 50	• Vocabulary Development, SE p. 487: oppressed, smite • Latin Root -press-, SE p. 492; TR Selection Support, p. 112	• Direct Address, SE p. 492; TR Selection Support, p. 113; WG Writing and Grammar, p. 696
from ***My Bondage and My Freedom***, Frederick Douglass, SE p. 496 Reading Level: Challenging	• Establishing a Purpose, SE p. 495; TR Selection Support, p. 118; TR Literary Analysis and Reading Transparencies, p. 55	• Autobiography, SE p. 495; TR Selection Support, p. 115; TR Literary Analysis and Reading Transparencies, p. 56	• Vocabulary Development, SE p. 495: congenial, benevolent, stringency, depravity, consternation, redolent • Latin Root -bene-, SE p. 504; TR Selection Support, p. 112	• Correlative Conjunctions, SE p. 504; TR Selection Support, p. 117; WG Writing and Grammar, p. 388
"An Occurrence at Owl Creek Bridge," Ambrose Bierce, SE p. 508 Reading Level: Average	• Identifying Chronological Order, SE p. 507; TR Selection Support, p. 122; TR Literary Analysis and Reading Transparencies, p. 53	• Point of View, SE p. 507; TR Selection Support, p. 123; TR Literary Analysis and Reading Transparencies, p. 54	• Vocabulary Development, SE p. 507: etiquette, deference, imperious, dictum, summarily, effaced, oscillation, apprised, malign, ineffable • Latin Root -summa-, SE p. 518; TR Selection Support, p. 120	• Semicolons in Compound Sentences, SE p. 518; TR Selection Support, p. 121; WG Writing and Grammar, p. 716
"The Gettysburg Address," Abraham Lincoln, SE p. 522; **"Second Inaugural Address,"** Abraham Lincoln, SE p. 523; **"Letter to His Son,"** Robert E. Lee, SE p. 525 Reading Level: Average, Challenging, Challenging	• Using Background Knowledge, SE p. 521; TR Selection Support, p. 126; TR Literary Analysis and Reading Transparencies, p. 55	• Diction, SE p. 521; TR Selection Support, p. 127; TR Literary Analysis and Reading Transparencies, p. 56	• Vocabulary Development, SE p. 521: consecrate, hallow, deprecated, insurgents, discern, scourge, malice, anarchy, redress • Greek Root -archy-, SE p. 528; TR Selection Support, p. 124	• Parallel Structure, SE p. 528; TR Selection Support, p. 125; WG Writing and Grammar, p. 154
Civil War Diaries, Journals, and Letters, SE p. 536 Reading Level: Average, Average, Average, Easy, Easy, Easy	• Distinguishing Fact From Opinion, SE p. 535; TR Selection Support, p. 130; TR Literary Analysis and Reading Transparencies, p. 57	• Diaries, Journals, and Letters, SE p. 535; TR Selection Support, p. 131; TR Literary Analysis and Reading Transparencies, p. 58	• Vocabulary Development, SE p. 535: capitulate, audaciously, foreboding, obstinate, imprecations, serenity • Latin Prefix ob-, SE p. 550; TR Selection Support, p. 128	• Capitalization of Proper Nouns, SE p. 550; TR Selection Support, p. 129; WG Writing and Grammar, p. 364
"The Boys' Ambition" from ***Life on the Mississippi,*** Mark Twain, SE p. 564; **"The Notorious Jumping Frog of Calaveras County,"** Mark Twain, SE p. 569 Reading Level: Average, Challenging	• Understanding Regional Dialect, SE p. 563; TR Selection Support, p. 136; TR Literary Analysis and Reading Transparencies, p. 59	• Humor, SE p. 563; TR Selection Support, p. 137; TR Literary Analysis and Reading Transparencies, p. 60	• Vocabulary Development, SE p. 563: transient, prodigious, eminence, garrulous, conjectured, monotonous, interminable, ornery • Greek Prefix mono-, SE p. 576; TR Selection Support, p. 134	• Double Negatives, SE p. 576; TR Selection Support, p. 135; WG Writing and Grammar, p. 642
"The Outcasts of Poker Flat," Bret Harte, SE p. 580 Reading Level: Average	• Questioning the Text, SE p. 579; TR Selection Support, p. 140; TR Literary Analysis and Reading Transparencies, p. 61	• Regionalism, SE p. 579; TR Selection Support, p. 141; TR Literary Analysis and Reading Transparencies, p. 62	• Vocabulary Development, SE p. 579: expatriated, anathema, bellicose, recumbent, equanimity, vociferation, vituperative, querulous • Latin Word Part -bel-, SE p. 592; TR Selection Support, p. 138	• Coordinating Conjunctions in Compound Sentences, SE p. 592; TR Selection Support, p. 139; WG Writing and Grammar, p. 388

Key to Program References: SE: Student Edition **TR:** Teaching Resources **WG:** Writing and Grammar

Unit 4 *Division, Reconciliation, and Expansion (1850–1914)*

Writing	Extension Activities	Assessment	Technology
• Writing Lesson: Reflective Essay, SE p. 493; WG Writing and Grammar, p. 58	• Listening and Speaking: Choral Reading, SE p. 493 • Research and Technology: Anthology, SE p. 493 • TR Extension Activities, p. 25	• Selection Test, TR Formal Assessment, pp. 122–124 • TR Open Book Test, pp. 73–75 • Rubric [for Writing Lesson], TR Performance Assess. and Portfolio Mgmt., p. 11	• Interest Grabber Video, Tape 4 • Listening to Literature, Audio-cassettes, Side 16; Audio CDs, CD 10 • Got It! Assessment Videotapes, Tape 3 • WG Writing and Grammar iText
• Writing Lesson: College Admission Essay, SE p. 505; WG Writing and Grammar, p. 56	• Listening and Speaking: Oral Presentation, SE p. 505 • Research and Technology: Multimedia Presentation, SE p. 505 • TR Extension Activities, p. 26	• Selection Test, TR Formal Assessment, pp. 125–127 • TR Open Book Test, pp. 76–78	• Interest Grabber Video, Tape 4 • Listening to Literature, Audio-cassettes, Side 17; Audio CDs, CD 11 • Got It! Assessment Videotapes, Tape 3 • WG Writing and Grammar iText
• Writing Lesson: Critical Essay, SE p. 519; WG Writing and Grammar, p. 309	• Listening and Speaking: Summary, SE p. 519 • Research and Technology: Visual Model, SE p. 519 • TR Extension Activities, p. 27	• Selection Test, TR Formal Assessment, pp. 128–130 • TR Open Book Test, pp. 79–81	• Interest Grabber Video, Tape 4 • Listening to Literature, Audio-cassettes, Side 17; Audio CDs, CD 11 • Got It! Assessment Videotapes, Tape 3 • WG Writing and Grammar iText
• Writing Lesson: Diary Entry, SE p. 529; WG Writing and Grammar, p. 129	• Listening and Speaking: Mock Supreme Court Hearing, SE p. 529 • Research and Technology: Internet Web Site, SE p. 529 • TR Extension Activities, p. 28	• Selection Test, TR Formal Assessment, pp. 131–133 • TR Open Book Test, pp. 82–84	• Interest Grabber Video, Tape 4 • Listening to Literature, Audio-cassettes, Sides 17 and 18; Audio CDs, CD 11 • Got It! Assessment Videotapes, Tape 3 • WG Writing and Grammar iText
• Writing Lesson: Problem-and-Solution Essay, SE p. 551; WG Writing and Grammar, p. 52	• Listening and Speaking: Dramatic Reading, SE p. 551 • Research and Technology: Model or Map of the Battlefield, SE p. 551 • TR Extension Activities, p. 29	• Selection Test, TR Formal Assessment, pp. 138–140 • TR Open Book Test, pp. 85–87 • Rubric [for Writing Lesson], TR Performance Assess. and Portfolio Mgmt., p. 10 • Rubric [for Listening and Speaking activity], TR Performance Assess. and Portfolio Mgmt., p. 31	• Interest Grabber Video, Tape 4 • Listening to Literature, Audio-cassettes, Side 18; Audio CDs, CD 11 • Got It! Assessment Videotapes, Tape 3 • WG Writing and Grammar iText
• Writing Lesson: Analytic Essay, SE p. 577; WG Writing and Grammar, p. 309	• Listening and Speaking: Interview, SE p. 577 • Research and Technology: Multimedia Report, SE p. 577 • TR Extension Activities, p. 30	• Selection Test, TR Formal Assessment, pp. 146–148 • TR Open Book Test, pp. 88–90 • Rubric [for Writing Lesson], TR Performance Assess. and Portfolio Mgmt., p. 23	• Interest Grabber Video, Tape 4 • Listening to Literature, Audio-cassettes, Side 19; Audio CDs, CD 12 • Got It! Assessment Videotapes, Tape 3 • WG Writing and Grammar iText
• Writing Lesson: Critical Review, SE p. 593; WG Writing and Grammar, p. 311	• Listening and Speaking: Eulogy, SE p. 593 • Research and Technology: Prospecting and Mining Report, SE p. 593 • TR Extension Activities, p. 31	• Selection Test, TR Formal Assessment, pp. 149–151 • TR Open Book Test, pp. 91–93 • Rubric [for Listening and Speaking activity], TR Performance Assess. and Portfolio Mgmt., p. 30	• Interest Grabber Video, Tape 4 • Listening to Literature, Audio-cassettes, Side 20; Audio CDs, CD 12 • Got It! Assessment Videotapes, Tape 3 • WG Writing and Grammar iText

PROGRAM PLANNER

Program Planner

Selection	Reading	Literary Analysis	Vocabulary	Grammar
"Heading West," Miriam Davis Colt, SE p. 596; **"I Will Fight No More Forever,"** Chief Joseph, SE p. 602 Reading Level: Easy, Easy	• Responding, SE p. 595; TR Selection Support, p. 144; TR Literary Analysis and Reading Transparencies, p. 63	• Tone, SE p. 595; TR Selection Support, p. 145; TR Literary Analysis and Reading Transparencies, p. 64	• Vocabulary Development, SE p. 595: genial, pervading, terra firma, emigrants, profusion, depredations, nonplused • Latin Term *terra firma*, SE p. 604; TR Selection Support, p. 142	• Sentence Fragments, SE p. 604; TR Selection Support, p. 143; WG Writing and Grammar, p. 492
"To Build a Fire," Jack London, SE p. 608 Reading Level: Average	• Predicting, SE p. 607; TR Selection Support, p. 148; TR Literary Analysis and Reading Transparencies, p. 65	• Conflict, SE p. 607; TR Selection Support, p. 149; TR Literary Analysis and Reading Transparencies, p. 66	• Vocabulary Development, SE p. 607: conjectural, unwonted, conflagration, peremptorily • Latin Root *-ject-*, SE p. 624; TR Selection Support, p. 146	• Adverb Clauses, SE p. 624; TR Selection Support, p. 147; WG Writing and Grammar, p. 458
"The Story of an Hour," Kate Chopin, SE p. 634 Reading Level: Average	• Recognizing Ironic Details, SE p. 633; TR Selection Support, p. 154; TR Literary Analysis and Reading Transparencies, p. 67	• Irony, SE p. 633; TR Selection Support, p. 155; TR Literary Analysis and Reading Transparencies, p. 68	• Vocabulary Development, SE p. 633: forestall, repression, elusive, tumultuously, importunities • Anglo Saxon Prefix *fore-*, SE p. 640; TR Selection Support, p. 152	• Appositives and Appositive Phrases, SE p. 640; TR Selection Support, p. 153; WG Writing and Grammar, p. 437
"April Showers," Edith Wharton, SE p. 644 Reading Level: Average	• Anticipating Events, SE p. 643; TR Selection Support, p. 158; TR Literary Analysis and Reading Transparencies, p. 69	• Elements of Plot, SE p. 643; TR Selection Support, p. 159; TR Literary Analysis and Reading Transparencies, p. 70	• Vocabulary Development, SE p. 643: admonitory, manuscript, retrospective, antagonism, contrition, commiseration • Latin Root *man-, -manu-*, SE p. 654; TR Selection Support, p. 156	• Gerund Phrases, SE p. 654; TR Selection Support, p. 157; WG Writing and Grammar, p. 442
"Douglass," Paul Laurence Dunbar, SE p. 658; **"We Wear the Mask,"** Paul Laurence Dunbar, SE p. 660 Reading Level: Average, Average	• Interpreting, SE p. 657; TR Selection Support, p. 162; TR Literary Analysis and Reading Transparencies, p. 71	• Rhyme, SE p. 657; TR Selection Support, p. 163; TR Literary Analysis and Reading Transparencies, p. 72	• Vocabulary Development, SE p. 657: salient, tempest, stark, guile, myriad • Forms of *guile*, SE p. 662; TR Selection Support, p. 160	• Punctuation of Interjections, SE p. 662; TR Selection Support, p. 161; WG Writing and Grammar, p. 394
"Luke Havergal," Edwin Arlington Robinson, SE p. 666; **"Richard Cory,"** Edwin Arlington Robinson, SE p. 668; **"Lucinda Matlock,"** Edgar Lee Masters, SE p. 669; **"Richard Bone,"** Edgar Lee Masters, SE p. 670 Reading Level: Average, Average, Average, Average	• Recognizing Attitudes, SE p. 665; TR Selection Support, p. 166; TR Literary Analysis and Reading Transparencies, p. 73	• Speaker, SE p. 665; TR Selection Support, p. 167; TR Literary Analysis and Reading Transparencies, p. 74	• Vocabulary Development, SE p. 665: imperially, repose, degenerate, epitaph • Latin Root *-pose-*, SE p. 672; TR Selection Support, p. 164	• Noun Clauses, SE p. 672; TR Selection Support, p. 165; WG Writing and Grammar, p. 454
"A Wagner Matinée," Willa Cather, SE p. 676 Reading Level: Challenging	• Clarifying, SE p. 675; TR Selection Support, p. 170; TR Literary Analysis and Reading Transparencies, p. 75	• Characterization, SE p. 675; TR Selection Support, p. 171; TR Literary Analysis and Reading Transparencies, p. 76	• Vocabulary Development, SE p. 675: reverential, tremulously, semi-somnambulant, inert, prelude, jocularity • Words From Music, SE p. 686; TR Selection Support, p. 168	• Reflexive and Intensive Pronouns, SE p. 686; TR Selection Support, p. 169; WG Writing and Grammar, p. 367

Key to Program References: SE: Student Edition **TR:** Teaching Resources **WG:** Writing and Grammar

Unit 4 *Division, Reconciliation, and Expansion (1850–1914)*

Writing	Extension Activities	Assessment	Technology
• Writing Lesson: Position Paper on Development, SE p. 605; WG Writing and Grammar, p. 132	• Listening and Speaking: Oral Interpretation, SE p. 605 • Research and Technology: Marketing Brochure, SE p. 605 • TR Extension Activities, p. 32	• Selection Test, TR Formal Assessment, pp. 161–163 • TR Open Book Test, pp. 97–99 • Rubric [for Listening and Speaking activity], TR Performance Assess. and Portfolio Mgmt., p. 30	• Interest Grabber Video, Tape 4 • Listening to Literature, Audio-cassettes, Side 20; Audio CDs, CD 12 • Got It! Assessment Videotapes, Tape 3 • WG Writing and Grammar iText
• Writing Lesson: Literary Analysis, SE p. 625; WG Writing and Grammar, p. 311	• Listening and Speaking: Enactment, SE p. 625 • Research and Technology: Booklet, SE p. 625 • TR Extension Activities, p. 33	• Selection Test, TR Formal Assessment, pp. 155–157 • TR Open Book Test, pp. 97–99 • Rubric [for Writing Lesson], TR Performance Assess. and Portfolio Mgmt., p. 23	• Interest Grabber Video, Tape 4 • Listening to Literature, Audio-cassettes, Sides 21 and 22; Audio CDs, CD 13 • Got It! Assessment Videotapes, Tape 3 • WG Writing and Grammar iText
• Writing Lesson: Reflective Essay, SE p. 641; WG Writing and Grammar, p. 52	• Listening and Speaking: Soliloquy, SE p. 641 • Research and Technology: Oral Report, SE p. 641 • TR Extension Activities, p. 34	• Selection Test, TR Formal Assessment, pp. 164–166 • TR Open Book Test, pp. 100–102 • Rubric [for Writing Lesson], TR Performance Assess. and Portfolio Mgmt., p. 11 • Rubric [for Listening and Speaking activity], TR Performance Assess. and Portfolio Mgmt., p. 30	• Interest Grabber Video, Tape 4 • Listening to Literature, Audio-cassettes, Side 23; Audio CDs, CD 13 • Got It! Assessment Videotapes, Tape 3 • WG Writing and Grammar iText
• Writing Lesson: Personal Narrative, SE p. 655; WG Writing and Grammar, p. 56	• Listening and Speaking: Speech, SE p. 655 • Research and Technology: Flowchart, SE p. 655 • TR Extension Activities, p. 35	• Selection Test, TR Formal Assessment, pp. 167–169 • TR Open Book Test, pp. 103–105 • Rubric [for Writing Lesson], TR Performance Assess. and Portfolio Mgmt., p. 11 • Rubric [for Listening and Speaking activity], TR Performance Assess. and Portfolio Mgmt., p. 30	• Interest Grabber Video, Tape 5 • Listening to Literature, Audio-cassettes, Side 29; Audio CDs, CD 16 • Got It! Assessment Videotapes, Tape 3 • WG Writing and Grammar iText
• Writing Lesson: Poem to Honor a Hero, SE p. 663; WG Writing and Grammar, p. 129	• Listening and Speaking: Oral Interpretation, SE p. 663 • Research and Technology: Report, SE p. 663 • TR Extension Activities, p. 36	• Selection Test, TR Formal Assessment, pp. 170–172 • TR Open Book Test, pp. 106–108 • Rubric [for Listening and Speaking activity], TR Performance Assess. and Portfolio Mgmt., p. 23	• Interest Grabber Video, Tape 4 • Listening to Literature, Audio-cassettes, Side 23; Audio CDs, CD 13 • Got It! Assessment Videotapes, Tape 3 • WG Writing and Grammar iText
• Writing Lesson: Firsthand Biography, SE p. 673; WG Writing and Grammar, p. 67	• Listening and Speaking: Class Discussion, SE p. 673 • Research and Technology: Illustrated Booklet, SE p. 673 • TR Extension Activities, p. 37	• Selection Test, TR Formal Assessment, pp. 173–175 • TR Open Book Test, pp. 109–111 • Rubric [for Writing Lesson], TR Performance Assess. and Portfolio Mgmt., p. 16	• Interest Grabber Video, Tape 4 • Listening to Literature, Audio-cassettes, Side 23; Audio CDs, CD 13 • Got It! Assessment Videotapes, Tape 3 • WG Writing and Grammar iText
• Writing Lesson: Editorial, SE p. 687; WG Writing and Grammar, p. 330	• Listening and Speaking: Monologues, SE p. 687 • Research and Technology: Musical Presentation, SE p. 687 • TR Extension Activities, p. 38	• Selection Test, TR Formal Assessment, pp. 176–178 • TR Open Book Test, pp. 112–114 • Rubric [for Listening and Speaking activity], TR Performance Assess. and Portfolio Mgmt., p. 30	• Interest Grabber Video, Tape 4 • Listening to Literature, Audio-cassettes, Side 24; Audio CDs, CD 14 • Got It! Assessment Videotapes, Tape 3 • WG Writing and Grammar iText

Program Planner

Selection	Reading	Literary Analysis	Vocabulary	Grammar
"The Love Song of J. Alfred Prufrock," T. S. Eliot, SE p. 718 Reading Level: Challenging	• Listening, SE p. 717; TR Selection Support, p. 176; TR Literary Analysis and Reading Transparencies, p. 77	• Dramatic Monologue, SE p. 717; TR Selection Support, p. 177; TR Literary Analysis and Reading Transparencies, p. 78	• Vocabulary Development, SE p. 717: insidious, digress, malingers, meticulous, obtuse • Greek Prefix *di-*, SE p. 724; TR Selection Support, p. 174	• Adjectival Modifiers, SE p. 724; TR Selection Support, p. 175; WG Writing and Grammar, p. 434
The Imagist Poets, SE p. 729 Reading Level: Challenging, Average, Easy, Average, Average, Average, Average, Average	• Engaging Your Senses, SE p. 728; TR Selection Support, p. 180; TR Literary Analysis and Reading Transparencies, p. 79	• Imagist Poetry, SE p. 728; TR Selection Support, p. 181; TR Literary Analysis and Reading Transparencies, p. 80	• Vocabulary Development, SE p. 728: voluminous, dogma, apparition • Forms of *appear,* SE p. 740; TR Selection Support, p. 178	• Concrete and Abstract Nouns, SE p. 740; TR Selection Support, p. 179; WG Writing and Grammar, p. 364
"Winter Dreams," F. Scott Fitzgerald, SE p. 744 Reading Level: Average	• Drawing Conclusions About Characters, SE p. 743; TR Selection Support, p. 184; TR Literary Analysis and Reading Transparencies, p. 81	• Characterization, SE p. 743; TR Selection Support, p. 185; TR Literary Analysis and Reading Transparencies, p. 82	• Vocabulary Development, SE p. 743: fallowness, preposterous, fortuitous, sinuous, mundane, poignant, pugilistic, somnolent • Latin Root *-somn-*, SE p. 764; TR Selection Support, p. 182	• Dashes, SE p. 764; TR Selection Support, p. 183; WG Writing and Grammar, p. 742
"The Turtle," John Steinbeck, SE p. 768 Reading Level: Average	• Finding Clues to Theme, SE p. 767; TR Selection Support, p. 188; TR Literary Analysis and Reading Transparencies, p. 83	• Theme, SE p. 767; TR Selection Support, p. 189; TR Literary Analysis and Reading Transparencies, p. 84	• Vocabulary Development, SE p. 767: embankment, protruded • Latin Prefix *pro-*, SE p. 772; TR Selection Support, p. 186	• Parallel Structure, SE p. 772; TR Selection Support, p. 187; WG Writing and Grammar, p. 504
"old age sticks," E. E. Cummings, SE p. 776; **"anyone lived in a pretty how town,"** E. E. Cummings, SE p. 777; **"The Unknown Citizen,"** W. H. Auden, SE p. 779 Reading Level: Challenging, Challenging, Average	• Relating Structure to Meaning, SE p. 775; TR Selection Support, p. 192; TR Literary Analysis and Reading Transparencies, p. 85	• Satire, SE p. 775; TR Selection Support, p. 193; TR Literary Analysis and Reading Transparencies, p. 86	• Vocabulary Development, SE p. 775: statistics, psychology • Greek Root *-psych-*, SE p. 782; TR Selection Support, p. 190	• Parentheses, SE p. 782; TR Selection Support, p. 191; WG Writing and Grammar, p. 746
"The Far and the Near," Thomas Wolfe, SE p. 786 Reading Level: Challenging	• Predicting, SE p. 785; TR Selection Support, p. 196; TR Literary Analysis and Reading Transparencies, p. 87	• Climax and Anticlimax, SE p. 785; TR Selection Support, p. 197; TR Literary Analysis and Reading Transparencies, p. 88	• Vocabulary Development, SE p. 785: tempo, sallow, sullen, timorous, visage • Latin Root *-temp-*, SE p. 792; TR Selection Support, p. 194	• Restrictive and Nonrestrictive Participial Phrases, SE p. 792; TR Selection Support, p. 195; WG Writing and Grammar, p. 442
"Of Modern Poetry," Wallace Stevens, SE p. 796; **"Anecdote of the Jar,"** Wallace Stevens, SE p. 797; **"Ars Poetica,"** Archibald MacLeish, SE p. 798; **"Poetry,"** Marianne Moore, SE p. 800 Reading Level: All Challenging	• Paraphrasing, SE p. 795; TR Selection Support, p. 200; TR Literary Analysis and Reading Transparencies, p. 89	• Simile, SE p. 795; TR Selection Support, p. 201; TR Literary Analysis and Reading Transparencies, p. 90	• Vocabulary Development, SE p. 795: suffice, insatiable, slovenly, dominion, palpable, derivative, literalists • Latin Root *-satis-*, SE p. 803; TR Selection Support, p. 198	• Subject Complements, SE p. 803; TR Selection Support, p. 199; WG Writing and Grammar, p. 425
"In Another Country," Ernest Hemingway, SE p. 809; **"The Corn Planting,"** Sherwood Anderson, SE p. 815; **"A Worn Path,"** Eudora Welty, SE p. 821 Reading Level: Average, Easy, Challenging	• Identifying With Characters, SE p. 808; TR Selection Support, p. 204; TR Literary Analysis and Reading Transparencies, p. 91	• Point of View, SE p. 808; TR Selection Support, p. 205; TR Literary Analysis and Reading Transparencies, p. 92	• Vocabulary Development, SE p. 808: invalided, grave, limber, obstinate • Latin Root *-val-*, SE p. 830; TR Selection Support, p. 202	• Punctuating Dialogue, SE p. 830; TR Selection Support, p. 203; WG Writing and Grammar, p. 724
"Chicago," Carl Sandburg, SE p. 838; **"Grass,"** Sandburg, SE p. 840 Reading Level: Easy, Average	• Responding, SE p. 837; TR Selection Support, p. 210; TR Literary Analysis and Reading Transparencies, p. 93	• Apostrophe, SE p. 837; TR Selection Support, p. 211; TR Literary Analysis and Reading Transparencies, p. 94	• Vocabulary Development, SE p. 837: brutal, wanton, cunning • Related Words: *brutal,* SE p. 842; TR Selection Support, p. 208	• Sentence Types, SE p. 842; TR Selection Support, p. 209; WG Writing and Grammar, p. 476

Key to Program References: SE: Student Edition **TR:** Teaching Resources **WG:** Writing and Grammar

Unit 5 *Disillusion, Defiance, and Discontent (1914–1946)*

Writing	Extension Activities	Assessment	Technology
• Writing Lesson: Character Analysis, SE p. 725; WG Writing and Grammar, p. 304	• Listening and Speaking: Role-Play, SE p. 725 • Research and Technology: Report, SE p. 725 • TR Extension Activities, p. 39	• Selection Test, TR Formal Assessment, pp. 185–187 • TR Open Book Test, pp. 115–117 • Rubric [for Writing Lesson], TR Performance Assess. and Portfolio Mgmt., p. 23	• Interest Grabber Video, Tape 5 • Got It! Assessment Videotapes, Tape 4 • WG Writing and Grammar iText
• Writing Lesson: An Editor's Review of Manuscript, SE p. 741; WG Writing and Grammar, p. 346	• Listening and Speaking: Informal Debate, SE p. 741 • Research and Technology: Illustration, SE p. 741 • TR Extension Activities, p. 40	• Selection Test, TR Formal Assessment, pp. 188–190 • TR Open Book Test, pp. 118–120 • Rubric [for Writing Lesson], TR Performance Assess. and Portfolio Mgmt., p. 23	• Interest Grabber Video, Tape 5 • Listening to Literature, Audio-cassettes, Sides 24 and 25; Audio CDs, CD 14 • Got It! Assessment Videotapes, Tape 4 • WG Writing and Grammar iText
• Writing Lesson: Character Analysis, SE p. 765; WG Writing and Grammar, p. 309	• Listening and Speaking: Presentation, SE p. 765 • Research and Technology: Report, SE p. 765 • TR Extension Activities, p. 41	• Selection Test, TR Formal Assessment, pp. 191–193 • TR Open Book Test, pp. 121–123	• Interest Grabber Video, Tape 5 • Listening to Literature, Audio-cassettes, Sides 25 and 26; Audio CDs, CDs 14 and 15 • Got It! Assessment Videotapes, Tape 4 • WG Writing and Grammar iText
• Writing Lesson: Essay About Historical Context, SE p. 773; WG Writing and Grammar, p. 257	• Listening and Speaking: Interview, SE p. 773 • Research and Technology: Cartoon Strip, SE p. 773 • TR Extension Activities, p. 42	• Selection Test, TR Formal Assessment, pp. 206–208 • TR Open Book Test, pp. 130–132	• Interest Grabber Video, Tape 5 • Listening to Literature, Audio-cassettes, Side 26; Audio CDs, CD 15 • Got It! Assessment Videotapes, Tape 4 • WG Writing and Grammar iText
• Writing Lesson: Introduction to a Poetry Reading, SE p. 783; WG Writing and Grammar, p. 304	• Listening and Speaking: Group Discussion, SE p. 783 • Research and Technology: Written Report, SE p. 783 • TR Extension Activities, p. 43	• Selection Test, TR Formal Assessment, pp. 197–199 • TR Open Book Test, pp. 127–129 • Rubric [for Writing Lesson], TR Performance Assess. and Portfolio Mgmt., p. 19	• Interest Grabber Video, Tape 5 • Listening to Literature, Audio-cassettes, Sides 26 and 27; Audio CDs, CD 15 • Got It! Assessment Videotapes, Tape 4 • WG Writing and Grammar iText
• Writing Lesson: Comparison-and-Contrast Essay, SE p. 793; WG Writing and Grammar, p. 166	• Listening and Speaking: Interview, SE p. 793 • Research and Technology: Written Report, SE p. 793 • TR Extension Activities, p. 44	• Selection Test, TR Formal Assessment, pp. 200–202 • TR Open Book Test, pp. 130–132	• Interest Grabber Video, Tape 5 • Listening to Literature, Audio-cassettes, Side 27; Audio CDs, CD 15 • Got It! Assessment Videotapes, Tape 4 • WG Writing and Grammar iText
• Writing Lesson: Definition, SE p. 804; WG Writing and Grammar, p. 788	• Listening and Speaking: Round-Table Discussion, SE p. 804 • Research and Technology: Collection of Poems, SE p. 804 • TR Extension Activities, p. 45	• Selection Test, TR Formal Assessment, pp. 203–205 • TR Open Book Test, pp. 133–135 • Rubric [for Listening and Speaking activity], TR Performance Assess. and Portfolio Mgmt., p. 55	• Interest Grabber Video, Tape 5 • Listening to Literature, Audio-cassettes, Side 27; Audio CDs, CD 15 • Got It! Assessment Videotapes, Tape 4 • WG Writing and Grammar iText
• Writing Lesson: Memorial Speech, SE p. 831; WG Writing and Grammar, p. 788	• Listening and Speaking: Sequel, SE p. 831 • Research and Technology: Research Report, SE p. 831 • TR Extension Activities, p. 46	• Selection Test, TR Formal Assessment, pp. 210–212 • TR Open Book Test, pp. 136–138	• Interest Grabber Video, Tape 5 • Listening to Literature, Audio-cassettes, Sides 27 and 28; Audio CDs, CDs 15 and 16 • Got It! Assessment Videotapes, Tape 4 • WG Writing and Grammar iText
• Writing Lesson: Essay Analyzing the Use of Repetition, SE p. 843; WG Writing and Grammar, p. 311	• Listening and Speaking: Stand-up Comedy Routine, SE p. 843 • Research and Technology: Report, SE p. 843 • TR Extension Activities, p. 47	• Selection Test, TR Formal Assessment, pp. 218–220 • TR Open Book Test, pp. 139–141	• Interest Grabber Video, Tape 5 • Listening to Literature, Audio-cassettes, Side 29; Audio CDs, CD 16 • Got It! Assessment Videotapes, Tape 4 • WG Writing and Grammar iText

Program Planner

Selection	Reading	Literary Analysis	Vocabulary	Grammar
"The Jilting of Granny Weatherall," Katherine Anne Porter, SE p. 846 Reading Level: Average	• Clarifying Sequence of Events, SE p. 845; TR Selection Support, p. 214; TR Literary Analysis and Reading Transparencies, p. 95	• Stream of Consciousness, SE p. 845; TR Selection Support, p. 215; TR Literary Analysis and Reading Transparencies, p. 96	• Vocabulary Development, SE p. 845: piety, frippery, dyspepsia • Greek Prefix *dys-*, SE p. 856; TR Selection Support, p. 212	• Imperative Sentences, SE p. 856; TR Selection Support, p. 213; WG Writing and Grammar, p. 476
"Race at Morning," William Faulkner, SE p. 860; **"Nobel Prize Acceptance Speech,"** Faulkner, SE p. 875 Reading Level: Average	• Breaking Down Long Sentences, SE p. 859; TR Selection Support, p. 218; TR Literary Analysis and Reading Transparencies, p. 97	• Dialect, SE p. 859; TR Selection Support, p. 219; TR Literary Analysis and Reading Transparencies, p. 98	• Vocabulary Development, SE p. 859: bayou, distillery, buck, moiling, switch, scrabbling, swag, glade • Latin Suffix *-ery*, SE p. 878; TR Selection Support, p. 216	• Correct Use of Irregular Verb Forms, SE p. 878; TR Selection Support, p. 217; WG Writing and Grammar, p. 520
The Poetry of Robert Frost, SE p. 882 Reading Level: Average, Average, Average, Easy, Average, Challenging	• Reading Blank Verse, SE p. 881; TR Selection Support, p. 222; TR Literary Analysis and Reading Transparencies, p. 99	• Blank Verse, SE p. 881; TR Selection Support, p. 223; TR Literary Analysis and Reading Transparencies, p. 100	• Vocabulary Development, SE p. 881: poise, rueful, luminary • Latin Root *-lum-*, SE p. 894; TR Selection Support, p. 220	• Uses of Infinitives, SE p. 894; TR Selection Support, p. 221; WG Writing and Grammar, p. 442
"The Night the Ghost Got In," James Thurber, SE p. 898; from **"Here Is New York,"** E. B. White, SE p. 903 Reading Level: Average, Easy	• Recognizing Hyperbole, SE p. 897; TR Selection Support, p. 226; TR Literary Analysis and Reading Transparencies, p. 101	• Informal Essay, SE p. 897; TR Selection Support, p. 227; TR Literary Analysis and Reading Transparencies, p. 102	• Vocabulary Development, SE p. 897: intuitively, blaspheming, aspiration, subterranean, claustrophobia, cosmopolitan • Latin Root *-terr-*, SE p. 908; TR Selection Support, p. 224	• Commas in Series, SE p. 908; TR Selection Support, p. 225; WG Writing and Grammar, p. 696
from **Dust Tracks on a Road,** Zora Neale Hurston, SE p. 914 Reading Level: Average	• Analyzing How a Writer Achieves Purpose, SE p. 913; TR Selection Support, p. 230; TR Literary Analysis and Reading Transparencies, p. 103	• Social Context in Autobiography, SE p. 913; TR Selection Support, p. 231; TR Literary Analysis and Reading Transparencies, p. 104	• Vocabulary Development, SE p. 913: foreknowledge, brazenness, caper, exalted, geography, avarice • Greek Root *-graph-*, SE p. 922; TR Selection Support, p. 228	• Parallelism in Coordinate Elements, SE p. 922; TR Selection Support, p. 229; WG Writing and Grammar, p. 504
"The Negro Speaks of Rivers," SE p. 926; **"Ardella,"** Langston Hughes, SE p. 927; **"Dream Variations,"** Hughes, SE p. 928; **"Refugee in America,"** Hughes, SE p. 929; **"The Tropics in New York,"** Claude McKay, SE p. 930 Reading Level: Challenging, Average, Challenging, Average, Challenging	• Drawing Inferences About the Speaker, SE p. 925; TR Selection Support, p. 234; TR Literary Analysis and Reading Transparencies, p. 105	• Speaker, SE p. 925; TR Selection Support, p. 235; TR Literary Analysis and Reading Transparencies, p. 106	• Vocabulary Development, SE p. 925: lulled, dusky, liberty • Latin Root *-lib-*, SE p. 932; TR Selection Support, p. 232	• Verb Tenses: Past and Present Perfect, SE p. 932; TR Selection Support, p. 233; WG Writing and Grammar, p. 532
"From the Dark Tower," Countee Cullen, SE p. 936; **"A Black Man Talks of Reaping,"** Arna Bontemps, SE p. 937; **"Storm Ending,"** Jean Toomer, SE p. 938 Reading Level: Average, Challenging, Average	• Connecting to Historical Context, SE p. 935; TR Selection Support, p. 238; TR Literary Analysis and Reading Transparencies, p. 107	• Metaphor, SE p. 935; TR Selection Support, p. 239; TR Literary Analysis and Reading Transparencies, p. 108	• Vocabulary Development, SE p. 935: increment, countenance, beguile, stark, reaping, glean • Latin Root *-cre-*, SE p. 940; TR Selection Support, p. 236	• Placement of Adjectives, SE p. 940; TR Selection Support, p. 237; WG Writing and Grammar, p. 696

Program Planner

Selection	Reading	Literary Analysis	Vocabulary	Grammar
"The Life You Save May Be Your Own," Flannery O'Connor, SE p. 973 Reading Level: Average	• Making Predictions, SE p. 971; TR Selection Support, p. 244; TR Literary Analysis and Reading Transparencies, p. 109	• Grotesque Characters, SE p. 971; TR Selection Support, p. 245; TR Literary Analysis and Reading Transparencies, p. 110	• Vocabulary Development, SE p. 971: desolate, listed, ominous, ravenous, morose, guffawing • Latin Root *-sol-*, SE p. 984; TR Selection Support, p. 242	• Subjunctive Mood, SE p. 984; TR Selection Support, p. 243; WG Writing and Grammar, p. 548

Key to Program References: SE: Student Edition **TR:** Teaching Resources **WG:** Writing and Grammar

Unit 5 *Disillusion, Defiance, and Discontent (1914–1946)*

Writing	Extension Activities	Assessment	Technology
• Writing Lesson: Stream-of-Consciousness Monologue, SE p. 857; WG Writing and Grammar, p. 82	• Listening and Speaking: Conversation, SE p. 857 • Research and Technology: Oral Report, SE p. 857 • TR Extension Activities, p. 48	• Selection Test, TR Formal Assessment, pp. 221–223 • TR Open Book Test, pp. 142–144 • Rubric [for Writing Lesson], TR Performance Assess. and Portfolio Mgmt., p. 15	• Interest Grabber Video, Tape 5 • Listening to Literature, Audio-cassettes, Side 30; Audio CDs, CD 17 • Got It! Assessment Videotapes, Tape 4 • WG Writing and Grammar iText
• Writing Lesson: Critical Review, SE p. 879; WG Writing and Grammar, p. 309	• Listening and Speaking: Broadcast, SE p. 879 • Research and Technology: Debate, SE p. 879 • TR Extension Activities, p. 49	• Selection Test, TR Formal Assessment, pp. 224–226 • TR Open Book Test, pp. 145–147 • Rubric [for Writing Lesson], TR Performance Assess. and Portfolio Mgmt., p. 23	• Interest Grabber Video, Tape 5 • Listening to Literature, Audio-cassettes, Side 31; Audio CDs, CD 17 • Got It! Assessment Videotapes, Tape 4 • WG Writing and Grammar iText
• Writing Lesson: Introduction to an Anthology, SE p. 895; WG Writing and Grammar, p. 37	• Listening and Speaking: Eulogy, SE p. 895 • Research and Technology: Interpretive Presentation, SE p. 895 • TR Extension Activities, p. 50	• Selection Test, TR Formal Assessment, pp. 241–243 • TR Open Book Test, pp. 154–156 • Rubric [for Listening and Speaking activity], TR Performance Assess. and Portfolio Mgmt., p. 30	• Interest Grabber Video, Tape 5 • Listening to Literature, Audio-cassettes, Sides 31 and 32; Audio CDs, CDs 17 and 18 • Got It! Assessment Videotapes, Tape 4 • WG Writing and Grammar iText
• Writing Lesson: Critical Response, SE p. 909; WG Writing and Grammar, p. 309	• Listening and Speaking: Role-Play, SE p. 909 • Research and Technology: Written Report, SE p. 909 • TR Extension Activities, p. 51	• Selection Test, TR Formal Assessment, pp. 230–232 • TR Open Book Test, pp. 151–153	• Interest Grabber Video, Tape 5 • Listening to Literature, Audio-cassettes, Side 32; Audio CDs, CD 18 • Got It! Assessment Videotapes, Tape 4 • WG Writing and Grammar iText
• Writing Lesson: Moment of Inspiration, SE p. 923; WG Writing and Grammar, p. 52	• Listening and Speaking: Campaign Speech, SE p. 923 • Research and Technology: Folk Tale Collection, SE p. 923 • TR Extension Activities, p. 52	• Selection Test, TR Formal Assessment, pp. 233–235 • TR Open Book Test, pp. 154–156	• Interest Grabber Video, Tape 5 • Listening to Literature, Audio-cassettes, Side 32; Audio CDs, CD 18 • Got It! Assessment Videotapes, Tape 4 • WG Writing and Grammar iText
• Writing Lesson: Poetry Comparison, SE p. 933; WG Writing and Grammar, p. 172	• Listening and Speaking: Presentation, SE p. 933 • Research and Technology: Posters, SE p. 933 • TR Extension Activities, p. 53	• Selection Test, TR Formal Assessment, pp. 236–238 • TR Open Book Test, pp. 157–159 • Rubric [for Writing Lesson], TR Performance Assess. and Portfolio Mgmt., p. 23	• Interest Grabber Video, Tape 5 • Listening to Literature, Audio-cassettes, Side 33; Audio CDs, CD 19 • Got It! Assessment Videotapes, Tape 4 • WG Writing and Grammar iText
• Writing Lesson: Comparison-and-Contrast Essay, SE p. 941; WG Writing and Grammar, p. 172	• Listening and Speaking: Dramatic Reading, SE p. 941 • Research and Technology: Research Report, SE p. 941 • TR Extension Activities, p. 54	• Selection Test, TR Formal Assessment, pp. 239–241 • TR Open Book Test, pp. 160–162 • Rubric [for Writing Lesson], TR Performance Assess. and Portfolio Mgmt., p. 23	• Interest Grabber Video, Tape 5 • Listening to Literature, Audio-cassettes, Side 33; Audio CDs, CD 19 • Got It! Assessment Videotapes, Tape 4 • WG Writing and Grammar iText

Unit 6 *Prosperity and Protest (1946–Present)*

Writing	Extension Activities	Assessment	Technology
• Writing Lesson: Deposition, SE p. 985; WG Writing and Grammar, p. 204	• Listening and Speaking: Reader's Theatre, SE p. 985 • Research and Technology: Body Language Presentation, SE p. 985 • TR Extension Activities, p. 55	• Selection Test, TR Formal Assessment, pp. 248–250 • TR Open Book Test, pp. 163–165 • Rubric [for Writing Lesson], TR Performance Assess. and Portfolio Mgmt., p. 20	• Interest Grabber Video, Tape 6 • Listening to Literature, Audio-cassettes, Side 33; Audio CDs, CD 19 • Got It! Assessment Videotapes, Tape 5 • WG Writing and Grammar iText

Program Planner

Selection	Reading	Literary Analysis	Vocabulary	Grammar
"The First Seven Years," Bernard Malamud, SE p. 988 Reading Level: Average	• Identifying With Characters, SE p. 987; TR Selection Support, p. 248; TR Literary Analysis and Reading Transparencies, p. 111	• Epiphany, SE p. 987; TR Selection Support, p. 249; TR Literary Analysis and Reading Transparencies, p. 112	• Vocabulary Development, SE p. 987: diligence, connivance, illiterate, unscrupulous, repugnant, discern • Latin Root -litera-, SE p. 998; TR Selection Support, p. 246	• Usage: who and whom, SE p. 998; TR Selection Support, p. 247; WG Writing and Grammar, p. 572
"The Brown Chest," John Updike, SE p. 1002 Reading Level: Average	• Breaking Down Long Sentences, SE p. 1001; TR Selection Support, p. 252; TR Literary Analysis and Reading Transparencies, p. 113	• Atmosphere, SE p. 1001; TR Selection Support, p. 253; TR Literary Analysis and Reading Transparencies, p. 114	• Vocabulary Development, SE p. 1001: mottled, assimilate, unfathomable, egregious, proprietorial, evanescent • Latin Root -sim-, SE p. 1010; TR Selection Support, p. 250	• Adverb Clauses, SE p. 1010; TR Selection Support, p. 251; WG Writing and Grammar, p. 454
"Hawthorne," Lowell, SE p. 1014; "Gold Glade," Penn Warren, SE p. 1017; "Traveling Through the Dark," Stafford, SE p. 1019; "The Light Comes Brighter," Roethke, SE p. 1021; "The Adamant," Roethke, SE p. 1022 Reading Level: Challenging, Challenging, Average, Easy, Challenging	• Paraphrasing, SE p. 1013; TR Selection Support, p. 256; TR Literary Analysis and Reading Transparencies, p. 115	• Style and Diction, SE p. 1013; TR Selection Support, p. 257; TR Literary Analysis and Reading Transparencies, p. 116	• Vocabulary Development, SE p. 1013: brooding, furtive, meditation, declivity, exhaust, vestiges • Related Words: exhaust, SE p. 1024; TR Selection Support, p. 254	• Subject and Verb Agreement, SE p. 1024; TR Selection Support, p. 255; WG Writing and Grammar, p. 584
"Average Waves in Unprotected Waters," Anne Tyler, SE p. 1028 Reading Level: Average	• Putting Events in Order, SE p. 1027; TR Selection Support, p. 260; TR Literary Analysis and Reading Transparencies, p. 117	• Foreshadowing, SE p. 1027; TR Selection Support, p. 261; TR Literary Analysis and Reading Transparencies, p. 118	• Vocabulary Development, SE p. 1027: orthopedic, transparent, stocky, staunch, viper • Latin Prefix trans-, SE p. 1038; TR Selection Support, p. 258	• Correct Use of Adjectives and Adverbs, SE p. 1038; TR Selection Support, p. 259; WG Writing and Grammar, p. 380
from The Names, N. Scott Momaday, SE p.1042; "Mint Snowball," Naomi Shihab Nye, SE p. 1047; "Suspended," Joy Harjo, SE p. 1049 Reading Level: All Easy	• Relating to Your Own Experiences, SE p. 1041; TR Selection Support, p. 264; TR Literary Analysis and Reading Transparencies, p. 119	• Anecdote, SE p. 1041; TR Selection Support, p. 265; TR Literary Analysis and Reading Transparencies, p. 120	• Vocabulary Development, SE p. 1041: supple, concocted, flamboyant, elixir, permeated, replicate, revelatory, confluence • Latin Prefix con-, SE p. 1052; TR Selection Support, p. 262	• Elliptical Clauses, SE p. 1052; TR Selection Support, p. 263; WG Writing and Grammar, p. 572
"Everyday Use," Alice Walker, SE p. 1056 Reading Level: Average	• Contrasting Characters, SE p. 1055; TR Selection Support, p. 268; TR Literary Analysis and Reading Transparencies, p. 121	• Character's Motivation, SE p. 1055; TR Selection Support, p. 269; TR Literary Analysis and Reading Transparencies, p. 122	• Vocabulary Development, SE p. 1055: furtive, lye, oppress, doctrines • Latin Root -doc-/-doct-, SE p. 1066; TR Selection Support, p. 266	• Sentence Fragments, SE p. 1066; TR Selection Support, p. 267; WG Writing and Grammar, p. 492
from The Woman Warrior, Maxine Hong Kingston, SE p. 1070 Reading Level: Average	• Applying Background Information, SE p. 1069; TR Selection Support, p. 272; TR Literary Analysis and Reading Transparencies, p. 123	• Memoirs, SE p. 1069; TR Selection Support, p. 273; TR Literary Analysis and Reading Transparencies, p. 124	• Vocabulary Development, SE p. 1069: hysterically, encampment, inaudibly, gravity, oblivious • Latin Root -aud-, SE p. 1078; TR Selection Support, p. 270	• Punctuating a Quotation Within a Quotation, SE p. 1078; TR Selection Support, p. 271; WG Writing and Grammar, p. 726
"Antojos," Julia Alvarez, SE p. 1082 Reading Level: Easy	• Identifying With a Character, SE p. 1081; TR Selection Support, p. 276; TR Literary Analysis and Reading Transparencies, p. 125	• Plot, SE p. 1081; TR Selection Support, p. 277; TR Literary Analysis and Reading Transparencies, p. 126	• Vocabulary Development, SE p. 1081: dissuade, loath, appease, machetes, collusion, docile, enunciated • Words From Spanish, SE p. 1094; TR Selection Support, p. 222	• Absolute Phrases, SE p. 1094; TR Selection Support, p. 275; WG Writing and Grammar, p. 442

Key to Program References: SE: Student Edition **TR:** Teaching Resources **WG:** Writing and Grammar

Unit 6 *Prosperity and Protest (1946–Present)*

Writing	Extension Activities	Assessment	Technology
• Writing Lesson: Personality Profile, SE p. 999; WG Writing and Grammar, p. 100	• Listening and Speaking: Presentation, SE p. 999 • Research and Technology: Cultural Research, SE p. 999 • TR Extension Activities, p. 56	• Selection Test, TR Formal Assessment, pp. 251–253 • TR Open Book Test, pp. 166–168 • Rubric [for Writing Lesson], TR Performance Assess. and Portfolio Mgmt., p. 16	• Interest Grabber Video, Tape 6 • Listening to Literature, Audio- cassettes, Side 34; Audio CDs, CD 19 • Got It! Assessment Videotapes, Tape 5 • WG Writing and Grammar iText
• Writing Lesson: Analysis of a Symbol, SE p. 1011; WG Writing and Grammar, p. 309	• Listening and Speaking: Conversation, SE p. 1011 • Research and Technology: Feature Article on Fashions, SE p. 1011 • TR Extension Activities, p. 57	• Selection Test, TR Formal Assessment, pp. 254–256 • TR Open Book Test, pp. 169–171 • Rubric [for Writing Lesson], TR Performance Assess. and Portfolio Mgmt., p. 23 • Rubric [for Listening and Speaking activity], TR Performance Assess. and Portfolio Mgmt., p. 30	• Interest Grabber Video, Tape 6 • Listening to Literature, Audio- cassettes, Side 34; Audio CDs, CD 19 • Got It! Assessment Videotapes, Tape 5 • WG Writing and Grammar iText
• Writing Lesson: Critical Response, SE p. 1025; WG Writing and Grammar, p. 309	• Listening and Speaking: Evaluation, SE p. 1025 • Research and Technology: Oral Presentation, SE p. 1025 • TR Extension Activities, p. 58	• Selection Test, TR Formal Assessment, pp. 257–259 • TR Open Book Test, pp. 172–174 • Rubric [for Writing Lesson], TR Performance Assess. and Portfolio Mgmt., p. 23 • Rubric [for Listening and Speaking activity], TR Performance Assess. and Portfolio Mgmt., p. 30	• Interest Grabber Video, Tape 6 • Listening to Literature, Audio- cassettes, Side 35; Audio CDs, CD 20 • Got It! Assessment Videotapes, Tape 5 • WG Writing and Grammar iText
• Writing Lesson: Social Worker's Report, SE p. 1039; WG Writing and Grammar, p. 204	• Listening and Speaking: Political Speech, SE p. 1039 • Research and Technology: Research Report, SE p. 1039 • TR Extension Activities, p. 59	• Selection Test, TR Formal Assessment, pp. 260–262 • TR Open Book Test, pp. 175–177 • Rubric [for Writing Lesson], TR Performance Assess. and Portfolio Mgmt., p. 20	• Interest Grabber Video, Tape 6 • Listening to Literature, Audio- cassettes, Side 35; Audio CDs, CD 20 • Got It! Assessment Videotapes, Tape 5 • WG Writing and Grammar iText
• Writing Lesson: Reflective Essay, SE p. 1053; WG Writing and Grammar, p. 56	• Listening and Speaking: Musical Analysis, SE p. 1053 • Research and Technology: Class Anthology, SE p. 1053 • TR Extension Activities, p. 60	• Selection Test, TR Formal Assessment, pp. 263–265 • TR Open Book Test, pp. 178–180 • Rubric [for Writing Lesson], TR Performance Assess. and Portfolio Mgmt., p. 11	• Interest Grabber Video, Tape 6 • Listening to Literature, Audio- cassettes, Sides 35 and 36; Audio CDs, CD 20 • Got It! Assessment Videotapes, Tape 5 • WG Writing and Grammar iText
• Writing Lesson: Review of a Short Story, SE p. 1067; WG Writing and Grammar, p. 309	• Listening and Speaking: Television Talk Show, SE p. 1067 • Research and Technology: African Languages Presentation, SE p. 1067 • TR Extension Activities, p. 61	• Selection Test, TR Formal Assessment, pp. 280–282 • TR Open Book Test, pp. 187–189	• Interest Grabber Video, Tape 6 • Listening to Literature, Audio- cassettes, Side 36; Audio CDs, CD 20 • Got It! Assessment Videotapes, Tape 5 • WG Writing and Grammar iText
• Writing Lesson: Character Analysis, SE p. 1079; WG Writing and Grammar, p. 800	• Listening and Speaking: Panel Discussion, SE p. 1079 • Research and Technology: Immigration Report, SE p. 1079 • TR Extension Activities, p. 62	• Selection Test, TR Formal Assessment, pp. 269–271 • TR Open Book Test, pp. 184–186 • Rubric [for Writing Lesson], TR Performance Assess. and Portfolio Mgmt., p. 23	• Interest Grabber Video, Tape 6 • Listening to Literature, Audio- cassettes, Side 36; Audio CDs, CD 20 • Got It! Assessment Videotapes, Tape 5 • WG Writing and Grammar iText
• Writing Lesson: New Version of the Story, SE p. 1095; WG Writing and Grammar, p. 82	• Listening and Speaking: Cause-and- Effect Flowchart, SE p. 1095 • Research and Technology: Multimedia Report, SE p. 1095 • TR Extension Activities, p. 63	• Selection Test, TR Formal Assessment, pp. 272–274 • TR Open Book Test, pp. 187–189 • Rubric [for Writing Lesson], TR Performance Assess. and Portfolio Mgmt., p. 15	• Interest Grabber Video, Tape 6 • Listening to Literature, Audio- cassettes, Side 37; Audio CDs, CD 21 • Got It! Assessment Videotapes, Tape 5 • WG Writing and Grammar iText

Program Planner

Selection	Reading	Literary Analysis	Vocabulary	Grammar
"Freeway 280," SE p.1098; "Who Burns for the Perfection of Paper," SE p. 1100; "Most Satisfied by Snow," SE p. 1101; "Hunger in New York City," SE p. 1102; "What For," SE p. 1103 Reading Level: Challenging, Easy, Average, Average, Challenging	• Summarizing, SE p. 1097; TR Selection Support, p. 280; TR Literary Analysis and Reading Transparencies, p. 127	• Voice, SE p. 1097; TR Selection Support, p. 281; TR Literary Analysis and Reading Transparencies, p. 128	• Vocabulary Development, SE p. 1097: crevices, pervade, automation, liturgy, conjure, calligraphy, trough • Greek Prefix auto-, SE p. 1107; TR Selection Support, p. 278	• Participial Phrases, SE p. 1107; TR Selection Support, p. 279; WG Writing and Grammar, p. 442
from The Mortgaged Heart, Carson McCullers, SE p. 1112; "Onomatopoeia," William Safire, SE p. 1115; "Coyote v. Acme," Ian Frazier, SE p. 1118 Reading Level: Challenging, Easy, Average	• Identifying Line of Reasoning, SE p. 1111; TR Selection Support, p. 284; TR Literary Analysis and Reading Transparencies, p. 129	• Essay, SE p. 1111; TR Selection Support, p. 285; TR Literary Analysis and Reading Transparencies, p. 130	• Vocabulary Development, SE p. 1111: pristine, corollary, aesthetic, maverick, contiguous, precipitate, caveat, tensile • Latin Root -ten-, SE p. 1124; TR Selection Support, p. 282	• Pronouns With Appositives, SE p. 1124; TR Selection Support, p. 283; WG Writing and Grammar, p. 562
"Straw Into Gold," Sandra Cisneros, SE p. 1128; "For the Love of Books," Rita Dove, SE p. 1133; "Mother Tongue," Amy Tan, SE p. 1136 Reading Level: Average, Easy, Average	• Evaluating a Writer's Message, SE p. 1127; TR Selection Support, p. 288; TR Literary Analysis and Reading Transparencies, p. 131	• Reflective Essay, SE p. 1127; TR Selection Support, p. 289; TR Literary Analysis and Reading Transparencies, p. 132	• Vocabulary Development, SE p. 1127: nomadic, transcribed, empirical, benign, semantic, quandary, nascent • Latin Root -scrib-, -script-, SE p. 1143; TR Selection Support, p. 286	• Varying Sentence Structure, SE p. 1143; TR Selection Support, p. 287; WG Writing and Grammar, p. 487
"The Rock Pile," James Baldwin, SE p. 1149 Reading Level: Average	• Identifying Cause and Effect, SE p. 1147; TR Selection Support, p. 292; TR Literary Analysis and Reading Transparencies, p. 133	• Setting, SE p. 1147; TR Selection Support, p. 293; TR Literary Analysis and Reading Transparencies, p. 134	• Vocabulary Development, SE p. 1147: intriguing, benevolent, decorously, latent, engrossed, jubilant, arrested, malevolence, perdition • Latin Prefix mal-, SE p. 1158; TR Selection Support, p. 290	• Restrictive and Nonrestrictive Adjective Clauses, SE p. 1158; TR Selection Support, p. 291; WG Writing and Grammar, p. 455
from Hiroshima, John Hersey, SE p. 1162; "Losses," Randall Jarrell, SE p. 1173; "The Death of the Ball Turret Gunner," Randall Jarrell, SE p. 1174 Reading Level: Challenging, Easy, Easy	• Drawing Inferences About Theme, SE p. 1161; TR Selection Support, p. 296; TR Literary Analysis and Reading Transparencies, p. 135	• Implied Theme, SE p. 1161; TR Selection Support, p. 297; TR Literary Analysis and Reading Transparencies, p. 136	• Vocabulary Development, SE p. 1161: evacuated, volition, rendezvous, philanthropies, incessant, convivial • Latin Root -vol-, SE p. 1176; TR Selection Support, p. 294	• Transitions and Transitional Phrases, SE p. 1176; TR Selection Support, p. 295; WG Writing and Grammar, p. 37
"Mirror," Plath, SE p. 1180; "In a Classroom," Rich, SE p. 1181; "The Explorer," Brooks, SE p. 1182; "Frederick Douglass," Hayden, SE p. 1183; "Runagate, Runagate," Hayden, SE p. 1184 Reading Level: Average, Challenging, Challenging Easy, Easy	• Interpreting, SE p. 1179; TR Selection Support, p. 300; TR Literary Analysis and Reading Transparencies, p. 137	• Theme, SE p. 1179; TR Selection Support, p. 301; TR Literary Analysis and Reading Transparencies, p. 138	• Vocabulary Development, SE p. 1179: preconceptions, meditate, din, wily • Latin Root -cep-/-cept-, SE p. 1188; TR Selection Support, p. 298	• Parallel Structure, SE p. 1188; TR Selection Support, p. 299; WG Writing and Grammar, p. 154
"For My Children," Colleen McElroy, SE p. 1192; "Bidwell Ghost," Louise Erdrich, SE p. 1195 Reading Level: Average, Average	• Reading in Sentences, SE p. 1191; TR Selection Support, p. 304; TR Literary Analysis and Reading Transparencies, p. 139	• Lyric Poetry, SE p. 1191; TR Selection Support, p. 305; TR Literary Analysis and Reading Transparencies, p. 140	• Vocabulary Development, SE p. 1191: shackles, heritage, effigies • Related Words: heritage, SE p. 1198; TR Selection Support, p. 302	• Sequence of Tenses, SE p. 1198; TR Selection Support, p. 303; WG Writing and Grammar, p. 532
"The Writer in the Family," E. L. Doctorow, SE p. 1202 Reading Level: Average	• Judging Characters' Actions, SE p. 1201; TR Selection Support, p. 308; TR Literary Analysis and Reading Transparencies, p. 141	• Static and Dynamic Characters, SE p. 1201; TR Selection Support, p. 309; TR Literary Analysis and Reading Transparencies, p. 142	• Vocabulary Development, SE p. 1201: bronchitis, cronies, barometer, authology • Greek Suffix -itis, SE p. 1216; TR Selection Support, p. 306	• Commonly Confused Words: affect and effect, SE p. 1216; TR Selection Support, p. 307; WG Writing and Grammar, p. 648

Key to Program References: SE: Student Edition **TR:** Teaching Resources **WG:** Writing and Grammar

Unit 6 *Prosperity and Protest (1946–Present)*

Writing	Extension Activities	Assessment	Technology
• Writing Lesson: Comparison-and-Contrast Essay, SE p. 1108; WG Writing and Grammar, p. 166	• Listening and Speaking: Interview, SE p. 1108 • Research and Technology: Anthology, SE p. 1108 • TR Extension Activities, p. 64	• Selection Test, TR Formal Assessment, pp. 275–277 • TR Open Book Test, pp. 190–192 • Writing Rubric [for Writing Lesson], TR Performance Assess. and Portfolio Mgmt., p. 19	• Interest Grabber Video, Tape 6 • Listening to Literature, Audio-cassettes, Side 37; Audio CDs, CD 21 • Got It! Assessment Videotapes, Tape 5 • WG Writing and Grammar iText
• Writing Lesson: Analytical Essay, SE p. 1125; WG Writing and Grammar, p. 37	• Listening and Speaking: Opening Statement, SE p. 1125 • Research and Technology: Essay, SE p. 1125 • TR Extension Activities, p. 65	• Selection Test, TR Formal Assessment, pp. 282–284 • TR Open Book Test, pp. 193–195 • Listening Rubric [for Listening and Speaking activity], TR Performance Assess. and Portfolio Mgmt., p. 26	• Interest Grabber Video, Tape 6 • Listening to Literature, Audio-cassettes, Side 37; Audio CDs, CD 21 • Got It! Assessment Videotapes, Tape 5 • WG Writing and Grammar iText
• Writing Lesson: Letter to the Author, SE p. 1144; WG Writing and Grammar, p. 311	• Listening and Speaking: Speech, SE p. 1144 • Research and Technology: Team Report, SE p. 1144 • TR Extension Activities, p. 66	• Selection Test, TR Formal Assessment, pp. 285–287 • TR Open Book Test, pp. 196–198 • Listening Rubric [for Listening and Speaking activity], TR Performance Assess. and Portfolio Mgmt., p. 55	• Interest Grabber Video, Tape 6 • Listening to Literature, Audio-cassettes, Side 38; Audio CDs, CD 22 • Got It! Assessment Videotapes, Tape 6 • WG Writing and Grammar iText
• Writing Lesson: Roy's Journal, SE p. 1159; WG Writing and Grammar, p. 309	• Listening and Speaking: Radio Play, SE p. 1159 • Research and Technology: Illustrated Report, SE p. 1159 • TR Extension Activities, p. 67	• Selection Test, TR Formal Assessment, pp. 291–293 • TR Open Book Test, pp. 199–201	• Interest Grabber Video, Tape 6 • Listening to Literature, Audio-cassettes, Side 38; Audio CDs, CD 22 • Got It! Assessment Videotapes, Tape 6 • WG Writing and Grammar iText
• Writing Lesson: Book Review, SE p. 1177; WG Writing and Grammar, p. 272	• Listening and Speaking: Dramatic Reading, SE p. 1177 • Research and Technology: Written Report, SE p. 1177 • TR Extension Activities, p. 68	• Selection Test, TR Formal Assessment, pp. 294–296 • TR Open Book Test, pp. 202–204	• Interest Grabber Video, Tape 6 • Listening to Literature, Audio-cassettes, Side 39; Audio CDs, CD 23 • Got It! Assessment Videotapes, Tape 6 • WG Writing and Grammar iText
• Writing Lesson: Literary Analysis, SE p. 1189; WG Writing and Grammar, p. 311	• Listening and Speaking: Debate, SE p. 1189 • Research and Technology: Multimedia Presentation, SE p. 1189 • TR Extension Activities, p. 69	• Selection Test, TR Formal Assessment, pp. 297–299 • TR Open Book Test, pp. 205–207 • Rubric [for Writing Lesson], TR Performance Assess. and Portfolio Mgmt., p. 23	• Interest Grabber Video, Tape 6 • Listening to Literature, Audio-cassettes, Side 39; Audio CDs, CD 23 • Got It! Assessment Videotapes, Tape 6 • WG Writing and Grammar iText
• Writing Lesson: Ghost Story, SE p. 1199; WG Writing and Grammar, p. 74	• Listening and Speaking: Dramatic Presentation, SE p. 1199 • Research and Technology: Multimedia Cultural Presentation, SE p. 1199 • TR Extension Activities, p. 70	• Selection Test, TR Formal Assessment, pp. 300–302 • TR Open Book Test, pp. 208–210 • Rubric [for Writing Lesson], TR Performance Assess. and Portfolio Mgmt., pp. 13, 15	• Interest Grabber Video, Tape 6 • Listening to Literature, Audio-cassettes, Side 40; Audio CDs, CD 23 • Got It! Assessment Videotapes, Tape 6 • WG Writing and Grammar iText
• Writing Lesson: Advice Column, SE p. 1217; WG Writing and Grammar, p. 226	• Listening and Speaking: Eulogy, SE p. 1217 • Research and Technology: Costume Proposal, SE p. 1217 • TR Extension Activities, p. 71	• Selection Test, TR Formal Assessment, pp. 303–305 • TR Open Book Test, pp. 211–213 • Rubric [for Writing Lesson], TR Performance Assess. and Portfolio Mgmt., p. 10	• Interest Grabber Video, Tape 6 • Listening to Literature, Audio-cassettes, Side 40; Audio CDs, CD 23 • Got It! Assessment Videotapes, Tape 6 • WG Writing and Grammar iText

PROGRAM PLANNER

Program Planner

Selection	Reading	Literary Analysis	Vocabulary	Grammar
"Camouflaging the Chimera," Yusef Komunyakaa, SE p. 1220; **"Ambush,"** from ***The Things They Carried,*** Tim O'Brien, SE p. 1222 Reading Level: Challenging, Average	• Picturing the Action, SE p. 1219; TR Selection Support, p. 312; TR Literary Analysis and Reading Transparencies, p. 143	• First-Person Narrator, SE p. 1219; TR Selection Support, p. 313; TR Literary Analysis and Reading Transparencies, p. 144	• Vocabulary Development, SE p. 1219: refuge, ambush, ammunition, muzzle, gape • Words From War, SE p. 1226; TR Selection Support, p. 310	• Noun Clauses, SE p. 1226; TR Selection Support, p. 311; WG Writing and Grammar, p. 460
The Crucible, Act I, Arthur Miller, SE p. 1233 Reading Level: Average	• Questioning the Characters' Motives, SE p. 1232; TR Selection Support, p. 316; TR Literary Analysis and Reading Transparencies, p. 145	• Dialogue and Stage Directions, SE p. 1232; TR Selection Support, p. 317; TR Literary Analysis and Reading Transparencies, p. 146	• Vocabulary Development, SE p. 1232: predilection, ingratiating, dessembling, calumny, inculcation, propitiation, licentious • Latin Root -grat-, SE p. 1265; TR Selection Support, p. 314	• Pronoun Case in Incomplete Constructions, SE p. 1265; TR Selection Support, p. 315; WG Writing and Grammar, p. 572
The Crucible, Act II, Arthur Miller, SE p. 1267 Reading Level: Average	• Reading Drama, SE p. 1266; TR Selection Support, p. 320; TR Literary Analysis and Reading Transparencies, p. 147	• Allusion, SE p. 1266; TR Selection Support, p. 321; TR Literary Analysis and Reading Transparencies, p. 148	• Vocabulary Development, SE p. 1266: pallor, ameliorate, avidly, base, deference, theology, quail, gingerly, abomination, blasphemy • Greek Suffix -logy, SE p. 1289; TR Selection Support, p. 318	• Commas After Introductory Words, SE p. 1289; TR Selection Support, p. 319; WG Writing and Grammar, p. 696
The Crucible, Act III, Arthur Miller, SE p. 1291 Reading Level: Average	• Categorizing Characters by Role, SE p. 1290; TR Selection Support, p. 324; TR Literary Analysis and Reading Transparencies, p. 149	• Dramatic and Verbal Irony, SE p. 1290; TR Selection Support, p. 325; TR Literary Analysis and Reading Transparencies, p. 150	• Vocabulary Development, SE p. 1290: contentious, deposition, imperceptible, deferentially, anonymity, prodigious, effrontery, confounded, incredulously, blanched • Concept Development: Legal Terms, SE p. 1317; TR Selection Support, p. 322	• Subject and Verb Agreement in Inverted Sentences, SE p. 1317; TR Selection Support, p. 323; WG Writing and Grammar, p. 584
The Crucible, Act IV, Arthur Miller, SE p. 1319 Reading Level: Average	• Applying Themes to Contemporary Events, SE p. 1318; TR Selection Support, p. 328; TR Literary Analysis and Reading Transparencies, p. 151	• Theme, SE p. 1318; TR Selection Support, p. 329; TR Literary Analysis and Reading Transparencies, p. 152	• Vocabulary Development, SE p. 1318: agape, conciliatory, beguile, floundering, retaliation, adamant, cleave, sibilance, tantalized, purged • Concept Development: Words From Myths, SE p. 1336; TR Selection Support, p. 326	• Commonly Confused Words: *raise* and *rise,* SE p. 1336; TR Selection Support, p. 327; WG Writing and Grammar, p. 520

Key to Program References: SE: Student Edition **TR:** Teaching Resources **WG:** Writing and Grammar

Unit 6 *Prosperity and Protest (1946–Present)*

Writing	Extension Activities	Assessment	Technology
• Writing Lesson: Newspaper Article, SE p. 1227; WG Writing and Grammar, p. 80	• Listening and Speaking: Interview, SE p. 1227 • Research and Technology: Multimedia Presentation, SE p. 1227 • TR Extension Activities, p. 72	• Selection Test, TR Formal Assessment, pp. 306–308 • TR Open Book Test, pp. 214–216	• Interest Grabber Video, Tape 6 • Listening to Literature, Audio-cassettes, Side 40; Audio CDs, CD 23 • Got It! Assessment Videotapes, Tape 6 • WG Writing and Grammar iText
• Writing Lesson: News Account, SE p. 1265	• Listening and Speaking: Oral Report, SE p. 1265 • TR Extension Activities, p. 73	• Selection Test, TR Formal Assessment, pp. 309–311 • TR Open Book Test, pp. 217–219	• Interest Grabber Video, Tape 6 • Got It! Assessment Videotapes, Tape 6 • WG Writing and Grammar iText
• Writing Lesson: Wanted Poster, SE p. 1289	• Listening and Speaking: Scene, SE p. 1289 • TR Extension Activities, p. 74	• Selection Test, TR Formal Assessment, pp. 312–314 • TR Open Book Test, pp. 220–222	• Interest Grabber Video, Tape 6 • Got It! Assessment Videotapes, Tape 6 • WG Writing and Grammar iText
• Writing Lesson: Character Sketch, SE p. 1317	• Listening and Speaking: Monologue, SE p. 1317 • TR Extension Activities, p. 75	• Selection Test, TR Formal Assessment, pp. 315–317 • TR Open Book Test, pp. 223–225	• Interest Grabber Video, Tape 6 • Got It! Assessment Videotapes, Tape 6 • WG Writing and Grammar iText
• Writing Lesson: Defense of a Character's Actions, SE p. 1337	• Listening and Speaking: Mock Trial, SE p. 1337 • Research and Technology: Comparison-and-Contrast Chart, SE p. 1337 • TR Extension Activities, p. 76	• Selection Test, TR Formal Assessment, pp. 318–320 • TR Open Book Test, pp. 226–228 • Rubric [for Writing Lesson], TR Performance Assess. and Portfolio Mgmt., p. 17	• Interest Grabber Video, Tape 6 • Got It! Assessment Videotapes, Tape 6 • WG Writing and Grammar iText

Unit Features

Unit	Writing About Literature	Reading Informational Materials	Writing Workshop	Listening and Speaking Workshop	Assessment Workshop
1 Beginnings to 1750	Analyze Literary Periods, p. 116	Web Sites: Locating Appropriate Information, p. 88	Narration: Autobiographical Narrative, p. 118	Delivering a Speech, p. 122	Summaries of Written Texts, p. 123
2 A Nation Is Born 1750–1800	Evaluate Literary Themes, p. 218	Newspaper Editorials: Analyzing Logical and Faulty Modes of Persuasion, p. 166	Exposition: Problem-and-Solution Essay, p. 220	Analyzing Persuasive Techniques, p. 224	Cause-and-Effect Relationships, p. 225
3 A Growing Nation 1800–1870	Compare and Contrast Literary Trends, p. 452	Memorandums: Analyzing Text Structures: Patterns of Organization, p. 296	Narration: Reflective Essay, p. 454	Analyzing Media, p. 458	Inferences and Generalizations, p. 459
4 Division, Reconciliation, and Expansion (1850–1914)	Compare and Contrast Literary Themes, p. 692	Public Documents: Analyzing an Author's Beliefs, p. 530	Research: Research Paper, p. 694	Critique Persuasive Arguments, p. 700	Context Clues, p. 701
5 Disillusion, Defiance, and Discontent (1914–1946)	Evaluate Literary Trends, p. 948	Public Relations Documents: Making Inferences, p. 942	Research: Multimedia Presentation, p. 950	Evaluating Communication Methods, p. 954	Sentence-Completion Questions, p. 955
6 Prosperity and Protest (1946–Present)	Analyze Literary Trends, p. 1342	Critical Commentaries: Interpreting an Author's Arguments, p. 1338	Workplace Writing: Job Portfolio, p. 1344	Analyzing the Impact of the Media, p. 1348	Punctuation, Usage, and Sentence Structure, p. 1349

FROM THE CLASSROOM: STRATEGIES FOR SUCCESS

How do we teach the literature we love and still prepare students for high-stakes standardized tests?

The recent emphasis on state and national standards has increased the demands on teachers. Language arts instructors face a daunting balancing act in the classroom. We asked teachers who use *Prentice Hall Literature* for practical advice on confronting this challenge. Here are some of their responses.

Using the Student Edition

✓ Make Cross-Curricular Connections Since I teach both world geography and world literature, my challenge is to open students' minds and hearts to diverse global viewpoints *while* preparing them to perform well on high-stakes standardized tests. In my classroom, I often pair Prentice Hall social studies texts with *Prentice Hall Literature*. The former points out how cultures are shaped by their geography; the latter provides thought-provoking excerpts from diverse classic works. What's more, Prentice Hall's well-rounded package of humanities enrichment materials adds depth and breadth to students' understanding of other cultures.

We must help students "read to understand" to succeed on standardized tests and to succeed in an integrated global society. Thanks to Prentice Hall, one does not have to be sacrificed for the other.

John Ludy
Fremont High School
Fremont, IN

✓ Develop Themes I divide state standards into categories of concepts and themes. I then develop units around these themes. Prentice Hall textbooks provide me with ideas and literature selections to include in each unit. I simply choose the one main concept I want to focus on and center the unit on that particular work. This process connects literary works to specific state standards, while also making these works relevant to students' lives.

Agathaniki (Niki) Locklear
Simon Kenton High School
Independence, KY

✓ Extend Learning I often use the Extension Activities in *Prentice Hall Literature* as resources for research and writing activities that connect with post-scholastic, "real world" problems. The challenge is to find an appropriate degree of difficulty for my students. I view the assignment in the Student Edition as a framework that I adjust to meet the identified objectives.

John Scott
Middlesex High School
Saluda, VA

✓ Maximize Resources Prentice Hall has developed a cohesive program of reading selections, connections to extend meaning, skills lessons, vocabulary study, and grammatical and literary studies that provide the teacher with everything needed to promote learning and ensure students' success on standardized tests.

Martha L. Wildman
Lynn Middle School
Las Cruces, NM

✓ Make Connections Prentice Hall's literary selections come complete with sidebars on reading strategies, literary analysis, critical viewing, vocabulary, and literature in context. I use these prompts as motivational hooks, mini-lessons, or assignment prompts. Such features help my students make meaningful connections in an effort to raise their test scores as well as their awareness of the world of ideas, language, and literature.

Charles E. Youngs
Bethel Park High School
Bethel Park, PA

✓ Use Poetry for Practice Here's an idea to try with students who need help with handling poetry on a standardized test. Put a poem on the overhead for the students to see. As a class, read the poem twice, and then give students 7 to 10 minutes to write about the poem's structure and the ideas it conveys. When students have finished writing, comment quickly on structural and thematic issues, asking students to jot down any important points that they did not include in their own responses. As the year goes on, ask students to write longer responses. All *Prentice Hall Literature* textbooks have dozens of useful poems for this literature/high-stakes testing exercise.

Helen Mundy Hudson
Crawfordsville High School
Crawfordsville, IN

STRATEGIES FOR SUCCESS

Using the Ancillaries

☑ **Monitor Progress** As a former language arts teacher, I have learned that familiarity doth breed . . . success! By using the Selection Tests in the *Formal Assessment* booklet, students become more comfortable with the accepted standardized test format—multiple choice. This workbook helps students not only learn to recognize the language of multiple-choice testing, but also to use the language to guide them in the process of elimination. Class time should be devoted to reviewing the test items and focusing on the specific language of the discriminators. This will increase students' comfort level and better prepare them for a variety of testing experiences.

In addition, the Literary Terms Handbook in the back of the Student Edition is a valuable resource that few make adequate use of.

Helen Spaith
Franklin Heights High School
Columbus, OH

☑ **Use Labels** An aspect of the Prentice Hall materials that I find very helpful is the labeling that accompanies the Thinking About the Selection questions in the Student Edition. These labels help students gain a better understanding of the language of standardized testing as it pertains to recalling, inferring, analyzing, evaluating, and extending information. Prentice Hall also provides materials for less proficient readers, allowing them to increase their level of understanding rather than struggling and becoming frustrated. Finally, Prentice Hall makes materials available on the Internet, allowing students to perform self-assessments and explore information without the time constraints of the classroom.

Holly Carr
Central Crossing High School
Grove City, OH

☑ **Review and Assess** Once students have read a selection in *Prentice Hall Literature* and we have reviewed the skills in focus, I assign the corresponding workbook pages in the *Selection Support: Skills Development Workbook.* Most of the time I allow students to work in pairs or groups. After students have completed the pages, we review and make any necessary corrections. Later these pages become study sheets for test preparation, as the pages can be easily removed from the workbook. Using the Resource Pro, I then design student tests. One of the best features of this portion of the CD-ROM is that the test questions include questions on the vocabulary, grammar, and literary analysis covered in the selection and practiced in the workbook.

Gail Hacker
North Charleston High School
North Charleston, SC

Using the Critical Viewing Questions

☑ **Practice Paragraph Development** One way that I help students prepare for standardized testing is to work on paragraph development. I use artwork in the Student Edition to give the students something to work from. The Critical Viewing question provides the writing prompt, and I show students on the overhead or the chalkboard how to turn the prompt into the topic sentence for a paragraph that answers the question. Then, I ask that students help me develop a paragraph that provides three pieces of evidence to support the topic sentence. This exercise can lead to stronger essays of the kind often asked for with free-responses or reading comprehension on state assessments.

Steve Thalheimer
Laurenceburg High School
Laurenceburg, IN

☑ **Use Picture Prompts** Although I have used *Prentice Hall Literature* consistently as a reading resource and teaching tool, I have found it useful in another invaluable way. The photographs and fine art in the Student Edition can be used as picture prompts, providing students with writing practice for standardized tests.

Linda Fund
Ezra L. Nolan Middle School
Jersey City, NJ

☑ **Analyze Art** Initially, one of the most challenging language arts standards for me to teach was viewing and representing. However, the fine art and Critical Viewing questions in *Prentice Hall Literature* have made this standard much more attainable. I select paintings from each unit in *Prentice Hall Literature* for my students to analyze critically. For example, my students view *Washington Crossing the Delaware* by Emanuel Gottlieb Leutze and answer questions about the setting, mood, and conflict. They then draw conclusions and make inferences about the action in the painting. This task covers an array of learning expectations and helps to prepare students for standardized tests. The questions for these assignments can be objective like most standardized tests or subjective to help students develop writing skills. Perhaps the best outcome is that my students now love "reading" art!

Cathy Robbs
Chattanooga Central High School
Harrison, TN

PRENTICE HALL
LITERATURE

Timeless Voices, Timeless Themes

THE AMERICAN EXPERIENCE

PEARSON

Prentice Hall

Upper Saddle River, New Jersey
Needham, Massachusetts

Copyright © 2005 by Pearson Education, Inc., publishing as Pearson Prentice Hall, Upper Saddle River, New Jersey 07458. All rights reserved. Printed in the United States of America. This publication is protected by copyright, and permission should be obtained from the publisher prior to any prohibited reproduction, storage in a retrieval system, or transmission in any form or by any means, electronic, mechanical, photocopying, recording, or likewise. For information regarding permission(s), write to: Rights and Permissions Department.

Pearson Prentice Hall™ is a trademark of Pearson Education, Inc.
Pearson® is a registered trademark of Pearson plc.
Prentice Hall® is a registered trademark of Pearson Education, Inc.

ISBN 0-13-180436-7
2 3 4 5 6 7 8 9 10   08 07 06 05 04

Cover: *Travel by Ox-Drawn Covered Wagons,* Artist unknown, Courtesy of the Bancroft Library, University of California, Berkeley

ACKNOWLEDGMENTS

Grateful acknowledgment is made to the following for copyrighted material:

Amistad Research Center, administered by Thompson and Thompson "From the Dark Tower" by Countee Cullen published in *Copper Sun,* Harper & Bros., © 1927, renewed 1954 by Ida Cullen. Copyrights held by the Amistad Research Center, administered by Thompson and Thompson, New York, NY. Used by permission.

Arte Público Press "To Walt Whitman" by Angela de Hoyos from *In Other Words: Literature by Latinas of the United States* (Houston: Arte Público Press, University of Houston, 1994).

The James Baldwin Estate "The Rockpile" is collected in *Going to Meet the Man,* (c) 1965 by James Baldwin. Copyright renewed. Published by Vintage Books. Used by arrangement with the James Baldwin Estate.

Peter Basch, Literary Agent "When Grizzlies Walked Upright" (Modoc) from *American Indian Myths and Legends,* selected and edited by Richard Erdoes and

Alfonso Ortiz, published by Pantheon Books. Copyright © 1984 by Richard Erdoes and Alfonso Ortiz.

Susan Bergholz Literary Services "Antojos" by Julia Alvarez, copyright © 1991 by Julia Alvarez. Later published in slightly different form in *How the Garcia Girls Lost Their Accents,* copyright © 1991 by Julia Alvarez. Published by Plume, an imprint of Dutton Signet, a division of Penguin USA, Inc., and originally in hardcover by Algonquin Books of Chapel Hill. "Straw into Gold" by Sandra Cisneros. Copyright © 1987 by Sandra Cisneros. First published in *The Texas Observer,* September 1987. Reprinted by permission of Susan Bergholz Literary Services, New York. All rights reserved.

(Acknowledgments continue on page R58, which constitutes an extension of this copyright page.)

PRENTICE HALL
LITERATURE

Timeless Voices, Timeless Themes

COPPER

BRONZE

SILVER

GOLD

PLATINUM

THE AMERICAN EXPERIENCE

THE BRITISH TRADITION

CONTRIBUTING AUTHORS

The contributing authors guided the direction and philosophy of *Prentice Hall Literature: Timeless Voices, Timeless Themes*. Working with the development team, they helped to build the pedagogical integrity of the program and to ensure its relevance for today's teachers and students.

Kate Kinsella

Kate Kinsella, Ed.D., is a faculty member in the Department of Secondary Education at San Francisco State University. A specialist in second-language acquisition and adolescent reading and writing, she teaches coursework addressing language and literacy development across the secondary curricula. She has taught high-school ESL and directed SFSU's *Intensive English Program* for first-generation bilingual college students. She maintains secondary classroom involvement by teaching an academic literacy class for second-language learners through the University's *Step to College* partnership program. A former Fulbright lecturer and perennial institute leader for TESOL, the California Reading Association, and the California League of Middle Schools, Dr. Kinsella provides professional development nationally on topics ranging from learning-style enhancement to second-language reading. Her scholarship has been published in journals such as the *TESOL Journal*, the *CATESOL Journal*, and the *Social Studies Review*. Dr. Kinsella earned her M.A. in TESOL from San Francisco State University and her Ed.D. in Second Language Acquisition from the University of San Francisco.

Kevin Feldman

Kevin Feldman, Ed.D., is the Director of Reading and Early Intervention with the Sonoma County Office of Education (SCOE). His career in education spans thirty-one years. As the Director of Reading and Early Intervention for SCOE, he develops, organizes, and monitors programs related to K–12 literacy and prevention of reading difficulties. He also serves as a Leadership Team Consultant to the California Reading and Literature Project and assists in the development and implementation of K–12 programs throughout California. Dr. Feldman earned his undergraduate degree in Psychology from Washington State University and has a Master's degree in Special Education, Learning Disabilities, and Instructional Design from U.C. Riverside. He earned his Ed.D. in Curriculum and Instruction from the University of San Francisco.

Colleen Shea Stump

Colleen Shea Stump, Ph.D., is a Special Education Supervisor in the area of Resource and Inclusion for Seattle Public Schools. She has served as a professor and chairperson for the Department of Special Education at San Francisco State University. She continues as a lead consultant in the area of collaboration for the California State Improvement Grant and travels the state of California providing professional development training in the areas of collaboration, content literacy instruction, and inclusive instruction. Dr. Stump earned her doctorate at the University of Washington, her M.A. in Special Education from the University of New Mexico, and her B.S. in Elementary Education from the University of Wisconsin–Eau Claire.

Joyce Armstrong Carroll

In her forty-year career, Joyce Armstrong Carroll, Ed. D., has taught on every grade level from primary to graduate school. In the past twenty years, she has trained teachers in the teaching of writing. A nationally known consultant, she has served as president of TCTE and on NCTE's Commission on Composition. More than fifty of her articles have appeared in journals such as *Curriculum Review, English Journal, Media & Methods, Southwest Philosophical Studies, English in Texas,* and the *Florida English Journal.* With Edward E. Wilson, Dr. Carroll co-authored *Acts of Teaching: How to Teach Writing* and co-edited *Poetry After Lunch: Poetry to Read Aloud.* She co-directs the New Jersey Writing Project in Texas.

Edward E. Wilson

A former editor of *English in Texas,* Edward E. Wilson has served as a high-school English teacher and a writing consultant in school districts nationwide. Wilson has served on both the Texas Teacher Professional Practices Commission and NCTE's Commission on Composition. Wilson's poetry appears in Paul Janeczko's anthology *The Music of What Happens.* With Dr. Carroll, he co-wrote *Acts of Teaching: How to Teach Writing* and co-edited *Poetry After Lunch: Poetry to Read Aloud.* Wilson co-directs the New Jersey Writing Project in Texas.

PROGRAM ADVISORS

The program advisors provided ongoing input throughout the development of *Prentice Hall Literature: Timeless Voices, Timeless Themes*. Their valuable insights ensure that the perspectives of the teachers throughout the country are represented within this literature series.

Diane Cappillo
English Department Chair
Barbara Goleman Senior High School
Miami, Florida

Anita Clay
Language Arts Instructor
Gateway Institute of Technology
St. Louis, Missouri

Ellen Eberly
Language Arts Instructor
Catholic Memorial High School
West Roxbury, Massachusetts

Nancy Fahner
L.A.M.P. Lansing Area Manufacturing
  Partnership
Ingham Intermediate School District
Mason, Michigan

Terri Fields
Instructor of Language Arts,
  Communication Arts, and Author
Sunnyslope High School
Phoenix, Arizona

Susan Goldberg
Language Arts Instructor
Westlake Middle School
Thornwood, New York

Margo L. Graf
English Department Chair, Speech,
  Yearbook, Journalism
Lane Middle School
Fort Wayne, Indiana

Christopher E. Guarraia
Language Arts Instructor
Lakewood High School
Saint Petersburg, Florida

V. Pauline Hodges
Teacher, Educational Consultant
Forgan High School
Forgan, Oklahoma

Karen Hurley
Language Arts Instructor
Perry Meridian Middle School
Indianapolis, Indiana

Lenore D. Hynes
Language Arts Coordinator
Sunman-Dearborn Community
  Schools
Sunman, Indiana

Linda Kramer
Language Arts Instructor
Norman High School North
Norman, Oklahoma

Thomas S. Lindsay
Assistant Superintendent of Schools
Manheim District 83
Franklin Park, Illinois

Agathaniki (Niki) Locklear
English Department Chair
Simon Kenton High School
Independence, Kentucky

Ashley MacDonald
Language Arts Instructor
South Forsyth High School
Cumming, Georgia

Mary Ellen Mastej
Language Arts Instructor
Scott Middle School
Hammond, Indiana

Nancy L. Monroe
English, Speed Reading Teacher
Bolton High School
Alexandria, Louisiana

Jim Moody
Language Arts Instructor
Northside High School
Fort Smith, Arkansas

David Morris
Teacher of English, Writing,
  Publications, Yearbook
Washington High School
South Bend, Indiana

Rosemary A. Naab
English Department Chair
Ryan High School
Archdiocese of Philadelphia
Philadelphia, Pennsylvania

Ann Okamura
English Teacher
Laguna Creek High School
Elk Grove, California

Tucky Roger
Coordinator of Languages
Tulsa Public Schools
Tulsa, Oklahoma

Jonathan L. Schatz
English Teacher/Team Leader
Tappan Zee High School
Orangeburg, New York

John Scott
Assistant Principal
Middlesex High School
Saluda, Virginia

Ken Spurlock
Assistant Principal, Retired
Boone County High School
Florence, Kentucky

Dr. Jennifer Watson
Secondary Language Arts
  Coordinator
Putnam City Schools
Oklahoma City, Oklahoma

Joan West
Assistant Principal
Oliver Middle School
Broken Arrow, Oklahoma

PART 3   The Puritan Influence

SKILLS WORKSHOPS

This selection is featured in
the *Reader's Companion* series.

UNIT 2 A Nation Is Born (1750–1800)

PART 3 Defining an American

SKILLS WORKSHOPS

RC This selection is featured in the *Reader's Companion* series.

UNIT 3

A Growing Nation (1800–1870)

RC This selection is featured in the *Reader's Companion* series.

UNIT 4

Division, Reconciliation, and Expansion (1850–1914)

This selection is featured in the *Reader's Companion* series.

UNIT 5

Disillusion, Defiance, and Discontent (1914–1946)

PART 3 From Every Corner of the Land

This selection is featured in the *Reader's Companion* series.

Contents ◆ xv

UNIT 5

Disillusion, Defiance, and Discontent (1914–1946) (continued)

UNIT 6

Prosperity and Protest (1946–Present)

This selection is featured in the *Reader's Companion* series.

Contents ◆ xvii

xvii

UNIT 6

Prosperity and Protest (1946–Present) (continued)

Skills Workshops

Resources

This selection is featured in the *Reader's Companion* series.

COMPARING LITERARY WORKS

READING INFORMATIONAL MATERIALS

CONNECTIONS: LITERATURE PAST AND PRESENT

WRITING WORKSHOPS

LISTENING AND SPEAKING WORKSHOPS

ASSESSMENT WORKSHOPS

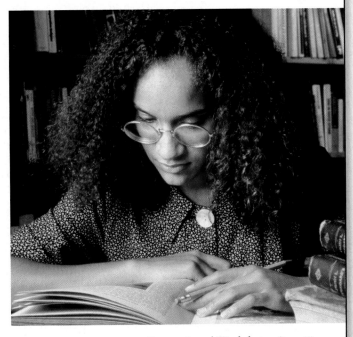

Unit Objectives

1. To read selections from the beginnings of the American literary tradition through 1750

2. To apply literal comprehension strategies appropriate for reading these selections

3. To analyze literary elements

4. To use a variety of strategies to read unfamiliar words and to build vocabulary

5. To learn elements of grammar, usage, and style

6. To use recursive writing processes to write in a variety of forms

7. To develop listening and speaking skills

8. To express and support responses to various types of texts

9. To prepare, organize, and present literary interpretation

Meeting the Objectives

With each selection, you will find instructional material and opportunities through which students can meet these objectives. You will find additional practice pages for reading strategies, literary elements, vocabulary, and grammar in the **Selection Support** booklet in the **Teaching Resources** box.

Background

Art

World Map, 1630

This map of the world in 1630 contains much detail. The Latin legend written across the top reads "New Geographic and Hydrographic Map of All the Lands of the Globe." The four elements—fire (Ignis), air (Aer), water (Aqua), and earth (Terra)—are depicted above and below the two large hemispheres. The portraits in the four corners (clockwise from top left) are of Julius Caesar, Ptolemy, Mercator, and Hondius.

1. How much of the New World had been explored by 1630?
   Answer: The outlines of South America and the Atlantic coastline of Central and North American are roughly accurate.

2. What name was given to the northeastern area of what is now the United States?
   Answer: Nova Britannia

World Map, 1630, The Huntington Library, Art Collections and Botanical Gardens, San Marino, CA

UNIT FEATURES

Connections	Reading Informational Materials
Every unit contains a feature that connects literature to a related topic, such as art, science, or history. Use the information and questions on the Connections page to help students enrich their understanding of the selections presented in the unit.	These selections will help students learn to analyze and evaluate informational materials, such as workplace documents, technical directions, and consumer materials. Students will learn about the organization and features unique to nonnarrative texts. In this unit, students will learn to read a site on the World Wide Web.

> **"** *We shall be as a City upon a Hill, the eyes of all people are upon us; so that if we shall deal falsely with our God in this work we have undertaken and so cause him to withdraw his present help from us, we shall be made a story and a by-word through the world.* **"**

—John Winthrop,
Governor of the Massachusetts
Bay Colony

ASSESSMENT RESOURCES

📖 **Selection Support:** Skills Development Workbook
📖 **Formal Assessment**
📖 **Open Book Tests**
📖 **Performance Assessment and Portfolio Management**
📖 **Extension Activities**

Assessing Student Progress

Listed below are tools to help you to measure the degree to which students meet the unit objectives.

Informal Assessment

The questions in the Review and Assess sections are a first level of response to the concepts and skills presented in the selections. Students' responses are a brief, informal measure of their grasp of the material. These responses can indicate where further instruction and practice are needed. Then follow up with the practice pages in the **Selection Support: Skills Development Workbook.**

Formal Assessment

The **Formal Assessment** workbook contains Selection Tests and Unit Tests.

- Selection Tests measure comprehension and skills acquisition for each selection or group of selections.
- Each Unit Test provides students with 30 multiple-choice questions and five essay questions designed to assess students' knowledge of the literature and skills taught in the unit.

The Open Book Tests ask students to demonstrate their ability to synthesize and communicate information from selections or groups of selections.

To assess students writing, you will find rubrics and scoring models in the **Performance Assessment and Portfolio Management** booklet. In this booklet you will also find scoring rubrics for listening and speaking activities.

Alternative Assessment

The **Extension Activities** booklet contains writing activities, listening and speaking activities, and research and technology activities that are appropriate for students with different ability levels. You may also use these activities as an alternative measurement of students' growth.

Using the Timeline

The timeline can serve a number of instructional purposes, as follows:

Getting an Overview

Use the timeline to help students get a quick overview of themes and events of the period. This approach will benefit all students but may be especially helpful for visually oriented students, English-language learners, and those less proficient in reading. (For strategies in using the timeline as an overview, see the bottom of this page.)

Thinking Critically

Have students answer critical-thinking questions about the timeline to help them establish the "so what" behind the "what happened." (For Critical Thinking and Critical Viewing questions, see the bottom and side columns of the facing page.)

Connecting to Selections

Have students refer back to the timeline when beginning to read individual selections. By consulting the timeline regularly, they will gain a better sense of the period's chronology. In addition, they will appreciate what was occurring in the world that gave rise to these works of literature.

Projects

Students can use the timeline as a launching pad for projects like these:

- **Customized Timeline** Have students create period timelines in their notebooks, adding key details as they read new selections. They can use dates from this timeline as a starting framework.

- **Special Report** Have students scan the timeline for items that interest them, research these further, and report on them to the class.

Timeline 1490–1750

| 1490 | 1542 | 1594 |

American Events

- **1492** Christopher Columbus lands in the Bahamas. ▼

- **1513** Juan Ponce de Léon lands on the Florida peninsula.
- **1515** Vasco Núñez de Balboa reaches the Pacific Ocean.
- **1540** Francisco Vázquez de Coronado explores the Southwest.

- **1565** St. Augustine, Florida: First permanent settlement in U.S., founded by Pedro Menendez.
- **1586** English colony at Roanoke Island disappears; known as the Lost Colony.
- **1590** Iroquois Confederacy established to stop warfare among the Five Nations.

- **1607** First permanent English settlement at Jamestown, Virginia.
- **1608** Captain John Smith writes *A True Relation . . . of Virginia.* ◄
- **1620** Pilgrims land at Plymouth, Massachusetts. ▼

- **1636** Harvard College founded in Massachusetts.
- **1639** First printing press in English-speaking North America arrives in Massachusetts.
- **1640** *Bay Psalm Book* published; first book printed in the colonies.

World Events

- **1499** England: 20,000 die in London plague.
- **1503** Italy: Leonardo da Vinci paints the *Mona Lisa.*
- **1508** Italy: Michelangelo paints ceiling of Sistine Chapel.
- **1518** Africa: Barbarossa drives the Spanish from most of Algeria.
- **1519** Spain: Chocolate introduced to Europe.
- **1520** Magellan sails around the world.
- **1520** Mexico: Cortez conquers Aztecs.
- **1531** Peru: Pizarro conquers Incas.

- **1558** England: Elizabeth I inherits throne. ▶
- **1560** Brazil: Smallpox epidemic kills millions.
- **1566** Belgium: Bruegel paints *The Wedding Dance.*
- **1580** France: Montaigne's *Essays* published.

- **1595** England: Shakespeare completes *A Midsummer Night's Dream.*
- **1605** Spain: Cervantes publishes Part I of *Don Quixote.*
- **1609** Italy: Galileo builds first telescope.
- **1630** Japan: All Europeans expelled.
- **1639** India: English establish settlement at Madras.
- **1642** Holland: Rembrandt paints *The Nightwatch.*
- **1642** England: Civil War begins.
- **1644** China: Ming Dynasty ends.

GETTING AN OVERVIEW OF THE PERIOD

Introduction To give students an overview of the period, indicate the span of dates along the top of the timeline. Point out the division of the timeline into American and World Events, and have students practice scanning the timeline to look at both categories. Finally, tell them that the events in the timeline represent beginnings, turning points, and endings. For example, European explorers first encountered Native Americans in 1492.

Key Events One story this timeline tells is that of the European discovery and colonization of the North American continent. Have students select items in the American Events section that help tell this story.
Possible answers: 1607, first permanent English settlement at Jamestown; 1647, Massachusetts establishes free public schools.

Have students look at American Events from 1698 to 1741 and identify trends.
Answer: The colonies were in the midst of a religious revival.

American and World Events

- **1647** Massachusetts establishes free public schools.
- **1650** Publication (in London) of Anne Bradstreet's *The Tenth Muse . . .*, a collection of poems.

- **1675** King Philip, chief of the Wampanoags, begins raiding New England frontier towns. ▲
- **1692** Salem witchcraft trials result in the execution of twenty people.

- **1652** South Africa: First Dutch settlers arrive.
- **1664** France: Molière's *Tartuffe* first performed.
- **1667** England: Milton publishes *Paradise Lost*.
- **1683** China: All ports opened to foreign trade.
- **1690** India: Calcutta founded by British.

- **1735** John Peter Zenger acquitted of libel, furthering freedom of the press.
- **1741** Great Awakening, a series of religious revivals, begins to sweep the colonies. ▼

- **1741** Jonathan Edwards first delivers his sermon *Sinners in the Hands of an Angry God*.

- **1702** England: First daily newspaper begins publication.
- **1719** England: Daniel Defoe publishes *Robinson Crusoe*.
- **1721** Germany: Bach composes *Brandenburg Concertos*.
- **1726** England: Jonathan Swift publishes *Gulliver's Travels*.
- **1727** Brazil: First coffee plants cultivated. ◄
- **1748** France: Montesquieu publishes *The Spirit of Laws*.

Analyzing the Timeline

1. **(a)** Name three explorers who helped open the North American continent to Europeans. **(b)** Judging by these names, which country took an especially active role in exploration?
   Answer: (a) Juan Ponce de Léon, Vasco Núñez de Balboa, Francisco Vásquez de Coronado **(b)** Spain

2. **(a)** How many years elapsed between the first European encounter with Native Americans and the first permanent European settlement? **(b)** What might account for this length of time?
   Answer: (a) 73 years
   (b) Possible answers: fear of the unknown; difficulty of journey across the ocean

3. **(a)** Name three key developments in colonial life. **(b)** Show how each indicates that life in the colonies improved steadily.
   Answer: (a) founding of Harvard University, first printing press, free public schools **(b)** These developments point to the spread of information and learning.

4. **(a)** What was the cause of the executions of 1692? **(b)** What does this event suggest about colonial life?
   Answer: (a) People were convicted of witchcraft.
   (b) The executions suggest that religious law superseded any other.

5. **(a)** What happened in the field of publishing in 1735? **(b)** What does this reveal?
   Answer: (a) John Peter Zenger was acquitted of libel charges.
   (b) Colonists had begun to recognize freedom of speech as valuable.

▶ **Critical Viewing**

1. What does Columbus's pose indicate?
   Answer: He seems triumphant. The flag shows that he is claiming the land for his country.

2. What does the picture of the Pilgrims' ship suggest about the voyage across the Atlantic?
   Answer: It was probably difficult and dangerous. The ship is small and appears to be tossing in rough water.

3. What does the picture of King Philip's raid suggest about life in the colonies?
   Answer: It suggests that colonists had violent conflicts with Native Americans.

4. What does the picture of the minister suggest about the Puritan style of preaching?
   Answer: The minister's gesture indicates a dramatic style of preaching.

3

Literature of the Period

- Students will encounter Native American works from several of the areas shown on the map on page 4. These works include an Onondaga origin myth "The World on Turtle's Back," p. 16, and an excerpt from *The Navajo Origin Legend*, p. 22 (Southwest).
- Students will gain greater insight into Puritan values and style as they read Anne Bradstreet's "To My Dear and Loving Husband," p. 102, and the excerpt from Jonathan Edwards's "Sinners in the Hands of an Angry God," p. 108.

▶ **Critical Viewing**

Answer: **(a)** any two of the following: Hopi, Pueblo, Navajo, Apache **(b)** Presence or absence of bodies of water, forests, and mountains would lead to different ways of adapting to the natural world and thus to different ways of life.

Beginnings to 1750

More than a century after European explorers first landed in North America, there were still no permanent settlements in the Western Hemisphere north of St. Augustine, Florida. By 1607, however, a small group of English settlers was struggling to survive on a marshy island in the James River in the present state of Virginia. In 1611, Thomas Dale, governor of the colony, wrote a report to the king expressing the colonists' determination to succeed. Despite disease and starvation, Jamestown did survive.

The first settlers were entranced by the native inhabitants they met. They did not at first realize that these earlier Americans, like Europeans, had cultural values and literary traditions of their own. Their literature was entirely oral, for the tribes of North America had not yet developed writing systems. This extensive oral literature, along with the first written works of the colonists, forms the beginning of the American literary heritage.

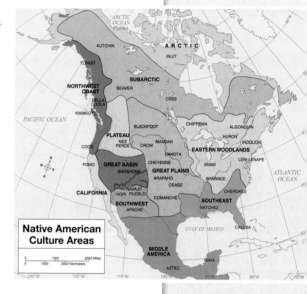

Native American Culture Areas

▲ **Critical Viewing**
As Native Americans spread out to populate North America, they developed varied cultures.
(a) Name two tribes in the Southwest culture area.
(b) What geographic features might have led to the development of different ways of life?
[Interpret]

Historical Background

When Christopher Columbus reached North America in 1492, the continent was already populated, though sparsely, by several hundred Native American tribes. Europeans did not encounter these tribes all at one time. Explorers from different nations came into contact with them at different times. As we now know, these widely dispersed tribes of Native Americans differed greatly from one another in language, government, social organization, customs, housing, and methods of survival.

The Native Americans No one knows for certain when or how the first Americans arrived in what is now the United States. It may have been as recently as 12,000 years ago or as long ago as 70,000 years. Even if the shorter estimate is correct, Native Americans have been on the continent thirty times longer than the Europeans. Colonists from Europe did not begin arriving on the east coast of North America until the late 1500s.

What were the earliest Americans doing for those many centuries? To a great extent, the answer is shrouded in mystery. No written story of the

---

🌟 **ENRICHMENT**

Social Studies Connection

Scholars now believe that "Native American" may be a misleading term, because these peoples actually originated in Asia. They came to this continent by way of a land bridge across the Bering Strait, migrating southward and eastward and eventually spreading over the entire continents of North South, and Central America. The different phases of this migration account for the different linguistic and cultural groups indicated on the map on this page. Remind students that Native Americans had probably been living in the Americas for thousands of years before Europeans arrived.

Native Americans exists. Archaeologists have deduced a great deal from artifacts, however, and folklorists have recorded a rich variety of songs, legends, and myths.

What we do know is that the Native Americans usually, but by no means always, greeted the earliest European settlers as friends. They instructed the newcomers in their agriculture and woodcraft and introduced them to maize, beans, squash, maple sugar, snowshoes, toboggans, and birch bark canoes. Indeed, many more of the European settlers would have succumbed to the bitter northeastern winters had it not been for the help of these first Americans.

▲ Critical Viewing
What Puritan values does this painting illustrate?
[Interpret]

Pilgrims and Puritans A small group of Europeans sailed from England on the *Mayflower* in 1620. The passengers were religious reformers—Puritans who were critical of the Church of England. Having given up hope of "purifying" the Church from within, they chose instead to withdraw from the Church. This action earned them the name Separatists; we know them as the Pilgrims. They landed in North America and established a settlement at what is now Plymouth, Massachusetts. With help from friendly tribes of Native Americans, the Plymouth settlement managed to survive the rigors of North America. The colony never grew very large, however. Eventually, it was engulfed by the Massachusetts Bay Colony, the much larger settlement to the north.

Like the Plymouth Colony, the Massachusetts Bay Colony was founded by religious reformers. These reformers, however, did not withdraw from the Church of England. Unlike the Separatists, they were Puritans who intended instead to reform the Church from within. In America, the Puritans hoped to establish what John Winthrop, governor of the Colony, called a "city upon a hill," a model community guided in all aspects by the Bible. Their form of government would be a theocracy, a state under the immediate guidance of God.

Among the Puritans' central beliefs were the ideas that human beings exist for the glory of God and that the Bible is the sole expression of God's will. They also believed in predestination—John Calvin's doctrine that God has already decided who will achieve salvation and who will not. Nevertheless, those who are to be saved cannot take their salvation for granted. For that reason, all devout Puritans searched their souls with great rigor and frequency for signs of grace. The Puritans felt that they could accomplish good only through continual hard work and self-discipline, a principle known today as the "Puritan ethic."

Background

History

Religion affected every aspect of Puritan life, although the Puritans were not always as stern and otherworldly as they are sometimes pictured. Their writings occasionally revealed a sense of humor, and the hardships of daily life forced them to be practical. In one sense, the Puritans were radical, since they demanded fundamental changes in the Church of England. In another sense, however, they were conservative. They interpreted the Bible literally and insisted on rigid standards for full church membership.

▶Critical Viewing

The painting illustrates the values of hard work, family and children, religion, and community.

CUSTOMIZE INSTRUCTION FOR UNIVERSAL ACCESS

For Less Proficient Readers	For English Learners	For Advanced Readers
Have students preview the art and illustrations for this period before reading "Historical Background." Have them write one or two questions about the illustrations and read the text to find the answers.	Have students use the art and illustrations on these pages to speculate about the era. Have them read the boldfaced heads and formulate questions based on these heads.	Have students use the evidence from "Historical Background" and the accompanying illustrations to draw conclusions about the daily life of colonial teenagers.

Background

Science

Europeans coming to North America for the first time encountered many plants and animals that were previously unknown to them. Among the new types of trees were the locust, the live oak, and the hickory. Fruits, vegetables, and nuts included eggplant, persimmons, pecans, sweet potatoes, and squash.

The colonists adopted the Indians' names for some animals, such as the skunk, the opossum, the chipmunk, the moose, and the raccoon. They made up their own names for others, such as the bullfrog, the garter snake, the mud hen, the potato bug, the groundhog, and the red bird.

Literature of the Period

- In reading Native American pieces like "When Grizzlies Walked Upright," p. 19, students should try to "hear" them as if they are being told aloud. This technique will help students remember that Native American literature was part of an oral tradition.

- In Jonathan Edwards's "Sinners in the Hands of an Angry God," p. 108, students will encounter the sermon, a type of literature that is characteristically Puritan.

▶Critical Viewing

Answer: (a) They both include chairs, tables, and utensils and dishes. **(b)** The landowner's living quarters are luxurious; the slave quarters are simple. The slave house is made of logs. The landowner's house includes ornaments such as pictures on the walls.

Puritanism was in decline throughout New England by the early 1700s, as more liberal Protestant congregations attracted followers. A reaction against this new freedom, however, set in around 1720. The Great Awakening, a series of religious revivals led by such eloquent ministers as Jonathan Edwards and George Whitefield, swept through the colonies. The Great Awakening attracted thousands of converts to many Protestant groups, but it did little to revive old-fashioned Puritanism. Nevertheless, Puritan ideals of hard work, frugality, self-improvement, and self-reliance are still regarded as basic American virtues.

The Southern Planters The Southern Colonies differed from New England in climate, crops, social organization, and religion. Prosperous coastal cities grew up in the South, just as in the North, but beyond the southern cities lay large plantations, not small farms. Despite its romantic image, the plantation was in fact a large-scale agricultural enterprise and a center of commerce. Up to a thousand people, many of them enslaved, might live and work on a single plantation.

The first black slaves were brought to Virginia in 1619, a year before the Pilgrims landed at Plymouth. The plantation system and the institution of slavery were closely connected from the very beginning, although slavery existed in every colony, including Massachusetts.

Most of the plantation owners were Church of England members who regarded themselves as aristocrats. The first generation of owners, the men who established the great plantations, were ambitious, energetic, self-disciplined, and resourceful, just as the Puritans were. The way of life on most plantations, however, was more sociable and elegant than that of any Puritan. By 1750, Puritanism was in decline everywhere, and the plantation system in the South was just reaching its peak.

▲ **Critical Viewing** These exhibition rooms in Colonial Williamsburg illustrate the living quarters of African slaves and white landowners. (a) What do these rooms have in common? (b) What are the major differences? **[Compare and Contrast]**

Literature of the Period

It was an oddly assorted group that established the foundations of American literature: the Native Americans with their oral traditions, the Puritans with their preoccupation with sin and salvation, enslaved and free African Americans, and the southern planters with their busy social lives. Indeed, much of the literature that the colonists read was not produced in the colonies—it came from England. Yet, by 1750, there were the clear beginnings of a native literature that would one day be honored throughout the English-speaking world.

Native American Tradition For a long time, Native American literature was viewed mainly as folklore. The consequence was that song lyrics, hero tales, migration legends, and accounts of the creation were studied more for their content than for their literary qualities. In an oral tradition, the telling of a tale may change with each speaker, and the words are almost sure to change over time. Thus, no fixed versions of such literary works exist. Still, in cases where the words of Native American lyrics or narratives have been captured in writing, the language is often poetic and moving. As might be expected in an oral setting, oratory was much prized among Native Americans. The names of certain orators, such as Logan and Red Jacket, were widely known.

The varied Native American cultures produced a diverse body of literature. However, while the myths, legends, and folk tales vary greatly, one common characteristic is the deep respect that Native American literature generally shows for nature. Tales and chants celebrate the wonders of the natural world and its interconnectedness with the world of the spirit.

The samples of Native American literature in this unit reveal the depth and power of those original American voices.

Explorers' Accounts No one knows when the first Europeans came to the Americas. However, archaeological evidence suggests that the seafaring northern Europeans known as Vikings set up small encampments on the islands of northeastern Canada beginning some time around A.D. 1000. Still, our knowledge about Viking settlements is largely speculative. Not until the late fifteenth century did Europe inaugurate an Age of Exploration in which its journeys to the Americas were well documented.

Christopher Columbus, an Italian living in Portugal, was convinced that he could reach Asia by sailing west. After receiving financial backing from Spain's Queen Isabella, he set sail in August of 1492 and landed on October 12 on an island in what is now the Bahamas. He wrote about his experience in his Journal of the First Voyage to America, in which he stressed the rich potential of the new lands that he still regarded as part of Asia.

Other explorers who wrote accounts of their voyages were the Spaniards Alvar Núñez Cabeza de Vaca and García López de Cárdenas. Cabeza de Vaca was one of four survivors of a 400-man expedition to Texas. In his narrative,

---

Background Native American Literature

Native American literature and language are closer to us than students usually realize. Tell them that they can find one-word examples of various tribal languages simply by looking at maps or road signs. A great number of American place names come from Native American words.

Background

Music

Play the "Navajo Night Chant" and "Psalm 100" from the **Listening to Music** Audio CD. Have students locate the Navajo on the map on page 4. Tell students that the "Navajo Night Chant" is performed on the final night of a three- to-seven-day healing ceremony meant to cure sickness by restoring the harmony among the individual, his or her people, and the universe.

Because Puritans believed that the melody of a religious song should not interfere with the message, the psalms were set to simple tunes.

Critical Thinking

1. What motives might have prompted the earliest European explorers to sail to North America?
   Answer: greed, curiosity, sense of adventure

2. What aspect of Native American literature might have caused the Europeans to overlook it?
   Answer: It wasn't written down; it wasn't in a language they could understand.

3. Were Puritan ideals especially suited to the task of colonizing New England? Explain.
   Answer: The Puritan commitment to hard work, frugality, and self-reliance is compatible with establishing a colony in a harsh wilderness.

4. In what way were the roots of the American Civil War planted during colonial times?
   Answer: Southern plantation owners relied more heavily on the labor of enslaved Africans than northerners did.

Background Literature

The Bay Psalm Book was published in Cambridge in 1640. Its full title was *The Whole Book of Psalms Faithfully Translated into English Metre.*

he describes a wilderness that is sometimes bountiful and sometimes very harsh. López de Cárdenas was the first European to see and describe the Grand Canyon, as we learn from Pedro de Castañeda's retelling.

Slave Narrative Olaudah Equiano, who lived about two hundred years later than these European explorers, came to America against his will as an enslaved African. However, he later purchased his freedom, settled in England, and worked to abolish slavery. As part of this effort, he wrote a two-volume autobiography entitled *The Interesting Narrative of the Life of Olaudah Equiano*. It contains a vivid and horrifying account of slaves journeying to America.

"In Adam's Fall/We Sinned All" Just as religion dominated the lives of the Puritans, it also dominated their writings—most of which would not be considered literary works by modern standards. Typically, the Puritans wrote theological studies, hymns, histories, biographies, and autobiographies. The purpose of such writing was to provide spiritual insight and instruction. When Puritans wrote for themselves in journals or diaries, their aim was the serious kind of self-examination they practiced in other aspects of their lives. The Puritans produced neither fiction nor drama because they regarded both as sinful.

A Writer's Voice

Lucy Terry, Earliest Known African American Poet

If Olaudah Equiano wrote the first slave narrative, Lucy Terry wrote what Henry Louis Gates, Jr., and Nellie Y. McKay have called "the earliest known poem by an African American." Like Equiano, Terry was kidnapped from Africa to serve as a slave in America. Also like him, she eventually gained her freedom.

Her 28-line poem entitled "Bars Fight" is the only poem she is known to have written. It describes an ambush by Indians of white families in a place in Massachusetts called "the Bars," meaning "meadows." Its rhythm indicates that it was probably meant to be sung. Transmitted orally for many years, the poem was finally published in 1855. Its first stanza appears below.

from "Bars Fight," by Lucy Terry

August, 'twas the twenty-fifth,
Seventeen hundred forty-six,
The Indians did in ambush lay,
Some very valiant° men to slay,   °valiant
5   The names of whom I'll not leave out:
Samuel Allen like a hero fout,°   °fought
And though he was so brave and bold,
His face no more shall we behold. . . .

✹ ENRICHMENT: Social Studies Connection

African-American Culture

African Americans made up the majority of the population of South Carolina and Georgia. They generally had contact with only a handful of European colonists. As a result, they were able to exercise greater control over their day-to-day existence than those enslaved in other colonies and to preserve many of their cultural traditions. Many had come to South Carolina and Georgia straight from Africa. They still practiced the crafts of their homeland, such as basket weaving and pottery, and they continued singing their music and telling the old stories from home. In some cases they maintained aspects of their native languages. The best-known example of this is Gullah, a combination of English and African. As late as the 1940s, speakers of Gullah were using 4,000 words from the languages of more than 21 separate West African languages. African Americans even preserved the African manner of burial.

The Puritans did write poetry, however, as a vehicle of spiritual enlightenment. Although they were less concerned with a poem's literary form than with its message, some writers were more naturally gifted than others. A few excellent Puritan poets emerged in the 1600s, among them Anne Bradstreet and Edward Taylor. Anne Bradstreet's moving, personal voice and Edward Taylor's devotional intensity shine through the conventional Puritanism of their themes.

The Puritans had a strong belief in education for both men and women. In 1636, they founded Harvard College to ensure a well-educated ministry. Three years later, they set up the first printing press in the colonies. In 1647, free public schools were established in Massachusetts. *The New England Primer,* first published around 1690, combined instruction in spelling and reading with moralistic teachings, such as "In Adam's fall/We sinned all."

One of the first books printed in the colonies was the *Bay Psalm Book,* the standard hymnal of the time. Richard Mather, one of the book's three authors, was the father of Increase Mather, who served for many years as pastor of the North Church in Boston. Increase Mather was also the author of more than 130 books. *Cases of Conscience Concerning Evil Spirits,* published in 1693, was a discourse on the Salem witchcraft trials of the previous year. The trials, conducted in an atmosphere of hysteria, resulted in the hanging of twenty people as witches.

Increase's eldest son, Cotton Mather, far exceeded his father's literary output, publishing at least 400 works in his lifetime. Cotton Mather, like his father, is remembered in part because of his connection with the Salem witchcraft trials. Although he did not actually take part in the trials, his works on witchcraft had helped to stir up some of the hysteria. Still, Cotton Mather was one of the most learned men of his time, a power in the state and a notable author. Although his writing was multifaceted, his theory of writing was simple: The more information a work contains, the better its style.

In fact, the Puritans in general had a theory about literary style. They believed in a plain style of writing, one in which clear statement is the

▲ **Critical Viewing**
The Puritans founded Harvard College at Newtowne in 1636. Three years later, they renamed the city Cambridge to honor the British city where many of the colonists had studied. What does this fact reveal about the group who fled England? **[Draw Conclusions]**

Background
History
As New Englanders took over more and more Indian lands, the Indians began attacking and burning colonial villages and kidnapping women and children for ransom. When Cotton Mather learned that settlers had captured the wife and son of a Native American leader and sold them into slavery, he declared, "It must be bitter as death to him to lose his wife and only son, for the Indians are marvelously fond and affectionate toward their children."

▶**Critical Viewing**
Possible answer: The colonists valued education and sought to re-create important educational institutions in their new country.

Background

Literature

Complied by Benjamin Harris, the *New England Primer* might have sold up to two million copies in the 1700s. It was the standard text from which most colonial children learned to read. Moral instruction was interwoven throughout the text, and letters of the alphabet were taught through inspirational couplets.

highest goal. An ornate or clever style would be a sign of vanity and, as such, would not be in accordance with God's will. Despite the restrictions built into their life and literature, the Puritans succeeded in producing a small body of excellent writing.

Southern Writers Considering the number of brilliantly literate statesmen who would later emerge in the South, especially in Virginia, it seems surprising that only a few notable southern writers appeared prior to 1750. As in Puritan New England, those who were educated produced a substantial amount of writing, but it was mostly of a practical nature. For example, John Smith, the leader of the settlement at Jamestown, Virginia, wrote *The General History of Virginia* to describe his experiences for Europeans. In addition to accounts like Smith's, letters written by southern planters also provide insight into this time period. Unlike the Puritans, southerners did not oppose fiction or drama, and the first theater in America opened in Williamsburg, Virginia, in 1716.

A Living Tradition

John Berryman and Anne Bradstreet

In the 1950s, the American poet John Berryman responded powerfully to the life and work of Puritan poet Anne Bradstreet, who had lived 300 years earlier. He wrote her a long poem of praise entitled "Homage to Mistress Bradstreet." In this adventurous poem, Berryman speaks both in his own voice and in the voice of Bradstreet herself. He also uses unusual sentence structures that seem to suggest the difficulty in contacting Bradstreet and the difficulty of life in the New World.

Speaking as himself in the beginning of the poem, he imagines the terrible "New World winters" that must have "stunned" Bradstreet and her Puritan companions. Berryman also addresses Bradstreet directly, indicating that he is more sympathetic to her poetry than was her busy husband, Simon Bradstreet.

from "Homage to Mistress Bradstreet" by John Berryman

Outside the New World winters in grand dark
white air lashing high thro' the virgin stands°   °unexplored forests

foxes down foxholes sigh,
surely the English heart quails, stunned.
5 I doubt if Simon than this blast, that sea,
spares from his rigor for your poetry
more. We are on each other's hands
who care. Both of our worlds unhanded us.
   Lie stark,

thy eyes look to me mild. Out of maize° & air   °Corn
10 your body's made, and moves. I summon, see,
from the centuries it. . . .

The Planter From Westover

The important literature of the pre-Revolutionary South can be summed up in one name: William Byrd. Byrd lived at Westover, a magnificent plantation on the James River bequeathed to him by his wealthy father. Commissioned in 1728 to survey the boundary line between Virginia and North Carolina, Byrd kept a journal of his experiences. That journal served as the basis for his book, *The History of the Dividing Line*, which was circulated in manuscript form among Byrd's friends in England. Published nearly a century after Byrd's death, the book was immediately recognized as a minor humorous masterpiece.

THE FIRST PRINTING PRESS BROUGHT TO AMERICA.

More of Byrd's papers were published later, establishing his reputation as the finest writer in the pre-Revolutionary South.

The writers whose work appears in this unit are not the great names in American literature. They are the founders, the men and women who laid the groundwork for the towering achievements that followed. The modest awakening of American literature seen in this unit had repercussions that echoed down the years.

▲ Critical Viewing
This is a picture of the first printing press in English-speaking North America. Judging by its appearance, how do you think it worked? **[Infer]**

A Writer's Voice

William Byrd, Writer with a Sense of Humor

Byrd's humor comes through in this anecdote he passes on to readers. It tells about a man from the north of England who out of curiosity explored the Dismal swamp, where Byrd later did his surveying.

from *The History of the Dividing Line* by William Byrd

. . . he, having no compass nor seeing the sun for several days together, wandered about till he was almost famished: but at last he bethought himself of a secret his countrymen make use of to pilot themselves in a dark day. He took a fat louse out of his collar and exposed it to the open day on a piece of white paper which he brought along with him for his journal. The poor insect, having no eyelids, turned himself about till he found the darkest part of the heavens and so made the best of his way toward the north. By this direction he steered himself safe out and gave such a frightful account of the monsters he saw and the distresses he underwent that no mortal since has been hardy enough to go upon the like dangerous discovery.

▶ Critical Viewing
Answer: The printing press probably pressed the inked type against the paper, creating a transfer.

Critical Thinking

1. Why do you think Puritans regarded fiction and drama as sinful?
   Answer: They may have viewed fiction and drama as forms of entertainment rather than of spiritual enlightenment.

2. Why do you think early Americans read so much work produced in England?
   Answer: They relied on what was familiar. Books from England were written in English, which was the language of many of the immigrants.

3. In what way are modern self-help books a reflection of Puritan values?
   Answer: Puritans stressed self-reliance, education, and hard work, as do many self-help books.

1. If the animal and plant species that settlers encountered in North America had been the same as those in Europe, how might American English have developed differently?
   Answer: The settlers probably wouldn't have adopted Indian names for the plants and animals.

2. What does the anglicizing of Native American names suggest about what happens when one language adopts terms from another?
   Answer: Adopted terms are usually altered to make them conform to the adopting language's rules of spelling and pronunciation.

Answers to Activities

1. The following states have Native American names:
   Alabama, Alaska, Arkansas, Arizona, Connecticut, Illinois, Hawaii, Iowa, Kansas, Kentucky, Massachusetts, Michigan, Minnesota, Mississippi, Missouri, Nebraska, North Dakota, Ohio, Oklahoma, South Dakota, Tennessee, Texas, Utah, Wisconsin, Wyoming.

   Different sources give different translations for some of these names. If students have trouble finding sources, suggest that they use an almanac.

2. Answers will vary depending on the area where students live. You might suggest that students use road maps to pick out names of local places. In searching out the origin of names, try consulting local historical societies or Native American organizations.

THE DEVELOPMENT OF AMERICAN ENGLISH
Our Native American Heritage

BY RICHARD LEDERER

If you had been one of the early explorers or settlers of North America, you would have found many things in your new environment unknown to you. The handiest way of filling voids in your vocabulary would have been to ask local Native Americans what words they used. The early colonists began borrowing words from friendly Native Americans almost from the moment of their first contact, and many of those shared words have remained in our everyday language.

ANGLICIZING

Pronouncing many of the Native American words was difficult for the early explorers and settlers. In many instances, they shortened and simplified the names. For example, *otchock* became "woodchuck," *rahaugcum* turned to "raccoon," and the smelly *segankw* transformed into a "skunk." The North American menagerie brought more new words into the English language, including caribou (Micmac), chipmunk (Ojibwa), moose (Algonquian), muskrat (Abenaki), and porgy (Algonquian).

THE POETRY OF PLACE NAMES

William Penn said he did not know "a language spoken in Europe that hath words of more sweetness and greatness." To Walt Whitman, *Monongahela* "rolls with venison richness upon the palate." Some of our loveliest place names—*Susquehanna, Shenandoah, Rappahannock*—began life as Native American words. Such names are the stuff of poetry.

If you look at a map of the United States, you will realize how freely settlers used words of Indian origin to name our states, cities, towns, mountains, lakes, rivers, and ponds. Five of our six Great Lakes and exactly half of our states have names that were borrowed from Native American words. Many other bodies of water and land have taken on names we have come to know as part of the American language.

Food	
squash (Natick)	pecan (Algonquian)
hominy (Algonquian)	pone (Algonquian)
pemmican (Cree)	succotash (Narraganset)

People	
sachem (Narraganset)	papoose (Narraganset)
squaw (Massachuset)	mugwump (Natick)

Native American life	
moccasin (Chippewa)	toboggan (Algonquian)
tomahawk (Algonquian)	wigwam (Abenaki)
tepee (Dakota)	caucus (Algonquian)
pow-wow (Narraganset)	wampum (Massachuset)
bayou (Choctaw)	potlatch (Chinook)
hogan (Navajo)	hickory (Algonquian)
kayak (Inuit)	totem (Ojibwa)

ACTIVITY

1. Brainstorm for a list of the states that have Native American names. Research the origin of each name.

2. With help from an encyclopedia or other source, find out which Native American tribes live—or once lived—in your part of the country. Do their languages survive in many place names? Pick out ten names of places in your state—cities, towns, mountains, or bodies of water—that have Native American names. Try to find their exact origins. What can you find out about the history of your state that will help explain why these names were chosen?

ENRICHMENT: Social Studies Connection

Linguistic Contributions of Immigrants

In addition to borrowing words from Native Americans, English colonists borrowed terms from the languages of various immigrant groups.

The Dutch, who colonized New York and the surrounding area before the English, contributed *cookie, cruller, boss, stoop*, and *scow*.

The French colonists in and around Canada, northern New York, the Ohio River, and New Orleans contributed *levee, cache, caribou, bayou, chowder,* and *portage*.

The Spaniards who first explored the Southwest, Florida, Texas, and the southeast contributed *alligator, armadillo, canoe*, and *maize*.

Meeting of Cultures

Oneida Chieftain Shikellamy, Unknown American Artist, Philadelphia Museum of Art

Selection Planning Guide

This section introduces students to the cultural groups that claimed a place in the early American wilderness. Columbus's *Journal of the First Voyage to America* describes the explorer's first encounter with local peoples. The origin myths and Iroquois constitution that follow offer a closer look at the culture of several Native American nations. The focus shifts to the Southwest with two accounts of Spanish quests to explore the New World. Olaudah Equino's "Interesting Narrative" offers a graphic, firsthand look at how enslaved Africans reached American soil. Part 1 closes with a contemporary short story and song lyrics that helps students relate the "meeting of cultures" theme to modern life.

Background

Art

Oneida Chieftain Shikellamy

Like other Iroquois tribes, the Oneida, who lived in what is now New York State, raised corn and formed permanent settlements. They lived together in longhouses that sheltered extended families. By the nineteenth century, most Oneida were living in either Oneida County, New York; Ontario, Canada; or Green Bay, Wisconsin. About 3,000 Oneida live in these three areas today.

1. What do you think the artist thought of Shikellamy? Why?
   Answer: The artist respected Shikellamy. He is shown full-length, which makes him look impressive and powerful. His posture makes him look commanding. There is nothing in the background to distract the viewer's attention from the chieftain.

2. What does this painting suggest about relations between Indians and Europeans?
   Answer: Shikellamy has a gun, which suggests that they traded with each other. The Europeans would have had to be interested in the Indians in order to paint their portraits. Enemies would not agree to pose for or paint each other; the existence of the portrait suggests that relations were cordial.

INSTRUCTION FOR UNIVERSAL ACCESS

the selections in Part 1, keep these factors in mind:

tle's Back," "When Grizzlies Walked e *Navajo Origin Legend,* and from stitution

accessible, and easy to read.

nstitution contains strong visual

"A Journey Through Texas" and "Boulders Taller than the Great Tower of Seville"

• Less proficient readers may need to break down lengthy sentences in "A Journey Through Texas."

The Earth on Turtle's Back ✦ When Grizzlies Walked Upright
from The Navaho Origin Legend ✦ *from* The Iroquois Constitution

Lesson Objectives

1. **To analyze and respond to literary elements**
   - Literary Analysis: Origin Myths
   - Comparing Literary Works:
2. **To read, comprehend, analyze, and critique myths**
   - Reading Strategy: Recognizing Cultural Details
   - Reading Check questions
   - Review and Assess questions
   - Assessment Practice (ATE)
3. **To develop word analysis skills, fluency, and systematic vocabulary**
   - Vocabulary Development Lesson: Latin Suffix: *-tion*
4. **To understand and apply written and oral language conventions**
   - Spelling Strategy
   - Grammar Lesson: Compound Sentences
5. **To understand and apply appropriate writing and research strategies**
   - Writing Lesson: Retelling of a Story
   - Extension Activity: Logo
6. **To understand and apply listening and speaking strategies**
   - Extension Activity: Dramatic Reenactment

STEP-BY-STEP TEACHING GUIDE	PACING GUIDE
PRETEACH	
Motivate Students and Provide Background	
Use the Motivation activity (ATE p. 14)	5 min.
Read and discuss Author and Background features (SE/ATE pp. 14, 16)	5 min.
Introduce the Concepts	
Introduce the Literary Analysis and Reading Strategy (SE/ATE p. 15)	15 min.
Pronounce the vocabulary words and read their definitions (SE p. 15)	5 min.
TEACH	
Monitor Comprehension	
Informally monitor comprehension by circulating while students read independently or in groups	25 min.
Monitor students' comprehension with the Reading Check notes (SE/ATE pp. 17, 19, 21, 25)	as students read
Develop vocabulary with Vocabulary notes (SE pp. 22, 23, 24, 26; ATE pp. 24)	as students read
Develop Understanding	
Develop students' understanding of origin myths with the Literary Analysis annotations (SE pp. 17, 19, 23, 24; ATE pp. 17, 18, 19, 23, 24)	5 min.
Develop students' ability to identify cultural details with the Reading Strategy annotations (SE pp. 17, 21, 22, 26; ATE pp. 17, 21, 22, 26)	5 min.
ASSESS	
Assess Mastery	
Assess students' mastery of the Reading Strategy and Literary Analysis by having them answer the Review and Assess questions (SE/ATE p. 27)	15–20 min.
Use one or more of the print and media Assessment Resources (ATE p. 28)	up to 45 min.
EXTEND	
Apply Understanding	
Have students complete the Vocabulary Development Lesson and the Grammar Lesson (SE p. 28)	20 min.
Apply students' ability to use effective repetition by using the Writing Lesson (SE/ATE p. 29)	45 min.
Apply students' understanding using one or more of the Extension Activities (SE p. 29)	20–90 min.

A **ACCELERATED INSTRUCTION:**
Use the strategies and activities identified with an **A**.

UNIVERSAL ACCESS
- ● = Below Level Students
- ▲ = On-Level Students
- ■ = Above Level Students

Time and Resource Manager

PRINT	TRANSPARENCIES	TECHNOLOGY
RESOURCES		
• **Beyond Literature,** Cultural Connection: Native American Myths, p. 1 ▲ ■		• **Interest Grabber Video,** Tape 1 ● ▲ ■
• **Selection Support Workbook:** ● ▲ ■ Literary Analysis, p. 4 Reading Strategy, p. 3 Build Vocabulary, p. 1	• **Literary Analysis and Reading Transparencies,** pp. 1 and 2 ● ▲ ■	
• **Adapted Reader's Companion** • **Reader's Companion**		• **Listening to Literature** ● ▲ ■ Audiocassettes, Side 1 Audio CDs, CD 1
• **English Learners' Companion** • **Literatura en español** ● ▲ • **Literary Analysis for Enrichment** ■	• **Fine Art Transparencies, Volume 1,** Art Transparency 1 ● ▲ ■	
• **Formal Assessment:** Selection Test, pp. 1–3 ● ▲ ■ • **Open Book Test,** pp. 1–3 ● ▲ ■ • **Performance Assessment and Portfolio Management,** p. 15 ● ▲ ■ • **PRENTICE HALL** ASSESSMENT *SYSTEM* ● ▲ ■	• **PRENTICE HALL** ASSESSMENT *SYSTEM* ● ▲ ■ Skills Practice Answers and Explanations on Transparencies	• **Test Bank Software** ● ▲ ■ • **Got It! Assessment Videotapes,** Tape 1 ● ▲
• **Selection Support Workbook:** ● ▲ ■ Build Grammar Skills, p. 2 • **Writing and Grammar,** Ruby Level ● ▲ ■ • **Extension Activities,** p. 1 ● ▲ ■	• **Daily Language Practice Transparencies** ● ▲ • **Writing Models and Graphic Organizers on Transparencies,** pp. 17–23 ● ▲ ■	• **Writing and Grammar iText CD-ROM** ● ▲ ■ 💻 *Take It to the Net* www.phschool.com

BLOCK SCHEDULING: Use one 90-minute class period to preteach the selection and have students read it. Use a second 90-minute class period to assess students' mastery of skills and have them complete one of the Extension Activities.

Step-by-Step Teaching Guide for pp. 14–15

Motivation

Ask students to imagine a time before people had developed much scientific knowledge about the world. Remind students that human beings asked the same questions— "Why am I here?" and "How did Earth come to be?"—that they ask today. Form small groups in which students can share any folklore they may know that seeks to explain natural phenomena such as the changing moon, the shifting ocean tides, and the beginnings of various life forms.

Let students know that this series of Native American myths provides insight into early peoples' thinking about the origins of life on Earth.

▣ Interest Grabber Video

As an alternative, you may wish to play "People of the Earth" on Tape 1 to engage students' interest.

❶ Background

More About the Authors

Joseph Bruchac is a novelist, poet, and storyteller of Abenaki descent. He lives in the foothills of New York's Adirondack Mountains, where his ancestors also lived.

The Modoc tale "When Grizzlies Walked Upright" was selected by Richard Erdoes and Alfonso Ortiz along with 165 other tales to appear in their anthology, *American Indian Myths and Legends.*

The Navajo migrated from northwestern Canada to the Southwest around 1300.

The Iroquois—who call themselves People of the Long House—are an alliance of North American tribes whose homelands range from the Atlantic coast westward to Lake Erie and from Ontario southward to North Carolina.

Prepare to Read

❶ The Earth on Turtle's Back ◆ When Grizzlies Walked Upright ◆ *from* The Navajo Origin Legend ◆ *from* The Iroquois Constitution

Onondaga

As one of the original five member nations, the Onondaga were an influential force in the Iroquois Confederation, a league of Iroquoian-speaking Native Americans in what is now the northeastern United States. The Onondaga lived in what is now central New York State, in villages of wood-and-bark long houses occupied by related families. The Onondaga were originally from Canada, where they acquired the French language. They practiced hospitality toward all people and did not believe in fighting. Following the breakup of the Iroquois Confederation after the American Revolution, factions of Onondaga scattered to various parts of the country, but the majority returned to their ancestral valley in New York where the Onondaga reservation now exists.

Modoc

The Modoc once lived in villages in the area of Oregon and Northern California, where they farmed, fished, and hunted. They also had a highly developed method of weaving. Though each village was independent and had its own leaders, in times of war they would band together. In the mid-nineteenth century, the Modoc were forced onto a reservation in Oregon. A band of Modoc, under the leadership of a subchief known as Captain Jack, later fled the reservation. The result was several years of hostilities with United States troops and the eventual relocation of Captain Jack's followers to Oklahoma. They were later allowed to return to the Oregon reservation, since dissolved.

Navajo

Today, the Navajo nation is the largest Native American nation in the United States and has more than 100,000 members. Many live on the Navajo reservation, which covers 24,000 square miles of Arizona, Utah, and New Mexico. Fierce warriors and hunters, the ancient Navajo settled in the Southwest about 1,000 years ago and eventually intermarried with the peaceful Pueblo people, who taught them to weave and raise crops. In 1864, after decades of fighting off encroaching American settlers, the Navajo were driven from their territory by the United States Army. They were eventually allowed to return to a reservation on Navajo land. Many Navajo still carry on native customs, living in earth-and-log structures and practicing the tribal religion.

Iroquois

The powerful Iroquois nation lived in what is now central New York State in the northeastern United States. During the sixteenth century, an Iroquoian mystic and prophet named Dekanawidah traveled from village to village urging the Iroquois-speaking people to stop fighting and band together in peace and brotherhood. Dekanawidah's efforts led to the formation of the Iroquois Confederation of the Five Nations, a league of five Iroquois tribes: Mohawk, Oneida, Seneca, Cayuga, and Onondaga. These tribes were democratic in process and composition, with leaders elected by their own people. The Iroquois tribes still exist today as self-governing bodies.

TEACHING RESOURCES

The following resources can be used to enrich or extend the instruction for pp. 14–15.

Motivation

▣ **Interest Grabber Video,** Tape 1 ▣

Background

▢ **Beyond Literature,** p. 1

▣ *Take It to the Net*
Visit www.phschool.com for Background and hotlinks for the selections.

Literary Analysis

▢ **Literary Analysis and Reading Transparencies,** Origin Myths, p. 2 ▣

▢ **Selection Support:** Literary Analysis, p. 4

Reading

▢ **Literary Analysis and Reading Transparencies,** Recognizing Cultural Details, p. 1 ▣

▣ **BLOCK SCHEDULING:** Resources marked with this symbol provide varied instruction during 90-minute blocks.

Preview

Connecting to the Literature

Just as you collect stories of your family history, cultures create stories to explain their world and place themselves in it. We share a fundamental desire to understand our origins—where we came from and our place in the world. In these stories, different cultures explain the world as they know it.

❷ Literary Analysis

Origin Myths

The need to explain how life began gave birth to myths and traditional stories that were passed down from generation to generation. These stories are called **origin myths.** Myths explain phenomena, including:

- customs, institutions, or religious rites;
- natural landmarks such as a great mountain;
- events beyond people's control.

Look for the roles that nature and animals play in Native American life, and note who or what is responsible for the start of life on Earth.

Comparing Literary Works

In cultures without a written language, the **oral tradition** captures a group's ideals. Stories, poems, and songs convey a people's values, concerns, and history by word of mouth. As you read these selections, compare the worlds they describe. Note what each culture values, fears, or determines important to pass on to its next generation.

❸ Reading Strategy

Recognizing Cultural Details

The Navajo Origin Legend excerpt opens with an image of the spirit men and women drying themselves with cornmeal. They call upon the gods, who appear carrying ears of corn. The references to corn reflect corn's importance to Navajo life.

Literature mirrors the culture that produces it. As you read, **recognize cultural details** by noticing references to objects, animals, or practices that signal how the people of a culture live, think, or worship. Use a chart like the one shown to record the details you find.

Details that signal how each group lives, thinks, or worships	
Onondaga	
Modoc	
Navajo	
Iroquois	

Vocabulary Development

ablutions (ab loo′ shənz) *n.* cleansing the body as part of a religious rite (p. 22)

protruded (prō trood′ id) *v.* jutted out (p. 23)

confederate (kən fed′ ər it) *adj.* united with others for a common purpose (p. 24)

disposition (dis′ pə zish′ ən) *n.* an inclination or tendency (p. 24)

deliberation (di lib′ ər ā′ shən) *n.* careful consideration (p. 26)

Turtle's Back / Grizzlies / from The Navajo Origin Legend / from The Iroquois Constitution ◆ 15

❷ Literary Analysis

Origin Myths

- Tell students that as they read the four selections in this lesson, they will focus on origin myths—traditional stories that recount the origins of life on Earth.
- Remind students that each selection is an example of one culture's origin myth.
- As students follow the narrative of each myth, have them try to recognize which ideas, landmarks, or events the narrative was designed to explain.
- Prepare students to read the selection by telling them that many characters in the narratives are gods, animals, or personified aspects of nature.
- You may wish to review personification with students; ask them to note the capitalization that is used to signify the names of such characters as the Duck.

❸ Reading Strategy

Recognizing Cultural Details

- Origin myths contain cultural details—such as references to objects, animals, or practices—that illuminate how the people of the culture live, think, and worship.
- Remind students that noting the cultural details that appear in each group's origin myth can help them gain insight into the Native American cultures to which these myths belong.
- Encourage students to think about the cultural details that may be evident in a traditional story from their own cultures.

Vocabulary Development

- Pronounce each vocabulary word for students, and read the definitions as a class. Have students identify any words with which they are already familiar.

 E-Teach

Visit E-Teach at www.phschool.com for teachers' essays on how to teach, with questions and answers.

CUSTOMIZE INSTRUCTION FOR UNIVERSAL ACCESS

For Special Needs Students	For Less Proficient Readers	For English Learners
Have students read the adapted version of "The Iroquois Constitution" in the **Adapted Reader's Companion.** This version provides basic-level instruction in an interactive format with questions and write-on lines. Completing the adapted version will prepare students to read the selection in the Student Edition.	Have students read "The Iroquois Constitution" in the **Reader's Companion.** This version provides basic-level instruction in an interactive format with questions and write-on lines. After students finish the selection in **Reader's Companion,** have them complete the questions and activities in the Student Edition.	Have students read the adapted version of "The Iroquois Constitution" in the **English Learner's Companion.** This version provides basic-level instruction in an interactive format with questions and write-on lines. Completing the adapted version will prepare students to read the selection in the Student Edition.

CUSTOMIZE INSTRUCTION
For Logical/Mathematical
Learners

When they read the excerpt from "The Navajo Origin Legend," have students look for number patterns and offer logical explanations for them. For instance, students may notice that the ceremony in this myth begins on the *twelfth* day. Twelve is a number often used in literature to indicate a year, a complete life cycle, or an indeterminate period of long waiting. Ask students to speculate about what the use of such number patterns meant to the myth's creators.

❶ About the Selection

This myth from the Onondaga people relates a story about the creation of the world. In this version, the Earth forms as an offshoot of a celestial place called Skyland.

❷ ▶ Critical Viewing

Answer: The marks on the turtle's shell are explained as muddy paw prints left by Muskrat.

❶ The Earth on Turtle's Back

(Onondaga-Northeast Woodlands)

Retold by Michael J. Caduto and Joseph Bruchac

Background

Native Americans have great respect for the natural world. They believe that each creature has its own power by which it maintains itself and affects others. Each Native American culture has its own name for this power, but many Native American cultures recognize a Great Spirit—an invisible power that is the source of life and good for humans. Many of the animals that helped feed and clothe the early Native Americans are also highly revered. Native American folklore, much of which portrays animals, reflects this great respect.

16 ◆ *Beginnings–1750*

TEACHING RESOURCES

The following resources can be used to enrich or extend the instruction for pp. 16–26.

Literary Analysis
📘 **Literary Analysis for Enrichment**, p. 2 ▧

Reading Strategy
📖 **Selection Support:** Reading Strategy, p. 3, Build Vocabulary, p. 1
🎧 **Listening to Literature Audiocassettes**, Side 1 ▧

💿 **Listening to Literature CDs**, CD 1

Extension
🖼 **Fine Art Transparencies, Volume 1,** Art Transparency 1 ▧

▧ **BLOCK SCHEDULING:** Resources marked with this symbol provide varied instruction during 90-minute blocks.

Before this Earth existed, there was only water. It stretched as far as one could see, and in that water there were birds and animals swimming around. Far above, in the clouds, there was a Skyland. In that Skyland there was a great and beautiful tree. It had four white roots which stretched to each of the sacred directions,[1] and from its branches all kinds of fruits and flowers grew.

There was an ancient chief in the Skyland. His young wife was expecting a child, and one night she dreamed that she saw the Great Tree uprooted. The next day she told her husband the story.

He nodded as she finished telling her dream. "My wife," he said, "I am sad that you had this dream. It is clearly a dream of great power and, as is our way, when one has such a powerful dream we must do all we can to make it true. The Great Tree must be uprooted."

Then the Ancient Chief called the young men together and told them that they must pull up the tree. But the roots of the tree were so deep, so strong, that they could not budge it. At last the Ancient Chief himself came to the tree. He wrapped his arms around it, bent his knees and strained. At last, with one great effort, he uprooted the tree and placed it on its side. Where the tree's roots had gone deep into the Skyland there was now a big hole. The wife of the chief came close and leaned over to look down, grasping the tip of one of the Great Tree's branches to steady her. It seemed as if she saw something down there, far below, glittering like water. She leaned out further to look and, as she leaned, she lost her balance and fell into the hole. Her grasp slipped off the tip of the branch, leaving her with only a handful of seeds as she fell, down, down, down, down.

Far below, in the waters, some of the birds and animals looked up. "Someone is falling toward us from the sky," said one of the birds.

"We must do something to help her," said another. Then two Swans flew up. They caught the Woman From The Sky between their wide wings. Slowly, they began to bring her down toward the water, where the birds and animals were watching.

"She is not like us," said one of the animals. "Look, she doesn't have webbed feet. I don't think she can live in the water."

"What shall we do, then?" said another of the water animals.

"I know," said one of the water birds. "I have heard that there is Earth far below the waters. If we dive down and bring up Earth, then she will have a place to stand."

So the birds and animals decided that someone would have to bring up Earth. One by one they tried.

The Duck dove first, some say. He swam down and down, far beneath the surface, but could not reach the bottom and floated back up. Then the Beaver tried. He went even deeper, so deep that

---

1. **the sacred directions** North, South, East, and West.

◀ **Critical Viewing** What characteristics of this turtle are explained in this origin myth? **[Connect]**

Literary Analysis
Origin Myths How do the opening words of this story identify it as an origin myth?

Reading Strategy
Recognizing Cultural Details What do the chief's words to his wife tell you about the beliefs of the Onondaga?

Reading Check
What does the Skyland Chief's wife dream?

The Earth on Turtle's Back ◆ *17*

---

❸ Literary Analysis
Origin Myths

- Explain to students that origin myths can be seen as a mixture of science and religion—they explain how the world and the things in it came to be.
- Read the story's first sentence aloud with students.
- Then, ask them the Literary Analysis question on p. 17: How do the opening words of this story identify it as an origin myth?
  Answer: The first sentence describes what existed before the creation of the earth.

❹ Reading Strategy
Recognizing Cultural Details

- Read the second and third paragraphs aloud with students.
- Then, write a list on the chalkboard as students identify cultural details or topics that appear in this passage. Encourage students to note the references to marriage, childbirth, respect for age, and the role of dreams.
- Then, ask students the Reading Strategy question on p. 17: What do the chief's words to his wife tell you about the beliefs of the Onondaga?
  Answer: The Onondaga believe that dreams are powerful, influential messages and that the dreams must be obeyed.

❺ ✔ Reading Check

Answer: She dreams that she sees the Great Tree uprooted.

CUSTOMIZE INSTRUCTION FOR UNIVERSAL ACCESS

For Less Proficient Readers	For Advanced Readers
Have students participate in a choral reading of this origin myth. Then, invite them to form groups in order to discuss what the myth reveals about the people who created it. How do students think the Onondaga viewed their environment?	Ask students to note details about how the Onondaga pictured the time before the creation of Earth. Have students discuss whether they know of any other origin stories that seem similar, such as that in the Bible's book of Genesis. Can students find further parallels between these narratives and scientific thinking about the formation of life on earth?

Origin Myths and Oral Tradition

- Read aloud with students the paragraphs in which various animals dive down in the ocean.

- Invite students to identify the unusual aspect of the animals' names. If necessary, draw students' attention to the "generic" quality of each name.

▶ Monitor Progress Ask students the Literary Analysis question on p. 18: In oral literature, why might characters have generic names like "Loon" or "Muskrat"?
Answer: Often, characters in oral literature are symbolic or archetypal figures that embody important cultural ideas rather than complex personalities.

Answers for p. 18

Review and Assess

1. Students may say that they would be obliged to take the dream seriously and follow tradition, as the chief did; others may say that they would not have let a dream persuade them to alter or remove a sacred tree.

2. **(a)** In trying to look down the hole left by the uprooted tree, she leans too far and falls into the hole. **(b)** After the animals rescue her, they realize that she cannot live in the water, as they do.

3. **(a)** Each animal attempts (and fails) to dive deep enough to retrieve some earth. **(b)** As they take these actions, the animals exhibit concern, kindness, generosity, and heroism. None of the animals is fearful or selfish.

4. **(a)** They credit the animals of the waters, as well as the Sky Woman. **(b)** The myth suggests that the Onondaga felt respect and even affection for nature. They recognize that the world belonged to the animals first.

5. Often substantive achievements require bold action. Society benefits by enjoying the results of such brave efforts.

---

it all was dark, but he could not reach the bottom, either. The Loon tried, swimming with his strong wings. He was gone a long long time, but he, too, failed to bring up Earth. Soon it seemed that all had tried and all had failed. Then a small voice spoke.

"I will bring up Earth or die trying."

❻ They looked to see who it was. It was the tiny Muskrat. She dove down and swam and swam. She was not as strong or as swift as the others, but she was determined. She went so deep that it was all dark, and still she swam deeper. She swam so deep that her lungs felt ready to burst, but she swam deeper still. At last, just as she was becoming unconscious, she reached out one small paw and grasped at the bottom, barely touching it before she floated up, almost dead.

When the other animals saw her break the surface they thought she had failed. Then they saw her right paw was held tightly shut.

"She has the Earth," they said. "Now where can we put it?"

"Place it on my back," said a deep voice. It was the Great Turtle, who had come up from the depths.

They brought the Muskrat over to the Great Turtle and placed her paw against his back. To this day there are marks at the back of the Turtle's shell which were made by the Muskrat's paw. The tiny bit of Earth fell on the back of the Turtle. Almost immediately, it began to grow larger and larger and larger until it became the whole world.

Then the two Swans brought the Sky Woman down. She stepped onto the new Earth and opened her hand, letting the seeds fall onto the bare soil. From those seeds the trees and the grass sprang up. Life on Earth had begun.

Review and Assess

Thinking About the Selection

1. **Respond:** If you had been the Great Chief, would you have pulled up the Great Tree? Explain your answer.

2. **(a) Recall:** Explain what happened to the wife of the chief when the young men uprooted the Great Tree. **(b) Interpret:** Why did this action generate concern among the animals?

3. **(a) Recall:** Describe the actions of the swans, the beaver, and the duck. **(b) Analyze:** How do these actions exhibit the best aspects of human nature?

4. **(a) Infer:** Whom do the Onondaga credit with bringing Earth into existence? **(b) Analyze:** From this myth, what can you conclude about the relationship between the Onondaga and their natural environment? Explain your answer.

5. **Generalize:** Muskrat makes a risky and desperate swim. How does society benefit from brave actions like this?

When Grizzlies Walked Upright

Modoc

Retold by Richard Erdoes and Alfonso Ortiz

Before there were people on earth, the Chief of the Sky Spirits grew tired of his home in the Above World, because the air was always brittle with an icy cold. So he carved a hole in the sky with a stone and pushed all the snow and ice down below until he made a great mound that reached from the earth almost to the sky. Today it is known as Mount Shasta.

Then the Sky Spirit took his walking stick, stepped from a cloud to the peak, and walked down to the mountain. When he was about halfway to the valley below, he began to put his finger to the ground here and there, here and there. Wherever his finger touched, a tree grew. The snow melted in his footsteps, and the water ran down in rivers.

The Sky Spirit broke off the small end of his giant stick and threw the pieces into the rivers. The longer pieces turned into beaver and otter; the smaller pieces became fish. When the leaves dropped from the trees, he picked them up, blew upon them, and so made the birds. Then he took the big end of his giant stick and made all the animals that walked on the earth, the biggest of which were the grizzly bears.

Now when they were first made, the bears were covered with hair and had sharp claws, just as they do today, but they walked on two feet and could talk like people. They looked so fierce that the Sky Spirit sent them away from him to live in the forest at the base of the mountain.

Pleased with what he'd done, the Chief of the Sky Spirits decided to bring his family down and live on earth himself. The mountains of snow and ice became their lodge. He made a big fire in the center of the mountain and a hole in the top so that the smoke and sparks could fly out. When he put a big log on the fire, sparks would fly up and the earth would tremble.

Late one spring while the Sky Spirit and his family were sitting round the fire, the Wind Spirit sent a great storm that shook the top of the mountain. It blew and blew and roared and roared. Smoke blown back into the lodge hurt their eyes, and finally the Sky Spirit

Literary Analysis
Origin Myths What natural phenomenon is explained here?

9 ✓ **Reading Check**
What is the biggest animal made by the Sky Spirit?

When Grizzlies Walked Upright ◆ 19

---

❼ About the Selection

This Modoc legend tells the story of the origin of all Native American people. After creating the world, the Chief of the Sky Spirits makes his home inside a mountain, where his daughter disobeys him and is stranded on the mountainside. Adopted and brought up by the grizzly bear people, who walk and talk, the spirit girl eventually marries a grizzly bear. When her father discovers her whereabouts, he curses the bears to walk on all fours and takes away their power of speech. The daughter's children with her grizzly husband are the ancestors of the Native American people.

❽ Literary Analysis

Origin Myths

- Explain to students that origin myths not only provided explanations for the formation of the natural world, but also provided entertainment.
- Read aloud with students the story's opening paragraph.
- Ask students the Literary Analysis question on p. 19: What natural phenomenon is explained here? **Answer:** This passage explains the origin of the volcano. Mount Shasta is a volcanic peak about fifty miles south of the Oregon border in present-day California.

▶ **Reteach** If students have difficulty understanding the explanation of natural phenomena in origin myths, have them reread the explanation of origin myths on page 15. Help students to recognize that Mt. Shasta was so much a part of the Modoc people's everyday lives that the story arose to explain its origin.

❾ ✓ **Reading Check**

Answer: The grizzly bear is the largest animal made by the Sky Spirit.

CUSTOMIZE INSTRUCTION FOR UNIVERSAL ACCESS

For Special Needs Students	For Gifted/Talented Students
Use the comparison/contrast chart in the **Writing Models and Graphic Organizers on Transparencies,** pp. 17–23 to help students contrast the way creation is presented in the Modoc myth and in the Onondaga myth. Help students understand that the Onondaga believe that existing animals were instrumental in creating Earth, whereas the Modoc believe that the Sky Spirit created both Earth and its creatures.	Ask students to relate this story to others in which people are rescued or raised by caring animals. Urge students to do research in order to collect two or three other examples of this narrative detail (such as those in the stories of Tarzan, Mowgli, and various other folktales). Students might make brief oral presentations in which they compare and contrast these tales and hypothesize about why this theme appears so often in literature.

19

Answer: The bear, feathers, paw print, and hides are part of the natural world; the shield and spear are the work of humans. The artwork reflects the Native Americans' sense of harmony with the natural world.

⑪ Background

Art

Dreamwalker by Nancy Wood Taber

Taber lives in the Manzano Mountains outside Albuquerque, New Mexico, where she creates detailed, lifelike paintings and colored pencil drawings of the birds and animals living in the wilderness near her home. She infuses her work with images relating to Native American lore.

This colored-pencil drawing—one in a series of works the artist calls "Spirit Shield"—shows a bear who has chosen "to take the earth walk among the two-leggeds." The bear's hibernation represents introspection and the quest for inner knowledge and strength. Use these questions for discussion:

1. In what way does the artist blend the natural and human worlds?
   Answer: Some of the objects, such as the shield and spear, are made by people using parts of animals.

2. What might the artist suggest about the bear by portraying it in the upright position?
   Answer: The artist is making a connection between this animal and humans, since humans also walk in an upright position.

◀Critical Viewing ⑩
Which elements of the natural world are included in this image? Which elements represent the human world? What is the effect of the presentation of both together? **[Assess]**

Dreamwalker, Nancy Wood Taber ⑪

said to his youngest daughter, "Climb up to the smoke hole and ask the Wind Spirit to blow more gently. Tell him I'm afraid he will blow the mountain over."

As his daughter started up, her father said, "But be careful not to stick your head out at the top. If you do, the wind may catch you by the hair and blow you away."

The girl hurried to the top of the mountain and stayed well inside the smoke hole as she spoke to the Wind Spirit. As she was about to climb back down, she remembered that her father had once said ⑫ you could see the ocean from the top of their lodge. His daughter wondered what the ocean looked like, and her curiosity got the better of her. She poked her head out of the hole and turned toward the west, but before she could see anything, the Wind Spirit caught her long hair, pulled her out of the mountain, and blew her down over the snow and ice. She landed among the scrubby fir trees at the edge of the timber and snow line, her long red hair trailing over the snow.

There a grizzly bear found the little girl when he was out hunting food for his family. He carried her home with him, and his wife brought her up with their family of cubs. The little red-haired girl and the cubs ate together, played together, and grew up together.

When she became a young woman, she and the eldest son of the grizzly bears were married. In the years that followed they had many children, who were not as hairy as the grizzlies, yet did not look exactly like their spirit mother, either.

All the grizzly bears throughout the forests were so proud of these new creatures that they made a lodge for the red-haired mother and her children. They placed the lodge near Mount Shasta—it is called Little Mount Shasta today.

After many years had passed, the mother grizzly bear knew that she would soon die. Fearing that she should ask of the Chief of the Sky Spirits to forgive her for keeping his daughter, she gathered all the grizzlies at the lodge they had built. Then she sent her eldest grandson in a cloud to the top of Mount Shasta, to tell the Spirit Chief where he could find his long-lost daughter.

When the father got this news he was so glad that he came down the mountainside in giant strides, melting the snow and tearing up the land under his feet. Even today his tracks can be seen in the rocky path on the south side of Mount Shasta.

As he neared the lodge, he called out, "Is this where my little daughter lives?"

He expected his child to look exactly as she had when he saw her last. When he found a grown woman instead, and learned that the strange creatures she was taking care of were his grandchildren, he became very angry. A new race had been created that was not of his making! He frowned on the old grandmother so sternly that she promptly fell dead. Then he cursed all the grizzlies:

"Get down on your hands and knees. You have wronged me, and from this moment all of you will walk on four feet and never talk again."

He drove his grandchildren out of the lodge, put his daughter over his shoulder, and climbed back up the mountain. Never again did he come to the forest. Some say that he put out the fire in the center of his lodge and took his daughter back up to the sky to live.

Those strange creatures, his grandchildren, scattered and wandered over the earth. They were the first Indians, the ancestors of all the Indian tribes.

That's why the Indians living around Mount Shasta would never kill a grizzly bear. Whenever a grizzly killed an Indian, his body was burned on the spot. And for many years all who passed that way cast a stone there until a great pile of stones marked the place of his death.

When Grizzlies Walked Upright ◆ 21

⓬ Reading Strategy

Recognizing Cultural Details What detail about the way Native American women wear their hair is revealed here?

⓭ Reading Strategy

Recognizing Cultural Details What does the mother grizzly bear's decision reveal about the culture's view of responsibility or guilt?

⓮ ✔Reading Check

What is the Spirit Chief's reaction to the mother grizzly bear's confession?

⓬ Reading Strategy

Recognizing Cultural Details

- Make sure that students don't overlook the significance of what they may think are minor details. Even a small detail can provide information about a particular culture.
- Have a student volunteer read aloud the paragraph in which the girl falls off the mountain.
- Ask students the first Reading Strategy question on p. 21: What detail about the way some Native American women wear their hair is revealed here?
  Answer: Some Native American women wear their hair long.

⓭ Reading Strategy

Recognizing Cultural Details

- Ask students the second Reading Strategy question on p. 21: What does the mother grizzly bear's decision reveal about the culture's view of responsibility or guilt?
  Answer: Her decision shows that the culture prizes a sense of personal responsibility.

⓮ ✔Reading Check

Answer: He is filled with gladness when he first hears the news of his daughter's whereabouts.

CUSTOMIZE INSTRUCTION FOR UNIVERSAL ACCESS

For Less Proficient Readers	For English Learners	For Gifted/Talented Students
Have students brainstorm a list of natural landmarks in their geographical region, such as lakes, valleys, cliffs, rivers, mesas, forests, plains, springs, or rock formations. Invite students to choose one and write (or narrate) a short myth that explains how this natural feature was created.	Invite students to share origin myths with which they may be familiar. First, have students compile English vocabulary lists for words that appear in their stories. Then, as they tell the stories, have them consult the lists to help them remember the vocabulary. Finally, have them add the vocabulary lists to their portfolios.	To illustrate how these stories functioned for Native Americans, have students recreate a tale-telling session. Invite them to perform this story for classmates, speaking expressively, making eye contact, and adding gestures. Have other students retell other origin myths from this collection or from other sources.

This creation story tells how the first Navajo man and woman were created from wind and ears of corn. The wind comes to represent life, an idea reflected in the fact that human beings breathe to survive. The legend illuminates the Navajo belief in the wind's sacredness, as well as other cultural details such as the importance of corn and deer as a source of sustenance.

16 Reading Strategy

Recognizing Cultural Details

• Remind students that myths often reflect important elements of a society's fundamental beliefs.

• Have a student volunteer read the opening paragraph and the first sentence of the second paragraph.

• Ask students the Reading Strategy question on p. 22: What does this description suggest about the role of deer in Navajo life?
Answer: The use of "sacred" buckskins in the ceremony suggests that deer are extremely important in Navajo life.

17 Critical Thinking

Hypothesize

• Have students read to the second sentence of the second paragraph.

• Then, ask students why, if the myth recounts the creation of the first people, the first sentence alludes to unnamed people washing and drying themselves with cornmeal?

Answer: Students will observe that in addition to these, the story's first paragraphs also refer to the Mirage People. Students should hypothesize that the Navajo creation myths regard many kinds of beings as "people," but that the story specifically refers to the creation of human beings.

15 *from* The Navajo Origin Legend

Navajo
Retold by Washington Matthews

On the morning of the twelfth day the people washed themselves well. The women dried themselves with yellow cornmeal; the men with white cornmeal. Soon after the <u>ablutions</u> were completed they heard the distant call of the approaching gods.[1] It was shouted, as before, four times—nearer and louder at each repetition—and, after the fourth call, the gods appeared. Blue **16** Body and Black Body each carried a sacred buckskin. White Body carried two ears of corn, one yellow, one white, each covered at the end completely with grains.

The gods laid one buckskin on the ground with the head to the west: on this they placed the two ears of corn, with their tips to the east, and over the corn they spread the other buckskin with its head to the east; under the white ear they put the feather of a white eagle, under the yellow ear the feather of a yellow eagle. Then they told the people to stand at a distance and allow the wind to enter. The white **17** wind blew from the east, and the yellow wind blew from the west, between the skins. While the wind was blowing, eight of the Mirage People[2] came and walked around the objects on the ground four

---

1. **the approaching gods** the four Navajo gods: White Body, Blue Body, Yellow Body, and Black Body.
2. **Mirage People** mirages personified.

ablutions (ab loo´ shənz) *n.* cleansing the body as part of a religious rite

Reading Strategy Recognizing Cultural Details What does this description suggest about the role of deer in Navajo life?

☀ ENRICHMENT: Social Studies

Origin Myths

Every culture has its own origin myths or *pourquoi* (the French word for "why?") tales that attempt to explain natural phenomena. Encourage interested students to find other examples of origin myths from around the world. Groups might select a trio of myths from three different cultures. Challenge them to find in that trio recurring themes or elements, unique explanations, and cultural details that both distinguish the myths and form common bonds among them. Students can present their findings in a multimedia presentation or as an oral or written report.

times, and as they walked the eagle feathers, whose tips <u>protruded</u> from between the buckskins, were seen to move. When the Mirage People had finished their walk the upper buckskin was lifted; the ears of corn had disappeared, a man and a woman lay there in their stead.

The white ear of corn had been changed into a man, the yellow ear into a woman. It was the wind that gave them life. It is the wind that comes out of our mouths now that gives us life. When this ceases to blow we die. In the skin at the tips of our fingers we see the trail of the wind; it shows us where the wind blew when our ancestors were created.

The pair thus created were First Man and First Woman (Atsé Hastin and Atsé Estsán). The gods directed the people to build an enclosure of brushwood for the pair. When the enclosure was finished, First Man and First Woman entered it, and the gods said to them: "Live together now as husband and wife."

protruded (prō trōōd´ id) *v.* jutted out

Literary Analysis
Origin Myths Why might the Navajo have viewed the wind as the source of life?

Review and Assess

Thinking About the Selections

1. **Respond:** What words would you use to describe the images in these tales and the impression they made on you?

2. **(a) Recall:** What do the grizzly bears do that angers the Chief of the Sky Spirit? **(b) Analyze:** What does his reaction tell you about him?

3. **(a) Recall:** What punishment does the Chief of the Sky Spirits levy against the grizzlies? **(b) Analyze Cause and Effect:** How does this action affect his grandchildren, the people of the Earth?

4. **(a) Recall:** Identify the stages of the Navajo creation ceremony. **(b) Analyze:** What do the order and ritual of the ceremony tell you about the Navajo people?

5. **(a) Recall:** What is the wind's role in the ceremony? **(b) Contrast:** How does the wind's role contrast with the order and ritual of the ceremony?

6. **(a) Compare and Contrast:** In what ways do the two tales differ in their attitude toward nature? **(b) Evaluate:** With which attitude do you most identify? Why?

from The Navajo Origin Legend ◆ 23

CUSTOMIZE INSTRUCTION FOR UNIVERSAL ACCESS

For Less Proficient Readers	For English Learners	For Gifted/Talented Students
Help students clarify the objects and actions described in this myth by suggesting that they create a storyboard or construct a simple model that shows various details in the myth's descriptions.	Draw students' attention to the items in the story that function as symbols. Encourage students to list the items—buckskins, ears of corn, and eagle feathers, as well as the colors white, yellow, blue, and black. On the lists, have students jot suggested explanations of the significance of these items to the Navajo.	Encourage students to research Native Americans' use of symbolism in other arts. For example, interested students might study the meanings of totems—carved and painted images on vertically mounted logs—that are constructed by the Indians of the Northwest Coast of the United States and Canada.

⓲ Literary Analysis

Origin Myths

- Read aloud with students the story's next-to-last paragraph.

- Ask students the Literary Analysis question on p. 23: Why might the Navajo have viewed the wind as the source of life? Answer: The wind is a major climatic force, so the Navajo may have come to ascribe many powers to the wind. Also, since breath and wind are both movements of air, and since breath sustains human and animal life, it makes sense to compare wind to breath.

Answers for p. 23

Review and Assess

1. The impressions created by the works will vary from tale to tale and student to student.

2. **(a)** They take in his daughter and marry her to their oldest son. **(b)** It reveals that he is proud as creator of the Earth and does not want to share his powers of creation.

3. **(a)** He forbids them to talk or to walk upright. **(b)** His action causes his grandchildren, the first Indians, to scatter and wander over the Earth.

4. **(a)** First stage—the spirit people cleanse and dry themselves and call forth the gods; second—gods appear and place corn and feathers on buckskin; third—Mirage People circle buckskins, wind blows and transforms ears into people. **(b)** The Navajo people value and rely on a sense of order and ritual in life.

5. **(a)** The wind transforms the ears of corn into human beings. **(b)** The wind's work is "magical," in contrast to the logical and precise actions taken by the spirit people in anticipation of the wind's arrival.

6. **(a)** The Navajo legend does not explain the formation of the Earth. Although animals play a key role in bringing human life to Earth in the first two myths, vegetation (corn) is the key to life in the Navajo tale. **(b)** Students' responses will vary and should be supported with references to one or more texts.

23

⑲ About the Selection

The Iroquois Constitution tells how and why representatives of the Iroquois nation should hold formal councils to discuss and decide issues of concern to all. When Dekanawidah presented his *Kaianerekowa*, or Great Law of Peace, much of the Iroquois world was beset by persecution, disease, and power struggles. His plan led to the most far-reaching and notable political unit north of the Aztec civilization. The Constitution's sense of mutual respect, cooperation, and ritual among the Iroquois nations may have served as a model for what became the Constitution of the United States of America.

⑳ Literary Analysis

Origin Myths and the Oral Tradition

- Explain to students that stories in an oral tradition are not only important for the values and ideas they contain, but also for their style and form. For example, word choice and descriptive language are very important features, as they can help the speaker to remember the text and the listener to visualize the text.

- Ask students the Literary Analysis question on p. 24: How would this visual description facilitate the oral transmission of this constitution?
Answer: The description of a majestic tree vividly conveys the unity and good will enjoyed by the members of the Five Nations.

㉑ Vocabulary Development

The Latin Suffix -tion

- Draw students' attention to the word *disposition* and its definition.

- Let students know that the suffix *-tion* forms a noun when added to a modified form of the verb.

- To show students how verbs may be made into nouns by using *-tion*, write the following on the chalkboard:

Anyone outside the Five Nations who *is disposed* to do so, may join.

- Then, show students how to form the noun using *-tion*:

Anyone outside the Five Nations who has the *disposition* to do so, may join.

⑲ *from*

The Iroquois Constitution

Iroquois

Translated by Arthur C. Parker

I am Dekanawidah and with the Five Nations[1] <u>confederate</u> lords I plant the Tree of the Great Peace. I name the tree the Tree of the Great Long Leaves. Under the shade of this Tree of the Great Peace we spread the soft white feathery down of the globe thistle as seats for you, Adodarhoh, and your cousin lords.

We place you upon those seats, spread soft with the feathery down of the globe thistle, there beneath the shade of the spreading branches of the Tree of Peace. There shall you sit and watch the council fire of the confederacy of the Five Nations, and all the affairs of the Five Nations shall be transacted at this place before you.

Roots have spread out from the Tree of the Great Peace, one to the north, one to the east, one to the south and one to the west. The name of these roots is the Great White Roots and their nature is peace and strength.

If any man or any nation outside the Five Nations shall obey the laws of the Great Peace and make known their <u>disposition</u> to the lords of the confederacy, they may trace the roots to the tree and if their minds are clean and they are obedient and promise to obey the wishes of the confederate council, they shall be welcomed to take shelter beneath the Tree of the Long Leaves.

We place at the top of the Tree of the Long Leaves an eagle who is able to see afar. If he sees in the distance any evil approaching or any

---

1. **Five Nations** the Mohawk, Oneida, Onondaga, Cayuga, and Seneca tribes. Together, these tribes formed the Iroquois Confederation.

confederate (kən fed′ ər it) *adj.* united with others for a common purpose

Literary Analysis
Origin Myths and the Oral Tradition How would this visual description facilitate the oral transmission of this constitution?

disposition (dis′ pə zish′ ən) *n.* an inclination or tendency danger threatening he will at once warn the people of the confederacy.

The smoke of the confederate council fire shall ever ascend and pierce the sky so that other nations who may be allies may see the council fire of the Great Peace . . .

Whenever the confederate lords shall assemble for the purpose of holding a council, the Onondaga lords shall open it by expressing their gratitude to their cousin lords and greeting them, and they shall make an address and offer thanks to the earth where men dwell, to the streams of water, the pools, the springs and the lakes, to the maize and the fruits, to the medicinal herbs and trees, to the forest trees for their usefulness, to the animals that serve as food and give their pelts for clothing, to the great winds and the lesser winds, to the thunderers, to the sun, the mighty warrior, to the moon, to the messengers of the Creator who reveal his wishes and to the Great Creator who dwells in the heavens above, who gives all the things useful to men, and who is the source and the ruler of health and life.

Then shall the Onondaga lords declare the council open . . .

All lords of the Five Nations' Confederacy must be honest in all things . . . It shall be a serious wrong for anyone to lead a lord into trivial affairs, for the people must ever hold their lords high in estimation out of respect to their honorable positions.

When a candidate lord is to be installed he shall furnish four strings of shells (or wampum)[2] one span in length bound together at one end. Such will constitute the evidence of his pledge to the confederate lords that he will live according to the constitution of the Great Peace and exercise justice in all affairs.

When the pledge is furnished the speaker of the council must hold the shell strings in his hand and address the opposite side of the council fire and he shall commence his address saying: "Now behold him. He has now become a confederate lord. See how splendid he looks." An address may then follow. At the end of it he shall send the bunch of shell strings to the opposite side

Red Jacket, George Catlin, The Thomas Gilcrease Institute of American History and Art, Tulsa, Oklahoma

22

---

2. **wampum** (wäm′ pəm) *n.* small beads made of shells.

23 ▲ **Critical Viewing**
What details or features of this portrait reflect a belief in the dignity and nobility of the Native Americans? **[Analyze]**

24 ☑ **Reading Check**
What does the speaker say is the nature of the Great White Roots?

from *The Iroquois Constitution* ◆ 25

22 **Background**
Art

Red Jacket, by George Catlin

George Catlin was born in Wilkes-Barre, Pennsylvania. To please his father, he practiced law until 1823, at which time he became intrigued by "the dignity and nobility of the Native Americans." It was then that Catlin decided to devote himself to art and to becoming a historian of Native American peoples.

This portrait depicts fiery Seneca orator Sagoyewatha, who reluctantly followed his people into an alliance with the British. He received a red coat from the British as a ritual gift. Although in this portrait he is not wearing the red coat that led to his English nickname, the viewer can see the large medal given to him by George Washington after the American Revolution. Use these questions for discussion:

1. What personality traits has the artist tried to capture in this portrait?
   Suggested answer: Strength, determination, and pride

2. How are these traits related to the values and ideas set forth in the Iroquois Constitution?
   Answer: The Constitution says a leader needs wisdom, patience, and a sense of duty—all of which require the inner strength and determination captured in the portrait.

23 ▶ **Critical Viewing**

Answer: The artist's portrayal of Red Jacket's serious, penetrating stare, defiant stance, face paint, and ceremonial objects—a tomahawk, a peace pipe, and a beaded belt—reflect the dignity and nobility of his subject.

24 ☑ **Reading Check**

Answer: The speaker says that the nature of the Great White Roots is "peace and strength."

CUSTOMIZE INSTRUCTION FOR UNIVERSAL ACCESS

For Advanced Readers	For Gifted/Talented Students
Assign students to compare and contrast the Iroquois Constitution and the Constitution of the United States of America. Have students read each text more than once before they begin to analyze the documents' similarities and differences. Encourage them to prepare a short presentation on the topic for the class.	Point out that the Iroquois Constitution began as an oral "document," and as such it needed to hold the attention of multiple listeners. Ask students to deliver the speech orally to classmates, to demonstrate how this literary work uses imagery and phrasing to create a memorable impression.

25 Reading Strategy

Recognizing Cultural Details

- Ask students why they think the antlers of a deer are used to crown the lords of the Five Nations Confederacy.
  Answer: Students may say it is because the deer live in peace, as the Iroquois do.

- Ask students the Reading Strategy question on p. 26: What can you learn about the Iroquois culture from the items mentioned here?
  Answer: The Iroquois show deep respect for the principles of just leadership.

Answers for p. 26

Review and Assess

1. Students are likely to say yes, that peace and strength in unity under a Constitution is very appealing.

2. **(a)** They plant the Tree of the Great Peace. **(b)** The roots symbolize strength and peace.

3. **(a)** They should thank one another and then "offer thanks to the earth where men dwell." **(b)** They respect each other and their environment and are conscious of their dependence on the earth.

4. **(a)** He uses the image of the Tree of the Long Leaves and its roots, the eagle, and the council fire. **(b)** They show that the Iroquois are conscious of creating a strongly rooted union that would shelter its members, be vigilant against threats from without, and welcome new members.

5. **(a)** A lord must be honest in all things, slow to anger, and full of peace, good will, and a desire for the welfare of his people. A lord's actions should always exhibit farsightedness, deliberation, and compassion. **(b)** Students' responses should include examples and supporting details.

6. Students should support their responses with clear reasoning.

---

and they shall be received as evidence of the pledge. Then shall the opposite side say:

"We now do crown you with the sacred emblem of the deer's antlers, the emblem of your lordship. You shall now become a mentor of the people of the Five Nations. The thickness of your skin shall be seven spans—which is to say that you shall be proof against anger, offensive actions and criticism. Your heart shall be filled with peace and good will and your mind filled with a yearning for the welfare of the people of the confederacy. With endless patience you shall carry out your duty and your firmness shall be tempered with tenderness for your people. Neither anger nor fury shall find lodgement in your **25** mind and all your words and actions shall be marked with calm <u>deliberation</u>. In all of your deliberations in the confederate council, in your efforts at law making, in all your official acts, self-interest shall be cast into oblivion. Cast not over your shoulder behind you the warnings of the nephews and nieces should they chide you for any error or wrong you may do, but return to the way of the Great Law which is just and right. Look and listen for the welfare of the whole people and have always in view not only the present but also the coming generations, even those whose faces are yet beneath the surface of the ground—the unborn of the future nation."

Reading Strategy
Recognizing Cultural Details What can you learn about the Iroquois culture from the items mentioned here?

deliberation (di lib′ ər ā′ shən) *n.* careful consideration

Review and Assess

Thinking About the Selection

1. **Respond:** If you were the chief of a Native American nation, would this speech persuade you to join the Confederation? Explain.

2. **(a) Recall:** What do the lords plant to commemorate their meeting? **(b) Analyze:** What do the roots of this plant symbolize?

3. **(a) Recall:** According to the Constitution, what must confederate lords do to open a council meeting? **(b) Infer:** What does this decree suggest about the Iroquois?

4. **(a) Analyze:** What three images from nature does Dekanawidah use in the Iroquois Constitution? **(b) Infer:** What do these references tell you about the Iroquois?

5. **(a) Summarize:** Summarize the qualities and conduct required of council lords by the Iroquois Constitution. **(b) Synthesize:** How well do these qualities apply to leaders in the modern world?

6. **Take a Position:** Do you agree with and support the ideas presented in *The Iroquois Constitution?* Why or Why not?

ASSESSMENT PRACTICE: Reading Comprehension

Summarizing Written Texts	(For more practice, see Test Preparation Workbook, p.1.)

Students will need to recognize accurate summaries on tests. Use this sample test item to help students practice:

The need to explain the origins of life and other great mysteries gave birth to myths, traditional stories, often about immortal beings, that are passed down from generation to generation. Myths often explain other phenomena, including customs, institutions, or religious rites.

Which of the following is the best summary of the passage?

A Myths are created to help explain things that can't be otherwise understood.

B Myths are created to explain religious rites.

C Myths explain how life begins.

D Myths are passed through the generations.

Choices *B, C,* and *D* offer accurate but incomplete information. Choice *A* is the best summary.

Review and Assess

Literary Analysis

Origin Myths

1. According to the Modoc **origin myth,** who formed the landscape and the creatures of the Earth?
2. (a) Review the selections and use a chart like the one shown here to record the roles nature plays in explaining and maintaining Native American life.

Aspect of Nature	Connection to Native American Life

   (b) What can you conclude from the details you have collected?
3. How do animals and natural objects portray aspects of human nature in these origin myths?
4. Origin myths explain natural phenomena, customs, and specific characteristics of animals. Cite examples from the myths.

One from each myth

Comparing Literary Works

5. In cultures with **oral traditions** such as these, in what ways do myths and stories instruct or share important values?
6. (a) Which culture sees the spirits as generous and kind? Explain. (b) Which culture sees them as vengeful? Explain.
7. (a) In what way does the language of the Iroquois Constitution differ from that of the other selections? (b) How does this contrast reflect the Constitution's purpose?

Reading Strategy

Recognizing Cultural Details

8. Identify two **cultural details** you learned from each selection. Then, describe what each selection reveals about the culture that created it.
9. What do the prevalent attitudes in the Iroquois Constitution reveal about the culture behind the literature?

Extend Understanding

10. **Social Studies Connection:** In what ways is the United States Constitution similar to the Iroquois Constitution? In what ways is it different?

Turtle's Back / Grizzlies / from The Navajo Origin Legend / from The Iroquois Constitution ◆ 27

Quick Review

Origin myths are stories passed from generation to generation to explain the creation of the world and all it holds.

In an **oral tradition,** people share their values, concerns, and history through verbal literature such as storytelling.

Cultural details are references to objects, animals, or practices that reflect aspects of daily life or prevalent attitudes.

 Take It to the Net
www.phschool.com
Take the interactive self-test online to check your understanding of these selections.

ENRICHMENT: Further Reading

Other Origin Myths

"The Coming of Gluscabi" (Abenaki), retold by Michael J. Caduto and Joseph Bruchac
Pictographs from the Walam Olum (Delaware)
Beginnings: Earth, Sky, Life, Death by Sophia Lyon Fahs and Dorothy T. Spoerl

Take It to the Net
Visit www.phschool.com for more information on the authors and translator.

Answers continued

9. The prevalent attitudes reveal that the culture prizes integrity, cooperation, peacefulness, compassion, thoughtfulness, and wisdom.
10. Students should make comparisons and contrasts about both the content and style of the two documents.

Answers for p. 27

Review and Assess

1. The Chief of the Sky Spirits formed the landscape and the creatures of Earth.
2. (a) Sample answers: Marks on turtle's back explain cooperation and toil necessary to form the world; grizzlies' muteness and need to walk on four legs explains ancestry of Indians; ears of corn becoming men and women explains centrality of this crop in Native American culture **(b)** The environment plays a central role in the traditions and beliefs of Native Americans.
3. Sample response: Animals in the Onondaga myth persevere, cooperate, and show compassion. The strings of shells in the Iroquois Constitution represent human loyalty.
4. Examples include the marks on a turtle's back ("The Earth on Turtle's Back"), the walking posture of grizzly bears ("When Grizzlies Walked Upright"), and the importance of deer ("The Navajo Origin Legend").
5. Elders instruct young people about their culture by passing along its myths and stories orally. The oral tradition allows sharing of traditions and cultural details.
6. (a) The spirits in the Navajo culture generously transform corn into human beings. **(b)** The Modoc culture sees the Sky Spirit as vengeful, as evidenced by his punishment of the grizzlies.
7. (a) The language of the Iroquois Constitution is more formal than the language in the other selections. **(b)** This formality reflects the serious purpose that the work describes.
8. Possible answers: <u>Onondaga</u>: Dreams are important; water and water animals are also central to their culture; <u>Modoc</u>: The Modoc live among mountains, valleys, rivers, and volcanoes; Mount Shasta is an important place to them; <u>Navajo</u>: Corn is central to Navajo life; the culture associates the wind with life; <u>Iroquois</u>: Trees and fire symbolize strength and community to the Iroquois; the Iroquois prize peace, obedience, honesty, patience, and goodwill.
continued

❶ **Vocabulary Development**

Word Analysis

1. constitution; The people's rights are spelled out in the Constitution.

2. estimation; The lords held Dekanawidah high in their estimation.

3. disposition; Only those with a peaceful disposition could remain in the group.

4. hesitation; The lord's hesitation to join almost cost him his place on the council.

3. inoculation; To prevent tetanus, doctors administer an inoculation.

Concept Development: Synonyms

1. b
2. c
3. b
4. c
5. a

Spelling Strategy

1. location; We could not identify the location of the treasure.

2. insulation; Thick insulation between the walls kept the cold air outside the house.

3. excavation; The excavation of the site uncovered an old burial site.

❷ **Grammar and Style**

Sample rewrite: Then the Beaver tried. He went even deeper into the darkness, but he could not reach the bottom, either. The loon dove next, swimming deep into the water. Even with his strong wings, he could not reach the bottom, and he floated back up. Then a voice spoke. "I will bring up Earth, or I will die trying."

Writing Application

Students' paragraphs should contain at least two compound sentences.

Integrate Language Skills

❶ **Vocabulary Development Lesson**

Word Analysis: Latin Suffix -tion

The word *deliberation* contains the Latin suffix *-tion*, which forms a noun when added to a verb. The literal meaning of *deliberation* is "the act of deliberating." Change the following verbs to nouns by adding the suffix *-tion*. Then, use each new word in a sentence.

1. constitute: to set up in a legal or official form; establish

2. estimate: to form an opinion or judgment based on preliminary information

3. dispose: to tend or incline; to place in a certain order

4. hesitate: to stop because of indecision; pause or delay

5. inoculate: to provide a vaccine that creates immunity

Concept Development: Synonyms

For each grouping, identify the word whose meaning does not match the other two.

1. (a) cleansings, (b) imaginings, (c) ablutions

2. (a) deliberation, (b) consideration, (c) commotion

3. (a) protruded, (b) dangled, (c) jutted

4. (a) disposition, (b) inclination, (c) assumption

5. (a) varied, (b) confederate, (c) united

Spelling Strategy

When you add the suffix *-tion* to a verb that ends in *te*, drop the *te*: deliberate + *-tion* = *deliberation*. Add *-tion* to the following verbs. Use the resulting nouns in sentences.

1. locate   2. insulate   3. excavate

❷ **Grammar and Style Lesson**

Compound Sentences

A main clause is a complete thought that contains a subject that tells who or what the sentence is about and a predicate that tells what the subject is or does.

In oral and written language, compound sentences provide a natural way to link ideas. A **compound sentence** has two or more main clauses linked by a semicolon or a comma and a coordinating conjunction such as *and*, *or*, or *but*. In the example, subjects are underlined and predicates are italicized.

> **Example:** Muskrat *dove down and brought up Earth*, and Earth *was placed on Turtle's back*.

Practice Rewrite the following paragraph so that it contains at least three compound sentences. You may need to add or change some words. Then, underline the subject and predicate in each clause.

> Then the Beaver tried. He went deeper into the darkness. He could not reach the bottom. Next, the loon dove into the water. Even he could not reach the bottom. He floated back up. Then a voice spoke, "I will bring up Earth or die trying."

Writing Application Write a paragraph about a natural landmark such as a river, cliff, or mountain in your state. In your writing, use at least two compound sentences.

W₆ Prentice Hall Writing and Grammar Connection: Chapter 19, Section 4

TEACHING RESOURCES

The following resources can be used to enrich or extend the instruction for pp. 28–29.

Vocabulary

📖 **Selection Support:** Build Vocabulary, p. 1

📖 **Vocabulary and Spelling Practice Book** 📖
(Use this booklet for skills enrichment.)

Grammar

📖 **Selection Support:** Grammar and Style, p. 2

W₆ **Writing and Grammar,** Ruby Level, pp. 466–467 📖

📖 **Daily Language Practice Transparencies**

Writing

W₆ **Writing and Grammar,** Ruby Level, p. 79 📖

📖 **Extension Activities**

📖 **Writing Models and Graphic Organizers on**

Transparencies pp. 17–23

💿 **Writing and Grammar iText CD-ROM**

📗 **BLOCK SCHEDULING:** Resources marked with this symbol provide varied instruction during 90-minute blocks.

❸ Writing Lesson

Retelling of a Story

Storytellers add something of their own when repeating stories. Select one of the myths presented here and retell it. Keep the structure and sequence of events, but rewrite the tale to appeal to your audience. For example, you might update the setting.

Prewriting Create a rough story outline based on the myth. Then, using a chart like the one shown, list elements of the myth that you will retain and elements that you will adapt.

Model: Gathering Details from the Original

Food	Clothing	Beliefs	Environment

Drafting Following your outline, create a rough draft. Consider using repetition of actions, phrases, or words to create drama and to heighten suspense.

Revising Read your tale aloud, listening carefully to your repetition. Make sure it includes vibrant words and dynamic actions that create dramatic and memorable effects.

W̶G Prentice Hall Writing and Grammar Connection: Chapter 5, Section 3

❹ Extension Activities

Listening and Speaking With a group, develop a **dramatic reenactment** of a council meeting called to install a new Iroquois lord.

- Create the roles outlined in "The Iroquois Constitution."
- Plan the staging to determine the physical movement of the reenactment.
- Rehearse your reenactment several times to learn your roles.

When you are ready, present your reenactment to the class. Then answer audience questions about the Constitution or reenactment. **[Group Activity]**

Research and Technology Using the images contained in the Iroquois Constitution for inspiration, design a **logo** representing the Iroquois Confederation. Be sure to include details in your design that relate to the culture and history of the Iroquois. Produce your logo, write a brief explanation of it, and share your work with classmates.

 Take It to the Net www.phschool.com

Go online for an additional research activity using the Internet.

Turtle's Back / Grizzlies / from The Navajo Origin Legend / from The Iroquois Constitution ◆ 29

❸ Writing Lesson

- Students' retellings should retain the major narrative elements of the original, though they may feature contemporary settings or characters. The basic motives of characters and the fundamental qualities of settings, however, should not change.

- Tell students that their retellings should be adapted to a particular contemporary audience. Encourage them to identify which existing elements will interest their audience and which will benefit from modification.

- Use the Writing Lesson, as well as Writing Process Model 4, pp. 17–23, in **Writing Models and Graphic Organizers on Transparencies**, to guide students in developing their retellings.

❹ Research and Technology

- Have students reread the text carefully before planning and designing their logos. Encourage them to think about interesting, effective logos they have seen. Let students know that often an effective logo conveys a single central feature of its subject.

- Ask students to select images that communicate the fundamental ideas of the Iroquois Constitution.

- Urge students to refine these images by making more than one version of their logos.

CUSTOMIZE INSTRUCTION
For Universal Access

To address different learning styles, use the following activities suggested in the **Extension Activities** booklet, p. 1.

- For Verbal/Linguistic and Musical/Rhythmic Learners, use Activity 5.

- For Interpersonal and Verbal/Linguistic Learners, use Activity 6.

ASSESSMENT RESOURCES

The following resources can be used to assess students' knowledge and skills.

Selection Assessment
- 📖 **Formal Assessment**, pp. 1–3
- 📖 **Open Book Test**, pp. 1–3
- 📼 **Got It! Assessment Videotapes**, Tape 1
- 💿 **Test Bank Software**

📶 **Take It to the Net**
Visit www.phschool.com for self-tests and additional questions on the selections.

Writing Rubric
- 📖 **Performance Assess. and Portfolio Mgmt.**, p. 15

PRENTICE HALL
ASSESSMENT *SYSTEM*
- 📖 **Workbook**
- 📖 **Skill Book**
- 🗄 **Transparencies**
- 💿 **CD-ROM**

A Journey Through Texas ✦ Boulders Taller Than the Great Tower of Seville

Lesson Objectives

1. **To analyze and respond to literary elements**
   - Literary Analysis: Exploration Narratives
   - Comparing Literary Works

2. **To read, comprehend, analyze, and critique nonfiction**
   - Reading Strategy: Recognizing Signal Words
   - Reading Check Questions
   - Review and Assess Questions
   - Assessment Practice (ATE)

3. **To develop word analysis skills, fluency, and systematic vocabulary**
   - Vocabulary Development Lesson: Latin Word Root: *-mort-*

4. **To understand and apply written and oral language conventions**
   - Spelling Strategy
   - Grammar Lesson: Past and Perfect Verb Tenses

5. **To understand and apply appropriate writing and research strategies**
   - Writing Lesson: Explorer's Journal
   - Extension Activity: Exploration Booklet

6. **To understand and apply listening and speaking strategies**
   - Extension Activity: Persuasive Speech

STEP-BY-STEP TEACHING GUIDE	PACING GUIDE
PRETEACH	
Motivate Students and Provide Background	
Use the Motivation activity (ATE p. 30)	5 min.
Read and discuss author and the background features (SE ATE pp. 30, 32)	5 min.
Introduce the Concepts	
Introduce the Literary Analysis and Reading Strategy (SE/ATE p. 31) A	15 min.
Pronounce the vocabulary words and read their definitions (SE p. 31)	5 min.
TEACH	
Monitor Comprehension	
Informally monitor comprehension by circulating while students read independently or in groups A	20 min.
Monitor students' comprehension with the Reading Check notes (SE/ATE pp. 33, 35, 37)	as students read
Develop vocabulary with Vocabulary notes (SE pp. 33, 34, 35, 36, 37; ATE p. 34)	as students read
Develop Understanding	
Develop students' understanding of exploration narratives with the Literary Analysis annotations (SE pp. 33, 35, 36, 37; ATE pp. 33, 35, 36, 37) A	5 min.
Develop students' ability to recognize signal words with the Reading Strategy annotations (SE pp. 34, 38; ATE pp. 34, 38)	5 min.
ASSESS	
Assess Mastery	
Assess students' mastery of the Reading Strategy and Literary Analysis by having them answer the Review and Assess questions (SE/ATE p. 39)	15 min.
Use one or more of the print and media Assessment Resources (ATE p. 41) A	up to 45 min.
EXTEND	
Apply Understanding	
Have students complete the Vocabulary Development Lesson and the Grammar Lesson (SE p. 40) A	20 min.
Apply students' ability to use precise details by using the Writing Lesson (SE/ATE p. 41) A	45 min.
Apply students' understanding of the selection using one or more of the Extension Activities (SE p. 41)	20–90 min.

A **ACCELERATED INSTRUCTION:**
Use the strategies and activities identified with an A.

UNIVERSAL ACCESS
● = Below Level Students
▲ = On-Level Students
■ = Above Level Students

Time and Resource Manager

Reading Level: Average, Average
Average Number of Instructional Days: 4

RESOURCES		
PRINT RESOURCES 📖	**TRANSPARENCY RESOURCES**	**TECHNOLOGY RESOURCES** 💿 🎧 📼
• **Beyond Literature,** Career Connection: Travel Writer, p. 2 ▲ ■		• **Interest Grabber Video,** Tape 1 ● ▲ ■
• **Selection Support Workbook:** ● ▲ ■ Literary Analysis, p. 8 Reading Strategy, p. 7 Build Vocabulary, p. 5	• **Literary Analysis and Reading Transparencies,** pp. 3 and 4 ● ▲ ■	
		• **Listening to Literature** ● ▲ ■ Audiocassettes, Sides 1 and 2 Audio CDs, CD 1
• **Literatura en español** ● ▲ • **Literary Analysis for Enrichment** ■		
• **Formal Assessment:** Selection Test, pp. 4–6 ● ▲ ■ • **Open Book Test,** pp. 4–6 ● ▲ ■ • **Performance Assessment and Portfolio Management,** p. 30 ● ▲ ■ • PRENTICE HALL **ASSESSMENT SYSTEM** ● ▲ ■	• PRENTICE HALL **ASSESSMENT SYSTEM** ● ▲ ■ Skills Practice Answers and Explanations on Transparencies	• **Test Bank Software** ● ▲ ■ • **Got It! Assessment Videotapes,** Tape 1 ● ▲
• **Selection Support Workbook:** ● ▲ ■ Build Grammar Skills, p. 6 • **Writing and Grammar,** Ruby Level ● ▲ ■ • **Extension Activities,** p. 2 ● ▲ ■	• **Daily Language Practice Transparencies** ● ▲ • **Writing Models and Graphic Organizers on Transparencies** pp. 13–16 ● ▲ ■	• **Writing and Grammar iText CD-ROM** ● ▲ ■ 💻 *Take It to the Net* www.phschool.com

BLOCK SCHEDULING: Use one 90-minute class period to preteach the selection and have students read it. Use a second 90-minute class period to assess students' mastery of skills and have them complete one of the Extension Activities.

30b

Step-by-Step Teaching Guide for pp. 30–31

Motivation

Invite students to imagine finding themselves in a strange land among people whose language and customs were unknown to them. What if they had no way of sending for help and no way of knowing exactly how to get back home? How would it feel to spend several years in this land with no apparent hope of returning home? On whom could they depend for help? Emphasize that Cabeza de Vaca and his followers spent eight years—many of them in enforced captivity—in just such a situation.

📼 Interest Grabber Video

As an alternative, play "The Grand Canyon" on Tape 1 to engage students' interest.

❶ Background

More About the Author

Alvar Núñez Cabeza de Vaca came to North America as treasurer of the Narváez expedition, the goal of which was to colonize lands north of Mexico. Cabeza de Vaca was shipwrecked on an island in the Gulf of Mexico with two other Spaniards and a slave. In a unique role reversal, the four became servants to the Cahoques Indians for about eight years. During this time, Cabeza de Vaca grew to understand the Native Americans as no other Spaniard had done before him.

Prepare to Read

❶ A Journey Through Texas ◆ Boulders Taller Than the Great Tower of Seville

Alvar Núñez Cabeza de Vaca (1490?–1557?)

In 1528, Pánfilo de Narváez and 400 Spanish soldiers landed near Tampa Bay and set out to explore Florida's west coast. Alvar Núñez Cabeza de Vaca (äl´ bär no͞on´ yes kä bā´ sä dä bä´ kä) was second in command. Beset by hostile natives, illness, and the prospect of starvation, Narváez and his men then set sail for Mexico in five flimsy boats, but he and most of the men drowned. Cabeza de Vaca and a party of about sixty survived and reached the Texas shore near present-day Galveston.

Shipwrecked without supplies, only fifteen of the group lived through the winter. In the end, Cabeza de Vaca and three others survived. They were captured by natives and spent the next several years in captivity. During that time, Cabeza de Vaca gained a reputation as a medicine man and trader. The four Spaniards finally escaped and wandered for eighteen months across the Texas plains. In 1536, the survivors finally reached Mexico City.

Invitation to Others Cabeza de Vaca's adventures and his reports on the richness of Texas sparked exploration of the region. In "A Journey Through Texas," he speaks of Estevanico, the first African to set foot in Texas.

In 1541, Cabeza de Vaca also led a 1,000-mile expedition through the south of present day Brazil to Asunción, the capital of Río de la Plata. He was appointed governor of the Río de la Plata region (now Paraguay), but he was ousted two years later as a result of revolt.

Through his journals, Cabeza de Vaca encouraged others, including Francisco Vásquez de Coronado, to explore America.

García López de Cárdenas (c. 1540)

García López de Cárdenas (gär sē´ ä lō´ pes dā kär´ dä näs) is best remembered as the first European to visit the Grand Canyon. As a leader of Francisco Vásquez de Coronado's expedition to New Mexico (1540–1542), Cárdenas was dispatched from Cibola (Zuni) in western New Mexico to see a river that the Moqui Native Americans of northeastern Arizona had described to one of Coronado's captains. The river was the Colorado. López de Cárdenas departed on August 25, 1540, reaching the Grand Canyon after a westward journey of about twenty days. He became the first explorer to view the canyon and its river, which from the vantage of the canyon's rim appeared to be a stream merely six feet wide! Unable to descend to the river, they took back to Europe descriptions that attempted to record the magnitude of the sight. López de Cárdenas reported that boulders in the Grand Canyon were taller than the 300-foot high Great Tower of Seville, one of the world's tallest cathedrals.

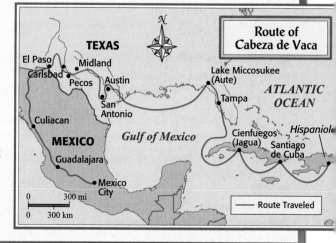

Route of Cabeza de Vaca

TEXAS — El Paso, Carlsbad, Midland, Pecos, Austin, San Antonio, Culiacan

MEXICO — Guadalajara, Mexico City

Gulf of Mexico

Lake Miccosukee (Aute), Tampa

ATLANTIC OCEAN

Cienfuegos (Jagua), Santiago de Cuba, Hispaniola

— Route Traveled

0   300 mi
0   300 km

TEACHING RESOURCES

The following resources can be used to enrich or extend the instruction for pp. 30–31.

Motivation

📼 Interest Grabber Video, Tape 1 ■

Background

📖 Beyond Literature, p. 2

💻 *Take It to the Net*

Visit www.phschool.com for Background and hotlinks for the selection.

Literary Analysis

📄 Literary Analysis and Reading Transparencies, Exploration Narrative, p. 4 ■

📖 Selection Support Workbook: Literary Analysis, p. 8

Reading

📄 Literary Analysis and Reading Transparencies, Recognizing Signal Words, p. 3

■ **BLOCK SCHEDULING:** Resources marked with this symbol provide varied instruction during 90-minute blocks.

Preview

Connecting to the Literature

The writers of these historical accounts describe places their readers could barely imagine. Think of the tales you would have told had you been among the first Europeans to travel to the southwest region of North America to meet the natives.

❷ Literary Analysis

Exploration Narratives

The Europeans who trailblazed the Americas recounted their experiences in **exploration narratives**—firsthand accounts of their travels. These accounts provided information to the people back home in Europe, so the explorers were careful to record in detail what they observed. For example, López de Cárdenas gives these details about the region.

> This region was high and covered with low and twisted pine trees; it was extremely cold, being open to the north . . .

As you read, look for details that provide descriptive images and insights about the regions these men explored.

Comparing Literary Works

These exploration narratives reflect two distinctly different **authors' styles,** or choices of words, details, and focus. Cabeza de Vaca uses descriptive details in his narrative. In contrast, López de Cárdenas avoids description and instead provides a detailed explanation of events. Create a Venn diagram like the one shown to compare and contrast the authors' styles.

❸ Reading Strategy

Recognizing Signal Words

To follow the order of events, pay close attention to **signal words**—words that highlight the relationships among ideas. Look at these examples:

- **time:** *After five days,* they had not *yet* returned.
- **contrast:** . . . *although* this was the warm season, no one could live in this canyon because of the cold.

As you read, take note of signal words and the relationships they indicate.

Vocabulary Development

entreated (en trēt´ id) *v.* begged; pleaded (p. 33)

feigned (fānd) *v.* pretended; faked (p. 33)

mortality (môr tal´ ə tē) *n.* death on a large scale (p. 34)

subsisted (səb sist´ id) *v.* remained alive; were sustained (p. 35)

traversed (trə vurst´) *v.* moved over, across, or through (p. 36)

dispatched (di spacht´) *v.* sent off on a specific assignment (p. 37)

[Cabeza de Vaca's Style]

[López de Cárdenas's Style]

---

❷ Literary Analysis

Exploration Narratives

- Let students know that many early explorers kept detailed records of their travels. Many of these records were composed for kings or other powerful people who had financed the journeys.

- As they read each exploration narrative, have students note general insights and descriptive details that the explorer includes in his account.

- Encourage students to relate to the explorers' experiences by using their own prior knowledge about the thoughts and feelings that arise when people, things, and places are utterly new and strange.

❸ Reading Strategy

Recognizing Signal Words

- Remind students that signal words tip off a reader about the relationships among ideas.

- Explain that there are several different types of relationships that signal words help readers to recognize: time order, cause-and-effect, level of importance, and contrast, for example.

- Encourage students to identify some of the signal words they know and the type of relationships expressed by these words.

- Point out to students that recognizing signal words is especially important in narratives.

Vocabulary Development

- Pronounce each vocabulary word for students, and read the definitions as a class. Have students identify any words with which they are already familiar.

CUSTOMIZE INSTRUCTION FOR UNIVERSAL ACCESS

For Less Proficient Readers	For English Learners	For Advanced Readers
Have students practice breaking down long sentences such as this one into two or three shorter sentences: "One night, I went away to sleep out in the field apart from them; but they soon came to where I was, and remained awake all night in great alarm, talking to me, saying how frightened they were."	These exploration narratives contain sentences characterized by archaic syntax and unfamiliar language. Guide English language learners to work with more fluent English speakers who can help them paraphrase or restate certain sentences to make them easier to understand.	To help students appreciate the stylistic characteristics of these exploration narratives, have them choose a single paragraph to rewrite in the most simple, direct way possible. Then, have pairs of students discuss what is lost or gained by rewriting the narrative in modern English.

 E-Teach

Visit E-Teach at www.phschool.com for teachers' essays on how to teach, with questions and answers.

Step-by-Step Teaching Guide for pp. 32–38

CUSTOMIZE INSTRUCTIONS
For Visual/Spatial Learners

Students may enjoy and benefit from referring to the map on p. 30, as well as to a contemporary map of the region in which the authors traveled. Have them use either map to orient themselves and try to trace Cabeza de Vaca's route from Cuba all the way to Mexico City.

❶ About the Selection

Cabeza de Vaca was a Spanish adventurer whose views and beliefs were dramatically altered by his extraordinary experiences living with Native Americans. This narrative describes his journey into what is now the state of Texas as he attempts to reach the Spanish settlements in Mexico City. Cabeza de Vaca came (albeit reluctantly) to understand and appreciate something of the people whose land he traveled through.

❷ ▶ Critical Viewing

Answer: Students may note that the landscape appears to be hot, sunny, and very dry. Such terrain would probably supply little food or water, and travelers might easily starve, dehydrate, or suffer heatstroke.

❶ A Journey Through Texas

Alvar Núñez Cabeza de Vaca

Background

Alvar Núñez Cabeza de Vaca and three countrymen wandered for months through Texas as they journeyed toward the Spanish settlement in Mexico City. In the course of his travels, Cabeza de Vaca healed a Native American by performing the first recorded surgery in Texas. His resulting fame attracted so many followers that Cabeza de Vaca noted in his journal, "The number of our companions became so large that we could no longer control them." As they continued traveling westward, the group was well received by the Native Americans they encountered.

❷ ▼ Critical Viewing
What details of a landscape like this one might pose difficulty for the expeditions that explored it? [Speculate]

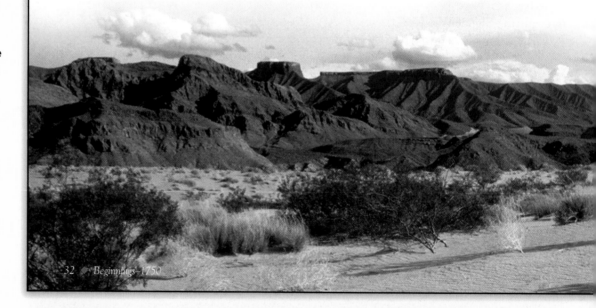

32   Beginnings–1750

TEACHING RESOURCES

The following resources can be used to enrich or extend the instruction for pp. 32–38.

Literary Analysis
📖 **Literary Analysis for Enrichment,** p. 4

Reading Strategy
📖 **Selection Support:** Reading Strategy, p. 7; Build Vocabulary, p. 5

🎧 **Listening to Literature Audiocassettes,** Sides 1, 2 ▦

💿 **Listening to Literature CDs,** CD 1 ▦

▦ **BLOCK SCHEDULING:** Resources marked with this symbol provide varied instruction during 90-minute blocks.

The same Indians led us to a plain beyond the chain of mountains, where people came to meet us from a long distance. By those we were treated in the same manner as before, and they made so many presents to the Indians who came with us that, unable to carry all, they left half of it. . . . We told these people our route was towards sunset, and they replied that in that direction people lived very far away. So we ordered them to send there and inform the inhabitants that we were coming and how. From this they begged to be excused, because the others were their enemies, and they did not want us to go to them. Yet they did not venture to disobey in the end, and sent two women, one of their own and the other a captive. They selected women because these can trade everywhere, even if there be war.

We followed the women to a place where it had been agreed we should wait for them. After five days they had not yet returned, and the Indians explained that it might be because they had not found anybody. So we told them to take us north, and they repeated that there were no people, except very far away, and neither food nor water. Nevertheless we insisted, saying that we wanted to go there, and they still excused themselves as best they could, until at last we became angry.

One night I went away to sleep out in the field apart from them; but they soon came to where I was, and remained awake all night in great alarm, talking to me, saying how frightened they were. They <u>entreated</u> us not to be angry any longer, because, even if it was their death, they would take us where we chose. We <u>feigned</u> to be angry still, so as to keep them in suspense, and then a singular[1] thing happened.

On that same day many fell sick, and on the next day eight of them died! All over the country, where it was known, they became so afraid that it seemed as if the mere sight of us would kill them. They besought[2] us not to be angry nor to procure the death of any

---

1. **singular** *adj.* strange.
2. **besought** *v.* (be sôt´) pleaded with.

Literary Analysis
Exploration Narratives
Why does Cabeza de Vaca include such detail about the conversation with the Indians in his narrative?

entreated (en trēt´ id) *v.* begged; pleaded

feigned (fānd) *v.* pretended; faked

⑤ ☑ Reading Check
Why do the Indians fear going on ahead?

A Journey Through Texas ◆ 33

❸ Literary Analysis
Exploration Narratives

- Draw students' attention to the way Cabeza de Vaca indirectly paraphrases, rather than reports word-for-word, the Native Americans' speech.

- Ask students what effect this has on the reader.
  Possible response: Students may say the effect is to emphasize the distance between the Spanish explorers and the Native Americans. They may note that no Native American emerges as an individual and none is named.

- Ask students the Literary Analysis question on p. 33: Why does Cabeza de Vaca include such details about the conversation with the Indians?
  Answer: With these details the author is able to heighten the drama of the apparent fearsomeness of the distant tribe.

❹ Critical Thinking
Making Inferences

- Explain to students that exploration narratives not only provide information about explorers' experiences, but also reveal information about the explorers themselves and the cultures from which they came.

- Ask students to describe the character of the Spanish explorers as shown by their interaction with the Native Americans.
  Answer: Students may call the Spaniards single-minded, uncompromising, or manipulative.

❺ ☑ Reading Check
Answer: Their enemies live there.

CUSTOMIZE INSTRUCTION FOR UNIVERSAL ACCESS

For Less Proficient Readers	For English Learners	For Advanced Readers
Help students recognize that the Spanish explorers probably infected the Native Americans with the illness of which eight of them died. Let students know that Europeans and Native Americans had no immunity to one another's diseases. Tragedies of this kind happened often, and contributed to distrust and hostility between the two groups.	Take advantage of this opportunity to invite English learners to share some of their insights about strategies people use to surmount language differences. Students might mention sign language, gestures, drawings, and so on, as techniques for communicating in the absence of a common spoken language.	Remind students to keep in mind the chronicler's purpose as they read. Have them consider whether the narrator knows he's making history. Though he must observe and record events carefully, he may also want to present his efforts and results in the best possible light. Do students see any evidence to this effect?

9

6 ▶Critical Viewing

Answer: Students may respond that the Native Americans seem respectful or even slightly in awe of the Spaniards. They bring their sick to the Spaniards, then give them room to work their healing.

7 Vocabulary Development

The Latin Word Root -mort-

• Draw students' attention to the word *mortality* and its definition. Let students know that the Latin word root *-mort-* means "death."

• Have students volunteer words containing this word root, and list them on the chalkboard.

Possibilities include: *mortal, immortal, mortuary, mortician.*

• Have students identify how the meaning of the word root *-mort-* contributes to the meanings of the words they volunteered.

8 Reading Strategy

Recognizing Signal Words

• Ask students to explain the function of signal words.

• Then, ask students the Reading Strategy question on p. 34: What words signal time or other relationships in this paragraph?

Answer: *when, already, as, So, and*

Painting of Cabeza de Vaca, Esteban, and their companions among various Texan Indian tribes, Tom Mirrat, The Institute of Texan Cultures, San Antonio, Texas

6 ▲ **Critical Viewing** What does this painting suggest about the relationship between Cabeza de Vaca and the Native Americans? Why? **[Infer]**

7 more of their number, for they were convinced that we killed them by merely thinking of it. In truth, we were very much concerned about it, for, seeing the great <u>mortality</u>, we dreaded that all of them might die or forsake us in their terror, while those further on, upon learning of it, would get out of our way hereafter. We prayed to God our Lord to assist us, and the sick began to get well. Then we saw something that astonished us very much, and it was that, while the parents, brothers and wives of the dead had shown deep grief at their illness, from the moment they died the survivors made no demonstration whatsoever, and showed not the slightest feeling; nor did they dare to go near the bodies until we ordered their burial. . . .

The sick being on the way of recovery, when we had been there already three days, the women whom we had sent out returned, saying that they had met very few people, nearly all having gone after the cows, as it was the season. So we ordered those who had been sick to remain, and those who were well to accompany us, and that, two days' travel from there, the same women should go with us and get people to come to meet us on the trail for our reception.

8

mortality (môr tal´ ə tē) *n.* death on a large scale, as from disease or war

Reading Strategy
Recognizing Signal Words What words signal time or other relationships in this paragraph?

34 ◆ *Beginnings–1750*

✸ **ENRICHMENT: Science**

Native Americans at the time of the arrival of the Europeans would have been little helped by the meager healing powers of the conquistadors. Many Native American groups knew how to use wild plants to restore health; some knew of the healing properties of more than 200 plants. They knew, for instance, that boiled sagebrush leaves cured headaches, simmered rabbit brush stems and leaves made an effective cough medicine, and boiled willow leaves rubbed into the scalp could cure dandruff. Furthermore, some Native Americans discovered the natural source of digitalis

and of salicylic acid, the active ingredient in aspirin.

Did Native Americans have a knowledge of herbal medicine that equaled or surpassed ours today, as some pharmacologists have claimed? Invite interested students to look into the matter and see what they can find out about Native American folk medicine.

The next morning all those who were strong enough came along, and at the end of three journeys we halted. Alonso del Castillo and Estevanico,[3] the negro, left with the women as guides, and the woman who was a captive took them to a river that flows between mountains, where there was a village, in which her father lived, and these were the first abodes we saw that were like unto real houses. Castillo and Estevanico went to these and, after holding parley[4] with the Indians, at the end of three days Castillo returned to where he had left us, bringing with him five or six of the Indians. He told how he had found permanent houses, inhabited, the people of which ate beans and squashes, and that he had also seen maize.

Of all things upon earth this caused us the greatest pleasure, and we gave endless thanks to our Lord for this news. Castillo also said that the negro was coming to meet us on the way, near by, with all the people of the houses. For that reason we started, and after going a league and a half met the negro and the people that came to receive us, who gave us beans and many squashes to eat, gourds to carry water in, robes of cowhide, and other things. As those people and the Indians of our company were enemies, and did not understand each other, we took leave of the latter, leaving them all that had been given to us, while we went on with the former and, six leagues beyond, when night was already approaching, reached their houses, where they received us with great ceremonies. Here we remained one day, and left on the next, taking them with us to other permanent houses, where they subsisted on the same food also, and thence on we found a new custom.

The people who heard of our approach did not, as before, come out to meet us on the way, but we found them at their homes, and they had other houses ready for us. . . . There was nothing they would not give us. They are the best formed people we have seen, the liveliest and most capable; who best understood us and answered our questions. We called them "of the cows," because most of the cows die near there, and because for more than fifty leagues up that stream they go to kill many of them. Those people go completely naked, after the manner of the first we met. The women are covered with deerskins, also some men, especially the old ones, who are of no use any more in war.

The country is well settled. We asked them why they did not raise maize, and they replied that they were afraid of losing the crops, since for two successive years it had not rained, and the seasons were so dry that the moles had eaten the corn, so that they did not dare to plant any more until it should have rained very hard. And they also begged us to ask Heaven for rain, which we promised to do. We also wanted to know from where they brought their maize, and they said it came from where the sun sets, and that

---

3. **Estevanico** (es´ tā vä nē´ kō) Of Moorish extraction, Estevanico was the first African man to set foot in Texas.
4. **holding parley** (pär´ lē) conferring.

Literary Analysis
Exploration Narratives
What specific details about the region does the writer provide here?

subsisted (səb sist´ id) v. remained alive; were sustained

✓ **Reading Check**
What prevents some of the expedition group from completing the planned trip?

CUSTOMIZE INSTRUCTION FOR UNIVERSAL ACCESS

For Special Needs Students	For Advanced Readers
Encourage students to create a graphic organizer that helps them distinguish among the various Native American peoples mentioned by Cabeza de Vaca. Students might create a cluster diagram for each group, using words and phrases from the text to characterize each. The author alludes to five groups. Ensure that students record details about each group and their relationships with other groups and with the explorers.	Between 1492 and 1540, exploration and expansion fever spread through western Europe. By the time Cabeza de Vaca landed in Texas, the Spanish had gained a solid foothold in the Caribbean basin and in Mexico; Ponce de León had explored the coasts of what is now Florida; Verrazano had been up the Atlantic coast to Newfoundland; and Magellan's ships had rounded South America and crossed the Pacific Ocean. Invite interested students to prepare a research report on one or more of these explorers.

---

❾ **Background**
Art

Painting of Cabeza de Vaca, Esteban, and their companions, by Tom Mirrat

This work portrays the encounter between the Spanish explorers and the sick Native Americans, as described in Cabeza de Vaca's journal. Use these questions for discussion:

1. How can you distinguish the Spaniards from the Native Americans?
   Answer: Students may say that the Spaniards are the ones with beards. Three Spaniards kneel beside sick Native Americans, and Esteban is the African man standing to the left.

2. What are the people in the picture doing?
   Answer: Students may say that the Spaniards are praying over the victims or offering sympathy or medical help, while some frightened and worried Native Americans stand aside looking on.

❿ **Literary Analysis**
Exploration Narratives

- Have students reread silently the first paragraph on p. 35.
- Then, ask them the Literary Analysis question on p. 35: What specific details about the region does the writer provide here?
  Answer: He provides details about the housing and diet of the Native Americans who inhabit the region.

▶ Monitor Progress Ask students to explain the primary purpose of Europeans' exploration narratives.
  Answer: Students should specify that these exploration narratives were intended to provide detailed information about places and experiences to the people back home.

⓫ ✓ **Reading Check**
Answer: Some of the group were beset by illness.

- Have students take turns reading
  the selection's final eight paragraphs aloud. Ask students to be
  alert for references to maize.

- Ask students the Literary Analysis
  question on p. 36: What might
  readers in Europe have thought
  about the group's determination
  to find maize?
  Answer: Students may say that
  readers would have believed the
  explorers thought maize was a
  valuable crop.

⑫ it was found all over that country, and the shortest way to it was in that direction. We asked them to tell us how to go, as they did not want to go themselves, to tell us about the way.

They said we should travel up the river towards the north, on which trail for seventeen days we would not find a thing to eat, except a fruit called *chacan*, which they grind between stones; but even then it cannot be eaten, being so coarse and dry; and so it was, for they showed it to us and we could not eat it. But they also said that, going upstream, we could always travel among people who were their enemies, although speaking the same language, and who could give us no food, but would receive us very willingly, and give us many cotton blankets, hides and other things; but that it seemed to them that we ought not to take that road.

In doubt as to what should be done, and which was the best and most advantageous road to take, we remained with them for two days. They gave us beans, squashes, and calabashes.[5] Their way of cooking them is so new and strange that I felt like describing it here, in order to show how different and queer are the devices and industries of human beings. They have no pots. In order to cook their food they fill a middle-sized gourd with water, and place into a fire such stones as easily become heated, and when they are hot to scorch they take them out with wooden tongs, thrusting them into the water of the gourd, until it boils. As soon as it boils they put into it what they want to cook, always taking out the stones as they cool off and throwing in hot ones to keep the water steadily boiling. This is their way of cooking.

After two days were past we determined to go in search of maize, and not to follow the road to the cows, since the latter carried us to the north, which meant a very great circuit, as we held it always certain that by going towards sunset we should reach the goal of our wishes.

So we went on our way and <u>traversed</u> the whole country to the South Sea,[6] and our resolution was not shaken by the fear of great starvation, which the Indians said we should suffer (and indeed suffered) during the first seventeen days of travel. All along the river, and in the course of these seventeen days we received plenty of cowhides, and did not eat of their famous fruit (*chacan*), but our food consisted (for each day) of a handful of deer-tallow, which for that purpose we always sought to keep, and so endured these seventeen days, at the end of which we crossed the river and marched for seventeen days more. At sunset, on a plain between very high mountains, we met people who, for one-third of the year, eat but powdered straw, and as we went by just at that time, had to eat it also, until, at the end of that journey we found some permanent houses, with plenty of harvested maize, of which and of its meal they gave us great quantities, also squashes and beans, and blankets of cotton. . . .

---

5. **calabashes** (kal´ ə bash´ əz) *n.* dried, hollow shells of gourds used to hold food or beverages.
6. **the South Sea** the Gulf of Mexico.

Literary Analysis
**Exploration Narratives
and Author's Style** What
might readers in Europe
have thought about the
group's determination
to find maize?

traversed (trə vurst´) *v.*
moved over, across, or
through

Boulders Taller Than the Great Tower of Seville

From an account by García López de Cárdenas
Retold by Pedro de Castañeda

*I*nformation was obtained of a large river and that several days down the river there were people with very large bodies. As Don Pedro de Tovar had no other commission, he returned from Tusayán and gave his report to the general. The latter at once <u>dispatched</u> Don García López de Cárdenas there with about twelve men to explore this river. When he reached Tusayán he was well received and lodged by the natives. They provided him with guides to proceed on his journey. They set out from there laden with provisions, because they had to travel over some uninhabited land before coming to settlements, which the Indians said were more than twenty days away. Accordingly when they had marched for twenty days they came to gorges of the river, from the edge of which it looked as if the opposite side must have been more than three or four leagues[1] away by air. This region was high and covered with low and twisted pine trees; it was extremely cold, being open to the north, so that, although this was the warm season, no one could live in this canyon because of the cold.

The men spent three days looking for a way down to the river; from the top it looked as if the water were a fathom[2] across. But, according to the information supplied by the Indians, it must have been half a league wide. The descent was almost impossible, but, after these three days, at a place which seemed less difficult, Captain Melgosa, a certain Juan Galeras, and another companion, being the most agile, began to go down. They continued descending within view of those on top until they lost sight of them, as they could not be seen from the top. They returned about four o'clock in the afternoon, as they could not reach the bottom because of the many obstacles they met, for

---

1. **leagues** (lēgz) *n.* units of measurement of approximately 3 miles.
2. **fathom** (fath´ əm) *n.* a unit of measurement of six feet.

dispatched (di spacht´) *v.* sent off on a specific assignment

Literary Analysis
Exploration Narratives
What impression of the group's efforts is López de Cárdenas trying to convey in his narrative?

⑮ ☑**Reading Check**
Who is dispatched to explore the river?

Boulders Taller Than the Great Tower of Seville ◆ 37

⑬ **About the Selection**
By the time of Coronado's expedition in 1540, the Spanish knew there was gold and silver in the Americas. Although Coronado's search for the Seven Cities of Cibola led only to impoverished villages in present-day New Mexico, the group he dispatched northward led to European discovery of the Grand Canyon. García López de Cárdenas, with the help of Hopi guides from nearby mesas, became the first European to see this natural wonder. Unable to find water or to cross the canyon, Cárdenas eventually left in frustration.

⑭ **Literary Analysis**
Exploration Narratives
• Review with students the purpose a writer brings to an exploration narrative: to convey information about a travel expedition to an audience.
• Point out to students that some exploration narratives may be thought of as reports to an employer.
• Ask students the Literary Analysis question on p. 37: What impression of the group's efforts is Lopez de Cárdenas trying to convey in his narrative?
Answer: By including details relating to the harsh landscape and the Spaniards' sober determination to explore it, the writer seems to wish to convey an impression of the group's physical and mental hardiness.

⑮ ☑**Reading Check**
Answer: Don García López de Cárdenas and approximately twelve other men are dispatched to explore the river.

CUSTOMIZE INSTRUCTION FOR UNIVERSAL ACCESS

For Less Proficient Readers	For Gifted/Talented Students
Cultural anthropologists observe peoples of the world: recording what they eat, how they dress, the roles of the young and elderly, relationships with neighbors and outsiders, their values and beliefs, and so on. Ask students to imagine that a cultural anthropologist from another culture is visiting your community. Challenge pairs of students to prepare a list of features of public and private life that would help that social scientist better understand your culture.	Within the boundaries of Grand Canyon National Park are about 2,000 sites once inhabited by the Anasazi—the name given to the Native American peoples who lived in settlements throughout the plateau country of the Southwest. Encourage students to read further in the library or on the Internet about the Anasazi people. Have students write a poem or a drama about the Anasazi, focusing on what they might have thought upon seeing the European explorers gazing across the Grand Canyon.

16 ## Reading Strategy

Recognizing Signal Words

- Ask students the Reading Strategy question on p. 38: What change do the words "up to that time" signal?

  Answer: This phrase signals a change in the course of the journey.

▶ Monitor Progress Ask a student volunteer to explain the three most common types of relationships between ideas that are indicated by signal words.

  Answer: Signal words most commonly indicate time relationships, connections of causality, and contrasts.

Answers for p. 38

Review and Assess

1. Students who have never visited the canyon may be surprised that the Spaniards were unable to descend.

2. (a) They wanted them to serve as guides. (b) The Native Americans may have been afraid of the Spaniards.

3. (a) They are afraid that the Native Americans will flee in terror and leave them stranded—and that other Native Americans will then avoid them. (b) They believe the Spaniards have the power to wish them dead.

4. (a) They are expecting to explore the Colorado River. (b) Possible reasons include meeting and learning about the people reputed to live near the river or exploring the river's possible use as a means of travel.

5. (a) It appears to be about six feet wide. (b) They are viewing the river from an extraordinary height.

6. The account might contain detailed descriptions of the canyon's impressive size and beauty in order to convince financial backers that exploration of the canyon could bring them fame, glory, and riches.

what from the top seemed easy, was not so, on the contrary, it was rough and difficult. They said that they had gone down one-third of the distance and that, from the point they had reached, the river seemed very large, and that, from what they saw, the width given by the Indians was correct. From the top they could make out, apart from the canyon, some small boulders which seemed to be as high as a man. Those who went down and who reached them swore that they were taller than the great tower of Seville.[3]

16 The party did not continue farther up the canyon of the river because of the lack of water. Up to that time they had gone one or two leagues inland in search of water every afternoon. When they had traveled four additional days the guides said that it was impossible to go on because no water would be found for three or four days, that when they themselves traveled through that land they took along women who brought water in gourds, that in those trips they buried the gourds of water for the return trip, and that they traveled in one day a distance that took us two days.

This was the Tizón river, much closer to its source than where Melchior Díaz and his men had crossed it. These Indians were of the same type, as it appeared later. From there Cárdenas and his men turned back, as that trip brought no other results.

---

3. **great tower of Seville** The Giralda, the tower on the Cathedral of Seville in Spain, rises above the cathedral more than twice its height.

Reading Strategy

Recognizing Signal Words What change do the words "up to that time" signal?

Review and Assess

Thinking About the Selections

1. **Respond:** How does López de Cárdenas's description compare with your knowledge of the Grand Canyon?

2. **(a) Recall:** Why do the Spaniards in "A Journey Through Texas" order the Native Americans to travel with them? **(b) Infer:** Why do the Native Americans obey the orders?

3. **(a) Recall:** In "A Journey Through Texas," why do the Spaniards become fearful when the Native Americans in their company die? **(b) Draw Conclusions:** What do the Native Americans believe is the cause of the sickness?

4. **(a) Recall:** What are López de Cárdenas and his men expecting to explore? **(b) Infer:** Why does Coronado send the group on this mission?

5. **(a) Recall:** How wide does the river appear from the edge? **(b) Hypothesize:** Why does the river seem narrow from above?

6. **Extend:** How might these accounts have been different if they had been written to secure further funding?

✏️ ASSESSMENT PRACTICE: Reading Comprehension

Grammar and Language (For more practice, see Test Preparation Workbook, p. 2.)

Some tests ask students to make revision suggestions to fix erroneous sentences. A working knowledge of the sequence of verb tenses will help students spot verb tense errors, as in this example:

The chart listed those who were still lost and <u>those that have been found</u>.

  A NO CHANGE
  B those who had been found
  C those who are found
  D the saved

A correct answer must use the past perfect tense. The correct answer is Choice *B*.

Review and Assess

Literary Analysis

Exploration Narratives

1. Why is the image of the great tower of Seville used to convey the size of the boulders?
2. How do López de Cárdenas's experiences with the rough Grand Canyon terrain affect which details he includes in his **narrative**?

Comparing Literary Works

3. Compare and contrast the reactions of Cabeza de Vaca and López de Cárdenas to the Native American culture they encounter in their explorations. Record them in a chart like the one shown here.

Writer	Landscape and Cultural Details	Writer's Reaction
Cabeza de Vaca		
López de Cárdenas		

4. (a) How are the **authors' styles** similar? (b) How do they differ?
5. Which narrative do you think is more effective? Explain.

Reading Strategy

Recognizing Signal Words

6. Determine the type of relationship (time, reason, or contrast) in each of the italicized **signal words** in these passages.
   a. *Nevertheless* we insisted, saying that we wanted to go there, and they still excused themselves as best they could, *until* at last we became angry.
   b. We feigned to be angry still, *so as* to keep them in suspense, and *then* a singular thing happened.
   c. The party did not continue farther up the canyon of the river *because of* a lack of water.

Extend Understanding

7. **Social Studies Connection:** What other searches have led to settlement of specific areas of what is now the United States?

A Journey Through Texas / Boulders Taller Than the Great Tower of Seville ◆ 39

Quick Review

Exploration narratives recount the firsthand expedition experiences of their authors.

An **author's style** reflects his choice and arrangement of words and details.

Signal words indicate relationships of time, reason, or contrast among ideas or events in a narrative.

 Take It to the Net
www.phschool.com

Take the interactive self-test online to check your understanding of these selections.

Answers for p. 39

Review and Assess

1. The awe-inspiring height of the great tower would have been well known to López de Cárdenas's contemporaries.

2. Because he cannot reach the Colorado River, Cárdenas must describe its appearance from above and the ruggedness of the surrounding terrain.

3. Though both writers seem to find the Native Americans friendly and cooperative, neither appears to consider them as equals. Cabeza de Vaca, however, interacts freely with the Native Americans and describes their diets, customs, and practices in greater detail than López de Cárdenas, who does not record his reactions to his Native American guides.

4. The authors' styles are similar in their straightforward, earnest tone. Of the two writers, Cabeza de Vaca seems to write from a more personal vantage point.

5. Students' responses should be supported with reasons and with examples from the texts.

6. **(a)** contrast; time **(b)** causality; time **(c)** causality

7. Suggested responses include: Ponce de León explored the land he named Florida. Cortés came upon the lower peninsula of California. Lewis and Clark explored westward from the Louisiana territory to the Oregon territory. Each of these explorations foretold European development of a part of North America.

☀ **ENRICHMENT: Further Reading**

Other Works by the Authors

Works by Alvar Núñez Cabeza de Vaca
"Relación," (other portions of the explorer's narrative)

Works by Pedro de Castañeda
The Narrative of the Expedition of Coronado, (the account from which the selection is taken)

Related Works

The Odyssey of Cabeza de Vaca, Morris Bishop

Wilderness at Dawn, Ted Morgan

 Take It to the Net
Visit www.phschool.com for more information on the authors.

Answers for p. 40

❶ Vocabulary Development

Word Analysis

Paragraphs should present a coherent narrative and use the four words correctly.

Spelling Strategy

Possible responses:

1. indirect
2. improper
3. independent
4. dishonest

Fluency: Words in Context

1. dispatched
2. entreated
3. feigned
4. traversed
5. subsisted
6. mortality

❷ Grammar and Style

Practice

1. past; past perfect
2. past
3. past
4. past perfect
5. past perfect

Writing Application

Students' descriptions should make proper use of both past and past perfect tenses in order to show time relationships among the various steps or processes involved in the activity.

Integrate Language Skills

❶ Vocabulary Development Lesson

Word Analysis: Latin Root -mort-

The word *mortality* includes the Latin root -*mort*-, meaning "death." With a small group, develop a paragraph about a modern-day space explorer who dies during the landing of a dangerous mission. Use the following words in your description.

mortally	mortuary
mortician	immortalized

Spelling Strategy

Prefixes do not change spellings. When you add a prefix to a word, keep all the letters of the original word: im- + mortality = immortality.

Add a prefix such as *in-*, *im-*, or *dis-* to each of the words listed below to create a new word.

1. __ direct
2. __ proper
3. __ dependent
4. __ honest

Fluency: Words in Context

Choose the word from the vocabulary list on page 31 that best completes each sentence.

1. The soldiers were _____?_____ by the expedition leader to find the river.
2. The Spaniards _____?_____ their guides to continue leading the way.
3. When pleading didn't work, they _____?_____ anger in order to intimidate their guides.
4. In the course of their seventeen-day march, they _____?_____ a barren stretch of land.
5. The starving travelers _____?_____ on mouthfuls of deer tallow.
6. The conquistadors were alarmed by the _____?_____ that befell the natives.

❷ Grammar and Style Lesson

Past and Perfect Verb Tenses

The **past tense** of a verb shows an action that began and ended at a given time in the past. The **past perfect tense** indicates an action that ended before another past action began. Verbs in the past perfect consist of *had*, followed by the past participle. In this example, the past tense verbs are in italicized text and the past perfect verbs are underlined.

> After five days they <u>had</u> not <u>returned</u> and the Indians *explained* that it might be because they <u>had</u> not <u>found</u> anybody.
> (The explorers *had not returned* and *had not found* before the Indians *explained*.)

Practice Identify the tense of the italicized verb where appropriate, and then indicate the sequence of the action.

1. We *followed* the woman to a place where it *had been agreed* we should wait for them.
2. Many *fell* sick.
3. On the next day, eight of them *died*!
4. They *had gone* down one third of the distance.
5. Until then, they *had gone* one or two leagues inland in search of water.

Writing Application Write a description of an activity that you had worked on for some time. Use both the past and past perfect tenses.

W̧G Prentice Hall Writing and Grammar Connection: Chapter 21, Section 2

TEACHING RESOURCES

The following resources can be used to enrich or extend the instruction for pp. 40–41.

Vocabulary
📖 **Selection Support:** Build Vocabulary, p. 5
📖 **Vocabulary and Spelling Practice Book**

Grammar
📖 **Selection Support:** Build Grammar, p. 6
W̧G **Writing and Grammar,** Ruby Level, pp. 532–545 ■

■ **Daily Language Practice Transparencies**

Writing
W̧G **Writing and Grammar,** Ruby Level, Chapter 4
📖 **Extension Activities**
■ **Writing Models and Graphic Organizers on Transparencies,** pp. 13–16
💿 **Writing and Grammar iText CD-ROM** ■

■ **BLOCK SCHEDULING:** Resources marked with this symbol provide varied instruction during 90-minute blocks.

❸ Writing Lesson

Explorer's Journal

Imagine that like Cabeza de Vaca and López de Cárdenas, you have begun to explore a territory where no one has gone before. Write a journal entry that provides precise details about your discoveries.

Prewriting	Choose a location to explore. Gather specific details, through research if necessary, so that your description will help others follow in your footsteps.
Drafting	Use precise details, identifying items as clearly and exactly as you can. Remember, your audience may be unfamiliar with these objects.
Revising	Ask a friend to read your draft. If your reader cannot "see" your description, highlight vague words and replace them with more precise details.

Model: Revising to Add Precise Details

stretched out   *Evergreen*

The narrow valley was nearly a mile from end to end. Trees dotted the

laurel

upper mountain slopes, giving way first to bushes and then to grassy

granite

areas pierced by outcroppings.

> Words like *evergreen*, *laurel*, and *granite* identify details with more precision.

WG *Prentice Hall Writing and Grammar Connection: Chapter 6, Section 4*

❹ Extension Activities

Listening and Speaking As a member of the party that explored the Grand Canyon with López de Cárdenas, give a **speech** to convince Coronado that the entire expedition should travel to view the canyon. Use these tips.

- Incorporate your personal experiences.
- Blend vivid description with well-supported persuasion.

Present your speech to the class.

Research and Technology In a group, create an **exploration booklet** covering either the Grand Canyon or the area between Austin and El Paso, Texas. Gather information from the selections and Internet sources. Use a desktop publishing program to blend these with your text.

Take It to the Net   www.phschool.com

Go online for an additional research activity using the Internet.

A Journey Through Texas / Boulders Taller Than the Great Tower of Seville ◆ 41

ASSESSMENT RESOURCES

The following resources can be used to assess students' knowledge and skills.

Selection Assessment

- 📖 **Formal Assessment,** pp. 4–6
- 📖 **Open Book Test,** pp. 4–6
- 📼 **Got It! Assessment Videotapes,** Tape 1
- 💿 **Test Bank Software**
- 💻 **Take It to the Net**
  Visit www.phschool.com for self-tests and additional questions on the selections.

Writing Rubric

- 📖 **Performance Assess. and Portfolio Mgmt.,** p. 9

Listening and Speaking Rubric

- 📖 **Performance Assess. and Portfolio Mgmt.,** p. 17

PRENTICE HALL **ASSESSMENT SYSTEM**

- 📖 **Workbook**
- 📖 **Skill Book**
- 🖨 **Transparencies**
- 💿 **CD-ROM**

---

❸ Writing Lesson

- Students' journal entries should contain a wealth of details that make the descriptions of places, things, and people as vivid and specific as possible.

- Remind students to consider their audience as they gather details and then begin to draft their journal entries. Urge them to ask themselves the question, "How will I make this clear and interesting to my readers?"

- Use the Writing Lesson, as well as Writing Process Model 3, pp. 13–16, in **Writing Models and Graphic Organizers on Transparencies,** to guide students in developing their explorer's journal entries.

- Use the Autobiographical Narrative Nonfiction rubric in **Performance Assessment and Portfolio Management,** p. 9, to evaluate students' journal entries.

❹ Listening and Speaking

- Ask students to recall López de Cárdenas's goal: to explore the river we know now as the Colorado. Then have students reread the entire narrative to sharpen their understanding of what the expedition did and did not accomplish.

- Encourage students to plan their speeches by brainstorming a list of items and ideas to include. Remind them that their audience is their superior officer, Coronado. Their speeches should contain concise and vivid descriptions and explanations of student explorers' ideas.

- Urge students to deliver their speeches to the class from outlines rather than from completely composed scripts.

- Have students use the Peer Assessment form for Persuasive Speech in **Performance Assessment and Portfolio Management,** p. 17.

CUSTOMIZE INSTRUCTION
For Universal Access

To address different learning styles, use the following activities suggested in the **Extension Activities** booklet, p. 2

For Verbal/Linguistic Learners, use Activity 5.

For Visual/Spatial Learners, use Activity 6.

from The Interesting Narrative of the Life of Olaudah Equiano

Lesson Objectives

1. **To analyze and respond to literary elements**
   - Literary Analysis: Slave Narratives
   - Connecting Literary Elements: Emotional Appeals

2. **To read, comprehend, analyze, and critique nonfiction**
   - Reading Strategy: Summarizing
   - Reading Check Questions
   - Review and Assess Questions
   - Assessment Practice (ATE)

3. **To develop word analysis skills, fluency, and systematic vocabulary**
   - Vocabulary Development Lesson: Latin Word Root: *-vid-*

4. **To understand and apply written and oral language conventions**
   - Spelling Strategy
   - Grammar and Style Lesson: Active and Passive Voice

5. **To understand and apply appropriate writing and research strategies**
   - Writing Lesson: Museum Placard
   - Extension Activity: Research Presentation

6. **To understand and apply listening and speaking strategies**
   - Extension Activity: Debate

STEP-BY-STEP TEACHING GUIDE	PACING GUIDE
PRETEACH	
Motivate Students and Provide Background	
Use the Motivation activity (ATE p. 42)	5 min.
Read and discuss the author and background features (SE/ATE pp. 42, 45)	5 min.
Introduce the Concepts	
Introduce the Literary Analysis and Reading Strategy (SE/ATE p. 43)	15 min.
Pronounce the vocabulary words and read their definitions (SE p. 43)	5 min.
TEACH	
Monitor Comprehension	
Informally monitor comprehension by circulating while students read independently or in groups A	20 min.
Monitor students' comprehension with the Reading Check notes (SE/ATE pp. 45, 47)	as students read
Develop vocabulary with Vocabulary notes (SE pp. 45, 48; ATE p. 45)	as students read
Develop Understanding	
Develop students' understanding of slave narratives with the Literary Analysis annotations (SE p. 46; ATE pp. 43, 46) A	5 min.
Develop students' understanding of summarizing with the Reading Strategy annotations (SE p. 48; ATE p. 43)	5 min.
ASSESS	
Assess Mastery	
Assess students' mastery of the Reading Strategy and Literary Analysis by having them answer the Review and Assess questions (SE/ATE p. 49)	15 min.
Use one or more of the print and media Assessment Resources (ATE p. 51) A	up to 45 min.
EXTEND	
Apply Understanding	
Have students complete the Vocabulary Development Lesson and the Grammar and Style Lesson (SE p. 50) A	20 min.
Apply students' ability to write using sequence of events using the Writing Lesson (SE/ATE p. 51) A	45 min.
Apply students' understanding using one or more of the Extension Activities (SE p. 51)	20–90 min.

A **ACCELERATED INSTRUCTION:**
Use the strategies and activities identified with an **A**.

UNIVERSAL ACCESS
● = Below Level Students
▲ = On-Level Students
■ = Above Level Students

Time and Resource Manager

Reading Level: Average
Average Number of Instructional Days: 4

RESOURCES		
PRINT 📖	**TRANSPARENCIES**	**TECHNOLOGY** 💿 🎧
• **Beyond Literature,** Media Connection: Film Portrayals of Slave Trade, p. 3 ▲ ■		• **Interest Grabber Video,** Tape 1 ● ▲ ■
• **Selection Support Workbook:** ● ▲ ■ Literary Analysis, p. 12 Reading Strategy, p. 11 Build Vocabulary, p. 9	• **Literary Analysis and Reading Transparencies,** pp. 5 and 6 ● ▲ ■	
• **Adapted Reader's Companion** • **Reader's Companion**		• **Listening to Literature** ● ▲ ■ Audiocassettes, Side 2 Audio CDs, CD 1
• **English Learner's Companion** • **Literatura en español** ● ▲ • **Literary Analysis for Enrichment** ■		
• **Formal Assessment:** Selection Test, pp. 7–9 ● ▲ ■ • **Open Book Test,** pp. 7–9 ● ▲ ■ • **Performance Assessment and Portfolio Management,** p. 26 ● ▲ ■ • **ASSESSMENT SYSTEM** ● ▲ ■	• **ASSESSMENT SYSTEM** ● ▲ ■ Skills Practice Answers and Explanations on Transparencies	• **Test Bank Software** ● ▲ ■ • **Got It! Assessment Videotapes,** Tape 1 ● ▲
• **Selection Support Workbook:** ● ▲ ■ Grammar and Style, p. 10 • **Writing and Grammar,** Ruby Level ● ▲ ■ • **Extension Activities,** p. 3 ● ▲ ■	• **Daily Language Practice Transparencies** ● ▲ • **Writing Models and Graphic Organizers on Transparencies,** pp. 95–97 ● ▲ ■	• **Writing and Grammar iText CD-ROM** ● ▲ ■ 💻 *Take It to the Net* Take it to the Net www.phschool.com

■ **BLOCK SCHEDULING:** Use one 90-minute class period to preteach the selection and have students read it. Use a second 90-minute class period to assess students' mastery of skills and have them complete one of the Extension Activities.

Motivation

Students are probably familiar with common expressions using the term *slave,* which inadvertently trivialize the horrors of slavery. You might ask students if they have ever heard—or used—expressions such as *to slave over homework* or *slave to fashion.*

Invite students to empathize with victims of slavery by imagining being forcibly captured and then hauled like cargo for many weeks in the dark and airless hold of a ship.

▭ Interest Grabber Video

As an alternative, you may wish to play "African Slave Trade" on Tape 1 to engage students' interest.

❶ Background

More About the Author

In the Ibo language, the author's name means "well-spoken leader," and after his years of slavery, Olaudah Equiano lived up to his name—not only publishing his acclaimed *Interesting Narrative,* but also playing a prominent role in the British abolitionist movement. Equiano lectured, protested, and personally petitioned the British Parliament to outlaw slavery.

Prepare to Read

❶ *from* The Interesting Narrative of the Life of Olaudah Equiano

Olaudah Equiano (1745–1797)

When published in 1789, the autobiography of Olaudah Equiano (ō lä ōō´ dä ek´ wē än´ ō) created a sensation. It was so widely acclaimed that by 1794 it had run through eight editions in England and one in the United States. *The Interesting Narrative of the Life of Olaudah Equiano* made society face the cruelties of slavery and contributed to the banning of the slave trade in both the United States and England.

Born to Leadership The son of a tribal elder in the powerful kingdom of Benin, Equiano might have followed in his father's footsteps had he not been sold into slavery. When Equiano was eleven years old, he and his sister were kidnapped from their home in West Africa and sold to British slave traders. Their circumstance was not unusual. About 15 million Africans were captured between 1500 and 1800 and shipped to the Western Hemisphere, where they became slaves. Historians estimate that nearly two million slaves died before reaching their destination.

The Middle Passage As Equiano reports, the conditions of the Atlantic voyage were atrocious. For six to ten weeks, the slaves were crammed below deck in spaces sometimes less than five feet high. Families were torn apart, with men and women placed in separate holds. The men were often shackled together in pairs. Because Equiano was so young at the time of his capture, however, he was allowed to remain on deck, unshackled. There, he observed the mariners using a compass-like instrument to determine the ship's heading.

Seeing Equiano's fascination with the device, the mariners allowed him to get a closer look. It was on that deck, perhaps, that Equiano first gained an interest in the sea.

The ship first anchored in Bridgetown, the capital of Barbados in the West Indies. Separated from his sister, Equiano was taken to Virginia, where he was purchased by a British captain and employed at sea.

Saving to Buy Liberty Renamed Gustavus Vassa, Equiano was enslaved for nearly ten years. After managing his Philadelphia master's finances and making his own money in the process, Equiano amassed enough to buy his freedom. In later years, he settled in England and devoted himself to the abolition of slavery. In 1787, he was named commissary of the slave ship *Vernon,* which held more than five hundred freed slaves who were taken to Freetown, Sierra Leone, to establish a settlement there.

Telling the Tale To publicize the plight of slaves, Equiano wrote his two-volume autobiography, *The Interesting Narrative. . . .* Although his writing raised concerns about the inhumane conditions of slavery, the U.S. slave trade was not abolished by law until 1808, nearly twenty years after its publication. In addition to his writings on American slavery, Equiano also lectured and rallied against the cruelty of British slave owners in Jamaica.

Equiano's writing demonstrates the important influence slave narratives have in documenting historic events. Encouraged by abolitionists, many other freed or escaped slaves published narratives in the years before the Civil War. Others told their stories in the first part of the twentieth century. Henry Louis Gates, Jr., professor of English and African American studies, notes that "No other group of slaves anywhere, at any other period in history, has left such a large repository of testimony about the horror of becoming the legal property of another human being."

42 ◆ *Beginnings–1750*

TEACHING RESOURCES

The following resources can be used to enrich or extend the instruction for pp. 42–43.

Motivation
▭ **Interest Grabber Video,** Tape 1

Background
📖 **Beyond Literature,** p. 3 ▪

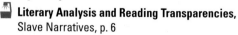
Take It to the Net

Visit www.phschool.com for Background and hotlinks for the selection.

Literary Analysis
📄 **Literary Analysis and Reading Transparencies,** Slave Narratives, p. 6

Reading
📄 **Literary Analysis and Reading Transparencies,** Summarizing, p. 5

📖 **Selection Support:** Reading Strategy, p. 11; Build Vocabulary, p. 9 ▪

BLOCK SCHEDULING: Resources marked with this symbol provide varied instruction during 90-minute blocks.

Preview

Connecting to the Literature

Imagine knowing that members of your family are valuable merchandise and could be shipped to a distant land to perform forced labor! If you lived in a world where slavery exists, you might develop a new attitude about the sweetness of freedom and the value of life.

❷ Literary Analysis

Slave Narratives

A uniquely American literary genre, a **slave narrative** is an autobiographical account of life as a slave. Often written to expose the horrors of human bondage, it documents a slave's experiences from his or her own point of view. In this example, Equiano describes the conditions on the ship.

> The shrieks of the women, and the groans of the dying, rendered the whole a scene of horror almost inconceivable.

As you read, look for other details that describe the horrors of the voyage.

Connecting Literary Elements

Equiano's narrative speaks persuasively against the slave trade by using deliberate **emotional appeals** to strengthen its impact. Writers create emotional appeals with words, such as "groans" and "shrieks," and details that trigger feelings of sympathy or outrage. For example, when Equiano describes the Africans begging for food, readers who have experienced hunger can likely sympathize with their plight. Notice how Equiano appeals to readers' emotions.

❸ Reading Strategy

Summarizing

As you read material published in another time period or written in an unfamiliar style, it is often helpful to **summarize** the main points. When you summarize, you state briefly in your own words the main ideas and key details of the text. Use a chart like the one shown which summarizes Equiano's first paragraph. As you read, write notes like these to help you summarize Equiano's ideas.

Main Point

The slaves were kept in unbearable conditions.

Detail
People were chained.

Detail
Disease ran rampant.

Detail
People were hungry.

Vocabulary Development

loathsome (lōth′ səm) *adj.* hateful; detestable (p. 45)

pestilential (pes′ tə len′ shəl) *adj.* likely to cause disease (p. 45)

copious (kō′ pē əs) *adj.* plentiful; abundant (p. 45)

improvident (im präv′ ə dənt) *adj.* shortsighted (p. 45)

avarice (av′ ə ris) *n.* greed for riches (p. 45)

pacify (pas′ ə fī) *v.* calm; soothe (p. 48)

from The Interesting Narrative of the Life of Olaudah Equiano ◆ 43

---

❷ Literary Analysis

Slave Narratives

- Tell students that they will focus on the characteristics of slave narratives as they read the following selection.

- As they read Olaudah Equiano's firsthand account of his experiences in slavery, have students consider his purpose for writing and reflect on how his tone affects their perceptions of the things he describes.

- Make sure to allow students sufficient time to discuss their personal responses to the selection.

❸ Reading Strategy

Summarizing

- Explain that summarizing can help students understand and remember a piece of writing.

- Remind students that summarizing requires that they identify and extract only the main ideas and most important details from their reading.

- Point out that summarizing can be especially useful in helping students master literary works that concern unfamiliar events, perspectives, and settings.

Vocabulary Development

- Pronounce each vocabulary word for students, and read the definitions as a class. Have students identify any words with which they are already familiar.

 E-Teach

Visit E-Teach at www.phschool.com for teachers' essays on how to teach, with questions and answers.

CUSTOMIZE INSTRUCTION FOR UNIVERSAL ACCESS

For Special Needs Students	For Less Proficient Readers	For English Learners
Have students read the adapted version of Equiano's narrative in the **Adapted Reader's Companion.** This version provides basic-level instruction in an interactive format with questions and write-on lines. Completing the adapted version will prepare students to read the selection in the Student Edition.	Have students read Equiano's narrative in the **Reader's Companion.** This version provides basic-level instruction in an interactive format with questions and write-on lines. After students finish the selection in **Reader's Companion,** have them complete the questions and activities in the Student Edition.	Have students read the adapted version of this selection in the **English Learner's Companion.** This version provides basic-level instruction in an interactive format with questions and write-on lines. Completing the adapted version will prepare students to read the selection in the Student Edition.

CUSTOMIZE INSTRUCTION
For Visual/Spatial and
Bodily/Kinesthetic Learners

To convey a modest approximation of the desperately crowded and deadly conditions on a slave ship, urge students to imagine the experience of being jammed tightly for weeks at a time into a rush-hour bus.

❶ About the Selection

Like Harriet Beecher Stowe's explosive, best-selling novel *Uncle Tom's Cabin* (1853), Equiano's work had a significant effect on the institution of slavery. By exposing the cruelty of slavery, both works contributed to its eventual demise in the United States. Unlike Stowe's work, *The Interesting Narrative* is a firsthand account of an actual event. Equiano communicates heinous details of the slave trade vividly but simply.

❷ Background

Art

Slaves Below Deck (detail), by Lt. Francis Meynell

This picture depicts a scene aboard a Spanish slave ship on its way to the West Indies.

• Do you think Meynell or Equiano more vividly captures the horror of the voyage? Explain.
  Possible response: Students may say Equiano's description seems more horrible than the scene portrayed in the painting because it tells of the stench, the pain of the shackles, and the mistreatment that slaves endured—none of which are immediately evident in the painting.

❸ ▶ Critical Viewing

Answer: Students may say that the painting is less dire than the scenes Equiano describes. Students may point to details such as the apparent lack of shackles and air and light reaching into the hold from the deck above.

❶ *from* **The Interesting Narrative
of the Life of**
Olaudah Equiano

Olaudah Equiano

Slaves Below Deck (detail), Lt. Francis Meynell, National Maritime Museum, Greenwich

❸ ▲ **Critical Viewing** The artist portrays conditions on a slave ship. Compare and contrast this image with the one that Equiano describes. **[Compare and Contrast]**

44 ◆ *Beginnings–1750*

TEACHING RESOURCES

The following resources can be used to enrich or extend the instruction for pp. 44–48.

Literary Analysis

📖 **Selection Support:** Literary Analysis
   p. 12

Reading Strategy

📖 **Reader's Companion**

📖 **English Learner's Companion**

🎧 **Listening to Literature Audiocassettes,** Side 2 ◼

💿 **Listening to Literature CDs,** CD 1 ◼

◼ **BLOCK SCHEDULING:** Resources marked with this symbol provide varied instruction during 90-minute blocks.

Background

In the first several chapters of his narrative, Olaudah Equiano describes how he and his sister were kidnapped by slave traders from their home in West Africa and transported to the African coast. During this six- or seven-month journey, Equiano was separated from his sister and held at a series of way stations. After reaching the coast, Equiano was shipped with other slaves to North America. The following account describes this horrifying journey.

❹ At last when the ship we were in, had got in all her cargo, they made ready with many fearful noises, and we were all put under deck, so that we could not see how they managed the vessel. But this disappointment was the least of my sorrow. The stench of the hold while we were on the coast was so intolerably <u>loathsome</u>, that it was dangerous to remain there for any time, and some of us had been permitted to stay on the deck for the fresh air; but now that the whole ship's cargo were confined together, it became absolutely <u>pestilential</u>. The closeness of the place, and the heat of the climate, added to the number in the ship, which was so crowded that each had scarcely room to turn himself, almost suffocated us. This produced <u>copious</u> perspirations, so that the air soon became unfit for respiration, from a variety of loathsome smells, and brought on a sickness among the slaves, of which many died—thus falling victims to the <u>improvident avarice</u>, as I may call it, of their purchasers. This wretched situation was again aggravated by the galling of the chains, now become insupportable, and the filth of the necessary tubs, into which the children often fell, and were almost suffocated. The shrieks of the women, and the groans of the dying, rendered the whole a scene of horror almost inconceivable. Happily perhaps, for myself, I was soon reduced so low here that it was thought necessary to keep me almost always on deck; and from my extreme youth I was not put in fetters.[1] In this situation I expected every hour to share the fate of my companions, some of whom were almost daily brought upon deck at the point of death, which I began to hope would soon put an end to my miseries. Often did I think many of the inhabitants of the deep much more happy than myself. I envied them the freedom they enjoyed, and as often wished I could change my condition for theirs. Every circumstance I met with, served only to render my state more painful, and heightened my apprehensions, and my opinion of the cruelty of the whites.

---

1. **fetters** (fet´ ərz) n. chains.

loathsome (lōth´ səm) adj. hateful; detestable

pestilential (pes´ tə len´ shəl) adj. likely to cause disease

copious (kō´ pē əs) adj. plentiful; abundant

improvident (im präv´ ə dənt) adj. shortsighted

avarice (av´ ə ris) n. greed for riches

❺ ✔ **Reading Check**
What conditions on the ship caused many of the slaves to die?

---

❹ ## Vocabulary Development
The Latin Root -vid-

- Call students' attention to the word *improvident* and its definition. Tell students that the Latin root -vid- comes from the Latin word *videre*, meaning "to see."
- Remind students that the prefix *im-* reverses (or negates) the meaning of *provident*, "to have foresight."
- Invite students to brainstorm a list of English words that contain the Latin root -vid-. Such words include *video* and all related terms (*videocassette*, *videotape*, *videodisk*).

❺ ## ✔ Reading Check

Answer: The author indicates that the foulness of the air causes respiratory problems that in turn cause some people to die.

CUSTOMIZE INSTRUCTION FOR UNIVERSAL ACCESS

For Special Needs Students	For English Learners
Help students focus on the text as they read Equiano's descriptions by having them use a graphic organizer to list sensory words and phrases. Students might use multiple cluster diagrams, sunbursts, or a basic five-column vertical chart. Students in pairs might take turns reading aloud and listing sensory images such as *fearful noises, stench,* and *almost suffocated.*	Have small groups of students listen to the recording of the selection on the **Listening to Literature Audiocassettes** or **Listening to Literature CDs** as they follow along in their texts. Have students pause the recording after each paragraph in order to discuss what they have heard and read. Encourage groups to end each discussion with a summary of the paragraph's most important ideas and details.

Answer: Students' estimates will vary and may be obtained by estimating the number of slaves per row and then multiplying by the number of rows. Although it is impossible for students to know what the artist thought and felt about slavery, they may surmise from the overcrowding that the ship's captain, owner, designer, or builder had little regard for its human cargo.

7 Literary Analysis

Slave Narratives and Emotional Appeal

- Read aloud with students the long sentence that starts the paragraph on p. 46. Encourage students to identify two distinct injustices that are presented in this passage.
  Answer: Injustices include the crew's throwing food overboard rather than allowing the slaves to eat it, and the crew's flogging some slaves for trying to get something to eat.

- Ask students the Literary Analysis question on p. 46: What is the effect of these floggings on the reader's emotions?
  Answer: Most readers will feel disgust, anger, or sadness while reading the report of these floggings.

6 ◀ Critical Viewing Estimate the number of slaves that this ship can carry. What do the drawings suggest about the ship designer's attitude toward slavery? **[Draw Conclusions]**

7 One day they had taken a number of fishes; and when they had killed and satisfied themselves with as many as they thought fit, to our astonishment who were on deck, rather than give any of them to us to eat, as we expected, they tossed the remaining fish into the sea again, although we begged and prayed for some as well as we could, but in vain; and some of my countrymen, being pressed by hunger, took an opportunity, when they thought no one saw them, of trying to get a little privately; but they were discovered, and the attempt procured them some very severe floggings. One day, when we had a smooth sea and moderate wind, two of my wearied countrymen who were chained together (I was near them at the time), preferring death

**Literary Analysis
Slave Narratives** What is the effect of these floggings on the reader's emotions?

✷ ENRICHMENT: FINE ARTS

Music

John Newton (1725-1807), a slave trader, experienced a total personal transformation after several voyages transporting slaves. He renounced what he now saw as his evil deeds and expressed his repentance in a musical composition, *Amazing Grace*, which was published in 1799. Reverend Newton dedicated his remaining years to the church. His inspiring song is still heard today at family gatherings and as a hymn sung in churches around the world.

You may wish to play a recording of this song or to invite a volunteer to sing it. Interested students can do research to learn more about the history and recordings of this song and of the unusual life of John Newton. In addition to library or Internet research, students may enjoy viewing the PBS video *Amazing Grace*, which presents background on Newton and explores the evolution and widespread social impact of his song.

to such a life of misery, somehow made through the nettings and jumped into the sea; immediately, another quite dejected fellow, who, on account of his illness, was suffered to be out of irons, also followed their example; and I believe many more would very soon have done the same, if they had not been prevented by the ship's crew, who were instantly alarmed. Those of us that were the most active, were in a moment put down under the deck; and there was such a noise and confusion amongst the people of the ship as I never heard before, to stop her, and get the boat out to go after the slaves. However, two of the wretches were drowned, but they got the other, and afterwards flogged him unmercifully, for thus attempting to prefer death to slavery. In this manner we continued to undergo more hardships than I can now relate, hardships which are inseparable from this accursed trade. Many a time we were near suffocation from the want of fresh air, which we were often without for whole days together. This, and the stench of the necessary tubs, carried off many.

During our passage, I first saw flying fishes, which surprised me very much; they used frequently to fly across the ship, and many of them fell on the deck. I also now first saw the use of the quadrant;[2] I had often with astonishment seen the mariners make observations with it, and I could not think what it meant. They at last took notice of my surprise; and one of them, willing to increase it, as well as to gratify my curiosity, made me one day look through it. The clouds appeared to me to be land, which disappeared as they passed along. This heightened my wonder; and I was now more persuaded than ever, that I was in another world, and that every thing about me was magic. At last, we came in sight of the island of Barbados, at which the whites on board gave a great shout, and made many signs of joy to us. We did not know what to think of this; but as the vessel drew nearer, we plainly saw the harbor, and other ships of different kinds an sizes, and we soon anchored amongst them, off Bridgetown.[3] Many merchants and planters now came on board, though it was in the evening. They

---

2. **quadrant** (kwä´ drənt) *n.* an instrument used by navigators to determine the position of a ship.
3. **Bridgetown** *n.* the capital of Barbados.

from *The Interesting Narrative of the Life of Olaudah Equiano* ◆ 47

Literature in context — Economics ⑧

The Slave Trade

While many people came to the new world in search of riches, many others were brought against their will to the Western Hemisphere to be sold as slaves. The map below indicates the major slave trade routes.

The Atlantic crossing, known as "the middle passage," was atrocious. For six to ten weeks, Africans were chained below decks in cramped, confining spaces. Overcrowding, disease, and despair claimed many lives. Some Africans mutinied, and others tried to starve themselves or jump overboard. Equiano's narrative describes his middle-passage experience.

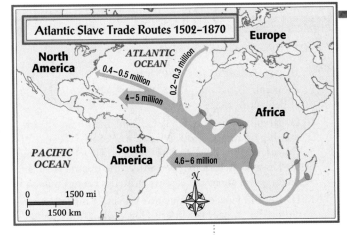

Atlantic Slave Trade Routes 1502–1870

Europe
North America
ATLANTIC OCEAN
0.4–0.5 million
0.2–0.3 million
4–5 million
Africa
PACIFIC OCEAN
South America
4.6–6 million

0   1500 mi
0   1500 km

⑨ ✔ Reading Check

What do some slaves do to escape the misery of the middle passage?

⑧ Background

The Slave Trade

Between 1500 and 1800, about 15 million Africans were captured and shipped as slaves to the Western Hemisphere. Historians estimate that nearly two million slaves died during the middle passage before reaching their destinations. You may wish to point out that Equiano and others were months in transit prior to boarding the ship itself—and that they then spent several weeks on board before setting sail. Often pairs of adult captives were chained together at the ankles and wrists, and the shackles were removed only when one of the pair became very sick or died.

⑨ ✔ Reading Check

Answer: Some slaves choose to jump into the ocean and drown themselves rather than continue to endure the torture of the middle passage.

CUSTOMIZE INSTRUCTION FOR UNIVERSAL ACCESS

For Less Proficient Readers	For Advanced Readers
Help students to make connections between the inset map and the information that appears in the Literature in Context box. Students should be able to recognize where the "middle passage" got its name and why it is so important to African Americans living in the United States.	Draw students' attention to the map, and point out that only a fraction of the total number of enslaved Africans came to what is now the United States. Encourage students to research the histories of these various populations of Africans and where their descendants live now.

⑩ Critical Thinking

Drawing Conclusions

Ask students to explain what the presence of a variety of languages indicates about the slave trade. **Answer:** Students should say that the slave trade was widespread throughout Africa.

Answers for p. 48

Review and Assess

1. Students may be impressed by Equiano's curiosity and eagerness to learn. They may also react to the high level of education that his writing shows he was able to obtain.

2. **(a)** Equiano believes that the traders' greed has led them to load the ships with more slaves than can comfortably fit. Thus their greed causes unsanitary conditions and illness. **(b)** The white crewmen view their captives as little more than cargo. **(c)** The captors do not seem to believe their cargo is human. They seem to believe that their captives' lives are only as valuable as the profit they bring.

3. **(a)** Equiano was granted certain privileges because of his age. For example, he was often kept on deck rather than in the cramped quarters below. **(b)** He probably felt lucky to be spared some of the degradation suffered by the other slaves.

4. **(a)** They preferred death to the misery aboard the ship. **(b)** The crew flogs newly rescued slaves to discourage others from attempting suicide.

5. Possible response: His strong constitution and instinct for survival are evident in his forceful prose.

6. Possible response: Through victims' recorded experiences, other people can understand history and learn how to prevent similar atrocities from recurring in the future.

---

put us in separate parcels,[4] and examined us attentively. They also made us jump, and pointed to the land, signifying we were to go there. We thought by this, we should be eaten by these ugly men, as they appeared to us; and, when soon after we were all put down under the deck again, there was much dread and trembling among us, and nothing but bitter cries to be heard all the night from these apprehensions, insomuch, that at last the white people got some old slaves from the land to <u>pacify</u> us. They told us we were not to be eaten, but ⑩ to work, and were soon to go on land, where we should see many of our country people. This report eased us much. And sure enough, soon after we were landed, there came to us Africans of all languages.

We were conducted immediately to the merchant's yard, where we were all pent up together, like so many sheep in a fold, without regard to sex or age. . . . We were not many days in the merchant's custody, before we were sold after their usual manner, which is this: On a signal given (as the beat of a drum), the buyers rush at once into the yard where the slaves are confined, and make choice of that parcel they like best. . . .

pacify (pas´ ə fī´) v. calm; soothe

---

4. **parcels** (pär´ səlz) n. groups.

Review and Assess

Thinking About the Selection

1. **Respond:** Based on his narrative, what is your impression of Equiano?

2. **(a) Recall:** Why does Equiano blame the illness aboard the ship on the "improvident avarice" of the traders?
   (b) Infer: How do the white crewmen view their captives?
   (c) Draw Conclusions: What does the treatment of the slaves reveal about the captors' attitudes toward human life?

3. **(a) Recall:** How does Equiano's age affect his experiences during the voyage? **(b) Infer:** How do you think he felt about his experience compared to the fate of other slaves on the ship?

4. **(a) Recall:** Why do some of the slaves jump overboard?
   (b) Infer: Why do you suppose the slaves who were rescued after jumping overboard got flogged?

5. **Analyze:** How does Equiano prove his great zest for life despite his assertion that he wants to die? Provide examples from the story.

6. **Generalize:** Why is it important for people who are victims of such human injustices to record their experiences?

✎ ASSESSMENT PRACTICE: Reading Comprehension

Summarizing Written Texts: Implied Main Idea   (For more practice, see Test Preparation Workbook, p. 3.)

When the main idea is not directly stated, students must infer the main focus of the passage. Some tests require students to identify the implied main idea of a reading passage. Have students reread p. 45. Then have them choose the implied main idea of the paragraph from the following responses:

A Most slaves were kept in the hold below the deck.

B Death seemed better than life to slaves on the African slave ships.

C Slave ships from Africa were filthy, overcrowded and cruelly managed, which caused many slaves to sicken and die.

D Equiano wrote a journal about life on an African slave ship.

Choice *A* is a supporting detail and choices *B* and *D* present background information. Choice *C* contains the implied main idea.

Review and Assess

Literary Analysis

Slave Narratives

1. According to Equiano's **slave narrative,** what was the general feeling of the slaves toward their situation?
2. Cite two examples of the slave traders' cruelty to the slaves.
3. Cite two examples that show the traders' concern for the slaves' well-being.
4. What might have motivated the traders' behavior toward their human cargo? Explain.

Connecting Literary Elements

5. (a) Using a chart like the one shown here, identify three examples of **emotional appeal** in Equiano's narrative. (b) What is the effect of these appeals on the reader?

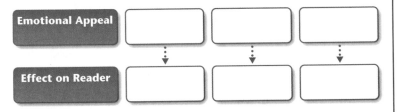

Emotional Appeal			

Effect on Reader			

6. What aspect of the conditions aboard ship does Equiano stress in his account?
7. Explain how emotional appeals might strengthen Equiano's position against the slave trade.

Reading Strategy

Summarizing

8. Identify at least three main ideas the author conveys about the voyage.
9. Summarize the events that occur after the ship reached Bridgetown.

Extend Understanding

10. **Social Studies Connection:** How does Equiano's voyage compare with those of explorers and colonists?

from *The Interesting Narrative of the Life of Olaudah Equiano* ◆ 49

Quick Review

A **slave narrative** is an autobiographical account of life as a slave.

Emotional appeals include vivid words and examples chosen for the feelings they inspire in readers.

To **summarize,** state main ideas and key details in your own words.

 Take It to the Net
www.phschool.com

Take the interactive self-test online to check your understanding of the selection.

☀ENRICHMENT: Further Reading

Other Works About the Middle Passage

The Middle Passage: White Ships, Black Cargo, Tom Feelings and John Henrick

Roots, Alex Haley

Middle Passage, Charles Johnson

 Take It to the Net
Visit www.phschool.com for more information on this subject.

Answers for p. 49

Review and Assess

1. The slaves felt complete despair. Many expressed a desire to die rather than endure conditions aboard the slave ship.

2. Possible response: The traders give the slaves very little living space on board ship. They routinely beat slaves to punish them.

3. The traders indulge Equiano's curiosity by allowing him to use the quadrant. They allow younger slaves to be kept out of chains and above deck.

4. The traders' main motivation is to make as much money as possible.

5. (a) Possible response: *so intolerably loathsome, absolutely pestilential,* and *wretched situation.* (b) These emotional appeals encourage the reader to empathize with the slaves.

6. Equiano stresses the unsanitary conditions.

7. Even eighteenth-century readers who accepted slavery as an economic idea might have been touched by Equiano's highly charged language. People's emotional reactions sometimes lead to changes in their opinions.

8. Summaries should include the following main points: Olaudah Equiano traveled across the Atlantic Ocean in a slave ship. The conditions on board were detestable; most slaves were confined to an overheated, cramped space. The crew treated the slaves as less than human, often flogging them for trespasses.

9. When the ship arrived on shore the frightened slaves were brought to auction and sold.

10. Possible response: Colonists and explorers did not know what they would find; however, they made the choice to take such a risk. Equiano's voyage is made against his will under horrible conditions.

❶ Vocabulary Development

Word Analysis

1. Evidence can establish guilt because others can see proof of what took place.

2. People using video phones might become more concerned with their appearance before making a call.

Spelling Strategy

1. immortal
2. imbalanced
3. impossible
4. imprecise

Concept Development:

1. synonyms
2. antonyms
3. antonyms
4. antonyms
5. synonyms
6. antonyms

❷ Grammar and Style

Practice

Suggested answers:

1. The crew permitted some of us to stay on the deck for fresh air.

2. The conditions soon reduced me so low.

3. The crew thought it necessary to keep me almost always on deck.

4. Crew members discovered them.

5. They saw flying fish.

Looking at Style

Answer: "We were conducted immediately . . ."; "We were all pent up together . . ."; "We were sold . . ." The passive voice emphasizes the helplessness and powerlessness of the slaves.

Integrate Language Skills

❶ Vocabulary Development Lesson

Word Analysis: Latin Root *-vid-*

The Latin root *-vid-*, from *videre*, means "to see." The word *provident* means "to have foresight." Considering the meaning of the root *-vid-*, answer these questions:

1. Why is *evidence* useful in establishing guilt?
2. How would *video* technology change telephone habits?

Spelling Strategy

Change the spelling of *in-*, a common prefix meaning "not," to *im-* when you add it to words beginning with *b, m,* or *p* (as in *improvident*). Using this strategy, spell the words described below:

1. not mortal
2. not balanced
3. not possible
4. not precice

Concept Development: Synonym or Antonym

Review the list of vocabulary words on page 43. Then, analyze the relationship between the words in each of the following pairs. Indicate whether the words are synonyms (words with similar meanings) or antonyms (words with opposite meanings).

1. loathesome, hateful
2. pestilential, sanitary
3. copious, sparse
4. improvident, cautious
5. avarice, greed
6. pacify, torment

❷ Grammar and Style Lesson

Active and Passive Voice

A verb is in the **active voice** when the subject of the sentence performs the action. A verb is in the **passive voice** when the subject receives the action.

> **Active Voice:** <u>They</u> *tossed* the remaining fish into the sea.
> (The subject, *they*, performs the action of the verb *tossed*.)
>
> **Passive Voice:** This <u>situation</u> *was aggravated* by the galling of the chains.
> (The subject, *situation*, receives the action of the verb *was aggravated*.)

Practice Rewrite the following sentences using the active voice. You may need to add words to indicate who performed the action.

1. Some of us had been permitted to stay on the deck for fresh air.
2. I was soon reduced so low here.
3. It was thought necessary to keep me almost always on deck.
4. They were discovered.
5. Flying fish were seen.

Looking at Style Find three examples of the passive voice in the final paragraph of the selection. What effect does the style have on your understanding of the slaves' experiences?

W̶G̶ Prentice Hall Writing and Grammar Connection: Chapter 21, Section 4

TEACHING RESOURCES

The following resources can be used to enrich or extend the instruction for pp. 50–51.

Vocabulary

📖 **Selection Support:** Build Vocabulary, p. 9
📖 **Vocabulary and Spelling Practice Book**

Grammar

📖 **Selection Support:** Grammar and Style, p. 10
W̶G̶ **Writing and Grammar,** Ruby Level, pp. 552–554
🖥 **Daily Language Practice Transparencies** ▪

Writing

W̶G̶ **Writing and Grammar,** Ruby Level, Chapter 10 ▪
📖 **Extension Activities**
🖥 **Writing Models and Graphic Organizers on Transparencies,** pp. 95–97
💿 **Writing and Grammar iText CD-ROM**

▪ **BLOCK SCHEDULING:** Resources marked with this symbol provide varied instruction during 90-minute blocks.

❸ Writing Lesson

Museum Placard

To educate today's audiences, museums present exhibits that document the slave trade of the 1800s. Write the introductory information for a large placard that visitors will read at an exhibit's beginning. Explain the sequence of events of the slave trade, from capture to slave auction.

Prewriting   Use library sources to gather facts. Organize your findings in sequence, perhaps by drawing a map to trace the routes or marking dates and other key details on a timeline.

Drafting   Create a timeline like the one shown to organize the events that occurred, listing them in chronological order. Begin with what happens first, and then continue in time order.

Model: Organizing Events in Chronological Order

| What happened first? How were the slaves captured? | What were the events during the voyage? | What events occurred after the ship landed? |

Revising   Check that your placard highlights the important stages of the slave trade. Eliminate any confusing shifts in time sequence, and add transitions to sharpen that sequence.

Prentice Hall Writing and Grammar Connection: Chapter 10, Section 3

❹ Extension Activities

Listening and Speaking   Can slavery exist in today's society? In a **debate** argue this question with a group of classmates, using these tips:

- Create "pro" and "con" teams.
- Develop key arguments.
- Find supporting evidence.
- Assign positions for introductory arguments, rebuttal and conclusion.

Stage the debate for the class, responding to questions from your audience. **[Group Activity]**

Research and Technology   Modern organizations such as Amnesty International work to increase awareness of injustices around the world. Use the Internet or the library to research the causes it publicizes. Develop charts or diagrams and give a **research presentation.**

 Take It to the Net   www.phschool.com

Go online for an additional research activity using the Internet.

from *The Interesting Narrative of the Life of Olaudah Equiano* ◆ 51

---

❸ Writing Lesson

- Students' placards should use clear prose to present factual information in chronological order. Each placard should contain the most important actions and events of the slave trade, as well as key descriptive details.

- Remind students to use appropriate transition words to show the time order of events.

- Use the Writing Lesson, as well as the Outline graphic organizer in **Writing Models and Graphic Organizers on Transparencies**, pp. 95–97, to guide students in developing their museum placards.

❹ Research and Technology

- Students can find a wealth of information on Amnesty International's official Web site: www.amnesty.org. *We strongly recommend that you preview this and related sites before you send students to them.*

- Amnesty International was begun in Britain in 1961 with the goal of helping to free individuals "imprisoned solely because of their political or religious beliefs, gender, or racial or ethnic origin," though they had "neither used nor advocated violence." In 1977, the organization won the Nobel Peace Prize for its work.

- Students might organize their presentations according to particular causes, individuals, time periods, or geographic regions.

CUSTOMIZE INSTRUCTION
For Universal Access

To address different learning styles, use the following activities suggested in the **Extension Activities** booklet, p. 3.

For Musical/Rhythmic and Verbal/Linguistic Learners, use Activity 4.

For Visual/Spatial Learners, use Activity 5.

For Bodily/Kinesthetic Learners, use Activity 6.

ASSESSMENT RESOURCES

The following resources can be used to assess students' knowledge and skills.

Selection Assessment
- 📖 **Formal Assessment**, pp. 7–9
- 📖 **Open Book Test** pp. 7–9
- 📼 **Got It! Assessment Videotapes**, Tape 1
- 📖 **Test Bank Software**

- 🖥 ***Take It to the Net***
  Visit www.phschool.com for self-tests and additional questions on the selection.

Writing Rubric
- 📖 **Performance Assess. and Portfolio Mgmt.**, p. 12

Listening and Speaking Rubric
- 📖 **Performance Assess. and Portfolio Mgmt.**, p. 26

PRENTICE HALL ASSESSMENT *SYSTEM*
- 📖 **Workbook**
- 📖 **Skill Book**
- 📖 **Transparencies**
- 💿 **CD-ROM**

Lesson Objectives

1. To explore how customs and traditions are passed from generation to generation
2. To make connection between Native American life today and the traditional Native American ways of life

Connection

In this selection, Native American writer Darryl Babe Wilson explores the challenge of preserving the cultures and traditions reflected in the Native American myths and legends at the beginning of this unit. Have students reread the Native American pieces after reading Wilson's narrative. How does knowledge of Native American folklore increase students' appreciation of the issues Wilson addresses?

Meeting of Cultures

- Give students the following advance assignment: If you could ask an ancestor—a great-grandparent, for example—a question about the past, what would you want to know? What knowledge has been lost that you feel should be preserved for future generations? Ask volunteers to share their responses.

- Explain that when cultures meet—including the cultures of older and newer generations—benefits emerge, yet other things may be lost forever.

- Darryl Babe Wilson was aware of this problem. He writes of his grandfather, "The volumes of knowledge that were buried with him are lost to my generation." Tell students that to rescue a part of his knowledge and experiences, Wilson's grandfather chose to share one very important tale from his past with his grandson. The story they are about to read describes how the elderly Native American ensures that at least one piece of his knowledge was preserved.

▶ Critical Viewing

Answers: Students may feel that the weathered look of the grandfather's face suggests that he has a wealth of experiences—some difficult—that have shaped him.

Though each is quite different, the works in Part 1 share one thing in common: They record impressions of the world, new experiences, and new people seen through the filter of the writers' experiences and cultures. The Native Americans saw nature as the source of earthly life. The conquistadors viewed new lands and people within the framework of European values. Olaudah Equiano vividly portrayed the consequences of one culture's belief in its right to dominate another.

Each of their stories contributes uniquely to our understanding of the country that would become the United States of America. Today, the distinct lines that separated these cultures have blurred into a shared "American experience." America is still celebrated as a melting pot of cultures from around the world, but there are those who feel that some of the values that once shaped the nation are in danger of being left behind.

Keeping the Flame Alive The last two centuries have also seen the gradual disappearance of many of the cultures and customs of Native American peoples. Darryl Babe Wilson preserves in writing the memories of Native American elders. He confronts the elders' fear that the younger generation of Native Americans is unenlightened about its ancestral heritage. Wilson strives to bring about a "meeting of cultures."

Photo of a Native American male (Wailaki tribe), Edward S. Curtis, Southwest Museum, Los Angeles

▶ Critical Viewing
In what way does this portrait convey the wisdom of the grandfather in the story? [Connect]

52 ◆ Beginnings–1750

Diamond Island: ALCATRAZ

Allisti Ti-Tanin-Miji (Rock Rainbow)

Darryl Babe Wilson

There was a single letter in the mailbox. Somehow it seemed urgent. The address, although it was labored over, could hardly be deciphered—square childlike print that did not complete the almost individual letters. Inside, five pages written on both sides. Blunt figures. Each word pressed heavily into the paper. I could not read it but I could feel the message. "Al traz" was in the first paragraph, broken and scattered, but there. At the very bottom of the final page—running out of space—he scrawled his name. It curved down just past the right-hand corner. The last letter of his name, *n*, did not fit: *Gibso*. It was winter, 1971. I hurried to his home.

Grandfather lived at Atwam, 100 miles east of Redding, California, in a little shack out on the flat land. His house was old and crooked just like in a fairy tale. His belongings were few and they, too, were old and worn. I always wanted to know his age and often asked some of the older of our people if they could recall when Grandfather was born. After silences that sometimes seemed more than a year, they always shook their silver-gray heads and answered: "I dunno. He was old and wrinkled with white hair for as long as I can remember. Since I was just a child." He must have been born between 1850 and 1870.

Thanksgiving weekend, 1989. It is this time of the year when I think about Grandfather and his ordeal. I keep promising myself that I will write his story down because it is time to give the island of Alcatraz a proper identity and a "real" history. It is easy for modern people to think that the history of Alcatraz began when a foreign ship sailed into the bay and a stranger named Don Juan Manuel de Ayala[1] observed the "rock" and recorded "Alcatraz" in a log book in 1775. That episode, that sailing and that recording was only moments ago.

Grandfather said that long ago the Sacramento Valley was a huge freshwater lake, that it was "as long as the land" (from the northern

---

1. **Don Juan Manuel de Ayala** (dän hwän män wel´ dä ä yä´ lä) an eighteenth-century Spanish explorer who was the first European to enter San Francisco Bay.

Thematic Connection
Why might the writer want to write his grandfather's story down?

Background

Places or events can hold different meanings and mysteries for different generations or cultures. The essayist offers his beliefs and attitudes as he shares a story his grandfather told him years earlier. A bold escape from Alcatraz a century before was a key event in the history of his people, yet is little known today. The writer wonders how and whether later generations will come to understand and appreciate their heritage.

Meeting of Cultures

Isla de los Alcatraces, or Isle of the Pelicans, was once home to thousands of birds. Early settlers drove the birds away; eventually, Anglo settlers remade the island as a fortress, a military prison, then a maximum security penitentiary. Strong, cold currents churn past "The Rock," supposedly making escape impossible. After 1963, when the prison closed, Alcatraz lay vacant, but for a caretaker. In 1969, a group of "Indians of All Nations" took over the old prison, claiming that unused federal property could be returned to reservation status. They hoped to establish a Native American cultural center there, but left the island in 1971. Today, Alcatraz is one of San Francisco's most popular tourist attractions.

Thematic Connection

Answer: He probably wants to do so to prevent the story from being lost.

Critical Thinking

Draw Conclusions

Ask students why Thanksgiving may remind the narrator of Grandfather's ordeal. What inferences can students draw from the use of the word *ordeal*?
Possible response: While Thanksgiving is often a time for reflection, it also celebrates the cooperative spirit between Native Americans and colonists. *Ordeal* suggests Grandfather has been through something terrible.

CUSTOMIZE INSTRUCTION FOR UNIVERSAL ACCESS

For Less Proficient Readers	For English Learners	For Advanced Readers
To help students decode the events described in the selection, present a simple chronology of "Diamond Island: Alcatraz." The piece, written in 1989, records a conversation held in 1971 about an event that happened sometime between 1850 and 1870.	Help students understand this passage by clarifying idiomatic phrases. Guide them to grasp the meaning of "been within the earth for many snows now," restated as "has been buried for many winters, or years." Explain that *original knowledge* refers to "an understanding of one's past, based on the stories of his or her heritage."	Challenge students by asking: How can the necklace be interpreted as a symbol of the clash between grandfather's culture and another? **Possible response:** Students may say that the necklace stands for the tradition of the past, which encircled the mother, and was broken as a result of persecution.

Meeting of Cultures

Cultures often disagree about how to describe a place or tell when and how it was first discovered or occupied. Ask students to summarize the point the author makes about cultural conflict in this passage.
Possible response: Students should notice the author's belief that Native Americans knew about Alcatraz and held it sacred generations before Ayala "discovered" it in 1775.

Thematic Connection

Possible response: By writing this tale down for modern readers, the author introduces traditional Native American culture to a contemporary audience. Even the mention of place names, such as the Sacramento Valley and San Francisco Bay, within the context of the traditional tale represents a meeting of cultures.

part of California to the southern), and that a great shaking of an angry spirit within the earth caused part of the coastal range to crumble into the outer-ocean. When the huge lake finally drained and the waves from the earthquake finally settled, there was the San Francisco Bay, and there, in isolation and containing a "truth," was Diamond Island (Alcatraz).

He told me the story one winter in his little one-room house in Atwam. It is bitter cold there during winters. I arrived late in the evening, tires of my truck spinning up his driveway. The driveway was a series of frozen, broken mudholes in a general direction across a field to his home. The headlights bounced out of control.

My old 1948 Chevy pickup was as cold inside as it was outside. The old truck kept going, but it was a fight to make it go in the winter. It was such a struggle that we called it "Mr. Miserable." Mr. Miserable and I came to a jolting halt against a snowbank that was the result of someone shoveling a walk in the front yard. We <u>expended</u> our momentum. The engine died with a sputtering cough. Lights flopped out.

It was black outside but the crusted snow lay like a ghost upon the earth and faded away in every direction. The night sky trembled with the fluttering of a million stars—all diamond blue. Wind whipped broken tumbleweeds across his neglected yard. The snow could not conceal the yard's chaos.

The light in the window promised warmth. Steam puffing from every breath, I hurried to his door. The snow crunched underfoot, sounding like a horse eating a crisp apple. The old door lurched open with a complaint. Grandfather's fatigued, centenarian[2] body a black silhouette against the brightness—bright although he had but a single shadeless lamp to light the entire house. I saw a skinned bear once. It looked just like Grandfather. Short, stout arms and bowed legs. Compact physique. Muscular—not fat. Thick chest. Powerful. Natural.

Old powder-blue eyes strained to see who was out there in the dark. "Hallo. You're just the man I'm lookin' for." Coffee aroma exploded from the open door. Coffee. Warmth!

Grandfather stood back and I entered the comfort of his jumbled little bungalow. It was cozy in there. He was burning juniper wood. Juniper, cured for a summer, has a clean, delicate aroma—a perfume. After a healthy handshake we huddled over steaming cups of coffee. Grandfather looked long at me. I think that he was not totally convinced that I was there. The hot coffee was good. It was not a fancy Colombian, aromatic blend, but it was so good!

We were surrounded by years of Grandfather's collections. It was like a museum. Everything was very old and worn. It seemed that every part of the clutter had a history—sometimes a history that remembered the origin of the earth, like the bent pail filled with

expended (ek spend´ id) v. to have spent or used by consuming

---

2. **centenarian** (sen´ tə ner´ ē ən) adj. at least one hundred years old.

obsidian[3] that he had collected from Glass Mountain many summers before, "just in case."

He also had a radio that he was talked into purchasing when he was a young working man in the 1920's. The radio cost $124. I think he got conned by that merchant and the episode magnified in mystery when he recalled that it was not until 1948 before he got the electric company to put a line to his home. By that time he forgot about the radio and he did not remember to turn it on until 1958. It worked. There was an odor of oldness—like a mouse that died then dried to a stiffness through the years—a <u>redolence</u> of old neglected newspapers.

The old person in the old house under the old moon began to tell the story of his escape from "the rock" long ago. He gathered himself together and reached back into a painful past. The silence was long and I thought that he might be crying silently. Then, with a quiver in his voice, he started telling the story that he wanted me to know:

"Alcatraz Island. Where the Pit River runs into the sea is where I was born, long ago. *Alcatraz*, that's the white man's name for it. To our people, in our legends, we always knew it as *Allisti Ti-tanin-miji* [Rock Rainbow], Diamond Island. In our legends, that's where the Mouse Brothers, the twins, were told to go when they searched for a healing treasure for our troubled people long, long ago. They were to go search at the end of *It A-juma* [Pit River]. They found it. They brought it back. But it is lost now. It is said, the 'diamond' was to bring goodness to all our people, everywhere.

"We always heard that there was a 'diamond' on an island near the great salt water. We were always told that the 'diamond' was a thought, or a truth. Something worth very much. It was not a jewelry. It sparkled and it shined, but it was not a jewelry. It was more. Colored lights came from inside it with every movement. That is why we always called it [Alcatraz] *Allisti Ti-Tanin-miji.*" With a wave of an ancient hand and words filled with enduring knowledge, Grandfather spoke of a time long past.

In one of the many raids upon our people of the Pit River country, his pregnant mother was taken captive and forced, with other Indians, to make the long and painful march to Alcatraz in the winter. At that same time, the military was "sweeping" California. Some of our people were "removed" to the Round Valley Reservation at Covelo; others were taken east by train in open cattle cars during the winter to Quapa, Oklahoma. Still others were taken out into the ocean at Eureka and thrown overboard into icy waters.

Descendants of those that were taken in chains to Quapa are still there. Some of those cast into the winter ocean at Eureka made it back to land and returned to Pit River country. A few of those defying confinement, the threat of being shot by "thunder sticks," and

---

3. **obsidian** (əb sid´ ē ən) *n.* hard, dark-colored or black volcanic glass.

redolence (red´ əl əns) *n.* scent; smell

Thematic Connection
What kind of meeting of cultures is described here?

Critical Thinking
Inferring

Ask students what kind of person Grandfather is, based on this anecdote and the other information the author has revealed so far.
Possible response: Students may say that Grandfather is uninterested in material things, and focuses more on daily survival; some may suggest that he leads a more spiritual life.

Critical Thinking
Speculate

Ask students to give a possible reason for Grandfather's apparently urgent need to tell his story.
Possible response: Students may say that Grandfather senses that his life is nearly over and that he wants to share a powerful family story with his grandson before it is too late.

Background

The Round Valley Reservation is in northern California, about twenty miles inland from the Pacific and about 175 miles north of San Francisco. Oklahoma, which has the biggest Native American population in the United States, was a destination for many Native Americans who were "removed" from their traditional lands.

Thematic Connection

This description captures a clash of cultures in which one dominates the other.

☀ ENRICHMENT: Cultural Connection

Native American Tradition

Respect for elders is a feature common to many cultures. Native Americans, and other cultures that have a long oral tradition, value elders as members of the group who can bridge the past and the future as they pass traditional wisdom from generation to generation. Not only do they keep alive a people's history, legends, myths, dances, songs, and customs, they also advise the young on how to live good and productive lives. Have students find out more about traditional Native American values. Challenge them to give examples of how the traditional wisdom is still applicable today.

Meeting of Cultures

Ask students to explain how Grandfather's efforts to recollect his tale for a grandson who "wrote things down on paper" represents a meeting of cultures.

Possible response: Grandfather realizes that his grandson's work is part of a written tradition, which can be used to preserve for others what he offers in his traditional oral manner.

Background

Art

San Francisco, 1849, by Joshua Pierce.

Little is known of American painter Joshua H. Pierce other than that he lived and worked in the San Francisco area from 1841 to 1859. His body of work consists of full-size paintings and miniatures (about the size of a playing card) of the San Francisco landscape. His works are valuable for their beauty and for the historical record they provide.

This oil painting shows San Francisco in 1849. In the harbor are sailing ships and Alcatraz Island. The scene would have looked much like this when Grandfather's family was imprisoned there.

Use this question for discussion:

• If Grandfather's ancestors were to view a current photograph of this same scene, do you think they would still recognize the site as Alcatraz Island? Why or why not?

Possible response: Students should note that the addition of the Golden Gate Bridge, skyscrapers, electric lights, cars, super-tankers, and so on, has dramatically changed the San Francisco Bay area.

dark winter nights of a cold Alcatraz-made-deadly by churning, freezing currents, made it back to Pit River country, too.

Grandfather said, "I was very small, too small to remember, but my grandmother remembered it all. The guards allowed us to swim around the rock. Every day, my mother swam. Every day, the people swam. We were not just swimming. We were gaining strength. We were learning the currents. We had to get home.

"When it was time, we were ready. We left at darkness. Grandmother said that I was a baby and rode my mother's back, clinging as she swam from Alcatraz to solid ground in night. My Grandmother remembered that I pulled so hard holding on that I broke my mother's necklace. It is still there in the water . . . somewhere." With a pointing of a stout finger southward, Grandfather indicated where "there" was.

Quivering with emotion, he hesitated. He trembled. "I do not remember if I was scared," Grandfather said, crooked, thick fingers rubbing a creased and wrinkled chin covered with white stubble. "I must have been."

When those old, cloudy eyes dripped tears down a leathery, crevassed[4] face, and long silences were between his sentences, often I trembled too. He softly spoke of his memory.

Our cups were long empty; *maliss* (fire) needed attention. The moon was suspended in the frozen winter night—round, bright, scratched and scarred—when Grandfather finally paused in his thinking. The old castiron heater grumbled and screamed when I slid open the top to drop in a fresh log. Sparks flew up into the darkness then disappeared. I slammed the top closed. Silence, again.

Grandfather continued, "There was not real diamonds on the island. At least I don't think so. I always thought the diamonds were not diamonds but some kind of understanding, some kind of good thought—or something." He shook a white, shaggy head and looked off into the distance into a time that was so long ago that the mountains barely remembered. For long moments he reflected, he gathered his thoughts. He knew that I "wrote things down on paper."

The night was thick. To the north a coyote howled. Far to the west an old coyote rasped a call to the black wilderness, a supreme presence beneath starry skies with icy freedom all around.

"When first I heard about the 'diamond,' I thought it might be a story of how we escaped. But after I heard that story so many times, I don't think so. I think there was a truth there that the Mouse Brothers were instructed to get and bring back long ago to help our people. I don't think that I know where that truth is now. Where can it be? It must be deep *inside Axo-Yet* [Mount Shasta][5] or *Sa Titt* [Medicine Lake]. It hides from our people. The truth

---

4. **crevassed** (krə vast´) *adj.* deeply cracked.
5. **Mount Shasta** (shas´ tə) a volcanic mountain in northern California.

San Francisco, 1849, Attributed to Joshua Pierce

▲ **Critical Viewing**
This painting shows Alcatraz as seen from a San Francisco hilltop at twilight. What mood is created by this depiction of the island? **[Describe]**

hides from us. It must not like us. It denies us."

The One-as-Old-as-the-Mountains made me wonder about this story. It seems incredible that there was such an escape from Alcatraz. Through American propaganda I have been trained to believe that it was impossible to escape from that isolated rock because of the currents and because of the freezing temperature as the powerful ocean and the surging rivers merged in chaos. I was convinced—until I heard Grandfather's story and until I realized that he dwelled within a different "time," a different "element." He dwelled within a spirituality of a natural source. In his world, I was only a foreign infant. It is true today that when I talk with the old people I feel like *nilladuwi*—(a white man). I feel like some domesticated creature addressing original royalty—knowing that the old ones were pure savage, born into the wild, free.

In his calm manner, Grandfather proceeded. "We wandered for many nights. We hid during the day. It is said that we had to go south for three nights before we could turn north. [My people landed at San Francisco and had to sneak to what is now San Jose, traveling at night with no food until they could turn northward.] They [the U.S. Army] were after us. They were after us all. We had to be careful. We had to be careful and not make mistakes. We headed north for two nights.

"We came to a huge river. We could not cross it. It was swift. My mother walked far upstream then jumped in. Everybody followed. The river washed us to the other shore [possibly the Benicia Straits]. We rested for two days eating dead fish that we found along the river. We could not build a fire because they would see the smoke and catch us so we must eat it [fish] raw. At night we traveled again. Again we traveled, this time for two nights also.

"There is a small island of mountains in the great valley [Sutter Buttes]. When we reached that place one of the young men climbed the highest peak. He was brave. We were all brave. It was during the sunlight. We waited for him to holler as was the plan. We waited

Thematic Connection
Why do you think it is so difficult for the writer to believe the story?

Thematic Connection
How does the language of Grandfather's story compare and contrast with García López de Cárdenas's account of the explanation of the Grand Canyon?

Meeting of Cultures

- Ask students to respond to the feelings the narrator expresses when he realizes how different he and his grandfather are. What does the narrator respect most? Possible response: The narrator most respects the oldest generation of Native Americans—those who were "born into the wild, free."

- Invite students to share any similar responses they may have had to family members or friends who come from other cultures.

▶ Critical Viewing

Answer: Students may say that Alcatraz Island seems isolated and mysterious, as it sits alone in the middle of the bay in the eerie purple twilight. They may also note that the island seems to form a boundary between the populated city in the foreground and the distant empty hills.

Thematic Connection

Answer: It seems difficult to believe because Alcatraz is supposed to be impossible to escape from.

Thematic Connection

Answer: Students may respond that the language used in the two stories is similar—direct and to the point.

Critical Thinking

Connect

Discuss with students what kinds of truths they believe that their generation seeks, or should seek, and how truths can set them free.

Answers

Connecting Literature Past and Present

1. **(a)** Wilson probably feels this way because he is much less in touch with the cultures and tradition of his people than are the elders. **(b)** Students may note that the contrast between cultures in the explorers' accounts are much greater than those in Wilson's.

2. **(a)** Student response will vary. **(b)** Student response will vary, but should be well-reasoned and refer to ideas from the selection about the meeting of cultures.

---

a long, long time. Then we heard: '*Axo-Yet! Axo-Yet! To-ho-ja-toki! To-ho-ja-toki Tanjan*' [Mount Shasta! Mount Shasta! North direction!]. Our hearts were happy. We were close to home. My mother squeezed me to her. We cried. I know we cried. I was there. So was my mother and grandmother."

Grandfather has been within the earth for many snows now. The volumes of knowledge that were buried with him are lost to my generation, a generation that needs original knowledge now more than ever, if we are to survive as a distinct and <u>autonomous</u> people. Perhaps a generation approaching will be more aware, more excited with tradition and custom and less satisfied to being off balance somewhere between the world of the "white man" and the world of the "Indian," and will seek this knowledge.

It is nearing winter, 1989. Snows upon *Axo-Yet* (Mount Shasta) are deep. The glaring white makes Grandfather's hair nearly yellow—now that I better recall the coarse strands that I often identified as "silver." That beautiful mountain. The landmark that caused the hunted warrior 140 years ago to forget the tragic episode that could have been the termination of our nation, and, standing with the sun shining full upon him, hollered to a frightened people waiting below: "*Axo-Yet! Axo-Yet! To-ho-ja-toki Tanjan!*"

Perhaps the approaching generation will seek and locate *Allisti Ti-tanin-miji* within the mountains. Possibly that generation will reveal many truths to this world society that is immense and confused in its immensity. An old chief of the Pit River country, "Charlie Buck," said often: "Truth. It is truth that will set us free." Along with Grandfather, I think that it was a "truth" that the Mouse Brothers brought to our land from Diamond Island long ago. A truth that needs to be understood, appreciated, and acknowledged. A truth that needs desperately to be found and known for its value.

Grandfather's letter is still in my files. I still can't read it, but if I could, I am sure that the message would be the same as this story that he gave to me as the moon listened and the winds whispered across a frozen Atwam, during a sparkling winter night long ago.

autonomous (ô tän´ ə məs) *adj.* independent

Darryl Babe Wilson

(b. 1939)

Darryl Babe Wilson is a Native American and short-story writer. He lives in California's San Francisco Bay area and teaches writing at two local colleges. Before moving to California in 1997, Wilson taught Native American studies at the University of Arizona, where he earned his Ph.D. in Comparative Culture and Literary Studies. Wilson often writes about the struggles of his people. For his book *Voices From the Earth*, he interviewed Native Americans from Barrow, Alaska, to the Mayan Peninsula of Mexico and Guatemala.

Connecting Literature Past and Present

1. **(a)** Why do you think Wilson says he feels like a domesticated creature or "white man" when he talks to the elders of his people? **(b)** In what way does Wilson's narrative account compare with the meeting of different cultures described by Alvar Núñez Cabeza de Vaca and García López de Cárdenas?

2. Describe a situation from your own life or observations that you feel represents a "meeting of cultures." **(a)** What are the "cultures" involved? **(b)** Is the meeting characterized by friendly exchange, or is it more a clash of cultures? Explain.

Focus on Literary Forms: Narrative Accounts

Building the Fort, Julien Binford,
The Jamestown/Yorktown Educational Trust

The settlers who journeyed across a hostile ocean and forged homes in a new land were generally far too busy just surviving to create poems and other types of literature that matched those of other areas of the world. The early settlers did succeed, however, in writing vivid narrative accounts—a literary form that has remained popular to this day.

Focus on Literary Forms: Narrative Accounts ◆ 59

Selection Planning Guide

This section explores narrative accounts, both as a literary form and as a firsthand look at the lives of some of America's first European settlers. Columbus's *Journal of the First Voyage to America* describes the explorer's first encounters with local natives. John Smith's *The General History of Virginia* is a colorful and subjective account of the establishment of Jamestown Colony. Smith's account is paired with William Bradford's modest, straight-forward retelling of the Pilgrims' plight in *Of Plymouth Plantation*. Though quite different in tone, all three accounts describe the Native Americans' important role in helping the settlers survive in the New World. The exploration of new worlds jumps to the space age in *The Right Stuff*, a contemporary account of the Mercury space program.

Background

Art

Building the Fort, Julien Binford

This oil painting depicts the building of the fort at the colony at Jamestown, Virginia, in May 1607. According to historical accounts, Captain John Smith ordered that the fort be built almost as soon as the colonists landed on shore. However, since most of the colonists had been gentlemen in England, they were reluctant to perform manual labor. During this early phase of construction, the colonists were taken by surprise by the natives' bow-and-arrow attacks, and a number of them died. This violence persuaded the men to finish the fort quickly and they became more willing to do whatever laborious tasks were required.

Use the following question for discussion:

• Looking at the image, would you say that the painter's attitude toward the Jamestown settlement was positive or negative? Why?
Possible responses: Most students will say that the painter's attitude was positive, based on such details as the warm colors in the painting and the sense of calm authority projected by the men who seem to be directing the work.

USTOMIZE INSTRUCTION FOR UNIVERSAL ACCESS

en assigning the selections in this part, keep in mind these factors:

m *Journal of the First Voyage America*

rief journal excerpt

ss proficient readers may need elp with diction.

from *The General History of Virginia*

• Difficult vocabulary

from *Of Plymouth Plantation*

• Firsthand accounts of New World settlement

• Readers may need help with language and long sentences.

from *The Right Stuff*

• High-interest, nonfiction account of space exploration

• Brief and accessible

• Some readers may need help with specialized vocabulary.

59

from Journal of the First Voyage to America

Lesson Objectives

1. **To analyze and respond to literary elements**
   - Literary Analysis: Journal
   - Connecting Literary Elements: Author's Point of View
2. **To read, comprehend, analyze, and critique a journal**
   - Reading Strategy: Recognizing Author's Purpose
   - Reading Check Questions
   - Review and Assess Questions
   - Assessment Practice (ATE)
3. **To develop word analysis skills, fluency, and systematic vocabulary**
   - Vocabulary Development Lesson: Latin Root *-flict-*
4. **To understand and apply written and oral language conventions**
   - Spelling Strategy
   - Grammar and Style Lesson: Action and Linking Verbs
5. **To understand and apply appropriate writing and research strategies**
   - Writing Lesson: Oral Report on the Voyage
   - Extension Activity: Chart
6. **To understand and apply listening and speaking strategies**
   - Extension Activity: Presentation

STEP-BY-STEP TEACHING GUIDE	PACING GUIDE
PRETEACH	
Motivate Students and Provide Background	
Use the Motivation activity (ATE p. 60)	5 min.
Read and discuss author and background features (SE p. 60; ATE p. 62)	5 min.
Introduce the Concepts	
Introduce the Literary Analysis and Reading Strategy (SE/ATE p. 61)	15 min.
Pronounce the vocabulary words and read their definitions (SE p. 61)	5 min.
TEACH	
Monitor Comprehension	
Informally monitor comprehension by circulating while students read independently or in groups	15 min.
Monitor students' comprehension with the Reading Check notes (SE/ATE p. 63)	as students read
Develop vocabulary with Vocabulary notes (SE pp. 62, 63, 64)	as students read
Develop Understanding	
Develop students' understanding of journals with the Literary Analysis annotations (SE/ATE p. 63)	5 min.
ASSESS	
Assess Mastery	
Assess students' mastery of the Reading Strategy and Literary Analysis by having them answer the Review and Assess questions (SE/ATE p. 65)	15 min.
Use one or more of the print and media Assessment Resources (ATE p. 67)	up to 45 min.
EXTEND	
Apply Understanding	
Have students complete the Vocabulary Development Lesson and the Grammar and Style Lesson (SE p. 66)	20 min.
Apply students' ability to use vivid elaboration using the Writing Lesson (SE/ATE p. 67)	45 min.
Apply students' understanding using one or more of the Extension Activities (SE p. 67)	20–90 min.

 ACCELERATED INSTRUCTION:
Use the strategies and activities identified with an .

UNIVERSAL ACCESS
● = Below Level Students
▲ = On-Level Students
■ = Above Level Students

Time and Resource Manager

RESOURCES		
PRINT 📖	**TRANSPARENCIES**	**TECHNOLOGY** 💿 🎧 📼
• **Beyond Literature,** Cross-Curricular Connection: Social Studies, p. 4 ▲ ■		• **Interest Grabber Video,** Tape 1 ● ▲ ■
• **Selection Support Workbook:** ● ▲ ■ Literary Analysis, p. 18 Reading Strategy, p. 17 Build Vocabulary, p. 15	• **Literary Analysis and Reading Transparencies,** pp. 7 and 8 ● ▲ ■	
		• **Listening to Literature** ● ▲ ■ Audiocassettes, Side 1 Audio CDs, CD 1
• **Literatura en español** ● ▲ • **Literary Analysis for Enrichment** ■		
• **Formal Assessment:** Selection Test, pp. 16–18 ● ▲ ■ • **Open Book Test,** pp. 10–12 ● ▲ ■ • **Performance Assessment and Portfolio Management,** p. 30 ● ▲ ■ **PRENTICE HALL ASSESSMENT SYSTEM**	**PRENTICE HALL ASSESSMENT SYSTEM** Skills Practice Answers and Explanations on Transparencies ● ▲ ■	• **Test Bank Software** ● ▲ ■ • **Got It! Assessment Videotapes,** Tape 1 ● ▲
• **Selection Support Workbook:** ● ▲ ■ Grammar and Style, p. 16 • **Writing and Grammar,** Ruby Level ● ▲ ■ • **Extension Activities,** p. 4 ● ▲ ■	• **Daily Language Practice Transparencies** ● ▲ • **Writing Models and Graphic Organizers on Transparencies,** p. 9–12 ● ▲ ■	• **Writing and Grammar iText CD-ROM** ● ▲ ■ 💻 *Take It to the Net* www.phschool.com

BLOCK SCHEDULING: Use one 90-minute class period to preteach the selection and have students read it. Use a second 90-minute class period to assess students' mastery of skills and have them complete one of the Extension Activities.

Step-by-Step Teaching Guide for pp. 60–61

Motivation

Prepare students to read the selection by asking them the following question: If someone agreed to finance a travel venture for them, where would they wish to go? Ask volunteers to share their responses with the class. Then, explain that students are about to read an account written by a man whose dream of finding a faster shipping route to the riches of the Indies led him to make a voyage to a place where no European had ever gone.

▭ Interest Grabber Video

As an alternative, play "European Explorers" on Tape 1 to engage student interest.

❶ Background

More About the Author

Christopher Columbus tried for years to finance his voyage. After rejections from the kings of Portugal, England, and France, he went to Spain in 1485. It took him two years even to get an audience with Ferdinand and Isabella and six more years to get their approval. In addition to assuring him ten percent of all valuables discovered, the deal between Columbus and the Spanish monarchs made him Governor General of any lands he discovered.

Prepare to Read

❶ *from* Journal of the First Voyage to America

Christopher Columbus (1451–1506)

Not much is known about the early life of Christopher Columbus, one of history's most famous explorers. In the late 1400s, Europeans had little knowledge about world geography, but Columbus left his home in Genoa, Italy, at a young age and went to sea. At age 25, he was shipwrecked off the coast of Portugal. Once back on land, Columbus studied mapmaking and navigation. He also learned Latin and read Marco Polo's account of the riches of Asia. Between 1480 and 1482, Columbus sailed to the Azores and to the Canary Islands off Africa. He then began to dream of more challenging voyages. Within ten years, he embraced the idea that led to his lifelong goal: reaching the fabled cities of Asia by sailing westward around the world.

First, Columbus tried to convince King John II of Portugal to fund a westward voyage. When his request was rejected there, he sought funding from other European rulers. After a series of unsuccessful attempts, Columbus won the support of Queen Isabella of Spain.

A Hard Bargain Queen Isabella and her husband, King Ferdinand, agreed to finance Columbus's first voyage in 1492. In forging the agreement, Columbus negotiated favorable terms. In addition to funding, he asked for and received the right to rule any lands he conquered. The agreement also noted that he would be entitled to 10 percent of all wealth from those lands.

The Famous Voyage On August 3, 1492, Columbus set sail from Palos, a small port in southwestern Spain, with his three ships—the *Niña*, the *Pinta*, and the *Santa Maria*. Although he knew how to measure latitude by using the North Star, Columbus had no navigational instruments. He used a compass to determine direction and an hourglass to estimate time. After more than a month at sea, his crews became disillusioned when they did not reach the islands Columbus had led them to expect. However, soon signs of life such as coastal seaweed and birds flying overhead indicated land was near, and the crew members' hopes were renewed. On October 12, Columbus reached one of the islands of Bahama, which he mistook for an island off India. He named the island San Salvador; he then continued to explore the Caribbean.

Linking East and West When Columbus reached these islands he had no idea there were millions of people living a short distance away in North and South America. He faced many challenges sailing the largely uncharted waters, but his voyages linked the Eastern and Western hemispheres. Over the next twelve years, he made three more transatlantic journeys, ever convinced that he had reached Asia and always hopeful of finding Marco Polo's fabled cities.

His Final Years Columbus was driven by his unrelenting desire to discover new territories, and he continued to sail until nearly the end of his life. His goal in his final voyage was to find a passage to the mainland of China. He set out from Cadiz, Spain, in 1502, traveling to Martinique and later east and south to the coasts of Honduras, Nicaragua, Costa Rica, Panama, and Jamaica. Suffering from exhaustion and malaria, he abandoned his search for China and returned to Spain in 1504. Although many scholars believe Columbus was poor at the time of his death, others say he died a wealthy man at the age of 54 in 1506. Today, he is recognized as one of the greatest mariners of all time.

TEACHING RESOURCES

The following resources can be used to enrich or extend the instruction for pp. 60–61.

Motivation

▭ **Interest Grabber Video**, Tape 1 ▭

Background

📖 **Beyond Literature**, p. 4

Take It to the Net
Visit www.phschool.com for Background and hotlinks for the selection.

Literary Analysis

▭ **Literary Analysis and Reading Transparencies**, Journal, p. 8

Reading

▭ **Literary Analysis and Reading Transparencies**, Recognizing Author's Purpose, p. 7 ▭

📖 **Selection Support Workbook:** Reading Strategy, p. 17; Build Vocabulary, p. 15

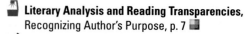
BLOCK SCHEDULING: Resources marked with this symbol provide varied instruction during 90-minute blocks.

Preview

Connecting to the Literature

Fulfilling the desire to circle the globe in a boat or discovering the cure for a deadly disease takes more than sheer will. A dreamer needs financial resources. To achieve his dream of circling the globe, Christopher Columbus had to persuade others to provide the funding. More often than not, people did not think it was worth the expense.

❷ Literary Analysis

Journal

The European expeditions in the Americas are recorded in the journals of the explorers. A **journal** is an individual's day-by-day account of events. As the example below shows, a journal provides valuable details that only a participant or an eyewitness can supply.

> . . . the inhabitants on discovering us abandoned their houses, and took to flight, carrying off their goods to the mountains.

As a record of personal reactions, a journal reveals as much about the writer as it does about events. As you read, look for details that reveal Columbus's values, hopes, and reactions.

Connecting Literary Elements

A journal is not necessarily a reliable record of the facts. The **author's point of view,** or attitudes about the topic or audience, may color the telling of events, particularly when the writer is a participant. Journals written for publication rather than private use are even less likely to be objective. While reading Columbus's journal, look for evidence that he was writing for an audience.

❸ Reading Strategy

Recognizing Author's Purpose

Columbus's purpose for writing his journal was to convince Queen Isabella and King Ferdinand to continue funding his explorations. **Recognizing the author's purpose** will help you to understand why a work was written, and it will also help you to understand Columbus's careful choice of words, details, and events to include in his journal. As you read, use a chart like this one to record Columbus's favorable descriptions and events. Then, explain his purpose for describing it that way.

Favorable Descriptions	Author's Purpose

Vocabulary Development

exquisite (eks´ kwi zit) *adj.* very beautiful; delicate; carefully wrought (p. 62)

affliction (ə flik´ shən) *n.* something causing pain or suffering (p. 63)

indications (in´ di kā´ shənz) *n.* signs; things that point out or signify (p. 64)

abundance (ə bun´ dəns) *n.* a great supply; more than enough (p. 64)

from Journal of the First Voyage to America ◆ 61

---

❷ Literary Analysis

Journal

- Explain that students will focus on a journal—an individuals' day-by-day account of events—as they read this selection.

- Ask whether students have ever kept a journal or diary of events in their own lives. Invite student volunteers to share their reflections about the process of keeping a journal. What are its rewards? What are its challenges or frustrations?

- Point out that a journal not only records events, but also reveals the ideas, beliefs, and feelings of its author.

- Encourage students to look for details in Columbus's journal that reveal his motives.

❸ Reading Strategy

Recognizing Author's Purpose

- Remind students that every writer has a purpose for writing, to entertain, inform, or persuade. Invite students to identify some common purposes for writing journal entries.

- Encourage students to reread details from the author biography about Columbus's efforts to secure funding for his explorations.

- Point out that in addition to a desire to record private impressions for his own personal use, Columbus also wanted to convince his benefactors that funding his explorations was money well spent.

- Urge students to look for passages in Columbus's journal in which this purpose is detectable.

Vocabulary Development

- Pronounce each vocabulary word for students, and read the definitions as a class. Have students identify any words with which they are familiar.

 E-Teach

Visit E-Teach at www.phschool.com for teachers' essays on how to teach, with questions and answers.

CUSTOMIZE INSTRUCTION FOR UNIVERSAL ACCESS

For Less Proficient Readers	For English Learners	For Advanced Readers
To help students work through the text, organize them into small groups. As you guide them through the single long paragraph, have students create a two-column vertical chart to distinguish key ideas from extraneous details.	Have students follow along in their texts as you read aloud to them or as they listen to a recording of the selection. On the chalkboard, list each key piece of information as it appears in the selection. For additional support, you may wish to provide a map showing Columbus's intended and actual journey.	Encourage students to think about (and discuss in small groups) how each of the key ideas in this selection relates to Columbus's overall purpose for writing this journal. Have students create a two-column chart to record details from the journal and the author's purpose in including them.

**CUSTOMIZE INSTRUCTION
For Verbal/Linguistic Learners**

Columbus uses archaic measurement terms such as *span*, *league*, and *quintal*. Have students use encyclopedias and dictionaries to learn more about the origins of these and more current terms of measurement, such as *inch*, *mile*, and *meter*. Have students record the words, together with their origins, in a chart.

❶ About the Selection

This excerpt from Christopher Columbus's journal conveys the explorer's observations and evaluations of San Salvador and its resources and states his plans for further exploration. Columbus appears to be taken with the natural beauty of the island and with the friendliness of its inhabitants. However, his choice of language and details make it clear that his purpose in writing is to impress Spain's king and queen, who were financing his expedition and expecting a return on their investment.

❷ ▶ Critical Viewing

Answer: Students should note that the astrolabe has a needle and markings around its perimeter similar to those of a navigational compass.

❶ *FROM* JOURNAL OF THE FIRST VOYAGE TO AMERICA

CHRISTOPHER COLUMBUS

Background

In the 1450s, the only way to India from Europe involved traveling through Turkey, but explorers in Portugal and Spain began to look at alternate sea routes. Columbus's search brought Europe into contact with North and South America. His voyages took him from Lisbon, Portugal, to Palos, Spain, and the Canary Islands before he crossed the Atlantic. He landed first on the island of San Salvador. This account begins nine days after Columbus landed there.

SUNDAY, OCT. 21ST [1492]. At 10 o'clock, we arrived at a cape of the island,[1] and anchored, the other vessels in company. After having dispatched a meal, I went ashore, and found no habitation save a single house, and that without an occupant; we had no doubt that the people had fled in terror at our approach, as the house was completely furnished. I suffered nothing to be touched, and went with my captains and some of the crew to view the country. This island even exceeds the others in beauty and fertility. Groves of lofty and flourishing trees are abundant, as also large lakes, surrounded and overhung by the foliage, in a most enchanting manner. Everything looked as green as in April in Andalusia.[2] The melody of the birds was so <u>exquisite</u> that one was never willing to part from the

2 ▲ Critical Viewing
The astrolabe was an invention that made the age of exploration possible. What features of this one suggest that it is an instrument of navigation? **[Support]**

exquisite (eks′ kwi zit) *adj.* very beautiful; delicate; carefully wrought

---

1. **the island** San Salvador.
2. **Andalusia** (an′ də lōō′ zhə) a region of Spain.

62 ◆ Beginnings–1750

TEACHING RESOURCES

The following resources can be used to enrich or extend the instruction for pp. 62–64.

Motivation

📼 **Interest Grabber Video**, Tape 1 🔲

Background

📖 **Beyond Literature**, p. 4

🖥 *Take It to the Net*
Visit www.phschool.com for Background and hotlinks for the selection.

📖 **Literary Analysis and Reading Transparencies,** Journals, p. 8 🔲

Reading

📖 **Selection Support Workbook:** Literary Analysis, p. 18; Build Vocabulary, p. 15

🔲 **BLOCK SCHEDULING:** Resources marked with this symbol provide varied instruction during 90-minute blocks.

spot, and the flocks of parrots obscured the heavens. The diversity in the appearance of the feathered tribe from those of our country is extremely curious. A thousand different sorts of trees, with their fruit were to be met with, and of a wonderfully delicious odor. It was a great <u>affliction</u> to me to be ignorant of their natures, for I am very certain they are all valuable; specimens of them and of the plants I have preserved. Going round one of these lakes, I saw a snake, which we killed, and I have kept the skin for your Highnesses; upon being discovered he took to the water, whither[3] we followed him, as it was not deep, and dispatched him with our lances; he was seven spans[4] in length; I think there are many more such about here. I discovered also the aloe tree, and am determined to take on board the ship tomorrow, ten quintals[5] of it, as I am told it is valuable. While we were in search of some good water we came upon a village of the natives about half a league from the place where the ships lay; the inhabitants on discovering us abandoned their houses, and took to flight, carrying off their goods to the mountain. I ordered that nothing which they had left should be taken, not even the value of a pin. Presently we saw several of the natives advancing towards our party, and one of them came up to us, to whom we gave some hawk's bells and glass beads, with which he was delighted. We asked him in return, for water, and after I had gone on board the ship, the natives

---

3. **whither** to which place.
4. **spans** *n.* units of measure, each equal to about nine inches.
5. **quintals** (kwin´ təlz) *n.* units of weight, each equal to 100 kilograms, or 220.46 pounds.

affliction (ə flik´ shən) *n.* something causing pain or suffering

Literary Analysis
Journal Why do you think Columbus relates the story of capturing and skinning the snake?

 Reading Check
Does Columbus encounter any people when he lands? Explain.

◄ **Critical Viewing** ❺
Evaluate the artist's interpretation of Columbus's landing in the Western Hemisphere. What aspects of the moment does he emphasize? **[Evaluate; Support]**

❻

from *Journal of the First Voyage to America* ◆ 63

❸ **Literary Analysis**
Journal
• Remind students that a journal is the product of an author with a particular point of view and a specific purpose for writing.
• Ask students the Literary Analysis question on p. 63: Why do you think Columbus relates the story of capturing and skinning the snake?
Answer: Students may suggest that Columbus wished to record any possible threats to subsequent explorers in the area.

❹ ✔ **Reading Check**
Answer: Immediately upon landing, Columbus encounters a furnished, but empty, house; later he discovers a similarly abandoned village. Finally he meets a few inhabitants of the village.

❺ ▶ **Critical Viewing**
Answer: Students may say that the artist emphasizes Columbus's role as the "discoverer" of America.

❻ **Background**
Art

Columbus Landing in the New World

The lithograph was made by an unknown artist. The lithography process was invented in the late 1700s and was used as an alternative to engraving for reproducing paintings and drawings for books. Use these questions for discussion:

1. Does this lithograph present a romanticized view of Columbus's landing? If so, how?
Answer: Students may say that the scene is romanticized because everyone is dressed in formal attire and the land seems beautiful and hospitable.

2. What can you learn about Columbus and his crew from this lithograph?
Answer: Students may cite the crew's religious inclinations, their formal dress, their sense of pageantry, and their seriousness.

CUSTOMIZE INSTRUCTION FOR UNIVERSAL ACCESS

For Special Needs Students	For Gifted/Talented Students
Point out to students that this part of Columbus's journal reads like a descriptive postcard sent home to Spain. Help students work through the selection a few sentences at a time. You might have students list sensory images of the New World in a five-column chart on the chalkboard as they encounter them.	You may not need to remind students that Columbus and other European explorers did not "discover" the Americas, since at the time of their arrival, Native Americans had lived in the hemisphere for thousands of years. Encourage students to prepare a research report on the Native American civilizations that preceded European discovery.

Answers for p. 64

Review and Assess

1. Students may say they would feel proud, intrigued, surprised, or wary after reading of Columbus's successes.

2. **(a)** Details such as *lofty and flourishing trees, wonderfully delicious odor,* and *exquisite . . . melody of the birds* convey Columbus's attitude toward the island.
(b) Columbus thinks that the landscape is beautiful and possibly contains things of great value.

3. **(a)** He trades glass beads and hawk's bells with the Native Americans. **(b)** The Native Americans are "delighted" with these items, and Columbus implies that this causes the Native Americans "great pleasure" in presenting the Europeans with water.

4. **(a)** Apparently Columbus respects the Native Americans. **(b)** He reveals his respect by ordering his men to touch nothing that belongs to the people and by trading honestly with them. **(c)** Possible response: Students may say that the clothing worn by Columbus and his men or the ships themselves may have frightened the island natives. In addition, Columbus and his men discover a house that is completely furnished, as though its inhabitant's had fled in haste without taking their belongings.

5. Possible responses: **(a)** A Native American's account probably would include more details that reveal concern, worry, shock, or fear about the foreign visitors. **(b)** Although a crew member also might be impressed by the landscape, a sailor's account might include more details about the Native Americans he met.

came down to the shore with their calabashes[6] full, and showed great pleasure in presenting us with it. I ordered more glass beads to be given them, and they promised to return the next day. It is my wish to fill all the water casks of the ships at this place, which being executed, I shall depart immediately, if the weather serve, and sail round the island, till I succeed in meeting with the king, in order to see if I can acquire any of the gold, which I hear he possesses. Afterwards I shall set sail for another very large island which I believe to be *Cipango*,[7] according to the <u>indications</u> I receive from the Indians on board. They call the Island *Colba*,[8] and say there are many large ships, and sailors there. This other island they name *Bosio*[9] and inform me that it is very large; the others which lie in our course, I shall examine on the passage, and according as I find gold or spices in <u>abundance</u>, I shall determine what to do; at all events I am determined to proceed on to the continent, and visit the city of Guisay[10] where I shall deliver the letters of your Highnesses to the *Great Can*,[11] and demand an answer, with which I shall return.

indications (in´ di kā´ shənz) *n.* signs; things that point out or signify

abundance (ə bun´ dəns) *n.* a great supply; more than enough

---

6. **calabashes** (kal´ ə bash´ əz) *n.* dried, hollow shells of gourds used as cups or bowls.
7. **Cipango** (si paŋ´ gō) old name for a group of islands east of Asia, probably what is now Japan.
8. **Colba** (kôl´ bə) Cuba.
9. **Bosio** (bō´ sē ō) probably the island on which the Dominican Republic and Haiti are now located.
10. **Guisay** (gē sā´) the City of Heaven, the name given by Marco Polo to the residence of Kublai Khan (kōō´ blī kän), the ruler of China from A.D. 1260–1294.
11. **Great Can** (kän) Kublai Khan.

Review and Assess

Thinking About the Selection

1. **Respond:** If you had sponsored Columbus's voyage, how would you feel upon reading this account of his experience?

2. **(a) Recall:** What details convey Columbus's attitude toward the tropical island? **(b) Interpret:** What is Columbus's reaction to the landscape?

3. **(a) Recall:** What items does Columbus trade with the natives? **(b) Generalize:** According to Columbus, how does this trade influence the success of the first meeting with the natives?

4. **(a) Infer:** How do you think Columbus views the natives? **(b) Support:** How does he reveal those views? **(c) Infer:** Why does Columbus think the natives fear him and his men?

5. **(a) Hypothesize:** How might this account be different if it were written by a Native American observing Columbus and his crew? **(b)** What might an account written by a crew member reveal?

64 ◆ *Beginnings–1750*

✒ ASSESSMENT PRACTICE: Reading Comprehension

Summarizing Written Texts	(For more practice, see Test Preparation Workbook, p. 1.)

Have students practice identifying the best summary of a passage.

In forging the agreement, Columbus had negotiated favorable terms. In addition to funding, he asked for and received the right to rule any lands he conquered. He would also be entitled to 10 percent of all wealth from those lands.

Which is the best summary of this passage?

A The agreement would make Columbus wealthy.

B Columbus expected to be a ruler.

C Columbus made an agreement that would bring him both wealth and the right to rule.

D Columbus was not only an explorer, but also was a shrewd politician.

Choice *C* is correct. Responses *A* and *B* contain accurate information but are incomplete. Choice *D* is an opinion.

Review and Assess

Literary Analysis

Journals

1. Use a chart like the one shown here to list three details from the **journal** that only an eyewitness or participant could provide.

2. Explain Columbus's thoughts and feelings about each of the details you have listed.
3. (a) What appears to have been Columbus's primary consideration in choosing "specimens" to send back to Spain? (b) What does this consideration reveal about his priorities?

Connecting Literary Elements

4. What can you guess about the **author's point of view** that would cause Columbus to say he hopes to find "gold or spices in abundance"?
5. What is Columbus's level of confidence in his ability to lead the expedition?
6. In what ways does Columbus's role as leader of the expedition affect the way he narrates events?

Reading Strategy

Recognizing Author's Purpose

7. How does the journal reflect the **author's purpose**—chronicling the voyage for his investors, the king and queen of Spain?
8. (a) Why do you think Columbus often refers to the monetary value of things he has seen? (b) Find two examples of this in the journal.
9. (a) What impression of the Americas does Columbus seem to be trying to convey? (b) Find three examples from the journal to support your answers.

Extend Understanding

10. **Science Connection:** How would this account be different if it were written by a botanist or other natural scientist?

from *Journal of the First Voyage to America* ◆ 65

Quick Review

A **journal** is an individual's day-by-day account of events.

An **author's point of view** or attitude toward the work's topic or audience may influence the facts or details a writer includes.

Recognizing the author's purpose helps you to understand the specific choice of words, details, and events.

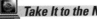 **Take It to the Net**
www.phschool.com

Take the interactive self-test online to check your understanding of the selection.

Answers for p. 65

Review and Assess

1. Possible response: Students' charts should accurately list details that only an eyewitness can provide.
2. Students should report details from the text that reveal Columbus's views about the details they listed.
3. (a) Columbus's primary considerations are value and novelty. (b) It reveals that he wants the new world to be of value to Spain and a subject of curiosity.
4. Columbus may wish to portray this new land as being potentially valuable to Spain, so that it will continue to fund voyages.
5. Columbus seems confident in his ability to lead the expedition.
6. Because he is the leader of the expedition, Columbus is obliged to present not only details about the places and people he encounters, but also an overview of the prospects for European profit from this part of the world.
7. Columbus includes many details that are likely to interest investors.
8. (a) Columbus includes monetary references to keep his financial supporters interested. (b) Two examples are the fruit he believes to be "valuable" and his wish to acquire gold from the island's king.
9. (a) Columbus describes a paradise where the landscape is beautiful and the people are friendly and helpful. (b) Three examples include the following: Columbus describes the land as beautiful and fertile; the melody of the birds is exquisite; the natives are timid but delighted with the Europeans' trinkets.
10. A natural scientist's observations of the island's landscape would be more precise and detailed.

☀ **ENRICHMENT: Further Reading**

Works About Columbus

Columbus Then and Now: A Life Reexamined, Miles H. Davidson

Christopher Columbus, Mariner, Samuel Eliot Morison

The Crown of Columbus, Michael Dorris and Louise Erdrich

 Take It to the Net

Visit www.phschool.com for more information on Christopher Columbus.

❶ Vocabulary Development

Word Analysis

1. Things that can be described as "conflicting" clash or strike against each other.

2. *Inflict* means to strike with something that causes pain.

3. Someone with an affliction is stricken with an illness or injury that causes suffering.

Spelling Strategy

1. acquaint

2. question, query, quiz

3. quench

Concept Development:

1. b

2. a

3. b

4. c

❷ Grammar and Style

Practice

1. linking; linking

2. action

3. linking

4. action; action

5. action

Writing Application

Students should discover that action verbs make writing more lively and that linking verbs make it less so.

Integrate Language Skills

❶ Vocabulary Development Lesson

Word Analysis: Latin Root -flict-

Words like *afflict*, *conflict*, and *inflict* build on the Latin root *-flict-*, meaning "to strike." The following words contain the root *-flict-*. Using the definitions, explain how the root contributes to the meaning of each word.

1. *conflicting*: fighting; battling

2. *inflict*: to give or cause pain

3. *affliction*: the condition of pain or suffering

Spelling Strategy

In some words, like *exquisite*, the *kw* sound is spelled with *qu*. Using the definitions below, write *qu* words that have the *kw* sound.

1. to familiarize yourself with

2. to ask

3. to satisfy thirst

Concept Development: Synonyms

Study the list of vocabulary words on page 61. Then, review each item below. In your notebook, write the letter of the synonym, or word that is closest in meaning, for the first word.

1. indication: (a) delight, (b) sign, (c) value, (d) contradiction, (e) pride

2. abundance: (a) overflow, (b) dearth, (c) preservation, (d) generosity, (e) anger

3. exquisite: (a) shocking, (b) beautiful, (c) sorrowful, (d) trustworthiness, (e) shoddy

4. affliction: (a) extension, (b) magnificence, (c) trouble, (d) institution, (e) perspective

❷ Grammar and Style Lesson

Action and Linking Verbs

Action verbs like *anchored*, *found*, and *saw* express physical or mental action.

Linking verbs such as *be*, *become*, and *look* express a state of being. Linking verbs are followed by a noun or pronoun that renames the subject or by an adjective that describes it.

Action Verbs: We *arrived* at a cape off the island.
The island *exceeds* the others in beauty.

Linking Verbs: Groves of trees *are* abundant.
Everything *looked* green.

Practice Indicate whether the italicized words are action or linking verbs.

1. I *am* very certain that they *are* all valuable.

2. Presently, we *saw* several of the natives. . .

3. This other island they *name* Bosio.

4. I *ordered* more glass beads to be given them and they *promised* to return the next day.

5. They *call* the island Colba.

Writing Application Write two descriptive paragraphs—one using only linking verbs and the other using only action verbs. Compare and contrast the different effects.

W͟G *Prentice Hall Writing and Grammar Connection: Chapter 17, Section 2*

66 ◆ *Beginnings–1750*

TEACHING RESOURCES

The following resources can be used to enrich or extend the instruction for pp. 66–67.

Vocabulary

📖 **Selection Support Workbook:** Build Vocabulary, p. 15

📖 **Vocabulary and Spelling Practice Book** (Use this booklet for skills enrichment.)

Grammar

📖 **Selection Support Workbook:** Grammar and Style, p. 16 ▦

W͟G **Writing and Grammar,** Ruby Level, p. 374

📘 **Daily Language Practice Transparencies** ▦

Writing

W͟G **Writing and Grammar,** Ruby Level, p. 788 ▦

📘 **Writing Models and Graphic Organizers on Transparencies,** pp. 9–12

💿 **Writing and Grammar iText CD-ROM**

▦ **BLOCK SCHEDULING:** Resources marked with this symbol provide varied instruction during 90-minute blocks.

❸ Writing Lesson

Oral Report on the Voyage

Columbus's funding depended on his ability to sell his experiences to an audience of readers who had not seen the lands he explored. Imitating Columbus's writing style, write an oral report that you would give to the king and queen of Spain upon your return to Europe.

Prewriting Imagine the landscape of the island Columbus visited. List the tropical sights, sounds, textures, smells, and tastes that he may have encountered.

Drafting As you describe the island, elaborate by including as many sensory details as you can. Instead of telling how lovely the island is, describe what you see, hear, feel, touch, or smell. Strive to imitate Columbus's style by choosing ornate words.

Model: Elaborating for Vividness

As we sailed the ocean, the sun sparkled on the water like translucent prisms of color. Yonder, we could see the different shades of lush, green foliage on the beach surrounded by many flowers of every hue.

> Sensory details such as *translucent prisms of color* and *different shades of lush green foliage* help readers imagine what they have never experienced.

Revising Add details to strengthen your images. Add smells to descriptions that appeal only to sight and sound; consider adding details about texture or taste where appropriate.

 Prentice Hall Writing and Grammar Connection: Chapter 8, Section 2

❹ Extension Activities

Listening and Speaking Many Native American cultures have artistic traditions. For a **humanities presentation** find pictures of Native American art forms, and compare them to European art from the same time period.

- Consider art, music, and dance.
- Determine the historical influences on the cultures.

Share your analysis with your class, including samples of the art you discuss.

Research and Technology With a group, use online newspapers and data banks for Columbus's presence in today's world. Create a **chart** of parks and public places named after him. Present your findings to the class. [**Group Activity**]

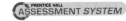 *Take It to the Net* www.phschool.com

Go online for an additional research activity using the Internet.

ASSESSMENT RESOURCES

The following resources can be used to assess students' knowledge and skills.

Selection Assessment

- 📖 **Formal Assessment,** pp. 16–18
- 📖 **Open Book Test,** pp. 10–12
- 📼 **Got It! Assessment Videotapes,** Tape 1
- 💿 **Test Bank Software**

🖥️ *Take It to the Net*
Visit www.phschool.com for self-tests and additional questions on the selection.

Listening and Speaking Rubric

- 📖 **Performance Assess. and Portfolio Mgmt.,** p. 30

PRENTICE HALL
ASSESSMENT SYSTEM

- 📖 **Workbook**
- 📄 **Transparencies**
- 📖 **Skill Book**
- 💿 **CD-ROM**

---

❸ Writing Lesson

- Students' oral reports should be written in Columbus's formal style and should contain a wealth of sensory details about the tropical landscape.

- Remind students to keep their audience and purpose in mind as they write. In other words, each sentence should appeal to their readers' interests and sensibilities about what is beautiful, interesting, beneficial, and profitable about this place.

- As they write and practice delivering their oral reports, students might find it helpful to imagine the king and queen of Spain sitting in the room and listening to their words.

- Use the Writing Lesson, as well as Writing Process Model 2, pp. 9–12 in **Writing Models and Graphic Organizers on Transparencies,** to guide students in developing their reports.

❹ Research and Technology

- You might encourage various groups to focus attention on different geographical areas. For instance, one group might research Columbus's presence within a fifty-mile radius of your school. Another group could research a neighboring county, state, or large city.

- Have students use the Self-Assessment form for Delivering a Speech, p. 30, in **Performance Assessment and Portfolio Management.**

CUSTOMIZE INSTRUCTION
For Universal Access

To address different learning styles, use the following activities suggested in the **Extension Activities** booklet, p. 4.

For Verbal/Linguistic Learners, use Activity 5.

For Interpersonal and Verbal/Linguistic Learners, use Activity 6.

Background

King Philip's War was the most savage of any war in American history, in proportion to the population. One of every sixteen men of fighting age were killed, in addition to the many men, women and children who died of starvation or exposure as a result of being kidnapped. Such a tremendous loss of life was a threat to the continued survival of New England. The war also brought the economy to the edge of disaster, costing nearly a hundred thousand pounds and destroying half the towns in the colony.

▶Critical Viewing

Answer: It suggests that King Philip was of high status and well respected.

A Closer Look

Captivity Narratives: Colonial Pulp Fiction

Mary Rowlandson was taken captive by Wampanoag Indians in 1676. The result was America's first bestseller, and a glimpse at Native American life.

Tensions were high in the Massachusetts Bay Colony near the end of the seventeenth century. The once-friendly relations between Native Americans and European settlers had broken down. While the peaceful Wampanoag tribe had shared its land and resources with the Massachusetts colonists for almost forty years, by the 1670s, cooperation between the two groups had failed.

Colonial troops began driving the Wampanoag from their land. As the winter of 1676 approached, the Wampanoag were cut off from the food they had stored for the harsh, snowy months. They were in desperate need of supplies, and they were angered by an attack on Wampanoag Indians in Rhode Island the previous December.

The Town Falls At sunrise on February 10, 1676, a group of Wampanoag Indians stormed the English frontier settlement of Lancaster, Massachusetts. It was perfect timing. Most of Lancaster's leaders were in Boston, seeking help in their struggle with the Indians from the royal governor. When gunshots rang out on that February morning, the settlement was virtually unguarded.

Mary Rowlandson, the forty-year-old wife of a Lancaster minister, huddled in her house and watched the battle. She saw friends and family cut down by gunfire. "The attack was launched not by human contestants in a struggle for land and power but by wolves . . . ," she later wrote. In all, twenty colonists were killed and twenty-four were taken captive, including Rowlandson and her son and daughter.

Thus began Rowlandson's three-month odyssey among the Wampanoag Indians. In May, Rowlandson and her children were ransomed back to her husband. After their release, she wrote an account of her captivity. The book, which has come to be called *A Narrative of the Captivity*, was originally published with a much longer title: *The Soveraignty & Goodness of God, Together with the Faithfulness of His Promises Displayed; Being a Narrative of the Captivity and Restauration of Mrs. Mary Rowlandson*. It was the first American bestseller written by a woman.

Rowlandson's book was so successful it spawned dozens of imitations. These other captivity narratives were largely fictional, though they claimed to be true. Immensely popular, they portrayed Native Americans as brutal savages, contributing to a stereotype that persisted for hundreds of years.

▲ Critical Viewing What does the beautiful bead work and design of this sash belonging to Wampanoag leader King Philip suggest about his status in his society? **[Interpret]**

✸ ENRICHMENT: Literature Connection

The Last of the Mohicans

The captivity narrative probably reached its literary high point in 1826 with the publication of *The Last of the Mohicans*, an adventure story by American novelist James Fenimore Cooper. Although it is a work of fiction, it includes all the ingredients that made Mary Rowlandson's narrative so popular—the clash between natural and civilized man, danger, battle, hairbreadth escapes, heroes, and villains.

The Last of the Mohicans is set in 1757, during the French and Indian wars. Two English girls, Alice and Cora Munro, are captured by Delaware and Huron tribes. Cora is eventually killed during the battle between the Indians and the rescue party.

Cooper portrays a variety of Indian personalities in his novel. Several of them are heroic, and even Magua, the Huron villain, wins the reader's sympathy as he speaks of the white man's greed and cruelty. Although all his characters seem clichéd to modern eyes, Cooper marks a turning point in the literary depiction of the Native American. Scholars consider Cooper America's first great social critic.

A Different Culture Ironically, though Rowlandson's book offered a one-sided and often negative view of Native Americans, her observations helped explain Indian culture to colonists. Native Americans had a rich oral tradition, but they had no literary tradition. They communicated their history, family genealogies, and religious beliefs through the spoken word. In most Native American communities, certain people were the designated storytellers. They learned all the tales that served as a repository for their tribe's traditions, values, and beliefs. They also chose and trained their successors. If there was one break in the cycle between generations, these stories—and the worldview they depicted—could vanish completely.

Rowlandson's narrative gave Europeans their first peek into Native American beliefs. Much of her story concerned details of the Indians' struggle for survival—how they ate beaver, foraged for other wild foods, and constructed rafts to cross rivers. Rowlandson describes how she knitted and sewed in exchange for food and asserted herself to receive better treatment. Some of the Indians were kind to her. She calls one of her captors her "best friend." Another found a Bible to comfort her.

Eventually, Rowlandson came to respect aspects of Native American culture. She admired their reverence for their elders, was impressed by the high status of women, and commended the close bonds between members of their community. She also noted details about Indian social hierarchy and government, reporting how the Indians credited their chief, or *sachem*, with great authority, but also used a "General Court to consult and determine."

In the latter years of her life, Rowlandson was widowed, and then remarried. She died in 1711. The Wampanoag, meanwhile, came close to extinction. By the summer of 1676, most of their warriors had been killed and their families sold into slavery. By the nineteenth century, the U.S. government abolished the tribe as a legal entity. Still, efforts were made to maintain Wampanoag traditions. Today, Rhode Island's Native American community has managed to preserve much of the tribe's culture, history, and language.

▼ **Critical Viewing**
What details on this early edition of Mary Rowlandson's book would be regarded as one-sided or inflammatory today? **[Analyze]**

Captivity Narratives: Colonial Pulp Fiction ◆ 69

▶**Critical Viewing**
Answer: The word "sufferings" in the subtitle, the illustration, and the phrases "barbarous and cruel" and "vile savages" below the illustration are all inflammatory.

Critical Thinking

1. Why do you think captivity narratives were so popular in early America?
   Answer: They were exciting stories. People enjoyed them for the adventure and suspense. The church approved their publication for their improving moral aspects, so people could buy and read them openly even if they weren't reading them for their instructive qualities.

2. Why do you think Mary Rowlandson chose to write about her experience?
   Possible answers: She was traumatized by the kidnapping and wrote the book as a form of therapy. She wanted to make some money. The book's original title suggests that she wanted to use her experience to preach to her readers.

from The General History of Virginia ✦ *from* Of Plymouth Plantation

Lesson Objectives

1. **To analyze and respond to literary elements**
   - Literary Analysis: Narrative Accounts
   - Comparing Literary Works

2. **To read, comprehend, analyze, and critique nonfiction**
   - Reading Strategy: Breaking Down Sentences
   - Reading Check Questions
   - Review and Assess Questions
   - Assessment Practice (ATE)

3. **To develop word analysis skills, fluency, and systematic vocabulary**
   - Vocabulary Development Lesson: Related Forms of *peril*

4. **To understand and apply written and oral language conventions**
   - Spelling Strategy
   - Grammar and Style Lesson: Singular and Plural Possessive Nouns

5. **To understand and apply appropriate writing and research strategies**
   - Writing Lesson: Comparison of Narratives
   - Extension Activity: Historic Menu

6. **To understand and apply listening and speaking strategies**
   - Extension Activity: Persuasive Speech

STEP-BY-STEP TEACHING GUIDE	PACING GUIDE
PRETEACH	
Motivate Students and Provide Background	
Use the Motivation activity (ATE p. 70)	5 min.
Read and discuss author and background features (SE p. 70; ATE p.70)	5 min.
Introduce the Concepts	
Introduce the Literary Analysis and Reading Strategy (SE/ATE p. 71)	15 min.
Pronounce the vocabulary words and read their definitions (SE p. 71)	5 min.
TEACH	
Monitor Comprehension	
Informally monitor comprehension by circulating while students read independently or in groups	25 min.
Monitor students' comprehension with the Reading Check notes (SE/ATE pp. 73, 75, 77, 79, 81, 83)	as students read
Develop vocabulary with Vocabulary notes (SE pp. 72, 73, 76, 78, 79, 81; ATE p. 78)	as students read
Develop Understanding	
Develop students' understanding of narrative accounts with the Literary Analysis annotations (SE pp. 74, 75, 76, 81, 82, 84; ATE pp. 74, 75, 76, 80, 81, 82, 84)	5 min.
Develop students' ability to break down long sentences with the Reading Strategy annotations (SE pp. 73, 75, 77, 78; ATE pp. 71, 73, 75, 76, 78)	5 min.
ASSESS	
Assess Mastery	
Assess students' mastery of the Reading Strategy and Literary Analysis by having them answer the Review and Assess questions (SE/ATE p. 85)	15 min.
Use one or more of the print and media Assessment Resources (ATE p. 87)	up to 45 min.
EXTEND	
Apply Understanding	
Have students complete the Vocabulary Development Lesson and the Grammar and Style Lesson (SE p. 86)	20 min.
Apply students' ability to use clear organization using the Writing Lesson (SE/ATE p. 87)	45 min.
Apply students' understanding using one or more of the Extension Activities (SE p. 87)	20–90 min.

A **ACCELERATED INSTRUCTION:**
Use the strategies and activities identified with an **A**.

UNIVERSAL ACCESS
- ● = Below Level Students
- ▲ = On-Level Students
- ■ = Above Level Students

Time and Resource Manager

Reading Level: Challenging, Challenging
Average Number of Instructional Days: 5 days

RESOURCES

PRINT 📖	TRANSPARENCIES	TECHNOLOGY 💿 🎧 📼
• **Beyond Literature,** Humanities Connection: Art, p. 5 ▲ ■		• **Interest Grabber Video,** Tape 1 ● ▲ ■
• **Selection Support Workbook:** ● ▲ ■ Literary Analysis, p. 22 Reading Strategy, p. 21 Build Vocabulary, p. 19	• **Literary Analysis and Reading Transparencies,** pp. 9 and 10 ● ▲ ■	
• **Adapted Reader's Companion** ● • **Reader's Companion** ●		• **Listening to Literature** ● ▲ ■ Audiocassettes, Sides 2–3 Audio CDs, CDs 1–2
• **English Learner's Companion** ● ▲ • **Literatura en español** ● ▲ • **Literary Analysis for Enrichment** ■		
• **Formal Assessment:** Selection Test, pp. 19–21 ● ▲ ■ • **Open Book Test,** pp. 13–15 ● ▲ ■ • **PRENTICE HALL ASSESSMENT SYSTEM** ● ▲ ■	**PRENTICE HALL ASSESSMENT SYSTEM** Skills Practice Answers and Explanations on Transparencies ● ▲ ■	• **Test Bank Software** ● ▲ ■ • **Got It! Assessment Videotapes,** Tape 1 ● ▲
• **Selection Support Workbook:** ● ▲ ■ Grammar and Style, p. 20 • **Writing and Grammar,** Ruby Level ● ▲ ■ • **Extension Activities,** p. 5 ● ▲ ■	• **Daily Language Practice Transparencies** ● ▲ • **Writing Models and Graphic Organizers on Transparencies** pp. 13–16 ● ▲ ■	• **Writing and Grammar iText CD-ROM** ● ▲ ■ 💻 *Take It to the Net* www.phschool.com

BLOCK SCHEDULING: Use one 90-minute class period to preteach the selection and have students read it. Use a second 90-minute class period to assess students' mastery of skills and have them complete one of the Extension Activities.

**Step-by-Step Teaching Guide
for pp. 70–71**

Motivation

Write the following "Help Wanted" advertisement on the chalkboard:

Wanted: Leader capable of governing people in life-threatening crisis. Ability to mediate disputes and maintain order in the face of chaos; good interpersonal and communication skills essential. Community outreach efforts require overcoming language and cultural barriers. Basic bookkeeping, homebuilding, farming, trading, and political skills a must. Salary cannot be guaranteed; no job security.

Ask students whether they would apply for this job and discuss their reactions to the description. Then, tell students that the two narratives they are about to read were written by men whose lives were the inspiration for this advertisement.

▥ Interest Grabber Video

As an alternative, play "European Explorers" and "The Jamestown Colony" on Tape 1.

❶ Background

More About the Authors

John Smith's expedition to America in 1607 was financed by wealthy English people who expected to profit from whaling and gold. However, the only objects of value that Smith and his fellow explorers netted were furs and fish for trade. While the trip's sponsors may have been disappointed, Smith conceived of the newly charted land (from Maine to Cape Cod) as an English colony.

Orphaned in the first year of life, William Bradford was trained by relatives to be a farmer. Receiving little formal education, he was forced to educate himself. Although *Of Plymouth Plantation* was not published until more than two hundred years after it was written, the book was known to the public (and even quoted by colonial historians) long before 1856.

Comparing Literary Works

Prepare to Read

**❶ *from* The General History of Virginia ◆
from Of Plymouth Plantation**

John Smith (1580–1631)

If John Smith were alive today, he would probably be starring opposite Arnold Schwarzenegger in blockbuster adventure films—at least, that might be where he would see himself. Adventurer, poet, mapmaker, and egotist are just a few of the labels that apply to Smith, who earned a reputation as one of England's most famous explorers by helping to lead the first successful English colony in America. Stories of his adventures, often embellished by his own pen, fascinated readers of his day and continue to provide details about the early exploration of the Americas.

Smith and a group of colonists landed in Virginia in 1607 and founded Jamestown. As president of the colony from 1608 to 1609, Smith helped to obtain food, enforce discipline, and deal with the local Native Americans. Although Smith returned to England in 1609, he made two more voyages to America and, in 1614, explored what he called New England. Using his skills as a mapmaker to chart his course, Smith mapped out the coast from Penobscot Bay, Maine, to Cape Cod, Massachusetts.

On a second voyage to further carve out new and chartered lands, Smith found himself in the dangerous company of pirates who held him against his will. Although Smith managed to escape, he returned to England without any money. In 1617, he made one final colonizing effort, but his ship was held back by wind gusts that lasted three months. After that, he never had a chance to set sail. Smith published several works in the course of his life, including *The General History of Virginia, New England,* and the *Summer Isles* (1624).

William Bradford (1590–1657)

Survival in North America was a matter of endurance, intelligence, and courage. William Bradford had all three. Thirteen years after the first permanent English settlement was established in Jamestown, Virginia, Bradford helped lead the Pilgrims to what is now Massachusetts.

Seeking Freedom Bradford, who was born in Yorkshire, England, joined a group of Puritans who believed that the Church of England was corrupt. This group wished to separate from the church. In the face of stiff persecution, they eventually fled to Holland and from there sailed to North America. In *Of Plymouth Plantation,* Bradford provides an account of the experiences of these early settlers. Historians consider this account to be accurate.

A Long Leadership After the death of the colony's first leader, the Pilgrims elected William Bradford governor. He was reelected thirty times. During his tenure, he organized the repayment of debts to financial backers, encouraged new immigration, and established good relations with the Native Americans, without whose help the colony never would have survived. He also instituted the town meeting within the colonies, a democratic process that continues to take place in state government today. Bradford was largely responsible for leading the infant colony through many hardships to success.

In 1630, Bradford began writing *Of Plymouth Plantation,* a firsthand account of the Pilgrims' struggle to endure, sustained only by courage and unbending faith. The work, written in the simple language known as Puritan Plain Style, was not published until 1856.

TEACHING RESOURCES

The following resources can be used to enrich or extend the instruction for pp. 70–71.

Motivation

▥ **Interest Grabber Video,** Tape 1 ▥

Background

📖 **Beyond Literature,** p. 5

💻 *Take It to the Net*
Visit www.phschool.com for Background and hotlinks for the selections.

Literary Analysis

▦ **Literary Analysis and Reading Transparencies,** Narrative Accounts, p. 10

📖 **Selection Support:** Literary Analysis, p. 22

Reading

▦ **Literary Analysis and Reading Transparencies,** Breaking Down Sentences, p. 9 ▥

▣ **BLOCK SCHEDULING:** Resources marked with this symbol provide varied instruction during 90-minute blocks.

Preview

Connecting to the Literature

You may remember a point in your life when you kept going even when everything seemed to be going against you. Consider the difficulties the early American colonists faced when they fought against all odds in their determination to cross the ocean and find a new homeland.

❷ Literary Analysis

Narrative Accounts

Narrative accounts tell the story of real-life events. Some historical narratives, including these, are firsthand accounts by people who lived through significant historic events. Others are secondhand accounts, written by people who researched the events but did not experience them. In the following passage, William Bradford provides a firsthand description.

> . . . after long beating at sea they fell with that land which is called Cape Cod; the which being made and certainly known to be it, they were not a little joyful.

Because of the writer's personal involvement, firsthand accounts are sometimes subjective.

Comparing Literary Works

John Smith and the settlers at Jamestown came to the New World in search of wealth. In contrast, Bradford and the Pilgrims sought religious freedom. As you read, compare and contrast the experiences of the two groups, and note how the different purposes of the two groups are reflected in the presentation of events.

❸ Reading Strategy

Breaking Down Sentences

You can analyze meaning by **breaking down sentences** and considering one section at a time. Look at a complex sentence, and separate its essential parts (the *who* and *what*) from the difficult language until you get to the main idea. As you read, use a diagram like the one shown to help you analyze and interpret the meaning of complex sentences.

Vocabulary Development

pilfer (pil´ fər) *v.* steal (p. 72)

palisades (pal´ə sādz´) *n.* large, pointed stakes set in the ground to form a fence used for defense (p. 73)

conceits (kən sēts´) *n.* strange or fanciful ideas (p. 73)

mollified (mäl´ ə fīd´) *v.* soothed; calmed (p. 76)

peril (per´əl) *n.* danger (p. 78)

loath (lōth) *adj.* reluctant, unwilling (p. 79)

sundry (sun´ drē) *adj.* various; different (p. 79)

recompense (rek´ əm pens´) *n.* reward; repayment (p. 81)

Whole Sentence

Who   **What**

Central Point

from *The General History of Virginia* / from *Of Plymouth Plantation* ◆ 71

---

❷ Literary Analysis

Narrative Accounts

- Tell students that they will focus on narrative accounts as they read the two prose selections in this lesson.

- Read aloud together the instruction about narrative accounts.

- With students, review the differences between firsthand and secondhand accounts.

- Clarify for students that although Smith's is a firsthand account, he chooses to refer to himself in the third person, as "Captain Smith." Explain that this convention was commonly used by those keeping narrative records about explorations or other group ventures.

- Invite students to look for evidence of subjectivity in the works of John Smith and William Bradford.

❸ Reading Strategy

Breaking Down Sentences

- Explain that most long or complicated sentences can be broken into sections or clauses. Analyzing each section individually can help readers distinguish the writer's main ideas from less crucial details.

- Point out that punctuation can guide students to logical places to break sentences for analysis.

- Remind students to look for signal words that indicate relationships among the ideas in various parts of a sentence.

Vocabulary Development

- Pronounce each vocabulary word for students, and read the definitions as a class. Have students identify any words with which they are already familiar.

CUSTOMIZE INSTRUCTION FOR UNIVERSAL ACCESS

For Special Needs Students	For Less Proficient Readers	For English Learners
Have students read the adapted version of "The General History of Virginia" in the **Adapted Reader's Companion**. This version provides basic level instruction in an interactive format with questions and write-on lines. Completing the adapted version will prepare students to read the selection in the Student Edition.	Have students read this selection in the **Reader's Companion**. This version provides basic level instruction in an interactive format with questions and write-on lines. After students finish the selection in Reader's Companion, have them complete the questions and activities in the Student Edition.	Have students read the adapted version of Smith's account in the **English Learners's Companion**. This version provides basic-level instruction in an interactive format with questions and write-on lines. Completing the adapted version will prepare students to read the selection in the Student Edition.

 E-Teach

Visit E-Teach at www.phschool.com for teachers' essays on how to teach with questions and answers.

71

**CUSTOMIZE INSTRUCTION
For Interpersonal Learners**

As students begin to read William Bradford's narrative (which follows John Smith's), have them form pairs to discuss the issues potentially hostile neighbors must work out to survive when living in such close proximity. Encourage students to consider the difficulties each party will face in such asituation.

❶ About the Selection

In this excerpt from *The General History of Virginia*, John Smith describes the rough beginning of the founding of Jamestown Colony. He emphasizes the ordeal the Europeans experienced in crossing the ocean, the struggle to find nourishment, and the challenge of living side by side with the Native Americans. The narrative, which contains the romantic tale of Smith's rescue by Pocahontas, is not always historically accurate, as it strives to present the writer's deeds in a favorable light. It is, however, a firsthand account of a significant event and provides a rare look at the life of a historical figure written in his own words.

▶Critical Viewing

Both the image and the text suggest the extreme exhaustion and despair of the Jamestown settlers.

---

❶ *from* The General History of Virginia
John Smith

The First Day at Jamestown, 14th May 1607, Augustus L. Mason, Library of Congress, Washington, D.C.

What Happened Till the First Supply

Being thus left to our fortunes, it fortuned[1] that within ten days, scarce ten amongst us could either go[2] or well stand, such extreme weakness and sickness oppressed us. And thereat none need marvel if they consider the cause and reason, which was this: While the ships stayed, our allowance was somewhat bettered by a daily proportion of biscuit which the sailors would <u>pilfer</u> to sell, give, or exchange with us for money, sassafras,[3] or furs. But when they departed, there remained neither tavern, beer house, nor place of relief but the common kettle.[4] Had we been as free from all sins as gluttony and drunkenness we might have been canonized for saints, but our President[5] would never have been admitted for engrossing to

▲ **Critical Viewing**
Contrast the feeling this image evokes with the details of the first sentence of Smith's account. **[Connect]**

pilfer (pil´ fər) *v.* steal

---

1. **fortuned** *v.* happened.
2. **go** *v.* be active.
3. **sassafras** (sas´ ə fras´) *n.* a tree, the root of which was valued for its supposed medicinal qualities.
4. **common kettle** communal cooking pot.
5. **President** Wingfield, the leader of the colony.

72 ◆ Beginnings–1750

TEACHING RESOURCES

The following resources can be used to enrich or extend the instruction for pp. 72–84.

Literary Analysis

📖 **Writing Models and Graphic Organizers on Transparencies**, pp. 13–16

Reading

📕 **Selection Support:** Reading Strategy, p. 21; Build Vocabulary, p. 19

🎧 **Listening to Literature Audiocassettes**
Sides 2, 3 ▪

💿 **Listening to Literature Audio CDs**, CDs 1, 2 ▪

▪ **BLOCK SCHEDULING:** Resources marked with this symbol provide varied instruction during 90-minute blocks.

his private,[6] oatmeal, sack,[7] oil, aqua vitae,[8] beef, eggs, or what not but the kettle; that indeed he allowed equally to be distributed, and that was half a pint of wheat and as much barley boiled with water for a man a day, and this, having fried some twenty-six weeks in the ship's hold, contained as many worms as grains so that we might truly call it rather so much bran than corn; our drink was water, our lodgings castles in the air.

With this lodging and diet, our extreme toil in bearing and planting <u>palisades</u> so strained and bruised us and our continual labor in the extremity of the heat had so weakened us, as were cause sufficient to have made us as miserable in our native country or any other place in the world.

From May to September, those that escaped lived upon sturgeon and sea crabs. Fifty in this time we buried; the rest seeing the President's projects to escape these miseries in our pinnace[9] by flight (who all this time had neither felt want nor sickness) so moved our dead spirits as we deposed him and established Ratcliffe in his place . . .

❷ But now was all our provision spent, the sturgeon gone, all helps abandoned, each hour expecting the fury of the savages; when God, the patron of all good endeavors, in that desperate extremity so changed the hearts of the savages that they brought such plenty of their fruits and provision as no man wanted.

And now where some affirmed it was ill done of the Council[10] to send forth men so badly provided, this incontradictable reason will show them plainly they are too ill advised to nourish such ill <u>conceits</u>: First, the fault of our going was our own; what could be thought fitting or necessary we had, but what we should find, or want, or where we should be, we were all ignorant and supposing to make our passage in two months, with victual to live and the advantage of the spring to work; we were at sea five months where we both spent our victual and lost the opportunity of the time and season to plant, by the unskillful presumption of our ignorant transporters that understood not at all what they undertook.

Such actions have ever since the world's beginning been subject to such accidents, and everything of worth is found full of difficulties, but nothing so difficult as to establish a commonwealth so far remote from men and means and where men's minds are so untoward[11] as neither do well themselves nor suffer others. But to proceed.

The new President and Martin, being little beloved, of weak judgment in dangers, and less industry in peace, committed the managing of all things abroad[12] to Captain Smith, who, by his own example,

---

6. **engrossing to his private** taking for his own use.
7. **sack** *n.* type of white wine.
8. **aqua vitae** (ak´ wə vi´ tə) brandy.
9. **pinnace** (pin´ is) *n.* small sailing ship.
10. **Council** the seven persons in charge of the expedition.
11. **untoward** *adj.* stubborn.
12. **abroad** *adv.* outside the palisades.

palisades (pal´ ə sādz´) *n.* large, pointed stakes set in the ground to form a fence used for defense

Reading Strategy
Breaking Down Sentences
In the long sentence beginning "But now" there is an important turn of events. Break the sentence down to understand its meaning.

conceits (kən sētz´) *n.* strange or fanciful ideas

❸ ✓**Reading Check**
Where do the pilgrims get food, once their supply runs out?

from *The General History of Virginia* ◆ 73

---

❷ **Reading Strategy**
Breaking Down Sentences
- Have two or three student volunteers take turns reading the sentence aloud.
- Write the entire sentence, with punctuation, on the chalkboard.
- Then, ask students the Reading Strategy feature on p. 73: Break the sentence down to understand its meaning.
  Answer: If necessary, help students see that a natural break occurs after the semicolon, that *the patron of all good endeavors* is an appositive referring to *God*, that *in that desperate extremity* refers to the situation described in the first part of the sentence, and that the writer attributes the change in the hearts of the Native Americans to God. This change prompts them to bring food to the settlers.

❸ ✓**Reading Check**
Answer: The Pilgrims receive gifts of food from the Native Americans.

CUSTOMIZE INSTRUCTION FOR UNIVERSAL ACCESS

For Special Needs Students	For Gifted/Talented Students
Encourage students to follow the written text as they listen to a recording of Smith's narrative. Stop the recording after each paragraph, discuss the topics Smith covers, reread the paragraph aloud with students, and then analyze the text sentence by sentence, so that students can distinguish main ideas.	The London Trading Company was the financial backer of the Jamestown expedition. It operated the settlement as a private venture from 1607 to 1624. The company expected to acquire land and eventually to export produce that could not be grown at home, such as tobacco. Unfortunately, the men who went to Jamestown were unfit for the task. Have students prepare a written or oral report on the fate of Jamestown, expanding on the history of the settlement.

❸ Background

Art

Founding of the First Permanent English Settlement in America, c. 19th century, by Asa Coolidge Warren

The engraving illustrates the moment when Pocahontas, Powhatan's daughter, came to the rescue of the English captive, John Smith.

1. Imagine that you were present at the scene depicted here. How would you describe it?
   Answer: Students' answers can include the looks of surprise and confusion many express, the eagerness of the young men to do Smith harm, and the body language of those in the scene.

2. The engraving describes Smith's account of the incident. Do you believe it happened this way? Did it happen at all?
   Answer: Students will have differing opinions about the accuracy of Smith's account; they should be prepared to explain the reasoning behind their answers.

❹ ▶Critical Viewing

Answer: Students may respond that the artist views Native Americans as being dangerous because some are shown as armed and hostile. Other students may point out that Pocahontas and the other women show compassion.

❺ Literary Analysis

Narrative Accounts

- Ask a student volunteer to read aloud this paragraph, as other students listen carefully for loaded words that indicate the author's bias toward Native Americans.

- Ask students the Literary Analysis question on p. 74: Which words in this paragraph alert you to the fact that Smith's account is not completely objective?
  Answer: Smith's use of the terms *barbarians* and *savages* indicates that his account is not completely objective. You may wish to engage students in a discussion of Europeans' general lack of understanding of Native American cultures.

Founding of the First Permanent English Settlement in America, A. C. Warren, New York Public Library

good words, and fair promises, set some to mow, others to bind thatch, some to build houses, others to thatch them, himself always bearing the greatest task for his own share, so that in short time he provided most of them lodgings, neglecting any for himself. . . .

Leading an expedition on the Chickahominy River, Captain Smith and his men are attacked by Indians, and Smith is taken prisoner.

When this news came to Jamestown, much was their sorrow for his loss, few expecting what ensued.

Six or seven weeks those barbarians kept him prisoner, many strange triumphs and conjurations they made of him, yet he so demeaned himself amongst them, as he not only diverted them from surprising the fort, but procured his own liberty, and got himself and his company such estimation amongst them, that those savages admired him.

❹
▲ **Critical Viewing**
What can you infer about the artist's attitude toward Native Americans from the way he depicts them? **[Infer]**

Literary Analysis
Narrative Accounts
Which words in this paragraph alert you to the fact that Smith's account is not completely objective?

✹ ENRICHMENT: Social Studies Connection

North American Colonies

In the early settling of North America there were four frontiers, or boundaries of settlement: the Spanish, French, English, and Dutch. There were Spanish settlements in present-day Florida and in the Southwest. The French settled in Quebec and explored the interior by sailing down the Mississippi River. The English hugged a narrow strip along the East Coast. In addition to frontiers in Jamestown, Virginia, and in Plymouth, Massachusetts, the English established colonies in Pennsylvania and in South Carolina. The Dutch briefly had settlements in New York.

You may wish to have some students conduct independent research to find a firsthand historical narrative describing life in a settlement other than Jamestown or Plymouth. Have them compare that narrative, in style and content, to those by Smith and Bradford.

The manner how they used and delivered him is as followeth:

The savages having drawn from George Cassen whither Captain Smith was gone, prosecuting that opportunity they followed him with three hundred bowmen, conducted by the King of Pamunkee,[13] who in divisions searching the turnings of the river found Robinson and Emry by the fireside; those they shot full of arrows and slew. Then finding the Captain, as is said, that used the savage that was his guide as his shield (three of them being slain and divers[14] others so galled),[15] all the rest would not come near him. Thinking thus to have returned to his boat, regarding them, as he marched, more than his way, slipped up to the middle in an oozy creek and his savage with him; yet dared they not come to him till being near dead with cold he threw away his arms. Then according to their compositions[16] they drew him forth and led him to the fire where his men were slain. Diligently they chafed his benumbed limbs.

He demanding for their captain, they showed him Opechancanough, King of Pamunkee, to whom he gave a round ivory double compass dial. Much they marveled at the playing of the fly and needle,[17] which they could see so plainly and yet not touch it because of the glass that covered them. But when he demonstrated by that globe-like jewel the roundness of the earth and skies, the sphere of the sun, moon, and stars, and how the sun did chase the night round about the world continually, the greatness of the land and sea, the diversity of nations, variety of complexions, and how we were to them antipodes[18] and many other such like matters, they all stood as amazed with admiration.

Notwithstanding, within an hour after, they tied him to a tree, and as many as could stand about him prepared to shoot him, but the King holding up the compass in his hand, they all laid down their bows and arrows and in a triumphant manner led him to Orapaks where he was after their manner kindly feasted and well used. . . .

At last they brought him to Werowocomoco, where was Powhatan, their Emperor. Here more than two hundred of those grim courtiers stood wondering at him, as he had been a monster, till Powhatan and his train had put themselves in their greatest braveries. Before a fire upon a seat like a bedstead, he sat covered with a great robe made of raccoon skins and all the tails hanging by. On either hand did sit a young wench of sixteen or eighteen years and along on each side the house, two rows of men and behind them as many women, with all their heads and shoulders painted red, many of their heads bedecked

---

13. Pamunkee Pamunkee River.
14. divers (dī´ vərz) *adj.* several.
15. galled *v.* wounded.
16. compositions *n.* ways.
17. fly and needle *n.* parts of a compass.
18. antipodes (an tip´ ə dēz´) *n.* two places on opposite sides of the Earth.

from *The General History of Virginia* ◆ 75

Reading Strategy
Breaking Down Sentences
Analyze the first sentence in this paragraph to determine who was killed.

Literary Analysis
Narrative Accounts
How does Smith portray himself in this description?

9 ☑**Reading Check**
What saves Smith from death after he is tied to a tree?

---

6 **Reading Strategy**
Breaking Down Sentences

• Have students analyze this long sentence by distinguishing these individuals or groups: the "savages," Cassen, Smith, three hundred bowmen led by the King of Pamunkee, and the pair "Robinson and Emry."

• After students have clarified that the Native Americans have left Cassen in search of Smith and in the process discover Robinson and Emry, ask them who is killed.
Answer: Robinson and Emry are killed.

7 **Critical Thinking**
Speculate

• Read aloud this passage with students. Invite a student volunteer to recall Smith's descriptions of the Native Americans during the first weeks of his captivity.

• Then, ask students to explain why the Native Americans let Smith live yet killed the others in his party.
Answer: Students might respond that they respect Smith for being a leader or that they are impressed by the way he defends himself.

8 **Literary Analysis**
Narrative Accounts

• Focus students' attention on the long sentence that ends the paragraph. As you read it aloud, invite students to visualize the scene between Smith and the Native Americans.

• ▶ Monitor Progress Then, ask students the Literary Analysis question on p. 75: How does Smith portray himself in this description?
Answer: Smith portrays himself as an intelligent, sophisticated authority in the process of dazzling the Native Americans with his knowledge.

9 ☑**Reading Check**
Answer: The King of Pamunkee holds Smith's compass in the air, and this gesture causes the other Native Americans to put down their bows and arrows.

Pocahontas

In 1609, after relations between the Virginian settlers and the Powhatan tribe had floundered, Pocahontas was kidnapped by the Virginian settlers under Captain Samuel Argall in the hope of using her to negotiate peace with the Powhatan. During her captivity Pocahontas not only converted to Christianity, but also fell in love with a settler named John Rolfe. Her father agreed to their marriage, and she was renamed and baptized Lady Rebecca. After returning to England with her husband and giving birth to a son, she died of smallpox in 1617.

⓫ Literary Analysis

Narrative Accounts

- Encourage students to be alert for words naming or describing Native Americans (*Powhatan, more like a devil than a man, some two hundred more as black as himself*).

- Ask students the Literary Analysis question on p. 76: What do you notice about the writer's attitudes toward people who are different from Europeans?
  Answer: When he is not mortally afraid of them, Smith seems to view Native Americans as curiosities.

⓬ Reading Strategy

Breaking Down Sentences

- Write the entire sentence on the chalkboard, and have several student volunteers read it aloud in its entirety as you graphically divide the sentence into sections.

- You might mark natural division points with slashes after the words *combustion* and *pinnace*. Then, use parentheses or a pair of slashes to separate *with the hazard of his life, with saker falcon and musket shot* from surrounding words.

- If necessary, help students to identify *they* as Jamestown settlers, to recall that a *pinnace* is a small sailing ship, and to understand that Smith threatened to sink the pinnace if the settlers did not quit preparing to flee in it.

---

with the white down of birds, but every one with something, and a great chain of white beads about their necks.

At his entrance before the King, all the people gave a great shout. The queen of Appomattoc was appointed to bring him water to wash his hands, and another brought him a bunch of feathers, instead of a towel, to dry them; having feasted him after their best barbarous manner they could, a long consultation was held, but the conclusion was, two great stones were brought before Powhatan: then as many as could, laid hands on him, dragged him to them, and thereon laid his head and being ready with their clubs to beat out his brains, Pocahontas,◆ the King's dearest daughter, when no entreaty could prevail, got his head in her arms and laid her own upon his to save him from death; whereat the Emperor was contented he should live to make him hatchets, and her bells, beads, and copper, for they thought him as well of all occupations as themselves.[19] For the King himself will make his own robes, shoes, bows, arrows, pots; plant, hunt, or do anything so well as the rest.

Two days after, Powhatan, having disguised himself in the most fearfulest manner he could, caused Captain Smith to be brought forth to a great house in the woods and there upon a mat by the fire to be left alone. Not long after, from behind a mat that divided the house, was made the most dolefulest noise he ever heard; then Powhatan more like a devil than a man, with some two hundred more as black as himself, came unto him and told him now they were friends, and presently he should go to Jamestown to send him two great guns and a grindstone for which he would give him the country of Capahowasic and forever esteem him as his son Nantaquond.

So to Jamestown with twelve guides Powhatan sent him. That night they quartered in the woods, he still expecting (as he had done all this long time of his imprisonment) every hour to be put to one death or other, for all their feasting. But almighty God (by His divine providence) had <u>mollified</u> the hearts of those stern barbarians with compassion. The next morning betimes they came to the fort, where Smith having used the savages with what kindness he could, he showed Rawhunt, Powhatan's trusty servant, two demiculverins[20] and a millstone to carry Powhatan; they found them somewhat too heavy, but when they did see him discharge them, being loaded with stones, among the boughs of a great tree loaded with icicles, the ice and branches came so tumbling down that the poor savages ran away half dead with fear. But at last we regained some conference with them and gave them such toys and sent to Powhatan, his women, and children such presents as gave them in general full content.

---

19. **as well . . . themselves** capable of making them just as well as they could themselves.
20. **demiculverins** (dem′ ē kul′ vər inz) large cannons.

❿ Literature in context — Social Studies Connection

◆ *Pocahontas*

Throughout American history, there has been much speculation about Pocahontas and John Smith. Smith's story of Pocahontas raises questions because of the subjectivity of his relationship with her and because there is no other documentation that substantiates his writing.

In early accounts of his capture, Smith never mentions that Pocahontas is only twelve or thirteen years old. He was twenty-eight at the time. In addition, Smith also speaks of other similar adventures with admiring women. This has led historians to question the accuracy of his account of Pocahontas. In addition, Smith wrote in third person. Historians suggest he may have chosen this style to distance himself from the writing and make it more believable.

mollified (mäl′ ə fīd′) v. soothed; calmed

Literary Analysis
Narrative Accounts and Historical Influences
What do you notice about the writer's attitudes toward people who are different from Europeans?

Now in Jamestown they were all in combustion,[21] the strongest preparing once more to run away with the pinnace; which, with the hazard of his life, with saker falcon[22] and musket shot, Smith forced now the third time to stay or sink.

Some, no better than they should be, had plotted with the President the next day to have him put to death by the Levitical law,[23] for the lives of Robinson and Emry; pretending the fault was his that had led them to their ends: but he quickly took such order with such lawyers that he laid them by their heels till he sent some of them prisoners for England.

Now every once in four or five days, Pocahontas with her attendants brought him so much provision that saved many of their lives, that else for all this had starved with hunger.

His relation of the plenty he had seen, especially at Werowocomoco, and of the state and bounty of Powhatan (which till that time was unknown), so revived their dead spirits (especially the love of Pocahontas) as all men's fear was abandoned.

Thus you may see what difficulties still crossed any good endeavor; and the good success of the business being thus oft brought to the very period of destruction; yet you see by what strange means God hath still delivered it.

---

21. **combustion** (kəm bus´ chən) *n.* tumult.
22. **saker falcon** small cannon.
23. **Levitical law** "He that killeth man shall surely be put to death" (Leviticus 24:17).

Review and Assess

Thinking About the Selection

1. **Respond:** If you faced a situation similar to Smith's, would you have returned to England at the earliest opportunity or stayed on at Jamestown? Why?

2. **(a) Recall:** Give one example of the way Smith praises his own good qualities. **(b) Infer:** What impression of Smith do you get from this account?

3. **(a) Recall:** What words does Smith use when he refers to himself? **(b) Draw Conclusions:** Why do you think he does this?

4. **(a) Interpret:** What is Smith's attitude toward the Native Americans? **(b) Analyze:** Do you think Smith's attitude changes after he gets to know them and they help him? Explain.

5. **Evaluate:** Do you think Smith's account is accurate? Why or why not?

6. **Take a Position:** Do you admire Smith? Why or why not?

from *The General History of Virginia* ◆ 77

Reading Strategy
Breaking Down Sentences
Break down the long sentence beginning "Now in Jamestown" to interpret its meaning.

Answers for p. 77

Review and Assess

1. Some students may point out that the voyage back to England might well have been just as dangerous as staying in Jamestown.

2. **(a)** Examples include *Captain Smith, who, by his own good example, good words, and fair promises, set some to mow, others to bind thatch . . . himself always bearing the greatest task for his own share. . . .*
   (b) Smith seems to think very well of himself and to be a resourceful, capable, and influential man.

3. **(a)** Smith uses the third person and refers to himself with the proper noun *Captain Smith* and the pronouns *he, him,* and *his.*
   (b) Smith may do this to distance himself from the writing and to make it seem less subjective.

4. **(a)** He calls them barbarians and savages but also observes that they can be kind.
   (b) His attitude doesn't appear to change dramatically, though he acknowledges the charitable acts of Pocahontas.

5. Students may suspect that Smith embellished and exaggerated some of his adventures.

6. Students should support their positions with solid reasons, examples, and details from Smith's narrative.

CUSTOMIZE INSTRUCTION FOR UNIVERSAL ACCESS

For Special Needs Students	For Gifted/Talented Students
Help students clarify the purpose and implications of the trip to Jamestown by having them make a graphic representation of the deal suggested by Powhatan. Have students write the names Powhatan and Smith on opposite sides of a sheet of paper. Using images or words, they can then show that Powhatan wants "two great guns and a grindstone"; in return he will give Smith "the country of Capahowasic" and his everlasting "esteem."	Encourage students to write short poems that capture the spirit of Smith's narrative using his language and tone. Prompt them to include descriptions and details that convey Smith's personality and the overall mood of his account. Have students share their poems when they finish. Do the poems reflect similar impressions of Smith?

13 About the Selection

William Bradford presents a firsthand description of the initial experiences of the Massachusetts settlers known to us as the Pilgrims. Historians consider this to be a factually accurate account. Bradford relates how this community of families, united in their goals and religious beliefs, begins the task of building a new settlement in the harsh wilderness. His account reflects religious faith, which he credits for the settlers' peaceful, beneficial relationship with their Native American neighbors.

14 Reading Strategy

Breaking Down Sentences

- Point out to students that Bradford's style is notable for its clarity. Despite the considerable length and apparent complexity of some sentences, students will probably find his prose easier to follow than John Smith's.

- Help students break down the sentence into sections. Draw students' attention to signal words (such as *after, and,* and *which*) that indicate relationships among ideas and events.

15 Vocabulary Development

Word Analysis: Related Forms of *Peril*

- Point out the word *peril* in the text, and let students know the word means "danger."

- Ask students to volunteer forms of the word such as *perilous* and *imperiled*, and write sentences using the words on the chalkboard.
  Possible answers: *Had the Pilgrims known of the perils associated with their voyage, they might have planned differently.*

The greatest peril that Captain John Smith encountered was probably being imprisoned by angry Native Americans.

History shows that most perilous element of settling the Americans was disease rather than violence.

13

from

P Of Plymouth Plantation

William Bradford

Background

In 1620, the Pilgrims made the difficult voyage to America aboard the tiny *Mayflower*. After fierce storms and the loss of lives, the Pilgrims landed near Cape Cod, Massachusetts, not in Virginia as intended. It was mid-December before they could build shelters and move ashore. Once ashore, the Pilgrims found the hardships of settling in a strange land worsened by a harsh winter. They struggled to make a new life in America.

Of Their Voyage and How They Passed the Sea; and of Their Safe Arrival at Cape Cod

14 After they had enjoyed fair winds and weather for a season, they were encountered many times with cross winds and met with many fierce storms with which the ship was shroudly[1] shaken, and her upper works made very leaky; and one of the main beams in the midships was bowed and cracked, which put them in some fear that the ship could not be able to perform the voyage. So some of the chief of the company, perceiving the mariners to fear the sufficiency of the ship as appeared by their mutterings, they entered into serious consultation with the master and other officers of the ship, to consider in time of the danger, and rather to return than to cast themselves into **15** a desperate and inevitable <u>peril</u>. And truly there was great distraction and difference of opinion amongst the mariners themselves: fain

Reading Strategy
Breaking Down Sentences
To better comprehend its meaning, break down the first sentence of this account.

peril (per´ el) *n.* danger

1. **shroudly** (shrōōd´ lē) *adv.* wickedly.

☀ ENRICHMENT: Culture Connection

Immigrants in America

The Pilgrims and the Jamestown colonists needed great fortitude to succeed in the New World. Discuss with students the idea that today's immigrants to the United States face their own (and different) kinds of hardships. Have groups discuss the opportunities and challenges that greet today's newcomers to America. These include overcoming language barriers, securing housing and jobs, dealing with different cultural traditions, facing discrimination, and adjusting to life in a new place. Have students compare and contrast the obstacles described by Smith and Bradford with the obstacles immigrants face today. Ask students to suggest and list the skills and strengths people must possess to overcome these difficulties. Some students may have firsthand knowledge of such as challenge. Invite any willing students to share personal or family experiences with you and their classmates.

would they do what could be done for their wages' sake (being now near half the seas over) and on the other hand they were <u>loath</u> to hazard their lives too desperately. But in examining of all opinions, the master and others affirmed they knew the ship to be strong and firm under water; and for the buckling of the main beam, there was a great iron screw the passengers brought out of Holland, which would raise the beam into his place; the which being done, the carpenter and master affirmed that with a post put under it, set firm in the lower deck and otherways bound, he would make it sufficient. And as for the decks and upper works, they would caulk them as well as they could, and though with the working of the ship they would not long keep staunch, yet there would otherwise be no great danger, if they did not overpress her with sails. So they committed themselves to the will of God and resolved to proceed.

In <u>sundry</u> of these storms the winds were so fierce and the seas so high, as they could not bear a knot of sail, but were forced to hull[2] for divers days together. And in one of them, as they thus lay at hull

---

2. **hull** *v.* drift with the wind.

loath (lōth) *adj.* reluctant; unwilling

sundry (sun′ drē) *adj.* various; different

18 ✔**Reading Check**

What happens to the ship in the storm?

The Coming of the Mayflower, N. C. Wyeth, from the Collection of the Metropolitan Life Insurance Company, New York City

16

17 ▲ **Critical Viewing** Is this an idealized or a realistic depiction of the *Mayflower's* Atlantic crossing? Explain your decision. **[Judge; Support]**

from *Of Plymouth Plantation* ◆ 79

16 ● **Background**

Art

The Coming of the Mayflower, by N. C. Wyeth

Wyeth (1882–1945) was a prolific American illustrator. His work appeared with many popular and well-known works of literature, and he also took up the difficult art of mural painting. Wyeth's last mural commission was a series of eight huge pieces that express the spirit and heritage of New England. *The Coming of the Mayflower* is one of this series. Wyeth died before completing the project, but his son, the artist Andrew Wyeth, and his son-in-law, John McCoy, finished the work for him. Use these questions for discussion:

1. **What viewpoint does Wyeth use to lend drama to the scene?**
   Possible response: The view is from land—perhaps the famous Plymouth Rock—toward which the ship appears to be headed. There is a sense of excitement and expectation.

2. **Wind plays a key role in the first part of Bradford's account. How does Wyeth demonstrate the power of wind in this mural?**
   Answer: Responses might point to the billowing sails, the listing ship, and the whitecaps in the choppy seas.

17 ▶ **Critical Viewing**

Answer: Students may respond that the colorful painting serves to glorify or romanticize the crossing because it does not portray the hardships endured by the ship's passengers. Others might say that the painting depicts realistically the rough seas the *Mayflower* faced.

18 ✔**Reading Check**

Answer: The ship is shaken and damaged by the wind and seas: in addition to leaks, the ship sustains a crack in a main beam amidships.

CUSTOMIZE INSTRUCTION FOR UNIVERSAL ACCESS

For Special Needs Students	For Gifted/Talented Students
Seeing a visual representation of the *Mayflower* will help students picture the repairs made to the ship. If possible, display a photograph, painting, or drawing of the *Mayflower,* the *Mayflower II,* or another similar vessel.	Challenge students to write a scene that dramatizes Bradford's decision to document his experiences in writing. Encourage students to depict Bradford discussing the Pilgrims' experiences with Myles Standish. Remind students to use what they have learned about writing dialogue, and encourage students to perform (or at least to read) their scenes to the class.

The Mayflower

Unfortunately, historians have been unable to locate any detailed description of the original *Mayflower*. The ship was intended to make the journey accompanied by a smaller ship, the *Speedwell*, but this vessel was forced to return to port in Southampton twice before finally being judged unseaworthy. Eventually, the *Mayflower* set off from England alone carrying some of the smaller ship's passengers and supplies.

⑳ Literary Analysis

Narrative Accounts

• Ask students to distinguish the characteristics of firsthand and secondhand narratives. Make sure they recognize that firsthand accounts are written by participants and that secondhand accounts are written by people who did not witness events directly.

▶ Monitor Progress Ask students this question: How does Bradford blur the line between firsthand and secondhand historical narrative?

Answer: Students can respond that Bradford blurs the line by using not only the pronoun *I* but also *they* and *them*; the former pronoun suggests a firsthand telling, and the latter two suggest a secondhand telling. Students may also point out that Bradford includes observations about how the sailors feel and inserts his own first-person comments in parentheses.

---

in a mighty storm, a lusty[3] young man called John Howland, coming upon some occasion above the gratings was, with a seel[4] of the ship, thrown into sea; but it pleased God that he caught hold of the topsail halyards[5] which hung overboard and ran out at length. Yet he held his hold (though he was sundry fathoms under water) till he was hauled up by the same rope to the brim of the water, and then with a boat hook and other means got into the ship again and his life saved. And though he was something ill with it, yet he lived many years after and became a profitable member both in church and commonwealth. In all this voyage there died but one of the passengers, which was William Butten, a youth, servant to Samuel Fuller, when they drew near the coast.

But to omit other things (that I may be brief) after long beating at sea they fell with that land which is called Cape Cod; the which being made and certainly known to be it, they were not a little joyful. After some deliberation had amongst themselves and with the master of the ship, they tacked about and resolved to stand for the southward (the wind and weather being fair) to find some place about Hudson's River for their habitation. But after they had sailed that course about half the day, they fell amongst dangerous shoals and roaring breakers, and they were so far entangled therewith as they conceived themselves in great danger; and the wind shrinking upon them withal,[6] they resolved to bear up again for the Cape and thought themselves happy to get out of those dangers before night overtook them, as by God's good providence they did. And the next day they got into the Cape Harbor[7] where they rid in safety.

Being thus arrived in a good harbor, and brought safe to land, they fell upon their knees and blessed the God of Heaven who had brought them over the vast and furious ocean, and delivered them from all the perils and miseries thereof, again to set their feet on the firm and stable earth, their proper element.

The Starving Time

But that which was most sad and lamentable was, that in two or three months' time half of their company died, especially in January and February, being the depth of winter, and wanting houses and

---

3. **lusty** *adj.* strong; hearty.
4. **seel** *n.* rolling.
5. **halyards** (haľ yərdz) *n.* ropes for raising or lowering sails.
6. **withal** (wi*th* ôl´) *adv.* also.
7. **Cape Harbor** now Provincetown Harbor.

⑲ *Literature*
in context History Connection

The Mayflower

The *Mayflower* was the British ship on which 102 Pilgrims sailed from Southampton, England, to North America during September, October, and November of 1620. In November, the Pilgrims disembarked at the tip of Cape Cod. Shortly before Christmas, they moved to the more protected site of Plymouth, Massachusetts. According to historians' estimates, the square-rigged *Mayflower* probably measured about 90 feet long and weighed 180 tons.

The Mayflower in Plymouth Harbor, William Halsall

other comforts: being infected with the scurvy[8] and other diseases which this long voyage and their inaccommodate[9] condition had brought upon them. So as there died sometimes two or three of a day in the foresaid time, that of one hundred and odd persons, scarce fifty remained. And of these, in the time of most distress, there was but six or seven sound persons who to their great commendations, be it spoken, spared no pains night or day, but with abundance of toil and hazard of their own health, fetched them wood, made them fires, dressed them meat, made their beds, washed their loathsome clothes, clothed and unclothed them. In a word, did all the homely[10] and necessary offices for them which dainty and queasy stomachs cannot endure to hear named; and all this willingly and cheerfully, without any grudging in the least, showing herein their true love unto their friends and brethren; a rare example and worthy to be remembered. Two of these seven were Mr. William Brewster, their reverend Elder, and Myles Standish, their Captain and military commander, unto whom myself and many others were much beholden in our low and sick condition. And yet the Lord so upheld these persons as in this general calamity they were not at all infected either with sickness or lameness. And what I have said of these I may say of many others who died in this general visitation,[11] and others yet living: that whilst they had health, yea, or any strength continuing, they were not wanting to any that had need of them. And I doubt not but their recompense is with the Lord.

But I may not here pass by another remarkable passage not to be forgotten. As this calamity fell among the passengers that were to be left here to plant, and were hasted ashore and made to drink water that the seamen might have the more beer, and one[12] in his sickness desiring but a small can of beer, it was answered that if he were their own father he should have none. The disease began to fall amongst them also, so as almost half of their company died before they went away, and many of their officers and lustiest men, as the boatswain, gunner, three quartermasters, the cook and others. At which the Master was something strucken and sent to the sick ashore and told the Governor he should send for beer for them that had need of it, though he drunk water homeward bound.

But now amongst his company there was far another kind of carriage[13] in this misery than amongst the passengers. For they that before had been boon[14] companions in drinking and jollity in the time of their health and welfare, began now to desert one another in this calamity, saying they would not hazard their lives for them, they

---

8. **scurvy** (skʉr′ vē) *n.* disease caused by vitamin C deficiency.
9. **inaccommodate** (in′ ə käm′ ə dāt′) *adj.* unfit.
10. **homely** (hōm′ lē) *adj.* domestic.
11. **visitation** *n.* affliction.
12. **one** William Bradford.
13. **carriage** *n.* behavior.
14. **boon** *adj.* close.

recompense (rek′ əm pens′) *n.* reward; repayment

Literary Analysis
Narrative Accounts
Do you think Bradford's illness would have been included in a secondhand narrative account? Explain.

 Reading Check
What did people like William Brewster and Miles Standish do to earn Bradford's respect?

㉑ Critical Thinking
Synthesize

- Ask students how Bradford's description of the few who are not afflicted by disease reflects his moral values.
  Answer: Bradford admires the virtue of self-sacrifice that arises from their religious beliefs and sense of community.

- Ask students what Bradford wants his readers to think about these people. What does he hope his readers will gain from learning of this experience?
  Answer: Students may assert that the care and concern the Pilgrims exhibit is a function of their strong religious beliefs and of the powerful sense of community they share. Bradford wants his readers to understand how the settlers' faith influenced their behavior toward one another.

㉒ Literary Analysis
Narrative Accounts

- Have students identify the first sentence that indicates that the author was one of the Pilgrims struck down by illness.

- If necessary, draw students' attention to the sentence that begins, *Two of these seven.*

- Ask students the Literary Analysis question on p. 81: Do you think Bradford's illness would have been included in a secondhand narrative account? Explain.
  Answer: Considering the many cases of extreme sickness in the colony, it is unlikely that a secondhand account would have included the minor incident Bradford describes.

㉓ ✓ Reading Check
Answer: They selflessly aided those around them who were ill.

CUSTOMIZE INSTRUCTION FOR UNIVERSAL ACCESS

For English Learners	For Advanced Readers
Invite students to listen carefully as you read a sentence aloud in a way that accentuates its overall rhythms and structure. Then, work with students to break down the sentence into parts for better understanding. Seeing the sectioning of the sentence will help students. You might consider other visual aids, as well, such as color-coding a sentence's nouns and verbs or its subject and predicate.	Have students do research in order to create brief biographical sketches of William Brewster and Myles Standish. Encourage students to share these summaries with the class in short oral presentations.

24 Literary Analysis

Narrative Accounts

- Students may be surprised at the behavior described in this long paragraph. Tell students that less than half of the 102 passengers on the *Mayflower* were Pilgrims. Forty people were recruited in England without regard to religious beliefs; there were also eighteen servants and three hired workers. In all, there were fifty men, twenty women, and thirty-two children.

- Ask students the Literary Analysis question on p. 82: What is revealed here about the Pilgrims' religious beliefs?
  Answer: Students will observe that Bradford's narrative reveals that the Pilgrims believed in showing compassion even to those who did not share their religious convictions.

should be infected by coming to help them in their cabins; and so, after they came to lie by it, would do little or nothing for them but, "if they died, let them die." But such of the passengers as were yet aboard showed them what mercy they could which made some of their hearts relent, as the boatswain (and some others) who was a proud young man and would often curse and scoff at the passengers. But when he grew weak, they had compassion on him and helped him; then he confessed he did not deserve it at their hands, he had abused them in word and deed. "Oh!" (saith he) "you, I now see, show your love like Christians indeed one to another, but we let one another lie and die like dogs." Another lay cursing his wife, saying if it had **24** not been for her he had never come this unlucky voyage, and anon cursing his fellows, saying he had done this and that for some of them; he had spent so much and so much amongst them, and they were now weary of him and did not help him, having need. Another gave his companion all he had, if he died, to help him in his weakness; he went and got a little spice and made him a mess[15] of meat once or twice. And because he died not so soon as he expected, he went amongst his fellows and swore the rogue would cozen[16] him, he would see him choked before he made him any more meat; and yet the poor fellow died before morning.

Indian Relations

All this while the Indians came skulking about them, and would sometimes show themselves aloof off, but when any approached near them, they would run away; and once they stole away their tools where they had been at work and were gone to dinner. But about the sixteenth of March, a certain Indian came boldly amongst them and spoke to them in broken English, which they could well understand but marveled at it. At length they understood by discourse with him, that he was not of these parts, but belonged to the eastern parts where some English ships came to fish, with whom he was acquainted and could name sundry of them by their names, amongst whom he had got his language. He became profitable to them in acquainting them with many things concerning the state of the country in the east parts where he lived, which was afterwards profitable unto them; as also of the people here, of their names, number and strength, of their situation and distance from this place, and who was chief amongst them. His name was Samoset. He told them also of another Indian whose name was Squanto, a native of this place, who had been in England and could speak better English than himself.

---

15. **mess** *n.* meal.
16. **cozen** (kuz´ en) *v.* cheat.

Literary Analysis

Narrative Accounts
What is revealed here about the Pilgrims' religious beliefs?

✸ ENRICHMENT: Social Studies Connection

Living Museums

Restoration villages are specific kinds of museums where people in period clothing attempt to recreate history for modern-day visitors. Plymouth Plantation in Massachusetts (pictured on p. 83) is one such place. In this reconstructed colonial village, costumed guides use period tools and materials to demonstrate seventeenth-century farming, homemaking, and survival skills. They even speak as the Pilgrims did. The *Mayflower II*, a full-size replica of the original 96-foot-long vessel, is moored nearby.

Encourage students to gather information about Plymouth Plantation and the Mayflower II by contacting the Plymouth Area Chamber of Commerce. They also can learn more about restoration villages closer to their area. In either case, students can request bibliographical material and information about summer jobs available to those interested in American history.

25 ▶ **Critical Viewing**
Answer: Students may respond that the photo indicates that life at the stark seaside plantation was hard. There is nothing lush or prosperous about the plain, unadorned buildings. Student responses should reflect the idea that the Pilgrims struggled to create a settlement within a rugged, unforgiving environment.

26 **Background**

History

Massasoit (c. 1580–1661), one of the most powerful Native American leaders in New England, was chief of the Wampanoag Indians. He faithfully observed the 1621 treaty with the Pilgrims.

English-speaking Squanto had been kidnapped by an English slave trader in 1615. When he finally returned to his people, the Patuxets, in 1619, he found that everyone had died of disease.

27 ☑ **Reading Check**

Answer: Samoset is an extraordinary Native American from lands east of Plymouth. He speaks basic English absorbed while living in the vicinity of European settlers. The Pilgrims meet Samoset after he approaches their settlement and addresses them.

Being, after some time of entertainment and gifts dismissed, a while after he came again, and five more with him, and they brought again all the tools that were stolen away before, and made way for the coming of their great Sachem,[17] called Massasoit. Who, about four or five days after, came with the chief of his friends and other attendance, with the aforesaid Squanto. With whom, after friendly entertainment and some gifts given him, they made a peace with him (which hath now continued this twenty-four years) in these terms:

1. That neither he nor any of his should injure or do hurt to any of their people.

25 ▲ **Critical Viewing**
What can you learn about the lifestyle at Plymouth Plantation from this photograph of an authentic re-creation of the settlement? **[Infer]**

27 ☑ **Reading Check**
Who is Samoset, and how do the Pilgrims meet him?

---

17. Sachem (sā´ chəm) Chief.

CUSTOMIZE INSTRUCTION FOR UNIVERSAL ACCESS

For English Learners	For Gifted/Talented Students
Pair students with more proficient English speakers to create picture cards for the key vocabulary words on these two pages. Students might illustrate and spell words such as *compassion, confess, companion, tools, friends, gifts,* and *people.*	Point out that readers of Bradford's text can gain a vivid sense of the time period and of the settlers' lives and can learn much about how they survived hardship and danger to start a new life in a new land. Encourage students as they read to put themselves in the place of a settler at Plymouth Plantation. After reading, have students write a diary page from the point of view of a settler.

28 **Literary Analysis**

Narrative Accounts

- Have a student volunteer read aloud the excerpt's final paragraph.

- Ask students the Literary Analysis question on p. 84: What does Bradford reveal about his religious beliefs in this description of Squanto as a "special instrument"? Answer: Students might note that Bradford's religious beliefs lead him to identify Squanto as an "instrument" of God. This suggests Bradford's belief that God is an active, benevolent presence in the Pilgrims' daily lives.

Answers for p. 84

Review and Assess

1. Students' answers should show an understanding of the settlers' hardships.

2. **(a)** On the ocean, the Pilgrims encounter fierce storms and their ship falls into disrepair. During the first winter, they lack shelter, warmth, and food. Many Pilgrims suffer from scurvy or die of other illnesses. **(b)** These troubles suggest that Plymouth's climate is harsh and that its landscape is rugged and unyielding.

3. **(a)** Bradford suggests that Squanto was sent to the Pilgrims by God to help them survive and thrive in the new world. **(b)** It suggests that the Pilgrims believed they were being guided and protected by God.

4. **(a)** Students might say that Bradford wishes to convey the idea that the Pilgrims' perseverance, courage, and faith in God allowed them to surmount enormous odds and to make a new life in a new world. **(b)** The message is universal in its assertion that human beings' inner resources strongly affect what they are able to endure and accomplish.

5. Bradford might have been more able to focus on matters other than basic survival.

6. Students may not have realized how hard the Pilgrims had to struggle to establish themselves in the new world.

2. That if any of his did hurt to any of theirs, he should send the offender, that they might punish him.

3. That if anything were taken away from any of theirs, he should cause it to be restored; and they should do the like to his.

4. If any did unjustly war against him, they would aid him; if any did war against them, he should aid them.

5. He should send to his neighbors confederates to certify them of this, that they might not wrong them, but might be likewise comprised in the conditions of peace.

6. That when their men came to them, they should leave their bows and arrows behind them.

28 After these things he returned to his place called Sowams, some 40 miles from this place, but Squanto continued with them and was their interpreter and was a special instrument sent of God for their good beyond their expectation. He directed them how to set their corn, where to take fish, and to procure other commodities, and was also their pilot to bring them to unknown places for their profit, and never left them till he died.

Review and Assess

Thinking About the Selection

1. **Respond:** If you had been making the journey on the *Mayflower*, what would you have done to prepare for life in America?

2. **(a) Recall:** What were some of the hardships the Pilgrims faced during their trip across the Atlantic and their first winter at Plymouth? **(b) Interpret:** What do their troubles suggest about the climate and landscape of Plymouth?

3. **(a) Recall:** How do the Pilgrims explain Squanto's role in their experience? **(b) Interpret:** What does this explanation suggest about the Pilgrims' religious convictions?

4. **(a) Draw Conclusions:** What do you think is the message that Bradford tries to convey in this narrative? **(b) Apply:** How might the message have meaning for people today?

5. **Hypothesize:** In what ways might this account have been different if the Pilgrims had successfully settled farther south?

6. **Evaluate:** How has this account changed your impression of the Pilgrims? Explain.

Literary Analysis
Narrative Accounts
What does Bradford reveal about his religious beliefs in this description of Squanto as a "special instrument"?

ASSESSMENT PRACTICE

Supporting Details (For more practice, see Test Preparation Workbook, p. 5.)

Many tests require students to recognize summaries by identifying main ideas and supporting details. Students should recognize which details are important to the main idea and which are not. Present the following sample test item:

With this lodging and diet, our extreme toil in bearing and planting palisades so strained and bruised us and our continual labor in the extremity of the heat had so weakened us, as were cause sufficient to have made us so miserable in our native country or any other place in the world.

Which of the following does NOT support the main idea that early Virginians were miserable in their new country?

A They were weak from planting their crops.

B They had little food.

C The heat was extreme.

D They were in conflict with the local Native Americans.

All of these support the main idea EXCEPT choice *D*.

Review and Assess

Literary Analysis

Narrative Accounts

1. Use a chart like the one shown to find examples of the key characteristics of **narrative accounts** in the selections.

What the Writer Saw	Factual Information
Selection	
What the Writer Heard	Subjective Bias

2. (a) What do you think Smith's purpose was in writing his narrative? (b) In what way was Bradford's purpose different?

Comparing Literary Works

3. Compare and contrast the relationship Smith and the Pilgrims had with the Native Americans.
4. In what way might political concerns have played a part in shaping John Smith's account of the Jamestown Colony's early days?
5. How might the Puritans' religious beliefs have influenced Bradford's account of the first experiences of the Massachusetts settlers?
6. (a) In what ways do the authors' presentations of events and the impressions they convey differ? (b) How do these differences reflect the purpose of each group's settlement?
7. Which account seems more reliable to you? Explain.

Reading Strategy

Breaking Down Sentences

8. Scan the narratives for three sentences that you found particularly challenging to interpret. Separating the complex language from the essential parts, analyze the sentences. Then, write the meaning of the sentences as you understand them.

Extend Understanding

9. **Social Studies Connection:** Do you feel that the changing attitudes of the settlers and the Native Americans reflect typical experiences with newcomers? Why or why not?

from *The General History of Virginia* / from *Of Plymouth Plantation* ◆ 85

Quick Review

A **narrative account** is a story about real-life experiences.

Breaking down sentences into simpler parts helps to interpret the meaning of lengthy and difficult sentences.

 Take It to the Net
www.phschool.com

Take the interactive self-test online to check your understanding of these selections.

✹ ENRICHMENT: Further Reading

Other Works by the Authors

Works by John Smith
The True Travels, Adventures and Observations of Captain J. Smith, John Smith

Works by William Bradford
Mourt's Relation, William Bradford

Take It to the Net
Visit www.phschool.com for more information on the authors.

Answers for p. 85

Review and Assess

1. Students should include specific textual references in their charts.
2. **(a)** Smith's purpose is to describe the settlement of Jamestown and to encourage others to join it. He also boasts about his own strength and cleverness. **(b)** Bradford wished to record a factual and modest account of the Pilgrims' experience. He wishes to credit God, rather than people, with the good things that happened to them.
3. Smith seems to find the Native Americans backward, ignorant, and dangerous. Bradford and the Pilgrims at first seem disapproving and curious about the Native Americans; later they befriend them and enjoy entertaining them.
4. Smith may have preferred that his financial backers see his deeds in the best possible light and shaped his account accordingly.
5. Students may say that Bradford may have seen the settler's hardships as a trial sent by God.
6. **(a)** Smith's account is in some ways the story of an individual because he repeatedly places himself in the foreground of the narrative; Bradford's sensibility seems more sober and wise, and his account has an authentic and authoritative ring. **(b)** Students may explain the difference by pointing to the authors' different motivations for writing: Smith seems interested in entertaining his readers and promoting his own heroism, and Bradford seems more interested in presenting the experience of the community.
7. Students should state opinions clearly and support ideas with examples from the texts.
8. Students should select appropriately complex or lengthy sentences and break them down into components that are more manageable or easily understood.
9. Sample response: Yes, at first strangers are usually apprehensive with one another. When they become familiar with one another, the fear and anxiety diminish.

❶ Vocabulary Development

Word Analysis

1. imperiled
2. perilously
3. perilous

Spelling Strategy

Possible responses:

1. Patting the baby's back pacified him.
2. The plan was modified so that my visiting sister could accompany us to dinner.
3. My friend testified in a criminal trial last week.

Concept Development

1. A	5. A
2. S	6. A
3. S	7. A
4. A	8. S

❷ Grammar and Style

Practice

Much to Bradford's amazement, Samoset spoke to the Pilgrims in broken English. Samoset convinced his fellow Indians to return the settlers' tools. He persuaded Massasoit to pay his respects to the Pilgrims and introduced them to one of his friends, Squanto.

Writing Application

Students' paragraphs should convey a realistic sense of the Pilgrims' arrival and should correctly use at least five plural and possessive nouns.

Integrate Language Skills

❶ Vocabulary Development Lesson

Word Analysis: Related Forms of *Peril*

The word *peril* comes from the Latin word *periculum*, which means "danger." Using your knowledge of the base word, fill in each blank with the word that best completes the sentence.

a. perilous **b.** perilously **c.** imperiled

1. Undertaking the risky voyage ___?___ the Pilgrims' lives.
2. The ship tossed ___?___ in the waves.
3. Building a new home in the wilderness was ___?___ as well.

Spelling Strategy

When you add *-ed* to a word that ends in the letters *-ify*, change the *y* to *i* before adding the suffix. For example, *mollify* becomes *mollified*. Write sentences using the past tense of each word.

1. pacify 2. modify 3. testify

Concept Development: Antonyms and Synonyms

Antonyms are words that have opposite meanings. **Synonyms** are words that have similar meanings. Decide whether the words in each of following pairs are antonyms or synonyms. Write A for *Antonym* or S for *Synonym*.

1. pilfer, donate
2. palisades, fences
3. conceits, fantasies
4. mollified, angered
5. peril, safety
6. loath, willing
7. sundry, single
8. recompense, reward

❷ Grammar and Style Lesson

Singular and Plural Possessive Nouns

The **possessive** form of nouns indicates kinship and ownership. Add an apostrophe and *-s* to form the **possessive singular** of most nouns. Add an apostrophe to form the **possessive of plural** nouns that end in *-s* or *-es*.

Singular: The *passenger's* spirits were low.

Plural: The *passengers'* spirits were low.

Do not use an apostrophe for simple plurals that do not show possession. Do not add an extra *s* for the possessive of plural nouns ending in *-s*.

Practice Rewrite this paragraph, correcting any mistakes in italicized plurals or possessives.

Much to *Bradfords* amazement, Samoset spoke to the *Pilgrims* in broken English. Samoset convinced his fellow *Indians'* to return the *settler's* tools. He persuaded Massasoit to pay his *respects* to the *Pilgrims* and introduced them to one of his *friend's*, Squanto.

Writing Application Write a paragraph about the Pilgrims' arrival in Plymouth, using at least five plural and possessive nouns.

𝒲𝒢 *Prentice Hall Writing and Grammar Connection: Chapter 27, Section 6*

TEACHING RESOURCES

The following resources can be used to enrich or extend the instruction for pp. 86–87.

Vocabulary

📖 **Selection Support:** Build Vocabulary, p. 19

📖 **Vocabulary and Spelling Practice Book**
(Use this booklet for skills enrichment.)

Grammar

📖 **Selection Support:** Grammar and Style, p. 20 ■

𝒲𝒢 **Writing and Grammar,** Ruby Level, p. 756

📠 **Daily Language Practice Transparencies**

Writing

𝒲𝒢 **Writing and Grammar,** Ruby Level, p. 166 ■

📖 **Extension Activities**

📠 **Writing Models and Graphic Organizers on Transparencies,** pp. 87–89

💿 **Writing and Grammar iText CD-ROM**

■ **BLOCK SCHEDULING:** Resources marked with this symbol provide varied instruction during 90-minute blocks.

❸ Writing Lesson

Comparison of Narratives

These narratives leave readers with the impression that Smith and Bradford held distinctly different outlooks on life. Write a comparison of these firsthand accounts.

Prewriting   Review the two narratives, noting each author's style, purpose, and objectivity. To help you gather and organize details, use a Venn diagram like the one shown.

Model: Gathering Details

Drafting   To keep your ideas clear for readers, choose a method of organization. You might discuss each aspect of your subjects in turn. For example, you could discuss Smith's tone and immediately contrast it with Bradford's tone. Alternatively, you might discuss all the qualities of one subject and then all the qualities of the other.

Revising   To clarify your comparison and contrast, consider transitions, such as *similarly* and *equally*, *to compare* and *in contrast*, and *instead* and *to contrast*. Be sure your conclusion effectively reinforces your ideas.

𝒲G   *Prentice Hall Writing and Grammar Connection: Chapter 9, Section 3*

❹ Extension Activities

Listening and Speaking   As Samoset, deliver a **persuasive speech** to make the case for fostering peace between the settlers and your tribe. Make your speech dramatic and convincing. To prepare, consider these questions:

- What personal experiences can you relate?
- What events prove your point?
- What are your greatest concerns?

Organize and review your notes before presenting your speech to your class.

Research and Technology   Many Pilgrims suffered from scurvy, a disease caused by a diet lacking in vitamin C. Research to learn about the foods the colonists ate and the crops they planted. Check the Internet or the library for colonial recipes. Then, plan a historically accurate **menu** for a typical day in the life of an early American colonist.

 Take It to the Net   www.phschool.com

Go online for an additional research activity using the Internet.

from *The General History of Virginia* / from *Of Plymouth Plantation* ◆ 87

Lesson Support for p. 87

❸ Writing Lesson

- Students' comparisons should analyze each narrative and discuss the similarities and differences between them.
- Regardless of which method of organization students choose to employ, their compositions should deal as thoroughly as possible with each writer's style, purpose, and level of objectivity.
- Use the Writing Lesson, as well as the Comparison and Contrast organizer in **Writing Models and Graphic Organizers on Transparencies,** pp. 87–89, to guide students in developing their comparisons.

❹ Research and Technology

- Encourage students to do research using traditional print sources (such as encyclopedias, biographies and journals, and social histories), as well as online resources.
- Students might also report on the ways in which the Pilgrims' dietary experiences in Virginia differed from those aboard the *Mayflower* and those in England.

CUSTOMIZE INSTRUCTION
For Universal Access

To address different learning styles, use the following activities suggested in the **Extension Activities** booklet, p. 5.

For Visual/Spatial Learners, use Activity 5.

For Verbal/Linguistic Learners, use Activity 6.

ASSESSMENT RESOURCES

The following resources can be used to assess students' knowledge and skills.

Selection Assessment

📘 **Formal Assessment,** pp. 19–21

📘 **Open Book Test,** pp. 13–15

📼 **Got It! Assessment Videotapes,** Tape 1

💿 **Test Bank Software**

🖥 *Take It to the Net*
   Visit www.phschool.com for self-tests and additional questions on the selections.

PRENTICE HALL ASSESSMENT SYSTEM

📘 **Workbook**   🖨 **Transparencies**

📘 **Skill Book**   💿 **CD-ROM**

Lesson Objectives

1. To locate appropriate information on a Web site
2. To learn how to read a home page

About Web Sites

- Write the term "Web sites" on the chalkboard. Have students share whatever they know about the different parts of a Web site. List specific terms such as "home page" and "URL" on the chalkboard as students mention them, and have students define these terms.

- Ask students to describe the kinds of information they find on specific Web sites they visit.
  Possible answers: Students might mention schedule information for sports teams or movies; historical information for research assignments; or the cost of an airline ticket.

Reading Strategy

Locating Appropriate Information

- Have students read and discuss the Reading Strategy information.

- Ask students to share strategies for locating Web sites. How do they narrow their searches?

- Make sure students understand the terms in the box labeled "Elements of Web Sites." If possible, demonstrate each term on an actual Web site in the classroom or the school library.

Web Sites

About Web Sites

A **Web site** is a collection of Web pages—text and graphics on a topic, accessible over the Internet through browser software. Each page has its own URL, or "address." Web sites feature underlined words that serve as links to other sites or pages. By clicking on these words, you can find more information.

The Web can be a wonderful tool. You can perform business transactions on the Web—for example, trading stocks or buying clothing. The Web also offers great ways to learn. Whether your interests are academic or recreational, you probably can locate several Web sites devoted to each of them.

Reading Strategy

Locating Appropriate Information

To get the most out of Internet research, learn how to locate appropriate information. Familiarize yourself with search engines on the Web. These services will list any page on the Web that contains text matching the search term that you type in. To use a search engine effectively, you need to select search terms with care. For instance, if you are looking for information on the Puritans who settled in America, you might use the word *Pilgrim*. Too broad a term, such as *colony*, will produce a list that is unmanageably long and cluttered with irrelevant listings, such as pages on space colonies.

Even a focused search term may yield irrelevant results. To further narrow down the list of sites, review the name of the sponsor that is listed on the search engine list, along with the brief excerpt from the site. You can eliminate sites in languages you do not speak, sites on unrelated topics, and, depending on your requirements, personal home pages.

When you arrive at a Web site, you usually will find that it offers many features. The box at right lists just a few of these elements. Not every feature will be appropriate to your search, so keep your purpose in mind as you explore.

Elements of Web Sites

- **Hotspotted text, buttons,** and other **navigation elements** help you move around the site quickly. Click on any area of the page over which your cursor changes to a hand, and you will be brought to a linked page.

- **A SEARCH function** helps you locate information anywhere on the site, using search terms.

- **Photos, videos, and audio clips** enrich many sites, providing audiovisual information or entertainment. You may need to download additional software to use these resources.

- **Links** connect you to related Web sites.

- **Contact information** tells you who sponsored the site. An e-mail address to which you may send questions or comments may be included.

Home Page

A home page is the "front door" of a Web site. It provides an overview of the site's information and features. From this home page of the Plimoth Plantation Web site, a user can learn about the museum in Plymouth, Massachusetts, that is devoted to the colonial history of the town. Using the home page, visitors can "navigate," or move to other pages within the site.

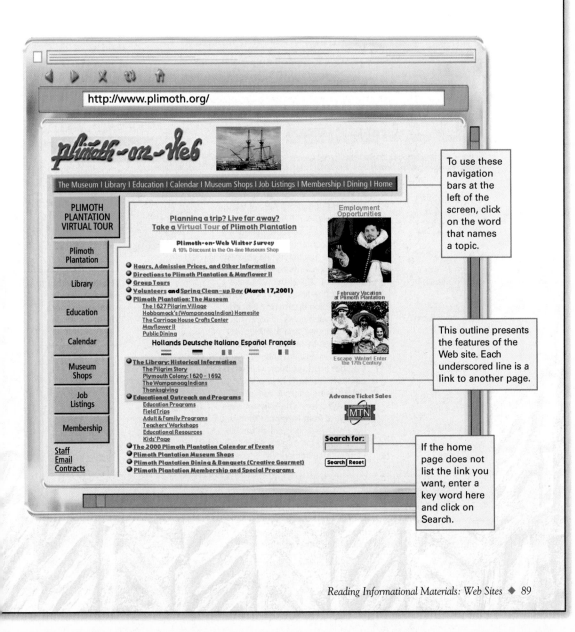

To use these navigation bars at the left of the screen, click on the word that names a topic.

This outline presents the features of the Web site. Each underscored line is a link to another page.

If the home page does not list the link you want, enter a key word here and click on Search.

Home Page

- Before discussing home pages, you might have some students volunteer to print out a home page and bring it to class. Preview the home pages before using them as visual aids in class discussions.

- Make sure students understand what a home page is. Have them examine the model home page in the textbook, identifying icons or items about which they have questions. If students have brought in copies of more home pages, have students examine these as well.

- Challenge students to formulate questions about Plimoth Plantation and indicate which links on the home page might lead them to answers.

CUSTOMIZE INSTRUCTION FOR UNIVERSAL ACCESS

For Less Proficient Readers	For English Learners
Make enlarged photocopies of the home page for "Plimoth-on-Web." Challenge students to mark up the photocopies, identifying each part of the home page and the purpose it serves. For instance, "Plimoth-on-Web" is the title of the site, and "Take a Virtual Tour of Plimoth Plantation" allows you to do just that. The underline indicates that the phrase is a "hotlink"; clicking on it will lead the computer user to a new screen.	Students may want to look for Web sites in languages other than English. Remind them that the World Wide Web is international, as its name suggests, and that it contains plenty of sites in many languages. The model on this page, for instance, offers its text in Dutch, German, Italian, Spanish, and French. Challenge each student to find a home page in a language of his or her choice, print it out, bring it to class, and explain his or her searching strategies.

Interior Page

- Point out that this interior page is called "1627 Pilgrim Village." It is highlighted in red in the left margin because it has been opened. The other interior pages listed in the left margin have not.

- Ask students why they think the navigation bar on the home page is also listed on this interior page. Answer: This allows the user to move easily from any page in the site to any other page.

- Ask students what they would do if they wanted more information about the Fort/Meetinghouse. Answer: Students would click on "Fort/Meetinghouse," a hotlink in the text.

Interior Page

Various pages within a Web site may offer passages of text, photographs, audio and video clips, and other related information. The page shown here presents an essay about the re-created village at Plimoth.

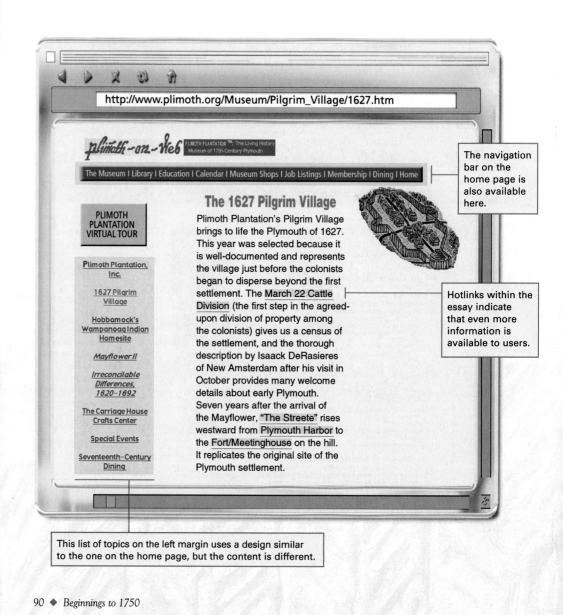

The navigation bar on the home page is also available here.

Hotlinks within the essay indicate that even more information is available to users.

This list of topics on the left margin uses a design similar to the one on the home page, but the content is different.

Check Your Comprehension

1. From the home page, what tool can you use to find Plimoth Plantation's calendar of events without knowing the URL for that page?
2. In the essay, why are the words *Plymouth Harbor* and *Fort / Meeting House* underlined and printed in blue?

Applying the Reading Strategy

Locating Appropriate Information

3. Using a chart like the one shown, indicate where you would expect to find the answers to each question—on the home page, the interior page, or in material found through a link from one of those pages.

Question	Location
When will the Holiday Fair at Plimouth be held?	
Do any early documents contain a census of the village?	
Why did the Pilgrims come to North America?	
What purpose or purposes did the Meetinghouse serve?	

Activity

Evaluating Information Online

Locate and explore another Web site relating to Plymouth Colony or the Pilgrims. Then, write an evaluation. Use these questions to guide you:

- What is the purpose of the site?
- Who are the site authors and what are the credentials of its sponsor? (Was the site developed by a university? A historical society? A college student?)
- What information and features does the site offer?
- Does the design complement the site's purpose and contents?

Compile your evaluation with those that classmates have completed. Together, prepare an annotated list of sites that you would recommend.

Contrasting Informational Materials

Web Sites and Other Reference Sources

What is the value of visiting a site like the one pictured in this feature instead of reading a book about Plymouth Colony? Jot down your ideas about the advantages and disadvantages of Web sites and more traditional reference sources, such as encyclopedias, atlases, and books. Then, write a conclusion based on your notes.

Answers for p. 91

Check Your Comprehension

1. Use the mouse to click on either the word "Calendar" in the navigation bar or the underlined phrase "The 2000 Plimoth Plantation Calendar of Events."

2. If you click on an underlined blue term, you will see a new screen with further information about it. These terms are called "hotlinks."

Applying the Reading Strategy

3. **(a)** On the home page, click on either the word "Calendar" in the navigation bar or the underlined phrase "The 2000 Plimoth Plantation Calendar of Events." **(b)** On the interior page, click on the underlined phrase "March 22 Cattle Division." **(c)** On the home page, click on "The Library: Historical Information" or on "The Pilgrim Story." **(d)** On the interior page, click on the underlined phrase "Fort/Meetinghouse."

Activity

Once students have handed in their lists, you may want to distribute them to different groups so that they can sample one another's recommendations. You might make this a homework assignment so that students can have a class discussion the next day about what constitutes a good, useful Web site.

Contrasting Informational Materials

Web Site: Remind students that the first rule when using the Web for research is to look at who created the site. Since anyone can post any information he or she chooses on the Web, many sites are not reliable sources of information.

Print Reference: Standards for accuracy in print references are usually much higher than standards for the Internet. Students should always check the resources listed in bibliographies. They should also check copyright dates. Unlike a Web site, a book cannot be updated once it is printed; changes have to wait for a new edition. Therefore, a book or journal article printed many years ago may be outdated, depending on its topic.

Lesson Objectives

1. To understand the connection between the pioneering spirits of the early American settlers and modern explorers

2. To compare and understand the difference between seventeenth-century and twentieth-century writing styles

Connections

John Smith and William Bradford speak of the Early American settlers' struggles in a new land, while Tom Wolfe describes the exploration of astronauts in a technological age and the need to fly higher, faster, and farther than anyone had before.

Ask students what Smith and Bradford might have defined as the "right stuff" to make a home in the American wilderness.

The Pioneer Spirit

- Play *The Right Stuff* film adaptation of the scene described in the selection. Ask students the following questions: What must Glenn have been thinking and feeling as he became the first person to orbit earth?
  Possible answer: Students will probably say that Glenn was elated or incredibly excited and proud.

- After students have shared their responses, tell them that the selection they are about to read paints a picture of space flight that is far more harrowing than they might think.

CONNECTIONS
Literature Past and Present
The Pioneer Spirit

The early American settlers struggled through rough seas, sickness, and starvation to carve out a home in a new land. The hunger for uncharted territory drove them to sail across the ocean and set foot on a forbidding continent. They were risking their lives for such things as religious freedom, economic opportunity, and political autonomy. That spirit kept Americans going for three more centuries as pioneers continued westward, blazing trails across the continent.

The New Pioneers In the new millennium, the frontier has given way to a network of highways, airports, and shopping malls. When the frontier disappeared, the pioneer spirit had nowhere to go but up. In the twentieth century, this spirit pushed Americans into tiny, cramped capsules. The new pioneers defied gravity and leapt upward into space. Tom Wolfe's book *The Right Stuff* documents this new American exploration.

Narrative Accounts John Smith, William Bradford, and Tom Wolfe all wrote historical narrative accounts—factual reports of notable events. You will notice clear differences between Wolfe's twentieth-century account of John Glenn's brief zooms around the planet and Smith's and Bradford's seventeenth-century chronicles of the colonists' struggles to survive. One obvious difference is in the style—the shift from the formal religious vocabulary of seventeenth-century men of authority to the more casual, slang-filled language of a twentieth-century journalist.

ENRICHMENT: Career Connection

Today's Pioneers

Who are today's pioneers? Students may identify them as computer wizards, medical researchers, astronomers, oceanographers, or avant-garde artists, among others. Have interested groups discuss what kind of "right stuff" modern-day pioneers need to succeed in breaking new ground in their particular field. Encourage each group to explore a different groundbreaking career, gathering information on education and skills requirements, qualifications, and job descriptions. Students can use library reference materials or the Internet to find this information, or they can interview family friends who work in related fields. Have students list key qualifications or characteristics that these "pioneers" share with pioneers of old. Each group can present its findings to the class in an oral report.

from The Right Stuff

Tom Wolfe

Background
First American Space Flight
On February 20, 1962, Lt. Col. John H. Glenn, Jr., became the first American to experience orbital space flight. A Mercury-Atlas-6 rocket shot the small capsule known as *Friendship 7,* with Glenn aboard, into space. He orbited the Earth three times, spending four hours and fifty-five minutes in space. In a then-remarkable feat of technology, millions of Americans watched his historic flight on their television sets.

Thematic Connection
Like the early settlers, John Glenn was also aware that he was making history with his first-ever American space flight. As a result, he probably wanted to document his experience as accurately and excitingly as possible for the television viewers at home and for his country.

▶ Critical Viewing
Answer: Students' responses should address the astronaut's unique perspective and sensations within the space capsule, with the very dramatic sight of the first rocket shooting into space experienced by those watching on the ground.

Here he is!—within twenty seconds of lift-off, and the only strange thing is how little adrenaline[1] is pumping when the moment comes . . . He can hear the rumble of the Atlas engines building up down there below his back. All the same, it isn't terribly loud. The huge squat rocket shakes a bit and struggles to overcome its own weight. It all happens very slowly in the first few seconds, like an extremely heavy elevator rising. They've lit the candle and there's no turning back, and yet there's no surge inside him. His pulse rises only to 110, no more than the minimum rate you should have if you have to deal with a sudden emergency. How strange that it should be this way! He has been more wound up for a takeoff in an F-102.[2]

"The clock is operating," he said, "We're underway."

It was all very smooth, much smoother than the centrifuge[3] . . . just as Shepard and Grissom said it would be. He had gone through the same g-forces[4] so many times . . . he hardly noticed them as they built up. It would have bothered him much more if they had been less. Nothing novel! No excitement, please! It took thirteen seconds for the huge rocket to reach

Thematic Connection
The early pioneers chronicled events because they knew they were making history. What parallels do you see between the purpose of their writing and the expectations for communication facing John Glenn?

---

1. **adrenaline** (ə dren´ ə lin´) *n.* stress-related hormone secreted by the adrenal gland. When released, it increases heartbeat and raises blood pressure.
2. **F-102** U.S. Air Force fighter plane.
3. **centrifuge** (sen´ trə fyo͞oj´) *n.* a machine using force to pull a rotating object outward from a center. This type of machine was used to train the astronauts for the effects of spaceflight.
4. **g-forces** *n.* units measuring inertial pressure on a body during rapid acceleration. Units represent multiples of the acceleration of gravity.

◀ Critical Viewing
In what ways might the astronauts' impressions of a liftoff differ from the views of spectators? **[Hypothesize]**

Connections: from The Right Stuff ◆ 93

CUSTOMIZE INSTRUCTION FOR UNIVERSAL ACCESS

For Less Proficient Readers	For English Learners	For Advanced Readers
To help students with this work, guide them to break apart long sentences into smaller segments to better follow the narrative.	This work is rich with technical terms and space jargon that may be unfamiliar to students who are English learners. To prepare students to read, use a model or photograph of a rocket to help them understand such terms as *liftoff, rocket, capsule, supersonic,* and *orbit,* in addition to the Vocabulary development and footnoted words.	Have students note the use of ellipses to create a suspension in thought and anticipation for the reader. After reading the selection, have students share other characteristics of the text that fulfilled their purpose for reading to be entertained.

Background

Draw Conclusions

Shephard and Grissom were among the original group of men selected for NASA's manned space program because they had "the right stuff." Alan B. Shepard, Jr., and Virgil I. "Gus" Grissom were the first and second Americans in space (May 5 and July 21, 1961), but neither went into earth orbit. Their flights were very brief—only fifteen minutes— but they provided the only firsthand experiences Glenn could draw upon during his own training.

▶ Critical Viewing

Answer: Presidents set policies and spending budgets. A president who has an interest in the space program would encourage and promote further exploration and allocate more money for it to ensure its success.

---

transonic speed. The vibrations started. It was just as Shepard and Grissom said: it was much gentler than the centrifuge. He was still lying flat on his back, and the g-forces drove him deeper and deeper into the seat, but it all felt so familiar. He barely noticed it. He kept his eyes on the instrument panel the whole time . . . All quite normal, every little needle and switch in the right place . . . No malevolent instructor feeding *Abort* problems into the loop . . . As the rocket entered the transonic zone, the vibration became intense. The vibrations all but obliterated the roar of the engines. He was entering the area of "*max q*," maximum aerodynamic pressure, in which the pressure of the shaft of the Atlas forcing its way through the atmosphere at supersonic speed would reach almost a thousand pounds per square foot. Through the cockpit window he could see the sky turning black. Almost 5 g's were driving him back into his seat. And yet . . . *easier than the centrifuge* . . . All at once he was through *max q*, as if through a turbulent strait, and the trajectory was smooth and he was supersonic and the rumble of the rocket engines was more muffled than ever and he could hear all the little fans and recorders and the busy little kitchen, the humming little shop . . . . The pressure on his chest reached 6 g's. The rocket pitched down. For the first time he could see clouds and the horizon. In a moment—*there it was*—the Atlas rocket's two booster engines shut down and were jettisoned from the side of the shaft and his body was slammed forward, as if he were screeching to a halt, and the g-forces suddenly dropped to 1.25, almost as if he were on earth and not accelerating at all, but the central sustainer engine and two smaller engines were still driving him up through the atmosphere . . . A flash of white smoke went up past the window. . . . *No! The escape tower was firing early—but the* JETTISON TOWER *light wasn't on!* . . . He didn't see the tower go . . . Wait a minute . . . There went the tower, on schedule . . . The JETTISON TOWER light came on green . . . The smoke must have been from the booster rockets as they left the shaft . . . The rocket pitched back up . . . going straight up . . . The sky was very black now . . . The g-forces began pushing him back into his seat again . . . 3 g's . . . 4 g's . . . 5 g's . . . Soon he would be forty miles up . . . the last critical moment of powered flight, as the capsule separated from the rocket and went into its orbital trajectory . . . or didn't . . . *Hey!* . . . All at once the whole capsule was whipping up and down, as if it were tied to the end of a diving board, a springboard. The g-forces built up and the capsule whipped up and down. Yet no sooner had it begun than Glenn knew what it was. The weight of the rocket on the launch pad had been 260,000 pounds, practically all of it rocket fuel, the liquid oxygen. This was being consumed at such a furious rate, about one ton per second, that the rocket was becoming merely a skeleton with a thin skin of metal stretched over it, a tube so long and light that it was flexing. The g-forces reached six and then he was weightless, just like that. The sudden release made him feel as if he were tumbling head over heels, as if he had been catapulted off the end of that same

malevolent (mə lev´ ə lənt) *adj.* mean-spirited; showing ill will

obliterated (ə blit´ ər āt´ id) *v.* blotted out; destroyed

trajectory (trə jek´ tə rē) *n.* the curved path of an object hurtling through space

jettisoned (jet´ ə sənd) *v.* thrown overboard to lighten the weight of a ship

▶ Critical Viewing
President John F. Kennedy inspects the Friendship 7 capsule in 1962. What effect would a president's interest in the space program have on its success? [**Analyze Cause and Effect**]

Connections: from *The Right Stuff* ◆ 95

Critical Thinking

Compare and Contrast

- Have students consider the preparatory training and knowledge Glenn had to acquire in advance of his pioneering flight.
- Ask them to compare his thorough preparation with the limited knowledge earlier travelers to the unknown, such as Christopher Columbus, John Smith, or William Bradford, might have had before their pioneering journeys.
- Debate whether advanced preparation minimizes, eliminates, or increases fears and concerns. How else can good preparation help a pioneer? What can it never do?

CUSTOMIZE INSTRUCTION FOR UNIVERSAL ACCESS

For Less Proficient Readers

Students will benefit from rereading part or all of the narrative account, and from watching the excerpt from the film adaptation of *The Right Stuff.* Help students focus on Glenn's responses to the events unfolding around him.

The Pioneer Spirit

Remind students that Columbus, the Puritans, and other early pioneers chronicled the events of their journeys because they were aware that they were making history. Have students draw parallels between their purposes for writing and the expectations for communication facing John Glenn during his flight.

Connecting Literature Past and Present

1. Both the early Settlers and Glenn were exploring new territories that posed many dangers and risks.

2. (a) Students may say Glenn had technological advantages and radio communications, but he also had concerns about his health and endurance in space. The settlers experienced a dangerous voyage and harsh weather conditions that made life difficult. (b) While the conditions may have enhanced Glenn's experience, there was still a threat for his safety and welfare. Students should support their responses based on their interpretations of Smith's, Bradford's, and Wolfe's accounts.

3. Student responses will depend on their assessments of the relative dangers faced by astronauts and settlers and by their degrees of preparation for what they might encounter.

springboard and was falling through the air doing forward rolls. But he had felt this same thing on the centrifuge when they ran the g-forces up to seven and then suddenly cut the speed. At the same moment, right on schedule . . . a loud report . . . the posigrade rockets fired, throwing the capsule free of the rocket shaft . . . the capsule began its automatic turnabout, and all the proper green lights went on in front of him, and he knew he was "through the gate," as they said.

"Zero-g and I feel fine," he said. "Capsule is turning around . . ."

Glenn knew he was weightless. From the instrument readings and through sheer logic he knew it, but he couldn't feel it, just as Shepard and Grissom had never felt it. The turnaround brought him up to a sitting position, vertical to the earth, and that was the way he felt. He was sitting in a chair, upright, in a very tiny cramped quiet little cubicle 125 miles above the earth, a little metal closet, silent except for the humming of its electrical system, the inverters, the gyros, the cameras, the radio . . . *the radio* . . . He had been specifically instructed to violate the Fighter Jock code of No Chatter. He was supposed to radio back every sight, every sensation, and otherwise give the taxpayers the juicy stuff they wanted to hear. Glenn, more than any of the others, was fully capable of doing the job. Yet it was an awkward thing. It seemed unnatural.

"Oh!" he said. "That view is tremendous!"

Well, it was a start. In fact, the view was not particularly extraordinary. It was extraordinary that he was up here in orbit about the earth. He could see the exhausted Atlas rocket following him. It was tumbling end over end from the force of the small rockets throwing the capsule free of it.

He could hear Alan Shepard, who was serving as capcom[5] in the Mercury Control Center at the Cape. His voice came in very clearly. He was saying, "You have a go, at least seven orbits."

"Roger," said Glenn. "Understand Go for at least seven orbits . . . This is *Friendship 7*. Can see clear back, a big cloud pattern way back across toward the Cape. Beautiful sight."

---

5. **capcom** (kap′ käm) *n. jargon* capsule communicator; person speaking directly to astronaut.

Connecting Literature Past and Present

1. In what ways is John Glenn's experience similar to that of the Europeans who crossed the Atlantic Ocean and settled in America?

2. (a) In what ways do twentieth-century advances make Glenn's experience different from that of the colonists? (b) Do you think these advances enhance Glenn's experience or diminish it? Why?

3. What takes more courage: riding in a capsule into space like the astronauts or making a new life in an uncharted land like the early settlers? Why?

Tom Wolfe

(b. 1930) Born in a Virginia far different from the one that John Smith knew, Tom Wolfe began his writing career working as a reporter and Latin America correspondent for the *Washington Post*. He then turned to magazine writing and eventually published essays, articles, and, later, full-length books that focused on the contemporary American scene. He described elements of popular culture in *The Kandy-Kolored Tangerine Flake Streamline Baby* and dissected the art world in *The Painted Word*. Many critics regard *The Right Stuff*, an account of the Mercury space program, as Wolfe's best work.

The Puritan Influence

Pilgrims Going to Church (detail)
George Henry Boughton
© Collection of The New York Historical Society

MIZE INSTRUCTION FOR UNIVERSAL ACCESS

gning the selections in this part, keep in mind these factors:

**ar and Loving
and "Huswifery"**

• poems

nguage

conveys marital and reli-
otion

onal learners relate to
evotion and dedication

"Sinner in the Hands of an Angry God"

• Excerpt from a sermon

• Help readers with language and imagery

• Fire and brimstone language evokes intense reactions

Selection Planning Guide

This section explores the Puritan influence on America's emerging literary identity. The poetry of Anne Bradstreet and Edward Taylor exemplifies the Puritan Plain Style, though Bradstreet's "To My Dear and Loving Husband" is unusual for its treatment of marital—rather than religious—love. Like the Puritans who first heard it, students are sure to find Jonathan Edwards's fiery sermon "Sinners in the Hands of an Angry God" to be an eye-opening look at Puritanism.

Background

Art

Pilgrims Going to Church, George Henry Boughton

George Henry Boughton (1833–1905) was born in Norwich, England. From 1852 to 1858, he lived in Albany, New York, concentrating on landscape painting. After a year in New York City, he went to Europe and settled back in England in the 1860s. Throughout his career, Boughton's work was exhibited in both England and the United States. He became known primarily as a painter of "subject pictures" like *Pilgrims Going to Church.*

Use these questions for discussion:

1. What does the way people are looking around and holding their guns tell you about their state of mind as they go to church? Why might they feel this way?
   Possible responses: They seem to be wary of some kind of danger. Perhaps there have been incidents in which colonists have been ambushed or attacked by animals, or perhaps they are afraid because they are in an unknown land, where anything might happen.

2. What do the details of the painting—the weather, the setting, the colors, the posture of the people—reveal about life in the early days of the Puritan settlement?
   Possible responses: The frozen landscape, the darkness at the edges of the painting, the stark colors, the watchful posture of the people all suggest that life among the Puritans was harsh, joyless, and possibly filled with danger.

97

Huswifery ✦ To My Dear and Loving Husband

Lesson Objectives

1. **To analyze and respond to literary elements**
   - Literary Analysis: The Puritan Plain Style
   - Comparing Literary Works

2. **To read, comprehend, analyze, and critique two poems**
   - Reading Strategy: Paraphrasing
   - Reading Check Questions
   - Review and Assess Questions
   - Assessment Practice (ATE)

3. **To develop word analysis skills, fluency, and systematic vocabulary**
   - Vocabulary Development Lesson: Anglo-Saxon Suffix: -fold

4. **To understand and apply written and oral language conventions**
   - Spelling Strategy
   - Grammar and Style Lesson: Direct Address

5. **To understand and apply appropriate writing and research strategies**
   - Writing Lesson: Reflective Essay
   - Extension Activity: Graphic Display

6. **To understand and apply listening and speaking strategies**
   - Extension Activity: Informal Debate

STEP-BY-STEP TEACHING GUIDE	PACING GUIDE
PRETEACH	
Motivate Students and Provide Background	
Use the Motivation activity (ATE p. 98)	5 min.
Read and discuss More About the Author and the Background information (SE/ATE p. 98) A	5 min.
Introduce the Concepts	
Introduce the Literary Analysis and Reading Strategy (SE/ATE p. 99) A	15 min.
Pronounce the vocabulary words and read their definitions (SE p. 99)	5 min.
TEACH	
Monitor Comprehension	
Informally monitor comprehension by circulating while students read independently or in groups A	10 min.
Develop vocabulary with Vocabulary notes (SE p. 102; ATE p. 102)	as students read
	as students read
Develop Understanding	
Develop students' understanding of Puritan plain style with the Literary Analysis annotations (SE p. 101; ATE p. 101) A	5 min.
Develop students' recognition of paraphrase with the Reading Strategy annotations (SE p. 102; ATE p. 102)	5 min.
ASSESS	
Assess Mastery	
Assess students' mastery of the Reading Strategy and Literary Analysis by having them answer the Review and Assess questions (SE/ATE p. 103)	15 min.
Use one or more of the print and media Assessment Resources (ATE p. 105) A	up to 45 min.
EXTEND	
Apply Understanding	
Have students complete the Vocabulary Development Lesson and the Grammar and Style Lesson (SE p. 104) A	20 min.
Apply students' ability to provide descriptive details by using the Writing Lesson (SE/ATE p. 105) A	45 min.
Apply students' understanding using one or more of the Extension Activities (SE p. 105)	20–90 min.

A **ACCELERATED INSTRUCTION:**
Use the strategies and activities identified with an **A**.

UNIVERSAL ACCESS
- ● = Below Level Students
- ▲ = On-Level Students
- ■ = Above Level Students

Time and Resource Manager

RESOURCES		
PRINT 📖	**TRANSPARENCIES**	**TECHNOLOGY**
• **Beyond Literature,** Cross-Curricular Connection: Performing Arts, p. 6 ▲■		• **Interest Grabber Video,** Tape 1 ● ▲ ■
• **Selection Support Workbook:** ● ▲ ■ Literary Analysis, p. 28 Reading Strategy, p. 27 Build Vocabulary, p. 25	• **Literary Analysis and Reading Transparencies,** pp. 11 and 12 ● ▲ ■	
• **Authors in Depth,** The American Experience, p. 5; p.17 ■		• **Listening to Literature** ● ▲ ■ Audiocassettes, Side 3 Audio CDs, CD 2
• **Literatura en español** ● ▲ • **Literary Analysis for Enrichment** ■		
• **Formal Assessment:** Selection Test, pp. 27–29 ● ▲ ■ • **Open Book Test,** pp. 16–18 ● ▲ ■ • **Performance Assessment and Portfolio Management,** p. 11 ● ▲ ■ • **PRENTICE HALL ASSESSMENT** *SYSTEM* ● ▲ ■	• **PRENTICE HALL ASSESSMENT** *SYSTEM* ● ▲ ■ Skills Practice Answers and Explanations on Transparencies	• **Test Bank Software** ● ▲ ■ • **Got It! Assessment Videotapes,** Tape 1 ● ▲
• **Selection Support Workbook:** ● ▲ ■ Grammar and Style, p. 26 • **Writing and Grammar,** Ruby Level ● ▲ ■ • **Extension Activities,** p. 6 ● ▲ ■	• **Daily Language Practice Transparencies** ● ▲ • **Writing Models and Graphic Organizers on Transparencies,** p. 9 ● ▲ ■	• **Writing and Grammar iText CD-ROM** ● ▲ ■ 💻 *Take It to the Net* www.phschool.com

BLOCK SCHEDULING: Use one 90-minute class period to preteach the selection and have students read it. Use a second 90-minute class period to assess students' mastery of skills and have them complete one of the Extension Activities.

Step-by-Step Teaching Guide for pp. 98–99

Motivation

As an advance homework assignment, ask students to think of one or two love songs they know and enjoy. Have them jot down the lyrics and/or bring recordings of the songs to class. Invite student volunteers to read the song lyrics or to play excerpts from the recordings. Ask students to explain why they find the songs interesting or involving.

On the chalkboard, write "If ever two were one, then surely we." You might identify the quotation as a line from a love poem not yet set to music. Ask students to respond to it and to state their opinion of its relevance today. Then, explain to students that the line was written by a Puritan woman more than three hundred years ago in a poem expressing her deep love for her husband.

Finally, invite students to think about a wider definition of the term "love song." Point out that certain gospel songs might be described as love songs celebrating the divine bond between a human being and God. Tell students that it is this type of love that a Puritan poet celebrates in "Huswifery."

▣ Interest Grabber Video

As an alternative, play "The Puritans" on Tape 1, to engage student interest.

❶ Background
More About the Authors

Edward Taylor's poetry expresses intensity, lyricism, and a love of language that contradicts the joyless Puritan creed. Taylor asked his heirs to refrain from publishing his works during his life, and it was only in 1883 that one of his descendants presented Taylor's "Poetical Works" to Yale University. In 1939 Taylor's verse was published for the first time.

Anne Dudley was sixteen when she married Simon Bradstreet. The couple emigrated to America and lived in North Andover, Massachusetts. Anne Bradstreet's best poems are those inspired by the rhythms of daily New England life. Her later poems reveal her spiritual growth as she came to embrace Puritan beliefs.

Prepare to Read

❶ Huswifery ◆ To My Dear and Loving Husband

Edward Taylor (1642–1729)

Puritanism was a religious reform movement that began in England in the sixteenth century. The Puritans sought to reform the Church of England, and to reshape English society according to their beliefs. These efforts led to both civil strife, and to government persecution of the Puritans. In response, many Puritans, including Edward Taylor, fled to the American colonies.

Before his emigration to America, Edward Taylor worked as a teacher in England. Upon arriving in Boston in 1668, Taylor entered Harvard College, graduating in 1671. He accepted the position of minister and physician in the small farming community of Westfield, Massachusetts, and then walked more than one hundred miles, much of it through snow, to his new home.

Harsh Life in a New World Life in Westfield was filled with hardships. Fierce battles between the Native Americans and the colonists left the community in constant fear. Taylor also experienced many personal tragedies. Five of his eight children died in infancy; then, his wife died while still a young woman. He remarried and had five or six more children. (Biographers differ on the exact number.)

Edward Taylor is now generally regarded as the best of the colonial poets. Yet, because Taylor thought of his poetry as a form of personal worship, he allowed only two stanzas to be published during his lifetime. In 1833, one of his descendants gave Taylor's writings to Yale University, and, in 1939, *The Poetical Works of Edward Taylor* was published. Most of Taylor's poetry, including "Huswifery," uses extravagant comparisons, intellectual wit, and subtle argument to explore religious faith and affection.

Anne Bradstreet (1612–1672)

Anne Bradstreet and her husband, Simon, arrived in the Massachusetts Bay Colony in 1630, when she was only eighteen. Armed with the convictions of her Puritan upbringing, she left behind her hometown of Northampton, England, to start afresh in America. It was not an easy life for Bradstreet, who raised eight children and faced many hardships.

A Private Writer Made Public Despite the difficulties she endured, Bradstreet was able to devote her spare moments to the very "unladylike" occupation of writing. She wrote for herself, not for publication. Nevertheless, in 1650, John Woodbridge, her brother-in-law, arranged for the publication in England of a collection of her scholarly poems, *The Tenth Muse Lately Sprung Up in America, By a Gentlewoman of Those Parts.* Generally considered to be the first collection of original poetry written in colonial America, the book examined the rights of women to learn and express themselves. Bradstreet's later poems, such as "To My Dear and Loving Husband," are more personal, expressing her feelings about the joys and difficulties of everyday Puritan life. In one, she wrote about her thoughts before giving birth. In another, she wrote about the death of a grandchild.

Bradstreet's poetry reflects the Puritans' knowledge of the stories and language of the Bible, as well as their concern for the relationship between earthly and heavenly life. Her work also exhibits some of the characteristics of the French and English poetry of her day.

In 1956, the poet John Berryman wrote "Homage to Mistress Bradstreet," a long poem that pays tribute to this first American poet.

TEACHING RESOURCES

The following resources can be used to enrich or extend the instruction for pp. 98–99.

Motivation
▣ **Interest Grabber Video**, Tape 1 ▣

Background
▣ **Beyond Literature**, p. 6

▣ *Take It to the Net*
Visit www.phschool.com for background and hotlinks for the selections.

Literary Analysis
▣ **Literary Analysis and Reading Transparencies,** The Puritan Plain Style, p. 12

▣ **Selection Support:** Literary Analysis, p. 28

Reading
▣ **Literary Analysis and Reading Transparencies,** Paraphrasing, p. 11 ▣

▣ **BLOCK SCHEDULING:** Resources marked with this symbol provide varied instruction during 90-minute blocks.

Preview

Connecting to the Literature

Unlike most of us today, the Puritans had few possessions, dressed uniformly, and frowned on creative expression. Because they left so few personal belongings behind, they remain a mystery. These poems provide us with glimpses into the poets' inner lives and show the universal emotions individual Puritans experienced within the confines of their culture.

❷ Literary Analysis

The Puritan Plain Style

The Puritans' writing style reflected the plain style of their lives—spare, simple, and straightforward. The **Puritan Plain Style** is characterized by short words, direct statements, and references to ordinary, everyday objects. Puritans believed that poetry should serve God by clearly expressing only useful or religious ideas. Poetry appealing to the senses or emotions was viewed as dangerous.

Comparing Literary Works

The poems by Taylor and Bradstreet are both expressions of devotion, but they are very different in the way they address the beloved. Taylor uses an **apostrophe**—a figure of speech in which a speaker directly addresses an absent person or a personified object, quality, or idea. For example:

> Line 1: Make me, O Lord, Thy spinning wheel complete.

> Line 8: And make Thy holy spirit, Lord, wind quills:

By contrast, the title of Bradstreet's poem indicates that the speaker is addressing her husband, but the poem contains no apostrophes. As you read, look for ways in which each poem reflects a distinct relationship between the speaker and his or her object of affection.

❸ Reading Strategy

Paraphrasing

Although these poems capture the simplicity of Puritan life, they are not necessarily simple to understand. To help you better absorb the meaning of each poem, take time to **paraphrase,** or restate in your own words, the ideas expressed by each poet. Because it helps to clarify meaning, paraphrasing will allow you to make accurate statements about each poet's ideas. Use a chart like the one shown to organize your paraphrases.

Vocabulary Development

recompense (rek´ əm pens´) *n.* repayment; something given or done in return for something else (p. 102)

manifold (man´ ə fōld´) *adv.* in many ways (p. 102)

persevere (pʉr´ sə vir´) *v.* persist; be steadfast in purpose (p. 102)

Poet's Version

My love is such that rivers cannot quench, Nor ought but love from thee, give recompense.

⋮

Restatement

My love is so strong that rivers cannot relieve its thirst; only your love will satisfy me.

---

❷ Literary Analysis

The Puritan Plain Style

- Tell students that as they read the two poems in this lesson, they will focus on the simple, spare, and straightforward writing of the Puritan Plain Style.

- Read the instruction about the Puritan Plain Style together as a class. Draw students' attention to the description of Puritan writers' use of short words, direct statements, and references to ordinary, everyday objects.

- As they read the poems, invite students to look for words and phrases that exemplify the Puritan Plain Style. Help them understand that the apparent "extravagance" of Taylor's extended metaphor is offset by the humble nature of the items he uses in his comparisons.

❸ Reading Strategy

Paraphrasing

- Make sure that students understand that paraphrasing means restating ideas or descriptions in one's own words.

- Point out that paraphrasing can be especially useful when students read literature from distant eras, since this type of writing often contains syntax and usage that is uncommon today.

- As they read the two poems, urge students to paraphrase whenever the underlying meaning of a line or idea is ambiguous to them.

Vocabulary Development

- Pronounce each vocabulary word for students, and read the definitions as a class. Have students identify any words with which they are already familiar.

CUSTOMIZE INSTRUCTION FOR UNIVERSAL ACCESS

For Less Proficient Readers	For English Learners	For Advanced Readers
Have students approach the poems in segments. Model how to break each poem into small chunks—stanzas for Taylor's poem, for instance, and couplets for Bradstreet's. Help students rephrase and summarize the meaning of each segment before proceeding.	As they read the poems, encourage students to keep a list of unfamiliar words. Have students note the line number of each new term. In addition, before reading the Taylor poem, students might benefit from looking at and labeling a diagram of a weaving loom.	In addition to examining the poems for their meaning and for examples of Puritan ideology, students might also write a brief composition in which they analyze each poem's formal elements—such as its syntax, rhyme scheme, and structure.

 E-Teach

Visit E-Teach at www.phschool.com for teachers' essays on how to teach, with questions and answers.

Step-by-Step Teaching Guide for pp. 100–102

CUSTOMIZE INSTRUCTION
For Intrapersonal Learners

As students read, have them look for the ways in which the poems' speakers convey their strong feelings about their subjects. Challenge students to list other ways in which people can demonstrate devotion to others.

❶ About the Selection

"Huswifery" compares the household task of making cloth with the gift of God's salvation. This extended metaphor expresses Edward Taylor's deep belief in God and celebrates the divine presence in daily life. The poem is like a prayer imploring God to guide the speaker to do His bidding. By submitting to God's will, the speaker hopes to achieve eternal glory.

❷ Background

Art

Crewel work chair seat cover

Although Puritan homes contained few works of art, Puritan women did produce artisanal crafts, such as embroidery and quilting, and men sometimes engaged in fine leather work, bookbinding, or metal smithing. Point out to students that the crewel work depicted on this page is attributed to Anne Bradstreet.

Use this question for discussion:

• How would you describe the subject of this image?
  Answer: In soft but definite colors, the work shows various forms of animal, insect, and plant life.

❸ ▶ Critical Viewing

Answer: The needlework was created around the same time as the poem. Moreover, it reflects the bright colors and "varnished flowers" of the needlework that Taylor describes in "Huswifery."

---

❶ Huswifery
Edward Taylor

Crewel work chair seat cover, Gift of Samuel Bradstreet, Museum of Fine Arts, Boston

❸ ▲ **Critical Viewing** What makes this sampler an effective illustration to accompany Taylor's poem? **[Make a Judgment]**

Background

Edward Taylor's work was generally unknown during his lifetime. Some believe that he chose not to publish his poems because their joyousness and delight in sensory experience ran counter to Puritan attitudes that poetry be for moral instruction only. The discovery in the 1930s of a stash of Taylor's poetry, including the poem that appears here, is considered one of the major literary finds of the twentieth century.

Although there were many writers of verse in Puritan times, few were women. Anne Bradstreet knew that writing was considered an unacceptable activity for women, but she persevered nonetheless, writing while children slept or in moments between household chores.

TEACHING RESOURCES

The following resources can be used to enrich or extend the instruction for pp. 100–102.

Reading

📖 **Selection Support:** Reading Strategy, p. 27; Build Vocabulary, p. 25

🎧 **Listening to Literature Audiocassettes,** Side 3 ▪

💿 **Listening to Literature Audio CDs,** CD 2 ▪

Extension

📖 **Authors in Depth, The American Experience** This collection includes three additional selections by Edward Taylor and four additional selections by Anne Bradstreet for extended reading. ▪

▪ **BLOCK SCHEDULING:** Resources marked with this symbol provide varied instruction during 90-minute blocks.

Make me, O Lord, Thy spinning wheel complete.
Thy holy word my distaff[1] make for me.
Make mine affections[2] Thy swift flyers[3] neat
And make my soul Thy holy spoole to be.
5 My conversation make to be Thy reel
And reel the yarn thereon spun of Thy wheel.

Make me Thy loom then, knit therein this twine:
And make Thy holy spirit, Lord, wind quills:[4]
Then weave the web Thyself. The yarn is fine.
10 Thine ordinances[5] make my fulling mills.[6]
Then dye the same in heavenly colors choice.
All pinked[7] with varnished flowers of paradise.

Then clothe therewith mine understanding, will,
Affections, judgment, conscience, memory
15 My words, and actions, that their shine may fill
My ways with glory and Thee glorify.
Then mine apparel shall display before Ye
That I am clothed in holy robes for glory.

1. **distaff** (dis´ taf´) *n.* staff on which flax or wool is wound for use in spinning.
2. **affections** (ə fek´ shənz) *n.* emotions.
3. **flyers** *n.* part of a spinning wheel that twists fibers into yarn.
4. **quills** *n.* weaver's spindles or bobbins.
5. **ordinances** (ôrd´ nəns əz) *n.* sacraments or religious rites.
6. **fulling mills** *n.* machines that shrink and thicken cloth to the texture of felt.
7. **pinked** *v.* decorated.

Review and Assess

Thinking About the Selection

1. **Respond:** *Huswifery* means "housekeeping." Given the title, were you surprised by the content of this poem? Explain.

2. **(a) Recall:** To what household objects and activities is the speaker compared in the first two stanzas? **(b) Analyze:** How do the images in the first two stanzas contribute to the idea of being "clothed in holy robes for glory," stated in the third stanza?

3. **(a) Interpret:** What images in this poem may have contradicted the Puritan requirement that clothing be dark and undecorated? **(b) Deduce:** What do these images suggest about the speaker's feelings about God?

4. **(a) Interpret:** What details in the final two lines convey Taylor's belief that religious grace comes as a gift from God? **(b) Analyze:** What seems to be the poem's overall purpose?

5. **Synthesize:** What household task or process might Taylor describe if he were writing this poem today?

Literary Analysis
Puritan Plain Style In what sense are the words *spinning wheel, distaff, flyers, spoole, reel,* and *yarn* symbolic of the Puritan Plain Style?

Huswifery ◆ 101

④ Literary Analysis

Puritan Plain Style

- Ask students to scour each stanza for nouns and verbs relating to cloth-making. Have a student volunteer make a list of these terms on the chalkboard.

▶ **Monitor Progress** Then, ask them the Literary Analysis question on p. 101: In what sense are the words *spinning wheel, distaff, flyers, spoole, reel,* and *yarn* symbolic of the Puritan Plain Style?
Answer: Each of these words names a part of a device, common in the seventeenth century, for making cloth.

- Point out that although this poem uses simple words to describe common household items, Taylor has created a rich, multi-layered metaphor. Increasingly complex connections—spinning wheel to yarn to loom to cloth to holy robes—represent steps the speaker hopes he can follow in life to glorify God and to achieve a state of grace.

Answers for p. 101

Review and Assess

1. Students should be specific in their explanations.

2. **(a)** The speaker is compared to a spinning wheel, distaff, flyers, spoole, reel, yarn, loom, twine, quills, fulling mills, and dyeing. **(b)** All of these images relate the speaker to the objects and process of clothmaking. By thinking and behaving in ways that serve and glorify God, the speaker figuratively wears "holy robes" that reflect divinity.

3. **(a)** *dye the same in heavenly colors choice; pinked with varnished flowers of paradise; their shine* **(b)** These images suggest that the speaker's feelings about God are deep, intense, and vivid.

4. **(a)** The lines describe the speaker offering himself to God in the hope of sharing in His grace. **(b)** Sample response: The poem's overall purpose is to convey to God (as a prayer might) the speaker's utter devotion.

5. Students' responses might identify such tasks or processes as cleaning, cooking, or caring for children.

CUSTOMIZE INSTRUCTION FOR UNIVERSAL ACCESS

For Special Needs Students	For Advanced Readers
Draw students' attention to the differences between abstract ideas, such as patriotism, and concrete images, such as saluting an American flag. With students' help, list a handful of abstract ideas on the chalkboard. Then, invite students to brainstorm concrete images that illustrate each of these ideas. Finally, explain to students that Taylor's poem contains numerous concrete images that serve to illustrate aspects of the speaker's love for God.	This version of Taylor's poem uses modern spelling and capitalization. During Taylor's day, the rules for spelling and capitalization were extremely flexible. Most of the time, varied use of such conventions reflected a writer's preferences. In some cases, however, they may also have added meaning to a work. Encourage students to locate and read a copy of Taylor's poem in its original form. Then, have them write a paragraph analyzing Taylor's use of uppercase letters in the original version.

❺ About the Selection

Simon Bradstreet was often away from home on business for months at a time, and Anne Bradstreet wrote this poem during one of his absences. In it, she expresses her deep love and admiration for her husband and her own spiritual conviction.

❻ Reading Strategy

Paraphrasing

• Ask a volunteer to define the term *paraphrase* and to explain how this skill can be used in reading. Answer: To paraphrase is "to restate in one's own words." Paraphrasing helps readers clarify obscure or difficult syntax.

• Have students read the first stanza silently. Then, ask a volunteer to read aloud the first two lines.

• Ask students the Reading Strategy question on p. 102: How would you paraphrase these first two lines? Possible response: We must be the ideal couple; you are the most beloved husband.

❼ Vocabulary Development

Anglo-Saxon Suffix -*fold*

• Draw students' attention to Bradstreet's use of the word *manifold*, and read its definition. Then, tell students that the suffix -*fold* means "a specific number of times or ways."

• Invite students to create three new words using the suffix -*fold*, and meaning *by ten times, by one hundred times,* and *by one thousand times.* Answers: tenfold; a hundredfold; a thousandfold

Answers for p. 102

Review and Assess

1. Students may express surprise at Bradstreet's passion, given her Puritan pedigree.

2. **(a)** Bradstreet repeats the phrase *if ever* and the words *were* and *then.* **(b)** Repetition suggests the strength of the speaker's feelings.

3. **(a)** She prizes her husband's love. **(b)** Other images include *riches, unquenchable rivers, I can no way repay.*

4. **(a)** The apparent contradiction is their "living" after their lives are over. **(b)** The last stanza indicates the Puritan belief in an afterlife.

5. Students should support their responses with clear reasoning and/or relevant personal observations and experiences.

102

---

❺ To My Dear and Loving Husband
Anne Bradstreet

Reading Strategy
Paraphrasing How would you paraphrase these first two lines?

❻ If ever two were one, then surely we.
If ever man were lov'd by wife, then thee;
If ever wife was happy in a man,
Compare with me ye women if you can.

5 I prize thy love more than whole mines of gold,
Or all the riches that the East doth hold.
My love is such that rivers cannot quench,
Nor ought[1] but love from thee, give recompense.
Thy love is such I can no way repay,

❼ The heavens reward thee manifold, I pray.
Then while we live, in love let's so persevere,[2]
That when we live no more, we may live ever.

recompense (rek´ em pens´) *n.* repayment; something given or done in return for something else

manifold (man´ e fōld´) *adv.* in many ways

persevere (pur´ se vir´) *v.* persist; be steadfast in purpose

---

1. **ought** (ôt) *n.* anything whatever.
2. **persevere** pronounced *per se´ ver* in the seventeenth century, and thus rhymed with the word *ever.*

Review and Assess

Thinking About the Selection

1. **Respond:** What is your image of Anne Bradstreet after reading this poem? Does she fit your concept of a Puritan? Explain.

2. **(a) Recall:** Note where Bradstreet uses repetition in the first stanza. **(b) Analyze:** How does her use of repetition suggest a growing emotional intensity?

3. **(a) Recall:** What does the speaker value more than "whole mines of gold"? **(b) Distinguish:** What other images suggest the richness and abundance of the love the speaker and her husband share?

4. **(a) Analyze:** What is the apparent contradiction in the last two lines? **(b) Draw Conclusions:** What does the last stanza reveal about Puritan beliefs in the afterlife?

5. **Apply:** Do you think personal devotion is as much esteemed today as it was in Bradstreet's day? Support your answer.

ASSESSMENT PRACTICE: Reading Comprehension

Summarizing Written Texts   (For more practice, see Test Preparation Workbook, p. 6.)

Some tests measure students' ability to identify the best summary of a passage. Explain that summarizing is especially useful when reading poetry. After students reread the poem on p. 102, have them pick the best summary from the choices below.

A The author wants to live forever with her husband.

B The author's love for her husband, which she values more than gold and riches, will never die.

C The author owes her husband money.

D The author wants heaven to reward her husband.

Choices *A* and *D* make only partially complete claims; *C* presents incorrect information. *B* is the best summary.

Review and Assess

Literary Analysis

Puritan Plain Style

1. Which words, phrases, and references in each poem reflect the plainness of the Puritans' lives? Use a chart like the one shown to organize your perceptions.

Concept		Perception
Thy spinning wheel complete	···▸	References to household objects reflect plain lives.

2. Which aspects of each poem are not typical of the **Puritan Plain Style**? Explain.
3. Compared to other poetry you know, how would you describe the effect of the Puritan Plain Style?

Comparing Literary Works

4. (a) Compare and contrast the emotions each of these speakers directs toward his or her subject. (b) What do these speakers want from the objects of their devotion? Explain.
5. How do both of these poems express emotions that are distinctly Puritan yet universally human?
6. Cite two lines from each of these poems that may have violated the Puritan prohibition against personal expression.
7. A **conceit** is an elaborate comparison between two very different subjects. (a) How does Taylor's use of conceit help to structure his poem? (b) By contrast, how does Bradstreet build the ideas in her poem?

Reading Strategy

Paraphrasing

8. **Paraphrase** these passages from the poems as though you were explaining their meaning to a friend: (a) "To My Dear and Loving Husband," lines 9–12, (b) "Huswifery," lines 9–12.

Extend Understanding

9. **History Connection:** (a) What was the Puritan attitude toward material wealth and spirituality? (b) In our culture today, what is the general view of the relationship between the two?

Quick Review

The **Puritan Plain Style** is a simple, direct style of writing characterized by the use of short, easily understood words common to seventeenth-century conversation.

When you **paraphrase**, you restate important ideas in your own words.

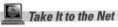 **Take It to the Net**
www.phschool.com
Take the interactive self-test online to check your understanding of these selections.

ENRICHMENT: Further Reading

Other Works by the Authors

Works by Edward Taylor
Poetical Works

Works by Anne Bradstreet
The Works of Anne Bradstreet, 1612–1672

Take It to the Net
Visit www.phschool.com for more information on the authors.

Answers for page 103
Review and Assess

1. **Taylor**—Concept: distaff, flyers, spoole, reel, yarn; Perceptions: ordinary objects. **Bradstreet**—Concept: I prize thy love more than...; Perceptions: love is more precious than wealth.

2. **Taylor**—extended use of metaphors and vivid images; **Bradstreet**—personal, emotional subject of love for husband.

3. Students should clearly describe their understanding of the effect of the Puritan Plain Style, and they should explain how this effect compares with that of other poetry.

4. **(a)** Taylor's speaker directs spiritual love and devotion toward God; Bradstreet's speaker directs conjugal love and devotion toward her husband. **(b)** Taylor's speaker wants to achieve eternal glory by serving God; Bradstreet's speaker wants her husband to share her love even after death.

5. Taylor's poem deals with the universal sentiments of love and devotion, yet the speaker's attitude is distinctly Puritan. Bradstreet's poem deals with the universal sentiment of romantic love expressed within the Puritan religious framework.

6. Possible response: Taylor—lines 17 and 18; Bradstreet—any two lines

7. **(a)** Taylor establishes the metaphor in the poem's first line; he adds details (different aspects of the same metaphor) to fill out the conceit. **(b)** Bradstreet establishes her main idea about marital love in the first stanza, develops it with figurative language in the second stanza and extends it by addressing the idea of the afterlife in the last stanza.

8. Possible responses: **(a)** Your love is so strong I can't repay it, so I pray heaven will reward you in many ways. **(b)** Weave the web yourself. The yarn is delicate. Your sacraments clean and thicken it. Then, dye it in heavenly colors, decorated with flowers of paradise.

Answers continued

9. Possible responses: **(a)** The Puritans regarded material wealth with suspicion, since they believed their duty lay in striving to serve God. **(b)** Our culture today is more accepting of material wealth—in fact, it might be said to celebrate it.

continued

❶ Vocabulary Development

Word Analysis

1. fourfold
2. threefold

Spelling Strategy

Taylor—*clothe, therewith;*
Bradstreet—*doth*

Fluency

1. b
2. c
3. b

❷ Grammar and Style

Practice

1. I beseech you, <u>O Muse</u>, to bring me inspiration!
2. And make Thy holy spirit, <u>Lord</u>, wind quills: / Then weave the web Thyself.
3. I could not love thee, <u>dear</u>, so much, / Loved I not honor more.
4. How can I repay, <u>my love</u>, the love you have given to me?
5. I see you in the holy work I strive to perform, <u>Lord</u>.

Writing Application

Students' letters should address a serious societal issue and should include at least one instance of direct address. For example, in the body of the letter, a student might write:

I hope you can focus the nation's attention on this problem, Senator Smith.

Integrate Language Skills

❶ Vocabulary Development Lesson

Word Analysis: Anglo-Saxon Suffix *-fold*

The Anglo-Saxon suffix *-fold*, meaning "a specific number of times or ways," is used to form both adjectives and adverbs. *Tenfold* means "ten times." Replace the italicized phrases with a word containing the suffix *-fold*.

1. Since having quadruplets, Sandy's laundry has grown *by four times*.
2. The savvy investor watched the value of his stock increase to *three times its size*.

Spelling Strategy

When the unvoiced *th* sound occurs at the end of a word, spell it with the letters *th*. When the voiced *th* sound occurs, include a final *e*. Find examples of each of these rules in these poems.

❷ Grammar and Style Lesson

Direct Address

When the speaker in a poem talks directly to someone or something, the form of speech is called a **direct address.** Commas are used to separate the word or phrase of the direct address from the rest of the sentence, regardless of its position in the sentence.

Middle: Make me, *O Lord*, Thy spinning wheel complete.

End: May you be rewarded for your love, *dear husband.*

WG *Prentice Hall Writing and Grammar Connection: Chapter 27, Section 2*

Fluency: Word Meaning

Identify the letter of the situation that best demonstrates the meaning of the italicized word or phrase.

1. *well-deserved recompense:* (a) getting a flat tire while taking your grandmother to the doctor, (b) getting a day off after working overtime, (c) cleaning a messy room after a long day
2. *increase manifold:* (a) to receive a twenty percent raise, (b) to add a drop of water to a full bucket, (c) to get a 300 percent return on an investment
3. *to persevere:* (a) to quit when you get tired, (b) to practice until you improve, (c) to argue with a referee

Practice Identify the word or phrase of direct address. Add punctuation where needed.

1. I beseech you O Muse to bring me inspiration!
2. And make Thy holy spirit Lord wind quills: / Then weave the web Thyself.
3. I could not love thee dear so much, / Loved I not honor more.
4. How can I repay my love the love you have given to me?
5. I see you in the holy work I strive to perform Lord.

Writing Application Write a letter to a political figure explaining your opinion about a subject of your choice. Use at least one direct address.

TEACHING RESOURCES

The following resources can be used to enrich or extend the instruction for pp. 104–105.

Vocabulary

📖 **Selection Support:** Build Vocabulary, p. 25
📖 **Vocabulary and Spelling Practice Book** ▪

Grammar

📖 **Selection Support:** Grammar and Style, p. 26
WG **Writing and Grammar,** Ruby Level, p. 696
▪ **Daily Language Practice Transparencies**

Writing

WG **Writing and Grammar,** Ruby Level, p. 100 ▪
📖 **Extension Activities,** p. 6
▪ **Writing Models and Graphic Organizers on Transparencies,** p. 9
◎ **Writing and Grammar iText CD-ROM**

▪ **BLOCK SCHEDULING:** Resources marked with this symbol provide varied instruction during 90-minute blocks.

❸ Writing Lesson

Reflective Essay

To write his poem, Edward Taylor had to understand the process by which clothes were made, from the spinning of the yarn to the sewing of a garment. The poem works on two different levels—as a description of an ordinary activity and as a comparison between that task and religious devotion. In an essay, describe a common household chore and then explain how that task suggests a larger meaning.

Prewriting   Identify a task to be completed in the average household. Note the steps involved in the process and the tools that might be used.

Drafting   Describe the task from beginning to end, incorporating details that appeal to the senses. Write a brief conclusion to address the larger meaning within this ordinary activity.

> #### Model: Providing Descriptive Details
>
> When I sort the clothes into darks and lights, I feel the roughness of denim and the smoothness of cotton. I smell the grass from mowing the lawn and pick out bits of leaves that found their way into folds of the cloth.

Specific details like *roughness of denim* and the smell of the grass help make writing vivid.

Revising   Invite a classmate to judge the vividness of your writing and to identify any points where the process is not described clearly. Evaluate whether or not the larger meaning makes sense.

 Prentice Hall Writing and Grammar Connection: Chapter 6, Section 2

❹ Extension Activities

Listening and Speaking Foremost among the Puritan values were a strong work ethic and devotion to God and family. Stage an **informal debate** to argue whether these values exist in today's society. Use these tips to prepare:

- Review a range of sources for evidence supporting either a pro or con stance.
- Anticipate opponents' arguments and prepare your defenses in advance.

When debating, speak clearly and slowly to make sure your ideas are heard. **[Group Activity]**

Research and Technology Research the process of spinning yarn and weaving cloth as it was practiced in the colonial era. Using available computer graphics, produce a **graphic display** that identifies the steps and tools referenced in "Huswifery," and write the corresponding line(s) of verse next to each.

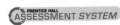 **Take It to the Net**   www.phschool.com
Go online for an additional research activity using the Internet.

Huswifery / To My Dear and Loving Husband ◆ 105

ASSESSMENT RESOURCES

The following resources can be used to assess students' knowledge and skills.

Selection Assessment

- **Formal Assessment,** pp. 27–29
- **Open Book Test,** pp. 16–18
- **Got It! Assessment Videotapes,** Tape 1
- **Test Bank Software**
- **Take It to the Net**
  Visit www.phschool.com for self-tests and additional questions on the selections.

Writing Rubric

- **Performance Assessment and Portfolio Management,** p. 11

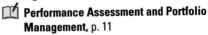 PRENTICE HALL ASSESSMENT *SYSTEM*

- **Workbook**
- **Skill Book**
- **Transparencies**
- **CD-ROM**

❸ Writing Lesson

- Students' reflective essays should present the steps involved in a common household task in a clear, detailed, and thorough way. Their essays should also suggest a larger meaning for this activity.

- After they have selected the household chore they wish to examine, encourage students to brainstorm for every possible step and detail involved in the completion of the task.

- Use the Writing Lesson, as well as Writing Process Model 2 in **Writing Models and Graphic Organizers on Transparencies,** p. 9, to guide students in developing their reflective essays.

- Use the Description rubric in **Performance Assessment and Portfolio Management,** p. 11, to evaluate students' reflective essays.

❹ Listening and Speaking

- Organize the class into at least two teams, and assign each team either a pro or a con stance.

- Encourage each team to spend time gathering ideas and evidence, and making careful records of all sources.

- Have each team write their ideas and supporting evidence on index cards, and organize the cards by category. This will allow for easier reference during the actual debate.

- Encourage each team to anticipate the opposing arguments and prepare responses ahead of time.

- As students debate, stop those who are speaking too quickly or unclearly. Have them pause and start again. Make sure students understand the importance of delivering their ideas in a slow, careful way, and with assurance.

CUSTOMIZE INSTRUCTION
For Universal Access

To address different learning styles, use the following activities suggested in the **Extension Activities** booklet, p. 6.

For Verbal/Linguistic and Intrapersonal Learners, use Activity 5.

For Verbal/Linguistic and Interpersonal Learners, use Activity 6.

from Sinners in the Hands of an Angry God

Lesson Objectives

1. **To analyze and respond to literary elements**
   - Literary Analysis: Sermon
   - Connecting Literary Elements: Oratory

2. **To read, comprehend, analyze, and critique nonfiction**
   - Reading Strategy: Using Context Clues
   - Reading Check Questions
   - Review and Assess Questions
   - Assessment Practice (ATE)

3. **To develop word analysis skills, fluency, and systematic vocabulary**
   - Vocabulary Development Lesson: Latin Prefix: *omni-*

4. **To understand and apply written and oral language conventions**
   - Spelling Strategy
   - Grammar and Style Lesson: Forms of Adjectives and Adverbs

5. **To understand and apply appropriate writing and research strategies**
   - Writing Lesson: Evaluation of Persuasion
   - Extension Activity: Puritan Handbook

6. **To understand and apply listening and speaking strategies**
   - Extension Activity: Oral Report

STEP-BY-STEP TEACHING GUIDE	PACING GUIDE
PRETEACH	
Motivate Students and Provide Background	
Use the Motivation activity (ATE p. 106)	10 min.
Read and discuss author and background information (SE/ATE p. 106) [A]	10 min.
Introduce the Concepts	
Introduce the Literary Analysis and Reading Strategy (SE/ATE p. 107) [A]	15 min.
Pronounce the vocabulary words and read their definitions (SE p. 107)	10 min.
TEACH	
Monitor Comprehension	
Informally monitor comprehension by circulating while students read independently or in groups [A]	35 min.
Monitor students' comprehension with the Reading Check notes (SE/ATE pp. 109, 111)	as students read
Develop vocabulary with Vocabulary notes (SE pp. 109, 110; ATE p. 109)	as students read
Develop Understanding	
Develop students' understanding of sermons with the Literary Analysis annotations (SE pp. 109, 111; ATE pp. 109, 111) [A]	5 min.
Develop students' recognition of context clues with the Reading Strategy annotations (SE p. 112; ATE p. 112)	5 min.
ASSESS	
Assess Mastery	
Assess students' mastery of the Reading Strategy and Literary Analysis by having them answer the Review and Assess questions (SE/ATE p. 113)	15 min.
Use one or more of the print and media Assessment Resources (ATE p. 115) [A]	up to 45 min.
EXTEND	
Apply Understanding	
Have students complete the Vocabulary Development Lesson and the Grammar and Style Lesson (SE p. 114) [A]	20 min.
Apply students' ability to write unified prose by using the Writing Lesson (SE/ATE p. 115) [A]	45 min.
Apply students' understanding using one or more of the Extension Activities (SE p. 115)	20–90 min.

 ACCELERATED INSTRUCTION:
Use the strategies and activities identified with an [A].

UNIVERSAL ACCESS
● = Below Level Students
▲ = On-Level Students
■ = Above Level Students

Time and Resource Manager

Reading Level: Challenging
Average Number of Instructional Days: 5

RESOURCES		
PRINT 📖	**TRANSPARENCIES**	**TECHNOLOGY** 💿 🎧 📼
• **Beyond Literature,** Workplace Skills: Persuasive Techniques, p. 7 ▲ ■		• **Interest Grabber Video,** Tape 1 ● ▲ ■
• **Selection Support Workbook:** ● ▲ ■ Literary Analysis, p. 32 Reading Strategy, p. 31 Build Vocabulary, p. 29	• **Literary Analysis and Reading Transparencies,** pp. 13 and 14 ● ▲ ■	
• **Adapted Reader's Companion** ● • **Reader's Companion** ●		• **Listening to Literature** ● ▲ ■ Audiocassettes, Side 3 Audio CDs, CD 2
• **English Learner's Companion** ● ▲ • **Literatura en español** ● ▲ • **Literary Analysis for Enrichment** ■		
• **Formal Assessment:** Selection Test, pp. 30–32 ● ▲ ■ • **Open Book Test,** pp. 19–21 ● ▲ ■ • **Performance Assessment and Portfolio Management,** p. 17 ● ▲ ■ • PRENTICE HALL **ASSESSMENT** *SYSTEM* ● ▲ ■	• PRENTICE HALL **ASSESSMENT** *SYSTEM* ● ▲ ■ Skills Practice Answers and Explanations on Transparencies	• **Test Bank Software** ● ▲ ■ • **Got It! Assessment Videotapes,** Tape 1 ● ▲
• **Selection Support Workbook:** ● ▲ ■ Grammar and Style, p. 30 • **Writing and Grammar,** Ruby Level ● ▲ ■ • **Extension Activities,** p. 7 ● ▲ ■	• **Daily Language Practice Transparencies** ● ▲ • **Writing Models and Graphic Organizers on Transparencies,** p. 25 ● ▲ ■	• **Writing and Grammar iText CD-ROM** ● ▲ ■ 💻 *Take It to the Net* www.phschool.com

BLOCK SCHEDULING: Use one 90-minute class period to preteach the selection and have students read it. Use a second 90-minute class period to assess students' mastery of skills and have them complete one of the Extension Activities.

Motivation

Most students are all too familiar with the persuasive power of advertising, of peer pressure, and of other methods people use to influence the actions or attitudes of others. Have small groups brainstorm for persuasive techniques that they find especially effective. Then, engage students' interest in Jonathan Edwards's persuasive sermon by reading the following passage to them:

"O, sinner! Consider the fearful danger you are in: it is a great furnace of wrath, a wide and bottomless pit, full of the fire of wrath, that you are held over in the hand of that God. . . "

Ask students to characterize Edwards's basic approach: is it emotional or intellectual? Invite other responses to this quotation, as well as speculation about how Edwards, a conservative Puritan preacher, might attempt to persuade a congregation to accept his message about their "wickedness."

◼ Interest Grabber Video

As an alternative, play "The Puritans" on Tape 1 to engage student interest.

❶ Background

More About the Author

As he toiled to strengthen Puritanism against what he saw as new waves of liberalism and rationalism, Jonathan Edwards deeply influenced American religious history. He wrestled continually with the theological issue of free will: if God determines all, how is human free will possible? Edwards concluded that since God gives people the power to choose, they hold responsibility for their acts and will earn God's praise or wrath accordingly. After Edwards left his preaching duties at Northampton, he ministered to the Housatonic Indians and to scattered frontier settlers in the area.

106

Prepare to Read

❶ *from* Sinners in the Hands of an Angry God

Jonathan Edwards
(1703–1758)

The sermons of Jonathan Edwards were so filled with "fire and brimstone"—a phrase symbolizing the torments of hell endured by sinners—that his name alone was enough to make many eighteenth-century Puritans shake in their shoes. Yet, Edwards was not merely a stone-faced religious zealot. He was also a man who believed in science and reason and who saw in the physical world the proof of God's presence and will.

A Preacher Born and Raised This great American theologian and powerful Puritan preacher was born in East Windsor, Connecticut, where he grew up in an atmosphere of devout discipline. As a young boy, he is said to have demonstrated his religious devotion by preaching sermons to his playmates from a makeshift pulpit he built behind his home. Edwards also displayed academic brilliance at an early age. By the time he was twelve, he had learned to speak Latin, Greek, and Hebrew and had written numerous philosophical and scientific essays. These essays, which include "Of Insects," and "Of the Rainbow," display Edwards's remarkable powers of observation and analysis. Edwards entered the Collegiate School of Connecticut (now Yale University) at the age of thirteen and graduated four years later as the valedictorian of his class. He went on to earn his master's degree in theology.

The Great Awakening Edwards began his preaching career in 1727 as assistant to his grandfather, Solomon Stoddard, pastor of the church at Northampton, Massachusetts, one of the largest and wealthiest Puritan congregations. Edwards became the church pastor two years later when his grandfather died. He also began preaching throughout New England. Committed to a return to the orthodoxy and fervent faith of the Puritan past, Edwards became one of the leaders of the Great Awakening, a religious revival that swept the colonies in the 1730s and 1740s. His sermons stimulated religious zeal and sparked conversions, often in a frenzied atmosphere.

Changing Attitudes As Pastor of the church at Northampton, Edwards had instituted disciplinary proceedings against members of his congregation for reading what he considered improper books. In his sermons he denounced by name those he considered sinners. Such actions, combined with the severity of his views, drew criticism. In 1750, a council representing ten congregations in the region dismissed Edwards as pastor.

Fall from Favor Edwards then moved to Stockbridge, Massachusetts, where he preached to the Native Americans. While in Stockbridge, Edwards wrote his most important theological works, including "A Careful and Strict Enquiry into . . . Notions of . . . Freedom of Will" (1754), in which he argued that human beings do not possess self-determination. The essay remains one of the most famous theological works ever written in America. Edwards continued to preach and write until his death in 1758, shortly after becoming president of the College of New Jersey (now Princeton University).

Although in most of his sermons, books, and essays Edwards appeals to reason and logic, his highly emotional sermon "Sinners in the Hands of an Angry God" is by far his most famous work. This sermon, which was delivered to a congregation in Enfield, Connecticut, in 1741 and is said to have caused listeners to rise from their seats in a state of hysteria, demonstrates Edwards's tremendous powers of persuasion and captures the religious fervor of the Great Awakening.

106 ◆ Beginnings–1750

TEACHING RESOURCES

The following resources can be used to enrich or extend the instruction for pp. 106–107.

Motivation

◼ **Interest Grabber Video**, Tape 1 ◼

Background

📖 **Beyond Literature**, p. 7

🖥 *Take It to the Net*
Visit www.phschool.com for Background and hotlinks for the selection.

Literary Analysis

📄 **Literary Analysis and Reading Transparencies**, Sermon, p. 14

Reading

📄 **Literary Analysis and Reading Transparencies**, Using Context Clues, p. 13 ◼

📖 **Selection Support:** Reading Strategy, p. 31; Build Vocabulary, p. 29

◼ **BLOCK SCHEDULING:** Resources marked with this symbol provide varied instruction during 90-minute blocks.

Preview

Connecting to the Literature

Suppose a friend is involved with the "wrong crowd" and you are concerned about his or her awful future. Jonathan Edwards had such concerns about his congregation. To turn his congregants toward repentance, Edwards filled his sermons with descriptions of the horrors that awaited those who did not mend their ways.

❷ Literary Analysis

Sermon

A **sermon** is broadly defined as a speech given from a pulpit in a house of worship. Like its written counterpart, the essay, a sermon conveys to an audience the speaker's message or point of view. In colonial America's religious atmosphere, the sermon flourished as a popular literary form.

Connecting Literary Elements

Sermons are one example of **oratory,** or formal public speaking. The best oratory almost always displays the following elements:

- It is persuasive, inspiring listeners to take action.
- It is emotionally appealing.
- It addresses the needs and concerns of its audience.
- It involves the use of colorful or rhythmic language.

Although oratory has become less common in American society, its lofty tones can still be heard in Senate chambers, courtrooms, and houses of worship. In Edwards's time, oratory played an important role in the lives of nearly all citizens of a community.

❸ Reading Strategy

Using Context Clues

Searching the **context**—the surrounding words, phrases, and sentences—for clues can help you understand the meaning of unfamiliar words. For example, look at the word *abominable* in this passage:

> You are ten thousand times more *abominable* in his [God's] eyes, than the most hateful venomous serpent is in ours. . . .

Edwards likens the way the sinner appears in God's eyes with our view of a snake. From this clue, you can determine that *abominable* must be close in meaning to *disgusting* or *horrible*. Use a chart like the one shown to define other difficult words by using context clues.

Vocabulary Development

omnipotent (äm nip′ ə tənt) *adj.* all-powerful (p. 109)

ineffable (in ef′ ə bəl) *adj.* inexpressible (p. 110)

dolorous (dō′ lər əs) *adj.* sad; mournful (p. 110)

Difficult Words

↓

Context Clues

↓

Meaning

from Sinners in the Hands of an Angry God ◆ 107

❷ Literary Analysis

Sermon

- Tell students that they will focus on sermons as they read this excerpt from one of the most famous sermons in American history, delivered two and a half centuries ago by Jonathan Edwards.

- As they read the sermon, students should remember that Edwards conceived the work as a piece of oratory—*spoken* text. Have a volunteer read the list of elements often found in oratory in the Connecting Literary Elements passage.

- Encourage students to look for examples of colorful or rhythmic language, including the use of repetition, alliteration, and other sound devices.

- As they read, invite students to imagine being one of Edwards's parishioners. Do his fiery words affect them emotionally? Encourage students to discuss the idea that the concepts of guilt, redemption, and mercy do not become outdated.

❸ Reading Strategy

Using Context Clues

- Remind students that every text that contains unfamiliar words also contains context clues. Readers can use these clues to unlock the meanings of difficult words.

- Point out that context clues can take several forms: a single word, a phrase, or a word group.

- Tell students that the use of context clues is not limited to literature. Point out that they can (and no doubt already *do*) use this skill in daily conversation. Encourage students to use context clues to determine the meanings of unfamiliar words every time they read.

Vocabulary Development

- Pronounce each vocabulary word for students, and read the definitions as a class. Have students identify any words with which they are already familiar.

 E-Teach

Visit E-Teach at www.phschool.com for teachers' essays on how to teach with questions and answers.

CUSTOMIZE INSTRUCTION FOR UNIVERSAL ACCESS

For Special Needs Students	For Less Proficient Readers	For English Learners
Have students read the adapted version of "Sinners in the Hands of an Angry God" in the **Adapted Reader's Companion.** This version provides basic-level instruction in an interactive format with questions and write-on lines. Completing the adapted version will prepare students to read the selection in the Student Edition.	Have students read the adapted version of the selection in the **Reader's Companion.** This version provides basic-level instruction in an interactive format with questions and write-on lines. After students finish the selection in **Reader's Companion,** have them complete the questions and activities in the Student Edition.	Have students read the adapted version of the selection in the **English Learner's Companion.** This version provides basic-level instruction in an interactive format with questions and write-on lines. Completing the adapted version will prepare students to read the selection in the Student Edition.

Step-by-Step Teaching Guide for pp. 108–112

CUSTOMIZE INSTRUCTION
For Verbal/Linguistic Learners

Invite volunteers to select a portion of this sermon to practice and deliver to classmates. After the presentations, encourage listeners to give constructive feedback about the effectiveness of the speakers' deliveries.

❶ About the Selection

The foundation of Edwards's sermon is the Puritan belief in a life of hard work, self-discipline, and religious devotion. The preacher intended to frighten his listeners into pursuing lives of humility and righteousness in the hope of achieving salvation. What Edwards's listeners probably found most dreadful was the idea of an omniscient God being indifferent to human misery. Moreover, the congregation was surely chilled by the realization that—though their only hope of salvation lay in observing divine laws to the letter— God might dole out mercy according to His whims.

❷ Background

Art

The Puritan, 1898, by Frank E. Schoonover

Frank Schoonover (1877–1922) was an American illustrator for magazines and books, such as *LaFitte, the Pirate of the Gulf,* and the *Hopalong Cassidy* series of westerns. His paintings show great precision and detail. This accurately illustrates Puritan garb, and conveys the subject's austere Puritan attitude. Use this question for discussion:

• This is a formal portrait, one in which the subject was posed by the artist. How does this concept echo Edwards's sermon?
Answer: The rigid pose suggests obedience to the will of the artist. Likewise, Edwards's sermon preaches a rigid obedience to the commands of God.

❶ from ***Sinners in the Hands of an Angry God***

Jonathan Edwards

Background

Surprisingly, Jonathan Edwards preached this famous fire-and-brimstone sermon in a quiet, restrained style. According to one account, he read the six-hour work in a level voice, staring over the heads of his congregation at the bell rope that hung against the back wall "as if he would stare it in two." Despite his calm demeanor, his listeners are said to have groaned and screamed in terror, and Edwards stopped several times to ask for silence.

This is the case of every one of you that are out of Christ:[1] That world of misery, that lake of burning brimstone, is extended abroad under you. There is the dreadful pit of the glowing flames of the wrath of God; there is Hell's wide gaping mouth open; and you have nothing to stand upon, nor anything to take hold of; there is nothing between you and Hell but the air; it is only the power and mere pleasure of God that holds you up.

You probably are not sensible of this; you find you are kept out of Hell, but do not see the hand of God in it; but look at other things, as the good state of your bodily constitution, your care of your own life, and the means you use for your own preservation. But indeed these things are nothing; if God should withdraw his hand, they would avail no more to keep you from falling than the thin air to hold up a person that is suspended in it.

---

1. out of Christ not in God's grace.

108 ◆ Beginnings–1750

TEACHING RESOURCES

The following resources can be used to enrich or extend the instruction for pp. 108–112.

Literary Analysis

📖 **Selection Support:** Literary Analysis, p. 32

Reading

📖 **Adapted Reader's Companion**

📖 **Reader's Companion**

📖 **English Learner's Companion**

🎧 **Listening to Literature Audiocassettes,** Side 3 ▪

💿 **Listening to Literature CDs,** CD 2 ▪

▪ **BLOCK SCHEDULING:** Resources marked with this symbol provide varied instruction during 90-minute blocks.

Your wickedness makes you as it were heavy as lead, and to tend downwards with great weight and pressure towards Hell; and if God should let you go, you would immediately sink and swiftly descend and plunge into the bottomless gulf, and your healthy constitution, and your own care and prudence, and best contrivance, and all your righteousness, would have no more influence to uphold you and keep you out of Hell, than a spider's web would have to stop a fallen rock. Were it not for the sovereign pleasure of God, the earth would not bear you one moment . . . The world would spew you out, were it not for the sovereign hand of Him who hath subjected it in hope. There are black clouds of God's wrath now hanging directly over your heads, full of the dreadful storm, and big with thunder; and were it not for the restraining hand of God, it would immediately burst forth upon you. The sovereign pleasure of God, for the present, stays[2] his rough wind; otherwise it would come with fury, and your destruction would come like a whirlwind, and you would be like the chaff of the summer threshing floor.

The wrath of God is like great waters that are dammed for the present; they increase more and more, and rise higher and higher, till an outlet is given; and the longer the stream is stopped, the more rapid and mighty is its course, when once it is let loose. It is true, that judgment against your evil works has not been executed hitherto; the floods of God's vengeance have been withheld; but your guilt in the meantime is constantly increasing, and you are every day treasuring up more wrath; the waters are constantly rising, and waxing more and more mighty; and there is nothing but the mere pleasure of God, that holds the waters back, that are unwilling to be stopped, and press hard to go forward. If God should only withdraw his hand from the floodgate, it would immediately fly open, and the fiery floods of the fierceness and wrath of God, would rush forth with inconceivable fury, and would come upon you with omnipotent power; and if your strength were ten thousand times greater than it is, yea, ten thousand times greater than the strength of the stoutest, sturdiest devil in Hell, it would be nothing to withstand or endure it.

The bow of God's wrath is bent, and the arrow made ready on the string, and justice bends the arrow at your heart, and strains the bow, and it is nothing but the mere pleasure of God, and that of an angry God, without any promise or obligation at all, that keeps the arrow one moment from being made drunk with your blood. Thus all you that never passed under a great change of heart, by the mighty power of the spirit of God upon your souls; all you that were never

2. **stays** (stāz) *v.* restrains.

from Sinners in the Hands of an Angry God ◆ 109

The Puritan, 1888, Frank E. Schoonover, Collection of the Brandywine River Museum

❸ ▲ Critical Viewing
What words from the text would you apply to describe the mood of this painting? **[Analyze]**

Literary Analysis
Sermon In what ways do these images of the fury of water help convey Edwards's message?

❹ omnipotent (äm nip´ ə tənt) *adj.* all-powerful

❻ ☑ Reading Check
What does Edwards say is the state of his congregation?

❸ ▶ Critical Viewing
Answer: Citations may include "your own care and prudence," "infinite gloom," "fierceness," "moral and strict, sober and religious," and "miserable condition that you are in."

❹ Vocabulary Development
Latin prefix *omni-*

• Draw students' attention to Edwards's use of the word *omnipotent*, and read its definition. Then, tell students that the prefix *omni-* means "all" or "every."

• Ask students why they might expect to find words beginning with the prefix *omni-* in a sermon.
Answer: The prefix *omni-* expresses the idea of encompassing all, a characteristic often attributed to God.

• Then, invite students to combine the prefix *omni-* with the word *present* to create another word Edwards might have used to describe God.

❺ Literary Analysis
Sermon

• Ask a student volunteer to read aloud the first two paragraphs on p. 109. Have students raise their hands when they hear images involving water. List these images on the chalkboard.

▶ Monitor Progress Ask students the Literary Analysis question on p. 109: In what ways do these images of the fury of water help convey Edwards's message?
Answer: The image of dammed water, rising in volume and power, serves as an effective metaphor for God's potential wrath. It is an image of the *possibility* of destruction. This is perfect for Edwards's purpose, as it checks his congregation's impulse to rationalize away the possibility of God's judgment.

❻ ☑ Reading Check
Answer: Edwards indicates that his congregation is poised above a "world of misery" and that at any moment God could let go and consign them to Hell forever.

CUSTOMIZE INSTRUCTION FOR UNIVERSAL ACCESS

For Special Needs Students	For Gifted/Talented Students
Students may benefit from a demonstration of how to use context clues. Invite them to identify a paragraph that includes one or more unfamiliar words or phrases. Write the passage on the board, underlining the difficult words. Then, circle the surrounding context clues that can help students determine the meanings of the unknown words. By reading the challenging words in relationship to the context clues, students may be able to interpret the meaning of the unfamiliar terms.	Ask students to find details that distinguish this piece as a sermon. They may cite Edwards's use of religious references or his use of repetition to heighten the sense of the congregants' peril. Also, have students look for examples of figurative language (such as the personification of hell's "wide gaping mouth"), which add poetic and dramatic impact to the sermon.

The King James Version of the Bible was preceded in English by Wyclif's Bible (1380), Tyndale's Bible (1525), Coverdale's Bible (1535), Matthew's Bible (1537), Taverner's Bible (1539), the Geneva Bible (1560), and the Bishops' Bible (1568). Also known as the "Authorized Version," the King James Version was composed from 1604 to 1611 by a group of scholars working for King James I. It is widely considered to be the most beautifully written translation of the Hebrew scriptures, and it has had an incalculable effect on English and American literary history.

born again, and made new creatures, and raised from being dead in sin, to a state of new, and before altogether unexperienced light and life, are in the hands of an angry God. However you may have reformed your life in many things, and may have had religious affections, and may keep up a form of religion in your families and closets,[3] and in the house of God, it is nothing but His mere pleasure that keeps you from being this moment swallowed up in everlasting destruction. However unconvinced you may now be of the truth of what you hear, by and by you will be fully convinced of it.

Those that are gone from being in the like circumstances with you, see that it was so with them; for destruction came suddenly upon most of them; when they expected nothing of it, and while they were saying, peace and safety: now they see, that those things on which they depended for peace and safety, were nothing but thin air and empty shadows.

The God that holds you over the pit of Hell, much as one holds a spider, or some loathsome insect over the fire, abhors you, and is dreadfully provoked: his wrath towards you burns like fire; he looks upon you as worthy of nothing else, but to be cast into the fire; he is of purer eyes than to bear to have you in his sight; you are ten thousand times more abominable in his eyes, than the most hateful venomous serpent is in ours. . . .

O sinner! Consider the fearful danger you are in: it is a great furnace of wrath, a wide and bottomless pit, full of the fire of wrath, that you are held over in the hand of that God, whose wrath is provoked and incensed as much against you, as against many of the damned in Hell. You hang by a slender thread, with the flames of divine wrath flashing about it, and ready every moment to singe it, and burn it asunder; and you have no interest in any mediator, and nothing to lay hold of to save yourself, nothing to keep off the flames of wrath, nothing of your own, nothing that you ever have done, nothing that you can do, to induce God to spare you one moment. . . .

When God beholds the <u>ineffable</u> extremity of your case, and sees your torment to be so vastly disproportioned to your strength, and sees how your poor soul is crushed, and sinks down, as it were, into an infinite gloom; he will have no compassion upon you, he will not forbear the executions of his wrath, or in the least lighten his hand; there shall be no moderation or mercy, nor will God then at all stay his rough wind; he will have no regard to your welfare, nor be at all careful lest you should suffer too much in any other sense, than only that you shall *not suffer beyond what strict justice requires.* . . .

God stands ready to pity you; this is a day of mercy; you may cry now with some encouragement of obtaining mercy. But once the day of mercy is past, your most lamentable and dolorous cries and shrieks will be in vain; you will be wholly lost and thrown away of

Good hates you

---

3. **closets** *n.* small, private rooms for meditation.

𝓛iterature in context History Connection

❼ *Biblical Imagery*

Jonathan Edwards's frightening imagery of God's potential for wrath and destruction recalls stories of fires, floods, and divine retribution in the Old Testament of the King James Bible. While this imagery terrified Edwards's audience, they would have found it quite familiar. In fact, in 1741, when Edwards delivered this sermon, the King James Bible had been in wide circulation for 130 years. The first English version of the Bible to include both the Old and New Testaments, the King James Bible had been produced at the express request of the Puritans in England in 1611. This Bible, with its haunting language and powerful imagery, would have been common daily reading for most of Edwards's listeners.

ineffable (in ef´ ə bəl) *adj.* inexpressible

dolorous (dō´ lər əs) *adj.* sad; mournful

❋ ENRICHMENT: Humanities Connection

The Afterlife

Edwards's apparent belief in an afterlife is typical of the followers of most major religions. According to the ancient Greeks, people who led a good life were sent to Elysium, a paradise filled with fields of flowers and sunlight. Ancient Egyptians also believed in the afterlife as an agricultural land of plenty. In Norse mythology, heroes slain in battle went to Valhalla, a golden palace in the gods' homeland where they would battle every morning and feast every noon forever. In Buddhism and in Hinduism, the soul is reincarnated (reborn in another body or form) until it achieves a state of spiritual perfection.

Encourage students to choose a religion or culture and investigate its beliefs about life after death. Students may also elect to examine the religious beliefs of two different cultures and compare and contrast their views of the afterlife. Have students examine the ways in which different religious beliefs express human values and emotions. Students can then report their findings in a presentation to the class.

God, as to any regard to your welfare. God will have no other use to put you to, but to suffer misery; you shall be continued in being to no other end; for you will be a vessel of wrath fitted to destruction; and there will be no other use of this vessel, but to be filled full of wrath. . . .

Thus it will be with you that are in an unconverted state, if you continue in it; the infinite might, and majesty, and terribleness of the omnipotent God shall be magnified upon you, in the ineffable strength of your torments. You shall be tormented in the presence of the holy angels, and in the presence of the Lamb,[4] and when you shall be in this state of suffering, the glorious inhabitants of Heaven shall go forth and look on the awful spectacle, that they may see what the wrath and fierceness of the Almighty is; and when they have seen it, they will fall down and adore that great power and majesty. . . .

It would be dreadful to suffer this fierceness and wrath of Almighty God one moment; but you must suffer it to all eternity. There will be no end to this exquisite horrible misery. When you look forward, you shall see a long forever, a boundless duration before you, which will swallow up your thoughts and amaze your soul; and you will absolutely despair of ever having any deliverance, any end, any mitigation, any rest at all. . . .

How dreadful is the state of those that are daily and hourly in the danger of this great wrath and infinite misery! But this is the dismal case of every soul in this congregation that has not been born again, however moral and strict, sober and religious, they may otherwise be. Oh that you would consider it, whether you be young or old! . . . Those of you that finally continue in a natural condition, that shall keep you out of Hell longest will be there in a little time! Your damnation does not slumber; it will come swiftly, and, in all probability, very suddenly upon many of you. You have reason to wonder that you are not already in Hell. It is doubtless the case of some whom you have seen and known, that never deserved Hell more than you, and that heretofore appeared as likely to have been now alive as you. Their case is past all hope; they are crying in extreme misery and perfect despair; but here you are in the land of the living and in the house of God, and have an opportunity to obtain salvation. What would not those poor damned hopeless souls give for one day's opportunity such as you now enjoy!

And now you have an extraordinary opportunity, a day wherein Christ has thrown the door of mercy wide open, and stands in calling and crying with a loud voice to poor sinners; a day wherein many are flocking to him, and pressing into the kingdom of God. Many are daily coming from the east, west, north and south; many that were very lately in the same miserable condition that you are in, are now in a happy state, with their hearts filled with love to him who has loved them, and washed them from their sins in his own blood, and

---

4. **the Lamb** Jesus.

from Sinners in the Hands of an Angry God ◆ 111

Literary Analysis
Sermon and Oratory
What action is this passage beginning "But this is the dismal case" designed to inspire?

9 ☑ **Reading Check**
What does Edwards say will happen when the day of mercy has passed?

8 Literary Analysis
Sermon and Oratory

- Invite students to explain the basic purpose of oratory.
  Answer: Oratory is intended to persuade listeners and to inspire them to take action.

- Ask a student volunteer to read the first three sentences of the third paragraph on p. 111.

▶ **Monitor Progress**

- Ask students the Literary Analysis question on p. 111: What action is the passage beginning "But this is the dismal case" designed to inspire?
  Answer: This passage is designed to inspire parishioners to repent for their sins and convert their hearts by becoming "born again."

9 ☑ **Reading Check**

Answer: He says that sinners "will be wholly lost and thrown away of God" and that "God will have no other use to put you to, but to suffer misery."

CUSTOMIZE INSTRUCTION FOR UNIVERSAL ACCESS	
For Less Proficient Readers	**For Gifted/Talented Students**
Invite students to engage in choral readings of parts of Edwards's sermon. (You might wish to alternate students' choral readings with your own reading aloud.) Choose short passages for students to read together, and encourage discussion after each passage of important images, symbols, and ideas. Encourage students to listen for repetition of words, phrases, or ideas.	Invite students to prepare oral interpretations of passages from Edwards's sermon. Have them consider various ways to make the work accessible to an audience, such as gestures, correct pronunciation, appropriate speaking rate, volume, pitch, and tone. Remind students that all of these elements must be properly utilized to achieve just the right mood for the sermon.

⑩ Reading Strategy

Using Context Clues

- Read aloud with students the selection's penultimate paragraph. Have them listen for images suggesting abundance.

- Invite a student volunteer to explain what it means to *feast*.

- Ask students the Reading Strategy question on p. 112: What clue does the reference to "feasting" provide to the meaning of *perishing*?
  Answer: Edwards sets up a series of opposites in this passage. Thus, knowing that *feasting* means "eating a rich and elaborate meal" suggests that *perishing* means "dying" as from lack of nourishment.

Answers for p. 112

Review and Assess

1. Possible responses: **(a)** fearful, humbled, and confused **(b)** shocked to learn of the Puritans' harsh religious beliefs **(c)** impressed by the power, and beauty of Edwards's oratory.

2. **(a)** the hand of God **(b)** His listeners mistakenly believe that their behavior keeps them from falling into Hell.

3. **(a)** The words *angry* and *sinners* suggest the emotional focus of Edwards's message. **(b)** He presents God as indifferent, contemptuous, and merciless, although capable of pity as well.

4. **(a)** mercy and salvation; **(b)** To obtain these things, sinners must repent.

5. **(a)** Sample response: black clouds hanging over the heads of sinners and dammed waters waiting to burst through the floodgate; **(b)** According to Edwards's creed, all of nature is controlled by God. Images of destructive and powerful nature thus become symbolic of God's own power.

6. Sample answer: Edwards's sermon was highly effective. Even contemporary readers can feel the sting of Edwards's threats.

7. **(a)** Students might mention subjects such as the perils of substance abuse. **(b)** Students should support their opinions with clearly stated reasons, examples, and details.

112

---

rejoicing in hope of the glory of God. How awful is it to be left behind ⑩ at such a day! To see so many others feasting, while you are pining and perishing! To see so many rejoicing and singing for joy of heart, while you have cause to mourn for sorrow of heart, and howl for vexation of spirit! . . .

Therefore, let everyone that is out of Christ now awake and fly from the wrath to come. The wrath of Almighty God is now undoubtedly hanging over a great part of this congregation: let everyone fly out of Sodom.[5] "Haste and escape for your lives, look not behind you, escape to the mountain, lest you be consumed."[6]

---

5. **Sodom** (säd´ em) In the Bible, a city destroyed by fire because of the sinfulness of its people.
6. **"Haste . . . consumed"** from Genesis 19:17, the angels' warning to Lot, the only virtuous man in Sodom, to flee the city before they destroy it.

Review and Assess

Thinking About the Selection

1. **Respond:** How might you have reacted to this sermon if you had been **(a)** a "Puritan," **(b)** a Native American, **(c)** another leader of the Great Awakening? Explain.

2. **(a) Recall:** According to the opening paragraph, what keeps sinners from falling into hell? **(b) Interpret:** According to Edwards, what do his listeners mistakenly feel keeps them from falling into hell?

3. **(a) Recall:** What words in the sermon's title suggest the emotional focus of Edwards's message? **(b) Analyze:** What additional traits does Edwards attribute to God as the sermon progresses?

4. **(a) Recall:** Toward the end of the sermon, what does Edwards say sinners can obtain? **(b) Analyze Cause and Effect:** What must sinners do to obtain these things?

5. **(a) Classify:** Note at least two images of natural destruction that Edwards uses to depict the wrath of God. **(b) Evaluate:** Why would images of the power of nature be particularly appropriate to Edwards's message?

6. **Evaluate:** Given his purpose and the audience of worshipers to whom he spoke, do you think Edwards's sermon was effective? Why or why not?

7. **(a) Extend:** For what other types of subjects might an appeal to an audience's fears be an effective persuasive technique? **(b) Judge:** Do you think it is right for a speaker to appeal to an audience's fears? Why or why not?

ASSESSMENT PRACTICE: Reading Comprehension

Summarizing Written Texts   (For more practice, see Test Preparation Workbook, p. 7.)

Many tests require students to identify the best summary of a written passage. Present the following sample, and ask students to choose the best summary.

However you may have reformed your life in many things, and may have had religious affections, and may keep up a form of religion in your families and closets, and in the house of God, it is nothing but his mere pleasure that keeps you from being this moment swallowed up in everlasting destruction.

A God can still condemn you even if you live virtuously, pray privately, and go to church.

B God will pardon you if you go to church.

C People should pray and lead virtuous lives.

D People should be religious in order to win God's approval.

B is accurate, but incomplete. C and D are misleading: praying and being religious don't necessarily secure God's grace. *A* is the best summary.

Review and Assess

Literary Analysis

Sermon

1. What point of view or message is Edwards conveying in this **sermon**?
2. (a) To what emotion does Edwards primarily appeal in his effort to motivate his congregation? (b) Considering Edwards's purpose, why is this an appropriate choice? Explain your answer.
3. (a) Use the chart shown here to identify the many symbols and images Edwards uses to describe God's wrath.

(b) How do these symbols and images add to the impact of Edwards's message?
4. What does Edwards seem to feel about those who maintain a "form of religion" or who seem "moral and strict"?

Connecting Literary Elements

5. What statements does Edwards make that indicate an understanding of the people he is addressing?
6. Why might Edwards's **oratory** have been less effective if he had not had a reputation as a brilliant spiritual leader?

Reading Strategy

Using Context Clues

7. Use **context clues** to define the italicized words:

(a) "you are every day treasuring up more wrath; the waters are constantly rising, and *waxing* more and more mighty. . . ."
(b) "The God that holds you over the pit of Hell, much as one holds a spider, or some loathsome insect over the fire, *abhors* you, and is dreadfully provoked. . . ."

Extend Understanding

8. **Cultural Connection:** In which situations, if any, is it justifiable to use fear to get a person to improve his or her behavior? Explain.

from Sinners in the Hands of an Angry God ◆ 113

Quick Review

A **sermon** is a speech that has a definite point of view and is delivered from the pulpit during a worship service.

Oratory is public speaking that is formal, persuasive, and emotionally appealing.

Using the **context**—the surrounding words or sentences—can be an effective way to unlock the meaning of an unfamiliar word.

 Take It to the Net
www.phschool.com
Take the interactive self-test online to check your understanding of the selection.

✺ ENRICHMENT: Further Reading

Other Works by Jonathan Edwards

A Faithful Narrative (1737)
Some Thoughts Concerning the Present Revival (1743)

Take It to the Net
Visit www.phschool.com for more information on Jonathan Edwards.

Answers for p. 113
Review and Assess

1. Edwards is trying to convince his audience of the need to repent in order to save themselves from damnation.

2. (a) He appeals to his listeners' sense of fear and uncertainty. (b) It is an appropriate choice because it taps into listeners' existing doubts about the strength of their faith and virtuousness of their behavior. Their fear of damnation might make them heed Edwards's message.

3. (a) Possible responses include *bow and arrow*, *fire*, and *rough wind*. (b) These symbols and familiar, concrete images reinforce the idea of God as a hostile force with a variety of means—both physical and psychological—to cause human suffering.

4. Edwards seems to feel that these individuals will nonetheless be viewed by God as contemptible.

5. Possible response: He appeals to their innate sense of fear and humility. He describes their religious beliefs accurately.

6. Edwards's reputation preceded him; it made people give greater credence to his message. Had he been less famous, the congregation might have doubted his motives or his techniques.

7. (a) *Waxing* means "growing or building." References to water that is "constantly increasing" and "constantly rising" and the words "more and more" indicate something that is getting larger in size. (b) *Abhors* means "detests or is disgusted by." If God feels towards the listener as he might toward a spider or "some loathsome insect," then *abhor* must be associated with feelings of hatred or disgust.

8. Students may say that scare tactics are justified in situations where someone's habits or actions endanger his or her health or well-being, or where attempts to reason with or educate the person are unsuccessful.

Answers for pp. 114–115

❶ Vocabulary Development

Word Analysis

1. b

2. a

3. c

Concept Development: Context

dolorous; ineffable; omnipotent

Spelling Strategy

1. provocation

2. preferable

3. opposite

❷ Grammar and Style

Practice

Sample rewrite: When we think of great preachers, Edwards is the name that most quickly comes to mind. Of the many Puritan sermonizers who rose to fame during the Great Awakening, Edwards is considered the most influential. Most of his writing appealed to reason; "Sinners" is his most emotional and most famous work.

Looking at Style

Sample response: " . . . ten thousand times greater than the strength of the stoutest, sturdiest devil in Hell . . . "—Edwards uses "greater" to compare a sinner's strength to that of a devil; he uses the superlatives "stoutest" and "sturdiest" to distinguish the particular devil among all devils.

Integrate Language Skills

❶ Vocabulary Development Lesson

Word Analysis: Latin Prefix *omni-*

The Latin prefix *omni-* means "all" or "every." *Omnipotent*, then, means "all-powerful." Each of the adjectives below contains the prefix *omni-*. Use the information in parentheses to match each adjective with the situation to which it best applies.

1. omniscient (*sciens* = knowing)
2. omnivorous (*vor* = to eat)
3. omnipotent (*potent* = powerful)

a. how a zoologist might describe an animal that eats both meat and plants
b. how a student might describe a brilliant teacher
c. how a prisoner might describe his jailer

❷ Grammar and Style Lesson

Forms of Adjectives and Adverbs

The **comparative** form of adjectives and adverbs is used to compare two things or ideas; the **superlative** form is used to compare more than two things or ideas. Many words follow the pattern below to indicate comparative and superlative degrees:

Regular form: Ann is *tall*.

Comparative: Yvette is *taller*.

Superlative: Miku is the *tallest*.

Other adjectives and adverbs use the words *more* or *most*, as in, "Ann is *more punctual* than Joe. Mina is the *most punctual* of all."

Concept Development: Context

Fill each blank in the following sentence with the appropriate word from the vocabulary list on page 107.

The citizens of Oz sighed with a ___?___ air, indicating their ___?___ sadness at learning that the Wizard they considered ___?___ was just an ordinary man, hiding behind a curtain.

Spelling Strategy

To decide how to spell the unstressed vowel sound represented by a schwa (ə), think of another form of the word in which the vowel is stressed. Then, use the same vowel. For example, think of *morality*, and you will know to use an *a* in *moral*. Correct the following misspelled words.

1. provacation   2. prefarable   3. oppasite

Finally, some forms such as "good, better, best" are irregular.

Practice Rewrite the following paragraph, correcting all errors in comparisons:

When we think of great preachers, Edwards is the name that quickliest comes to mind. Of the many Puritan sermonizers who rose to fame during the Great Awakening, Edwards is considered the more influential. Most of his writing appealed to reason; "Sinners" is his most emotional and more famous work.

Looking at Style Review the sermon, and find an adjective and an adverb in each form. Explain how Edwards uses each one to create a powerful image.

WG *Prentice Hall Writing and Grammar Connection: Chapter 24, Section 1*

114 ◆ Beginnings–1750

TEACHING RESOURCES

The following resources can be used to enrich or extend the instruction for pp. 114–115.

Vocabulary

📖 **Selection Support Workbook:** Build Vocabulary, p. 29

📖 **Vocabulary and Spelling Practice Book**

Grammar

📖 **Selection Support:** Grammar and Style, p. 30 ▪

WG **Writing and Grammar,** Ruby Level, p. 620

📖 **Daily Language Practice Transparencies**

Writing

WG **Writing and Grammar,** Ruby Level, p. 309 ▪

💿 **Writing and Grammar iText CD-ROM**

📖 **Writing Models and Graphic Organizers on Transparencies,** p. 25

▪ **BLOCK SCHEDULING:** Resources marked with this symbol provide varied instruction during 90-minute blocks.

❸ Writing Lesson

Evaluation of Persuasion

A speaker's choice of persuasive techniques should depend on the audience and the occasion. Write an evaluation of the persuasive techniques of imagery and theme that Edwards uses. Discuss the response he evokes and the ways he achieves it. Your evaluation will have greater clarity and strength if its elements work together to form a unified effect.

Prewriting To help focus your writing, jot down examples of Edwards's uses of imagery and identify his specific themes. Then, evaluate their effectiveness in a clearly defined statement.

Drafting Use the statement you wrote as the basis for a strong, focused opening paragraph. Support your main point in the paragraphs that follow.

> **Model: Building Unity**
>
> Jonathan Edwards appealed to his audience's vulnerability by using powerful, elemental images of nature run amok. His images of air, water, and fire terrified his audience by summoning up mental pictures of unlimited natural destruction.

> A general statement followed by specific examples builds unity.

Revising Read your evaluation as though you were seeing it for the first time. Eliminate any information that is unrelated to the main idea.

 Prentice Hall Writing and Grammar Connection: Chapter 14, Section 3

❹ Extension Activities

Listening and Speaking Sermons like those of Dr. Martin Luther King, Jr., still have the power to inspire us. With a group, research Dr. King's sermons and their role in the civil rights movement. Give a brief **oral report** on your findings. To increase your listeners' interest, include the following:

- direct quotes from Dr. King's sermons
- quotes from reports in the media.

If possible, include a short video or audio tape of Dr. King as part of your report. **[Group Activity]**

Research and Technology Because of their religious beliefs, Puritans developed a strong sense of the importance of work. Gather information about Puritan doctrine and the famous "work ethic." Create a **handbook** that includes guidelines and rules for living and working as a proper Puritan.

 Take It to the Net www.phschool.com

Go online for an additional research activity using the Internet.

from Sinners in the Hands of an Angry God ◆ 115

ASSESSMENT RESOURCES

The following resources can be used to assess students' knowledge and skills.

Selection Assessment

 Formal Assessment, pp. 30–32

📖 **Open Book Test**, pp. 19–21

📼 **Got It! Assessment Videotapes**

⊙ **Test Bank Software**

💻 *Take It to the Net*
Visit www.phschool.com for self-tests and additional questions on the selection.

Listening and Speaking Rubric

📖 **Performance Assess. and Portfolio Mgmt.**, p. 17

 PRENTICE HALL
ESSMENT *SYSTEM*

📖 **Workbook**   📕 **Transparencies**

📖 **Skill Book**   ⊙ **CD-ROM**

---

❸ Writing Lesson

- Students' evaluations should express a clear and definite view of Edwards's achievement in this excerpt from *Sinners in the Hands of an Angry God*. Remind students that the effectiveness of the sermon is related directly to Edwards's Puritan audience, not to a contemporary American one.

- Students should not only identify Edwards's principal themes, but should also explain how these themes interrelate. Similarly, students should cite the sermon's key images and symbols and explain how they reinforce each other.

- Use the Writing Lesson, as well as Writing Process Model 5 in **Writing Models and Graphic Organizers on Transparencies**, p. 25 to guide students in developing their evaluations of persuasion.

❹ Listening and Speaking

- Encourage students to use various types of research sources. Possible print sources include biographies of Dr. King, oral histories of the civil rights movement, encyclopedias, and newspaper and magazine articles. In addition, students may be able to locate audio recordings of King's sermons and speeches, as well as video documentaries such as *Eyes on the Prize*. Lastly, students might use the Internet to gather additional information.

- For their oral presentations, encourage students to provide written transcripts of certain passages of sermons so that their classmates might follow along with the text as they listen to Dr. King's speaking style.

- Have students use the Peer Assessment form for Speech, p. 17 in **Performance Assessment and Portfolio Management.**

CUSTOMIZE INSTRUCTION
For Universal Access

To address different learning styles, use the following activities suggested in the **Extension Activities** booklet, p. 7.

For Verbal/Linguistic Learners, use Activity 5.

For Verbal/Linguistic and Bodily/Kinesthetic Learners, use Activity 6.

Objectives

1. To write an analytic essay on literary periods
2. To use writing strategies to generate ideas and to plan, organize, evaluate, and revise writing

Prewriting

- Have a class discussion on the ways in which the writers represented in this unit respond to their circumstances and their world. This discussion should help students find ideas for topics.

- Suggest that students take notes on the three selections they will explore in their essays. They can record their notes in the Argument Organizer on p. 75 of **Writing Models and Graphic Organizers on Transparencies.**

- When constructing their thesis statements, students should focus on common threads they find in their notes.

Writing About Literature

Analyze Literary Periods

Although the forms and context of earliest American literature are diverse, much of it deals with people's attempts to cope with the world around them. Strategies included everything from trying to overcome hunger and disease, to trying to set up a workable government, to trying to please an angry God. Writers' concerns reflected both their own belief systems and the circumstances in which they found themselves. Using the assignment outlined in the yellow box, write an analytical essay about this period in American literature.

Prewriting

Review the selections. Look for ways in which the writers try to cope with the world. Use these questions as a guide:

- Does the writer focus on the physical world?
- Does the writer focus on other people?
- Does the writer discuss political and social systems?
- Does the writing explain how the world was created?

Use index cards to note details of people's efforts to cope. On each card, identify the title of the selection and the page number, details describing people's actions or reactions, and the conclusions you draw from these details.

Conclusion: The urge to explore was limited by obstacles within the environment. This account shows that some newcomers survived by following the advice of local inhabitants.

Model: Drawing Conclusions Based on Evidence

"Boulders Taller Than the Great Tower of Seville"

p. 34 Two of the explorers descend the canyon, determining that the terrain is rough and the river is as wide as was previously reported by Indians.

p. 34 The explorers do not travel farther up the canyon because of the lack of water reported by their Indian guides.

Find a focus. Review your notes to find a working thesis that expresses the main idea you want to explore. Write the idea in one sentence, and use this sentence as a working thesis.

Gather details. Once you have your working thesis, focus on the relevant selections. Return to your index cards to gather more details. Then, identify the ideas that will best support your thesis statement.

116 ◆ Beginnings–1750

Assignment: Living in This World

Write an analytical essay that explores the way the earliest Americans (both Native Americans and European immigrants) tried to cope with their world.

Criteria:

- Include a thesis statement that draws on information from at least three different selections in the unit.
- Support your thesis with details from specific selections.
- Approximate length: 1,500 words.

📖 **Read to Write**
Reread the texts and focus on the motivation behind the individuals' questions, explanations, and struggles. Take notes to discover how those individuals attempted to cope with the world.

TEACHING RESOURCES

The following resources can be used to enrich or extend the instruction for pages 116–117.

𝒲𝒢 **Writing and Grammar,** Ruby Level, Chapter 12, pp. 242–260

📖 **Performance Assessment and Portfolio Management,** p. 21

📊 **Writing Models and Graphic Organizers on Transparencies,** p. 75

💿 **Writing and Grammar iText CD-ROM**

Students can use the following tools as they complete their comparison-contrast essays:

- Cause and Effect
- Topic Bank
- Unity and Coherence

Drafting

Organize into paragraphs. You might want to write a separate paragraph for each selection that illustrates your thesis, or you might choose to devote each paragraph to a unique concept that all the selections you have identified support.

Two Approaches to Paragraph Organization

By Selection		Selection One	Selection Two
Survival required • getting food and shelter. • overcoming enemy attacks.	····▶	Discuss all the ways in which this selection supports your thesis.	Discuss all the ways in which this selection supports your thesis.

By Subject		Aspect One	Aspect Two
Survival was threatened by hostilities between old and new arrivals.	····▶	Analyze all of the selections that illustrate this idea.	Analyze all of the selections that illustrate this idea.

Develop each paragraph. Develop each paragraph, supplying details from the selections that clearly support your ideas.

Revising and Editing

Review content: Check the relevance of details. Review each paragraph, evaluating the connection between the main idea and the support. Confirm that details are relevant, and delete those that do not further your analysis.

Review style and format: Replace unclear pronouns. Improve your writing by checking for unclear pronouns. Review your essay, circling each pronoun and checking that the word to which it refers will be clear to your readers.

Vague Referent: The *guides* told the *Spaniards* that the terrain was

dry and difficult, so (they) turned back.

Clarify the sentence above by replacing the pronoun with a noun that clearly refers to the Spaniards, such as *the European explorers*.

Publishing and Presenting

Hold a panel discussion. In today's world, we still have to figure out how to adapt to our environment and one another if we are to live successfully. Hold a panel discussion in which you and your classmates identify the selections that had the wisest lessons for today's reader.

W︠G Prentice Hall Writing and Grammar Connection: Chapter 14

✎ Write to Learn

Writing can help you transform vague ideas into a clear analysis.

✎ Write to Explain

Help your reader understand your reasoning by making clear connections between details from the selections and the conclusions you have drawn.

Drafting

Make sure students understand the two methods of organization: by selection and by subject. Students should choose the method that helps to make their essay clear.

Revising and Editing

Students may want to exchange papers with partners. Partners can help identify irrelevant details and unclear pronoun references. Students' ideas may be clear to them, but may not be clear to their readers.

Publishing and Presenting

You may want to organize students so that each selection is represented in each group, rather than grouping students who wrote about the same selection.

CUSTOMIZE INSTRUCTION FOR UNIVERSAL ACCESS

For Less Proficient Writers	For English Learners	For Advanced Writers
Have students identify their main arguments and list the supporting details. Remind them to return to the text for quotations that support their arguments.	Encourage students to include quotations from the selections in their essays. Students should be careful to copy these quotations exactly. They should look up any unfamiliar words to be sure the quotations support their ideas.	Encourage students to review their essays, making sure they have explained the relevance of each quotation, rather than simply including it in the text.

Lesson Objectives

1. To write an autobiographical narrative

2. To use writing strategies to generate ideas and to plan, organize, evaluate, and revise writing

Model from Literature

The Interesting Narrative of the Life of Olaudah Equiano, p. 44, is a gripping autobiographical narrative that conveys both a factual account of events and a record of the writer's emotions.

Prewriting

- Have students look at the topics of the autobiographical narratives in Unit 1. Point out that Columbus, Cabeza de Vaca, and Equiano all write about journeys. Suggest that students consider writing about journeys they have taken.

- Discuss occasions on which students will have to do some research. Explain that research will be needed only if students refer to factual events with details they do not recall, or if they need to clarify the context in which they are writing for their readers.

- Before students draft their essays, have them review the Rubric for Self-Assessment (p. 121) so they know what is expected.

Writing WORKSHOP

Narration: Autobiographical Narrative

An **autobiographical narrative** is a work in which a writer relates an experience from his or her life. In this workshop, you will write an autobiographical narrative that tells a story from your life.

Assignment Criteria Your autobiographical narrative should have the following characteristics:

- The writer as the main character
- A sequence of events that leads to an insight gained by the writer
- Action that incorporates shifts in time and mood
- Concrete details that locate and describe the sights, sounds, and smells of scenes and incidents
- Personal feelings, thoughts, and views of the writer

To preview the criteria on which your autobiographical narrative may be assessed, see the Rubric on page 121.

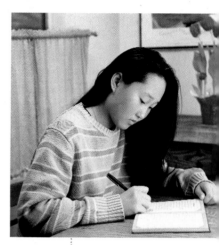

Prewriting

Choose a topic. For an entire day, keep an **idea notebook** that records your activities and thoughts. Consider these personal experiences as possible topics for exploration in your autobiographical narrative.

Isolate an episode. Once you have chosen your topic, list all the events related to it. Review the list, and choose a significant moment that you can develop into an effective piece of autobiographical narrative.

Add factual information. Some autobiographical incidents may require more information than is available to you through your memory or powers of observation. For such incidents, you will need to conduct research. For example, if you are describing an incident in a region or climate unknown to most people, you may have to add facts that place your experience in context. In the example shown here, factual details are italicized.

> **Example:** We flew *200 miles* to the nearest village. Throughout Antarctica, *planes are the primary mode of transportation.* I shook with fear for most of the flight.

Model: Isolating an Episode

- My mother's nocturnal schedule.
- The effect of the schedule on our relationship: We watched old TV shows, I saw mom reading books.
- I asked about a book of poems.
- I experienced "Patty Poem."
- I discovered the power of poetry.
- This event changed my life.

TEACHING RESOURCES

The following resources can be used to enrich or extend the instruction for pages 118–121.

WG **Writing and Grammar,** Ruby Level, Chapter 4, pp. 48–66

Performance Assessment and Portfolio Management, p. 9

Writing Models and Graphic Organizers on Transparencies, p. 13

Writing and Grammar iText CD-ROM

Students can use the following tools as they complete their autobiographical narratives:

- Topic Bank
- Self-Interview
- Timeline

Student Model

Before you begin to write, read this student model and review the characteristics of effective autobiographical narrative.

Branden Boyer-White
Palm Springs, California

Discovering Poetry

My mother was a night owl. She worked nights as a nurse at the hospital. She liked it; the schedule suited her. The nights she was off, she maintained her nocturnal routine—active at night and asleep in the early part of the day.

One early morning, I went into the living room to find my mother reading a thick book called *Best Loved Poems to Read Again and Again.* My interest was piqued solely by the fact that the word *Poems* appeared in big, hot pink letters.

	Branden uses concrete details to set the scene.

"Is it good?" I asked her.

"Yeah," she answered. "There's one you'll really like."

She began to thumb through the grainy white pages. She finally stopped and asked, "Ready?" I certainly was! I leaned forward.

"'Patty Poem,'" she read the title. *Who is Patty?* my mind buzzed. The poem began:

> *She never puts her toys away,*
> *Just leaves them scattered where they lay, . . .*

The poem was just three short stanzas. The final one came quickly:

> *When she grows and gathers poise,*
> *I'll miss her harum-scarum noise,*
> *And look in vain for scattered toys,*
> *And I'll be sad.*

	The inclusion of excerpts from the poem allows readers to understand the writer's emotional reaction.

A terrible sorrow washed over me. Whoever Patty was, she was a dreadful, mean girl. Then, the bombshell.

"It's you, honey," my mother sentimentalized.

To my mother, the poem captured a parent's nostalgic love when her child grows up and leaves. To me, the "she" in the poem was a horror. It was *my* mama who would be sad. It was so terrible I burst into tears.

"What's wrong?" my mother asked.

"Oh Mama," I babbled. "I don't want to grow up *ever*!"

	Dialogue makes the narrative more realistic and poignant.

She smiled. "Honey, it's okay. You're not growing up anytime soon. And when you do, I'll still love you, okay?"

"Okay," I hiccuped. My panic had subsided. But I could not stop thinking about that silly poem. After what seemed like a safe amount of time, I read the poem again, and was mystified. It all fit so well together, like a puzzle. The language was simple, so simple I could plainly understand its meaning, yet it was still beautiful. I was now transfixed by the idea of poetry, words that had the power to make or break a person's world. . . .

I have since fallen in love with other poems, but "Patty Poem" remains my poem. It was my first, and it will be mine to the end, because it brought me my love for poetry. This is a great testimony to the poignancy of the art. After all, "Patty Poem" gave me my love for poetry not because it was the verse that lifted my spirits, but because it was the one that hurt me the most.

	Branden clearly demonstrates the importance of this experience.

Student Model

- Explain that the Student Model is a sample. Students' own essays may be longer than this model.
- Have students read the model silently. Point out that Branden has centered her narrative around a crucial event that happened in her childhood. This may give students ideas for topics of their own.
- Have students discuss the details with which Branden sets the scene. Have them list specific details they will use in their own essays.
- Ask students how the essay would have been affected if Branden hadn't quoted from the poem. Answer: Point out that being able to read the poem themselves makes readers much more likely to identify with Branden's reaction to it.
- Have a student read the essay's final paragraph aloud. Help students see that Branden states the reason she chose her topic and that she connects her experience to a broader statement about human life with a reference to "the poignancy of art."

Real-World Connection

Autobiographical narratives in the real world: Tell students that most college applications ask students to write an essay on a given topic. Frequently, these essay topics are autobiographical. Cover letters for job applications are concise autobiographical essays, which include only certain relevant details.

CUSTOMIZE INSTRUCTION FOR UNIVERSAL ACCESS

For Less Proficient Writers	For English Learners	For Advanced Writers
Have students share with partners the stories they will use as the basis for their essays. Telling their stories orally as a prewriting activity will help students organize their ideas, eliminate irrelevant details and events, and shape the plots of their narratives.	During the prewriting stage, meet with students individually to discuss their topics. Encourage them to tackle subjects that will not pose the difficulty of too many new and unfamiliar words. Remind them that Hemingway and others wrote masterpieces in simple language.	Point out that in the next-to-last sentence of his essay, Branden links his experience to the universal human reaction to art, thus giving his essay an overall theme beyond its literal meaning. Challenge students to include thematic statements like this in their essays.

Drafting

- Because the climax of a story is its most interesting or suspenseful moment, it is the most important point in a story. Therefore, all the details that come before the climax should lead clearly to it.

- Students may find it helpful to write out the main events of their narratives in chronological order. They can then expand this list of events into an outline as they add the details that will flesh out the story.

Revising

- If time permits, let students wait 24 hours before they begin to revise their drafts. A little time away from a piece of writing helps the writer see his or her work with fresh eyes and renewed attention and energy.

- Reassure students that they need not force dialogue into their essays if it isn't a natural fit. Some essays, for example, may not include more than one character. If students' essays don't lend themselves to dialogue passages, have them think about other ways in which they might clarify a point or make it more effective.

(continued on p. 121)

120

Writing WORKSHOP *continued*

Drafting

Organize significant events. As you write, add the most significant events to your story, and order them in a logical sequence. Identify the climax, or point of highest interest. Then, arrange the other events to fit the structure of an event diagram as shown here.

Provide details. For each event in your narrative, provide concrete details that enrich the story and make it more vivid. Types of details include the following:

- Sights, sounds, and smells of a scene or incident
- Specific actions, movements, and gestures of key characters
- Locations where events occurred

Elaborate your feelings. As you draft, note where you could include more information about your thoughts or feelings at the time of the event. Jot these ideas down. If necessary, you can incorporate such details later, when you revise.

Climax: The conflict is greatest.

The conflict develops.

Suspense and tension decrease.

Exposition— The scene is set.

Resolution

Revising

Revise to add dialogue and description. Read your draft, and highlight points in the narrative that might be made clearer or more emotionally effective with the inclusion of dialogue or description. Pay special attention to those parts of your story in which emotions are most intense, as well as to points at which one character's actions directly affect another character. Jot down these details on a separate piece of paper, and incorporate them into your revised draft.

Model: Adding Dialogue

To my mother, the poem captured a parent's nostalgic love

when her child grows up and leaves. To me, the "she" in the poem

was a horror. It was *my* mama who would be sad. It was so terrible

I burst into tears.

"What's wrong?" my mother asked.

~~My mother seemed concerned, and asked me what was wrong.~~

"Oh, Mama," I babbled. "I don't want to grow up ever!"

~~I told her that I did not want to grow up.~~

The use of dialogue makes a narrative more vivid and interesting to read.

USING TECHNOLOGY IN WRITING

When they reach the revision stage, students working on word processors may want to print out double-spaced copies of their drafts. They can mark up these copies with pens and highlighters, noting changes they plan to make. A double-spaced text allows plenty of room to write between the lines, and the hard copy allows students to spread the pages out and look at the essay as a whole, rather than seeing only a few lines of it at once on a screen. Students can use these marked-up copies to make the changes on the computer. Encourage them to save their drafts so that they can compare them to the revised version.

Revise word choice. To bring your narrative to life for your readers, use active language rather than vague or general words. Choose vivid action verbs, precise adjectives, and specific nouns to convey your meaning.

Vague: There *were* lightning and wind all night.

Vivid: Lightning *crashed,* and wind *gusted* all night.

Compare the model and the non-model. Why is the model more effective than the non-model?

Nonmodel	Model
"Okay," I said. My fear had gone. But I could not stop thinking about that poem.	"Okay," I hiccuped. My panic had subsided. But I could not stop thinking about that silly poem.

Publishing and Presenting

Share your writing with a wider audience by presenting your narrative to your classmates.

Deliver an oral presentation. Practice reading your autobiographical narrative aloud. Mark a copy of your finished draft, underlining any dialogue, thoughts, quotations, or descriptions. As you present the narrative to your classmates, emphasize those passages.

Produce an Illustrated Anthology. With classmates, combine several essays in a single binder. To enhance each narrative, include photographers or artwork that capture the mood the writing achieves.

WG Prentice Hall Writing and Grammar Connection: Chapter 4

Rubric for Self-Assessment

Evaluate your autobiographical narrative using the following criteria and rating scale:

Criteria	Rating Scale				
	Not very				Very
How well established is the writer as the main character?	1	2	3	4	5
How effectively organized is the sequence of events?	1	2	3	4	5
How well does the action accommodate shifts in time and mood?	1	2	3	4	5
How powerfully are concrete and sensory details used to describe events?	1	2	3	4	5
How well does the narrative convey the feelings of the writer?	1	2	3	4	5

TEST-TAKING TIP

When students encounter test prompts that ask them to write autobiographical essays, remind them not to waste too much time agonizing over a topic. Students should read the test prompt carefully to determine whether it sets any limits to the topic. Then, they should choose a topic they know well, and move ahead to the prewriting phase. Remind them to leave enough time to reread their essays and to revise them with requirements given in the prompt in mind.

Revising *(continued)*

• Challenge students to eliminate linking verbs from their essays. Go over the model on this page to show them how to do this. Then, write a few sentences with linking verbs on the chalkboard and challenge students to make them active and interesting.

Examples

1. The crowd was noisy. (The crowd roared and cheered.)

2. He was angry. (His eyes narrowed, his lips grew tight, and he clenched his fists.)

3. Miles was a musician. (Miles coaxed gorgeous melodies out of his battered saxophone.)

Publishing and Presenting

• Have students discuss how they might revise their essays if they planned to share them with an audience other than their classmates. What changes might they have to make?

• Have students try telling their stories from memory rather than reading their essays aloud. Since the narratives are autobiographical, students should easily be able to do this. Have students discuss the differences between the written and oral versions of the stories. How are they different? Why are they different?

Assessment

• Go over the assessment criteria with the class before they begin the revision stage of the essay. The points in the chart are things students will want to consider as they revise their drafts.

• You may want to have students exchange papers with partners and score one another's essays. If students disagree strongly, they should debate their reasons for disagreeing.

• The rubric on this page, and another rubric in an alternative format, can be found on pp. 9 and 34 of **Performance Assessment and Portfolio Management.**

Lesson Objectives

1. To prepare, rehearse, and deliver a speech

2. To modify a speech to fit an audience

3. To perform and present a speech effectively

Organizing Content

- A speech's main idea is its most important point. Communicating this main idea to the audience is the goal of the speech. Students should state the main idea at least twice in the course of the speech, preferably at the beginning and at the end.

- Remind students to include necessary background information depending on their audience. If they speak to their classmates on an issue relating to the school, for instance, they need not include background information. If they give the same speech to a gathering of outside citizens, they might need to provide some background.

- Remind students to keep their language appropriate to their audience.

Giving the Speech

- Students should go over their speeches frequently before delivering them, making sure that they are familiar with the main points and supporting details. They need not memorize the text word for word, but they should be very familiar with it so they can make eye contact with the audience rather than reading the whole speech from their notes.

- Do not require students to use visuals or sound effects. These may not be appropriate to every speech. Remind them that Lincoln's *Gettysburg Address* and Martin Luther King's "I Have a Dream" speech were delivered with no special effects but have proved unforgettable nonetheless.

Whether you are recounting an autobiographical incident while accepting an award or explaining the new student-government rules, delivering speeches offers a unique opportunity to convey ideas. The following speaking strategies can help you master the components of **speech delivery**.

Organizing Content

Before you begin rehearsing your speech, spend time planning and refining the content you will present.

Focus on purpose. Determine whether your purpose is narrative or informative. Then, choose and develop main points and details that suit your purpose.

Modify to fit your audience. Keep the knowledge level and interest of your audience in mind when you organize content. With a general audience, for example, plan frequent pauses to refer to explanatory visual material. Choose examples and illustrations, such as personal anecdotes and common experiences, that will draw your audience in.

Craft the speech. Using numbered index cards like the ones shown here, outline your main ideas. Then, choose from techniques such as rhetorical questions, figurative language, and dialogue to convey your ideas. You can keep the interest level high by choosing and combining informal expressions, Standard English, and technical language as dictated by your material.

Giving the Speech

Effective speakers use appropriate rehearsal and delivery strategies to keep audiences engaged.

- **Performance details** Memorize main ideas so that you can refer only briefly to notes, and maintain eye contact with the audience.
- **Special effects** Use sound or visual effects, graphics, and background music to enhance your presentation.
- **Artistic staging** Choose movements and gestures that support the speech content and suit the occasion.

Activity: Prepare and Deliver a Speech
Choose a situation, audience, and purpose for which you might deliver a speech. Then, prepare, rehearse, and deliver a three-minute speech. Use index cards to highlight and sequence key ideas. Ask classmates for feedback so you can improve your public speaking skills.

122 ◆ Beginnings–1750

I NEW STUDENT GOVERNMENT

Announce new government

A. Format and Rules
B. Offices

II GOALS FOR SCHOOL YEAR

A. Develop priorities and clear vision
B. Focus on 5 key projects
C. Raise necessary funds

III HOW TO GET INVOLVED

A. Come to meetings
B. Join project committees
C. Help raise funds

CUSTOMIZE INSTRUCTION FOR UNIVERSAL ACCESS

For English Learners

Giving a speech is a good opportunity for these students to practice their spoken English. Give them plenty of time to rehearse their speeches. Suggest that, if possible, they deliver their speeches in advance before an audience, such as a friend or family member. Remind students that speaking clearly and intelligibly is very important. If students are shy because they speak with strong foreign accents, reassure them that the United States is full of regional accents: Abraham Lincoln and Martin Luther King had very well-defined regional accents. Remind students that they will have their written speeches in front of them; they need not memorize the text.

Assessment WORKSHOP

Summaries of Written Texts

The reading sections of some tests often require you to identify the implied main idea in a passage. They may also require you to choose the best summary of a passage. Use these strategies to help you answer test questions on these skills:

- As you read, identify the sentence in the text that best expresses the main idea of the passage.
- If you are having difficulty identifying the implied main idea, ask yourself, "What general idea is the writer expressing?"

Test Taking Strategies

- Look for the details in the passage that will help you identify the main idea.
- Taking notes as you read is an active way to organize and condense the material.

Sample Test Item

Directions: Read the passage, and then answer the question that follows.

Haiku are three-line poems in which the first and third lines contain five syllables and the second line contains seven syllables. This form of poetry, which originated in Japan, reflects Japanese views of simplicity and nature. Matsuo Bashō, a seventeenth-century Japanese poet, is credited with making haiku an important art form.

1. Which of the following choices best expresses the main idea implied in the first paragraph?

   A Haiku originated in Japan.

   B Bashō was the first great haiku poet.

   C Haiku is a unique and important art form in Japan.

   D People have been writing haiku for 300 years.

Answer and Explanation

The correct answer is *C*. Answers A, B, and D give background information. C contains the implied main idea.

▶ Practice

Directions: Read the passage, and then answer the question that follows.

Born into a wealthy family in the seventeenth century, Bashō left home to study Zen Buddhism, history, and classical Chinese poetry. His nomadic life increased the popularity of haiku—a concise style of lyric poetry—as he shared his verse in the communities through which he passed. Most literary historians agree that he was influential in building the recognition of haiku as a poetic form.

1. Which of the following is the best summary of this paragraph?

   A Uniquely Japanese, haiku is a concise poetic form popularized by the seventeenth-century poet Bashō.

   B Most literary historians agree that Bashō was an important poet.

   C Haiku would never have developed as a separate form were it not for wandering poets.

   D Bashō, a seventeenth-century poet, popularized haiku.

Assessment Workshop ◆ *123*

Lesson Objective
To summarize written texts in standardized-test situations

Applying Reading Strategies
Remind students that a summary expresses the main idea of a paragraph. When students are dealing with a brief text like a paragraph, the summary and the main idea are the same thing.

Test-Taking Skills

- Have students read the sample test item. Ask them to identify the main idea of the paragraph. Answer: Haiku are Japanese poems about nature.
- Have students vote for the correct answer. If any students choose incorrect answers, challenge them to reread the paragraph to find the correct answer.

Answer

The correct answer is *D*. Choices A, B, and C include information not stated in the paragraph.

TEACHING RESOURCES

The following resources can be used to enrich or extend the instruction on page 123.

 PRENTICE HALL
 ASSESSMENT *SYSTEM*

 Workbook   **Transparencies**

 Skill Book   **CD-ROM**

Unit Objectives

1. To read selections from the American literary tradition written between 1750 and 1800

2. To apply a variety of reading strategies, particularly strategies for constructing meaning, to these selections

3. To analyze literary elements

4. To use a variety of strategies to build vocabulary

5. To learn elements of grammar, usage, and style

6. To use recursive writing processes to write in a variety of forms

7. To develop listening and speaking skills

8. To express and support responses to various types of texts

9. To prepare, organize, and present literary interpretations

Meeting the Objectives

With each selection, you will find instructional material and opportunities through which students can meet these objectives. You will find additional practice pages for reading strategies, literary analysis, vocabulary, and grammar in the **Selection Support: Skills Development Workbook** in your **Teaching Resources**.

Background

Art

Washington Crossing the Delaware, by Emanuel Gottleib Leutze

On Christmas night, 1776, 2,400 American soldiers crossed the Delaware River from Pennsylvania to Trenton, New Jersey. George Washington commanded that campfires be left burning on the Pennsylvania side to fool the German-born Hessian mercenaries. The Hessians had celebrated the holiday and were asleep when the Americans attacked the next morning.

Which figure in the painting is George Washington? How do you know?

Answer: He is the man just to the left of the center, in the hat and red-lined cloak. Since his head is the highest in the painting, this is probably the commander.

124

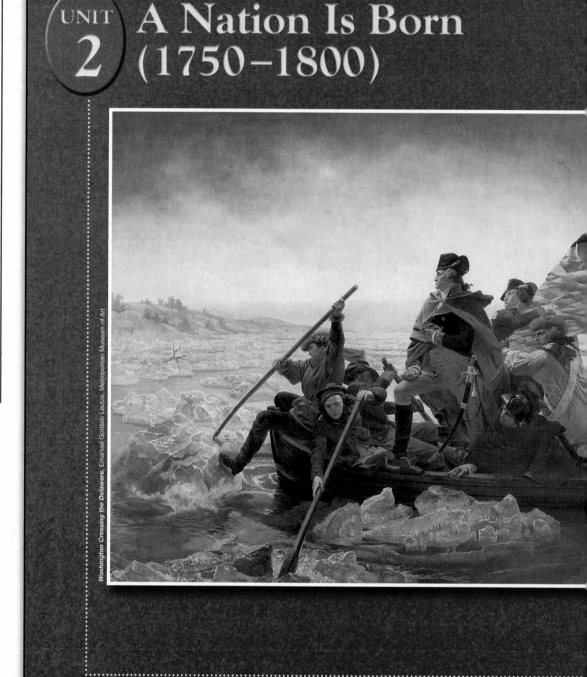

UNIT 2 A Nation Is Born (1750–1800)

Washington Crossing the Delaware, Emanuel Gottlieb Leutze, Metropolitan Museum of Art

UNIT FEATURES

Connections

Every unit contains a feature that connects literature to a related topic, such as art, science, or history. In this unit, students will connect literature from the past to literature from the present day.

Use the information and questions on the Connections page to help students enrich their understanding of the selections presented in the unit.

Reading Informational Materials

These selections will help students learn to analyze and evaluate informational materials, such as workplace documents, technical directions, and consumer materials. They will expose students to the organization and features unique to nonnarrative texts.

In this unit, students will learn to read newspaper editorials.

66 *The fate of unborn millions will now depend, under God, on the courage and conduct of this army. Our cruel and unrelenting enemy leaves us only the choice of brave resistance, or the most abject submission. We have, therefore, to resolve to conquer or die.* *99*

—George Washington,
addressing the Continental Army before
the battle of Long Island, August 27, 1776

ASSESSMENT RESOURCES

- 📖 **Selection Support: Skills Development Workbook**
- 📖 **Formal Assessment**
- 📖 **Open Book Tests**
- 📖 **Performance Assessment and Portfolio Management**
- 📖 **Extension Activities**

Assessing Student Progress

Listed below are the tools that are available to measure the degree to which students meet the unit objectives.

Informal Assessment

The questions in the Review and Assess sections are a first level of response to the concepts and skills presented within the selections. Students' responses are a brief, informal measure of their grasp of the material. These responses can indicate where further instruction and practice are needed. Then follow up with the practice pages in the **Selection Support: Skills Development Workbook.**

Formal Assessment

The **Formal Assessment** workbook contains Selection Tests and Unit Tests.

- Selection Tests measure comprehension and skills acquisition for each selection or group of selections.
- Each Unit Test provides students with 30 multiple-choice questions and five essay questions designed to assess students' knowledge of the literature and skills taught in the unit.

The **Open Book Tests** ask students to demonstrate their ability to synthesize and communicate information from selections or groups of selections.

To assess student writing, you will find rubrics and scoring models in the **Performance Assessment and Portfolio Management** booklet. In this booklet you will also find scoring rubrics for listening and speaking activities.

Alternative Assessment

The **Extension Activities** booklet contains writing activities, listening and speaking activities, and research and technology activities that are appropriate for students with different ability levels. You may also use these activities as an alternative measurement of students' growth.

Using the Timeline

The timeline can serve a number of instructional purposes, as follows:

Getting an Overview

Use the timeline to help students get a quick overview of themes and events of the period. This approach will benefit all students but may be especially helpful for visually oriented students, English learners, and those less proficient in reading. (For strategies in using the timeline as an overview, see the bottom of this page.)

Thinking Critically

Questions are provided on the facing page. Use these questions to have students review the events, discuss their significance, and examine the *so what* behind the *what happened.*

Connecting to Selections

Have students refer to the timeline when beginning to read individual selections. By consulting the timeline regularly, they will gain a better sense of the period's chronology. In addition, they will appreciate world events that gave rise to these works of literature.

Projects

Students can use the timeline as a launching pad for projects such as these:

- **Customized Timeline** Have students create period timelines in their notebooks, adding key details as they read new selections. They can use dates from this timeline as a starting framework.

- **Special Report** Have students scan the timeline for items that interest them, research these further, and report on them to the class.

126

Timeline 1750–1800

1750   1760   1770

American Events

- **1748** Benjamin Franklin retires from the printing business after 26 years. ▶

- **1752** Benjamin Franklin conducts his kite-and-key experiment with lightning. ▲
- **1753** African American Benjamin Banneker constructs the first striking clock with all parts made in America.
- **1754** French and Indian War begins.

Poor Richard, 1733.
AN
Almanack
For the Year of Christ
1733,

Being the First after LEAP YEAR:

By RICHARD SAUNDERS, Philom.
PHILADELPHIA:
Printed and sold by B. FRANKLIN, at the New Printing-Office near the Market.

- **1759–63** France gives up claims to North American territory.
- **1765** Stamp Act passed by British Parliament; colonists protest bitterly
- **1767** Townshend Acts impose new taxes, angering colonists further.

- **1773** Parliament's Tea Act prompts Boston Tea Party.
- **1773** Phillis Wheatley's *Poems on Various Subjects* published in England. ▶
- **1774** First Continental Congress meets in Philadelphia.
- **1775** The American Revolution begins.
- **1776** Second Continental Congress adopts Declaration of Independence. ▼

World Events

- **1755** France: School for deaf opens in Paris.
- **1755** England: Samuel Johnson publishes *Dictionary of the English Language.*
- **1759** France: Voltaire publishes *Candide,* satirizing optimism of the philosopher Leibniz.

- **1762** France: Jean Jacques Rousseau states his political philosophy in *The Social Contract.*
- **1763** Seven Years' War ends.
- **1769** Scotland: James Watt invents an improved steam engine.
- **1769** England: Richard Arkwright invents a frame for spinning; helps bring about factory system.

- **1770** Germany: Ludwig von Beethoven is born.
- **1774** England: Joseph Priestley discovers oxygen, named later by Lavoisier.
- **1779** South Africa: First of Kaffir wars between blacks and whites breaks out.

126 ◆ A Nation Is Born (1750–1800)

✴ ENRICHMENT: Getting an Overview of the Period

Introduction	Key Events
To give students an overview of the period, indicate the span of dates along the top of the timeline. Next, point out the division of the timeline into American and World Events, and have students practice scanning the timeline to look at both categories. Finally, tell them that the events in the Timeline represent beginnings, turning points, and endings.	This timeline tells the story of how America won its independence from Great Britain. Have students select items in the American Events section that help tell this story. **Possible answers:** Students might mention 1765, 1767, imposition of Stamp Acts and Townshend Acts; and 1774, meeting of First Continental Congress. What events after the Revolution show how the nation's identity was developing? **Possible answer:** Students might mention the election of George Washington in 1789 and the first census in 1790.

American and World Events

- **1781** General Cornwallis surrenders British army to George Washington at Yorktown. ▼

- **1783** Noah Webster's *Spelling Book* first appears; 60 million copies would be sold.
- **1783** Revolutionary War ends.
- **1787** Constitutional Convention meets in Philadelphia to draft Constitution.
- **1789** George Washington elected first President of United States.

- **1781** England: William Herschel discovers planet Uranus.
- **1786** Scotland: Robert Burns is widely acclaimed for his first book of poems.
- **1786** Austria: Wolfgang Amadeus Mozart creates the comic opera *The Marriage of Figaro.*
- **1789** France: Storming of Bastille in Paris sets off French Revolution.

- **1790** First federal U.S. census shows approximately 757,208 blacks in the U.S., nearly 20% of the total population. 59,557 are free.

- **1793** Eli Whitney invents cotton gin. ▶

- **1791** England: James Boswell publishes *The Life of Samuel Johnson.*
- **1793** France: King Louis XVI and Marie Antoinette executed.
- **1796** France: Napoleon Bonaparte comes to power in France. ▶
- **1798** England: William Wordsworth and Samuel Taylor Coleridge publish *Lyrical Ballads.*

- **1800** Second U.S. census shows a total population of 5,308,483.
- **1801** Thomas Jefferson, principal author of Declaration of Independence, elected President.
- **1804** Federalist leader Alexander Hamilton killed in a duel with Aaron Burr.

- **1800** Germany: Ludwig von Beethoven composes *First Symphony.*

Introduction ◆ 127

---

continued from right column

▶Critical Viewing

1. What does the picture reveal about Franklin's experiment with lightning?
   Answer: He used a kite to get a bolt of lightning to strike a key.

2. How do the writing implements shown with the entry on the Declaration of Independence help you imagine the writing of that document?

   Answer: The implements suggest that Jefferson wrote the Declaration with a quill pen. The pen appears to be dipped in an inkwell.

3. What does the picture indicate about the British surrender?
   Answer: It was conducted with a great deal of ceremony.

Analyzing the Timeline

1. **(a)** Which two entries between 1750 and 1760 mention Benjamin Franklin? **(b)** What do these entries reveal about Franklin's interests?
   Answer: **(a)** 1748, Franklin retires from the printing business. 1752, Franklin conducts kite-and-key experiment. **(b)** His interests were varied. Some were literary, and some were scientific.

2. **(a)** What did France give up between 1759 and 1763? **(b)** Suggest some causes for France's decision.
   Answer: **(a)** France gave up claims to territory in North America. **(b)** France may have engaged in a contest for it, probably with the British. France's giving up this territory suggests it lost the conflict.

3. **(a)** Which actions did Congress take between 1770 and 1780? **(b)** What ongoing story does this suggest?
   Answer: **(a)** Congress appointed Washington commander in chief of the American army and adopted the Declaration of Independence. **(b)** These events show America declaring her independence and preparing to fight for it.

4. **(a)** Name two technological developments that occurred in England in 1769. **(b)** How might these developments have affected people's lives?
   Answer: **(a)** An improved steam engine and the spinning jenny were invented. **(b)** These developments made possible mass-produced goods and the factory system. They probably drew people to work in cities.

5. **(a)** When was the first federal census taken? **(b)** What does it indicate about the status of blacks in the United States?
   Answer: **(a)** It was taken in 1790. **(b)** Blacks made up 20% of the total population. More than 90% of them were enslaved.

continued

- In "Speech to the Virginia Convention," p. 186, Patrick Henry demonstrates the fiery oratorical style that helped inspire Americans to revolutionary fervor.

- In selections such as "The Declaration of Independence," p. 156, and the excerpt from *The Crisis*, p. 160, students will find eloquent expression of the American wish for independence.

▶ **Critical Viewing**

Answer: The thirteen colonies enjoyed the strategic advantage of a long coastline. With several major ports, such as New York and Philadelphia, they could easily receive shipments of goods and troop transports.

A Nation Is Born
(1750–1800)

Historical Background

It is easy to forget how long the thirteen original states had been colonies. By 1750, there were fourth- and fifth-generation Americans of European descent living in Virginia and New England. These people were English subjects, and, on the whole, they were well satisfied with that status. In fact, as late as the early 1760s, few Americans had given much thought to the prospect of independence.

Between the mid-1760s and the mid-1770s, however, attitudes changed dramatically. King George III and Parliament imposed a number of regulations that threatened the liberties of the colonists. With each succeeding measure, the outrage in America grew, finally erupting into war.

The Age of Reason Great upheavals in history occur when circumstances are ripe. The American Revolution was such an upheaval, and the groundwork for it had been laid by European writers and thinkers as well as by the English king and Parliament. The eighteenth century is often characterized as the Enlightenment, or the Age of Reason. Spurred by the work of many seventeenth-century thinkers— such as scientists Galileo and Sir Isaac Newton, philosophers Voltaire and Jean-Jacques Rousseau, and political theorist John Locke—the writers and thinkers of the Enlightenment valued reason over faith. Unlike the Puritans, they had little interest in the hereafter, believing instead in the power of reason and science to further human progress. They spoke of a social contract that forms the basis of government. Above all, they believed that people are by nature good, not evil. A perfect society seemed to them to be more than just an idle dream.

The American statesmen of the Revolutionary period were themselves figures of the Enlightenment. No history of the period would be complete without mention of the ideas and writings of Benjamin Franklin, Thomas Paine, and Thomas Jefferson. These Americans not only expressed the ideas of the Age of Reason but also helped to put them spectacularly into practice.

North America in 1753

Claimed by Britain
Claimed by France
Claimed by Spain
= French forts

▲ Critical Viewing
On the eve of the French and Indian War, France still had claim to a majority of the interior of North America. What strategic advantage did the thirteen colonies enjoy because of their geographic location? **[Interpret]**

✳ ENRICHMENT: Social Studies Connection

The French and Indian War

The French and Indian War paved the way for the American Revolution. It strained the previously good relations between the colonies and the home country. The arrogance displayed by the British officers offended American military leaders such as Washington, and many New Englanders were shocked by what they regarded as the immorality of British soldiers.

During the years before the Revolution, the colonists began to develop their own identity—not English but American. They felt that though their manners were less formal than those of the British, their morals were superior. They began thinking of the British as corrupt people who had departed from the path of righteousness.

Toward a Clash of Arms The American Revolution was preceded by the French and Indian War, a struggle between England and France for control of North America. The conflict broke out in 1754 and continued for nearly a decade. When the war officially ended in 1763, defeated France gave up its claims to North American territory. There was general jubilation in the thirteen English colonies.

The good feelings were short-lived, however. The British government, wanting to raise revenue in the colonies to pay its war debt, passed the Stamp Act in 1765. Colonial reaction to the Stamp Act, which required the buying and affixing of stamps to each of 54 ordinary items, was swift and bitter. Stamps were burned. Stamp distributors were beaten and their shops destroyed. Eventually, the Stamp Act was repealed.

Other acts and reactions followed. The Townshend Acts of 1767 taxed paper, paint, glass, lead, and tea. When the colonists organized a boycott, the British dissolved the Massachusetts legislature and sent two regiments of British troops to Boston. In 1770, these Redcoats fired into a taunting mob, causing five fatalities. This so-called Boston Massacre further inflamed colonial passions. Parliament repealed the Townshend duties except for the tax on tea, but a separate Tea Act giving an English company a virtual monopoly soon greeted the colonists. Furious, a group of Bostonians dressed as Mohawks dumped a shipment of tea into Boston harbor. As punishment for this Boston Tea Party, the English Parliament passed the Coercive Acts. Because these laws shut down the port of Boston, forbade meetings other than annual town meetings, and insisted that British troops could be housed in colonists' homes, colonists immediately dubbed them the Intolerable Acts.

In September 1774, colonial leaders, although not speaking openly of independence, met in Philadelphia for the First Continental Congress. The British, their authority slipping away, appointed General Thomas Gage governor of Massachusetts. The stage was set for war.

"The Shot Heard Round the World" On April 19, 1775, 700 British troops met some 70 colonial minutemen on the Lexington green. A musket shot was fired (from which side, no one knows), and before the shooting that followed was over, eight Americans lay dead. The British marched west to Concord, where another skirmish took place. The encounters at Lexington and Concord, a landmark in American history, have been referred to as "the shot heard round the world." The American Revolution had begun, and there would be no turning back.

▲ **Critical Viewing**
Paul Revere's engraving of the Boston Massacre played a major role in whipping up colonial fury against the British. Revere purposefully distorted the events. Which details suggest the artist was pro-colonist? **[Analyze]**

Background
Art

The Boston Massacre, by Paul Revere

A group of Bostonians began taunting the British sentries and threw snowballs and perhaps stones at them. The soldiers ordered the colonists to back off and fired on them when they refused. Paul Revere, the Boston engraver, silversmith, and patriot, does not show this in his famous engraving of the event, copies of which were seen all over Boston and soon all over the colonies.

1. Compare and contrast Revere's engraving with what actually happened.
   Answer: The Bostonians provoked the quarrel. Only five people were killed. The quarrel was simply a street fight that escalated, not the slaughter of a defenseless group of peaceful citizens as the engraving suggests.

2. Why might Revere have chosen to distort the reality of the situation?
   Answer: He wanted to stir up fury against England.

▶**Critical Viewing**

Answer: The soldiers are armed, and they are shooting from close range. The colonists are unarmed, and some have already fallen. The calm dog in the foreground creates sympathy for the colonists.

Background
John Adams

The British soldiers arrested after the Boston Massacre asked future president John Adams, then a young Boston lawyer, to defend them. Adams, a fierce patriot, knew that it might cost him friends and respect to appear on the side of England. He also believed that any accused person, no matter who, deserved a fair trial. He agreed to defend them. The case came to trial in October, and all the soldiers were acquitted. Adams had acted on an important principle of the future American government—that everyone was equal under the law.

CUSTOMIZE INSTRUCTION FOR UNIVERSAL ACCESS

For Less Proficient Readers	For English Learners	For Advanced Readers
Have students preview the art and illustrations for this period before reading "A Nation Is Born." Have them make up questions based on the illustrations, and then read the text to find the answers.	Have students use the art and illustrations on these pages to speculate about the era. Have them read the boldfaced heads and formulate questions based on these heads. Then, they can read the text to find the answers.	Have students consider this question: Did the political revolution in America have a counterpart in literature? Explain. Students can use selections from this unit and from Unit 1 to support their answers.

129

Background

Revolutionary War Battles

At the Concord skirmish on April 19, 1775, two Americans fell, as did three redcoats. The British commander ordered a retreat to Boston. American snipers fired on the British troops all the way back, killing a total of 273 men.

In June, the Americans killed or wounded more than a thousand British soldiers at the Battle of Bunker Hill. Although all the fighting up to this point had occurred in Massachusetts, the revolt involved all of the colonies. Two days before Bunker Hill, the Second Continental Congress in Philadelphia had selected Virginian George Washington as commander in chief of the Continental Army.

The Battle of Saratoga in the fall of 1777 marked a turning point in the war. The British were surrounded and forced to surrender more than 5,000 men. When news of this victory reached Paris, the French government formally recognized the independence of the United States. Soon afterward, France began to commit troops to the American cause.

In June, the Americans killed or wounded more than a thousand British soldiers at the Battle of Bunker Hill. Although the fighting up to this point had taken place in Massachusetts, the revolt involved all the colonies. Two days before Bunker Hill, the Second Continental Congress, meeting in Philadelphia, had named a commander in chief of the official American army. He was George Washington of Virginia.

More than a year would pass before the colonies declared their independence. More than six years would pass before the war ended, although the Battle of Saratoga, in the fall of 1777, marked a turning point. At Saratoga, in upstate New York, the British were surrounded and 5,700 of them were forced to surrender. When news of the American victory reached Paris, the government of France formally recognized the independence of the United States. Soon afterward, France began to commit troops to aid the American cause.

After six years of fighting, the war finally came to an end at Yorktown, Virginia, on October 19, 1781. Aided by the French army and navy, and enlisting the service of African American soldiers, General Washington's army bottled up the 8,000-man British force under General Cornwallis. Seeing that escape was impossible, General Cornwallis surrendered.

Close-up on History

African Americans and Women in the Revolution

In 1776, more than a half million African Americans lived in the colonies. At first, the Continental Congress did not permit enslaved or free African Americans to join the American army. However, when the British offered to free any male slave who fought for the king, George Washington changed American policy and allowed free African Americans to enlist.

About 5,000 African Americans fought against the British. As this eyewitness account demonstrates, they fought with great courage:

> Three times in succession, [African American soldiers] were attacked . . . by well-disciplined and veteran [British] troops, and three times did they successfully repel the assault, and thus preserve our army from capture.

Women also helped in the struggle for independence. When men went off to war, they took on added work. They planted and harvested the crops that fed the army. They also made shoes and wove cloth for blankets and uniforms. Many women joined their soldier-husbands at the front, where they washed, cooked, and cared for the wounded.

A few women actually took part in battle. In 1778, Mary Ludwig Hays carried water to her husband and other soldiers. The soldiers called her Moll of the Pitcher or Molly Pitcher. When her husband was wounded, she took his place, loading and firing a cannon. Another woman, Deborah Sampson of Massachusetts, dressed as a man and fought in several battles. Later, she wrote about her experiences in the army.

ENRICHMENT: Social Studies Connection

A People's War

About 200,000 fighters served at one time or another in the American cause. Most of them were young, relatively poor men. They and their officers were paid badly, if at all, and poorly fed and clothed.

Some 5,000 African American men took part in the war, on both sides. African American and white women served on both sides as well. Many women followed husbands, lovers, or fathers into battle, cared for them, and nursed them. A few women actually fought in battles. Deborah Sampson, for example, disguised herself as a man, calling herself Robert Shurtleff, and served from May, 1782 to October, 1783. Her husband became the only man to receive a pension as a "widow" of a veteran!

The New Nation The path to self-government was not always smooth. After the Revolution, the Articles of Confederation established a "league of friendship" among the new states. This arrangement did not work well. The federal Constitution that replaced the Articles required many compromises and was ratified only after a long fight. Even then, a Bill of Rights had to be added to placate those who feared the centralized power that the Constitution conferred.

The old revolutionaries, by and large, remained true to their principles and continued their public duties. George Washington became the nation's first president. John Adams, a signer of the Declaration of Independence, succeeded him in that office. Then, in 1800, Americans elected as their president the brilliant statesman who had drafted the Declaration, one of the heroes of the Enlightenment, Thomas Jefferson.

▲ Critical Viewing
Patrick Henry criticized the Stamp Act in the Virginia House of Burgesses, and Virginia became the first colony officially to protest the new tax law. Based on this painting, what type of citizen do you think was generally elected to serve in the Virginia House of Burgesses? **[Draw Conclusions]**

Literature of the Period

A Time of Crisis In contrast to the private soul-searching of the Puritans of New England, much of what was produced during the Revolutionary period was public writing. By the time of the War for Independence, nearly thirty newspapers had been established in the coastal cities. At the time of Washington's inauguration, there were nearly forty magazines. Almanacs were popular from Massachusetts to Georgia.

The mind of the nation was on politics. Journalists and printers provided a forum for the expression of ideas. After 1763, those ideas were increasingly focused on relations with Great Britain and, more broadly, on the nature of government. As the literature presented in this unit testifies, the writing of permanent importance from the Revolutionary era is mostly political writing.

Politics as Literature The writing and speaking of American statesmen in two tumultuous decades, the 1770s and 1780s, helped to reshape not only the nation but also the world. James Otis of Massachusetts defended colonial rights vigorously in speeches and pamphlets. Otis is credited with giving Americans their rallying cry: "Taxation without representation is tyranny."

Patrick Henry was a spellbinding orator whose speech against the Stamp Act in the Virginia House of Burgesses brought cries of "Treason!" Ten years later, his electrifying speech to the Virginia Convention expressed the rising sentiment for independence.

Thomas Paine was perhaps more influential than any other in swaying public opinion in favor of independence. His 1776 pamphlet *Common Sense* swept the colonies, selling 100,000 copies in three months.

▶Critical Viewing
Answer: The men in the illustration look wealthy and educated.

Historical Background
Critical Thinking

1. Why did the Enlightenment idea that people have a right to happiness prove a spur to revolution?
   Answer: If happiness is a natural right, then any form of government that makes people suffer must be wrong. People are therefore justified in changing their government.

2. In what way did the French and Indian War sow the seeds of the American Revolution?
   Answer: The British war debt was the immediate cause for raising colonial taxes.

3. How were the colonists able to defeat England, a great world power?
   Answer: The colonists were fighting on familiar ground; the British were in an unknown land. The colonists used effective guerrilla tactics to which the British were unaccustomed.

Background

History

When Thomas Paine wrote *Common Sense*, he was a recent immigrant from England. Nevertheless, he was able to capture the revolutionary mood in the colonies. His pamphlet sold about 500,000 copies, compared to the few hundred copies most political pamphlets averaged.

During the Revolution, Paine wrote 16 pamphlets that were collectively called *The Crisis* (see p. 160 for an excerpt from *The Crisis, Number 1*). These pamphlets also sold widely.

Shortly after the Revolution, Paine returned to England. There he wrote a tract called *The Rights of Man*, which was a defense of the French Revolution. In this work, Paine argued that people enjoy natural rights and that governments have an obligation to guarantee these rights.

A Writer's Voice

Thomas Paine and the Age of Reason

The Age of Reason was not necessarily reasonable or moderate. Indeed, a chief characteristic of reason during this era was that it led some writers very far past old customs and institutions. Questioning the way things were, these writers reasoned their way to revolution.

You can see this link between reason and revolution in Thomas Paine's *Common Sense*. Even the title is an appeal to everyday logic, and throughout this pamphlet, Paine uses what George Washington called "unanswerable reasoning" to make the case for dramatic political changes.

from *Common Sense*

In the following pages I offer nothing more than simple facts, plain arguments, and common sense; and have no other preliminaries to settle with the reader than that he will divest himself of prejudice and prepossession [preconceived ideas] and suffer [allow] his reason and his feelings to determine for themselves. . . .

. . . it is not in the power of Britain to do this continent justice: The business of it will soon be too weighty, and intricate, to be managed with any tolerable degree of convenience, by a power so distant from us, and so very ignorant of us; for if they cannot conquer us, they cannot govern us. To be always running 3000 or 4000 miles with a tale or a petition, waiting four or five months for an answer, which when obtained required five or six more to explain it in, will in a few years be looked upon as folly and childishness—there was a time when it was proper, and there is a proper time for it to cease. . . .

The Declaration of Independence was first drafted by Thomas Jefferson in June 1776. The finished document is largely his work, although a committee of five statesmen, including Benjamin Franklin, was involved in its creation. The Declaration, despite some exaggerated charges against King George III, is one of the most influential political statements ever made.

Another Revolutionary-period document written by committee that has stood the test of time is the Constitution of the United States, drafted in 1787. The framers, whose new nation boasted about four million people, hoped that the Constitution would last at least a generation. It still survives, amended only 27 times, as the political foundation of a superpower of 50 states and more than 250 million people. However, not everyone in 1787 was pleased with the Constitution. Alexander Hamilton called it a "weak and worthless fabric," and Benjamin Franklin supported it only because, as he said, "I expect no better."

The doubts of the framers were reflected in the controversy over ratification. Delaware ratified the Constitution within three months, thus becoming the first state in the Union. However, the ratification of nine states was necessary before the document could go into effect. The last few states proved difficult. The contest between supporters and opponents was especially

132 ◆ A Nation Is Born (1750–1800)

 ENRICHMENT: Architecture Connection

Planning a Capital City

At Congress's request, George Washington himself chose the site of the capital city that would bear his name—the banks of the Potomac and Anacostia rivers. French engineer and architect Pierre Charles L'Enfant designed the city plan, inspired by his beloved Paris. Broad boulevards radiate from the circular drives surrounding important sites like the Capitol building and the lawns of the presidential mansion. Quarrels over details resulted in L'Enfant's replacement by African-American engineer Benjamin Banneker, who in turn had

to step down after three months owing to illness.

Many years passed before Washington became the gracious, majestic city today's tourists flock to visit. In 1842, Charles Dickens's reaction to Washington was, "Such as it is, it is likely to remain." In 1901, President Theodore Roosevelt appointed a commission that included landscaper Frederick Law Olmstead and architect Charles McKim to spruce up the city, make the Mall a permanent lawn, and build the monumental Union Station.

hard-fought in New York. Alexander Hamilton, who did not think highly of the Constitution, nevertheless wanted to see it pass in his home state. With James Madison and John Jay, he wrote a series of essays that were first published as letters to three New York newspapers. These essays, collected as *The Federalist*, served their immediate purpose. New York ratified the Constitution by a vote of 30 to 27. Over time, these essays have come to be recognized as authoritative statements on the principles of American government.

The Cultural Scene While politics dominated the literature of the Revolutionary period, not every writer of note was a statesman. Verse appeared in most of the newspapers, and numerous broadside ballads were published. (A broadside ballad is a single sheet of paper, printed on one or both sides, dealing with a current topic.) One of the most popular broadside ballads was called "The Dying Redcoat," supposedly written by a British sergeant mortally wounded in the Revolution. The sergeant in the ballad realizes too late that his sympathy lies with the American cause:

> Fight on, America's noble sons,
> Fear not Britannia's thundering guns:
> Maintain your cause from year to year,
> God's on your side, you need not fear.

One poet of the time whose works were more sophisticated than the broadside ballads was Philip Freneau, a 1771 graduate of Princeton. A journalist and newspaper editor, Freneau wrote poetry throughout his life. Several of his poems, such as "The Indian Burying Ground," earned him a reputation as America's earliest important lyric poet.

Two other poets of the day were Joel Barlow and Phillis Wheatley. Barlow, a 1778 Yale graduate, is best remembered for "The Hasty Pudding," a mock-heroic tribute to cornmeal mush. Phillis Wheatley, born in Africa and brought to Boston in childhood as a slave, showed early signs of literary genius. A collection of her poems was published in England while she was still a young woman.

Another writer of the Revolutionary period recorded his impressions of everyday American life. Born into an aristocratic French family, Michel-Guillaume Crèvecoeur became a soldier of fortune, a world traveler, and a farmer. For fifteen years, he owned a plantation in Orange County, New York, and his impressions of life there were published in London in 1782 as *Letters From an American Farmer*.

▲ Critical Viewing
This painting captures the writing of the Declaration of Independence. What do the many papers on the floor of the room suggest about the writing of the document? **[Draw Conclusion]**

Background

History

Help students identify the figures in the painting. Benjamin Franklin is seated at the left, John Adams is in the center, and Jefferson stands at the right. These three men, along with Robert Livingston of New York and Roger Sherman of Connecticut, had been assigned to a congressional committee to write a declaration of independence. The committee members agreed that Jefferson, considered by Adams the best writer in Congress, would write the document.

Contrary to the suggestion made by the painting, Jefferson's fellow committee members were pleased with his work and suggested no changes. However, the full Congress debated Jefferson's wording for three days, making numerous minor changes and one major change—the deletion of Jefferson's reference to slavery as "cruel war against human nature." Dismayed at this reaction to what he considered a brilliant expression of the American mind, John Adams hotly contested every suggested change.

▶**Critical Viewing**

Answer: The numerous crumpled papers suggest that the document underwent many revisions and that writing it was very hard work.

► Critical Viewing

Answer: The government's income was $4,418,000. It owed $81,497,000.

Perhaps the best-known writing of the period outside the field of politics was done by Benjamin Franklin. His *Poor Richard's Almanack* became familiar to most households in the colonies. In addition to information on the calendar and the weather common to most almanacs, it contained such sayings as these:

No man e'er was glorious, who was not laborious.
Make haste slowly.
Little Strokes, fell great Oaks.

A statesman, printer, author, inventor, and scientist, Franklin was a true son of the Enlightenment. His *Autobiography*, covering only his early years, is regarded as one of the finest autobiographies in any language.

Culture and Art During the Revolutionary period, America began to establish a cultural identity of its own. Theaters were built from New York to Charleston. Yet despite the energy invested in these enterprises, the plays produced were often little more than pale imitations of dramas that had achieved success in Britain. The first play written by an author born in America was Thomas Godfrey's tragedy *The Prince of Parthia* (1767). However, no truly American characters appeared in a play before Royall Tyler featured American types in his comedy *The Contrast* (1787). That play also dealt with a theme that would be popular in many early American dramas: the victory of honest Americans over deceitful foreigners. It is not hard to see how that theme might appeal to audiences who had lived through the Revolution.

A number of new colleges were established after the war, especially in the South. For example, what is today the University of Tennessee, Knoxville, was founded in 1794 as Blount College, and the University of North Carolina, Chapel Hill, opened its doors in 1795.

Several outstanding painters were at work in the colonies and the young republic. Among them were John Singleton Copley, Gilbert Stuart, John Trumbull, and Charles Willson Peale. Patience Wright, famous in the colonies as a sculptor of wax portraits, moved to London before the war. While there, she acted as a Revolutionary spy. In music, William Billings produced *The New England Psalm-Singer* and a number of patriotic hymns. Billings earned his living as a tanner and taught himself music. Among his friends were such revolutionary activists as Samuel Adams and Paul Revere. This was a turbulent time—a time of action—and its legacy was cultural as well as political.

▼ Critical Viewing
As the first secretary of the treasury, Alexander Hamilton had to develop a financial plan for the government. (a) What was the government's income in 1789? (b) How much did it owe? [Analyze]

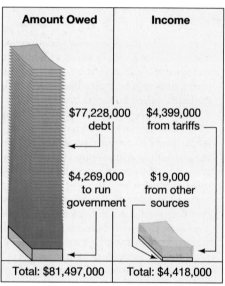

Money Problems of the New Nation, 1789–1791

Amount Owed	Income
$77,228,000 debt	$4,399,000 from tariffs
$4,269,000 to run government	$19,000 from other sources
Total: $81,497,000	Total: $4,418,000

Source: *Historical Statistics of the United States*

Art in the Historical Context

Gilbert Stuart, Portraitist

After Americans won the Revolution in 1781, one might have expected to see painters portray some of the most dramatic battle scenes—for example, the Battle of Bunker Hill or the surrender at Yorktown, Virginia. Most of the country's best-known painters, however, produced portraits.

Gilbert Stuart was among the most distinguished of these portraitists. He had studied with Benjamin West, a famous American painter who lived and worked in London. When Stuart did several paintings of the country's first citizen, George Washington, it was as if he were painting a portrait of the Revolution itself. Perhaps believing that the ideals of that struggle could be read in Washington's features and personality, Stuart focused on the upper part of Washington's body, especially his face, and he did not include any props or scenery.

George Washington (Vaughan portrait), Gilbert Stuart, Photograph © Board of Trustees, National Gallery of Art, Washington, D.C.

▶ **Make an Inference** What impression of Washington—and, by extension, of the American Revolution—does this portrait convey? Explain.

American Literature at Daybreak By the early 1800s, America could boast a small body of national literature. The Native Americans had contributed haunting poetry and legends through their oral traditions. The Puritans had written a number of powerful, inward-looking works. The statesmen of the Revolutionary period had produced political documents for the ages. A few poets and essayists had made a permanent mark on the literature of the young republic. There were, however, no American novels or plays of importance, and the modern short story had yet to be invented.

As the eighteenth century came to a close, however, the raw materials for a great national literature were at hand, waiting to be used. The nation stood on the threshold of a territorial and population explosion unique in the history of the world. It would take almost exactly a century to close the frontier of the vast and varied continent beyond the Appalachians. During that century, American literature would burst forth with a vitality that might have surprised even the farsighted founders of the nation. The colonial age ended with a narrow volume of memorable literature. The nineteenth century would close with a library of works that form a major part of America's literary heritage.

Continued from right column

Possible answers: Americans were hesitant to compete with established European authors. Much of America was still a frontier farming society, and the American character was still in its formative stages.

▶**Critical Viewing**

Answer: Washington looks serious, focused, and determined. This might be a reflection of the colonists' determination to win independence from Britain.

Literature of the Period
Comprehension Check

1. In what way was the writing produced during this period different from that produced by the Puritans?
   Answer: The Puritans were concerned with private soul-searching, while writing of the Revolutionary era discussed political, public issues.

2. Name three important speakers and writers of this era.
   Possible answers: Thomas Jefferson, John Adams, Benjamin Franklin, Patrick Henry, James Madison, Michel-Guillaume Crèvecoeur, and Thomas Paine were important speakers and writers of this era.

3. Name two political documents of the era whose final text was the result of committee debate.
   Answer: The Declaration of Independence and the Constitution were the result of committee debate.

4. Outside the field of politics, which writer was most widely read?
   Answer: Benjamin Franklin was most widely read.

5. As the eighteenth century came to a close, which types of literature were still largely untried by American writers?
   Answer: Novels, short stories, and plays were largely untried.

Critical Thinking

1. Why do you think most of the important writing of the period was political?
   Answer: The colonists' minds were on political matters because the country was going through a momentous revolutionary struggle.

2. Why is it important to remember that the Declaration of Independence and the Constitution are the result of long hours of debate by many men?
   Answer: Many opinions were needed to ensure that all areas and interests in the colonies would be represented in the final documents.

3. Why do you think American writers of this era produced no plays or novels?

continued

Critical Thinking

1. Why do you think Washington called on Noah Webster?
Answer: He wanted to meet the man who was struggling to "declare independence" for American English.

2. Why do you think Webster traveled across America?
Answer: He knew that vocabulary, pronunciation, and definition varied by region, and he wanted his dictionary to represent everyone.

3. In what ways do Webster's efforts reflect a drive to standardize and innovate?
Answer: He wanted to standardize American spellings, but he also wanted to change them from British spellings.

4. What can you deduce from the spelling changes Webster introduced?
Answer: He wanted to spell words more simply. He deleted extra letters that don't affect pronunciation, such as the *u* in *honour*.

Activity

1. Answers will vary depending on the words students choose. You might photocopy an entry from the OED and take students through it, showing them how it tells the history of a word in chronological order.

2. (a) suspenders **(d)** gasoline
   (b) elevator **(e)** television
   (c) truck

Additional words:

British	American
boot (of car)	trunk
mobile	cell phone
loo	bathroom
biscuit	cookie
tin	can

THE DEVELOPMENT OF AMERICAN ENGLISH

Noah Webster and the American Language

BY RICHARD LEDERER

Travel back in time to May 1787 to the city of Philadelphia. It is thronged with important visitors, including Benjamin Franklin, Alexander Hamilton, James Madison, and the brightest of these luminaries—George Washington. They have come to attend the Constitutional Convention "in order to form a more perfect Union" of states that have recently won a surprising military victory.

On the evening of May 26, 1787, General Washington pays a visit to talk about education with a 28-year-old New Englander who is teaching school in Philadelphia. His name is Noah Webster.

AMERICA'S SCHOOLMASTER

Why did Washington call on a young man scarcely half his age who was neither a Revolutionary War hero nor a Convention delegate? One reason was that Noah Webster was the author, publisher, and salesman of *The Blue-Backed Speller*, a book that was then more widely read in the United States than any other except the Bible.

WEBSTER AND THE AMERICAN DICTIONARY

On top of such an amazing achievement, Webster devoted thirty years to creating the first great American dictionaries. The fact that the name *Webster* and the word *dictionary* are practically synonymous indicates the enduring brightness of Webster's reputation.

Throughout his life, Noah Webster was afire with the conviction that the United States should have its own version of the English language. In 1789, he wrote:

As an independent nation, our honor requires us to have a system of our own, in language as well as government. Great Britain, whose children we are and whose language we speak, should no longer be our standard.

In putting this theory into practice, Noah Webster traveled throughout the East and South, listening to the speech of American people, and taking endless notes. He included in his dictionaries an array of shiny new American words, among them *applesauce, bullfrog, chowder, handy, hickory, succotash, tomahawk*—and *skunk:* "a quadruped remarkable for its smell."

In shaping the American language, Noah Webster also taught a new nation a new way to spell.

British	Webster's
honour	honor
humour	humor
musick	music
publick	public
centre	center
theatre	theater
plough	plow

ACTIVITY

1. Dictionary-makers are the biographers of words. Pick a word from the *Oxford English Dictionary* and write its "biography"—when the word was born and how it acquired new meanings over the course of its life.

2. Give the American equivalent of each of the following British words:
(a) braces, **(b)** lift, **(c)** lorry, **(d)** petrol, **(e)** telly.
Identify additional words that distinguish Americans from British citizens.

✸ ENRICHMENT: History Connection

Noah Webster

It is difficult for us fully to appreciate the impact that Noah Webster had on American English, and especially on spelling. His *Blue-Backed Speller* sold about one million copies every year starting in 1850, when the population of the country was about 23 million.

Webster's schoolbooks sold so well that he was able to devote the latter part of his life to compiling dictionaries. *The American Dictionary of the English Language,* which appeared in 1828, achieved annual sales of about 300,000. In addition to providing definitions of some 70,000 words, it helped teach Americans how to pronounce these words in a uniform way.

Voices for Freedom

Miss Liberty, artist unknown. Abby Aldrich Rockefeller Folk Art Center, Williamsburg, VA

Liberty and Independence.   Ever Glorious Memory.
UNITED STATES AMERICA. 1776.

Selection Planning Guide

This section introduces students to some of colonial America's greatest revolutionary voices. The excerpt from *The Autobiography* presents Franklin's self-disciplined, practical wisdom. In *The Crisis, Number 1*, the voice of Thomas Paine rings with a call to fight for freedom. The final text of Thomas Jefferson's Declaration of Independence as passed by Congress contains some of the most stirring prose on the rights of man ever written. Two poems by Phillis Wheatley, an African American, pay tribute to General Washington and reflect on the restorative powers of night and sleep. Part 1 ends with an excerpt from Martin Luther King's *Letter from Birmingham City Jail*, where this twentieth-century fighter for freedom was confined at the start of the civil rights movement.

Background

Art

Miss Liberty, artist unknown

Folk art like *Miss Liberty* was produced by untrained artists. The stiff, doll-like appearance of the figure and the bright red spots on the cheeks are hallmarks of American folk art of the period. Abstract concepts like Truth and Justice had been personified in painting and sculpture for centuries, but they were usually shown as goddesses. *Miss Liberty* shows the new twist of portraying such a concept as an ordinary woman.

The red farmer's cap atop *Miss Liberty's* staff and the sheaf in her hand indicate the large role farmers played in the American Revolution.

1. Why do you think the artist personified Liberty as a young woman?
   Answer: The artist wanted to emphasize the naturalness and innocence of liberty.

INSTRUCTION FOR UNIVERSAL ACCESS

he selections in Part 1, keep these factors in mind:

tobiography

cient readers may need help with
vocabulary and unusual sentence

isis, Number 1

onal call to arms will appeal to
ents.

The Declaration of Independence

- Difficult vocabulary may cause problems for less proficient readers.

"To His Excellency, General Washington"

- Difficult vocabulary and sentence structure may cause problems for less proficient readers.

from The Autobiography ✦ *from* Poor Richard's Almanack

Lesson Objectives

1. **To analyze and respond to literary elements**
   - Literary Analysis: Autobiography
   - Comparing Literary Works

2. **To read, comprehend, analyze, and critique nonfiction**
   - Reading Strategy: Drawing Conclusions
   - Reading Check questions
   - Review and Assess questions
   - Assessment Practice (ATE)

3. **To develop word analysis skills, fluency, and systematic vocabulary**
   - Vocabulary Development Lesson: Latin Word Root: *-vigil-*

4. **To understand and apply written and oral language conventions**
   - Spelling Strategy
   - Grammar and Style Lesson: Pronoun Case

5. **To understand and apply appropriate writing and research strategies**
   - Writing Lesson: Autobiographical Account
   - Extension Activity: Travel Brochure

6. **To understand and apply listening and speaking strategies**
   - Extension Activity: Class Improvement Plan

STEP-BY-STEP TEACHING GUIDE	PACING GUIDE
PRETEACH	
Motivate Students and Provide Background	
Use the Motivation activity (ATE p. 138)	5 min.
Read and discuss the author and the background features (SE p. 140/ATE p. 138) **A**	5 min.
Introduce the Concepts	
Introduce the Literary Analysis and Reading Strategy (SE/ATE p. 139) **A**	15 min.
Pronounce the vocabulary words and read their definitions (SE p. 139)	5 min.
TEACH	
Monitor Comprehension	
Informally monitor comprehension by circulating while students read independently or in groups **A**	20 min.
Monitor students' comprehension with the Reading Check notes (SE/ATE pp. 141, 143, 145, 147)	as students read
Develop vocabulary with Vocabulary notes (SE pp. 141, 142, 144, 145, 147, 148; ATE p. 142)	as students read
Develop Understanding	
Develop students' understanding of autobiography with the Literary Analysis annotations (SE pp. 141, 143, 144; ATE pp. 141, 143, 144) **A**	5 min.
Develop students' ability to draw conclusions with the Reading Strategy annotations (SE p. 142; ATE p. 142)	5 min.
ASSESS	
Assess Mastery	
Assess students' mastery of the Reading Strategy and Literary Analysis by having them answer the Review and Assess questions (SE/ATE p. 149)	15 min.
Use one or more of the print and media Assessment Resources (ATE p. 151) **A**	up to 45 min.
EXTEND	
Apply Understanding	
Have students complete the Vocabulary Development Lesson and the Grammar and Style Lesson (SE p. 150) **A**	20 min.
Apply students' ability to show cause and effect by using the Writing Lesson (SE/ATE p. 151) **A**	45 min.
Apply students' understanding using one or more of the Extension Activities (SE p. 151)	20–90 min.

 ACCELERATED INSTRUCTION:
Use the strategies and activities identified with an **A**.

UNIVERSAL ACCESS
● = Below Level Students
▲ = On-Level Students
■ = Above Level Students

Time and Resource Manager

Reading Level: Challenging, Challenging
Average Number of Instructional Days: 4

RESOURCES

PRINT 📖	TRANSPARENCIES 📑	TECHNOLOGY 💿 🎧 📼
• **Beyond Literature,** Workplace Skills: Multiple Careers, p. 8 ▲ ■		• **Interest Grabber Video,** Tape 2 ● ▲ ■
• **Selection Support Workbook:** ● ▲ ■ Literary Analysis, p. 36 Reading Strategy, p. 35 Build Vocabulary, p. 33	• **Literary Analysis and Reading Transparencies,** pp. 23 and 24 ● ▲ ■	
• **Adapted Reader's Companion** ● • **Reader's Companion** ● • **Authors In Depth,** The American Experience ■		• **Listening to Literature** ● ▲ ■ Audiocassettes, Side 4 Audio CDs, CD 2
• **English Learner's Companion** ● ▲ • **Literatura en español** ● ▲ • **Literary Analysis for Enrichment** ■		
• **Formal Assessment:** Selection Test, pp. 38–40 ● ▲ ■ • **Open Book Test,** pp. 22–24 ● ▲ ■ • **Performance Assessment and Portfolio Management,** p. 9 ● ▲ ■ • **PRENTICE HALL** ASSESSMENT *SYSTEM* ● ▲ ■	**PRENTICE HALL** ASSESSMENT *SYSTEM* ● ▲ ■ Skills Practice Answers and Explanations on Transparencies	• **Test Bank Software** ● ▲ ■ • **Got It! Assessment Videotapes,** Tape 1 ● ▲
• **Selection Support Workbook:** ● ▲ ■ Grammar and Style, p. 34 • **Writing and Grammar,** The American Experience ● ▲ ■ • **Extension Activities,** p. 8 ● ▲ ■	• **Daily Language Practice Transparencies** ● ▲ • **Writing Models and Graphic Organizers on Transparencies,** p. 91 ● ▲ ■	• **Writing and Grammar iText CD-ROM** ● ▲ ■ 💻 *Take It to the Net* www.phschool.com

■ **BLOCK SCHEDULING:** Use one 90-minute class period to preteach the selection and have students read it. Use a second 90-minute class period to assess students' mastery of skills and have them complete one of the Extension Activities.

Motivation

Write the following quotation by Benjamin Franklin on the chalkboard: "I wished to live without committing any fault at any time." Ask students whether they believe they have committed any "faults" in the past twenty-four hours. Discuss reasons it would be difficult to live without committing any faults. Ask students to look for the difficulties Franklin may have faced in achieving this goal.

▣ Interest Grabber Video

As an alternative, you may wish to play "*The Autobiography*: Ben Franklin on Moral Perfection" on Tape 2 to engage student interest.

❶ More About the Author

No other colonial American more closely embodied the promise of America than did Benjamin Franklin. Through hard work, dedication, and ingenuity, Franklin rose out of poverty to become a wealthy, famous, and influential person. Although he never received a formal education, Franklin made important contributions in science, literature, journalism, and education. In addition, as a statesman, he is the only American to sign the four documents that established the nation: the Declaration of Independence, the treaty of alliance with France, the peace treaty with England, and the Constitution.

Prepare to Read

from The Autobiography ◆ *from* Poor Richard's Almanack

❶ Benjamin Franklin (1706–1790)

From his teen years until his retirement at forty-two, Benjamin Franklin worked as a printer. Franklin got his start as an apprentice to his brother, James Franklin, a Boston printer. By the time he was sixteen, he was not only printing, but writing parts of his brother's newspaper. Using the name "Silence Dogood," Franklin satirized daily life and politics in Boston.

When he was seventeen, Franklin left Boston and traveled to Philadelphia, intending to open his own print shop. This move gave birth to one of Franklin's most popular and enduring contributions to American culture, *Poor Richard's Almanack*. This annual publication, which Franklin published from 1732 to 1757, contained information, observations, and advice and was very popular with readers of his day.

The "Write Reputation" Just as he had signed "Silence Dogood" to the letters he wrote for his brother's paper, Franklin created for the *Almanack* a fictitious author/editor, the chatty Richard Saunders (and his wife, Bridget). Although Poor Richard's early appearances in the *Almanack* present him as a dull and foolish astronomer, his character developed over the years, becoming more thoughtful, pious, and humorous. Despite the fact that Franklin published under a pseudonym, the *Almanack* earned him a reputation as a talented writer.

Secret to Success Like most almanacs, Franklin's contained practical information about the calendar, the sun and moon, and the weather. *Poor Richard's Almanack* also featured a wealth of homespun sayings and observations, many of which are still quoted today. It was these aphorisms, with their characteristic moral overtones, that made the *Almanack* a bestseller. Franklin put an aphorism at the top or bottom of most pages of his almanacs. The wit and brevity of these sayings allowed Franklin to include many moral messages in very little space, while also entertaining his readers.

Man of Science When Franklin was forty-two, he retired from the printing business to devote himself to science. He proved to be as successful a scientist as he had been a printer. Over the course of his lifetime, Franklin was responsible for inventing the lightning rod, bifocals, and a new type of stove; confirming the laws of electricity; and contributing to the scientific understanding of earthquakes and ocean currents. In spite of all these achievements, Franklin is best remembered for his career in politics.

Statesman and Diplomat Franklin played an important role in drafting the Declaration of Independence, enlisting French support during the Revolutionary War, negotiating a peace treaty with Britain, and drafting the United States Constitution. In his later years, he was ambassador first to England and then to France. Even before George Washington, Franklin was considered to be "the father of his country."

The Story Behind the Story Franklin wrote the first section of *The Autobiography* in 1771 at the age of sixty-five. At the urging of friends, he wrote three more sections—the last shortly before his death—but succeeded in bringing the account of his life only to the years 1757 to 1759. Though never completed, his *Autobiography*, filled with his opinions and suggestions, provides not only a record of his achievements but also an understanding of his character.

TEACHING RESOURCES

The following resources can be used to enrich or extend the instruction for pp. 138–139.

Motivation

▣ **Interest Grabber Video**, Tape 2 ▣

Background

📖 **Beyond Literature**, p. 8

🖥 *Take It to the Net*
Visit 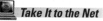www.phschool.com for background and hotlinks for the selections.

Literary Analysis

📄 **Literary Analysis and Reading Transparencies**, Autobiography, p. 24 ▣

Reading

📖 **Selection Support Workbook:** Reading Strategy, p. 35; Build Vocabulary, p. 33

📄 **Literary Analysis and Reading Transparencies**, Drawing Conclusions, p. 23

▣ **BLOCK SCHEDULING:** Resources marked with this symbol provide varied instruction during 90-minute blocks.

Preview

Connecting to the Literature

Autobiographies of historical figures such as Franklin allow us a closer look at world-shaping events and can be just as gripping as great fiction.

❷ Literary Analysis

Autobiography

Benjamin Franklin's *Autobiography* set the standard for what was then a new genre. Usually written in the first person, **autobiographies** present life events as the writer sees them. They also provide a view of history that is more personal than accounts in history books. Use a chart like the one shown to record details from Franklin's *Autobiography* that paint a portrait of the man, his attitudes, and the world he inhabited.

Comparing Literary Works

Franklin's interest in self-improvement is evident both in this excerpt from *The Autobiography* and in the **aphorisms**—short sayings with a message—he wrote for the *Almanack:*

> If you would know the value of money, try to borrow some.

In *The Autobiography*, Franklin examines his own life and applies higher standards to his behavior. By contrast, the aphorisms offer witty advice to the general public. As you read these selections, examine how they each convey messages of moral self-improvement, but with very different effects.

❸ Reading Strategy

Drawing Conclusions

Franklin vividly describes his life and goals, letting you form an impression of his character. To form an impression, **draw conclusions** based on evidence from the text and your own experience. For example:

Detail: Franklin makes lists to organize his plan.

Personal Experience: You make "to do" lists, too.

Conclusion: Franklin likes to plan ahead.

Draw conclusions about Franklin's character as you read these works.

Vocabulary Development

arduous (är′ jōō əs) *adj.* difficult (p. 141)

avarice (av′ ə ris) *n.* greed (p. 141)

vigilance (vij′ ə ləns) *n.* watchfulness (p. 142)

disposition (dis′ pə zish′ ən) *n.* management (p. 144)

foppery (fäp′ ər ē) *n.* foolishness (p. 145)

felicity (fə lis′ i tē) *n.* happiness; bliss (p. 145)

squander (skwän′ dər) *v.* spend or use wastefully (p. 147)

fasting (fast′ iŋ) *v.* eating very little or nothing (p. 148)

from *The Autobiography* / from *Poor Richard's Almanack* ◆ *139*

- Details of Franklin's life
- Franklin's attitudes
- Portrait of the times

---

❷ Literary Analysis

Autobiography

- Tell students that as they read the excerpt from *The Autobiography*, they will focus on its literary genre, or form. *Autobiography* is a first-person account of the writer's own life.

- Have a volunteer read aloud the description of autobiography. Point out the special view of events that autobiographies offer readers.

- Emphasize that Benjamin Franklin's autobiography reveals up-close information about U.S. history that students might not know.

- Highlight the chart, and remind students that completing it as they read it will help them get to know Franklin better.

❸ Reading Strategy

Drawing Conclusions

- Remind students that when they draw conclusions, they use both clues from the text and their own experiences to make reasonable statements about what they read.

- Then, tell students that drawing conclusions can help them paint a more complete picture of Franklin. As they read his autobiography, they can use hints from his style and language to help answer their questions.

- For example, point out that Franklin's detailed list of virtues might lead students to draw the conclusion that he is very serious about living without "fault."

Vocabulary Development

- Pronounce each vocabulary word for students, and read the definitions as a class. Have students identify any words with which they are already familiar.

CUSTOMIZE INSTRUCTION FOR UNIVERSAL ACCESS

For Less Proficient Readers	For English Learners	For Special Needs Students
Have students read the selection in the **Reader's Companion**. This version provides basic-level instruction in an interactive format with questions and write-on lines. After students finish the selection in **Reader's Companion**, have them complete the questions and activities in the Student Edition.	Have students read the adapted version of the selection in the **English Learner's Companion**. This version provides basic-level instruction in an interactive format with questions and write-on lines. Completing the adapted version will prepare students to read the selection in the Student Edition.	Have students read the adapted version of Franklin's autobiography in the **Adapted Reader's Companion**. This version provides basic-level instruction in an interactive format with questions and write-on lines. Completing the adapted version will prepare students to read the selection in the Student Edition.

 E-Teach

Visit E-Teach at www.phschool.com for teachers' essays on how to teach, with questions and answers.

Step-by-Step Teaching Guide for pp. 140–148

CUSTOMIZE INSTRUCTION for Verbal/Linguistic Learners

Tell students that this selection contains many words chosen by Franklin for their particular connotations. Remind students that a word's connotation is the set of ideas associated with it, in addition to its explicit meaning. For example, the noun *frugality* denotes a quality of thriftiness or economy, generally perceived as a positive quality. The word *stinginess*, which denotes the same thing, carries negative connotations. Have students note and discuss the positive, negative, or neutral connotation of other words as they read.

❶ About the Selection

This excerpt shows Franklin's struggle to reach moral perfection, a subject he writes about with the fervent hope that others will imitate the effort. Naming thirteen virtues, Franklin focuses on one at a time, the perfection of one leading to ease of perfecting the next. As years pass, he devotes more time to attaining each virtue before advancing to the next. In telling his story, Franklin displays his fastidious nature, detailed mind, logic in addressing the virtues, daily organization, and harsh self-evaluations. Finally, he claims the result of his life-long struggle has been happiness.

❷ ▶ Critical Viewing

Answer: In the painting, students may note discipline in the worshippers' attention, their head coverings, the separation of sexes, and their row seats. Similarly, in *The Autobiography*, students may note that Franklin shows discipline in his use of the little book and of daily schedules.

---

❶ *from* The Autobiography
Benjamin Franklin

Background

Benjamin Franklin arrived in the city of Philadelphia in 1723 at the age of 17. He knew no one, and he had little money and fewer possessions. However, his accomplishments shaped the city in ways that are still visible today. He helped establish Philadelphia's public library and fire department, as well as its first college. In addition, through his efforts, Philadelphia became the first city in the colonies to have street lights. While Franklin was a brilliant man, some of his success can be attributed to sheer self-discipline, which is evident in this excerpt from his *Autobiography*.

Quaker Meeting, British, fourth quarter 18th century or first quarter 19th century, Museum of Fine Arts, Boston

❸ ▲ **Critical Viewing** Relate this picture to *The Autobiography*. What does each suggest about discipline and order? **[Draw Conclusions]**

TEACHING RESOURCES

The following resources can be used to enrich or extend the instruction for pp. 140–148

Literary Analysis

📖 **Selection Support Workbook:** Literary Analysis, p. 36

Reading

📖 **Reader's Companion**

📖 **English Learner's Companion**

🎧 **Listening to Literature Audiocassettes,** Side 4 ▪

💿 **Listening to Literature Audio CDs,** CD 2 ▪

Extension

📖 **Authors In Depth,** The American Experience (The collection includes three additional selections by Benjamin Franklin for extended reading.) ▪

▪ **BLOCK SCHEDULING:** Resources marked with this symbol provide varied instruction during 90-minute blocks.

It was about this time I conceived the bold and arduous project of arriving at moral perfection. I wished to live without committing any fault at any time; I would conquer all that either natural inclination, custom, or company might lead me into. As I knew, or thought I knew, what was right and wrong, I did not see why I might not always do the one and avoid the other. But I soon found I had undertaken a task of more difficulty than I had imagined. While my care was employed in guarding against one fault, I was often surprised by another; habit took the advantage of inattention; inclination was sometimes too strong for reason. I concluded, at length, that the mere speculative conviction that it was our interest to be completely virtuous was not sufficient to prevent our slipping; and that the contrary habits must be broken, and good ones acquired and established, before we can have any dependence on a steady, uniform rectitude of conduct. For this purpose I therefore contrived the following method.

In the various enumerations of the moral virtues I had met with in my reading, I found the catalog more or less numerous, as different writers included more or fewer ideas under the same name. Temperance, for example, was by some confined to eating and drinking, while by others it was extended to mean the moderating every other pleasure, appetite, inclination, or passion, bodily or mental, even to our avarice and ambition. I proposed to myself, for the sake of clearness, to use rather more names, with fewer ideas annexed to each, than a few names with more ideas; and I included under thirteen names of virtues all that at that time occurred to me as necessary or desirable, and annexed to each a short precept, which fully expressed the extent I gave to its meaning.

These names of virtues, with their precepts, were:

1. TEMPERANCE Eat not to dullness; drink not to elevation.
2. SILENCE Speak not but what may benefit others or yourself; avoid trifling conversation.
3. ORDER Let all your things have their places; let each part of your business have its time.
4. RESOLUTION Resolve to perform what you ought; perform without fail what you resolve.
5. FRUGALITY Make no expense but to do good to others or yourself; i.e., waste nothing.
6. INDUSTRY Lose no time; be always employed in something useful; cut off all unnecessary actions.
7. SINCERITY Use no hurtful deceit; think innocently and justly, and, if you speak, speak accordingly.
8. JUSTICE Wrong none by doing injuries, or omitting the benefits that are your duty.
9. MODERATION Avoid extremes; forebear resenting injuries so much as you think they deserve.
10. CLEANLINESS Tolerate no uncleanliness in body, clothes, or habitation.

arduous (är´ jōō əs) *adj.* difficult

Literary Analysis
Autobiography What does Franklin's goal of moral "perfection" suggest about the values of the time period?

avarice (av´ ə ris) *n.* greed

5 ☑ Reading Check
What prompts Franklin to make his list?

from The Autobiography ◆ 141

❸ Background
Art
Quaker Meeting, artist unknown
Dating from the late 18th or early 19th century, this British painting is based on a print of a Quaker meeting by Egbert van Heemkirk of London (c. 1670). The painting, which now belongs to Haverford College's Quaker collection, depicts a sense of Quaker order and virtue. Use these questions for discussion.

1. What contributes to the severe mood of the painting?
   Answer: The lack of bright colors, the dark background, the parallel rows, and the worshippers' somber expressions and shaded eyes all contribute to the mood.

2. In what ways do the people shown in the painting seem to be following Benjamin Franklin's approach to life?
   Possible response: The worshippers are silent and orderly.

❹ Literary Analysis
Autobiography

• Have students paraphrase Franklin's attitude toward moral perfection, and write it on the chalkboard.
  Possible response: Franklin believes that moral perfection is desirable and can be achieved through hard work.

• Ask students the Literary Analysis question on p. 141: What does Franklin's goal of moral "perfection" suggest about the values of the time period?
  Answer: It suggests that people of the time period valued hard work and moral behavior very highly.

❺ ☑ Reading Check
Answer: He makes a list to clarify his definitions of the virtues.

CUSTOMIZE INSTRUCTION FOR UNIVERSAL ACCESS

For Less Proficient Readers	For English Learners	For Advanced Readers
To help students develop a rounded picture of Benjamin Franklin, have them create a character web. Demonstrate how to create such a web, placing Franklin's name in the center cell and creating outer cells labeled to describe Franklin's views, actions, and words.	Have students use dictionaries to define each of Franklin's listed virtues. Then, demonstrate the use of a word web to help students understand these concepts. Place the virtue in the center cell, and use outer cells for Franklin's examples and definitions. Help students to complete the outer cells with information from the text.	Challenge students to explore the advantages and disadvantages of each virtue that Franklin describes. Demonstrate the use of a web in which the center cell contains the virtue and two outer rings of cells contain either advantages or disadvantages. Have students work in pairs to complete webs for each virtue.

❻ Background

Social Studies

Socrates wrote nothing of his own, so we are dependent on the writings of his contemporaries for information about his life. Some of the best sources of information are the early dialogues of his student Plato, who attempted to provide a full picture of Socrates' teaching methods. Socrates became well known for using a method of critical inquiry that explored and often undermined widely held beliefs.

❼ Vocabulary Development

Latin Word Root: *-vigil-*

- Draw students' attention to the word *vigilance* and its definition, "watchfulness."

- Explain that the root *-vigil-* means "the act or period of remaining awake so as to guard or observe something."

- Ask students to name situations in which people might hold a vigil.

❽ Reading Strategy

Drawing Conclusions

- Ask students to give examples of goals they have worked hard to reach. Discuss how they developed systems or schedules for attaining intermediate goals or for keeping on track. Ask students why they developed these systems.

  Possible answer: When goals are important to us, we take great care to ensure we will reach them.

- Invite students to answer the question on p. 142: What does Franklin's methodical approach, described in this passage, suggest about his dedication to his plan for self-improvement?

  Answer: He is dedicated to his plan and wants to do everything he can to ensure its success.

 Monitor Progress As students continue to read, have them make a list of details that reveal Franklin's dedication to his plan.

142

---

11. TRANQUILLITY Be not disturbed at trifles, or at accidents common or unavoidable.
12. CHASTITY
13. HUMILITY Imitate Jesus and Socrates♦.

My intention being to acquire the *habitude* of all these virtues, I judged it would be well not to distract my attention by attempting the whole at once but to fix it on one of them at a time; and, when I should be master of that, then to proceed to another, and so on, till I should have gone through the thirteen; and, as the previous acquisition of some might facilitate the acquisition of certain others, I arranged them with that view, as they stand above. *Temperance* first, as it tends to procure that coolness and clearness of head, which is so necessary where ❼ constant <u>vigilance</u> was to be kept up, and guard maintained against the unremitting attraction of ancient habits and the force of perpetual temptations. This being acquired and established, *Silence* would be more easy; and my desire being to gain knowledge at the same time that I improved in virtue, and considering that in conversation it was obtained rather by the use of the ears than of the tongue, and therefore wishing to break a habit I was getting into of prattling, punning, and joking, which only made me acceptable to trifling company, I gave *Silence* the second place. This and the next, *Order*, I expected would allow me more time for attending to my project and my studies. *Resolution*, once become habitual, would keep me firm in my endeavors to obtain all the subsequent virtues; *Frugality* and *Industry* freeing me from my remaining debt and producing affluence and independence, would make more easy the practice of *Sincerity* and *Justice*, etc., etc. Conceiving then, that, agreeably to the advice of Pythagoras[1] in his *Golden Verses*, daily examination would be necessary, I contrived the following method for conducting that examination.

I made a little book, in which I allotted a page for each of the virtues. I ruled each page with red ink, so as to have seven columns, one for each day of the week, marking each column with a letter for the day. I crossed these columns with thirteen red lines, marking the ❽ beginning of each line with the first letter of one of the virtues, on which line and in its proper column I might mark, by a little black spot, every fault I found upon examination to have been committed respecting that virtue upon that day.

I determined to give a week's strict attention to each of the virtues successively. Thus, in the first week, my great guard was to avoid every[2] the least offense against *Temperance*, leaving the other virtues

---

1. **Pythagoras** (pi *thag*´ ə rəs) Greek philosopher and mathematician who lived in the sixth century B.C.
2. **every** even.

142 ◆ *A Nation Is Born (1750–1800)*

---

❻ ♦ Socrates

A Greek philosopher and teacher who lived in the fifth century B.C., Socrates pioneered the kind of self-reflection that Benjamin Franklin undertakes with his moral improvement plan. Socrates held self-knowledge dear, believing that only through knowledge can people achieve moral virtue. He led many in Athens in searching for moral truth and defining rules for right conduct. Nonetheless, Socrates' criticism of Athenian government resulted in his execution.

vigilance (vij´ ə ləns) *n.* watchfulness

Reading Strategy
Drawing Conclusions
What does Franklin's methodical approach, described in this passage, suggest about his dedication to his plan for self-improvement?

✴ ENRICHMENT: Social Studies

Franklin in Philadelphia

Benjamin Franklin greatly influenced daily life in colonial Philadelphia. He helped establish the city's public library and fire department, as well as its first college. In addition, through his efforts, Philadelphia became the first city in the colonies to have street lights.

Philadelphia was an important center of activity during the period leading up to the American Revolution. It was there that the Declaration of Independence, which established the United States as an independent nation, was written and signed.

In Philadelphia today, you can still walk down cobblestone streets and visit historic sites. Independence Hall (where the Declaration of Independence was signed), the Liberty Bell, and the home of Betsy Ross are within walking distance of one another for tourists and history enthusiasts.

to their ordinary chance, only marking every evening the faults of the day. Thus, if in the first week I could keep my first line, marked *T.* clear of spots, I supposed the habit of that virtue so much strengthened, and its opposite weakened, that I might venture extending my attention to include the next, and for the following week keep both lines clear of spots. Proceeding thus to the last, I could go through a course complete in thirteen weeks, and four courses in a year. And like him who, having a garden to weed, does not attempt to eradicate all the bad herbs at once, which would exceed his reach and his strength, but works on one of the beds at a time, and, having accomplished the first, proceeds to a second, so I should have, I hoped, the encouraging pleasure of seeing on my pages the progress I made in virtue, by clearing successively my lines of their spots, till in the end, by a number of courses, I should be happy in viewing a clean book, after a thirteen weeks' daily examination. . . .

The precept of *Order* requiring that *every part of my business should have its allotted time*, one page in my little book contained the following scheme of employment for the twenty-four hours of a natural day.

THE MORNING.	5	Rise, wash, and
Question. What good shall I do this day?	6	address *Powerful Goodness!* Contrive day's business, and take the resolution of the day;
	7	prosecute the present study, and breakfast.
	8	
	9	Work.
	10	
	11	
NOON.	12	Read, or overlook
	1	my accounts, and dine.
	2	
	3	Work.
	4	
	5	
EVENING.	6	Put things in their places. Supper.
Question. What good have I done today?	7	Music or diversion, or conversation.
	8	Conversation. Examination of
	9	the day.
	10	
	11	
	12	
NIGHT.	1	Sleep.
	2	
	3	
	4	

Literary Analysis
Autobiography What insight into Franklin's character does this list provide?

10 ☑ **Reading Check**
Which virtue did Franklin hope to achieve by planning each day's activities?

from *The Autobiography* ◆ 143

---

9 **Literary Analysis**
Autobiography

- Read the bracketed passage on p. 143. Confirm that students understand what it shows.
  Answer: It shows Franklin's daily schedule with guiding questions to organize his day.

- Focus students' attention on Franklin's guiding questions, pointing out that these highlight the author's desire to use his time for good deeds.

- Have volunteers read aloud the items under 6 a.m. and 6 p.m. Discuss ways that these are similar.
  Answer: Both reflect Franklin's desire for order and accomplishment.

- Ask students to answer the Literary Analysis question on p. 143: What insight into Franklin's character does this list provide?
  Possible response: It suggests that he does not like to waste time and that he has a disciplined and purposeful way of living.

10 ☑ **Reading Check**
Answer: He hoped to achieve the virtue of *Order* by planning the day's activities.

CUSTOMIZE INSTRUCTION FOR UNIVERSAL ACCESS

For Less Proficient Readers	For Special Needs Students	For Gifted/Talented Students
Focus students' attention on Franklin's two organizers: the list on p. 141 and the daily calendar on p. 143. Help students understand these two organizers by clarifying their structure and defining any unfamiliar terms.	Have students add to the character webs they began on p. 141 using details from pp. 142–143. Encourage them to keep adding to their webs as they finish reading Franklin's autobiographical reflections.	Have students read the additional excerpt from Franklin's *Autobiography*, found in **Authors In Depth**, The American Experience, p. 27. Discuss ways that the excerpt compares and contrasts with the excerpt included here.

① Background

Art

Benjamin Franklin as a Young Printer in Philadelphia

While most people are familiar with the grandfatherly, spectacled image of Franklin, this engraving provides a rare glimpse of Benjamin Franklin in his youth. Here we see the young Franklin carrying the tools of his trade, that of a printer. Discuss with students the calm confidence that radiates from Franklin's posture and expression. Use these questions for discussion:

1. What can we learn about Franklin from this picture?
   Answer: We can learn about Franklin's occupation, personality traits, and the era in which he lived.

2. How is this picture related to the selection?
   Answer: The picture shows a hard-working, self-disciplined Franklin, just the sort of person who might reach for moral perfection.

⑫ ▶Critical Viewing

Answer: The expression suggests that Franklin is a calm, confident, and serious individual.

⑬ Literary Analysis

Autobiography

- With students, read aloud the bracketed passage on pp. 144–145.

- Ask the Literary Analysis question on p. 145: What does this anecdote about the man with the axe reveal Franklin's sense of humor?
  Possible response: The anecdote reveals that Franklin understands that some of his goals are unrealistic.

▶ Monitor Progress Remind students that, as they read an autobiography, they can learn about the writer based on the details and anecdotes that he or she decides to include.

① I entered upon the execution of this plan for self-examination, and continued it with occasional intermissions for some time. I was surprised to find myself so much fuller of faults than I had imagined; but I had the satisfaction of seeing them diminish. To avoid the trouble of renewing now and then my little book, which, by scraping out the marks on the paper of old faults to make room for new ones in a new course, became full of holes, I transferred my tables and precepts to the ivory leaves of a memorandum book, on which the lines were drawn with red ink that made a durable stain, and on those lines I marked my faults with a black-lead pencil, which marks I could easily wipe out with a wet sponge. After a while I went through one course only in a year, and afterward only one in several years, till at length I omitted them entirely, being employed in voyages and business abroad, with a multiplicity of affairs that interfered; but I always carried my little book with me.

My scheme of *Order* gave me the most trouble; and I found that, though it might be practicable where a man's business was such as to leave him the <u>disposition</u> of his time, that of a journeyman printer, for instance, it was not possible to be exactly observed by a master, who must mix with the world and often receive people of business at their own hours. *Order*, too, with regard to places for things, papers, etc., I found extremely difficult to acquire. I had not been early accustomed to it, and, having an exceeding good memory, I was not so sensible of the inconvenience attending want of method. This article, therefore, cost me so much painful attention, and my faults in it vexed me so much, and I made so little progress in amendment, and had such frequent relapses, that I was almost ready to give up the attempt, and content myself with a

Benjamin Franklin as a Young Printer in Philadelphia, The Granger Collection, New York

⑫ ▲ Critical Viewing
What does the expression on Franklin's face suggest about his personality? **[Infer]**

disposition (dis′ pə zish′ ən) *n.* management

CUSTOMIZE INSTRUCTION FOR UNIVERSAL ACCESS

For Advanced Readers

Suggest that students read additional works by Benjamin Franklin, such as those listed in the Enrichment box, ATE p. 149. You may also wish to use **Authors In Depth**, The American Experience, which contains the following selections:

- from *The Autobiography* (nonfiction, pp. 27–30)

- "Information to Those Who Would Remove to America" (nonfiction, pp. 31–32)

- "Speech in the Convention on the Subject of Salaries" (nonfiction, pp. 33–40)

After students have read these or other works by Franklin, ask them whether or not the body of his work conforms to an overall and consistent image of his character. Invite students to answer this question in a brief oral report containing quotations from the works.

faulty character in that respect, like the man who, in buying an ax of a smith, my neighbor, desired to have the whole of its surface as bright as the edge. The smith consented to grind it bright for him if he would turn the wheel; he turned, while the smith pressed the broad face of the ax hard and heavily on the stone, which made the turning of it very fatiguing. The man came every now and then from the wheel to see how the work went on, and at length would take his ax as it was, without farther grinding. "No," said the smith, "turn on, turn on; we shall have it bright by and by; as yet, it is only speckled." "Yes," says the man, "*but I think I like a speckled ax best.*" And I believe this may have been the case with many, who, having, for want of some such means as I employed, found the difficulty of obtaining good and breaking bad habits in other points of vice and virtue, have given up the struggle, and concluded that "*a speckled ax was best*"; for something, that pretended to be reason, was every now and then suggesting to me that such extreme nicety as I exacted of myself might be a kind of foppery in morals, which, if it were known, would make me ridiculous; that a perfect character might be attended with the inconvenience of being envied and hated; and that a benevolent man should allow a few faults in himself, to keep his friends in countenance.

In truth, I found myself incorrigible with respect to *Order*; and now I am grown old, and my memory bad, I feel very sensibly the want of it. But, on the whole, though I never arrived at the perfection I had been so ambitious of obtaining, but fell far short of it, yet I was, by the endeavor, a better and a happier man than I otherwise should have been if I had not attempted it; as those who aim at perfect writing by imitating the engraved copies, though they never reached the wished-for excellence of those copies, their hand is mended by the endeavor, and is tolerable while it continues fair and legible.

It may be well my posterity should be informed that to this little artifice, with the blessing of God, their ancestor owed the constant felicity of his life, down to his seventy-ninth year in which this is written. What reverses may attend the remainder is in the hand of Providence; but, if they arrive, the reflection on past happiness enjoyed ought to help his bearing them with more resignation. To *Temperance* he ascribes his long-continued health, and what is still left to him of a good constitution; to *Industry* and *Frugality*, the early easiness of his circumstances and acquisition of his fortune, with all that knowledge that enabled him to be a useful citizen, and obtained for him some degree of reputation among the learned; to *Sincerity* and *Justice*, the confidence of his country, and the honorable employs it conferred upon him; and to the joint influence of the whole mass of the virtues, even in the imperfect state he was able to acquire them, all that evenness of temper, and that cheerfulness in conversation, which makes his company still sought for, and agreeable even to his younger acquaintance. I hope, therefore, that some of my descendants may follow the example and reap the benefit.

Literary Analysis
Autobiography What does this anecdote about the man with the axe reveal about Franklin's sense of humor?

foppery (fäp´ ər ē) *n.* foolishness

felicity (fə lis´ i tē) *n.* happiness; bliss

15 ✓**Reading Check**
Did Franklin consider his moral improvement plan successful? Explain.

14 Critical Thinking
Analyze
- Have students read the bracketed passage. Point out that Franklin admits to the motivation of wanting to look good in the eyes of his descendents. He also wants to show that he produced some positive results in his life.
- Ask students to describe Franklin's final message to his readers.
  Answer: He wants others to follow in his footsteps.

15 ✓**Reading Check**
Possible response: Franklin considered his plan generally successful in that it led to moral improvements and to his overall happiness. He acknowledges, however, that it did not lead to moral perfection.

CUSTOMIZE FOR UNIVERSAL ACCESS

For Less Proficient Readers	For English Learners	For Gifted/Talented Students
Review the selection with students, asking them to identify passages they found especially difficult. Using these passages to demonstrate, show students how to break long sentences into shorter units of thought by using punctuation—especially commas and semicolons—as a guide.	When they finish reading, have students write a summary of the selection. Then, have them compare their summary with the one in the **English Learner's Companion**. Discuss any discrepancies, making sure students understand the main ideas in the selection.	Using the knowledge they've gained about Benjamin Franklin from his *Autobiography*, invite students to portray Franklin in a character study. Encourage students to return to the text and images for details about Franklin's character, mannerisms, and speech style.

16 About the Selection

By providing practical wisdom through aphorisms, Benjamin Franklin teaches valuable lessons in brief and easy-to-remember sayings.

17 Background

Art

Cover, *Poor Richard's Almanack*, by Benjamin Franklin

Like most almanacs, Poor Richard's contained practical information about the calendar, the sun and moon, and the weather. It also contained a wealth of homespun sayings and observations, many of which are still used today. Use these questions for discussion:

1. What makes the original page more difficult to read than the reprinted excerpt?
Answer: On the original page, the letter *s* is printed differently.

2. Would the information in this almanac have been accurate for the people where you live?
Answer: The information is appropriate for areas near Philadelphia—from Newfoundland to South Carolina.

18 ▶Critical Viewing

Answer: Students may speculate that *philomath* means "a love of learning," since the Greek prefix *philo* means "love" and *mathē* means "learning."

16 *from*

Poor Richard's Almanack

Benjamin Franklin

17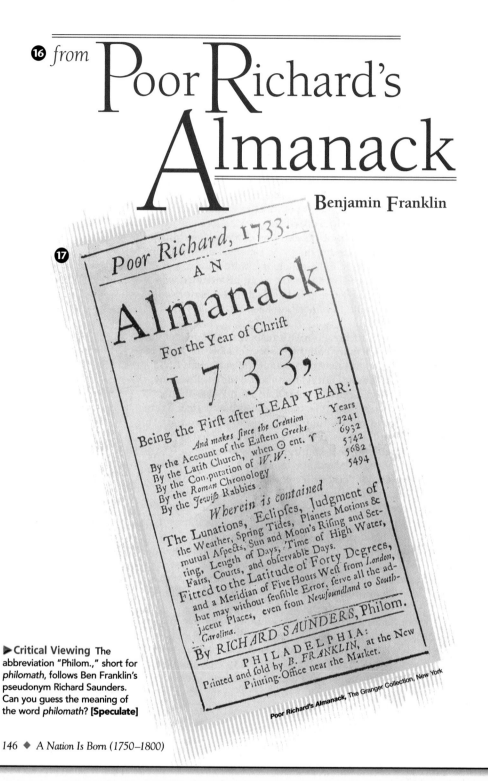

Poor Richard's Almanack, The Granger Collection, New York

18 ▶Critical Viewing The abbreviation "Philom.," short for *philomath*, follows Ben Franklin's pseudonym Richard Saunders. Can you guess the meaning of the word *philomath*? **[Speculate]**

✹ ENRICHMENT: Language Connection

Aphorisms

The aphorisms, or witty sayings, in *Poor Richard's Almanack* still circulate in modern conversation. An aphorism is a short, concise statement expressing a wise or clever observation or general truth. It usually reflects the setting and the time in which it was created. A variety of devices make aphorisms easy to remember. Some contain rhymes or repeated words or sounds; others use parallel structure to present contrasting ideas. The aphorism "no pain, no gain," for instance, uses rhyme, repetition, and parallel structure.

Ask students to name aphorisms they have heard. Discuss the language devices each uses to make a memorable impression on readers. Then, challenge students to check a dictionary of quotations to identify the source of each aphorism. Together, calculate how many come from Franklin's almanac.

Fools make feasts, and wise men eat them.

Be slow in choosing a friend, slower in changing.

Keep thy shop, and thy shop will keep thee.

Early to bed, early to rise, makes a man healthy,
wealthy, and wise.

Three may keep a secret if two of them are dead.

God helps them that help themselves.

The rotten apple spoils his companions.

An open foe may prove a curse; but a pretended
friend is worse.

Have you somewhat to do tomorrow, do it today.

A true friend is the best possession.

A small leak will sink a great ship.

No gains without pains.

'Tis easier to prevent bad habits than to break them.

Well done is better than well said.

 Dost thou love life? Then do not <u>squander</u> time; for
that's the stuff life is made of.

Write injuries in dust, benefits in marble.

A slip of the foot you may soon recover, but a
slip of the tongue you may never get over.

If your head is wax, don't walk in the sun.

A good example is the best sermon.

Hunger is the best pickle.

Genius without education is like silver in the mine.

Literature in context — Cultural Connection

⑲ Proverbs

Most of Franklin's aphorisms are adapted from traditional or folk sayings, known as proverbs. Franklin, who believed that clarity and brevity were two of the most important characteristics of good prose, rewrote many proverbs, crafting short, witty sayings that taught a lesson.

Proverbs are nearly as old as language itself, and exist in all societies. They reflect each culture's view of the world, conveying feelings about fate, the seasons, the natural world, work and effort, love, death, and other universal experiences. These memorable bits of wisdom have survived for centuries, perhaps because they reflect unchanging truths about human nature.

squander (skwän′ dər) v. spend or use wastefully

㉑ ✓Reading Check
Which aphorisms offer advice about using time wisely?

from Poor Richard's Almanack ◆ 147

⑲ Background

Culture

Share with students the following proverbs. Have them discuss their meanings and whether they think Franklin would agree or disagree with each one.

- "Brevity is the soul of wit."
  —William Shakespeare
- "Everything should be made as simple as possible, but not simpler."
  —Albert Einstein
- "Reading makes a full man, conference makes a ready man, and writing makes an exact man."
  —Francis Bacon

⑳ Critical Thinking

Apply

- Read aloud the bracketed aphorism. Then, ask students to paraphrase it.
  Answer: Time is precious and shouldn't be wasted.
- Invite volunteers to discuss how this aphorism relates to their own experiences.
  Possible response: Students should discuss how they handle the various demands on their time, and how they choose to spend their free time.

㉑ ✓Reading Check

Answer: Students might mention these aphorisms: "Have you somewhat to do tomorrow, do it today"; "Dost thou love life? Then do not squander time; for that's the stuff life is made of"; and "Haste makes waste."

CUSTOMIZE INSTRUCTION FOR UNIVERSAL ACCESS

For Less Proficient Readers	For English Learners	For Advanced Readers
Because of their metaphoric quality, aphorisms may be difficult for less proficient readers to understand. Begin with a contemporary aphorism, such as "Life is like a box of chocolates." Discuss its metaphoric meaning so that students see how to draw their own comparisons as they read Franklin's aphorisms.	Have students concentrate on the multiple meanings of words in Franklin's aphorisms. For instance, "Fish and visitors smell in three days" includes a double meaning of "smell." As they read the aphorisms, encourage students to list and define words with multiple meanings.	Challenge students to distill the meaning from Franklin's aphorisms. Then, have them write their own aphorisms that convey the same message. Have volunteers compile their work and create a class booklet of aphorisms.

Answers for p. 148

Review and Assess

1. Possible answer: Temperance, or moderation, seems to be the most important virtue because it governs one's approach to all the other virtues.

2. **(a)** He makes a daily calendar with tasks and times outlined. **(b)** He does not succeed, finding that sometimes he must order tasks around others' and that he cannot change his own habit of relying on memory. **(c)** It illustrates the overwhelming effort involved in the struggle for order, as well as its likely impossibility.

3. **(a)** He probably felt very determined and optimistic. **(b)** As he gets older, Franklin learns the difficulty of attaining moral perfection, but he also realizes that the effort is more important than the goal. **(c)** Possible answer: Perfection is probably unreasonable, but the desire to work hard to improve oneself is not.

4. **(a)** The following aphorisms concern friendship: "An open foe may prove a curse; but a pretended friend is worse"; "Be slow in choosing a friend, slower in changing"; and "A true friend is the best possession." **(b)** Yes, he says that friendship is precious and needs care.

5. **(a)** He will die of fasting. **(b)** If hope keeps people from taking action, it can be highly impractical and ultimately dangerous. **(c)** He might suggest effort or planning.

6. Possible answer: It can highlight counterproductive behavior for change.

7. **(a)** Most express timeless values. **(b)** Students should support their answers with reasons. **(c)** Students should support their answers with reasons.

For want of a nail the shoe is lost; for want of a shoe
   the horse is lost; for want of a horse the rider is lost.

Haste makes waste.

The doors of wisdom are never shut.

Love your neighbor; yet don't pull down your hedge.

He that lives upon hope will die <u>fasting</u>.

fasting (fast´ in) v. eating very little or nothing

Review and Assess
Thinking About the Selections

1. **Respond:** Which virtue on Franklin's list strikes you as being the most important? Explain.

2. **(a) Recall:** According to his *Autobiography*, what efforts does Franklin make to become more orderly? **(b) Infer:** Is he successful? Explain. **(c) Analyze:** What aspect of his attempt to become more orderly is illustrated by the anecdote of the man with the speckled ax?

3. **(a) Interpret:** When Franklin began his project, he was a young man. How do you think he felt at the time about his chances of attaining moral "perfection"? **(b) Compare and Contrast:** What insights does Franklin gain about the importance of achieving moral perfection as he gets older? **(c) Take a Position:** Do you think the goal of achieving moral perfection is reasonable? Explain.

4. **(a) Recall:** Note three aphorisms that deal directly with friendship. **(b) Analyze:** Is Franklin's message about friendship consistent? Explain.

5. **(a) Recall:** According to the aphorisms from *Poor Richard's Almanack*, what happens to a person who "lives upon hope"? **(b) Infer:** Why might Franklin see hope as impractical or even dangerous? **(c) Speculate:** What more reliable value would Franklin say a person can successfully "live upon"?

6. **Generalize:** In what ways can analyzing one's own behavior contribute to personal growth?

7. **(a) Generalize:** Which of Franklin's aphorisms express values that are still widely held in America? Explain. **(b) Evaluate:** With which of Franklin's aphorisms do you most strongly agree? Why? **(c) Evaluate:** With which of Franklin's aphorisms do you disagree? Why?

ASSESSMENT PRACTICE: Reading Comprehension

Cause and Effect   (For more practice, see Test Preparation Workbook, p. 8)

In many tests, students will have to identify causes and effects. Use the following sample test item to demonstrate.

   I proposed to myself, for the sake of clearness, to use rather more names [for virtues], with fewer ideas annexed to each, than a few names with more ideas; and I included under thirteen names of virtues all that at that time occurred to me as necessary or desirable . . . .

Why did Franklin name more virtues instead of fewer?

   A He wanted to be clear.
   B He wanted to measure the virtue of his friends.
   C He thought thirteen was a lucky number.
   D He decided there were only thirteen virtues.

Choices *B* and *C* do not contain any information from the passage. Students may be tempted by choice *D*, but should recognize that *A* is the best answer.

Review and Assess

Literary Analysis

Autobiography

1. What does Franklin's concern with moral virtue reveal about the period in which he lived?
2. (a) Do you think Franklin achieved the virtue of humility? (b) Do you find any evidence of pride—humility's opposite—in this account of his life?
3. How do you think the *Autobiography* would be different if it were written about Franklin rather than by him?

Comparing Literary Works

4. (a) Are Franklin's struggles to improve himself related to the advice he offers in the **aphorisms**? (b) Do these aphorisms seem to be written by the same person who wrote the *Autobiography*? Why, or why not?
5. Use a chart like the one below to match aphorisms with virtues from the *Autobiography*. Explain each choice.

Reading Strategy

Drawing Conclusions

6. Franklin made adjustments to his record-keeping system as his plan progressed. What **conclusion** can you draw about his character from these adjustments? Explain.
7. (a) What conclusions can you draw from Franklin's statement that people dislike perfection in others? (b) Do you agree? Explain.

Extend Understanding

8. **Cultural Connection:** Franklin's aphorism, "If your head is wax, don't walk in the sun," is similar to a Russian proverb that advises, "One who sits between two chairs may easily fall down." (a) What do these proverbs mean? (b) How are they similar? (c) Why do different cultures preserve similar kinds of wisdom?

from The Autobiography / from Poor Richard's Almanack ◆ 149

Quick Review

An **autobiography** is a person's account of his or her own life, usually written in the first person.

An **aphorism** is a short saying with a message.

A **conclusion** is a reasonable statement you develop from details in the text and your own life experience.

 Take It to the Net

www.phschool.com

Take the interactive self-test online to check your understanding of these selections.

Answers for p. 149

Review and Assess

1. His concern suggests that people of his time period cared a great deal about moral behavior.

2. (a) Possible response: He did not achieve this goal, because at the end of the selection he is still hoping to impress his descendants with his character. (b) Yes, he seems quite proud of his little book, lists, and daily calendar.

3. Another writer would not have been able to write as much about what Franklin was thinking at the time. Another writer might have pointed out contradictions between Franklin's aims and instances where he did not live up to these ideals. Another writer might have presented Franklin in a less positive light.

4. Possible response: (a) Yes, both reflect concerns for moral behavior and moral consequences. (b) Students' answers should be supported by the texts.

5. Students' charts should show insight into how Franklin's aphorisms teach the reader about moral virtues.

6. Franklin is willing to examine and change his behavior. He is capable of self-analysis and of growth.

7. (a) He understands people well and appreciates their human desire to avoid criticism. (b) Students should support their answers with evidence from personal experience.

8. Possible responses: (a) These proverbs mean that problems result when you don't pay attention to what you are doing. (b) Both describe inattentive behavior that can lead to injury. (c) People everywhere encounter many of the same problems.

 ENRICHMENT: Further Reading

Other Works by Benjamin Franklin

The Autobiography of Benjamin Franklin and Other Writings, L. Jesse Lemisch, ed.

Benjamin Franklin's The Art of Virtue: His Formula for Successful Living, George L. Rogers, ed.

Letters to the Press, 1758–1775, Verner W. Crane, ed.

Take It to the Net

Visit www.phschool.com for more information on Benjamin Franklin.

❶ Vocabulary Development

Word Analysis

1. watchful

2. A group of people watching out for the public good; a volunteer who without authority assumes police powers such as pursuing and punishing criminal suspects.

Spelling Strategy

1. faddish

2. punning

3. snobbery

4. mapped

Concept Development: Analogies

1. avarice

2. foppery

3. vigilance

4. felicity

5. arduous

6. disposition

7. squander

8. fasting

❷ Grammar and Style

1. me

2. us

3. they

4. We

5. he

Writing Application

When they finish, have students exchange papers and check each other's use of pronoun cases.

Integrate Language Skills

❶ Vocabulary Development Lesson

Word Analysis: Word Root -vigil-

The word *vigilance*, meaning "watchfulness," contains the root -*vigil*-, which means "the act or period of remaining awake so as to guard or observe something." Write a definition of the italicized word in each sentence below.

1. He was *vigilant* in his efforts to reform.

2. To restore safety, members of a *vigilante* group patrolled the streets at night.

Spelling Strategy

When you add a suffix that begins with a vowel to a one-syllable word that ends with a consonant, double the consonant: *fop* + -*ery* = *foppery*. Add the indicated suffixes to the following words.

1. fad + -*ish*   3. snob + -*ery*

2. pun + -*ing*   4. map + -*ed*

Concept Development: Analogies

In each item, match the relationship between the first two words by selecting a word from the vocabulary list on page 139.

1. *Permission* is to *authorization* as _____?_____ is to *greed*.

2. *Danger* is to *peril* as _____?_____ is to *silliness*.

3. *Tragedy* is to *comedy* as _____?_____ is to *negligence*.

4. *Order* is to *chaos* as _____?_____ is to *sadness*.

5. *Rare* is to *common* as _____?_____ is to *easy*.

6. *Error* is to *mistake* as _____?_____ is to *arrangement*.

7. *Cruelty* is to *kindness* as _____?_____ is to *generosity*.

8. *Sloth* is to *industry* as _____?_____ is to *indulgence*.

❷ Grammar and Style Lesson

Pronoun Case

Pronouns are words that replace nouns. **Pronoun case** refers to the form that a pronoun takes to indicate its function in a sentence. Always use pronouns in the case reflecting their function.

Subjective case pronoun, also called **nominative** pronouns—*I, we, you, he, she, it, they*, are used when the pronoun is the subject of the sentence.

Objective case pronouns—*me, us, him, her, it, them*—are used when the pronoun receives the action of the verb or is the object of a preposition.

SUBJ. CASE	OBJ. CASE
I always carried my little book with *me*.	

Practice Choose the correct pronoun to complete each sentence below.

1. At length a fresh difference arose between my brother and (I, me).

2. It was time for (we, us) to leave that place.

3. Though I did not give them any dissatisfaction, (they, them) dismissed me from my position.

4. (We, Us) two undertook to move to Boston.

5. Wilson and (he, him) took care to prevent my getting employment anywhere else.

Writing Application Write an account of a time when you made a conscious effort at self-improvement, using pronoun cases correctly.

℘G *Prentice Hall Writing and Grammar Connection: Chapter 22, Section 1*

150 ◆ A Nation Is Born (1750–1800)

TEACHING RESOURCES

The following resources can be used to enrich or extend the instruction for pp. 150–151

Vocabulary

📖 **Selection Support Workbook,** Build Vocabulary, p. 33

📖 **Vocabulary and Spelling Practice Book** (Use this booklet for skills enrichment.) ▪

Grammar

📖 **Selection Support Workbook,** Grammar and Style, p. 34

℘G **Writing and Grammar,** Ruby Level, p. 562

▪ **Daily Language Practice Transparencies** ▪

Writing

℘G **Writing and Grammar,** Ruby Level, p. 58

💿 **Writing and Grammar iText CD-ROM**

▪ **Writing Models and Graphic Organizers on Transparencies,** p. 91

▪ **BLOCK SCHEDULING:** Resources marked with this symbol provide varied instruction during 90-minute blocks.

❸ Writing Lesson

Autobiographical Account

With your activities, friendships, family and school events, successes and failures, you have a vast amount of material to build your autobiography. Choose an important experience and discuss it. Tell what made this experience memorable and describe what you have learned from it.

Prewriting   Brainstorm for a list of details from the experience. Note what happened, what you felt, and what you learned. Include specific details that will help your readers understand your experience better.

Drafting   As you draft, incorporate details that will make the event and its significance clear to readers. Remember to show the cause-and-effect relationship between the event or experience and your life.

Revising   When you revise, pay attention to cause-and-effect relationships. Add transition words to make these relationships more obvious.

Model: Revising to Show Cause and Effect

I pivoted the wrong way. The ball bounced off Alec's back, and

ricocheted into the goal. I had scored a goal for the other team!
                                             as a result of my mistake
The buzzer sounded. The game was over, we had lost.
                                                   ∧

> Transition words and phrases such as *as a result* highlight cause-and-effect relationships.

 Prentice Hall Writing and Grammar Connection: Chapter 4, Section 4

❹ Extension Activities

Listening and Speaking Think of a few areas in which the students in your class would like to improve. In small groups, consider specific action steps you can take, and write a **class improvement plan.** Be sure to identify the following elements of a plan:

- how you will define the steps to be taken
- how you will record your efforts
- what your time frame will be

Each group should then present its plan in brief oral reports. **[Group Activity]**

Research and Technology With a group, create a **travel brochure** for tourists visiting Philadelphia. Use the Internet and electronic reference sources to gather information and obtain appropriate pictures, maps, or lists. If possible, blend your text and images in one file using a desktop publishing program.

Take It to the Net   www.phschool.com

Go online for an additional research activity using the Internet.

from The Autobiography / from Poor Richard's Almanack ◆ 151

ASSESSMENT RESOURCES

The following resources can be used to assess students' knowledge and skills.

Selection Assessment
- **Formal Assessment,** pp. 38–40
- **Open Book Test,** pp. 22–24
- **Got It! Assessment Videotapes,** Tape 1
- **Test Bank Software**
- **Take It to the Net**
  Visit www.phschool.com for self-tests and additional questions on the selection.

Writing Rubric
- **Performance Assess. and Portfolio Mgmt.,** p. 9

PRENTICE HALL ASSESSMENT *SYSTEM*
- **Workbook**
- **Skill Book**
- **Transparencies**
- **CD-ROM**

---

❸ Writing Lesson

- Remind students of the features of an autobiography by rereading the definition on p. 139.
- Tell students that when they write autobiographies, they should try to develop a fully rounded picture of their experiences by including details that help readers envision both situations and emotions.
- Have students use the Cause-and-Effect organizer from **Writing Models and Graphic Organizers on Transparencies,** p. 91, to help them show the effects that an experience had on their life.
- Use the Writing Lesson to guide students in developing their autobiography.
- Use the Autobiographical Narrative rubric in **Performance Assessment and Portfolio Management,** p. 9, to evaluate students' autobiographies.

❹ Research and Technology

- Encourage students to examine travel brochures in the school library to get a sense of the features they commonly include.
- Have students focus on three to five important historic sites, rather than trying to cover all of Philadelphia.
- As students research these sites, remind them to gather both text and images so they can create a brochure that is not only informative but also visually appealing.

CUSTOMIZE INSTRUCTION
For Universal Access

To address different learning styles, use the following activities suggested in the **Extension Activities** booklet, p. 8.

For Visual/Spatial and Interpersonal Learners, use Activity 5.

For Bodily/Kinesthetic Learners, use Activity 6.

A Closer Look

▶Critical Viewing

Answer: The audience seems
unemotional. They are attentive and
interested.

A Closer Look

All the News That's Fit to Print

Colonial Newspapers Paved the Way for a Free Press

"EXTRA! EXTRA! Read all about it! Newspapers banned! Journalists Jailed! Americans Fight for a Free Press!" Those might have been the headlines blaring from a local newspaper if you had lived in America in the eighteenth century. Might have been, that is, if colonial newspapers had headlines. America's earliest newspapers bore little resemblance to the publications we know today. They were crudely printed on wooden hand presses, and contained only a clumsy illustration or two. Most were just one or two pages, and their stories were often no more involved than a listing of ship arrivals. Despite the primitive character of these early newspapers, they laid the groundwork for a uniquely American phenomenon: a free press that could criticize the government.

▲ Critical Viewing In this image portraying the trial of Peter Zenger, with what emotions does the audience seem to be reacting to the lawyer's argument? [Interpret]

Trailblazers The first American newspaper was printed on September 25, 1690. Titled *Publick Occurrences, Both Foreign and Domestick*, the Boston-based paper filled three of four pages, leaving the last page blank for readers' notes. It contained no headlines, and mixed news and editorials into the same stories. The remarkable thing about *Publick Occurrences* was that it existed at all. England had no history of a free and independent press. All British publications were licensed by the King. If a newspaper criticized the crown, it could be shut down with no legal recourse. Yet *Publick Occurrences* was published without British approval, and printed stories that the Massachusetts royal governor found offensive. As a result, it lasted exactly one issue.

Americans waited 14 more years for another newspaper. In 1704, the Boston *News-Letter*, appeared. The *News-Letter* contained financial and foreign news as well as records of births and deaths. Approved by the governor of the Massachusetts Bay Colony, the *News-Letter* was little more than a British mouthpiece, careful not to offend colonial authorities.

The Franklin Brothers In contrast, other papers sought controversy. For example, the New England *Courant*, first published in 1721 by James Franklin, appeared without British approval. The paper jabbed mercilessly at the royal governor, and eventually landed Franklin in jail. While serving his sentence,

JOIN, or DIE.

James Franklin handed control of the paper to his 16-year-old brother, Benjamin—someone who would play his own significant role in our nation's history. The following year, Ben ran away to New York, and later to Philadelphia.

In 1729, Benjamin Franklin founded another newspaper, the Pennsylvania *Gazette*. The *Gazette* was the first newspaper to carry weather reports, interviews, and cartoons, and it immediately became the most successful publication of its kind in the colonies.

Freedom of the Press is Born A landmark legal case helped establish freedom of the press in America. In 1733, John Peter Zenger, a German immigrant, began publishing the *New York Weekly Journal*. The paper immediately ran afoul of the royal governor by publishing articles critical of his policies. One year after the newspaper was founded, Zenger was thrown in jail for libel.

In his 1735 trial, Zenger's lawyer, Andrew Hamilton, argued that while Zenger had indeed printed material offensive to the governor, the material was true and, therefore, not libelous. Under British law, such a concept had never been argued. British law held that even true statements against the government could be legally silenced. Hamilton made an impassioned plea to the jury to defend the "cause of liberty . . . the liberty both of exposing and opposing arbitrary power . . . by speaking and writing truth."

The jury found Zenger innocent. As a result of the Zenger case, the British refrained from prosecuting American journalists, even when their criticisms of the government grew intense in the years leading up to the American Revolution.

Revolutionary Journalists Most historians agree that the American Revolution would not have happened when it did without the efforts of colonial newspapers. Newspapers stoked the flames of revolution, coining phrases like "taxation without representation" and influencing public perception of England as an enemy. When the British Stamp Act of 1765 imposed a heavy tax on all printed materials, the press denounced the legislation and refused to pay the tax. Even though the Stamp Act was repealed in 1766, it united editors and publishers in support of independence. Indeed, in 1776, most newspapers printed the Declaration of Independence on their front page.

During the Revolution, newspapers brought accounts of military developments to an eager readership. By the time the war was over, newspapers had gained enormous strength. American newspapers represented something the world had never before seen: a press committed to telling the truth, not pleasing the government.

▲ **Critical Viewing** This image was created by Benjamin Franklin for his newspaper in 1754. What does it suggest about the impact of the French war on colonial unity? **[Analyze]**

▼ **Critical Viewing** What does this image of Ben Franklin's printing press show about the physical labor of printing in colonial America? **[Infer]**

All the News That's Fit to Print ◆ 153

▶**Critical Viewing**

Answer: Franklin suggests that the colonies are a natural unit and if they separate they will perish. The image of the snake as well as the brief warning "join or die" underscores this idea.

▶**Critical Viewing**

Answer: It suggests that printing was hard physical work, even for a newspaper with a limited circulation.

Critical Thinking

1. Why do you think newspapers were so popular in early America?

   Answer: American newspapers were not censored. People liked reading about news and opinions, just as they do today. People who did not have time to catch up on news with their friends might have time to glance at a paper. Newspapers attacked unpopular politicians, and readers enjoyed these attacks.

2. What role did newspapers play in the Revolution?

   Answers: They spread popular ideas and opinions. They informed readers about new Parliamentary edicts and taxes. They helped everyone keep abreast of the political situation. Their editorials urged people to rebel against the king and the royal governors. They helped to create and maintain a revolutionary mood and keep readers informed about events.

The Declaration of Independence ✦ *from* The Crisis

Lesson Objectives

1. **To analyze and respond to literary elements**
   - Literary Analysis: Persuasion
   - Comparing Literary Works
2. **To read, comprehend, analyze, and critique speeches**
   - Reading Strategy: Recognizing Charged Words
   - Reading Check Questions
   - Review and Assess Questions
   - Assessment Practice (ATE)
3. **To develop word analysis skills, fluency, and systematic vocabulary**
   - Vocabulary Development Lesson: Word Analysis: Latin Root: *-fid-*
4. **To understand and apply written and oral language conventions**
   - Spelling Strategy
   - Grammar and Style Lesson: Parallelism
5. **To understand and apply appropriate writing and research strategies**
   - Writing Lesson: A Proposal to the Principal
   - Extension Activity: Write a Précis
6. **To understand and apply listening and speaking strategies**
   - Extension Activity: News Reports

STEP-BY-STEP TEACHING GUIDE	PACING GUIDE
PRETEACH	
Motivate Students and Provide Background	
Use the Motivation activity (ATE p. 154)	5 min.
Read and discuss author and the background features (SE/ATE pp. 154, 156) **A**	5 min.
Introduce the concepts	
Introduce the Literary Analysis and Reading Strategy (SE/ATE p. 155) **A**	15 min.
Pronounce the vocabulary words and read their definitions (SE p. 155)	5 min.
TEACH	
Monitor Comprehension	
Informally monitor comprehension by circulating while students read independently or in groups **A**	35 min.
Monitor students' comprehension with the Reading Check notes (SE/ATE pp. 157, 161)	as students read
Develop vocabulary with Vocabulary notes (SE pp. 156, 158, 159, 161; ATE p. 161)	as students read
Develop Understanding	
Develop students' understanding of persuasion with the Literary Analysis annotations (SE pp. 156, 157, 158; ATE pp. 156, 157, 158) **A**	5 min.
Develop students' ability to recognize charged words with with the Reading Strategy annotations (SE p. 161; ATE p. 161)	5 min.
ASSESS	
Assess Mastery	
Assess students' mastery of the Reading Strategy and Literary Analysis by having them answer the Review and Assess questions (SE/ATE p. 163)	15 min.
Use one or more of the print and media Assessment Resources (ATE p. 165) **A**	up to 45 min.
EXTEND	
Apply Understanding	
Have students complete the Vocabulary Development Lesson and the Grammar and Style Lesson (SE p. 164) **A**	20 min.
Apply students' ability to use forceful words by using the Writing Lesson (SE/ATE p. 165) **A**	45 min.
Apply students' understanding using one or more of the Extension Activities (SE p. 165)	20–90 min.

 ACCELERATED INSTRUCTION:
Use the strategies and activities identified with an **A**.

UNIVERSAL ACCESS
- ● = Below Level Students
- ▲ = On-Level Students
- ■ = Above Level Students

Time and Resource Manager

RESOURCES		
PRINT 📖	**TRANSPARENCIES** 🖼	**TECHNOLOGY** 💿 🎧 📼
• **Beyond Literature,** Community Connection: Local Newspaper Editorial, p. 9 ▲ ■		• **Interest Grabber Video,** Tape 2 ● ▲ ■
• **Selection Support Workbook:** ● ▲ ■ Literary Analysis, p. 40 Reading Strategy, p. 39 Build Vocabulary, p. 37	• **Literary Analysis and Reading Transparencies,** pp. 17 and 18 ● ▲ ■	
• **Adapted Reader's Companion** ● • **Reader's Companion** ●		• **Listening to Literature** ● ▲ ■ Audiocassettes, Side 5 Audio CDs, CD 3
• **English Learner's Companion** ● ▲ • **Literatura en español** ● ▲ • **Literary Analysis for Enrichment** ■		
• **Formal Assessment:** Selection Test, pp. 39–40 ● ▲ ■ • **Open Book Test,** pp. 25–27 ● ▲ ■ • **Performance Assessment and Portfolio Management,** p. 17 ● ▲ ■ • **PRENTICE HALL ASSESSMENT SYSTEM** ● ▲ ■	• **PRENTICE HALL ASSESSMENT SYSTEM** ● ▲ ■ Skills Practice Answers and Explanations on Transparencies	• **Test Bank Software** ● ▲ ■ • **Got It! Assessment Videotapes,** Tape 1 ● ▲
• **Selection Support Workbook:** ● ▲ ■ Grammar and Style, p. 38 • **Writing and Grammar,** Ruby Level ● ▲ ■ • **Extension Activities,** p. 9 ● ▲ ■	• **Daily Language Practice Transparencies** ● ▲ • **Writing Models and Graphic Organizers on Transparencies,** pp. 79, 95 ● ▲ ■	• **Writing and Grammar iText CD-ROM** ● ▲ ■ 💻 *Take It to the Net* www.phschool.com

■ **BLOCK SCHEDULING:** Use one 90-minute class period to preteach the selection and have students read it. Use a second 90-minute class period to assess students' mastery of skills and have them complete one of the Extension Activities.

Step-by-Step Teaching Guide
for pp. 154–155

❶ Motivation

Jefferson and Paine wrote inspirational words that roused colonial Americans to action. Set the following scene for students. They are soldiers dressed in ragged clothes. It's winter; snow and ice surround them. A few have light jackets; some are barefoot. All are hungry, huddled in tents without floors. Badly defeated in the last battle, they think of home.

What spoken words could keep these desperate soldiers fighting for independence? Have students answer in their journals, writing in the first person as a soldier in the Revolutionary war. Discuss their responses. Then explain that they are about to read two writing selections that inspired those soldiers.

📼 Interest Grabber Videotapes

As an alternative, you may wish to play "The Declaration of Independence: Two Documents That Define the United States" on Tape 1.

More About the Authors

Though he spent nearly all his life in public service, Thomas Jefferson actually preferred life on his farm. He loved to read and owned a library of 6,400 books.

Thomas Paine's words aroused much passion in the hearts of his listeners. Not all of it was positive, however. Many hated Paine. Some found his personality offensive. Others disagreed with his views on religion. Perhaps it was Paine's dislike for compromise that earned him the most enemies.

Prepare to Read

❶ The Declaration of Independence ◆ *from* The Crisis, Number 1

Thomas Jefferson (1743–1826)

When you look at all of Thomas Jefferson's achievements, it seems there was virtually nothing that he couldn't do. Not only did he help our nation win its independence and serve as its third president, but he also founded the University of Virginia, helped establish the public school system, designed his own home, invented a type of elevator for sending food from floor to floor, and created the decimal system for American money. He was a skilled violinist, an art enthusiast, and a brilliant writer.

Revolutionary Leader Born into a wealthy Virginia family, Jefferson attended the College of William and Mary and went on to earn a law degree. While serving in the Virginia House of Burgesses, he became an outspoken defender of American rights. When conflict between the colonists and the British erupted into revolution, Jefferson emerged as a leader in the effort to win independence.

Valued Statesman When the war ended, Jefferson served as the American minister to France for several years. He then served as the nation's first secretary of state and second vice president before becoming president in 1801. While in office, Jefferson nearly doubled the size of the nation by authorizing the purchase of the Louisiana Territory from France.

On the morning of July 4, 1826, the fiftieth anniversary of the Declaration of Independence, Jefferson died at the age of 83. John Adams, Jefferson's fellow contributor to the Declaration of Independence, died only several hours after his longtime friend. Adams's last words were "Thomas Jefferson still survives."

Thomas Paine (1737–1809)

Thomas Paine met Benjamin Franklin in London, and the introduction changed his life—and American history. Paine emigrated to the colonies from England in 1774. With a letter of introduction from Franklin, Paine began a career as a journalist. In January 1776, he published *Common Sense*, in which he argued that Americans must fight for independence. The pamphlet created a national mood for revolution.

Inspiring Essayist Paine enlisted in the American army toward the end of 1776. At that time, the army had just suffered a crushing defeat by the British in New Jersey and had retreated into Pennsylvania. The soldiers were suffering from freezing weather, a shortage of provisions, and low morale. Paine was writing the first of a series of essays entitled *The American Crisis*. Washington ordered Paine's essay read to his troops before they crossed the Delaware River to defeat the Hessians at the Battle of Trenton.

In 1787, several years after the end of the American Revolution, Paine traveled to Europe and became involved with the French Revolution. Though he wrote in support of the revolutionary cause in *The Rights of Man* (1791–1792), he was imprisoned for pleading against the execution of the overthrown French king. While in prison, he began writing *The Age of Reason* (1794), an attack on organized religion. The book turned American public opinion against him, and when he died in 1809, he was a broken man. Years later, however, Paine was once again recognized as a hero of the Revolution.

154 ◆ *A Nation Is Born (1750–1800)*

TEACHER RESOURCES

The following resources can be used to enrich or extend the instruction for pp. 154–155.

Motivation

📼 **Interest Grabber Video**, Tape 2 ▪

Background

📖 **Beyond Literature**, p. 9

💻 *Take It to the Net*
Visit www.phschool.com for background and hotlinks for the selections.

Literary Analysis

📔 **Selection Support Workbook:** Literary Analysis, p. 40

📄 **Literary Analysis and Reading Transparencies,** Persuasion, p. 18 ▪

Reading

📄 **Literary Analysis and Reading Transparencies,** Compare Literary Works, p. 17

▪ **BLOCK SCHEDULING:** Resources marked with this symbol provide varied instruction during 90-minute blocks.

Preview

Connecting to the Literature

Today, we witness armed struggles for freedom through reports in the news media. The best way to experience what our own revolution was like, however, is to read documents, like these by Jefferson and Paine.

❷ Literary Analysis

Persuasion

Persuasion is writing meant to convince readers to think or act in a certain way. A persuasive writer appeals to emotions or reason, offers opinions, and urges action. The writer must also back up his or her points with evidence. For example, to support his argument for independence, Jefferson presents a list of offenses committed by the British king.

> He has dissolved representative houses repeatedly, for opposing with manly firmness his invasions of the rights of the people.

In these works, notice how each writer appeals to both reason and emotion to persuade readers of the rightness of his position.

Comparing Literary Works

Jefferson's and Paine's writings argue in support of independence. They were, however, written for different **audiences**. Jefferson wrote to the British king, while Paine wrote for a broad colonial readership. As you read, look for the ways in which different audiences shape each document's message.

❸ Reading Strategy

Recognizing Charged Words

Charged words are likely to produce a strong emotional response. For example, a word like *tyranny*, which means "oppressive power," may evoke feelings of outrage. To avoid being swayed by charged words, look for support to back up the words. Use a chart like the one shown to record charged words and their connotations, or the ideas they suggest.

Vocabulary Development

unalienable (un āl′ yən ə bəl) *adj.* not to be taken away (p. 156)

usurpations (yōō′ sər pā′ shənz) *n.* unlawful seizures of rights or privileges (p. 156)

perfidy (pʉr′ fə dē) *n.* betrayal of trust (p. 158)

redress (ri dres′) *n.* compensation for a wrong done (p. 158)

magnanimity (mag′ nə nim′ ə tē) *n.* ability to rise above pettiness or meanness (p. 158)

acquiesce (ak′ wē es′) *v.* agree without protest (p. 159)

consanguinity (kän′ saŋ gwin′ ə tē) *n.* kinship (p. 159)

impious (im′ pē əs) *adj.* lacking reverence for God (p. 161)

infidel (in′ fə dəl′) *n.* person who holds no religious belief (p. 161)

The Declaration of Independence / from The Crisis, Number 1 ◆ 155

---

❷ Literary Analysis

Persuasion

- Tell students that in reading these selections by Jefferson and Paine, they will focus on persuasion, or writing meant to convince readers to think or act a certain way.

- After reading aloud the instruction, have a volunteer read the quotation from Jefferson on page 155. Then read this Paine excerpt to students: "...if a thief breaks into my house, burns and destroys my property, and kills or threatens to kill me...am I to suffer it?" Discuss how both excerpts appeal to reason and emotion.

- Use the instruction for Comparing Literary Works to highlight other similarities and differences between the two selections.

- Use the Persuasion transparency in **Literary Analysis and Reading Transparencies,** p. 18, to demonstrate for students how to identify persuasive techniques.

❸ Reading Strategy

Recognizing Charged Words

- Remind students that charged words inspire an emotional response. Usually these words carry strong connotations, or associated meanings.

- Point out to students that charged words can greatly advance a writer's persuasive goals by appealing to listeners' emotions. Demonstrate this by completing the chart from the student page using the word *tyranny*.

- Instruct students to complete their own charts as they read, inserting charged words from the selection and then identifying the connotations and emotions each inspires.

Vocabulary Development

- Pronounce each vocabulary word for students, and read the definition as a class. Have students identify any words with which they are already familiar.

 E-Teach

Visit E-Teach at www.phschool.com for teachers' essays on how to teach, with questions and answers.

CUSTOMIZE INSTRUCTION FOR UNIVERSAL ACCESS

For Special Needs Students	For Less Proficient Readers	For English Learners
Have students read the adapted version of "The Crisis" in the **Adapted Reader's Companion.** This version provides basic-level instruction in an interactive format with questions and write-on lines. Completing the adapted version will prepare them to read the selection in the Student Edition.	Have students read "The Crisis" in the **Reader's Companion.** This version provides basic-level instruction in an interactive format with questions and write-on lines. After students finish the selection in **Reader's Companion,** have them complete the questions and activities in the Student Edition.	Have students read the adapted version of this selection in the **English Learner's Companion.** This version provides basic-level instruction in an interactive format with questions and write-on lines. Completing the adapted version will prepare them to read the selection in the Student Edition.

Step-by-Step Teaching Guide
For pp. 156–162

CUSTOMIZE INSTRUCTION
For Visual/Spatial Learners

For each point that Jefferson makes about King George and his treatment of the colonies, direct students to create one or more index cards. On each card, students can record each point and the evidence Jefferson uses to support it. Using various colors of either index cards or highlighter pens, students can organize the information for easy reference.

❶ About the Selection

Perhaps the most influential document in American history, *The Declaration of Independence* details the philosophy of the colonial revolutionaries and outlines their experiences with what they call a tyrannical king.

In this famous battlecry of freedom, Jefferson identifies what he calls "self-evident" truths, pointing out the equality of men and the tenuous contract of government. Then, in a list of the objectionable acts of King George III, arranged from least offensive to most, Jefferson outlines the reasons that the colonials are dissatisfied with their government. Jefferson reaches the reasoned conclusion that every rational means of reaching détente with Britain has failed, and, therefore, the United States of America must become independent of Britain.

❷ Literary Analysis

Persuasion

• Draw students' attention to the bracketed passage. Have students paraphrase the long sentence.

   Possible response: Because it isn't wise to change governments without serious reasons, people are likely to just go along with things even if they aren't entirely fair.

• Then ask students the Literary Analysis question on page 156: Why does Jefferson introduce the ideas that one does not change a government for "light" causes?

   Answer: Jefferson is arguing that the colonists' reasons for declaring independence are very serious.

156

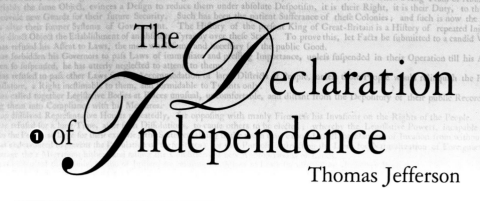

The Declaration
❶ of Independence
Thomas Jefferson

Background

In 1776, Jefferson was chosen (with Franklin, Adams, and others) to write a declaration of the colonies' independence. The draft presented to the Second Continental Congress was largely Jefferson's work. To his disappointment, however, Congress made changes before approving the document. They dropped Jefferson's condemnation of the British for tolerating a corrupt Parliament, and they struck out a strong statement against slavery.

When in the course of human events, it becomes necessary for one people to dissolve the political bands which have connected them with another, and to assume among the powers of the earth, the separate and equal station to which the laws of nature and of nature's God entitle them, a decent respect to the opinions of mankind requires that they should declare the causes which impel them to the separation.

We hold these truths to be self-evident: that all men are created equal; that they are endowed by their Creator with certain <u>unalienable</u> rights; that among these are life, liberty and the pursuit of happiness; that to secure these rights, governments are instituted among men, deriving their just powers from the consent of the governed; that whenever any form of government becomes destructive of these ends, it is the right of the people to alter or to abolish it, and to institute new government, laying its foundation on such principles and organizing its powers in such form, as to them shall seem most likely to effect their safety and happiness. Prudence, indeed, will dictate that governments long established should not be changed for light and transient causes; ❷ and accordingly all experience hath shown, that mankind are more disposed to suffer while evils are sufferable than to right themselves by abolishing the forms to which they are accustomed. But when a long train of abuses and <u>usurpations</u>, pursuing invariably the same object, evinces a design to reduce them under absolute despotism,[1] it is their

---

1. **despotism** (des′ pət iz′ əm) *n.* tyranny.

156 ◆ *A Nation Is Born (1750–1800)*

---

unalienable (un āl′ yən ə bəl) *adj.* not to be taken away

Literary Analysis
Persuasion Why does Jefferson introduce the idea that one does not change a government for "light" causes?

usurpations (yōō′ sər pā′ shənz) *n.* unlawful seizures of rights or privileges

---

TEACHING RESOURCES

The following resources can be used to enrich or extend the instruction for pp. 156–162.

Literary Analysis
▢ **Writing Models and Graphic Organizers on Transparency**, p. 95 ▪

Reading
▢ **Reader's Companion**
▢ **English Learner's Companion**
▢ **Selection Support:** Reading Strategy, p. 39; Build Vocabulary, p. 37

▢ **Adapted Reader's Companion**
◯ **Listening to Literature Audiocassettes**, Side 5
◉ **Listening to Literature Audio CDs**, CD 3 ▪

▪ **BLOCK SCHEDULING:** Resources marked with this symbol provide varied instruction during 90-minute blocks.

right, it is their duty, to throw off such government, and to provide new guards for their future security. Such has been the patient sufferance of these colonies; and such is now the necessity which constrains them to alter their former systems of government. The history of the present king of Great Britain is a history of repeated injuries and usurpations, all having in direct object the establishment of an absolute tyranny over these states. To prove this, let facts be submitted to a candid world.

He has refused his assent to laws the most wholesome and necessary for the public good.

He has forbidden his governors to pass laws of immediate and pressing importance, unless suspended in their operation till his assent should be obtained; and when so suspended, he has utterly neglected to attend to them.

He has refused to pass other laws for the accommodation of large districts of people, unless those people would relinquish the right of representation in the legislature, a right inestimable to them and formidable to tyrants only.

He has called together legislative bodies at places unusual, uncomfortable, and distant from the depository of their public records, for the sole purpose of fatiguing them into compliance with his measures.

He has dissolved representative houses repeatedly, for opposing with manly firmness his invasions on the rights of the people.

He has refused for a long time after such dissolutions to cause others to be elected, whereby the legislative powers, incapable of annihilation, have returned to the people at large for their exercise, the state remaining in the mean time exposed to all the dangers of invasion from without, and convulsions within.

He has endeavored to prevent the population of these states; for that purpose obstructing the laws for naturalization of foreigners, refusing to pass others to encourage their migration hither, and raising the conditions of new appropriations of lands.

He has obstructed the administration of justice, by refusing his assent to laws for establishing judiciary powers.

He has made judges dependent on his will alone, for the tenure of their offices, and the amount and payment of their salaries.

He has erected a multitude of new offices, and sent hither swarms of officers to harass our people and eat out their substance.

He has kept among us in times of peace standing armies without the consent of our legislatures.

The Declaration of Independence, John Trumbull, Yale University Art Gallery

Literary Analysis
Persuasion What does the statement about submitting facts to a "candid world" suggest about the intended audience?

5 ▲**Critical Viewing**
What is the mood of this painting? In what ways does the mood suit the occasion? **[Relate]**

6 ☑**Reading Check**
Why did Jefferson write this long list of facts?

The Declaration of Independence ◆ 157

CUSTOMIZE INSTRUCTION FOR UNIVERSAL ACCESS

For Special Needs Students	For Less Proficient Readers	For Gifted/Talented Students
As volunteers take turns reading aloud Jefferson's list of grievances, work with others to paraphrase and decode difficult language. Use the outline organizer in **Writing Models and Graphic Organizers**, p. 95, to help students record the meaning of each grievance. As they reread, have students identify Jefferson's persuasive evidence.	To help students understand Jefferson's list of grievances against King George III, model the use of an outline organizer from **Writing Models and Graphic Organizers on Transparency**, p. 95. Direct students to insert a subtopic name for each grievance, then list the supporting evidence Jefferson provides.	Have students read Jefferson's list of grievances, directing their attention to its paragraph structure. As they complete the outline organizer from **Writing Models and Graphic Organizers on Transparency**, p. 95, discuss how Jefferson's use of parallel structure adds impact to his writing.

3 **Literary Analysis**
Persuasion

- Write the bracketed text from p. 157 on the chalkboard. Review with students the meaning of the word *candid* and emphasize that Jefferson uses the word in the sense of "unbiased."
- Ask students the Literary Analysis question on p. 157: What does the statement about submitting facts to a "candid world" suggest about the intended audience?
  Possible response: It suggests that Jefferson believed he was speaking to the world and that he believed the world would judge his words fairly and honestly.

4 **Background**
Art

The Declaration of Independence
by John Trumbull

This painting is only thirty inches wide yet it contains forty-eight figures! Trumbull's placement of his subjects' heads and the sweep of banners in the background add action and excitement to the composition. Use these questions for discussion:

1. How does this painting add to your knowledge of the events surrounding Jefferson's work?
   Possible response: It shows that Jefferson spoke for many.

2. How does the composition of the painting heighten the impact of Jefferson's writing?
   Possible response: The dignity with which the figures are posed shows how important Jefferson's writing was to them.

5 ▶**Critical Viewing**

Answer: The mood of this painting is dignified, stately, and triumphant, which suits the historic occasion.

6 ☑**Reading Check**

Answer: He wanted to build a strong case against King George III in order to show that the colonists had no choice but to seek independence.

Jefferson echoed Locke's views about natural rights with his phrase "unalienable rights." Like Locke, Jefferson advanced the idea that government has no right to give or take away such rights. Instead, the social contract allows communities to grant certain individuals the power to govern. If a ruler fails to act in the community's best interest, he has broken the social contract and should be removed from power.

❽ Literary Analysis

Persuasion

- Identify for students the bracketed text on p. 158 and the earlier portion of the list on p. 157. Have students explain how each listed item is similar.
  Answer: They are all descriptions of how George III has mistreated the colonists.

- Invite students to recap Jefferson's main point in the selection's opening paragraph.
  Answer: When one people decides it must separate itself from the rule of another, it should explain why.

▶ **Monitor Progress** Ask students the Literary Analysis question on p. 158: What support does this catalog of offenses provide for Jefferson's argument?
Answer: By showing the king as an unfit ruler who has imposed a series of unjust and oppressive measures on the colonists, Jefferson answers any argument readers may advance in favor of remaining loyal to Britain.

He has affected to render the military independent of, and superior to, the civil power.

He has combined with others to subject us to a jurisdiction foreign to our constitution and unacknowledged by our laws, giving his assent to their acts of pretended legislation: for quartering large bodies of armed troops among us; for protecting them by a mock trial from punishment for any murders which they should commit on the inhabitants of these states; for cutting off our trade with all parts of the world; for imposing taxes on us without our consent; for depriving us, in many cases, of the benefits of trial by jury; for transporting us beyond seas to be tried for pretended offenses; for abolishing the free system of English laws in a neighboring province,[2] establishing therein an arbitrary government, and enlarging its boundaries, so as to render it at once an example and fit instrument for introducing the same absolute rule into these colonies; for taking away our charters, abolishing our most valuable laws, and altering fundamentally the forms of our governments; for suspending our own legislatures, and declaring themselves invested with power to legislate for us in all cases whatsoever.

He has abdicated government here, by declaring us out of his protection and waging war against us.

He has plundered our seas, ravaged our coasts, burned our towns, and destroyed the lives of our people.

He is at this time transporting large armies of foreign mercenaries to complete the works of death, desolation, and tyranny, already begun with circumstances of cruelty and perfidy scarcely paralleled in the most barbarous ages, and totally unworthy the head of a civilized nation.

He has constrained our fellow citizens taken captive on the high seas to bear arms against their country, to become the executioners of their friends and brethren, or to fall themselves by their hands.

He has excited domestic insurrections amongst us, and has endeavored to bring on the inhabitants of our frontiers, the merciless Indian savages, whose known rule of warfare is an undistinguished destruction of all ages, sexes, and conditions.

In every stage of these oppressions we have petitioned for redress in the most humble terms. Our repeated petitions have been answered only by repeated injury.

A prince whose character is thus marked by every act which may define a tyrant is unfit to be the ruler of a free people.

Nor have we been wanting in attentions to our British brethren. We have warned them from time to time of attempts by their legislature to extend an unwarrantable jurisdiction over us. We have reminded them of the circumstances of our emigration and settlement here. We have appealed to their native justice and magnanimity and we

---

2. **neighboring province** Quebec.

158 ◆ A Nation Is Born (1750–1800)

Jefferson, Locke, and the Social Contract

In writing the Declaration of Independence, Jefferson drew on a theory of government devised by earlier European political thinkers, especially the Englishman John Locke (1632–1704). Locke argued that all people are born with certain *natural rights*. According to Locke, these rights are not the property of governments. Rather, these rights belong to people simply because they are human. Locke's ideas also contributed to Jefferson's notion that governments derive their power from "the consent of the governed." Locke called this concept the *social contract*. According to Locke, and Jefferson after him, when a ruler like King George III breaks the social contract by acting abusively, the people have the right to revolt against his unjust rule. In 1776, that is what the American colonists did.

perfidy (pur´ fə dē) *n.* betrayal of trust

redress (ri dres´) *n.* compensation for a wrong done

Literary Analysis
Persuasion What support does this catalog of offenses provide for Jefferson's argument?

magnanimity (mag´ nə nim´ ə tē) *n.* ability to rise above pettiness or meanness

---

✹ **ENRICHMENT: Social Studies Connection**

A Spreading Flame of Freedom

When representatives from the thirteen colonies signed the Declaration of Independence, they were forging a path that other nations would soon follow. France, who helped the colonists defeat Great Britain, soon found itself amidst revolution against tyranny from within. The French Revolution began in 1789 and soon led to overthrow of the monarchy and to the establishment of democracy. In Latin America, a campaign for independence from Spain, led by Simón Bolívar, took shape early in the nineteenth century. His dream was to create a nation of united excolonies, a kind of United States of Central and South America.

For this reason, Bolívar is sometimes called "the George Washington of South America."

Ironically, although the French Revolution inspired many new independence movements, it was France's usurpation of the Spanish throne that prompted Bolívar to raise an army to liberate what are now the countries of Venezuela, Colombia, Ecuador, Peru, and Bolivia from Spanish rule.

have conjured[3] them by the ties of our common kindred to disavow these usurpations which would inevitably interrupt our connections and correspondence. They too have been deaf to the voice of justice and of consanguinity. We must therefore acquiesce in the necessity which denounces our separation and hold them, as we hold the rest of mankind, enemies in war, in peace friends.

We, therefore, the representatives of the United States of America in general congress assembled, appealing to the Supreme Judge of the world for the rectitude of our intentions, do in the name and by authority of the good people of these colonies, solemnly publish and declare that these united colonies are and of right ought to be free and independent states; that they are absolved from all allegiance to the British Crown, and that all political connection between them and the state of Great Britain is and ought to be totally dissolved; and that as free and independent states, they have full power to levy war, conclude peace, contract alliances, establish commerce, and to do all other acts and things which independent states may of right do.

And for the support of this declaration, with a firm reliance on the protection of divine providence, we mutually pledge to each other our lives, our fortunes and our sacred honor.

consanguinity (kän′ saŋ gwin′ ə tē) *n.* kinship

acquiesce (ak′ wē es′) *v.* agree without protest

---

3. **conjured** *v.* solemnly appealed to.

Review and Assess
Thinking About the Selection

1. **Respond:** How would you have responded to the Declaration if you were (a) the king of England, (b) someone from a nation lacking in human rights, or (c) a Native American?

2. **(a) Recall:** What points about human rights does Jefferson make at the beginning of the Declaration? **(b) Analyze:** Why does he begin with these observations before addressing the colonists' situation?

3. **(a) Recall:** What does Jefferson claim has happened at "every stage of these oppressions"? **(b) Interpret:** What is Jefferson's purpose in presenting this information?

4. **(a) Evaluate:** What is the most convincing evidence that Jefferson cites to support his points? Explain. **(b) Evaluate:** How would you rate the overall effectiveness of his argument? Why?

5. **Synthesize:** The period in which this document was written is often referred to as the Age of Reason because of the emphasis on logic and discipline at the time. What elements of Jefferson's Declaration reflect a faith in reason?

The Declaration of Independence ◆ 159

ASSESS

Answers for p. 159
Review and Assess

1. **Possible responses: (a)** I would have been insulted and angered as the Declaration paints me in a very negative light; **(b)** I would be first astonished and then envious that Americans believed themselves entitled to these rights; **(c)** I would have been angered by the hypocrisy toward my people suggested in the Declaration. It neither grants my people inalienable rights nor acknowledges that the colonists stole America's land from my people.

2. **Possible response: (a)** He says that some human rights are unalienable. **(b)** He wants to appeal to feelings about justice in the minds of listeners.

3. **(a)** At every stage the colonists have petitioned the king for redress. **(b)** He wants to show the colonists as reasonable and thereby justify their final decision to seek independence.

4. **Possible response: (a)** Jefferson's most convincing evidence is the last item about the king's dissolution of colonial representative houses when these oppose him. **(b)** Jefferson's argument is overwhelmingly effective. He first appeals to ideas about justice and humanity. Then he paints the king as an abusive ruler and the colonists as highly reasonable subjects. This contrast supports his argument that George III left the colonists no alternative but to seek independence.

5. Jefferson's detailed explanation of Great Britain's wrongs against the colonies set up a rational justification for the revolution. He clearly expects the reader to follow his reasonings.

CUSTOMIZE INSTRUCTION FOR UNIVERSAL ACCESS

For Special Needs Students	For Less Proficient Readers
Have students work through the selection paragraph by paragraph to find the key ideas in each. Help students identify unfamiliar words or usage *before* they address the content of each paragraph.	Encourage students to break down Jefferson's long sentences. One way to do this is by separating clauses. Using a random complex sentence, demonstrate how to identify and separate clauses. Ask students to paraphrase each clause. Then help them compose their own sentences using the paraphrasing.

⑨ About the Selection

Paine's rhetoric, designed to build morale among the soldiers, promises that the severity of their situation makes triumph more glorious. He also vows that God would never desert those who fight for just causes. He criticizes Tories for being short sighted, because he believes revolution to be inevitable. He praises those who stand fast in their opposition to England and calls on all the states to put forth their best efforts to resist English rule. He labels those who step aside as evil, cold-hearted, cowardly, and unprincipled and concludes with an extended metaphor comparing the British to theives who must be punished.

⑩ Background

Art

Recruiting for the Continental Army by William T. Ranney

Ranney has captured what must have been the energy of the moment through artistic dramatization and excitement. The image resonates with patriotism. Since a recruit was paid less than seven dollars a month, from which the cost of his clothing was deducted, an appeal to patriotism was a chief recruiting strategy.

Use these questions for discussion:

1. How could Thomas Paine have used this painting to advance his position?
   Possible response: He could use it to show weary soldiers that many support them, even at cost to themselves, and that patriotic fervor remains strong.

2. Why is this painting an appropriate choice to illustrate Paine's essay?
   Possible response: The artist assumes the same fervor as Paine does in depicting the noble act of signing to fight for independence.

⑪ ▶ Critical Viewing

Answer: By placing a single recruit in the center and strongly lighting him and by placing the recruiter in an elevated position with his arms raised toward the heavens, the artist conveys the solemnity and intense feelings surrounding the revolutionary cause.

160

⑨ from *The Crisis* *Number 1*

Thomas Paine

Recruiting for the Continental Army, c. 1857-59, William T. Ranney, Munson-Williams-Proctor Institute, Museum of Art, Utica, New York

*T*hese are the times that try men's souls.
The summer soldier and the sunshine patriot will in this crisis, shrink from the service of his country; but he that stands it now, deserves the love and thanks of man and woman. Tyranny, like hell, is not easily conquered; yet we have this consolation with us, that the harder the conflict, the more glorious the triumph. What we obtain too cheap, we esteem too lightly; 'tis dearness only that gives everything its value. Heaven knows how to put a proper price upon its goods; and it would be strange indeed, if so celestial an article as FREEDOM should not be highly rated. Britain, with an army to enforce

160 ◆ A Nation Is Born (1750–1800)

⑪ ▲ Critical Viewing
What details in this image capture the patriotic fervor of Paine's essay? **[Connect]**

✸ **ENRICHMENT: Social Studies Connection**

Revolutionary Blockbuster

Colonists began noticing Thomas Paine's extraordinary talents as a communicator nearly a year before the dark winter of his *Crisis* essay. Paine's pamphlet *Common Sense*, which in early 1776 had helped set the revolutionary mood, made a dramatic impact on colonists. The pamphlet spoke out fervently and frankly for independence, brooking no compromises or halfway measures—advocating only complete independence. Further, Paine criticized the entire concept of monarchy and called for the abolition of inherited class status. He said, "the birthday of a new world is at hand" and so it was.

her tyranny, has declared that she has a right (*not only* to TAX) but "to BIND *us in* ALL CASES WHATSOEVER," and if being *bound in that manner*, is not slavery, then is there not such a thing as slavery upon earth. Even the expression is <u>impious</u>, for so unlimited a power can belong only to God . . .

I have as little superstition in me as any man living, but my secret opinion has ever been, and still is, that God Almighty will not give up a people to military destruction, or leave them unsupportedly to perish, who have so earnestly and so repeatedly sought to avoid the calamities of war, by every decent method which wisdom could invent. Neither have I so much of the <u>infidel</u> in me, as to suppose that he has relinquished the government of the world, and given us up to the care of devils; and as I do not, I cannot see on what grounds the king of Britain can look up to heaven for help against us: a common murderer, a highwayman, or a housebreaker, has as good a pretense as he . . .

I once felt all that kind of anger, which a man ought to feel, against the mean[1] principles that are held by the Tories:[2] a noted one, who kept a tavern at Amboy, was standing at his door, with as pretty a child in his hand, about eight or nine years old, as I ever saw, and after speaking his mind as freely as he thought was prudent, finished with this unfatherly expression, "*Well! give me peace in my day.*" Not a man lives on the continent but fully believes that a separation must some time or other finally take place, and a generous parent should have said, "*If there must be trouble let it be in my day, that my child may have peace*"; and this single reflection, well applied, is sufficient to awaken every man to duty. Not a place upon earth might be so happy as America. Her situation is remote from all the wrangling world, and she has nothing to do but to trade with them. A man can distinguish himself between temper and principle, and I am as confident, as I am that God governs the world, that America will never be happy till she gets clear of foreign dominion. Wars, without ceasing, will break out till that period arrives, and the continent must in the end be conqueror; for though the flame of liberty may sometimes cease to shine, the coal can never expire . . .

I turn with the warm ardor of a friend to those who have nobly stood, and are yet determined to stand the matter out: I call not upon a few, but upon all; not on *this* state or *that* state, but on *every* state; up and help us; lay your shoulders to the wheel; better have too much force than too little, when so great an object is at stake. Let it be told to the future world, that in the depth of winter, when nothing but hope and virtue could survive, that the city and the country, alarmed at one common danger, came forth to meet and to repulse it. Say not that thousands are gone, turn out your tens of thousands; throw not the burden of the day upon Providence, but "*show your faith by your*

---
1. **mean** *adj.* here, small-minded.
2. **Tories** colonists who remained loyal to Great Britain.

impious (im′ pē əs) *adj.* lacking reverence for God

infidel (in′ fə dəl′) *n.* a person who holds no religious belief

Reading Strategy
Recognizing Charged Words In what ways might the word "foreign" help Paine inspire the colonists to fight against Great Britain?

⑭ ✓Reading Check
Whom does Paine call to arms?

⑫ Vocabulary Development

The Latin Word Root *-fid-*

- Draw students' attention to Paine's use of the word *infidel*, and tell students that the root *-fid-* comes from the Latin word *fides*, which means "faith."
- Remind students that the prefix "in-" adds the meaning of "not" or "without" to a word.
- Guide students to see that Paine uses the word to mean specifically "one who is unfaithful to his religion."
- Let students know that the root *-fid-* appears in many words containing the idea of faith or trust, such as *fidelity* (faithfulness) and *confidence* (faith in the self).

⑬ Reading Strategy

Recognizing Charged Words

- Invite a volunteer to stand and speak the words of the bracketed passage on p. 161. Encourage the volunteer to put special emphasis on the word *foreign*.
- Ask students what associations they have with the word *foreign*, reminding students to be honest but sensitive in their responses. **Possible response:** Students may acknowledge associating the word *foreign* with things that are strange or alien to them but also with things that are exciting and interesting.

▶ Monitor Progress Ask students the Reading Strategy question on p. 161: In what ways might the word "foreign" help Paine inspire the colonists to fight against Great Britain? **Possible response:** With it, Paine casts the British as outsiders, when in fact most colonists were of British stock. By distancing the colonists' from their adversary, Paine appeals to the colonists' sense of themselves as an emerging nation. Casting Great Britain as a foreign power rather than as the colonists' legal government helps colonists avoid any sense of disloyalty.

⑭ ✓Reading Check

Answer: He calls on every colonist in every state to help with this important cause.

CUSTOMIZE INSTRUCTION FOR UNIVERSAL ACCESS

For Less Proficient Readers	For English Learners	For Advanced Learners
Point out to students the many places in Paine's essay where he uses either all capital letters or italicized letters. Explain that Paine used these techniques to emphasize certain ideas. Thus, when students encounter a phrase such as "*not only* to TAX" they can use the special treatment of the letters to help them construct meaning.	Tell students that Paine uses figurative speech—words that have meaning beyond their literal definition—throughout his essay. Model how to decode this figurative language, using the example of the "summer soldier" and the "sunshine patriot." Then invite volunteers to take turns restating figurative language.	In a May 1777 address to the Continental Congress, George Washington said, "I am wearied to death. I think the game is pretty near up." Have students write a speech as if they were Washington, conveying their thoughts *after* hearing Paine's essay. Challenge them to quote from Paine's essay, and to express a renewed dedication to the revolution.

Review and Assess

1. **Possible response:** A Tory would probably be angered by Paine's remarks and would consider him a traitor to the crown.

2. **(a)** He says the king is as bad as a common murderer, a highwayman, or burglar. **(b)** It is exaggerated for effect. **(c)** Some students might find Paine a trustworthy reporter because he conveys the emotional immediacy of events. Others might argue that Paine is too committed to one side to give a balanced account.

3. **(a)** He says that the harder a goal is to achieve, the more worthy it is and that Britian's colonial policy amounts to slavery. **(b)** He refers to people who are available only when times are easy and who desert the cause in bleak, harsh, difficult circumstances.

4. **Possible responses: (a)** He appeals to the emotions of resentment and anger. **(b)** He appeals more to emotions. For example, he uses many charged words, such as *crisis, tyranny, hell, heaven, freedom,* and *slavery.*

5. **(a)** The main idea of the essay is that the colonists are fighting for a just cause; thus they should endure the difficult times and not lose sight of their purpose. **(b) Possible response:** He cites oppressive British policy; he suggests that separation from Britain is inevitable, and should be resolved now. **(c) Possible response:** Paine's vivid descriptions of the American predicament and his comparisons between British behavior and the actions of common criminals make his argument very persuasive.

6. **Possible response:** The image of America as a champion of freedom over tyranny still holds true today.

---

works," that God may bless you. It matters not where you live, or what rank of life you hold, the evil or the blessing will reach you all. The far and the near, the home counties and the back, the rich and the poor, will suffer or rejoice alike. The heart that feels not now, is dead: the blood of his children will curse his cowardice, who shrinks back at a time when a little might have saved the whole, and made *them* happy. (I love the man that can smile at trouble; that can gather strength from distress, and grow brave by reflection.) 'Tis the business of little minds to shrink; but he whose heart is firm, and whose conscience approves his conduct, will pursue his principles unto death. My own line of reasoning is to myself as straight and clear as a ray of light. Not all the treasures of the world, so far as I believe, could have induced me to support an offensive war, for I think it murder; but if a thief breaks into my house, burns and destroys my property, and kills or threatens to kill me, or those that are in it, and to "*bind me in all cases whatsoever*," to his absolute will, am I to suffer it? What signifies it to me, whether he who does it is a king or a common man: my countryman, or not my countryman; whether it be done by an individual villain or an army of them? If we reason to the root of things we shall find no difference; neither can any just cause be assigned why we should punish in the one case and pardon in the other.

Review and Assess

Thinking About the Selection

1. **Respond:** If you were a colonist who had remained loyal to the British how would you react to Paine's argument?

2. **(a) Recall:** In the second paragraph, what terms does Paine use to describe the British king? **(b) Analyze:** Is this description realistic or exaggerated? Explain. **(c) Draw Conclusions:** Is Paine trustworthy as a reporter of historical events? Explain.

3. **(a) Recall:** In the first paragraph, with what ideas does the author justify the struggle of revolution? **(b) Interpret:** What does Paine mean when he refers to "the summer soldier" and the "sunshine patriot"?

4. **(a) Classify:** Name two emotions to which Paine appeals in this essay. **(b) Make a Judgment:** Does Paine appeal more to emotion or to reason in this essay? Support your answer.

5. **(a) Interpret:** What is the main idea of this essay? **(b) Support:** What persuasive techniques does Paine use to develop his main idea? **(c) Evaluate:** In your opinion, how persuasive is Paine's essay?

6. **Connect:** Which of Paine's images of the American Revolution still hold true today? Why?

✐ ASSESSMENT PRACTICE

Recognize Cause and Effect　　　　　　　　　　　**(For more practice, see test Preparation Workbook, p. 9.)**

To help students understand cause-and-effect relationships, have them reread pp. 156–157. Then ask:

Which of the following actions of the British king was NOT a cause of the American colonists' Declaration of Independence?

A His refusal to pass laws created by the colonists

B His dissolution of colonial houses of representatives

C His interference with the American justice system

D His personal visit to the thirteen colonies

Choices *A, B,* and *C* contributed to the Americans' decision to declare independence from Britain. Choice *D* is the correct choice, because it was NOT a cause of the revolution.

■ **BLOCK SCHEDULING:** Resources marked with this symbol provide varied instruction during 90-minute blocks.

Review and Assess

Literary Analysis

Persuasion

1. (a) Why does Jefferson present such a long list of grievances? (b) Does this list make his argument more or less convincing? Why?

2. What strategy does Jefferson use to organize his list of grievances—for example, time order, order of severity, or order of importance—and why do you think he chose this organization?

3. An **aphorism** is a brief, pointed statement expressing a wise or clever observation. Use a chart like the one shown to identify three aphorisms Paine uses and to analyze how each one contributes to his overall message.

Aphorism	Meaning	Purpose
What we obtain too cheap, we esteem too lightly.	We value only those things that cost us dearly.	to emphasize the point that the struggle for freedom is worth it

Comparing Literary Works

4. (a) Who is the intended **audience** for each of these works? (b) What kinds of supporting evidence would you expect to see in writing meant for each audience? (c) Does each writer offer the type of support that is most convincing for his audience? Explain.

5. In what ways does the language of each document reflect its intended audience?

Reading Strategy

Recognizing Charged Words

6. These authors carefully selected **charged words** to stir readers' emotions. What responses do each of these words evoke in you?

   a. liberty   **b.** justice   **c.** honor   **d.** barbarous

7. In describing the colonists' British rulers, how does Paine's use of the word *thief* evoke a different response than would the word *supporters*?

Extend Understanding

8. **Social Studies Connection:** The Declaration of Independence has been a source of inspiration throughout the world, and Paine's essay contains many frequently quoted sayings. Why do you think these documents have had such a lasting impact?

The Declaration of Independence / from The Crisis, Number 1 ◆ 163

Quick Review

Persuasion is writing meant to convince readers to think or act in a certain way.

The **audience** of a literary work is the person or group of people the author intends to reach.

Charged words contain strong connotations likely to produce an emotional response.

 Take It to the Net

www.phschool.com

Take the interactive self-test online to check your understanding of these selections.

⁂ **ENRICHMENT: Further Reading**

Other Works by Jefferson and Paine

The Complete Jefferson, Saul K. Padover, ed.

Common Sense, The Rights of Man, and Other Essential Writing of Thomas Paine

 Take It to the Net

Visit www.phschool.com for more information on the authors.

Answers for p. 163

Review and Assess

1. Possible responses: **(a)** He wants to make it clear that the colonists are justified in their position. **(b)** It makes his argument more convincing by showing how much the colonists have already tolerated.

2. Possible response: He organizes them in order of severity, from least offensive to most offensive. He chose that organization to build the intensity of his argument.

3. Students' charts should contain aphorisms from the text.

4. **(a)** Jefferson speaks to the world, while Paine speaks more specifically to those colonists already fighting and those who he hopes will fight. **(b)** Possible response: I would expect to see carefully constructed rational arguments in writing for the British king and the world stage, but more emotional and highly charged writing for soldiers in the field. **(c)** Yes, they do. Although both documents are moving, Jefferson's is more closely argued whereas Paine's is more rousing, aimed at the heart rather than the head.

5. Possible response: Jefferson uses the language of diplomacy while Paine uses more familiar language as if he were addressing readers personally.

6. Possible responses: **(a)** *Liberty* suggests an ideal life characterized by freedom. **(b)** *Justice* can be associated with fairness, freedom, and equality. **(c)** *Honor* evokes a sense of morality and dignity. **(d)** *Barbarous* suggests cruel and animalistic behavior.

7. Possible response: *Supporters* is a kinder word that suggests care-taking, while *thief* suggests a negative image of Britain.

8. Possible response: These documents have had a lasting impact because they express ideals of freedom, equality, and justice, which are enduringly appealing. Also, both men use convincing arguments and employ memorable language in strong appeals to human emotion.

❶ Vocabulary Development

Word Analysis

1. *confident*: certain; self-assured
2. *fidelity*: faithful devotion
3. *confidential*: maintaining a trust

Spelling Strategy

1. acquaint
2. acknowledge
3. acquittal
4. acquire
5. acquiesce

Fluency: True or False

1. True
2. True
3. True
4. False
5. False
6. False
7. False
8. False
9. False

❷ Grammar and Style

1. Jefferson was patriotic, intelligent, imaginative, and courageous.
2. He wrote the Declaration of Independence, designed his home, and co/founded a university.
3. Henry was a great speaker, Jefferson was a gifted writer, and Washington was a talented military leader.
4. Paine was passionate, eloquent, inspiring, and persuasive.
5. The Declaration accused King George III of tyranny, unfair taxation, military occupation, and bullying the legislature.

Writing Application

Students' opinions should be supported by facts and contain at least two examples of parallelism.

Integrate Language Skills

Vocabulary Development Lesson

Word Analysis: Latin Root -fid-

The Latin root *-fid-* means "faith" or "trust." An *infidel* is a person without faith, and *perfidy* is a betrayal of trust. Use your understanding of this root to define the following words.

    1. confident   2. fidelity   3. confidential

Spelling Strategy

When you join the prefix *ac-* to a word or root beginning with *q*, *k*, or hard *c*, retain the *c*, as in *acclaim*. Add *ac-* to each of the words or roots below.

    1. -quaint
    2. -knowledge
    3. -quittal
    4. -quire
    5. -quiesce

Grammar and Style Lesson

Parallelism

Parallelism refers to the repeated use of phrases, clauses, or sentences that are similar in structure or meaning.

> **Example:** He has *plundered our seas, ravaged our coasts, burned our towns*, and *destroyed the lives of our people.* (parallel verb phrases: *verb-our-object*)

Practice Rewrite each sentence to correct errors in parallel structure.

    1. Jefferson was patriotic, intelligent, imaginative, and he had courage.

WG *Prentice Hall Writing and Grammar Connection: Chapter 20, Section 6*

164 ◆ *A Nation Is Born (1750–1800)*

Fluency: True or False

Indicate which of the statements below are true and which are false. Explain your answers.

1. If a child *acquiesces* about being put to bed, she accepts her bedtime.
2. Leaders should have *magnanimity*.
3. There is no need for *redress* if no wrong has been committed.
4. American citizens would not be right to protest *usurpations* of their property.
5. Enemies have *consanguinity* toward one another.
6. The quality of *perfidy* is honorable.
7. *Unalienable* rights must be agreed upon annually.
8. *Infidels* observe certain religious holidays.
9. A pastor's *impious* behavior would be celebrated by his parishioners.

2. He wrote the Declaration, designed his home, and was one of the people who founded a university.
3. Henry was a great speaker, Jefferson was a gifted writer, and the talented military leader was Washington.
4. Paine was passionate, eloquent, inspiring, and he was persuasive.
5. The Declaration accused King George III of tyranny, of unfair taxation, of military occupation, and it said he bullied the legislature.

Writing Application Write your opinion on an issue about which you have strong feelings. Use two examples of parallelism to emphasize ideas.

TEACHING RESOURCES

The following resources can be used to enrich or extend the instruction for pp. 164–165.

Vocabulary

📖 **Selection Support Workbook:** Build Vocabulary, p. 37

📖 **Vocabulary and Spelling Practice Book** (Use this booklet for skills enrichment.) ▪

Grammar

📖 **Selection Support Workbook:** Build Grammar Skills, p. 38

WG **Writing and Grammar,** Ruby Level, p. 504

▪ **Daily Language Practice Transparencies** ▪

Writing

WG **Writing and Grammar,** Ruby Level, p. 118

💿 **Writing and Grammar iText CD-ROM**

▪ **Writing Models and Graphic Organizers on Transparencies,** p. 95

▪ **BLOCK SCHEDULING:** Resources marked with this symbol provide varied instruction during 90-minute blocks.

Writing Lesson

A Proposal to the Principal

Like Jefferson and Paine, you can change your world with the persuasive use of words. Choose a problem or troubling situation in your school. Then, draft a proposal to the principal explaining why the situation needs attention and how you think it should be corrected. Use parallelism to emphasize your ideas.

Prewriting List the reasons that the situation in your school should be changed. Write details—facts, examples, explanations—supporting each reason. Keep word connotations in mind as you choose evidence.

Drafting Use language with positive connotations to present ideas you would like your audience to accept; use language with negative connotations to present ideas you would like your audience to reject. Remember, however, that because you are writing for the principal, you should demonstrate respect.

Model: Drafting with Forceful Language

Separate lounges for upper-and lowerclassmen reflect superior planning. Wise thinkers recognize that each group needs a place to pursue age-appropriate activities.

> Terms such as *superior* and *wise* reinforce the soundness of this proposal.

Revising Review your proposal and revise any statements that seem unreasonable. Check that you have offered evidence in addition to using forceful language to support your argument.

 Prentice Hall Writing and Grammar Connection: Chapter 7, Section 4

Extension Activities

Listening and Speaking With a group, write and deliver two **news reports**. First, recount the signing of the Declaration. Then, present the version of the story that might have appeared on London television. For each, remember these tips:

- Include the facts of the events.
- Consider what the news means to each specific audience.

Present both reports to classmates. **[Group Activity]**

Research and Technology A **précis** is a concise summary of essential points or statements. Research Thomas Paine's life, using library and Internet sources to gather information about his philosophies and activities. Then, write a précis detailing Paine's contributions to the Revolutionary cause.

 Take It to the Net www.phschool.com

Go online for an additional research activity using the Internet.

The Declaration of Independence / from The Crisis, Number 1 ◆ *165*

ASSESSMENT RESOURCES

The following resources can be used to assess students' knowledge and skills.

Selection Assessment

- **Formal Assessment,** pp. 39–40
- **Open Book Test,** pp. 25–27
- **Got It! Assessment Videotapes,** Tape 1
- **Test Bank Software**
- **Take It to the Net**
  Visit www.phschool.com for self-tests and additional questions on the selections.

Writing Rubric

- 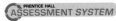 **Performance Assessment and Portfolio Mgmt.,** p. 17

 ASSESSMENT *SYSTEM*

- **Workbook**
- **Skill Book**
- **Transparencies**
- **CD-ROM**

---

❸ Writing Lesson

- Have students use the Problem/Solution Organizer in **Writing Models and Graphic Organizers on Transparencies,** p. 79; to organize their prewriting details. Remind them to organize their evidence for the greatest impact as Jefferson did with his list of grievances.
- Use the Writing Lesson to guide students in developing their proposals.
- Adapt the Persuasive Speech rubric in **Performance Assessment and Portfolio Management,** p. 17, to evaluate students' proposals.

❹ Listening and Speaking

- Divide each group into two teams. Have one team focus on the colonial news report and the other focus on the British report. Then, have the teams discuss the facts and events they want to include in their reports.
- Suggest some typical television news elements that students might want to include in their reports—for example, video footage, still photographs, voice-over narration, and mood music.
- Encourage students to create a script or storyboard for their report, noting how each visual will work with the spoken text.
- Have students rehearse their reports before making their final presentation to the class.

CUSTOMIZE INSTRUCTION
For Universal Access

To address different learning styles, use the activities suggested in the **Extension Activities** booklet p. 9.

For Visual/Spatial Learners, use Activity 5.

For Bodily/Kinesthetic and Verbal/Linguistic Learners, use Activity 6.

For Verbal/Linguistic and Intrapersonal Learners, use Activity 7.

Lesson Objectives

1. To analyze logical and faulty modes of persuasion
2. To understand the nature and purpose of newspaper editorials

About Newspaper Editorials

- Write the word *editor* on the chalkboard and explain that it comes from the Latin verb *edere*, which means "to give out, to publish." Editorials give out the publisher's point of view.

- Bring in the editorial page from a major newspaper such as *The New York Times*. Point out that newspapers publish editorials written by their own editorial boards, as well as editorials sent in by independent writers.

Reading Strategy

Analyzing Logical and Faulty Modes of Persuasion

- Review the types of supporting details listed under the Reading Strategy head. Challenge students to examine editorials in a school or local newspaper and find an example of each type of supporting detail.

- Have students go over the list of faulty methods of persuasion and explain why each one is faulty.

Newspaper Editorials

About Newspaper Editorials

In addition to the news, newspapers also offer opinions on the issues they report. Opinions appear primarily on the editorial page and may include political cartoons, letters to the editor, and editorials.

An **editorial** is a persuasive essay that addresses a current topic on which public opinion may be divided, and it presents the editor's or publisher's point of view. Occasionally, a newspaper may pair two editorials representing opposing points of view, creating a debate of sorts. In the editorials you are about to read, the newspaper presents two opposing viewpoints on the benefits of *pro bono* work—services donated "for the public good."

Reading Strategy

Analyzing Logical and Faulty Modes of Persuasion

To achieve its persuasive purpose, an editorial's argument requires factual support. Such support may include:

- *statistics*, or numerical data.
- *anecdotes*, or brief stories that illustrate the writer's point.
- *quotations* from expert sources.
- *facts* that are well researched and that support the writer's view.

Faulty modes of persuasion, on the other hand, twist facts or use nonfactual methods in an attempt to persuade. Review the chart below for a list of these commonly used—but faulty—techniques.

Faulty Modes of Persuasion

Type	Definition	Example
loaded language	using words with strongly negative or positive connotations	"The firm's *horse-and-buggy* attitudes *tyrannize* mothers."
bandwagon appeal	urging readers to adopt a course of action because "everyone is doing it"	"*Every other high school* in the county has a soccer team; we need one, too."
circular reasoning	supporting a point by merely stating it in other words	"The law *should be amended* because it needs *changing*."
post hoc, ergo propter hoc argument	assuming that because one event occurs after another, the first causes the second	"Since she became CEO, the value of our stock has fallen. It's time for her to resign."

September 25, 2000

Lawyers Leave Poor Behind

Our View: Volunteerism in legal profession drops as salaries rise.

For weeks, the head of the Arizona Civil Liberties Union has been asking law firms to represent, on a volunteer basis, a client in a free-speech case against the state government. And for weeks, Eleanor Eisenberg has been turned down.

Eisenberg knows firsthand what national statistics are now showing: Law firms are bucking the national trend toward charity and doing less "pro bono" work than in the past. As a result, there aren't enough lawyers willing to represent the poor and disenfranchised when they have legal trouble.

According to a recent survey by *The American Lawyer* magazine, lawyers average 40 minutes of pro bono work per week on lawsuits. That's 35% less unpaid legal work than in 1992.

Lawyers aren't even keeping their own standards. During the same period that 20% more Americans took up volunteer work, attorneys at 82 of the USA's top 100 law firms averaged fewer than the 50 hours a year of pro bono that the American Bar Association (ABA) recommends.

But instead of offering solutions for the disenfranchised, the bar association gives excuses. ABA pro bono committee chairman Robert Weiner says the top firms' record isn't as bad as it looks, and predicts it will improve as young, idealistic new hires demand to do charitable work and change the culture of their offices.

That view glibly skips over the real problem: To cover wildly increasing salaries, lawyers at many firms have been told to work more hours—2,000 per year in some cases—to bring in more revenue, according to findings from the Pro Bono Institute at Georgetown University.

Some firms in Washington, D.C., Texas, and California have stopped or cut back on counting pro bono hours as part of their lawyers' work time, institute president Esther Lardent says. With management creating that sort of an atmosphere, it's no surprise that charitable work at all but a dozen of the nation's biggest firms gets short shrift.

The ABA's own statistics show that 80% of the nation's poor are forced to go without legal help when they really need it. And the association is in the perfect position to lead efforts to ensure that the poor are treated equally.

For a start, it should encourage greater donations to legal-aid charities and insist that pro bono hours be counted as part of a lawyer's performance. A toughly worded rule could influence state bar associations, which often have the power to enforce standards.

Last winter, the Minnesota state bar was defeated in its effort to force lawyers to report fully the amount of pro bono work they do. Similar measures in Massachusetts and Colorado were also defeated.

Yet reforms do work. In Florida, a court forced lawyers to disclose their pro bono hours, and the ABA says their record subsequently improved.

The late Supreme Court Justice Louis Brandeis once noted that the legal profession "is an occupation which is pursued largely for others and not merely for one's self."

The ABA needs to remind law firms of that standard—forcefully.

An editorial expresses the official view of the publication.

In order to be persuasive, editorials often include factual support, such as statistics (numerical data).

As a part of its persuasive strategy, this editorial anticipates and answers opposition arguments.

This quote by a revered member of the legal profession eloquently supports the editorial position.

- Point out that the title and subhead of the editorial summarize its argument. Not all editorials summarize their viewpoints with a subhead like the one shown here, but most have descriptive titles.
- Have students identify examples of the four types of supporting details described on p. 166.
- Have students read the editorial and try to identify examples of both logical and faulty methods of persuasion. Remind them that they may not find examples of both types of persuasion.
- After students have read the editorial, have them discuss whether they were persuaded to its viewpoint. If so, which parts of the argument convinced them? If not, why not?

CUSTOMIZE INSTRUCTION FOR UNIVERSAL ACCESS

For Gifted/Talented Students

Challenge pairs of students to come up with a topic on which they disagree. They might choose an issue that currently faces the school or the community. Each student can then write an editorial supporting his or her position. Have partners read each other's editorials and identify the strongest opposing argument. Then, have them revise their own editorials, adding a refutation of the opposition's argument. Students can share their work with classmates, who can determine whether the arguments are logical or faulty.

Pro Bono Work Still Valued

- Draw students' attention to the editorial's subhead: "Idealistic new lawyers will lead way in boosting service to poor." Make sure they understand that the viewpoint of this editorial opposes the one on p. 167.

- After they read this editorial, have the class discuss which editorial they find more convincing, and why.

- Point out the writer's name and credentials at the end of the editorial. Explain that these credentials constitute a supporting argument for the editorial. The writer shows that he is the chairman of a committee that deals with the subject of his editorial. Therefore, he probably has an informed opinion on this topic.

- Point out that the writer's credentials may also work against his persuasiveness, because it is clearly in his own interest to defend a committee on which he sits. The fact that he is on this committee may make readers doubt his ability to be objective.

September 25, 2000

Pro Bono Work Still Valued

Opposing View:
Idealistic new lawyers will lead way in boosting service to poor.

By Robert N. Weiner

The writer begins with a quote from an expert source that will frame the ideas to follow.

The great judge, Learned Hand, once identified the central commandment in a democracy, "Thou shalt not ration justice." As caretakers of our system of justice, lawyers have a special obligation to ensure access to justice for those who cannot afford legal fees.

The legal profession has embraced its obligation to serve the poor. Our model code of ethics instructs that "A lawyer should aspire to render at least 50 hours of pro bono public legal services per year," primarily to persons of limited means.

This editorial writer uses numerical data to support his argument.

The legal profession can be proud of its record. The recent survey indicating a drop in pro bono hours covers only some large firms, not the profession as a whole. The largest 500 firms donated more than 2 million pro bono hours in 1999. Moreover, the vast majority of lawyers do not practice in large firms. These lawyers, including government attorneys and corporate counsel, also do valuable pro bono work, serving as the last best hope of the least fortunate among us.

The writer answers critics by noting that the issue is more complex than it seems at first glance.

Indeed, many lawyers, from every corner of the profession, have toiled with great dedication on behalf of the poor. The American Bar Association (ABA), for example, launched an effort to obtain representation for disabled children denied Social Security benefits. Thousands of lawyers responded. In addition, with numerous projects ranging from rural pro bono to child custody to immigration and asylum, ABA has worked with state and local programs linking many thousands of lawyers with even more clients.

Nonetheless, we meet less than 20% of the legal needs of the poor, far short of ensuring access to justice. In addition to pro bono efforts, federal funding of the Legal Services Corp. remains critical.

The paradox here is that prosperity—higher billable hours—indeed has put pressure on pro bono time. But this will not last. Firms must compete for the best law students. They remain idealistic, and a prime area of competition is the firms' pro bono programs. We expect that this new generation of lawyers will reinforce our profession's commitment to its most basic values.

Robert N. Weiner is chairman of the American Bar Association's Standing Committee on Pro Bono and Public Service.

The editorial also uses anecdotal information that illustrates the writer's position.

Check Your Comprehension

1. According to the first editorial, how well do lawyers meet the standard for *pro bono* work set by the American Bar Association?

2. According to the second editorial, how should the legal profession feel about its record regarding *pro bono* work?

3. What does the writer of that editorial believe will increase law firms' involvement in *pro bono* work?

Apply the Reading Strategy

Analyzing Logical and Faulty Modes of Persuasion

4. Using a chart like the one shown here, analyze the persuasive techniques at work in each editorial.

Mode of Persuasion	Editorial 1	Editorial 2
Statistics		
Quotations		
Anecdotes		
Faulty Modes?		

5. Which editorial is more persuasive? Explain your response.

Activity

Evaluating Editorials

In a group, read and analyze several newspaper editorials on an issue that interests you. Use these questions to guide your analysis:

• What is the proposition or main idea that each editorial supports?

• What supporting evidence does each writer provide?

• What arguments, facts, or details are omitted? Why?

To complete your evaluation, rate the editorials from most to least persuasive. Explain your ratings to the class.

Comparing Informational Materials

Editorials and Advertisements

Like an editorial, an advertisement often includes factual details to support its "pitch." Look through a magazine or newspaper, and find three advertisements that catch your attention. Then, analyze their persuasive approaches. For each advertisement, decide whether the central persuasive technique is logical or faulty.

Answers for p. 169

Check Your Comprehension

1. Lawyers at 82 of the top 100 American law firms fail to meet the standard of 50 hours per year.

2. Lawyers should be proud of their contribution because most of them put in many hours of *pro bono* work.

3. Idealistic young lawyers will force law firms to increase their involvement in *pro bono* work.

Applying the Reading Strategy

4. Editorial 1: Statistics: 35% less pro bono work than in 1992, 80% of the nation's poor can't afford legal help. Quotations: Supreme Court Justice Brandeis. Anecdotes: The story of Eleanor Eisenberg. Faulty modes: Investigates only the nation's top firms; ignores smaller firms, government attorneys, and corporate counsel. Editorial 2: Statistics: Largest 500 firms donated 2 million hours in 1999. Quotations: Judge Hand. Anecdotes: ABA representing disabled children. Faulty modes: none.

5. Students may find the second editorial less persuasive because it is in the author's own interest to defend his committee.

Activity

Encourage groups to read editorials about issues they find interesting. This way, they will be more motivated to analyze the editorials with care.

Comparing Informational Materials

Remind students to examine visual images as well as words when analyzing advertisements. Like words, visuals are chosen very carefully to convey a certain message.

169

An Hymn to the Evening ✦ To His Excellency, General Washington

Lesson Objectives

1. **To analyze and respond to literary elements**
   - Literary Analysis: Personification
   - Comparing Literary Works
2. **To read, comprehend, analyze, and critique two poems**
   - Reading Strategy: Clarifying Meaning
   - Reading Check Questions
   - Review and Assess Questions
   - Assessment Practice (ATE)
3. **To develop word analysis skills, fluency, and systematic vocabulary**
   - Vocabulary Development Lesson: Latin Prefix: *re-*
4. **To understand and apply written and oral language conventions**
   - Spelling Strategy
   - Grammar Lesson: Subject and Verb Agreement
5. **To understand and apply appropriate writing and research strategies**
   - Writing Lesson: Inscription for a Monument
   - Extension Activity: Graphic Display
6. **To understand and apply listening and speaking strategies**
   - Extension Activity: Dramatic Reading

STEP-BY-STEP TEACHING GUIDE	PACING GUIDE
PRETEACH	
Motivate Students and Provide Background	
Use the Motivation activity (ATE p. 170)	5 min.
Read and discuss author and background features (SE/ ATE p. 170)	5 min.
Introduce the Concepts	
Introduce the Literary Analysis and Reading Strategy (SE/ATE p. 171)	15 min.
Pronounce the vocabulary words and read their definitions (SE p. 171)	5 min.
TEACH	
Monitor Comprehension	
Informally monitor comprehension by circulating while students read independently or in groups	15 min.
Monitor students' comprehension with the Reading Check notes (SE/ATE p. 175)	as students read
Develop vocabulary with Vocabulary notes (SE pp. 172, 175, 176; ATE p. 171)	as students read
Develop Understanding	
Develop students' understanding of personification with the Literary Analysis annotations (ATE pp. 171, 172, 175)	5 min.
Develop students' ability to clarify meanings with the Reading Strategy annotations (ATE p. 171)	5 min.
ASSESS	
Assess Mastery	
Assess students' mastery of the Reading Strategy and Literary Analysis by having them answer the Review and Assess questions (SE/ATE p. 177)	15 min.
Use one or more of the print and media Assessment Resources (ATE p. 179)	up to 45 min.
EXTEND	
Apply Understanding	
Have students complete the Vocabulary Development Lesson and the Grammar Lesson (SE p. 178)	20 min.
Apply students' ability to use a persuasive tone by using the Writing Lesson (SE/ATE p. 179)	45 min.
Apply students' understanding using one or more of the Extension Activities (SE p. 179)	20–90 min.

A **ACCELERATED INSTRUCTION:**
Use the strategies and activities identified with an **A**.

UNIVERSAL ACCESS
● = Below Level Students
▲ = On-Level Students
■ = Above Level Students

Time and Resource Manager

Reading Level: Average, Challenging
Average Number of Instructional Days: 4

RESOURCES		
PRINT 📖	**TRANSPARENCIES** 🔖	**TECHNOLOGY** 💿 🎧
• **Beyond Literature,** Humanities Connection: Fine Art, p. 10 ▲ ■		• **Interest Grabber Video,** Tape 2 ● ▲ ■
• **Selection Support Workbook:** ● ▲ ■ Literary Analysis, p. 44 Reading Strategy, p. 43 Build Vocabulary, p. 41	• **Literary Analysis and Reading Transparencies,** pp. 19 and 20 ● ▲ ■	
• **Authors In Depth,** The American Experience ■		• **Listening to Literature** ● ▲ ■ Audiocassettes, Side 5 Audio CDs, CD 3
• **Literatura en español** ● ▲ • **Literary Analysis for Enrichment** ■		
• **Formal Assessment:** Selection Test, pp. 42–44 ● ▲ ■ • **Open Book Test,** pp. 28–30 ● ▲ ■ • *PRENTICE HALL* **ASSESSMENT** *SYSTEM* ● ▲ ■	*PRENTICE HALL* **ASSESSMENT** *SYSTEM* Skills Practice Answers and Explanations on Transparencies ● ▲ ■	• **Test Bank Software** ● ▲ ■ • **Got It! Assessment Videotapes,** Tape 1 ● ▲
• **Selection Support Workbook:** ● ▲ ■ Build Grammar Skills, p. 42 • **Writing and Grammar,** Ruby Level ● ▲ ■ • **Extension Activities,** p. 10 ● ▲ ■	• **Daily Language Practice Transparencies** ● ▲ • **Writing Models and Graphic Organizers on Transparencies,** p. 67 ● ▲ ■	• **Writing and Grammar iText CD-ROM** ● ▲ ■ 🖥 *Take It to the Net* www.phschool.com

■ **BLOCK SCHEDULING:** Use one 90-minute class period to preteach the selection and have students read it. Use a second 90-minute class period to assess students' mastery of skills and have them complete one of the Extension Activities.

Step-by-Step Teaching Guide for pp. 170–171

Motivation

Understanding Wheatley's poems depends on students' ability to recognize personification. Write a list of common items on the board, such as rubber band, wind, table, cloud, car, newspaper, snow, rock, sparrow, leaf, and book. In small groups, ask students to provide sentences that give each item a human characteristic, such as "The *wind* gripped the tree and shook it violently." Put each group's sentences on the chalkboard. Compare the effect of various instances of personification. For instance, a leaf that dances in the wind takes on a different characteristic than one that hangs on tenaciously, shouldering the brutal buffeting of the wind.

▣ Interest Grabber Video

As an alternative, play "To His Excellency, General Washington: Phillis Wheatley" on Tape 1.

❶ More About the Author

Wheatley's prominent Massachusetts supporters—led by Governor Thomas Hutchinson—had administered an oral examination to her to persuade themselves of her intellectual and creative capacity. Impressed by her answers, they drafted a two-paragraph letter to the public stating, in part:

We. . .assure the World, that the POEMS specified in the following Page, were (as we verily believe) written by PHILLIS, a young Negro Girl, who was but a few Years since, brought. . .from *Africa*.

Prepare to Read

❶ An Hymn to the Evening ◆ To His Excellency, General Washington

Phillis Wheatley (1753?–1784)

Although she was an enslaved African whose native language was not English, Phillis Wheatley achieved success as a poet at an early age and went on to become one of the finest American poets of her day. This was an amazing feat, considering that few women in the colonies and even fewer slaves could read or write.

Born in West Africa, Wheatley was brought to America on a slave ship when she was about eight years old. She was purchased by John Wheatley, a Boston merchant, in 1761, probably as a gift for his wife Susannah. The Wheatleys gave Phillis their name and converted her to Christianity. They also recognized the girl's high intelligence and taught her to read and write. She avidly read the Bible, Latin and Greek classics, and works by contemporary English poets. At age thirteen, she saw her first poem published.

Fame Abroad at an Early Age In 1770, when she published a poem about the death of George Whitehead, a celebrated English clergyman, Wheatley became famous. Two years later, Wheatley met several British aristocrats who admired her poetry and helped her to publish *Poems on Various Subjects: Religious and Moral* in London in 1773. This was probably the first published work by an African in the colonies.

In a foreword to the book, the publisher claimed that persons who had read the poems felt that "Numbers would be ready to suspect they were not really the Writings of Phillis."

Therefore, he offered an "attestation" to their authorship, which was signed by eighteen prominent Massachusetts men, among them John Hancock. Phillis Wheatley was well received by London society, and Benjamin Franklin visited her there. However, *Poems on Various Subjects: Religious and Moral* was not published in the United States until 1786, two years after her death.

The Story Behind the Poem During the Revolutionary War, Wheatley wrote a poem addressed to the commander of the American forces, George Washington. In October 1775, Wheatley sent the poem to Washington. He responded:

I thank you most sincerely for your polite notice of me in the elegant lines you enclosed; and however undeserving I may be of such encomium [high praise] and panegyric [tribute], the style and manner exhibit a striking proof of your poetical talents; in honor of which, and as a tribute justly due you, I would have published the poem, had I not been apprehensive that, while I only meant to give the world this new instance of your genius, I might have incurred the imputation of vanity. . . .

Slide From Glory Though she was freed in 1773, the last several years of Wheatley's life were filled with hardship and sorrow. Three of her children died in infancy, her husband was jailed for debt, and she fell into obscurity as a poet. Though she assembled a second collection of her poetry, the manuscript was lost before it could be published. With her husband in jail and her fame having faded, Phillis Wheatley died alone and impoverished in 1784.

In the centuries since Wheatley's death, her star has again risen. She is now seen as an important forerunner—the first writer of African origin to gain a voice in the United States.

170 ◆ A Nation Is Born (1750–1800)

TEACHING RESOURCES

The following resources can be used to enrich or extend the instruction for pp. 170–171.

Motivation
▣ **Interest Grabber Video**, Tape 2 ▣

Background
▣ **Beyond Literature**, p. 10

▣ *Take It to the Net*
Visit www.phschool.com for Background and hotlinks for the selections.

Literary Analysis
▣ **Literary Analysis and Reading Transparencies,** Personification, p. 20 ▣

▣ **Selection Support:** Literary Analysis, p. 44

Reading
▣ **Literary Analysis and Reading Transparencies,** Clarify Meaning, p. 19

▣ **BLOCK SCHEDULING:** Resources marked with this symbol provide varied instruction during 90-minute blocks.

Preview
Connecting to the Literature

A movie, a haircut, a joke—you may informally praise several things or people every day. At times you may express praise in a more formal way—in a song, essay, or poem—as Phillis Wheatley does in these selections.

❷ Literary Analysis
Personification

Personification is the attribution of human powers or qualities to something that is not human, such as an inanimate object, an aspect of nature, or an abstract idea. For instance, note the way Phillis Wheatley describes the ocean in these lines:

> *Enwrapp'd in tempest and a night of storms;*
> *Astonish'd ocean feels the wild uproar . . .*

Here, the poet personifies the sea by giving it a human emotion and sensibility. In both poems, notice how Wheatley uses personification to portray her subjects in human terms.

Comparing Literary Works

Beginning with the earliest epic poems, the **poem of praise** has had a long history in literature. Some poems of praise celebrate the deeds of a hero, others celebrate the natural world, and others celebrate ordinary objects. Though both of Wheatley's poems are tributes, their subjects are very different. As you read, think about how the subject matter leads Wheatley to use distinct descriptive language and to create very different moods and meaning in each poem.

❸ Reading Strategy
Clarifying Meaning

When reading poetry, you may need to **clarify the meaning** of passages that at first seem unclear. In these poems, Wheatley often inverts common sentence order by placing a verb before its subject. Clarify meaning by rephrasing unusual word orders and checking the definitions of unfamiliar words. Use a chart like the one shown to aid your understanding.

Vocabulary Development

placid (plas´ id) *adj.* tranquil; calm; quiet (p. 172)

scepter (sep´ tər) *n.* a rod or staff held by rulers as a symbol of sovereignty (p. 172)

celestial (sə les´ chəl) *adj.* of the heavens (p. 175)

refulgent (ri ful´ jənt) *adj.* radiant; shining (p. 175)

propitious (prō pish´ əs) *adj.* favorably inclined or disposed (p. 175)

refluent (ref´ lo͞o ənt) *adj.* flowing back (p. 175)

pensive (pen´ siv) *adj.* thinking deeply or seriously (p. 176)

> **Original Sentence**
> See mother earth her offspring's fate bemoan.

> **Define Words**
> ↓
> offspring=children
> bemoan=grieve
> ↓

> **Reordered and Clarified Sentence**
> See mother earth grieve over her children's fate.

An Hymn to the Evening / To His Excellency, General Washington ◆ 171

CUSTOMIZE INSTRUCTION FOR UNIVERSAL ACCESS

For Less Proficient Readers	For English Learners	For Advanced Readers
Have students work in pairs to paraphrase the poems. Make sure they attack ideas sentence by sentence, using the reading strategy to clarify meaning. If you wish, use the Clarify Meaning transparency from **Literary Analysis and Reading Transparencies,** p. 19, as a tool. Have students share their paraphrases with the class.	With a dictionary and a thesaurus, have students generate a glossary for the poems, listing any unfamiliar words next to simpler synonyms. Then use the Clarify Meaning transparency from **Literary Analysis and Reading Transparencies,** p. 19, as a tool to model the Reading Strategy.	Challenge students to complete the Clarify Meaning transparency from **Literary Analysis and Reading Transparencies,** p. 19, *without* reference to a dictionary. Encourage them to use context and their shared knowledge to define unfamiliar words. If necessary, refer students to a dictionary.

---

❷ Literary Analysis
Personification

- Tell students that as they read Phillis Wheatley's poems, they will focus on personification, the attribution of human powers or qualities to something that is not human.

- Have students read the instruction about personification.

- Ask students to recall the Motivation activity and then ask what human qualities Wheatley attributes to the sea in the excerpt on p. 171.
  Answer: She gives it the capacity to feel astonishment and to experience *wild uproar.*

- Use the instruction for Comparing Literary Works to prepare students to read two very different Wheatley poems.

- Use the Personification transparency in **Literary Analysis and Reading Transparencies,** p. 20, to model for students how to decode personification.

❸ Reading Strategy
Clarifying Meaning

- Help students recognize that they can clarify unusual poetic wording by focusing on word meaning and word order.

- Suggest that students begin by identifying and then defining unfamiliar words in the poems.

- Then, have students look for words that appear out of their usual order. Have students experiment with a variety of word orders and see which best clarifies the meaning.

- Model the clarification process using the diagram on the student page, and direct students to use their own diagrams as they read.

Vocabulary Development

- Pronounce each vocabulary word for students, and read the definitions as a class. Have students identify any words with which they are already familiar.

🖥 E-Teach

Visit E-Teach at www.phschool.com for teachers' essays on how to teach, with questions and answers.

CUSTOMIZE INSTRUCTION
For Visual/Spatial Learners

To acquaint students with personification, have them find a picture of a statue of the goddess Columbia. You might remind them that a statue of Columbia sits atop the dome of the Capitol in Washington, D.C. When they read "To His Excellency, General Washington," ask students to compare a sculptor's interpretation with Wheatley's.

❶ About the Selection

In "An Hymn to the Evening," Wheatley directs her attention to the close of day by describing a sunset and the night's restorative powers. Beginning after sunrise, storms have shaken the earth. After the rain, however, the aroma of blossoms, the sound of water in streams and the songs of birds make music. By evening, the western sky is the most beautiful—a deep red. Grateful to God for the light, the narrator asks for a peaceful night of sleep and to awaken the next morning refreshed and ready for the day's tasks.

❷ Literary Analysis

Personification

• Read the bracketed text on p. 172 aloud for students, pausing at punctuation to give the lines their proper rhythm.

• Have students paraphrase the lines if they can.
  Possible response: The west wind brings the scent of flowers on the air.

• Ask students the following question: How is the wind personified in these lines?
  Answer: The wind breathes and exhales incense.

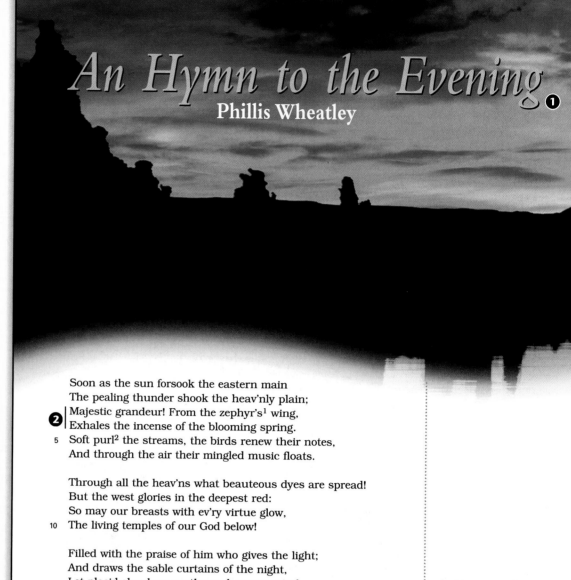

An Hymn to the Evening
Phillis Wheatley ❶

Soon as the sun forsook the eastern main
The pealing thunder shook the heav'nly plain;
❷ Majestic grandeur! From the zephyr's[1] wing,
Exhales the incense of the blooming spring.
5 Soft purl[2] the streams, the birds renew their notes,
And through the air their mingled music floats.

Through all the heav'ns what beauteous dyes are spread!
But the west glories in the deepest red:
So may our breasts with ev'ry virtue glow,
10 The living temples of our God below!

Filled with the praise of him who gives the light;
And draws the sable curtains of the night,
Let <u>placid</u> slumbers soothe each weary mind,
At morn to wake more heav'nly, more refined;
15 So shall the labours of the day begin
More pure, more guarded from the snares of sin.

Night's leaden <u>scepter</u> seals my drowsy eyes,
Then cease, my song, till far *Aurora* rise.

---

1. **zephyr's** (zef´ ərz) *n.* belonging to the west wind.
2. **purl** (pʉrl) *v.* to move in ripples or with a murmuring sound.

172 ◆ A Nation Is Born (1750–1800)

placid (plas´ id) *adj.* tranquil; calm; quiet

scepter (sep´ tər) *n.* a rod or staff held by rulers as a symbol of sovereignty

---

TEACHING RESOURCES

The following resources can be used to enrich or extend the instruction for pp. 172–176.

Literary Analysis

📘 **Literary Analysis and Reading Transparencies**, p. 20

Reading

📖 **Selection Support:** Reading Strategy, p. 43; Build Vocabulary, p. 41

🎧 **Listening to Literature Audiocassettes**, Side 5 ▪

💿 **Listening to Literature Audio CDs,** CD 3

Extension

📖 **Authors In Depth,** The American Experience (The collection includes four additional selections by Phillis Wheatley for extended reading.) ▪

▪ **BLOCK SCHEDULING:** Resources marked with this symbol provide varied instruction during 90-minute blocks.

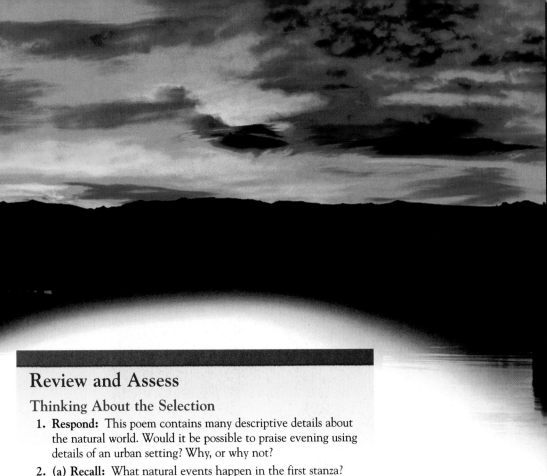

Review and Assess

Thinking About the Selection

1. **Respond:** This poem contains many descriptive details about the natural world. Would it be possible to praise evening using details of an urban setting? Why, or why not?

2. **(a) Recall:** What natural events happen in the first stanza? **(b) Interpret:** What specific words suggest the speaker's feelings about the scene she observes?

3. **(a) Recall:** What natural phenomenon does the poet describe in lines 7–8? **(b) Analyze:** What image does the poet use to make a transition from describing the natural world to describing a spiritual state of being? **(c) Draw Conclusions:** According to the poet, what are the "living temples of our God below"?

4. **(a) Recall:** What descriptive details does Wheatley use to describe the evening? **(b) Recall:** What details does she use to describe the morning? **(c) Compare and Contrast:** What mood or feeling does the poet connect with each time of day?

5. **(a) Recall:** When, according to Wheatley, are human beings more pure? **(b) Evaluate:** In your view, how accurate is Wheatley's contrast of a person's state of mind at night and in the morning?

An Hymn to the Evening ◆ *173*

Answers for p. 173

Review and Assess

1. **Possible answer:** Yes, one can praise evening with urban details. For example, one can describe the changing light reflecting in buildings.

2. **(a)** On a spring afternoon, a brief thundershower occurs; the aroma of flowers is blown through the air by the wind; the sounds of streams and birds blend together. **(b)** The words "majestic grandeur" and "music" suggest Wheatley's positive feelings about the scene.

3. **(a)** She describes a sunset. **(b)** She uses the image of people glowing with virtue just as the sky glows with light. **(c)** People are "the living temples of our God below."

4. **(a)** Wheatley uses descriptive details such as "beauteous dyes" and "deepest red." **(b)** Wheatley describes people waking in a state of mind that is more "heav'nly, more refined" and "more pure, more guarded." **(c) Possible response:** She connects evening with an ability to soothe and refresh; morning with a feeling of purity.

5. **(a)** They are more pure in the morning. **(b) Possible response:** Students may cite their own experiences with the refreshing power of sleep.

CUSTOMIZE INSTRUCTION FOR UNIVERSAL ACCESS

For Special Needs Students	For Less Proficient Readers	For English Learners
To help students clarify the meaning of difficult lines, use this strategy: Suggest that students write out any difficult lines and then use different colored markers to circle the subject, underline the verb, and double underscore the object of the verb. Afterward, suggest that they write the sentence again, reordering the words.	Students might have an easier time understanding the meaning of this poem by making a chart in which they list the different parts of the day the poem mentions—the daylight hours, sunset, and night—as well as the corresponding line numbers of the poem. Students can then record details from the poem about these times of day.	Students will need help with Wheatley's use of apostrophes. For example, point out the words "heav'ns," "ev'ry," and "heav'nly." Explain that the apostrophes indicate missing letters. Then, help students complete each word and read the pertinent lines of the poem to reinforce comprehension.

❸ **About the Selection**

This poem glorifies the bravery and goodness of the revolutionary cause by personifying America as the goddess Columbia. The poet pictures Columbia as a daughter of Mother Earth, who sympathizes with her daughter's fight as she faces her enemies. The poem then praises George Washington as "first in peace and honors," famous for both his bravery and goodness, the perfect leader for a nation defended by heaven, a leader who has the moral support of other nations that hope America will win the war against Britain. The poem asks Washington to proceed, guided by the goddess; and Wheatley suggests that he will be rewarded with a crown, a mansion, and a golden throne.

❹ **Background**

Art

Liberty and Washington

This folk art image glorifies Washington in many of the same ways as Wheatley's poem does. The light bathes the statue of George Washington and the woman standing above him as if to suggest their purity and inner light. Use these questions for discussion:

1. How do the words on the pedestal reflect Phillis Wheatley's attitude toward George Washington?
   Answer: They reinforce her admiration of Washington as a military leader, diplomat, and national hero.

2. What elements from the poem can you find in the painting?
   Possible responses: The painting displays a crown, a wreath of laurels, a flag, and the female goddess who suggests the figure of Columbia.

❺ ▶**Critical Viewing**

Answer: Students may note that the goddess tramples the British crown underfoot while she places the laurel wreath, a symbol of victory, on Washington's head. This suggests Washington's leadership in the colonists' victory over England.

---

❸ *To His Excellency, General Washington*

PHILLIS WHEATLEY

❹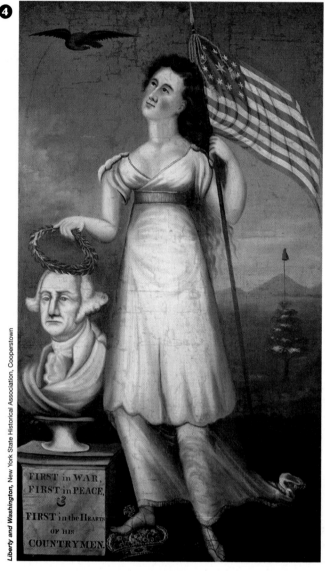

Liberty and Washington, New York State Historical Association, Cooperstown

FIRST in WAR, FIRST in PEACE, & FIRST in the HEARTS OF HIS COUNTRYMEN.

❺ ◀**Critical Viewing**
Noting the symbols of the Revolutionary conflict, explain the action of the painting.
[Interpret]

174 ◆ *A Nation Is Born (1750–1800)*

CUSTOMIZE INSTRUCTION FOR UNIVERSAL ACCESS

For Advanced Readers

Suggest that students read additional works by Phillis Wheatley. Provide students with the titles listed in the Enrichment box, ATE p. 177. You may also wish to use **Authors In Depth**, The American Experience, which contains the following selections:

- "To the Right Honorable William, Earl of Dartmouth, His Majesty's Principal Secretary of State for North America" (poem, p. 41)
- "To S.M., a Young African Painter, on Seeing His Works" (poem, p. 43)

- "On Imagination" (poem, p. 44)
- "Letter" by John Wheatley (nonfiction, p. 46)

After students have read these or other works by Wheatley, review the instruction on Comparing Literary Works. Discuss whether the additional works students read are **poems of praise**. Invite students to provide specific details from the poems, such as descriptive language, to support their interpretation.

Culture

The publication of Phillis Wheatley's work merits special note for several reasons. First, she was female; few female authors anywhere had gained recognition by the eighteenth century. Second, she was African American; that group, too, had been denied literary recognition. Third, she was a slave; slaves generally could neither read nor write. Thus, Wheatley earned many "firsts." Nevertheless, for years she stood alone as an African American female author before other African American women joined the literary ranks.

⑥ Background

Phillis Wheatley was the first poet to personify America as the goddess Columbia. By giving the country's muse a name based on the explorer Columbus, Wheatley added to the new nation's mythology. The image caught on. In fact, a statue of Columbia sits atop the dome of the Capitol building in Washington, D.C.

Celestial choir! enthron'd in realms of light,
    Columbia's scenes of glorious toils I write.
While freedom's cause her anxious breast alarms,
She flashes dreadful in refulgent arms.
5 See mother earth her offspring's fate bemoan,
And nations gaze at scenes before unknown!
See the bright beams of heaven's revolving light
Involved in sorrows and the veil of night!
    The goddess comes, she moves divinely fair,
10 Olive and laurel binds her golden hair:
Wherever shines this native of the skies,
Unnumber'd charms and recent graces rise.
    Muse![1] bow propitious while my pen relates
How pour her armies through a thousand gates,
15 As when Eolus[2] heaven's fair face deforms,
Enwrapp'd in tempest and a night of storms;
Astonish'd ocean feels the wild uproar,
The refluent surges beat the sounding shore;
Or thick as leaves in Autumn's golden reign,
20 Such, and so many, moves the warrior's train.
In bright array they seek the work of war,
Where high unfurl'd the ensign[3] waves in air.
Shall I to Washington their praise recite?
Enough thou know'st them in the fields of fight.
25 Thee, first in peace and honors,—we demand
The grace and glory of thy martial band.
Fam'd for thy valor, for thy virtues more,
Hear every tongue thy guardian aid implore!

---

1. **Muse** A Greek goddess, in this case Erato, who is thought to inspire poets. She is one of nine muses presiding over literature, the arts, and the sciences.
2. **Eolus** (ē´ ə ləs) the Greek god of the winds.
3. **ensign** (en´ sin) flag.

celestial (sə les´ chəl) *adj.* of the heavens

refulgent (ri ful´ jənt) *adj.* radiant; shining

propitious (prō pish´ əs) *adj.* favorably inclined or disposed

refluent (ref´ lōō ənt) *adj.* flowing back

⑧

✔**Reading Check**

What army is the poet celebrating?

⑦ **Literary Analysis**

Personification

- Have students read the bracketed text on p. 175 aloud. Ask them to paraphrase the lines.
  Possible response: Strong winds and storms cause ocean turbulence and heavy surf.

▶ Monitor Progress Ask students how heaven, the ocean, and autumn are personified in the bracketed lines.
Answer: Heaven has a "fair face"; the ocean is "astonished" by the wind's "wild uproar"; autumn has a "golden reign."

⑧ ✔**Reading Check**

Answer: She is celebrating the American Revolutionary army.

CUSTOMIZE FOR UNIVERSAL ACCESS

For Less Proficient Readers	For Gifted/Talented Students
Increase students' access and their enjoyment of Wheatley's poem by playing the **Listening to Literature Audiocassettes/Audio CDs.** Encourage students to first listen to the poem with their eyes closed, trying to picture Wheatley's images. Then, have students listen again as they read along silently. Tell students that they can appreciate the mood and emotions these visual images evoke even when they don't entirely understand a poem's words or meaning.	In "To His Excellency, General Washington," Phillis Wheatley personifies elements of nature, such as the ocean, autumn, and the earth. Have students choose an object or idea of their own to personify. It might be something in nature or an abstract idea such as freedom. Encourage students to communicate their personification in performance or in art.

Answers for p. 176

Review and Assess

1. Possible answer: Columbia and Washington are worthy of praise because both stand for something invaluable—freedom.

2. **(a)** She is described as beautiful (fair), charming, and graceful with golden hair bound by olive and laurel. **(b)** America is beautiful and gracious.

3. **(a)** The army is compared to the constant beating of waves on the shore during a storm and to the continuous shower of leaves during autumn. **(b)** Possible response: They suggest that the American military forces are powerful and numerous.

4. **(a)** Possible responses: She uses the words "heaven-defended race," "a crown, a mansion, and a throne," and "heaven's revolving light."
(b) Possible response: God supports the American cause.

5. **(a)** Possible response: They suggest that the new nation will create a government on the model of Britain's monarchy.
(b) He will be its king.
(c) It hints at a conflict between those seeking a monarchy and those desiring democracy.

6. **(a)** Students' answers will vary depending upon current events and their own points of view.
(b) Students may select any person who seems worthy of such a tribute.

One century scarce perform'd its destined round,
30　When Gallic[4] powers Columbia's fury found;
And so may you, whoever dares disgrace
The land of freedom's heaven-defended race!
Fix'd are the eyes of nations on the scales,
For in their hopes Columbia's arm prevails.
35　Anon Britannia[5] droops the <u>pensive</u> head,
While round increase the rising hills of dead.
Ah! cruel blindness to Columbia's state!
Lament thy thirst of boundless power too late.
　　Proceed, great Chief, with virtue on thy side,
40　Thy ev'ry action let the goddess guide.
A crown, a mansion, and a throne that shine,
With gold unfading, WASHINGTON! be thine.

pensive (pen´ siv) *adj.* thinking deeply or seriously

---

4. **Gallic** (gal´ ik) French. The colonists, led by Washington, defeated the French in the French and Indian War (1754–1763).
5. **Britannia** England.

Review and Assess

Thinking About the Selection

1. **Respond:** Do you think that Columbia and General Washington are worthy subjects of the poet's praise? Explain.

2. **(a) Recall:** In lines 9–12, how is Columbia described? **(b) Deduce:** What does this image of Columbia suggest about the speaker's view of America?

3. **(a) Recall:** In lines 13–20, to what natural phenomenon is the American army compared? **(b) Interpret:** What does this comparison suggest about the power of American military forces in battle?

4. **(a) Recall:** Note three instances where Wheatley indicates a relationship between God and the American cause. **(b) Analyze:** What is the nature of this relationship?

5. **(a) Infer:** What details in the last two lines reflect the influence of the British political system? **(b) Deduce:** What position in a new government does the speaker assume Washington will occupy? **(c) Synthesize:** Which details in this depiction of Washington suggest the debate about the kind of government to be established after the war?

6. **(a) Relate:** If you were to write a poetic tribute, how would you personify the spirit of the United States today? **(b) Synthesize:** Whom would you choose for the subject of such a poetic tribute? Explain your choice.

ASSESSMENT PRACTICE: Reading Comprehension

Predict Outcomes   **(For more practice, see Test Preparation Workbook, p. 10.)**

Have students answer this sample test item.

Brought to America from West Africa on a slave ship when she was eight years old, Phillis Wheatley quickly learned to speak, read, and write English. She avidly read classic works, as well as those by contemporary English poets. When publishers did not believe she wrote the poems she claimed to have written, they gave her a test.

Phillis most likely—

A failed the test.
B passed the test.
C refused to take the test.
D was too nervous to take the test.

Choices *A, C,* and *D* are possible outcomes, but they are not supported by textual evidence. Choice *B* is the most likely outcome based on the text.

Review and Assess

Literary Analysis

Personification

1. (a) In lines 9–12 of "To His Excellency, General Washington," how does the poet characterize Columbia? (b) What details does she use to describe Columbia's appearance?

2. Use a chart like the one shown to analyze other examples of **personification** that appear in "To His Excellency . . .".

Object/Idea	Human Qualities		Poet's Meaning
Eolus heaven's fair face deforms	The sky has a face.	···▶	Wind makes the sky turbulent

3. Compare and contrast Wheatley's personification of America as the goddess Columbia with the common personification of the United States as Uncle Sam.

Comparing Literary Works

4. Compare the two poems in this section. Without seeing her name, could you tell they are by the same poet? Explain.

5. In what ways does the descriptive language and mood of each **poem of praise** reflect its distinct subject?

6. Both of these poems are written in **couplets**—two consecutive lines of poetry that rhyme. Do you think the couplet works equally well in both of these poems? Why, or why not?

Reading Strategy

Clarifying Meaning

7. **Clarify** lines 11–14 of "To His Excellency, General Washington" by explaining the meaning of *unnumber'd* and *graces* and reordering the sentence parts.

8. What effect does the inverted subject and verb order have on the reader of today?

Extend Understanding

9. **Social Studies Connection:** How might a historian's treatment of the British-American conflict differ from Wheatley's treatment of the same subject in "To His Excellency, General Washington"?

An Hymn to the Evening / To His Excellency, General Washington ◆ 177

Quick Review

Personification is the attribution of human powers or qualities to something that is not human.

Poems of praise are often written in tribute to heroes, the natural world, or even ordinary objects.

To **clarify the meaning** of poetry, define unfamiliar words and rephrase unusual word orders.

 Take It to the Net

www.phschool.com

Take the interactive self-test online to check your understanding of these selections.

✦ ENRICHMENT: Further Reading

Other Works by Phillis Wheatley

Life and Works of Phillis Wheatley

Memoir and Poems of Phillis Wheatley

Take It to the Net

Visit www.phschool.com for more information on Phillis Wheatley.

Answers for p. 177

Review and Assess

1. (a) Columbia is characterized as a powerful, flashing, resplendent goddess. (b) The goddess moves divinely; her hair is gold and bound by olive and laurel leaves.

2. Students may cite Wheatley's personification of the United States as the goddess Columbia or any other use of personification in the poem.

3. Possible response: In personifying America as a goddess, Wheatley elevates the nation to a higher plane. She presents it as divinely featured and blessed. The image of America as Uncle Sam conjures a more everyday persona for the nation.

4. Possible response: Yes, the personification, references to classical literary figures, and inverted word orders mark both these poems as Wheatley's.

5. In "An Hymn to the Evening," Wheatley's descriptive language is highly sensual and largely natural. The mood is peaceful. In "To His Excellency, General Washington," Wheatley uses military descriptive language and the mood is celebratory.

6. Students may feel that the couplets work better in "To His Excellency, General Washington" because they echo the marching rhythm of an army.

7. The word *unnumber'd* means "numerous" and *graces* means "beauties." *Wherever this native of the skies shines, unnumber'd charms and recent graces rise. Muse! bow propitious while my pen relates how her armies pour through a thousand gates.*

8. It makes the poetry more difficult for today's reader to understand. It also seems more flowery, more poetic, and less straightforward.

9. Possible response: A scholarly historian would probably rely almost entirely on facts and would attempt to avoid bias and the appearance of nationalism.

177

❶ Vocabulary Development

Word Analysis

1. c
2. b
3. a

Spelling Strategy

1. theater
2. center
3. meager

Concept Development: Antonyms

1. b
2. a
3. c
4. a
5. c
6. b
7. a

❷ Grammar and Style

1. thunder: shakes
2. powers: find
3. breasts: glow
4. slumbers: soothe
5. hills; increase

Integrate Language Skills

❶ Vocabulary Development Lesson

Word Analysis: Latin Prefix *re-*

The prefix *re-*, which means "again" or "back," can help you define many words. The Latin word *fluere* means "to flow," and *refluent* can be defined as "flowing back." *Refulgent*, from the Latin word *refulgere*—"to flash back"—means "brilliant." Match each word in the left column with its definition in the right column.

1. revolve   a. repeat from memory
2. relate   b. link back to; connect
3. recite   c. turn or roll again and again

Spelling Strategy

The *-re* ending in British words like *sceptre* is usually spelled *-er* in American English: *scepter*. Rewrite each of these words with the correct American English spelling.

1. theatre   2. centre   3. meagre

Concept Development: Antonyms

Identify the word whose meaning is most nearly opposite that of the first word:

1. celestial: (a) heavenly, (b) earthbound, (c) windy
2. refulgent: (a) tarnished, (b) sparkling, (c) colorful
3. propitious: (a) evil, (b) lucky, (c) inopportune
4. refluent: (a) surging, (b) stagnant, (c) ebbing
5. pensive: (a) reflective, (b) mournful, (c) carefree
6. placid: (a) unfettered, (b) agitated, (c) generous
7. scepter: (a) trinket, (b) emblem, (c) wand

❷ Grammar and Style Lesson

Subject and Verb Agreement

Even in poetry, the rules of **subject-verb agreement** apply. Verbs become either singular or plural to agree with their subject in number. Singular subjects take singular verb forms; plural subjects take plural verb forms.

> **Singular:** *She* <u>flashes</u> dreadful . . .
> **Plural:** And *nations* <u>gaze</u> at scenes . . .

Practice Identify the subject in each sentence. Then, choose the correct form of the verb in parentheses.

1. The thunder (shake, shakes) the heavenly plain.
2. When Gallic powers Columbia's fury (find, finds).
3. So may our breasts with every virtue (glow, glows).
4. Slumbers (soothe, soothes) each weary mind.
5. While round (increase, increases) the rising hills of dead.

Writing Application Write a paragraph describing a visit you made to a site of historic importance. Circle at least three instances where you use correct subject-verb agreement.

W̶G̶ Prentice Hall Writing and Grammar Connection: Chapter 23, Section 1

TEACHING RESOURCES

The following resources can be used to enrich or extend the instruction for pp. 178–179.

Vocabulary

📖 **Selection Support,** Build Vocabulary, p. 41

📖 **Vocabulary and Spelling Practice Book** (Use this booklet for skills enrichment.) ▪

Grammar

📖 **Selection Support,** Grammar and Style, p. 42

W̶G̶ **Writing and Grammar,** Ruby Level, p. 584

📄 **Daily Language Practice Transparencies** ▪

Writing

W̶G̶ **Writing and Grammar,** Ruby Level, p. 131

💿 **Writing and Grammar iText CD-ROM**

📄 **Writing Models and Graphic Organizers on Transparency,** p. 67

▪ **BLOCK SCHEDULING:** Resources marked with this symbol provide varied instruction during 90-minute blocks.

❸ Writing Lesson

Inscription for a Monument

Choose a figure from history whom you admire. Imagine you have been hired to write an inscription for a monument honoring this individual. Using Wheatley's poems as a model, convey the heroic qualities of this historical figure.

Prewriting Briefly research your chosen historical subject. Make a list of specific accomplishments and notable qualities—personal and professional—to persuade readers of your subject's historical importance.

Drafting Choose language that emphasizes the subject's greatness. Use forceful nouns (*trailblazer* instead of *worker*) and adjectives (*tireless* in place of *good*) that have positive connotations.

> **Model: Drafting with a Persuasive Tone**
>
> A man of supreme courage and skill, George Washington was an inspiring general, a true patriot, and a fearless leader. . . .
>
> Charged words like *supreme* and *patriot* emphasize heroic qualities.

Revising Look for opportunities to be more economical, precise, and persuasive with word choices. Check to be sure you have included the figure's most important accomplishments.

Prentice Hall Writing and Grammar Connection: Chapter 7, Section 4

❹ Extension Activities

Listening and Speaking When read aloud, poems gain richness because sound devices such as rhyme, meter, alliteration, and assonance become fully animated. Choose one of Wheatley's poems and prepare a **dramatic reading.** Use these tips to guide your rehearsal:

- Read the poem several times aloud to hear and identify the elements that make it musical.
- Mark a copy of the poem with notes about where to pause, and where to change the tone of your voice.

As you present the poem to classmates, use body language and eye contact for dramatic effect.

Research and Technology Team up with two classmates to research George Washington's military career, political life, and youth. Using computer graphics software, create a **graphic display** that highlights important events from his life. With your classmates, integrate the displays into a fold-out presentation poster. **[Group Activity]**

 Take It to the Net www.phschool.com

Go online for an additional research activity using the Internet.

An Hymn to the Evening / To His Excellency, General Washington ◆ 179

❸ Writing Lesson

- Refer students to the inscription in the painting on SE p. 174 for an example.
- Read through the Writing Lesson steps with students and clarify any confusion.
- Have students use the Branching Organizer in **Writing Models and Graphic Organizers on Transparencies**, p. 67, to organize their subject's accomplishments and notable qualities.
- Encourage students to work in pairs to brainstorm for powerful nouns and adjectives.
- Adapt the Description rubric in **Performance Assessment and Portfoilio Management**, p. 16, to evaluate students' inscription.

❹ Research and Technology

- Help students divide up the research tasks, either by the listed aspects of Washington's life or, if students prefer, by source type.
- Encourage students to address no more than three or four events in each category. Suggest that they focus on events that lend themselves to visual representation, for example, important battles.
- Direct students to sketch out their presentation poster before developing the computerized material.
- Have each team present a guided tour of their poster for the class.

**CUSTOMIZE INSTRUCTION
For Universal Access**

To address different learning styles, use the activities suggested in the **Extension Activities** booklet, p. 10.

For Interpersonal and Visual/Spatial Learners, use Activity 5.

For Musical/Rhythmic Learners, use Activity 6.

For Intrapersonal and Verbal/Linguistic Learners, use Activity 7.

ASSESSMENT RESOURCES

The following resources can be used to assess students' knowledge and skills.

Selection Assessment
- 📖 **Formal Assessment**, pp. 42–44
- 📖 **Open Book Test**, pp. 28–30
- 📺 **Got It! Assessment Videotapes**, Tape 1
- 💿 **Test Bank Software**

🖥 **Take It to the Net**
Visit www.phschool.com for self-tests and additional questions for Wheatley's poetry.

Writing Rubric
- 📖 **Performance Assess. and Portfolio Mgmt.**, p. 16

PRENTICE HALL ASSESSMENT *SYSTEM*
- 📖 **Workbook**
- 📖 **Skill Book**
- 🖥 **Transparencies**
- 💿 **CD-ROM**

Lesson Objectives

To understand the connection between the fight for American independence and the Civil Rights movement

Connections

Like the "Speech to the Virginia Convention" and the Declaration of Independence, the "Letter from Birmingham City Jail" urges readers to fight for the freedom to which all human beings have a natural right. Have students read these documents and find themes common to all three selections.

Voices for Freedom

- Make sure students understand that the Declaration of Independence did not specifically guarantee rights for black Americans, who were not considered citizens. Jefferson's message that "all men are created equal" has come to mean "all human beings," but it was not so interpreted in the 1770s.

- In many speeches during the Civil War era, President Lincoln insisted that Jefferson meant literally that all people, black and white, were created equal under the law. However, a century after Lincoln's death, African Americans were still fighting for their legal and human rights.

- As students read this selection, ask them to look for evidence to support King's statement that the "goal" of both Birmingham and America is freedom. Do students believe that the "Speech to the Virginia Convention" and the Declaration of Independence suggest that America's goal is freedom?

The voices that cried out for freedom during the revolutionary period began a tradition that has carried on to this day. In recent years, Americans have raised insistent voices in the name of personal, social, and political freedoms. Among the most eloquent voice for freedom was that of Martin Luther King, Jr.

Twentieth-Century Echoes Martin Luther King, Jr. and other American civil rights leaders of the 1950s and 1960s shared similar ideas of freedom expressed by early Americans such as Thomas Paine, Thomas Jefferson, and Phillis Wheatley. King addressed some of the same themes as did his revolutionary forebears—freedom, the fundamental importance of justice, and strategies for fighting oppression. Like Paine's, King's language was vivid; like Wheatley's, his words alluded to deities and heroes; and like Jefferson's, his voice called for boldness, wisdom, and morality.

In 1963, King was arrested for protesting racial segregation in Birmingham, Alabama. As he sat in jail, he read a newspaper article in which eight white clergymen chastised him for "unwise and untimely" demonstrations. Without proper writing paper, King drafted a response—the "Letter from Birmingham City Jail"—in the cramped margins of that newspaper. A few months later, King led the March on Washington. On this occasion, more than 200,000 Americans of all races gathered around the Lincoln Memorial and heard his voice ring out again for the causes of racial justice and freedom.

from Letter from Birmingham City Jail

Dr. Martin Luther King, Jr.

I hope the church as a whole will meet the challenge of this decisive hour. But even if the church does not come to the aid of justice, I have no despair about the future. I have no fear about the outcome of our struggle in Birmingham, even if our <u>motives</u> are presently misunderstood. We will reach the goal of freedom in Birmingham and all over the nation, because the goal of America is freedom. Abused and scorned though we may be, our destiny is tied up with the destiny of America. Before the Pilgrims landed at Plymouth we were here. Before the pen of Jefferson etched across the pages of history the majestic words of the

motives (mōt′ ivz) *n.* reasons for action; inner drives

✹ ENRICHMENT: History Connection

The Civil Rights Movement

King was thrust into the leadership of the Montgomery [Alabama] Improvement Association (MIA) in 1955, when Rosa Parks famously refused to relinquish her seat on a Montgomery bus to a white passenger. The MIA was a group of mostly black citizens of Montgomery who sponsored a boycott of city buses intended to guarantee fair treatment for blacks, who made up 75% of the city's bus passengers. Despite their dependence on public transportation, African Americans held to the boycott with remarkable solidarity. MIA leaders arranged car pools, and black taxi drivers charged only the ten-cent bus fare to transport black passengers. The boycott lasted for a little over a year; finally, the bus company and the city agreed to desegregate the buses. By this time Dr. King had become a front-page name and was viewed as the spokesman of the civil rights movement.

Declaration of Independence, we were here. For more than two centuries our foreparents labored in this country without wages; they made cotton king; and they built the homes of their masters in the midst of brutal injustice and shameful humiliation—and yet out of a bottomless <u>vitality</u> they continued to thrive and develop. If the inexpressible cruelties of slavery could not stop us, the opposition we now face will surely fail. We will win our freedom because the sacred heritage of our nation and the eternal will of God are embodied in our echoing demands.

I must close now. But before closing I am <u>impelled</u> to mention one other point in your statement that troubled me profoundly. You warmly commended the Birmingham police force for keeping "order" and "preventing violence." I don't believe you would have so warmly commended the police force if you had seen its angry violent dogs literally biting six unarmed, nonviolent Negroes. I don't believe you would so quickly commend the policemen if you would observe their ugly and inhuman treatment of Negroes here in the city jail; if you would watch them push and curse old Negro women and young Negro girls; if you would see them slap and kick old Negro men and young Negro boys; if you will observe them, as they did on two occasions, refuse to give us food because we wanted to sing our grace together. I'm sorry that I can't join you in your praise for the police department.

It is true that they have been rather disciplined in their public handling of the demonstrators. In this sense they have been rather publicly "nonviolent." But for what purpose? To preserve the evil system of segregation. Over the last few years I have consistently preached that nonviolence demands that the means we use must be as pure as the ends we seek. So I have tried to make it clear that it is wrong to use immoral means to attain moral ends. But now I must affirm that it is just as wrong, or even more so, to use moral means to preserve immoral ends. Maybe Mr. Connor and his policemen have been rather publicly nonviolent, as Chief Pritchett was in Albany, Georgia, but they have used the moral means of nonviolence to maintain the immoral end of <u>flagrant</u> racial injustice. T. S. Eliot has said that there is no greater treason than to do the right deed for the wrong reason.

I wish you had commended the Negro sit-inners and demonstrators of Birmingham for their sublime courage, their willingness to suffer and their amazing discipline in the midst of the most inhuman provocation. One day the South will recognize its real heroes. They will be the James Merediths, courageously and with a majestic sense of purpose facing jeering and hostile mobs and the agonizing loneliness that characterizes the life of the pioneer. They will be old, oppressed, battered Negro women, symbolized in a seventy-two-year-old woman of Montgomery, Alabama, who rose up with a sense of dignity and with her people decided not to ride the segregated buses, and responded to one who inquired about

vitality (vī tal′ ə tē) *n.* power to endure or survive; life force

impelled (im peld′) *v.* moved; forced

flagrant (flā′ grənt) *adj.* glaring, outrageous

▼ **Critical Viewing**
To prevent others from joining this African American sitting at a "whites only" lunch counter, the other seats were piled with linen supplies. Basing your response on their posture and activity, what might the customer and the waitress be feeling? **[Hypothesize]**

Connections: from Letter From Birmingham City Jail ◆ 181

▶ **Critical Viewing**
Answer: The man at the counter appears to be engaged in his book; it is possible that he feels vulnerable because he is alone, but his posture seems relaxed. The waitress seems to be busying herself with her chores—perhaps she finds the situation awkward and would prefer to focus on her work.

CUSTOMIZE INSTRUCTION FOR UNIVERSAL ACCESS

For Less Proficient Readers	For English Learners	For Advanced Readers
Make sure students understand the situation that prompted King to write this letter. Ask them these questions: Where is King? Why is he there? To whom is he writing? What events does his letter address?	As students read, have them look up unfamiliar words in the dictionary and record the words and definitions in their notebooks. Then, have them reread the letter using their notebooks as a reference source.	Have students discuss why King disagrees with the priests for commending the Birmingham police. Why does he believe it is dangerous to "use moral means to preserve immoral ends"?

Answers

Connecting Literature Past and Present

1. During the 1770s, colonists died for the cause of freedom. King was jailed for the same cause.

2. In both cases, groups of people fought an establishment that denied them important rights. The American colonists fought for representation in government; when they realized that this would not be possible, they fought for freedom from Britain. African Americans in the 1960s fought for the freedom they were guaranteed in the Constitution—full equality as first-class citizens of their country. During the 1770s, the conflict led to war; during the 1960s, the conflict led to both peaceful and violent forms of protest.

her tiredness with ungrammatical profundity: "My feet is tired, but my soul is rested." They will be the young high school and college students, young ministers of the gospel and a host of their elders courageously and nonviolently sitting-in at lunch counters and willingly going to jail for conscience's sake. One day the South will know that when these disinherited children of God sat down at lunch counters they were in reality standing up for the best in the American dream and the most sacred values in our Judeo-Christian heritage, and thusly, carrying our whole nation back to those great wells of democracy which were dug deep by the Founding Fathers in the formulation of the Constitution and the Declaration of Independence.

Never before have I written a letter this long (or should I say a book?). I'm afraid that it is much too long to take your precious time. I can assure you that it would have been much shorter if I had been writing from a comfortable desk, but what else is there to do when you are alone for days in the dull monotony of a narrow jail cell other than write long letters, think strange thoughts, and pray long prayers?

If I have said anything in this letter that is an overstatement of the truth and is indicative of an unreasonable impatience, I beg you to forgive me. If I have said anything in this letter that is an understatement of the truth and is indicative of my having a patience that makes me patient with anything less than brotherhood, I beg God to forgive me.

I hope this letter finds you strong in the faith. I also hope that circumstances will soon make it possible for me to meet each of you, not as an integrationist or a civil rights leader, but as a fellow clergyman and a Christian brother. Let us all hope that the dark clouds of racial prejudice will soon pass away and the deep fog of misunderstanding will be lifted from our fear-drenched communities and in some not too distant tomorrow the radiant stars of love and brotherhood will shine over our great nation with all of their scintillating beauty.

Yours for the cause of Peace
and Brotherhood,
Martin Luther King, Jr.

profundity (prō fun′ də tē) *n.* intellectual depth

monotony (mə nät′ ən ē) *n.* tiresome, unchanging sameness; lack of variety

scintillating (sint′ əl āt′ iŋ) *adj.* sparkling

Martin Luther King, Jr.

(1929–1968)

A charismatic Baptist minister and civil rights leader, Martin Luther King, Jr. struggled to bring African Americans into the political and economic mainstream of American life in the 1950s and 1960s. King drew inspiration from Christian ideals and insisted, like Indian leader Mohandas K. Gandhi, that political and social freedoms were attainable through nonviolent actions.

King led boycotts, marches, and sit-ins to protest segregation and organized the March on Washington, speaking out against discrimination. Although King stressed nonviolence, he became an American martyr for freedom when he was assassinated at the age of 39. His widow, Coretta Scott King, works to keep King's message and achievements alive.

Connecting Literature Past and Present

1. How is King's imprisonment related to "those great wells of democracy which were dug deep by the founding fathers in the formulation of the Constitution and the Declaration of Independence"?

2. Both "Letter from Birmingham City Jail" and "To His Excellency, General Washington" glorify freedom. What similarities and differences can you identify between the war for independence and the struggle for civil rights?

PART 2

Focus on Literary Forms: Speeches

George Washington Standing on the Platform,
Pennsylvania State Capitol, Harrisburg

The colonial period of American history witnessed speeches and oratory powerful enough to start the Revolution. In speeches that rang through the halls of government, speakers such as Patrick Henry and Benjamin Franklin turned away from colonial loyalty toward a spirit of independence.

Focus on Literary Forms: Speeches ◆ 183

CUSTOMIZE INSTRUCTION FOR UNIVERSAL ACCESS

When assigning the selections in this part, keep in mind these factors:

"Speech in the Convention"
- Complex reasoning within this speech may challenge some readers.

"Speech in the Virginia Convention"
- Fiery spirit will appeal to most students.
- Unfamiliar vocabulary may cause some difficulties.

"Inaugural Address"
- A modern appeal for freedom at home and abroad will engage student interest.

Selection Planning Guide

The selections in this section feature three of the finest orators in American history. In his famous "Speech in the Virginia Convention," Patrick Henry rouses his countrymen to battle for freedom. Benjamin Franklin then shows how the wisdom that comes with age can help resolve a clashing of the minds in "Speech in the Convention." This part concludes with an example of a modern inspirational speech, President John F. Kennedy's Inaugural Address.

Background

Art

George Washington Standing on the Platform

This painting depicts George Washington as President of the Constitutional Convention that met in the Pennsylvania State House in May, 1787. The words arching over the painting are taken from Washington's address to the Convention, in which he told the delegates to forge a worthy document that they could strongly support. Four months later, in September, 1787, the Constitution was signed by a majority of the men who had met to draft it.

Use these questions for discussion:

1. Compare the image of George Washington in this painting to that in Leutze's *Washington Crossing the Delaware* (page 124). What elements in this painting suggest that Washington will be a successful leader for the new nation?
   Possible response: His posture suggests confidence and vision. As in the Leutze painting, no head is higher than Washington's, and several of the delegates to the Convention have turned their heads to listen to him.

2. What is the effect of showing Washington's words as they are arranged here, arching over the speaker and his audience?
   Possible response: The painter suggests that these words in particular go to the heart of Washington's address and that they have become immortal.

183

Speech in the Virginia Convention ✦ Speech in the Convention

Lesson Objectives

1. **To analyze and respond to literary elements**
   - Literary Analysis: Speeches
   - Comparing Literary Works
2. **To read, comprehend, analyze, and critique speeches**
   - Reading Strategy: Evaluating Persuasive Appeals
   - Reading Check Questions
   - Review and Assess Questions
   - Assessment Practice (ATE)
3. **To develop word analysis skills, fluency, and systematic vocabulary**
   - Vocabulary Development Lesson: Latin suffix: *-ity*
4. **To understand and apply written and oral language conventions**
   - Spelling Strategy
   - Grammar and Style Lesson: Double Negatives
5. **To understand and apply appropriate writing and research strategies**
   - Writing Lesson: Commentary on a Speech
   - Extension Activity: Display
6. **To understand and apply listening and speaking strategies**
   - Extension Activity: Debate

STEP-BY-STEP TEACHING GUIDE	PACING GUIDE
PRETEACH	
Motivate Students and Provide Background	
Use the Motivation activity (ATE p. 184)	5 min.
Read and discuss the author and background features (SE/ATE p. 184)	5 min.
Introduce the Concepts	
Introduce the Literary Analysis and Reading Strategy (SE/ATE p. 185)	15 min.
Pronounce the vocabulary words and read their definitions (SE p. 185)	5 min.
TEACH	
Monitor Comprehension	
Informally monitor comprehension by circulating while students read independently or in groups	20 min.
Monitor students' comprehension with the Reading Check notes (SE/ATE pp. 187, 189 ,191)	as students read
Develop vocabulary with Vocabulary notes (SE pp. 188, 189, 191, 192; ATE p. 191)	as students read
Develop Understanding	
Develop students' understanding of speeches with the Literary Analysis annotations (SE pp. 187, 188; ATE pp. 187, 188)	5 min.
Develop students' ability to evaluate persuasive appeals with the Reading Strategy annotations (SE p. 189; ATE pp. 189, 191)	5 min.
ASSESS	
Assess Mastery	
Assess students' mastery of the Reading Strategy and Literary Analysis by having them answer the Review and Assess questions (SE/ATE p. 193)	15 min.
Use one or more of the print and media Assessment Resources (ATE p. 195)	up to 45 min.
EXTEND	
Apply Understanding	
Have students complete the Vocabulary Development Lesson and the Grammar and Style Lesson (SE p. 194)	20 min.
Apply students' ability to evaluate speeches by using the Writing Lesson (SE/ATE p. 195)	45 min.
Apply students' understanding using one or more of the Extension Activities (SE p. 195)	20–90 min.

A ACCELERATED INSTRUCTION:
Use the strategies and activities identified with an **A**.

UNIVERSAL ACCESS
● = Below Level Students
▲ = On-Level Students
■ = Above Level Students

Time and Resource Manager

Reading Level: Challenging, Challenging
Average Number of Instructional Days: 5

RESOURCES

PRINT 📖	TRANSPARENCIES	TECHNOLOGY 💿 🎧
• **Beyond Literature,** Workplace Skills: Persuasion, p. 11 ▲ ■		
• **Selection Support Workbook:** ● ▲ ■ Literary Analysis, p. 50 Reading Strategy, p. 49 Build Vocabulary, p. 47	• **Literary Analysis and Reading Transparencies,** pp. 21 and 22 ● ▲ ■	
• **Adapted Reader's Companion** ● • **Reader's Companion** ● • **Authors In Depth,** The American Experience ■		• **Listening to Literature** ● ▲ ■ Audiocassettes, Sides 5, 6 Audio CDs, CDs 3, 4
• **English Learner's Companion** ● ▲ • **Literatura en español** ● ▲ • **Literary Analysis for Enrichment** ■		
• **Formal Assessment:** Selection Test, pp. 51–53 ● ▲ ■ • **Open Book Test,** pp. 31–33 ● ▲ ■ **Performance Assessment and Portfolio Management,** p. 17 ● ▲ ■ • **PRENTICE HALL ASSESSMENT SYSTEM** ● ▲ ■	**PRENTICE HALL ASSESSMENT SYSTEM** ● ▲ ■ Answers and Explanations on Transparencies ● ▲ ■	• **Test Bank Software** ● ▲ ■ • **Got It! Assessment Videotapes,** Tape 1 ● ▲
• **Selection Support Workbook:** ● ▲ ■ Build Grammar Skills, p. 48 • **Writing and Grammar,** Ruby Level ● ▲ ■ • **Extension Activities,** p. 11 ● ▲ ■	• **Daily Language Practice Transparencies** ● ▲ • **Writing Models and Graphic Organizers on Transparencies** pp. 25–31 ● ▲ ■	• **Writing and Grammar iText CD-ROM** ● ▲ ■ 💻 **Take It to the Net** www.phschool.com

BLOCK SCHEDULING: Use one 90-minute class period to preteach the selection and have students read it. Use a second 90-minute class period to assess students' mastery of skills and have them complete one of the Extension Activities.

Step-by-Step Teaching Guide for pp. 184–185

Motivation

Patrick Henry concluded his speech with the famous words, "Give me liberty or give me death." Write these words on the board. Have students spend six or seven minutes freewriting in their journals in response to this question: What is worth dying for? Encourage students to share their thoughts, and then discuss the circumstances under which Henry spoke these words. Have students imagine that they were members of the Virginia Convention. Ask them what else Henry would have to say to convince them that they too should be willing to die for liberty.

❶ Background

More About the Authors

Patrick Henry was no stranger to conflict with the Crown. In 1765 he had been accused of treason when he delivered his fiery denunciation of the Stamp Act. On that occasion, Henry had referred to two leaders who had been killed for political reasons and declared that King George III might "profit by their example." This shocked the members of the audience so much that they screamed out, accusing Henry of treason. Henry is reported to have made the memorable reply, "If this be treason, make the most of it!"

It is difficult for many people to believe that Benjamin Franklin—scientist, journalist, educator, and statesman—started out as a penniless runaway in the English colonies. At age 12, Franklin had been apprenticed to his brother James, who operated a printing shop in Boston. James, however, often beat his brother when upset by his work. Franklin ran away, first traveling to New York and then on to Philadelphia. There, he found work as a printer's assistant. In a few years, he was able to open his own printing shop.

Prepare to Read

❶ Speech in the Virginia Convention ◆ Speech in the Convention

Patrick Henry (1736–1799)

It was said that Patrick Henry could move his listeners to anger, fear, or laughter more easily than the most talented actor. Remembered most for his fiery battle cry— "Give me liberty or give me death"—Henry is considered to be the most powerful orator of the American Revolution. He helped to inspire colonists to unite in an effort to win their independence from Britain.

Voice of Protest In 1765, Henry was elected to the Virginia House of Burgesses. Shortly after his election, he delivered one of his most powerful speeches, declaring his opposition to the Stamp Act. The Stamp Act, which was passed by the British Parliament, required American colonists to pay a tax on every piece of printed paper they used. Legal documents, newspapers, and even playing cards were all subject to the tax. Over the protests of some of its most influential members, the Virginia House adopted Henry's resolutions.

A Call to Arms In 1775, Henry delivered his most famous speech at the Virginia Provincial Convention. While most of the speakers that day argued that the colony should seek a compromise with the British, Henry boldly urged armed resistance to England. His speech had a powerful impact on the audience, feeding the revolutionary spirit that led to the signing of the Declaration of Independence.

In the years that followed, Henry continued to be an important political leader, serving as governor of Virginia and member of the Virginia General Assembly.

Benjamin Franklin (1706–1790)

No other colonial American better embodied the promise of America than Benjamin Franklin. Through hard work, dedication, and ingenuity, Franklin was able to rise out of poverty to become a wealthy, famous, and influential person. Although he never received a formal education, Franklin made important contributions in the fields of literature, journalism, science, diplomacy, education, and philosophy.

A Persuasive Diplomat Franklin was a leader in the movement for independence. In 1776, Congress sent him to France to enlist aid for the American Revolution. Franklin's persuasive powers proved effective, as he was able to achieve his goal—a pivotal breakthrough that may have been the deciding factor in the war.

Helping Forge a Nation In 1783, Franklin signed the peace treaty that ended the war and established the new nation. He returned home to serve as a delegate to the Constitutional Convention in Philadelphia. There, as politicians clashed over plans for the new government, Franklin worked to resolve conflicts and ensure ratification of the Constitution.

In spite of his other contributions, Franklin is best remembered as a statesman and diplomat. He was the only American to sign all four documents that established the nation: the Declaration of Independence, the treaty of alliance with France, the peace treaty with England, and the Constitution. (For more on Franklin, see p. 138.)

184 ◆ A Nation Is Born (1750–1800)

TEACHING RESOURCES

The following resources can be used to enrich or extend the instruction for pp. 184–185.

Background

 Beyond Literature, p. 11

 Take It to the Net
Visit www.phschool.com for Background and hotlinks for the selections.

Literary Analysis

 Literary Analysis and Reading Transparencies, Speeches, p. 22

Reading

Selection Support: Reading Strategy, p. 49; Build Vocabulary, p. 47

Literary Analysis and Reading Transparencies, Evaluating Persuasive Appeals, p. 21

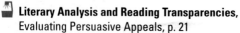 **BLOCK SCHEDULING:** Resources marked with this symbol provide varied instruction during 90-minute blocks.

Preview

Connecting to the Literature

Speeches, like Martin Luther King's "I have a dream," have helped to shape the American identity by expressing our goals as a people. As you read these speeches, think about the vital American principles they express.

❷ Literary Analysis

Speeches

Speeches are written works that are delivered orally. An effective speaker uses a variety of techniques to emphasize key points:

- *Restatement:* repeating an idea in a variety of ways
- *Repetition:* restating an idea using the same words
- *Parallelism:* repeating grammatical structures
- *Rhetorical question:* asking a question whose answer is self-evident

Watch for examples of these techniques in these speeches.

Comparing Literary Works

Speeches from the same time period, even those addressing related topics, may sound very different. One reason for this is that a speaker's **diction**—the choice and arrangement of words—creates a personal stamp. Diction may be casual, formal, simple, or sophisticated, and is often altered to address the aims of the speech. Compare the diction of these speeches, evaluating how well each speaker's word choices support his purposes.

❸ Reading Strategy

Evaluating Persuasive Appeals

To stir an audience, speakers may appeal to people's emotions, or to a sense of reason. When you read a persuasive speech, **evaluate** the **persuasive appeals** that the speaker makes. Assess the speaker's motivation in evoking emotions. Note the arguments and evidence offered, and evaluate how well the appeals suit the audience and occasion. Use a diagram like the one shown to record each speaker's persuasive appeals.

Appeals to Emotion

Appeals to Reason

Henry

Franklin

Appeals to Emotion

Appeals to Reason

Vocabulary Development

arduous (är′ jōō əs) *adj.* difficult (p. 188)

insidious (in sid′ ē əs) *adj.* deceitful; treacherous (p. 188)

subjugation (sub′ jə gā′ shən) *n.* the act of conquering (p. 188)

vigilant (vij′ ə lənt) *adj.* alert to danger (p. 189)

infallibility (in fal′ ə bil′ ə tē) *n.* inability to be wrong; reliability (p. 191)

despotism (des′ pət iz′ əm) *n.* absolute rule; tyranny (p. 191)

salutary (sal′ yōō ter′ ē) *adj.* beneficial; promoting a good purpose (p. 192)

unanimity (yōō′ nə nim′ ə tē) *n.* complete agreement (p. 192)

posterity (päs ter′ ə tē) *n.* all succeeding generations (p. 192)

manifest (man′ ə fest′) *adj.* evident; obvious; clear (p. 192)

Speech in the Virginia Convention / Speech in the Convention ◆ 185

---

❷ Literary Analysis

Speeches

- Tell students they will read two speeches about critical issues in the birth of the United States. Remind students that speeches are written works that are meant to be delivered orally in front of an audience.

- Read the instruction about the different techniques used by speakers to emphasize key points. Encourage students to offer examples of each technique.

- Use the instruction from Comparing Literary Works to help students understand the importance of a speaker's choice of words.

- Use the Speeches transparency in **Literary Analysis and Reading Transparencies,** p. 22, to demonstrate the different techniques used in both speeches.

❸ Reading Strategy

Evaluating Persuasive Appeals

- Explain to students that effective speakers use a variety of persuasive appeals in order to convince their audiences to believe in something or follow a particular course of action.

- Remind students that a speaker can persuade an audience by appealing to listeners' sense of reason or can sway them through emotional appeals.

- Then, discuss with students how a speaker might make this decision. Ask them to consider such things as the speaker's objective, the occasion, and the audience in evaluating the speaker's persuasive appeals.

- Instruct students to create charts like the one shown to record the different appeals each speaker makes as they read the selections.

Vocabulary Development

- Pronounce each vocabulary word for students, and read the definitions as a class. Have students identify any words with which they are already familiar.

 E-Teach

Visit E-Teach at www.phschool.com for teachers' essays on how to teach, with questions and answers.

CUSTOMIZE INSTRUCTION FOR UNIVERSAL ACCESS

For Special Needs Students	For Less Proficient Readers	For English Readers
Have students read the adapted version of "Speech in the Virginia Convention" in the **Adapted Reader's Companion.** This version provides basic-level instruction in an interactive format with questions and write-on lines. Completing the adapted version will prepare students to read the selection in the Student Edition.	Have students read "Speech in the Virginia Convention" in the **Reader's Companion.** This version provides basic-level instruction in an interactive format with questions and write-on lines. After students finish the selection in **Reader's Companion,** have them complete the questions and activities in the Student Edition.	Have students read the adapted version of this selection in the **English Learner's Companion.** This version provides basic-level instruction in an interactive format with questions and write-on lines. Completing the adapted version will prepare students to read the selection in the Student Edition.

185

Step-By-Step Teaching Guide for pp. 186–192

CUSTOMIZE INSTRUCTION
Verbal/Linguistic Learners

Have students listen to the speech on **Listening to Literature Audiocassettes,** Sides 5 and 6. Then, have students rehearse and deliver one or two paragraphs of Henry's speech to the class. Have the class offer suggestions on ways to make each student's delivery more dramatic and persuasive.

❶ About the Selection

Patrick Henry's speech in the convention played a key role in turning colonial sentiment against negotiation with England and toward armed rebellion. He begins the speech with a respectful rebuttal to the previous speeches. He then defends his call for independence.

Henry argues that colonists have tried every argument but discussion is useless in averting the coming conflict. By establishing that the British are preparing for war, he asserts the war has already begun, undercutting any arguments for peaceful compliance.

❷ Background

Art

Patrick Henry Before the Virginia House of Burgesses,
by Peter F. Rothermel

In the mid-1800s Philadelphia had its own group of painters of historical subjects. The leader of these artists was Rothermel. In this painting, Rothermel presents his interpretation of Patrick Henry delivering his famous address.

Use this question for discussion:

> How has the artist created a dramatic atmosphere in this painting?
>
> Answer: Henry is on a raised platform; his lighted face is set against a dark background; his listeners are responding with animated expressions; the character in the foreground grips the chair and table; a glove lies forgotten on the floor.

Patrick Henry Before the Virginia House of Burgesses, Peter F. Rothermel, Red Hill, The Patrick Henry National Memorial

❸ ▲ **Critical Viewing** Patrick Henry's dramatic speeches swayed sentiment away from loyalty to the British crown and toward armed resistance. What details in this painting convey the power of Henry's oratory? **[Analyze]**

186 ◆ *A Nation Is Born (1750–1800)*

TEACHING RESOURCES

The following resources can be used to enrich or extend the instruction for pp. 186–192.

Literary Analysis

- 📑 **Writing Models and Graphic Organizers on Transparencies,** pp. 25–31
- 📖 **Selection Support:** Literary Analysis, p. 50

Reading

- 📖 **Adapted Reader's Companion**
- 📖 **Reader's Companion**
- 📖 **English Learner's Companion**

- 🎧 **Listening to Literature Audiocassettes,** Sides 5, 6 ▪
- 💿 **Listening to Literature Audio CDs,** CDs 3, 4 ▪

▪ **BLOCK SCHEDULING:** Resources marked with this symbol provide varied instruction during 90-minute blocks.

Speech in the Virginia Convention

Patrick Henry

Background

In this speech, delivered in 1775, Patrick Henry publicly denounces the British king and urges the colonists to fight for independence. Making such a declaration took tremendous bravery. England was the world's most powerful country at the time, and the odds against the colonists were overwhelming. If the colonies had failed to win independence, Henry could have been executed for treason.

Mr. President: No man thinks more highly than I do of the patriotism, as well as abilities, of the very worthy gentlemen who have just addressed the house. But different men often see the same subject in different lights; and, therefore, I hope it will not be thought disrespectful to those gentlemen, if, entertaining, as I do, opinions of a character very opposite to theirs, I shall speak forth my sentiments freely and without reserve. This is no time for ceremony. The question before the house is one of awful moment[1] to this country. For my own part, I consider it as nothing less than a question of freedom or slavery. And in proportion to the magnitude of the subject ought to be the freedom of the debate. It is only in this way that we can hope to arrive at truth, and fulfill the great responsibility which we hold to God and our country. Should I keep back my opinions at such a time, through fear of giving offense, I should consider myself as guilty of treason toward my country, and of an act of disloyalty toward the Majesty of Heaven, which I revere above all earthly kings.

1. **moment** importance.

Literary Analysis
Speeches and Diction
Identify three phrases from this section that show Henry's use of sophisticated diction.

5 ✓**Reading Check**
Does Henry agree or disagree with those who spoke before him?

Speech in the Virginia Convention ◆ 187

3 ▶**Critical Viewing**
Answer: Some students may say that the painting shows dramatic impact, with the speech causing incredulous characters to talk among themselves or to rise in reaction. Other students may classify those same depictions as examples of inattention.

4 **Literary Analysis**
Speeches and Diction
• Remind students that diction is a writer's (or speaker's) choice of words. A speaker's word choice often depends on his or her subject, the occasion, and the audience.
• Ask students to identify both the speaker's purpose and his audience. Then, in view of these, ask students to discuss what diction they would expect the speaker to use.
Answer: Henry is trying to persuade listeners to fight for independence. His audience is made up of Virginia statesmen. Henry's diction would most likely be formal and sophisticated.

▶ Monitor Progress Have students answer the Literary Analysis question on p. 187: Identify three phrases from this section that show Henry's use of sophisticated diction.
Possible responses: "No man thinks more highly than I do . . . "; "I shall speak forth my sentiments . . . "; " . . . in proportion to the magnitude of the subject ought to be the freedom of the debate"

5 ✓**Reading Check**
Answer: Henry disagrees with those who spoke before him.

CUSTOMIZE INSTRUCTION FOR UNIVERSAL ACCESS

For Special Needs Students	For Gifted/Talented Students
Have students work in pairs to read through the speech, stopping at the end of each paragraph to review Henry's oratory techniques. Students can fill in the Speeches transparency in **Literary Analysis and Reading Strategy Transparencies**, p. 22, by finding examples of each technique as they read.	Challenge students to write a speech to be delivered in the United States Congress on an important contemporary issue. Suggest that students write a persuasive speech that appeals to both reason and emotion and deliver it to the class in much the same way Patrick Henry may have delivered his speech.

❻ Literary Analysis

Speeches

• Remind students that asking
a rhetorical question is one
technique a speaker can use in
a speech. Rhetorical questions
are questions to which the answer
is evident. Because the answer
is evident, these questions are
often used to stir the emotions
of listeners.

• Have a volunteer read aloud the
bracketed passage. Encourage
students to think about how these
questions make them feel as they
listen to them.

• Then, ask students the Literary
Analysis question on p. 188: What
is the effect of the five rhetorical
questions in this paragraph?
Answer: These questions counter
any possible argument from those
who still hesitate about going to
war. They also help to stir up the
indignation and frustration of the
listeners.

Mr. President, it is natural to man to indulge in the illusions of
hope. We are apt to shut our eyes against a painful truth, and listen
to the song of that siren till she transforms us into beasts.[2] Is this
the part of wise men, engaged in a great and arduous struggle for
liberty? Are we disposed to be of the number of those who having
eyes see not, and having ears hear not,[3] the things which so nearly
concern their temporal salvation? For my part, whatever anguish of
spirit it may cost, I am willing to know the whole truth; to know the
worst and to provide for it.

I have but one lamp by which my feet are guided, and that is the
lamp of experience. I know of no way of judging of the future but by the
past. And judging by the past, I wish to know what there has been in
the conduct of the British ministry for the last ten years to justify those
hopes with which gentlemen have been pleased to solace themselves
and the house? Is it that insidious smile with which our petition
has been lately received? Trust it not, sir; it will prove a snare to
your feet. Suffer not yourselves to be betrayed with a kiss.[4] Ask
yourselves how this gracious reception of our petition comports
with those warlike preparations which cover our waters and darken
our land. Are fleets and armies necessary to a work of love and reconciliation? Have we shown ourselves so unwilling to be reconciled
that force must be called in to win back our love? Let us not deceive
ourselves, sir. These are the implements of war and subjugation—the
last arguments to which kings resort.

I ask gentlemen, sir, what means this martial array, if its purpose
be not to force us to submission? Can gentlemen assign any other
possible motive for it? Has Great Britain any enemy in this quarter
of the world, to call for all this accumulation of navies and armies?
No, sir, she has none. They are meant for us: they can be meant for
no other. They are sent over to bind and rivet upon us those chains
which the British ministry have been so long forging.

❻ And what have we to oppose to them? Shall we try argument? Sir,
we have been trying that for the last ten years. Have we anything new
to offer upon the subject? Nothing. We have held the subject up in
every light of which it is capable; but it has been all in vain. Shall we
resort to entreaty and humble supplication? What terms shall we find
which have not been already exhausted? Let us not, I beseech you, sir,
deceive ourselves longer. Sir, we have done everything that could be
done to avert the storm which is now coming on. We have petitioned;
we have remonstrated; we have supplicated; we have prostrated ourselves before the throne, and have implored its interposition[5] to arrest
the tyrannical hands of the ministry and Parliament. Our petitions

arduous (är′ jōō əs) *adj.*
difficult

insidious (in sid′ ē əs) *adj.*
deceitful; treacherous

subjugation (sub′ jə gā′
shən) *n.* the act of
conquering

**Literary Analysis
Speeches** What is
the effect of the five
rhetorical questions
in this paragraph?

---

2. **listen . . . beasts** In Homer's *Odyssey*, the enchantress Circe transforms men into
swine after charming them with her singing.
3. **having eyes . . . hear not** In Ezekiel 12:2, those "who have eyes to see, but see not,
who have ears to hear, but hear not" are addressed.
4. **betrayed with a kiss** In Luke 22:47–48, Jesus is betrayed with a kiss.
5. **interposition** intervention.

✹ ENRICHMENT: Social Studies

The Year 1775

The year 1775 was a momentous one in American
history. It was on March 23 of 1775 that Patrick Henry
rose to address the Virginia Convention. The issue
before the legislative body was whether to arm the
Virginia Militia in order to be ready to fight Great
Britain. Less than a month after Henry's speech, on
April 19, British troops marched to Lexington and
Concord in search of hidden colonial arms and leaders. Before the year was over, the colonists appointed
George Washington as Commander-in-Chief of the
Continental Army. In Virginia, the local militia forced
the Royal Governor to flee to the safety of a British
warship off the coast. By the end of the year, it was
clear to colonial leaders that there was no turning
back. Patrick Henry's call for freedom or death had
become reality.

have been slighted; our remonstrances have produced additional violence and insult; our supplications have been disregarded; and we have been spurned with contempt from the foot of the throne! In vain, after these things, may we indulge the fond[6] hope of peace and reconciliation. There is no longer any room for hope. If we wish to be free, if we mean to preserve inviolate those inestimable privileges for which we have been so long contending, if we mean not basely to abandon the noble struggle in which we have been so long engaged, and which we have pledged ourselves never to abandon until the glorious object of our contest shall be obtained—we must fight! I repeat it, sir, we must fight! An appeal to arms and to the God of Hosts is all that is left us!

They tell us, sir, that we are weak—unable to cope with so formidable an adversary. But when shall we be stronger? Will it be the next week, or the next year? Will it be when we are totally disarmed, and when a British guard shall be stationed in every house? Shall we gather strength by irresolution and inaction? Shall we acquire the means of effectual resistance by lying supinely on our backs and hugging the delusive phantom of hope until our enemies shall have bound us hand and foot? Sir, we are not weak, if we make a proper use of those means which the God of nature hath placed in our power. Three millions of people, armed in the holy cause of liberty, and in such a country as that which we possess, are invincible by any force which our enemy can send against us. Besides, sir, we shall not fight our battles alone. There is a just God who presides over the destinies of nations and who will raise up friends to fight our battles for us. The battle, sir, is not to the strong alone;[7] it is to the <u>vigilant</u>, the active, the brave. Besides,

AMERICA TRIUMPHANT and BRITANNIA in DISTRESS

EXPLANATION.

I America sitting on that quarter of the globe with the Flag of the United States displayed over her head; holding in one hand the Olive branch, inviting the ships of all nations to partake of her commerce; and in the other hand the Cap of Liberty.
II Fame proclaiming the joyful news to all the world.
III Britannia weeping at the loss of the trade of America, attended with an evil genius.
IV The British flag struck, on her strong Fortresses.
V French, Spanish, Dutch, &c shipping in the harbours of America.
VI A view of New York, wherein is exhibited the Traitor Arnold, taken with remorse for selling his country, and Judas like hanging himself.

---

6. **fond** foolish.
7. **The battle . . . alone** "The race is not to the swift, nor the battle to the strong." (Ecclesiastes 9:11)

Speech in the Virginia Convention ◆ 189

7 ▲ **Critical Viewing**
What details in this political cartoon convey the artist's opinion? [Analyze]

vigilant (vij′ ə lənt) *adj.* alert to danger

9 ☑ **Reading Check**
What measures, short of war, have the colonists tried?

7 ► Critical Viewing
The depiction of Britain with an "evil genius," and America with an olive branch are two elements that reveal the artist's opinion.

8 Reading Strategy
Evaluating Persuasive Appeals
• Direct students' attention to Henry's use of the words *God* and *destinies*. Ask students to analyze what Henry is saying here.
Possible response: Henry argues that God, who is on the side of the just, will favor their cause.

► Monitor Progress Have students evaluate Henry's emotional appeal. How well do students think this appeal suits his audience and occasion?
Possible response: Students may say that listeners who foresaw the establishment of a new nation would have responded well to Henry's appeal.

9 ☑ Reading Check
Answers: The colonists have tried organizing protests and petitioning the king for justice.

CUSTOMIZE INSTRUCTION FOR UNIVERSAL ACCESS

For Less Proficient Readers	For English Learners	For Advanced Readers
Direct students' attention to the paragraph on page 188 that begins "I ask gentlemen . . . ." Have the students work in pairs to use context clues to find out the meaning of *martial* and *forging*. Direct them to use *armies and navies* and *implements of war* to find the meaning of *martial,* and to use *chains* and *rivet* to find the meaning of *forging*.	Have students use each of the following vocabulary words in a sentence: *arduous, insidious, subjugation,* and *vigilant*. Then, have students work in pairs to write a paragraph about the American colonies in which they use each word.	Have students work in pairs to write a speech in rebuttal to Patrick Henry's. Have students do historical research to develop point-by-point rebuttals and encourage them to develop their own persuasive appeals, which should include appeals to emotion.

Review and Assess

1. Students may say they would be swayed by the power of Henry's rhetoric and logic. They should refer to the historical context and Henry's powerful appeals to patriotism and the love of freedom.

2. (a) Henry says he thinks highly of their patriotism and abilities. (b) Henry wants to give the impression that he has listened to and has considered their arguments.

3. (a) Henry says they have "petitioned," "remonstrated," "supplicated," "prostrated," and "implored" the throne. (b) The crown has shown it will not compromise and is intent on using force to gain the colonists submission.

4. (a) He wants the colonists to prepare for war. (b) He says that any delay will only allow the British to grow stronger.

5. (a) Students may say that Henry was deeply committed to the cause of independence. In making that statement, in the context of the times, he was bringing a death sentence on himself if the colonists failed to win the war. (b) Students may say it shows Henry was a man of courage who cared deeply about his country. (c) Students' responses will vary but probably will follow how well they are able to understand the historical context of the speech.

6. Students should recognize that many people with a close emotional connection to England were likely to support the Tory cause.

❿ About the Selection

In an interesting coda to his career as an American statesman, Benjamin Franklin uses his years of experience to urge his fellow colleagues to accept the United States Constitution. Franklin admits that he does not entirely approve of the newly framed Constitution but that he recognizes the limitations of any such document. He says that any legal document created by committee will have some inherent weaknesses although the government will more likely fail because of the people who administer it than because of the document that established it. This speech paves the way for the acceptance of one of America's most important and lasting documents.

190

---

sir, we have no election;[8] if we were base enough to desire it, it is now too late to retire from the contest. There is no retreat but in submission and slavery! Our chains are forged! Their clanging may be heard on the plains of Boston! The war is inevitable—and let it come! I repeat it, sir, let it come!

It is in vain, sir, to extenuate the matter. Gentlemen may cry, "Peace, peace"—but there is no peace. The war is actually begun! The next gale that sweeps from the north[9] will bring to our ears the clash of resounding arms! Our brethren are already in the field! Why stand we here idle? What is it that gentlemen wish? What would they have? Is life so dear, or peace so sweet, as to be purchased at the price of chains and slavery? Forbid it, Almighty God! I know not what course others may take; but as for me, give me liberty or give me death!

---

8. **election** choice.
9. **The next gale . . . north** In Massachusetts, some colonists had already shown open resistance to the British.

Review and Assess

Thinking About the Selection

1. **Respond:** If you had been in the audience, how would you have responded to Henry's speech? Why?

2. (a) **Recall:** What does Henry say about the previous speakers? (b) **Infer:** What does he hope to accomplish by commenting on the earlier speakers?

3. (a) **Recall:** What measures does Henry say the colonists have already tried in their dealings with England? (b) **Analyze:** What examples does Henry provide to support his position that compromise with the British is not a workable solution?

4. (a) **Infer:** What course of action does Henry want the colonists to take? (b) **Draw Conclusions:** What is Henry's answer to the objection that the colonists are not ready to fight against the British?

5. (a) **Speculate:** Do you think Henry was prepared to stand behind his words when he exclaimed, "Give me liberty or give me death"? Why, or why not? (b) **Deduce:** What does his willingness to make such an assertion reveal about his character? (c) **Extend:** If you had been in his place, would you have made such an assertion? Why, or why not?

6. **Speculate:** What types of people living in the colonies at the time of Henry's speech might have reacted negatively to his words? Why?

✳ ENRICHMENT: Social Studies Connection

The Constitution

Following the American Revolution, the newly independent states created their own constitution that gave most of the power to each state's elected legislative officials.

Congress was able to pass limited laws, but it had no power to tax the states or to regulate issues regarding trade and boundaries between states. These problems and other weaknesses inherent in the confederation resulted in the states sending delegates to a Constitutional Convention. This convention gave national government more power.

During the debate over ratification, two major sides emerged: the Federalists and anti-Federalists. Anti-Federalists were worried that the Constitution would give too much power to the federal government. The Federalists promised to add a Bill of Rights, which helped win ratification.

Speech in the Convention

Benjamin Franklin

Mr. President,

I confess, that I do not entirely approve of this Constitution at present; but, Sir, I am not sure I shall never approve it; for, having lived long, I have experienced many instances of being obliged, by better information or fuller consideration, to change my opinions even on important subjects, which I once thought right, but found to be otherwise. It is therefore that, the older I grow, the more apt I am to doubt my own judgment of others. Most men, indeed, as well as most sects in religion, think themselves in possession of all truth, and that wherever others differ from them, it is so far error. . . . Though many private Persons think almost as highly of their own <u>infallibility</u> as of that of their Sect, few express it so naturally as a certain French Lady, who, in a little dispute with her sister, said, "But I meet with nobody but myself that is *always* in the right." "*Je ne trouve que moi qui aie toujours raison.*"

In these sentiments, Sir, I agree to this Constitution, with all its faults,—if they are such;—because I think a general Government necessary for us, and there is no form of government but what may be a blessing to the people, if well administered; and I believe, farther, that this is likely to be well administered for a course of years, and can only end in <u>despotism</u>, as other forms have done before it, when the people shall become so corrupted as to need despotic government, being incapable of any other. I doubt, too, whether any other Convention we can obtain, may be able to make a better constitution; for, when you assemble a number of men, to have the advantage of their joint wisdom, you inevitably assemble with those men all their prejudices, their passions, their errors of opinion, their local interests, and their selfish views. From such an assembly can a *perfect* production be expected? It therefore astonishes me, Sir, to find this system approaching so near to perfection as it does; and I think it will astonish our enemies, who are waiting with confidence to hear, that our councils are confounded like those of the builders of Babel, and that our States are on the point of separation, only to meet hereafter for the purpose of cutting one another's throats. Thus I consent, Sir, to this Constitution, because I expect no better, and because I am

infallibility (in fal´ ə bil´ ə tē) *n.* inability to be wrong; reliability

despotism (des´ pət iz´ əm) *n.* absolute rule; tyranny

⓭ ✔ **Reading Check**

Why is Franklin so astonished by the high quality of the Constitution?

CUSTOMIZE INSTRUCTION FOR UNIVERSAL ACCESS

For Advanced Readers

Suggest that students read additional works by Benjamin Franklin. Provide students with titles listed in the Enrichment box, ATE, p. 193. You may also wish to direct students to **Authors In Depth,** The American Experience, which contains the following selections:

• from *The Autobiography* (nonfiction, p. 27)

• "Information to Those Who Would Remove to America" (nonfiction, p. 31)

• "Speech in the Convention on the Subject of

Salaries" (nonfiction, p. 33)

After students have read these or other works by Franklin, have them form discussion groups in which they compare and contrast the selections they have read. Suggest criteria for comparison, such as author's purpose or persuasive writing. To extend the activity, have volunteers read the speeches to the class, and then ask the class to analyze Franklin's effectiveness.

⓫ Reading Strategy

Evaluating Persuasive Appeals

• Have students read the bracketed passage to themselves. Then, have them paraphrase the passage's meaning.

• Ask students to identify Franklin's main points in this passage.
Answer: Franklin says that he does not entirely approve of the Constitution. He also says that the older he gets, the more he doubts his judgements of others.

• Ask students to describe the appeal Franklin uses in this passage.
Answer: Franklin appeals to his listeners' fears of making a grave error in voting to ratify the Constitution. By admitting to his own fallibility and the impossibility of perfect judgment, he neutralizes such fears, leaving his listeners free to compromise.

⓬ Vocabulary Development

The Latin suffix -ity

• Draw students' attention to Franklin's use of the word *infallibility*, and read its definition.

• Have students suggest other words containing the suffix *-ity*, and write their suggestions on the chalkboard.
Possible answers: *creativity, ingenuity, possibility*

• Break the suggested words down into their base word plus suffix. For example, creativity becomes creative + *-ity*. Based on these words, have students infer the meaning of the suffix *-ity*.
Answer: When added to an adjective, the suffix *-ity* creates a noun indicating a state of being.

⓭ ✔ **Reading Check**

Answer: Franklin is astonished because he believes that when you assemble a group of people, their prejudices, passions, personal views, and selfish interests will color any achievements. A perfect product cannot come out of such an assembly. However, he believes that the Constitution is as close to perfect as one can get.

Answers for p. 192

Review and Assess

1. Possible response: In the spirit of pragmatism, students will likely agree that it was the best document available at the time and has certainly stood the test of time.

2. (a) He confesses that he does not entirely approve of the Constitution. (b) Students should see he disarms opponents by showing he is not rigid or inflexible.

3. (a) Unanimity will show citizens and the world that conflicting political interests do not prevent the nation's officials from working together. (b) Franklin does not want factions to arise as a result of lingering objections to this or that aspect of the Constitution's provisions.

4. (a) A committee brings not just its strengths but its weaknesses together. (b) Franklin implies that people have shortcomings as well as strengths in their character and abilities.

5. (a) The reasons he gives include that a general government is necessary; that no other convention could make a better constitution; and that enemies of the nation hope for a disagreement among the separate states. (b) Franklin effectively establishes positive reasons for approving the Constitution and eliminates any reasons for withholding approval. He does so by pointing out the impossibility of creating a perfect document by a committee and by stressing the importance of showing unanimity to Americans and the world.

6. Student responses will probably reflect the presence or absence of doubts that many people have about the political system.

---

not sure that it is not the best. The opinions I have had of its *errors* I sacrifice to the public good. I have never whispered a syllable of them abroad. Within these walls they were born, and here they shall die. If every one of us, in returning to our Constituents, were to report the objections he has had to it, and endeavour to gain Partisans in support of them, we might prevent its being generally received, and thereby lose all the <u>salutary</u> effects and great advantages resulting naturally in our favour among foreign nations, as well as among ourselves, from our real or apparent <u>unanimity</u>. Much of the strength and efficiency of any government, in procuring and securing happiness to the people, depends on *opinion*, on the general opinion of the goodness of that government, as well as of the wisdom and integrity of its governors. I hope, therefore, for our own sakes, as a part of the people, and for the sake of our <u>posterity</u>, that we shall act heartily and unanimously in recommending this Constitution, wherever our Influence may extend, and turn our future thoughts and endeavors to the means of having it *well administered*.

On the whole, Sir, I cannot help expressing a wish, that every member of the Convention who may still have objections to it, would with me on this occasion doubt a little of his own infallibility, and, to make <u>*manifest*</u> our *unanimity*, put his name to this Instrument.

salutary (sal´ yoo ter´ ē) *adj.* beneficial; promoting a good purpose

unanimity (yoo´ nə nim´ ə tē) *n.* complete agreement

posterity (päs ter´ ə tē) *n.* all succeeding generations

manifest (man´ ə fest´) *adj.* evident; obvious; clear

Review and Assess

Thinking About the Selection

1. **Respond:** Based on Franklin's argument, would you have ratified the Constitution? Why or why not?

2. (a) **Recall:** What confession does Franklin make in the first paragraph? (b) **Interpret:** What effect does Franklin achieve with this "confession"?

3. (a) **Recall:** Why does Franklin feel that unanimity among the delegates is essential to the success of the United States? (b) **Analyze:** What is Franklin's purpose in suppressing his "opinions" for the "public good"?

4. (a) **Recall:** Why, according to Franklin, would any document created by a committee be faulty? (b) **Draw Conclusions:** What is Franklin implying about human nature?

5. (a) **Recall:** What three reasons does Franklin give for finally agreeing to accept the Constitution? (b) **Evaluate:** How effectively does he convey the thought process that brought him from doubt about the Constitution to a decision to accept it? Explain.

6. **Take a Position:** Franklin says that government depends in part on the wisdom and integrity of its leaders. Do you agree? Explain.

192 ◆ A Nation Is Born (1750–1800)

⬦ STANDARDIZED TEST APPLICATION: Reading Comprehension

Predict Outcomes   **(For more practice, see Test Preparation Workbook, p. 11.)**

Practice predicting with this sample test item:

> Have we [colonists] shown ourselves so unwilling to be reconciled that [English] force must be called in to win back our love? These are implements of war and subjugation—the last arguments to which kings resort.

Based on this passage, what will happen if the British assemble their armies and navies?

A The British will remain peaceful.

B The colonists will monitor the British military to avoid armed conflict.

C The British will decrease their show of strength after they threaten the colonists.

D The British will use force against the colonists, and the two sides will go to war.

Based on the text, *D* is the most likely choice.

Review and Assess

Literary Analysis

Speeches

1. Use a chart like the one shown to analyze each speaker's use of persuasive techniques.

	Example	Effect
Restatement		
Repetition		
Parallelism		

2. In what way does each speaker use "concession," or the acknowledgment of opposition arguments, to advance his position?

3. Based on this **speech,** do you think Henry's reputation as a great orator was deserved? Explain.

Comparing Literary Works

4. (a) To analyze the **diction** used by each speaker, find an example of ornate language from each speech. (b) Rewrite the passage in plain language. (c) Explain how the diction helps convey the message.

5. (a) Compare and contrast the endings of these speeches and weigh their impact on an audience. (b) Which do you think is more effective? Explain.

6. (a) What words does each speaker use to refer to the country's future? (b) How does each man see his responsibility—and that of his audience—to that future?

7. (a) How is Franklin's experience as a diplomat reflected in his speech? (b) How is Henry's experience as a lawyer reflected in his?

Reading Strategy

Evaluating Persuasive Appeals

8. Considering the purpose of Henry's speech, why are **persuasive appeals** to both emotions and reason appropriate?

9. What arguments does Franklin use to back up his emotional appeals?

Extend Understanding

10. **Social Studies Connection:** At times of crisis, what role can political speeches like those of Henry and Franklin play in public life? Explain.

Speech in the Virginia Convention / Speech in the Convention ◆ 193

Quick Review

Speeches are works of writing delivered orally. They often include techniques such as restatement, repetition, parallelism, and rhetorical questions.

Diction refers to a writer's choice and arrangement of words, and is often described as being either ornate or simple.

Persuasive techniques include appeals to both the audience's emotions and to their reason.

 Take It to the Net
www.phschool.com
Take the interactive self-test online to check your understanding of these selections.

ENRICHMENT: Further Reading

Other Works by the Authors

Works about Patrick Henry
Patrick Henry: Life, Correspondence, and Speeches, W. W. Henry

Works about Benjamin Franklin
Letters to the Press, 1758–1775, V. W. Crane, editor

 Take It to the Net
Visit www.phschool.com for more information about the authors.

Answers for page 193

Review and Assess

1. Sample response:
   (Henry) Restatement
   Mr. President, it is natural to indulge in the illusions of hope. We are apt to shut our eyes against a painful truth.
   Effect: It reinforces the point.

2. Possible response: Henry's "concession" to former speakers' patriotism and good intentions establishes his voice as one of considerate reasonableness pushed to extremes. Franklin's concession that those who oppose ratification have some valid arguments reinforces his position that some compromise is needed.

3. Possible response: Henry's reputation is deserved. The speech has dynamic imagery, powerful emotional appeals, and eloquent diction.

4. Possible response: **(a)** Students should choose effective and characteristic language from each speech. **(b)** Students' paraphrases should retain the meaning of the originals. **(c)** Students should recognize how the speakers use rhetorical devices to emphasize their points.

5. **(a)** Henry builds to an emotional climax with the final line. Franklin closes with a reasoned conclusion. **(b)** Possible response: Students will recognize that both accomplish their purposes.

6. **(a)** Franklin refers to *posterity,* and to the government's future administration. Henry speaks less directly about the future, but does refer to the great responsibility he and the others hold to achieve their aim of freedom. **(b)** Both men recognize that the future of the country hinges on decisions they and their peers will make.

7. **(a)** Possible response: Franklin's speech is logical, restrained, and respectful. **(b)** Henry's emotional appeal might sway a jury.

8. Possible response: Henry's well-educated audience needed a blend of reason and emotion to prompt them to act.

continued

Answers continued

9. Possible response: Franklin appeals to the delegates' pride and vanity when he describes the Constitution as a document "so near to perfection."

10. Possible response: Speeches like these can unite people in a common cause.

193

❶ Vocabulary Development

Word Analysis

1. the quality of being complicated
2. the quality of being flexible; either changing shape or being receptive to change
3. the quality of being anonymous or unknown
4. the quality of being adaptable or changing to meet a situation

Spelling Strategy

1. legibility
2. acceptability
3. reliability

Fluency: Definitions

1. b   6. i
2. e   7. c
3. f   8. a
4. g   9. k
5. d   10. j

❷ Grammar and Style

1. Don't sign anything until you hear from me.
2. correct
3. I don't think you'll want anything from me.
4. correct
5. It wouldn't make any difference to me if they cancelled the meeting.

Writing Application

See that students relate the revolutionary spirit to contemporary events. Also, make sure they include at least three double negatives in their paragraph, exchange papers with a classmate, and correct the errors.

Integrate Language Skills

❶ Vocabulary Development Lesson

Word Analysis: Latin Suffix -ity

The Latin suffix -ity turns adjectives into nouns. Added to the adjective *infallible*, meaning "incapable of error," it creates the noun *infallibility*, meaning "the state of being infallible."

Define each of the following words:

1. complexity   3. anonymity
2. flexibility   4. adaptability

Spelling Strategy

When you add the suffix -ity to a word that ends in -able or -ible, drop the final e and insert i between the b and l (infallible + -ity = infallibility).

Add the suffix -ity to each word below.

1. legible   2. acceptable   3. reliable

Fluency: Definitions

Match the vocabulary word with its definition.

1. insidious   a. evident; clear
2. subjugation   b. deceitful; treacherous
3. vigilant   c. complete agreement
4. infallibility   d. tyranny
5. despotism   e. the act of conquering
6. salutary   f. alert to danger
7. unanimity   g. reliability
8. manifest   i. beneficial
9. arduous   j. succeeding generations
10. posterity   k. very difficult

❷ Grammar and Style Lesson

Double Negatives

Although it is no longer considered acceptable style, orators in the Revolutionary period sometimes used **double negatives**—two negatives where only one is needed—to stress their opinions. Look at these incorrect and correct examples. In both, the negatives are italicized:

> **Incorrect:** I *don't hardly* know where to begin.
>
> **Correct:** I *don't* know where to begin.

In the first example, there are two negatives. Remember to use only one negative to make a negative sentence.

Practice Revise each sentence that contains a double negative. If a sentence is correct, write "correct."

1. Don't sign nothing until you hear from me.
2. You don't have enough information.
3. I don't think you'll want hardly anything from me.
4. I didn't have any idea that he wouldn't show up.
5. It wouldn't make no difference to me if they cancelled the meeting.

Writing Application Write a paragraph in which you explain how the spirit of revolutionary Americans like Henry and Franklin does or does not still exist today. Use double negatives at least three times. Then, exchange your speech with a classmate and correct each other's mistakes.

W̸G Prentice Hall Writing and Grammar Connection: Chapter 25, Section 1

194 ◆ A Nation Is Born (1750–1800)

TEACHING RESOURCES

The following resources can be used to enrich or extend the instruction for pp.194–195.

Vocabulary
📖 **Selection Support:** Build Vocabulary, p. 47 ▦

Grammar
📖 **Selection Support:** Grammar and Style, p. 48
W̸G **Writing and Grammar,** Ruby Level, p. 642 ▦
▦ **Daily Language Practice Transparencies**

Writing
W̸G **Writing and Grammar,** Ruby Level, p. 310 ▦
💿 **Writing and Grammar iText CD-ROM**

▦ **BLOCK SCHEDULING:** Resources marked with this symbol provide varied instruction during 90-minute blocks.

❸ Writing Lesson

Commentary on a Speech

Choose a speech by a skilled modern orator and write a commentary that evaluates the way in which the speaker leads an audience to agree with his or her ideas.

Prewriting   Review the speech to outline the speaker's key points and to note the persuasive techniques used. Then, critically analyze how well the speaker has supported his or her key points and how effectively he or she has used persuasive techniques.

Drafting   Focus each paragraph on a single point—for example, one paragraph might focus on the speaker's appeals to emotions, another on the speaker's appeals to reason.

Revising   Review your commentary to make sure you have adequately supported your ideas. Identify places in your draft where you might strengthen your analysis with direct quotations from the speech.

Model: Revising to Add Quotations

In his speech on the occasion of the Challenger space shuttle

(add quote)

disaster, President Reagan spoke first as a private man, and

(add quote)

second as a political leader.

A caret identifies places where direct quotation would support the thesis.

𝒲𝒢 *Prentice Hall Writing and Grammar Connection: Chapter 28, Section 1*

❹ Extension Activities

Listening and Speaking With a group, prepare a **debate** about the value of independence or the ratification of the Constitution. Keep the following tips in mind:

- Choose evidence that supports your persuasive purpose.
- Include logical, ethical, and emotional appeals.

Present the debate to classmates.

Research and Technology Using electronic and online encyclopedias as sources, collect speeches from different periods of history. Incorporate photographs and audiotaped recordings of the speeches. Create a **display** highlighting key passages from the speeches.

 Take It to the Net   www.phschool.com

Go online for an additional research activity using the Internet.

Speech in the Virginia Convention / Speech in the Convention ◆ 195

---

❸ Writing Lesson

- Model a speech for students by reading John F. Kennedy's Inaugural Address on pp. 196–200.
- Show students how Kennedy uses many of the same techniques as Henry and Franklin do—restatement, repetition, and parallelism—to reinforce his points.
- Analyze the persuasive appeals Kennedy uses to make his points.
- Show students how direct quotations can be used to illustrate points in support of their arguments.
- Have students use the Written Evaluation transparency, pp. 25–31 in **Writing Models and Graphic Organizers on Transparencies** to complete their commentaries.

❹ Research and Technology

- Have students brainstorm for a list of possible research topics. If they have difficulties, suggest that they focus on famous presidents (Washington, Lincoln, Theodore and Franklin Roosevelt, Woodrow Wilson) and other statesmen (Winston Churchill, Daniel Webster, Henry Clay, John C. Calhoun).
- Divide the class into groups and assign each group a research topic to pursue.
- Encourage students to research the context and historical situation in which each speech was made.
- Have students share their findings with the rest of the class.

**CUSTOMIZE INSTRUCTION
For Universal Access**

To address different learning styles, use the following activities suggested in the **Extension Activities** booklet, p. 11.

For Visual/Spatial Learners, use Activity 5.

For Bodily/Kinesthetic Learners use Activity 6.

For Interpersonal and Verbal/Linguistic Learners, use Activity 7.

ASSESSMENT RESOURCES

The following resources can be used to assess students' knowledge and skills.

Selection Assessment

📖 **Formal Assessment**, pp. 51–53

📖 **Open Book Test**, pp. 31–33

📼 **Got It! Assessment Videotapes**, Tape 1

💻 **Take It to the Net**

Visit www.phschool.com for self-tests and additional questions on the selections.

Writing Rubric

📖 **Performance Assessment and Portfolio Management**, p. 17

PRENTICE HALL *ASSESSMENT SYSTEM*

📖 **Workbook**   📄 **Transparencies**

📖 **Skill Book**   💿 **CD-ROM**

Lesson Objectives

1. To understand the connection between early and modern American speeches
2. To compare the use of rhetorical devices in early and modern American speeches

Connections

Have students reread Patrick Henry's "Speech to the Virginia Convention" and Jefferson's Declaration of Independence. Like those selections, Kennedy's inaugural address discusses problems and presents solutions. Like them, it is a political document. Challenge students to identify similar messages in all three selections.

American Speechmaking

- Point out the word "Inaugural" on p. 197. Explain that when a president begins or inaugurates his term of office, he speaks to the American people, accepting the challenge of the presidency and outlining his plans for the next four years.

- Inaugural addresses are generally optimistic and celebratory in tone, because each speech marks a fresh start for the country. Sometimes a president takes office in a time of great national trouble: Abraham Lincoln's second inaugural address, which students will read in Unit 3, was made during the last months of the Civil War. Have students read the information on this page about Kennedy's times, and have them make predictions about the content and the tone of Kennedy's speech.

CONNECTIONS
Literature Past and Present
American Speechmaking

"Give me liberty or give me death!" "Four score and seven years ago . . . " "We have nothing to fear but fear itself." "I have a dream ..." All of these lines from famous speeches cry out from the pages of American history, forming an important part of our nation's identity. Public speaking has been an important American tradition from the Revolutionary period to the present. Speeches provide a valuable record of the events and issues that have been pivotal in shaping our nation.

Many of our nation's most memorable speeches were delivered in difficult or troubled times. Patrick Henry's speech was delivered at a time when the colonies were on the brink of war with England. Benjamin Franklin's speech was presented during the heated struggle to forge our Constitution.

A Modern Orator When John F. Kennedy took office in 1961, the United States was locked in a potentially explosive stalemate with the Soviet Union and its allies. Fierce adversaries, the United States and the Soviet Union were stockpiling nuclear weapons, creating the possibility of a disastrous war that could destroy the Earth. In his now-famous inaugural address, Kennedy addressed our nation's fears and reached out to our adversaries, while reaffirming our nation's strength.

Inaugural Address

John F. Kennedy

Vice President Johnson, Mr. Speaker, Mr. Chief Justice, President Eisenhower, Vice President Nixon, President Truman,[1] *reverend clergy, fellow citizens,* we observe today not a victory of party, but a celebration of freedom—symbolizing an end, as well as a beginning—signifying renewal, as well as change. For I have sworn before you and Almighty God the same solemn oath our forebears prescribed nearly a century and three quarters ago.

The world is very different now. For man holds in his mortal hands the power to abolish all forms of human poverty and all forms of human life. And yet the same revolutionary beliefs for which our forebears fought are still at issue around the globe—the belief that the rights of man come not from the generosity of the state, but from the hand of God.

We dare not forget today that we are the <u>heirs</u> of that first revolution. Let the word go forth from this time and place, to friend and foe alike, that the torch has been passed to a new generation of Americans—born in this century, tempered by war, disciplined by a hard and bitter peace, proud of our ancient heritage—and unwilling to witness or permit the slow undoing of those human rights to which this Nation has always been committed, and to which we are committed today at home and around the world.

Let every nation know, whether it wishes us well or ill, that we shall pay any price, bear any burden, meet any hardship, support any friend, oppose any foe, in order to assure the survival and the success of liberty.

This much we pledge—and more.

To those old allies whose cultural and spiritual origins we share, we pledge the loyalty of faithful friends. United, there is little we cannot do in a host of cooperative ventures. Divided, there is little we can do—for we dare not meet a powerful challenge at odds and split asunder.[2]

---

1. **Vice President . . . Truman** Present at Kennedy's inauguration were Lyndon B. Johnson, Kennedy's vice president; 34th president Dwight D. Eisenhower and his vice president, Richard M. Nixon; and 33rd president Harry S. Truman.
2. **United . . . Divided . . . split asunder** Kennedy echoes the famous lines from Abraham Lincoln's second inaugural address: "United we stand . . . divided we fall."

heirs (erz) *n.* people who carry on the tradition of predecessors

Thematic Connection
What characteristics of this sentence echo Patrick Henry's and Benjamin Franklin's speeches?

Connections: Inaugural Address ◆ 197

Background

History
Give students the text of the presidential oath of office: "I, John Fitzgerald Kennedy, do solemnly swear that I will faithfully execute the office of President of the United States, and will, to the best of my ability, preserve, protect, and defend the Constitution of the United States." Explain that the wording of this oath is in the Constitution and that every president has sworn the oath before taking office.

Thematic Connection
Answer: Kennedy's statement, like Henry's and Franklin's, uses parrallelism to underscore an important idea.

CUSTOMIZE INSTRUCTION FOR UNIVERSAL ACCESS

For Less Proficient Readers	For English Learners	For Advanced Readers
Point out the short paragraph "This much we pledge—and more" on this page. Have students note, in outline form, what "more" the speech goes on to pledge.	Students may have difficulty with metaphors such as "the beachhead of cooperation" and "the jungle of suspicion." Have them list metaphors that they find puzzling and work with partners to figure out what the metaphors mean.	Have students reread Patrick Henry's "Speech to the Virginia Convention" and write essays comparing and contrasting the two speeches. Which is more effective, and why? Which is more inspirational, and why? What are the key similarities and differences in style?

Thematic Connection

Answer: Both speeches convey a sense of fearlessness in the face of forces that threaten freedom.

American Speechmaking

- Remind students that parallelism is the placement of equal ideas in words, phrases, clauses, or sentences of similar types. Explain that parallelism is often used to emphasize an idea.

- Point out that the first five paragraphs on this page begin with similar prepositional phrases. This is an example of parallelism.

- Have students point out other instances of parallelism in both speeches and explain why they are effective.

  Sample answers: Kennedy: The phrase "Let both sides [verb]" begins or appears in several paragraphs of the speech. Henry: "We have petitioned; we have remonstrated; we have supplicated; we have prostrated. . . ." Each is effective because it emphasizes points in a list: Kennedy lists what he wants to accomplish; Henry lists the good-faith attempts of the colonists to avoid war.

To those new States whom we welcome to the ranks of the free, we pledge our word that one form of colonial control shall not have passed away merely to be replaced by a far more iron <u>tyranny</u>. We shall not always expect to find them supporting our view. But we shall always hope to find them strongly supporting their own freedom—and to remember that, in the past, those who foolishly sought power by riding the back of the tiger ended up inside.

To those peoples in the huts and villages across the globe struggling to break the bonds of mass misery, we pledge our best efforts to help them help themselves, for whatever period is required—not because the Communists may be doing it, not because we seek their votes, but because it is right. If a free society cannot help the many who are poor, it cannot save the few who are rich.

To our sister republics south of our border, we offer a special pledge—to convert our good words into good deeds—in a new <u>alliance</u> for progress—to assist free men and free governments in casting off the chains of poverty. But this peaceful revolution of hope cannot become the prey of hostile powers. Let all our neighbors know that we shall join with them to oppose aggression or subversion anywhere in the Americas. And let every other power know that this Hemisphere intends to remain the master of its own house.

To that world assembly of sovereign states, the United Nations, our last best hope in an age where the instruments of war have far outpaced the instruments of peace, we renew our pledge of support—to prevent it from becoming merely a forum for <u>invective</u>—to strengthen its shield of the new and the weak—and to enlarge the area in which its writ may run.

Finally, to those nations who would make themselves our <u>adversary</u>, we offer not a pledge but a request: that both sides begin anew the quest for peace, before the dark powers of destruction[3] unleashed by science engulf all humanity in planned or accidental self-destruction.

We dare not tempt them with weakness. For only when our arms are sufficient beyond doubt can we be certain beyond doubt that they will never be employed.

But neither can two great and powerful groups of nations take comfort from our present course—both sides overburdened by the cost of modern weapons, both rightly alarmed by the steady spread of the deadly atom, yet both racing to alter that uncertain balance of terror that stays the hand of mankind's final war.

So let us begin anew—remembering on both sides that civility is not a sign of weakness, and sincerity is always subject to proof. Let us never negotiate out of fear. But let us never fear to negotiate.

Let both sides explore what problems unite us instead of belaboring those problems which divide us.

---

3. **dark powers of destruction** nuclear war.

tyranny (tir´ ə nē) *n.* oppressive and unjust government

alliance (ə lī´ əns) *n.* union of nations for a specific purpose

invective (in vek´ tiv) *n.* verbal attack; strong criticism

adversary (ad´ vər ser´ ē) *n.* opponent; enemy

Thematic Connection
In what way does the reference to "fear" compare with Henry's statement, "Give me liberty or give me death"?

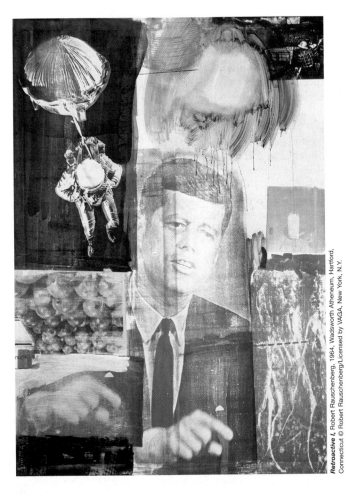

Retroactive I, Robert Rauschenberg, 1964, Wadsworth Atheneum, Hartford, Connecticut. © Robert Rauschenberg/Licensed by VAGA, New York, N.Y.

◀ Critical Viewing
What do the images in this montage—and the unfinished quality of the upper right corner—suggest about Kennedy? [Infer]

Let both sides, for the first time, formulate serious and precise proposals for the inspection and control of arms—and bring the absolute power to destroy other nations under the absolute control of all nations.

Let both sides seek to <u>invoke</u> the wonders of science instead of its terrors. Together let us explore the stars, conquer the deserts, <u>eradicate</u> disease, tap the ocean depths, and encourage the arts and commerce.

Let both sides unite to heed in all corners of the earth the command of Isaiah—to "undo the heavy burdens . . . and to let the oppressed go free."[4]

And if a beachhead of cooperation may push back the jungle of suspicion, let both sides join in creating a new endeavor, not a new balance of power, but a new world of law, where the strong are just and the weak secure and the peace preserved.

invoke (in vōk´) *v.* call on for help, inspiration, or support

eradicate (e rad´ i kāt´) *v.* get rid of; wipe out; destroy

---

4. Isaiah the quotation refers to the passage in Isaiah 58:6.

Connections: Inaugural Address ◆ 199

Background

Art

Retroactive I, 1964, by Robert Rauschenberg

Born in Texas in 1925, Rauschenberg experimented with different combinations of various materials and techniques. In the early 1960s, he began to combine media images with printmaking techniques to create striking works like the one shown here. Use these questions for discussion.

1. What impression does *Retroactive I* give you of the Kennedy era?
   Answer: It suggests that the Kennedy era was a chaotic time in America.

2. Does the work capture the mood and content of the inaugural address? Explain.
   Answer: The speech refers to many of the world's ills and to many causes of fear—for example, poverty and "instruments of war." However, the speech is confident and strong. In the same way, the chaotic images of the painting are dominated by the strong, confident image of Kennedy.

▶ Critical Viewing

Answer: The images suggest that Kennedy was in control of a variety of issues. The unfinished corner may allude to his unfinished term of office.

CUSTOMIZE INSTRUCTION FOR UNIVERSAL ACCESS

For Gifted/Talented Students

Share the following reactions to Kennedy's speech:

". . . his inaugural address really inspired people; it was a feeling of renewal."

". . . that business of bearing any burden and taking on any foe was great at the time, but looking back on it, I think it was really quite arrogant."

Challenge students to write essays supporting one of these two reactions. Remind them to use specific evidence from the speech and from their knowledge of history to support their arguments. If students disagree with both views, have them articulate and support their own reactions.

199

Answers

Connecting Literature Past and Present

1. Kennedy's speech was broadcast over radio and television, reaching millions of people all over the world.
2. Any of the settings mentioned would emphasize presidential authority and power.
3. All three speakers allude to great events of the past and convey the sense that they are taking part in making history.

All this will not be finished in the first 100 days. Nor will it be finished in the first 1,000 days, nor in the life of this Administration, nor even perhaps in our lifetime on this planet. But let us begin.

In your hands, my fellow citizens, more than in mine, will rest the final success or failure of our course. Since this country was founded, each generation of Americans has been summoned to give testimony to its national loyalty. The graves of young Americans who answered the call to service surround the globe.

Now the trumpet summons us again—not as a call to bear arms, though arms we need; not as a call to battle, though embattled we are—but a call to bear the burden of a long twilight struggle, year in and year out, "rejoicing in hope, patient in tribulation"[5]—a struggle against the common enemies of man: tyranny, poverty, disease, and war itself.

Can we forge against these enemies a grand and global alliance, North and South, East and West, that can assure a more fruitful life for all mankind? Will you join in that historic effort?

In the long history of the world, only a few generations have been granted the role of defending freedom in its hour of maximum danger. I do not shrink from this responsibility—I welcome it. I do not believe that any of us would exchange places with any other people or any other generation. The energy, the faith, the devotion which we bring to this endeavor will light our country and all who serve it—and the glow from that fire can truly light the world.

And so, my fellow Americans: ask not what your country can do for you—ask what you can do for your country.

My fellow citizens of the world: ask not what America will do for you, but what together we can do for the freedom of man.

Finally, whether you are citizens of America or citizens of the world, ask of us the same high standards of strength and sacrifice which we ask of you. With a good conscience our only sure reward, with history the final judge of our deeds, let us go forth to lead the land we love, asking His blessing and His help, but knowing that here on earth God's work must truly be our own.

---

5. **"rejoicing . . . tribulation"** from Romans 12:12. In Paul's letter to the Romans, he enjoins people to work together in love and mutual respect.

Connecting Literature Past and Present

1. Henry and Franklin gave speeches that were heard only by an immediate audience. What advances in technology have changed the way speeches like Kennedy's are received? Explain.
2. How does setting—the Oval Office, the Capitol steps, or the halls of Congress—affect the way a speech is prepared and received?
3. Do you think a sense of history influenced Henry's, Franklin's, and Kennedy's speech writing? Explain.

John F. Kennedy

(1917–1963)

Elected thirty-fifth president of the United States, John Fitzgerald Kennedy was the youngest person ever to serve in that office. The era over which Kennedy presided during his brief presidency witnessed events as diverse as the launch of the first communication satellite, Telstar, and the signing of the first nuclear nonproliferation treaty with the Soviet Union. The United States teetered on the brink of nuclear war during the Cuban missile crisis and put its first astronaut into orbit around the Earth. Tragically, Kennedy was assassinated on November 22, 1963, after serving only two years and ten months in office.

✹ ENRICHMENT: History Connection

The Assassination of President Kennedy

Lee Harvey Oswald, a supporter of Communist Cuba, was quickly arrested for shooting President Kennedy. During a transfer between jails, Oswald was fatally shot by a nightclub owner named Jack Ruby, who soon thereafter died of cancer. Neither man lived to stand trial.

Newly sworn-in President Lyndon Johnson immediately ordered a special investigation into the assassination. The Warren Commission found no evidence of a conspiracy to assassinate the President. Perhaps because Oswald was never tried and found guilty, many have refused to accept the commission's conclusions. Conspiracy theories continue to be advanced in books, films, and talk shows. However, no person has ever confessed to involvement in such a conspiracy, nor has any hard evidence contradicted the Warren Commission's conclusions.

Defining an American

Eighteenth-century New England needlework Colonial Williamsburg Foundation

---

CUSTOMIZE INSTRUCTION FOR UNIVERSAL ACCESS

When assigning the selections in this part, keep in mind these factors:

"Letter to Her Daughter From the New White House"

- The vignette of the White House under construction will appeal to most students.

"Letters From an American Farmer"

- Difficult vocabulary may challenge some readers.
- Background on life in Europe during the period can aid students' understanding.

from *Roots*

- Accessible, high-interest autobiographical account

Selection Planning Guide

The selections in this section illustrate the American character that began to emerge in the eighteenth century. Abigail Adams's "Letter to Her Daughter from the New White House" illustrates both literally and figuratively that the United States was a country under construction. "Letters from an American Farmer" defines a new kind of person, an American. This section ends with an excerpt from *Roots*, a contemporary work that traces the history of Americans of African descent.

Background
Art

Eighteenth-century New England needlework

This needlework was made in the 1700s by a woman in New England. Help students see that the bright colors and loving detail of the work suggest the charm the creator saw in the land around her. The land is green, fertile, and abundant in both plant and animal life. The couple are happily reaping grain and picnicking. The natural scene—complete with serpent—recalls paradise in its beauty and innocence, suggesting America might be viewed as a New Eden.

Use these questions for discussion:

1. According to this needlework, what things were important to eighteenth-century Americans?
   Possible responses: This needlework suggests that Americans valued the beauty of their land, its ability to provide for them, the animals that they encountered, both wild and domestic, their homes, and their family life.

2. Give this needlework a title appropriate to the idea of a new nation.
   Possible responses: "A New Eden"; "A Day in an American Life"; "Adam and Eve in the New World."

Letter to Her Daughter From the New White House ✦
from Letters From an American Farmer

Lesson Objectives

1. **To analyze and respond to literary elements**
   - Literary Analysis: Private and Public Letters (Epistles)
   - Comparing Literary Works

2. **To read, comprehend, analyze, and critique nonfiction**
   - Reading Strategy: Distinguishing Between Fact and Opinion
   - Reading Check Questions
   - Review and Assess Questions
   - Assessment Practice (ATE)

3. **To develop word analysis skills, fluency, and systematic vocabulary**
   - Vocabulary Development Lesson: Etymologies

4. **To understand and apply written and oral language conventions**
   - Spelling Strategy
   - Grammar and Style Lesson: Semicolons

5. **To understand and apply appropriate writing and research strategies**
   - Writing Lesson: Personal Letter
   - Extension Activity: Advertisements

6. **To understand and apply listening and speaking strategies**
   - Extension Activity: Interview

STEP-BY-STEP TEACHING GUIDE	PACING GUIDE
PRETEACH	
Motivate Students and Provide Background	
Use the Motivation activity (ATE p. 202)	5 min.
Read and discuss More author and background features (SE p. 205; ATE, p. 202) **A**	5 min.
Introduce the Concepts	
Introduce the Literary Analysis and Reading Strategy (SE/ATE p. 203) **A**	15 min.
Pronounce the vocabulary words and read their definitions (SE p. 203)	5 min.
TEACH	
Monitor Comprehension	
Informally monitor comprehension by circulating while students read independently or in groups **A**	20 min.
Monitor students' comprehension with the Reading Check notes (SE/ATE pp. 205, 209)	as students read
Develop vocabulary with Vocabulary notes (SE pp. 205, 206, 208, 210; ATE p. 205)	as students read
Develop Understanding	
Develop students' understanding of private and public letters with the Literary Analysis annotations (SE pp. 206, 209; ATE pp. 206, 209) **A**	5 min.
Develop students' recognition of fact and opinion with the Reading Strategy annotations (SE p. 209; ATE p. 209)	5 min.
ASSESS	
Assess Mastery	
Assess students' mastery of the Reading Strategy and Literary Analysis by having them answer the Review and Assess questions (SE/ATE p. 215)	15 min.
Use one or more of the print and media Assessment Resources (ATE p. 213) **A**	up to 45 min.
EXTEND	
Apply Understanding	
Have students complete the Vocabulary Development Lesson and the Grammar Lesson (SE p. 212) **A**	20 min.
Apply students' ability to use necessary context and background by using the Writing Lesson (SE/ATE p. 213) **A**	45 min.
Apply students' understanding using one or more of the Extension Activities (SE p. 213)	20–90 min.

 ACCELERATED INSTRUCTION:
Use the strategies and activities identified with an **A**.

UNIVERSAL ACCESS
● = Below Level Students
▲ = On-Level Students
■ = Above Level Students

Time and Resource Manager

Reading Level: Average, Challenging
Average Number of Instructional Days: 4

RESOURCES

PRINT 📝	TRANSPARENCIES	TECHNOLOGY 💿 🎧 📼
• **Beyond Literature,** Workplace Skills: Writing A Business Letter, p. 12 ▲ ■		• **Interest Grabber Video,** Tape 2 ● ▲ ■
• **Selection Support Workbook:** ● ▲ ■ Literary Analysis, p. 56 Reading Strategy, p. 55 Build Vocabulary, p. 53	• **Literary Analysis and Reading Transparencies,** pp. 23 and 24 ● ▲ ■	
• **Adapted Reader's Companion** ● • **Reader's Companion** ●		• **Listening to Literature** ● ▲ ■ Audiocassettes, Side 6 Audio CDs, CD 4
• **English Learner's Companion** ● ▲ • **Literatura en español** ● ▲ • **Literary Analysis for Enrichment** ■		
• **Formal Assessment:** Selection Test, pp. 59–61 ● ▲ ■ • **Open Book Test,** pp. 34–36 ● ▲ ■ • **Performance Assessment and Portfolio Management,** p. 9 ● ▲ ■ • **PRENTICE HALL ASSESSMENT SYSTEM** ● ▲ ■	• **PRENTICE HALL ASSESSMENT SYSTEM** Skills Practice Answers and Explanations on Transparencies ● ▲ ■	• **Test Bank Software** ● ▲ ■ • **Got It! Assessment Videotapes,** Tape 1 ● ▲
• **Selection Support Workbook:** ● ▲ ■ Grammar and Style, p. 54 • **Writing and Grammar,** The American Experience ● ▲ ■ • **Extension Activities,** p. 12 ● ▲ ■	• **Daily Language Practice Transparencies** ● ▲ • **Writing Models and Graphic Organizers on Transparencies,** pp. 9–12 ● ▲ ■	• **Writing and Grammar iText CD-ROM** ● ▲ ■ 💻 *Take It to the Net* www.phschool.com

BLOCK SCHEDULING: Use one 90-minute class period to preteach the selection and have students read it. Use a second 90-minute class period to assess students' mastery of skills and have them complete one of the Extension Activities.

Step-by-Step Teaching Guide for pp. 202–203

Motivation

Inform students that the selections provide windows through which they can catch a glimpse of early America. Ask students to imagine themselves receiving letters from early America. Have students make a list in response to the following questions:

For Adams: What is the new White House like?

For Crèvecoeur: What do you want to learn about American life?

Have students share their lists with the class. Discuss how such lists can be the basis of an informative letter.

▪▪ Interest Grabber Video

As an alternative, you may wish to play "Early American Farmers" on Tape 1 to engage student interest.

❶ Background

More About the Authors

Abigail Adams was born Abigail Smith, in Weymouth, Mass., on Nov. 11, 1744, the second of four children of Rev. William and Elizabeth Quincy Smith. Delicate in health, she never went to school. She married John Adams, a young Braintree lawyer, in 1764 when she was twenty, and bore him five children: two daughters, one of whom died as an infant, and three sons.

When Michel-Guillaume Jean de Crèvecoeur published *Letters From an American Farmer* he captured the imagination of downtrodden Europeans hungry for a better life. Life in America, however, was far from idyllic.

Because the country needed hard workers, not those seeking an easy life, it is no wonder that some American leaders worried about the effects of Crèvecoeur's glowing descriptions. George Washington himself called *Letters* "rather too flattering."

Prepare to Read

❶ Letter to Her Daughter From the New White House ◆
from Letters From an American Farmer

Abigail Smith Adams (1744–1818)

Wife, mother, writer, first lady, revolutionary, women's rights pioneer—Abigail Smith Adams was all these and more. As the intelligent, outspoken wife of John Adams, the second president of the United States, and the mother of John Quincy Adams, the sixth president, Abigail Adams was one of the most influential women of her time.

Unequal Education Abigail Smith was born in Weymouth, Massachusetts. Although her father was a well-to-do minister and her mother came from an upper-class family, Abigail had no formal schooling. She often excused this shortcoming by saying that she was ill as a child. However, as a mother, she made sure that her daughter received as thorough an education as her four sons did—a privilege allotted to few American girls. Throughout her life, Adams vigorously supported women's rights to an education equal to the one men received.

A Political Wife At the age of twenty, Abigail married John Adams, whose political duties during and after the Revolution kept him from home for the better part of ten years. Abigail, therefore, became an avid correspondent, penning hundreds of letters to her husband and relatives and discussing everything from her opposition to slavery to her belief in women's rights. During the war, she even kept her husband posted on the movements of British troops.

Abigail Adams died in 1818. Twenty-two years after her death, her letters were collected and published. Today, she is a celebrated writer who is widely recognized as a pioneer of the American women's movement.

Michel-Guillaume Jean de Crèvecoeur (1735–1813)

The first writer to compare America to a melting pot, French aristocrat Michel-Guillaume Jean de Crèvecoeur (mē shel′ gē yōm zhän də krev kur) chronicled his experiences as a European immigrant adjusting to life in America. His idealistic descriptions confirmed a common vision of America as a land of great promise.

A Famous Farmer Born into a wealthy French family, Crèvecoeur emigrated to Canada and served for several years as a member of the French army in Quebec. After spending ten years traveling the colonies as a land surveyor and Indian trader, he married and settled on a farm in New York, where he began writing about his experiences in America. In 1780, Crèvecoeur sailed to London, where his *Letters From an American Farmer* was published two years later. This book, which was translated into several languages, made Crèvecoeur famous.

Returning To America In 1783, after visiting France, Crèvecoeur returned to America as a French Consul. Upon his return, he discovered that his farm had been burned, his wife killed, and his children sent to live with foster parents. When the French Revolution began in 1789, Crèvecoeur was obliged to return to Paris. He later fled to his family home in Normandy, where he continued to write about the adoptive country that he would never see again.

As France and the rest of Europe descended into the turmoil of the Napoleonic Wars, interest in the New World waned. Crèvecoeur spent the last years of his life largely forgotten amid the political turbulence.

202 ◆ A Nation Is Born (1750–1800)

TEACHING RESOURCES

The following resources can be used to enrich or extend the instruction for pp. 202–203.

Motivation

▪▪ **Interest Grabber Video**, Tape 2

Background

 Beyond Literature, p. 12

 Take It to the Net

Visit www.phschool.com for Background and hotlinks for Abigail Adams and Michel-Guillaume Jean de Crèvecoeur

Literary Analysis

 Literary Analysis and Reading Transparencies, Private and Public Letters (Epistles), p. 24

Reading

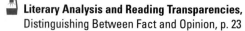 **Selection Support Workbook:** Build Vocabulary, p. 53; Reading Strategy, p. 57 ▪

Literary Analysis and Reading Transparencies, Distinguishing Between Fact and Opinion, p. 23

▪ **BLOCK SCHEDULING:** Resources marked with this symbol provide varied instruction during 90-minute blocks.

Preview

Connecting to the Literature

Today, fewer and fewer people reach for pen and paper when they want to get in touch with someone. These selections, however, come from an era when letters were the only means of communicating over distances.

❷ Literary Analysis

Private and Public Letters (Epistles)

Personal or **private letters** tend to be spontaneous, conversational, and intended only for the reader(s) to whom they are addressed. For example, Abigail Adams's language is conversational in this letter to her daughter:

> You must keep all this to yourself, and when asked how I like it, say that I write you the situation is beautiful, which is true.

By contrast, Crèvecoeur's *Letters* are **public letters** intended for a wide audience. Such literary works—essays written in letter form—are called **epistles.** By writing his essays in this form, Crèvecoeur maintains a personal approach while arguing public ideas.

Comparing Literary Works

The letters by Adams and the epistle by Crèvecoeur are both **primary source documents**—nonfiction accounts that reflect and comment upon the era in which they are written. Some primary source documents, like the Declaration of Independence, speak solely to issues of public concern. Others reveal information about the private life of the writer. Compare and contrast the ways in which these letters detail the challenges of life in a new country.

❸ Reading Strategy

Distinguishing Between Fact and Opinion

- A **fact** is something that can be proved or observed.
- An **opinion** is a personal belief that can be supported but not proved. Opinions are usually indicated by words like "I think" or "it seems," suggesting individual judgment.

By **distinguishing between fact and opinions,** you can interpret the meaning of a literary work with greater accuracy. Use a chart like the one shown to record your observations about facts and opinions in these letters.

Vocabulary Development

extricate (eks´ tri kāt´) *v.* set free (p. 205)

agues (ā´ gyōōz) *n.* fits of shivering (p. 206)

asylum (ə sī´ ləm) *n.* place of refuge (p. 208)

penury (pen´ yə rē) *n.* lack of money, property, or necessities (p. 208)

despotic (des pät´ ik) *adj.* harsh; cruel; unjust (p. 210)

subsistence (səb sis´ təns) *n.* means of support (p. 210)

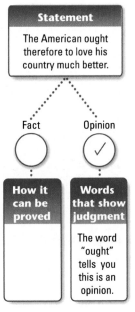

Statement

The American ought therefore to love his country much better.

Fact — Opinion ✓

How it can be proved

Words that show judgment

The word "ought" tells you this is an opinion.

Letter to Her Daughter . . . / from Letters From an American Farmer ◆ 203

---

❷ Literary Analysis

Private and Public Letters (Epistles)

- Explain to students that in addition to private letters, with which students will be familiar, there are also public letters, known as epistles, which are written as an essay in the form of a letter to a general audience.
- Read the description of private letters and epistles together as a class. Draw students' attention to the examples provided.
- Use the instruction for Comparing Literary Works to familiarize students with primary source documents.
- Use the **Literary Analysis and Reading Transparency,** p. 24, to give students practice in comparing the two types of letters.

Reading Strategy

Distinguishing Between Fact and Opinion

- Review the definitions for fact and opinion with students.
- Explain the examples offered in the text, ensuring that students understand that factual statements are not necessarily true but they must be subject to proof.
- As they read the selections, have students use a chart like the one shown to record facts and opinions and to help them distinguish between the two.

Vocabulary Development

- Pronounce each vocabulary word for students, and read the definitions as a class. Have students identify any words with which they are unfamiliar.

CUSTOMIZE INSTRUCTION FOR UNIVERSAL ACCESS

For Less Proficient Readers	For English Learners	For Special Needs Students
Have students read these letters in the Reader's Companion. This version provides basic level instruction in an interactive format with questions and write-on lines. After students finish the selection in Reader's Companion, have them complete the questions and activities in the Student Edition.	Have students read the adapted version of these letters in the English Learner's Companion. This version provides basic level instruction in an interactive format with questions and write-on lines. Completing the adapted version will prepare students to read the selection in the Student Edition.	Have students read the adapted version of Adams's and Crevecoeur's letters in the Adapted Reader's Companion. These versions provide basic level instruction in an interactive format with questions and write-on lines. Completing the adapted versions will prepare students to read the selections in the Student Edition.

 E-Teach

Visit E-Teach at www.phschool.com for teachers' essays on how to teach, with questions and answers.

Step-By-Step Teaching Guide for pp. 204–210

CUSTOMIZE INSTRUCTION
For Verbal/Linguistic Learners

Abigail Adams' letters provide vivid firsthand accounts of history. Have students use Internet or library resources to find letters that capture the spirit of a period of history. Have students choose a letter and write a paragraph about what the letter reveals about the time in which it was written. Have students read their paragraphs aloud to the class. Students may also make the letters available to the class.

❶ About the Selection

This letter provides an opportunity to examine the thoughts and feelings of the First Lady to occupy the White House. The beginning of the letter describes the difficulty Mrs. Adams's traveling party has in finding the way from Baltimore to Washington, a town made up at this time of nothing more than a few public buildings with crude residences scattered widely around it. The unfinished White House is huge but ill-equipped for living: there are thirty servants but no bells to ring for them, little firewood, and no fence or yard. Mrs. Adams, however, asks her daughter to keep these complaints between the two of them and to tell others only that the new White House and its city are beautiful. The first lady also shares with her daughter her active social life, including an invitation from Mrs. George Washington to visit Mount Vernon.

❷ ▶ Critical Viewing

Possible response: With a sense of history, Abigail Adams may have expressed pride to be the first occupant of the White House. At the same time, she might have had some reservations about moving into an unfinished house without any conveniences in a town that was still under construction.

Building the First White House, N. C. Wyeth, White House Historical Association

❷ ▲ **Critical Viewing** With what emotions might Abigail Adams have reacted to this scene? **[Speculate]**   ❸

204 ◆ *A Nation Is Born (1750–1800)*

TEACHING RESOURCES

The following resources can be used to enrich or extend the instruction for pp. 204–210.

Literary Analysis

📖 **Writing Models and Graphic Organizers on Transparencies,** pp. 9–12 ▪

📕 **Selection Support Workbook:** Literary Analysis, p. 56

Reading

📕 **Reader's Companion**

📕 **English Learner's Companion**

🎧 **Listening to Literature Audiocassettes,** Side 6 ▪

💿 **Listening to Literature Audio CD,** CD 4 ▪

▪ **BLOCK SCHEDULING:** Resources marked with this symbol provide varied instruction during 90-minute blocks.

❶ *Letter to Her Daughter from the*
New White House

— **ABIGAIL ADAMS** —

Background

When John Adams was elected president of the United States, he and Abigail became the first couple to live in the White House. At the time, the city of Washington consisted of a few public buildings and a scattered collection of crude residences. This letter to Adams's daughter describes the unfinished White House and captures the essence of life in the new nation.

Washington, 21 November, 1800

My Dear Child:

I arrived here on Sunday last, and without meeting with any accident worth noticing, except losing ourselves when we left Baltimore and going eight or nine miles on the Frederick road, by which means we were obliged to go the other eight through woods, where we wandered two hours without finding a guide or the path. Fortunately, a straggling black came up with us, and we engaged him as a guide to <u>extricate</u> us out of our difficulty; but woods are all you see from Baltimore until you reach the *city*, which is only so in name. Here and there is a small cot, without a glass window, interspersed amongst the forests, through which you travel miles without seeing any human being. In the city there are buildings enough, if they were

❹ **extricate** (eks´ tri kāt´) *v.* set free

❺ ☑**Reading Check**

What kind of terrain does Adams encounter on her trip?

Letter to Her Daughter From the New White House ◆ 205

CUSTOMIZE INSTRUCTION FOR UNIVERSAL ACCESS

For Less Proficient Readers	For Gifted/Talented Students
Students may have difficulty with some of Adams's longer sentences. Encourage students to break down these long sentences to clarify their meaning. You may wish to model this process for students with the first sentence of the selection. Ask students to list events that Adams reports in each sentence segment: • arrived last Sunday • got lost leaving Baltimore • went the wrong way on the Frederick road • wandered for two hours in the woods	Remind students that newspapers were few and far between, and all communications had to travel by horse and wagon. Explain to students that letters were the lifeline through which early Americans sent and received personal, professional, and political information. Have students analyze what the letters of Adams and Crévecoeur tell the reader about what it meant to be an American during our nation's early years.

---

❸ Background
Art

Building the First White House, 1930, N.C. Wyeth

Newell Convers Wyeth was a famous and prolific American illustrator. One of his first commercial illustration commissions was to commemorate the Washington bicentennial year for the Pennsylvania Railroad. On May 1, 1930, the railroad advertised that "historical posters in full color, dealing with patriotic subjects have been designed by a well-known painter." In 1971 this painting appeared on the Christmas cards sent by then-President and Mrs. Nixon. Use the following questions for discussion:

1. What details in the painting clarify the time period?
   Answer: The lack of any other buildings in the vicinity, the clothes that the figures are wearing, and the wagon clarify the time period.

2. What effect does the placement of the figures have on the viewer?
   Answer: The figures help draw attention to the White House, especially the two figures standing in the center.

❹ Vocabulary Development
Word Analysis Etymologies

• Draw students' attention to the word *extricate* on page 205, and to its definition.
• Remind students that the Latin prefix *ex-* means *away from*, or *out of.*
• Let students know that the Latin root *tricae* means "a vexation or difficulty."
• Show students how from these definitions the meaning of the word can be inferred, "to remove or set free from a trouble or difficulty."

❺ ☑Reading Check
Answer: Adams travels through woods.

205

- Point out to students that the unfavorable comparison of Georgetown to Milton is a personal expression of opinion that would be entirely impolite to make in a public letter, especially as the author was the First Lady.

- Ask students the Literary Analysis question on p. 206: Why would this comment about "ladies" be found only in a private letter, never in an epistle?
  Answer: Adams's reports of her social visits are personal and would not appear in an epistle.

7 Literary Analysis

Letters and Primary Source Documents

- Explain to students that in 1800, Washington, D.C., was mostly rural. Adams was coming from Boston, one of the oldest and most developed of American cities.

- Encourage students to infer from the text what conveniences Adams had been accustomed to in her previous homes.

- Then, ask students the Literary Analysis question on p. 206: How does this statement about coming into a "new country" suggest a moment in time that is both historically and personally significant?
  Answer: Historically, the United States was a very young country and had a brand-new capital. Personally, the move to Washington was an adventure for Adams, and represented a very different kind of life than she had had in refined, cultivated Boston.

---

compact and finished, to accommodate Congress and those attached to it; but as they are, and scattered as they are, I see no great comfort for them. The river, which runs up to Alexandria,[1] is in full view of my window, and I see the vessels as they pass and repass. The house is upon a grand and superb scale, requiring about thirty servants to attend and keep the apartments in proper order, and perform the ordinary business of the house and stables; an establishment very well proportioned to the President's salary. The lighting of the apartments, from the kitchen to parlors and chambers, is a tax indeed; and the fires we are obliged to keep to secure us from daily <u>agues</u> is another very cheering comfort. To assist us in this great castle, and render less attendance necessary, bells are wholly wanting, not one single one being hung through the whole house, and promises are all you can obtain. This is so great an inconvenience, that I know not what to do, or how to do. The ladies from Georgetown[2] and in the city have many of them visited me. Yesterday I returned fifteen visits—but such a place as Georgetown appears—why, our Milton is beautiful.

But no comparisons—if they will put me up some bells and let me have wood enough to keep fires, I design to be pleased. I could content myself almost anywhere three months; but, surrounded with forests, can you believe that wood is not to be had because people cannot be found to cut and cart it? Briesler entered into a contract with a man to supply him with wood. A small part, a few cords only, has he been able to get. Most of that was expended to dry the walls of the house before we came in, and yesterday the man told him it was impossible for him to procure it to be cut and carted. He has had recourse to coals; but we cannot get grates made and set. We have, indeed, come into a *new country*.

You must keep all this to yourself, and, when asked how I like it, say that I write you the situation is beautiful, which is true. The house is made habitable, but there is not a single apartment finished, and all withinside, except the plastering, has been done since Briesler came. We have not the least fence, yard, or other convenience without and the great unfinished audience room I make a drying-room of, to hang up the clothes in. The principal stairs are not up, and will not be this winter. Six chambers are made comfortable; two are occupied by the President and Mr. Shaw; two lower rooms, one for a common parlor, and one for a levee room. Upstairs there is the oval room, which is designed for the drawing room, and has the crimson furniture in it. It is a very handsome room now; but, when completed, it will be beautiful. If the twelve years, in which this place has been considered as the future seat of government had been improved, as they would have been if in New England, very many of the present inconveniences would have been removed. It is a beautiful spot,

---

1. **Alexandria** city in northeastern Virginia.
2. **Georgetown** section of Washington, D.C.

agues (āʹ gyo͞oz) *n.* fits of shivering

Literary Analysis
Private and Public Letters (Epistles) Why would this comment about "ladies" be found only in a private letter, never in an epistle?

Literary Analysis
Letters and Primary Source Documents In what ways does this statement about coming into a "new country" suggest a moment in time that is both historically and personally significant?

✸ ENRICHMENT: SOCIAL STUDIES CONNECTION

Adams and Women's Rights

In an era when most people believed that women needed little education, the Reverend William Smith saw to it that his daughter Abigail had the free use of his library. Under her father's guidance, she absorbed history, literature, philosophy, religion—and politics. John Adams was impressed with young Abigail's independent mind, and she became his wife and his chief advisor. In 1776 Abigail wrote to her husband of her vision of a new independence for women. "And by the way, in the new code of laws, which I suppose it will be necessary for you to make, I desire you would remember the ladies . . . Do not put such unlimited power into the hands of the husbands. Remember, all men would be tyrants if they could." Her complaint reflected her acute awareness that the era's law dictated that a married woman's rights were subsumed in her husband's; she could not vote, and any property she had when she married became her husband's absolutely.

capable of every improvement, and, the more I view it, the more I am delighted with it.

Since I sat down to write, I have been called down to a servant from Mount Vernon,[3] with a billet[4] from Major Custis, and a haunch of venison, and a kind, congratulatory letter from Mrs. Lewis, upon my arrival in the city, with Mrs. Washington's love, inviting me to Mount Vernon, where, health permitting, I will go before I leave this place.

Affectionately, your mother,
Abigail Adams

---

3. **Mount Vernon** home of George Washington, located in northern Virginia.
4. **billet** (bil´ it) *n.* brief letter.

Review and Assess

Thinking About the Selection

1. **Respond:** What, if anything, surprised you about Adams's description of the White House and the surrounding area?

2. **(a) Recall:** What details does Adams use to describe the area surrounding the White House? **(b) Generalize:** What does Adams's letter suggest about the difficulties facing those who were setting up a centralized national government?

3. **(a) Recall:** What does Adams instruct her daughter to tell those who ask about the White House? **(b) Speculate:** Why might Adams be greatly concerned about the opinions of others?

4. **(a) Classify:** Name two character traits that Adams exhibits as she faces the difficulties of life in her new home. **(b) Evaluate:** Adams is often referred to as a remarkable figure in our nation's history. Which character traits exhibited in this letter contribute to that assessment?

5. **(a) Apply:** Today, how are the White House and the city of Washington, D.C., different from the way they were when Adams lived there? **(b) Synthesize:** What do these differences tell you about changes in the United States since the eighteenth-century?

6. **Analyze:** In what ways does the construction of a home for its Presidents help the young nation to establish (a) its identity on the world stage, (b) symbolism, (c) tradition?

7. **Evaluate:** Is the continuity of the Presidential residence— the fact that every U.S. President lives in the White House— valuable? Explain.

Letter to Her Daughter From the New White House ◆ 207

CUSTOMIZE INSTRUCTION FOR UNIVERSAL ACCESS

For Special Needs Students	For English Learners	For Gifted/Talented Students
Have students use the visual details in Adams's letter as the basis of a sketch or drawing of either the White House or her journey through the forest. Ask students to copy the details from the letter that they have illustrated on the bottom of their picture.	Have students choose a paragraph of the letter and identify the facts and opinions that Adams writes. For each fact and opinion, ask students to explain why they have identified each as such. Have students use the Distinguishing Between Fact and Opinion transparency in **Literary Analysis and Reading Strategy Transparencies**, p. 23.	John Adams's term as president was filled with controversy, as was the election of 1800 that was finally decided by the House of Representatives. Have students choose among the following issues on which to research and write a brief report: the XYZ Affair, the Alien and Sedition Acts, or the development of political parties.

Answers for page 207

Review and Assess

1. Students may have been surprised by the degree to which the White House was unfinished. For example, students may be amused by the account of Abigail Adams drying laundry in the White House reception hall.

2. **(a)** The surrounding area is mostly wooded with just a few cottages interspersed throughout the forests, which are largely uninhabited. **(b)** Students should infer that those setting up the national government would not be able to show the world a national capital with the pomp and grandeur of other world cities.

3. **(a)** She tells her to say that the White House is located in a beautiful area. **(b)** Students should infer that as First Lady, Adams was in a political position in which the opinions of others carried great weight.

4. **(a)** She is plucky and flexible in adjusting to the situation. **(b)** She displays her intelligence, tact, and awareness of the difficulties of constructing the new nation's capital.

5. **(a)** Washington today is a modern, elegant city and the White House a beautifully preserved mansion. **(b)** The United States is now an established, developed nation.

6. **(a)** It shows the world that the country believes in a leader elected by the people who thus lives in the people's house. **(b)** It establishes a concrete image of the White House as the seat of American democracy and power. **(c)** It fixes a specific location for the presidential residence, thus establishing a sense of history and ongoing tradition.

7. Students should infer that it is appropriate that the President, who is elected by and should serve the people, lives during his term of office in the people's house.

❽ About the Selection

In this essay, Crèvecoeur celebrates America as the land of opportunity. He describes the experience of immigrants to America, suffering from discrimination and poverty in Europe but finding opportunity and fair treatment in the United States.

❾ Background

Art

Independence (Squire Jack Porter)
1858, by Frank Blackwell Mayer

Frank Blackwell Mayer (1827–1899) was born in Baltimore and studied in Paris. Because of his realistic portrayal of subjects from everyday life, Mayer was known as a genre painter.

This painting is a portrait of a prosperous farmer in western Maryland. The title suggests that Mayer wished to illustrate the American ideal discussed in Crèvecoeur's epistle. In the picture, a prospering landowner enjoys his hard-earned leisure. Use the following questions for discussion:

1. Although this painting was not created to illustrate *Letters from an American Farmer,* how does it relate to the text?
 Possible response: The painting shows a person who has obtained economic independence, as Crèvecoeur says that immigrants may do.

2. How would you define the mood of the painting?
 Possible response: The mood is one of quiet satisfaction.

❿ ▶ Critical Viewing

Answer: Students may note that the artist depicts a well-dressed gentleman-farmer at ease. In that respect, the painting correlates with Crèvecoeur's idyllic description of the American colonists.

❽ *from*
Letters from an American Farmer

Michel-Guillaume Jean de Crèvecoeur

Independence (Squire Jack Porter), 1858, Frank Blackwell Mayer, National Museum of American Art, Smithsonian Institution

❿ ▲ Critical Viewing What connections do you see between this painting and Crèvecoeur's *Letters from an American Farmer?* **[Connect]**

In this great American <u>asylum</u>, the poor of Europe have by some means met together, and in consequence of various causes; to what purpose should they ask one another what countrymen they are? Alas, two thirds of them had no country. Can a wretch who wanders about, who works and starves, whose life is a continual scene of sore affliction or pinching <u>penury</u>, can that man call England or any other kingdom his country? A country that had no bread for him, whose fields

asylum (ə sī´ ləm) *n.* place of refuge

penury (pen´ yə rē) *n.* lack of money, property, or necessities

208 ◆ *A Nation Is Born (1750–1800)*

⬡ ENRICHMENT: Cultural Connection

Immigrants

Crèvecoeur's letter shows that even in colonial times, immigrants came to America from a variety of countries. During the 1600s and 1700s, settlers came to the colonies from many parts of Europe, and enslaved Africans were taken to the Americas against their will.

In the 1840s a potato famine in Ireland drove one-and-a-half million people to America's shores, and Chinese immigrants arrived in the 1860s to work on the transcontinental railroad.

In the 1870s immigrants from Germany and Scandinavia came to the Great Plains as farmers or to the East as skilled workers. Another wave of immigrants came between 1880 and 1914.

By 1929 laws had reduced the annual quota of immigrants to 154,000. Immigration restrictions eased after World War II, however, as new prosperity increased the demand for labor. The United States continues to be a nation of immigrants.

procured him no harvest, who met with nothing but the frowns of the rich, the severity of the laws, with jails and punishments; who owned not a single foot of the extensive surface of this planet? No! Urged by a variety of motives, here they came. Everything has tended to regenerate them; new laws, a new mode of living, a new social system; here they are become men: in Europe they were as so many useless plants, wanting vegetative mold[1] and refreshing showers; they withered, and were mowed down by want, hunger, and war; but now by the power of transplantation, like all other plants they have taken root and flourished!

Formerly they were not numbered in any civil lists[2] of their country, except in those of the poor; here they rank as citizens. By what invisible power has this surprising metamorphosis been performed? By that of the laws and that of their industry. The laws, the indulgent laws, protect them as they arrive, stamping on them the symbol of adoption; they receive ample rewards for their labors; these accumulated rewards procure them lands; those lands confer on them the title of freemen, and to that title every benefit is affixed which men can possibly require. This is the great operation daily performed by our laws. From whence proceed these laws? From our government. Whence the government? It is derived from the original genius and strong desire of the people ratified and confirmed by the crown. . . .

What attachment can a poor European emigrant have for a country where he had nothing? The knowledge of the language, the love of a few kindred as poor as himself, were the only cords that tied him: his country is now that which gives him land, bread, protection, and consequence: *Ubi panis ibi patria*[3] is the motto of all emigrants. What then is the American, this new man? He is either a European, or the descendant of a European, hence that strange mixture of blood, which you will find in no other country. I could point out to you a family whose grandfather was an Englishman, whose wife was Dutch, whose son married a French woman, and whose present four sons have now four wives of different nations. *He* is an American, who, leaving behind him all his ancient prejudices and manners, receives new ones from the new mode of life he has embraced, the new government he obeys, and the new rank he holds. He becomes an American by being received in the broad lap of our great *Alma Mater.*[4] Here individuals of all nations are melted into a new race of men, whose labors and posterity will one day cause great changes in the world. Americans are the western pilgrims, who are carrying along with them that great mass of arts, sciences, vigor, and industry which began long since in the east; they will finish the great circle. The Americans were once scattered all over Europe: here they

---

1. **vegetative mold** enriched soil.
2. **civil lists** lists of distinguished persons.
3. **Ubi . . . patria** (ū´ bē pä´ nis ib´ ē pä´ trē ə) "Where there is bread, there is one's fatherland" (Latin).
4. **Alma Mater** (al´ mə mät´ ər) "Fostering mother." Here, referring to America; usually used in reference to a school or college (Latin).

**Literary Analysis
Private and Public Letters (Epistles)** Does this passage describing Europeans coming to the "American asylum" address a public or a private concern?

**Reading Strategy
Distinguishing Between Fact and Opinion** By referencing a family with roots in many nations, does the writer present a fact or an opinion? Explain.

✓ **Reading Check**
What kind of lives did Europeans have in their homelands?

from Letters From an American Farmer ◆ 209

**11 Literary Analysis
Private and Public Letters (Epistles)**

- Ask students to list the reasons that Crèvecoeur gives for Europeans coming to America.
- Then, ask students the Literary Analysis question on p. 209: How does this passage describing Europeans coming to the "American asylum" address a public rather than a private concern?
  Answer: Crèvecoeur addresses social issues, such as poverty and famine, that provide motivation for coming to America. These are public, not private, concerns.

▶ **Monitor Progress** Ask students how this passage might have been different if Crèvecoeur had been writing a private letter.

**12 Reading Strategy
Distinguishing Between Fact and Opinion**

- Remind students that a fact can be proven true or false.
- Ask students the Reading Strategy question on p. 209: By referencing a family with roots in many nations, does the writer present a fact or an opinion? Explain.
  Answer: The description of the family is a factual statement because it can be proved whether such a family exists.

**13 Reading Strategy
Distinguishing Between Fact and Opinion**

- Direct students' attention to the bracketed passage. Ask them if they think Crèvecoeur's statement about the population of America is a fact or an opinion.
- Then, ask students the following question: Which words indicate Crèvecoeur's expression of opinion in his discussion of the "finest systems of population?"
  Answer: finest, ever appeared, which will become distinct

14 ✓ Reading Check
Answer: Europeans suffered without land or liberty.

CUSTOMIZE INSTRUCTION FOR UNIVERSAL ACCESS

For Less Proficient Readers	For English Learners	For Advanced Readers
Have students use a comparison chart to help sort details of Crèvecoeur's contrast of life in Europe and America. Have students draw two columns down a page and write *Europe* on top of one column and *America* on top of the other. Then have them make entries on the chart as they read through the letter.	Volunteers might work in a group to discuss their own experiences about emigration or living in a different land and culture than the one in which their family originated. Do they agree or disagree with Crèvecoeur's main points?	Encourage students to write a cause-and-effect essay discussing the advantages and disadvantages of an open-door immigration policy. Have students gather background information by researching United States immigration history on the Internet or at the library. Remind students to take into account that circumstances have changed substantially since the eighteenth century.

Answers for page 210

Review and Assess

1. Students should find that the letter is persuasive in establishing the opportunities that exist in America. They may cast doubt, however, on how accurately Crèvecoeur portrays the situation in Europe.

2. **(a)** Crèvecoeur compares the Europeans to withering plants lacking fertilizer and water that are mowed down by poverty and war. **(b)** Students should infer that the problem is not Europeans' abilities but the impoverished environment from which they fled.

3. **(a)** "New laws, a new mode of living, [and] a new social system" have regenerated the European immigrant. **(b)** Students should infer that Crèvecoeur would define a citizen as someone who not only lives in a place but contributes through his or her labor and earns his or her own living.

4. **(a)** The average European is impoverished and without rights, power, or dignity; Americans are free, productive citizens who through intermarriage have created a new race of people. **(b)** He believes Americans will continue the advance of civilization that began in the East and continued on to Europe.

5. **(a)** Possible response: An American is someone who has initiated a new social system through labor, industry, and self-interest. **(b)** Students should understand that in a very different world, there are many other things that make one an American, including living and participating in a social and political American milieu. **(c)** Students may point out that because the Americas stretch from Canada to Cape Horn, a single definition of an American is difficult to agree upon.

6. Students should understand that while the world has changed, some things remain the same, including many immigrants' desire for freedom and opportunity.

210

---

are incorporated into one of the finest systems of population which has ever appeared, and which will hereafter become distinct by the power of the different climates they inhabit. The American ought therefore to love this country much better than that wherein either he or his forefathers were born. Here the rewards of his industry follow with equal steps the progress of his labor; his labor is founded on the basis of nature, *self-interest*; can it want a stronger allurement? Wives and children, who before in vain demanded of him a morsel of bread, now, fat and frolicsome, gladly help their father to clear those fields whence exuberant crops are to arise to feed and to clothe them all; without any part being claimed, either by a <u>despotic</u> prince, a rich abbot,[5] or a mighty lord. Here religion demands but little of him; a small voluntary salary to the minister, and gratitude to God; can he refuse these? The American is a new man, who acts upon new principles; he must therefore entertain new ideas, and form new opinions. From involuntary idleness, servile dependence, penury, and useless labor, he has passed to toils of a very different nature, rewarded by ample <u>subsistence</u>—This is an American.

despotic (des pät′ ik) *adj.* harsh; cruel; unjust

subsistence (səb sis′ təns) *n.* means of support

---

5. **abbot** *n.* the head of a monastery.

Review and Assess

Thinking About the Selection

1. **Respond:** If you were an eighteenth-century European, would this essay motivate you to relocate to the United States? Why or why not?

2. **(a) Recall:** To what natural objects does Crèvecoeur compare impoverished Europeans? **(b) Assess:** What is suggested through this imagery about Europeans' capacity to thrive in a new environment?

3. **(a) Recall:** What are the sources of the "invisible power" that is responsible for transforming humble Europeans into esteemed American "citizens"? **(b) Define:** How do you think Crèvecoeur would define a "citizen"?

4. **(a) Compare and Contrast:** How does the American population differ from that of Europe? **(b) Explain:** In what ways does Crèvecoeur believe the world will be invigorated by Americans?

5. **(a) Define:** How would you summarize Crèvecoeur's definition of an American? **(b) Evaluate:** Does Crèvecoeur's definition still hold true today? Explain. **(c) Take a Position:** Do you think that there can be a single definition of an American? Why or why not?

6. **Apply:** Do you think that eighteenth-century immigrants to America had the same goals as immigrants of today? Explain.

✑ ASSESSMENT PRACTICE: Reading Comprehension

Recognize Cause and Effect

Successful readers understand that causal relationships are sometimes signaled by transitions such as "since" or "because." Use the following example to help students identify signal words as they look for causal relationships.

. . . if they will . . . let me have wood enough to keep fires, I design to be pleased. I could content myself almost anywhere three months; but surrounded with forests, can you believe that wood is not to be had

because people cannot be found to cut and cart it?

Why does Abigail Adams lack firewood?

A There were no forests nearby.

B There was no one to cut the wood.

C People did not use firewood in Washington.

D Abigail Adams preferred coal.

Choices *A, C,* and *D* contain inaccurate information. *B* states the correct cause as it is given in the text.

Review and Assess

Literary Analysis

Private and Public Letters (Epistles)

1. Use a chart like the one shown to explore ways in which you might rewrite Adams's **private letter** for a public audience.

Letter	Words suggesting private purpose	Revision
Surrounded with forests, can you believe that wood is not to be had?	Can you believe	We are surrounded by dense forest, but wood is not readily available.

2. What kinds of information would Crèvecoeur have included in a private letter to a friend that are inappropriate for an **epistle**?

3. How does the epistle form allow Crèvecoeur to be more persuasive than a regular essay would permit?

Comparing Literary Works

4. (a) What character traits does Crèvecoeur hold up as being both typically American and admirable? (b) Are these character traits evident in Adams's descriptions? Explain.

5. (a) Which writer presents a more idealized view of America? Explain. (b) Which presents a more realistic view? Explain.

Reading Strategy

Distinguishing Between Fact and Opinion

6. Identify the **facts** and **opinions** in this statement.

   "The house is made habitable, but there is not a single apartment finished, and all withinside, except the plastering, has been done since Briesler came."

7. Identify at least one fact Crèvecoeur uses to support the following opinion: "here they are become men: in Europe they were as so many useless plants."

Extend Understanding

8. **Social Studies Connection:** Crèvecoeur implies that self-interest is valuable because it motivates people to work harder. Does modern society regard self-interest as a desirable quality? Explain your answer.

Letter to Her Daughter . . . / from Letters From an American Farmer ◆ 211

Quick Review

Private letters are intended only for the reader to whom they are addressed.

Epistles, written in the form of personal letters, are created for general publication.

Primary source documents are nonfiction literary works that comment upon events taking place at the time they were written.

A **fact** is a statement that can be proved. An **opinion** expresses a belief, feeling, or judgment.

 Take It to the Net
www.phschool.com
Take the interactive self-test online to check your understanding of these selections.

❋ ENRICHMENT: Further Reading

Other Works by the Authors

Other Works by Adams
New Letters of Abigail Adams, 1788–1801, Stewart Mitchell, ed.

Other Works by Crèvecoeur
Journey into Northern Pennsylvania and the State of New York

Take It to the Net
Visit www.phschool.com for more information on the authors.

Answers for page 211

Review and Assess

1. Be sure students' charts contain specific sentences from Adams's letter and, for each sentence, a phrase suggesting private purpose as well as a suitable revision of that phrase.

2. Possible response: Crèvecoeur might have included personal comments, opinions, and complaints.

3. By using the form of the letter, Crèvecoeur can be persuasive in an intimate and personal manner. When reading a letter, readers have the sense that the author is speaking directly to them, which makes his words more persuasive.

4. (a) Crèvecoeur believes that Americans are hard workers who enjoy the fruits of their labors. Americans have initiated a new social system through labor, industry, and self-interest. (b) These traits are not evident in Adams's descriptions. Her letter describes all the things that are unfinished and missing in and around the White House. She even observes that the site had been chosen for the White House twelve years earlier yet little progress has been made.

5. Crèvecoeur offers a more idealized view of life in America. He feels that any industrious person can make a better life here. (b) Adams presents a more sober view by detailing all the problems she faces moving into the nation's new capital.

6. **Facts:** "not a single apartment finished"; "all withinside except the plastering has been done." **Opinion:** "The house is made habitable, . . ."

7. Possible response: In Europe, men were incapacitated by poverty, hunger, and war.

8. Students' responses will vary. Some will say that modern society regards self-interest as a desirable quality because it is seen as one important way of getting ahead. Others will say that society does not see self-interest as an admirable quality because it encourages people to be selfish and uncaring.

❶ Vocabulary Development

Word Analysis

1. *inter* (among) and *spargere* (scattered)

2. to scatter or distribute among other things

Spelling Strategy

1. observance

2. confidence

3. intelligence

Fluency: Word Matching

1. e

2. b

3. d

4. f

5. a

6. c

❷ Grammar and Style

Practice

1. The travelers sought help finding Baltimore; the woods blocked their view of the city.

2. Six rooms were completed; two were not.

3. Adams thought she could be happy; however, the shortages caused her distress.

4. Crèvecoeur presents America as a land of opportunity; in fact, he shows how European immigrants have prospered.

5. Crèvecoeur wrote convincingly about the land; nevertheless, some felt he created an unrealistic picture of the quality of life.

Writing Application

Each sentence should present an opinion about, or insight into, America; there should be a semicolon in each of the four sentences.

Integrate Language Skills

❶ Vocabulary Development Lesson

Word Analysis: Etymologies

You can learn how words evolved by using a dictionary that shows etymologies, or word histories. Use this etymology for the word *interspersed* to answer the questions that follow.

> < *interspersus*, pp. of *interspergere* < *inter-*, among + *spargere*, to scatter

1. *Interspersed* can be traced back to what two words or word parts?

2. What is the meaning of *interspersed*?

Spelling Strategy

The suffixes *-ance* and *-ence* are used to form nouns from adjectives. *Evident* becomes *evidence*, and *significant* becomes *significance*. Write the noun form of each adjective:

1. observant   2. confident   3. intelligent

Fluency: Word Matching

Match each numbered word with the best lettered description.

1. extricate
2. agues
3. asylum
4. penury
5. subsistence
6. despotic

a. a minimal income

b. what people who live in drafty houses suffer from

c. how you might describe an evil dictator

d. the quiet privacy of your room

e. to work your way out of an argument

f. the condition in which most homeless people live

❷ Grammar and Style Lesson

Semicolons

The **semicolon** can replace a comma and a coordinating conjunction to signal closely connected ideas. The semicolon can also be used to join independent clauses separated by a conjunctive adverb or a transitional expression.

> **Semicolon with conjunctive adverb:**
> Crèvecoeur was the first to express the concept of America as a melting pot; **however,** the term was not used until the twentieth century.

Practice Rewrite the following sentences, adding semicolons where needed.

1. The travelers sought help finding Baltimore the woods blocked their view of the city.

2. Six rooms were completed two were not.

3. Adams thought she could be happy however, the shortages caused her distress.

4. Crèvecoeur presents America as a land of opportunity in fact he shows how European immigrants have prospered.

5. Crèvecoeur wrote convincingly about the land nevertheless some felt he created an unrealistic picture of the quality of life.

Writing Application Write four sentences reflecting on what America means to you. Use a semicolon in each sentence.

$\mathcal{W}_G$ *Prentice Hall Writing and Grammar Connection: Chapter 27, Section 3*

TEACHING RESOURCES

The following resources can be used to enrich or extend the instruction for pp. 212–213.

Vocabulary

📖 **Selection Support Workbook:** Build Vocabulary, p. 53

📖 **Vocabulary and Spelling Practice Book,** (Use this booklet for skills enrichment.) ▦

Grammar

📖 **Selection Support Workbook:** Grammar and Style, p. 54

$\mathcal{W}_G$ **Writing and Grammar,** Ruby Level, p. 716

📖 **Daily Language Practice Transparencies**

Writing

$\mathcal{W}_G$ **Writing and Grammar,** Ruby Level, p.153

◉ **Writing and Grammar iText CD-ROM** ▦

▦ **BLOCK SCHEDULING:** Resources marked with this symbol provide varied instruction during 90-minute blocks.

❸ Writing Lesson

Personal Letter

In a personal letter to either Adams or Crèvecoeur, provide an update on how an area of interest to the recipient has changed since his or her lifetime. Like a foreign pen pal, your reader lives in a different country—the country of the past—and will need help understanding your world.

Prewriting Decide on an appropriate subject for your letter. Outline the developments you will cover. Then, decide what background information your reader will need to understand your points.

Drafting Make sure to address the person to whom you are writing. You will need to include necessary context and background—the information a reader needs in order to make sense of the information you provide.

Model: Providing Context and Background
Unlike your contemporaries, who rarely worked outside the home, women today have many choices, Ms. Adams. While some stay home to raise children, others have full-time jobs.

> Comparison-and-contrast examples establish context.

Revising Review your letter and decide whether the recipient would be able to understand the references you make. If necessary, add more detail to explain and prove your point.

 Prentice Hall Writing and Grammar Connection: Chapter 9, Section 2

❹ Extension Activities

Research and Technology With a group of your classmates, use a drawing software program to design **advertisements** that might have attracted immigrants to America in the late eighteenth century. As you plan, think about these questions:

- Who would have been the target group for such ads?
- What messages and images would have convinced them to make the journey to a new land?

Display your ads for the class. [**Group Activity**]

Listening and Speaking Interview a recent immigrant to find out why and how he or she came to this country. Prepare your questions in advance, and ask follow-up questions as the interview progresses. With your subject's permission, you might take photographs of him or her as well. Record your **interview,** and then share it with your class.

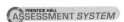 **Take It to the Net** www.phschool.com

Go online for an additional research activity using the Internet.

Letter to Her Daughter . . . / from Letters From an American Farmer ◆ 213

---

❸ Writing Lesson

- Tell students that when they have selected a recipient for their letters, they should focus on an area of interest. Discourage students from addressing too many topics or areas of interest in their letter.

- Help students choose and narrow a topic, ensuring that the topic is one with sufficient context and background to meet the needs of the assignment.

- Use the Writing Lesson to guide students through the assignment.

- When students have finished their letters, have them read the letters to the class.

You may wish to use the writing model for Descriptive and Observational Writing in **Writing Models and Graphic Organizers on Transparencies,** pp. 9–12.

❹ Listening and Speaking

- Have students work together to prepare questions. Encourage them to prepare general, open-ended questions to encourage their interviewee to feel more comfortable.

- If students record the interview, see that they have the proper equipment and know how to operate it. Instruct them to do a sample test at the interview site to make sure recording is taking place.

CUSTOMIZE INSTRUCTION
For Universal Access

To address different learning styles, use the following activities suggested in the **Extension Activities** booklet, p. 12.

For Visual/Spatial Learners, use Activity 5.

For Bodily Kinesthetic Learners use Activity 6.

For Musical/Rhythmic Learners, use Activity 7.

ASSESSMENT RESOURCES

The following resources can be used to assess students' knowledge and skills.

Selection Assessment

- 📖 **Formal Assessment,** pp. 59–63
- 📖 **Open Book Test,** pp. 34–36
- 📼 **Got It! Assessment Videotapes,** Tape 1

ASSESSMENT SYSTEM *PRENTICE HALL*

- 📖 **Workbook**
- 📖 **Skill Book**
- 📖 **Transparencies**
- 💿 **CD-ROM**

 Take It to the Net

Visit www.phschool.com for self-tests and additional questions on the selections.

Connections

Franklin's American aims for moral aptitude; Adams' American concerns himself or herself with national issues and personal challenges; and Crevecoeur's American renounces his European heritage to join the American melting pot. Haley adds a new defining element to answer the question "what is an American?": that of an African American whose sense of identity is firmly rooted in an African ancestry. While discovering his own particular forebear, Haley realizes his own search would be "a symbolic saga of all African-descent people." In a larger sense, his quest is symbolic of everyone's search for ancestral roots. When we define our roots, we also define ourselves.

CONNECTIONS
Literature Past and Present

Defining an American

What is an American? The works in Part 3 offer a telling look at a young nation consciously struggling with this question. At the time, neither Abigail Adams, nor Michel-Guillaume Jean de Crèvecoeur could have foreseen the impact that descendants of enslaved Africans would one day have on America's answer. Those writers could not have known that a book written by an African American in the twentieth-century would influence the way in which millions of Americans defined their identities. That book is *Roots*.

An Educational Blockbuster Published in 1976 and followed by a television miniseries of the same name, *Roots* changed the nation's perception of itself as only very powerful events can. A fictionalized tale of the author Alex Haley's search for his African ancestors and the story of his family's history from their beginnings in Africa to emancipation, the book focused America's attention on the richness of the African cultural heritage. Civil rights leader Vernon Jordan called the television miniseries based on Haley's book "the single most spectacular educational experience in race relations in America." African Americans everywhere followed Haley's example by renewing ties with their African ancestry. Thanks to a single book, the identities of millions of Americans expanded to include a new awareness of rich roots firmly planted in another time and place.

214 ◆ *A Nation is Born (1750–1800)*

from
ROOTS

Alex Haley

Alex Haley's search for his African roots takes him to the small village of Juffure, located in the country in western Africa now known as The Gambia. The elderly village historian honors the American visitor by relating for him the ancestral history of the Kinte clan.

The old *griot*[1] had talked for nearly two hours up to then, and perhaps fifty times the narrative had included some detail about someone whom he had named. Now after he had just named those four sons, again he appended a detail, and the interpreter translated—

"About the time the King's soldiers came"—another of the *griot's* time-fixing references— "the oldest of these four sons, Kunta, went away from his village to chop wood . . . and he was never seen again. . . ." And the *griot* went on with his narrative.

I sat as if I were carved of stone. My blood seemed to have <u>congealed</u>. This man whose lifetime had been in this back-country African village had no way in the world to know that he had just echoed what I had heard all through my boyhood years on my grandma's front porch in Henning, Tennessee . . . of an African who always had insisted that his name was "Kin-tay"; who had called a guitar a *"ko,"* and a river within the state of Virginia, "Kamby Bolongo";[2] and who had been kidnaped into slavery while not far from his village, chopping wood, to make himself a drum.

I managed to fumble from my duffelbag my basic notebook, whose first pages containing grandma's story I showed to an interpreter. After briefly reading, clearly astounded, he spoke rapidly while showing it to the old *griot*, who became agitated; he got up, exclaiming to the people, gesturing at my notebook in the interpreter's hands, and *they* all got agitated.

---

1. **griot** (grē′ ō) *n.* the village oral historian, generally an elderly man who recites histories of famous heroes and families on special occasions.
2. **"Kamby Bolongo"** (käm′ bē bō lôn̄′ gō) "Gambia River" in the Mandinka language of western Africa.

congealed (kən jēld′) *v.* thickened or solidified

Thematic Connection
How might growing up with this story have influenced Haley's perception of his American identity?

Defining an American

• Tell students that they are about to read a passage from the book that made a lasting impression on the face of American culture— and American television—in the late 1970s.

• To introduce students to Alex Haley's epic tale, play your choice of scenes from the television mini-series.

• Afterward, ask students to discuss their impressions of what they saw. Prompt them to speculate about why the book and mini-series have had such an effect on our understanding of what it means to be an American.

Thematic Connection

Answer: Students should note that Haley learned from a young age that he was descended from African ancestry; this knowledge was a big part of his identify as a person and as an African American.

Critical Thinking

Speculate

Ask students to speculate about what might have prompted the woman to hand her baby to Haley.
Answer: Student speculations will vary. Some may say that the women may have considered it an honor to have the special visitor hold their babies.

Background

Art

This painting, *Dance Africa* by Synthia Saint James, was created to promote the 1996 national tour of Dance African America, a North Carolina-based dance company. Each year, founding director Chuck Davis travels with his students to Africa so that they can learn the authentic African rhythms and dances that are the hallmark of the company's electrifying performances. In this painting, Davis, the central male figure, is represented in the role of *griot*—a village historian and storyteller—the keeper of a village's history and culture.

Self-taught artist and author Synthia Saint James (b. 1949) is an internationally recognized artist whose works can be found on the covers of more than 40 books. She has created commissioned works of art for dozens of major organizations including UNICEF. In 1997, she designed the first official Kwanzaa stamp issued by the United States Postal Service.

Ask students: How is the portrayal of the male figure symbolic of his role as the griot?
Answer: He unites the figures in the painting, just as the griot is the keeper of a clan's shared history.

▶ Critical Viewing

Answer: Students may respond that the people in the painting appear animated and vibrant, as do the people that Haley describes in his piece.

I don't remember hearing anyone giving an order, I only recall becoming aware that those seventy-odd people had formed a wide human ring around me, moving counterclockwise, chanting softly, loudly, softly; their bodies close together, they were lifting their knees high, stamping up reddish puffs of the dust. . . .

The woman who broke from the moving circle was one of about a dozen whose infant children were within cloth slings across their backs. Her jet-black face deeply contorting, the woman came charging toward me, her bare feet slapping the earth, and snatching her baby free, she thrust it at me almost roughly, the gesture saying "Take it!" . . . and I did, clasping the baby to me. Then she snatched away her baby; and another woman was thrusting her baby, then another, and another . . . until I had embraced probably a dozen babies. I wouldn't learn until maybe a year later, from a Harvard University professor, Dr. Jerome Bruner, a scholar of such matters, "You didn't know you were participating in one of the oldest ceremonies of humankind, called 'The laying on of hands'! In their way, they were telling you 'Through this flesh, which is us, we are you, and you are us!'"

Later the men of Juffure[3] took me into their mosque[4] built of bamboo and thatch, and they prayed around me in Arabic. I remember thinking, down on my knees, "After I've found out where I came from, I can't understand a word they're saying." Later the <u>crux</u> of their prayer was translated for me: "Praise be to Allah for one long lost from us whom Allah has returned."

Since we had come by the river, I wanted to return by land. As I sat beside the wiry young Mandingo driver who was leaving dust pluming behind us on the hot, rough, pitted, back-country road toward Banjul, there came from somewhere into my head a staggering awareness . . . that *if* any black American could be so blessed as I had been to know only a few ancestral clues—could he or she know *who* was either the paternal or maternal African ancestor or ancestors, and about *where* that ancestor lived when taken, and finally about *when* the ancestor was taken—then only those few clues might well see that black American able to locate some wizened old black *griot* whose narrative could reveal the black American's ancestral clan, perhaps even the very village.

In my mind's eye, rather as if it were mistily being projected on a screen, I began envisioning descriptions I had read of how collectively millions of our ancestors had been enslaved. Many thousands were individually kidnaped, as my own forebear Kunta had been, but into the millions had come awake screaming in the night, dashing out into

crux (kruks) *n.* essential point

Dance Africa, Synthia Saint James, Third World Art Exchange

▲ Critical Viewing
What details of this image suit Haley's description of the African village he visits? **[Connect]**

---

3. **Juffure** (jōō´ fōō rā)
4. **mosque** (mäsk) *n.* Muslim temple or place of worship.

the bedlam of raided villages, which were often in flames. The captured able survivors were linked neck-by-neck with thongs into processions called "coffles," which were sometimes as much as a mile in length. I envisioned the many dying, or left to die when they were too weak to continue the torturous march toward the coast, and those who made it to the beach were greased, shaved, probed in every orifice, often branded with sizzling irons; I envisioned them being lashed and dragged toward the longboats; their spasms of screaming and clawing with their hands into the beach, biting up great choking mouthfuls of the sand in their desperation efforts for one last hold on the Africa that had been their home; I envisioned them shoved, beaten, jerked down into slave ships' stinking holds and chained onto shelves, often packed so tightly that they had to lie on their sides like spoons in a drawer. . . .

My mind reeled with it all as we approached another, much larger village. Staring ahead, I realized that word of what had happened in Juffure must have left there well before I did. The driver slowing down, I could see this village's people thronging the road ahead; they were weaving, amid their <u>cacophony</u> of crying out something; I stood up in the Land-Rover, waving back as they seemed grudging to open a path for the Land-Rover.

I guess we had moved a third of the way through the village when it suddenly registered in my brain what they were all crying out . . . the wizened, robed elders and younger men, the mothers and the naked tar-black children, they were all waving up at me; their expressions buoyant, beaming, all were crying out together, *"Meester Kinte! Meester Kinte!"*

Let me tell you something: I am a man. A sob hit me somewhere around my ankles; it came surging upward, and flinging my hands over my face, I was just bawling, as I hadn't since I was a baby. *"Meester Kinte!"* I just felt like I was weeping for all of history's incredible atrocities against fellowmen, which seems to be mankind's greatest flaw. . . .

Flying homeward from Dakar, I decided to write a book. My own ancestors would automatically also be a symbolic saga of all African-descent people—who are without exception the seeds of someone like Kunta who was born and grew up in some black African village, someone who was captured and chained down in one of those slave ships that sailed them across the same ocean, into some succession of plantations, and since then a struggle for freedom.

cacophony (kə käf′ ə nē) *n.* harsh, jarring sound

Alex Haley

(1921–1992) Alex Haley spent twenty years in the Coast Guard as a journalist before deciding to become a freelance writer. His first big success came with his highly praised *The Autobiography of Malcolm X*. His greatest and best-known accomplishment, however, is *Roots: The Saga of an American Family.* The book was an immediate bestseller and within two years had won more than 200 awards. The television miniseries based on the book was viewed by 130 million people. About the success of *Roots*, Haley said, "When you start talking about family, about lineage and ancestry, you are talking about every person on earth. We all have it; it's a great equalizer. . . . I think the book has touched a strong, subliminal chord."

Connecting Literature Past and Present

1. How do you think Alex Haley might answer the question, What is an American?
2. Which of the beliefs expressed by other writers in this section do you think Haley might share? Why?

Critical Thinking

Speculate

Ask students: If the villagers had treated Haley as an outsider rather than as a kinsman, how might his search for his heritage have been affected?

Answer: He may not have been as interested in pursuing his search for his family's African roots.

Critical Thinking

Evaluate

Tell students that critics have suggested that *Roots* blurs the lines between fact and fiction, and that Haley may have presented fictional segments of the story as fact. Ask students whether they think that this blurring detracts from the book's value.

Answer: Some may feel the awareness of African heritage created by the book means more than the accuracy of its contents. Others may argue that distortion diminishes the value of the work.

Answers

Connecting Literature Past and Present

1. Possible Answer: Haley would point out that the American identity encompasses many cultural backgrounds, including the various cultural heritages that evolved in Africa.

2. Students may note that Crevecoeur would probably have shared Haley's view, since he saw the United States as a unique nation that blended many cultures.

Objectives

1. To write an analytical essay on literary themes

2. To develop a list of criteria by which to judge literary works

3. To evaluate literary works using precise and varied terms

4. To use writing strategies to generate ideas and to plan, organize, evaluate, and revise a piece of writing

Prewriting

- Review the assignment with the class.

- Then, write the titles of the selections that appear in this unit on the chalkboard, and invite comments about each one.

- Ask students to briefly state the message about freedom each selection presents. Then, ask them to state which selections they responded to most strongly. In the course of discussion, help students develop a list of criteria by which to judge the success of the selections in their arguments for freedom.

- Encourage students to write about the selections to which they responded most intensely, whether in a positive or a negative way.

- Draw students' attention to the model chart on this page. Have students use a similar chart to develop their analyses of the selections, and to formulate a working thesis.

- Remind students that the purpose of this assignment is to evaluate the literary works. This requires them to make and support judgments, not simply present an analysis.

Writing About Literature

Evaluate Literary Themes

The writers of the Revolutionary period believed that they could—and should—take control of their destinies, both as individuals and as Americans. Belief in personal and political freedom gave these writers an enormous sense of optimism and energy. They saw all problems, from those of poor personal habits to those of political tyranny, as obstacles to be overcome rather than as circumstances to accept. In many respects, this sense of revolutionary optimism continues to characterize American political discourse. Review the literature in this unit to complete the assignment outlined in the box at right.

Prewriting

Judge the selections. To evaluate literary works, follow these steps:

- First, determine the criterion upon which to base the evaluation.
- Second, analyze the authors' messages and methods.
- Finally, make judgments about the works in light of the stated criterion.

In this essay, your criterion is the success of the author's arguments in favor of freedom. Therefore, when you analyze each selection, focus on references to personal and political liberty.

Formulate a thesis. Use a chart like the one shown to organize your analysis of the references to freedom made by a number of authors. Then, state your judgment about the success with which the authors have argued for the rights of individuals to direct their own lives. Write your assessment in one sentence. Use this sentence as a working thesis.

> **Assignment:**
> **A Matter of Persuasion**
>
> Write an analytical essay that evaluates the success with which the authors in this unit make their cases for personal and/or political freedom.
>
> **Criteria:**
> - Include a thesis statement that states your opinion.
> - Support your opinion with examples from the selections.
> - Approximate length: 1,500 words.

Read to Write

Reread the texts, looking for the precise methods that the writers use to make their points about personal liberty.

Model: Charting to Develop a Thesis

Thesis: Jefferson and his colleagues are cautious men moved to radical action by extreme circumstances.

Selection	Reference	Method/Message
The Declaration of Independence	"Prudence, indeed, will dictate that governments long established should not be changed for light and transient causes."	Jefferson highlights idea of prudence, implying that reasons for declaring independence are not trivial.

Select powerful examples. Some of the selections you have analyzed will support your thesis better than others will. Pick the examples that most powerfully support your thesis statement.

TEACHING RESOURCES

The following resources can be used to extend the instruction for pp. 218–219.

𝒲𝒢 **Writing and Grammar,** Ruby Level, Chapter 14

📖 **Performance Assessment and Portfolio Management,** p. 23

📑 **Writing Models and Graphic Organizers on Transparencies,** p. 75

💿 **Writing and Grammar iText CD-ROM**

Students can use the following tools as they complete their evaluation essays:

- Listing Tool
- Sensory Word Bin
- Sentence Openers Variety Revising Tools

Drafting

Write an introduction. In your introduction, state your subject matter and purpose, and identify the works you will be evaluating—in this case, literature from the formative years of the United States. Then, assert your opinion of the success or failure of this literature in its argument that individuals should determine their own futures.

Present examples in order. Follow your introduction with the example that best supports your opinion. For example, if you think the writers in this unit fail to make a strong case for individual liberty, quote the argument that most clearly supports your point. Then, explain the reasons for your opinion.

Revising and Editing

Review content: Make sure that you are evaluating your material. To be successful, an evaluative essay must assert a judgment about a subject, not just report on it. To make sure you are actually evaluating the literature, review each paragraph of your essay. Jot down the ideas you present in each paragraph. Then, use a highlighter to mark the sentences that contain evaluations. If you see too few highlighted sentences, go back and add well-supported judgments.

Write to Learn

You may find a selection to be more or less effective than you had originally thought. Allow for such changes in opinion; the writing process has given you a new perspective.

Write to Explain

It is not sufficient to judge a work in a casual way. Instead, justify your evaluations with examples from the selection.

Model: Revising to Add Evaluation

Paragraph
1. Jefferson wrote the Declaration as a message to the British king.
2. He portrays the colonists as cautious men who do not want to rebel, but feel they have no choice.
3. He says that the signers of the Declaration stake their lives and sacred honors on this document.
4. *This strategy is persuasive because it shows that freedom matters more than anything, including wealth or life itself.*

Review style: Use a variety of evaluative terms. An evaluative essay contains value-laden terms such as *effective, clear, convincing,* and *persuasive.* Review your draft, and underline your use of such terms. Replace vague adjectives, such as *good,* with more precise alternatives. If you have used certain words too often, replace them with synonyms.

Publishing and Presenting

Generate a literary magazine. With classmates, publish your essays in a literary magazine. Select a title for your magazine that indicates the scope and subject matter of the essays.

𝒲𝒢 *Prentice Hall Writing and Grammar Connection: Chapter 14*

Writing About Literature ◆ 219

Drafting

- Encourage students to create informal outlines of their essays, including complete introductions followed by brief lists of the ideas they will develop, and the examples they will use as support.
- Briefly check each student's informal outline before he or she begins to draft. Make sure that each introduction clearly states a thesis, and that the list of ideas and examples follows logically from that point.

Revising and Editing

- If you wish, have students share papers and apply the activity described under "Review Content" to their partner's work.
- To clarify the idea of using precise evaluative terms, write two columns of words on the chalkboard. In column A, write a list of general evaluative words, such as *good, bad, okay,* and *nice.* In column B, write a list of precise evaluative terms, such as *reasonable, effective, powerful,* and *convincing.*
- Ask students which column lists more effective word choices, and to explain why these words are better. **Answer:** Column B lists more effective words. They are better word choices because they are precise. The words in Column A are vague.
- As students review each other's work, encourage them to make sure their use of evaluative terms is varied and precise.

Publishing and Presenting

- Organize students into small groups. To each group assign the responsibility for a specific element of the magazine. For example, one group should handle design—the size, font choices, and overall layout of the magazine. Another group should select appropriate illustrations and graphics. Another group should determine the best method of printing and binding the magazine. The last group should organize the magazine's distribution or sale.
- Encourage students to develop procedures that will allow all the groups to work together to create the best possible product.
- Conduct a brainstorming session with the class as a whole to choose a suitable title for the magazine.

CUSTOMIZE INSTRUCTION FOR UNIVERSAL ACCESS

For Less Proficient Readers	For English Learners	For Advanced Readers
Work with students to develop criteria by with which to judge the selections. Hold a discussion about freedom as a principle in their daily lives. What does freedom mean to them personally? As they speak, help them to identify those writers whose work most directly addresses their feelings about freedom.	The value of personal freedom is not unique to America, but it is highly emphasized here. Invite students to discuss whether or not their cultures of origin share this value. Have students use these cultural comparisons to frame their ideas and make judgments about the selections in this unit.	Invite students to research European philosophers, such as John Locke, who inspired writers in this unit. Urge them to examine the ways in which American revolutionary writers both drew and departed from the Europeans. Have students consider this question: Do the writers in this unit express a distinctly American sensibility?

219

Lesson Objectives

1. To write a problem-and-solution essay

2. To use writing strategies to generate ideas and to plan, organize, evaluate, and revise the composition

Model From Literature

Patrick Henry's "Speech in the Virginia Convention," p. 187, states the problems of the colonies' relationship to England and suggests a solution—a war for independence.

Prewriting

- Have students discuss Patrick Henry's speech. Point out that the problem Henry wants to solve is an issue of national concern. Suggest that students consider writing about national or international issues that they think are of great importance.

- Students may or may not be able to interview people about their topics. Instead, they may want to do research in a library or on the Internet.

- Before students draft their essays, have them review the Rubric for Self-Assessment (p. 223) so they know what is expected.

Writing WORKSHOP

Exposition: Problem-and-Solution Essay

A **problem-and-solution essay** identifies and explains a problem and then offers a practical solution. In this workshop, you will plan, draft, and revise a problem-and-solution essay.

Assignment Criteria Your problem-and-solution essay should have the following characteristics:

- A statement of a problem that is clear enough to develop fully and support in an essay
- A proposed solution that is practical
- Facts, statistics, or expert testimony that illustrates the scope of the problem and the practicality of the solution
- Language appropriate to the knowledge level of the audience
- A logical organization that establishes the relationship between problem and solution

To preview the criteria on which your problem-and-solution essay may be assessed, refer to the Rubric on page 223.

Prewriting

Choose a topic. Write your problem-and-solution essay about an issue of interest to you. To find a subject, **watch or listen to the news** on television or radio, and create a chart like the one shown to assess the problems reported. Then, review your chart to select a problem for which you can offer a viable solution.

Problem List

Problem	Personal Experience	Can I Provide a Solution?
Forest Fires	No direct experience.	No.
Pedestrian traffic accidents	Yes. Sister almost hit by car on Main Street.	Yes, but not that interested.
Teen Stress	A lot of personal experience	Yes. I could use my own advice.

Analyze your audience. When you write a problem-and-solution essay, keep a specific audience in mind: readers who have the ability to implement your suggestions. Ask yourself the following questions to customize your essay to your audience's needs:

- Who is my audience?
- What does my audience already know about my topic?
- What information do I need to provide?
- In what ways can I stir my audience's interest in this problem?
- Does my audience have the power and authority to implement the solution I suggest?

Gather details. To collect the information you will need, make a list of details, facts, and examples that prove there is a problem. To gather additional information, conduct interviews with people who have been frustrated by the situation your essay will address.

220 ◆ A Nation Is Born (1750–1800)

TEACHING RESOURCES

The following resources can be used to enrich or extend the instruction for pages 220–223.

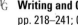 **Writing and Grammar,** Ruby Level, Chapter 11, pp. 218–241; Chapter 14, pp. 298–325

 Performance Assessment and Portfolio Management, p. 10

 Writing Models and Graphic Organizers on Transparencies, p. 79

 Writing and Grammar iText CD-ROM

Students can use the following tools as they complete their problem-and-solution essays:

- Audience Profile
- Topic Bank
- Comparatives

Student Model

Before you begin writing, read this student model and review the characteristics of an effective problem-and-solution essay.

Katie Burcham
Florence, Kentucky

Rat Race Tips: Surviving Student Stress

William Henry Davies once wrote, "A poor life this is, full of care; we have no time to stand and stare." Due to the high amount of stress our society creates, this quotation accurately portrays the quality of life for many teenagers. Stress is a leading cause of health problems, including depression, a major issue among teenagers.

> Katie tells readers why they should care about her subject.

A recent study by Reuters [http://www.intelihealth.com, 27 Oct. 1999] reported that one third of American teens say they feel "stressed out" every day. The study also reports that one source of all this stress is unrealistic expectations which parents have for their children.

> She then provides evidence attesting to the magnitude of the problem.

Parental Expectations Parental stress can play out in comparisons that make teens feel inadequate. For me, parental stress means comparison to siblings. One sister was valedictorian, and another sister was salutatorian. An air of expectation returns every time my report card arrives: "Will Katie do as well as her sisters?" This motivates me, but it creates stress.

College Admissions Teens know that college admissions are more competitive than ever. However, paying for college can place financial pressures on a family. Teens become frantic to create the type of profile that scholarship committees love—one packed with activities, top grades, volunteer jobs, and part-time work. These activities create an unmanageable schedule, and a lot of stress.

> This logical point-by-point form of organization, with main points called out by subheads, is effective in a problem-and-solution essay.

Self-Inflicted Stress Often, students will overextend themselves, resolving to stay up longer and study harder. But the "cramming" that overachievers resort to—an activity that can involve pulling all-nighters, and skipping meals—usually backfires. Studies show that the stress linked with this frenzied preparation actually impairs the memory [http:///www.cgi.cnn.com/HEALTH/9808/19/stress.memory, Aug. 19, 1998].

Solutions How can teenagers combat stress? Experts have these suggestions:

- *Learn relaxation and breathing techniques.* When the body relaxes, the emotions follow [http://www.aacap.org/publications/factsfam/66.htm, 21 Jan. 2001].
- *Say no.*
- *Take one thing at a time.*
- *Have fun!* Laughter is a proven stress reducer.

> Katie provides reasonable solutions supported by evidence.

Some might say that if teens do not push themselves, they will lose out on opportunities, and that stress is just a part of striving. To that, I can only say that everything suffers when an individual is overextended, and eventually the teen will burn out, not achieve. Instead, by being selective about their activities, approaching projects in small steps, and learning to laugh, teenagers can live rewarding lives—not stress free, but manageable.

> Katie anticipates and answers possible objections.

Student Model

- Explain that the Student Model is a sample. Students' own essays may be longer than this model.
- Have students read the model silently. Point out that Katie has chosen to discuss an issue with which she has direct personal experience. This may give students ideas for topics of their own.
- Point out the boldface heads with which Katie begins each new section of her essay. These heads highlight the main ideas of the paragraphs they set off. Have students discuss other effective ways of organizing an essay.
- Ask students why Katie includes the Internet addresses for the studies to which she refers. **Answer:** With this information, a reader can check the studies to see whether Katie's interpretation is accurate, and to read more about the topic.
- Point out that in the final paragraph, Katie refutes a possible objection to her main argument. Ask students why she does this. **Answer:** A reader might make this argument and assume that Katie failed to take it into account. By bringing it up herself, she gives herself a chance to answer it.

Real-World Connection

Problem-and-solution essays in the real world: Many jobs require people to propose solutions to problems. As Patrick Henry's speech shows, politicians routinely have to make speeches outlining problems and proposing solutions. Mathematics and archaeology are other fields in which researchers are faced with problems of interpretation that they have to solve.

CUSTOMIZE INSTRUCTION FOR UNIVERSAL ACCESS

For Less Proficient Readers	For English Learners	For Advanced Readers
Have students use an outline form to organize their ideas from the prewriting stage. They can state their main argument, list supporting details, and then list opposing arguments and their refutations of these.	During the prewriting stage, meet with students individually to discuss their topics. Encourage students to choose familiar problems that they have the vocabularies to discuss in writing.	Challenge students to write about a problem from the period of history covered in this unit. Students can reread the selections for information and also do some research. Here is one example of a historical problem: How might the Continental Congress have eliminated slavery and still satisfied the needs of the southern colonies?

Drafting

- Explain that a problem-and-solution essay can be organized in a number of ways. In "Speech to the Virginia Convention," Patrick Henry takes a question-and-answer approach. Students should experiment to see which pattern of organization seems most natural for their topics.

- Remind students that supporting details will vary in type depending on their topics. Patrick Henry appealed directly to his listeners' own experiences by referring to current events that they had all lived through. In the student model, Katie cited her own experience of the pressures of being a teenager; she also referred to professional studies of these pressures.

Revising

- Remind students to include at least one opposing argument. If they don't anticipate the arguments of the opposition, they leave themselves open to being dismissed. If they mention opposing arguments, they give themselves an opportunity to refute them.

- Students may want to ask partners to read their essays. Partners can help each other spot difficult or obscure terms that might need explaining. Students can either substitute easier synonyms or provide context clues or definitions.

(continued on p. 223)

Writing WORKSHOP continued

Drafting

Choose an organization. Your problem-and-solution essay must achieve two goals: It must define a problem, and it must identify and develop a workable solution. Review the following forms of organization and determine which will work best for the problem you have chosen:

- **Point-by-Point:** This organizational strategy breaks down the main problem into an array of smaller problems, and then addresses each one, point by point, offering small-scale solutions.
- **Block:** This organizational strategy lays out the problem as a whole, and then proposes a comprehensive solution to the entire problem.

Provide evidence. Support all statements with facts, statistics, personal experiences, and any other documentation that will persuade your audience of the soundness of your ideas. Use a chart like the one shown to guide your selection of evidence.

Address readers' concerns. Convince those who may not approve of your solution by anticipating objections and demonstrating that you have taken them into account. Address each objection with explanations and evidence that prove your solution is the best plan.

Revising

Revise by taking the opposing view. Look for places where a critic might disagree with your ideas, and answer their likely objections. A few common objections are listed below, along with strategies that may be used to answer them. Use these strategies to guide your revision.

- **Why should I care?** Include information to show how the problem affects your audience.
- **Why should I do it?** Use language that makes your audience see that their participation is a critical part of the solution.
- **This solution is too difficult.** Show how the solution can be completed easily, or stress that a complicated solution is necessary because of the complexity of the problem.

Collect Types of Evidence

Type of Evidence	
Fact	Anxiety obstructs memory.
Statistic	One third of American teens say they feel "stressed out" on a daily basis.
Anecdote	I am compared to my high-achieving sisters.
Expert Testimony	Teens should learn to say "no."

Model: Address the Opposition

Due to the high amount of stress our society creates, this quotation accurately portrays the quality of life for many teenagers.

Stress is a leading cause of health problems, including depression, a major issue among teenagers.

Katie added information to reinforce the importance of her topic.

USING TECHNOLOGY IN WRITING

After students working on word processors have drafted their essays, they can print out copies to read through before they revise their work on the screen. Word processors allow students to move large blocks of text around within a document. As they revise their essays, students should concentrate on the logical order of the paragraphs. They can renumber them on the printed draft and then move the paragraphs within the revised version. Students can also use the organizing tools and revision checkers on the **Writing and Grammar iText CD-ROM**.

Revise for word choice. Review your draft as if you were a member of your intended audience. Circle terms that need to be defined, or vocabulary that seems too easy for your readers. For example, in the following passage, the word *hybridization* is defined to make sense to a general audience.

Without definition: The plants feature a genetic *hybridization* that modifies their color.

With definition: The plants feature a genetic hybridization, or *blending,* that modifies their color.

Compare the model and the non-model. Why is the model more effective?

Nonmodel	Model
But the "cramming" that overachievers resort to usually backfires.	But the "cramming" that overachievers resort to—an activity that can involve pulling all-nighters, and skipping meals—usually backfires.

Publishing and Presenting

Consider the following activity to share your writing with classmates or a wider audience.

Deliver an oral presentation. Read your problem-and-solution essay aloud for your class. When you have finished, invite comments and questions. Determine whether or not your classmates are convinced that your solution is the best answer to the problem.

 Prentice Hall Writing and Grammar Connection: Chapter 11

Rubric for Self-Assessment

Evaluate your problem-and-solution essay using the following criteria and rating scale:

Criteria	Rating Scale				
	Not very				Very
Is the problem stated clearly enough to be fully developed and supported?	1	2	3	4	5
How practical is the suggested solution?	1	2	3	4	5
How effective are facts, statistics, and details that illustrate the problem and the solution?	1	2	3	4	5
Is the language appropriate to the audience's knowledge level?	1	2	3	4	5
How well is the material organized?	1	2	3	4	5

Writing Workshop: Problem-and-Solution Essay ◆ *223*

- Have students read the model and the nonmodel. Then, have them explain why the model is more effective.
  Answer: The model not only explains the term "cramming," but makes clear the reasons that it usually backfires.

Publishing and Presenting

- Have students discuss how they might revise their essays if they planned to share them with an audience other than their classmates. What changes might they have to make?
- Have students try presenting their essays from memory rather than reading them aloud. Students can make note cards to aid them during their presentations. Have them discuss the differences between the written and oral versions of the essays. How are they different? Why are they different?

Assessment

- Review the assessment criteria with the class before they begin the revision stage of the essay. The points in the chart are things students will want to consider and correct as they revise their drafts.
- Have students exchange papers with partners and score one another's essays. If partners disagree strongly, they should debate their reasons for disagreeing.
- The rubric on this page, and another rubric in an alternative format, can be found on pp. 10 and 40 of **Performance Assessment and Portfolio Management**.

TEST-TAKING TIP

When students encounter a test prompt that asks them to write problem-and-solution essays, they should brainstorm for a list of solutions to the problem they have chosen to address. If they can't think of two or three feasible solutions, students might consider writing about a different problem.

Lesson Objectives

1. To analyze persuasive techniques

2. To analyze the purpose of a persuasive speech based on the evidence presented by the speaker

3. To evaluate the support that a speaker provides for his or her claims

---

Analyze Persuasive Purposes

• Review with students the bulleted list under "Analyze Persuasive Purposes." Make sure they understand each type of proposition on the list.

• Ask students to name instances when they've encountered or used one of the four types of propositions.
Possible answer: Students might have encountered propositions of value in televised advertisements about political candidates. They might have used propositions in policy when talking with their parents about changes in household rules.

Evaluate Support

• Have students read the three questions for evaluating a speaker's support.

• Tell students that it might be helpful to take notes while listening to a persuasive speech. That way, they can thoroughly evaluate the speaker's evidence after the speech has ended.

• Encourage students to ask questions of the speaker when they encounter what is unclear or illogical.

Listening and Speaking WORKSHOP

Analyze Persuasive Techniques

When speakers want to convince you to accept their ideas, they can use a variety of **persuasive techniques**. The strategies noted below will help you recognize and evaluate four kinds of speech.

Analyze Persuasive Purposes

Persuasive speakers seek to convince audiences using one or more of these four types of ideas:

• **Proposition of fact:** The speaker wants listeners to accept a claim as either true or false.

• **Proposition of value:** The speaker wants listeners to accept a claim as either good or bad.

• **Proposition to illuminate a problem:** The speaker asks listeners to share a concern.

• **Proposition of policy:** The speaker wants listeners to agree to a change in policy regarding an issue.

As you listen to a persuasive speech, identify the speaker's main purpose.

Identify evidence. Each type of persuasive speech offers distinct kinds of evidence: For a proposition of fact, evidence should include hard data, examples, or testimony. For a proposition of value, evidence should include both facts and appeals to emotion, and will indicate the speaker's sense of values. For a proposition to illuminate a problem, the speaker must establish the existence of a threat or obstacle. Lastly, in a proposition of policy, the speaker must persuade listeners to take specific action.

As you listen to a speech, identify the evidence presented, note whether it is suited to the speaker's purpose, and weigh its strength.

Evaluate Support

Use these questions to evaluate the support a speaker provides:

• **Proof:** Does the speaker's proof pertain directly to the thesis?

• **Persuasive Language:** Does the speaker use strong language that urges agreement, and clear language that ensures understanding?

• **Reasoning:** Is the speaker's reasoning sound and logical?

Use a form like the one shown to assess the effectiveness of a speech.

(Activity:)
Speak and Respond — In a group of four, present speeches of each type on a topic familiar to group members. Evaluate the effectiveness of each speech's organization and support.

Evaluating Persuasive Techniques

Rating System
+ = excellent   ✔ = average   – = weak

Goals and Organization
Purpose clearly presented _____
Thesis statement is clear _____
Logical organization of supporting material _____
Clear link to audience _____

Support
Proofs match speech type _____
Proofs support thesis _____
Language is compelling _____
Language is persuasive _____
Reasoning is sound _____

Answer the following questions:
Which type of persuasive speech did you find most compelling?

Which persuasive techniques did you find most effective?

CUSTOMIZE INSTRUCTION FOR UNIVERSAL ACCESS

For Less Proficient Readers	For Gifted/Talented Students
Give students some practice with the terms on this page by having them analyze the persuasive selections in Unit 2 and identify which types of ideas and evidence are represented in each. Students can identify the purpose of each speech and discuss how successfully each writer supported his or her ideas.	Have students analyze the purpose and evaluate the support of the persuasive messages around them. For example, they might examine local billboards or current advertisements on television or the radio. Which ads are well supported, and which simply have the appearance of being so?

Assessment WORKSHOP

Cause-and-Effect Relationships

The reading sections of some tests often require you to recognize cause-and-effect relationships and to predict probable outcomes based on the content of a passage. Use the following strategies to answer test questions on these skills:

- As you read, clarify the connections among events to help you identify the cause-and-effect relationships.
- Remember that a single cause can have many effects, and a single effect can have many causes.
- While other causes may be stated or implied, concentrate on the cause that has the most direct influence on the outcome.
- Look for words that indicate cause and effect, such as *causes, produces, affects, because of, as a result,* or *for this reason.*

Test-Taking Strategy

Identify connections between causes (an event or condition that produces a result) and effects (the result).

Sample Test Item

Directions: Read the passage, and then answer the question that follows.

The increasing growth of weeds in Cabot Lake threatens to turn it into a stagnant swamp. Ira North, a researcher for the Cabot Institute, cites an increase in phosphorus-based lawn fertilizers as the primary factor in the growth of lake weeds. "When it rains, fertilizer runs into the lake, causing aquatic plants to grow rapidly. Phosphorus-laden water from washing machines and dishwashers also contributes to the problem."

1. What is the main cause of weed over-growth in Cabot Lake?

   A the fertilizing properties of phosphorus

   B rainwater runoff

   C lawn fertilizers

   D dishwashers and washing machines

Answer and Explanation

The correct answer is *C*. Answers *A, B,* and *D* all play a role in lake weed growth. *C*, however, is the "primary factor."

▶ Practice

Directions: Read the passage, and then answer the question that follows.

At this point, more than one third of Cabot Lake is overrun by lake weeds and is unsuitable for swimming. North says that as more people build homes in the area, the use of phosphorus-based lawn fertilizers will increase dramatically. The number of dishwashers and washing machines in use will also go up, putting additional strain on the ecosystem. North predicts that if nothing is done to control development and fertilizer use, the lake will be fully overrun with weeds within twenty-five years.

1. Why is one third of Cabot Lake unsuitable for swimming?

   A an increased number of lawns in the area

   B an overgrowth of weeds in the lake

   C more roads, increasing rainwater runoff

   D more people buying fertilizer for their lawns

Lesson Objective

To recognize cause-and-effect relationships in test situations

Applying Reading Strategies

Review the clue words indicating cause-and-effect relationships. Have students suggest other clue words that they may encounter.

Test-Taking Skills

- Have students read the sample test item. Ask them to identify words and phrases that indicate cause-and-effect relationships. Answer: Students should mention "primary factor in the growth of lake weeds," and "also contributes to the problem."

- Have students vote for the correct answer. If any students choose incorrect answers, have them reread the passage and identify the sentence that reveals the correct answer.

Answer

1. The correct answer is *B*. The weed growth is the direct cause of people's inability to swim in the lake.

TEACHING RESOURCES

The following resources can be used to enrich or extend the instruction on page 225.

PRENTICE HALL
ASSESSMENT *SYSTEM*

- **Workbook**
- **Skill Book**
- **Transparencies**
- **CD-ROM**

Unit Objectives

1. To read selections from the American literary tradition written between 1800 and 1870

2. To apply critical-reading strategies to these selections

3. To analyze literary elements

4. To use a variety of strategies to read unfamiliar words and build vocabulary

5. To learn elements of grammar, usage, and style

6. To use recursive writing processes to write in a variety of forms

7. To develop listening and speaking skills

8. To express and support responses to various types of texts

9. To prepare, organize, and present literary interpretations

Meeting the Objectives

With each selection, you will find instructional material and opportunities through which students can meet these objectives. You will find additional practice pages for reading strategies, literary elements, vocabulary, and grammar in the **Selection Support** booklet in the **Teaching Resources** box.

Background

Art

Niagara Falls, by Thomas Chambers

Niagara Falls is a typical example of the Hudson River School of painting, born in New York City in 1825 when Thomas Cole exhibited several paintings done on a sketching trip along the Hudson River into New York State. Hudson River School paintings featured rugged, Romantic landscapes not only of New York state but also of Canada, the Arctic, and the American West.

• How does this painting convey the theme of a growing nation?
Answer: It shows a person in the foreground and houses along the bank in the background, suggesting that Americans are spreading out and settling more and more land.

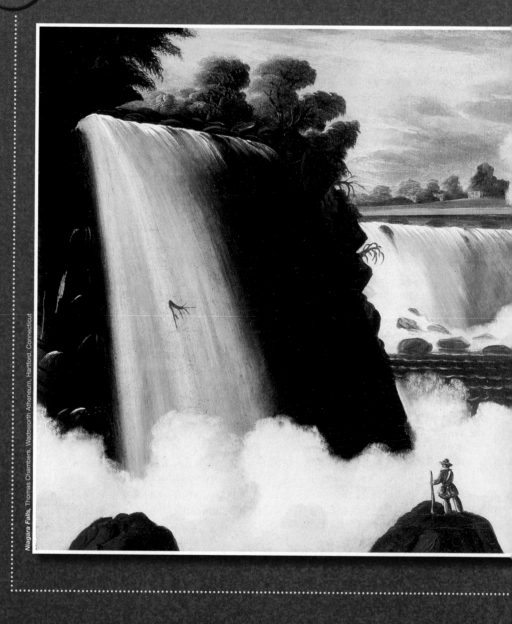

Niagara Falls, Thomas Chambers, Wadsworth Atheneum, Hartford, Connecticut

UNIT 3 A Growing Nation (1800–1870)

UNIT FEATURES

Connections	Reading Informational Materials

Every unit contains a feature that connects literature to a related topic, such as art, science, or history. In this unit, students will connect literature from the past to literature from the present day.
 	
   Use the information and questions on the Connections page to help students enrich their understanding of the selections presented in the unit.
	These selections will help students learn to analyze and evaluate informational materials, such as workplace documents, technical directions, and consumer materials. They will expose students to the organization and features unique to nonnarrative texts.
	
	   In this unit, students will learn to read memorandums.

66 *America is a land of wonders, in which everything is in constant motion and every change seems an improvement. . . . No natural boundary seems to be set to the efforts of man; and in his eyes what is not yet done is only what he has not yet attempted to do* 99

— Alexis de Tocqueville

ASSESSMENT RESOURCES

- **Selection Support:** Skills Development Workbook
- **Formal Assessment**
- **Open Book Tests**
- **Performance Assess. and Portfolio Mgmt.**
- **Extension Activities**

Assessing Student Progress

Listed below are the tools that are available to measure the degree to which students meet the unit objectives.

Informal Assessment

The questions in the Review and Assess sections are a first level of response to the concepts and skills presented in the selections. Students' responses are a brief, informal measure of their grasp of the material. These responses can indicate where further instruction and practice are needed. Then follow up with the practice pages in the **Selection Support: Skills Development Workbook.**

Formal Assessment

The **Formal Assessment** workbook contains Selection Tests and Unit Tests.

- Selection Tests measure comprehension and skills acquisition for each selection or group of selections.
- Each Unit Test provides students with 30 multiple-choice questions and five essay questions designed to assess students' knowledge of the literature and skills taught in the unit.

The **Open Book Tests** ask students to demonstrate their ability to synthesize and communicate information from selections or groups of selections.

To assess students writing, you will find rubrics and scoring models in the **Performance Assessment and Portfolio Management** booklet. In this booklet you will also find scoring rubrics for listening and speaking activities.

Alternative Assessment

The **Extension Activities** booklet contains writing activities, listening and speaking activities, and research and technology activities that are appropriate for students with different ability levels. You may also use these activities as an alternative measurement of students' growth.

Using the Timeline

The timeline can serve a number of instructional purposes, as follows:

Getting an Overview

Use the timeline to help students get a quick overview of themes and events of the period. This approach will benefit all students but may be especially helpful for visually oriented students, English-language learners, and those less proficient in reading. (For strategies in using the Timeline as an overview, see the bottom of this page.)

Thinking Critically

Have students answer critical-thinking questions about the timeline to help them establish the "so what" behind the "what happened." (For Critical Thinking and Critical Viewing questions, see the bottom and side columns of the facing page.)

Connecting to Selections

Have students refer back to the timeline when beginning to read individual selections. By consulting the timeline regularly, they will gain a better sense of the period's chronology. In addition, they will appreciate what was occurring in the world that gave rise to these works of literature.

Projects

Students can use the timeline as a launching pad for projects like these:

- **Annotated Map** Have students use this timeline and other sources to create annotated maps in their notebooks. Maps can show the growth of America from 1800 to 1870, with notes indicating when each state was added to the country.
- **Headline History** Have students scan the American Events section of the timeline for ten especially newsworthy items. Then ask them to write headlines dramatizing each of these items for readers living at the time.

Timeline 1800–1870

1800   1810   1820

American Events

- **1803** Louisiana Purchase extends nation's territory to the Rocky Mountains.
- **1804** Lewis and Clark begin expedition exploring and mapping vast regions of the West. ▼

- **1807** Robert Fulton's steamboat makes first trip from New York City to Albany.

- **1812** U.S. declares war on Great Britain; early battles in War of 1812 are at sea.
- **1814** Bombardment of Fort McHenry inspires Francis Scott Key to write "The Star-Spangled Banner." ▼

- **1817** William Cullen Bryant publishes early draft of "Thanatopsis" in a Boston magazine.

- **1820** Missouri Compromise bans slavery in parts of new territories.

- **1825** Completion and success of Erie Canal spurs canal building throughout the nation. ▲
- **1827** Edgar Allan Poe publishes *Tamerlane,* his first collection of poems.

World Events

- **1804** France: Napoleon Bonaparte proclaims himself emperor. ▼

- **1813** England: Jane Austen publishes *Pride and Prejudice.*
- **1815** Belgium: French army under Napoleon routed at Waterloo.
- **1815** Austria: Congress of Vienna redraws map of Europe following Napoleon's downfall.
- **1816** France: René Läennec invents the stethoscope.
- **1818** England: Mary Wollstonecraft Shelley creates a legend with *Frankenstein.*

- **1829** England: George Stephenson perfects a steam locomotive for Liverpool-Manchester Railway. ▼

228 ◆ A Growing Nation (1800–1870)

GETTING AN OVERVIEW OF THE PERIOD

Introduction To give students an overview of the period, indicate the span of dates along the top of the timeline. Point out the division of the timeline into American and World Events, and have students practice scanning the timeline to look at both categories. Finally, tell them that the events in the timeline represent beginnings, turning points, and endings.

Key Events Have students select items in the American Events section that help tell the story of American expansion.
Possible answers: 1803, Louisiana Purchase; 1850, California admitted to the Union

American and World Events

- **1831** Cyrus McCormick invents mechanical reaper. ▼

MᶜCORMICK.

REAPING MACHINE.

- **1837** Samuel F. B. Morse patents electromagnetic telegraph.
- **1838** U.S. Army marches Cherokees of Georgia on long "Trail of Tears" to Oklahoma. ▶

- **1831** France: Victor Hugo publishes *Notre Dame de Paris*. ▼

- **1841** Antarctica: First explored by Englishman James Ross.
- **1842** Asia: Hong Kong becomes a British colony.
- **1845** Ireland: Famine results from failure of potato crop.
- **1847** Italy: Verdi's opera *Macbeth* first performed.
- **1847** England: Emily Brontë publishes *Wuthering Heights*.
- **1848** Belgium: Karl Marx and Friedrich Engels publish *The Communist Manifesto*.

- **1846** Mexican War begins.
- **1846** Abraham Lincoln first elected to Congress.
- **1848** Mexican War ends; United States expands borders.
- **1848** California Gold Rush begins.
- **1848** Women's Rights Convention held in Seneca Falls, New York.

- **1850** Nathaniel Hawthorne publishes *The Scarlet Letter*.
- **1850** California admitted to the Union. ▼

- **1851** Herman Melville publishes *Moby-Dick*.
- **1851** Nathaniel Hawthorne publishes *The House of the Seven Gables*.
- **1852** Harriet Beecher Stowe publishes *Uncle Tom's Cabin*.

- **1850** France: Life insurance introduced.
- **1850** England: Elizabeth Barrett Browning publishes *Sonnets from the Portuguese*.
- **1851** Australia: Gold discovered in New South Wales.
- **1853** Europe: Crimean War begins.
- **1854** Japan: Ports open to trade.
- **1855** England: Robert Browning publishes *Men and Women*.
- **1856** Crimean War ends.

Introduction ◆ 229

Critical Thinking

1. **(a)** Which event between 1800 and 1810 greatly increased the size of the United States? **(b)** How would the United States have been different if this event had not taken place?
   Answer: (a) 1803, Louisiana Purchase **(b)** The United States would not have been as powerful without the natural resources of the region.

2. **(a)** Which event between 1820 and 1830 affected the issue of slavery? **(b)** How was this event a harbinger of future conflict?
   Answer: (a) 1820, Missouri Compromise banned slavery in new territories. **(b)** This foreshadowed future disputes over slavery.

3. **(a)** Indicate a date that relates to the invention of the telegraph. **(b)** Describe the effect the telegraph had on communication.
   Answer: 1837, Morse patented his idea for telegraph. For the first time, people could send messages quickly over long distances.

4. **(a)** When were the words for "The Star-Spangled Banner" written? **(b)** Why was it an appropriate choice for the national anthem?
   Answer: (a) The words were written in 1814. **(b)** Its description of the flag in the midst of battle made it the prefect choice for a national anthem.

▶ **Critical Viewing**

1. What does the illustration of the Lewis and Clark expedition reveal about the American West?
   Answer: It indicates the vastness and great natural beauty of the region.

2. What impression does his portrait give you of Napoleon?
   Answer: He seems to have forgotten his revolutionary ideas and begun to think of himself as an absolute monarch.

3. What does the illustration of the forced march of the Cherokee suggest about government policy toward Native Americans?
   Answer: The government forcibly removed whole peoples from their homelands in order to make way for white settlers.

Literature of the Period

- As Alexis de Tocqueville proclaimed that America had produced few writers of distinction, Washington Irving was writing tales that would bring him international distinction. One of these tales appears on p. 242.

- The Louisiana Purchase was a key event of this period. Lewis's "Crossing the Great Divide," which describes the expedition's journey across this new territory, appears on p. 286.

▶Critical Viewing

Answer: The small chunk of present-day southern Arizona and New Mexico called the Gadsden Purchase was the last region to be added to the United States.

A Growing Nation
(1800–1870)

In 1831, the Frenchman Alexis de Tocqueville, sent to report on America's prisons, ultimately wrote about something far more interesting: a bustling new nation full of individuals optimistically pursuing their destinies. His *Democracy in America* observed that Americans had "a lively faith in the perfectibility of man," believing "what appears to them today to be good may be superseded by something better tomorrow."

The bustling spirit that had enchanted Tocqueville in 1831 would make for a turbulent "tomorrow" in the decades to come: By 1870, industrialism, explosive population and economic growth, and the Civil War had all aged the nation's spirit. American literature also matured during this time. In 1831, Tocqueville wrote, "America has produced very few writers of distinction. . . . [The literature of England] still darts its rays into the forests of the New World." By 1870, America had produced many "writers of distinction": Irving, Cooper, Bryant, Poe, Emerson, Thoreau, Hawthorne, Melville, Dickinson, and Whitman—all of whom eventually shone their unmistakably American light into and far beyond "the forests of the New World."

CANADA (Ceded by Britain, 1818)

OREGON COUNTRY (Agreement with Britain, 1846)

LOUISIANA PURCHASE (Purchased from France, 1803)

THE UNITED STATES, 1783

MEXICAN CESSION (Treaty of Guadalupe-Hidalgo, 1848)

ORIGINAL 13 STATE

PACIFIC OCEAN

TEXAS ANNEXATION (Annexed by Congress, 1845)

ATLA OCE

GADSDEN PURCHASE (Purchased from Mexico, 1853)

FLORIDA (Ceded by Spain, 1819)

MEXICO

GULF OF MEXICO

Growth of the United States to 1853

Present-day state boundaries

| 0 | 400 | 800 Miles |

| 0 | 400 | 800 Kilometers |

▲ **Critical Viewing** By 1848, the United States stretched from the Atlantic Ocean to the Pacific Ocean. What region of the map was the last to be added to the United States? **[Read a Map]**

Historical Background

In 1800, the United States consisted of sixteen states clustered near the east coast. In 1803, Thomas Jefferson doubled the nation's size by signing the Louisiana Purchase. The rapid growth of the nation inspired an upsurge in national pride and self-awareness. Improved transportation helped bind the old and the new states together. Canals, turnpikes, and railroads boomed during this period. Steamboats and sailing packets helped speed people and goods to their destinations.

⚜ ENRICHMENT: Social Studies Connection

Old New York

In 1800, New York City had a population of 60,000, making it the second-largest city in the United States. A decade later, New York became the largest city, a rank it holds to this day. By 1840, New York was as heavily populated as Philadelphia and Boston combined.

The Dutch first settled the southern tip of Manhattan Island. By 1820, the city extended as far north as 14th Street. The buildings of the day were rarely more than four stories high.

Despite New York's prosperity, it was not looked on as a cultural capital. Alexis de Tocqueville saw it as "a center of all our greatest vices, without any of those interests which counteract their baleful influence."

The Growth of Democracy at Home: 1800–1840 As the nation expanded, Americans began to take more direct control of their government. The 1828 election of Andrew Jackson, "the People's President," ushered in the era of the common man, as property requirements for voting began to be eliminated. The democratic advances of the time, however, were confined to white males. Scant political attention was paid to women, and most African Americans remained enslaved. One of the most tragic policies of this period was "Indian removal," the forced westward migration of Native Americans from confiscated tribal lands—as in the 1838 "Trail of Tears," in which 4,000 of 15,000 Cherokee perished on the trek from Georgia to Oklahoma.

Young Nation on the World Stage Despite all this, the first decades of the 1800s were, on the whole, hopeful ones. The young republic seemed able to weather any storm.

The War of 1812 convinced Europeans that the United States was on the world stage to stay. In the Monroe Doctrine of 1823, President James Monroe warned Europe not to intervene in the new Latin American nations. In the 1830s, the U.S. became embroiled in a conflict over the secession of Texas from Mexico; in 1836, the Mexican Army made its

---

Close-up on History

Sacajawea, Guide for Lewis and Clark

Here is a sad contradiction: A Shoshone Indian woman named Sacajawea helped Lewis and Clark explore the territories bought in the Louisiana Purchase, but the westward movement inspired by this expedition eventually led to "Indian removal" and the confiscation of Indian lands.

In 1804, Sacajawea was staying with the Mandan Indians near present-day Bismarck, North Dakota. Meriwether Lewis and William Clark, who had been asked by President Thomas Jefferson to explore the new western lands, were overwintering with the Mandans. They worried about how they would cross the Rocky Mountains when they continued the expedition in the spring. Fortunately, Sacajawea offered to guide them. The Shoshones lived in the Rockies, and she knew the region well. She could also translate for them in their encounters with different Indian tribes.

Sacajawea contributed greatly to the success of the expedition, gathering wild vegetables and advising the men where to fish and hunt game. She also knew about the healing qualities of different herbs. When the party reached the mountains, Sacajawea recognized the lands of her people. Soon, she was reunited with her brother, and she persuaded her relatives to support the expedition with the food and horses it needed to continue.

After successfully crossing the Rockies, the explorers reached the west coast and returned to St. Louis in 1806. Thanks in large part to Sacajawea, their relations with Indians had been almost entirely peaceful. However, in the westward expansion to come, such peaceful relations were an early casualty.

Background

History

James Marshall found gold at Sutter's Mill in California in January of 1848. In a few days, word of the gold strike spread to San Francisco. Carpenters threw down their tools, bakers left their loaves to burn, and schools emptied as teachers joined the rush to the gold fields.

The news quickly spread outward from San Francisco. More than 80,000 Americans, Europeans, and South Americans made the long journey to California in 1849. They became known as Forty-Niners.

CUSTOMIZE INSTRUCTION FOR UNIVERSAL ACCESS

For Less Proficient Readers	For English Learners	For Advanced Readers
Ask each student to become an expert on a particular section of "A Growing Nation" by reading it several times and devising a comprehension test on it.	Draw a rough outline of the United States on the chalkboard. As students read about each new surge of expansion, shade in and date newly-acquired territory, so that students can see the course of growth.	Challenge students to find links between this historical period and their own times. Students can look for parallels or cause-and-effect relationships. For example, why might people have hesitated to settle in the western frontier before the Louisiana Purchase?

Critical Thinking

1. In what way is the story of this period the story of westward expansion?

Answer: The Louisiana Purchase made westward expansion possible. Settlers continued spreading westward as the population grew. The war with Mexico resulted from westward expansion.

2. What link exists between westward expansion and conflicts over slavery?

Answer: Some people moving to new territories wanted slaves; others were against any expansion of slavery.

▶ **Critical Viewing**

The poster depicts slavery as a brutal and terrifying experience.

▲ **Critical Viewing** Harriet Beecher Stowe's novel *Uncle Tom's Cabin* (1851–1852) stirred anti-slavery sentiment in the North. What message regarding slavery is conveyed by this poster for an 1881 theatrical production of the novel? **[Analyze]**

famous assault on the Alamo, in which every Texan defender was killed. When Texas was admitted to the Union in 1845, the resulting war with Mexico (1846–1848) ended in a U.S. victory, which added more territory to the nation, including California. Soon after, the Gold Rush of 1849 drew hundreds of thousands to this new land of promise.

The Way West and Economic Growth In a sense, the entire course of American history can be seen as a pageant rolling ever westward, as new territories opened up and transportation improved. The first white settlers sailed west from Europe, establishing their homes on the East Coast of the New World. All thirteen original states were on the eastern seaboard, hemmed in by mountain barriers blocking easy access to the interior. As late as 1845 the most western state in the Union was Texas. The last of the fifty states, Hawaii, lying far to the west of the North American continent, was at the time an independent kingdom.

During the early decades of the 1800s, transportation was steadily changing and improving. The Erie Canal, completed in New York in 1825, set off a wave of canal building. In the 1850s, the "iron horse"—the railroad—began to dominate long-distance American travel; by 1869, rail lines linked east and west coasts.

Advances in technology spurred social change. Factories sprang up all over the Northeast. The steel plow and reaper encouraged frontier settlement by making farming practical on the vast, sod-covered grasslands. The telegraph facilitated almost instant communication across great distances. Inventor Samuel F. B. Morse's message from Washington to Baltimore in 1844 could serve as the motto for this era: "What hath God wrought!"

Winds of Change It was evident to even the most cheerful observer that the United States at mid-century faced trouble as well as bright promise. The new prosperity unleashed fierce competition, leading to the creation of factories scarred by child labor and unsafe working conditions. In 1840, most women could not vote or file a lawsuit. The 1840s and 1850s saw an outburst of efforts promoting women's rights, notably the 1848 Seneca Falls Convention. Above all, the centuries-old institution of slavery bitterly divided the nation. The conflict between abolitionists, who opposed slavery, and the advocates of states' rights, who argued that the federal government could not bend states to its will, sharpened in the 1850s. The gathering storm finally burst into war in 1861, but it was a storm that had been building for 250 years, ever since the first slave was brought in chains to this continent.

✳ ENRICHMENT: Science Connection

Francis Lowell and American Industry

Britain's War of 1812 blockade of the United States provided a boost to American industry. Cut off from foreign suppliers, Americans had to produce more goods themselves.

As in Britain, advances occurred in the textile industry. A Boston merchant named Francis Cabot Lowell had toured the British textile mills, where he saw that workers at one factory spun thread while workers at another wove it into cloth. Lowell thought it would be more efficient to combine the spinning and weaving tasks under one roof.

Lowell and several partners built a textile mill in Waltham, Massachusetts. The nearby Charles River powered the machines that turned the raw cotton into finished cloth. Lowell died in 1817. In time, his company built an entire factory town on the Merrimack River and named it in his honor. By 1836, Lowell was a thriving town of more than 10,000 people.

Literature of the Period

American Literature Comes of Age Before 1800, American writers were not widely read—not even in America—but that situation soon began to change. The writers of this period would define the American voice—personal, idiosyncratic, bold—and its primary theme: the quest of the individual to define him- or herself.

Romanticism Despite their unmistakable differences, the writers of the early nineteenth century—Washington Irving, James Fenimore Cooper, William Cullen Bryant, and Edgar Allan Poe—can all be described as Romantics.

Romanticism was an artistic movement that dominated Europe and America during the nineteenth century. The name Romanticism can be a bit misleading because Romantics do not necessarily write about love. Romantic writers elevated the imagination over reason and intuition over fact. Washington Irving, the first American to be read widely overseas, made his mark with his *History of New York* (1809), which is not a dry historical record but a rollicking narrative that alters facts at will.

Point/Counterpoint

Edgar Allan Poe, Immature Genius or Mature Craftsman?

Was Edgar Allan Poe an immature genius who appeals to our childish love of mysteries and puzzles, or was he a mature craftsman who knew exactly what he wanted to achieve with every effect? Two critics—one of them, T.S. Eliot, a major poet himself—disagree about Poe's worth and craftsmanship.

An Immature Genius "That Poe had a powerful intellect is undeniable: but it seems to me the intellect of a highly gifted young person before puberty. The forms which his lively curiosity takes are those in which a pre-adolescent mentality delights: . . . puzzles and labyrinths, mechanical chess players . . . The variety and ardor of his curiosity delight and dazzle; yet in the end the eccentricity and lack of coherence of his interests tire. There is just that lacking which gives dignity to the mature man: a consistent view of life."

—**T.S. Eliot,** *To Criticize the Critic*

A Mature Craftsman "In the new picture of Poe, then, . . . we see somewhat less 'mad genius' and somewhat more 'commercial craftsman.' More wit, erudition, and philosophical consistency are evident in the new Poe, and far less compulsion. If we cannot entirely do away with the popular image of guttering candles and circling bats, in short, we should at least be able to point to craftsmanship, detachment, and humor . . . his brilliance is indisputable and his contribution to American and world literature, enormous."

—**Stuart Levine,** Introduction to *The Short Fiction of Edgar Allan Poe*

Background
Music

While the United States was forging a national literature, it also began establishing its own identity in the field of music. Among the Americans to contribute to this field was Frank Johnson (1792–1844).

One of the first of many prominent, successful African-American musicians, Johnson formed a woodwind band in the 1820s. In addition to playing throughout the United States, Johnson's band traveled to England and performed for the Queen.

Background

Social Studies

Transcendentalism was not essentially a religious movement; it was a philosophical movement with religious overtones. Even though 100 years had passed since the death of Calvinist minister Jonathan Edwards, his teachings continued to influence people. William Ellery Channing, minister of Boston's Federal Street Church, had recently broken with Calvinist ideas like Edwards's. Channing had become the apostle of Unitarianism. His sermons and essays, promoting more tolerant religious attitudes and encouraging people to work in various social causes, helped to lay the groundwork for Transcendentalism.

▶ Critical Viewing

The motto, "The birds and beasts will teach thee!" and a glowing, floating book inscribed "Nature" illustrate the Transcendental tenet that the natural world can teach people to see the presence of the "Over-Soul" in the creation.

The Romantics reveled in nature. William Cullen Bryant is best known for his lyric poems rejoicing in the healing powers of nature. Irving's "Rip Van Winkle" and "The Legend of Sleepy Hollow" sparked an interest in his beloved Hudson River Valley. James Fenimore Cooper's four *Leatherstocking Tales* feature the exploits of Natty Bumppo in the frontier forests of upstate New York. A man of absolute moral integrity, Natty Bumppo preferred nature over civilization, establishing the pattern for countless American heroes to come.

Romantic writing often accented the fantastic aspects of human experience. The tortured genius Edgar Allan Poe remains popular to this day for his haunting poems and suspenseful stories whose characters, as one biographer has said, "are either grotesques or the inhabitants of another world than this."

New England Renaissance: 1840–1855 In 1837, Ralph Waldo Emerson, a former Boston minister, delivered his famous oration "The American Scholar," calling for American intellectual independence from Europe. Emerson believed that American writers should begin to interpret their own culture in new ways. As if in response to Emerson's call, an impressive burst of literary activity took place in and around Boston between 1840 and 1855. This "flowering of New England" would produce an array of great writers and enduring literature.

Transcendentalism Most, if not all, of these writers were influenced by the Transcendental movement then flourishing in New England. Emerson and Thoreau were the best-known Transcendentalists, but the ferment of Transcendental ideas affected many other writers.

Transcendentalism demands careful definition, yet it is very hard to define. It has many facets, many sources, and encompasses a range of beliefs whose specific principles depend on the individual writer or thinker. The term itself and some of the ideas came from the German philosopher Immanuel Kant. In his *Critique of Practical Reason* (1788), Kant defines the "transcendental" as the understanding a person gains intuitively because it lies beyond direct experience. American Transcendentalism drew on other thinkers as well: the ancient Greek philosopher Plato, the French mathematician Pascal,

▲ Critical Viewing
Above is a ticket to Charles Willson Peale's museum, which he ran to teach Americans how to learn by observing nature. How does this effort reflect Transcendentalist beliefs? **[Connect]**

the Swedish mystic and scientist Swedenborg, and the anti-materialism of Buddhist thought. Philosophy, religion, and literature all merged in New England Transcendentalism producing a native blend that was romantic, intuitive, mystical, and considerably easier to recognize than to explain.

For Transcendentalists the point was that the real truths, the most fundamental truths lie outside the experience of the senses, residing instead, as Emerson put it, in the "Over-Soul . . . a universal and benign omnipresence. . . ." If that seems a bit obscure, so did the essays in *The Dial*, the quarterly magazine of New England Transcendentalism. Published from 1840 to 1844, *The Dial* was first edited by Margaret Fuller, a dominant personality and zealous feminist who was an accepted member of the Transcendentalist group.

Walden The most influential expression of Transcendental philosophy came from Emerson and his younger friend and protégé, Henry David Thoreau, who withdrew from society to live by himself on the shores of Walden Pond. Thoreau undertook this way of life because he felt intensely the Transcendentalists' reverence for nature. He begins *Walden*, his account of this experience, by writing, "When I wrote the following pages . . . I lived alone, in the woods, a mile from any neighbor, in a house which I had built myself, on the shore of Walden Pond, in Concord, Massachusetts, and earned my living by the labor of my hands only." Published in 1854, *Walden* consists of eighteen essays about matters ranging from a battle between red and black ants to the individual's relation to society. Thoreau's observations of nature reveal his philosophy of individualism, simplicity, and passive resistance to injustice.

A Living Tradition

Walden Pond and Tinker Creek

About 120 years after Thoreau set himself the experiment of living "alone, in the woods . . . on the shore of Walden Pond," Annie Dillard undertook a similar experiment with nature and solitude: "I live by a creek, Tinker Creek, in a valley in Virginia's Blue Ridge." Just as Thoreau wrote *Walden* to describe his experiences, she, too, wrote a book about what she saw and thought, the best-selling *Pilgrim at Tinker Creek*. Near the beginning of the book, she describes the home base for her observations:

"An anchorite's hermitage [hermit's secluded retreat] is called an anchor-hold; some anchor-holds were simple sheds clamped to the side of a church like a barnacle to a rock. I think of this house clamped to the side of Tinker Creek as an anchor-hold. It holds me at anchor to the rock bottom of the creek itself and it keeps me steadied in the current, as a sea anchor does, facing the stream of light pouring down. It's a good place to live; there's a lot to think about. The creeks—Tinker and Carvin's—are an active mystery, fresh every minute."

Literature of the Period

• To gain a better understanding of Transcendentalism, students can read the excerpt from *Nature* by Ralph Waldo Emerson on p. 388.

• Students can read Thoreau's own description of his plan to live by Walden Pond in the excerpt from *Walden*, p. 403.

✸ ENRICHMENT: Music Connection

American Music, New England Style

While American literature was blossoming in New England, Lowell Mason (1792–1872) of Boston and other New England musicians were reshaping American music. Determined to bring about universal musical literacy, Mason organized the Boston Academy of Music and added music to the curriculum of Boston public schools. Mason also prompted a change in the style of American church music by emphasizing the selection of easy and solemn songs that all members of a congregation could sing in harmony. He wrote thousands of musical pieces, including many hymns that have remained popular.

Background

Literature

The friendship between Hawthorne and Melville happened almost by accident. In his early thirties, Melville moved from New York City to Pittsfield, Massachusetts, where he wrote his monumental novel *Moby Dick*. It was published in 1851, a year after Hawthorne's *The Scarlet Letter*. Hawthorne's novel was an immediate success, but Melville's would not receive its due until many years later. Melville approached Hawthorne, seeking solace and friendship. The two men became and remained friends.

▶ Critical Viewing

The years between 1855 and 1860 saw the greatest growth in railroads, an increase of some 10,000 miles of track.

The Possibility of Evil Not everyone shared the Transcendentalists' optimistic views. Nathaniel Hawthorne and Herman Melville expressed the darker vision of those who, in Hawthorne's words, "burrowed into the depths of our common nature" and found the area not always shimmering, but often "dusky." Hawthorne's Puritan heritage was never far from his consciousness. His masterpiece, *The Scarlet Letter* (1850), set in Boston in the seventeenth century, deals with sin, concealed guilt, hypocrisy, and humility. In *The House of the Seven Gables*, he delves into seventeenth-century witchcraft, insanity, and a legendary curse.

Hawthorne became a kind of mentor to Melville. Depressed about the negative critical response to his novel *Moby-Dick* (1851), Melville approached the older, more successful writer. Both men saw human life in grim terms, but their personalities were quite different. Hawthorne, despite a tendency toward solitude, was stable and self-possessed, a shrewd man without illusions. Melville, by contrast, was a man at odds with the world, a tortured and cryptic personality. For a large part of his career, he raged against his fate, much as Captain Ahab in *Moby-Dick* unleashed his fury against the white whale that had maimed him.

At Home in Amherst While Thoreau was planting beans next to Walden Pond, Emily Dickinson was growing up in the nearby town of Amherst, Massachusetts. Her startling, intensely focused poetry catapulted her into the company of the greatest American poets—although not in her lifetime. A recluse for the second half of her life, Dickinson did not write for publication, or even for her family, but rather from a personal need to wrestle with questions about death, immortality, and the soul—questions unresolved by conventional religion.

Beyond New England Meanwhile, the quintessential American poet was tramping about the countryside, laboring at odd jobs to finance his poetry. In 1855, New Yorker Walt Whitman published his groundbreaking series of poems, *Leaves of Grass*, proudly broadcasting his "barbaric yawp" from Brooklyn to the universe. Most American readers ignored the irregular forms and frank language of this revolutionary poet, but Emerson knew an American original when he saw one and praised Whitman's work. Of all the poets of the period between 1800 and 1870, Whitman would have the most lasting effect on American literature—despite the fact that the first edition of *Leaves* sold fewer than twenty copies.

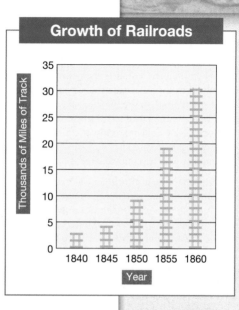

Growth of Railroads

▲ **Critical Viewing**
Railroads expanded rapidly after 1840. According to this graph, what five-year period saw the greatest growth in railroads?
[Read a Graph]

Fireside Poets Those were the literary giants of the period, as singled out by twentieth-century scholars. In 1850, however, the American reading public would probably have pointed instead to four other New England writers, known as the Fireside Poets: Henry Wadsworth Longfellow, a Harvard professor and tremendously popular poet; John Greenleaf Whittier, from a hardworking Quaker farm family; James Russell Lowell, born to wealth and position; and Oliver Wendell Holmes, a poet-physician and the unofficial laureate of the group.

After the Flowering As the war clouds gathered, the great burst of creativity in the Northeast began to subside. Antislavery writers, such as Emerson, Melville, Whittier, and Lowell, strongly supported the northern effort in the Civil War. Thoreau and Hawthorne died before the war ended. Whitman worked as a nurse in the war and incorporated war poems in his later editions of *Leaves of Grass*. Dickinson ignored the war in her poetry.

Oliver Wendell Holmes, energetic and cheerful, outlasted the rest of his renowned generation. He became "the last leaf upon the tree," to quote words he himself had written about Melville's grandfather, an old Revolutionary War veteran, in a poem published in 1831, when the poet and his country were still young.

▼ **Critical Viewing**
In this image, a freight train delivers ore to a foundry where it will be turned into steel. The railroad was a key to the growth of industry in the North. What other effects do you think the growth of the railroads had on northern life? **[Form a Hypothesis]**

Critical Thinking

1. In what way was Transcendentalism a response to Puritanism?
   Answer: Transcendentalism replaced Puritan severity with optimism and tolerance.

2. Why is *Walden* an especially meaningful book today?
   Possible answers: Thoreau's deep feeling for nature has influenced many and is embraced by today's environmental movement.

3. Where did most of America's great writers of this period live? Why?
   Answer: Most were from New England or the Mid-Atlantic states. This was the first area of the country to be settled by Europeans and was therefore the most civilized and sophisticated area of the new country.

▶ **Critical Viewing**

It would have greatly increased people's mobility, allowing suburbs to grow. It would also have contributed to the development of air pollution, from trains and from foundries.

Critical Thinking

1. Why do you think Americans are so fond of abbreviations?
   Answer: Americans are informal and like to save time.
2. What does the origin of the expression O.K. suggest about the relationship between new words and politics?
   Answer: Since people remember an expression from a political campaign, it suggests that Americans are fascinated by politics and that they pay attention to campaigns.

Answers to Activities

1. **(a)** Anno Domini, Latin for "in the year of our Lord"/"before Christ" **(b)** also known as **(c)** Grand Old Party, meaning the Republican Party **(d)** in radio, amplitude modulation/frequency modulation **(e)** compact disk **(f)** Equal Rights Amendment **(g)** ante meridiem/post meridiem, Latin for "before/after noon" **(h)** intelligence quotient **(i)** postscript **(j)** requiescat in pace, Latin for "rest in peace" **(k)** répondez, s'il vous plaît, French for "please reply" **(l)** unidentified flying object

2. Sample answers: ASAP, as soon as possible; PE, physical education; ID, identification; HQ, headquarters; COD, collect on delivery; PJs, pajamas; NBA, National Basketball Association; AWOL, absent without official leave; OJ, orange juice; DA, district attorney

THE DEVELOPMENT OF AMERICAN ENGLISH
The Truth About O.K.

BY RICHARD LEDERER

Martin Van Buren

We Americans seem to have a passion for stringing initial letters together. We use *a.m.* and *p.m.* to separate light from darkness and B.C. and A.D. to identify vast stretches of time. We may listen to a deejay or veejay on *ABC*, *CBS*, *NBC*, or *MTV* or a crusading *DA* on *CNN*, *NPR*, or *PBS*.

Perhaps the most widely understood American word in the world is O.K. The explanations for its origin have been as imaginative as they have been various. Some have claimed that O.K. is a version of the Chocktaw affirmative *okeh*. Others have asserted that it is short for the Greek *olla kalla* ("all good") or *Orrin Kendall* crackers or *Aux Kayes* rum, or the name of chief *Old Keokuk*.

The truth is more politically correct than any of these theories.

———◆———

In the 1830s in New England, there was a craze for initialisms, in the manner of the currently popular *T.G.I.F.* and *F.Y.I.* The fad went so far as to generate letter combinations of intentional misspellings: *K.G.* for "know go," *K.Y.* for "know use," and *O.W.* for "oll wright." *O.K.* for "oll korrect" naturally followed.

Of all the loopy initialisms and misspellings of the time, *O.K.* alone survived. That's because of a presidential nickname that consolidated the letters in the national memory.

Martin Van Buren, elected our eighth president in 1836, was born in Kinderhook, New York, and, early in his political career, was dubbed "Old Kinderhook." Echoing the "Oll Korrect" initialism, *O.K.* became the rallying cry of the Old Kinderhook Club, a political organization supporting Van Buren during the 1840 campaign.

The coinage did Van Buren no good, and he was defeated in his bid for reelection. But the word honoring his name today remains what H. L. Mencken identified as "the most shining and successful Americanism ever invented."

ACTIVITIES

1. In a dictionary, research what each of these initialisms stand for:
   (a) A.D./B.C.
   (b) aka
   (c) GOP
   (d) A.M./F.M.
   (e) CD
   (f) ERA
   (g) a.m./p.m.
   (h) IQ
   (i) PS
   (j) RIP
   (k) RSVP
   (l) UFO

2. Identify ten additional initialisms and the words each represents.

Fireside and Campfire

Fredericksburg Refugee Family at Campfire, D. E. Henderson, Gettysburg National Military Park Museum

Selection Planning Guide

The selections in this section reflect the literary and territorial expansion of the United States in the nineteenth century. Ralph Waldo Emerson's *Nature* introduces students to the Transcendentalist movement. They will enjoy reading "The Devil and Tom Walker" by Washington Irving, one of the first of a new breed of purely American writers. The popular works of the Fireside Poets—Longfellow, Holmes, Lowell, and Whittier—break new ground in American literature. "Crossing the Great Divide" and "The Most Sublime Spectacle on Earth" recount Lewis and Clark's exploration of the frontier. The excerpt from *Pilgrim at Tinker Creek* invites students to parallel the nineteenth-century view of nature with the views of twentieth-century naturalist Annie Dillard.

Background

Art

Untitled, by D. Henderson

This genre painting shows a refugee family around a campfire after the Civil War Battle of Fredericksburg, Virginia, which took place on December 13, 1862. The defeated Union forces, which outnumbered the Southern troops by two to one, continued to threaten Fredericksburg even after the battle. Although General Lee's Confederate troops held firm, the threat of more fighting persisted for months. The painting is a reminder of the terrible toll the war took on civilians in the South, where most of the battles were fought.

Use the following question for discussion:

From what might the people in the painting be running?
Answer: Their home may have been in the middle of a battle. Enemy soldiers might have commandeered their home for barracks, or might have burned it down. They may have lost everything they had.

OMIZE INSTRUCTION FOR UNIVERSAL ACCESS

ssigning the selections in Part 1, keep these factors in mind:

vil and Tom Walker"

uated language may challenge less proficient rs and English learners.

m of Life," "The Tide Rises, The Tide Falls"

ssible poems filled with ocean imagery

"Thanatopsis," "Old Ironsides," "The First Snowfall," from *Snowbound*

• Four poems varying in difficulty

• Challenge more advanced students to interpret "Thanatopsis."

"Crossing the Great Divide," "The Most Sublime Spectacle on Earth"

• Vocabulary may require clarification.

The Devil and Tom Walker

Lesson Objectives

1. **To analyze and respond to literary elements**
   - Literary Analysis: Third-Person Omniscient Point of View
   - Connecting Literary Elements: Characterization

2. **To read, comprehend, analyze, and critique a short story**
   - Reading Strategy: Infering Cultural Attitudes
   - Reading Check questions
   - Review and Assess questions
   - Assessment Practice (ATE)

3. **To develop word analysis skills, fluency, and systematic vocabulary**
   - Vocabulary Development Lesson: Latin Prefix: *ex-*

4. **To understand and apply written and oral language conventions**
   - Spelling Strategy
   - Grammar and Style Lesson: Adjective Clauses

5. **To understand and apply appropriate writing and research strategies**
   - Writing Lesson: Updating a Story
   - Extension Activity: Exhibition

6. **To understand and apply listening and speaking strategies**
   - Extension Activity: Enactment

STEP-BY-STEP TEACHING GUIDE	PACING GUIDE
PRETEACH	
Motivate Students and Provide Background	
Use the Motivation activity (ATE p. 240)	5 min.
Read and discuss more author and the background features (SE p. 242; ATE p. 240) **A**	5 min.
Introduce the Concepts	
Introduce the Literary Analysis and Reading Strategy (SE/ATE p. 241) **A**	15 min.
Pronounce the vocabulary words and read their definitions (SE p. 241)	5 min.
TEACH	
Monitor Comprehension	
Informally monitor comprehension by circulating while students read independently or in groups **A**	45 min.
Monitor students' comprehension with the Reading Check notes (SE/ATE pp. 243, 245, 247, 249, 251)	as students read / as students read
Develop vocabulary with Vocabulary notes (SE pp. 246, 249, 250; ATE p. 249)	
Develop Understanding	
Develop students' understanding of the omniscient narrator with the Literary Analysis annotations (SE pp. 243, 244, 247, 250; ATE pp. 243, 244, 246, 247, 248, 250) **A**	5 min.
Develop students' ability to infer cultural attitudes with the Reading Strategy annotations (SE pp. 243, 244, 250; ATE pp. 243, 244, 250)	5 min.
ASSESS	
Assess Mastery	
Assess students' mastery of the Reading Strategy and Literary Analysis by having them answer the Review and Assess questions (SE/ATE p. 253)	15 min.
Use one or more of the print and media Assessment Resources (ATE p. 255) **A**	up to 45 min.
EXTEND	
Apply Understanding	
Have students complete the Vocabulary Development Lesson and the Grammar and Style Lesson (SE p. 254) **A**	20 min.
Apply students' ability to include audience-appropriate details in their writing by using the Writing Lesson (SE/ATE p. 255) **A**	45 min.
Apply students' understanding using one or more of the Extension Activities (SE p. 255)	20–90 min.

 ACCELERATED INSTRUCTION:
Use the strategies and activities identified with an **A**.

UNIVERSAL ACCESS
● = Below Level Students
▲ = On-Level Students
■ = Above Level Students

RESOURCES		
PRINT 📖	**TRANSPARENCIES** 🖍	**TECHNOLOGY** 💿 🎧 📼
• **Beyond Literature**, Media Connection: Narrative Point of View, p. 13 ▲ ■		• **Interest Grabber Video**, Tape 3 ● ▲ ■
• **Selection Support Workbook:** ● ▲ ■ Literary Analysis, p. 62 Reading Strategy, p. 61 Build Vocabulary, p. 59	• **Literary Analysis and Reading Transparencies,** pp. 25 and 26 ● ▲ ■	
		• **Listening to Literature** ● ▲ ■ Audiocassettes, Side 7 Audio CDs, CD 5
• **Literatura en español** ● ▲ • **Literary Analysis for Enrichment** ■		
• **Formal Assessment:** Selection Test, pp. 67–69 ● ▲ ■ • **Open Book Test**, pp. 37–39 ● ▲ ■ • **Performance Assessment and Portfolio Management**, p. 15 ● ▲ ■ • (PRENTICE HALL ASSESSMENT SYSTEM) ● ▲ ■	• (PRENTICE HALL ASSESSMENT SYSTEM) ● ▲ ■ Skills Practice Answers and Explanations on Transparencies	• **Test Bank Software** ● ▲ ■ • **Got It! Assessment Videotapes**, Tape 2 ● ▲
• **Selection Support Workbook:** ● ▲ ■ Grammar and Style, p. 60 • **Writing and Grammar**, Ruby Level ● ▲ ■ • **Extension Activities**, p. 13 ● ▲ ■	• **Daily Language Practice Transparencies** ● ▲ • **Writing Models and Graphic Organizers on Transparencies**, pp. 17–23, 95 ● ▲ ■	• **Writing and Grammar iText CD-ROM** ● ▲ ■ 💻 *Take It to the Net* www.phschool.com

BLOCK SCHEDULING: Use one 90-minute class period to preteach the selection and have students read it. Use a second 90-minute class period to assess students' mastery of skills and have them complete one of the Extension Activities.

Step-by-Step Teaching Guide for pp. 240–241

Motivation

Dim the lights in the classroom and read aloud the paragraph on page 243 of "The Devil and Tom Walker," beginning "One day that . . ." The passage contains a detailed description of the gloomy swamp where Tom first encounters the Devil. Ask students to discuss the mood created by the description. What do they think will happen to Tom? Have students discuss their responses to the passage and make predictions about the story.

▦ Interest Grabber Video

As an alternative, play "Washington Irving: His Life and Times" on Tape 3 to engage student interest.

❶ Background

More About the Author

Although Irving's comic look at New York—usually referred to as *Knickerbocker's History of New York*—made him famous, it also offended many leading families by poking fun at their ancestors and heritage. Perhaps hoping to alleviate American criticism about his time spent abroad, Irving went to work for the U.S. government in Europe. He served as a U.S. diplomat first in Spain and later in London.

Prepare to Read

❶ The Devil and Tom Walker

Washington Irving (1783–1859)

Named after President George Washington, Washington Irving became the first American writer to achieve an international reputation. He was born into a wealthy family and began studying law at the age of sixteen. Although he had planned to be a lawyer, he found he was more interested in travel and writing. He spent a great deal of time exploring New York's Hudson Valley. He also traveled throughout Europe and enjoyed European literature.

A Writing Career Blooms Irving wrote satirical essays using the pen name Jonathan Oldstyle. When he was twenty-four, he and his brother anonymously began publishing the magazine *Salmagundi* (the name of a spicy appetizer), which carried humorous sketches and essays about New York society.

In 1809, using the pseudonym Diedrich Knickerbocker, he published his first major work, *A History of New York From the Beginning of the World to the End of the Dutch Dynasty*. The book, a humorous examination of New York during colonial times, was well received and made Irving famous.

Tour of Europe From 1815 to 1832, Irving lived in Europe. There, he traveled extensively and learned about European customs, traditions, and folklore. Inspired by the European folk heritage, Irving created two of his most famous stories, "The Legend of Sleepy Hollow" and "Rip Van Winkle." Both stories transform two traditional German tales into distinctly American narratives set in the Hudson Valley. Both Ichabod Crane, the nervous school teacher who hunts the headless horseman in Sleepy Hollow, and Rip Van Winkle, the colonist who sleeps for decades, have become classic figures of American literature. When Irving published these two stories in the *Sketchbook* (1820) under the pseudonym Geoffrey Crayon, writers and critics throughout Europe and United States responded enthusiastically.

While in Europe, Irving completed three other books, including *Tales of a Traveler*, which contains "The Devil and Tom Walker." In this story ill-gotten wealth, Irving reshaped a German folk tale about a man who sells his soul to the Devil for earthly gain. Irving's adaptation of the story was timely in New England during the 1720s when the Puritan belief of devoting one's life to God was being replaced by materialism and the desire for personal gain.

A Devoted American Because of the amount of time he spent abroad, some questioned Irving's patriotism. Irving offered this response:

> I am endeavoring to serve my country. Whatever I have written has been written with the feelings and published as the writing of an American. Is that renouncing my country? How else am I to serve my country—by coming home and begging an office of it: which I should not have the kind of talent or the business habits requisite to fill?—If I can do any good in this world it is with my pen.

Irving continued to publish after returning to the United States, and, like the original folk tales which inspired his work, his stories have remained popular for generations. His writing has become an important part of the American literary heritage.

TEACHING RESOURCES

The following resources can be used to enrich or extend the instruction for pp. 240–241.

Motivation

▦ **Interest Grabber Video,** Tape 3 ▦

Background

📖 **Beyond Literature,** p. 13

🖥 *Take It to the Net*

Visit www.phschool.com for Background and hotlinks for "The Devil and Tom Walker."

Literary Analysis

📄 **Literary Analysis and Reading Transparencies,** Third-Person Omniscient Point of View, p. 26 ▦

📖 **Selection Support Workbook:** Literary Analysis, p. 62

📄 **Literary Analysis and Reading Transparencies,** Infer Cultural Attitudes, p. 25

▦ **BLOCK SCHEDULING:** Resources marked with this symbol provide varied instruction during 90-minute blocks.

Preview

Connecting to the Literature

Most of us know people who are consumed with making money. In this story, you will meet a character who is so filled with the desire for wealth that he will do virtually anything to attain it.

❷ Literary Analysis

Third-Person Omniscient Point of View

"The Devil and Tom Walker" uses a **third-person omniscient point of view** in which an all-knowing narrator relates the events of the story. Stories told using this perspective have the following characteristics:

- A narrator who stands outside the action
- Details about the thoughts and feelings of all the characters
- The narrator's commentary about the events of the story

As you read the story, notice how Irving's use of the omniscient narrator allows you to see the conflicts in the story from several angles.

Connecting Literary Elements

Irving uses **characterization** to reveal the personality traits of his characters. In stories told using the third-person point of view, characterization is achieved in two primary ways.

- In **direct characterization,** the narrator tells the reader what the character is like.
- In **indirect characterization,** personality traits are revealed through the words, thoughts, and actions of the characters.

Notice how Irving makes use of both characterization methods.

❸ Reading Strategy

Inferring Cultural Attitudes

This story reveals the **cultural attitudes** of New Englanders during the 1720s. Irving suggests these attitudes through descriptive details, the narrator's comments, and dialogue, and leaves it up to you to **make inferences,** or draw conclusions, based on these elements. For example, the colonists' belief in the Devil and the reference to Native Americans as "savages" reveal cultural attitudes. As you read, record details in a chart like the one shown, and draw conclusions about the cultural attitudes they represent.

Detail	Cultural Attitude

Vocabulary Development

avarice (av´ ər is) *n.* greed (p. 246)

usurers (yōō´ zhər rərz) *n.* money-lenders who charge very high interest (p. 249)

extort (eks tôrt´) *v.* to obtain by threat or violence (p. 249)

ostentation (äs´ tən tā´ shən) *n.* boastful display (p. 250)

parsimony (pär´ sə mō´ nē) *n.* stinginess (p. 250)

The Devil and Tom Walker ◆ 241

CUSTOMIZE INSTRUCTION FOR UNIVERSAL ACCESS

For Less Proficient Readers	For English Learners	For Advanced Readers
Have students pause at key scenes in the story in order to record events up to that point. Encourage students to jot down these main events on a time line as they read. They can use the time line to help them complete the Writing Lesson at the end of the selection.	Direct students to watch for signal words that can help them keep the story events in sequence. For example, language such as *one day, late in the dusk,* and *at length* indicate the passage of time. As students identify these signal phrases, have them record key story events on a time line.	Point out that Irving retraces his chronology several times in telling the story. This allows him to recount alternate versions of the same events or recount events happening simultaneously in different locations. Have students create a multilayered time line that shows the author's retracing.

---

❷ Literary Analysis

Third-Person Omniscient Point of View

- Tell students that "The Devil and Tom Walker," is written from the third-person omniscient point of view. Explain to students that an omniscient narrator knows the characters' thoughts, feelings, and experiences.

- Point out that omniscient narration provides a writer with great flexibility and gives the reader access to all the characters and events in a story in a way that other types of narration cannot.

- Use the instruction for Connecting Literary Elements to point out that the third-person omniscient point of view greatly widens Irving's ability to use direct, as well as indirect, characterization.

- Use the Third-Person Omniscient Point of View transparency in **Literary Analysis and Reading Transparencies,** p. 26, to model for students how to record character information from the story's omniscient narrator.

❸ Reading Strategy

Inferring Cultural Attitudes

- Remind students that making inferences means drawing reasoned conclusions from the available evidence.

- To infer cultural attitudes, readers must focus on text clues about beliefs and values expressed in the story. Tell students that in this story, the characters' attitudes about money, for example, directly influence their behavior.

- Direct students to the chart on p. 241. Urge them to record story details or descriptions that reveal cultural attitudes in a chart like the one shown.

Vocabulary Development

- Pronounce each vocabulary word for students, and read the definitions as a class. Have students identify any words with which they are unfamiliar.

 E-Teach

Visit E-Teach at www.phschool.com for teachers' essays on how to teach, with questions and answers.

Step-by-Step Teaching Guide for pp. 242–252

CUSTOMIZE INSTRUCTION
For Logical/Mathematical Learners

Tell students that in this story characters make bargains—with themselves and with others. In each case, something is offered and something is expected in return. As students read the story, have them summarize each bargain on a two-column chart headed *Offered* and *Expected*. Have students discuss the terms of each bargain.

❶ About the Selection

Set in colonial Massachusetts, this story is Irving's retelling of the Faust legend. The miser Tom Walker, faced with an opportunity to acquire wealth, makes a pact with the Devil, whom he encounters in a swampy forest. Like other fictional characters who sell their souls, he obtains his heart's desire in exchange. The pact causes Walker to become even greedier, and he begins a campaign to fleece his neighbors of their property. Despite his tremendous wealth, Tom is just as stingy and miserly as ever. Although Tom later regrets his deal and attempts to reform his life, his efforts to save his soul are in vain; he cannot escape his terrible bargain, and must pay his inevitable debt to the Devil. The story illustrates the degree to which people may be overcome by greed and underlines the potentially devastating consequences of such an obsession.

The Devil and ❶ Tom Walker

Washington Irving

Background

"The Devil and Tom Walker" is a variation of the Faust legend—a tale about a man who sells his soul to the Devil for earthly benefits. The legend was inspired by a real person, a wandering scholar and conjurer named Faust who lived in early sixteenth-century Germany. *Faustbach*, the first printed version of a Faust legend, was published in 1587. That story proposed that Faust had made a pact with the Devil for knowledge and power on Earth. Over the years, many variations of the Faust legend have appeared. Each retelling involves a person who trades his soul for experience, knowledge, or treasure. Adaptations do not share the same ending—in some, the protagonist is doomed; in others, he is redeemed.

A few miles from Boston in Massachusetts, there is a deep inlet, winding several miles into the interior of the country from Charles Bay, and terminating in a thickly wooded swamp or morass. On one side of this inlet is a beautiful dark grove; on the opposite side the land rises abruptly from the water's edge into a high ridge, on which grow a few scattered oaks of great age and immense size. Under one of these gigantic trees, according to old stories, there was a great amount of treasure buried by Kidd the pirate.[1] The inlet allowed a facility to bring the money in a boat secretly and at night to the very foot of the hill; the elevation of the place permitted a good look-out to be kept that no one was at hand; while the remarkable trees formed good landmarks by which the ❷ place might easily be found again. The old stories add, moreover,

1. **Kidd the pirate** Captain William Kidd (1645-1701).

TEACHING RESOURCES

The following resources can be used to enrich or extend the instruction for pp. 242–252.

Literary Analysis

📘 **Writing Models and Graphic Organizers on Transparencies,** pp. 17–23

📘 **Literary Analysis and Reading Transparencies,** p. 25

Reading

📖 **Selection Support Workbook:** Reading Strategy, p. 61; Build Vocabulary, p. 59

🎧 **Listening to Literature Audiocassettes,** Side 7 ▤

💿 **Listening to Literature Audio CDs,** CD 5 ▤

▤ **BLOCK SCHEDULING:** Resources marked with this symbol provide varied instruction during 90-minute blocks.

that the Devil presided at the hiding of the money, and took it under his guardianship; but this it is well known he always does with buried treasure, particularly when it has been ill-gotten.

Be that as it may, Kidd never returned to recover his wealth; being shortly after seized at Boston, sent out to England, and there hanged for a pirate.

About the year 1727, just at the time that earthquakes were prevalent in New England, and shook many tall sinners down upon their knees, there lived near this place a meager, miserly fellow, of the name of Tom Walker. He had a wife as miserly as himself: they were so miserly that they even conspired to cheat each other. Whatever the woman could lay hands on, she hid away; a hen could not cackle but she was on the alert to secure the new-laid egg. Her husband was continually prying about to detect her secret hoards, and many and fierce were the conflicts that took place about what ought to have been common property. They lived in a forlorn-looking house that stood alone, and had an air of starvation. A few straggling savin trees, emblems of sterility, grew near it; no smoke ever curled from its chimney; no traveler stopped at its door. A miserable horse, whose ribs were as articulate as the bars of a gridiron, stalked about a field, where a thin carpet of moss, scarcely covering the ragged beds of puddingstone, tantalized and balked his hunger; and sometimes he would lean his head over the fence, look piteously at the passerby, and seem to petition deliverance from this land of famine.

The house and its inmates had altogether a bad name. Tom's wife was a tall termagant,[2] fierce of temper, loud of tongue, and strong of arm. Her voice was often heard in wordy warfare with her husband; and his face sometimes showed signs that their conflicts were not confined to words. No one ventured, however, to interfere between them. The lonely wayfarer shrunk within himself at the horrid clamor and clapperclawing;[3] eyed the den of discord askance; and hurried on his way, rejoicing, if a bachelor, in his celibacy.

One day that Tom Walker had been to a distant part of the neighborhood, he took what he considered a shortcut homeward, through the swamp. Like most shortcuts, it was an ill-chosen route. The swamp was thickly grown with great gloomy pines and hemlocks, some of them ninety feet high, which made it dark at noonday, and a retreat for all the owls of the neighborhood. It was full of pits and quagmires, partly covered with weeds and mosses, where the green surface often betrayed the traveler into a gulf of black, smothering mud; there were also dark and stagnant pools, the abodes of the tadpole, the bullfrog, and the watersnake; where the trunks of pines and hemlocks lay half-drowned, half-rotting, looking like alligators sleeping in the mire.

Tom had long been picking his way cautiously through this treacherous forest; stepping from tuft to tuft of rushes and roots, which

---

2. **termagant** (tʉr′ mə gənt) *n.* quarrelsome woman.
3. **clapperclawing** (klap′ ər klô′ iŋ) *n.* clawing or scratching.

Reading Strategy
Inferring Cultural Attitudes What does this reference to the Devil and money suggest about cultural attitudes toward wealth?

Literary Analysis
Third-Person Omniscient Point of View What do you learn about Tom and his wife through this description?

✓**Reading Check**
Summarize what you have learned about the Walkers.

---

❷ **Reading Strategy**
Inferring Cultural Attitudes

- Have students paraphrase the bracketed passage.
  Possible response: Legend says the Devil loves money, especially if obtained illegally or immorally.

- Ask students whether they think that Irving's linking the figure of the Devil with money is a form of social commentary on wealth.

- Then, ask students the Reading Strategy question on p. 243: What does this reference to the Devil and money suggest about cultural attitudes toward wealth?
  Answer: People in New England colonial society regarded a preoccupation with money as immoral and hence linked it with the Devil.

❸ **Literary Analysis**
Third-Person Omniscient Point of View

- Have students read the bracketed passage. Ask them to note the details that they learn about Tom and his wife in this passage.

- Ask students the Literary Analysis question on p. 243: What do you learn about Tom and his wife through this description?
  Possible response: They fight a lot. She picks on him verbally and physically. He suffers in these arguments.

▶ Monitor Progress Invite students to discuss how they know that this passage is told from the third-person omniscient point of view.
  Answer: The narrator uses third-person pronouns such as *her*, *them*, *his*, and *himself*. The narrator knows not only intimate details about the Walkers' relationship, but how others responded to them.

❹ ✓**Reading Check**

Answer: The Walkers are miserly, stingy people with a great love of money. They are unhappy, both individually and together. They fight a lot; no one likes them.

CUSTOMIZE INSTRUCTION FOR UNIVERSAL ACCESS

For Less Proficient Readers	For English Learners	For Advanced Readers
Students may have difficulty with this long selection. Help sustain interest and concentration by encouraging students to summarize paragraphs. Remind them that in a summary, they should state the main idea in their own words and include only the most important information.	The dialogue includes words and expressions rarely used in modern conversation—for example, "Look yonder, and see how Deacon Peabody is faring." Using a two-column chart, have students jot down each unfamiliar term or expression and its meaning. Check students' understanding, clarifying as necessary.	Encourage students to identify and analyze the symbolic language that Irving uses in his story. Have them share their observations and interpretations with the rest of the class.

⑤ Reading Strategy
Inferring Cultural Attitudes

- Point out the word *savages* and ask students to share their associations with this word. Ask them what they associate with the ritual of making sacrifices.
  Answer: Most students will associate the word *savages* with animalistic, inhuman people. Most will associate the custom of making sacrifices with cultures that are called primitive.

- Ask students the Reading Strategy question on p. 244: What does the sentence beginning "Anyone but he" reveal about the colonists' attitudes toward Native Americans?
  Answer: The colonists saw the Native Americans as warlike savages who practiced unholy religious ceremonies characterized by magical chants and sacrifice.

⑥ Literary Analysis
Third-Person Omniscient Point of View

- Read the bracketed passage aloud, instructing students to pay particular attention to the use of the words *he* and *his*. Tell them to listen to determine the antecedents to (or nouns replaced by) these pronouns.
  Answer: *He* and *him* refer first to Tom Walker and then to the man Tom meets.

- Ask students the Literary Analysis question on p. 244: Whose thoughts and feelings—if anyone's—are revealed in this paragraph?
  Answer: The passage reveals Tom's thoughts and feelings. However, it also reveals details of the man's appearance.

---

afforded precarious footholds among deep sloughs; or pacing carefully, like a cat, along the prostrate trunks of trees; startled now and then by the sudden screaming of the bittern, or the quacking of a wild duck, rising on the wing from some solitary pool. At length he arrived at a piece of firm ground, which ran out like a peninsula into the deep bosom of the swamp. It had been one of the strongholds of the Indians during their wars with the first colonists. Here they had thrown up a kind of fort, which they had looked upon as almost impregnable, and had used as a place of refuge for their squaws and children. Nothing remained of the old Indian fort but a few embankments, gradually sinking to the level of the surrounding earth, and already overgrown in part by oaks and other forest trees, the foliage of which formed a contrast to the dark pines and hemlocks of the swamp.

⑤ It was late in the dusk of evening when Tom Walker reached the old fort, and he paused there awhile to rest himself. Anyone but he would have felt unwilling to linger in this lonely, melancholy place, for the common people had a bad opinion of it, from the stories handed down from the time of the Indian wars; when it was asserted that the savages held incantations here, and made sacrifices to the evil spirit.

Tom Walker, however, was not a man to be troubled with any fears of the kind. He reposed himself for some time on the trunk of a fallen hemlock, listening to the boding cry of the tree toad, and delving with his walking staff into a mound of black mold at his feet. As he turned up the soil unconsciously, his staff struck against something hard. He raked it out of the vegetable mold, and lo! a cloven skull, with an Indian tomahawk buried deep in it, lay before him. The rust on the weapon showed the time that had elapsed since this deathblow had been given. It was a dreary memento of the fierce struggle that had taken place in this last foothold of the Indian warriors.

"Humph!" said Tom Walker, as he gave it a kick to shake the dirt from it.

"Let that skull alone!" said a gruff voice. Tom lifted up his eyes, and beheld a great black man seated directly opposite him, on the stump of a tree. He was exceedingly surprised, having neither heard nor seen anyone approach; and he was still more perplexed on observing, as well as the gathering gloom would permit, that the ⑥ stranger was neither Negro nor Indian. It is true he was dressed in a rude half-Indian garb, and had a red belt or sash swathed round his body; but his face was neither black nor copper color, but swarthy and dingy, and begrimed with soot, as if he had been accustomed to toil among fires and forges. He had a shock of coarse black hair, that stood out from his head in all directions, and bore an ax on his shoulder.

He scowled for a moment at Tom with a pair of great red eyes.

"What are you doing on my grounds?" said the black man, with a hoarse growling voice.

"Your grounds!" said Tom with a sneer, "no more your grounds than mine; they belong to Deacon Peabody."

Reading Strategy
Inferring Cultural Attitudes What does the sentence begining "Anyone but he" reveal about the colonists' attitudes toward Native Americans?

Literary Analysis
Third-Person Omniscient Point of View Whose thoughts and feelings—if anyone's—are revealed in this paragraph?

✺ ENRICHMENT: Social Studies Connection

The Massachusetts Bay Colony

The Puritans obtained a royal charter and established the Massachusetts Bay Colony in the Boston area in 1629. The successful colony grew and expanded into Massachusetts and Connecticut. The settlers soon began creating a new life without interference from England. However, they came into conflict with Native Americans already living in the region, whom they regarded as heathen obstacles to progress. Puritan and Native American ways of life contrasted dramatically.

In addition, the Puritans faced criticism for their treatment of Native Americans from the Quakers. This innovative religious sect believed in pacifism, justice, charity, and spiritual equality for all, including Native Americans. For these beliefs, they were persecuted in the colony, where four were executed. In Pennsylvania, however, Quakers prospered.

"Deacon Peabody be d—d," said the stranger, "as I flatter myself he will be, if he does not look more to his own sins and less to those of his neighbors. Look yonder, and see how Deacon Peabody is faring."

Tom looked in the direction that the stranger pointed, and beheld one of the great trees, fair and flourishing without, but rotten at the core, and saw that it had been nearly hewn through, so that the first high wind was likely to blow it down. On the bark of the tree was scored the name of Deacon Peabody, an eminent man, who had waxed wealthy by driving shrewd bargains with the Indians. He now looked round, and found most of the tall trees marked with the name of some great man of the colony, and all more or less scored by the ax. The one on which he had been seated, and which had evidently just been hewn down, bore the name of Crowninshield: and he recollected a mighty rich man of that name, who made a vulgar display of wealth, which it was whispered he had acquired by buccaneering.

"He's just ready for burning!" said the black man, with a growl of triumph. "You see I am likely to have a good stock of firewood for winter."

"But what right have you," said Tom, "to cut down Deacon Peabody's timber?"

"The right of a prior claim," said the other. "This woodland belonged to me long before one of your white-faced race put foot upon the soil."

"And pray, who are you, if I may be so bold?" said Tom.

"Oh, I go by various names. I am the wild huntsman in some countries; the black miner in others. In this neighborhood I am known by the name of the black woodsman. I am he to whom the red men consecrated this spot, and in honor of whom they now and then roasted a white man, by way of sweet-smelling sacrifice. Since the red men have been exterminated by you white savages, I amuse myself by presiding at the persecutions of Quakers and Anabaptists;[4] I am the great patron and prompter of slave dealers, and the grandmaster of the Salem witches."

"The upshot of all which is, that, if I mistake not," said Tom, sturdily, "you are he commonly called Old Scratch."

---

4. **Quakers and Anabaptists** two religious groups that were persecuted for their beliefs.

The Devil and Tom Walker, 1856, John Quidor, The Cleveland Museum of Art

▲ **Critical Viewing** ❽
This painting is called *The Devil and Tom Walker.* In what ways do the lighting and details reflect the mood of Irving's story? **[Analyze]**

❾
✓ **Reading Check**
Who does Tom encounter in the woods?

The Devil and Tom Walker ◆ 245

❼ **Background**
Art

The Devil and Tom Walker, by John Quidor

This oil painting by American artist John Quidor (1801–1881) depicts Tom's initial meeting with the Devil in the swampy forest. The skull on the ground and the grinning, half-clothed creature holding an ax indicate that Tom's meeting is not a typical encounter. Use these questions for discussion:

1. What does the painting reveal about the story's setting?
   Answer: It highlights the dark, gloomy, wooded setting where Tom Walker first meets the Devil.

2. What does the painting reveal about the story's main character?
   Answer: It reveals the clothing worn during the time of the story and that Walker's physical appearance in the painting fits with his characterization as a greedy miser.

❽ ▶ **Critical Viewing**

Answer: The gloomy lighting and sinister setting reflect the mood of the story, particularly the scenes set in the swamp. Students may note that although Tom is brightly lit, the Devil is in the shadows, symbolizing his association with evil.

❾ ✓ **Reading Check**

Answer: Walker encounters the Devil in the woods.

CUSTOMIZE INSTRUCTION FOR UNIVERSAL ACCESS

For Special Needs Students	For English Language Learners	For Gifted/Talented Students
To clarify students' understanding of the selection, ask them to draw the scene described in the bracketed passage. Use their sketches to assess their comprehension of descriptive details. If you find that students have omitted details, have them revise their drawings.	Point out the word *impregnable,* line 8 on p. 244. Tell students to try to determine its meaning from context clues. Guide students to recognize that phrases such as "strongholds of the Indians during their wars," and "a kind of fort," all convey that *impregnable* means "not capable of being captured."	Ask students to identify the features that mark this character as the Devil. They can, for example, point to the coarse, animal-like hair; the soot from the fires of hell; and the red eyes. Have students suggest other physical features by which the Devil is represented in literature and in art.

Speculate

- Read aloud the bracketed passage. Discuss with students any speculations they can make about the fate of Mr. Crowninshield.

- Ask: Do you think Crowninshield, too, had dealings with Old Scratch?
  Answer: Most students will probably say that he did, based on Mr. Crowninshield's wealth and attitude toward it, as well as on the tree marked with Mr. Crowninshield's name and on the Devil's earlier reference to Mr. Crowninshield burning.

⑪ Literary Analysis

Third-Person Omniscient Point of View

- Have students create a two-column chart headed *Tom* and *Mrs. Walker*. Read the bracketed passage aloud to them as they jot down details related to each character in the appropriate column.

- Point out that in this paragraph the narrator reveals both Tom's thoughts and his wife's attitudes.

- Ask students what they learn here about the relationship between Tom and his wife.
  Possible response: Both were selfish and untrusting, and neither had any interest in pleasing the other.

"The same, at your service!" replied the black man, with a half-civil nod.

Such was the opening of this interview, according to the old story; though it has almost too familiar an air to be credited. One would think that to meet with such a singular personage, in this wild, lonely place, would have shaken any man's nerves; but Tom was a hard-minded fellow, not easily daunted, and he had lived so long with a termagant wife, that he did not even fear the Devil.

It is said that after this commencement they had a long and earnest conversation together, as Tom returned homeward. The black man told him of great sums of money buried by Kidd the pirate, under the oak trees on the high ridge, not far from the morass. All these were under his command, and protected by his power, so that none could find them but such as propitiated his favor. These he offered to place within Tom Walker's reach, having conceived an especial kindness for him; but they were to be had only on certain conditions. What these conditions were may easily be surmised, though Tom never dis-closed them publicly. They must have been very hard, for he required time to think of them, and he was not a man to stick at trifles where money was in view. When they had reached the edge of the swamp, the stranger paused—"What proof have I that all you have been telling me is true?" said Tom. "There is my signature," said the black man, pressing his finger on Tom's forehead. So saying, he turned off among the thickets of the swamp, and seemed, as Tom said, to go down, down, down, into the earth, until nothing but his head and shoulders could be seen, and so on, until he totally disappeared.

When Tom reached home, he found the black print of a finger, burnt, as it were, into his forehead, which nothing could obliterate.

⑩ The first news his wife had to tell him was the sudden death of Absalom Crowninshield, the rich buccaneer. It was announced in the papers with the usual flourish, that "A great man had fallen in Israel."[5]

Tom recollected the tree which his black friend had just hewn down, and which was ready for burning, "Let the freebooter roast," said Tom, "who cares!" He now felt convinced that all he had heard and seen was no illusion.

He was not prone to let his wife into his confidence; but as this was an uneasy secret, he willingly shared it with her. All her <u>avarice</u> ⑪ was awakened at the mention of hidden gold, and she urged her husband to comply with the black man's terms and secure what would make them wealthy for life. However Tom might have felt disposed to sell himself to the Devil, he was determined not to do so to oblige his

---

5. **A . . . Israel** a reference to II Samuel 3:38 in the Bible. The Puritans often called New England "Israel."

Walking stick, King Georges County, Virginia, 1846, Abby Aldrich Rockefeller Folk Art Center, Williamsburg, Virginia

avarice (av´ ə ris) *n.* greed

 ENRICHMENT: Culture Connection

The Devil Across Cultures

In legend and literature, from the Bible to modern fiction, the Devil has appeared in many guises and under many names. Examples include Beelzebub, Mephistopheles, Satan, and Lucifer.

A pact with the Devil is a common theme in the folklore of many cultures. Although the Devil may go by different names, most cultures have their own tales about human encounters with an embodiment of evil. For some Native Americans, evil enters this world as a creature that can change shape and size at will. For example, Native American heroes from many various groups have been afraid of the water monster known as Unktehi in Nebraska and the Dakotas; others fear No Body, the Great Rolling Head of the prairies and mountains.

wife; so he flatly refused, out of the mere spirit of contradiction. Many and bitter were the quarrels they had on the subject, but the more she talked, the more resolute was Tom not to be damned to please her.

At length she determined to drive the bargain on her own account, and if she succeeded, to keep all the gain to herself. Being of the same fearless temper as her husband, she set off for the old Indian fort towards the close of a summer's day. She was many hours absent. When she came back, she was reserved and sullen in her replies. She spoke something of a black man, whom she had met about twilight, hewing at the root of a tall tree. He was sulky, however, and would not come to terms: she was to go again with a propitiatory offering, but what it was she forbore to say.

The next evening she set off again for the swamp, with her apron heavily laden. Tom waited and waited for her, but in vain; midnight came, but she did not make her appearance: morning, noon, night returned, but still she did not come. Tom now grew uneasy for her safety, especially as he found she had carried off in her apron the silver teapot and spoons, and every portable article of value. Another night elapsed, another morning came; but no wife. In a word, she was never heard of more.

What was her real fate nobody knows, in consequence of so many pretending to know. It is one of those facts which have become confounded by a variety of historians. Some asserted that she lost her way among the tangled mazes of the swamp, and sank into some pit or slough; others, more uncharitable, hinted that she had eloped with the household booty, and made off to some other province; while others surmised that the tempter had decoyed her into a dismal quagmire, on the top of which her hat was found lying. In confirmation of this, it was said a great black man, with an ax on his shoulder, was seen late that very evening coming out of the swamp, carrying a bundle tied in a checked apron, with an air of surly triumph.

The most current and probable story, however, observes that Tom Walker grew so anxious about the fate of his wife and his property, that he set out at length to seek them both at the Indian fort. During a long summer's afternoon he searched about the gloomy place, but no wife was to be seen. He called her name repeatedly, but she was nowhere to be heard. The bittern alone responded to his voice, as he flew screaming by; or the bullfrog croaked dolefully from a neighboring pool. At length, it is said, just in the brown hour of twilight, when the owls began to hoot, and the bats to flit about, his attention was attracted by the clamor of carrion crows hovering about a cypress tree. He looked up, and beheld a bundle tied in a checked apron, and hanging in the branches of the tree, with a great vulture perched hard by, as if keeping watch upon it. He leaped with joy; for he recognized his wife's apron, and supposed it to contain the household valuables.

Teapot, Yale University Art Gallery, New Haven

Literary Analysis
Third-Person Omniscient Point of View What does the narrator reveal about Mrs. Walker's thoughts and feelings here?

13 ▲ **Critical Viewing**
Tom Walker's wife packs up her valuables to take into the forest. Why might a teapot like this one be considered valuable? **[Support]**

14 ☑ **Reading Check**
What action does Tom's wife take?

The Devil and Tom Walker ◆ 247

12 Literary Analysis
Third-Person Omniscient Point of View

- Call on a volunteer to read aloud the bracketed passage. Have students paraphrase its meaning.
  Answer: Tom's wife planned to make her own deal with the Devil but to exclude Tom from its benefits. She went to the old Indian fort but would not discuss what occurred there.

- Ask students the Literary Analysis question on p. 247: What does the narrator reveal about Mrs. Walker's thoughts and feelings here?
  Answer: The narrator reveals that Tom's wife will stop at nothing when money is at stake.

▶ Monitor Progress Ask students to discuss how the story would be different if it were told only from Tom's point of view.

13 ▶ **Critical Viewing**
Possible response: The teapot appears to be made of a metal such as silver or pewter, which was costly for people like the Walkers.

14 ☑ **Reading Check**
Answer: Tom's wife collects the family valuables and brings them with her to bargain with the Devil.

CUSTOMIZE INSTRUCTION FOR UNIVERSAL ACCESS

For English Learners	For Advanced Readers	For Gifted/Talented Students
Tell students that Irving's very long sentences may be difficult to understand. Point out, however, that Irving frequently uses semicolons to link clauses. Encourage students to break down long sentences into their several parts by separating them at the semicolons. They can read each clause for meaning before proceeding to the next clause.	Point out Tom Walker's last comment on p. 247. Then share with student's the following critic's remark: "One of Washington Irving's great gifts to prose is his ability to find humor even in the most grotesque circumstances." Have students write an essay about the selection in which they identify and discuss the effect of humorous elements such as this line.	Challenge students to deliver an unrehearsed speech about the dangers of greed, using details from Mrs. Walker's experience as supporting evidence. Invite students to present their speeches to the class, if possible without reference to notes. Afterward, have students share their experience of extemporaneous, or ad-libbed, speaking.

Third-Person Omniscient Point of View

- Remind students of the opening descriptions from p. 243 about the attitudes Tom and Mrs. Walker hold toward money and the relationship they have with each other. Then have students read the bracketed passage to themselves.

- Have students identify the losses to which the author alludes.
  Answer: Tom has lost his wife and the household's considerable valuable property.

- Ask students what the narrator reveals here about Tom's feelings.
  Answer: The narrator makes it clear that Tom is resigned to the loss of his goods only because it also means the loss of his wife, for which he feels no grief.

16 ▶Critical Viewing

Possible response: Students can surmise that she is dead because her apron is attended by a vulture, a symbol of death.

"Let us get hold of the property," said he, consolingly to himself, "and we will endeavor to do without the woman."

As he scrambled up the tree, the vulture spread its wide wings, and sailed off screaming into the deep shadows of the forest. Tom seized the checked apron, but woeful sight! found nothing but a heart and liver tied up in it!

Such, according to the most authentic old story, was all that was to be found of Tom's wife. She had probably attempted to deal with the black man as she had been accustomed to deal with her husband; but though a female scold is generally considered a match for the Devil, yet in this instance she appears to have had the worst of it. She must have died game, however; for it is said Tom noticed many prints of cloven feet deeply stamped about the tree, and found handfuls of hair, that looked as if they had been plucked from the coarse black shock of the woodsman. Tom knew his wife's prowess by experience. He shrugged his shoulders, as he looked at the signs of a fierce clapperclawing. "Egad," said he to himself, "Old Scratch must have had a tough time of it!"

15 Tom consoled himself for the loss of his property, with the loss of his wife, for he was a man of fortitude. He even felt something like gratitude towards the black woodsman, who, he considered, had done him a kindness. He sought, therefore, to cultivate a further acquaintance with him, but for some time without success; the old blacklegs played shy, for whatever people may think, he is not always to be had for calling for: he knows how to play his cards when pretty sure of his game.

At length, it is said, when delay had whetted Tom's eagerness to the quick, and prepared him to agree to anything rather than not gain the promised treasure, he met the black man one evening in his usual woodsman's dress, with his ax on his shoulder, sauntering along the swamp, and humming a tune. He affected to receive Tom's advances with great indifference, made brief replies, and went on humming his tune.

By degrees, however, Tom brought him to business, and they began to haggle about the terms on which the former was to have the pirate's treasure. There was one condition which need not be mentioned, being generally understood in all cases where the Devil grants favors; but there were others about which, though of less importance, he was inflexibly obstinate. He insisted that the money found through his means should be employed in his service. He proposed, therefore, that Tom should employ it in the black traffic; that is to say, that he should

16 ▲ **Critical Viewing**
The narrator describes "a great vulture perched hard by" and a checked apron hanging in the tree. What do you think happened to Tom Walker's wife? **[Infer]**

✳ ENRICHMENT: Math Connection

Loan Practices

Although usury such as that practiced by Tom Walker is illegal today, the legitimate financial services industry has a useful purpose and its loan practices are strictly monitored. Banks lend money to businesses and individuals for home mortgages, cars, tuition, renovations, and other large expenses. Rates for various loans are regulated by federal and state law.

In general, interest is charged at an annual percentage of the amount borrowed. For example, a loan of $100 at the 2% interest rate requires a repayment of $102 after a year. However, in Irving's story, the Devil seeks a rate of 2% a month, or 24% a year, which is an exorbitant rate. Tom Walker's rates, which add up to 48% a year, are even more extreme.

fit out a slave ship. This, however, Tom resolutely refused: he was bad enough in all conscience, but the Devil himself could not tempt him to turn slave-trader.

Finding Tom so squeamish on this point, he did not insist upon it, but proposed, instead, that he should turn usurer; the Devil being extremely anxious for the increase of <u>usurers</u>, looking upon them as his peculiar[6] people.

usurers (yoo′ zhər ərz) *n.* moneylenders who charge very high interest

To this no objections were made, for it was just to Tom's taste.

"You shall open a broker's shop in Boston next month," said the black man.

"I'll do it tomorrow, if you wish," said Tom Walker.

"You shall lend money at two per cent a month."

"Egad, I'll charge four!" replied Tom Walker.

"You shall <u>extort</u> bonds, foreclose mortgages, drive the merchant to bankruptcy—"

extort (eks tôrt′) *v.* to obtain by threat or violence

"I'll drive him to the D——l," cried Tom Walker.

"You are the usurer for my money!" said the blacklegs with delight. "When will you want the rhino?"[7]

"This very night."

"Done!" said the Devil.

"Done!" said Tom Walker. So they shook hands and struck a bargain.

A few days' time saw Tom Walker seated behind his desk in a countinghouse in Boston.

His reputation for a ready-moneyed man, who would lend money out for a good consideration, soon spread abroad. Everybody remembers the time of Governor Belcher,[8] when money was particularly scarce. It was a time of paper credit. The country had been deluged with government bills; the famous Land Bank[9] had been established; there had been a rage for speculating; the people had run mad with schemes for new settlements, for building cities in the wilderness; land jobbers[10] went about with maps of grants, and townships, and El Dorados,[11] lying nobody knew where, but which everybody was ready to purchase. In a word, the great speculating fever which breaks out every now and then in the country, had raged to an alarming degree, and everybody was dreaming of making sudden fortunes from nothing. As usual the fever had subsided; the dream had gone off, and the imaginary fortunes with it; the patients were left in doleful plight, and the whole country resounded with the consequent cry of "hard times."

At this propitious time of public distress did Tom Walker set up as usurer in Boston. His door was soon thronged by customers. The needy

---

6. **peculiar** particular; special.
7. **rhino** (rī′nō) slang term for money.
8. **Governor Belcher** Jonathan Belcher, the governor of Massachusetts Bay Colony from 1730 through 1741.
9. **Land Bank** a bank that financed transactions in real estate.
10. **land jobbers** people who bought and sold undeveloped land.
11. **El Dorados** (el′ də rä′ dōz) *n.* places that are rich in gold or opportunity. El Dorado was a legendary country in South America sought by early Spanish explorers for its gold and precious stones.

19 ✓ **Reading Check**

What is Tom's new occupation?

The Devil and Tom Walker ◆ 249

---

17 Reading Strategy

Inferring Cultural Attitudes

- Have two students read aloud the conversation between the Devil and Tom Walker. Ask students to share any prior knowledge they have about colonial attitudes toward brokers and usurers.

- Have students determine what the bracketed dialogue reveals about colonial attitudes toward brokers and usurers.

▶ **Monitor Progress** If students have difficulty contributing to the discussion, post the graphic organizer from p. 241. Help students list details about Tom and the Devil that suggest colonial attitudes. Charts should look similar to the one shown below.

Detail or Description	Cultural Attitude
Devil suggests usury; greedy Tom is eager to be a usurer; the word *extort*	colonists frowned on usury, considering it the work of the Devil

18 Vocabulary Development

Word Analysis: Latin Prefix *ex-*

- Draw students' attention to the word *extort* and its definition on page 249.

- Let students know that the Latin prefix *ex-* means "out." Show students how together with the Latin root *torquere*, which means "to twist," the prefix forms a word meaning literally "to twist (something) out."

- Have students volunteer other words containing the prefix *ex-*. Possibilities include: exhale, expand, exude, excel, and excess.

- Then, have students infer how the prefix contributes to the meanings of these words. The prefix *ex-* of the word "exhale" shows that the word means, "breathe out."

- Finally, if students cannot infer the significance of the prefix in the meanings of the listed words, have them look up the explanations in a dictionary.

19 ✓ Reading Check

Answer: Tom has become a loan shark who charges exceptionally high rates because he lends money to people who cannot borrow it anywhere else.

CUSTOMIZE INSTRUCTION FOR UNIVERSAL ACCESS

For Less Proficient Readers	For Advanced Readers
Direct students to the text bracketed at 17. Guide students to understand that here Irving points out that the Devil embodies a range of bad qualities, that he is sly and manipulative. Ask students to note that the Devil and Tom Walker seem to agree well together. Emphasize to students that Irving wishes the reader to recognize that the two characters have much in common.	Have students write a character comparison/contrast of Tom Walker and the Devil. To get students started, pose questions such as these: In what ways are the two similar? Why, for example, would the Devil bargain with Tom but not with Mrs. Walker?

- Stress to students that people often have mixed feelings about money. Remind students, for example, that their discusssion of p. 243 included how colonists linked money with the Devil. Point out, however, that here Irving seems to suggest that parsimony is no more admirable than ostentation.

- Ask students the Reading Strategy question on p. 250: From the paragraph beginning "As Tom waxed old," what can you infer about the attitudes of the day about money?
  Answer: Tom's onrush of guilt about his ill-gotten gains—and his consequent bout of church-going—indicate that the people of the day took literally the biblical idea that the love of money is the root of all evil.

21 Literary Analysis

Third-Person Omniscient Point of View and Characterization

- Have students read the bracketed passage carefully. Help them list topics about which Tom Walker cares deeply, whether positively or negatively.
  Possible response: He hates his wife passionately, he desires money above all else, he becomes rigidly religious.

- Ask students the Literary Analysis question on p. 250: What do you learn about Tom's character from the narrator's description of his religious zeal?
  Possible response: You learn that he is as rigid, narrow-minded, and cold-hearted in his religiosity as he is in his money-making.

▶ Monitor Progress Encourage students to discuss whether this passage is an example of direct characterization, indirect characterization, or both.

and adventurous, the gambling speculator, the dreaming land jobber, the thriftless tradesman, the merchant with cracked credit, in short, everyone driven to raise money by desperate means and desperate sacrifices, hurried to Tom Walker.

Thus Tom was the universal friend of the needy, and acted like a "friend in need"; that is to say, he always exacted good pay and good security. In proportion to the distress of the applicant was the hardness of his terms. He accumulated bonds and mortgages; gradually squeezed his customers closer and closer, and sent them at length, dry as a sponge, from his door.

In this way he made money hand over hand, became a rich and mighty man, and exalted his cocked hat upon 'Change.[12] He built himself, as usual, a vast house, out of <u>ostentation</u>; but left the greater part of it unfinished and unfurnished, out of <u>parsimony</u>. He even set up a carriage in the fullness of his vainglory, though he nearly starved the horses which drew it; and as the ungreased wheels groaned and screeched on the axletrees, you would have thought you heard the souls of the poor debtors he was squeezing.

As Tom waxed old, however, he grew thoughtful. Having secured the good things of this world, he began to feel anxious about those of the next. He thought with regret on the bargain he had made with his black friend, and set his wits to work to cheat him out of the conditions. He became, therefore, all of a sudden, a violent churchgoer. He prayed loudly and strenuously, as if heaven were to be taken by force of lungs. Indeed, one might always tell when he had sinned most during the week, by the clamor of his Sunday devotion. The quiet Christians who had been modestly and steadfastly traveling Zionward,[13] were struck with self-reproach at seeing themselves so suddenly outstripped in their career by this new-made convert. Tom was as rigid in religious as in money matters; he was a stern supervisor and censurer of his neighbors, and seemed to think every sin entered up to their account became a credit on his own side of the page. He even talked of the expediency of reviving the persecution of Quakers and Anabaptists. In a word, Tom's zeal became as notorious as his riches.

Still, in spite of all this strenuous attention to forms, Tom had a lurking dread that the Devil, after all, would have his due. That he might not be taken unawares, therefore, it is said he always carried a small Bible in his coat pocket. He had also a great folio Bible on his countinghouse desk, and would frequently be found reading it when people called on business; on such occasions he would lay his green spectacles in the book, to mark the place, while he turned round to drive some usurious bargain.

Some say that Tom grew a little crackbrained in his old days, and that fancying his end

---

12. **'Change** exchange where bankers and merchants did business.
13. **Zionward** (zī´ ən wərd) toward heaven.

ostentation (äs´ tən tā´ shən) n. boastful display

parsimony (pär´ sə mō´ nē) n. stinginess

Reading Strategy
Inferring Cultural Attitudes From the paragraph beginning "As Tom waxed old," what can you infer about the attitudes of the day about money?

Literary Analysis
Third-person Omniscient Point of View and Characterization What do you learn about Tom's character from the narrator's description of his religious zeal?

✸ **ENRICHMENT: Social Studies Connection**

Changing Views

Washington Irving wrote this story in the early nineteenth century, but the story's setting is 100 years earlier. As a result, Irving's attitudes about certain key cultural issues contrast sharply with those of his characters. For example, by 1824, antislavery and abolitionist attitudes had grown strong in the Northeast. Thus, when Tom Walker refuses to turn slave-trader, his attitude reflects the abolitionist sentiments of Irving and his northern contemporaries more than the mores of eighteenth-century colonists.

Irving's distance from Tom Walker's time allowed him to comment critically on that culture. He knew that in the early eighteenth century, many colonists were beginning to replace Puritanism with a philosophy of commercialism and capitalism. Thus, when Tom Walker first meets the Devil and sees his wealthy neighbors' names scored into the trees, Irving can satirize the hypocrisy of those Puritans who used their prominence to amass wealth. He continues by describing Tom's own ostentatious behavior once he becomes wealthy.

approaching, he had his horse newly shod, saddled and bridled, and buried with his feet uppermost; because he supposed that at the last day the world would be turned upside down, in which case he should find his horse standing ready for mounting, and he was determined at the worst to give his old friend a run for it. This, however, is probably a mere old wives' fable. If he really did take such a precaution, it was totally superfluous; at least so says the authentic old legend, which closes his story in the following manner.

One hot summer afternoon in the dog days, just as a terrible black thunder-gust was coming up, Tom sat in his counting-house in his white linen cap and India silk morning gown. He was on the point of foreclosing a mortgage, by which he would complete the ruin of an unlucky land speculator for whom he had professed the greatest friendship. The poor land jobber begged him to grant a few months' indulgence. Tom had grown testy and irritated, and refused another day.

"My family will be ruined and brought upon the parish," said the land jobber.

"Charity begins at home," replied Tom; "I must take care of myself in these hard times."

"You have made so much money out of me," said the speculator.

Tom lost his patience and his piety—"The Devil take me," said he, "if I have made a farthing!"

Just then there were three loud knocks at the street door. He stepped out to see who was there. A black man was holding a black horse, which neighed and stamped with impatience.

"Tom, you're come for," said the black fellow, gruffly. Tom shrunk back, but too late. He had left his little Bible at the bottom of his coat pocket, and his big Bible on the desk buried under the mortgage he was about to foreclose: never was sinner taken more unawares. The black man whisked him like a child into the saddle, gave the horse the lash, and away he galloped, with Tom on his back, in the midst of the thunderstorm. The clerks stuck their pens behind their ears, and stared after him from the windows. Away went Tom Walker, dashing down the streets, his white cap bobbing up and down, his morning gown fluttering in the wind, and his steed striking fire out of the pavement at every bound. When the clerks turned to look for the black man he had disappeared.

Tom Walker never returned to foreclose the mortgage. A countryman who lived on the border of the swamp, reported that in the height of the thunder-gust he had heard a great clattering of hoofs and a howling along the road, and running to the window caught sight of a figure, such as I have described, on a horse that galloped like mad across the fields, over the hills and down into the black hemlock swamp towards the old Indian fort; and that shortly after a thunderbolt falling in that direction seemed to set the whole forest in a blaze.

The American Experience

21 The European Influence on American Literature

Washington Irving lived in Europe for many years, joining a trend of American writers and artists who left home to study or travel abroad. This trend was sparked by an American desire to maintain ties to European roots, to model English style, and to find publishers and readers abroad. Through their travels, Irving, and other writers such as Nathaniel Hawthorne and the Fireside Poets, brought new themes and ideas to American literature. Under the pseudonym Geoffrey Crayon, Irving later wrote,

"... Europe held for the charms of storied and poetical association. There were to be seen the masterpieces of art, the refinements of highly cultivated society, the quaint peculiarities of ancient and local custom. My native country was full of youthful promise; Europe was rich in the accumulated treasures of age."

22 Reading Check

According to legend, how does the Devil catch up with Tom?

The Devil and Tom Walker ◆ 251

22 Background

The European Influence on American Literature

European influence appeared in many of Irving's works. In addition to the German folktale behind this story, Irving explored Italian folk themes in other *Tales of a Traveller*. Later, while serving the United States in Spain, Irving focused on Spanish literary themes. There he produced works such as *The Conquest of Granada* (1829) and *The Alhambra* (1832). In his later years, however, Irving apparently decided that America's promise was worthy of study. His final work—historical and biographical rather than fictional—followed the life of American hero George Washington.

23 Reading Check

Answer: Tom calls up the Devil by using him to prove his own truthfulness, even though he is in fact lying.

CUSTOMIZE INSTRUCTION FOR UNIVERSAL ACCESS

For Less Proficient Readers	For English Learners	For Advanced Readers
Students will benefit from rereading all or parts of the story and filling in any missing elements of their story time lines. In reviewing the story, prompt students to focus on specific elements, such as cultural attitudes, Tom Walker's attitudes, or how the third-person omniscient point of view narrator contributes to the story.	Explain that a farthing was equal to about a fourth of a cent in American money. Then explain that Tom speaks figuratively. He refers to the Devil taking him as an example of something that would never happen in order to stress that he is speaking the truth. Help students recognize the irony of the statement.	Ask students to identify the scary details in the description of Tom's capture and contrast them with those that are sardonic. Suggest that they list their contrasting details in a two-column chart with the headings *Scary* and *Sardonic*.

Answers for p. 252

Review and Assess

1. Possible response: No. He behaves quite characteristically throughout, showing his single-mindedness and self-absorbtion.

2. **(a)** He offers to make Tom Walker rich by giving him the pirate's treasure. **(b)** The Devil's conditions are hard and Tom wants to think about them before accepting.

3. **(a)** The Devil kills her. **(b)** Possible response: You learn that he cares more about money than about people.

4. **(a)** Tom agrees to sell his soul to the Devil in exchange for the pirate's treasure and also to use the treasure as a moneylender in the Devil's service. **(b)** Possible response: He begins to regret his bargain and hopes that religious zeal will protect him from the Devil.

5. **(a)** He prays loudly and strenuously. **(b)** He becomes a stern supervisor of the spiritual accounts of his neighbors and is willing to persecute other sects, just as he harasses his debtors.

6. Possible response: They were selfish, greedy, and callous. All their actions were self-serving, whether in seeking money or in seeking escape from a bargain.

7. **(a)** Possible response: Anyone willing to bargain with the Devil deserves his fate. **(b)** Possible response: One might think this to be a more acceptable bargain because knowledge seems more worthy. On reflection, however, any bargain in which someone sells his or her soul will likely prove dangerous in the end.

The good people of Boston shook their heads and shrugged their shoulders, but had been so much accustomed to witches and goblins and tricks of the Devil, in all kind of shapes from the first settlement of the colony, that they were not so much horror struck as might have been expected. Trustees were appointed to take charge of Tom's effects. There was nothing, however, to administer upon.

On searching his coffers all his bonds and mortgages were found reduced to cinders. In place of gold and silver his iron chest was filled with chips and shavings; two skeletons lay in his stable instead of his half-starved horses, and the very next day his great house took fire and was burned to the ground.

Such was the end of Tom Walker and his ill-gotten wealth. Let all griping money brokers lay this story to heart. The truth of it is not to be doubted. The very hole under the oak trees, whence he dug Kidd's money, is to be seen to this day; and the neighboring swamp and old Indian fort are often haunted in stormy nights by a figure on horseback, in morning gown and white cap, which is doubtless the troubled spirit of the usurer. In fact, the story has resolved itself into a proverb, and is the origin of that popular saying, so prevalent throughout New England, of "The Devil and Tom Walker."

Review and Assess

Thinking About the Selection

1. **Respond:** Were you surprised by Tom's actions in this story? Why or why not?

2. **(a) Recall:** What does the Devil offer Tom Walker? **(b) Analyze:** What factors contribute to Tom's initial refusal?

3. **(a) Recall:** What happens to Tom's wife? **(b) Interpret:** What do you learn about Tom, based on his reaction to the loss of his wife?

4. **(a) Recall:** What agreement does Tom Walker ultimately make with the Devil? **(b) Draw Conclusions:** As the story progresses, why do you think Tom begins to go to church and carry a Bible around with him at all times?

5. **(a) Recall:** What does Tom do to cause the narrator to call him a "violent churchgoer"? **(b) Interpret:** In what way is Tom's approach to religion similar to his approach to financial dealings?

6. **Evaluate:** What kind of people do you think Tom Walker and his wife are? Explain.

7. **(a) Take a Position:** Do you feel that Tom Walker deserved his fate? Why or why not? **(b) Defend:** Would you have felt more sympathy for Tom if he had sold his soul for knowledge instead of money? Explain.

STANDARDIZED TEST APPLICATION: Reading Comprehension

Make Inferences and Generalizations (For more practice, see **Test Preparation Workbook, p. 15.**)

An inference is a reasonable guess based on facts. Use this sample test item._____

A miserable horse, whose ribs were as articulated as the bars of a gridiron, stalked about a field . . . and sometimes he would lean his head over the fence . . . and seem to petition deliverance from this land of famine.

According to the passage, why is the horse so miserable?

A He misses his former owner.
B He is kept in the barn all day.
C He lives in the country.
D He is starving.

The excerpt makes no mention of any information found in choices *A*, *B*, and *C*. The horse's ribs show, and the author describes a "land of famine." Students should infer that the horse is not well fed and choose *D*.

Review and Assess

Literary Analysis

Third-Person Omniscient Point of View

1. Using a diagram like the one shown, give two examples in which the **third-person omniscient point of view narrator** reveals the thoughts and feelings of the characters in the story.

2. Find two places in the story where the narrator reveals Tom Walker's plans.
3. Find one place in the story where the narrator reveals the thoughts or unspoken plans of Tom Walker's wife.

Connecting Literary Elements

4. Identify three things you learn about Tom through **direct characterization.**
5. (a) Characterize Tom's wife based on the narrator's comments. (b) What do you learn about the relationship of Tom and his wife through **indirect characterization**? Explain.
6. What does the narrator's description of the Walker's house and the condition of their horse tell you about their personalities?

Reading Strategy

Inferring Cultural Details

7. What inferences can you draw about the **cultural attitudes** of New Englanders during the 1720s, especially in the area of religion? Explain.
8. (a) What can you infer about the attitudes of people toward moneylenders in Tom Walker's time? (b) Which details in the story lead you to draw this inference?

Extend Understanding

9. **Career Connection:** In what way might a banker today respond to Irving's suggestion that moneylenders are greedy?

Quick Review

In a story told through **third-person omniscient point of view**, a narrator is all-knowing, stands outside the action, and relates the thoughts and feelings of all the characters.

Characterization is the art of revealing character. With **direct characterization,** a writer simply states what a character is like. With **indirect characterization,** a writer reveals personality traits through the characters' thoughts, words, and actions, and through what other characters say about them.

By drawing conclusions about the details describing people in a story, you can **infer cultural attitudes.**

 Take It to the Net

www.phschool.com

Take the interactive self-test online to check your understanding of the selection.

The Devil and Tom Walker ◆ 253

✸ ENRICHMENT: Further Reading

Other Works by Washington Irving

Bracebridge Hall

The Alhambra

A Chronicle of the Conquest of Granada

Take It to the Net

Visit www.phschool.com for more information on Washington Irving.

Answers for p. 253

Review and Assess

1. **Possible response:** Tom Walker: is greedy for money; attends church and reads the Bible out of fear. Mrs. Walker: dislikes her husband; wants money more than anything else. The Devil: lies and manipulates people; exacts his due no matter what.

2. **Possible responses:** The narrator states that Tom seeks to cultivate a further acquaintance with the Devil. Later the narrators states that Tom plans to avoid the consequences of his bargain through his religious behavior.

3. **Possible response:** The narrator states that she decided to drive a bargain with the Devil and to keep all the gain for herself.

4. **Possible response:** You learn that he is crafty, selfish, and greedy.

5. **(a) Possible response:** She is greedy, with a violent temper, a nasty manner, and distorted values. **(b) Possible response:** That they fight is learned from the reactions of passers-by and neighbors who avoid the Walkers' home at all costs.

6. The description shows that the Walkers are too miserly and too mean to care for their house and field or to feed their horse.

7. **Possible response:** New Englanders prided themselves on their piety and religious faith. They regarded worldly success as possibly being of the Devil.

8. **Possible response: (a)** People of Tom Walker's time saw money-lenders as people who took advantage of people's weakness. **(b)** The author's ironic tone, the Devil's delight at Tom's willingness to be a money lender, and Tom's own guilty conscience show that money lending was not admired.

9. A banker would probably object to Irving's implications. Today's bankers are employees of financial institutions and do not personally profit from lending; banking and lending are carefully regulated industries.

Answers for p. 254

❶ Vocabulary Development

Word Analysis

1. b
2. d
3. a
4. e
5. c

Spelling Strategy

1. excerpt
2. ex-marine
3. excavate

Fluency: Words in Context

1. usurers
2. extort
3. parsimony
4. ostentation
5. avarice

❷ Grammar and Style

1. which ran out like a peninsula into the . . . deep bosom of the swamp; modifies *ground*

2. who would lend money out for a good consideration; modifies *man*

3. whom she had met about twilight; modifies *man*

4. that stood out from his head in all directions; modifies *hair*

5. which is doubtless the troubled spirit of the usurer; modifies *figure*

Writing Application

Paragraphs should contain at least three adjective clauses with *who, whom, whose, which,* or *that* in them.

Integrate Language Skills

❶ Vocabulary Development Lesson

Word Analysis: Latin Prefix *ex-*

The Latin prefix *ex-* means "out," as in *extort,* which means "to squeeze out." Match the words on the left with their definitions on the right.

1. exceed   **a.** elevate; glorify
2. exact   **b.** go beyond normal limits
3. exalt   **c.** look out; look forward
4. expedite   **d.** wring; pry out
5. expect   **e.** speed up; hasten

Spelling Strategy

When the prefix *ex-* means "out," do not use a hyphen after it: *extort, export, extract.* When it means "former," use a hyphen: *ex-president, ex-wife.* Add the prefix *ex-* to the following words, using a hyphen if it is needed.

1. cerpt   2. marine   3. cavate

❷ Grammar and Style Lesson

Adjective Clauses

An **adjective clause** is a subordinate clause that modifies a noun or a pronoun. Adjective clauses are introduced with relative pronouns: *who* or *whom, whose, which,* or *that.*

> Adjective Clause
> **Example:** A miserable horse, *whose ribs stuck out,* stalked about a field. (modifies *horse*)

Practice Identify the adjective clause and the word it modifies in each of the following sentences.

1. At length he arrived at a piece of firm ground, which ran out like a peninsula into the . . . deep bosom of the swamp.

Fluency: Words in Context

Select the word from the vocabulary list on page 241 that best completes each sentence.

1. Unfortunately, we had borrowed money from ___?___, who charged an excessive rate of interest.

2. He would ___?___ money by threatening to harm victims if they did not pay.

3. Her ___?___ led her to refuse to send for a doctor—even when she was ill.

4. The house was such a model of ___?___ that visitors speculated about its excessive cost.

5. A main characteristic of Mrs. Walker's personality was ___?___ .

2. His reputation for a ready-moneyed man, who would lend money out for a good consideration, soon spread abroad.

3. She spoke something of a black man, whom she had met about twilight . . .

4. He had a shock of coarse black hair, that stood out from his head in all directions . . .

5. The . . . swamp and the old Indian fort are often haunted . . . by a figure on horseback, which is doubtless the troubled spirit of the usurer.

Writing Application Write a paragraph about another character who makes a deal at a high price. Use three adjective clauses that contain the relative pronouns *who, whom, whose, which,* or *that.*

WG *Prentice Hall Writing and Grammar Connection: Chapter 19, Section 3*

254 ◆ *A Growing Nation (1800–1870)*

TEACHING RESOURCES

The following resources can be used to enrich or extend the instruction for pp. 254–255.

Vocabulary

📖 **Selection Support Workbook:** Build Vocabulary, p. 59

📖 **Vocabulary and Spelling Practice Book** (Use this booklet for skills enrichment.) ▪

Grammar

📖 **Selection Support Workbook:** Grammar and Style, p. 60

WG **Writing and Grammar,** Ruby Level, p. 454

▪ **Daily Language Practice Transparencies** ▪

Writing

WG **Writing and Grammar,** Ruby Level, p. 76

💿 **Writing and Grammar iText CD-ROM**

▪ **Writing Models and Graphic Organizers on Transparencies,** pp. 17–23, 95

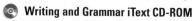 **BLOCK SCHEDULING:** Resources marked with this symbol provide varied instruction during 90-minute blocks.

❸ Writing Lesson

Modern Retelling of a Story

Write an updated version of Irving's story with new plot elements and character details. Use your story to convey the same message as Irving, but in a way that addresses a modern audience.

Prewriting Outline the plot of the original story. Consider the best way to update each plot event you list. For example, instead of meeting in a forest, Tom Walker might encounter the Devil at the mall.

Drafting Write your story, making sure your characters' dialogue, dress, and actions reflect modern times. Include references to food, clothes, and current events.

Writing Model: Updating a Story

Tom sitting at his computer, and downloading promissory notes. Suddenly, he saw a pair of beady eyes glaring at him from the screen. Then, pixel by pixel, a strange-looking face took shape.

> While maintaining the intent of the story, modern elements such as "pixel" and "computer" update the setting.

Revising Confirm that your draft balances the original story elements with the new details that update it. Check to see that the conflict and the message are the same, but make sure the language and setting reflect today's world.

 Prentice Hall Writing and Grammar Connection: Chapter 5, Section 2

❹ Extension Activities

Listening and Speaking Speculate about what happens when Mrs. Walker meets the Devil. Prepare an **enactment** of the scene as you think it would occur.

- Write dialogue to show what might take place between the two characters.
- Choose a classmate to perform the scene with you.

Practice the scene; then perform it for your class. [Group Activity]

Research and Technology In addition to providing the basis for this story, the Faust legend has inspired plays, operas, and even a Broadway musical. Research these works, and write an **essay** reporting your findings. Include photographs, illustrations, and other art with your essay.

 Take It to the Net www.phschool.com

Go online for an additional research activity using the Internet.

The Devil and Tom Walkert ◆ 255

ASSESSMENT RESOURCES

The following resources can be used to assess students' knowledge and skills.

Selection Assessment

- 📖 **Formal Assessment,** pp. 67–69
- 📖 **Open Book Test,** pp. 37–39
- 📼 **Got It! Assessment Videotapes,** Tape 2
- 💿 **Test Bank Software**
- **Take It to the Net**
  Visit www.phschool.com for self-tests and additional questions on the selections.

Writing Rubric

- 📖 **Performance Assessment and Portfolio Mgmt.,** p. 15

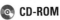 PRENTICE HALL ASSESSMENT *SYSTEM*

- 📖 **Workbook**
- 📖 **Skill Book**
- 📄 **Transparencies**
- 💿 **CD-ROM**

---

❸ Writing Lesson

- Remind students that a story must have a beginning, a middle, and an end. Review the central conflict and message in Irving's story.
- To aid prewriting, have students use the Story Map in **Writing Models and Graphic Organizers on Transparencies,** pp. 17–23, to outline the original story plot.
- Read through the Writing Lesson steps with students and clarify any confusion.
- Urge students to use descriptive detail to set the scene in modern times and to use both direct and indirect characterization to develop their characters.
- Use the Narration rubric in **Performance Assessment and Portfolio Management,** p. 15, to evaluate students' stories.

❹ Research and Technology

- Help students choose a manageable number of works to research. Add poetry and novels to the list of genre choices.
- Encourage students to focus on topic headings before conducting their research. Logical topics might include author background, audience reception, basic story line, story outcome.
- Direct students to outline their essay before writing, using the Outline Transparency in **Writing Models and Graphic Organizers on Transparencies,** p. 95.

CUSTOMIZE INSTRUCTION
For Universal Access

To address different learning styles, use the activities suggested in the **Extension Activities** booklet, p. 13.

For Interpersonal and Visual/Spatial Learners, use Activity 5.

For Musical/Rhythmic Learners, use Activity 6.

For Bodily/Kinesthetic Learners, use Activity 7.

A Psalm of Life ✦ The Tide Rises, the Tide Falls

Lesson Objectives

1. **To analyze and respond to literary elements**
   - Literary Analysis: Stanza Form
   - Comparing Literary Works

2. **To read, comprehend, analyze, and critique two poems**
   - Reading Strategy: Associating Images With Life
   - Reading Check questions
   - Review and Assess questions
   - Assessment Practice (ATE)

3. **To develop word analysis skills, fluency, and systematic vocabulary**
   - Vocabulary Development Lesson: Latin Word Root: -face-

4. **To understand and apply written and oral language conventions**
   - Spelling Strategy
   - Grammar and Style Lesson: Inverted Word Order

5. **To understand and apply appropriate writing and research strategies**
   - Writing Lesson: Analytical Essay
   - Extension Activity: Research Essay

6. **To understand and apply listening and speaking strategies**
   - Extension Activity: Recording

STEP-BY-STEP TEACHING GUIDE	PACING GUIDE
PRETEACH	
Motivate Students and Provide Background	
Use the Motivation activity (ATE p. 256)	5 min.
Read and discuss More author and background features (SE p. 258; ATE p. 256)	5 min.
Introduce the Concepts	
Introduce the Literary Analysis and Reading Strategy (SE/ATE p. 257) Ⓐ	15 min.
Pronounce the vocabulary words and read their definitions (SE p. 257)	5 min.
TEACH	
Monitor Comprehension	
Informally monitor comprehension by circulating while students read independently or in groups Ⓐ	10 min.
Develop vocabulary with Vocabulary notes (SE pp. 258, 259, 260)	as students read as students read
Develop Understanding	
Develop students' understanding of stanza forms with the Literary Analysis annotations (SE p. 258; ATE p. 258) Ⓐ	5 min.
Develop students' ability to associate images with life by using the Reading Strategy annotations (SE p. 259; ATE p. 259)	5 min.
ASSESS	
Assess Mastery	
Assess students' mastery of the Reading Strategy and Literary Analysis by having them answer the Review and Assess questions (SE/ATE p. 261)	15 min.
Use one or more of the print and media Assessment Resources (ATE p. 263) Ⓐ	up to 45 min.
EXTEND	
Apply Understanding	
Have students complete the Vocabulary Development Lesson and the Grammar and Style Lesson (SE p. 262) Ⓐ	20 min.
Apply students' ability to use persuasive tone by using the Writing Lesson (SE/ATE p. 263) Ⓐ	45 min.
Apply students' understanding using one or more of the Extension Activities (SE p. 263)	20–90 min.

Ⓐ ACCELERATED INSTRUCTION:
Use the strategies and activities identified with an Ⓐ.

UNIVERSAL ACCESS
- ● = Below Level Students
- ▲ = On-Level Students
- ■ = Above Level Students

Time and Resource Manager

Reading Level: Average, Easy
Average Number of Instructional Days: 3

	RESOURCES	
PRINT 🖺	**TRANSPARENCIES** 🎒	**TECHNOLOGY** 💿 🎧 📼
• **Beyond Literature,** Cross-Curricular Connection: Science, p. 14 ▲ ■		• **Interest Grabber Video,** Tape 3 ● ▲ ■
• **Selection Support Workbook:** ● ▲ ■ Literary Analysis, p. 66 Reading Strategy, p. 65 Build Vocabulary, p. 63	• **Literary Analysis and Reading Transparencies,** pp. 27 and 28 ● ▲ ■	
• **Adapted Reader's Companion** ● • **Reader's Companion** ●		• **Listening to Literature** ● ▲ ■ Audiocassettes, Side 7 Audio CDs, CD 5
• **English Learner's Companion** ● ▲ • **Literatura en español** ● ▲ • **Literary Analysis for Enrichment** ■		
• **Formal Assessment:** Selection Test, pp. 70–72 ● ▲ ■ • **Open Book Test,** pp. 40–42 ● ▲ ■ • **Performance Assessment and Portfolio Management,** p. 11 ● ▲ ■ • **PRENTICE HALL ASSESSMENT** *SYSTEM* ● ▲ ■	**PRENTICE HALL ASSESSMENT** *SYSTEM* ● ▲ ■ Skills Practice Answers and Explanations on Transparencies	• **Test Bank Software** ● ▲ ■ • **Got It! Assessment Videotapes,** Tape 2 ● ▲
• **Selection Support Workbook:** ● ▲ ■ Grammar and Style, p. 64 • **Writing and Grammar,** Ruby Level ● ▲ ■ • **Extension Activities,** p. 14 ● ▲ ■	• **Daily Language Practice Transparencies** ● ▲ • **Writing Models and Graphic Organizers on Transparencies,** pp. 37–40 ● ▲ ■	• **Writing and Grammar iText CD-ROM** ● ▲ ■ 💻 *Take It to the Net* www.phschool.com

BLOCK SCHEDULING: Use one 90-minute class period to preteach the selection and have students read it. Use a second 90-minute class period to assess students' mastery of skills and have them complete one of the Extension Activities.

Step-by-Step Teaching Guide for pp. 256–257

Motivation

To help set the mood for Longfellow's poetry, ask students to close their eyes and imagine the smell of ocean air and the sound of waves washing across the sand. If possible, play a tape of ocean sounds. Then discuss why authors, poets, artists, and lyricists are so fascinated by the sea. Write "Footprints on the sands of time" on the chalkboard and tell students that they will be reading the poem in which this famous line appears.

▄▄ Interest Grabber Video

As an alternative, play "Henry Wadsworth Longfellow" on Tape 3 to engage student interest.

❶ Background

More About the Author

Longfellow showed his literary promise early. He published his first poem when he was only 13 and entered Bowdoin College at age 15. In a letter written from college to his father, Longfellow declared his wish to spend his life writing.

Longfellow's childhood home in Portland, Maine, was located at the seashore. Perhaps this explains the poet's lifelong knowledge of and interest in the sea. "The Tide Rises, The Tide Falls" is only one of several poems Longfellow wrote about the sea.

Comparing Literary Works

Prepare to Read

❶ A Psalm of Life ◆ The Tide Rises, the Tide Falls

Henry Wadsworth Longfellow (1807–1882)
Henry Wadsworth Longfellow once wrote, "Music is the universal language of mankind—poetry their universal pastime and delight."
During the latter half of the nineteenth century, Longfellow's poetry certainly was a "universal pastime and delight"; his work was translated into two dozen languages and read by millions.

The Teaching Years Longfellow was born and raised in Portland, Maine. He attended Bowdoin College, where one of his classmates was Nathaniel Hawthorne. After graduating in 1825, Longfellow spent three years in Europe before returning to Bowdoin as a professor of modern languages. After five years, he left the college to spend another year in Europe before accepting a position at Harvard University, where he taught for eighteen years.

A Teacher and an Editor Longfellow often wrote and published his own textbooks since no others were available. The translation of foreign literature, especially poetry, was very important to him. For many years, his translations outnumbered his original poems. Although Longfellow began translating to provide material for his college students, it is clear that he also found in the foreign poetry inspirational models for his own work.

Tragedy Strikes Longfellow suffered the tragic deaths of two wives. His first wife, Mary, died in Europe in 1835 from an infection following a miscarriage. Eight years later, after a long courtship, Longfellow married Frances Appleton of Boston. Their happy marriage ended tragically when Frances was fatally burned in a household accident. Longfellow's attempts to beat out the flames left him badly burned. The resulting scars prevented him from shaving, and he grew the long, flowing beard so familiar to generations of his readers.

Poet to the People Longfellow enjoyed a long and successful career as a poet, publishing his first collection of poems, *Voices in the Night*, in 1839. By writing poetry that soothed and encouraged readers, Longfellow became the first American poet to reach a wide audience and create a national interest in poetry. His popular anthology *The Poets and Poetry of Europe*, published in 1845, accomplished his goal of bringing non-English poetry to the ordinary American reader.

Longfellow experimented with adapting traditional European verse forms and themes to uniquely American subjects. Many of his narrative poems, such as *Evangeline* (1847), *The Song of Hiawatha* (1855), *The Courtship of Miles Standish* (1858), and "Paul Revere's Ride" (1860), gave a romanticized view of America's early history and democratic ideals.

Longfellow's Legacy Longfellow's poetry has been criticized for being overly optimistic and sentimental. Yet it was his optimism and sentimentality that made Longfellow the most popular poet of his time. He became known as one of the "Fireside Poets." Families gathered around the fireplace would spend evenings reading and discussing their favorite poems by Longfellow, just as many of today's families are likely to gather around the television set to watch a favorite program.

Longfellow was so popular in his time that his seventy-fifth birthday was celebrated as if it were a national holiday. Indeed, the last years of Longfellow's life were filled with honors, both in the United States and abroad. He was given honorary degrees at Oxford and Cambridge, and invited to audiences with royalty. "Of all the suns of the New England morning," wrote the literary historian Van Wyck Brooks after the poet's death, "he was the largest in his golden sweetness."

256 ◆ *A Growing Nation (1800–1870)*

TEACHING RESOURCES

The following resources can be used to enrich or extend the instruction for pp. 256–257.

Motivation
▄▄ **Interest Grabber Video**, Tape 3 ▪

Background
📖 **Beyond Literature**, p. 14

🖥 *Take It to the Net*
Visit www.phschool.com for Background and hotlinks for the selections.

Literary Analysis
📖 **Literary Analysis and Reading Transparencies,** Stanza Form, p. 28 ▪

Reading
📖 **Literary Analysis and Reading Transparencies,** Associating Images With Life, p. 27
📖 **Selection Support Workbook:** Reading Strategy, p. 65; Build Vocabulary, p. 63

▪ **BLOCK SCHEDULING:** Resources marked with this symbol provide varied instruction during 90-minute blocks.

Preview

Connecting to the Literature

In each stage of our lives, we leave marks by which others remember us: breaking a school basketball record, performing acts of charity, or even establishing close friendships. In these poems, Longfellow explores the passage of time and the human desire to leave a mark on the world.

❷ Literary Analysis

Stanza Form

Longfellow wrote his poems in **stanzas**—units of two or more lines arranged in patterns of rhythm (or meter) and rhyme. Like a paragraph, each stanza develops a single main idea. Unlike paragraphs, however, stanzas are often a fixed length and share the same rhythm. Stanzas are named according to the number of lines they contain.

- A two-line stanza is a **couplet.**
- A four-line stanza is a **quatrain.**
- A five-line stanza is a **cinquain.**

Note which stanza form Longfellow uses in each poem.

Comparing Literary Works

In these poems, Longfellow reflects on two different periods of his life. "A Psalm of Life" was written when he was thirty-one years old, after the tragic death of his wife and child. In contrast, "The Tide Rises, The Tide Falls" was written nearly forty years later, when Longfellow was in his seventies. By this time, he had endured many hardships and learned many of life's lessons. As you read, compare the two poems and look for the prevailing **mood** and sentiment in each of them to see how they represent a difference of forty years.

❸ Reading Strategy

Associating Images With Life

Poets often use images that take on greater significance when we consider them as symbols of the journey of life. To **associate images with life,** think about what each image means in a broader context. For example, when Longfellow describes the end of the day with "The twilight darkens, the curlew calls," he may also be describing the end of a life. Use a chart like the one shown to help you interpret images in these poems.

Vocabulary Development

bivouac (biv′ wak) *n.* temporary encampment (p. 259)

sublime (sə blīm′) *adj.* noble; inspiring (p. 259)

efface (ə fās′) *v.* erase; wipe out (p. 260)

Poetic Image

Twilight darkens

Broader Meaning

Life itself will soon come to an end.

A Psalm of Life / The Tide Rises, The Tide Falls ◆ 257

CUSTOMIZE INSTRUCTION FOR UNIVERSAL ACCESS

For Special Needs Students	For Less Proficient Readers	For English Learners
Have students read the adapted version of "A Psalm of Life" in the Adapted Reader's Companion. These versions provide basic level instruction in an interactive format with questions and write-on lines. Completing the adapted versions will prepare students to read the selections in the Student Edition.	Have students read Longfellow's poem in the Reader's Companion. This version provides basic level instruction in an interactive format with questions and write-on lines. After students finish the selection in Reader's Companion, have them complete the questions and activities in the Student Edition.	Have students read the adapted version of the poem in the English Learner's Companion. This version provides basic level instruction in an interactive format with questions and write-on lines. Completing the adapted version will prepare students to read the selection in the Student Edition.

❷ Literary Analysis

Stanza Form

- Read aloud the literary analysis instruction. Stress the analogy between a stanza and a paragraph, encouraging students to read stanzas for their central idea. Review and confirm understanding of the stanza types.

- Use the instruction for **Comparing Literary Works** to prepare students for reading two very different Longfellow poems.

- Demonstrate how to analyze stanza form. The Stanza Form transparency in **Literary Analysis and Reading Transparencies,** p. 28 provides examples.

❸ Reading Strategy

Associating Images With Life

- Remind students that associating images with life can help them understand a poet's views about the human experience.

- Explain to students that this strategy is not necessarily the same as connecting what they read with their own lives. Here, they will explore the broader meanings of poetic images as they relate to human existence.

- To help students respond to Longfellow's images, tell them to jot down notes of their first associations with an image. By exploring these notes, students can develop links between the image and a broader meaning. Use the chart on the student page as an example of this technique.

- Direct students to use their own diagrams to continue this process as they read Longfellow's poetry.

Vocabulary Development

- Pronounce each vocabulary word for students, and read the definitions as a class. Have students identify any words with which they are familiar.

 E-Teach

Visit E-Teach at www.phschool.com for teachers' essays on how to teach, with questions and answers.

257

Step-by-Step Teaching Guide for pp. 258–260

CUSTOMIZE INSTRUCTION
For Verbal/Linguistic Learners

Play the **Listening to Literature Audiocassettes** (Side 7)/**Audio CDs** (CD 5) for students. Have students listen carefully to the cadence and rhythm of the two poems. In particular talk with students about the refrain in "The Tide Rises, The Tide Falls." Ask how the refrain emphasizes Longfellow's main points.

❶ About the Selections

Longfellow wrote "A Psalm of Life" after he had finally recovered from the death of his first wife. In it, he urges readers to accept the idea that, despite grief, sorrow, and death, they should live enthusiastically, take action to make a mark on the world, and realize that strength and comfort come from the pursuit of an active, productive life.

The mysterious sea, with its endless cycle of tides, is the setting for "The Tide Rises, The Tide Falls," which suggests or implies the idea that, though a person may die, life continues. The recurring pauses, frequent repetition of words, and refrain combine with strong metrical rhythm to create a rising and falling rhythm, like the breaking of waves on the shore.

❷ Literary Analysis

Stanza Form

- To distinguish among the different stanza forms, students can use their knowledge of root words and prefixes: a *couplet* has a "couple" of lines, a *quatrain* has four lines (from the French word for four, *quatre*), and a *cinquain* has five lines (from the French word for five, *cinque*).

- Read aloud the first stanza of the poem. Point out that the remaining stanzas reflect the same stanza form as does this first paragraph.

- Give students the Literary Analysis instruction on p. 258: Identify the stanza form used in this poem. **Answer:** The poem's stanza form is the quatrain.

---

❶ A Psalm of Life

Henry Wadsworth Longfellow

Background

Longfellow wrote "A Psalm of Life" in 1838 after suffering through the tragic death of his first wife, Mary, coupled with the loss of the baby they were happily expecting. Longfellow intended the poem as an inspiration to himself and others to overcome the misfortunes of the past and to live productively in the present. In contrast, "The Tide Rises, The Tide Falls" was penned when Longfellow was in his early seventies. That poem reveals the poet's acceptance of the inevitability of death.

> Tell me not, in mournful numbers,[1]
>   Life is but an empty dream!—
> For the soul is dead that slumbers,
>   And things are not what they seem.
>
> 5 Life is real! Life is earnest!
>   And the grave is not its goal:
> Dust thou art, to dust returnest,
>   Was not spoken of the soul.
>
> Not enjoyment, and not sorrow,
> 10   Is our destined end or way;
> But to act, that each tomorrow
>   Find us farther than today.
>
> Art is long, and Time is fleeting,
>   And our hearts, though stout and brave,
> 15 Still, like muffled drums, are beating
>   Funeral marches to the grave.

1. **numbers** verses.

Literary Analysis
Stanza Form Identify the stanza form used in this poem.

TEACHING RESOURCES

The following resources can be used to enrich or extend the instruction for pp. 258–260.

Literary Analysis

📖 **Writing Models and Graphic Organizers on Transparencies,** pp. 37–40

📖 **Selection Support:** Literary Analysis, p. 66

Reading

📖 **Adapted Reader's Companion**

📖 **English Learner's Companion**

🎧 **Listening to Literature Audiocassettes,** Side 7 ▪

💿 **Listening to Literature Audio CDs,** CD 5 ▪

▪ **BLOCK SCHEDULING:** Resources marked with this symbol provide varied instruction during 90-minute blocks.

In the world's broad field of battle,
    In the <u>bivouac</u> of Life,
Be not like dumb, driven cattle!
20   Be a hero in the strife!

Trust no Future, howe'er pleasant!
    Let the dead Past bury its dead!
Act—act in the living Present!
    Heart within, and God o'erhead!

25 Lives of great men all remind us
    We can make our lives <u>sublime</u>,
❸ And, departing, leave behind us
    Footprints on the sands of time;

Footprints, that perhaps another,
30   Sailing o'er life's solemn main,[2]
A forlorn and shipwrecked brother,
    Seeing, shall take heart again.

Let us, then, be up and doing,
    With a heart for any fate;
35 Still achieving, still pursuing,
    Learn to labor and to wait.

---

2. main open sea.

bivouac (biv´ wak´) *n.* temporary encampment

sublime (sə blīm´) *adj.* noble; inspiring

Reading Strategy
Associating Images With Life What does the poet mean by encouraging people to "leave behind us / Footprints in the sands of time"?

Review and Assess

Thinking About the Selection

1. **Respond:** What "footprints" would you like to leave "on the sands of time"?
2. **(a) Recall:** What attitude or idea does the speaker challenge in the first two stanzas? **(b) Evaluate:** Is the attitude the poet expresses positive or negative?
3. **(a) Recall:** In the third stanza, what does the speaker warn against? **(b) Interpret:** What is the speaker's attitude concerning individuality and self-reliance?
4. **(a) Recall:** According to the poem, how can our lives influence future generations? **(b) Interpret:** What is the poet calling readers to do?
5. **(a) Draw Conclusions:** Summarize the speaker's view of life. **(b) Evaluate:** What is the message of this poem? Do you agree with the poet's ideas?

A Psalm of Life ◆ 259

---

❸ Reading Strategy
Associating Images With Life

- Invite a volunteer to read aloud the bracketed lines on p. 259. Discuss possible paraphrases.
  Possible response: After death, our influence or presence in the world may still be felt.

- Ask students the Reading Strategy question on p. 259: What does the poet mean by encouraging readers to "leave behind us/Footprints in the sands of time"?
  Possible response: He means that people should seek accomplishments that will leave lasting impressions on the world even after their death.

Answers for p. 259

Review and Assess

1. Students should cite the personal goals they hope to achieve.
2. **(a)** He challenges the idea that life is a meaningless and empty journey toward the grave. **(b)** It is finally positive.
3. **(a)** He warns against focusing on the emotions of the moment. **(b)** He suggests that it is important to be an individual, not a passive member of the herd.
4. **(a)** We can live in such a way that our personal achievements inspire others. **(b)** Work hard so that they make a mark future generations will recall.
5. **(a)** Life is real and best lived in the here and now. We have an obligation to make something of our lives, both for ourselves and for those who come after us. **(b)** Possible response: Life is a profound and real challenge, not a wispy, meaningless dream. We are obliged to find a way to be equal to that challenge through achievements that will inspire others.

CUSTOMIZE INSTRUCTION FOR UNIVERSAL ACCESS

For Special Needs Students	For English Language Learners	For Gifted/Talented Students
Provide visual images to help students gain insight into Longfellow's poems, such as footprints in the sand or waves breaking on the beach. Clarify for students that the poet uses the image of footprints in the sand to suggest different things in the two poems; first, a lasting record, then a fleeting impression.	Longfellow's shorter poems have long been favorites for memorization. Reciting them can provide good public speaking practice. Encourage students to recite "The Tide Rises, The Tide Falls" aloud. Students working in pairs or small groups can deliver the poem in unison or antiphonally.	Have students listen to the beat of "The Tide Rises, The Tide Falls" as you read it aloud. Then challenge them to create a piece of music, choreograph a dance, or develop a piece of visual art to accompany the poem.

Review and Assess

1. Possible response: It evoked images of waves breaking on the beach.

2. **(a)** The tide rises and falls; evening brings darkness; a night bird calls; a traveler approaches a town. **(b)** Possible response: The darkening of the sky and sound of the night suggest the ending of a life. **(c)** Darkness has settled, and the waves have erased the traveler's footprints.

3. **(a)** "And the tide rises, the tide falls" is repeated. **(b)** Mirroring the repeated motion of the tide reminds the reader of the never-ending cycle of life on earth.

4. **(a)** Possible responses: The day returns, but the traveler does not. **(b)** Humans come and go, but the rhythms of nature endure. Humans are mortal; nature is eternal.

5. **(a)** Possible response: Longfellow seems to view the life and death of a single human being as a small part of a vast, timeless cycle of nature. In this poem, Longfellow evokes the relative insignificance of a single human life against the background of the long, slow turning of time and tide.

❶

The Tide Rises, The Tide Falls

Henry Wadsworth Longfellow

The tide rises, the tide falls.
The twilight darkens, the curlew[1] calls;
Along the sea sands damp and brown
The traveler hastens toward the town,
5   And the tide rises, the tide falls.

Darkness settles on roofs and walls,
But the sea, the sea in the darkness calls:
The little waves, with their soft, white hands,
<u>Efface</u> the footprints in the sands,
10   And the tide rises, the tide falls.

The morning breaks; the steeds in their stalls
Stamp and neigh, as the hostler[2] calls:
The day returns, but nevermore
Returns the traveler to the shore,
15   And the tide rises, the tide falls.

efface (ə fās´) v. erase; wipe out

---

1. **curlew** (kur´ lōō´) n. large wading bird associated with the evening.
2. **hostler** (häs´ lər) n. person who tends horses at an inn or stable.

Review and Assess

Thinking About the Selection

1. **Respond:** What images did this poem evoke for you?
2. **(a) Recall:** Which events occur in the first stanza? **(b) Interpret:** Which details suggest that the traveler is nearing death? **(c) Support:** Which details suggest that he has died?
3. **(a) Recall:** Which line does the speaker repeat throughout the poem? **(b) Evaluate:** What effect does this repetition have on the message of the poem?
4. **(a) Contrast:** In the third stanza, what is the difference between the traveler and the day? **(b) Draw Conclusions:** What does the poem suggest about humanity and nature?
5. **Evaluate:** What do you think Longfellow's outlook on life and death was when he wrote this poem? Explain.

✒ ASSESSMENT PRACTICE: Reading Comprehension

Make Inferences and Generalizations	(For more practice, see Test Preparation Workbook, p. 16.)

A generalization is a broad statement based on a series of observations. Use this sample item to give students practice.

Which of the following best describes the mood of "A Psalm of Life"?

A pessimistic
B inspirational
C hopeless
D ironic

Choices *A* and *C* are incorrect, because the poem celebrates hope and strength in the face of adversity. The poem supports seeing the future clearly and matter-of-factly, so *D* is incorrect. *B* is the correct choice.

Review and Assess

Literary Analysis

Stanza Forms

1. Describe the **stanza form** of (a) "A Psalm of Life" and (b) "The Tide Rises, The Tide Falls."

2. With only one exception, every stanza in "A Psalm of Life" develops a separate idea and can stand alone. Which stanza is dependent on the one before for its meaning?

3. How does the stanza form in "The Tide Rises, The Tide Falls" allow Longfellow to emphasize the repetition of nature's cycles?

Comparing Literary Works

4. (a) Describe the overall **mood** in "A Psalm of Life." (b) Describe the mood in "The Tide Rises, The Tide Falls."

5. In what ways, if any, does Longfellow's attitude toward life change between the first poem and the one he wrote forty years later?

6. In what ways do the images in each poem and the moods they evoke connect with the circumstances of Longfellow's life? Explain.

Reading Strategy

Associating Images With Life

7. Identify three **images** in these poems that suggest a broader meaning about the journey of life.

8. How do the images contribute to the overall meaning of each poem? Using a chart like the one shown, select five images and explain how they relate to life.

Image	How It Relates to Life
1. Footprints on the sands of time	

Extend Understanding

9. **Philosophy Connection:** What are the similarities and differences in the philosophies of life expressed in both poems?

A Psalm of Life / The Tide Rises, The Tide Falls ◆ 261

Quick Review

A **stanza** is a unit of two or more lines arranged in a pattern of rhythm (or meter) and rhyme.

The **mood** is the overall tone or feeling evoked from a literary work.

To **associate images with life,** discover a deeper meaning by thinking about the image in the broader context of life.

 Take It to the Net
www.phschool.com

Take the interactive self-test online to check your understanding of these selections.

ENRICHMENT: Further Reading

Other Works by Henry Wadsworth Longfellow

"The Song of Hiawatha"
"The Courtship of Miles Standish"
"Evangeline"

 Take It to the Net
Visit www.phschool.com for more information on Henry Wadsworth Longfellow.

Answers for p. 261

Review and Assess

1. (a) "A Psalm of Life" contains quatrains: line 1 and 3, and lines 2 and 4 of each stanza rhyme. (b) "The Tides Rises, The Tide Falls" contains cinquains: lines 1, 2, and 5, and lines 3 and 4 of each stanza rhyme.

2. The eighth stanza ("Footprints, that perhaps another . . .) can be understood only when read in conjunction with the seventh stanza, which introduces the footprints described in stanza eight.

3. The use of the cinquain allows Longfellow to include the line "And the tide rises, the tide falls" in each stanza.

4. Possible responses: (a) inspirational (b) accepting

5. Possible response: He is somewhat more accepting of life's brevity and perhaps insignificance in the later poem than he is in the earlier work.

6. Possible response: The first poem might refer to his struggle to accept his first wife's death and to turn his efforts away from grieving and toward living. The second poem might reflect the acceptance and wisdom Longfellow had acquired at the end of a long life.

7. Possible responses: footprints on the sands of time; the sea in the darkness calls; nevermore returns the traveler to the shore.

8. Sample response: Image: footprints on the sands of time; How It Relates to Life: Each person leaves his or her mark on the world.

9. Possible response: "Psalm of Life" seems to reflect the philosophy of a man in the prime of life who is actively striving to make his mark on the world; "The Tide Rises, the Tide Falls" seems to reflect a much older man's sober reflections on the powerlessness and brevity of a single human life in the context of the larger natural world.

Answer for p. 262

❶ Vocabulary Development

Word Analysis

1. b
2. e
3. a
4. c
5. d

Concept Development: Analogies

1. efface
2. bivouac
3. sublime

Spelling Strategy

1. psaltery
2. pseudonym
3. psychology

❷ Grammar and Style

1. complement-verb-subject
2. Using the phrases *not enjoyment* and *not sorrow* rather than "Neither enjoyment nor sorrow" gives the line greater emphasis.
3. Our destined end or way is not enjoyment and is not sorrow.
4. The rhythm is completely different from, and is no longer consistent with, the rest of the poem.
5. The image is a three-way fork in the road.

Writing Application

Stanzas should be written in poetic format and should include at least two examples of inverted word order. They should also be free of major grammatical and mechanical errors.

Integrate Language Skills

❶ Vocabulary Development Lesson

Word Analysis: Latin Root -face-

The root *-face-* means "appearance or outward aspect." To *efface* a footprint is to remove any trace of its presence. Use your knowledge of the meaning of the root *-face-* to match each word with its definition. Then, use a dictionary to check your answers.

1. facade   **a.** to ruin the appearance of
2. interface   **b.** the front of a building
3. deface   **c.** the exterior of an object
4. surface   **d.** to precede or come before
5. preface   **e.** to come in contact with

Concept Development: Analogies

Complete each analogy with a word from the vocabulary list on page 257. Write your answers on a separate sheet of paper.

1. *Raise* is to *lower* as *inscribe* is to ___?___.
2. *Hut* is to *shack* as *campsite* is to ___?___.
3. *Aggravated* is to *calm* as *humble* is to ___?___.

Spelling Strategy

Several English words that come from Greek roots begin with a silent *p* before the *s*, as in *psalm* or *psychiatrist*. It is best simply to memorize these spellings. Complete each of the following words.

1. A __altery is a flat, stringed instrument.
2. A false or fictitious name is a __eudonym.
3. __ychology is the science of the mind.

❷ Grammar and Style Lesson

Inverted Word Order

To achieve a rhyme or maintain a rhythm, poets may **invert** the normal English word order of subject-verb-complement. Longfellow sometimes used inverted word order for effect, as in this example from "The Tide Rises, The Tide Falls":

> **Example:** ". . . nevermore / Returns the traveler to the shore."

Longfellow places the verb, *returns*, before the subject, *the traveler*, which is an inversion of typical subject-verb order.

You can also invert the structure of a prose sentence to emphasize a particular word or idea.

Looking at Style Answer these questions about lines 9 and 10 of "A Psalm of Life."

> Not enjoyment, and not sorrow,
> Is our destined end or way

1. What word order is shown in these lines?
2. What effect does the word order have on the meaning of the lines? Explain.
3. Rewrite the lines in conventional order.
4. What do you notice about the rhythm of the new lines when read aloud?
5. What imagery does the new order create?

Writing Application Using inverted word order, write a stanza describing how you would like to leave your mark on the world.

W͜G *Prentice Hall Writing and Grammar Connection: Chapter 20, Section 3*

TEACHING RESOURCES

The following resources can be used to enrich or extend the instruction for pp. 262–263.

Vocabulary

📖 **Selection Support Workbook:** Build Vocabulary, p. 63

📖 **Vocabulary and Spelling Practice Book** (Use this booklet for skills enrichment.) ▪

Grammar

📖 **Selection Support Workbook:** Grammar and Style, p. 64

W͜G **Writing and Grammar,** Ruby Level, p. 490

💿 **Daily Language Practice Transparencies** ▪

Writing

W͜G **Writing and Grammar,** Ruby Level, p. 177

💿 **Writing and Grammar iText CD-ROM**

📀 **Writing Models and Graphic Organizers on Transparencies,** p. 37–40

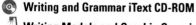

▪ **BLOCK SCHEDULING:** Resources marked with this symbol provide varied instruction during 90-minute blocks.

❸ Writing Lesson

Analytical Essay

A German proverb says: "Look not mournfully into the Past. It comes not back again. Wisely improve the Present. It is thine. Go forth to meet the shadowy Future, without fear, and with a manly heart." Write an essay that explains whether "A Psalm of Life" reflects these sentiments, comparing the poem to the proverb.

Prewriting   Reread the poem and the proverb, looking for similar symbols, imagery, or messages. Use a chart like the one shown to note words, lines, and stanzas you will compare, with the poem on one side and the proverb on the other.

Model: Gathering Details

A Psalm of Life	German Proverb
The soul is dead that slumbers Be a hero in the strife	Go forth to meet the shadowy Future . . . without fear and with a manly heart

Drafting   Organize your comparison, analyzing each section of the poem against the relevant portion of the proverb. Consider including paraphrases of both to ensure readers' understanding. Quote accurately to make logical comparisons.

Revising   Review your essay and make sure you have presented your ideas convincingly. Review your conclusion to determine whether you have made a strong connection between the poem and the proverb.

𝒲𝒢 *Prentice Hall Writing and Grammar Connection: Chapter 9, Section 3*

❹ Extension Activities

Listening and Speaking Play a **recording** of ocean sounds for the class. Discuss the ideas and emotions you associate with the sea. Consider the following questions:

- What images do crashing waves convey?
- What do you associate with the ocean?
- Does the recording enhance the poem?

Follow by having classmates discuss why Longfellow selected ocean imagery to communicate his ideas. [**Group Activity**]

Research and Technology Use library resources and the Internet to gather information about Henry Wadsworth Longfellow, and his life, family and children. Write a **research essay,** comparing the circumstances of his life to his writing to see whether there is a relationship between the two. Present your essay to the class.

 Take It to the Net   www.phschool.com

Go online for an additional research activity using the Internet.

Lesson Support for p. 263

❸ Writing Lesson

- Review the German proverb with students, asking them to paraphrase its meaning.
- Remind students of the Reading Strategy and encourage them to use it in searching for appropriate imagery.
- Tell students to use comparison transition words such as *also, similarly,* and *like* to link their ideas.

❹ Research and Technology

- Encourage students to read additional works by Longfellow in order to broaden their basis for comparison. Refer them to the works listed on TE p. 261.
- Suggest that students choose a few poems on which to focus and try to date the writing of these poems. Then students can read biographical information in search of pertinent facts.

CUSTOMIZE INSTRUCTION
For Universal Access

To address different learning styles, use the activities suggested in the **Extension Activities** booklet, p. 14.

For Intrapersonal Learners, use Activity 5.

For Visual/Spatial and Interpersonal Learners, use Activity 6.

For Musical/Rhythmic Learners, use Activity 7.

ASSESSMENT RESOURCES

The following resources can be used to assess students' knowledge and skills.

Selection Assessment

- 📖 **Formal Assessment,** pp. 70–72
- 📖 **Open Book Test,** pp. 40–42
- 📼 **Got It! Assessment Videotapes,** Tape 2
- 💿 **Test Bank Software**

- 💻 **Take It to the Net**
  Visit www.phschool.com for self-tests and additional questions on the selections.

PRENTICE HALL ASSESSMENT SYSTEM

- 📖 **Workbook**
- 📖 **Skill Book**
- 📄 **Transparencies**
- 💿 **CD-ROM**

Thanatopsis ✦ Old Ironsides ✦ The First Snowfall
from Snowbound

Lesson Objectives

1. **To analyze and respond to literary elements**
   - Literary Analysis: Meter
   - Comparing Literary Works

2. **To read, comprehend, analyze, and critique four poems**
   - Reading Strategy: Summarizing
   - Reading Check questions
   - Review and Assess questions
   - Assessment Practice (ATE)

3. **To develop word analysis skills, fluency, and systematic vocabulary**
   - Vocabulary Development Lesson: Latin Word root: *-patr-*

4. **To understand and apply written and oral language conventions**
   - Spelling Strategy
   - Grammar and Style Lesson: Participles as Adjectives

5. **To understand and apply appropriate writing and research strategies**
   - Writing Lesson: Précis
   - Extension Activity: Oral Presentation

6. **To understand and apply listening and speaking strategies**
   - Extension Activity: Dramatic Reading

STEP-BY-STEP TEACHING GUIDE	PACING GUIDE
PRETEACH	
Motivate Students and Provide Background	
Use the Motivation activity (ATE p. 264)	5 min.
Read and discuss author and background features (SE/ATE p. 264 and 265) Ⓐ	5 min.
Introduce the Concepts	
Introduce the Literary Analysis and Reading Strategy (SE/ATE p. 266) Ⓐ	15 min.
Pronounce the vocabulary words and read their definitions (SE p. 266)	5 min.
TEACH	
Monitor Comprehension	
Informally monitor comprehension by circulating while students read independently or in groups Ⓐ	50 min.
Monitor students' comprehension with the Reading Check notes (SE/ATE pp. 267, 275, 277, 279)	as students read
Develop vocabulary with Vocabulary notes (SE pp. 268, 272, 275, 276, 278; ATE p. 278)	as students read
Develop Understanding	
Develop students' understanding of meter with the Literary Analysis annotations (SE pp. 268, 271, 272, 273, 276, 277, 279; ATE pp. 268, 271, 272, 273, 275, 276, 277, 279, 280) Ⓐ	5 min.
Develop students' ability to summarize with the Reading Strategy annotations (SE pp. 268, 269, 271, 277, 278, 279; ATE pp. 268, 269, 270, 277, 278, 279)	5 min.
ASSESS	
Assess Mastery	
Assess students' mastery of the Reading Strategy and Literary Analysis by having them answer the Review and Assess questions (SE/ATE p. 281)	15 min.
Use one or more of the print and media Assessment Resources (ATE p. 283) Ⓐ	up to 45 min.
EXTEND	
Apply Understanding	
Have students complete the Vocabulary Development Lesson and the Grammar and Style Lesson (SE p. 282) Ⓐ	20 min.
Apply students' ability to use a clear beginning, middle, and end in their writing by using the Writing Lesson (SE/ATE p. 283) Ⓐ	45 min.
Apply students' understanding using one or more of the Extension Activities (SE p. 283)	20–90 min.

Ⓐ **ACCELERATED INSTRUCTION:**
Use the strategies and activities identified with an Ⓐ.

UNIVERSAL ACCESS
● = Below Level Students
▲ = On-Level Students
■ = Above Level Students

Time and Resource Manager

Reading Level: Challenging, Average, Easy, Average
Average Number of Instructional Days: 5

RESOURCES		
PRINT 📖	**TRANSPARENCIES** 🗄	**TECHNOLOGY** 💿 🎧 📼
• **Beyond Literature,** Humanities Connection: Fine Art, p. 15 ▲ ■		• **Interest Grabber Video,** Tape 3 ● ▲ ■
• **Selection Support Workbook:** ● ▲ ■ Literary Analysis, p. 70 Reading Strategy, p. 69 Build Vocabulary, p. 67	• **Literary Analysis and Reading Transparencies,** pp. 29 and 30 ● ▲ ■	
		• **Listening to Literature** ● ▲ ■ Audiocassettes, Sides 7–8 Audio CDs, CD 5
• **Literatura en español** ● ▲ • **Literary Analysis for Enrichment** ■		
• **Formal Assessment:** Selection Test, pp. 73–75 ● ▲ ■ • **Open Book Test,** pp. 43–45 ● ▲ ■ • (ASSESSMENT *SYSTEM*) ● ▲ ■	• (PRENTICE HALL ASSESSMENT *SYSTEM*) ● ▲ ■ Skills Practice Answers and Explanations on Transparencies	• **Test Bank Software** ● ▲ ■ • **Got It! Assessment Videotapes,** Tape 2 ● ▲
• **Selection Support Workbook:** ● ▲ ■ Grammar and Style, p. 68 • **Writing and Grammar,** Ruby Level ● ▲ ■ • **Extension Activities,** p. 15 ● ▲ ■	• **Daily Language Practice Transparencies** ● ▲ • **Writing Models and Graphic Organizers on Transparencies,** p. 67 ● ▲ ■	• **Writing and Grammar iText CD-ROM** ● ▲ ■ 🖥 *Take It to the Net* www.phschool.com

▪ **BLOCK SCHEDULING:** Use one 90-minute class period to preteach the selection and have students read it. Use a second 90-minute class period to assess students' mastery of skills and have them complete one of the Extension Activities.

Step-by-Step Teaching Guide for pp. 264–275

Motivation

Have some students bring to class a recording of or lyrics to a contemporary song that has special meaning to them. Ask volunteers to share their songs. Discuss how some musical artists give voice to the concerns and ideals of an entire generation of listeners. To which musical artists do students feel such a connection? Explain to students that the poets whose work they are about to read popularized poetry as a family entertainment long before families could turn to CDs, radio, television, movies, or other technological diversions. They expressed the values, emotions, and concerns of those who lived in earlier eras.

▣ Interest Grabber Video

As an alternative, play "Old Ironsides: Reading and Student Response" on Tape 3 to engage student interest.

❶ Background

More About the Authors

William Cullen Bryant helped to establish an American literary tradition by producing poems that were a match for the work of the best European poets of his day. Perhaps his early lessons in Greek and Latin, taught by his country doctor father, gave him added linguistic dexterity. Certainly his father helped launch Bryant's career by submitting "Thanatopsis" and another poem to a Boston magazine. Shocked that an American could draft such compelling verse, the magazine nonetheless published Bryant's poem in its first version—minus some of the introductory lines and the final stanza.

Prepare to Read

❶ Thanatopsis ◆ Old Ironsides ◆ The First Snowfall ◆ *from* Snowbound

William Cullen Bryant (1794–1878)

As a journalist and political activist, William Cullen Bryant fought to ensure that industrialization did not obscure America's democratic values. Bryant began writing poetry at the age of nine and drafted the first version of "Thanatopsis," his most famous poem, when he was only nineteen. To support himself, Bryant practiced law for ten years while continuing to write poetry in his spare time. In 1825, he moved to New York City and became a journalist; by 1829, he had become editor-in-chief and part owner of the New York newspaper the *Evening Post*.

Voice for Justice Bryant used his position as an influential journalist to defend human rights and personal freedoms. He was an outspoken advocate of women's rights and a passionate foe of slavery. Bryant was the first American poet to win worldwide critical acclaim, and his work helped establish the Romantic Movement in America.

Oliver Wendell Holmes (1809–1894)

Oliver Wendell Holmes made important contributions to both literature and medicine. A descendant of seventeenth-century poet Anne Bradstreet (p. 98), he briefly studied law and then moved on to study medicine. Holmes completed a medical degree at Harvard University in 1836, the same year his first collection of poetry, *Poems*, was published.

Holmes enjoyed a long teaching career at Harvard, becoming a leading medical researcher and continuing his literary pursuits. Along with James Russell Lowell, Holmes founded *The Atlantic Monthly*. His love of exaggeration, colorful expressions, and quotable statements made his essays popular with readers.

In 1830, Holmes wrote "Old Ironsides" to protest the planned destruction of the battleship *Constitution*, nicknamed "Old Ironsides" for its ability to withstand British attacks during the War of 1812. The poem saved the ship and earned Holmes national recognition as a poet.

James Russell Lowell (1819–1891)

James Russell Lowell may have been the most talented of the Fireside Poets. However, his literary career was disrupted by personal tragedies, including the deaths of three of his four children. Following the death of his wife in 1853, he lost much of his focus and was never able to match his earlier work, but he still made important literary contributions as a poet, editor, and critic.

Lowell published his first book of poetry, *A Year's Life*, in 1841. His literary career reached its peak in 1848 with the publication of three highly successful works—*A Fable for Critics*, *The Bigelow Papers*, and *The Vision of Sir Launfal*—that gained him international fame.

Later in his life, Lowell pursued other interests. He wrote editorials supporting the abolition of slavery. He succeeded Longfellow as professor of languages at Harvard, and he helped found *The Atlantic Monthly*, serving as its first editor.

264 ◆ A Growing Nation (1800–1870)

TEACHING RESOURCES

The following resources can be used to enrich or extend the instruction for pp. 264–265.

Motivation

▣ **Interest Grabber Video**, Tape 3 ▣

Background

▢ **Beyond Literature**, p. 15

 Take It to the Net
Visit www.phschool.com for background and hotlinks for the selections.

Literary Analysis

▨ **Literary Analysis and Reading Transparencies**, Meter, p. 30 ▣

▢ **Selection Support Workbook:** Literary Analysis, p. 70

Reading

▨ **Literary Analysis and Reading Transparencies**, Summarizing, p. 29 ▣

▣ **BLOCK SCHEDULING:** Resources marked with this symbol provide varied instruction during 90-minute blocks.

John Greenleaf Whittier (1807–1892)

John Greenleaf Whittier was born in poverty. As a child, he worked on his family's debt-ridden farm near Haverhill, Massachusetts and received virtually no formal education. As a Quaker, Whittier believed in hard work, simplicity, pacifism, religious devotion, and social justice.

Whittier was more deeply involved in the social issues of his day than were his fellow poets.

He was elected to the Massachusetts State Legislature in 1835. For twenty-five years, he worked diligently for the abolition of slavery. Because of his devotion to the abolitionist cause, he did not gain national prominence until after the Civil War. When the Civil War ended, Whittier focused on writing poetry, earning national fame with the 1866 publication of *Snowbound*, which depicts the simple warmth of rural New England life. In the poem, Whittier remembers with fondness the life he spent as a boy in his family's farmhouse. As the way of life captured in Whittier's poetry disappeared, the popularity of his poems grew.

Background

Until the third decade of the nineteenth century, America had little real literature to call its own. The Fireside Poets—Henry Wadsworth Longfellow, Oliver Wendell Holmes, James Russell Lowell, and John Greenleaf Whittier—represented a literary coming of age for the young country. This first generation of acclaimed American poets took their name from the popularity of their works, which were widely read both as fireside family entertainment and in the schoolroom, where generations of children memorized them.

The four poets—all New England born and bred—chose uniquely American settings and subjects. Their themes, meter, and imagery, however, borrowed heavily from the English tradition. Though their reliance on conservative literary styles prevented them from being truly innovative, the Fireside Poets were literary giants of their day. In their own time, and for decades afterward, they ranked as America's most read and best-loved poets.

The Four Seasons of Life, Currier & Ives

Thanatopsis / Old Ironsides / The First Snowfall / from Snowbound ◆ 265

Although nationally recognized for his poetry, Oliver Wendell Holmes took greater pride in his medical achievements. In particular, his ideas about improving medical practices in childbirth—doctors began to wash their hands and wear sterile clothing to deliver babies—saved many lives. Holmes's medical students loved him as much as did the readers of his poetry. As a result, he always taught his classes at times when students would be most tired—Holmes's witty style kept them interested!

Few of James Russell Lowell's works remain well read today, although in his own time they were immensely popular. The two-volume *Biglow Papers* has endured as a humorous social criticism. In the first volume, Lowell attacks U.S. involvement in the Mexican War; in the second, he targets slavery and the Civil War Confederacy. Both featured Hosea Biglow, whose brilliantly rendered rural New England dialect perhaps single-handedly earned Lowell his reputation as a humorous writer.

John Greenleaf Whittier expressed his passionate antislavery views through his poetry, as well as his political activities. In one poem, "Massachusetts to Virginia," he criticizes Virginia for forgetting the democratic ideals on which America had been founded. In another, "Ichabod," Whittier upbraids a U.S. senator for supporting legislation that would return runaway slaves to their owners. These political poems, contrasting with his more sentimental New England poems, added depth to Whittier's reputation.

CUSTOMIZE INSTRUCTION FOR UNIVERSAL ACCESS

For Less Proficient Readers	For English Learners	For Advanced Readers
Have volunteers read a section of poem silently and then identify phrases or words that are confusing. Demonstrate how to rearrange inverted word order or break down stanzas and lines to decipher these confusing elements. Then encourage students to read the section again to comprehend it fully.	To help students' comprehension invite groups to preread to identify unusual or unfamiliar words. Examples might include "the *insensible* rock," "wore *ermine too dear* for an earl," and "shook his *sage* head." Help students define the words or find synonyms for them; then reread the poems.	Allow students to read the poems independently. Then challenge them to identify poetic word uses, in particular sound devices, sensory details, figurative language, and symbols. Ask students to explain how they think each enhances the meaning or music of the poem or a reader's appreciation of it.

- Tell students that as they read the poems, they should focus on meter, that is, the systematic arrangement of stressed and unstressed syllables in poetry.

- Read aloud the instruction about meter. Then read aloud the *Snowbound* example and help students hear its meter.

- Use the Meter transparency in **Literary Analysis and Reading Transparencies,** p. 30 to model the process of identifying meter. Explain to students that reading aloud a poem can help them identify its meter.

- Discuss the instruction under Comparing Literary Works and invite students to give some examples of mood in other poetry they have read.

❸ Reading Strategy
Summarizing

- Remind students that summarizing can help them understand a poet's key points.

- Explain that readers can summarize by identifying main ideas and key details. Use the Summarizing transparency in **Literary Analysis and Reading Transparencies,** p. 29, to demonstrate.

- Direct students to use charts like the one on the student page to summarize as they read the poems of the Fireside Poets.

Vocabulary Development

- Pronounce each vocabulary word for students, and read the definitions as a class. Have students identify any words with which they are familiar.

E-Teach

Visit E-Teach at www.phschool.com for teacher's essays on how to teach, with questions and answers.

Preview
Connecting to the Literature

Do the lyrics or attitudes of your favorite musicians reflect *your* feelings, and *your* views? Gifted musicians and writers often give voice to a generation. Similarly, in the early nineteenth century, the Fireside Poets gave voice to the sentiments of their age.

❷ Literary Analysis
Meter

In poetry, a systematic arrangement of stressed (´) and unstressed (˘) syllables is called **meter.** The basic unit of meter is the foot, which usually consists of one stressed and one or more unstressed syllables. The most frequently used foot in American verse is the *iamb*—one unstressed syllable followed by a stressed syllable. The type and number of feet in the lines of a poem determine its meter. For example, a pattern of four iambs per line, as in this excerpt from *Snowbound*, is known as iambic tetrameter.

> Thĕ sún thăt bríef Dĕcémbĕr dáy
> Rŏse chéerlĕss óvĕr hílls ŏf gráy

Read each poem aloud to discover its meter, listening for metrical patterns that repeat.

Comparing Literary Works

While these poems were written during the same period in history, they each present a different mood. **Mood,** or atmosphere, is the feeling created in a reader by a literary work or passage. Setting, tone, subject, or events can influence mood. As you read, notice the similarities and differences in the mood of each poem and how each poem makes you feel.

❸ Reading Strategy
Summarizing

To check your understanding of what you have read, **summarize** the work or parts of the work by briefly stating the main ideas and supporting details in your own words. Use an organizer like the one shown to summarize each poem.

Vocabulary Development

sepulcher (sep´əl kər) *n.* tomb (p. 268)

pensive (pen´ siv) *adj.* expressing deep thoughtfulness (p. 268)

venerable (ven´ ər ə bəl) *adj.* worthy of respect (p. 268)

gloaming (glōm´ iŋ) *n.* evening dusk; twilight (p. 272)

ominous (äm´ ə nəs) *adj.* threatening (p. 275)

querulous (kwer´ yōō ləs) *adj.* complaining (p. 276)

patriarch (pā´ trē ärk´) *n.* the father and ruler of a family or tribe (p. 278)

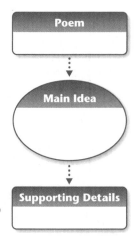

TEACHING RESOURCES

The following resources can be used to enrich or extend the instruction for pp. 267–280.

Literary Analysis

📖 **Writing Models and Graphic Organizers on Transparencies,** p. 67

📖 **Literary Analysis and Reading Transparencies,** p. 30

Reading

📖 **Selection Support Workbook:** Reading Strategy, p. 71; Build Vocabulary, p. 67

🎧 **Listening to Literature Audiocassettes,** Sides 7, 8 ▪

💿 **Listening to Literature Audio CDs,** CD 5 ▪

BLOCK SCHEDULING: Resources marked with this symbol provide varied instruction during 90-minute blocks.

➊ Thanatopsis

William Cullen Bryant

Kindred Spirits, Asher B. Durand, New York Public Library

➋

To him who in the love of Nature holds
Communion with her visible forms, she speaks
A various language; for his gayer hours
She has a voice of gladness, and a smile
5 And eloquence of beauty, and she glides
Into his darker musings, with a mild
And healing sympathy, that steals away
Their sharpness, ere[1] he is aware. When thoughts
Of the last bitter hour come like a blight
10 Over thy spirit, and sad images
Of the stern agony, and shroud, and pall,
And breathless darkness, and the narrow house,[2]
Make thee to shudder, and grow sick at heart—
Go forth, under the open sky, and list
15 To Nature's teachings, while from all around—
Earth and her waters, and the depths of air—

---

1. **ere** before.
2. **narrow house** coffin.

➌ ▲ **Critical Viewing** This painting pays tribute to the friendship between the poet Bryant and landscape painter Thomas Cole. What does the painting suggest about the two men's shared interests? **[Infer]**

➍ ☑ **Reading Check**

Who has "a voice of gladness" and a "healing sympathy"?

Thanatopsis ◆ 267

TEACH

Step-by-Step Teaching Guide for pp. 267–280

CUSTOMIZE INSTRUCTION For Visual/Spatial Learners

Tell students that the way of living recorded in *Snowbound* has largely disappeared. To convey a visual image of this time, bring in copies of paintings of mid-nineteenth-century America. The prints of Currier and Ives and the watercolor paintings of Winslow Homer are appropriate examples.

➊ About the Selection

"Thanatopsis" presents the poet's thoughts on death and its links to nature. Nature brings joy and comfort to those who love it. When people think of death, nature teaches them that everyone and everything must die and become part of the earth again. As all of nature is intertwined, so are the bodies and spirits of all who die. Death need not be feared or despised.

➋ Background

Art

Kindred Spirits, by Asher B. Durand

This portrait-in-nature shows artist Thomas Cole and poet William Cullen Bryant. Durand, Cole, and Bryant were close friends who encouraged and supported one another's work. Use this question for discussion: What inspirations might Bryant have taken from this scene?
Answer: Perhaps he developed ideas for poems on nature or friendship.

➌ ▶ Critical Viewing

Answer: Because Cole was a landscape painter, he, like Bryant, must have had deep feelings about nature. The two, standing on a rock overlooking a beautiful valley might be sharing their views on the relationship between nature and art.

➍ ☑ Reading Check

Answer: Nature has a voice of gladness and a healing sympathy.

CUSTOMIZE INSTRUCTION FOR UNIVERSAL ACCESS

For Less Proficient Readers	For Special Needs Students	For Gifted/Talented Students
Students may find the poetic language of these poems challenging. Point out some examples in lines 8 and 14 (*ere* and *list*, meaning "before" and "listen"). Explain that poetic language—language used in some older, traditional poetry but not in speech—includes words such as these, which poets include for the sake of rhyme or meter.	To help students appreciate this poem, focus on its rhythm before addressing its meaning. Have students listen to Bryant's poem on **Listening to Literature Audiocassettes,** Side 7 or **Audio CDs,** CD 5. Discuss students' reactions to hearing the poem. Then guide them in reading the poem for meaning.	Tell students that the painting on p. 267 belongs to the Hudson River School. Although this group of artists received little respect, their skill in portraying the wilderness helped make landscape an honorable subject in American art. Encourage students to complete the Research and Technology Extension Activity on p. 283.

267

- Invite a volunteer to read aloud the bracketed text.

- Have students identify the main idea and the details that support this idea.

- Tell students to do the Reading Strategy task on p. 268: Summarize the meaning of lines 22–30.
  Possible response: We return to nature when we die.

❻ Literary Analysis

Meter and Mood

- Before addressing the text, have students review the instruction about meter and mood on p. 266.

- Ask students to identify the mood of the poem up to line 30. Then, draw their attention to the word *Yet* in line 31. Tell students that this signal word indicates a shift in the poem's mood.

- In the bracketed text, focus students' attention on words such as *magnificent, kings, wise,* and *good.* Urge them to think about the mood these words suggest.

- Have students respond to the Literary Analysis direction on p. 268: Describe the shift in mood in lines 31–35.
  Possible response: Here the mood becomes hopeful and positive as the poet describes an eternal resting place, in contrast to the previous lines in which the mood was somber and even grim in discussing earthly burial.

Comes a still voice—Yet a few days, and thee
The all-beholding sun shall see no more
In all his course; nor yet in the cold ground,
20　Where thy pale form was laid, with many tears,
Nor in the embrace of ocean, shall exist
Thy image. Earth, that nourished thee, shall claim
Thy growth, to be resolved to earth again,
And, lost each human trace, surrendering up
25　Thine individual being, shalt thou go
To mix forever with the elements,
To be a brother to the insensible rock
And to the sluggish clod, which the rude swain[3]
Turns with his share,[4] and treads upon. The oak
30　Shall send his roots abroad, and pierce thy mold.

　　Yet not to thine eternal resting place
Shalt thou retire alone, nor couldst thou wish
Couch[5] more magnificent. Thou shalt lie down
With patriarchs of the infant world—with kings,
35　The powerful of the earth—the wise, the good,
Fair forms, and hoary seers of ages past,
All in one mighty sepulcher. The hills
Rock-ribbed and ancient as the sun—the vales
Stretching in pensive quietness between;
40　The venerable woods—rivers that move
In majesty, and the complaining brooks
That make the meadows green; and, poured round all,
Old Ocean's gray and melancholy waste—
Are but the solemn decorations all
45　Of the great tomb of man. The golden sun,
The planets, all the infinite host of heaven,
Are shining on the sad abodes of death,
Through the still lapse of ages. All that tread
The globe are but a handful to the tribes
50　That slumber in its bosom. Take the wings
Of morning,[6] pierce the Barcan[7] wilderness,
Or lose thyself in the continuous woods
Where rolls the Oregon,[8] and hears no sound,
Save his own dashings—yet the dead are there:
55　And millions in those solitudes, since first
The flight of years began, have laid them down

---

3. **swain** country youth.
4. **share** plowshare.
5. **couch** bed.
6. **Take . . . morning** allusion to Psalm 139:9.
7. **Barcan** (bär´ kən) referring to Barca, a desert region in North Africa.
8. **Oregon** river flowing between Oregon and Washington, now known as the Columbia River.

268 ◆ A Growing Nation (1800–1870)

Reading Strategy
Summarizing Summarize the meaning of lines 22–30.

Literary Analysis
Meter and Mood Describe the shift in mood in lines 31–35.

sepulcher (sep´əl kər) *n.* tomb

pensive (pen´ siv) *adj.* expressing deep thoughtfulness

venerable (ven´ər ə bəl) *adj.* worthy of respect

✹ ENRICHMENT: Culture Connection

Cultural Views of Death

Many cultures have looked upon death with as much interest as William Cullen Bryant does in this poem. In many ancient civilizations, death was seen as a passage to another life. The Egyptians built huge pyramids as tombs for their pharaohs and stocked them with all the comforts needed for the afterlife, including pets and servants.

The position in which the dead are buried also has significance. In some African cultures, men are buried on their right side, facing east, so the rising sun will wake them in the afterlife to hunt and farm. Women are buried facing west, so the setting sun will remind them to prepare the evening meal.

In their last sleep—the dead reign there alone.
So shalt thou rest, and what if thou withdraw
In silence from the living, and no friend
60 Take note of thy departure? All that breathe
Will share thy destiny. The gay will laugh
When thou art gone, the solemn brood of care
Plod on, and each one as before will chase
His favorite phantom; yet all these shall leave
65 Their mirth and their employments, and shall come
And make their bed with thee. As the long train
Of ages glide away, the sons of men,
The youth in life's green spring, and he who goes
In the full strength of years, matron and maid,
70 The speechless babe, and the gray-headed man—
Shall one by one be gathered to thy side,
By those, who in their turn shall follow them.

       So live, that when thy summons comes to join
The innumerable caravan, which moves
75 To that mysterious realm, where each shall take
His chamber in the silent halls of death,
Thou go not, like the quarry-slave at night,
Scourged to his dungeon, but, sustained and soothed
By an unfaltering trust, approach thy grave,
80 Like one who wraps the drapery of his couch
About him, and lies down to pleasant dreams.

Reading Strategy
Summarizing How would
you restate the poet's
message in the final
stanza?

Review and Assess

Thinking About the Selection

1. **Respond:** Did this poem make you think of nature in a new way? Explain.
2. **(a) Recall:** Identify the various languages Nature speaks to those who love her. **(b) Interpret:** How does the speaker find comfort in Nature's "various language"?
3. **(a) Recall:** According to the "still voice" introduced in line 17 what will happen to the individual being? **(b) Interpret:** In what ways do the images in lines 27–30 reinforce this idea?
4. **(a) Recall:** In the end, who shares the individual being's destiny? **(b) Draw Conclusions:** How would you summarize the poet's attitudes toward life and death?
5. **(a) Connect:** The title combines the Greek words *thanatos* (death) and *opsis* (a vision). Explain the title's connection to the poem. **(b) Apply:** In what ways can Nature provide insight into the mysteries of life and death?

Thanatopsis ◆ 269

❼ Reading Strategy
Summarizing

• Read aloud the bracketed text, striving to convey the poem's meter and to create its uplifting final mood.

• Ask students the Reading Strategy question on p. 269: How would you restate the poet's message in the final stanza? **Possible response:** Be aware that death is a natural process that comes to all, and you can accept it peacefully when it comes.

Answers for p. 269

Review and Assess

1. Responses should reflect new insights gained in students' reading.

2. **(a)** Nature has a voice of gladness and a still voice. **(b)** Nature can rejoice with us when we are happy and comfort us when we are sad.

3. **(a)** He or she will die, be buried, and become part of nature's elements. **(b)** They describe a buried body's return to the earth.

4. **(a)** "All that breathe"—anyone who lives—share that destiny. **(b)** The poet seems to have accepted his place in the life cycle. He recognizes that it is his destiny to return to the earth at death so that his mortal body may in some way become part of nature's immortality.

5. **(a)** The poet is examining his beliefs about death and man's place in the world. He conveys his own philosophy or "vision" of death: that mortal man must die and become part of immortal nature. **(b) Possible response:** In life, nature comforts and heals us. Through nature, we come to understand our place in the life cycle and how, with our deaths, our bodies return to it.

CUSTOMIZE INSTRUCTION FOR UNIVERSAL ACCESS

For Less Proficient Readers	For English Language Learners	For Advanced Readers
Point out Bryant's extensive use of figurative language. Review the definition of metaphor: a thing is spoken of as though it were something else. For example, the poet describes the earth metaphorically as "the great tomb of man." Help students locate and decipher other metaphors in "Thanatopsis."	Tell students that Bryant personifies Earth, nature, and ocean in this poem. Review with students that in using personification, poets attribute human qualities to inanimate objects. Help students understand that with personification, Bryant can portray Earth having feelings or taking actions that it cannot really have or take.	Challenge students to develop a character analysis of Nature as Bryant portrays her. What feelings does he ascribe to her? Is she seen as beautiful and inviting or as threatening? Ask volunteers to read their analyses aloud for the class. Poll the class to see how many students agree with each writer's interpretation of the poem.

❽ **About the Selection**

Written when the War of 1812 was still a living memory, the poem "Old Ironsides" pays homage to the valiant role the ship U.S.S. *Constitution* played in American history. The poet pleads to let it sink at sea rather than suffer ignominious demolition.

❾ ▶**Critical Viewing**

Answer: Students may cite lines 2–4 and lines 9–14.

❽ OLD IRONSIDES

Oliver Wendell Holmes

❾ ▲**Critical Viewing** To celebrate the 200th anniversary of her October 1797 launch, the U.S.S. *Constitution* took a five-hour sail around Massachusetts Bay in July 1997. Before that date, the ship had not sailed under its own power in more than 116 years. Which lines from the poem still apply to "Old Ironsides" today?

270 ◆ A Growing Nation (1800–1870)

✹ ENRICHMENT: Social Studies Connection

The U.S.S. *Constitution*

America has always been proud of the great ships its workers have built. Certain ships stand out as praiseworthy examples of this complex craft. The U.S.S. *Constitution*, nicknamed "Old Ironsides," is foremost among them. This 44-gun warship, ordered by President George Washington and completed in 1797, first won fame battling Barbary pirates in Tripoli, a victory celebrated in the Marine Corps hymn. The *Constitution* is probably best remembered for its role in the War of 1812, when it outsailed British ships to win

several decisive battles for the U.S. Navy.

Though Oliver Wendell Holmes helped win the war to save the *Constitution* from peril, a century later it was in peril again. The deteriorating ship was in need of major repairs. This time, America's schoolchildren came to the rescue, by contributing money that they had collected to restore the ship to its original conditions. The restored *Constitution* is still on display at Charlestown Navy Yard, Charlestown, Massachusetts.

Ay, tear her tattered ensign down!
    Long has it waved on high,
And many an eye has danced to see
    That banner in the sky;
5 Beneath it rung the battle shout,
    And burst the cannons roar;—
The meteor of the ocean air
    Shall sweep the clouds no more.

Her deck, once red with heroes' blood,
10   Where knelt the vanquished foe,
When winds were hurrying o'er the flood,
    And waves were white below,
No more shall feel the victor's tread,
    Or know the conquered knee;—
15 The harpies[1] of the shore shall pluck
    The eagle of the sea!

Oh, better that her shattered hulk
    Should sink beneath the wave;
Her thunders shook the mighty deep,
20   And there should be her grave;
Nail to the mast her holy flag.
    Set every threadbare sail,
And give her to the god of storms,
    The lightning and the gale!

Literary Analysis
Meter Why do you think Holmes occasionally alters the meter in "Old Ironsides"?

Reading Strategy
Summarizing Summarize the last stanza of the poem.

1. **harpies** (här′ pēz) In Greek mythology, hideous, half-woman, half bird monsters.

Review and Assess

Thinking About the Selection

1. **Respond:** If you had been alive in 1830, would this poem have inspired you to protest the ship's demolition? Explain.
2. **(a) Recall:** In the first stanza, what does the speaker suggest doing with the ship? **(b) Infer:** Is he being sincere?
3. **(a) Recall:** By what names does the speaker refer to the ship? **(b) Infer:** What do these names imply?
4. **(a) Draw Conclusions:** Which do you think is more important to the speaker—the ship itself or its historic role? Explain. **(b) Analyze:** In what ways does the poet appeal to the American sense of patriotism?
5. **Evaluate:** This poem was instrumental in saving *Old Ironsides*. Could a poem have such an effect today? Explain.

Old Ironsides ◆ 271

CUSTOMIZE INSTRUCTION FOR UNIVERSAL ACCESS

For Less Proficient Readers	For English Learners	For Advanced Readers
Provide students with the Summarizing transparency in **Literary Analysis and Reading Strategy Transparencies,** p. 29. Help them complete similar organizers for each stanza of "Old Ironsides." Then lead a class discussion on the poem's overall message.	Help students visualize the action Holmes evokes. Help them make sketches of the ship's flag, the cannon fire, the battling sailors and vanquished foes. Then, have them use the photograph on page 270 as a guide to sketch the sinking ship as Holmes describes it.	Invite interested students to learn more about the 200th birthday sail of the *Constitution* on July 21, 1997. That was the first time since 1881 that the nation's oldest commissioned warship sailed under its own power. Students might prepare a presentation about the event for the class.

⑩ Literary Analysis

Meter

- Have volunteers identify which lines vary the meter.
  Possible response: line 13

- Ask students the Literary Analysis question on p. 271: Why do you think Holmes occasionally alters the meter in "Old Ironsides"?
  Possible response: Holmes may have varied the meter to capture readers' attention and thus stress an important idea.

⑪ Reading Strategy

Summarizing

- Have students read the bracketed passage several times.

- Then, offer students the Reading Strategy prompt on p. 271: Summarize the last stanza of the poem.
  Possible response: Let the ship go down in a storm to a dignified death.

Answers for p. 271

Review and Assess

1. Students should support their responses with well-reasoned explanations.

2. **(a)** He suggests tearing down the ship's ragged flag. **(b)** No, he is being ironic.

3. **(a)** He calls it "the meteor of the ocean air" and "the eagle of the sea." **(b)** Possible response: They imply that the *Constitution* was a swift ship.

4. **(a)** His references to the important battles in which the ship took part show that he thinks of the ship as an American symbol. **(b)** He reminds the reader of important battles in which the ship played a key role.

5. Possible response: Because fewer people now read poetry, a poem probably would not have so powerful an effect.

❷ About the Selection

In this poem, inspired by the death of Lowell's own child, a silent, pristine snowfall reminds a still-grieving father of the untimely loss of his young daughter.

❸ Literary Analysis

Meter

- Have a volunteer read aloud the first five stanzas of the poem. If necessary, read it aloud yourself to convey the appropriate meter.

- Review meter with students, using the Meter transparency in **Literary Analysis and Reading Transparencies,** p. 30.

- Ask students the Literary Analysis question on p. 272: In what way does the meter of this poem help to convey the speaker's feelings?
  Possible response: The poem's meter does not vary, creating a chantlike rhythm reminiscent of prayer. This suggests the speaker's great sadness.

The First Snowfall

James Russell Lowell

The snow had begun in the <u>gloaming</u>,
   And busily all the night
Had been heaping field and highway
   With a silence deep and white.

5   Every pine and fir and hemlock
      Wore ermine too dear for an earl
   And the poorest twig on the elm tree
      Was ridged inch deep with pearl.

   From sheds new-roofed with Carrara[1]
10   Came Chanticleer's[2] muffled crow
   The stiff rails softened to swan's-down,
      And still fluttered down the snow.

   I stood and watched by the window
      The noiseless work of the sky,
15   And the sudden flurries of snowbirds.
      Like brown leaves whirling by.

   I thought of a mound in sweet Auburn[3]
      Where a little headstone stood;
   How the flakes were folding it gently,
20   As did robins the babes in the wood.

   Up spoke our own little Mabel,
      Saying, "Father, who makes it snow?"
   And I told of the good All-Father
      Who cares for us here below.

gloaming (glōm´ iŋ) *n.* evening dusk; twilight

Literary Analysis
Meter In what way does the meter of this poem help to convey the speaker's feelings?

---

1. **Carrara** (kə rär´ ə) *n.* fine, white marble.
2. **Chanticleer's** (chan´ ti klirz´) referring to a rooster.
3. **Auburn** Mt. Auburn Cemetery in Cambridge, Massachusetts.

✹ ENRICHMENT: Science Connection

Infant and Maternal Mortality

Lowell's daughter Blanche (his only child up to that time) died in March 1847, when she was little more than a year old. His daughter Mabel, to whom he speaks in the poem, was born in the fall of that year. Mabel was the only one of his four children to survive infancy. In Lowell's time the infant mortality rate was much higher than it is today. Even at the middle of the twentieth century, infant mortality rates in the United States were about 25 percent overall. At the turn of the twenty-first century, improved medical care had low- ered these rates to around 7 percent overall. In Lowell's time, the work of his fellow Fireside Poet, Oliver Wendell Holmes, also helped reduce rates of maternal death linked to childbirth. Holmes's break-through ideas about cleanliness during childbirth dramatically reduced the incidence of puerperal fever, an infection that once claimed the lives of countless delivering mothers.

> 25 Again I looked at the snowfall,
>   And thought of the leaden sky
>   That arched o'er our first great sorrow,
>   When that mound was heaped so high.
>
>   I remembered the gradual patience
> 30   That fell from that cloud like snow,
>   Flake by flake, healing and hiding
>   The scar that renewed our woe.
>
>   And again to the child I whispered,
>   "The snow that husheth all,
> 35 Darling, the merciful Father
>   Alone can make it fall!"
>
>   Then, with eyes that saw not, I kissed her:
>   And she, kissing back, could not know
>   That my kiss was given to her sister,
> 40   Folded close under deepening snow.

Literary Analysis
Meter and Mood What mood is conveyed in the stanza beginning "Again I looked at the snowfall"? Explain.

Review and Assess

Thinking About the Selection

1. **Respond:** Which natural events trigger personal memories for you? Explain.

2. **(a) Recall:** Of what does the snowfall make the speaker think? **(b) Draw Conclusions:** Why do you think the snowfall reminds the speaker of this event?

3. **(a) Recall:** How does the speaker first respond to his daughter's question about the snow? **(b) Connect:** What does he later add to his response?

4. **(a) Analyze:** In lines 29–32, in what way does the snowfall act as a healer? **(b) Infer:** What do lines 34–36 suggest about the source of emotional healing?

5. **(a) Analyze:** What does the falling snow symbolize, or represent? **(b) Extend:** In what way could such symbolism provide comfort for someone grieving the loss of a loved one?

6. **Speculate:** How might the high infant mortality rate of the nineteenth century have affected the attitudes and values of the day?

7. **Evaluate:** Do you think this poem realistically conveys a parent's pain over a lost child? Explain.

The First Snowfall ◆ 273

⓮ Literary Analysis
Meter and Mood

- Have a volunteer read aloud the bracketed stanza. Urge students to listen for the mood conveyed by the text.

- Have students identify words and details that help to convey the mood of this poem.

- Then, ask students the Literary Analysis question on p. 273: What mood is conveyed by the stanza beginning "Again I looked at the snowfall"? Explain.
  Possible response: The mood is sad, as evoked by words such as *leaden* and *great sorrow*.

Answers for p. 273

Review and Assess

1. Students may cite thunderstorms, rainbows, or similar natural occurrences.

2. **(a)** The snowstorm makes him think of his daughter's death and her burial place. **(b)** The snow buries the earth just as he buried his daughter.

3. **(a)** At first he answers that the "good All-Father who cares for us" makes it snow. **(b)** He adds that only the "merciful Father" can make it fall.

4. **(a)** It can cover the burial mound of his daughter's grave. **(b)** They suggest that God is the source of the healing that eventually allows us to bury our grief.

5. **(a)** It represents the passage of time and the cycles of nature. **(b)** It suggests that time will heal the grief by gently covering it.

6. **Possible response:** People may have been more accustomed to death, accepting it as a natural part of life. They may have better understood life's fragility.

7. **Possible response:** The speaker may seem to accept the pain more easily than is believable. Some students may observe that the sentiments expressed are typical of Lowell's era.

CUSTOMIZE INSTRUCTION FOR UNIVERSAL ACCESS

For Less Proficient Readers	For Advanced Readers	For Gifted/Talented Students
Direct students' attention to lines 9–12. Clarify the reference to Carrara by reading the footnote. Then, be sure students understand that sheds commonly do not have marble roofs. Here, the poet uses a metaphor to compare the smooth white layer of snow to fine, white marble.	Focus students' attention on lines 13–16. Guide them to identify this as a transitional stanza in the poem. Help them recognize that in these lines, the poet shifts the poem's focus from the outer landscape to the speaker's perceptions.	Cemetaries tell stories about patterns of life and death. Students might use information gleaned from headstones and from research into local history to suggest possible research topics about local families, community leaders, or events such as epidemics or natural disasters.

273

15

15 About the Selection

This narrative poem commemorates a way of life and a close-knit family. A December snowstorm isolates a family on a New England farm. Despite extra efforts they must make to care for their animals and keep warm, the family relishes its cozy home and the beauties of nature's artistry.

16 Background

Art

Old Holley House, Cos Cob, by John Henry Twachtman

The artist uses soft colors in this painting. At first glance, the picture seems flat, but closer examination reveals depth and vibrancy, such as might be seen on the bright snowy day after Whittier's snowstorm. Use these questions for discussion:

1. How do the artist and the poet use color to describe snow?
   Answer: The artist uses shades of blue, white, gray, pink, and purple while Whittier mostly refers to the snow as either white or crystalline (clear).

2. What words from the poem also describe this picture?
   Possible response: *Hills of gray, white drift, glistening, dazzling crystal, snow-mist,* and *frost line*

17 ▶Critical Viewing

Answer: Students may say that the mood inside the speaker's home is cozy, warm, merry, and content. The painting conveys an exterior that is cold, lonely, and unwelcoming.

16

Old Holley House, Cos Cob, John Henry Twachtman, Cincinnati Art Museum

17 ▲ **Critical Viewing** At the end of this poem, the speaker describes the inside of his home. Contrast that interior with the exterior of the house in this painting. **[Contrast]**

274 ◆ *A Growing Nation (1800–1870)*

CUSTOMIZE INSTRUCTION FOR UNIVERSAL ACCESS

For Advanced Readers

In his poem "A Fable for Critics," James Russell Lowell wrote about his contemporary, John Greenleaf Whittier. Read these lines to students:

> There was ne'er a man born who had more of the swing
>
> Of the true lyric bard and all that kind of thing;
>
> And his failures arise (though he seem not to know it)

> From the very same cause that has made him a poet,—

Challenge students to find the complete poem and read it independently. Then, lead a brief discussion in which you invite students to ask questions if there are lines or passages they don't understand. Finally, have them answer the following question in their journals: Do you think Lowell's criticism of Whittier is reasonable or unreasonable? Why or why not?

from
15 SNOWBOUND

John Greenleaf Whittier

A Winter Idyll

18

    The sun that brief December day
Rose cheerless over hills of gray,
And, darkly circled, gave at noon
A sadder light than waning moon.
5 Slow tracing down the thickening sky
Its mute and <u>ominous</u> prophecy,

    A portent seeming less than threat,
It sank from sight before it set.
A chill no coat, however stout,
10 Of homespun stuff could quite shut out,
A hard, dull bitterness of cold,
That checked, mid-vein, the circling race
Of lifeblood in the sharpened face,
The coming of the snowstorm told.
15 The wind blew east; we heard the roar
Of Ocean on his wintry shore,
And felt the strong pulse throbbing there
Beat with low rhythm our inland air.

    Meanwhile we did our nightly chores—
20 Brought in the wood from out of doors,
Littered the stalls, and from the mows
Raked down the herd's-grass for the cows:
Heard the horse whinnying for his corn;
And, sharply clashing horn on horn,
25 Impatient down the stanchion[1] rows
The cattle shake their walnut bows;
While, peering from his early perch

ominous (ăm´ ə nəs) *adj.*
threatening

---

1. **stanchion** (stan´ chən) restraining device fitted around the neck of a cow to confine it to its stall.

19 ✔ **Reading Check**
What signals the coming
of the snowstorm?

---

18 **Literary Analysis**
Meter and Mood

- Have students read bracketed text to themselves.
- Encourage students to reflect on their emotional responses to the text, focusing on such words and phrases as *brief December day*, *cheerless*, *grey hills*, *darkly circled*, *sadder light*, and *ominous*.
- Ask students to identify the mood of these six lines.
  Answer: The mood is ominous, threatening, and gloomy.

19 ✔ **Reading Check**

Answer: The sky's thickening, the gray light, a chill in the air, the hard and dull cold, the wind blowing east and a sound like the sea all signal the coming snowstorm.

CUSTOMIZE INSTRUCTION FOR UNIVERSAL ACCESS

For Less Proficient Readers

To help students understand this lengthy poem, treat the selection in sections. You may divide the poem as follows:

1. Signs of the coming storm (lines 1–3)

2. Description of the storm and the family's response to it (lines 31–115)

3. Lighting a fire in the fireplace (lines 116–142)

4. Description of the outside world (lines 143–154)

5. Description of the world inside (lines 155–174)

    As they read each section, have students note how the poet appeals to the senses. They might make a graphic organizer in which they list sense imagery.

⑳ Literary Analysis

Meter

- Read aloud lines 35–36. Have students comment on both the meter and the action of these lines.

- Have students identify what is being described in these lines.
  Answer: The movement of the snow in the wind is being described.

- Ask students the Literary Analysis question on p. 276: The pattern of meter changes at lines 35 and 36. In what ways does this change in meter correspond with the action described in these lines?
  Answer: The changing meter suggests the back and forth movement of snow in the wind.

▶ Monitor Progress Have students use the Meter transparency in **Literary Analysis and Reading Transparencies,** p. 30, to review scansion and to help them track the meter of these lines. Then point out words such as *zigzag, to and fro,* and *crossed and recrossed* that indicate the action of the lines.

Upon the scaffold's pole of birch,
The cock his crested helmet bent
30   And down his querulous challenge sent.

Unwarmed by any sunset light
The gray day darkened into night,
A night made hoary with the swarm
And whirl-dance of the blinding storm,
35   As zigzag, wavering to and fro,
Crossed and recrossed the winged snow:
And ere the early bedtime came
The white drift piled the window frame,
And through the glass the clothesline posts
40   Looked in like tall and sheeted ghosts.

So all night long the storm roared on:
The morning broke without a sun;
In tiny spherule[2] traced with lines
Of Nature's geometric signs,
45   in starry flake, and pellicle,[3]
All day the hoary meteor fell;

querulous (kwerˊ ə ləs) *adj.* complaining

Literary Analysis

Meter The pattern of the meter changes at lines 35 and 36. In what ways does this change correspond with the action described in these lines?

2. **spherule** (sferˊ o͞ol) small sphere.
3. **pellicle** (pelˊ i kəl) thin film of crystals.

✸ ENRICHMENT: Music Connection

Musical "Descriptions"

Many of the wintry descriptions John Greenleaf Whittier created with words, the Italian composer Antonio Vivaldi (1678–1741) created with music. His famous *Four Seasons* concerto is rich with dynamic, tonal, and rhythmic effects. This piece, based on a cycle of four sonnets that Vivaldi himself may have written, offers musical images of spring, summer, autumn, and winter.

Play "Winter" for the class. Challenge students to

listen for musical illustrations of icy snow, chilling winds, and chattering teeth. Discuss the musical devices Vivaldi used to convey his imagery.

And, when the second morning shone,
We looked upon a world unknown,
On nothing we could call our own.
50 Around the glistening wonder bent
The blue walls of the firmament,
No cloud above, no earth below—
A universe of sky and snow!
The old familiar sights of ours
55 Took marvelous shapes; strange domes and towers
Rose up where sty or corncrib stood,
Or garden wall, or belt of wood;
A smooth white mound the brush pile showed,
A fenceless drift what once was road;
60 The bridle post an old man sat
With loose-flung coat and high cocked hat;
The wellcurb had a Chinese roof;
And even the long sweep,[4] high aloof,
In its slant splendor, seemed to tell
65 Of Pisa's leaning miracle.[5]

A prompt, decisive man, no breath
Our father wasted: "Boys, a path!"
Well pleased (for when did farmer boy
Count such a summons less than joy?)
70 Our buskins[6] on our feet we drew;
With mittened hands, and caps drawn low,
To guard our necks and ears from snow,

---

4. **sweep** pole with a bucket at one end, used for raising water from a well.
5. **Pisa's leaning miracle** famous leaning tower of Pisa in Italy.
6. **buskins** high-cut leather shoes or boots.

Literary Analysis
Meter and Mood What mood is conveyed in the morning light? Which words create this mood?

Reading Strategy
Summarizing Why are the boys so excited by their father's order to make a path through the snow?

23 ✔**Reading Check**
What does the family discover on the second morning?

from *Snowbound* ◆ 277

CUSTOMIZE INSTRUCTION FOR UNIVERSAL ACCESS

For Special Needs Students	For Less Proficient Readers	For Advanced Readers
Students may more easily visualize the playful, stunning imagery of the snow-covered farm by sketching the scene Whittier describes in lines 50–65. Before students begin their sketching, work through each line word by word to define and explore the meanings of Whittier's highly evocative language.	To help students access Whittier's description of the snowbound setting, remind them to use the Reading Strategy: Summarizing. Explain that by summarizing the main ideas and key details of Whittier's description, they can build a clear visual image of the setting. Model this process on lines 50–65.	Revisit the Literary Analysis question on p. 272 to remind students of the impact mood has on a setting description. Then challenge students to compare and contrast the setting Whittier describes in lines 50–65 with the snowy setting of James Russell Lowell's "The First Snowfall."

21 Literary Analysis
Meter and Mood

- After students read the bracketed text silently, call on a volunteer to read aloud the lines. Urge the other students to close their eyes as they listen and to visualize the new morning.

- Encourage students to identify the feelings they associate with the following words and phrases: *glistening wonder*, *universe of sky and snow*, *marvelous shapes*, and *slant splendor*.

- Then, ask students the Literary Analysis questions on p. 277: What mood is conveyed in the morning light? Which words create this mood?
Answer: The mood is one of wonder and fascination at the transformation wrought by the snow. Words such as *glistening wonder*, *universe of sky and snow*, *marvelous*, *strange*, *splendor*, and *miracle* all contribute to this mood.

22 Reading Strategy
Summarizing

- Have students reread the bracketed text. Then ask them to summarize its contents.
Answer: The father asks his sons to make a path through the snow. They eagerly get warmly dressed to tackle the task.

- Ask students the Reading Strategy question on p. 277: Why are the boys so excited by their father's order to make a path through the snow?
Answer: This is not a typical farm chore; it evokes a sense of excitement and mystery and stimulates their imaginations.

23 ✔Reading Check

Answer: They discover that their farm has been transformed by the heavy snowfall.

㉔ Vocabulary Development

The Latin Word Root -patr-

- Call students' attention to the word *patriarch* and its definition. Let students know that the root comes from the Latin word for father, *pater*.

- Ask students to volunteer any other words they may know that incorporate this word root. Possibilities include: patronage, paternal, and patriot.

- Have students write short explanations of how the idea of fatherhood influenced the formation of words such as *patronage* and *patriot*.

㉕ Reading Strategy

Summarizing

- Direct students' attention to the bracketed text. As they read it, urge students to note words that describe or convey sound. Possible answers: The words *no welcome sound, sharpest ear, could not hear, music, almost human tone* connote sound.

- Ask the Reading Strategy question on p. 278: How do the sounds of the world change as a result of the snowstorm? Answer: The wind shrieks, boughs moan, sleet beats against the window. Also, the snow's blanket quiets certain sounds such as those of church bells or the brook.

▶ Monitor Progress Have students make an organizer like the one shown on p. 266 to record the main idea and supporting details of this passage.

We cut the solid whiteness through.
And, where the drift was deepest, made
75 A tunnel walled and overlaid
With dazzling crystal: we had read
Of rare Aladdin's[7] wondrous cave,
And to our own his name we gave,
With many a wish the luck were ours
80 To test his lamp's supernal powers.
We reached the barn with merry din,
And roused the prisoned brutes within,
The old horse thrust his long head out,
And grave with wonder gazed about;
85 The cock his lusty greeting said,
And forth his speckled harem led;
The oxen lashed their tails, and hooked,
And mild reproach of hunger looked;
The hornèd patriarch of the sheep,
90 Like Egypt's Amun[8] roused from sleep,
Shook his sage head with gesture mute,
And emphasized with stamp of foot.

All day the gusty north wind bore
The loosening drift its breath before:
95 Low circling round its southern zone,
The sun through dazzling snow-mist shone.
No church bell lent its Christian tone
To the savage air, no social smoke
Curled over woods of snow-hung oak
100 A solitude made more intense
By dreary-voicèd elements,
The shrieking of the mindless wind,
The moaning tree boughs swaying blind,
And on the glass the unmeaning beat
105 Of ghostly fingertips of sleet.
Beyond the circle of our hearth
No welcome sound of toil or mirth
Unbound the spell, and testified
Of human life and thought outside.
110 We minded that the sharpest ear
The buried brooklet could not hear,
The music of whose liquid lip
Had been to us companionship,
And, in our lonely life, had grown
115 To have an almost human tone.

---

7. **Aladdin's** referring to Aladdin, a boy in *The Arabian Nights* who found a magic lamp and through its powers discovered a treasure in a cave.
8. **Amun** Egyptian god with a ram's head.

㉔ patriarch (pā´ trē ärk´) *n.* the father and ruler of a family or tribe

Reading Strategy
Summarizing How do the sounds of the world change as a result of the snowstorm?

As night drew on, and, from the crest
Of wooded knolls that ridged the west,
The sun, a snow-blown traveler, sank
From sight beneath the smothering bank,
120 We piled, with care, our nightly stack
Of wood against the chimney back—
The oaken log, green, huge, and thick,
And on its top the stout backstick;
The knotty forestick laid apart,
125 And filled between with curious art
The ragged brush; then, hovering near,
We watched the first red blaze appear,
Heard the sharp crackle, caught the gleam
On whitewashed wall and sagging beam,
130 Until the old, rude-furnished room
Burst, flowerlike, into rosy bloom;
While radiant with a mimic flame
Outside the sparkling drift became,
And through the bare-boughed lilac tree
135 Our own warm hearth seemed blazing free.
The crane and pendent trammels[9] showed,
The Turks' heads[10] on the andirons glowed;
While childish fancy, prompt to tell
The meaning of the miracle,
140 Whispered the old rhyme: *"Under the tree,*
When fire outdoors burns merrily,
There the witches are making tea."

The moon above the eastern wood
Shone at its full; the hill range stood
145 Transfigured in the silver flood,
Its blown snows flashing cold and keen,
Dead white, save where some sharp ravine
Took shadow, or the somber green
Of hemlocks turned to pitchy black
150 Against the whiteness at their back.
For such a world and such a night
Most fitting that unwarming light,
Which only seemed where'er it fell
To make the coldness visible.

155 Shut in from all the world without,
We sat the clean-winged hearth[11] about,

---

9. **trammels** (tram′ əlz) *n.* adjustable pothooks hanging from the movable arm, or crane, attached to the hearth.
10. **Turks' heads** turbanlike knots at the top of the andirons.
11. **clean-winged hearth** a turkey wing was used for the hearth broom.

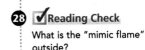

Literary Analysis
Meter and Mood What mood is conveyed by nightfall, the crackling fire, and the warm hearth?

27 **Reading Strategy**
Summarizing Summarize the action in lines 116–142

28 ☑ **Reading Check**
What is the "mimic flame" outside?

from Snowbound ◆ 279

---

26 **Literary Analysis**
Meter and Mood

• Play the Listening to **Literature Audiocassette,** Side 8, or **Audio CDs,** CD 5, so that students can hear the bracketed lines read aloud. Encourage students to visualize the speaker's surroundings as they listen.

• Invite volunteers to highlight especially evocative words from the bracketed text.
Possible responses: *snow-blown traveler; nightly stack; first red blaze; sharp crackle; burst, flowerlike, into rosy bloom; radiant with a mimic flame; warm hearth*

• Ask students the Literary Analysis question on p. 279: What mood is conveyed by nightfall, the crackling fire, and the warm hearth?
Answer: a mood of warmth and coziness

27 **Reading Strategy**
Summarizing

• Make sure students understand that a summary, whether for an entire work or part of a work, should include only the main idea and any important details that support this idea.

• Remind students of the audio reading they listened to when responding to the Literary Analysis question above. Then ask students to respond to the Reading Strategy prompt on p. 279: Summarize the action in lines 116–142.
Possible response: Night falls as the family gathers wood for the night, builds a fire, and warms the house's interior against the storm.

28 ☑ **Reading Check**
Answer: The speaker is describing the reflection of the hearth flames in the windowpanes.

CUSTOMIZE INSTRUCTION FOR UNIVERSAL ACCESS

For English Learners

Help students gain oral proficiency by having them read aloud lines 116–142 and then lines 143–154. After they read, lead a comparison discussion about the colors the speaker mentions in the two stanzas. Make sure that students know the colors named, using classroom objects or photographs to indicate examples. Then point out that the speaker uses color imagery to contrast the mood of the two stanzas, using white, silver, and black to describe the outdoors and rose, red, and gold to describe the indoors. Help stu- dents assign moods to these color groups as a way of understanding the text. For example, the outside colors are cold colors that suggest a stark, cold, detached mood. The inside colors are warm, glowing colors that suggest an embracing, welcoming mood.

Literary Analysis

Meter and Mood

- After students read the bracketed text, ask them what feelings the lines evoke in the reader.
  Possible responses: security, warmth

- Ask students what the lasting mood of the final lines of this poem is?
  Answer: happy, contented

Answers for p. 280

Review and Assess

1. Students may reply that it might be fun for a short time; others may not like the idea of being confined to their homes.

2. **(a)** There is hardly any sun, and the sky is thickening. **(b)** They hint at the possibility of danger.

3. **(a)** They contain and feed the animals; they gather wood. **(b)** They suggest that the family lives in harmony with nature.

4. **(a)** Possible response: "Shut in from all the world without" and "the red logs before us beat/The frost line back with tropic heat" convey these feelings. **(b)** Possible responses: "No cloud above, no earth below" and "Around the glistening wonder bent/The blue walls of firmament" show the narrator's sense of wonder. **(c)** They enjoy the time to step outside daily routine and be together.

5. **(a)** People today may more often feel that a snowbound day is an inconvenience. **(b)** Possible response: When such storms occur, people might avail themselves of snow blowers, SUVs, and other equipment to cope with the severe conditions. Likewise, people might communicate with neighbors and government agencies through the use of the telephone or Internet. **(c)** Possible response: Some students may observe that people are much less affected by weather than in Whittier's day. Others may point out that most people today cannot cook or heat their homes without electricity, and that a blizzard may therefore leave many at nature's mercy.

Content to let the north wind roar
In baffled rage at pane and door,
While the red logs before us beat
160 The frost line back with tropic heat;
And ever, when a louder blast
Shook beam and rafter as it passed,
The merrier up its roaring draft
The great throat of the chimney laughed;
165 The house dog on his paws outspread
Laid to the fire his drowsy head.
The cat's dark silhouette on the wall
A couchant tiger's seemed to fall:
And, for the winter fireside meet,
170 Between the andirons' straddling feet.
The mug of cider simmered slow.
The apples sputtered in a row.
And, close at hand, the basket stood
With nuts from brown October's wood.

Review and Assess

Thinking About the Selection

1. **Respond:** Would you find it pleasant to be isolated, like the narrator and his family, by a powerful snowstorm? Why or why not?

2. **(a) Recall:** What weather conditions forewarn the narrator of the approaching snowstorm? **(b) Connect:** In what way do these "previews" build suspense in the poem?

3. **(a) Recall:** In what ways does the family prepare for and cope with the storm? **(b) Draw Conclusions:** What do these responses to the storm suggest about the family's relationship with nature?

4. **(a) Recall:** Which details in the poem convey a sense of warmth, security, and family closeness? **(b) Analyze:** Which descriptive details in lines 47–80 convey the narrator's sense of wonder upon viewing the snow-covered landscape? **(c) Infer:** What are the family's feelings about being snowbound?

5. **(a) Assess:** In what ways has life changed since *Snowbound* was written in 1865? **(b) Extend:** Today, influenced as we are by modern technologies, how would people cope with the consequences such a storm could pose? **(c) Take a Position:** Are people still at the mercy of nature, as they were in Whittier's day? Explain your answer.

ASSESSMENT PRACTICE: Reading Comprehension

| **Make Inferences and Generalizations** | **(For more practice, see Test Preparation Workbook, p. 17.)** |

Many tests require students to make valid generalizations based on specific evidence in a text. Explain that a valid generalization is supported by information found in the passage. Use this sample test item:

Which of the following most accurately describes Old Ironsides's record of service?

A inactive
B unremarkable
C distinguished
D brief

A, B, and *D* are not supported by the poem. The ship survived difficult battles and won many victories at sea. Therefore, *C* is correct.

Review and Assess

Literary Analysis

Meter

1. Copy these lines from "Thanatopsis" and mark the stressed and unstressed syllables of the **meter:** So shalt thou rest, and what if thou withdraw / In silence from the living, and no friend.

2. Copy these lines from *Snowbound*. Mark the stressed and unstressed syllables: Beyond the circle of our hearth / No welcome sound of toil or mirth.

3. (a) In the second stanza of "Old Ironsides," which lines are in iambic tetrameter (four iambs)? (b) Which are iambic trimeter (three iambs)?

Comparing Literary Works

4. (a) Contrast the **moods** of the two poems set in winter—"The First Snowfall" and the excerpt from *Snowbound*. (b) How does the situation in each poem contribute to these moods?

5. (a) What shift in mood occurs in line 31 of "Thanatopsis"? (b) How does this mood shift offer comfort?

6. Which of the other poems in this grouping best matches the mood of "Thanatopsis"? Why?

Reading Strategy

Summarizing

7. Using a chart like the one shown, write a **summary** of the first two stanzas of the excerpt from *Snowbound*.

Key Details	Summary
Stanza 1	
Stanza 2	

8. Summarize the main idea of "Thanatopsis." Consider your summary as a prereading guide for someone who is unfamiliar with the poem.

Extend Understanding

9. **Cultural Connection:** What value do historical monuments and symbols have to American society?

Thanatopsis / Old Ironsides / The First Snowfall / from Snowbound ◆ 281

Quick Review

Meter in poetry is a systematic arrangement of stressed and unstressed syllables.

Mood, or atmosphere, is the feeling created in a reader by a literary work or passage.

To **summarize,** briefly state the main ideas and supporting details in your own words.

 Take It to the Net
www.phschool.com
Take the interactive self-test online to check your understanding of these selections.

Answers for p. 281

Review and Assess

1. So shalt thou rest, and what if thou withdraw In silence from the living, and no friend

2. Beyond the circle of our hearth No welcome sound of toil or mirth

3. (a) Lines 9, 11, 13, and 15 are in iambic tetrameter. (b) Lines 10, 12, 14, and 16 are in iambic trimeter.

4. (a) "The First Snowfall" has a sad and somber mood while *Snowbound* conveys a cozy, festive mood. (b) "The First Snowfall" discusses a grieving father's sadness while *Snowbound* discusses an exciting snowstorm.

5. (a) Possible response: The mood shifts from grim to exalted. (b) The new mood offers comfort to those grieving or facing death.

6. "The First Snowfall," which speaks of finding comfort despite death, most closely matches the mood of "Thanatopsis."

7. Possible responses: Students should cite key details from stanzas 1 and 2 in writing their summaries.

8. Possible response: In "Thanatopsis," the speaker details his thoughts about death and man's place in the world. He begins by exploring the role of nature, stating that nature's cycle naturally includes man's death, and his resulting return to nature. Finally, the speaker urges people to live fully so that they can accept death peacefully.

9. Historical monuments remind us of our rich history.

※ **ENRICHMENT: Further Reading**

Other Works by the Authors

Other works by William Cullen Bryant
Picturesque America: Or, The Land We Live In

Other works by Oliver Wendell Holmes
The Autocrat of the Breakfast Table
"The Chambered Nautilus"

Other works by James Russell Lowell
"The Vision of Sir Launfal"
"A Fable for Critics"

Other works by John Greenleaf Whittier
"Hampton Beach"
"The Barefoot Boy"

 Take It to the Net
Visit www.phschool.com for more information on the authors.

Answers for p. 282

❶ Vocabulary Development

Word Analysis

1. patriots
2. paternal
3. patronage

Spelling Strategy

1. dividable
2. sensible
3. usable

Concept Development: Antonyms or Synonyms?

1. synonyms
2. antonyms
3. antonyms
4. antonyms
5. synonyms
6. antonyms
7. synonyms

❷ Grammar and Style

1. *circled* modifies *sun; waning* modifies *moon*
2. *resting* modifies *place*
3. *healing* modifies *sympathy*
4. *all-beholding* modifies *sun*
5. *shattered* modifies *hulk*

Writing Application

Possible response:

The *dazzling* snow reflected the sunlight from every *crusted* branch and *drifted* slope. As I squinted into the *chilling* wind, I could barely make out the *ice-coated* snow bank that used to be my front steps.

Integrate Language Skills

❶ Vocabulary Development Lesson

Word Analysis: Latin Root *-patr-*

The Latin root *-patr-*, comes from the word *pater*, meaning "father." This root is found in many English words, including *patriarch*. Complete each sentence by writing one of the *-patr-* words listed below in the blank.

patronage   paternal   patriot

1. People who love their fatherland are called ___?___.
2. My father's mother is my ___?___ grandmother.
3. The mayor has the authority to give out certain ___?___ jobs to his supporters.

Concept Development: Antonyms or Synonyms?

Decide whether the words in each pair are *antonyms* (opposites) or *synonyms* (similar).

1. sepulcher, tomb
2. pensive, frivolous
3. venerable, contemptible
4. gloaming, sunlight
5. ominous, forbidding
6. querulous, content
7. patriarch, father

Spelling Strategy

The suffix *-able / -ible* is used to form adjectives, such as *biodegradable* and *visible*. Use the roots below to write adjectives that end with *-able / -ible*.

1. divide   2. sense   3. use

❷ Grammar and Style Lesson

Participles as Adjectives

A **participle** is a verb form that can act as an adjective and answers the question *What kind?* or *Which one?* about the noun or pronoun it modifies. **Present participles** end in *-ing*, as in *dazzling*. **Past participles**, like *walled* and *overlaid*, may end in *-ed*, *-d*, *-t*, or *-en*. Notice the participles in this example.

Example: "A tunnel *walled* and *overlaid* / With *dazzling* crystal . . . "

Practice Identify the participles in each item, along with the noun each participle modifies.

1. The sun . . . / Rose cheerless . . . , / And, darkly circled, gave at noon / A sadder light than waning moon.

2. Yet not to thine eternal resting place / Shalt thou retire alone, . . .

3. Into his darker musings, with a mild / And healing sympathy, . . .

4. . . .Yet a few days, and thee / The all-beholding sun shall see no more / In all his course; . . .

5. Oh, better that her shattered hulk / Should sink beneath the wave; . . .

Writing Application Write three sentences describing a snow-covered landscape. Use participial forms of the following verbs as adjectives: *dazzle, coat, crust, drift, chill*. Draw arrows from the participles to the words they modify.

Prentice Hall Writing and Grammar Connection: Chapter 19, Section 2

282 ◆ *A Growing Nation (1800–1870)*

TEACHING RESOURCES

The following resources can be used to enrich or extend the instruction for pp. 282–283.

Vocabulary

📖 **Selection Support Workbook:** Build Vocabulary, p. 67

📖 **Vocabulary and Spelling Practice Book** (Use this booklet for skills enrichment.)

Grammar

📖 **Selection Support Workbook:** Grammar and Style, p. 68

📖 **Writing and Grammar,** Ruby Level, p. 442

📖 **Daily Language Practice Transparencies**

Writing

📖 **Writing and Grammar,** Ruby Level, p. 857

💿 **Writing and Grammar iText CD-ROM**

📖 **Writing Models and Graphic Organizers on Transparencies**, p. 67

BLOCK SCHEDULING: Resources marked with this symbol provide varied instruction during 90-minute blocks.

❸ Writing Lesson

Précis

Write a précis (prā sē′)—a concise abridgment or brief summary of a longer work—of the selection from *Snowbound*. Include all the main ideas and key details a reader would need in order to understand the events in the poem. Your summary should have a clear beginning, middle, and end.

Prewriting For each stanza of the poem, list the main ideas and key details you will include in your précis. Try to convey a series of details with a single phrase or sentence.

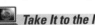

Model: Identifying Beginning, Middle, and End

Beginning	Middle	End
Darkening December sky, cold, windy . . .	Chores, blizzard starts, roars through night . . .	

> A clear beginning, middle, and end are especially important to a précis, which should reflect the structure or progression of the original work.

Drafting Set the mood for the poem's impending storm by summarizing the poem's opening stanza. Refer to your prewriting notes to avoid confusing the sequence of events as you draft the middle and end.

Revising Evaluate whether your précis accurately reflects the phases of the storm. Add details to convey the wonder of the snowy landscape and the coziness of the farmhouse hearth.

𝒲𝒢 *Prentice Hall Writing and Grammar Connection: Chapter 31, Section 1*

Extension Activities

❹ **Listening and Speaking** Convey Holmes's patriotic fervor in a **dramatic reading** of "Old Ironsides." As you rehearse:

- Work to achieve command of text and meter.
- Use a tone and pace suited to the work.
- Present the poem in a way that will persuade and move the audience.

Ask classmates to critique your reading.

Research and Technology The painting on page 267 depicts William Cullen Bryant and Thomas Cole. Research Cole and the Hudson River School of artists to determine the basis for Cole's claim to kinship with Bryant. Present your findings in an **oral presentation.**

🖥 **Take It to the Net** www.phschool.com

Go online for an additional research activity using the Internet.

Thanatopsis / Old Ironsides / The First Snowfall / from Snowbound ◆ 283

❸ Writing Lesson

- Review the Reading Strategy: Summarizing instruction on p. 266 with students.

- After discussing the steps in the Writing Lesson, emphasize the importance of careful detail selection. Stress that students should select enough details to convey the feel of the poem but not so many that their writing becomes cluttered.

- Have students use the Branching Organizer in **Writing Models and Graphic Organizers on Transparencies,** p. 67, to list main ideas and details for each section of the poem. Model how to add a third branch to the organizer's second tier.

❹ Listening and Speaking

- Organize students in groups to summarize and discuss Holmes's poem and the emotions it conveys. Urge students to build on the discussion as they prepare their readings.

- Pair students to rehearse. Partners can take turns prompting each other with the words or suggesting possible places for emphasis.

CUSTOMIZE INSTRUCTION For Universal Access

To address different learning styles, use the activities suggested in the Extension Activities booklet, p. 15.

For Intrapersonal and Verbal/Linguistic Learners, use Activity 5.

For Intrapersonal Learners, use Activity 6.

For Visual/Spatial Learners, use Activity 7.

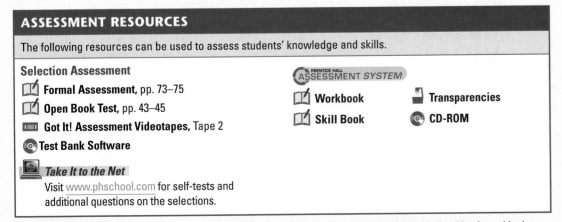

ASSESSMENT RESOURCES

The following resources can be used to assess students' knowledge and skills.

Selection Assessment

📖 **Formal Assessment,** pp. 73–75

📖 **Open Book Test,** pp. 43–45

📼 **Got It! Assessment Videotapes,** Tape 2

💿 **Test Bank Software**

🖥 **Take It to the Net**
Visit www.phschool.com for self-tests and additional questions on the selections.

PRENTICE HALL ASSESSMENT SYSTEM

📖 **Workbook**

📖 **Skill Book**

📖 **Transparencies**

💿 **CD-ROM**

◼ **BLOCK SCHEDULING:** Resources marked with this symbol provide varied instruction during 90-minute blocks.

Crossing the Great Divide ✦ The Most Sublime Spectacle on Earth

Lesson Objectives

1. **To analyze and respond to literary elements**
   - Literary Analysis: Description
   - Comparing Literary Works
2. **To read, comprehend, analyze, and critique nonfiction**
   - Reading Strategy: Noting Spatial Relationships
   - Reading Check questions
   - Review and Assess questions
   - Assessment Practice (ATE)
3. **To develop word analysis skills, fluency, and systematic vocabulary**
   - Vocabulary Development Lesson: Latin Prefix: *multi-*
4. **To understand and apply written and oral language conventions**
   - Spelling Strategy
   - Grammar and Style Lesson: Participial Phrases
5. **To understand and apply appropriate writing and research strategies**
   - Writing Lesson: Description of a Natural Wonder
   - Extension Activity: Expedition Map
6. **To understand and apply listening and speaking strategies**
   - Extension Activity: Tourism Presentation

STEP-BY-STEP TEACHING GUIDE	PACING GUIDE
PRETEACH	
Motivate Students and Provide Background	
Use the Motivation activity (ATE p. 284)	5 min.
Read and discuss the author and the background information (SE p. 287; ATE p. 284)	5 min.
Introduce the Concepts	
Introduce the Literary Analysis and Reading Strategy (SE/ATE p. 285) A	15 min.
Pronounce the vocabulary words and read their definitions (SE p. 285)	5 min.
TEACH	
Monitor Comprehension	
Informally monitor comprehension by circulating while students read independently or in groups A	20 min.
Monitor students' comprehension with the Reading Check notes (SE/ATE pp. 287, 289, 291)	as students read
Develop vocabulary with Vocabulary notes (SE pp. 288, 289, 290, 291; ATE p. 291)	as students read
Develop Understanding	
Develop students' understanding of description with the Literary Analysis annotations (ATE p. 289) A	5 min.
Develop students' ability to note spatial relationships with the Reading Strategy annotations (SE p. 288; ATE pp. 287, 290)	5 min.
ASSESS	
Assess Mastery	
Assess students' mastery of the Reading Strategy and Literary Analysis by having them answer the Review and Assess questions (SE/ATE p. 293)	15 min.
Use one or more of the print and media Assessment Resources (ATE p. 295) A	up to 45 min.
EXTEND	
Apply Understanding	
Have students complete the Vocabulary Development Lesson and the Grammar and Style Lesson (SE p. 294) A	20 min.
Apply students' ability to use transitions by using the Writing Lesson (SE/ATE p. 295) A	45 min.
Apply students' understanding of the selection using one or more of the Extension Activities (SE p. 295)	20–90 min.

A ACCELERATED INSTRUCTION:
Use the strategies and activities identified with an A.

UNIVERSAL ACCESS
- ● = Below Level Students
- ▲ = On-Level Students
- ■ = Above Level Students

Time and Resource Manager

Reading Level: Average, Average
Average Number of Instructional Days: 4

RESOURCES

PRINT 📖	TRANSPARENCIES 📄	TECHNOLOGY 💿 🎧 📼
• **Beyond Literature,** Cross-Curricular Connection: Social Studies, p. 16 ▲ ■		• **Interest Grabber Video,** Tape 3 ● ▲ ■
• **Selection Support Workbook:** ● ▲ ■ Literary Analysis, p. 74 Reading Strategy, p. 73 Build Vocabulary, p. 71	• **Literary Analysis and Reading Transparencies,** pp. 31 and 32 ● ▲ ■	
		• **Listening to Literature** ● ▲ ■ Audiocassettes, Side 8 Audio CDs, CD 5
• **Literatura en español** ● ▲ • **Literary Analysis for Enrichment** ■	• **Fine Art Transparencies, Volume 1,** Transparency 2 ● ▲ ■	
• **Formal Assessment:** Selection Test, pp. 76–78 ● ▲ ■ • **Open Book Test,** pp. 46–48 ● ▲ ■ • **Performance Assessment and Portfolio Management,** p. 16 ● ▲ ■ • **PRENTICE HALL ASSESSMENT SYSTEM** ● ▲ ■	• **PRENTICE HALL ASSESSMENT SYSTEM** ● ▲ ■ Skills Practice Answers and Explanations on Transparencies	• **Test Bank Software** ● ▲ ■ • **Got It! Assessment Videotapes,** Tape 2 ● ▲
• **Selection Support Workbook:** ● ▲ ■ Grammar and Style, p. 72 • **Writing and Grammar,** Ruby Level ● ▲ ■ • **Extension Activities,** p. 16 ● ▲ ■	• **Daily Language Practice Transparencies** ● ▲ • **Writing Models and Graphic Organizers on Transparencies,** pp. 9–12 ● ▲ ■	• **Writing and Grammar iText CD-ROM** ● ▲ ■ 💻 *Take It to the Net* www.phschool.com

BLOCK SCHEDULING: Use one 90-minute class period to preteach the selection and have students read it. Use a second 90-minute class period to assess students' mastery of skills and have them complete one of the Extension Activities.

Prepare to Read

**❶ Crossing the Great Divide ◆
The Most Sublime Spectacle on Earth**

Meriwether Lewis (1774–1809)

Meriwether Lewis, along with William Clark and a team of hearty former soldiers, completed a two-year, 8,000-mile expedition across the uncharted territory that the United States acquired in the Louisiana Purchase. Between 1804 and 1806, Lewis and Clark traveled from St. Louis up the Missouri River to its source, then across Rocky Mountain passes to the Pacific coast. When they returned to St. Louis, they brought back valuable information about the Pacific Northwest and the other lands through which they had passed.

An American Expedition Captain Lewis's efforts were sponsored by President Thomas Jefferson, for whom Lewis had served as personal secretary. Jefferson gave Lewis and his team a rigorous assignment: map a passage to the Pacific Ocean, collect scientific information about the regions he traveled, trace the boundaries of the Louisiana territory, and claim the Oregon territory for the United States.

Along his journey, Lewis documented plants, animals, and minerals. To complement Lewis's naturalist interests, Clark provided strong map skills and created detailed sketches of the regions they crossed. The men also encountered a variety of Indian nations on the frontier with whom they traded gifts and information.

Mixed Results When Meriwether Lewis returned to Washington, D.C., after the expedition had concluded, he was received as a national hero. However, because he had not found what Jefferson sought—an all-water route to the Pacific Ocean—he himself thought the journey was a failure.

John Wesley Powell (1834–1902)

As a Union soldier fighting in the Civil War, John Wesley Powell lost an arm at the Battle of Shiloh. Despite this injury, he was the first to navigate and chart the Colorado River and the Grand Canyon.

Exploring the Grand Canyon Powell was a geologist who conducted a daring and dangerous three-month journey on the Colorado River in 1869. Financed by the Smithsonian Institution and Congress, Powell led a party of ten men in four boats. In a reflective moment before he entered the canyon, Powell described the experience ahead of him as "an unknown distance yet to run; an unknown river yet to explore." Entering the Grand Canyon by boat, the explorers faced raging rapids, towering waterfalls, and dangerously sharp rock formations. Once in the canyon, Powell's expedition party split up. Those who had become too terrified of the river went overland at "Separation Rapids" and eventually perished. Powell and the others who remained on the river survived and completed the expedition.

An Early Conservationist Later, in other expeditions, Powell surveyed the Rocky Mountains and the canyons of the Green River. In the 1870s, he directed a federal geographic survey of western lands in the public domain, urging the government to develop plans for using the land. Powell had a profound understanding of the American West, and he warned the government of the hazards of economic exploitation of the region. He spent the rest of his life trying to communicate his message of responsible development of that magnificent but arid, unpredictable, and fragile land.

Step-by-Step Teaching Guide for pp. 284–285

Motivation

Show students a portion of the PBS *Nova* episode entitled "Rafting Through the Grand Canyon" (which includes several excerpts from John Wesley Powell's journal) or any other documentary program about the canyon. Then ask students to write a brief postcard from the Grand Canyon describing to a friend what they have just seen. Have volunteers share their postcard messages. Ask students to discuss how it would feel to be the first person to see such a sight. Explain that the journals that they are about to read are the literary equivalent of post-cards from the American frontier.

▣ Interest Grabber Video

As an alternative, play "Lewis and Clark's Expedition" on Tape 3 to engage student interest.

❶ Background

More About the Authors

Despite Captain Lewis's sense of failure about the expedition, historians credit Lewis and Clark with great leadership skills. They led the expedition across thousands of miles, through the lands of many different Native American peoples, and returned to tell about it. As a reward for the journey, President Jefferson made Lewis governor of the Louisiana Territory. Nonetheless, Lewis did not feel satisfied. Recent research suggests that Lewis's fatal gunshot wound in 1809 was probably self-inflicted.

As a result of his journeys to study the geology of the west, John Wesley Powell developed a profound interest in the Native Americans living on those lands. In fact, he was the first to truly study and classify Native American languages. His expertise contributed to a new government department, the U.S. Bureau of Ethnology, of which he was the first director.

TEACHING RESOURCES

The following resources can be used to enrich or extend the instruction for pp. 284–285.

Motivation

▣ **Interest Grabber Video,** Tape 3 ▣

Background

▣ **Beyond Literature,** p. 16

▣ *Take It to the Net*
Visit www.phschool.com for background and hotlinks for the selections.

Literary Analysis

▣ **Literary Analysis and Reading Transparencies,** Description, p. 32 ▣

Reading

▣ **Literary Analysis and Reading Transparencies,** Noting Spatial Relationships, p. 31

▣ **Selection Support Workbook:** Reading Strategy, p. 73; Build Vocabulary, p. 71

▣ **BLOCK SCHEDULING:** Resources marked with this symbol provide varied instruction during 90-minute blocks.

Preview

Connecting to the Literature

If you have ever had an outdoor adventure while backpacking or mountain climbing, you know how exciting it is to experience the power of nature. Imagine what it would have been like to chart new territory like the adventurers who blazed a trail across the western frontier.

❷ Literary Analysis

Description

Description in writing captures the physical sensations of sight, sound, smell, taste, and touch. Consider this example from Powell's journal:

> But form and color do not exhaust all the divine qualities of the Grand Canyon. It is the land of music. The river thunders in perpetual roar . . .

Look for similar examples of descriptive language that bring scenes to life in these selections. Use a chart like the one shown to record descriptive details.

Descriptions	
Sight	
Sound	
Smell	
Taste	
Touch	

Comparing Literary Works

Both of the men who wrote these selections were working under government commissions to explore uncharted lands. In writing these journals, both explorers sought to describe the amazing sights and experiences of their expeditions to readers in cities and towns far away. While their motives for writing were similar, their styles differ greatly. As you read, note the effects of each **writer's style**—word choice, level of formality, and imagery—on your perception of his experiences.

❸ Reading Strategy

Noting Spatial Relationships

Noting spatial relationships as you read can help to clarify the size, distance, and location of the features being described. Using this information will help you form an accurate mental picture of the subject. Note the spatial relationships in these selections to gain a better understanding of the features they describe.

Vocabulary Development

conspicuous (kən spik´ yōō əs) *adj.* obvious; easy to see or perceive (p. 288)

sublime (sə blīm´) *adj.* inspiring awe or admiration through grandeur or beauty (p. 289)

labyrinth (lab´ə rinth´) *n.* intricate network of winding passages; maze (p. 289)

excavated (eks´ kə vāt´ id) *v.* dug out; made a hole (p. 289)

demarcation (dē´ mär kā´ shən) *n.* separation (p. 290)

multifarious (mul´ tə far´ ē əs) *adj.* having many parts; diverse (p. 291)

multitudinous (mul´ tə tōōd´ 'n əs) *adj.* numerous (p. 291)

Crossing the Great Divide / The Most Sublime Spectacle on Earth ◆ 285

---

❷ Literary Analysis

Description

- Tell students that as they read these journal entries, they will focus on description, writing that captures the physical sensations of an experience or setting.
- Have a volunteer read aloud the excerpted text from Powell's journal. Help students identify sensory words in the excerpt.
- Use the instruction for Comparing Literary Works to prepare students to appreciate the writers' styles in two very different journal excerpts.
- Instruct students to complete the sensory details chart on the student page. Model its use by placing details from the Powell excerpt in the correct place.

❸ Reading Strategy

Noting Spatial Relationships

- Remind students that noting spatial relationships can help them track events and visualize settings.
- Draw students' attention to the three types of spatial relationships mentioned: size, distance, and location. Remind them to pay attention to all three as they read.
- Tell students to jot down spatial relationship clues under the headings *Size, Distance,* and *Location.*

Vocabulary Development

- Pronounce each vocabulary word for students, and read the definitions as a class. Have students identify any words with which they are familiar.

CUSTOMIZE INSTRUCTION FOR UNIVERSAL ACCESS

For Less Proficient Readers	For English Learners	For Advanced Readers
Use the Noting Spatial Relationships transparency in **Literary Analysis and Reading Transparencies,** p. 31, to highlight examples of spatial relationship clues. Invite students to help you demonstrate each type of clue, identifying classroom objects by size, location, and distance.	With a dictionary and with pantomime or visual clues, make sure that students understand the meaning of spatial clues such as *down, below, as far as, to the west, up, headfirst,* and *over the walls.* Use the Noting Spatial Relationships transparency from **Literary Analysis and Reading Transparencies,** p. 31, as a source of examples.	Provide students with an uncompleted copy of the Noting Spatial Relationships transparency from **Literary Analysis and Reading Transparencies,** p. 31. Challenge them to complete it by listing clue words to spatial relationships. Then have students use their own words to describe the settings in the excerpts.

 E-Teach

Visit E-Teach at www.phschool.com for teacher's essays on how to teach, with questions and answers.

**Step-by-Step Teaching Guide
for pp. 286–292**

CUSTOMIZE INSTRUCTION
For Musical/Rhythmic Learners

Students can enhance their appreciation of Powell's journal entry by listening to music composed to celebrate the Grand Canyon. For example, they can listen to *Grand Canyon Suite* by Ferdi Grofé or *Canyon Trilogy* by the Navajo-Ute flutist Carlos Nakai.

❶ About the Selection

Lewis kept an intermittent but very detailed, descriptive, and informative journal of his expedition. Here he describes one of the expedition's many interactions with Native Americans. It is characteristic of Lewis's efforts to persuade Native Americans of the powers of his government and of the advantages of cooperating with him in his mission to reach the Pacific.

❷ Background

Art

Lewis and Clark With Sacagawea at the Great Falls of the Missouri, by Olaf Seltzer

This painting depicts a scene that took place some time during the spring of 1805. Sacagawea, a Shoshone teenager, served as a guide to Lewis and Clark. The fourth figure, York, was Clark's slave and lifelong companion. Use this question for discussion:

• If you were Lewis, how might you describe the landscape in your journal?
Possible response: Students may mention the barren, treeless, rugged landscape; the brown, rocky bluffs; and the white mesas far in the distance that suggest a desertlike terrain.

❸ ▶Critical Viewing

Answer: Students should note that the figures in the painting appear to be at ease with one another. The text, which describes the explorers' friendship with and dependence on the Native Americans, is reflected in the painting.

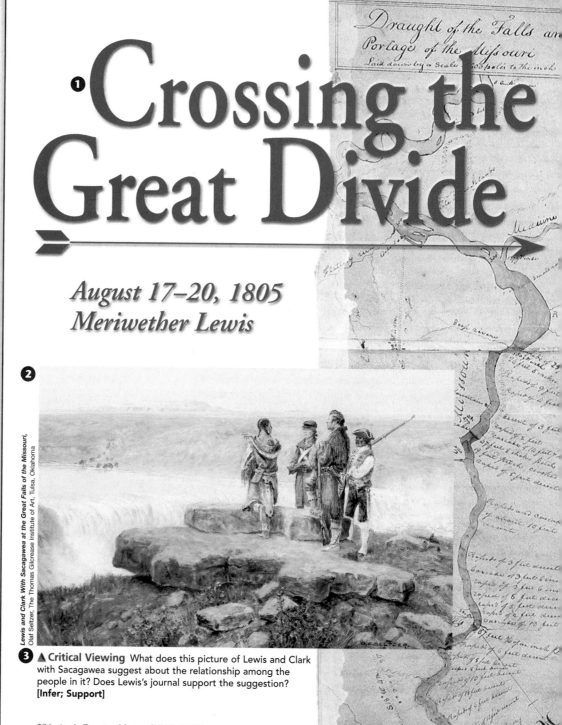

❶ ◦Crossing the Great Divide

*August 17–20, 1805
Meriwether Lewis*

*Lewis and Clark With Sacagawea at the Great Falls of the Missouri,
Olaf Seltzer, The Thomas Gilcrease Institute of Art, Tulsa, Oklahoma*

❸ ▲ **Critical Viewing** What does this picture of Lewis and Clark with Sacagawea suggest about the relationship among the people in it? Does Lewis's journal support the suggestion? **[Infer; Support]**

286 ◆ A Growing Nation (1800–1870)

TEACHING RESOURCES

The following resources can be used to enrich or extend the instruction for pp. 286–292.

Literary Analysis

📓 **Writing Models and Graphic Organizers on Transparencies,** pp. 9–12

📖 **Selection Support:** Literary Analysis, p. 74

Reading

🎧 **Listening to Literature Audiocassettes,** Side 8 ■

💿 **Listening to Literature Audio CDs,** CD 5 ■

Extension

📓 **Fine Art Transparencies, Volume 1,** Art Transparency 2 (Have students speculate about how the pictured discusssion might have influenced Lewis's decisions about his route.) ■

■ **BLOCK SCHEDULING:** Resources marked with this symbol provide varied instruction during 90-minute blocks.

Background

In 1803, the United States doubled the amount of territory it controlled with a single purchase of land from the French. Looking for money to finance its wars against other European nations, France sold land to the United States for a total price of $15 million—less than three cents an acre. Known as the Louisiana Purchase, the acquisition began an era of westward expansion that lasted for nearly a century. These accounts detail what the explorers found in the newly purchased territory.

Saturday, August 17th, 1805

This morning I arose very early and dispatched Drewyer and the Indian down the river. Sent Shields to hunt. I made McNeal cook the remainder of our meat which afforded a slight breakfast for ourselves and the Chief. Drewyer had been gone about 2 hours when an Indian who had straggled some little distance down the river returned and reported that the white men were coming, that he had seen them just below. They all appeared transported with joy, and the chief repeated his fraternal hug. I felt quite as much gratified at this information as the Indians appeared to be. Shortly after Capt. Clark arrived with the Interpreter Charbono, and the Indian woman, who proved to be a sister of the Chief Cameahwait. The meeting of those was really affecting, particularly between Sah-ca-ga-we-ah and an Indian woman, who had been taken prisoner at the same time with her, and who had afterwards escaped from the Minnetares and rejoined her nation. At noon the canoes arrived, and we had the satisfaction once more to find ourselves all together, with a flattering prospect of being able

4 ◄ Critical Viewing What do visuals like maps and illustrations add to the narrative of exploration accounts? **[Interpret]**

5 ▲ Critical Viewing
What does the placement and size of this sketch in Clark's journal reveal about his purpose in creating it? **[Infer]**

6 ☑ Reading Check
What information does the Indian bring to Lewis and his group?

Crossing the Great Divide ◆ 287

4 ▶ Critical Viewing

Answer: In an age before photography, detailed drawings provided the only way to present visual descriptions of the new people, places, and things Lewis encountered in his travels. The maps also provided valuable documentation of the terrain for the use of future travelers and traders.

5 ▶ Critical Viewing

Answer: The size of the sketch suggests that Clark wished to make the image large enough to show details. The placement of the image inside the journal's text reveals that he needed to use each piece of paper fully, since he could not obtain more.

6 ☑ Reading Check

Answer: He has seen a small part of their group, including both Capt. Clark and his interpreters, on the way back to the main camp.

CUSTOMIZE INSTRUCTION FOR UNIVERSAL ACCESS

For Less Proficient Readers	For Special Needs Students	For Advanced Readers
Help students identify familiar words used in unfamiliar ways. Examples include *affecting* ("emotionally moving") and *flattering* ("favorable"). Have volunteers read aloud the sentences from p. 287 that contain each word. Guide students to use context clues to determine the meanings of each usage.	Point out that Lewis's writing—even in a journal—is more formal than most modern writing. Draw students' attention to words such as *gratified*, which simply means "pleased." Help students work through the text on p. 287 word by word to find synonyms for challenging terms. Encourage the use of a dictionary and thesaurus.	Have students identify vocabulary on this page that reflects Lewis's era either through archaic word usage or especial formality. Then challenge students to list as many synonyms or paraphrases for these words or phrases as they can. Have students share these keys to comprehension with the class.

- Read the bracketed passage with students.

- Ask students the Reading Strategy question on p. 288: Which words help readers gain a clearer picture of the campsite? Answer: Words such as *just below*, *Lard. side*, *here*, *on shore*, and *in the ground* help readers get a clear picture.

▶ **Monitor Progress** Have students sketch the scene described in the bracketed text, identifying the words and details they used to help them determine the spatial relationships between the objects mentioned in the passage.

Answers for p. 288

Review and Assess

1. Possible response: Some students might observe that Lewis disguised his real motives.

2. **(a)** He is pleased and relieved. **(b)** He now has hopes of obtaining enough horses to continue the voyage by land if necessary.

3. **(a)** He tells them his goal is to improve trade routes for the Indians' benefit. **(b)** Possible response: Lewis is not being completely candid. Lewis hints at how he misled the Indians when he says that he "gave them as a reason . . . to examine and find out a more direct way to bring merchandise to them."

4. **(a)** He told them to expect trade, defense, and comfort. **(b)** Possible response: He wants them to understand their dependence on the U.S. for certain goods, and to appreciate the government's strength. Thus, he hopes to obtain their help.

5. **(a)** He expected friendliness, horses, guidance through unfamiliar territory, supplies. **(b)** Possible response: He is very persuasive in his bid to convince the Native Americans to cooperate.

---

to obtain as many horses shortly as would enable us to prosecute our voyage by land should that by water be deemed unadvisable.

We now formed our camp just below the junction of the forks on the Lard. side[1] in a level smooth bottom covered with a fine turf of greensward. Here we unloaded our canoes and arranged our baggage on shore; formed a canopy of one of our large sails and planted some willow brush in the ground to form a shade for the Indians to sit under while we spoke to them, which we thought it best to do this evening. Accordingly about 4 P.M. we called them together and through the medium of Labuish, Charbono and Sah-ca-ga-we-ah, we communicated to them fully the objects which had brought us into this distant part of the country, in which we took care to make them a <u>conspicuous</u> object of our own good wishes and the care of our government. We made them sensible of their dependence on the will of our government for every species of merchandise as well for their defense and comfort; and apprised them of the strength of our government and its friendly dispositions towards them. We also gave them as a reason why we wished to penetrate the country as far as the ocean to the west of them was to examine and find out a more direct way to bring merchandise to them. That as no trade could be carried on with them before our return to our homes that it was mutually advantageous to them as well as to ourselves that they should render us such aids as they had it in their power to furnish in order to hasten our voyage and of course our return home.

---

1. **Lard. side** abbreviation for larboard, the port side of a ship. From their perspective, they camped on the left side of the river.

---

conspicuous (kən spik´ yo͞o əs) *adj.* obvious; easy to see or perceive

---

Review and Assess

Thinking About the Selection

1. **Respond:** What did you think of the way Lewis negotiated with the Indians? Explain.

2. **(a) Recall:** How did Lewis feel about being reunited with his party? **(b) Analyze:** What were his reasons for feeling as he did?

3. **(a) Recall:** What did Lewis tell the Indians was the reason for the expedition? **(b) Infer:** Was he being candid in his explanation? Explain.

4. **(a) Recall:** What did Lewis tell the Indians to expect from the United States government? **(b) Speculate:** Why do you think he told the Indians the things he did?

5. **(a) Generalize:** What did Lewis expect from the Indians? **(b) Evaluate:** How would you rate Lewis as a negotiator?

✹ ENRICHMENT: Social Studies Connection

A Formidable Landscape

In 1804, President Thomas Jefferson and his advisers knew almost nothing about the lands Lewis was to explore. For one thing, they thought that there was an all-water route to the Pacific. For another, they thought Lewis and Clark might encounter mastodons. Geographically, all they really knew was the latitude and longitude of the mouth of the Columbia River, St. Louis, and the Mandan peoples' villages along the Missouri River. With so much yet to discover, Jefferson made choices. For example, he chose not to seek gold or silver. Instead, he instructed Lewis to focus on the possibility of establishing trade with the Native Americans.

❽ The Most Sublime Spectacle on Earth

John Wesley Powell

The Grand Canyon of the Colorado is a canyon composed of many canyons. It is a composite of thousands, of tens of thousands, of gorges. In like manner, each wall of the canyon is a composite structure, a wall composed of many walls, but never a repetition. Every one of these almost innumerable gorges is a world of beauty in itself. In the Grand Canyon there are thousands of gorges like that below Niagara Falls, and there are a thousand Yosemites. Yet all these canyons unite to form one grand canyon, the most <u>sublime</u> spectacle on the earth. Pluck up Mt. Washington by the roots to the level of the sea and drop it headfirst into the Grand Canyon, and the dam will not force its waters over the walls. Pluck up the Blue Ridge and hurl it into the Grand Canyon, and it will not fill it.

The carving of the Grand Canyon is the work of rains and rivers. The vast <u>labyrinth</u> of canyon by which the plateau region drained by the Colorado is dissected is also the work of waters. Every river has <u>excavated</u> its own gorge and every creek has excavated its gorge. When a shower comes in this land, the rills carve canyons—but a little at each storm; and though storms are far apart and the heavens above are cloudless for most of the days of the year, still, years are plenty in the ages, and an intermittent rill called to life by a shower can do much work in centuries of centuries.

sublime (sə blīm´) *adj.* inspiring admiration

labyrinth (lab´ ə rin*th*´) *n.* network of passages; maze

excavated (eks´ kə vāt´ id) *v.* dug out; made a hole

❿ **Reading Check**

What is "the most sublime spectacle" on Earth?

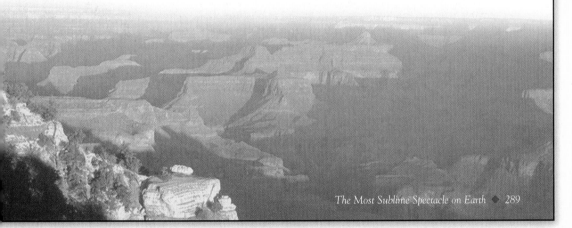

The Most Sublime Spectacle on Earth ◆ 289

CUSTOMIZE INSTRUCTION FOR UNIVERSAL ACCESS

For Less Proficient Readers

Increase students' comprehension by providing the following context: Powell is attempting a written description of a vast and constantly changing landscape that his original readers have never seen. To convey his awestruck impression, he invites the reader to imagine various details of geologic phenomena, sights, and sounds. He imparts information by giving readers statistics, comparisons, and detailed descriptions of colors, sounds, and movements. Help students access this multilayered descriptive text by suggesting that they take time to imagine the visual images and the sounds the author provides. Direct students to specific descriptions on p. 289, such as the comparison of the Canyon to familiar landmarks or the image of water carving out gorges a little at a time. Help students practice visualizing.

❽ About the Selection

In this excerpt, Powell provides a rich description of the grandeur of the Grand Canyon. He writes of its size, the many different layers and formations of rock, its colors, and its shapes. In his attempt to describe its majesty to people who have never seen anything like it, Powell admits to the inadequacy of words.

❾ Literary Analysis

Description

• After students read the text on p. 289, have them reread it, looking for ways in which Powell uses description to help readers appreciate the size and grandeur of the Grand Canyon.

• Ask students to identify the descriptive strategies that Powell uses to help readers appreciate the size and grandeur of the Grand Canyon.

Answer: Powell uses relative sizes, for example, by saying "thousands, tens of thousands, of gorges"; he uses recognizable landmarks such as Niagara Falls to provide benchmarks for readers; he uses vivid sensory details to paint a picture of the place for readers.

▶ **Monitor Progress** Have students complete the graphic organizer from p. 285 with details from these paragraphs to explore the sensory imagery that Powell uses to describe the Grand Canyon.

❿ ✓ Reading Check

Answer: The Grand Canyon is the "most sublime spectacle" on Earth.

❶❶ Background

The Hudson River School

Also known as Romantic Realists, the artists of the Hudson River school loved the untainted and untamed American wilderness. They combined detailed panoramic landscapes with the moral messages found in the literature of the time. The style of the Hudson River artists led to the creation of the National Academy of Design. An 1836 exhibit held by the academy was praised by writers such as William Cullen Bryant and James Fenimore Cooper.

❶❷ Reading Strategy

Noting Spatial Relationships

- Invite a volunteer to read aloud the bracketed passage. Urge students to jot down spatial word clues as they hear them.
- Ask students to identify the words or phrases that help them visualize the rock formations and other geologic features of the grand vista Powell describes.

Possible responses: below, the foundation, crowned, covered, from below, seem to graduate, a portion, vast, wall to wall, spanning, blended, vast

The erosion represented in the canyons, although vast, is but a small part of the great erosion of the region, for between the cliffs blocks have been carried away far superior in magnitude to those necessary to fill the canyons. Probably there is no portion of the whole region from which there have not been more than a thousand feet degraded, and there are districts from which more than 30,000 feet of rock have been carried away. Altogether, there is a district of country more than 200,000 square miles in extent from which on the average more than 6,000 feet have been eroded. Consider a rock 200,000 square miles in extent and a mile in thickness, against which the clouds have hurled their storms and beat it into sands and the rills have carried the sands into the creeks and the creeks have carried them into the rivers and the Colorado has carried them into the sea. We think of the mountains as forming clouds about their brows, but the clouds have formed the mountains. Great continental blocks are upheaved from beneath the sea by internal geologic forces that fashion the earth. Then the wandering clouds, the tempest-bearing clouds, the rainbow-decked clouds, with mighty power and with wonderful skill, carve out valleys and canyons and fashion hills and cliffs and mountains. The clouds are the artists sublime.

In winter some of the characteristics of the Grand Canyon are emphasized. The black gneiss[1] below, the variegated quartzite, and the green or alcove sandstone form the foundation for the mighty red wall. The banded sandstone entablature is crowned by the tower limestone. In winter this is covered with snow. Seen ❶❷ from below, these changing elements seem to graduate into the heavens, and no plane of <u>demarcation</u> between wall and blue firmament[2] can be seen. The heavens constitute a portion of the facade and mount into a vast dome from wall to wall, spanning the Grand canyon with empyrean blue. So the earth and the heavens are blended in one vast structure.

When the clouds play in the canyon, as they often do in the rainy season, another set of effects is produced. Clouds creep out of canyons and wind into other canyons. The heavens seem to be alive, not moving as move the heavens over a plain, in one direction with the wind, but following the multiplied courses of these gorges. In this manner the little clouds seem to be individualized, to have wills and souls of their own, and to be going on diverse errands—a vast assemblage of self-willed clouds, faring here and there, intent upon purposes hidden in their own breasts. In the imagination the clouds belong to the sky, and when they are in the canyon the skies come

---

1. **gneiss** (nīs) *n.* coarse-grained metamorphic rock resembling granite, consisting of alternating layers of minerals such as feldspar, quartz, and mica and having a banded appearance.
2. **firmament** (furm´ ə mənt) *n.* sky.

290 ◆ *A Growing Nation (1800–1870)*

❶❶ The Hudson River School

Writers and explorers were not the only ones who responded to the beauty of the American landscape—artists were inspired by it as well. In 1825, British-born American painter Thomas Cole founded the Hudson River school, a group of artists who painted strikingly beautiful images of the Hudson River Valley and America's wilderness and western frontier. These paintings—such as the one shown on page 291—featured the effects of sunsets and dramatic weather on mountains, ravines, and rivers. Cole and his fellow artists searched for exciting and uniquely American images and helped to create an artistic identity for the young nation.

demarcation (dē´ mär kā´ shən) *n.* separation

☀ ENRICHMENT: Science Connection

The Grand Canyon

Located in northwest Arizona, the Grand Canyon is nearly one mile deep, up to 18 miles wide, and 277 miles long.

Around 6 million years ago, the Colorado River began carving its way through the rock to form the Grand Canyon. The warping of Earth's crust steepened the river's path, increasing the water's velocity and volume. The rushing river, which carried large amounts of abrasive mud, sand, and gravel, wore away the soft rock, cutting sharp, deep channels. The almost rainless climate preserved the steep pitch of the canyon walls, which otherwise would have been softened or even entirely eroded by rain wash, leaving only gentle hills behind.

The layers of rock in the canyon's walls contain a historical record of geological events. The oldest rocks at the bottom of the canyon may be as many as four billion years old.

down into the gorges and cling to the cliffs and lift them up to immeasurable heights, for the sky must still be far away. Thus they lend infinity to the walls.

The wonders of the Grand Canyon cannot be adequately represented in symbols of speech, nor by speech itself. The resources of the graphic art are taxed beyond their powers in attempting to portray its features. Language and illustration combined must fail. The elements that unite to make the Grand Canyon the most sublime spectacle in nature are <u>multifarious</u> and exceedingly diverse. The Cyclopean forms which result from the sculpture of tempests through ages too long for man to compute, are wrought into endless details, to describe which would be a task equal in magnitude to that of describing the stars of the heavens or the <u>multitudinous</u> beauties of the forest with its traceries of foliage presented by oak and pine and poplar, by beech and linden and hawthorn, by tulip and lily and rose, by fern and moss and lichen. Besides the elements of form, there are elements of color, for here the colors of the heavens are rivaled by the colors of the rocks. The rainbow is not more replete with hues. But form and color do not exhaust all the divine qualities of the Grand Canyon. It is the land of music. The river thunders in perpetual roar, swelling in floors of music when the storm gods play upon the rocks and fading away in soft and low murmurs when the infinite blue of heaven is unveiled. With the melody of the great tide rising and falling, swelling and vanishing forever, other melodies are heard in the gorges of the lateral[3] canyons, while the waters plunge in the rapids among the rocks or leap in great cataracts. Thus the Grand Canyon is a land of song. Mountains of music swell in the rivers, hills of music billow in the creeks, and meadows of music murmur in the rills that ripple over the rocks. Altogether it is a symphony of multitudinous melodies. All this is the music of waters. The adamant foundations of the earth have been wrought into a sublime harp, upon which the clouds of the heavens play with mighty tempests or with gentle showers.

The glories and the beauties of form, color, and sound unite in the Grand Canyon—forms unrivaled even by the mountains, colors that

---

3. **lateral** (lat′ ər əl) *adj.* of, from, or at the sides.

Grand Canyon With Rainbow, 1912 (detail), Thomas Moran, Fine Arts Museum of San Francisco

15

14 ▲ **Critical Viewing**
Compare Powell's description with the painter's interpretation of the same natural wonder. [**Compare**]

multifarious (mul′ tə far′ ē əs) *adj.* having many parts; diverse **13**

multitudinous (mul′ tə tōōd′ 'n əs) *adj.* numerous

16 ✓ **Reading Check**
Why does Powell describe the Grand Canyon as the "land of song"?

The Most Sublime Spectacle on Earth ◆ 291

---

13 **Vocabulary Development**
The Latin prefix *multi-*

• Call students' attention to the word *multifarious* on page 291 and to its definition. Let students know that the prefix *multi-* derives from the Latin word *multus* meaning "much" or "many."

• Ask students to volunteer words with which they are familiar that begin with this prefix.
Possibilities include: multiple, multilingual, multimedia, multimillionaire, and multicultural.

• List student words on the chalkboard as they are mentioned. When the list is complete, erase the prefix *multi-* from the words. Guide students to recognize how the addition of the prefix adds the idea of "many" to nouns.

14 ▶ **Critical Viewing**
Answer: Students may respond that the painting vividly captures the beautiful colors, forms, and unusual cloud formations Powell describes. The painting does not, however, convey how the scene changes under different conditions, nor does it convey the "music" of the canyon's waters—both of which are important parts of Powell's written description of the Grand Canyon.

15 **Background**
Art

Grand Canyon With Rainbow, by Thomas Moran

English immigrant Thomas Moran traveled to Yellowstone Park in 1871 and—like Powell—was captivated by its natural beauty. In this powerful landscape painting, Moran captures the vivid colors and beauty of the Grand Canyon. Use this question for discussion:

• Would Powell have approved of this painting as an illustration for his journal passage? Explain.
Possible response: He probably would have approved of the painting because it captures the striking colors and forms that he describes in such detail.

16 ✓ **Reading Check**
Answer: Powell hears many sounds of nature in the Grand Canyon.

CUSTOMIZE INSTRUCTION FOR UNIVERSAL ACCESS

For Less Proficient Readers	For English Learners	For Advanced Readers
Help students build background for reading Powell's journal. Read the Enrichment: Science Connection information on TE p. 290 to students, answering any questions they have. Then model for students how to use the Cause and Effect transparency from **Writing Models and Graphic Organizers on Transparencies**, p. 91 to track the canyon's formation.	Distribute the Cause and Effect organizer in **Writing Models and Graphic Organizers on Transparencies**, pp. 91–93. Instruct students to enter "Formation of the Grand Canyon" under "Major Event." Then, have students carefully reread pages 290–291, identifying causes of the formation of the canyon and entering them in the appropriate boxes.	Have students look into current ecological issues related to the Grand Canyon, specifically, the effects of the Glen Canyon Dam. Provide students with Cause and Effect transparency from **Writing Models and Graphic Organizers on Transparencies**, p. 91, as a framework in which to organize their findings.

Answers for p. 292

Review and Assess

1. **Possible responses: (a)** Powell was driven by the need to make the reader understand the scope and magnificence of the Grand Canyon. **(b)** He was inspired by the sight of the Grand Canyon.

2. **(a)** He describes the form, color, and sounds of the canyon. **(b)** He appeals to sight and to hearing.

3. **(a)** One effect is the blending of canyon walls into sky in the winter; the other is the effect of clouds playing in the canyons during the rainy season. **(b)** Powell effectively conveys the varied sights, sounds, and ever-changing quality of these features of the Grand Canyon.

4. **(a)** The details that make up the beauty of the Grand Canyon are too many and too varied for language or illustration to adequately describe. **(b)** Powell's journey seems to have been an awe-inspiring experience.

5. **(a) Possible response:** A painting can capture the colors, the forms, and the play of light and shadow in a way that words cannot. **(b)** A description can convey changes that take place over time, as well as the sounds that are part of the Grand Canyon experience.

6. **Possible responses: (a)** They would effectively convey the size and grandeur of the Grand Canyon, as well as its varied physical features. **(b)** What kind of animals live there? What peoples, if any, make their home along the river's edge?

---

vie with sunsets, and sounds that span the diapason[4] from tempest to tinkling raindrop, from cataract to bubbling fountain. But more: it is a vast district of country. Were it a valley plain it would make a state. It can be seen only in parts from hour to hour and from day to day and from week to week and from month to month. A year scarcely suffices to see it all. It has infinite variety, and no part is ever duplicated. Its colors, though many and complex at any instant, change with the ascending and declining sun; lights and shadows appear and vanish with the passing clouds, and the changing seasons mark their passage in changing colors. You cannot see the Grand Canyon in one view, as if it were a changeless spectacle from which a curtain might be lifted, but to see it you have to toil from month to month through its labyrinths. It is a region more difficult to traverse than the Alps or the Himalayas, but if strength and courage are sufficient for the task, by a year's toil a concept of sublimity can be obtained never again to be equaled on the hither side of Paradise.

---

4. **diapason** (dī´ ə pā´ zən) *n.* entire range of a musical instrument.

Review and Assess

Thinking About the Selection

1. **Respond: (a)** Why do you think Powell says much about the Grand Canyon but almost nothing about his journey? **(b)** What do you think that says about him?

2. **(a) Recall:** List three aspects of the Grand Canyon that Powell describes at length. **(b) Analyze:** To what senses does Powell appeal in those descriptions?

3. **(a) Recall:** Powell describes two special visual effects that are produced seasonally. What are they? **(b) Evaluate:** What is effective about the descriptions?

4. **(a) Interpret:** What point does he make when he writes that, in portraying the Grand Canyon, "Language and illustration combined must fail"? **(b) Draw Conclusions:** What do you think it meant to Powell to explore the Grand Canyon?

5. **(a) Compare and Contrast:** What might a painting of the Grand Canyon show that a description cannot? **(b) Compare and Contrast:** What can a description include that a painting cannot?

6. **(a) Assess:** If you were reading this description without any prior knowledge of the Grand Canyon, what would Powell's words effectively convey? **(b) Criticize:** What further questions might you have?

292 ◆ *A Growing Nation (1800–1870)*

✐ ASSESSMENT PRACTICE: Reading Comprehension

Make Inferences and Generalizations	**(For more practice, see Test Preparation Workbook, p. 18.)**

Many tests ask students to make inferences about implied information. After students read "Crossing the Great Divide," ask: Why does Lewis emphasize the U.S. government's "friendly disposition" toward the Indians in his meeting with them?

  A He wants them to help his expedition.
  B He wants to join their community.
  C He wants them to join the United States.
  D He wants to take their land.

B, C, and *D* are not supported by the passage. Lewis explains that if the Indians help the explorers reach the Pacific Ocean and then return home, the government will provide them with many benefits. Thus, choice *A* is correct.

Review and Assess

Literary Analysis

Description

1. (a) Choose three passages of **description** in "The Most Sublime Spectacle on Earth." (b) What makes each one effective?
2. Lewis is not as descriptive as Powell, but he does include some descriptive elements in his writing. Identify a passage in Lewis's journal that helps readers see his camp.

Comparing Literary Works

3. Based on these accounts, what differences do you see in the **writers' styles**?
4. Judging by the amount of description each writer includes, what would you guess is the purpose of each piece? Support your answer with references from the selections.
5. Considering Lewis's word choice, tone, and level of formality, how would you categorize his style of writing?
6. Which of the two accounts do you find more effective, and why? Support your answer with evidence from the selections.

Reading Strategy

Noting Spatial Relationships

7. **Noting relationships** of space and size as Powell describes them, determine which is greater—the erosion of the canyons or the erosion of the region? Explain.
8. Using a chart like the one shown, note details that indicate size and spatial relationships of the Grand Canyon. Then, describe these relationships in your own words.

Description	Spatial Relationships	In My Own Words

Extend Understanding

9. **Social Studies Connection:** Where are some unexplored areas in the world today? Upon which of these do you think we should focus the most attention? Why?

Crossing the Great Divide / The Most Sublime Spectacle on Earth ◆ 293

Quick Review

Description is language or writing that uses sensory details to create a word picture.

A **writer's style** includes such elements as word choice, tone, level of formality, figurative language, imagery, and sentence structure.

To **note spatial relationships,** pay attention to the description of sizes, distances, and locations of features.

 Take It to the Net
www.phschool.com
Take the interactive self-test online to check your understanding of these selections.

✳ ENRICHMENT: Further Reading

Other Works by the Authors

Other Works about Powell

Exploration of the Colorado River of the West and Its Tributaries

Other Works by Lewis

The Journals of the Lewis and Clark Expedition, ed. G. E. Moulton

 Take It to the Net
Visit www.phschool.com for more information on the authors.

Answers for p. 293

Review and Assess

1. **(a)** Students should choose passages that are rich in descriptive imagery. **(b)** Examples of what makes passages descriptive should include vivid sensory details and clear spatial orientation.
2. Possible responses: Students should identify a passage that describes Lewis's camp.
3. Possible response: Lowell occasionally uses phrases or incomplete sentences, in true journal format, while Powell writes more formally in longer and more complex sentences.
4. Possible response: Lewis seems more focused on portraying a view of himself while Powell wants only to describe his surroundings.
5. Possible response: His style is factual; it conveys information rather than emotions.
6. Most students will probably find Powell's account more effective because of its detailed description.
7. Answer: The erosion of the region is greater. Powell states that one is greater than the other.
8. Possible responses: Description: Powell's description of the behavior of clouds in the Grand Canyon during rain. Spatial Relationships: Out of canyons, into other canyons, over a plain, in one direction, multiplied courses, vast, here and there, the skies come down, lift them up, far away, infinity. In My Own Words: During the rainy season, the canyon is filled with clouds that spread into all its crevices. Because clouds are usually seen in the sky, this image of the canyon makes it look as if the sky had come down into the canyon and as if its walls stretched upward forever.
9. Possible response: Antarctica is largely unexplored, as are many parts of the ocean. Both these places merit exploration.

❶ Vocabulary Development

Word Analysis

1. multiply: increase something many times

2. multicultural: having or characterized by many different cultures

3. multimedia: a combination of many different types of media, such as television, radio, print, and photography

Spelling Strategy

1. vision
2. explosion
3. examination
4. situation
5. dimension
6. explanation

Fluency: Clarify Word Meaning

1. Yes, because they are obvious.

2. It probably is not, because a rainstorm might delay or curtail graduation celebrations.

3. To be prepared, one should have a compass, pencil and paper to make a map, and enough food to last for some time.

4. A bucket and a shovel are usually used to dig out a sandbox.

5. Yes it is, because it clearly defines and separates adjoining spaces.

6. Possible response: Yes; I like to wear many different types of clothes.

7. Yes, anthills are occupied by swarms of ants.

❷ Grammar and Style

1. "described by Powell" modifies *sights*

2. "known as Sacagawea" modifies *woman*

3. "Begun in 1804" modifies *expedition*

4. "deeply moved by what he saw" modifies *Powell*

5. "published years after his visit" modifies *description*

Writing Application

Paragraphs should be free of major mechanical errors and should contain at least three participial phrases.

Integrate Language Skills

❶ Vocabulary Development Lesson

Word Analysis: Latin Prefix *multi-*

The word *multitudinous* contains the common Latin prefix *multi-*, which means "many" or "much." The word "multitudinous" means "numerous." Write definitions for each of the following words.

1. multiply
2. multicultural
3. multimedia

Spelling Strategy

In general, use *-tion* to spell the sound of *shun*, as in *portion*. Use *-sion* to spell the sound of *zhun*, as in *erosion*. Complete each word with: *-tion* or *-sion*.

1. vi__
2. explo__
3. examina__
4. situa__
5. dimen__
6. explana__

Fluency: Clarify Word Meaning

Review the vocabulary list on p. 285. Then, answer the following questions. Explain each answer, referring to the meaning of italicized word in the question.

1. Are *conspicuous* omissions easy to find?

2. Is a graduation-day rainstorm a *sublime* experience?

3. How would you prepare before entering an unexplored *labyrinth*?

4. What tools are used to *excavate* a sandbox?

5. Is a fence a sign of *demarcation*?

6. Is your wardrobe *multifarious*?

7. Are the inhabitants of an anthill *multitudinous*?

❷ Grammar and Style Lesson

Participial Phrases

A **participial phrase** consists of a participle (a verb form used as an adjective to modify a noun or pronoun) and its complements and modifiers. Participial phrases can add details to descriptions.

> **Past Participle:** The Grand Canyon is a canyon <u>composed of many canyons</u>. (modifies *canyon*)

Practice Identify each participial phrase, and explain the word it modifies.

1. Sights described by Powell can be seen today.

2. Lewis's expedition would fail without the woman known as Sacagawea.

3. Begun in 1804, the expedition to explore uncharted territories of the United States took two years.

4. Deeply moved by what he saw, Powell produced a poetic description.

5. Powell's description of the Grand Canyon, published years after his visit, set off a wave of tourism.

Writing Application Write a paragraph describing something that you recently witnessed. In your writing, include sensory images and at least three participial phrases.

W̶G̶ *Prentice Hall Writing and Grammar Connection: Chapter 19, Section 2*

TEACHING RESOURCES

The following resources can be used to enrich or extend the instruction for pp. 294–295.

Vocabulary

📖 **Selection Support Workbook:** Build Vocabulary, p. 71

📖 **Vocabulary and Spelling Practice Book** (Use this booklet for skills enrichment.) ▪

Grammar

📖 **Selection Support Workbook:** Grammar and Style p. 72

W̶G̶ **Writing and Grammar,** Ruby Level, p. 442

📄 **Daily Language Practice Transparencies** ▪

Writing

W̶G̶ **Writing and Grammar,** Ruby Level, p. 100

💿 **Writing and Grammar iText CD-ROM**

📄 **Writing Models and Graphic Organizers on Transparencies,** pp. 9–12

📄 **Fine Art Transparencies, Volume 1,** Art Transparency 2

▪ **BLOCK SCHEDULING:** Resources marked with this symbol provide varied instruction during 90-minute blocks.

❸ Writing Lesson

Description of a Natural Wonder

Have you ever seen a natural wonder—something so amazing that it leaves you searching for words to describe it? Choose a natural wonder that you have observed directly, learned about through research, or seen on film. Like Powell, write a description of it, using sensory images so that your readers can share your experience.

Prewriting   Picture the natural wonder you are going to describe. Create a rough sketch of your subject, and jot down some details. Also jot down the feelings your subject evoked in you.

Drafting   Decide which feature you will describe first, and continue logically and spatially from that point. Use transitions such as *behind, next to, in front of,* or *at the bottom* to show the relationship of details in your description.

> ### Model: Using Transitions to Show Place
>
> The solitary rock, as tall as a skyscraper, stood guard *at the foot* of the canyon, *just to the east* of the rushing river. We looked past the lone sentinel, *up the canyon,* to the plateau *in the distance.*

The transitions *at the foot, just to the east, past, up,* and *in the distance* aid and enhance the description by clarifying spatial relationships.

Revising   Review your work, adding or changing your sensory details to make the description more clear. Look for places where you can add transitions to clarify the spatial relationships.

 Prentice Hall Writing and Grammar Connection: Chapter 6, Section 2

❹ Extension Activities

Listening and Speaking In a small group, create a **tourism presentation** about a Grand Canyon sightseeing tour by raft. Address the following aspects of the tour:

- Present a vivid description of the sights.
- Provide an explanation of what rafting through the Grand Canyon will be like.
- Offer a list of the clothing and equipment to take along.

Use slides and photos of the canyon to enrich your presentation. **[Group Activity]**

Research and Technology Prepare a map showing Lewis and Clark's expedition route from its start in St. Louis, Missouri, to its conclusion at the Oregon coast. Use the Internet to gather details about the journey. If possible, use a desktop publishing program to produce an **expedition map** and an informative brochure to accompany it.

Take It to the Net   www.phschool.com

Go online for an additional research activity using the Internet.

ASSESSMENT RESOURCES

The following resources can be used to assess students' knowledge and skills.

Selection Assessment

- **Formal Assessment,** pp. 76–78
- **Open Book Test,** pp. 46–48
- **Got It! Assessment Videotapes,** Tape 2
- **Test Bank Software**

 Take It to the Net
Visit www.phschool.com for self-tests and additional questions on the selections.

Writing Rubric

- **Performance Assess. and Portfolio Mgmt.,** p. 16

PRENTICE HALL ASSESSMENT SYSTEM

- **Workbook**
- **Skill Book**
- **Transparencies**
- **CD-ROM**

---

❸ Writing Lesson

- Reread a portion of Powell's description to remind students of its descriptive elements.
- Offer students the scene in **Fine Art Transparencies,** Volume 1, Art Transparency 2, as an alternative visual stimulus or provide books depicting the world's great natural wonders.
- Read through the Writing Lesson steps with students and clarify any confusion.
- Use the Writing Process Model 2: Descriptive and Observational Writing, **Writing Models and Graphic Organizers on Transparencies,** pp. 9–12, to introduce the elements of descriptive writing.
- Use the Description rubric in **Performance Assessment and Portfolio Management,** p. 16, to evaluate students' descriptions.

❹ Research and Technology

- Help students identify likely research avenues, for example, historical sites or even those from government geological or historical departments. Historical atlases are also rich information sources.
- Provide students with sample maps of the complexity level you expect to see from them. These maps should be relatively simple with political boundaries and very major geographical landmarks labeled.
- Direct students to sketch their maps before they attempt to create a computerized version.
- Have each student present his or her map and brochure to the class in a guided tour.

CUSTOMIZE INSTRUCTION
For Universal Access

To address different learning styles, use the activities suggested in the Extension Activities booklet, p. 15.

For Intrapersonal Learners, use Activity 5.

For Musical/Rhythmic Learners, use Activity 6.

For Visual/Spatial Learners, use Activity 7.

Lesson Objectives

1. To analyze patterns of organization within texts

2. To learn how to read a memorandum

About Memorandums

- Write the word *memorandum* on the chalkboard. Underline the first five letters and point out the link to the words *memory* and *remember*. A memorandum is a note that will help the recipient remember something of importance.

- Ask students to list situations in which memorandums might be useful.
  Possible answers: Any time you have to remember something, it's good to have a written record of it. Memorandums of agreements made in meetings are important so that there can't be any disagreement afterwards.

Reading Strategy

Analyzing Text Structure: Patterns of Organization

- Have students read and discuss the paragraphs under the Reading Strategy head at the right.

- Challenge students to come up with at least one more type of writing for each pattern of organization listed in the chart.
  Answer: Chronological order: minutes from a meeting. Order of importance: instructions for carrying out a number of tasks of varying importance. Enumeration: instructions for carrying out tasks of equal importance.

Memorandums

About Memorandums

You may already have a job, or you may be planning for your career. Either way, you are likely to read memorandums, or memos, in your workplace.

In today's workplace, the average memorandum is brief and rather informal in tone. It usually contains a heading beginning with these recognizable lines:

    TO: (naming the recipient (s) of the memo)

    FROM: (naming the sender)

    DATE:

    TOPIC:

The body of the note contains only a few facts—for example, an announcement of a time change for a staff meeting or a reminder about a deadline.

The memorandums that you read today may differ from those written in the past. Historical memorandums may be more formal, longer, and more detailed. You will find these qualities in the following memorandum, written by President Thomas Jefferson when he assigned Meriwether Lewis to undertake the exploration of the Missouri River.

Reading Strategy

Analyzing Text Structures: Patterns of Organization

Informative writing of any length can follow several different patterns of organization. Three patterns are described below.

Common Patterns of Organization

Pattern of Organization	Structure	Type of writing in which it is found
Chronological Order	Details appear in the sequence in which they occur.	do-it-yourself instructions
Order of Importance	Information is arranged so that ideas flow from most to least important, or build from least to most important.	persuasive writing
Enumeration	Supporting details are provided in list form.	brochures or sales documents

Commission of Meriwether Lewis

Thomas Jefferson
Historic memorandum

June 20, 1803

To Meriwether Lewis, esquire, captain of the first regiment of infantry of the United States of America: Your situation as secretary of the president of the United States, has made you acquainted with the objects of my confidential message of January 18, 1803, to the legislature; you have seen the act they passed, which, though expressed in general terms, was meant to sanction those objects, and you are appointed to carry them into execution.

. . .

The object of your mission is to explore the Missouri river, and such principal streams of it, as, by its course and communication with the waters of the Pacific ocean, whether the Columbia, Oregan [*sic*], Colorado, or any other river, may offer the most direct and practicable water-communication across the continent, for the purposes of commerce.

Beginning at the mouth of the Missouri, you will take observations of latitude and longitude, at all remarkable points on the river, and especially at the mouths of rivers, at rapids, at islands, and other places and objects distinguished by such natural marks and characters, of a durable kind, as that they may with certainty be recognized hereafter. The courses of the river between these points of observation may be supplied by the compass, the log-line, and by time, corrected by the observations themselves. The variations of the needle, too, in different places, should be noticed.

The interesting points of the portage between the heads of the Missouri, and of the water offering the best communication with the Pacific Ocean, should also be fixed by observation; and the course of that water to the ocean, in the same manner as that of the Missouri.

Your observations are to be taken with great pains and accuracy; to be entered distinctly and intelligibly for others as well as yourself; to comprehend all the elements necessary, with the aid of the usual tables, to fix the latitude and longitude of the places at which they were taken; and are to be rendered to the war-office, for the purpose of having the calculations made concurrently by proper persons within the United States. Several copies of these, as well as of your other notes, should be made at leisure times, and put into the care of the most trustworthy of your attendants to guard, by multiplying them against the accidental losses to which they will be exposed. A further guard would be, that one of these copies be on the cuticular membranes of the paper-birch, as less liable to injury from damp than common paper.

The commerce which may be carried on with the people inhabiting the line you will pursue, renders a knowledge of those people important. You will therefore endeavor to make yourself acquainted, as far as a diligent pursuit of your journey shall admit, with the names of the nations and their numbers;

The extent and limits of their possessions;

Their relations with other tribes or nations;

Their language, traditions, monuments;

Their ordinary occupations in agriculture, fishing, hunting, war, arts, and the implements for these;

Their food, clothing, and domestic accommodations;

The diseases prevalent among them, and the remedies they use;

Moral and physical circumstances which distinguish them from the tribes we know;

> Although this historical memorandum does not have the same format as a modern memorandum, it still begins with the date and the name of the recipient.

> Jefferson takes the time in this memorandum to explain not only what is required but also why it is required.

Commission of Meriwether Lewis

- Point out that Jefferson lays out in specific detail what he expects Lewis to do.
- Point out the phrase "as far as a diligent pursuit of your journey shall admit" (a little over halfway down the right column). Ask students what this implies about the main purpose of Lewis's assignment.
  Answer: The main purpose is to find a waterway across the continent. Gathering information about the Indians is a secondary purpose, to be accomplished as far as his time allows.

CUSTOMIZE INSTRUCTION FOR UNIVERSAL ACCESS

For Less Proficient Readers	For Advanced Readers
Challenge students to find the main idea of each section of the memo and then to go on and identify supporting or contributing details. Students should work with peer tutors who read easily and fluently, since Jefferson's language may pose difficulties in comprehension.	Challenge students to locate and read Jefferson's complete instructions to Lewis, and then to dip into the journals kept by Lewis and Clark. Students can evaluate how well the journals comply with Jefferson's instructions and note the plans of organization evident in the journal entries.

Commission of Meriwether Lewis
(continued)

- Point out the lists of what Lewis is to note about the Indians and about the landscape. Ask students why lists like these are useful to the recipient of a memorandum. **Answer:** They are helpful because they highlight important points. If the listed items were written in running text, they would be harder to notice and remember.

- Ask students why Jefferson wrote this memorandum in order of importance with Lewis's most important task first. Why did he not write it in chronological order? **Answer:** He wrote it in order of importance with the most important task first so that Lewis would understand what the main purpose of his journey was. It couldn't have been written in chronological order because Lewis and his party will have to accomplish all of their tasks concurrently: they will meet Indians and take notes on the landscape during their search for the Pacific.

Peculiarities in their laws, customs, and dispositions;

And articles of commerce they may need or furnish, and to what extent.

And, considering the interest which every nation has in extending and strengthening the authority of reason and justice among the people around them, it will be useful to acquire what knowledge you can of the state of morality, religion, and information among them; as it may better enable those who may endeavor to civilize and instruct them, to adapt their measures to the existing notions and practices of those on whom they are to operate.

Other objects worthy of notice will be—The soil and face of the country, its growth and vegetable productions, especially those not of the United States;

The animals of the country generally, and especially those not known in the United States;

The remains and accounts of any which may be deemed rare or extinct;

The mineral productions of every kind, but more particularly metals, limestone, pit-coal, and saltpeter; salines and mineral waters, noting the temperature of the last, and such circumstances as may indicate their character;

Volcanic appearances;

Climate, as characterized by the thermo-meter, by the proportion of rainy, cloudy, and clear days; by lightning, hail, snow, ice; by the access and recess of frost; by the winds prevailing at different seasons; the dates at which particular plants put forth, or lose their flower or leaf; times of appearance of particular birds, reptiles or insects.. . .

In all your [dealings] with the natives, treat them in the most friendly and conciliatory manner which their own conduct will admit; allay all jealousies as to the object of your journey; satisfy them of its innocence; make them acquainted with the position, extent, character, peaceable and commercial dispositions of the United States; of our

wish to be neighborly, friendly, and useful to them, and of our dispositions to a commercial [relationship] with them; confer with them on the points most convenient as mutual emporiums, and the articles of most desirable interchange for them and us. If a few of their influential chiefs, within practicable distance, wish to visit us, arrange such a visit with them, and furnish them with authority to call on our officers on their entering the United States, to have them conveyed to this place at the public expense. If any of them should wish to have some of their young people brought up with us, and taught such arts as may be useful to them, we will receive, instruct, and take care of them. Such a mission, whether of influential chiefs, or of young people, would give some security to your own party. Carry with you some matter of the kine-pox; inform those of them with whom you may be of its efficacy as a preservative from the small-pox, and instruct and encourage them in the use of it. This may be especially done wherever you winter.

As it is impossible for us to foresee in what manner you will be received by those people, whether with hospitality or hostility, so is it impossible to prescribe the exact degree of perseverance with which you are to pursue your journey. We value too much the lives of citizens to offer them to probable destruction. Your numbers will be sufficient to secure you against the unauthorized opposition of individuals, or of small parties; but if a superior force, authorized, or not authorized, by a nation, should be arrayed against your further passage, and inflexibly determined to arrest it, you must decline its further pursuit and return. In the loss of yourselves we should lose also the information you will have acquired. By returning safely with that, you may enable us to renew the essay with better calculated means. To your own discretion, therefore, must be left the degree of danger you may risk, and the point at which you should decline, only saying, we wish you to err on the side of your safety, and to bring back your party safe, even if it be with less information. . . .

Like today's memorandums, this historical memorandum focuses on precise facts.

Check Your Comprehension

1. Why does Jefferson want Lewis to explore the Missouri River?
2. What information does Jefferson consider so important that he wants Lewis to make multiple copies of it?
3. How is Lewis to treat Native Americans whom he meets?

Applying the Reading Strategy

Analyzing Text Structures: Patterns of Organization

4. Copy this chart below, leaving room to make notes. Complete the chart by naming one example of each type of organization in this historical memorandum.

Pattern of Organization	Examples
Chronological Order	
Order of Importance	
Enumeration	

Activity

Writing a Modern Memorandum

In Jefferson were to write "Commission of Meriwether Lewis" today, he probably would compose several different memorandums, each with its own date and special focus. Choose one topic that Jefferson covers and write one such memorandum. Use modern language to share the information clearly and concisely, following the format shown in the example.

TO: Meriwether Lewis
FROM: Thomas Jefferson
DATE: June 15, 1803
TOPIC: Animals and Vegetables

Contrasting Informational Materials

Patterns of Organization

Part of Lewis's job would have been to turn Jefferson's commission into day-to-day instructions for the expedition. Today, a handbook would present such material. If Lewis had prepared a handbook, what kind of information would he have presented in chronological order? In order of importance? Through enumeration? Give an example of each.

Check Your Comprehension

1. He wants Lewis to find a waterway to the Pacific Ocean and to take accurate notes of everything he encounters along the way.

2. He wants all Lewis' notes copied, but especially the latitude and longitude of the places he sees.

3. He is to be "friendly and conciliatory."

Apply the Reading Strategy

4. Chronological order: not used in this memorandum. Order of importance: This is the overall plan of the entire memo, in which the most important objective is to find the waterway to the Pacific, then to collect data for accurate maps, then to observe and befriend Indians, then to observe the landscape. Enumeration: lists of what Lewis is to note about the Indians and about the landscape.

Activity

Check students' work to be sure that they have included all the important details of Jefferson's original.

Comparing Informational Materials

Handbook: Point out that instructions would vary by the day, depending on whether the Lewis and Clark party were in an area where there were Indians living, whether they were crossing a river or crossing land, and so on. Lewis would probably follow Jefferson's methods of organization in his instructions to the other members of his party.

Connections

Have students reread Lewis' and Powell's descriptions of nature, on pp. 286–292. Like them, Dillard writes to express her sense of wonder at the beauties of nature. Have students discuss what these excerpts have in common.

Fireside and Campside: Views of Nature

- Have students discuss their own reactions to the natural world. Have them share experiences they have had while camping, hiking, walking by the fields, and so on. Have students compare their own reactions to those of Lewis, Powell, and Dillard.

CONNECTIONS
Literature Past and Present

Fireside and Campfire: Views of Nature

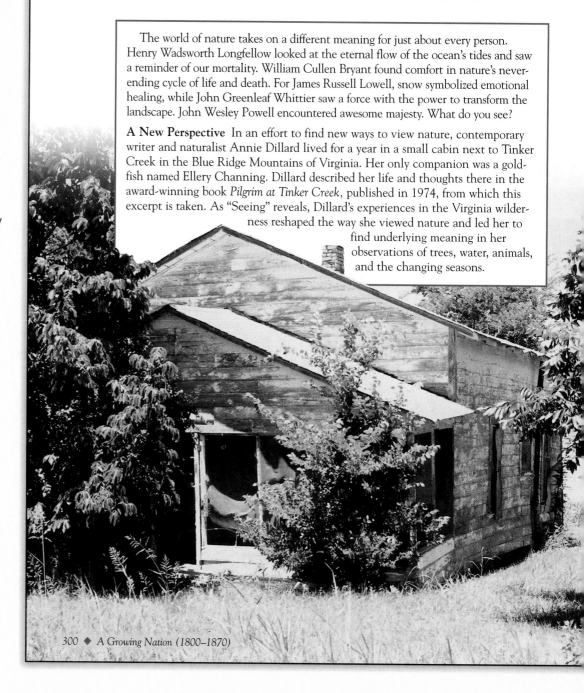

The world of nature takes on a different meaning for just about every person. Henry Wadsworth Longfellow looked at the eternal flow of the ocean's tides and saw a reminder of our mortality. William Cullen Bryant found comfort in nature's never-ending cycle of life and death. For James Russell Lowell, snow symbolized emotional healing, while John Greenleaf Whittier saw a force with the power to transform the landscape. John Wesley Powell encountered awesome majesty. What do you see?

A New Perspective In an effort to find new ways to view nature, contemporary writer and naturalist Annie Dillard lived for a year in a small cabin next to Tinker Creek in the Blue Ridge Mountains of Virginia. Her only companion was a goldfish named Ellery Channing. Dillard described her life and thoughts there in the award-winning book *Pilgrim at Tinker Creek*, published in 1974, from which this excerpt is taken. As "Seeing" reveals, Dillard's experiences in the Virginia wilderness reshaped the way she viewed nature and led her to find underlying meaning in her observations of trees, water, animals, and the changing seasons.

from Pilgrim at Tinker Creek
Seeing
Annie Dillard

When I was six or seven years old, growing up in Pittsburgh, I used to take a precious penny of my own and hide it for someone else to find. It was a curious compulsion; sadly, I've never been seized by it since. For some reason I always "hid" the penny along the same stretch of sidewalk up the street. I would cradle it at the roots of a sycamore, say, or in a hole left by a chipped-off piece of sidewalk. Then I would take a piece of chalk and, starting at either end of the block, draw huge arrows leading up to the penny from both directions. After I learned to write I labeled the arrows: SURPRISE AHEAD or MONEY THIS WAY. I was greatly excited, during all this arrow drawing, at the thought of the first lucky passerby who would receive in this way, regardless of merit, a free gift from the universe. But I never lurked about, I would go straight home and not give the matter another thought until, some months later, I would be gripped by the impulse to hide another penny.

It is still the first week in January, and I've got great plans. I've been thinking about seeing. There are lots of things to see, unwrapped gifts and free surprises. The world is fairly studded and strewn with pennies cast broadside from a generous hand. But—and this is the point—who gets excited by a mere penny? If you follow one arrow, if you crouch motionless on a bank to watch a tremulous ripple thrill on the water and are rewarded by the sight of a muskrat kit paddling from its den, will you count that sight a chip of copper only, and go your rueful way? It is dire poverty indeed when a man is so malnourished and fatigued that he won't stoop to pick up a penny. But if you cultivate a healthy poverty and simplicity, so that finding a penny will literally make your day, then, since the world is in fact planted in pennies, you have with your poverty bought a lifetime of days. It is that simple. What you see is what you get.

I used to be able to see flying insects in the air. I'd look ahead and see, not the row of hemlocks across the road, but the air in front of it. My eyes would focus along that column of air, picking out flying insects. But I lost interest, I guess, for I dropped the habit. Now I can see birds.

✔**Reading Check**
What did Dillard do when she was a child?

Connections: from Pilgrim at Tinker Creek, *Seeing* ◆ 301

- Write the following sentence from the essay on the chalkboard: "The world is fairly studded and strewn with pennies cast broadside by a generous hand." As students continue reading the essay, have them explain what Dillard means. What do the pennies symbolize? Answer: Dillard is speaking figuratively. She compares the joy of finding a copper coin unexpectedly to the joy of seeing a mockingbird, a butterfly, or some other small beauty of nature.

✔**Reading Check**
Answer: She hid pennies for other people to find.

CUSTOMIZE INSTRUCTION FOR UNIVERSAL ACCESS

For Less Proficient Readers	For English Learners	For Advanced Readers
Challenge students to find the main idea of Dillard's essay and to compare and contrast it with the main ideas of Lewis and Powell's pieces.	Have students note the many animal species mentioned in the essay and look up their pictures in nature guides or the encyclopedia as they learn these names.	Have students identify the main theme of Dillard's essay and compare and contrast it with the main themes of Lewis and Powell's pieces. What broad statement about life is each writer trying to make?

Fireside and Campside: Views of Nature (continued)

- Discuss with students why the ease with which the blackbirds hide surprises Dillard so much. **Answer:** She can't believe that so many of them can be so still and quiet that they are invisible.

- Dillard restates her idea that the ability to see the world around us is not just a matter of having good eyesight. Which other senses must we use to observe nature? **Answer:** We must listen to the sounds made by wind, rain, birds, and animals. We should smell the scents in the air.

Thematic Connection

Answer: Dillard and Bryant both locate their love of nature in the act of seeing it and thus (in Bryant's words) "holding communion" with it.

Probably some people can look at the grass at their feet and discover all the crawling creatures. I would like to know grasses and sedges—and care. Then my least journey into the world would be a field trip, a series of happy recognitions. Thoreau, in an expansive mood, exulted, "What a rich book might be made about buds, including, perhaps, sprouts!" It would be nice to think so. I cherish mental images of three perfectly happy people. One collects stones. Another—an Englishman, say—watches clouds. The third lives on a coast and collects drops of seawater, which he examines microscopically and mounts. But I don't see what the specialist sees, and so I cut myself off, not only from the total picture, but from the various forms of happiness.

Unfortunately, nature is very much a now-you-see-it, now-you-don't affair. A fish flashes, then dissolves in the water, before my eyes like so much salt. Deer apparently ascend bodily into heaven; the brightest oriole fades into leaves. These disappearances stun me into stillness and concentration; they say of nature that it conceals with a grand nonchalance, and they say of vision that it is a deliberate gift, the revelation of a dancer who for my eyes only flings away her seven veils. For nature does reveal as well as conceal: now you don't see it, now you do. For a week last September, migrating red-winged blackbirds were feeding heavily down by the creek at the back of the house. One day I went out to investigate the racket; I walked up to a tree, an Osage orange, and a hundred birds flew away. They simply materialized out of the tree. I saw a tree, then a whisk of color, then a tree again. I walked closer, and another hundred blackbirds took flight. Not a branch, not a twig budged: the birds were apparently weightless as well as invisible. Or it was as if the leaves of the Osage orange had been freed from a spell in the form of red-winged blackbirds: they flew from the tree, caught my eye in the sky, and vanished. When I looked again at the tree, the leaves had reassembled as if nothing had happened. Finally I walked directly to the trunk of the tree, and a final hundred, the real diehards, appeared, spread, and vanished. How could so many hide in the tree without my seeing them? The Osage orange, unruffled, looked just as it had looked from the house, when three hundred red-winged blackbirds cried from its crown. I looked downstream where they flew, and they were gone. Searching, I couldn't spot one. I wandered downstream to force them to play their hand, but they'd crossed the creek and scattered. One show to a customer. These appearances catch at my throat; they are the free gifts, the bright coppers at the roots of trees.

It's all a matter of keeping my eyes open. Nature is like one of those line drawings of a tree that are puzzles for children: Can you find hidden in the leaves a duck, a house, a boy, a bucket, a zebra, and a boot? Specialists can find the most incredibly well-hidden things. A book I read when I was young recommended an easy way to

Thematic Connection
Compare Dillard's message of "seeing" with Bryant's "visible forms" in the first two lines of "Thanatopsis."

find caterpillars to rear: you simply find some fresh caterpillar droppings, look up, and there's your caterpillar. Most recently an author advised me to set my mind at ease about those piles of cut stems on the ground in grassy fields. Field mice make them; they cut the grass down by degrees to reach the seeds at the head. It seems that when the grass is tightly packed, as in a field of ripe grain, the blade won't topple at a single cut through the stem; instead the cut stem simply drops vertically, held in the crush of grain. The mouse severs the bottom again and again, the stem keeps dropping an inch at a time, and finally the head is low enough for the mouse to reach the seeds. Meanwhile, the mouse is positively littering the field with its little piles of cut stems, into which, presumably, the author of the book is constantly stumbling.

If I can't see these minutiae,[1] I still try to keep my eyes open. I'm always on the lookout for ant lion traps in sandy soil, monarch pupae near milkweed, skipper larvae in locust leaves. These things are utterly common, and I've not seen one. I bang on hollow trees near water, but so far no flying squirrels have appeared. In flat country I watch every sunset in hopes of seeing the green ray. The green ray is a seldom-seen streak of light that rises from the sun like a spurting fountain at the moment of sunset; it throbs into the sky for two seconds and disappears. One more reason to keep my eyes open.

A photography professor at the University of Florida just happened to see a bird die in midflight; it jerked, died, dropped, and smashed on the ground. I squint at the wind because I read Stewart Edward White: "I have always maintained that if you looked closely enough you could *see* the wind—the dim, hardly-made-out, fine débris fleeing high in the air." White was an excellent observer, and devoted an entire chapter of *The Mountains* to the subject of seeing deer: "As soon as you can forget the naturally obvious and construct an artificial obvious, then you too will see deer."

But the artificial obvious is hard to see. My eyes account for less than one percent of the weight of my head; I'm bony and dense; I *see* what I expect. I once spent a full three minutes looking at a bullfrog that was so unexpectedly large I couldn't see it even though a dozen enthusiastic campers were shouting directions.

Finally I asked, "What color am I looking for?" and a fellow said, "Green." When at last I picked out the frog, I saw what painters are up against: the thing wasn't green at all, but the color of wet hickory bark.

The lover can see, and the knowledgeable. I visited an aunt and uncle at a quarter-horse ranch in Cody, Wyoming. I couldn't do much of anything useful, but I could, I thought, draw. So as we all sat around the kitchen table after supper, I produced a sheet of paper and drew a horse. "That's one lame horse," my aunt volunteered. The rest of the family joined in: "Only place to saddle that one is his neck"; "Looks like we better shoot the poor thing, on account of those terrible growths."

---

1. minutiae (mi noo′ shē ĭ) *n.* small or relatively unimportant details.

Thematic Connection
Compare Dillard's message about observing nature with John Wesley Powell's success in doing so.

✔**Reading Check**
According to the author, how does one see nature?

Connections: from Pilgrim at Tinker Creek, Seeing ◆ *303*

Thematic Connection

Answer: Both writers agree that a person has to observe closely and be interested enough in nature to look carefully.

Reading Check

Answer: She says one must keep one's eyes open.

- What conclusions can students draw from the Donald Carr quotation on this page?
  Answer: There is always something more to see if one knows what to look for.

Connecting Literature Past and Present

1. She sees beauty, variety, and power.

2. Dillard suggests that people who don't notice things in nature miss them because they aren't interested enough to observe. Students choices of poems will vary. Make sure they support their answers with well reasoned explanations.

Meekly, I slid the pencil and paper down the table. Everyone in that family, including my three cousins, could draw a horse. Beautifully. When the paper came back, it looked as though five shining, real quarter horses had been corraled by mistake with a papier-mâché moose; the real horses seemed to gaze at the monster with a steady, puzzled air. I stay away from horses now, but I can do a creditable goldfish. The point is that I just don't know what the lover knows; I just can't see the artificial obvious that those in the know construct. The herpetologist[2] asks the native, "Are there snakes in the ravine?" "Nosir." And the herpetologist comes home with, yessir, three bags full. Are there butterflies on that mountain? Are the bluets in bloom, are there arrowheads here, or fossil shells in the shale?

Peeping through my keyhole, I see within the range of only about 30 percent of the light that comes from the sun; the rest is infrared and some little ultraviolet, perfectly apparent to many animals, but invisible to me. A nightmare network of ganglia,[3] charged and firing without my knowledge, cuts and splices what I do see, editing it for my brain. Donald E. Carr points out that the sense impressions of one-celled animals are not edited for the brain: "This is philosophically interesting in a rather mournful way, since it means that only the simplest animals perceive the universe as it is."

A fog that won't burn away drifts and flows across my field of vision. When you see fog move against a backdrop of deep pines, you see not the fog itself but streaks of clearness floating across the air in dark shreds. So I see only tatters of clearness through a pervading obscurity. I can't distinguish the fog from the overcast sky; I can't be sure if the light is direct or reflected. Everywhere darkness and the presence of the unseen appalls. We estimate now that only one atom dances alone in every cubic meter of intergalactic space. I blink and squint. What planet or power yanks Halley's Comet out of orbit? We haven't seen that force yet; it's a question of distance, density, and the pallor of reflected light. We rock, cradled in the swaddling band of darkness. Even the simple darkness of night whispers suggestions to the mind.

---

2. **herpetologist** (hur′ pə täl′ ə jist) one who practices the study of reptiles and amphibians.

3. **ganglia** (gan′ glē ə) masses of nerve cells that serve as centers from which nerve impulses are transmitted.

Connecting Literature Past and Present

1. What does Dillard see when she looks at nature?

2. What enables some people to see things in nature that go unnoticed by others? Name two poems in Part 1 in which the speakers share the appreciation of nature expressed in "Seeing." Explain your choices.

Annie Dillard

(b. 1945)

As a child in Pittsburgh, Pennsylvania, Annie Dillard loved reading, drawing, and observing the natural world.

She attended Hollins College in Roanoke, Virginia, and graduated with a B.A. and later an M.A in English. Her exploration of a Virginia valley during her years at Hollins led to the publication of *Pilgrim at Tinker Creek* (1974), which won the Pulitzer Prize for Nonfiction in 1975. Since then, she has published ten other books, including the memoir *An American Childhood* (1987) and *The Living* (1992), a novel.

Shadows of the Imagination

Mysterious Night, ca. 1895, Daingerfield, Morris Museum of Art, Georgia

The selections in this section deal with the ominous side of human emotions. Here we find characters who are tortured individuals ruled by the menacing shadows of their imaginations. "The Fall of the House of Usher" introduces Roderick Usher, a physically deteriorating person who knows he is losing his mind and tries anything, including burying his twin sister alive, to escape death. In "The Raven," Poe presents a man whose grief for his deceased beloved knows no bounds. His wounded psyche proves far too fragile to survive the shattering blows of the single negative word uttered repeatedly by an uninvited guest. The next selection provides a close-up of obsession at its most dangerous. In an excerpt from the novel *Moby-Dick*, Captain Ahab is driven to revenge at any cost, including the lives of most of his crew and himself. Part 2 ends with "Where *Is* Here?" a story about an anguished soul who visits his childhood home and haunts his hosts with suggestions of deep, dark secrets in the shadows of his past.

Background

Art

Mysterious Night,
Elliott Daingerfield

Ask students what they see in this painting, and generate a list of possibilities on the board for students to compile situations from. Then use these questions to spark discussion.

1. Imagine that a person lurks underneath the white shape on the right. Make up a story idea explaining what he or she is doing out on this foggy night.
   Possible response: He is waiting to meet someone who has the other half of a treasure map.

2. Describe the mood of this painting. What details and elements contribute most to this mood?
   Possible response: The mood of the painting is mysterious, haunting, ominous. Details that contribute to the mood include the fog or mist; the large, shadowy tree; the pool of light in the middle of the painting.

...IZE INSTRUCTION FOR UNIVERSAL ACCESS

...gning the selections in this part, keep in mind these factors:

...the House of Usher"

...ntences may present challenges for some
...

...s may need help with obscure words and ...nconventional sentence structure.

...er's Black Veil"

...ound information about symbolism will aid

student comprehension of this story.

from *Moby Dick*

- English language learners may have difficulty with Captain Ahab's thick dialect.

"Where *Is* Here?"

- This tale of the unknown will capture students' interest.

The Fall of The House of Usher ✦ The Raven

Lesson Objectives

1. **To analyze and respond to literary elements**
   - Literary Analysis: Single Effect
   - Comparing Literary Works

2. **To read, comprehend, analyze, and critique a short story and a poem**
   - Reading Strategy: Breaking Down Long Sentences
   - Reading Check Questions
   - Review and Assess Questions
   - Assessment Practice (ATE)

3. **To develop word analysis skills, fluency, and systematic vocabulary**
   - Vocabulary Development Lesson: Latin Word Root: -voc-

4. **To understand and apply written and oral language conventions**
   - Spelling Strategy
   - Grammar and Style Lesson: Coordinate Adjectives

5. **To understand and apply appropriate writing and research strategies**
   - Writing Lesson: Literary Criticism
   - Extension Activity: Movie Analysis

6. **To understand and apply listening and speaking strategies**
   - Extension Activity: Dramatic Reading

STEP-BY-STEP TEACHING GUIDE	PACING GUIDE
PRETEACH	
Motivate Students and Provide Background	
Use the Motivation activity (ATE p. 306)	5 min.
Read and discuss the author and background information (SE/ATE pp. 306, 308)	5 min.
Introduce the Concepts	
Introduce the Literary Analysis and Reading Strategy (SE/ATE p. 307) [A]	20 min.
Pronounce the vocabulary words and read their definitions (SE p. 307)	10 min.
TEACH	
Monitor Comprehension	
Informally monitor comprehension by circulating while students read independently or in groups [A]	60 min.
Monitor students' comprehension with the Reading Check notes (SE/ATE pp. 311, 313, 315, 317, 319, 321, 323, 327, 329)	as students read
Develop vocabulary with Vocabulary notes (SE pp. 310, 311, 314, 318, 327; ATE p. 311)	as students read
Develop Understanding	
Develop students' understanding of a single effect with the Literary Analysis annotations (SE/ATE pp. 308, 311, 313, 314, 315, 317, 318, 320, 321, 322, 324, 326, 329) [A]	5 min.
Develop students' ability to break down long sentences with the Reading Strategy annotations (SE/ATE pp. 310, 312, 313, 318, 319, 324, 327, 329)	10 min.
ASSESS	
Assess Mastery	
Assess students' mastery of the Reading Strategy and Literary Analysis by having them answer the Review and Assess questions (SE/ATE p. 331)	25 min.
Use one or more of the print and media Assessment Resources (ATE p. 333) [A]	up to 45 min.
EXTEND	
Apply Understanding	
Have students complete the Vocabulary Development Lesson and the Grammar and Style Lesson (SE p. 332) [A]	20 min.
Apply students' ability to write appropriately for a medium by using the Writing Lesson (SE/ATE p. 333) [A]	45 min.
Apply students' understanding using one or more of the Extension Activities (SE p. 333)	20–90 min.

 ACCELERATED INSTRUCTION: Use the strategies and activities identified with an [A].

UNIVERSAL ACCESS
● = Below Level Students
▲ = On-Level Students
■ = Above Level Students

Time and Resource Manager

Reading Level: Challenging, Average
Average Number of Instructional Days: 7

RESOURCES

PRINT 📖	TRANSPARENCIES 💾	TECHNOLOGY 💿 🎧 📼
• **Beyond Literature,** Media Connection: Film Versions of Edgar Allen Poe Stories, p. 17 ▲ ■		• **Interest Grabber Video,** Tape 3 ● ▲ ■
• **Selection Support Workbook:** ● ▲ ■ Literary Analysis, p. 80 Reading Strategy, p. 79 Build Vocabulary, p. 77	• **Literary Analysis and Reading Transparencies,** pp. 33 and 34 ● ▲ ■	
• **Adapted Reader's Companion** ● • **Reader's Companion** ● • **Authors In Depth,** The American Experience, p. 53 ■		• **Listening to Literature** ● ▲ ■ Audiocassettes, Side 9–10 Audio CDs, CD 6
• **English Learner's Companion** ● ▲ • **Literatura en español** ● ▲ • **Literary Analysis for Enrichment** ■		
• **Formal Assessment:** Selection Test, pp. 85–87 ● ▲ ■ • **Open Book Test,** pp. 49–51 ● ▲ ■ • **Performance Assessment and Portfolio Management,** p. 23 ● ▲ ■ • 🔘 **PRENTICE HALL** ASSESSMENT *SYSTEM* ● ▲ ■	• 🔘 **PRENTICE HALL** ASSESSMENT *SYSTEM* ● ▲ ■ Skills Practice Answers and Explanations on Transparencies	• **Test Bank Software** ● ▲ ■ • **Got It! Assessment Videotapes,** Tape 2 ● ▲
• **Selection Support Workbook:** ● ▲ ■ Grammar and Style Skills, p. 78 • **Writing and Grammar,** Ruby Level ● ▲ ■ • **Extension Activities,** p. 17 ● ▲ ■	• **Daily Language Practice Transparencies** ● ▲ • **Writing Models and Graphic Organizers on Transparencies,** pp. 37–40 ● ▲ ■	• **Writing and Grammar iText CD-ROM** ● ▲ ■ 🖥️ *Take It to the Net* www.phschool.com

BLOCK SCHEDULING: Use one 90-minute class period to preteach the selection and have students read it. Use a second 90-minute class period to assess students' mastery of skills and have them complete one of the Extension Activities.

Step-by-Step Teaching Guide for pp. 306–307

Motivation

The odd deterioration of Roderick Usher and the madness of the narrator of "The Fall of the House of Usher" are shrouded in as much mystery and horror as any psychological thriller students may have encountered on the page or screen. Engage students' interest in Poe by writing the following passages on the chalkboard:

"Having deposited our mournful burden . . . within this region of horror, we partially turned aside the yet unscrewed lid of the coffin, and looked upon the face of the tenant."

"Deep into that darkness peering, long I stood there wondering, fearing,

Doubting, dreaming dreams no mortal ever dared to dream before . . . ."

Have students use the passages to make predictions about the story and poem.

▪▪ Interest Grabber Video

As an alternative, play "Raven As Trickster in Literature" on Tape 3 to engage student interest.

❶ Background

More About the Author

Edgar Allan Poe's writing contains a fascinating duality. On one hand, Poe was an idealist whose sensitivity led him to write touching lyrics, most notably "Annabel Lee." Yet he was intrigued by dark escapes from reality as well. He was irresistibly drawn to eerie thoughts, impulses, and fears in writing his daring tales of wickedness, anguish, crime, and death.

Prepare to Read

❶ The Fall of the House of Usher ◆ The Raven

Edgar Allan Poe (1809–1849)

When Edgar Allan Poe died, Rufus Griswold wrote a slanderous obituary of the eccentric writer. He claimed that Poe had been expelled from college, that he had neither good friends nor good qualities, and that he committed flagrant acts of plagiarism. Suspicious of this unconventional obituary, some have speculated that Poe orchestrated the death notice himself to keep his name in the public eye. Yet, Poe's real life was almost as dark and dismal as the possibly false obituary described it.

A Troubled Childhood Poe was born in Boston in 1809, the son of impoverished traveling actors. Shortly after Poe's birth, his father deserted the family; a year later, his mother died. Young Edgar was taken in—though never formally adopted—by the family of John Allan, a wealthy Virginia merchant. Poe lived with the Allans in England from 1815 to 1820, when they returned to the United States. It was from John Allan that Poe received his middle name. The Allans also provided for Poe's education; however, when his stepfather refused to pay Poe's large gambling debts at the University of Virginia, the young man was forced to leave the school.

Building a Literary Career In 1827, after joining the army under an assumed name, Poe published his first volume of poetry, *Tamerlane and Other Poems*. Two years later, he published a second volume, *Al Aaraaf*. In 1830, John Allan helped Poe win an appointment to the United States Military Academy at West Point. Within a year, however, Poe was expelled for academic violations,

and his dismissal resulted in an irreparable break with his stepfather.

An Unhappy Ending During the second half of his short life, Poe pursued a literary career in New York, Richmond, Philadelphia, and Baltimore, barely supporting himself by writing and working as an editor for several magazines. After his third volume of poetry, *Poems* (1831), failed to bring him either money or acclaim, he turned from poetry to fiction and literary criticism. Five of his short stories were published in newspapers in 1832, and in 1838 he published his only novel, *The Narrative of Arthur Gordon Pym*. Although his short stories gained him some recognition and his poem "The Raven" (1845) was greeted with enthusiasm, Poe could never escape from poverty. He suffered from bouts of depression and madness. Then, in 1849, two years after the death of his beloved wife, Virginia, Poe died in Baltimore, alone and unhappy.

A Legacy Since his death, Poe's work has been a magnet for attention. Poe is widely accepted as the inventor of the detective story, and his psychological thrillers have been imitated by scores of modern writers. His work has been translated into nearly every language, and dozens of film adaptations have been made of his stories. Although critics have not always agreed about Poe, the Mystery Writers of America have honored their best and brightest by conferring upon them the "Edgar" award for great achievement in mystery writing.

Poe's work has provoked intense critical debate. Some scholars have harshly criticized his writing, while others have celebrated his use of vivid imagery and sound effects, as well as his tireless exploration of altered mental states and the dark side of human nature. Despite Poe's uncertain status among critics, his work has remained extremely popular among generations of American readers.

TEACHING RESOURCES

The following resources can be used to enrich or extend the instruction for pp. 306–307.

Motivation

▪▪ **Interest Grabber Video**, Tape 3 ▪

Background

📖 **Beyond Literature**, p. 17

🖥 ***Take It to the Net***

Visit www.phschool.com for background and hotlinks for the selection.

Literary Analysis

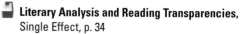

📄 **Literary Analysis and Reading Transparencies**, Single Effect, p. 34

📖 **Selection Support Workbook:** Literary Analysis, p. 80

Reading

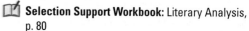

📄 **Literary Analysis and Reading Transparencies**, Breaking Down Long Sentences, p. 33 ▪

▪ **BLOCK SCHEDULING:** Resources marked with this symbol provide varied instruction during 90-minute blocks.

Preview

Connecting to the Literature

It is natural to feel anxiety, but in extreme circumstances, "nerves" can become a destructive part of a person's personality. Such is the case for the characters in the selections that follow.

② Literary Analysis

Single Effect

Poe argued that a short story should be constructed to achieve "a certain unique or **single effect.**" He believed that every character, incident, and detail should contribute to this effect. As you read, examine the ways in which Poe heeds his own advice.

Comparing Literary Works

Although one is a story and the other a poem, both "The Fall of the House of Usher" and "The Raven" exemplify the literary genre known as **gothic.** The gothic style is characterized by the following elements:

- The story is set in bleak or remote places.
- The plot involves macabre or violent incidents.
- Characters are in psychological and/or physical torment.
- A supernatural or otherworldly element is often present.

As you read, examine how both the story and the poem emphasize different elements of the gothic style.

③ Reading Strategy

Breaking Down Long Sentences

Long, intricate sentences can challenge your understanding. It may help to **break down long sentences** into logical parts. First, look for a sentence's core: its subject and verb. Then, look for clues in punctuation, conjunctions, and modifying words. Use a chart like the one shown to break down Poe's lengthy sentences into more manageable parts.

Vocabulary Development

importunate (im pôr´ choo nit) *adj.* insistent (p. 310)

munificent (myoo nif´ ə sənt) *adj.* generous (p. 310)

equivocal (ē kwiv´ ə kəl) *adj.* having more than one possible interpretation (p. 311)

appellation (ap´ ə lā´ shən) *n.* name or title (p. 311)

specious (spē´ shəs) *adj.* seeming to be good or sound without actually being so (p. 311)

anomalous (ə näm´ ə ləs) *adj.* abnormal (p. 314)

sentience (sen´ shəns) *n.* capacity of feeling (p. 318)

obeisance (ō bā´ səns) *n.* gesture of respect (p. 327)

craven (krā´ vən) *adj.* very cowardly (p. 327)

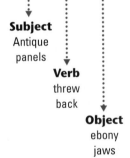

Sentence

As if . . . there had been found the potency of a spell, the huge antique panels to which the speaker pointed threw slowly back, upon the instant, their ponderous and ebony jaws.

Subject
Antique panels

Verb
threw
back

Object
ebony jaws

The Fall of the House of Usher / The Raven ◆ 307

---

② Literary Analysis
Single Effect

- Explain to students that as they read the two selections, they will focus on the single effect that Poe believed should be achieved by a short story.

- Let students know that Edgar Allan Poe was the first writer to define the short story as a distinct literary genre and to argue that it deserved the same status as a poem or a novel.

- Read the instruction on single effect together as a class. Point out that Poe believed not only that every character and incident should contribute to this effect but also each detail in every sentence. If not, Poe wrote, "then [the writer] has failed."

- Invite students as they read to identify and characterize the particular effect Poe set out to achieve in each of these works.

③ Reading Strategy
Breaking Down Long Sentences

- Read aloud with students the instruction on breaking down long sentences. Point out that Poe's style is notable for its use of long, complicated sentences.

- Point out that rereading a challenging sentence several times can help readers appreciate its structure, as well as its main idea.

- Also encourage students to read aloud difficult sentences to allow them to *hear* the sentence's essential meaning.

- Remind students that identifying a sentence's subject and predicate can help them distinguish the sentence's main idea from various details. Suggest that students use a chart like the one shown as they read the selections.

Vocabulary Development

- Pronounce each vocabulary word for students, and read the definitions as a class. Have students identify any words with which they are already familiar.

 E-Teach

Visit E-Teach at www.phschool.com for teachers' essays on how to teach, with questions and answers.

CUSTOMIZE INSTRUCTION FOR UNIVERSAL ACCESS

For Special Needs Students	For Less Proficient Readers	For English Learners
Have students read the adapted version of "The Raven" in the **Adapted Reader's Companion**. This version provides basic-level instruction in an interactive format with questions and write-on lines. Completing the adapted version will prepare students to read the selection in the Student Edition.	Have students read "The Raven" in the **Reader's Companion**. This version provides basic-level instruction in an interactive format with questions and write-on lines. After students finish the selection in the **Reader's Companion**, have them complete the questions and activities in the Student Edition.	Have students read the adapted version of this poem in the **English Learner's Companion**. This version provides basic-level instruction in an interactive format with questions and write-on lines. Completing the adapted version will prepare students to read the selection in the Student Edition.

Step-by-Step Teaching Guide for pp. 308–330

CUSTOMIZE INSTRUCTION
for Visual/Spatial Learners

Invite students to compare and contrast the descriptions of the Usher house at the beginning and end of the tale in order to identify a crucial example of the story's total effect. Encourage students to take special note of descriptive details such as the unusual lighting effects, the vast house standing alone in shadow, the fissure in the wall, and the sullen silence with which the waters of the tarn close over the ruins of the House of Usher.

❶ About the Selection

In Poe's classic journey into the inner reaches of a decaying mind, the narrator honors a request from a boyhood friend to visit him during an oppressive illness. The narrator arrives at a remote, gloomy mansion next to a dark lake and finds Roderick Usher in poor physical and mental health. Usher is not unaware that his mind is disintegrating. After the apparent death of his twin sister, Usher and the narrator bear a coffin containing her body to a vault in the lower reaches of the mansion. After several days of unexplained sounds emanating from the vault, Usher admits that she may have been buried alive. On a subsequent stormy night, she escapes the vault, appears in the doorway before them, and (with Roderick) suddenly dies. The narrator flees the house as it collapses into the dark lake.

❷ Literary Analysis

Single Effect

- Write a list on the chalkboard of students' ideas about what words and phrases in this sentence create a distinct atmosphere. Students' responses might include *dull dark, soundless, clouds hung oppressively low, alone, dreary, shades, evening,* and *melancholy.*

- Ask students the Literary Analysis question on p. 308: What single effect does Poe create in the very first sentence?

  Answer: The first sentence establishes the gloominess of the story's setting.

---

❶ The Fall of the House of Usher

Edgar Allan Poe

Background

In 1839, Poe lived in Philadelphia and became coeditor of *Burton's Gentleman's Magazine,* a journal that published essays, fiction, reviews, and poems, as well as articles on sailing, hunting, and cricket. Poe's articles ran the gamut of topics. He explained the parallel bars, mused about the mysteries of Stonehenge, and reviewed more than eighty books on a variety of topics. It was in this magazine, in 1839, that Poe first published "The Fall of the House of Usher."

Son Coeur est un luth suspendu:
Sitôt qu'on le touche il résonne.[1]

❷ During the whole of a dull, dark, and soundless day in the autumn of the year, when the clouds hung oppressively low in the heavens, I had been passing alone, on horseback, through a singularly dreary tract of country, and at length found myself, as the shades of evening drew on, within view of the melancholy House of Usher. I know not how it was—but, with the first glimpse of the building, a sense of insufferable gloom pervaded my spirit. I say insufferable; for the feeling was unrelieved by any of that half-pleasurable, because poetic, sentiment, with which the mind usually receives even the sternest natural images of the desolate or terrible. I looked upon the scene before me—upon the mere house, and the simple landscape features of the domain—upon the bleak walls—upon the vacant eyelike windows—upon a few rank sedges[2]—and upon a few white trunks of decayed trees—with an utter

---

1. **Son . . . résonne** "His heart is a lute strung tight: As soon as one touches it, resounds." From "Le Refus" by Pierre Jean de Béranger (1780–1857).
2. **sedges** (sej´ iz) *n.* grasslike plants.

308 ◆ *A Growing Nation (1800–1870)*

Literary Analysis
Single Effect What single effect does Poe create in the very first sentence?

TEACHING RESOURCES

The following resources can be used to enrich or extend the instruction for pp. 308–330.

Reading Strategy

📖 **Selection Support Workbook: Reading Strategy,** p. 79; Build Vocabulary, p. 77

📖 **Reader's Companion**

📖 **English Learner's Companion**

🎧 **Listening to Literature Audiocassettes,** Sides 9, 10 ■

💿 **Listening to Literature Audio CDs,** CD 6 ■

Extension

📖 **Authors In Depth, The American Experience**
This collection includes five additional selections by Edgar Allan Poe for extended reading.

■ **BLOCK SCHEDULING:** Resources marked with this symbol provide varied instruction during 90-minute blocks.

"I at length...." Edgar Allan Poe's Tales of Mystery and Imagination, Arthur Rackham, The New York Public Library

④ ▲ Critical Viewing What mood does the artist's choice of shapes and colors create in this painting? Which details of the story's opening paragraph does the painter convey? **[Analyze]**

The Fall of the House of Usher ◆ 309

❸

❸ Background

Art

"I at length . . ." Edgar Allan Poe's Tales of Mystery and Imagination, 1935, by Arthur Rackham

London-born Arthur Rackham (1867–1939) was one of the best known illustrators of his day, and his work is still familiar to millions of readers. Some of his most famous works are the illustrations for *Grimm's Fairy Tales* (1900) and for limited editions of German legends and Christmas stories. Rackham's imaginative, fanciful style was well suited to whimsical, grotesque, and gruesome subjects. For example, his use of form and color in this illustration for "The Fall of the House of Usher" dramatically captures the tortured mood of the story.

1. How does Rackham's rendition of this scene compare with the image Poe creates?
   Suggested answer: The scene is gloomy, remote, and eerie, much as Poe describes it.

2. Often Rackham's trees have twisted or otherwise misshapen trunks. How do the trees contribute to the overall effect of this scene?
   Answer: Students may say that the trees suggest death and distortion.

❹ ▶ Critical Viewing

Answer: The artist's choice of shapes and colors creates a gloomy and forbidding mood. Details from the story's opening paragraph that appear in the picture include the dark sky, the narrator on horseback, the House of Usher's bleak walls and vacant windows, and the decayed trees.

CUSTOMIZE INSTRUCTION FOR UNIVERSAL ACCESS

For English Learners	For Gifted/Talented Students
Help students to orient themselves at the start of Poe's story by pointing out and discussing key words in the story's opening sentences. After discussing the definitions of words such as *oppressively, melancholy, gloom, insufferable,* and *decayed,* invite students to create picture cards for each term. Explain that understanding the meaning of these few words puts readers on track to understand the single effect sought by the author.	Have students speculate on why Poe opens the story with the French couplet from "Le Rufus." Why might he have chosen this particular quotation? As they read, have students try to determine which character the author intends to evoke with the quotation. Is it the narrator or Roderick Usher who is extraordinarily sensitive to impressions? Students might also do research to learn more about Pierre Jean de Béranger and his literary works.

Breaking Down Long Sentences

- Have two student volunteers read aloud the sentence beginning "It was possible, I reflected . . . ."

- Ask students the first Reading Strategy question on p. 310: What are the subjects and verbs in the sentence beginning "It was possible, I reflected"?
  Answer: The sentence's subjects and predicates are as follows: *It/was; I/reflected; arrangement/would be.*

▶ Monitor Progress Ask students to paraphrase the meaning of this sentence.
  Possible response: I thought that maybe if the house and its surroundings were looked at from another point of view they might look less grim; but when I looked at them reflected in the tarn they looked even worse.

❻ Reading Strategy

Breaking Down Long Sentences

- Read aloud the sentence beginning "It was the manner" two or three times with students.

- Encourage students to momentarily ignore the nonessential parts of this sentence (for example, "and much more," as well as the phrase marked off by dashes), to help them focus on the core of the sentence.

- Then, ask students the second Reading Strategy question on p. 310: What is the core of the sentence beginning "It was the manner"?
  Answer: The core of the sentence is "It was the manner in which all of this was said which allowed me no room for hesitation."

---

depression of soul, which I can compare to no earthly sensation more properly than to the afterdream of the reveler upon opium—the bitter lapse into everyday life—the hideous dropping off of the veil. There was an iciness, a sinking, a sickening of the heart—an unredeemed dreariness of thought which no goading of the imagination could torture into aught[3] of the sublime. What was it—I paused to think—what was it that so unnerved me in the contemplation of the House of Usher? It was a mystery all insoluble; nor could I grapple with the shadowy fancies that crowded upon me as I pondered. I was forced to fall back upon the unsatisfactory conclusion, that while, beyond doubt, there are combinations of very simple natural objects which have the power of thus affecting us, still the analysis of this power lies among considerations beyond our depth. It was possible, I reflected, that a mere different arrangement of the particulars of the scene, of the details of the picture, would be sufficient to modify, or perhaps to annihilate its capacity for sorrowful impression; and, acting upon this idea, I reined ❺ my horse to the precipitous brink of a black and lurid tarn[4] that lay in unruffled luster by the dwelling, and gazed down—but with a shudder even more thrilling than before—upon the remodeled and inverted images of the gray sedge, and the ghastly tree stems, and the vacant and eyelike windows.

Nevertheless, in this mansion of gloom I now proposed to myself a sojourn of some weeks. Its proprietor, Roderick Usher, had been one of my boon companions in boyhood; but many years had elapsed since our last meeting. A letter, however, had lately reached me in a distant part of the country—a letter from him—which, in its wildly importunate nature, had admitted of no other than a personal reply. The MS[5] gave evidence of nervous agitation. The writer spoke of acute bodily illness—of a mental disorder which oppressed him—and of an earnest desire to see me, as his best and indeed his only personal friend, with a view of attempting, by the cheerfulness of my society, some alleviation of his malady. It was the manner in which all this, and much more, was said—it was the apparent *heart* that went with his request—which allowed me no room for hesitation; and I ❻ accordingly obeyed forthwith what I still considered a very singular summons.

Although, as boys, we had been even intimate associates, yet I really knew little of my friend. His reserve had been always excessive and habitual. I was aware, however, that his very ancient family had been noted, time out of mind, for a peculiar sensibility of temperament, displaying itself, through long ages, in many works of exalted art, and manifested, of late, in repeated deeds of munificent yet unobtrusive charity, as well as in a passionate devotion to the intricacies, perhaps even more than to the orthodox and easily recognizable

---

3. **aught** (ôt) anything.
4. **tarn** (tärn) *n.* small lake.
5. **MS.** *abbr.* manuscript.

Reading Strategy
Breaking Down Long Sentences What is the subject and what are the verbs in the sentence beginning "It was possible, I reflected"?

importunate (im pôr′ chə nit) *adj.* insistent

Reading Strategy
Breaking Down Long Sentences What is the core of the sentence beginning "It was the manner"?

munificent (myōō nif′ ə sənt) *adj.* generous

beauties, of musical science. I had learned, too, the very remarkable fact, that the stem of the Usher race, all time-honored as it was, had put forth, at no period, any enduring branch: in other words, that the entire family lay in the direct line of descent, and had always, with very trifling and very temporary variations, so lain. It was this deficiency, I considered, while running over in thought the perfect keeping of the character of the premises with the accredited character of the people, and while speculating upon the possible influence which the one, in the long lapse of centuries, might have exercised upon the other—it was this deficiency, perhaps of collateral issue,[6] and the consequent undeviating transmission, from sire to son, of the patrimony[7] with the name, which had, at length, so identified the two as to merge the original title of the estate in the quaint and equivocal appellation of the "House of Usher"—an appellation which seemed to include, in the minds of the peasantry who used it, both the family and the family mansion.

I have said that the sole effect of my somewhat childish experiment—that of looking down within the tarn—had been to deepen the first singular impression. There can be no doubt that the consciousness of the rapid increase of my superstition—for why should I not so term it?—served mainly to accelerate the increase itself. Such, I have long known, is the paradoxical law of all sentiments having terror as a basis. And it might have been for this reason only, that, when I again uplifted my eyes to the house itself, from its image in the pool, there grew in my mind a strange fancy—a fancy so ridiculous, indeed, that I but mention it to show the vivid force of the sensations which oppressed me. I had so worked upon my imagination as really to believe that about the whole mansion and domain there hung an atmosphere peculiar to themselves and their immediate vicinity—an atmosphere which had no affinity with the air of heaven, but which had reeked up from the decayed trees, and the gray wall, and the silent tarn—a pestilent and mystic vapor, dull, sluggish, faintly discernible and leaden-hued.

Shaking off from my spirit what *must* have been a dream, I scanned more narrowly the real aspect of the building. Its principal feature seemed to be that of an excessive antiquity. The discoloration of ages had been great. Minute fungi overspread the whole exterior, hanging in a fine tangled web-work from the eaves. Yet all this was apart from any extraordinary dilapidation. No portion of the masonry had fallen; and there appeared to be a wild inconsistency between its still perfect adaptation of parts, and the crumbling condition of the individual stones. In this there was much that reminded me of the specious totality of old woodwork which has rotted for long years in some neglected vault, with no disturbance from the breath of the

---

6. **collateral** (kə lat′ ər əl) **issue** descended from the same ancestors but in a different line.
7. **patrimony** (pat′ rə mō′ nē) *n.* property inherited from one's father.

equivocal (i kwiv′ ə kəl) *adj.* having more than one possible interpretation

appellation (ap′ ə lā′ shən) *n.* name or title

specious (spē′ shəs) *adj.* seeming to be good or sound without actually being so

Reading Check
What is the physical condition of the House of Usher?

❼ **Vocabulary Development**
The Latin Word Root -voc-
- Call students' attention to the word *equivocal* and its definition. Tell students that the Latin word root -voc- comes from the Latin word for "voice," *vox.*
- Ask students to volunteer words or phrases that contain this root, and list them on the blackboard. Possibilities include: vocal, vocation, vocabulary
- Have students discuss how the meaning of the root -voc- contributes to the definitions of words such as *vocation* and *equivocate.*

❽ **Literary Analysis**
Single Effect
- Have a student volunteer read aloud this paragraph. Ask the class to think about what single effect Poe aims to achieve as the volunteer reads this passage.
- Read the paragraph aloud a second time. Help students recognize that Poe describes the house as an old, decaying wreck whose "barely perceptible fissure" suggests a fatal flaw.
- Discuss how the author repeatedly emphasizes the isolation of the house. Encourage students to think about what these clues may suggest about the inhabitants.

❾ **Reading Check**
Answer: The house is notable for its extreme age, its rotting and discolored shell, and the evidence of decay in many of the individual stones of which its walls are made up.

CUSTOMIZE INSTRUCTION FOR UNIVERSAL ACCESS

For Special Needs Students	**For Advanced Readers**
Have students in small groups listen as you read the story's opening paragraphs. Point out that despite all of the gloom described in the opening passages, the narrator plans to stick to his decision to stay for some weeks. Have students discuss why he makes this choice. Encourage them to see that he may feel loyalty to his old friend, that he may not want to let the gloom frighten him away, or that his curiosity may compel him to stay on.	Challenge students to trace and analyze a common theme in Poe's work: a narrator preyed upon by malevolent outside forces, as well as by his own disordered or obsessive thoughts or those of another character. Have students look for examples of such outside forces in this story and in the poem that follows.

311

⑩ Background

Poe and the Gothic Tradition

Despite the fact that British writers established the Gothic novel and produced most of its famous examples—including Mary Shelley's *Frankenstein* and Bram Stoker's *Dracula*—the form took hold in the United States as well. Several notable writers set about the task of discovering Gothic effects in the newly explored American landscape.

Edgar Allan Poe and Nathaniel Hawthorne are the two best-known American authors who fashioned tales using dark, mysterious, and sometimes ghastly subjects and settings. Yet before either of these men was born, Charles Brockden Brown crafted full-length Gothic narratives such as *Wieland, or The Transformation* (1798) and *Edgar Huntly* (1799). Sometimes called "the father of the American novel," Brown wove into his tales eerie topics and grisly special effects (prefiguring later American works ranging from Poe's to John Carpenter's) such as mass murder, religious mania, spontaneous combustion, ventriloquism, and psychological terror.

⑪ Reading Strategy

Breaking Down Long Sentences

- Write the bracketed sentence on the chalkboard. Have a volunteer read aloud this sentence.

- Show students that they can omit the nonessential phrases and clauses in order to clarify its meaning. On the chalkboard, cross out "Upon my entrance," "on which he had been lying at full length," "which had much in it," "I at first thought," and "of the constrained effort of the *ennuyé* man of the world."

- Lead students to see that the sentence's essential meaning is as follows: *Usher got up to greet me with too much warmth.*

---

external air. Beyond this indication of extensive decay, however, the fabric gave little token of instability. Perhaps the eye of a scrutinizing observer might have discovered a barely perceptible fissure, which, extending from the roof of the building in front, made its way down the wall in a zigzag direction, until it became lost in the sullen waters of the tarn.

Noticing these things, I rode over a short causeway to the house. A servant in waiting took my horse, and I entered the Gothic[8] archway of the hall. A valet, of stealthy step, then conducted me, in silence, through many dark and intricate passages in my progress to the studio of his master. Much that I encountered on the way contributed, I know not how, to heighten the vague sentiments of which I have already spoken. While the objects around me—while the carvings of the ceilings, the somber tapestries of the walls, the ebon blackness of the floors, and the phantasmagoric[9] armorial trophies which rattled as I strode, were but matters to which, or to such as which, I had been accustomed from my infancy—while I hesitated not to acknowledge how familiar was all this—I still wondered to find how unfamiliar were the fancies which ordinary images were stirring up. On one of the staircases, I met the physician of the family. His countenance, I thought, wore a mingled expression of low cunning and perplexity. He accosted me with trepidation and passed on. The valet now threw open a door and ushered me into the presence of his master.

The room in which I found myself was very large and lofty. The windows were long, narrow, and pointed, and at so vast a distance from the black oaken floor as to be altogether inaccessible from within. Feeble gleams of encrimsoned light made their way through the trellised panes, and served to render sufficiently distinct the more prominent objects around; the eye, however, struggled in vain to reach the remoter angles of the chamber, or the recesses of the vaulted and fretted[10] ceiling. Dark draperies hung upon the walls. The general furniture was profuse, comfortless, antique, and tattered. Many books and musical instruments lay scattered about, but failed to give any vitality to the scene. I felt that I breathed an atmosphere of sorrow. An air of stern, deep, and irredeemable gloom hung over and pervaded all.

⑪ Upon my entrance, Usher arose from a sofa on which he had been lying at full length, and greeted me with a vivacious warmth which had much in it, I at first thought, of an overdone cordiality—of the constrained effort of the *ennuyé*[11] man of the world. A glance, however, at his countenance convinced me of his perfect sincerity.

---

8. **Gothic** high and ornate.
9. **phantasmagoric** (fan taz´ mə gôr´ ik) *adj.* fantastic or dreamlike.
10. **fretted** (fret´ id) *v.* ornamented with a pattern of small, straight, intersecting bars.
11. *ennuyé* (än´ wē ā´) *adj.* bored (French).

The American Experience

⑩ *Poe and the Gothic Tradition*

Gothic fiction first appeared on the literary scene in England in the late 1700s in works like *Castle of Otranto* (1765) by Horace Walpole and *The Mysteries of Udolpho* (1794) by Ann Radcliffe. It has never gone away.

The word *gothic* was borrowed from architecture, where it is used to describe buildings that were created during the late Middle Ages. To later generations, their cold chambers and secret passages held mysteries—dark tales of vengeance and passion. Gothic novels, which were often set in such buildings, were populated by the insane, the lovelorn, the terrified, and, often, the dead, thus promising reading experiences of intense emotion.

Edgar Allan Poe translated the imagery and atmosphere of British gothic into an American landscape. His work paved the way for an American gothic tradition that has been a mainstay of popular culture. Contemporary writers like Stephen King, Anne Rice, and Ray Bradbury are in a direct line of descent from Poe, and many of Hollywood's most successful filmmakers owe their inspiration—and their fortunes—to his legacy.

✦ ENRICHMENT: Art Connection

Gothic Architecture

Introduce students to the characteristics of Gothic architecture—as found in European cathedrals built between the twelfth and sixteenth centuries—such as interior pillars, side aisles, radiating chapels, soaring ceilings, flying buttresses, and luminous windows. If possible, display pictures of famous Gothic structures, such as the cathedrals of Notre Dame (Paris), Chartres, Reims, and Amiens in France; the cathedrals of Salisbury, Gloucester, and Canterbury, as well as Westminster Abbey (London) in England; the cathedrals of Avila, Barcelona, Toledo, and Palma da Majorca in Spain; the cathedrals of Santa Croce (Florence) and Milan in Italy; and Town Hall in Brussels, Belgium. Discuss how these structures affect people who approach or enter them, and make an effort to link these responses to students' responses to Poe's work.

We sat down; and for some moments, while he spoke not, I gazed upon him with a feeling half of pity, half of awe. Surely, man had never before so terribly altered, in so brief a period, as had Roderick Usher! It was with difficulty that I could bring myself to admit the identity of the wan being before me with the companion of my early boyhood. Yet the character of his face had been at all times remarkable. A cadaverousness of complexion; an eye large, liquid, and luminous beyond comparison; lips somewhat thin and very pallid, but of a surpassingly beautiful curve; a nose of a delicate Hebrew model, but with a breadth of nostril unusual in similar formations; a finely molded chin, speaking, in its want of prominence, of a want of moral energy; hair of a more than weblike softness and tenuity—these features, with an inordinate expansion above the regions of the temple, made up altogether a countenance not easily to be forgotten. And now in the mere exaggeration of the prevailing character of these features, and of the expression they were wont to convey, lay so much of change that I doubted to whom I spoke. The now ghastly pallor of the skin, and the now miraculous luster of the eye, above all things startled and even awed me. The silken hair, too, had been suffered to grow all unheeded, and as, in its wild gossamer texture, it floated rather than fell about the face, I could not, even with effort, connect its Arabesque[12] expression with any idea of simple humanity.

In the manner of my friend I was at once struck with an incoherence—an inconsistency; and I soon found this to arise from a series of feeble and futile struggles to overcome an habitual trepidancy—an excessive nervous agitation. For something of this nature I had indeed been prepared, no less by his letter than by reminiscences of certain boyish traits, and by conclusions deduced from his peculiar physical conformation and temperament. His action was alternately vivacious and sullen. His voice varied rapidly from a tremulous indecision (when the animal spirits seemed utterly in abeyance) to that species of energetic concision—that abrupt, weighty, unhurried, and hollow-sounding enunciation—that leaden, self-balanced, and perfectly modulated guttural utterance, which may be observed in the lost drunkard, or the irreclaimable eater of opium, during the periods of his most intense excitement.

It was thus that he spoke of the object of my visit, of his earnest desire to see me, and of the solace he expected me to afford him. He entered, at some length, into what he conceived to be the nature of his malady. It was, he said, a constitutional and a family evil and one for which he despaired to find a remedy—a mere nervous affection,[13] he immediately added, which would undoubtedly soon pass off. It displayed itself in a host of unnatural sensations. Some of these, as he detailed them, interested and bewildered me; although, perhaps, the terms and the general manner of their narration had their weight. He

---

12. **Arabesque** (ar′ ə besk′) *adj.* of complex and elaborate design.
13. **affection** affliction.

Reading Strategy
Breaking Down Long Sentences In your own words, restate the meaning of the sentence beginning "His voice varied."

Reading Check
In what ways has Roderick Usher changed since the speaker last saw him?

The Fall of the House of Usher ◆ 313

CUSTOMIZE INSTRUCTION FOR UNIVERSAL ACCESS

For Less Proficient Readers	For Gifted/Talented Students
Help students infer the kind of background or upbringing the narrator has had based on his comments and observations. Students may notice the narrator's awareness of and familiarity with elements of wealth and finery to which "[he has] been accustomed from [his] infancy." They can conclude that he has been raised in a well-to-do family.	Challenge students to write dialogue for the scene on this page between the speaker and Roderick Usher. Suggest that students reread the text several times to develop dialogue that reveals the characters' backgrounds, personalities, and present emotions as described in the narrative. Allow interested students to perform their dialogue for the class.

---

12 Literary Analysis
Single Effect

• Slowly read aloud this detailed description of Roderick Usher's appearance.

• Help students with the complexity of Poe's descriptive prose by encouraging them to keep close track of the focus on Usher's features and on the effect created by these details.

• Invite students to find parallels between the descriptions of Roderick Usher and those of the house. Explain to students that this likeness is another manifestation of Poe's use of single effect. **Possible responses:** Usher's web-like hair is like the tangled web of fungi on the house; the ghastly pallor of his skin is like the house's bleak walls.

13 Reading Strategy
Breaking Down Long Sentences

• Have a student volunteer read the sentence beginning "His voice varied."

• Draw students' attention to the fact that the sentence is designed to distinguish two styles of speaking.

• Have students copy the sentence onto a piece of paper. Ask them to break down the sentence by writing each of the sentence's parts on a separate line. Students can then recognize the meaning of these shorter parts in order to understand the main idea of the sentence.

• Then, ask students to respond to the Reading Strategy instruction on p. 313: In your own words, restate the meaning of the sentence beginning "His voice varied." **Possible response:** His voice alternated quickly between an uncertain, halting quality and an unnaturally deliberate, hollow, heavy quality.

14 Reading Check

Answer: Usher has grown "wan," and each of his facial features has been exaggerated by time. Especially notable are Usher's "ghastly pallor," the " miraculous luster of the eye," and disheveled "silken hair."

313

- Ask one or more student volunteers to summarize Roderick Usher's mental state. Students' responses should focus on his nervousness, distraction, hypersensitivity, and apparent weakness of spirit.

- Then, have one or more other students characterize the condition and appearance of the Usher house in a single sentence. Students' responses might focus on the grimness of the building and its situation, the layer of moss covering the entire house, and so forth.

▶ **Monitor Progress** Ask students the Literary Analysis question on p. 314: In what ways do Usher's mental state and the house itself typify a work of Gothic literature?

Answer: Both are characterized by gloom and decay, as is Gothic literature itself.

---

suffered much from a morbid acuteness of the senses; the most insipid food was alone endurable; he could wear only garments of certain texture; the odors of all flowers were oppressive; his eyes were tortured by even a faint light; and there were but peculiar sounds, and these from stringed instruments, which did not inspire him with horror.

To an <u>anomalous</u> species of terror I found him a bounden slave. "I shall perish," said he, "I *must* perish in this deplorable folly. Thus, thus, and not otherwise, shall I be lost. I dread the events of the future, not in themselves, but in their results. I shudder at the thought of any, even the most trivial, incident, which may operate upon this intolerable agitation of soul. I have, indeed, no abhorrence of danger, except in its absolute effect—in terror. In this unnerved, in this pitiable, condition I feel that the period will sooner or later arrive when I must abandon life and reason together, in some struggle with the grim phantasm, FEAR."

15 I learned, moreover, at intervals, and through broken and equivocal hints, another singular feature of his mental condition. He was enchained by certain superstitious impressions in regard to the dwelling which he tenanted, and whence, for many years, he had never ventured forth—in regard to an influence whose supposititious[14] force was conveyed in terms too shadowy here to be restated—an influence which some peculiarities in the mere form and substance of his family mansion had, by dint of long sufferance, he said, obtained over his spirit—an effect which the physique of the gray walls and turrets, and of the dim tarn into which they all looked down, had at length, brought about upon the morale of his existence.

He admitted, however, although with hesitation, that much of the peculiar gloom which thus afflicted him could be traced to a more natural and far more palpable origin—to the severe and long-continued illness—indeed to the evidently approaching dissolution—of a tenderly beloved sister, his sole companion for long years, his last and only relative on earth. "Her decease," he said, with a bitterness which I can never forget, "would leave him (him, the hopeless and the frail) the last of the ancient race of the Ushers." While he spoke, the lady Madeline (for so was she called) passed through a remote portion of the apartment, and, without having noticed my presence, disappeared. I regarded her with an utter astonishment not unmingled with dread; and yet I found it impossible to account for such feelings. A sensation of stupor oppressed me as my eyes followed her retreating steps. When a door, at length, closed upon her, my glance sought instinctively and eagerly the countenance of the brother; but he had buried his face in his hands, and I could only perceive that a far more than ordinary wanness had overspread the emaciated fingers through which trickled many passionate tears.

The disease of the lady Madeline had long baffled the skill of her physicians. A settled apathy, a gradual wasting away of the person,

---

14. **supposititious** (sə päz′ ə tish′ əs) *adj.* supposed.

anomalous (ə näm′ ə ləs) *adj.* abnormal

Literary Analysis

Single Effect and Gothic Style In what ways do Usher's mental state and the house itself typify a work of gothic literature?

✳ ENRICHMENT: Music Connection

Carl Maria von Weber

Poe mentions the music of German Romantic composer Carl Maria von Weber (1786–1826). Play excerpts of his work, such as the overtures from his operas *Der Freischütz* (The Free-shooter) and *Oberon*. Tell students that von Weber had a great influence on later Romantic composers, much like Poe had on writers who followed him. Or you might play the works of other Romantic composers such as Frédéric Chopin, Franz Liszt, Robert Schumann, and Hector Berlioz. Have students respond to the moods evoked by musical works such as these. Ask students whether they think Romantic music is designed to evoke a strong emotional response. Help them recognize that the melodious—and at times poignant—aspects of much Romantic music seem intended to elicit a strong emotional response in listeners.

and frequent although transient affections of a partially cataleptical[15] character were the unusual diagnosis. Hitherto she had steadily borne up against the pressure of her malady, and had not betaken herself finally to bed; but on the closing in of the evening of my arrival at the house, she succumbed (as her brother told me at night with inexpressible agitation) to the prostrating power of the destroyer; and I learned that the glimpse I had obtained of her person would thus probably be the last I should obtain—that the lady, at least while living, would be seen by me no more.

For several days ensuing, her name was unmentioned by either Usher or myself; and during this period I was busied in earnest endeavors to alleviate the melancholy of my friend. We painted and read together, or I listened, as if in a dream, to the wild improvisations of his speaking guitar. And thus, as a closer and still closer intimacy admitted me more unreservedly into the recesses of his spirit, the more bitterly did I perceive the futility of all attempt at cheering a mind from which darkness, as if an inherent positive quality, poured forth upon all objects of the moral and physical universe in one unceasing radiation of gloom.

I shall ever bear about me a memory of the many solemn hours I thus spent alone with the master of the House of Usher. Yet I should fail in any attempt to convey an idea of the exact character of the studies, or of the occupations, in which he involved me, or led me the way. An excited and highly distempered ideality[16] threw a sulfureous[17] luster over all. His long improvised dirges will ring forever in my ears. Among other things, I hold painfully in mind a certain singular perversion and amplification of the wild air of the last waltz of von Weber.[18] From the paintings over which his elaborate fancy brooded, and which grew, touch by touch, into vaguenesses at which I shuddered the more thrillingly, because I shuddered knowing not why—from these paintings (vivid as their images now are before me) I would in vain endeavor to educe more than a small portion which should lie within the compass of merely written words. By the utter simplicity, by the nakedness of his designs, he arrested and overawed attention. If ever mortal painted an idea, that mortal was Roderick Usher. For me at least, in the circumstances then surrounding me, there arose out of the pure abstractions which the hypochondriac contrived to throw upon his canvas, an intensity of intolerable awe, no shadow of which felt I ever yet in the contemplation of the certainly glowing yet too concrete reveries of Fuseli.[19]

---

15. **cataleptical** (kat´ əl ep´ tik əl) *adj.* in a state in which consciousness and feeling are suddenly and temporarily lost and the muscles become rigid.
16. **ideality** (ī dē al´ i tē) *n.* something that is ideal and has no reality.
17. **sulfureous** (sul fyŏŏr´ ē əs) *adj.* greenish-yellow.
18. **von Weber** (fôn vā´ bər) Karl Maria von Weber (1786–1826), a German Romantic composer whose music was highly emotional and dramatic.
19. **Fuseli** (fŏŏ ze´ lē) Johann Hinrich Fuseli (1741–1825), also known as Henry Fuseli, Swiss-born painter who lived in England and was noted for his depictions of dreamlike and sometimes nightmarish images.

Literary Analysis
Single Effect In what way does Madeline's surrender on this night contribute to a single effect?

Reading Check
What conclusion does the narrator draw about Usher's mental state?

The Fall of the House of Usher ◆ 315

16 Literary Analysis
Single Effect

- Have students reread the two paragraphs beginning "The disease of the Lady Madeline." Make sure students understand that Madeline's disease is mysterious, even to her physicians.
- With students, write on the chalkboard a list of the disease's symptoms and characteristics.
- Ask students the Literary Analysis question on p. 315: In what way does Madeline's surrender on this night contribute to a single effect? Answer: Students may say that her mysterious (and apparently final) appearance in the house adds to the narrator's sense of anxiety and foreboding.

17 ✓ Reading Check
Answer: The narrator concludes that Usher is agitated, terrified, melancholic, and hypochondriacal. He correlates Usher's mental state both with the condition and atmosphere of the house and with the condition of his sister.

CUSTOMIZE INSTRUCTION FOR UNIVERSAL ACCESS

For Less Proficient Readers	For Gifted/Talented Students
Read aloud with students the paragraphs beginning "For several days" and "I shall ever bear." Help students focus on the activities that the narrator and Roderick Usher perform together—reading, playing music, and painting. Then lead students in a discussion of the narrator's conclusion that Usher is so deeply rooted in gloom that not even gestures of friendship can cheer him up. Students may say that a person so fraught with emotional turmoil is unlikely to change—even with the attentions of a devoted friend.	Have students read carefully the two last paragraphs on p. 315. Invite them to create a work of art, for example a lyric or musical composition fitting the term *dirge* ("a song of grief") or a painting fitting Poe's description of Usher's work. Encourage students to share their finished works with classmates. Interested students might research the paintings of Johann Hinrich Fuseli and compare them with their own work.

315

18 Background

"The Haunted Palace"

Tell students that Poe's poem that appears here, "The Haunted Palace," was published separately five months before it appeared in this short story (in fact, it is possible that the poem inspired the tale). In one of his letters, Poe says that the palace in the poem's title symbolizes the human mind: " . . . by the Haunted Palace I mean to imply a mind haunted by phantoms—a disordered brain." Invite students to use this detail to interpret the poem and then to relate its meaning to the theme of the story.

One of the phantasmagoric conceptions of my friend, partaking not so rigidly of the spirit of abstraction, may be shadowed forth, although feebly, in words. A small picture presented the interior of an immensely long and rectangular vault or tunnel, with low walls, smooth, white and without interruption or device. Certain accessory points of the design served well to convey the idea that this excavation lay at an exceeding depth below the surface of the earth. No outlet was observed in any portion of its vast extent, and no torch or other artificial source of light was discernible; yet a flood of intense rays rolled throughout, and bathed the whole in a ghastly and inappropriate splendor.

I have just spoken of that morbid condition of the auditory nerve which rendered all music intolerable to the sufferer, with the exception of certain effects of stringed instruments. It was, perhaps, the narrow limits to which he thus confined himself upon the guitar which gave birth, in great measure, to the fantastic character of his performances. But the fervid facility of his impromptus could not be so accounted for. They must have been, and were, in the notes, as well as in the words of his wild fantasias (for he not unfrequently accompanied himself with rhymed verbal improvisations), the result of that intense mental collectedness and concentration to which I have previously alluded as observable only in particular moments of the highest artificial excitement. The words of one of these rhapsodies I have easily remembered. I was, perhaps, the more forcibly impressed with it as he gave it because, in the under or mystic current of its meaning, I fancied that I perceived, and for the first time, a full consciousness on the part of Usher of the tottering of his lofty reason upon her throne. The verses, which were entitled "The Haunted Palace," ran very nearly, if not accurately, thus:

20 ▲ Critical Viewing In what ways do the colors and shapes in this image suggest Roderick Usher's tormented mental condition? **[Interpret]**

I

In the greenest of our valleys,
    By good angels tenanted,
Once a fair and stately palace—
    Radiant palace—reared its head.
In the monarch Thought's dominion—
    It stood there!
Never seraph[20] spread a pinion
    Over fabric half so fair.

---

20. **seraph** (ser´ əf) angel.

II

Banners yellow, glorious, golden,
 On its roof did float and flow
(This—all this—was in the olden
 Time long ago)
And every gentle air that dallied,
 In that sweet day,
Along the ramparts plumed and pallid,
 A winged odor went away.

III

Wanderers in that happy valley
 Through two luminous windows saw
Spirits moving musically
 To a lute's well-tunéd law;
Round about a throne, where sitting
 (Porphyrogene!)[21]
In state his glory well befitting,
 The ruler of the realm was seen.

IV

And all with pearl and ruby glowing
 Was the fair palace door,
Through which came flowing, flowing, flowing
 And sparkling evermore,
A troop of Echoes whose sweet duty
 Was but to sing,
In voices of surpassing beauty,
 The wit and wisdom of their king.

V

But evil things, in robes of sorrow,
 Assailed the monarch's high estate;
(Ah, let us mourn, for never morrow
 Shall dawn upon him, desolate!)
And, round about his home, the glory
 That blushed and bloomed
Is but a dim-remembered story
 Of the old time entombed.

VI

And travelers now within that valley,
 Through the red-litten[22] windows see

---

21. **Porphyrogene** (pôr fer ō jēn´) born to royalty or "the purple."
22. **litten** lighted.

Literary Analysis
Single Effect Which details of this poem contribute to the story's style effect?

21 ☑ **Reading Check**
What is "The Haunted Palace"?

CUSTOMIZE INSTRUCTION FOR UNIVERSAL ACCESS

For Special Needs Students	For English Learners
These students might gain greater appreciation of "The Haunted Palace" if they accompany the words with music, as was done by Roderick Usher. Groups of students might do a choral reading of the words accompanied by a recording of appropriate—melancholy or softly moody—background music. Students can evaluate whether the music enhances the mood of the words.	Help students read the poem stanza by stanza, identifying subjects and verbs and analyzing unusual sentence structures. Encourage students to color-code rhyming words at the ends of lines and to take note of Poe's use of sound devices (such as the many examples of repetition and alliteration). Finally, invite students to work in pairs to read the poem aloud. Partners might proceed by reading alternate stanzas.

⓳ Literary Analysis

Single Effect

- Remind students that the narrator identifies these stanzas as the lyrics to a song sung by Roderick Usher.
- Guide students to notice in what ways the poem reflects the same atmosphere and emotions as those in the story. In this way the verse augments Poe's intended single effect.
- Ask students the Literary Analysis question on p. 317: Which details of this poem contribute to the story's style effect?
  Answer: Examples include the reference to a lute (stanza III), which echoes the opening French couplet, and the words "But evil things, in robes of sorrow,/ Assailed the monarch's high estate" (stanza V), which mirror the eerie mood at the Usher mansion.

⓴ ▶ Critical Viewing

Answer: The artist's use of dark colors and twisted shapes reflects Roderick Usher's melancholia and distorted thinking.

㉑ ☑ Reading Check

Answer: "The Haunted Palace" is a song sung by Roderick Usher. The lyrics of the song describe the mysterious, desolate palace of a doomed king.

Reading Strategy

Breaking Down Long Sentences

- Read aloud with students the sentence beginning "But, in his disordered fancy."

- Help students identify the sentence's subject (*idea*) and its compound predicate (*had assumed, [had] trespassed*).

- Then, have students identify and paraphrase key words and phrases, such as *disordered fancy, more daring character, trespassed,* and *kingdom of inorganization.*

▶ Monitor Progress Ask students to restate the meaning of the entire sentence.

Sample Answer: Usher's confused mind has led him to believe that not only *living* things but also inanimate objects possess the ability to think and feel.

ⓚ Literary Analysis

Single Effect

- Ask students to summarize the single effect Poe sets out to achieve in this story.

- Then, ask students to recall how (earlier in the story) Poe linked Roderick Usher and the house in which he lives. If necessary, review passages in which the man and the structure are described as having similar characteristics.

- Finally, ask students the Literary Analysis question on p. 318: What details of this philosophical discussion contribute to the story's single effect?

Answer: Students should note that Usher's delusions about the stones, the fungus on them, the decayed trees, and the house's reflection in the tarn link the house even more closely with the decay of its inhabitants.

ⓛ Background

Octavo

An octavo edition is a book whose page size is six by nine inches. A quarto Gothic book has a page size of about nine by twelve inches; the words appear in Gothic type.

Vast forms that move fantastically
To a discordant melody;
While, like a rapid ghastly river,
Through the pale door,
A hideous throng rush out forever,
And laugh—but smile no more.

I well remember that suggestions arising from this ballad led us into a train of thought wherein there became manifest an opinion of Usher's which I mention not so much on account of its novelty (for other men have thought thus), as on account of the pertinacity with which he maintained it. This opinion, in its general form, was that of the <u>sentience</u> of all vegetable things. But, in his disordered fancy the idea had assumed a more daring character, and trespassed, under certain conditions, upon the kingdom of inorganization.[23] I lack words to express the full extent, or the earnest abandon of his persuasion. The belief, however, was connected (as I have previously hinted) with the gray stones of the home of his forefathers. The conditions of the sentience had been here, he imagined, fulfilled in the method of collocation of these stones—in the order of their arrangement, as well as in that of the many fungi which overspread them, and of the decayed trees which stood around—above all, in the long undisturbed endurance of this arrangement, and in its reduplication in the still waters of the tarn. Its evidence—the evidence of the sentience—was to be seen, he said (and I here started as he spoke), in the gradual yet certain condensation of an atmosphere of their own about the waters and the walls. The result was discoverable, he added, in that silent yet importunate and terrible influence which for centuries had molded the destinies of his family, and which made him what I now saw him—what he was. Such opinions need no comment, and I will make none.

Our books—the books which, for years, had formed no small portion of the mental existence of the invalid—were, as might be supposed, in strict keeping with this character of phantasm. We pored together over such works as the *Ververt et Chartreuse*[24] of Gresset; the *Belphegor* of Machiavelli; the *Heaven and Hell* of Swedenborg; the *Subterranean Voyage of Nicholas Klimm* by Holberg; the *Chiromancy* of Robert Flud, of Jean D'Indaginé and of De la Chambre; the *Journey into the Blue Distance* of Tieck; and the *City of the Sun* of Campanella. One favorite volume was a small octavo edition of the *Directorium Inquisitorium,* by the Dominican Eymeric de Gironne; and there were passages in Pomponius Mela, about the old African Satyrs and Œgipans, over which Usher would sit dreaming for hours. His chief delight, however, was found in the perusal of an exceedingly rare and curious book in quarto

---

23. **inorganization** (in´ ôr gə ni zā´ shən) *n.* inanimate objects.
24. ***Ververt et Chartreuse,*** **etc.** All the books listed deal with magic or mysticism.

sentience (sen´ shəns) *n.* capacity of feeling

Literary Analysis
Single Effect Which details of this philosophical discussion contribute to the story's single effect?

✸ **ENRICHMENT: Cultural Connection**

Film Adaptations of Poe's Work

The vivid images in Edgar Allan Poe's stories and poems and his exploration of macabre, gruesome, and chilling themes have made his literary works appealing to filmmakers, and some works have been adapted more than once. Films based on Poe's works include *The Raven* (1935, 1963), *The Tell-Tale Heart* (1962), *The Fall of the House of Usher* (1982), *Murders in the Rue Morgue* (1932, 1971, 1986), *The Masque of the Red Death* (1964, 1989), and *The Pit and the Pendulum* (1961).

Invite interested students to read the original poem or tale and then to watch a film adaptation of it. Then, have students write a critical essay that analyzes the strengths and weaknesses of the film version.

318

Gothic—the manual of a forgotten church—the *Vigilae Mortuorum secundum Chorum Ecclesiae Maguntinae.*

I could not help thinking of the wild ritual of this work, and of its probable influence upon the hypochondriac, when, one evening, having informed me abruptly that the lady Madeline was no more, he stated his intention of preserving her corpse for a fortnight (previously to its final interment), in one of the numerous vaults within the main walls of the building. The worldly reason, however, assigned for this singular proceeding, was one which I did not feel at liberty to dispute. The brother had been led to his resolution (so he told me) by consideration of the unusual character of the malady of the deceased, of certain obtrusive and eager inquiries on the part of her medical men, and of the remote and exposed situation of the burial ground of the family. I will not deny that when I called to mind the sinister countenance of the person whom I met upon the staircase, on the day of my arrival at the house, I had no desire to oppose what I regarded as at best but a harmless, and by no means an unnatural precaution.

At the request of Usher, I personally aided him in the arrangements for the temporary entombment. The body having been encoffined, we two alone bore it to its rest. The vault in which we placed it (and which had been so long unopened that our torches, half smothered in its oppressive atmosphere, gave us little opportunity for investigation) was small, damp, and entirely without means of admission for light; lying, at great depth, immediately beneath that portion of the building in which was my own sleeping apartment. It had been used, apparently, in remote feudal times, for the worst purposes of a donjon-keep, and, in later days, as a place of deposit for powder, or some other highly combustible substance, as a portion of its floor, and the whole interior of a long archway through which we reached it, were carefully sheathed with copper. The door, of massive iron, had been, also, similarly protected. Its immense weight caused an unusually sharp, grating sound, as it moved upon its hinges.

Having deposited our mournful burden upon trestles within this region of horror, we partially turned aside the yet unscrewed lid of the coffin, and looked upon the face of the tenant. A striking similitude between the brother and sister now first arrested my attention; and Usher, divining, perhaps, my thoughts, murmured out some few words from which I learned that the deceased and himself had been twins, and that <u>sympathies of a scarcely intelligible nature</u> had always existed between them. Our glances, however, rested not long upon the dead—for we could not regard her unawed. The disease which had thus entombed the lady in the maturity of youth, had left, as usual in all maladies of a strictly cataleptical character, the mockery of a faint blush upon the bosom and the face, and that <u>suspiciously lingering smile upon the lip</u> which is so terrible in death. We replaced and screwed down the lid, and, having secured the door of iron, made our way, with toil, into the scarcely less gloomy apartments of the upper portion of the house.

they very similar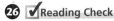

heard she got out

Reading Strategy
Breaking Down Long Sentences Clarify the main idea of the sentence beginning "The vault in which we placed it."

26 ✓**Reading Check**
What does the narrator notice about Madeline's appearance in her coffin?

The Fall of the House of Usher ◆ 319

---

25 **Reading Strategy**
Breaking Down Long Sentences

- Begin by reading aloud each of this paragraph's first two sentences, encouraging students to visualize Poe's descriptions of physical actions and other details. Make sure students understand the difference between a *coffin* and a *vault* ("a burial chamber or other underground storage compartment").

- Invite one or more students to read aloud the sentence beginning "The vault in which we placed it."

- Direct students to respond to the Reading Strategy instruction on p. 319: Clarify the main idea of the sentence beginning "The vault in which we placed it."
  Answer: The vault where Madeline's body will be temporarily entombed is dark, small, damp, and long unused. Students may also note the location of the vault directly below the room where the narrator sleeps.

26 ✓**Reading Check**
Answer: The narrator notices her close resemblance to her brother, as well as the way the corpse retains a slight smile on her mouth and small patches of color on her skin.

CUSTOMIZE INSTRUCTION FOR UNIVERSAL ACCESS

For Gifted/Talented Students

Have students do research for an essay on the Gothic novel. Point out that they will need to use a variety of literary resources. Have students brainstorm for ideas about what they want to find out, how they might find resources, and the ways in which they will conduct their research. Ideas should include using the library, the Internet, and other print and non-print resources.

Have students generate a list of questions related to the history of the Gothic novel, for example:

- How and where did the Gothic novel originate?
- Who were the first authors of Gothic novels, and how did this genre grow in Europe and in the United States?
- What Gothic novels are still popular?

Suggest that students organize information in an outline that includes dates for important literary works.

- Ask students to recall and discuss Roderick Usher's behavior and appearance earlier in the story. Students will probably note his nervousness and apparent ill health.

- Read aloud the paragraph beginning "And now, some days of bitter grief." Invite students to speculate on what may have caused this deterioration.
Answer: Students may say that grief has overwhelmed him, that his twin's death has made him fear for his own life, and that he is harboring a terrible secret that torments him.

28 Critical Thinking

Analyze Cause and Effect

- Draw students' attention to the fact that the narrator says that he is not only terrified but also "infected" by Usher's condition.

- Ask students this question: How might one "catch" another's mood?
Answer: Students might say that being with someone for a number of days could influence one's emotional state.

29 Literary Analysis

Single Effect and Gothic Style

- Have a student volunteer read aloud the paragraph beginning "It was, especially." Encourage other students to listen carefully for descriptions of the narrator's physical and mental condition.

- Then ask students the Literary Analysis question on p. 320: Which elements of Gothic literature do the narrator's physical and mental state reflect?
Answer: The narrator is feeling a growing psychological and physical torment. Moreover, his physical and mental symptoms have begun to feed one another in a destructive cyclical manner. This repetitive process is echoed by the narrator's pacing back and forth across the floor.

---

27 And now, some days of bitter grief having elapsed, an observable change came over the features of the mental disorder of my friend. His ordinary manner had vanished. His ordinary occupations were neglected or forgotten. He roamed from chamber to chamber with hurried, unequal, and object-less step. The pallor of his countenance had assumed, if possible, a more ghastly hue—but the luminousness of his eye had utterly gone out. The once occasional huskiness of his tone was heard no more; and a tremulous quaver, as if of extreme terror, habitually characterized his utterance. There were times, indeed, when I thought his unceasingly agitated mind was laboring with some oppressive secret, to divulge which he struggled for the necessary courage. At times, again, I was obliged to resolve all into **28** the mere inexplicable vagaries[25] of madness, for I beheld him gazing upon vacancy for long hours, in an attitude of the profoundest attention, as if listening to some imaginary sound. It was no wonder that his condition terrified—that it infected me. I felt creeping upon me, by slow yet uncertain degrees, the wild influences of his own fantastic yet impressive superstitions.

It was, especially, upon retiring to bed late in the night of the seventh or eighth day after the placing of the lady Madeline within the donjon, that I experienced the full power of such feelings. Sleep came not near my couch—while the hours waned and waned away. I struggled to reason off the nervousness which had dominion over me. I endeavored to believe that much, if not all of what I felt, was due to the bewildering influence of the gloomy furniture of the room—of the dark and tattered draperies, which, tortured into motion by the breath of a rising tempest, swayed fitfully to and fro upon the walls, and rustled uneasily about the decorations of the bed. But my efforts were fruitless. An irrepress- **29** ible tremor gradually pervaded my frame; and, at length, there sat upon my very heart an incubus[26] of utterly causeless alarm. Shaking this off with a gasp and a struggle, I uplifted myself upon the pillows, and, peering earnestly within the intense darkness of the chamber, heark- ened—I know not why, except that an instinctive spirit prompted me— to certain low and indefinite sounds which came, through the pauses of the storm, at long intervals, I knew not whence. Overpowered by an intense sentiment of horror, unaccountable yet unendurable, I threw on my clothes with haste (for I felt that I should sleep no more during the night), and endeavored to arouse myself from the pitiable condition into which I had fallen by pacing rapidly to and fro through the apartment.

I had taken but few turns in this manner, when a light step on an adjoining staircase arrested my attention. I presently recognized it as that of Usher. In an instant afterward he rapped, with a gentle touch, at my door, and entered, bearing a lamp. His countenance was, as usual, cadaverously wan—but, moreover, there was a species of mad hilarity in his eyes—an evidently restrained hysteria in his whole demeanor. His

---

25. **vagaries** (vā′ ger ēz) *n.* odd, unexpected actions or notions.
26. **incubus** (iŋ′ kyə bəs) *n.* something nightmarishly burdensome.

air appalled me—but anything was preferable to the solitude which I had so long endured, and I even welcomed his presence as a relief.

"And you have not seen it?" he said abruptly, after having stared about him for some moments in silence—"you have not then seen it?—but, stay! you shall." Thus speaking, and having carefully shaded his lamp, he hurried to one of the casements, and threw it freely open to the storm.

The impetuous fury of the entering gust nearly lifted us from our feet. It was, indeed, a tempestuous yet sternly beautiful night, and one wildly singular in its terror and its beauty. A whirlwind had apparently collected its force in our vicinity; for there were frequent and violent alterations in the direction of the wind; and the exceeding density of the clouds (which hung so low as to press upon the turrets of the house) did not prevent our perceiving the lifelike velocity with which they flew careering from all points against each other, without passing away into the distance. I say that even their exceeding density did not prevent our perceiving this—yet we had no glimpse of the moon or stars, nor was there any flashing forth of the lightning. But the under surfaces of the huge masses of agitated vapor, as well as all terrestrial objects immediately around us, were glowing in the unnatural light of a faintly luminous and distinctly visible gaseous exhalation which hung about and enshrouded the mansion.

Literary Analysis
Single Effect In what way does the description of the storm contribute to the growing sense of terror?

"You must not—you shall not behold this!" said I, shuddering, to Usher, as I led him, with a gentle violence, from the window to a seat. "These appearances, which bewilder you, are merely electrical phenomena not uncommon—or it may be that they have their ghastly origin in the rank miasma[27] of the tarn. Let us close this casement:—the air is chilling and dangerous to your frame. Here is one of your favorite romances. I will read, and you shall listen:—and so we will pass away this terrible night together."

The antique volume which I had taken up was the *Mad Trist* of Sir Launcelot Canning;[28] but I had called it a favorite of Usher's more in sad jest than in earnest; for, in truth, there is little in its uncouth and unimaginative prolixity which could have had interest for the lofty and spiritual ideality of my friend. It was, however, the only book immediately at hand; and I indulged a vague hope that the excitement which now agitated the hypochondriac, might find relief (for the history of mental disorder is full of similar anomalies) even in the extremeness of the folly which I should read. Could I have judged, indeed, by the wild overstrained air of vivacity with which he hearkened, or apparently hearkened, to the words of the tale, I might well have congratulated myself upon the success of my design.

I had arrived at that well-known portion of the story where Ethelred, the hero of the Trist, having sought in vain for peaceable admission into the dwelling of the hermit, proceeds to make good an

Reading Check
Which odd or unnatural sight does the narrator see when the curtains are opened?

---

27. **miasma** (mī az´ me) *n.* unwholesome atmosphere.
28. *Mad Trist* **of Sir Launcelot Canning** fictional book and author.

⬤30 Literary Analysis
Single Effect

- Invite a student volunteer to summarize Edgar Allan Poe's theory about a single effect in literary works. If necessary, remind students that Poe's theory asserts that every character, incident and description in a story must contribute to the single effect being achieved in the story.

- Ask students the Literary Analysis question on p. 321: In what way does the description of the storm contribute to the growing sense of terror?
Answer: Students may say that Poe describes the storm with many of the same words he used to describe the mansion and Roderick Usher, such as *agitated, luminous, ghastly, rank, chilling,* and *dangerous.*

⬤31 ✓Reading Check

Answer: The narrator sees strangely dense clouds, whirlwinds, and other effects of a terrible storm taking place on this "sternly beautiful night."

CUSTOMIZE INSTRUCTION FOR UNIVERSAL ACCESS

For Advanced Readers

Tell students that whirlpools and whirlwinds are recurring symbols in Poe stories. Because they draw things toward their center, they stand for destructive collapse. Poe believed that the universe was destined to collapse in on itself. He wrote about his theories of cosmology in his book *Eureka*. His ideas about the origin and end of the universe are remarkable because they anticipated the Big Bang theory by many years.

Have students read and report on another piece of

Poe's short fiction that uses whirlpool or whirlwind imagery, such as "A Descent Into the Maelstrom." Encourage students to give short oral presentations in which they summarize the story and explain how this particular imagery relates to the story's plot, themes, or characters.

- Have three or four student volunteers read these four paragraphs as classmates listen to and record Poe's descriptive details.

- Ask students the Literary Analysis question on p. 322: Which words and details from this description of the unusual sounds add to the single effect?

  Answer: Words and details include: *echo; cracking and ripping sound; coincidence; rattling; increasing storm; disturbed; shriek so horrid and harsh; piercing; dreadful noise; wild amazement; low and apparently distant . . . grating sound;* and *dragon's unnatural shriek.*

entrance by force. Here, it will be remembered, the words of the narrative run thus:

"And Ethelred, who was by nature of a doughty heart, and who was now mighty withal, on account of the powerfulness of the wine which he had drunken, waited no longer to hold parley with the hermit, who, in sooth, was of an obstinate and maliceful turn, but feeling the rain upon his shoulders, and fearing the rising of the tempest, uplifted his mace outright, and, with blows, made quickly room in the plankings of the door for his gauntleted hand; and now pulling therewith sturdily, he so cracked, and ripped, and tore all asunder, that the noise of the dry and hollow-sounding wood alarumed and reverberated throughout the forest."

 At the termination of this sentence I started and, for a moment, paused; for it appeared to me (although I at once concluded that my excited fancy had deceived me)—it appeared to me that, from some very remote portion of the mansion, there came, indistinctly to my ears, which might have been, in its exact similarity of character, the echo (but a stifled and dull one certainly) of the very cracking and ripping sound which Sir Launcelot had so particularly described. It was, beyond doubt, the coincidence alone which had arrested my attention; for, amid the rattling of the sashes of the casements, and the ordinary commingled noises of the still increasing storm, the sound, itself, had nothing, surely, which should have interested or disturbed me. I continued the story:

"But the good champion Ethelred, now entering within the door, was sore enraged and amazed to perceive no signal of the maliceful hermit; but, in the stead thereof, a dragon of a scaly and prodigious demeanor, and of a fiery tongue, which sate in guard before a palace of gold, with a floor of silver; and upon the wall there hung a shield of shining brass with this legend enwritten—

> *Who entereth herein, a conqueror*
> *hath bin;*
> *Who slayeth the dragon, the shield*
> *he shall win.*

And Ethelred uplifted his mace, and struck upon the head of the dragon, which fell before him, and gave up his pasty breath, with a shriek so horrid and harsh, and withal so piercing, that Ethelred had fain to close his ears with his hands against the dreadful noise of it, the like whereof was never before heard."

Here again I paused abruptly, and now with a feeling of wild amazement—for there could be no doubt whatever that, in this instance, I did actually hear (although from what direction it proceeded I found it impossible to say) a low and apparently distant, but harsh, protracted, and most unusual screaming or grating sound—the exact counterpart of what my fancy had already conjured up for the dragon's unnatural shriek as described by the romancer.

322 ◆ *A Growing Nation (1800–1870)*

Literary Analysis
Single Effect Which words and details from this description of the unusual sounds add to the single effect?

✷ ENRICHMENT: Cultural Connection

Dragons

In the story within this tale, Poe describes a dragon slain by Ethelred. Though dragons are imaginary creatures that appear in myths and legends of many cultures, not all dragons are alike. In the Chinese and Japanese cultures, dragons symbolize wisdom, power, and the mysteries of the universe. They possess courage, impart knowledge, and are assumed to be fabulously rich. Their strength is thought to explain forces of nature such as lightning and wind.

Unlike the benevolent Eastern dragon, the typical Western dragon is unmercifully evil. This dragon has a hideous, scaly body with angular wings. Its breath is so foul that the stench—or the blast of red-hot fire—from its mouth can kill. Western legends place dragons in habitats such as caves or underground in tunnels, cellars, or wells. Some live above ground in trees, fields, or mountains. Like Eastern dragons, some Western dragons live in or near lakes, rivers, swamps, or oceans.

Separation, 1896, Edvard Munch, Munch Museet, Oslo, Norway

Oppressed, as I certainly was, upon the extraordinary coincidence, by a thousand conflicting sensations, in which wonder and extreme terror were predominant, I still retained sufficient presence of mind to avoid exciting, by an observation, the sensitive nervousness of my companion. I was by no means certain that he had noticed the sounds in question; although, assuredly, a strange alteration had, during the last few minutes, taken place in his demeanor. From a position fronting my own, he had gradually brought round his chair; so as to sit with his face to the door of the chamber; and thus I could but partially perceive his features, although I saw that his lips trembled as if he were murmuring inaudibly. His head had dropped upon his breast—yet I knew that he was not asleep, from the wide and rigid opening of the eye as I caught a glance of it in profile. The motion of his body, too, was at

34 ▲ Critical Viewing
Describe the ways in which this painting conveys the same unnatural sense of terror Poe creates in the story.
[Analyze]

35 ☑ Reading Check
What unusual sounds does the narrator hear?

The Fall of the House of Usher ◆ 323

CUSTOMIZE INSTRUCTION FOR UNIVERSAL ACCESS

For Advanced Readers

The French poet Charles Baudelaire saw Poe as both an outlaw and a hero. In an essay published in the *Paris Review* in 1852, Baudelaire observed:

"Poe usually suppresses the minor details or gives them a minimal value. Because of this harsh severity, the generating idea is more evident and the subject stands out vividly against the bare background. In Poe's books the style is condensed, tightly linked. The ill will or laziness of the reader cannot slip through the mesh of this logically woven net. All ideas, like obedient arrows, fly to the same target."

Read aloud Baudelaire's critique and work with students to paraphrase it. Then have students discuss or write about the following question:

Does Poe "suppress the minor details"? Explain. Which details might he have suppressed in "The Fall of the House of Usher"?

33 Background

Art

Separation, 1896, by Edvard Munch

Edvard Munch (1863–1944) was a painter and graphic artist who studied in Paris, as well as in his native Norway. Munch's complex psychological style is considered one of the earliest manifestations of Expressionism, a movement in art marked by the use of symbols and images that are distorted to convey emotion and inner experience. Like Poe, Munch drew his identity as an artist from an obsession with depression, fear, and death; his exploration of these dark themes infuses his art with a harrowing power.

Like so many of Munch's works, *Separation* focuses on the emotional effects of a situation. The dark colors and drawn expression of the person in the foreground create a mood of despair. Use these questions for discussion:

1. How does the artist create contrast in the painting?
   Answer: Students may note that one person is dressed in dark clothes and is stationary. The other figure's dress is light; she is in motion; and her face and fingers are only suggested. Students may also point out the painting's contrasting settings.

2. In what ways is the image related to Poe's tale?
   Answer: Roderick Usher is a man in despair; his sister Madeline is isolated by illness. The story describes their "separation."

34 ▶ Critical Viewing

Answer: The painting shows two people. One seems to have a troubled expression; the other appears to be a faceless ghost. Both the painting and Poe's story evoke a sense of supernatural dread and anguish.

35 ☑ Reading Check

Answer: The narrator hears a "cracking and ripping sound," "a shriek so horrid and harsh," and "a low and apparently distant, but harsh, protracted, and most unusual screaming or grating sound."

323

36 Reading Strategy

Breaking Down Long Sentences

- Read aloud for students the paragraph beginning "And now, the champion." Remind students that these words likewise are being read aloud to Roderick Usher by the narrator from a book called *Mad Trist*.

- Direct students to respond to the Reading Strategy question on p. 324: Summarize the action of the paragraph-long sentence beginning "And now, the champion." Possible response: Ethelred thinks of the magical shield, removes the dragon's corpse, and walks toward the shield hanging on the castle wall, during which time the shield crashes to the floor at his feet.

37 Critical Thinking

Draw Conclusions

- Read aloud this passage, in which Roderick Usher claims—excitedly and repeatedly—that he did not dare to speak of his fearful realization.

- Ask students why Usher may have been unable to speak out, given that he took careful precautions to ensure that he did not bury his sister alive. Answer: Students may say that Roderick feels guilty about what he has done but fears exposing the gruesome act to his one friend or that he intentionally kept silent because he wanted his sister to be dead.

38 Literary Analysis

Single Effect and Gothic Style

- Read aloud the paragraph beginning "As if in the superhuman energy."

- Ask students the Literary Analysis question on p. 324: What elements of Gothic literature are evident in this passage about Madeline Usher? Answer: This passage features elements such as macabre or violent plot details (*blood upon her white robes, some bitter struggle, violent and now final death agonies*), characters in physical or psychological torment (Madeline and Roderick), and the presence of a supernatural or otherworldly element (*superhuman energy*).

324

---

variance with this idea—for he rocked from side to side with a gentle yet constant and uniform sway. Having rapidly taken notice of all this, I resumed the narrative of Sir Launcelot, which thus proceeded:

36 "And now, the champion, having escaped from the terrible fury of the dragon, bethinking himself of the brazen shield, and of the breaking up of the enchantment which was upon it, removed the carcass from out of the way before him, and approached valorously over the silver pavement of the castle to where the shield was upon the wall; which in sooth tarried not for his full coming, but fell down at his feet upon the silver floor, with a mighty great and terrible ringing sound."

No sooner had these syllables passed my lips, than—as if a shield of brass had indeed, at the moment, fallen heavily upon a floor of silver—I became aware of a distinct, hollow, metallic, and clangorous, yet apparently muffled, reverberation. Completely unnerved, I leaped to my feet; but the measured rocking movement of Usher was undisturbed. I rushed to the chair in which he sat. His eyes were bent fixedly before him, and throughout his whole countenance there reigned a stony rigidity. But, as I placed my hand upon his shoulder, there came a strong shudder over his whole person; a sickly smile quivered about his lips; and I saw that he spoke in a low, hurried, and gibbering murmur, as if unconscious of my presence. Bending closely over him I at length drank in the hideous import of his words.

37 "Not hear it?—yes, I hear it, and have heard it. Long—long—long—many minutes, many hours, many days, have I heard it—yet I dared not—oh, pity me, miserable wretch that I am!—I *dared* not—I dared not speak! *We have put her living in the tomb!* Said I not that my senses were acute? I *now* tell you that I heard her first feeble movement in the hollow coffin. I heard them—many, many days ago—yet I dared not—*I dared not speak!* and now—tonight—Ethelred—ha! ha!—the breaking of the hermit's door, and the death cry of the dragon, and the clangor of the shield—say, rather, the rending of her coffin, and the grating of the iron hinges of her prison, and her struggles within the coppered archway of the vault! Oh! wither shall I fly? Will she not be here anon? Is she not hurrying to upbraid me for my haste? Have I not heard her footstep on the stair? Do I not distinguish that heavy and horrible beating of her heart? Madman!"—here he sprang furiously to his feet, and shrieked out his syllables, as if in the effort he were giving up his soul—*"Madman! I tell you that she now stands without the door!"*

As if in the superhuman energy of his utterance there had been found the potency of a spell, the huge antique panels to which the speaker pointed threw slowly back, upon the instant, their ponderous and ebony jaws. It was the work of the rushing gust—but then without **38** those doors there *did* stand the lofty and enshrouded figure of the lady Madeline of Usher. There was blood upon her white robes, and the evidence of some bitter struggle upon every portion of her emaciated frame. For a moment she remained trembling and reeling to and fro upon the threshold—then, with a low moaning cry, fell heavily inward upon the person of her brother, and in her violent and now final

324 ◆ *A Growing Nation (1800–1870)*

Reading Strategy
Breaking Down Long Sentences Summarize the action of the paragraph-long sentence beginning "And now, the champion."

Literary Analysis
Single Effect and Gothic Style Which elements of gothic literature are evident in this passage about Madeline Usher?

❋ **ENRICHMENT: Career Connection**

Literary Critics

A literary critic reads, analyzes, evaluates, and comments on literature for both general and specialized audiences. He or she does so on-line, in magazines or newspapers, on radio or television, or in professional journals. Have students read some literary criticism about Edgar Allan Poe's "The Fall of the House of Usher" or "The Raven" to get a better grasp of a critic's objectives and style of writing. Tell students that literary critics usually support their opinions—whether positive or negative—about a literary work with citations from the text.

Invite students to brainstorm for a list of traits that a good literary critic should possess. Students who have an interest in this field might be encouraged to submit their own literary reviews to a school newspaper.

death agonies, bore him to the floor a corpse, and a victim to the terrors he had anticipated.

From that chamber, and from that mansion, I fled aghast. The storm was still abroad in all its wrath as I found myself crossing the old causeway. Suddenly there shot along the path a wild light, and I turned to see whence a gleam so unusual could have issued; for the vast house and its shadows were alone behind me. The radiance was that of the full, setting, and bloodred moon, which now shone vividly through that once barely discernible fissure, of which I have before spoken as extending from the roof of the building, in a zigzag direction, to the base. While I gazed, this fissure rapidly widened—there came a fierce breath of the whirlwind—the entire orb of the satellite burst at once upon my sight—my brain reeled as I saw the mighty walls rushing asunder—there was a long tumultuous shouting sound like the voice of a thousand waters—and the deep and dank tarn at my feet closed sullenly and silently over the fragments of the *"House of Usher."*

Review and Assess

Thinking About the Selection

1. **Respond:** In this story, the narrator barely escapes being drawn into Roderick's fantasy world. Were you drawn into the fantasy world of the story? Explain.

2. **(a) Recall:** Why has the narrator gone to visit Usher?
   (b) Assess: Does the narrator succeed in his purpose?
   (c) Analyze: What is the significance of the detail that the narrator finds himself becoming affected by Usher's condition?

3. **(a) Analyze:** In the description of the exterior of the house, which words suggest the presence of decay in the structure itself? **(b) Connect:** In what ways does this description foreshadow, or hint at, the ending of the story?

4. **(a) Interpret:** Which descriptive details of the interior of the house suggest that the narrator has entered a realm that is quite different from the ordinary world? **(b) Infer:** Which details in Usher's appearance suggest that he has been cut off from the outside world for many years? **(c) Connect:** In what ways is the appearance of the interior of the house related to Usher's appearance and to the condition of his mind?

5. **(a) Speculate:** Poe chose to characterize Roderick and Madeline as twins, not simply as brother and sister. Why do you think he made this choice? **(b) Support:** What evidence is there to support the claim of some critics who have argued that Madeline and Roderick are actually physical and mental components of the same being?

Review and Assess

1. Students may say that they *were* drawn into the fantasy world. The unbroken span of terror in this story may have made students imagine the frightening scene all too clearly.

2. **(a)** The narrator arrives to lessen the effects of the "malady" of Usher, his boyhood friend. **(b)** He is powerless to stop Usher's descent into madness and death. **(c)** It indicates that a person can become infected by another person's psychological maladies.

3. **(a)** Students might point to words such as *excessive antiquity, discoloration of ages, minute fungi overspread the whole exterior, crumbling condition of individual stones, barely perceptible fissure . . . extending from the roof . . . down the wall in a zigzag fashion.* **(b)** Especially the final detail hints that the house may be vulnerable to collapse.

4. **(a)** Students might cite details such as *dark and intricate passages; phantasmagoric armorial trophies; feeble beams of encrimsoned light;* and *an air of stern, deep, and irredeemable gloom.* **(b)** Possible responses include *overdone cordiality, cadaverousness of complexion, ghastly pallor of the skin, silken hair . . . suffered to grow all unheeded.* **(c)** Like Usher's physical appearance, the house is in a state of decay; like his mind, the house is gloomy and full of sorrow.

5. **(a)** Possible response: Making the Ushers twins increases the horror of Roderick's inability (or unwillingness) to save his sister; moreover it suggests a self-destructive or suicidal impulse in Roderick. **(b)** Suggested response: Roderick seems always to know what Madeline is experiencing; he does not attempt to rescue her because he knows they are both doomed; he mentions the extremely intuitive feelings that have always been between them.

39 About the Selection

39 About the Selection

On one level, "The Raven" tells of a man who grieves for his lost love, Lenore. A mysterious talking raven appears at the speaker's door, prompting him to question the bird about Lenore. The raven responds to each question—including the question of whether the speaker will ever see Lenore again—with the single word *Nevermore*, leaving the speaker broken and devoid of hope. On another level, the poem explores how grief and loneliness can turn to madness. Poe depicts a mind going to pieces—and watching itself in the process.

40 Critical Thinking

Infer

• Help students to infer from the clues in these five lines what kind of person the speaker is.

• As they discuss this issue and return to the text for evidence, encourage students to consider every part of both lines—not just the adjectives that describe the speaker directly.
Response: Students may say that the speaker is prone to melancholy and self-absorption or that he seems to be lonely.

41 Literary Analysis

Single Effect

• Tell students that poets use sound devices—such as alliteration, assonance, consonance, repetition, internal rhyme, and onomatopoeia—to give a musical quality to their writing. Sound devices please the ear and reinforce meaning by emphasizing key sounds, ideas, words, or images.

• Ask students the Literary Analysis question on p. 326: In what way does Poe's use of sound devices contribute to the creation of a single effect?
Answer: Poe's use of all of these devices creates a hypnotic effect that draws readers into the speaker's world. As a result, Poe persuades readers temporarily to abandon their notions of reality to accept the speaker's demented vision.

The Raven

Edgar Allan Poe

> **O**nce upon a midnight dreary, while I pondered, weak and weary,
> Over many a quaint and curious volume of forgotten lore—
> **40** While I nodded, nearly napping, suddenly there came a tapping,
> As of some one gently rapping, rapping at my chamber door.
> 5 "'Tis some visitor," I muttered, "tapping at my chamber door—
>   Only this, and nothing more."
>
> Ah, distinctly I remember it was in the bleak December;
> And each separate dying ember wrought its ghost upon the floor.
> **41** Eagerly I wished the morrow;—vainly I had sought to borrow
> 10 From my books surcease[1] of sorrow—sorrow for the lost Lenore—
> **42** For the rare and radiant maiden whom the angels name Lenore—
>   Nameless *here* for evermore.
>
> And the silken, sad, uncertain rustling of each purple curtain
> Thrilled me—filled me with fantastic terrors never felt before;
> 15 So that now, to still the beating of my heart, I stood repeating
> "'Tis some visitor entreating entrance at my chamber door—

---

1. **surcease** (sur sēs´) end.

326 ◆ *A Growing Nation (1800–1870)*

Literary Analysis
Single Effect In what ways does Poe's use of sound devices contribute to the creation of a single effect?

☀ ENRICHMENT: Cultural Connection

The Raven

Point out that when Edgar Allan Poe wrote this poem, he drew from a long tradition that viewed the raven as a bird of ill omen. Yet, in some cultures, the raven enjoys a more positive image. In the Bible, ravens feed the prophet Elijah in the desert; Christian art depicts ravens as symbols of God's providence. When Vikings were lost at sea, they would set free a raven and the bird would fly toward land, leading the Vikings to safety. The Vikings prized ravens highly and featured them on their flags.

Discuss with students the symbolic meanings, both positive and negative, of ravens and other birds in various cultures. You might speak of such birds as the albatross, bluebird, crow, nightingale, owl, and parrot. Individual students might be assigned to research the symbolism of one type of bird and to report their findings to the class.

Some late visitor entreating entrance at my chamber door;—
                  This it is and nothing more."

Presently my soul grew stronger; hesitating then no longer,
20 "Sir," said I, "or Madam, truly your forgiveness I implore;
But the fact is I was napping, and so gently you came rapping,
And so faintly you came tapping, tapping at my chamber door,
That I scarce was sure I heard you"—here I opened wide the door;—
                  Darkness there and nothing more.

25 Deep into that darkness peering, long I stood there wondering,
    fearing,
Doubting, dreaming dreams no mortal ever dared to dream before;
But the silence was unbroken, and the stillness gave no token,
And the only word there spoken was the whispered word, "Lenore?"
This I whispered, and an echo murmured back the word, "Lenore!"
30   Merely this and nothing more.

Back then into the chamber turning, all my soul within me
    burning,
Soon again I heard a tapping somewhat louder than before.
"Surely," said I, "surely that is something at my window lattice;
Let me see, then, what thereat is, and this mystery explore—
35 Let my heart be still a moment and this mystery explore;—
              'Tis the wind and nothing more!"

Open here I flung the shutter, when, with many a flirt and flutter,
In there stepped a stately Raven of the saintly days of yore;
Not the least <u>obeisance</u> made he; not a minute stopped or
    stayed he;
40 But, with mien of lord or lady,² perched above my chamber door—
Perched upon a bust of Pallas² just above my chamber door—
        Perched, and sat, and nothing more.

Then this ebony bird beguiling³ my sad fancy into smiling,
By the grave and stern decorum of the countenance⁴ it wore,
45 "Though thy crest be shorn and shaven, thou," I said, "art sure
    no <u>craven</u>,
Ghastly grim and ancient Raven wandering from the Nightly shore—
Tell me what thy lordly name is on the Night's Plutonian⁵ shore!"
        Quoth the Raven, "Nevermore."

---

2. **Pallas** (pal´ əs) Pallas Athena, the ancient Greek goddess of wisdom.
3. **beguiling** (bi gīl´ iŋ) *part.* charming.
4. **countenance** (koun´ tə nəns) *n.* facial expression.
5. **Plutonian** (ploō tō´ nē ən) *adj.* like the underworld or infernal regions; refers to Pluto, Greek and Roman god of the underworld.

Reading Strategy
Breaking Down Long Sentences Summarize the action of the stanza-long sentence beginning "Presently my soul grew stronger."

obeisance (ō bā´ səns) *n.* gesture of respect

craven (krā´ vən) *adj.* very cowardly

Reading Check

What is the speaker's first reaction to the Raven?

The Raven ◆ 327

42 Background

Poe's Maidens

In his poems and fictional prose works, Poe often depicts the death of a beautiful young woman. He considered this to be the greatest tragic theme, perhaps as a result of his wife's fragile health or his mother's early death.

43 Reading Strategy

Breaking Down Long Sentences

• Have students listen to the fourth stanza read aloud by a classmate, by you, or by a professional reader (on the **Listening to Literature** Audiotapes or CD).

• Direct students to respond to the Reading Strategy task on p. 327: Summarize the action of the stanza-long sentence beginning "Presently my soul grew stronger." Answer: The speaker feels bolder, stops hesitating, and speaks to his undiscovered visitor. Then he opens the door and sees nothing but darkness.

44 ✔Reading Check

Answer: The speaker smiles at its apparent "grave and stern decorum."

CUSTOMIZE INSTRUCTION FOR UNIVERSAL ACCESS

For Special Needs Students	For Advanced Readers
Encourage students to choose a stanza—or even a single line—and to identify in it examples of repeated sounds or letter sequences. In line 37, for instance, students might note the three words beginning with the letters *fl*, the two words containing the sequence of letters *u-t-t-e-r*, and the two words starting with *w*. Have students listen to the line (or stanza) spoken aloud more than once, and have them practice saying it themselves.	Have students identify examples of Poe's use of assonance, consonance, and alliteration. Students might point to the repetition of vowel sounds in the words *flung, shutter,* and *flutter* as an example of assonance; the repetition of consonant sounds in the words *shutter, flirt,* and *flutter* is an example of consonance; the repetitions of initial consonant sounds in the words *when* and *with* and *flirt* and *flutter* are examples of alliteration. These devices give the poem a driving rhythm and a musical flair.

Art

The Raven, 1845, by Edmund Dulac

This picture of a raven features bold lines that give the bird a frenzied or disheveled quality while at the same time symbolically evoking a troubled or discordant mind.

Use these questions for discussion:

1. What images from the poem does the artist evoke?
   Answer: Students may say that the raven sits on a bust; its open mouth suggests speech; its ruffled appearance fits the line about the "ungainly fowl"; the brightness behind it recalls "lamp-light o'er him streaming."

2. Why is the raven off-center?
   Answer: Students may say that the unbalanced scene suggests the speaker's unbalanced mind.

46 ▶ Critical Viewing

Answer: The lines going at many angles convey the feeling of chaos or frenzy. The shading lets the raven stand out from the vortex-like background at the same time that it is clearly part of it. The mood of the illustration—that of brooding or lurking evil—clearly matches that of the poem.

45 *The Raven*, Edmund Dulac

Much I marveled this ungainly fowl to hear discourse so plainly,
50 Though its answer little meaning—little relevancy bore;
For we cannot help agreeing that no living human being
Ever yet was blessed with seeing bird above his chamber door—
Bird or beast upon the sculptured bust above his chamber door,
             With such name as "Nevermore."

55 But the Raven, sitting lonely on the placid bust, spoke only
That one word, as if his soul in that one word he did outpour.
Nothing farther than he uttered—not a feather then he fluttered—
Till I scarcely more than muttered, "Other friends have flown before—
On the morrow *he* will leave me, as my Hopes have flown before."
60   Then the bird said, "Nevermore."

46 ▲ Critical Viewing
Explain the effect produced by the lines and shading of this drawing. Does the mood of the illustration match that of the poem? Explain. **[Assess]**

CUSTOMIZE INSTRUCTION FOR UNIVERSAL ACCESS

For Advanced Readers

Suggest that students read additional works by Edgar Allan Poe. Provide students with the titles listed in the Enrichment box on ATE p. 331. You may also wish to use **Authors In Depth**, The American Experience, which contains the following selections:

• Preface from *Lyrical Ballads*

• from "Chapter of Suggestions"

• "Alone"

• "Eldorado"

• "To Helen"

After students read these or other works by Poe, have them form discussion groups in which they compare and contrast the selections they have read. Suggest criteria for comparison, such as setting, theme, characters, and mood. To extend the activity, have volunteers present to the class brief oral reports on their favorite Poe selections.

Startled at the stillness broken by reply so aptly spoken,
"Doubtless," said I, "what it utters is its only stock and store
Caught from some unhappy master whom unmerciful Disaster
Followed fast and followed faster till his songs one burden bore—
65   Till the dirges of his Hope that melancholy burden bore
                    Of 'Never—nevermore.'"

But the Raven still beguiling my sad fancy into smiling,
Straight I wheeled a cushioned seat in front of bird, and bust
    and door;
Then, upon the velvet sinking, I betook myself to linking
70   Fancy unto fancy, thinking what this ominous[6] bird of yore—
What this grim, ungainly, ghastly, gaunt, and ominous bird of yore
                  Meant in croaking "Nevermore."

This I sat engaged in guessing, but no syllable expressing
To the fowl whose fiery eyes now burned into my bosom's core;
75   This and more I sat divining, with my head at ease reclining
On the cushion's velvet lining that the lamp-light gloated o'er,
But whose velvet-violet lining with the lamp-light gloating o'er,
                  She shall press, ah, nevermore!

Then, methought, the air grew denser, perfumed from an unseen
    censer
80   Swung by seraphim whose foot-falls tinkled on the tufted floor.
"Wretch," I cried, "thy God hath lent thee—by these angels he
    hath sent thee
Respite—respite and nepenthe[7] from thy memories of Lenore;
Quaff, oh quaff this kind nepenthe and forget this lost Lenore!"
                Quoth the Raven, "Nevermore."

85   "Prophet!" said I, "thing of evil!—prophet still, if bird or devil!—
Whether Tempter sent, or whether tempest tossed thee here
    ashore,
Desolate yet all undaunted, on this desert land enchanted—
On this home by Horror haunted—tell me truly, I implore—
Is there—*is* there balm in Gilead?[8]—tell me—tell me, I implore!"
90   Quoth the Raven, "Nevermore."

"Prophet!" said I, "thing of evil!—prophet still, if bird or devil!
By that Heaven that bends above us—by that God we both adore—
Tell this soul with sorrow laden if, within the distant Aidenn,[9]

---

6. **ominous** (äm´ ə nəs) *adj.* threatening; sinister.
7. **nepenthe** (ni pen´ thē) *n.* drug that the ancient Greeks believed could relieve sorrow.
8. **balm in Gilead** (gil´ ē əd) in the Bible, a healing ointment made in Gilead, a region of ancient Palestine.
9. **Aidenn** (ā´ den) Arabic for Eden or heaven.

Literary Analysis
Single Effect and Gothic Style Which aspects of the gothic style are evident in the speaker's relationship to the Raven?

49 ✔**Reading Check**
What does the speaker want the Raven to tell him?

The Raven ◆ 329

47 ❷ **Reading Strategy**
Breaking Down Long Sentences
- To aid in students' understanding, suggest that students break down long sentences into phrases that tell about the key ideas: who, what, and why. Using this visual device will help students focus on the ideas for restatement:

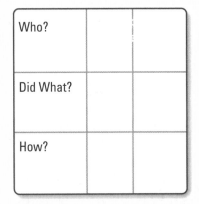

Who?		
Did What?		
How?		

- Explain that by separating out the nonessential information or details, students can more easily restate a passage in their own words.
- Have students use the organizer to break down lines 67–78 into phrases or segments of information. Then have students summarize the text in their own words.

48 ❷ **Literary Analysis**
Single Effect and Gothic Style
- Have students pair up and review stanzas 7–15 of the poem, noting how the speaker and the Raven interact and how the Raven affects the speaker's thoughts and emotions.
- Ask students the Literary Analysis question on p. 329: What aspects of the Gothic style are evident in the speaker's relationship to the Raven? **Answer:** Students may note the macabre effect of the Raven's repetition of the word *nevermore*, the psychological torment the speaker feels because of the Raven's implacability, and the otherworldly overtones in the creature's presence in the speaker's chamber.

49 ✔**Reading Check**
Answer: The speaker wants the Raven to say whether there is "balm in Gilead"—in other words, whether there is a prospect of relief from his grief.

Review and Assess

1. Students might suggest that many generations of readers have responded to the poem's sound effects and rhythm, as well as to its fantastic elements, especially the enigmatic and maddening utterances of the raven.

2. **(a)** He is reading to forget his sadness about the death of his lover. **(b)** The speaker is sad, tired, and abstracted.

3. **(a)** At first the speaker is amused by the creature. **(b)** The speaker marvels that the bird can speak; he tries to understand its meaning; he begins to believe that the bird is a messenger from heaven; then he thinks it is evil; finally he becomes angry and orders the bird to leave. **(c)** The speaker grows increasingly agitated by the Raven's use of this word—because of the unvarying quality of its response, as well as because the speaker's queries to the bird grow more and more important as the poem progresses.

4. **(a)** He orders the Raven to leave. **(b)** Students might say that the Raven has, in fact, never left the chamber—or that the creature so disturbed the speaker's mind that now he believes the Raven is still there, although actually it has departed.

5. **(a)** The effect of the Raven's visit, symbolized by its shadow, has been to permanently darken the speaker's soul. **(b)** It comes to represent the speaker's permanent state of madness and despair.

6. Most students will say that normally grief abates with time.

It shall clasp a sainted maiden whom the angels name Lenore—
95 Clasp a rare and radiant maiden whom the angels name Lenore."
Quoth the Raven, "Nevermore."

"Be that word our sign of parting, bird or fiend!" I shrieked, upstarting—
"Get thee back into the tempest and the Night's Plutonian shore!
Leave no black plume as a token of that lie thy soul hath spoken!
100 Leave my loneliness unbroken!—quit the bust above my door!
Take thy beak from out my heart, and take thy form from off my door!"

Quoth the Raven, "Nevermore."

And the Raven, never flitting, still is sitting, *still* is sitting
On the pallid bust of Pallas just above my chamber door;
105 And his eyes have all the seeming of a demon's that is dreaming;
And the lamp-light o'er him streaming throws his shadow on the floor;
And my soul from out that shadow that lies floating on the floor
Shall be lifted—nevermore!

Review and Assess

Thinking About the Selection

1. **Respond:** This poem has been popular for more than one hundred years. Explain why you think the poem does or does not merit this continued attention.

2. **(a) Recall:** Why is the speaker reading at the beginning of the poem? **(b) Assess:** What is his emotional state as the poem begins?

3. **(a) Recall:** With what emotion does the speaker first greet the Raven? **(b) Interpret:** During the course of the poem, how does the speaker's attitude toward the Raven change? **(c) Analyze Cause and Effect:** In what way is the word *nevermore* related to these emotional changes?

4. **(a) Recall:** What does the speaker eventually order the Raven to do? **(b) Analyze:** At the end of the poem, what does the speaker mean when he says the Raven "still is sitting" above the door?

5. **(a) Interpret:** What is the relationship between the raven's shadow and the speaker's soul at the end of the poem? **(b) Analyze:** What does the Raven finally come to represent?

6. **Apply:** Do you think grief can truly cause a person to permanently lose the ability to reason? Explain.

 ASSESSMENT PRACTICE: Reading Comprehension

| Make Inferences and Generalizations | (For more practice, see Test Practice Workbook, p. 17.) |

Many tests require students to make inferences—to fill in information not stated by the author—about written texts. Students can practice making inferences by completing the following exercise:

While he spoke, the lady Madeline . . . passed through a remote portion of the apartment, and without having noticed my presence, disappeared. I regarded her with an utter astonishment not unmingled with dread . . . .

In this passage, Madeline most resembles

A a movie star
B a ghost
C a dancer
D a servant

A and *D* are incorrect. Madeline silently enters, then "disappears," causing a feeling of dread in the speaker. *B* is correct.

Review and Assess

Literary Analysis

Single Effect

1. Describe the ways in which the following elements contribute to the **single effect** of a growing sense of terror in "The Fall of the House of Usher": (a) the description of the house, (b) Madeline's entombment, (c) the storm.

2. In "The Raven," how do both the tapping and the Raven's fiery eyes contribute to the speaker's deteriorating emotional state?

Comparing Literary Works

3. Use a chart like the one shown to compare the **gothic** elements in both the story and the poem. Is one of these works more typical of the gothic style than the other? Explain.

Gothic Element	House of Usher	Raven
Setting		
Violence		
Characterization		
The Supernatural		

4. Are the narrators of these works reliable or unreliable? Explain.

5. (a) When Madeline appears at the end of the story, is she there in actuality or is she a hallucination? Explain. (b) At the end of "The Raven," do you think the bird is actually still in the room? Why or why not?

Reading Strategy

Breaking Down Long Sentences

6. Break down this sentence from the story and restate it in your own words.

   At times, again, I was obliged to resolve all into the mere inexplicable vagaries of madness, for I beheld him gazing upon vacancy for long hours, in an attitude of the profoundest attention, as if listening to some imaginary sound.

Extend Understanding

7. **Psychology Connection:** Both this story and this poem suggest that the imagination is capable of producing false perceptions of reality. Do you agree with this suggestion? Why or why not?

The Fall of the House of Usher / The Raven ◆ 331

Quick Review

In writing constructed to achieve a **single effect,** every character, incident, and detail contributes to an overall impression.

The **gothic style** is characterized by remote settings, violent or macabre acts, tormented characters, and, often, the presence of supernatural elements.

To **break down a long sentence,** identify logical parts and analyze the relationship of these parts.

 Take It to the Net
www.phschool.com
Take the interactive self-test online to check your understanding of these selections.

Answers

Review and Assess

1. **(a)** The description of the house gives the story an ominous start and establishes a mood of gloom and bleakness. **(b)** Madeline's entombment provides a sense of the ultimate horror for Roderick (as well as for many readers)—the fear of being buried alive. **(c)** The storm reinforces the growing terror inside the house and eventually accompanies the story's climax.

2. The increasing volume of the tapping emphasizes an increasingly acute sensitivity to sensory stimuli. The detail of the Raven's "fiery eyes" shows that the speaker is now attributing unlikely expressions (in the form of otherworldly effects) to the bird's eyes.

3. Students should fill their charts with specific details and textual references. They may assert that the poem's occasional (albeit dark) humor makes it less typical of the Gothic style than the story.

4. Given that the speaker of the poem descends into madness, clearly he is unreliable. The narrator of the story *seems* largely reliable, though he admits being influenced by Roderick Usher's melancholy and mental illness.

5. **(a)** There is no way of knowing for certain. Students should support either conclusion with clear reasoning and textual citations. **(b)** Students should support either interpretation with reasons and with details taken from the text.

6. Possible response: "Sometimes I thought that everything was just the quirks of insanity, because I saw him looking at nothing for hours in rapt attention, as if listening to an imaginary sound."

7. Students should support their answers with clear explanations, reasons, and examples.

✳ **ENRICHMENT: Further Reading**

Other Works by Edgar Allan Poe

"The Black Cat"

"The Pit and the Pendulum"

"The Bells"

"The Cask of Amontillado"

 Take It to the Net
Visit www.phschool.com for more information on Edgar Allan Poe.

331

❶ Vocabulary Development

Word Analysis

1. vocal—"uttered or produced by the *voice*"

2. equivocate—"to *voice* vague terms to deceive or mislead"

3. vociferous—"using a loud or vehement *voice* in making one's feelings known"

4. vocation—"a call, or *voice*; a feeling of being summoned to enter a certain career"

Spelling Strategy

1. gracious

2. mention

3. suspicion

4. malicious

Concept Development

1. antonyms

2. synonyms

3. synonyms

4. synonyms

5. antonyms

6. synonyms

7. synonyms

8. antonyms

9. synonyms

❷ Grammar and Style

1. *Correct*

2. He gazed longingly at the clear, placid lake.

3. She marveled at the low, smooth, white walls of the tunnel.

4. The guests noticed her wild, theatrical manner.

5. The dry, hollow-sounding wood splintered and crashed.

Integrate Language Skills

❶ Vocabulary Development Lesson

Word Analysis: Latin Root *-voc-*

The word *equivocal* contains the Latin root *-voc-*, which derives from the Latin word *vox*, meaning "voice." *Equivocal* can be defined as "equal voices" or "having two or more interpretations."

Explain how the root *-voc-* influences the meaning of each of the following words.

1. vocal
2. equivocate
3. vociferous
4. vocation

Spelling Strategy

The sound of *sh* is sometimes spelled *ci*, as in *specious*, or *ti*, as in *sentience*. Complete each word with the correct spelling of the *sh* sound.

1. gra__ous
2. men__on
3. suspi__on
4. mali__ous

Concept Development: Synonyms or Antonyms?

Identify each of the following pairs of words as either synonyms (words with similar meanings) or antonyms (words with opposite meanings).

1. anomalous, normal
2. appellation, title
3. craven, weak
4. equivocal, ambiguous
5. importunate, yielding
6. munificent, charitable
7. obeisance, reverence
8. specious, sound
9. sentience, emotion

❷ Grammar and Style Lesson

Coordinate Adjectives

Coordinate adjectives are adjectives of equal rank that separately modify the noun they precede. They should always be separated by commas. To determine whether adjectives are coordinate, switch their order or add *and* between them. If the sentence still makes sense, the adjectives are coordinate.

> **Example:** During the whole of a *dull, dark,* and *soundless* day . . .
>
> **Example:** . . . about the whole mansion and domain there hung an atmosphere . . . a pestilent and mystic vapor, *dull, sluggish, faintly discernible*, and *leaden-hued*.

Practice In each item, identify which adjectives are coordinate. Then, insert commas where necessary. If a sentence needs no commas, write *Correct*.

1. I was his only personal friend.
2. He gazed longingly at the clear placid lake.
3. She marveled at the low smooth white walls of the tunnel.
4. The guests noticed her wild theatrical manner.
5. The dry hollow-sounding wood splintered and crashed.

Writing Application Write an obituary of Roderick Usher. Include at least two sentences that contain coordinate adjectives.

W̸G Prentice Hall Writing and Grammar Connection: Chapter 27, Section 2

TEACHING RESOURCES

The following resources can be used to enrich or extend the instruction for pp. 332–333.

Vocabulary

📖 **Selection Support Workbook:** Build Vocabulary, p. 77

📖 **Vocabulary and Spelling Practice Book** (Use this booklet for skills enrichment.)

Grammar and Style

📖 **Selection Support Workbook:** Grammar and Style, p. 78 ▪

W̸G **Writing and Grammar,** Ruby Level, p. 304

▪ **Daily Language Practice Transparencies**

Grammar

W̸G **Writing and Grammar,** Ruby Level, p. 16 ▪

🔘 **Writing and Grammar iText CD-ROM**

▪ **Writing Models and Graphic Organizers on Transparencies,** pp. 37–40

 BLOCK SCHEDULING: Resources marked with this symbol provide varied instruction during 90-minute blocks.

❸ Writing Lesson

Literary Criticism

Since its publication in 1839, "The Fall of the House of Usher" has prompted many critical views. Some say it is the narrator who is insane, not Usher. Others say that each character represents a separate aspect of human psychology—the conscious mind, the unconscious mind, and the soul. Write an essay in which you defend or refute one of these critical views.

Prewriting   Reread the story, noting passages and details that support your critical interpretation.

Drafting   In your introduction, note the critical viewpoint you will address, and state whether or not you agree with it. Elaborate upon your reasoning in each body paragraph, using details from the text.

> #### Model: Refuting an Argument
>
> The idea that the narrator of Poe's famous story is himself insane is compelling. After all, that would explain the story's strangeness: It is all in the narrator's mind. Unfortunately, that view is unconvincing.

> The writer shows an understanding of the opinion being critiqued. The essay to follow will support the analysis.

Revising   Review your draft, making sure you have supported your ideas with details from the text. Note places where you might address readers who hold opposing viewpoints.

WG Prentice Hall Writing and Grammar Connection: Chapter 14, Section 2

❹ Extension Activities

Listening and Speaking Present a **dramatic reading** of "The Raven" that captures the poem's tension and brings to life its unique rhymes and rhythms. Use the following technique to prepare:

- Record yourself on audio- or videotape, and review your presentation for possible lack of clarity or dramatic effect.
- Use body language to help convey the poems meaning.

As you perform, speak clearly, and allow your voice to reflect the poem's rising emotion.

Research and Technology In a group, watch a film by director Alfred Hitchcock. Then, lead a **discussion** in which you analyze the techniques Hitchcock uses to produce suspense and fear, and compare Hitchcock's techniques with Poe's. With classmates, discuss whether print or film is a better medium for horror. [**Group Activity**]

 Take It to the Net   www.phschool.com

Go online for an additional research activity using the Internet.

The Fall of the House of Usher / The Raven ◆ 333

---

❸ Writing Lesson

- Students' critical essays should present one of the noted critical views of "The Fall of the House of Usher" and then defend or refute this view clearly, logically, and thoroughly. If students choose to refute a view, their essay should indicate a more convincing interpretation.

- Encourage students to use an outline to organize the main ideas of their critical essay. Details culled from the text can be indicated briefly on these outlines.

- Use the Writing Lesson, as well as Writing Process Model 7, pp. 37–40 in **Writing Models and Graphic Organizers on Transparencies,** to guide students in developing their critical essays.

- Use the rubric for Response to Literature in **Performance Assessment** and **Portfolio Management**, p. 23 to evaluate students' essays.

❹ Listening and Speaking

- You might have students photocopy the text so that they have wide margins in which to write notes and instructions to themselves.

- Encourage students to identify the exposition, the rising action, the climax, and the resolution. Explain that knowing how Poe structured his poem will help them make decisions about how to interpret the poem orally.

CUSTOMIZE INSTRUCTION
For Universal Access

To address different learning styles, use the following activities suggested in the **Extension Activities** booklet, p. 17.

For Intrapersonal and Spatial/Visual Learners, use Activity 5.

For Musical/Rhythmic Learners, use Activity 6.

For Verbal/Linguistic Learners, use Activity 7.

ASSESSMENT RESOURCES

The following resources can be used to assess students' knowledge and skills.

Selection Assessment
- 📖 **Formal Assessment**, pp. 85–87
- 📖 **Open Book Test**, pp. 49–51
- 📼 **Got It! Assessment Videotapes**, Tape 2
- 💿 **Test Bank Software**
- **Take It to the Net**
  Visit www.phschool.com for self-tests and additional questions on the selections.

Writing Rubric
- 📖 **Performance Assessment and Portfolio Mgmt.,** p. 23

PRENTICE HALL
ⒶSSESSMENT *SYSTEM*
- 📖 **Workbook**
- 📖 **Skill Book**
- 📄 **Transparencies**
- 💿 **CD-ROM**

333

The Minister's Black Veil

Lesson Objectives

1. **To analyze and respond to literary elements**
   - Literary Analysis: Parable
   - Connecting Literary Elements: Symbol

2. **To read, comprehend, analyze, and critique a short story**
   - Reading Strategy: Drawing Inferences About Meaning
   - Reading Check questions
   - Review and Assess questions
   - Assessment Practice (ATE)

3. **To develop word analysis skills, fluency, and systematic vocabulary**
   - Vocabulary Development Lesson: Latin Word Root: *equi-*

4. **To understand and apply written and oral language conventions**
   - Spelling Strategy
   - Grammar and Style Lesson: Varying Sentence Openers

5. **To understand and apply appropriate writing and research strategies**
   - Writing Lesson: Response to a Short Story
   - Extension Activity: Oral Presentation

6. **To understand and apply listening and speaking strategies**
   - Extension Activity: Monologue

STEP-BY-STEP TEACHING GUIDE	PACING GUIDE
PRETEACH	
Motivate Students and Provide Background	
Use the Motivation activity (ATE p. 334)	5 min.
Read and discuss the author and background information (SE pp. 334, 336/ATE p. 336)	5 min.
Introduce the Concepts	
Introduce the Literary Analysis and Reading Strategy (SE/ATE p. 335) Ⓐ	15 min.
Pronounce the vocabulary words and read their definitions (SE p. 335)	10 min.
TEACH	
Monitor Comprehension	
Informally monitor comprehension by circulating while students read independently or in groups Ⓐ	50 min.
Monitor students' comprehension with the Reading Check notes (SE/ATE pp. 337, 339, 341, 343, 345, 347	as students read
Develop vocabulary with Vocabulary notes (SE pp. 338, 339; 340, 341, 342, 343 ATE p. 339)	as students read
Develop Understanding	
Develop students' understanding of parables with the Literary Analysis annotations (SE pp. 338, 342, 344, 345, 346, 347; ATE pp. 338, 342, 344, 345, 346, 347) Ⓐ	10 min.
Develop students' ability to draw inferences about meaning with the Reading Strategy annotations (SE pp. 339, 341, 343, 345; ATE pp. 339, 341, 343, 345)	10 min.
ASSESS	
Assess Mastery	
Assess students' mastery of the Reading Strategy and Literary Analysis by having them answer the Review and Assess questions (SE/ATE p. 349)	20 min.
Use one or more of the print and media Assessment Resources (ATE p. 351) Ⓐ	up to 50 min.
EXTEND	
Apply Understanding	
Have students complete the Vocabulary Development Lesson and the Grammar and Style Lesson (SE p. 350) Ⓐ	20 min.
Apply students' ability to use exact quotations by using the Writing Lesson (SE/ATE p. 351) Ⓐ	45 min.
Apply students' understanding using one or more of the Extension Activities (SE p. 351)	20–90 min.

Ⓐ **ACCELERATED INSTRUCTION:** Use the strategies and activities identified with an Ⓐ.

UNIVERSAL ACCESS
- ● = Below Level Students
- ▲ = On-Level Students
- ■ = Above Level Students

Time and Resource Manager

Reading Level: Challenging
Average Number of Instructional Days: 5

RESOURCES

PRINT 📖	TRANSPARENCIES	TECHNOLOGY 💿 🎧 📼
• **Beyond Literature,** Cross-Curricular Connection: Art, p. 18 ▲ ■		• **Interest Grabber Video,** Tape 3 ● ▲ ■
• **Selection Support Workbook:** ● ▲ ■ Literary Analysis, p. 84 Reading Strategy, p. 83 Build Vocabulary, p. 81	• **Literary Analysis and Reading Transparencies,** pp. 35 and 36 ● ▲ ■	
		• **Listening to Literature** ● ▲ ■ Audiocassettes, Side 11 Audio CDs, CD 7
• **Literatura en español** ● ▲ • **Literary Analysis for Enrichment** ■		
• **Formal Assessment:** Selection Test, pp. 88–90 ● ▲ ■ • **Open Book Test,** pp. 52–54 ● ▲ ■ • **Performance Assessment and Portfolio Management,** p. 17 ● ▲ ■ • PRENTICE HALL **ASSESSMENT** *SYSTEM* ● ▲ ■	• PRENTICE HALL **ASSESSMENT** *SYSTEM* ● ▲ ■ Skills Practice Answers and Explanations on Transparencies	• **Test Bank Software** ● ▲ ■ • **Got It! Assessment Videotapes,** Tape 2 ● ▲
• **Selection Support Workbook:** ● ▲ ■ Grammar and Style Skills, p. 82 • **Writing and Grammar,** Ruby Level ● ▲ ■ • **Extension Activities,** p. 18 ● ▲ ■	• **Daily Language Practice Transparencies** ● ▲ • **Writing Models and Graphic Organizers on Transparencies,** pp. 37–40 ● ▲ ■	• **Writing and Grammar iText CD-ROM** ● ▲ ■ 💻 *Take It to the Net* www.phschool.com

BLOCK SCHEDULING: Use one 90-minute class period to preteach the selection and have students read it. Use a second 90-minute class period to assess students' mastery of skills and have them complete one of the Extension Activities.

Step-by-Step Teaching Guide
for pp. 334–335

Motivation

Write the following quotation on the chalkboard:

"But what has good Parson Hooper got upon his face?" cried the sexton in astonishment.

When Parson Hooper appears one day wearing a black veil, it causes quite a stir among his congregation. Invite students to imagine that someone they know appears unexpectedly wearing a mask. Ask them to predict how they would react. What might they wish to ask or say to this person?

▭ Interest Grabber Video

As an alternative, play "Literary Symbolism" on Tape 3 to engage student interest.

❶ Background

More About the Author

Nathaniel Hawthorne was a master of symbolism and allegory. He wrote throughout his life, nearly always with the same result—critical acclaim coupled with monetary failure. The literary critic Edward H. Davidson has written: "That a century after he lived he should be included in a collection of major writers of America would have baffled Hawthorne . . . Hawthorne himself had been so consistently ignored, that to be a subject for literary study . . . and to be termed a 'classic' among American writers, would have seemed nothing short of grotesque . . . Indeed, his literary reputation has maintained its high place more steadily than that of any other major American writer."

Prepare to Read

❶ The Minister's Black Veil

Nathaniel Hawthorne (1804–1864)

Along with Herman Melville, Nathaniel Hawthorne is sometimes referred to as an Anti-Transcendentalist. Although he lived at a time when many intellectuals glorified the power of the human spirit, as it was described by Transcendentalists like Ralph Waldo Emerson, Hawthorne found it impossible to adopt such an optimistic worldview. Despite his admiration for Emerson, Hawthorne believed that evil was a dominant force in the world, and his fiction expresses a gloomy vision of human affairs.

Inherited Guilt Born in Salem, Massachusetts, Hawthorne was descended from a prominent Puritan family. One of Hawthorne's ancestors was a Puritan judge who played a key role in the Salem witchcraft trials. Another ancestor was a judge known for his persecution of Quakers. Both Hawthorne's character and his focus as a writer were shaped by a sense of inherited guilt. He was haunted by the intolerance and cruelty of these ancestors, even though he himself was not a Puritan and was born 112 years after the Salem witchcraft trials.

The Long Seclusion After graduation from Maine's Bowdoin College in 1825, Hawthorne secluded himself at his mother's house in Salem and wrote a novel, *Fanshawe*. Soon after the book's anonymous publication in 1828, the young author was seized by shame and abruptly burned most available copies of it. During the nine years that followed, Hawthorne single-mindedly honed his writing skills, working in a room he called "the dismal chamber" on the third floor of his mother's house. These labors resulted in a collection of stories entitled *Twice-Told Tales*, which was published in 1837. Although the book sold poorly, it established Hawthorne as a respected writer and gave him sufficient resources and encouragement to continue his writing.

Moving in Transcendentalist Society After moving out of his mother's house, Hawthorne lived briefly at Brook Farm, the utopian community designed by the Transcendentalists. Then, in 1842, he married Sophia Peabody and moved to the Old Manse at Concord, Massachusetts, where Emerson had once lived. During his years in Concord, Hawthorne spent time with both Emerson and Henry David Thoreau, but their vastly different spiritual philosophies remained an obstacle to deeper friendship. While in Concord, Hawthorne published a second collection of stories, *Mosses From an Old Manse* (1846), and celebrated the birth of his first daughter, Una.

Man of Letters When he was appointed surveyor at the Salem customhouse, Hawthorne moved with his family back to his birthplace. In 1850, after a change in administration forced him out of office, he published his masterpiece, *The Scarlet Letter*, a powerful novel about sin and guilt among early Puritans. The book was extremely successful, earning its author international fame. He soon wrote two more novels, *The House of the Seven Gables* (1851) and *The Blithedale Romance* (1852).

When his college friend Franklin Pierce became president, Hawthorne was named the American consul at Liverpool, England. He spent several years in England and traveled through Italy before returning to Massachusetts. He used his Italian experiences in the novel *The Marble Faun* (1860). Hawthorne died in his sleep four years later, while on a carriage tour in New Hampshire. He left four unfinished novels among his belongings.

TEACHING RESOURCES

The following resources can be used to enrich or extend the instruction for pp. 334–335

Motivation
▭ Interest Grabber Video, Tape 3 ▭

Background
▭ Beyond Literature, p. 18

 Take It to the Net
Visit www.phschool.com for Background and hotlinks for "The Minister's Black Veil."

Literary Analysis
▭ Literary Analysis and Reading Transparencies, Parable, p. 36 ▭

Reading
▭ Literary Analysis and Reading Transparencies, Drawing Inferences About Meaning, p. 35 ▭

▭ Selection Support Workbook: Reading Strategy, p. 83

 BLOCK SCHEDULING: Resources marked with this symbol provide varied instruction during 90-minute blocks.

Preview

Connecting to the Literature

A secret, when kept too long, can take on mysterious significance. If unrevealed, it can cause people to fill in the missing story and draw their own untrue conclusions. In "The Minister's Black Veil," a Puritan parson keeps a secret from an entire village for his whole life.

❷ Literary Analysis

Parable

A **parable** is a simple, usually brief, story that teaches a moral lesson. Unlike a fable, which features animal characters, a parable is populated by human beings. In subtitling this story "A Parable," Hawthorne indicates that the moral message it conveys is important. As you read, think about the lesson Hawthorne wants his story to communicate.

Connecting Literary Elements

The veil that Mr. Hooper vows never to remove is a **symbol**—something that has meaning in itself while also standing for something greater. To understand the message expressed in Hawthorne's parable, you must analyze the veil's symbolic meaning, which is revealed through the responses of the parishioners and in the minister's own deathbed explanation:

"I look around me, and, lo! on every visage a Black Veil!"

To discover the veil's symbolic meaning, notice Hawthorne's descriptions of the veil and its effects on the characters in the story.

❸ Reading Strategy

Drawing Inferences About Meaning

When the message of a work of fiction is conveyed indirectly, as it is in this symbolic story, the reader must **draw inferences,** or conclusions, by looking closely at details, especially description and dialogue. Use a chart like the one shown to draw inferences about the story's characters and events.

Description/ Dialogue
"He has changed himself into something awful, only by hiding his face."

↓

Inference
Villagers are frightened by the veil.

Vocabulary Development

venerable (ven´ ər ə bəl) *adj.* commanding respect (p. 338)

iniquity (i nik´ wi tē) *n.* sin (p. 339)

indecorous (in dek´ ə rəs) *adj.* improper (p. 339)

ostentatious (äs´ tən tā´ shəs) *adj.* intended to attract notice (p. 339)

sagacious (sə gā´ shəs) *adj.* shrewd (p. 339)

vagary (və ger´ ē) *n.* unpredictable occurrence (p. 340)

tremulous (trem´ yoo ləs) *adj.* characterized by trembling (p. 341)

waggery (wag´ ər ē) *n.* mischievous humor (p. 341)

impertinent (im purt´ ən ənt) *adj.* not showing proper respect (p. 342)

obstinacy (äb´ stə nə sē) *n.* stubbornness (p. 343)

The Minister's Black Veil ◆ 335

CUSTOMIZE INSTRUCTION FOR UNIVERSAL ACCESS

For Less Proficient Readers	For English Learners	For Advanced Readers
Discuss the use of masks as a literary device. Tell students that in this story, a minister refuses to explain the mask he wears. Encourage students to use their prior experiences (for instance, at Halloween) to recall how it feels to wear a mask and to see other masked people.	Help these students by breaking down or rephrasing long, sentences and by summarizing difficult passages. You might paraphrase the description of the veil on page 338 as follows: *He wore a thin black cloth on his face. Although he could see through it, it covered his forehead, eyes, and nose.*	Point out how the veil functions in two ways: it conceals Hooper's face and eyes from others' view, and it alters (shades) everything that Hooper sees. Then, ask students whether Hawthorne believes Hooper's actions are essentially true and worthy of imitation or merely reflective of an unhealthy society.

❷ Literary Analysis

Parable

- Tell students that they will focus on the parable as they read Hawthorne's short story.

- Read the instruction about parables together as a class. Lead students in a discussion of other stories they have read that carry a moral lesson. What topics are writers likely to touch on as they convey moral messages to readers?

- Help students understand that because its purpose is moral instruction, a parable often contains some characters and events that are more symbolic than realistic.

- As they read, invite students to relate to the views and feelings of Parson Hooper (as well as of other Milford residents), using their own prior knowledge about clashes between private belief and public reputation.

❸ Reading Strategy

Drawing Inferences About Meaning

- Remind students that drawing inferences is a way of interpreting a character's behavior, statements, or an author's message. You might wish to point out that Hawthorne delights in presenting people and situations that are cloaked in ambiguity. Thus it is imperative that readers draw inferences about his meaning.

- Explain the importance of focusing special attention on characters' words and on descriptions of characters' actions as students attempt to draw inferences about the story. Often a reader can find meaning in the disparity between characters' words and their actions.

Vocabulary Development

- Pronounce each vocabulary word for students, and read the definitions as a class. Have students identify any words with which they are already familiar.

 E-Teach

Visit E-Teach at www.phschool.com for teachers' essays on how to teach, with questions and answers.

CUSTOMIZE INSTRUCTION
for Visual/Spatial Learners

Invite students to create a picture that evokes the eerie atmosphere of this story. Have the students draw or paint a scene such as a chance meeting between the minister and a parishioner on a village street. Remind students to decide what emotion the person will feel when confronted by the veiled minister: Will he or she betray feelings of fear, surprise, curiosity, or terror?

❶ About the Selection

In this parable, Mr. Hooper, a highly respected minister in a small Puritan community, suddenly appears wearing a black veil, a mask he vows never to remove. The veil has a powerful, gloomy effect on his parishioners; they are stunned and unable to ask him directly why he is wearing it. Even Hooper's fiancée turns from him because of the veil. The veil's symbolic meaning—a reminder of the secret sins each soul carries to the grave—is revealed through the speech and actions of Hooper and his parishioners, as well as in his deathbed explanation.

❶ The MINISTER'S BLACK VEIL
A PARABLE

Nathaniel Hawthorne

Background

Set in the 1600s, in a typical village of Puritan New England, this story reflects Hawthorne's deep awareness of his Puritan ancestry. The Puritans lived stern lives, emphasizing hard work and religious devotion. They believed that only certain people were predestined by God to go to heaven. This belief led Puritans to search their souls continually for signs that God had chosen them. At the same time, those who behaved unusually were often thought to be controlled by evil forces. This attitude contributed to the Salem witchcraft trials of 1692, during which at least twenty accused witches were executed. In this story, Hawthorne explores how such attitudes probably led to other, more commonplace acts of cruelty.

The sexton[1] stood in the porch of Milford meetinghouse, pulling busily at the bell rope. The old people of the village came stooping along the street. Children, with bright faces, tripped merrily beside their parents, or mimicked a graver gait, in the conscious dignity of their Sunday clothes. Spruce bachelors looked sidelong at the pretty maidens, and fancied that the Sabbath sunshine made them prettier than on weekdays. When the throng had mostly streamed into the porch, the sexton began to toll the bell, keeping his eye on the

1. **sexton** (seks´ tən) *n.* person in charge of the maintenance of a church.

TEACHING RESOURCES

The following resources can be used to enrich or extend the instruction for pp. 336–348

Literary Analysis

📖 **Selection Support Workbook:** Literary Analysis, p. 84

📄 **Writing Models and Graphic Organizers on Transparencies,** pp. 37–40

Reading Strategy

📖 **Selection Support Workbook:** Build Vocabulary, p. 81

🎧 **Listening to Literature Audiocassettes,** Side 11 ▪

💿 **Listening to Literature CDs,** CD 7 ▪

▪ **BLOCK SCHEDULING:** Resources marked with this symbol provide varied instruction during 90-minute blocks.

Reverend Mr. Hooper's door. The first glimpse of the clergyman's figure was the signal for the bell to cease its summons.

"But what has good Parson Hooper got upon his face?" cried the sexton in astonishment.

All within hearing immediately turned about, and beheld the semblance of Mr. Hooper, pacing slowly his meditative way towards the meetinghouse. With one accord they started, expressing more wonder than if some strange minister were coming to dust the cushions of Mr. Hooper's pulpit.

"Are you sure it is our parson?" inquired Goodman[2] Gray of the sexton.

"Of a certainty it is good Mr. Hooper," replied the sexton. "He was to have exchanged pulpits with Parson Shute, of Westbury; but Parson Shute sent to excuse himself yesterday, being to preach a funeral sermon."

---

2. **Goodman** title of respect similar to "Mister."

2 ✓ **Reading Check**

As the story begins, what weekly event is about to take place?

3 ▼ **Critical Viewing**

Identify the elements or details of this painting that correspond to those in Hawthorne's story. **[Connect]**

Winter Sunday in Norway, Maine, Unidentified artist, New York State Historical Association, Cooperstown

The Minister's Black Veil ◆ 337

4

2 ✓ **Reading Check**

Answer: Reverend Hooper's regular Sunday church service is about to begin at Milford meetinghouse.

3 ▶ **Critical Viewing**

Answer: Students can point to the painting's cold, gray, and gloomy setting, as well as to the stiff, proper appearance of the people.

4 **Background**

Art

Winter Sunday in Norway, Maine, artist unidentified

This painting is by an anonymous folk artist. Folk artists provide a link between the past and the present by reflecting social history. Folk art paintings offer intimate views of events through the eyes of ordinary people. Thus, images in folk art tend to be simple, homey, deeply felt, and untutored. Folk art incorporates common scenes and materials, native designs, and artisanship. Use these questions for discussion:

1. How would you describe the mood of this scene?
   Answer: Students may say that it is a dreary, somber winter day in a small town where the church plays a prominent role. Students may notice that the insides of the church and houses are as colorless as the bleak landscape.

2. What seems to be missing from this scene?
   Answer: Students may notice that no smoke comes from the chimneys and that there appears to be a lack of warmth inside and out.

CUSTOMIZE INSTRUCTION FOR UNIVERSAL ACCESS

For Special Needs Students	For English Learners	For Advanced Readers
Students will benefit from hearing dialogue read aloud; in many cases it will help them to hear a passage read aloud more than once. Point out how Hawthorne uses dialogue skillfully for dramatic effect. For example, the veil is first mentioned and the minister's identity first questioned in the story's initial line of dialogue.	Encourage students to create a graphic organizer to track characters and dialogue. Have them record the name of each character as it is mentioned in the text, together with notes about their actions and dialogue. Students should also note new vocabulary and definitions that appear in the story.	To help students make inferences about the story, encourage them to speculate about the thoughts of Milford residents as they read. Have students use a two-column graphic organizer. Have students note characters' spoken words in one column and jot down speculations about their inner thoughts in the other.

Parable

- Slowly read aloud the first paragraph on this page. Encourage students to listen for descriptive details about Mr. Hooper, the veil, and the reactions of townspeople.

- Ask students the Literary Analysis question on p. 338: What does this first detailed description of the veil indicate about its effect on the community?
  Answer: The description makes the veil seem strange and significant.

6 Literary Analysis

Parable and Symbol

- Remind students that when an object takes on significance outside itself and stands for something greater, it is being used as a symbol.

- Ask one or more student volunteers to read aloud carefully the passage beginning "That mysterious emblem." Urge students to take note of how Hawthorne has chosen to describe the effect of the veil.

- Ask students the second Literary Analysis question on p. 338: The passage beginning "That mysterious emblem" is the first suggestion that the veil is a symbol. What might the veil symbolize?
  Answer: Hawthorne's descriptions delineate how the veil creates an "unnatural" separation between Hooper and the subject of his current attention (speaking the psalm, reading the page of the Bible, looking up to God). Thus the veil may symbolize something that has come between the minister and ordinary life.

---

5 The cause of so much amazement may appear sufficiently slight. Mr. Hooper, a gentlemanly person, of about thirty, though still a bachelor, was dressed with due clerical neatness, as if a careful wife had starched his band, and brushed the weekly dust from his Sunday's garb. There was but one thing remarkable in his appearance. Swathed about his forehead, and hanging down over his face, so low as to be shaken by his breath, Mr. Hooper had on a black veil. On a nearer view it seemed to consist of two folds of crape,[3] which entirely concealed his features, except the mouth and chin, but probably did not intercept his sight, further than to give a darkened aspect to all living and inanimate things. With this gloomy shade before him, good Mr. Hooper walked onward, at a slow and quiet pace, stooping somewhat, and looking on the ground, as is customary with abstracted men, yet nodding kindly to those of his parishioners who still waited on the meetinghouse steps. But so wonderstruck were they that his greeting hardly met with a return.

"I can't really feel as if good Mr. Hooper's face was behind that piece of crape," said the sexton.

"I don't like it," muttered an old woman, as she hobbled into the meetinghouse. "He has changed himself into something awful, only by hiding his face."

"Our parson has gone mad!" cried Goodman Gray, following him across the threshold.

A rumor of some unaccountable phenomenon had preceded Mr. Hooper into the meetinghouse, and set all the congregation astir. Few could refrain from twisting their heads towards the door; many stood upright, and turned directly about; while several little boys clambered upon the seats, and came down again with a terrible racket. There was a general bustle, a rustling of the women's gowns and shuffling of the men's feet, greatly at variance with that hushed repose which should attend the entrance of the minister. But Mr. Hooper appeared not to notice the perturbation of his people. He entered with an almost noiseless step, bent his head mildly to the pews on each side, and bowed as he passed his oldest parishioner, a white-haired great-grandsire, who occupied an armchair in the center of the aisle. It was strange to observe how slowly this <u>venerable</u> man became conscious of something singular in the appearance of his pastor. He seemed not fully to partake of the prevailing wonder, till Mr. Hooper had ascended the stairs, and showed himself in the pulpit, face to face with his congregation, except for the black veil. That mysterious emblem was never once withdrawn.
6 It shook with his measured breath, as he gave out the psalm; it threw its obscurity between him and the holy page, as he read the Scriptures; and while he prayed, the veil lay heavily on his uplifted countenance. Did he seek to hide it from the dread Being whom he was addressing?

Such was the effect of this simple piece of crape, that more than one woman of delicate nerves was forced to leave the meetinghouse.

---

3. **crape** (krāp) *n.* piece of black cloth worn as a sign of mourning.

Literary Analysis
Parable What does this first detailed description of the veil indicate about its effect on the community?

venerable (ven′ ər ə bəl) *adj.* commanding respect

Literary Analysis
Parable and Symbol The passage beginning "That mysterious emblem" is the first suggestion that the veil is a symbol. What might the veil symbolize?

 ENRICHMENT: Cultural Connection

Veils

A veil can be defined as "a piece of light fabric, as of net or gauze, worn especially by women over the face or head or draped from a hat to conceal, protect, or enhance the face." Traditionally veils have been worn for a variety of reasons in different cultures. Often they are worn at weddings, funerals, and other religious ceremonies. People may wear veils to express modesty or mourning.

Have students do research to find out more about why, when, how, and by whom veils are worn in different cultures. When students complete their research, they may share their findings with their classmates during a class discussion.

Yet perhaps the palefaced congregation was almost as fearful a sight to the minister, as his black veil to them.

Mr. Hooper had the reputation of a good preacher, but not an energetic one: he strove to win his people heavenward by mild, persuasive influences, rather than to drive them thither by the thunders of the Word. The sermon which he now delivered was marked by the same characteristics of style and manner as the general series of his pulpit oratory. But there was something, either in the sentiment of the discourse itself, or in the imagination of the auditors, which made it greatly the most powerful effort that they had ever heard from their pastor's lips. It was tinged, rather more darkly than usual, with the gentle gloom of Mr. Hooper's temperament. The subject had reference to secret sin, and those sad mysteries which we hide from our nearest and dearest, and would fain conceal from our own consciousness, even forgetting that the Omniscient[4] can detect them. A subtle power was breathed into his words. Each member of the congregation, the most innocent girl, and the man of hardened breast, felt as if the preacher had crept upon them, behind his awful veil, and discovered their hoarded <u>iniquity</u> of deed or thought. Many spread their clasped hands on their bosoms. There was nothing terrible in what Mr. Hooper said, at least, no violence; and yet, with every tremor of his melancholy voice, the hearers quaked. An unsought pathos came hand in hand with awe. So sensible were the audience of some unwonted attribute in their minister, that they longed for a breath of wind to blow aside the veil, almost believing that a stranger's visage would be discovered, though the form, gesture, and voice were those of Mr. Hooper.

At the close of the services, the people hurried out with <u>indecorous</u> confusion, eager to communicate their pent-up amazement, and conscious of lighter spirits the moment they lost sight of the black veil. Some gathered in little circles, huddled closely together, with their mouths all whispering in the center; some went homeward alone, wrapt in silent meditation; some talked loudly, and profaned the Sabbath day with <u>ostentatious</u> laughter. A few shook their <u>sagacious</u> heads, intimating that they could penetrate the mystery; while one or two affirmed that there was no mystery at all, but only that Mr. Hooper's eyes were so weakened by the midnight lamp, as to require a shade. After a brief interval, forth came good Mr. Hooper also, in the rear of his flock. Turning his veiled face from one group to another, he paid due reverence to the hoary heads, saluted the middle-aged with kind dignity as their friend and spiritual guide, greeted the young with mingled authority and love, and laid his hands on the little children's heads to bless them. Such was always his custom on the Sabbath day. Strange and bewildered looks repaid him for his courtesy. None, as on former occasions, aspired to the honor of walking by their pastor's side. Old Squire Saunders, doubtless by an

---

4. **Omniscient** (äm ni′ shənt) all-knowing God.

The Minister's Black Veil ◆ 339

Reading Strategy
Drawing Inferences About Meaning Has Mr. Hooper truly changed? What inferences can you draw based on this description of his sermon?

iniquity (i nik′ wi tē) *n.* sin

indecorous (in dek′ ə rəs) *adj.* improper

ostentatious (äs′ tən tā′ shəs) *adj.* intended to attract notice

sagacious (sə gā′ shəs) *adj.* shrewd

✓ Reading Check
What change has occurred in Mr. Hooper's appearance?

❼ Reading Strategy
Drawing Inferences About Meaning

- Ask a students to summarize how readers can determine meanings in a work of fiction when the author's message is conveyed indirectly.
  Answer: The reader must draw inferences after examining textual details, particularly the writer's use of description and dialogue.
- Invite students to listen closely to an oral reading of the first paragraph on p. 339.
- Then, ask them the Reading Strategy questions on p. 339: Has Mr. Hooper truly changed? What inferences can you draw based on this description of his sermon?
  Possible answer: Some students may feel that Mr. Hooper has changed, and point to the choice of sermon and the reaction of parishioners. Others may feel that the sight of the veil is causing the villagers' response.

❽ Vocabulary Development
Latin Root -*equi*-

- Point out the word *iniquity* in the bracketed sentence. Explain that this word means "sin."
- Tell students that the Latin word root -*equi*- means "equal." Have students use a dictionary to find out how the meaning of this root word comes to bear on the word *iniquity*.
  Answer: *Iniquity* means "uneven" or "unjust" and has come to be defined as "wickedness" or "sin."
- Have students identify other words that contain this Latin word root.
  Possibilities include: *equable*, *equity*, *equivocate*, *equinox*, and *equilateral*.

❾ ✓ Reading Check
Answer: Mr. Hooper has draped a black veil across his face from his forehead.

CUSTOMIZE INSTRUCTION FOR UNIVERSAL ACCESS

For Less Proficient Readers	For Advanced Readers
Help students draw inferences about meaning by drawing their attention to the three lines of dialogue on p. 338. Point out the strong reactions, both verbal and physical, that the townspeople have toward the veil. Ask students to think about what these reactions reveal about Hooper's parishioners. Help students appreciate that these reactions reveal the parishioners' superstitious thoughts, as well as their inability to accept change or tolerate differences.	Hawthorne's focus on the superstitious character of the Puritans provides much of the mystery and tension in his stories. Guide students to recognize the elements of tension Hawthorne uses to build suspense throughout "The Minister's Black Veil." Then, remind students that mystery is created both by description and by information that is deliberately omitted. Urge students to identify both of these strategies in Hawthorne's story.

In *Jonathan Edwards, Pastor,* author Patricia Tracy discusses how Edwards achieved the "terrifying effects" of his sermon: "Although it conveys the reek of brimstone, the sermon does not say that God will hurl man into everlasting fires—on the contrary, doom will come from God's indifference . . . He holds man above the pit as by a spider's thread, and should He become weary of protecting worthless man, that abominable insect will *drop of his own weight.* Man's preservation lay in God's whim of mercy, and the terror of this message derived from the insecurity of being temporarily protected by an all-powerful being who had an infinite anger. (Was the control of such strong feelings something that Edwards's audience found difficult to understand or to trust?)" Tracy suggests that because the Puritans held such a dim view of human beings' ability to control their feelings, they were all the more anxious about God's ability to control His anger.

accidental lapse of memory, neglected to invite Mr. Hooper to his table, where the good clergyman had been wont to bless the food, almost every Sunday since his settlement. He returned, therefore, to the parsonage, and, at the moment of closing the door, was observed to look back upon the people, all of whom had their eyes fixed upon the minister. A sad smile gleamed faintly from beneath the black veil, and flickered about his mouth, glimmering as he disappeared.

"How strange," said a lady, "that a simple black veil, such as any woman might wear on her bonnet, should become such a terrible thing on Mr. Hooper's face!"

"Something must surely be amiss with Mr. Hooper's intellects," observed her husband, the physician of the village. "But the strangest part of the affair is the effect of this vagary, even on a sober-minded man like myself. The black veil, though it covers only our pastor's face, throws its influence over his whole person, and makes him ghostlike from head to foot. Do you not feel it so?"

"Truly do I," replied the lady; "and I would not be alone with him for the world. I wonder he is not afraid to be alone with himself!"

"Men sometimes are so," said her husband.

The afternoon service was attended with similar circumstances. At its conclusion, the bell tolled for the funeral of a young lady. The relatives and friends were assembled in the house, and the more distant acquaintances stood about the door, speaking of the good qualities of the deceased, when their talk was interrupted by the appearance of Mr. Hooper, still covered with his black veil. It was now an appropriate emblem. The clergyman stepped into the room where the corpse was laid, and bent over the coffin, to take a last farewell of his deceased parishioner. As he stooped, the veil hung straight down from his forehead, so that, if her eyelids had not been closed forever, the dead maiden might have seen his face. Could Mr. Hooper be fearful of her glance, that he so hastily caught back the black veil? A person who watched the interview between the dead and living, scrupled not to affirm, that, at the instant when the clergyman's features were disclosed, the corpse had slightly shuddered, rustling the shroud and muslin cap, though the countenance retained the composure of death. A superstitious old woman was the only witness of this prodigy. From the coffin Mr. Hooper passed into the chamber of the mourners, and thence to the head of the staircase; to make the funeral prayer. It was a tender and heart-dissolving prayer, full of sorrow, yet so imbued with celestial hopes, that the music of a heavenly harp, swept by the fingers of the dead, seemed faintly to be heard among the saddest accents of the minister. The people trembled, though they but darkly understood him when he prayed that they, and himself, and all of mortal race, might be ready,

The American Experience

⑩ Jonathan Edwards, Puritans, and Sermons of Fear

The congregation's fear of Mr. Hooper's veil recalls Jonathan Edwards, one of the greatest preachers of the colonial period. Edwards used his sermons to inspire fear of eternal damnation in the minds of his listeners. He insisted that the evidence they saw as proof of God's grace in their lives was false. According to Edwards, personal comfort, success, health, and a sense of being a good person were no proof that one was saved. Rather, these satisfactions in the earthly realm were mere distractions, providing comfort, but no substance, to the ignorant.

Though Hawthorne describes Mr. Hooper as a mild and benevolent preacher—certainly no spouter of fire-and-brimstone like Edwards—his veil inspires a similar fear and trembling among the villagers. You can read an excerpt of Jonathan Edwards's "Sinners in the Hands of an Angry God" on page 108.

vagary (və ger´ ē) *n.* unpredictable occurrence

⚜ ENRICHMENT: Career Connection

The Clergy

Like most members of the clergy—such as ministers, rabbis, and priests—Mr. Hooper is a central figure in his community. In addition to offering religious instruction and counseling to their congregations, the clergy preside over weddings, funerals, and other rites of passage. Many are involved in education and social service. Today, as in Hooper's time, a minister is a public figure whose words and actions are observed by all.

Have students interview members of the clergy in your area to find out how they view the breadth of their responsibilities. Students might ask them to describe various interactions with their congregations and with other members of their communities. Students can compare notes to identify characteristics that are shared by effective clergy and to gain a better understanding of their leadership roles.

as he trusted this young maiden had been, for the dreadful hour that should snatch the veil from their faces. The bearers went heavily forth, and the mourners followed, saddening all the street, with the dead before them, and Mr. Hooper in his black veil behind.

"Why do you look back?" said one in the procession to his partner.

"I had a fancy," replied she, "that the minister and the maiden's spirit were walking hand in hand."

"And so had I, at the same moment," said the other.

That night, the handsomest couple in Milford village were to be joined in wedlock. Though reckoned a melancholy man, Mr. Hooper had a placid cheerfulness for such occasions, which often excited a sympathetic smile where livelier merriment would have been thrown away. There was no quality of his disposition which made him more beloved than this. The company at the wedding awaited his arrival with impatience, trusting that the strange awe, which had gathered over him throughout the day, would now be dispelled. But such was not the result. When Mr. Hooper came, the first thing that their eyes rested on was the same horrible black veil, which had added deeper gloom to the funeral, and could portend nothing but evil to the wedding. Such was its immediate effect on the guests that a cloud seemed to have rolled duskily from beneath the black crape, and dimmed the light of the candles. The bridal pair stood up before the minister. But the bride's cold fingers quivered in the <u>tremulous</u> hand of the bridegroom, and her deathlike paleness caused a whisper that the maiden who had been buried a few hours before was come from her grave to be married. If ever another wedding were so dismal, it was that famous one where they tolled the wedding knell.[5] After performing the ceremony, Mr. Hooper raised a glass of wine to his lips, wishing happiness to the new-married couple in a strain of mild pleasantry that ought to have brightened the features of the guests, like a cheerful gleam from the hearth. At that instant, catching a glimpse of his figure in the looking glass, the black veil involved his own spirit in the horror with which it overwhelmed all others. His frame shuddered, his lips grew white, he spilt the untasted wine upon the carpet, and rushed forth into the darkness. For the Earth, too, had on her Black Veil.

The next day, the whole village of Milford talked of little else than Parson Hooper's black veil. That, and the mystery concealed behind it, supplied a topic for discussion between acquaintances meeting in the street, and good women gossiping at their open windows. It was the first item of news that the tavernkeeper told to his guests. The children babbled of it on their way to school. One imitative little imp covered his face with an old black handkerchief, thereby so affrighting his playmates that the panic seized himself, and he well nigh lost his wits by his own <u>waggery</u>.

---

5. **If . . . knell** reference to Hawthorne's short story "The Wedding Knell." A knell is the slow ringing of a bell, as at a funeral.

Reading Strategy
Drawing Inferences About Meaning What inferences can you draw from this dialogue about the veil's intensifying impact on the villagers?

tremulous (trem′ yŏŏ ləs) *adj.* characterized by trembling

waggery (wag′ ər ē) *n.* mischievous humor

13 ✓ Reading Check

Why is the black veil an appropriate emblem for a funeral?

The Minister's Black Veil ◆ 341

11 Reading Strategy

Drawing Inferences About Meaning

- Have two students read this dialogue in quiet, discreet voices.
- Encourage students to pay attention to the reference to the spirit of the dead maiden. Have them consider why the villager might have made this statement.
- Then ask students the Reading Strategy question on p. 341: What inferences can you draw from this dialogue about the veil's increasing impact on the villagers? Answer: A reader might infer that the veil has started to work on villagers' imaginations. Though the minister has said nothing yet regarding the meaning of the veil, parishioners are creating increasingly detailed scenarios that might explain the veil and Hooper's behavior.

12 Critical Thinking

Compare and Contrast

- Ask students to brainstorm a list of words, phrases, ideas, and feelings they associate with the word *wedding*.
- Ask students: Why might the fearful effect of the black veil be more intense at the wedding than at the funeral? Possible response: People expect such dismal attire (as well as sadness) at a funeral. A wedding, however, is ordinarily a time of joy. Therefore, the minister's black veil at the wedding inverts everyone's sense of normalcy and makes the veil's effect even more upsetting than it would be at a funeral.

13 ✓ Reading Check

Answer: In the context of a funeral, a black veil is appropriate as a symbol of mourning.

CUSTOMIZE INSTRUCTION FOR UNIVERSAL ACCESS

For Less Proficient Readers	For Advanced Readers
Have students reread the dialogue near the top of p. 341, in order to discuss whether the lines suggest a link between the maiden's death and Mr. Hooper's wearing the veil. Help them understand that the mourners are only gossiping and that the remarks are pure speculation. You may wish to explain that Hawthorne may be invoking the Salem witch trials, in which innocent people were condemned by the specious and hysterical testimony of neighbors.	Hawthorne's short story "The Wedding Knell" is one of the pieces Hawthorne chose to include in his first published volume, *Twice-Told Tales*. Have students choose another of Hawthorne's short stories to read and analyze. Tales that are especially interesting in comparison and contrast to "The Minister's Black Veil" include "The Maypole of Merry Mount," "The Birthmark," "Rappaccini's Daughter," and "Ethan Brand."

⓮ Literary Analysis

Parable

- Encourage students to look carefully for details that reveal the character of Mr. Hooper's fiancée.

- Then, ask students to identify any possible connections between these details and the symbolism represented by the veil.

- Ask students the Literary Analysis question on p. 342: What might these details about Mr. Hooper's fiancée add to the parable's moral?

Answer: The description of how directly and simply Hooper's fiancée approaches the topic of the veil and the revelation that the minister refuses to explain his reasons even to her reinforce the symbolic power of the veil.

It was remarkable that of all the busybodies and <u>impertinent</u> people in the parish, not one ventured to put the plain question to Mr. Hooper, wherefore he did this thing. Hitherto, whenever there appeared the slightest call for such interference, he had never lacked advisers, nor shown himself averse to be guided by their judgment. If he erred at all, it was by so painful a degree of self-distrust that even the mildest censure would lead him to consider an indifferent action as a crime. Yet, though so well acquainted with this amiable weakness, no individual among his parishioners chose to make the black veil a subject of friendly remonstrance. There was a feeling of dread, neither plainly confessed nor carefully concealed, which caused each to shift the responsibility upon another, till at length it was found expedient to send a deputation of the church, in order to deal with Mr. Hooper about the mystery, before it should grow into a scandal. Never did an embassy so ill discharge its duties. The minister received them with friendly courtesy, but became silent, after they were seated, leaving to his visitors the whole burden of introducing their important business. The topic, it might be supposed, was obvious enough. There was the black veil swathed round Mr. Hooper's forehead, and concealing every feature above his placid mouth, on which, at times, they could perceive the glimmering of a melancholy smile. But that piece of crape, to their imagination, seemed to hang down before his heart, the symbol of a fearful secret between him and them. Were the veil but cast aside, they might speak freely of it, but not till then. Thus they sat a considerable time, speechless, confused, and shrinking uneasily from Mr. Hooper's eye, which they felt to be fixed upon them with an invisible glance. Finally, the deputies returned abashed to their constituents, pronouncing the matter too weighty to be handled, except by a council of the churches, if, indeed, it might not require a general synod.[6]

⓮ But there was one person in the village unappalled by the awe with which the black veil had impressed all beside herself. When the deputies returned without an explanation, or even venturing to demand one, she, with the calm energy of her character, determined to chase away the strange cloud that appeared to be settling round Mr. Hooper, every moment more darkly than before. As his plighted wife,[7] it should be her privilege to know what the black veil concealed. At the minister's first visit, therefore, she entered upon the subject with a direct simplicity, which made the task easier both for him and her. After he had seated himself, she fixed her eyes steadfastly upon the veil, but could discern nothing of the dreadful gloom that had so overawed the multitude: it was but a double fold of crape, hanging down from his forehead to his mouth, and slightly stirring with his breath.

"No," said she aloud, and smiling, "there is nothing terrible in this piece of crape, except that it hides a face which I am always glad to

---

6. **synod** (sin´ əd) *n.* high governing body in certain Christian churches.
7. **plighted wife** fiancée.

impertinent (im purt´ 'n ənt) *adj.* not showing proper respect

Literary Analysis
Parable What might these details about Mr. Hooper's fiancée add to the parable's moral?

look upon. Come, good sir, let the sun shine from behind the cloud. First lay aside your black veil; then tell me why you put it on."

Mr. Hooper's smile glimmered faintly.

"There is an hour to come," said he, "when all of us shall cast aside our veils. Take it not amiss, beloved friend, if I wear this piece of crape till then."

"Your words are a mystery, too," returned the young lady. "Take away the veil from them, at least."

"Elizabeth, I will," said he, "so far as my vow may suffer me. Know, then, this veil is a type and a symbol, and I am bound to wear it ever, both in light and darkness, in solitude and before the gaze of multitudes, and as with strangers, so with my familiar friends. No mortal eye will see it withdrawn. This dismal shade must separate me from the world: even you, Elizabeth, can never come behind it!"

"What grievous affliction hath befallen you," she earnestly inquired, "that you should thus darken your eyes forever?"

"If it be a sign of mourning," replied Mr. Hooper, "I, perhaps, like most other mortals, have sorrows dark enough to be typified by a black veil."

"But what if the world will not believe that it is the type of an innocent sorrow?" urged Elizabeth. "Beloved and respected as you are, there may be whispers that you hide your face under the consciousness of secret sin. For the sake of your holy office, do away this scandal!"

The color rose into her cheeks as she intimated the nature of the rumors that were already abroad in the village. But Mr. Hooper's mildness did not forsake him. He even smiled again—that same sad smile, which always appeared like a faint glimmering of light, proceeding from the obscurity beneath the veil.

"If I hide my face for sorrow, there is cause enough," he merely replied; "and if I cover it for secret sin, what mortal might not do the same?"

And with this gentle, but unconquerable obstinacy did he resist all her entreaties. At length Elizabeth sat silent. For a few moments she appeared lost in thought, considering, probably, what new methods might be tried to withdraw her lover from so dark a fantasy, which, if it had no other meaning, was perhaps a symptom of mental disease. Though of a firmer character than his own, the tears rolled down her cheeks. But in an instant, as it were, a new feeling took the place of sorrow: her eyes were fixed insensibly on the black veil, when, like a sudden twilight in the air, its terrors fell around her. She arose, and stood trembling before him.

"And do you feel it then, at last?" said he mournfully.

She made no reply, but covered her eyes with her hand, and turned to leave the room. He rushed forward and caught her arm.

"Have patience with me, Elizabeth!" cried he, passionately. "Do not desert me, though this veil must be between us here on earth. Be mine, and hereafter there shall be no veil over my face, no darkness

Reading Strategy
Drawing Inferences About Meaning In his reply to Elizabeth, what does Mr. Hooper suggest about the veil's meaning?

obstinacy (äb′ stə nə sē) *n.* stubbornness

16 ✔ **Reading Check**
Are the villagers able to confront Mr. Hooper directly about the veil? Why or why not?

The Minister's Black Veil ◆ 343

15 Reading Strategy
Drawing Inferences About Meaning

- Ask two students to read aloud the dialogue between Mr. Hooper and his fiancée.

- Then ask students the Reading Strategy question on p. 343: In his reply to Elizabeth, what does Mr. Hooper suggest about the veil's meaning?
  Possible response: He suggests that the veil possesses a deep, serious, and universal meaning. Moreover, he implies that its meaning relates to the contrast between his relationship with God and his relationship with human society.

 Monitor Progress Ask students to explain what Mr. Hooper's responses say about Hawthorne's view of humanity.
  Answer: Hawthorne seems to believe that people everywhere know sorrow, but more importantly, that they live burdened with secret sins.

16 ✔ Reading Check

Answer: The villagers see the veil as "the symbol of a fearful secret between him and them" and so are unable to confront him directly about it.

CUSTOMIZE INSTRUCTION FOR UNIVERSAL ACCESS

For Special Needs Students

These students may need help focusing the central ideas underlying this pivotal scene between Elizabeth and Mr. Hooper. Read aloud the scene, stopping to clarify and discuss how Elizabeth tries to elicit an explanation from Hooper first by using a simple, direct approach based on her position as his beloved and fiancée and secondly by suggesting that a scandal may result if some people are led to believe that he is hiding a secret sin.

Then spend time discussing with students Mr. Hooper's question "what mortal might not do the same?" Help students see that Hooper expresses the belief (no doubt Hawthorne's own) that people everywhere carry the consciousness of their own sins with them.

❿ Background

Art

Cemetery, 1970, by Peter McIntyre

Peter McIntyre (1910–) was born in New Zealand. He studied art in London, where he became involved in illustrating books and magazines, as well as in stage design. He was an "Official War Artist" during World War II. He served in that capacity in Greece, Crete, North Africa, and Italy. *Cemetery* was completed during a trip to the United States and published in the book *Peter McIntyre's West.* Use this question for discussion:

• How do you think the artist's perspective and his feelings about this place suggest that he has attempted to achieve more than a photographic likeness?
Answer: Students may point to the vivid contrast between the menacing, overgrown, disorderly graveyard and the serene village in the background, and they may say that the artist creates the impression that there may be something ominous in the town's past—or perhaps its future.

❽ ▶Critical Viewing

Answer: Students may say that the artist has created a gloomy atmosphere in which death and dying hover menacingly over a sleepy village. In Hawthorne's story, an atmosphere of gloom, mistrust, and foreboding blankets the village.

❾ Literary Analysis

Parable

• Read aloud the passage beginning "But even amid his grief."

• Ask students the Literary Analysis question on p. 344: What message is conveyed by the passage beginning "But even amid his grief"?
Answer: Hawthorne's pessimistic view of human nature is revealed. Marital bliss is denied the minister and his fiancée because of his refusal to provide a direct answer about the veil. Thus, a "material emblem" destroys happiness. Hawthorne may be suggesting that true happiness is impossible in this imperfect material world.

Cemetery, Peter McIntyre, Courtesy of the artist

❽ ▲ Critical Viewing In what ways does the atmosphere in this painting reflect the mood of the story? **[Connect]**

between our souls! It is but a mortal veil—it is not for eternity! O! you know not how lonely I am, and how frightened, to be alone behind my black veil. Do not leave me in this miserable obscurity forever!"

"Lift the veil but once, and look me in the face," said she.

"Never! It cannot be!" replied Mr. Hooper.

"Then farewell!" said Elizabeth.

She withdrew her arm from his grasp, and slowly departed, pausing at the door, to give one long shuddering gaze, that seemed almost to penetrate the mystery of the black veil. But, even amid his grief, Mr. Hooper smiled to think that only a material emblem had separated him from happiness, though the horrors, which it shadowed forth,

Literary Analysis
Parable What message is conveyed by the passage beginning "But, even amid his grief"?

✹ ENRICHMENT: Literary Connection

Hawthorne

"The Minister's Black Veil" reflects Hawthorne's intense awareness of the distrustfulness and intolerance of his Puritan ancestors. You may wish to share with students this excerpt from Hawthorne's celebrated introduction to *The Scarlet Letter*:

It is nearly two centuries and a quarter since the original Briton, the earliest emigrant of my name, made his appearance in the wild and forest-bordered settlement . . . The figure of that first ancestor, invested by family tradition with a dim and dusky grandeur, was

present to my boyish imagination, as far back as I can remember. It still haunts me, and induces a sort of home-feeling with the past . . . He was a soldier, legislator, judge; he was a ruler in the Church; he had all the Puritanical traits, both good and evil. He was likewise a bitter persecutor . . . His son, too, inherited the persecuting spirit, and made himself so conspicuous in the martyrdom of the witches, that their blood may fairly be said to have left a stain upon him . . .

must be drawn darkly between the fondest of lovers. From that time no attempts were made to remove Mr. Hooper's black veil, or, by a direct appeal, to discover the secret which it was supposed to hide. By persons who claimed a superiority to popular prejudice, it was reckoned merely an eccentric whim, such as often mingles with the sober actions of men otherwise rational, and tinges them all with its own semblance of insanity. But with the multitude, good Mr. Hooper was irreparably a bugbear.[8] He could not walk the street with any peace of mind, so conscious was he that the gentle and timid would turn aside to avoid him, and that others would make it a point of hardihood to throw themselves in his way. The impertinence of the latter class compelled him to give up his customary walk at sunset to the burial ground; for when he leaned pensively over the gate, there would always be faces behind the gravestones, peeping at his black veil. A fable went the rounds that the stare of the dead people drove him thence. It grieved him, to the very depth of his kind heart, to observe how the children fled from his approach, breaking up their merriest sports, while his melancholy figure was yet afar off. Their instinctive dread caused him to feel more strongly than aught else, that a preternatural[9] horror was interwoven with the threads of the black crape. In truth, his own antipathy to the veil was known to be so great that he never willingly passed before a mirror, nor stooped to drink at a still fountain, lest, in its peaceful bosom, he should be affrighted by himself. This was what gave plausibility to the whispers, that Mr. Hooper's conscience tortured him for some great crime too horrible to be entirely concealed, or otherwise than so obscurely intimated. Thus, from beneath the black veil, there rolled a cloud into the sunshine, an ambiguity of sin or sorrow, which enveloped the poor minister, so that love or sympathy could never reach him. It was said that ghost and fiend consorted with him there. With self-shudderings and outward terrors, he walked continually in its shadow, groping darkly within his own soul or gazing through a medium that saddened the whole world. Even the lawless wind, it was believed, respected his dreadful secret, and never blew aside the veil. But still good Mr. Hooper sadly smiled at the pale visages of the worldly throng as he passed by.

Among all its bad influences, the black veil had the one desirable effect, of making its wearer a very efficient clergyman. By the aid of his mysterious emblem—for there was no other apparent cause—he became a man of awful power over souls that were in agony for sin. His converts always regarded him with a dread peculiar to themselves, affirming, though but figuratively, that, before he brought them to celestial light, they had been with him behind the black veil. Its gloom, indeed, enabled him to sympathize with all dark affections. Dying sinners cried aloud for Mr. Hooper, and would not yield their

---

8. **bugbear** *n.* something causing needless fear.
9. **preternatural** (prēt′ ər nāch′ ər əl) *adj.* supernatural.

Reading Strategy
Drawing Inferences About Meaning What can you infer about the people in the community based on their fear of Mr. Hooper's veil?

Literary Analysis
Parable Why is it significant that nature, as represented by the wind, respects the veil?

 Reading Check
How does Mr. Hooper feel about the veil?

The Minister's Black Veil ◆ 345

⓴ Reading Strategy

Drawing Inferences About Meaning

- Have a student volunteer read the first three sentences of the paragraph beginning "She withdrew her arm from his grasp." Then help students summarize the reactions of various townspeople and acquaintances of Hooper, as described by Hawthorne so far.

- Ask students the Reading Strategy question on p. 345: What can you infer about the people in the community based on their fear of Mr. Hooper's veil?
  Possible response: One might infer that Milford residents are guilt ridden, superstitious, or reluctant to admit the possibility of shame or sin in themselves or in those around them.

ⓡ Literary Analysis

Parable

- Read aloud with students the passage beginning "In truth, his own antipathy." Ask students to listen in order to identify Hawthorne's use of nature imagery. If necessary, draw students' attention to the words *cloud into the sunshine*, *shadow*, and *lawless wind*.

- Ask students the Literary Analysis question on p. 345: Why is it significant that nature, as represented by the wind, respects the veil?
  Possible response: If even such a powerful and "lawless" force as Nature respects the veil, one might feel confident inferring that Hooper is hiding a secret or sin of great significance.

ⓢ Reading Check

Answer: He feels such horror and loathing toward the veil that he avoids any situation in which he might be confronted with a reflection of himself.

CUSTOMIZE INSTRUCTION FOR UNIVERSAL ACCESS

For Special Needs Students	For Advanced Readers
Students may need help to understand why the black veil makes Mr. Hooper "a very efficient clergyman." After reading aloud the paragraph beginning "Among all its bad influences," use discussion to guide students to understand the effect the veiled minister has upon people who suffer from overwhelming guilt. For these people, the minister's veil symbolizes their own sense of sin, suffering, and shame.	Point out that Parson Hooper is a religious leader commanding the utmost respect. Yet his action throws the village into confusion and anxiety. Invite students to stage a debate on whether a leader has the right to take such an action. Should a leader publicly acknowledge his or her own wrongdoing while continuing to serve in an official capacity? Students may wish to conduct research to support their viewpoints. History provides ample evidence for and against the rights and responsibilities of leaders.

- Spend time reading aloud and discussing the final paragraph on p. 346. Help students recognize that Hawthorne is setting the stage for the story's climactic scene.

- Ask students the Literary Analysis question on p. 346: What message is Hawthorne conveying in his description of the veil as a partition, setting Mr. Hooper off from "cheerful brotherhood"?
  Possible response: Hawthorne highlights an awful irony; although Mr. Hooper wears a veil symbolizing the guilt and sin that all people share, the veil separates him from humanity.

breath till he appeared; though ever, as he stooped to whisper consolation, they shuddered at the veiled face so near their own. Such were the terrors of the black veil, even when Death had bared his visage! Strangers came long distances to attend service at his church, with the mere idle purpose of gazing at his figure, because it was forbidden them to behold his face. But many were made to quake ere they departed! Once, during Governor Belcher's[10] administration, Mr. Hooper was appointed to preach the election sermon. Covered with his black veil, he stood before the chief magistrate, the council, and the representatives, and wrought so deep an impression that the legislative measures of that year were characterized by all the gloom and piety of our earliest ancestral sway.

In this manner Mr. Hooper spent a long life, irreproachable in outward act, yet shrouded in dismal suspicions; kind and loving, though unloved, and dimly feared; a man apart from men, shunned in their health and joy, but ever summoned to their aid in mortal anguish. As years wore on, shedding their snows above his sable veil, he acquired a name throughout the New England churches, and they called him Father Hooper. Nearly all his parishioners, who were of mature age when he was settled, had been borne away by many a funeral: he had one congregation in the church, and a more crowded one in the churchyard; and having wrought so late into the evening, and done his work so well, it was now good Father Hooper's turn to rest.

Several persons were visible by the shaded candlelight, in the death chamber of the old clergyman. Natural connections[11] he had none. But there was the decorously grave, though unmoved physician, seeking only to mitigate the last pangs of the patient whom he could not save. There were the deacons, and other eminently pious members of his church. There, also, was the Reverend Mr. Clark, of Westbury, a young and zealous divine, who had ridden in haste to pray by the bedside of the expiring minister. There was the nurse, no hired handmaiden of death, but one whose calm affection had endured thus long in secrecy, in solitude, amid the chill of age, and would not perish, even at the dying hour. Who, but Elizabeth! And there lay the hoary head of good Father Hooper upon the death pillow, with the black veil still swathed about his brow, and reaching down over his face, so that each more difficult gasp of his faint breath caused it to stir. All through life that piece of crape had hung between him and the world: it had separated him from cheerful **23** brotherhood and woman's love, and kept him in that saddest of all prisons, his own heart; and still it lay upon his face, as if to deepen the gloom of his darksome chamber, and shade him from the sunshine of eternity.

---

10. **Governor Belcher** Jonathan Belcher (1682–1757), the royal governor of the Massachusetts Bay Colony, from 1730 to 1741.
11. **Natural connections** relatives.

Literary Analysis
Parable What message is Hawthorne conveying in his description of the veil as a partition, setting Mr. Hooper off from "cheerful brotherhood"?

For some time previous, his mind had been confused, wavering doubtfully between the past and the present, and hovering forward, as it were, at intervals, into the indistinctness of the world to come. There had been feverish turns, which tossed him from side to side, and wore away what little strength he had. But in his most convulsive struggles, and in the wildest vagaries of his intellect, when no other thought retained its sober influence, he still showed an awful solicitude lest the black veil should slip aside. Even if his bewildered soul could have forgotten, there was a faithful woman at his pillow, who, with averted eyes, would have covered that aged face, which she had last beheld in the comeliness of manhood. At length the death-stricken old man lay quietly in the torpor of mental and bodily exhaustion, with an imperceptible pulse, and breath that grew fainter and fainter, except when a long, deep, and irregular inspiration seemed to prelude the flight of his spirit.

The minister of Westbury approached the bedside.

"Venerable Father Hooper," said he, "the moment of your release is at hand. Are you ready for the lifting of the veil that shuts in time from eternity?"

Father Hooper at first replied merely by a feeble motion of his head; then, apprehensive, perhaps, that his meaning might be doubtful, he exerted himself to speak.

"Yea," said he, in faint accents, "my soul hath a patient weariness until that veil be lifted."

"And is it fitting," resumed the Reverend Mr. Clark, "that a man so given to prayer, of such a blameless example, holy in deed and thought, so far as mortal judgment may pronounce; is it fitting that a father in the church should leave a shadow on his memory, that may seem to blacken a life so pure? I pray you, my venerable brother, let not this thing be! Suffer us to be gladdened by your triumphant aspect as you go to your reward. Before the veil of eternity be lifted, let me cast aside this black veil from your face!"

And thus speaking, the Reverend Mr. Clark bent forward to reveal the mystery of so many years. But, exerting a sudden energy, that made all the beholders stand aghast, Father Hooper snatched both his hands from beneath the bedclothes, and pressed them strongly on the black veil, resolute to struggle, if the minister of Westbury would contend with a dying man.

"Never!" cried the veiled clergyman. "On earth, never!"

"Dark old man!" exclaimed the affrighted minister, "with what horrible crime upon your soul are you now passing to the judgment?"

Father Hooper's breath heaved; it rattled in his throat; but, with a mighty effort, grasping forward with his hands, he caught hold of life, and held it back till he should speak. He even raised himself in bed; and there he sat, shivering with the arms of death around him, while the black veil hung down, awful, at that last moment, in the gathered terrors of a lifetime. And yet the faint, sad smile, so often

Literary Analysis
Parable and Symbol
What does the minister of Westbury's question suggest about the veil's symbolic meaning?

Reading Check
On his deathbed, does Mr. Hooper wish the veil to be removed?

The Minister's Black Veil ◆ 347

24 Literary Analysis
Parable and Symbol

- Read aloud the bracketed passage to students. Ask them what they think the minister of Westbury means when he says that the moment of Mr. Hooper's "release" is near.

Answer: Mr. Hooper is about to die.

- Spend time discussing the question the minister asks Mr. Hooper, "Are you ready for the lifting of the veil that shuts in time from eternity?" Help students realize that in this solemn moment he alludes to the lifting of the veil between life and death—"time and eternity"—more than he does to the physical veil worn by Mr. Hooper.

- Ask students the Literary Analysis question on page 347: What does the minister of Westbury's question suggest about the veil's symbolic meaning?

Possible responses: Students may say that it suggests that the veil symbolizes the division or veil between life and death.

25 Reading Check

Answer: Hooper musters all his strength to resist having the veil removed from his face before death.

CUSTOMIZE INSTRUCTION FOR UNIVERSAL ACCESS

For English Learners	For Advanced Readers
Read aloud the key sentence beginning "Nearly all his parishioners" on p. 346. Help students work through and paraphrase the sentence. Help students recognize the use of metaphor in Hawthorne's description of Hooper's "congregations," alive and dead. Tell students that Hawthorne's reference to Hooper's having "wrought so late into the evening" is a way of comparing his life to a single working day. Hooper is very old and about to die.	Remind students that Hawthorne's writing reflects his preoccupation with the superstitions, cruelty, and character flaws of his Puritan ancestors. Invite students to identify and analyze examples of this preoccupation in "The Minister's Black Veil." Also, point out that Hawthorne incorporated his keen awareness of human flaws into his work. Encourage students to keep these ideas in mind as they read.

Answers for p. 348

Review and Assess

1. (a) Some students may say that they would have reacted to the veil with fear or shock. Others may say that they would not have been alarmed by the veil. **(b)** Students may say that as a Puritan clergyman, they would have tried to persuade Hooper (much as Reverend Clark did) to remove the veil and bring to an end the mystery, gossip, suspicions, and sense of dread that had infected the village.

2. (a) His congregation held him in high esteem. **(b)** The veil separates him from them; they grow fearful of him and of his apparent secret. Also the performance of his ordinary duties as a minister begins to have a greater and keener impact on the members of his congregation.

3. (a) The sermon's subject is secret sin. **(b)** His sermon arouses feelings of guilt, fear, and remorse. **(c)** The minister's wearing of an unexplained black veil is shocking and provocative, and it causes his listeners to react in unexpected, dramatic ways.

4. (a) It makes him a very efficient clergyman. **(b)** Students may say that the veil impels Hooper's listeners to question why he wears the veil, to relate the words of his sermon to his wearing the veil, and to relate both the sermon and the veil to their private knowledge about their own secret sins.

5. (a) The veil has a powerful effect on people because it reminds them of their secret sins. **(b)** Students may respond that they do agree with the suggestion, because all people have some thoughts and concerns that they feel they have to keep to themselves.

6. Students may say that guilt could have benefits for a person if it led him or her to admit fault or to change destructive behavior.

---

there, now seemed to glimmer from its obscurity, and linger on Father Hooper's lips.

"Why do you tremble at me alone?" cried he, turning his veiled face round the circle of pale spectators. "Tremble also at each other! Have men avoided me, and women shown no pity, and children screamed and fled, only for my black veil? What, but the mystery which it obscurely typifies, has made this piece of crape so awful? When the friend shows his inmost heart to his friend; the lover to his best beloved; when man does not vainly shrink from the eye of his Creator, loathsomely treasuring up the secret of his sin; then deem me a monster, for the symbol beneath which I have lived, and die! I look around me, and, lo! on every visage a Black Veil!"

While his auditors shrank from one another, in mutual affright, Father Hooper fell back upon his pillow, a veiled corpse, with a faint smile lingering on the lips. Still veiled, they laid him in his coffin, and a veiled corpse they bore him to the grave. The grass of many years has sprung up and withered on that grave, the burial stone is moss-grown, and good Mr. Hooper's face is dust; but awful is still the thought that it moldered beneath the Black Veil!

Review and Assess

Thinking About the Selection

1. **Respond:** How would you have reacted to the veil if you had been (a) a member of Mr. Hooper's congregation or (b) another Puritan clergyman?

2. **(a) Recall:** How did his congregation regard Mr. Hooper before he began wearing the veil? **(b) Analyze:** In what ways does the veil affect Mr. Hooper's relationship with his congregation?

3. **(a) Recall:** What is the subject of Mr. Hooper's sermon on the day he first wears the veil? **(b) Compare and Contrast:** What emotions does Mr. Hooper evoke in his congregation that he never did before? **(c) Draw Conclusions:** To what do you attribute Mr. Hooper's new found ability to affect his listeners?

4. **(a) Recall:** According to the narrator, what is the veil's "one desirable effect"? **(b) Infer:** Why does the veil make Mr. Hooper a more effective minister?

5. **(a) Interpret:** Why does the veil have such a powerful effect on people? **(b) Synthesize:** Hawthorne suggests that all people carry secrets they choose not to reveal to anyone. Do you agree or disagree with this suggestion? Explain.

6. **Take a Position:** At some point in our lives, most human beings will feel guilty about something. Do you think that guilt is ever beneficial? Explain.

ASSESSMENT PRACTICE: Reading Comprehension

Make Inferences and Generalizations (For more practice, see Test Preparation Workbook, p. 20.)

Many tests require students to make generalizations—that is, general statements based on specific information from the written passage. A generalization is a general idea that is supported by textual evidence. Use the following sample question about Hawthorne's story to show students how to make generalizations about a written text:

What effect does the appearance of Minister Hooper's black veil have on his congregation?

A They are afraid and confused.
B They are indifferent.
C They are quietly supportive.
D They are angry and violent.

Choices *B, C,* and *D* contain information not found in the text. *A* is correct. The veil is mysterious and makes Mr. Hooper appear more threatening and powerful.

Review and Assess

Literary Analysis

Parable

1. In what ways does this **parable** convey the message that people possess the potential for both good and evil?
2. Why do you think Hawthorne does not reveal the reason Parson Hooper begins wearing the veil?
3. The Anti-Transcendentalists believed that the truths of existence are both elusive and disturbing. What disturbing truth does Hawthorne convey through Parson Hooper and his black veil?

Connecting Literary Elements

4. (a) With what emotions does Elizabeth regard the veil at first and later on? (b) What do her reactions suggest about the veil as a **symbol**?
5. (a) Use a chart like the one shown to analyze the emotional associations contained in three descriptions of the veil. (b) Is the veil symbolic of a single idea, or does it offer a range of possible interpretations?

Descriptive Detail	Emotional Associations	Symbolic Meaning

6. On his deathbed, Mr. Hooper says, "I look around me, and lo! on every visage a Black Veil!" What does this statement suggest about the veil's symbolic meaning?

Reading Strategy

Drawing Inferences About Meaning

7. Based on the villagers' reactions to Parson Hooper, **draw inferences** about human nature as Hawthorne sees it.
8. What can you infer about the author's attitude toward the Puritans from this story? Support your answer.

Extend Understanding

9. **Cultural Connection:** (a) Do you think a community's expectations that its leaders be without any guilt are realistic? (b) Are they fair? Explain.

Quick Review

A **parable** is a short, simple story with a moral message.

A **symbol** is something that has meaning in and of itself and also stands for something else.

To **draw inferences about meaning,** use details from the text as clues to an author's larger purpose.

 Take It to the Net
www.phschool.com

Take the interactive self-test online to check your understanding of the selection.

The Minister's Black Veil ◆ 349

ENRICHMENT: Further Reading

Other Works by Nathaniel Hawthorne

"Young Goodman Brown"

"The May-Pole of Merry Mount"

"Dr. Heidegger's Experiment"

"Rappaccini's Daughter"

"The Antique Ring"

The Scarlet Letter

The House of the Seven Gables

The Marble Faun

 Take It to the Net
Visit www.phschool.com for more information on Nathaniel Hawthorne.

Answers

Review and Assess

1. **Possible responses:** The behavior and actions of Parson Hooper alone show that human beings have the potential for both evil (his implied albeit unspecified "secret sin") and good (his lifetime of honesty and good works). The actions and behavior of Elizabeth and of the other townspeople also show the potential for good and evil, respectively.

2. By not revealing Hooper's motive, Hawthorne creates ambiguity and forces the reader to infer the reason by examining the evidence in the story.

3. All people have committed some acts that they regret as sinful, and all put some barriers between themselves and others.

4. **(a)** She regards the veil with determination, embarrassment, sorrow, and finally fear. **(b)** Her reactions suggest that the veil is a symbol characterized by ambiguity and great power.

5. **(a)** Students' charts should contain accurate details drawn from the story, and insightful inferences about emotional associations and symbolic meanings.

   (b) The veil takes on different meanings and associations at various times during the story.

6. It suggests that the veil symbolizes the secret sin that lies in the heart of every human being.

7. Hawthorne seems to see human nature as marked by negative characteristics such as suspicion, pettiness, ignorance, and cowardice.

8. One can infer that Hawthorne took a negative view of the Puritans, because many characters are hypocritical and lack compassion.

9. **(a and b)** Students should support their responses with clear reasoning and examples.

❶ Vocabulary Development

Word Analysis

1. *equidistant*—equally distant
2. *equivalent*—equal in value, quantity, force, meaning, etc.
3. *equate*—to make equal
4. *equilibrium*—a state of balance or equality between opposing forces

Spelling Strategy

1. impertinent
2. iniquity
3. indecorous
4. impassive

Concept Development

1. c
2. f
3. g
4. j
5. a
6. d
7. e
8. i
9. b
10. h

❷ Grammar and Style

Looking at Style

Answers should include the following: **(1)** two paragraphs from the selection; **(2)** a list of the types of openers of the sentences; **(3)** two rewritten paragraphs, both with sentences containing the same type of opener; **(4)** an explanation of the ineffectiveness of the rewritten paragraphs.

Writing Application

Students' paragraphs should engage readers and use a variety of sentence openers.

Integrate Language Skills

❶ Vocabulary Development Lesson

Word Analysis: Latin Root *-equi-*

The Latin root *-equi-* means "equal." The spelling of the root changes slightly in the word **iniquity,** meaning "sin or gross injustice." Using your knowledge of this root, define the following words:

1. equidistant
2. equivalent
3. equate
4. equilibrium

Spelling Strategy

The prefix *in-,* meaning "not," as in *indecorous,* changes to *im-* before many words beginning with *p,* such as *impersonal,* or with *m,* such as *immature.* Complete the words below by adding the correct prefix.

1. __pertinent (impolite)
2. __iquity (evil)
3. __decorous (vulgar)
4. __passive (emotionless)

Concept Development: Synonyms

Review the vocabulary list on page 335. Then, select the letter of the best synonym for each numbered word.

1. venerable   **a.** wise
2. iniquity   **b.** rude
3. indecorous   **c.** honorable
4. ostentatious   **d.** whim
5. sagacious   **e.** timid
6. vagary   **f.** evil
7. tremulous   **g.** uncouth
8. waggery   **h.** stubbornness
9. impertinent   **i.** humor
10. obstinacy   **j.** showy

❷ Grammar and Style Lesson

Varying Sentence Openers

By **varying sentence openers,** Hawthorne helps readers follow the story, from detail to detail and event to event. For example, some sentences begin with prepositional phrases; others begin with transitions. Look at these examples from the story:

> **Prepositional Phrase:** *Among all its bad influences,* the black veil had the one desirable effect . . .
>
> **Transition:** *Though reckoned a melancholy man,* Mr. Hooper had a placid cheerfulness for such occasions . . .

Looking at Style Review the story, and select two paragraphs that contain at least three different types of sentence openers. Identify the type of opener used in each sentence. Then, rewrite the two paragraphs so that all of the sentences have the same type of opener. Finally, explain why the rewritten paragraphs are less effective than the original ones.

Writing Application Write the opening paragraph to a short story. Engage readers, and lead them from detail to detail by using a variety of sentence openers.

W̶G *Prentice Hall Writing and Grammar Connection: Chapter 20, Section 3*

TEACHING RESOURCES

The following resources can be used to enrich or extend the instruction for pp. 350–351.

Vocabulary

📖 **Selection Support Workbook:** Build Vocabulary, p. 81

📖 **Vocabulary and Spelling Practice Book** (Use this booklet for skills enrichment.)

Grammar and Style

📖 **Selection Support Workbook:** Grammar and Style, p. 82 ▪

W̶G **Writing and Grammar,** Ruby Level, p. 489

▪ **Daily Language Practice Transparencies**

Writing

W̶G **Writing and Grammar,** Ruby Level, p. 304 ▪

💿 **Writing and Grammar iText CD-ROM**

📖 **Writing Models and Graphic Organizers on Transparencies,** pp. 37–40

 BLOCK SCHEDULING: Resources marked with this symbol provide varied instruction during 90-minute blocks.

❸ Writing Lesson

Response to a Short Story

Some aspects of this dark and powerful story probably made a distinct impression on you. Perhaps you were fascinated by the spectacle of the veil or upset by Parson Hooper's (or the villagers') behavior. Write a short paper in which you present your response to an element of the story. Support your response with specific details from the story.

Prewriting   Review the story, and note your thoughts and feelings about the characters, setting, plot, and symbols. Choose one element to address. Then, find details that you can use to help explain your reactions.

Drafting   In an introductory paragraph, identify the element on which you are focusing and explain your reaction to it. Then, explain the role of this element in the story, citing specific details for support.

Revising   Revise your response to make certain that you have included enough passages and details from the story to explain your reaction.

> *, which Hawthorne describes as a "gloomy shade,"*

Model: Using Exact Quotations

Hawthorne never tells us why Parson Hooper decides to wear the veil. We know only that the veil conceals his entire face except for his chin and mouth.

> The most effective way to cite details from a literary work is to use word-for-word quotations.

 Prentice Hall Writing and Grammar Connection: Chapter 14, Section 2

❹ Extension Activities

Listening and Speaking   As Elizabeth, plan and present a **monologue** in which you appeal to your fiancé to remove his black veil.

- Use a familiar tone of address.
- Maintain an appropriately Puritan air of restraint.
- Refer to Elizabeth's history with Mr. Hooper and her hopes for their future.

Give a dramatic presentation to the class.

Research and Technology   Read "The Wedding Knell"—another story in Hawthorne's *Twice-Told Tales*. Compare and contrast it with "The Minister's Black Veil." Then, prepare and deliver an **oral presentation** in which you discuss the two stories.

Take It to the Net   www.phschool.com

Go online for an additional research activity using the Internet.

The Minister's Black Veil ◆ *351*

ASSESSMENT RESOURCES

The following resources can be used to assess students' knowledge and skills.

Selection Assessment

- **Formal Assessment,** pp. 88–90
- **Open Book Test,** pp. 52–54
- **Got It! Assessment Video,** Tape 2
- **Test Bank Software**
- **Take It to the Net**
  Visit www.phschool.com for self-tests and additional questions on "The Minister's Black Veil."

Listening and Speaking Rubric

- **Performance Assessment and Portfolio Mgmt.,** p. 17

 ASSESSMENT SYSTEM

- **Workbook**
- **Skill Book**
- **Transparencies**
- **CD-ROM**

---

❸ Writing Lesson

- Students' responses should focus on Hawthorne's use of a literary element. Their papers should include not only explanations and descriptions of their responses, but also a variety of supporting textual details.

- Use the Writing Lesson, as well as Writing Process Model 7, pp. 37–40, in **Writing Models and Graphic Organizers on Transparencies,** to guide students in developing their responses to Hawthorne's short story.

❹ Listening and Speaking

- Urge students to reread carefully each of the two scenes in which Elizabeth plays a role. They should take special note of her dialogue, in order to clarify its content and familiarize themselves with the style of her words.

- Pairs of students might benefit from improvising dialogue between Elizabeth and Hooper. If students record some of these improvisations, they may discover material that can be used later in their monologues.

- Have students use the Peer Assessment form for Persuasive Speech, p. 17, in **Performance Assessment and Portfolio Management.**

CUSTOMIZE INSTRUCTION
For Universal Access

To address different learning styles, use the following activities suggested in the **Extension Activities** booklet, p. 18.

For Intrapersonal and Spatial/Visual Learners, use Activity 5.

For Bodily/Kinesthetic and Musical/Rhythmic Learners, use Activity 6.

For Verbal/Linguistic Learners, use Activity 7.

from Moby-Dick

Lesson Objectives

1. **To analyze and respond to literary elements**
   - Literary Analysis: Symbol
   - Connecting Literary Elements: Theme
2. **To read, comprehend, analyze, and critique an excerpt from a novel**
   - Reading Strategy: Recognizing Symbols
   - Reading Check questions
   - Review and Assess questions
   - Assessment Practice (ATE)
3. **To develop word analysis skills, fluency, and systematic vocabulary**
   - Vocabulary Development Lesson: Latin Prefix: *mal-*
4. **To understand and apply written and oral language conventions**
   - Spelling Strategy
   - Grammar and Style Lesson: Agreement With Collective Nouns
5. **To understand and apply appropriate writing and research strategies**
   - Writing Lesson: A Character Study
   - Extension Activity: Report
6. **To understand and apply listening and speaking strategies**
   - Extension Activity: Monologue

STEP-BY-STEP TEACHING GUIDE	PACING GUIDE
PRETEACH	
Motivate Students and Provide Background	
Use the Motivation activity (ATE p. 352)	5 min.
Read and discuss the author and background information (SE/ATE pp. 352, 354)	5 min.
Introduce the Concepts	
Introduce the Literary Analysis and Reading Strategy (SE/ATE p. 353)	15 min.
Pronounce the vocabulary words and read their definitions (SE p. 353)	5 min.
TEACH	
Monitor Comprehension	
Informally monitor comprehension by circulating while students read independently or in groups	60 min.
Monitor students' comprehension with the Reading Check notes (SE/ATE pp. 355, 357, 359, 361, 363, 365, 367, 369)	as students read
Develop vocabulary with Vocabulary notes (SE pp. 358, 360, 364, 366; ATE p. 360)	as students read
Develop Understanding	
Develop students' understanding of symbol with the Literary Analysis annotations (SE/ATE pp. 355, 357, 358, 360, 362, 365, 366, 367, 368)	10 min.
Develop students' ability to recognize symbols with the Reading Strategy annotations (SE pp. 356, 361, 365, 367; ATE pp. 356, 361, 363, 364, 365, 367)	10 min.
ASSESS	
Assess Mastery	
Assess students' mastery of the Reading Strategy and Literary Analysis by having them answer the Review and Assess questions (SE/ATE p. 371)	15 min.
Use one or more of the print and media Assessment Resources (ATE p. 373)	up to 45 min.
EXTEND	
Apply Understanding	
Have students complete the Vocabulary Development Lesson and the Grammar and Style Lesson (SE p. 372)	20 min.
Apply students' ability to write a summary by using the Writing Lesson (SE/ATE p. 373)	45 min.
Apply students' understanding using one or more of the Extension Activities (SE p. 373)	20–90 min.

A ACCELERATED INSTRUCTION:
Use the strategies and activities identified with an **A**.

UNIVERSAL ACCESS
● = Below Level Students
▲ = On-Level Students
■ = Above Level Students

Time and Resource Manager

RESOURCES

PRINT 📖	TRANSPARENCIES	TECHNOLOGY 💿 🎧 📼
• **Beyond Literature,** Cross-Curricular Connection: Art, p. 19 ▲ ■		• **Interest Grabber Video,** Tape 3 ● ▲ ■
• **Selection Support Workbook:** ● ▲ ■ Literary Analysis, p. 88 Reading Strategy, p. 87 Build Vocabulary, p. 85	• **Literary Analysis and Reading Transparencies,** pp. 37 and 38 ● ▲ ■	
• **Adapted Reader's Companion** ● • **Reader's Companion** ●		• **Listening to Literature** ● ▲ ■ Audiocassettes, Side 12 Audio CDs, CD 8
• **English Learner's Companion** ● ▲ • **Literatura en español** ● ▲ • **Literary Analysis for Enrichment** ■		
• **Formal Assessment:** Selection Test, pp. 91–93 ● ▲ ■ • **Open Book Test,** pp. 55–57 ● ▲ ■ • **Performance Assessment and Portfolio Management,** p. 30 ● ▲ ■ • **PRENTICE HALL ASSESSMENT SYSTEM** ● ▲ ■	• **PRENTICE HALL ASSESSMENT SYSTEM** ● ▲ ■ Skills Practice Answers and Explanations on Transparencies	• **Test Bank Software** ● ▲ ■ • **Got It! Assessment Videotapes,** Tape 2 ● ▲
• **Selection Support Workbook:** ● ▲ ■ Grammar and Style, p. 86 • **Writing and Grammar,** Ruby Level ● ▲ ■ • **Extension Activities,** p. 19 ● ▲ ■	• **Daily Language Practice Transparencies** ● ▲ • **Writing Models and Graphic Organizers on Transparencies,** p. 37–40 ● ▲ ■	• **Writing and Grammar iText CD-ROM** ● ▲ ■ 💻 *Take It to the Net* www.phschool.com

BLOCK SCHEDULING: Use one 90-minute class period to preteach the selection and have students read it. Use a second 90-minute class period to assess students' mastery of skills and have them complete one of the Extension Activities.

**Step-by-Step Teaching Guide
for pp. 352–353**

Motivation

Ahab says, "Death to Moby-Dick! God hunt us all, if we do not hunt Moby-Dick to his death!" After reading this quotation, tell students that Ahab is a man obsessed. Invite students to think of people (or fictional characters) they know who have worked intensely to reach a goal. You might mention people like Midori, Tiger Woods, and Gary Kasparov, as well as world-class ice skaters, musicians, gymnasts, and others whose intense, single-minded efforts began at an early age. Ask students whether they see a distinction between concentrated effort and obsession. Does one need to be obsessed to reach lofty goals?

▣ Interest Grabber Video

As an alternative, play "The Making of a Classic" on Tape 3 to engage student interest.

❶ Background

More About the Author

After an unsuccessful job search and a brief stint as a teacher, Melville sailed on the whaler *Acushnet* to the South Seas in 1841, anchoring in the Marquesas Islands. On this voyage, he joined an uprising that landed him in a Tahitian jail. After escaping, Melville roamed throughout French Polynesia, during which time he became deeply embittered at the mistreatment of native Polynesian peoples by colonists and missionaries.

In addition to his novels and short stories, Melville wrote verse. His first volume of poetry, *Battle-Pieces and Aspects of the War* (1866), concerned the Civil War. His last prose work, *Billy Budd, Foretopman*, was not published until 1924.

Prepare to Read

❶ *from* Moby-Dick

Herman Melville
(1819–1891)

Herman Melville is one of America's greatest novelists. Unfortunately, his work was never fully appreciated during his lifetime, and he lived a life that was often filled with frustration and despair.

Melville was born in New York City, the son of a wealthy merchant. His family's comfortable financial situation changed drastically in 1830, however, when his father's import business failed. Two years later, Melville's father died, leaving the family in debt. Forced to leave school, Melville spent the rest of his childhood working as a clerk, a farmhand, and a teacher to help support his family.

Whaling in the South Pacific Melville became a sailor at the age of nineteen and spent several years working on whaling ships and exploring the South Pacific. He returned to the United States in 1844, after a brief period of service in the navy.

Soon thereafter, Melville began his career as a writer, using his adventures in the South Seas as material for his fiction. He quickly produced two popular and financially successful novels, *Typee* (1846) and *Omoo* (1847), both set in the Pacific islands. His third novel, *Mardi* (1849), was considerably more abstract and symbolic. When readers rejected the book and his fame began to fade, Melville grew increasingly melancholy. He continued writing, however, turning out two more novels, *Redburn* (1849) and *White-Jacket* (1850), over the next two years.

Writing in the Berkshires Using the profits from his popular novels, Melville bought a farm, known as Arrowhead, near Pittsfield, Massachusetts. There, he befriended the author Nathaniel Hawthorne, who lived in a neighboring village. Greatly encouraged by Hawthorne's interest and influenced by his reading of Shakespeare, Melville redoubled his own creative energies. He began producing deeper and more sophisticated works. In 1851, he published his masterpiece, *Moby-Dick*, under the title *The Whale*.

Moby-Dick is a complex novel with several layers of meaning. On the surface, it is the story of the fateful voyage of a whaling ship. On another level, it is the story of a bitter man's quest for vengeance and truth. On still another level, it is a philosophical examination of humanity's relationship to the natural world and the conflict between creativity and cruelty.

A Moment of Pride When he finished the book, Melville sensed the magnitude of his achievement. Unfortunately, his pleasure in his work was short-lived. Unable to appreciate the novel's depth, nineteenth-century readers responded unfavorably to *Moby-Dick*. It did not attract a wide audience.

Audiences also rejected his next two novels, *Pierre* (1852) and *The Confidence Man* (1857). Melville fell into debt and was forced to accept a job as an inspector at the New York customs house. Some of the short stories Melville published between 1852 and 1855—including "Bartleby the Scrivener," "The Encantadas," and "Benito Cereno"—reflect the author's circumstances at the time, including his contempt for hypocrisy and materialism.

Rediscovered Disillusioned and bitter, Melville turned away from writing fiction during the latter part of his life. He privately published several volumes of poetry. He also produced a handful of short stories and the moving novella *Billy Budd*. Melville died in 1891, unappreciated and unnoticed. In the 1920s, however, his novels and tales were rediscovered and hailed by scholars, and he finally received the recognition he deserved. Today, *Moby-Dick* is widely regarded as one of the finest novels in all of American literature.

TEACHING RESOURCES

The following resources can be used to enrich or extend the instruction for pp. 352–353.

Motivation

▣ **Interest Grabber Video,** Tape 3 ▣

Background

📖 **Beyond Literature,** p. 19

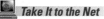
💻 *Take It to the Net*
Visit www.phschool.com for background and hotlinks for the selection.

Literary Analysis

📄 **Literary Analysis and Reading Transparencies,** Symbol, p. 38

Reading

📖 **Selection Support Workbook:** Reading Strategy, p. 87; Build Vocabulary, p. 85

📄 **Literary Analysis and Reading Transparencies,** Recognizing Symbols, p. 37 ▣

▣ **BLOCK SCHEDULING:** Resources marked with this symbol provide varied instruction during 90-minute blocks.

Preview

Connecting to the Literature

Some situations demand fierce concentration. However, as this excerpt from one of literature's most famous works of fiction illustrates, when one focuses *too* intensely on a goal, attention can become obsession.

❷ Literary Analysis

Symbol

A **symbol** is a person, place, or thing that has its own meaning and also represents something larger. The white whale of Melville's *Moby-Dick* is an extremely complex symbol. To understand its meaning, examine every aspect of the whale's behavior and appearance.

- Moby-Dick is massive, threatening, and awe-inspiring yet beautiful.
- Moby-Dick seems unpredictable but is controlled by natural laws.
- Moby-Dick seems immortal and indifferent to human suffering.

Analyzed in this way, Moby-Dick seems to symbolize all that is mysterious and uncontrollable in life.

Connecting Literary Elements

A **theme** is a central message revealed by a literary work, and is often expressed through the use of symbols, as well as characters' actions, descriptions, and imagery. In *Moby-Dick*, Melville explores the enormous theme of the mysteries of existence. As you read, look for points at which Melville addresses such ideas as good, evil, sacrifice, and revenge.

❸ Reading Strategy

Recognizing Symbols

To **recognize symbols,** look for characters, places, or objects that are mentioned repeatedly or linked to larger concepts. For example, Ahab's description of Moby-Dick gives the whale symbolic meaning:

> I see in him outrageous strength, with an inscrutable malice sinewing it. That inscrutable malice is chiefly what I hate . . .

From this description, you might guess that Moby-Dick symbolizes nature's destructive power. Use a chart like the one shown to recognize and interpret symbols.

Vocabulary Development

inscrutable (in skrōōt´ ə bəl) *adj.* not able to be easily understood (p. 358)

maledictions (mal´ ə dik´ shənz) *n.* curses (p. 360)

prescient (presh´ ənt) *adj.* having foreknowledge (p. 364)

pertinaciously (pʉr´ tə na´ shəs lē) *adv.* holding firmly to some purpose (p. 366)

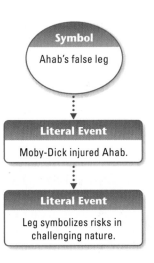

Symbol
Ahab's false leg

Literal Event
Moby-Dick injured Ahab.

Literal Event
Leg symbolizes risks in challenging nature.

from Moby-Dick ◆ 353

❷ Literary Analysis

Symbol

- Tell students that they will focus on symbol as they read the excerpts from *Moby-Dick* in this selection. You may want students to review what they learned about symbols when they read Hawthorne's "The Minister's Black Veil."

- Urge students to analyze each symbol to identify its literal meaning, as well as its deeper or larger meaning.

- Before they begin reading, you might wish to encourage students to use prior knowledge to list and reflect on some common symbols in our culture today. Examples include flags; colors; fashions; vehicles; cellular phones; fences, walls, and bridges; and so on.

❸ Reading Strategy

Recognizing Symbols

- As they read Melville's narrative, have students take note of characters, places, objects, images, and actions that are mentioned repeatedly, explained in detail, or linked to larger concepts.

- Explain that symbols can range from relatively simple to very complex. Point out that Melville portrays the great white whale in such a way that it takes on many shades of symbolic meaning.

- Have students use a chart like the one shown to help them recognize and interpret the symbols as they read the excerpt from *Moby-Dick*.

Vocabulary Development

- Pronounce each vocabulary word for students, and read the definitions as a class. Have students identify any words with which they are already familiar.

 E-Teach

Visit E-Teach at www.phschool.com for teachers' essays on how to teach, with questions and answers.

CUSTOMIZE INSTRUCTION FOR UNIVERSAL ACCESS

For Special Needs Students	For Less Proficient Readers	For English Learners
Have students read the adapted version of the excerpt from *Moby Dick* in the **Adapted Reader's Companion**. This version provides basic-level instruction in an interactive format with questions and write-on lines. Completing the adapted version will prepare students to read the selection in the Student Edition.	Have students read Melville's fiction in the **Reader's Companion**. This version provides basic-level instruction in an interactive format with questions and write-on lines. After students finish the selection in **Reader's Companion**, have them complete the questions and activities in the Student Edition.	Have students read the adapted version of the selection in the **English Learner's Companion**. This version provides basic-level instruction in an interactive format with questions and write-on lines. Completing the adapted version will prepare students to read the selection in the Student Edition.

**CUSTOMIZE INSTRUCTION
for Intrapersonal Learners**

To promote active reading, invite students to keep a reader's response journal. Guide them to focus their observations about Ahab's desire for revenge and on Starbuck's responses to Ahab. Encourage them to record their own opinions of Ahab's quest and the reactions of the other sailors.

❶ About the Selection

Widely regarded as one of the finest American novels ever written, *Moby-Dick* expresses the view that, despite people's desire to do so, they will never be able to control nature or understand it completely. In "The Quarter-Deck," one of the novel's key early chapters, Ahab becomes the novel's dominant character, and Melville reveals Ahab's vengeful, obsessive personality and his conflict with Moby-Dick. At this turning point, readers and sailors alike learn the true purpose of the *Pequod's* voyage. "The Chase—Third Day" is the book's last chapter. There the novel reaches its climax in the final catastrophic contest with Moby-Dick.

❷ Background

In Melville's day, the captain of a ship had unlimited authority—and all aboard ship knew this to be the case. Failing to follow orders brought harsh and perhaps arbitrary punishment, and most crew members were careful not to challenge the captain directly.

❶ **FROM**

MOBY-DICK

Herman Melville

Background

Moby-Dick is the story of a man's obsession with the dangerous and mysterious white whale that years before had taken off one of his legs. The man, Captain Ahab, guides the *Pequod*, a whaling ship, and its crew in relentless pursuit of this whale, Moby-Dick. Among the more important members of the crew are Starbuck, the first mate; Stubb, the second mate; Flask, the third mate; Queequeg, Tashtego, and Daggoo, the harpooners; and Ishmael, the young sailor who narrates the book.

When the crew signed aboard the *Pequod*, the voyage was to be nothing more than a business venture. However, in the following excerpt, Ahab makes clear to the crew that his purpose is to seek revenge against Moby-Dick.

from The Quarter-Deck

❷ One morning shortly after breakfast, Ahab, as was his wont, ascended the cabin gangway to the deck. There most sea captains usually walk at that hour, as country gentlemen, after the same meal, take a few turns in the garden.

❸ Soon his steady, ivory stride was heard, as to and fro he paced his old rounds, upon planks so familiar to his tread, that they were all over dented, like geological stones, with the peculiar mark of his walk. Did you fixedly gaze, too, upon that ribbed and dented brow;

TEACHING RESOURCES

The following resources can be used to enrich or extend the instruction for pp. 354–370.

Literary Analysis

📖 **Writing Models and Graphic Organizers on Transparencies,** pp. 37–40

📓 **Selection Support Workbook:** Literary Analysis, p. 88

Reading

📓 **Reader's Companion**

📖 **English Learner's Companion**

🎧 **Listening to Literature Audiocassettes,** Side 12 ▦

💿 **Listening to Literature CDs,** CD 8 ▦

▦ **BLOCK SCHEDULING:** Resources marked with this symbol provide varied instruction during 90-minute blocks.

there also, you would see still stranger footprints—the footprints of his one unsleeping, ever-pacing thought.

But on the occasion in question, those dents looked deeper, even as his nervous step that morning left a deeper mark. And, so full of his thought was Ahab, that at every uniform turn that he made, now at the mainmast and now at the binnacle,[1] you could almost see that thought turn in him as he turned, and pace in him as he paced; so completely possessing him, indeed, that it all but seemed the inward mold of every outer movement.

"D'ye mark him, Flask?" whispered Stubb; "the chick that's in him pecks the shell. 'Twill soon be out."

The hours wore on—Ahab now shut up within his cabin; anon, pacing the deck, with the same intense bigotry of purpose[2] in his aspect.

It drew near the close of day. Suddenly he came to a halt by the bulwarks, and inserting his bone leg into the auger hole there, and with one hand grasping a shroud, he ordered Starbuck to send everybody aft.

"Sir!" said the mate, astonished at an order seldom or never given on shipboard except in some extraordinary case.

"Send everybody aft," repeated Ahab. "Mastheads, there! come down!"

When the entire ship's company were assembled, and with curious and not wholly unapprehensive faces, were eyeing him, for he looked not unlike the weather horizon when a storm is coming up, Ahab, after rapidly glancing over the bulwarks, and then darting his eyes among the crew, started from his standpoint; and as though not a soul were nigh him resumed his heavy turns upon the deck. With bent head and half-slouched hat he continued to pace, unmindful of the wondering whispering among the men; till Stubb cautiously whispered to Flask, that Ahab must have summoned them there for the purpose of witnessing a pedestrian feat. But this did not last long. Vehemently pausing, he cried:

"What do ye do when ye see a whale, men?"

"Sing out for him!" was the impulsive rejoinder from a score of clubbed voices.

"Good!" cried Ahab, with a wild approval in his tones; observing the hearty animation into which his unexpected question had so magnetically thrown them.

"And what do ye next, men?"

"Lower away, and after him!"

"And what tune is it ye pull to, men?"

"A dead whale or a stove[3] boat!"

More and more strangely and fiercely glad and approving, grew the countenance of the old man at every shout; while the mariners began to

---

1. **binnacle** (bin´ ə kəl) *n.* case enclosing a ship's compass.
2. **bigotry of purpose** complete single-mindedness.
3. **stove** *v.* broken; smashed.

Literary Analysis
Symbol What might the "dents" on Ahab's furrowed brow symbolize?

❹ ✓ Reading Check
Why are the *Pequod's* planks dented?

from Moby-Dick ◆ 355

❸ Literary Analysis
Symbol

- Have a student volunteer read aloud the paragraph beginning "Soon his steady, ivory stride was heard." Make sure students understand the cause of the "dents" mentioned by Melville's narrator; these are the dents in the wooden planks of the ship's deck caused by Ahab's peg leg.

- Point out that the repetition of the image of dents indicates the presence of a symbol. Draw students' attention to the language Melville uses—*the footprints of his one unsleeping, ever-pacing thought*—to describe the wrinkles in Ahab's brow.

- In addition, point out the connection Melville draws between Ahab's dented brow and the deeper marks left by Ahab's "nervous" steps.

- Ask students the Literary Analysis question on p. 355: What might the "dents" on Ahab's furrowed brow symbolize?
Answer: The dents might symbolize psychological injuries Ahab has suffered in his battle with the great whale.

❹ ✓ Reading Check

Answer: Ahab has dented them walking back and forth with his "bone leg."

CUSTOMIZE INSTRUCTION FOR UNIVERSAL ACCESS

For Less Proficient Readers	For English Learners
Discuss with students why the men are curious and apprehensive. The reasons include that it is unusual for the men to be gathered on this particular deck (the "aft" deck at the stern, or rear, of the ship). Also, the men are wary of Ahab's peculiar behavior as he continues to pace about as if not noticing them. Point out how Melville establishes early on an atmosphere of psychological tension, together with the idea that Ahab is a man with powerful feelings.	Draw students' attention to Melville's use of metaphor and simile to describe Ahab's growing tension (a chick pecking the shell, a stormy horizon). Also draw their attention to possibly confusing descriptive phrasing in the text ("not wholly unapprehensive"). Explain that these writing techniques were common in the nineteenth century. Encourage students to read slowly and carefully and to paraphrase the story whenever possible.

❺ Background

Art

Captain Ahab on the Deck of the Pequod, 1930, by Rockwell Kent

Rockwell Kent made many pen-and-ink drawings, including those that appear in this selection, for the 1930 Lakeside Press edition of *Moby-Dick*, published by Random House, Chicago. Kent was a painter, printmaker, author, illustrator, explorer, and political activist. Use the following question for discussion:

• What evidence of symbolism can you find in this image?
  Possible answer: Ahab's looming shadow might symbolize the destructive effects of his obsession with Moby-Dick.

❻ ▶Critical Viewing

Answer: Students may say that the illustration captures Ahab's implacable, obssesive nature very well.

❼ Reading Strategy

Recognizing Symbols

• Point out that the narrator mentions several times a gold coin brandished by Ahab.

• Ask students the Reading Strategy question on p. 356: What does Ahab's treatment of the gold coin suggest about its presence as a symbol?
  Answer: Ahab's nailing of the coin to the mast of the *Pequod* ensures its central and continual presence throughout the voyage. The gold, worth a fortune to the sailors, thus symbolizes the value that the quest has for Ahab, and the extreme nature of his desire for vengeance.

356

---

gaze curiously at each other, as if marveling how it was that they themselves became so excited at such seemingly purposeless questions.

But, they were all eagerness again, as Ahab, now half-revolving in his pivot hole, with one hand reaching high up a shroud,[4] and tightly, almost convulsively grasping it, addressed them thus:

"All ye mastheaders have before now heard me give orders about a white whale. Look ye! d'ye see this Spanish ounce of gold?"—holding up a broad bright coin to the sun—"it is a sixteen-dollar piece, men. D'ye see it? Mr. Starbuck, hand me yon topmaul."

❼ While the mate was getting the hammer, Ahab, without speaking, was slowly rubbing the gold piece against the skirts of his jacket, as if to heighten its luster, and without using any words was meanwhile lowly humming to himself, producing a sound so strangely muffled and inarticulate that it seemed the mechanical humming of the wheels of his vitality in him.

Receiving the topmaul from Starbuck, he advanced towards the mainmast with the hammer uplifted in one hand, exhibiting the gold with the other, and with a high raised voice exclaiming: "Whosoever of ye raises me a white-headed whale with a wrinkled brow and a crooked jaw; whosoever of ye raises me that white-headed whale, with three holes punctured in his starboard fluke[5]—look ye, whosoever of ye raises me that same white whale, he shall have this gold ounce, my boys!"

"Huzza! huzza!" cried the seamen, as with swinging tarpaulins they hailed the act of nailing the gold to the mast.

"It's a white whale, I say," resumed Ahab, as he threw down the topmaul: "a white whale. Skin your eyes for him, men; look sharp for white water; if ye see but a bubble, sing out."

All this while Tashtego, Daggoo, and Queequeg had looked on with even more intense interest and surprise than the rest, and at the mention of the wrinkled brow and crooked jaw they had started as if each was separately touched by some specific recollection.

"Captain Ahab," said Tashtego, "that white whale must be the same that some call Moby-Dick."

"Moby-Dick?" shouted Ahab. "Do ye know the white whale then, Tash?"

❽ "Does he fantail[6] a little curious, sir, before he goes down?" said the Gay-Header deliberately.

---

4. **shroud** *n.* set of ropes from a ship's side to the masthead.
5. **starboard fluke** (flōōk) *n.* right half of a whale's tail.
6. **fantail** *v.* to spread the tail like a fan.

Captain Ahab on the Deck of the Pequod, Rockwell Kent

❻ ▲ **Critical Viewing**
In what ways does this portrait of Ahab compare or contrast with your mental image of him? **[Compare and Contrast]**

Reading Strategy
Recognizing Symbols
What does Ahab's treatment of the gold coin suggest about its presence as a symbol?

☀ ENRICHMENT: Social Studies Connection

Nantucket

The *Pequod* sails from the island of Nantucket, which is situated in the Atlantic Ocean off the southern coast of Massachusetts, about twenty miles south of Cape Cod and just east and south of Martha's Vineyard. In the late 1700s and early 1800s, Nantucket was one of the world's major whaling centers. At one point during this period, well over one hundred whaling ships used the island as their main port. In the mid-1800s, the whaling industry began to decline and the island developed its other resources.

Invite students to do research on the Internet and elsewhere to find whaling museums or restored seaports that feature whaling ships, tools, and other objects associated with the whaling industry. You might have students send for brochures on various items and exhibits. Such institutions include the Kendall Whaling Museum in Sharon, Massachusetts; the New Bedford Whaling Museum in New Bedford, Massachusetts; and the Cold Spring Harbor Whaling Museum in Cold Spring Harbor, New York.

"And has he a curious spout, too," said Daggoo, "very bushy, even for a parmacetty,[7] and mighty quick, Captain Ahab?"

"And he have one, two, tree—oh! good many iron in him hide, too, Captain," cried Queequeg disjointedly, "all twiske-tee betwisk, like him—him—" faltering hard for a word, and screwing his hand round and round as though uncorking a bottle— "like him—him—"

"Corkscrew!" cried Ahab, "aye, Queequeg, the harpoons lie all twisted and wrenched in him; aye, Daggoo, his spout is a big one, like a whole shock of wheat, and white as a pile of our Nantucket wool after the great annual sheepshearing; aye, Tashtego, and he fantails like a split jib in a squall. Death and devils! men, it is Moby-Dick ye have seen—Moby-Dick— Moby-Dick!"

"Captain Ahab," said Starbuck, who, with Stubb and Flask, had thus far been eyeing his superior with increasing surprise, but at last seemed struck with a thought which somewhat explained all the wonder. "Captain Ahab, I have heard of Moby-Dick—but it was not Moby-Dick that took off thy leg?"

"Who told thee that?" cried Ahab; then pausing, "Aye, Starbuck; aye, my hearties all round; it was Moby-Dick that dismasted me; Moby-Dick that brought me to this dead stump I stand on now. Aye, aye," he shouted with a terrific, loud, animal sob, like that of a heart-stricken moose; "Aye, aye! it was that accursed white whale that razeed me; made a poor pegging lubber[8] for me forever and a day!" Then tossing both arms, with measureless imprecations he shouted out: "Aye, aye! and I'll chase him round Good Hope, and round the Horn, and round the Norway Maelstrom, and round perdition's flames before I give him up. And this is what ye have shipped for, men! to chase that white whale on both sides of land, and over all sides of earth, till he spouts black blood and rolls fin out. What say ye, men, will ye splice hands on it, now? I think ye do look brave."

"Aye, aye!" shouted the harpooneers and seamen, running closer to the excited old man: "A sharp eye for the white whale; a sharp lance for Moby-Dick!"

"God bless ye," he seemed to half sob and half shout. "God bless ye, men. Steward! go draw the great measure of grog. But what's this long face about, Mr. Starbuck; wilt thou not chase the white whale? art not game for Moby-Dick?"

"I am game for his crooked jaw, and for the jaws of Death too, Captain Ahab, if it fairly comes in the way of the business we follow; but I came here to hunt whales, not my commander's vengeance. How many barrels will thy vengeance yield thee even if thou gettest it, Captain Ahab? it will not fetch thee much in our Nantucket market."

---

7. **parmacetty** (pär´mə set´ ē) *n.* dialect for spermaceti, the formal term for a sperm whale, which has a blunt snout.

8. **lubber** (lub´ ər) *n.* slow, clumsy person.

Literary Analysis
Symbol What image of Moby-Dick is created in this discussion?

10 ✓Reading Check
What does Ahab say is his real purpose for making the voyage?

from *Moby-Dick* ◆ 357

8 Literary Analysis
Symbol

• Invite listeners to focus on the details about Moby-Dick that are offered by each speaker. Suggest that students use a graphic organizer like one shown on p. 353 to record these details.

• Ask students the Literary Analysis question on p. 357: What image of Moby-Dick is created in this discussion?
Possible answer: The image of Moby-Dick as an almost super-natural being is created.

9 Background
Whaling Ships

Discuss with students why Ahab's command would surprise the crew. Point out that sailors on a whaler signed on for a share of the net profits. Although some probably hoped for adventure, most sailors simply hoped to capture as many whales as possible so they could sell the valuable whale oil, whalebone, and other whale byproducts. It would be understandable if Ahab's crew were to show reluctance to chase a single whale.

10 ✓Reading Check

Answer: The real purpose is to chase and kill the great white whale, Moby-Dick.

CUSTOMIZE INSTRUCTION FOR UNIVERSAL ACCESS

For Less Proficient Readers	For English Learners
To help students comprehend the text, have them list and discuss the physical traits that Ahab and the crew members say distinguish Moby-Dick from other whales. These include his white color; his unique way of fanning his tail before submerging; his unusual, large, and "bushy" spout; his quickness; and his hide, which contains several iron harpoons.	Help improve students' comprehension with the Identify Chain of Events page in **English Learner's Companion.** Use this page to help students connect the events in the story.

⑪ Literary Analysis

Symbol and Theme

- Have students read this passage and identify references to money and commerce (*Nantucket market, money's, accountants, computed, countinghouse, guineas, premium*).

- Then, ask students how they know Ahab is using business metaphors to emphasize the strength of his desire to catch and kill Moby-Dick. If necessary, point out his explicit reference to "my vengeance" and his physical indication of his heart.

- Ask students the first Literary Analysis question on p. 358: What do Ahab's comments say about the value of money compared with great desire?
  Answer: Ahab views desire—even if it is considered "vengeance"—as far more valuable than money.

⑫ Literary Analysis

Symbol

- Read aloud the passage more than once, so that students can focus on the key ideas of Ahab's speech.

- Help students understand Ahab's references to masks. These tell the reader that the captain believes that the whale's behavior shows it to be acting in response to a mind and will, rather than by animal instincts.

- Ask students the second Literary Analysis question on p. 358: What insights into the whale's symbolic meaning can you gain from a close reading of this passage?
  Answer: Close reading indicates that Ahab (and the reader) must view the whale on both real and symbolic levels. Ahab declares here that he does not care whether the whale acts on its own out of malice or at the direction of another greater will ("Talk not to me of blasphemy, man; I'd strike the sun if it insulted me"). Indeed, the unknowability of the whale's—and by implication God's—motives are the very thing Ahab hates. Because it is hate that drives Ahab, his quest is cast symbolically in this passage as *hubris*, or the placing of the self above the will of God as revealed in nature, including the white whale.

"Nantucket market! Hoot! But come closer, Starbuck; thou requirest a little lower layer. If money's to be the measurer, man, and the accountants have computed their great countinghouse the globe, by girdling it with guineas, one to every three parts of an inch; then, let me tell thee, that my vengeance will fetch a great premium *here!*"

"He smites his chest," whispered Stubb, "what's that for? methinks it rings most vast, but hollow."

"Vengeance on a dumb brute!" cried Starbuck, "that simply smote thee from blindest instinct! Madness! To be enraged with a dumb thing, Captain Ahab, seems blasphemous."

"Hark ye yet again—the little lower layer. All visible objects, man, are but as pasteboard masks. But in each event—in the living act, the undoubted deed—there, some unknown but still reasoning thing puts forth the moldings of its features from behind the unreasoning mask. If man will strike, strike through the mask! How can the prisoner reach outside except by thrusting through the wall? To me, the white whale is that wall, shoved near to me. Sometimes I think there's naught beyond. But 'tis enough. He tasks me; he heaps me; I see in him outrageous strength, with an <u>inscrutable</u> malice sinewing it. That inscrutable thing is chiefly what I hate; and be the white whale agent, or be the white whale principal, I will wreak that hate upon him. Talk not to me of blasphemy, man; I'd strike the sun if it insulted me. For could the sun do that, then could I do the other; since there is ever a sort of fair play herein, jealousy presiding over all creations. But not my master, man, is even that fair play. Who's over me? Truth hath no confines. Take off thine eye! more intolerable than fiends' glarings is a doltish stare! So, so; thou reddenest and palest; my heat has melted thee to anger-glow. But look ye, Starbuck, what is said in heat, that thing unsays itself. There are men from whom warm words are small indignity. I meant not to incense thee. Let it go. Look! see yonder Turkish cheeks of spotted tawn—living, breathing pictures painted by the sun. The pagan leopards—the unrecking and unworshiping things, that live, and seek, and give no reasons for the torrid life they feel! The crew, man, the crew! Are they not one and all with Ahab, in this matter of the whale? See Stubb! he laughs! See yonder Chilean! he snorts to think of it. Stand up amid the general hurricane, thy one tossed sapling cannot, Starbuck! And what is it? Reckon it. 'Tis but to help strike a fin; no wondrous feat for Starbuck. What is it more? From this one poor hunt, then, the best lance out of all Nantucket, surely he will not hang back, when every foremasthand has clutched a whetstone. Ah! constrainings seize thee; I see! the billow lifts thee! Speak, but speak!—Aye, aye! thy silence, then, that voices thee. *(Aside)* Something shot from my dilated nostrils, he has inhaled it in his lungs. Starbuck now is mine; cannot oppose me now, without rebellion."

"God keep me!—keep us all!" murmured Starbuck, lowly.

But in his joy at the enchanted, tacit acquiescence of the mate, Ahab did not hear his foreboding invocation; nor yet the low laugh

Literary Analysis
Symbol and Theme What do Ahab's comments say about the value of money compared with great desire?

inscrutable (in skrōōt′ ə bəl) *adj.* not able to be easily understood

Literary Analysis
Symbol What insights into the whale's symbolic meaning can you gain from a close reading of this passage?

✳ ENRICHMENT: Culture Connection

Hunting Rituals

Ahab gathers his crew on the quarter-deck to begin the hunt for Moby-Dick. The gathering has ceremonial aspects that echo the tradition of centuries of pre-hunt rituals. Tell students that ever since the earliest Americans drummed and sang to address the animal spirits before a hunt, many peoples have believed in the power of ritual to aid their success. For example, before buffalo hunts, the Blackfeet and other Plains Indians held celebrations in which they prayed, danced, sang, smoked, and made offerings to ensure

that the animals would come near enough to be taken.

Have students find out more about pre-hunt rituals in North America or elsewhere. Have them look for similarities and differences among them. Invite students to make class presentations of their findings.

from the hold; nor yet the presaging vibrations of the winds in the cordage; nor yet the hollow flap of the sails against the masts, as for a moment their hearts sank in. For again Starbuck's downcast eyes lighted up with the stubbornness of life; the subterranean laugh died away; the winds blew on; the sails filled out; the ship heaved and rolled as before. Ah, ye admonitions and warnings! why stay ye not when ye come? But rather are ye predictions than warnings, ye shadows! Yet not so much predictions from without, as verifications of the fore-going things within. For with little external to constrain us, the innermost necessities in our being, these still drive us on.

"The measure! the measure!" cried Ahab.

Receiving the brimming pewter, and turning to the harpooneers, he ordered them to produce their weapons. Then ranging them before him near the capstan,[9] with their harpoons in their hands, while his three mates stood at his side with their lances, and the rest of the ship's company formed a circle round the group; he stood for an instant searchingly eyeing every man of his crew. But those wild eyes met his, as the bloodshot eyes of the prairie wolves meet the eye of their leader, ere he rushes on at their head in the trail of the bison; but, alas! only to fall into the hidden snare of the Indian.

"Drink and pass!" he cried, handing the heavy charged flagon to the nearest seamen. "The crew alone now drink. Round with it, round! Short drafts—long swallows, men; 'tis hot as Satan's hoof. So, so; it goes round excellently. It spiralizes in ye; forks out at the serpent-snapping eye. Well done; almost drained. That way it went, this way it comes. Hand it me—here's a hollow! Men, ye seem the years; so brimming life is gulped and gone. Steward, refill!

"Attend now, my braves. I have mustered ye all round this capstan; and ye mates, flank me with your lances; and ye harpooneers, stand there with your irons; and ye, stout mariners, ring me in, that I may in some sort revive a noble custom of my fishermen fathers before

---

9. **capstan** (kap´ sten) *n.* large cylinder, turned by hand, around which cables are wound.

Literature
in context History Connection

⓭

The Legend of the White Whale

Herman Melville's whaling experiences in the South Pacific provided him with rich material for his writing. While working aboard the whaling ship *Acushnet*, he often heard stories about an elusive, monstrous white whale. Melville expanded this legend—adding his knowledge of the day-to-day workings of a whaler—into his best-known work, *Moby-Dick*.

⓮ ✔**Reading Check**

With whom does Ahab share a drink? For what purpose?

from Moby-Dick ◆ 359

⓭ **Background**

Melville

When the *Acushnet* rounded Cape Horn and crossed the Pacific Ocean to the Marquesas Islands in 1842, Melville deserted the ship and headed inland. There he encountered the Typees, an island tribe rumored to be cannibals. To Melville's surprise, the people were peaceful and generous. He was to use this experience later as the basis for his 1846 novel *Typee*.

⓮ ✔**Reading Check**

Answer: Ahab shares a pre-hunt drink with his crew in order to get them to pledge their success in the hunt for Moby-Dick.

CUSTOMIZE INSTRUCTION FOR UNIVERSAL ACCESS

For Less Proficient Readers	For Advanced Readers
Moby-Dick is a huge novel, and when it is read in its entirety, the characters grow in detail and fullness before the reader's eyes. In excerpts like these, students may need help delineating the characters. For especially challenging passages, have students read each paragraph twice—once silently and once aloud. Help students identify any fragments of dialogue or description that seem important or suggestive about a particular character.	Point out that Ahab could be described as suffering what the Greeks called *hubris*, or excessive pride. Invite these students to define the term, to identify other tragic heroes who share this character trait, and to lead the class in a discussion of how hubris might be said to apply to Ahab.

Symbol

- Encourage students to visualize or model what the harpooners are doing here, as well as what Ahab has in mind for them.

- If necessary, help students understand that the harpooners are removing the iron part of their harpoons and up-ending the sockets to use as cups, which Ahab will fill with drink.

▶ Monitor Progress Ask students the Literary Analysis question on p. 360: What is Ahab's symbolic purpose in having his harpooners drink from their weapons?

Answer: Ahab may wish them to participate in a pre-hunt ritual that symbolizes a common mission and allegiance. The act of drinking from their weapons symbolically binds them together as extensions of Ahab's vision and vengeance. Students may mention that the drinking from the "chalices" is reminiscent of parts of many religious rituals in which people drink wine or holy water to sanctify a blessing or rite.

16 Vocabulary Development

Latin Prefix mal-

- Point out the word *maledictions* in the bracketed sentence. Tell students that this prefix means "bad."

- Have students look up this word in a dictionary to find its literal meaning.

- As a class, have students suggest other words that contain this prefix.

- Possibilities include: malicious, malign, malodorous, maladroit Have them define each word, using a dictionary for any unfamiliar words.

---

me. O men, you will yet see that—Ha! boy, come back? bad pennies come not sooner. Hand it me. Why, now, this pewter had run brimming again, wer't not thou St. Vitus' imp[10]—away, thou ague![11]

"Advance, ye mates! cross your lances full before me. Well done! Let me touch the axis." So saying, with extended arm, he grasped the three level, radiating lances at their crossed center; while so doing, suddenly and nervously twitched them; meanwhile glancing intently from Starbuck to Stubb; from Stubb to Flask. It seemed as though, by some nameless, interior volition, he would fain have shocked into them the same fiery emotion accumulated within the Leyden jar[12] of his own magnetic life. The three mates quailed before his strong, sustained, and mystic aspect. Stubb and Flask looked sideways from him; the honest eye of Starbuck fell downright.

"In vain!" cried Ahab; "but, maybe, 'tis well. For did ye three but once take the full-forced shock, then mine own electric thing, *that* had perhaps expired from out me. Perchance, too, it would have dropped ye dead. Perchance ye need it not. Down lances! And now, ye mates, I do appoint ye three cupbearers to my three pagan kinsmen there—yon three most honorable gentlemen and noblemen, my valiant harpooneers. Disdain the task? What, when the great Pope washes the feet of beggars, using his tiara for ewer? Oh, my sweet cardinals! your own condescension, that shall bend ye to it. I do not order ye; ye will it. Cut your seizings and draw the poles, ye harpooneers!"

Silently obeying the order, the three harpooneers now stood with the detached iron part of their harpoons, some three feet long, held, barbs up, before him.

"Stab me not with that keen steel! Cant them; cant them over! know ye not the goblet end? Turn up the socket! So, so; now, ye cupbearers, advance. The irons! take them; hold them while I fill!" Forthwith, slowly going from one officer to the other, he brimmed the **15** harpoon sockets with the fiery waters from the pewter.

"Now, three to three, ye stand. Commend the murderous chalices! Bestow them, ye who are now made parties to this indissoluble league. Ha! Starbuck! but the deed is done! Yon ratifying sun now waits to sit upon it. Drink, ye harpooneers! drink and swear, ye men that man the deathful whaleboat's bow—Death to Moby-Dick! God hunt us all, if we do not hunt Moby-Dick to his death!" The long, barbed steel goblets were lifted; and to cries and <u>maledictions</u> against **16** the white whale, the spirits were simultaneously quaffed down with a hiss. Starbuck paled, and turned, and shivered. Once more, and finally, the replenished pewter went the rounds among the frantic crew; when, waving his free hand to them, they all dispersed; and Ahab retired within his cabin.

---

10. **St. Vitus' imp** offspring of St. Vitus, the patron saint of people stricken with the nervous disorder chorea, which is characterized by irregular, jerking movements.
11. **ague** (ā′ gyo͞o) *n.* a chill or fit of shivering.
12. **Leyden** (līd′ ən) **jar** *n.* glass jar coated inside and out with tinfoil and having a metal rod connected to the inner lining; used to condense static electricity.

Literary Analysis
Symbol What is Ahab's symbolic purpose in having his harpooners drink from their weapons?

maledictions (mal′ ə dik′ shənz) *n.* curses

✺ ENRICHMENT: Literature Connection

Moby-Dick

Moby-Dick is a long and complex novel that can be divided into five parts. In the first part, the reader meets Ishmael, the story's narrator, and learns of his relationship with the harpooner Queequeg. The chapter "The Quarter-Deck" appears in the next part of the book, the section that develops the character of Ahab and the conflict between Ahab and Moby-Dick. Parts three and four are concerned with the business of the *Pequod* and the general subject of whales and whaling. "The Chase—Third Day" is the last chapter

of the fifth and final part, in which Melville focuses on the search for—and confrontation with—the great whale. In a one-page epilogue, Ishmael tells how he survived to tell his tale: He was rescued by another ship, the *Rachel*, "that in her retracing search after her missing children, only found another orphan."

Melville's reference is to the Bible's book of Jeremiah in which Rachel is said to be weeping for her children, "because they were not."

Moby-Dick, Rockwell Kent

⓱

After Moby-Dick has been sighted in the Pacific Ocean, the Pequod's boats pursue the whale for two days. One of the boats has been sunk, and Ahab's ivory leg has been broken off. However, as the next day dawns, the chase continues.

The Chase—Third Day

The morning of the third day dawned fair and fresh, and once more the solitary night man at the foremasthead was relieved by crowds of the day-light lookouts, who dotted every mast and almost every spar.

"D'ye see him?" cried Ahab; but the whale was not yet in sight.

"In his infallible wake, though; but follow that wake, that's all. Helm there; steady, as thou goest, and hast been going. What a lovely day again! were it a new-made world, and made for a summerhouse to the angels, and this morning the first of its throwing open to them, a fairer day could not dawn upon that world. Here's food for thought, had Ahab time to think; but Ahab never thinks; he only feels, feels, feels; that's tingling enough for mortal man! to think's audacity. God only has that right and privilege. Thinking is, or ought to be, a coolness and a calmness; and our poor hearts throb, and our poor brains beat too much for that. And yet, I've sometimes thought my brain was very calm—frozen calm, this old skull cracks so, like a glass in which the contents turned to ice, and shiver it. And still this hair is growing now; this moment growing, and heat must breed it; but no, it's like that sort of common grass that will grow anywhere, between the earthy clefts of Greenland ice or in Vesuvius lava. How the wild winds blow it; they whip it about me as the torn shreds of split sails lash the tossed ship they cling to. A vile wind that has no doubt blown ere this through prison corridors and cells, and wards of hospitals, and ventilated them, and now comes blowing hither as innocent as fleeces.[13] Out upon it!—it's tainted. Were I the wind, I'd blow no more on such a wicked, miserable world. I'd crawl somewhere to a cave, and slink there. And yet, 'tis a noble and heroic thing, the wind! who ever conquered it? In every fight it has the last and bitterest blow. Run tilting at it, and you but run through it. Ha! a coward wind that strikes stark-naked men, but will not stand to receive

13. **fleeces** (flēs´ ez) *n.* sheep.

⓳

▲ **Critical Viewing**
Draw an inference about the size of the whale pictured. On what details do you base your inference? **[Infer]**

Reading Strategy
Recognizing Symbols
What does the wind symbolize to Ahab?

✓ **Reading Check**
For how long has the *Pequod* pursued Moby-Dick?

from *Moby-Dick* ◆ 361

⓱ Background

Art

Moby-Dick, 1930, by Rockwell Kent

Throughout his life, Kent tested his devotion to nature. He spent extended time in some of the planet's coldest and most remote, severe environments. Kent captured these experiences in his drawings, paintings, illustrations, and prints in some of the most authentic evocations of nature's power in twentieth-century art. Use the following question for discussion:

• What evidence of symbolism can you find in this image? **Possible answer:** The small whales are fleeing Moby-Dick as the giant surfaces. The act of surfacing might represent the destiny of the whale in this novel.

⓲ ▶ Critical Viewing

Answer: Students may infer that the whale pictured here is huge. Their inference might be based on the proximity of three small whales. If these are swimming in the vicinity of the large one, then the latter is indeed enormous.

⓳ Reading Strategy

Recognizing Symbols

• Have a student volunteer read this passage as you—or students—write on the chalkboard words and phrases that Melville uses to characterize the wind.

• Lead students to see that these images include *wild winds, vile wind, tainted, noble and heroic thing, coward wind, bodiless, most special . . . most cunning, glorious and gracious,* and so on.

▶ **Monitor Progress** Ask students the Reading Strategy question on p. 361: What does the wind symbolize to Ahab? **Answer:** The wind symbolizes the maddening, sometimes ineffable, noble, and glorious power of nature. He absolves it of malice, however, unlike Moby-Dick.

⓴ ✓ Reading Check

Answer: The *Pequod* is in its third day of pursuing Moby-Dick.

CUSTOMIZE INSTRUCTION FOR UNIVERSAL ACCESS

For Special Needs Students

These students may benefit from seeing some or all of a dramatized version of Melville's sprawling story. Of course, *Moby-Dick* has all the elements of a blockbuster movie—compelling characters, exotic locations, and one of the largest movie "villains" imaginable—and filmmakers have tried a number of times to bring to the screen Melville's tale of the great white whale.

One of the best attempts was made by director John

Huston, who cast Gregory Peck as Ahab in the 1956 film *Moby Dick.* Screen a video of this production for students. Have students view one or more scenes in order to help them appreciate the characterizations of Ahab, Starbuck, and Ishmael; the evocations of the whale as a symbol of nature's power and of the untamable; and the various conflicts that drive the story forward.

361

Literature in Context

In the biblical tale, the great fish is portrayed as the embodiment of evil. Jonah is sent by God to the city of Ninevah to prophesy about the city's wickedness. To escape God's order, Jonah heads in the opposite direction. However, his ship is engulfed by an extraordinary storm. Knowing that his disobedience has caused the storm, Jonah asks to be thrown overboard. He is swallowed by a "great fish," stays inside it for three days and nights, and is finally vomited onto land. The ninth chapter of Melville's *Moby-Dick* addresses the story of Jonah directly.

22 Literary Analysis

Symbol

• Have a student volunteer read this passage in which Ahab addresses the masthead and then begins to compare himself to it.

• Ask students the Literary Analysis question on p. 363: What symbolic meaning do you find in the comparison between Ahab and the mast?

• As students consider the question, you might list words and phrases from their responses in a Venn diagram on the chalkboard. This diagram can help students see the similarities and differences between Ahab and the masthead. **Answer:** Students may say that to Ahab the mast represents his resolve in his quest for Moby-Dick. The mast stands alone, tall, strong, and long lasting, as he does in his single-mindedness.

a single blow. Even Ahab is a braver thing—a nobler thing than *that*. Would now the wind but had a body but all the things that most exasperate and outrage mortal man, all these things are bodiless, but only bodiless as objects, not as agents. There's a most special, a most cunning, oh, a most malicious difference! And yet, I say again, and swear it now, that there's something all glorious and gracious in the wind. These warm trade winds, at least, that in the clear heavens blow straight on, in strong and steadfast, vigorous mildness; and veer not from their mark, however the baser currents of the sea may turn and tack, and mightiest Mississippis of the land swift and swerve about, uncertain where to go at last. And by the eternal poles! these same trades that so directly blow my good ship on; these trades, or something like them—something so unchangeable, and full as strong, blow my keeled soul along! To it! Aloft there! What d'ye see?"

"Nothing, sir."

"Nothing! and noon at hand! The doubloon[14] goes a-begging! See the sun! Aye, aye, it must be so. I've oversailed him. How, got the start? Aye, he's chasing me now; not I, him—that's bad; I might have known it, too. Fool! the lines—the harpoons he's towing.

Aye, aye, I have run him by last night. About! about! Come down, all of ye, but the regular lookouts! Man the braces!"

Steering as she had done, the wind had been somewhat on the Pequod's quarter, so that now being pointed in the reverse direction, the braced ship sailed hard upon the breeze as she rechurned the cream in her own white wake.

"Against the wind he now steers for the open jaw," murmured Starbuck to himself, as he coiled the new-hauled main brace upon the rail. "God keep us, but already my bones feel damp within me, and from the inside wet my flesh. I misdoubt me that I disobey my God in obeying him!"

"Stand by to sway me up!" cried Ahab, advancing to the hempen basket.[15] "We should meet him soon."

"Aye, aye, sir," and straightway Starbuck did Ahab's bidding, and once more Ahab swung on high.

A whole hour now passed; gold-beaten out to ages. Time itself now held long breaths with keen suspense. But at last, some three points off the weather bow, Ahab descried the spout again, and instantly from the three mastheads three shrieks went up as if the tongues of fire had voiced it.

"Forehead to forehead I meet thee, this third time, Moby-Dick! On deck there!—brace sharper up; crowd her into the wind's eye. He's too far off to lower yet, Mr. Starbuck. The sails shake! Stand over that helmsman with

---

14. **doubloon** (du blōōn´) *n.* old Spanish gold coin. (Ahab offered it as a reward to the first man to spot the whale.)

15. **hempen basket** rope basket. (The basket was constructed earlier by Ahab, so that he could be raised, by means of a pulley device, to the top of the mainmast.)

Literature in context Humanities C

21 *The Whale as Archetype*

An archetype is a basic or primordial image that recurs so consistently across cultures and time that it is considered universal. The term comes from the writings of Swiss psychologist Carl Jung (1875–1961), who believed that certain human experiences have been transferred through generations. According to Jung, it is this shared genetic memory, or "collective unconscious," that explains why archetypes evoke similar strong feelings in people of all cultures.

The whale had made many appearances in myth, folklore, literature, and art well before Melville used it as a central symbol in *Moby-Dick*. Perhaps the most famous is the biblical tale in which Jonah is swallowed by a whale and then cast ashore. Because the whale is the largest of all earthly creatures, its image evokes emotions of fear, awe, and respect, as well as a sense of the enormity of nature. In *Moby-Dick*, Melville understood and used these archetypal associations to create fiction of enduring power.

☀ **ENRICHMENT: Science Connection**

Whales

In existence for over ten million years, whales are among the world's most ancient and intelligent animals. They also are the largest: The blue whale is heavier and longer than any known dinosaur. Invite students to find out more about these amazing mammals. They can find interesting information as they work to answer questions like these:

1. How do whales keep warm? How deep do they dive?

2. How are the swimming methods of whales and of fish different? How far can whales swim?

3. What is the world's whale population today? Are whales in danger of extinction?

4. How do whales, porpoises, and dolphins differ?

5. How do whales communicate with one another?

Invite students to share their findings.

a topmaul! So, so; he travels fast, and I must down. But let me have one more good round look aloft here at the sea; there's time for that. An old, old sight, and yet somehow so young; aye, and not changed a wink since I first saw it, a boy, from the sand hills of Nantucket! The same!—the same!—the same to Noah as to me. There's a soft shower to leeward. Such lovely leewardings! They must lead somewhere—to something else than common land, more palmy than the palms. Leeward! the white whale goes that way; look to windward, then; the better if the bitterer quarter. But good-bye, good-bye, old masthead! What's this?—green? aye, tiny mosses in these warped cracks. No such green weather stains on Ahab's head! There's the difference now between man's old age and matter's. But aye, old mast, we both grow old together; sound in our hulls, though, are we not, my ship? Aye, minus a leg, that's all. By heaven this dead wood has the better of my live flesh every way. I can't compare with it; and I've known some ships made of dead trees outlast the lives of men made of the most vital stuff of vital fathers. What's that he said? he should still go before me, my pilot; and yet to be seen again? But where? Will I have eyes at the bottom of the sea, supposing I descend those endless stairs? and all night I've been sailing from him, wherever he did sink to. Aye, aye, like many more thou told'st direful truth as touching thyself, O Parsee; but, Ahab, there thy shot fell short. Good-bye, masthead—keep a good eye upon the whale, the while I'm gone. We'll talk tomorrow, nay, tonight, when the white whale lies down there, tied by head and tail."

He gave the word; and still gazing round him, was steadily lowered through the cloven blue air to the deck.

In due time the boats were lowered; but as standing in his shallop's stern, Ahab just hovered upon the point of the descent, he waved to the mate—who held one of the tackle ropes on deck—and bade him pause.

"Starbuck!"

"Sir?"

"For the third time my soul's ship starts upon this voyage, Starbuck."

"Aye, sir, thou wilt have it so."

"Some ships sail from their ports, and ever afterwards are missing, Starbuck!"

"Truth, sir: saddest truth."

"Some men die at ebb tide; some at low water; some at the full of the flood—and I feel now like a billow that's all one crested comb, Starbuck. I am old—shake hands with me, man."

Their hands met; their eyes fastened; Starbuck's tears the glue.

"Oh, my captain, my captain!—noble heart—go not—go not!—see, it's a brave man that weeps; how great the agony of the persuasion then!"

"Lower away!"—cried Ahab, tossing the mate's arm from him. "Stand by the crew!"

In an instant the boat was pulling round close under the stern.

"The sharks! the sharks!" cried a voice from the low cabin window there; "O master, my master, come back!"

Literary Analysis
Symbol What symbolic meaning do you find in the comparison between Ahab and the mast?

✓Reading Check
What does Starbuck beg Ahab to do?

from *Moby-Dick* ◆ 363

㉓ Background
Parsee
The Parsee is a Persian sailor who disappeared in the previous chapter of the novel. Earlier in the book, a prediction was made that he would die before Ahab but that Ahab would see him once more before his own death.

㉔ Critical Thinking
Analyze
- Have three students—playing Ahab, Starbuck, and the narrator—read aloud this passage.
- Ask students to explain what is happening in this exchange between Ahab and Starbuck. **Answer:** Students may respond that Ahab is expressing fear and apprehension prior to this (his next attempt to kill Moby-Dick) and that Starbuck is making one last futile effort to persuade Ahab to forgo the quest.

㉕ ✓Reading Check
Answer: Starbuck begs Ahab not to pursue Moby-Dick in a small harpooning boat.

26 Reading Strategy

Recognizing Symbols

- As you read aloud this passage, ask students to think about the possible symbolic meaning of the sharks that surround Ahab and follow him in his small boat.

- Help students understand that the sharks separate Ahab further from his crew. Moreover, they suggest in a symbolic way that Ahab's pursuit of the white whale is foolish and doomed. The sharks add an extra element of danger; they are harbingers of death.

27 Background

Art

Moby-Dick, 1930, by Rockwell Kent

This is another of Rockwell's pen-and-ink drawings for the Lakeside Press edition of *Moby-Dick.* Use the following question for discussion.

- What evidence of symbolism can you find in this image? **Possible answer:** Although the whale is largely out of sight, it is responsible for the chaos and destruction portrayed in the image. The whale's partial concealment beneath the sea may symbolize the "masked," "inscrutable" malice that Ahab sees in Moby-Dick's actions.

28 ▶ Critical Viewing

Answer: Students may respond that the artist used many details from *Moby-Dick* to create this illustration, among them the descriptions of the boats, harpoons, and lines, as well as the descriptions of the size, speed, and power of Moby-Dick as he dives and surfaces.

29 Reading Strategy

Recognizing Symbols

- Tell students that three is a traditional symbol echoing the trinity in Christian belief. The third number often represents finality.

- Ask students to explain the significance of Starbuck's reference to the number three here. **Answer:** Usually the voice of practicality, Starbuck now recognizes the grim meaning of the three-day chase. Ahab and the crew are now in the third day, and Starbuck seems to sense a mystical significance in the length of time the chase has taken.

But Ahab heard nothing; for his own voice was high-lifted then; and the boat leaped on.

Yet the voice spake true; for scarce had he pushed from the ship, **26** when numbers of sharks, seemingly rising from out the dark waters beneath the hull, maliciously snapped at the blades of the oars, every time they dipped in the water; and in this way accompanied the boat with their bites. It is a thing not uncommonly happening to the whaleboats in those swarming seas; the sharks at times apparently following them in the same <u>prescient</u> way that vultures hover over the banners of marching regiments in the east. But these were the first sharks that had been observed by the *Pequod* since the White Whale had been first descried; and whether it was that Ahab's crew were all such tiger-yellow barbarians, and therefore their flesh more musky to the senses of the sharks—a matter sometimes well known to affect them—however it was, they seemed to follow that one boat without molesting the others.

"Heart of wrought steel!" murmured Starbuck gazing over the side, and following with his eyes the receding boat—"canst thou yet ring boldly to that sight?—lowering thy keel among ravening sharks, and fol-**29** lowed by them, open-mouthed to the chase; and this the critical third day?—For when three days flow together in one continuous intense pursuit; be sure the first is the morning, the second the noon, and the third the evening and the end of that thing—be that end what it may. Oh! my God! what is this that shoots through me, and leaves me so deadly calm, yet expectant—fixed at the top of a shudder! Future things swim before me, as in empty outlines and skeletons; all the past is somehow grown dim. Mary, girl; thou fadest in pale glories behind me; boy! I seem to see but thy eyes grown wondrous blue.[16] Strangest problems of life seem clearing; but clouds sweep between—Is my journey's end coming? My legs feel faint; like his who has footed it all day. Feel thy heart—beats it yet? Stir thyself, Starbuck!—stave it off—move, move! speak aloud!—Masthead there! See ye my boy's hand on the hill?—Crazed—aloft there!—keep thy keenest eye upon the boats—mark well the whale!—Ho! again!—drive off that hawk! see! he pecks—he tears the vane"—pointing to the red flag flying at the maintruck—"Ha,

---

16. Mary . . . blue reference to Starbuck's wife and son.

prescient (presh′ənt) *adj.* having foreknowledge

Moby-Dick, Rockwell Kent

28 ▲ **Critical Viewing** What details from *Moby-Dick* did the artist probably use to create this illustration? **[Hypothesize]**

☀ ENRICHMENT: Music Connection

Whale Songs

Some people—scientists and musicians alike—are fascinated by the mysterious, mournful, musical sounds whales make as they communicate with one another. Their groans, yips, and wails can carry many miles through and across the water. Humpback whales, in particular, are skillful performers: Each male sings its own unique song (which can last for up to thirty-five minutes) over and over again.

Obtain recordings of whale songs to play for students. For example, on the Judy Collins album *Whales and Nightingales,* the traditional sea song "Farewell to Tarwathie" incorporates melodies of the humpback whale. Invite students to freewrite in response to the sounds they hear.

he soars away with it!—Where's the old man now? see'st thou that sight, oh Ahab!—shudder, shudder!"

The boats had not gone very far, when by a signal from the mast-heads—a downward pointed arm, Ahab knew that the whale had sounded; but intending to be near him at the next rising, he held on his way a little sideways from the vessel; the becharmed crew maintaining the profoundest silence, as the head-beat waves hammered and hammered against the opposing bow.

"Drive, drive in your nails, oh ye waves! to their uttermost heads drive them in! ye but strike a thing without a lid; and no coffin and no hearse can be mine:—and hemp only can kill me! Ha! ha!"

Suddenly the waters around them slowly swelled in broad circles; then quickly upheaved, as if sideways sliding from a submerged berg of ice, swiftly rising to the surface. A low rumbling sound was heard; a subterraneous hum; and then all held their breaths; as bedraggled with trailing ropes, and harpoons, and lances, a vast form shot lengthwise, but obliquely from the sea. Shrouded in a thin drooping veil of mist, it hovered for a moment in the rainbowed air; and then fell swamping back into the deep. Crushed thirty feet upwards, the waters flashed for an instant like heaps of fountains, then brokenly sank in a shower of flakes, leaving the circling surface creamed like new milk round the marble trunk of the whale.

"Give way!" cried Ahab to the oarsmen, and the boats darted forward to the attack; but maddened by yesterday's fresh irons that corroded in him, Moby-Dick seemed combinedly possessed by all the angels that fell from heaven. The wide tiers of welded tendons overspreading his broad white forehead, beneath the transparent skin, looked knitted together; as head on, he came churning his tail among the boats; and once more flailed them apart; spilling out the irons and lances from the two mates' boats, and dashing in one side of the upper part of their bows, but leaving Ahab's almost without a scar.

While Daggoo and Queequeg were stopping the strained planks; and as the whale swimming out from them, turned, and showed one entire flank as he shot by them again; at that moment a quick cry went up. Lashed round and round to the fish's back; pinioned in the turns upon turns in which, during the past night, the whale had reeled the involutions of the lines around him, the half-torn body of the Parsee was seen; his sable raiment frayed to shreds; his distended eyes turned full upon old Ahab.

The harpoon dropped from his hand.

"Befooled, befooled!"—drawing in a long lean breath—"Aye, Parsee! I see thee again—Aye, and thou goest before; and this, this then is the hearse that thou didst promise. But I hold thee to the last letter of thy word. Where is the second hearse? Away, mates, to the ship! those boats are useless now; repair them if ye can in time, and return to me; if not, Ahab is enough to die—Down, men! the first thing that but offers to jump from this boat I stand in, that thing I harpoon. Ye are not other men, but my arms and my legs; and so obey me—Where's the whale? gone down again?"

Literary Analysis
Symbol What symbolic meaning is suggested by the description of the whale's behavior as he breaks the water's surface?

Reading Strategy
Recognizing Symbols What does Ahab realize when he sees Parsee's body lashed to Moby-Dick?

☑ **Reading Check**
What happens to Parsee?

from *Moby-Dick* ◆ 365

---

30 Literary Analysis
Symbol

- If necessary, draw students' attention to the import of what is about to happen: Moby-Dick is about to surface. Point out that—given the symbolic associations Melville has established already for the white whale—the descriptive details of the whale's appearance are bound to carry symbolic meaning.

- Ask students the Literary Analysis question on p. 365: What symbolic meaning is suggested by the description of the whale's behavior as he breaks the water's surface?
  Answer: The description of the whale's behavior, rising slowly at first so that the water shows mysterious portents of his presence, then bursting from the sea into the air and seeming to hang suspended there, symbolizes Moby-Dick's near-supernatural status as Ahab's nemesis.

31 Reading Strategy
Recognizing Symbols

- If necessary, remind students of the identity of the Parsee and of his prophecy regarding his own and Ahab's death (see p. 363).

- Ask students the Reading Strategy question on p. 365: What does Ahab realize when he sees the Parsee's body lashed to Moby-Dick?
  Answer: He realizes that his own death is at hand.

32 ☑ Reading Check
Answer: He has died and remains lashed to the body of Moby-Dick.

CUSTOMIZE INSTRUCTION FOR UNIVERSAL ACCESS

For Less Proficient Readers	For English Learners
The paragraph beginning "Suddenly the waters" marks the start of the dramatic final clash with Moby-Dick. Encourage students to pause here to picture the sudden appearance of the whale and its powerful movements. Invite them to imagine the spray, the sounds, and the changing textures of the surface of the water as the giant emerges from, and then dives back into, the depths. You might encourage students to draw their own illustrations of this dramatic passage.	Encourage students to use the illustrations accompanying the selection to help them picture and understand the action. Have them note key details that they find in the illustrations that add meaning to what they encounter in the text. Then have students share and discuss these details with other students.

Symbol and Theme

- Remind sudents that every symbol functions on two levels—a literal meaning and a larger meaning—and that a theme is one of a literary work's central messages.

- Ask students the Literary Analysis question on p. 366: What does Melville mean when he describes Ahab as being tormented by "far other hammers?"
Possible response: He means that Ahab briefly feels a stab of regret and remorse when he passes the *Pequod* and sees his men working hard to repair damage Moby-Dick has done.

34 Critical Thinking

Speculate

- Read this passage aloud and ask students to identify the surprising idea that the narrator seems to be suggesting. If necessary, point out that Ishmael is suggesting that Moby-Dick may be giving up the fight.

- Invite students to say what they think will happen next.
Answer: Students might respond that because of what has happened up to this point, the fight with Moby-Dick is far from over. In fact, catastrophe may yet result.

But he looked too nigh the boat; for as if bent upon escaping with the corpse he bore, and as if the particular place of the last encounter had been but a stage in his leeward voyage, Moby-Dick was now again steadily swimming forward; and had almost passed the ship—which thus far had been sailing in the contrary direction to him, though for the present her headway had been stopped. He seemed swimming with his utmost velocity, and now only intent upon pursuing his own straight path in the sea.

"Oh! Ahab," cried Starbuck, "not too late is it, even now, the third day, to desist. See! Moby-Dick seeks thee not. It is thou, thou, that madly seekest him!"

Setting sail to the rising wind, the lonely boat was swiftly impelled to leeward, by both oars and canvas. And at last when Ahab was sliding by the vessel, so near as plainly to distinguish Starbuck's face as he leaned over the rail, he hailed him to turn the vessel about, and follow him, not too swiftly, at a judicious interval. Glancing upwards he saw Tashtego, Queequeg, and Daggoo, eagerly mounting to the three mast-heads; while the oarsmen were rocking in the two staved boats which had just been hoisted to the side, and were busily at work in repairing them, one after the other, through the portholes, as he sped, he also caught flying glimpses of Stubb and Flask, busying themselves on deck among bundles of new irons and lances. As he saw all this; as he heard the hammers in the broken boats; far other hammers seemed driving a nail into his heart. But he rallied. And now marking that the vane or flag was gone from the main masthead, he shouted to Tashtego, who had just gained that perch, to descend again for another flag, and a hammer and nails, and so nail it to the mast.

Whether fagged by the three days' running chase, and the resistance to his swimming in the knotted hamper he bore; or whether it was some latent deceitfulness and malice in him: whichever was true, the White Whale's way now began to abate, as it seemed, from the boat so rapidly nearing him once more; though indeed the whale's last start had not been so long a one as before. And still as Ahab glided over the waves the unpitying sharks accompanied him; and so <u>pertinaciously</u> stuck to the boat; and so continually bit at the plying oars, that the blades became jagged and crunched, and left small splinters in the sea, at almost every dip.

"Heed them not! those teeth but give new rowlocks to your oars. Pull on! 'tis the better rest, the sharks' jaw than the yielding water."

"But at every bite, sir, the thin blades grow smaller and smaller!"

"They will last long enough! pull on!—But who can tell"—he muttered—"whether these sharks swim to feast on the whale or on Ahab?—But pull on! Aye, all alive, now—we near him. The helm! take the helm! let me pass"—and so saying, two of the oarsmen helped him forward to the bows of the still flying boat.

At length as the craft was cast to one side, and ran ranging along with the White Whale's flank, he seemed strangely oblivious of its advance—as the whale sometimes will—and Ahab was fairly within

Literary Analysis
Symbol and Theme
What does Melville mean when he describes Ahab as being tormented by "far other hammers?"

pertinaciously (pu̇r´ tə nā´ shəs lē) *adv.* holding firmly to some purpose

---

❁ ENRICHMENT: Career Connection

Cetology

Cetology is the branch of zoology that deals with the study of cetaceans, a mammalian order that includes whales and dolphins. Oceanography is the study of the ocean environments, including analysis of the water, ocean depths, sea beds, animals, and plants. Invite interested students to research what kinds of work scientists at the cutting edge of these branches of science are doing currently. To research today's cetology or oceanography issues, students can use the Internet, books, scientific journals, or magazines such as *Nature* or *Natural History*. Students might even interview scientists who are doing research in either field. Suggest that students get started on their research by talking with their science teachers about the best research paths to follow.

the smoky mountain mist, which, thrown off from the whale's spout, curled round his great Monadnock[17] hump; he was even thus close to him; when, with body arched back, and both arms lengthwise high-lifted to the poise, he darted his fierce iron, and his far fiercer curse into the hated whale. As both steel and curse sank to the socket, as if sucked into a morass, Moby-Dick sidewise writhed; spasmodically rolled his nigh flank against the bow, and, without staving a hole in it, so suddenly canted the boat over, that had it not been for the elevated part of the gunwale to which he then clung, Ahab would once more have been tossed into the sea. As it was, three of the oarsmen—who foreknew not the precise instant of the dart, and were therefore unprepared for its effects—these were flung out; but so fell, that, in an instant two of them clutched the gunwale again, and rising to its level on a combing wave, hurled themselves bodily inboard again; the third man helplessly dropping astern, but still afloat and swimming.

Almost simultaneously, with a mighty volition of ungraduated, instantaneous swiftness, the White Whale darted through the weltering sea. But when Ahab cried out to the steersman to take new turns with the line, and hold it so; and commanded the crew to turn round on their seats, and tow the boat up to the mark; the moment the treacherous line felt that double strain and tug, it snapped in the empty air!

"What breaks in me? Some sinew cracks!—'tis whole again; oars! oars! Burst in upon him!"

Hearing the tremendous rush of the sea-crashing boat, the whale wheeled round to present his blank forehead at bay; but in that evolution, catching sight of the nearing black hull of the ship; seemingly seeing in it the source of all his persecutions; bethinking it—it may be—a larger and nobler foe; of a sudden, he bore down upon its advancing prow, smiting his jaws amid fiery showers of foam.

Ahab staggered; his hand smote his forehead. "I grow blind; hands! stretch out before me that I may yet grope my way. Is't night?"

"The whale! The ship!" cried the cringing oarsmen.

"Oars! oars! Slope downwards to thy depths. O sea that ere it be forever too late, Ahab may slide this last, last time upon his mark! I see: the ship! the ship! Dash on, my men! will ye not save my ship?"

But as the oarsmen violently forced their boat through the sledge-hammering seas, the before whale-smitten bow-ends of two planks burst through, and in an instant almost, the temporarily disabled boat lay nearly level with the waves; its half-wading, splashing crew, trying hard to stop the gap and bale out the pouring water.

Meantime, for that one beholding instant, Tashtego's masthead hammer remained suspended in his hand; and the red flag, half wrapping him as with a plaid, then streamed itself straight out from him, as his own forward-flowing heart; while Starbuck and Stubb, standing upon the bowsprit beneath, caught sight of the down-coming monster just as soon as he.

---

17. **Monadnock** (mə nad′ näk) mountain in New Hampshire.

Literary Analysis
Symbol What symbolic connection between his own body and the boat does Ahab seem to feel?

Reading Strategy
Recognizing Symbols What is symbolized by the red flag streaming out from Tashtego?

 Reading Check
What happens to the boat carrying Ahab when it nears Moby-Dick?

from Moby-Dick ◆ 367

35 Literary Analysis
Symbol

- Have students note the rapid chain of events in the bracketed passage: Moby-Dick, having nearly turned the boat over, swims swiftly away. Ahab orders the line connecting the boat to the whale to be pulled taut, to pull the boat closer to the whale. The rope snaps in two, and Ahab cries out.
- Then, ask students the Literary Analysis question on p. 367: What symbolic connection between his own body and the boat does Ahab seem to feel?
  Answer: Ahab seems to feel as though the boat is an extension of his body.

36 Reading Strategy
Recognizing Symbols

- Draw students' attention back to the passage on p. 366 in which Ahab instructs Tashtego to nail another flag to the main masthead, since a hawk has torn down the other and flown away with it.
- Ask students the Reading Strategy question on p. 367: What is symbolized by the red flag streaming out from Tashtego?
  Answer: Students might say that the flag symbolizes the passionate desire of Tashtego, the crew, and Ahab's to vanquish the white whale; others might say that the flag symbolizes Ahab's life, which is about to be lost to the vast ocean.

37 Reading Check
Answer: The boat is nearly capsized by the whale's rolling motion.

CUSTOMIZE INSTRUCTION FOR UNIVERSAL ACCESS

For Gifted/Talented Students	For Advanced Readers
Students might enjoy acting out part of the exciting action of this chapter. Have students prepare a script, using correct conventions and style to indicate dialogue and stage directions. Use page 91 in **Writing and Grammar**, Ruby Level, to help students draft their scripts. Guide students to rehearse lines and actions before performing their scenes for the class. If possible, have students include props to make their performances more realistic.	Guide students to appreciate that the action is becoming increasingly kaleidoscopic. Have them notice that readers now catch only brief bits of the action, much as a sailor at the scene would do in the midst of the chaos of battle. Also help students note that Ahab's statements become increasingly disjointed. Aside from the frantic chase of the white whale, what do students think is causing Ahab's strange, sometimes incomprehensible statements?

38 Literary Analysis

Symbol

- Point out that Ahab himself articulates the symbolic nature of the great whale in a conversation with Starbuck (see p. 358): "I see in him outrageous strength, with an inscrutable malice sinewing it."

- After reteaching symbol, read aloud with students the bracketed passage and ask students the first Literary Analysis question on p. 368: What details in this paragraph suggest that the whale has become a symbol of retribution?
  Answer: Students may point to details such as the whale's "swift vengeance" and the "eternal malice [of] his whole aspect."

- Remind students that it is the narrator, Ishmael, who is telling the story. Ask students what is suggested by Ishmael's description of the whale as malicious and vengeful.
  Possible response: Students may point out that Ishmael's account suggests that he has joined Ahab in his view of the whale as a deliberate agent of destruction.

39 Literary Analysis

Symbol and Theme

- Read aloud this stirring speech, or play the recording of it on the **Listening to Literature** Audiocassettes or Audio CDs.

- Ask students the second Literary Analysis question on p. 368: What thematic elements come together in Ahab's climactic speech?
  Possible response: In Ahab's speech, Melville touches on thematic elements such as personal loyalty, death, humanity's search for meaning in life, the mysteries of nature, and good and evil.

"The whale, the whale! Up helm, up helm! Oh, all ye sweet powers of air, now hug me close! Let not Starbuck die, if die he must, in a woman's fainting fit. Up helm I say—ye fools, the jaw! the jaw! Is this the end of all my bursting prayers? all my lifelong fidelities? Oh, Ahab, Ahab, lo, thy work. Steady! helmsman, steady. Nay, nay! Up helm again! He turns to meet us! Oh, his unappeasable brow drives on towards one, whose duty tells him he cannot depart. My God, stand by me now!"

"Stand not by me, but stand under me, whoever you are that will now help Stubb; for Stubb, too, sticks here. I grin at thee, thou grinning whale! Who ever helped Stubb, or kept Stubb awake, but Stubb's own unwinking eye? And now poor Stubb goes to bed upon a mattress that is all too soft; would it were stuffed with brushwood! I grin at thee, thou grinning whale! Look ye, sun, moon, and stars! I call ye assassins of as good a fellow as ever spouted up his ghost. For all that, I would yet ring glasses with thee, would ye but hand the cup! Oh, oh! oh, oh! thou grinning whale, but there'll be plenty of gulping soon! Why fly ye not, O Ahab! For me, off shoes and jacket to it; let Stubb die in his drawers! A most moldy and oversalted death, though—cherries! cherries! cherries! Oh, Flask, for one red cherry ere we die!"

"Cherries? I only wish that we were where they grow. Oh, Stubb, I hope my poor mother's drawn my part-pay ere this; if not, few coppers will now come to her, for the voyage is up."

From the ship's bows, nearly all the seamen now hung inactive; hammers, bits of plank, lances, and harpoons, mechanically retained in their hands, just as they had darted from their various employments; all their enchanted eyes intent upon the whale, which from side to side strangely vibrating his predestinating head, sent a broad band of overspreading semicircular foam before him as he rushed. Retribution, swift vengeance, eternal malice were in his whole aspect, and spite of all that mortal man could do, the solid white buttress of **38** his forehead smote the ship's starboard bow, till men and timbers reeled. Some fell flat upon their faces. Like dislodged trucks, the heads of the harpooneers aloft shook on their bull-like necks. Through the breach, they heard the waters pour, as mountain torrents down a flume.

"The ship! The hearse!—the second hearse!" cried Ahab from the boat; "its wood could only be American!"

Diving beneath the settling ship, the whale ran quivering along its keel; but turning under water, swiftly shot to the surface again, far off the other bow, but within a few yards of Ahab's boat, where, for a time, he lay quiescent.

"I turn my body from the sun. What ho, Tashtego! let me hear thy hammer. Oh! ye three unsurrendered spires of mine; thou uncracked keel; and only god-bullied hull; thou firm deck, and haughty helm, **39** and Polepointed prow—death-glorious ship! must ye then perish, and without me? Am I cut off from the last fond pride of meanest ship-wrecked captains? Oh, lonely death on lonely life! Oh, now I feel my

Literary Analysis
Symbol What details in this paragraph suggest that the whale has become a symbol of retribution?

Literary Analysis
Symbol and Theme What thematic elements come together in Ahab's climactic speech?

368 ◆ *A Growing Nation (1800–1870)*

✸ ENRICHMENT: Science Connection

Impacts on Whale Hunting

A decade after *Moby-Dick* was published, a Norwegian whaling captain developed two inventions that revolutionized the whaling industry. One was a new harpoon tipped with an exploding bomb to kill whales more quickly; the other was a faster, steam-powered whaling boat. As a result, more whales were killed in the first forty years of the twentieth century than in the four preceding centuries.

For humanitarian reasons, many nations, including

the United States, Canada, and most of Europe, have stopped hunting whales. Japan and the former Soviet Union still do hunt, although international pressure to outlaw whaling increases each year. Have students find out what whale products are used today and the current size of the world's whale population. Ask them to give and support their opinion on whether or not whaling should be prohibited internationally.

topmost greatness lies in my topmost grief. Ho, ho! from all your furthest bounds, pour ye now in, ye bold billows of my whole foregone life, and top this one piled comber of my death! Towards thee I roll, thou all-destroying but unconquering whale; to the last I grapple with thee; from hell's heart I stab at thee; for hate's sake I spit my last breath at thee. Sink all coffins and all hearses to one common pool! and since neither can be mine, let me then tow to pieces, while still chasing thee, though tied to thee, thou damned whale! *Thus,* I give up the spear!"

The harpoon was darted; the stricken whale flew forward; with igniting velocity the line ran through the groove;—ran foul. Ahab stooped to clear it; he did clear it; but the flying turn caught him round the neck, and voicelessly as Turkish mutes bowstring their victim, he was shot out of the boat, ere the crew knew he was gone. Next instant, the heavy eye splice in the rope's final end flew out of the stark-empty tub, knocked down an oarsman, and smiting the sea, disappeared in its depths.

For an instant, the tranced boat's crew stood still; then turned. "The ship? Great God, where is the ship?" Soon they through dim, bewildering mediums saw her sidelong fading phantom, as in the gaseous fata morgana,[18] only the uppermost masts out of water: while fixed by infatuation, or fidelity, or fate, to their once lofty perches, the pagan harpooneers still maintained their sinking lookouts on the sea. And now, concentric circles seized the lone boat itself, and all its crew, and each floating oar, and every lance pole, and spinning, animate and inanimate, all round and round in one vortex, carried the smallest chip of the *Pequod* out of sight.

But as the last whelmings intermixingly poured themselves over the sunken head of the Indian at the mainmast, leaving a few inches of the erect spar yet visible, together with long streaming yards of the flag, which calmly undulated, with ironical coincidings, over the destroying billows they almost touched—at that instant, a red arm and a hammer hovered backwardly uplifted in the open air, in the act of nailing the flag faster and yet faster to the subsiding spar. A sky hawk that tauntingly had followed the main-truck down-wards from its natural home among the stars, pecking at the flag, and

18. **fata morgana**
(fät′ ə môr gän′ ə) *n.*
mirage seen at sea.

41 ☑ **Reading Check**
What happens to the *Pequod*?

40 ▼ **Critical Viewing**
In this image from a film version of Moby-Dick, how do the filmmakers use a sense of scale to suggest the whale's overwhelming power? **[Analyze]**

from Moby-Dick ◆ 369

40 ▶ **Critical Viewing**
Answer: The filmmakers show Moby-Dick's huge jaw closing upon Ahab's tiny boat, which will clearly be barely a mouthful for the great whale.

41 ☑ **Reading Check**
Answer: The *Pequod* sinks in a vortex of swirling water.

CUSTOMIZE INSTRUCTION FOR UNIVERSAL ACCESS

For Less Proficient Readers	For Gifted/Talented Students
Using repeated oral readings, help students understand how Ahab dies. Guide them to see that he is caught around the neck by the harpoon line and jerked from the boat. He dies throwing a harpoon into a fleeing Moby-Dick and declaring his eternal hatred of the animal. Have students use the same technique to recognize the fate of the *Pequod*.	Invite students to review the text in order to create a glossary of nautical and other technical terms for readers of *Moby-Dick*. Students' entries might include such terms as *capstan, harpoon,* and *keel*.

Review and Assess

1. Students should support their responses with clear reasons and examples from the text.

2. **(a)** Ahab offers a Spanish coin made from one ounce of gold. **(b)** He may sense that it would be impossible for them to feel as strong a motivation as he does to hunt down this particular whale.

3. **(a)** He lost one of his legs. **(b)** It reveals that he is a stubborn, angry, and bitter man. **(c)** Starbuck is practical and realistic and is disturbed by Ahab's obsession; in contrast, Ahab is obsessive and volatile.

4. **(a)** Starbuck sees the obsession as vengeance against a dumb animal. **(b)** Starbuck obeys because he is loyal and has served Ahab a long time; Starbuck also cares about Ahab, and may unwillingly admire his courage.

5. **(a)** Ahab is caught by the fouled, or tangled, harpoon line, is yanked out of the boat and disappears; with the harpoon in him, Moby-Dick disappears; the *Pequod* sinks. **(b)** Possible response: Nature endures in the face of human mortality and is indifferent to human suffering.

6. **(a)** He surfaces and then disappears. **(b)** In his obsession, Ahab feels pursued and tormented by Moby-Dick; in reality, Moby-Dick is trying to escape his pursuers.

7. **(a)** Ahab means that he—like many human beings—is powerless to resist following his emotions. Ahab implies that thought is a "higher" process that is best left to God. **(b)** Students should support their opinions with evidence from the selection.

8. Many students may agree with this assessment, given that the last years of Ahab's life are dedicated to his journey to find and kill Moby-Dick.

incommoding Tashtego there: this bird now chanced to intercept its broad fluttering wing between the hammer and the wood: and simultaneously feeling that ethereal thrill, the submerged savage beneath, in his deathgasp, kept his hammer frozen there: and so the bird of heaven, with archangelic shrieks, and his imperial beak thrust upwards, and his whole captive form folded in the flag of Ahab, went down with his ship, which, like Satan, would not sink to hell till she had dragged a living part of heaven along with her, and helmeted herself with it.

Now small fowls flew screaming over the yet yawning gulf; a sullen white surf beat against its steep sides; then all collapsed, and the great shroud of the sea rolled on as it rolled five thousand years ago.

Review and Assess

Thinking About the Selection

1. **Respond:** Do you admire, despise, or pity Captain Ahab? Explain.

2. **(a) Recall:** What does Ahab offer to the crew member who spots Moby-Dick? **(b) Infer:** Why does Ahab feel it necessary to offer this incentive to his crew?

3. **(a) Recall:** What happened to Ahab in his previous encounter with Moby-Dick? **(b) Interpret:** What does Ahab's obsession with Moby-Dick reveal about his character? **(c) Compare and Contrast:** In what ways is Starbuck different from Ahab?

4. **(a) Recall:** How does Starbuck interpret Ahab's obsession with Moby-Dick? **(b) Analyze:** Why does Starbuck obey Ahab even though he disagrees with him?

5. **(a) Recall:** What happens to Ahab, Moby-Dick, and the *Pequod* at the end? **(b) Analyze:** What does the final paragraph indicate about the relationship between humanity and nature?

6. **(a) Recall:** What is Moby-Dick's reaction when the *Pequod* first approaches his flank? **(b) Compare and Contrast:** How does Moby-Dick's reaction to the ship illuminate the differences between the whale in reality and in Ahab's imagination?

7. **(a) Interpret:** What does Ahab mean when he says, "Ahab never thinks; he only feels, feels, feels; that's tingling enough for mortal man! to think's audacity." **(b) Evaluate:** Do you think Ahab's beliefs about human nature are true? Explain.

8. **Take a Position:** This novel has been called a "voyage of the soul." Would you agree or disagree with that assessment? Explain.

ASSESSMENT PRACTICE: Reading Comprehension

Make Inferences and Generalizations　　　(For more practice, see Test Preparation Workbook, p. 19.)

Many tests require students to make generalizations about a written passage. Use this sample test item:

... to and fro he paced his old rounds, upon planks so familiar to his tread, that they were all over dented, like geological stones, with the peculiar mark of his walk. Did you fixedly gaze, too, upon that ribbed and dented brow; there also, you would see still stranger footprints—the footprints of his one unsleeping, ever-pacing thought.

Based on this passage, which of the following best describes Ahab?

A rational and energetic

B calm and powerful

C reverent and self-effacing

D tormented and obsessed

A, B, and *C* are not supported by the text. Ahab's pacing shows he is obsessed with Moby-Dick and tormented by the attack. *D* is correct.

Review and Assess

Literary Analysis

Symbol

1. What omens appear (a) as Ahab's whaleboat pulls away from the *Pequod* and (b) when Moby-Dick surfaces? (c) What is Ahab's reaction to these omens?

2. The color white is often used as a **symbol** for innocence, as well as for absence and death. What contradictory symbolic meanings does the whale's whiteness convey?

3. If the crew of the *Pequod* symbolizes humanity and Moby-Dick symbolizes nature, what do you think the ship's voyage symbolizes?

Connecting Literary Elements

4. (a) Use a chart like the one shown to compare and contrast the characters of Starbuck and Ahab. (b) What **theme** is Melville expressing through these contrasting characters?

5. Considering the journey's symbolic meaning and its terrible outcome, speculate about the novel's overall theme, or central idea.

Reading Strategy

Recognizing Symbols

6. Identify events, dialogue, or descriptions that lead you to **recognize** Moby-Dick as a **symbol** of (a) nature's beauty, (b) nature's power, and (c) nature's immortality. Explain your reasoning.

7. How does this statement by Ishmael suggest a way to look at the symbolic nature of the events he describes:

   "Ah, ye admonitions and warnings! why stay ye not when ye come? But rather are ye predictions than warnings, ye shadows! Yet not so much predictions from without, as verifications of the foregoing things within."

Extend Understanding

8. **Psychology Connection:** (a) With what goals are people obsessed today? (b) In what cases, if any, are obsessions helpful?

Quick Review

A **symbol** is a person, place, or thing that has meaning in itself and also represents something larger.

A **theme** is a central message or insight revealed by a literary work.

To **recognize symbols,** look for characters, places, or objects that are stressed, mentioned repeatedly, or linked to larger ideas.

 Take It to the Net
www.phschool.com
Take the interactive self-test online to check your understanding of the selection.

from Moby-Dick ◆ *371*

✳ ENRICHMENT: Further Reading

Other Works by Herman Melville

Typee

"Bartleby the Scrivener"

Benito Cereno

Billy Budd, Foretopman

Take It to the Net
Visit www.phschool.com for more information on Herman Melville.

Answers for p. 371

Review and Assess

1. **(a)** Sharks appear and surround his boat; Starbuck sees visions of his family. **(b)** Ahab sees the corpse of the Parsee. **(c)** Though he acknowledges each omen, he says that the last part of the omen has not been seen, and he continues to pursue the whale.

2. Sample answer: Despite Ahab's obsession with avenging what he sees as the whale's evil action, Moby-Dick is innocent: He is merely a creature following its instincts. On the other hand, the whale's whiteness represents death not only for Ahab, but also for the entire crew of the *Pequod*—with the exception of Ishmael.

3. The ship's voyage may symbolize humanity's efforts to explain and control nature.

4. **(a)** Whereas Starbuck is practical, realistic, and thoughtful, Ahab is stubborn, angry, and bitter. **(b)** Sample answer: With these contrasting characters, Melville touches on themes such as good vs. evil, loyalty, and sacrifice.

5. Possible response: The *Pequod*'s journey suggests that the most impassioned and determined human will is dwarfed and easily subdued by the vast, mysterious powers of nature.

6. **(a)** One example might be "There's a soft shower to leeward. Such lovely leewardings! They must lead somewhere—to something else than common land, more palmy than the palms. Leeward! the white whale goes that way; look to windward, then . . ." **(b)** One example might be " . . . it was Moby-Dick that dismasted me; Moby-Dick that brought me to this dead stump I stand on now . . . ." **(c)** Students may mention Moby-Dick's disappearance—but not death—at the end of the fight with Ahab.

7. Sample answer: Ishmael's comments suggest that humanity is itself responsible for much of what it sees as tragic or evil in the world.

8. Many people are obsessed with attaining financial prosperity; many others focus on getting political power or fame.

continued

Answers continued

Students may mention that obsession could be helpful insofar as it keeps a person focused on a goal; the danger is that obsession can throw a person's sense of judgment out of balance.

❶ Vocabulary Development

Word Analysis

1. d
2. c
3. e
4. b
5. a

Concept Development: Synonyms

1. b
2. d
3. a
4. c

Spelling Strategy

1. *ss*
2. *sk*
3. *sh*

❷ Grammar and Style

Practice

1. crew *line up*
2. team *draws*
3. crew *is*
4. flock *glides*
5. crowd *gathers*

Writing Application

Possible responses:
The audience is utterly silent./The house manager would prefer that the audience enter through several doors simultaneously.
A herd of mustangs could be seen in the distance./The herd ranges from one-day-old foals to twenty-five-year-old stallions.
The foreman said, "The jury finds the defendant not guilty."/The jury spend much of their time sequestered in their rooms at the hotel.

Integrate Language Skills

Vocabulary Development Lesson

Word Analysis: Latin Prefix *mal-*

The Latin prefix *mal-* means "bad" or "badly." The word *malady* means illness and the word *maladjusted* means "badly adjusted." Select the letter of the definition that best matches each word below.

1. malcontent
2. malevolent
3. malign
4. malignant
5. malice

a. active ill will
b. likely to cause death
c. wishing harm to others
d. dissatisfied
e. to slander

Concept Development: Synonyms

Select the best synonym from the column on the right for each vocabulary word.

1. maledictions
2. prescient
3. pertinaciously
4. inscrutable

a. tenaciously
b. curses; bad words
c. mysterious
d. prophetic

Spelling Strategy

The letters *sc* usually make the sound of *sk*, as in *describe*. Sometimes, however, *sc* makes the sound of *sh*, as in *prescient*, or *s*, as in *science*. Indicate the sound *sc* makes in each of these words.

1. muscles   2. mascot   3. omniscient

Grammar and Style Lesson

Agreement With Collective Nouns

Collective nouns—such as *team* or *flock*—name a group of people or things. A collective noun may be either singular or plural, depending on whether the group it names is seen as a unit (singular) or as a collection of individuals (plural). The verb must always agree in number with the intended meaning of the collective noun.

> **Plural:** When the entire ship's company *were* assembled . . .
> **Singular:** The company *consists* of 150 sailors.

Practice Identify the collective noun in each sentence. Then, write the verb form that agrees with it.

1. The crew _____?_____ up. (lines, line)

2. A team of horses _____?_____ the hearse. (draws, draw)

3. The crew of the whaling ship _____?_____ composed of fine, experienced sailors from all over the world. (is, are)

4. A flock of gulls _____?_____ over the ship. (glides, glide)

5. A curious and horrified crowd _____?_____ quickly near the site of the grisly accident. (gathers, gather)

Writing Application Use each of these collective nouns—*audience, herd, jury*—in two different sentences. In the first, construct a situation that calls for a singular verb; in the second, construct a sentence that requires a plural verb.

𝒲𝒢 *Prentice Hall Writing and Grammar Connection: Chapter 23, Section 1*

TEACHING RESOURCES

The following resources can be used to enrich or extend the instruction for pp. 372–373.

Vocabulary

📖 **Selection Support Workbook:** Build Vocabulary, p. 85

📖 **Vocabulary and Spelling Practice Book** (Use this booklet for skills enrichment.)

Grammar and Style

📖 **Selection Support Workbook:** Grammar and Style, p. 86 ■

𝒲𝒢 **Writing and Grammar,** Ruby Level, p. 584

📲 **Daily Language Practice Transparencies**

Writing

𝒲𝒢 **Writing and Grammar,** Ruby Level, p. 304

📲 **Writing Models and Graphic Organizers on Transparencies,** pp. 37–40

💿 **Writing and Grammar iText CD-ROM**

■ **BLOCK SCHEDULING:** Resources marked with this symbol provide varied instruction during 90-minute blocks.

Writing Lesson

Character Study

For some readers, Ahab's obsession with Moby-Dick borders on madness. For others, his persistence borders on greatness. Write an essay in which you make your own judgement of Ahab's character. To ensure that your readers understand your ideas, include a brief summary of the story.

Prewriting   Gather and interpret details about Ahab. Organize your interpretations into a statement of opinion. This will serve as your working thesis.

Drafting   Include information from the beginning, middle, and end of the story to create a brief summary. Then, state your thesis in your introduction. Use one body paragraph to develop each of your supporting ideas about Ahab's character.

> **Model: Writing a Summary**
>
> **Beginning:** The *Pequod* sets out.
> **Middle:** Ahab tells the crew that he will kill Moby-Dick.
> **End:** In a struggle with Moby-Dick, the ship is destroyed.
> **Summary:** In Ahab's search for Moby-Dick, the *Pequod* is destroyed, and most of her crew killed.

To write an effective summary, select key elements from the beginning, middle, and end of a text.

Revising   Review your essay, making sure that your summary provides the necessary context, and that your opinion is supported by the text.

 Prentice Hall Writing and Grammar Connection: Chapter 14, Section 2

Extension Activities

Listening and Speaking Present a **monologue** that Ishmael might have spoken to the whalers who rescued him. As you prepare, pay attention to the following elements:

- Use nautical terms like Melville's.
- Replicate Ishmael's tone.
- Describe the order of events clearly.
- Add descriptive details about the characters.

Write a monologue that is clear, dramatic, and forceful. Then, share it with the class.

Research and Technology Write a **report** concerning the species of whales that face possible extinction today and what efforts, if any, are being made to save them. Use a series of clear questions to direct your research. Locate answers using field studies, interviews, and news reports from written and electronic sources.

 Take It to the Net   www.phschool.com

Go online for an additional research activity using the Internet.

ASSESSMENT RESOURCES

The following resources can be used to assess students' knowledge and skills.

Selection Assessment

- **Formal Assessment,** pp. 91–93
- **Open Book Test,** pp. 55–57
- **Got It! Assessment Videotapes,** Tape 2
- **Test Bank Software**
- *Take It to the Net*
  Visit www.phschool.com for self-tests and additional questions on the selection.

Listening and Speaking Rubric

- **Performance Assess. and Portfolio Mgmt.,** p. 30

 SYSTEM

- **Workbook**
- **Skill Book**
- **Transparencies**
- **CD-ROM**

Lesson Support for p. 373

❸ Writing Lesson

- Students' character studies should include a brief summary of the story, as well as establish and explain their ideas and insights about Ahab's character.

- Remind students to take into account Ahab's position as the captain of the *Pequod* as they develop their theses. Point out, also, that students should support their theses by citing Ahab's actions, behavior, and speech.

- Use the Writing Lesson, as well as Writing Process model 7, pp. 37–40, in **Writing Models and Graphic Organizers on Transparencies,** to guide students in developing their character studies.

❹ Listening and Speaking

- You might recommend that students begin by sketching out the order of events first as a reference point. Then, they might consider whether Ishmael would place more emphasis on certain events and less emphasis on others as he speaks to his rescuers.

- Encourage students to reread a variety of narrative passages from the selection to re-familiarize themselves with Ishmael's tone.

- Have students attempt to capture the rhythm and style of Ishmael's account. Urge them to rehearse their monologues as a way of making decisions about how to revise them.

- Have students use the Peer Assessment form for Delivering a Speech p. 30, in **Performance Assessment and Portfolio Management.**

CUSTOMIZE INSTRUCTION
For Universal Access

To address different learning styles, use the following activities suggested in the **Extension Activities** booklet, p. 19.

For Intrapersonal and Bodily/Kinesthetic Learners, use Activity 5.

For Verbal/Linguistic Learners, use Activity 6.

For Visual/Spatial Learners, use Activity 7.

Connections

Students might reread "The Fall of the House of Usher" and the excerpts from *Moby Dick*. Like those selections, Oates' story contains mysteries and takes place in an atmosphere of gloom and foreboding. Have students identify similarities in the mood, atmosphere, and tone of the three works.

Shadows of the Imagination

- Have students discuss the role imagination plays in "The Fall of the House of Usher" and *Moby Dick*. Have them think about imagination as they read "Where Is Here?" Whose imagination is most important in this story—the writer's, the characters', or the reader's?

- Have students recall how Poe and Melville aroused fear and horror in their readers. Have them note ways in which Oates does the same. Do the three writers use different or similar techniques to create a frightening atmosphere?

CONNECTIONS
Literature Past and Present
Shadows of the Imagination

Edgar Allan Poe, Nathaniel Hawthorne, and Herman Melville are towering figures in American literature. They were fascinated by human behavior, especially that exhibited in extreme situations. Each portrays characters acting in disturbing or extraordinary ways because of an internal conflict or a crisis. Using their powerful imaginations, these writers transform realistic details of daily life into ambiguous, shadowy, and precarious worlds.

In Edgar Allan Poe's work, for instance, gloomy heroes like Roderick Usher languish as their mental equilibrium teeters and the outside world—which once seemed orderly and healthful—collapses. Likewise, many of Nathaniel Hawthorne's characters hold some secret, shadowy knowledge that leads them to behave in unsettling and unaccountable ways; often Hawthorne focuses on the odd ways human beings think and act when they are struggling with dark emotions such as guilt.

Modern Gothic In the twentieth century, only a few American writers have been inclined to embrace the dusky themes, characters, and atmospheres that stamped the work of their Gothic forebears. One of these writers is Joyce Carol Oates. Many of Oates's novels and stories concern individuals whose ordinary lives are suddenly upset by mysterious forces beyond their control. Much of the suspense and emotional power in Oates's fiction can be traced to her depiction of common people who seem powerless to save their identities from alteration or destruction by some shadowy force.

Where *Is* Here?
Joyce Carol Oates

For years they had lived without incident in their house in a quiet residential neighborhood when, one November evening at dusk, the doorbell rang, and the father went to answer it, and there on his doorstep stood a man he had never seen before. The stranger apologized for disturbing him at what was probably the dinner hour and explained that he'd once lived in the house— "I mean, I was a child in this house"—and since he was in the city on business he thought he would drop by. He had not seen the house since January 1949 when

►Critical Viewing

Answer: The trees cluster against the house as if they were trying to guard or hide it. They also hide the house's immediate surroundings, suggesting that there may be something lurking there. Flaking paint on the building's facade make it appear dilapidated.

he'd been eleven years old and his widowed mother had sold it and moved away but, he said, he thought of it often, dreamt of it often, and never more powerfully than in recent months. The father said, "Would you like to come inside for a few minutes and look around?" The stranger hesitated, then said firmly, "I think I'll just poke around outside for a while, if you don't mind. That might be sufficient." He was in his late forties, the father's approximate age. He wore a dark suit, conservatively cut; he was hatless, with thin silver-tipped neatly

▲ **Critical Viewing**
What details in this photograph lend an air of mystery—even menace— to an ordinary house? **[Analyze]**

CUSTOMIZE INSTRUCTION FOR UNIVERSAL ACCESS

For Less Proficient Readers	For English Learners	For Advanced Readers
Have students identify three of the four short story elements—main characters, setting, and main events of the plot. Have them use these three elements to try to establish the story's theme or themes.	Have students diagram the story's plot. Remind them that plot consists of exposition, rising action, climax, falling action, and resolution. Can students find all five stages in this story, or do they think it is missing one or more stages? Which ones?	Have students discuss which narrative element—plot, character, setting, or theme—is most important to this story. Have them explain their answers in brief essays.

Answer: The characters in both stories are disturbed because the visitor and the minister both behave in unexpected, unconventional ways. The characters don't know how to react to this out-of-the-ordinary behavior.

• Point out that the narrator in "The Fall of the House of Usher" is unnamed, and that all the characters in Oates' story are unnamed. Ask students what effect this has on both stories.

Answer: Each reader of "The Fall of the House of Usher" can identify with the unnamed narrator precisely because he is unnamed; the reader enters into this character and experiences the story through his eyes. In "Where Is Here," the lack of names makes the characters generic. They might be any family. Oates implies that something like this could happen at any time to any family.

• Have students compare the house in this story to the Ushers' house. How are both places described? What are they like to live in? How do Poe and Oates make the houses function as characters in the stories? What are their personalities like? Have a class discussion on this topic, encouraging students to support their arguments with specific descriptive details from both stories.

---

combed hair; a plain, sober, intelligent face and frowning eyes. The father, reserved by nature, but _genial_ and even _gregarious_ when taken unaware, said amiably, "Of course we don't mind. But I'm afraid many things have changed since 1949."

So, in the chill, damp, deepening dusk, the stranger wandered around the property while the mother set the dining room table and the father peered covertly out the window. The children were upstairs in their rooms. "Where is he now?" the mother asked. "He just went into the garage," the father said. "The garage! What does he want in there!" the mother said uneasily. "Maybe you'd better go out there with him." "He wouldn't want anyone with him," the father said. He moved stealthily to another window, peering through the curtains. A moment passed in silence. The mother, paused in the act of setting down plates, neatly folded paper napkins, and stainless-steel cutlery, said impatiently, "And where is he now? I don't like this." The father said, "Now he's coming out of the garage," and stepped back hastily from the window. "Is he going now?" the mother asked. "I wish I'd answered the door." The father watched for a moment in silence then said, "He's headed into the backyard." "Doing what?" the mother asked. "Not _do_ing anything, just walking," the father said. "He seems to have a slight limp." "Is he an older man?" the mother asked. "I didn't notice," the father confessed. "Isn't that just like you!" the mother said.

She went on worriedly, "He could be anyone, after all. Any kind of thief, or mentally disturbed person, or even a murderer. Ringing our doorbell like that with no warning and you don't even know what he looks like!"

The father had moved to another window and stood quietly watching, his cheek pressed against the glass. "He's gone down to the old swings. I hope he won't sit in one of them, for memory's sake, and try to swing—the posts are rotted almost through." The mother drew breath to speak but sighed instead, as if a powerful current of feeling had surged through her. The father was saying, "Is it possible he remembers those swings from his childhood? I can't believe they're actually that old." The mother said vaguely, "They were old when we bought the house." The father said, "But we're talking about forty years or more, and that's a long time." The mother sighed again, involuntarily. "Poor man!" she murmured. She was standing before her table but no longer seeing it. In her hand were objects—forks, knives, spoons—she could not have named. She said, "We can't bar the door against him. That would be cruel." The father said, "What? No one has barred any door against anyone." "Put yourself in his place," the mother said. "He told me he didn't _want_ to come inside," the father said. "Oh—isn't that just like you!" the mother said in exasperation.

Without a further word she went to the back door and called out for the stranger to come inside, if he wanted, when he had finished looking around outside.

genial (jēn′ yəl) _adj._ cheerful; friendly

gregarious (grə ger′ ē əs) _adj._ sociable

covertly (kō vərt′ lē) _adv._ secretly; surreptitiously

Thematic Connection
Both the villagers in "The Minister's Black Veil" and the couple in this story are unnerved by the sudden appearance of something mysterious. Compare the reactions each writer describes.

They introduced themselves rather shyly, giving names, and forgetting names, in the confusion of the moment. The stranger's handshake was cool and damp and tentative. He was smiling hard, blinking moisture from his eyes; it was clear that entering his childhood home was enormously exciting yet intimidating to him. Repeatedly he said, "It's so nice of you to invite me in—I truly hate to disturb you—I'm really so grateful, and so—" But the perfect word eluded him. As he spoke his eyes darted about the kitchen almost like eyes out of control. He stood in an odd stiff posture, hands gripping the lapels of his suit as if he meant to crush them. The mother, meaning to break the awkward silence, spoke warmly of their satisfaction with the house and with the neighborhood, and the father concurred, but the stranger listened only politely, and continued to stare, and stare hard. Finally he said that the kitchen had been so changed—"so modernized"— he almost didn't recognize it. The floor tile, the size of the windows, something about the position of the cupboards—all were different. But the sink was in the same place, of course; and the refrigerator and stove; and the door leading down to the basement—"That *is* the door leading down to the basement, isn't it?" He spoke strangely, staring at the door. For a moment it appeared he might ask to be shown the basement but the moment passed, fortunately—this was not a part of their house the father and mother would have been comfortable showing to a stranger.

Finally, making an effort to smile, the stranger said, "Your kitchen is so—pleasant." He paused. For a moment it seemed he had nothing further to say. Then, "A—controlled sort of place. My mother—When we lived here—" His words trailed off into a dreamy silence and the mother and father glanced at each other with carefully neutral expressions.

On the windowsill above the sink were several lushly blooming African violet plants in ceramic pots and these the stranger made a show of admiring. Impulsively he leaned over to sniff the flowers— "Lovely!"—though African violets have no smell. As if embarrassed he

▲ **Critical Viewing**
How does the writer create mystery and suspense from ordinary domestic items like these? **[Connect]**

✔**Reading Check**
What is the stranger doing in the house?

Shadows of the Imagination

- Ask students to give their impressions of the stranger so far. Have them compare and contrast their impressions of him with their reactions to Roderick Usher.
  Answer: Students should note that both men behave oddly and inexplicably. They probably felt on their guard against Usher and probably find the stranger equally alarming.

- Have students compare and contrast the mother's and father's reactions to the stranger. How would students have reacted in their place? Why?
  Answer: Students may say that fears for their own safety or that of their children would have prevented them from inviting the man inside. Others may say that friendliness and compassion would have made them ask him in.

▶**Critical Viewing**
Answer: The juxtaposition of ordinary people and ordinary domestic items with extraordinary occurrences is the source of the mystery and suspense. The stranger's behavior might not seem so eerie in a less bland setting.

✔**Reading Check**
Answer: The stranger has been invited in to see the house in which he used to live as a boy.

CUSTOMIZE INSTRUCTION FOR UNIVERSAL ACCESS

For English Learners	For Gifted/Talented Students
In this story, the occupants of the house reluctantly invite a stranger into their home because they do not wish to appear rude or cruel. Ideals of hospitality vary from culture to culture. In some cultures, guests bring gifts to honor their hosts, while in other cultures the reverse is true. Some cultures consider it dishonorable *not* to offer hospitality, even to total strangers or enemies. Encourage students to compare customs in the United States with those of their first cultures.	Challenge students to collaborate on a one-act play version of this story. Students can work together to write the script, memorize the lines, and stage the play for the class. Have them consider how they will convey the descriptive details in dialogue. Will they write new dialogue, have a narrator to read the descriptive details from the story, or solve the problem in some other way? Work with students as adviser and director and give them plenty of time to prepare before they perform for the class.

Thematic Connection

Answer: In many stories, darkness symbolizes the bad, evil, or negative aspects of life. Because human beings perceive the world around them more through their eyesight than any other sense, darkness is especially threatening to us—we can't see in it. Darkness conceals information from people and therefore creates fear and uncertainty.

said, "Mother too had plants on this windowsill but I don't recall them ever blooming."

The mother said tactfully, "Oh they were probably the kind that don't bloom—like ivy."

In the next room, the dining room, the stranger appeared to be even more deeply moved. For some time he stood staring, wordless. With fastidious slowness he turned on his heel, blinking, and frowning, and tugging at his lower lip in a rough gesture that must have hurt. Finally, as if remembering the presence of his hosts, and the necessity for some display of civility, the stranger expressed his admiration for the attractiveness of the room, and its coziness. He'd remembered it as cavernous, with a ceiling twice as high. "And dark most of the time," he said wonderingly. "Dark by day, dark by night." The mother turned the lights of the little brass chandelier to their fullest: shadows were dispersed like ragged ghosts and the cut-glass fruit bowl at the center of the table glowed like an exquisite multifaceted jewel. The stranger exclaimed in surprise. He'd extracted a handkerchief from his pocket and was dabbing carefully at his face, where beads of perspiration shone. He said, as if thinking aloud, still wonderingly, "My father was a unique man. Everyone who knew him admired him. He sat *here*," he said, gingerly touching the chair that was in fact the father's chair, at one end of the table. "And Mother sat *there*," he said, merely pointing. "I don't recall my own place or my sister's but I suppose it doesn't matter. . . . I see you have four place settings, Mrs. . . .? Two children, I suppose?" "A boy eleven, and a girl thirteen," the mother said. The stranger stared not at her but at the table, smiling. "And so too *we* were—I mean, there were two of us: my sister and me."

The mother said, as if not knowing what else to say, "Are you—close?"

The stranger shrugged, distractedly rather than rudely, and moved on to the living room.

This room, cozily lit as well, was the most carefully furnished room in the house. Deep-piled wall-to-wall carpeting in hunter green, cheerful chintz drapes, a sofa and matching chairs in nubby heather green, framed reproductions of classic works of art, a gleaming gilt-framed mirror over the fireplace: wasn't the living room impressive as a display in a furniture store? But the stranger said nothing at first. Indeed, his eyes narrowed sharply as if he were confronted with a disagreeable spectacle. He whispered, "Here too! Here too!"

He went to the fireplace, walking, now, with a decided limp; he drew his fingers with excruciating slowness along the mantel as if testing its materiality. For some time he merely stood, and stared, and listened. He tapped a section of wall with his knuckles—"There used to be a large water stain here, like a shadow."

"Was there?" murmured the father out of politeness, and "Was there!" murmured the mother. Of course, neither had ever seen a water stain there.

Then, noticing the window seat, the stranger uttered a soft surprised cry, and went to sit in it. He appeared delighted: hugging his knees like a child trying to make himself smaller. "This was one of my happy places! At least when Father wasn't home. I'd hide away here for hours, reading, daydreaming, staring out the window! Sometimes Mother would join me, if she was in the mood, and we'd plot together—oh, all sorts of fantastical things!" The stranger remained sitting in the window seat for so long, tears shining in his eyes, that the father and mother almost feared he'd forgotten them. He was stroking the velvet fabric of the cushioned seat, gropingly touching the leaded windowpanes. Wordlessly, the father and mother exchanged a glance: who was this man, and how could they tactfully get rid of him? The father made a face signaling impatience and the mother shook her head without seeming to move it. For they couldn't be rude to a guest in their house.

The stranger was saying in a slow, dazed voice, "It all comes back to me now. How could I have forgotten! Mother used to read to me, and tell me stories, and ask me riddles I couldn't answer. 'What creature walks on four legs in the morning, two legs at midday, three legs in the evening?' 'What is round, and flat, measuring mere inches in one direction, and infinity in the other?' 'Out of what does our life arise? Out of what does our consciousness arise? Why are we here? Where *is* here?' "

The father and mother were perplexed by these strange words and hardly knew how to respond. The mother said uncertainly, "Our daughter used to like to sit here too, when she was younger. It *is* a lovely place." The father said with surprising passion, "I hate riddles—they're moronic some of the time and obscure the rest of the time." He spoke with such uncharacteristic rudeness, the mother looked at him in surprise.

Hurriedly she said, "Is your mother still living, Mr. . . .?" "Oh no. Not at all," the stranger said, rising abruptly from the window seat, and looking at the mother as if she had said something mildly preposterous. "I'm sorry," the mother said. "Please don't be," the stranger said. "We've all been dead—*they've* all been dead—a long time."

The stranger's cheeks were deeply flushed as if with anger and his breath was quickened and audible.

The visit might have ended at this point but so clearly did the stranger expect to continue on upstairs, so purposefully, indeed almost defiantly, did he limp his way to the stairs, neither the father nor the mother knew how to dissuade him. It was as if a force of nature, benign at the outset, now uncontrollable, had swept its way into their house! The mother followed after him saying nervously, "I'm not sure what condition the rooms are in, upstairs. The children's rooms especially—" The stranger muttered that he did not care in the slightest about the condition of the household and continued on up without a backward glance.

The father, his face burning with resentment and his heart accelerating as if in preparation for combat, had no choice but to follow the stranger and the mother up the stairs. He was flexing and unflexing his fingers as if to rid them of stiffness.

☑**Reading Check**

What does the stranger recall about the window seat?

Background

Riddles

The riddle the visitor recites— "What goes on four legs in the morning, two legs at midday, and three legs in the evening?"—is the riddle of the Sphinx, who killed every passerby who could not answer her question. Oedipus was the first to guess the correct answer—man, who crawls on all fours as a baby, walks on two legs as a youth, and uses a cane in old age. The round, flat object that measures inches in one direction and infinity in another is a clock—only a few inches across but capable of measuring time, which is infinite.

☑**Reading Check**

Answer: He remembers that he liked to sit there and daydream.

CUSTOMIZE INSTRUCTION FOR UNIVERSAL ACCESS

For Advanced Readers

Two recurring themes that critics have noted in Oates' writing are the violence that underpins much of her fiction, and the melancholy that is often present in her characters.

Share the following quotation from Joyce Carol Oates:

A melancholy vision, a tragic vision, is inevitable. . . . Uplifting endings and resolutely cheery world views are appropriate to television commercials but misleading elsewhere. It is not only wicked to pretend otherwise; it is futile.

Have students give their reactions to this quotation. Have them apply it to the Poe and Hawthorne stories from this unit and to *Moby Dick*. Would these authors have agreed with Oates? Does her story support the view she expresses? Have students explain their answers.

Shadows of the Imagination

- On page 375, Oates says that the stranger and the father are about the same age. Now she adds that they are the same height. What does this resemblance suggest to students?

Answer: It suggests that the stranger may be the son's ghost or spirit; that his visit portends things to come. It adds to the sense of mystery in the story.

▶ **Critical Viewing**

Answer: The stranger might compare the neat bedroom to what it looked like when he was a child in the house.

On the landing, the stranger halted abruptly to examine a stained-glass fanlight—"My God, I haven't thought of this in years!" He spoke excitedly of how, on tiptoe, he used to stand and peek out through the diamonds of colored glass, red, blue, green, golden yellow: seeing with amazement the world outside so *altered.* "After such a lesson it's hard to take the world on its own terms, isn't it?" he asked. The father asked, annoyed, "On what terms should it be taken, then?" The stranger replied, regarding him levelly, with a just perceptible degree of disdain, "Why, none at all."

It was the son's room—by coincidence, the stranger's old room—the stranger most wanted to see. Other rooms on the second floor, the "master" bedroom in particular, he decidedly did not want to see. As he spoke of it, his mouth twisted as if he had been offered something repulsive to eat.

The mother hurried on ahead to warn the boy and to straighten up his room a bit. No one had expected a visitor this evening! "So you have two children," the stranger murmured, looking at the father with a small quizzical smile. "Why?" The father stared at him as if he hadn't heard correctly. "'Why'?" he asked. "Yes. *Why?*" the stranger repeated. They looked at each other for a long strained moment, then the stranger said quickly, "But you love them—of course." The father controlled his temper and said, biting off his words, "Of course."

"Of course, of course," the stranger murmured, tugging at his necktie and loosening his collar, "otherwise it would all come to an end." The two men were of approximately the same height but the father was heavier in the shoulders and torso; his hair had thinned more severely so that the scalp of the crown was exposed, flushed, damp with perspiration, sullenly alight.

With a stiff <u>avuncular</u> formality the stranger shook the son's hand. "So this is your room, now! So you live here, now!" he murmured, as if the fact were an astonishment. Not used to shaking hands, the boy was stricken with shyness and cast his eyes down. The stranger limped past him, staring. "The same!—the same!—walls, ceiling,

avuncular (ə vuŋ´ kyo͞o lər) *adj.* having traits considered typical of uncles: jolly, indulgent, stodgy

▼ **Critical Viewing**
What might the stranger say about a scene like the one shown here?
[Hypothesize]

floor—window—" He drew his fingers slowly along the windowsill; around the frame; rapped the glass, as if, again, testing materiality; stooped to look outside—but it was night, and nothing but his reflection bobbed in the glass, ghostly and insubstantial. He groped against the walls, he opened the closet door before the mother could protest, he sat heavily on the boy's bed, the springs creaking beneath him. He was panting, red-faced, dazed. "And the ceiling overhead," he whispered. He nodded slowly and repeatedly, smiling. "And the floor beneath. That is what *is*."

He took out his handkerchief again and fastidiously wiped his face. He made a visible effort to compose himself.

The father, in the doorway, cleared his throat and said, "I'm afraid it's getting late—it's almost six."

The mother said, "Oh yes I'm afraid— I'm afraid it *is* getting late. There's dinner, and the children have their homework—"

The stranger got to his feet. At his full height he stood for a precarious moment swaying, as if the blood had drained from his head and he was in danger of fainting. But he steadied himself with a hand against the slanted dormer ceiling. He said, "Oh yes!—I know!—I've disturbed you terribly! —you've been so *kind*." It seemed, surely, as if the stranger *must* leave now, but, as chance had it, he happened to spy, on the boy's desk, an opened mathematics textbook and several smudged sheets of paper, and impulsively offered to show the boy a mathematical riddle—"You can take it to school tomorrow and surprise your teacher!"

So, out of dutiful politeness, the son sat down at his desk and the stranger leaned familiarly over him, demonstrating adroitly with a ruler and a pencil how "what we call 'infinity' " can be contained within a small geometrical figure on a sheet of paper. "First you draw a square; then you draw a triangle to fit inside the square; then you draw a second triangle, and a third, and a fourth, each to fit inside the square, but without their points coinciding, and as you continue—here, son, I'll show you—give me your hand, and I'll show you—the border of the triangles' common outline gets more complex and measures larger, and larger, and larger—and soon you'll need a magnifying glass to see the details, and then you'll need a microscope, and so on and so forth, forever, laying triangles neatly down to fit inside the original square *without their points coinciding*—!" The stranger spoke with increasing fervor; spittle gleamed in the corners of his mouth. The son stared at the geometrical shapes rapidly materializing on the sheet of paper before him with no seeming comprehension but with a rapt staring fascination as if he dared not look away.

After several minutes of this the father came abruptly forward and dropped his hand on the stranger's shoulder. "The visit is over," he said calmly. It was the first time since they'd shaken hands that the two men had touched, and the touch had a galvanic effect upon the stranger: he dropped ruler and pencil at once, froze in his stooped posture, burst into frightened tears.

galvanic (gal van′ ik) *adj.* startling; stimulating as if by electric current

✔**Reading Check**

What room in the house does the stranger most want to see? Why?

Connections: Where Is Here? ◆ 381

Shadows of the Imagination

- Ask why the stranger bursts into tears at the father's speech and gesture at the end of this page.
  Possible answer: The stranger is reminded of his own parents' harshness.

- Have students go back through the story looking for references to the stranger's parents. Have them discuss what they think happened in the house when the stranger was a child.
  Answer: Students should note that the parents kept the house dark and tormented their son with sophisticated riddles he couldn't possibly answer. Students may think that the parents killed their son or perhaps that he killed them. They might point out the stranger's comfort in concrete objects like the "ceiling overhead and the floor beneath" (p. 381) and contrast this with the abstract concepts of riddles and infinity that he associates with his parents.

✔**Reading Check**

Answer: He wanted to see the son's room, which had been his room when he lived there.

381

Answers

Connecting Literature Past and Present

1. Oates' story is mysterious because she doesn't explain directly who the stranger is, because his behavior is extraordinary, and because none of the characters has a name. The mystery in her story works to make a familar scene—a suburban home—strange and unfamiliar, allowing the reader to envision new and unsettling possibilities.

2. (a) The minister and the stranger are the central characters in the stories. They both do extraordinary things that repel everyone around them.
(b) Because they don't explain themselves, their behavior makes everyone else imagine things.

Now the visit truly was over; the stranger, at last, *was* leaving, having wiped away his tears and made a stoical effort to compose himself; but on the doorstep, to the father's astonishment, he made a final, preposterous appeal—he wanted to see the basement. "Just to sit on the stairs? In the dark? For a few quiet minutes? And you could close the door and forget me, you and your family could have your dinner and—"

The stranger was begging but the father was resolute. Without raising his voice he said, "No. *The visit is over.*"

He shut the door, and locked it.

Locked it! His hands were shaking and his heart beat angrily.

He watched the stranger walk away—out to the sidewalk, out to the street, disappearing in the darkness. Had the streetlights gone out?

Behind the father the mother stood apologetic and defensive, wringing her hands in a classic stance. "Wasn't that *sad!* Wasn't that—*sad!* But we had no choice but to let him in, it was the only decent thing to do." The father pushed past her without comment. In the living room he saw that the lights were flickering as if on the brink of going out; the patterned wallpaper seemed drained of color; a shadow lay upon it shaped like a bulbous cloud or growth. Even the robust green of the carpeting looked faded. Or was it an optical illusion? Everywhere the father looked, a pulse beat mute with rage. "*I* wasn't the one who opened the door to that man in the first place," the mother said, coming up behind the father and touching his arm. Without seeming to know what he did the father violently jerked his arm and thrust her away.

"Shut up. We'll forget it," he said.

"But—"

"*We'll forget it.*"

The mother entered the kitchen walking slowly as if she'd been struck a blow. In fact, a bruise the size of a pear would materialize on her forearm by morning. When she reached out to steady herself she misjudged the distance of the door frame—or did the door frame recede an inch or two—and nearly lost her balance.

In the kitchen the lights were dim and an odor of sourish smoke, subtle but unmistakable, made her nostrils pinch.

She slammed open the oven door. Grabbed a pair of pot holders with insulated linings. "*I* wasn't the one, . . ." she cried, panting, "and you know it."

Joyce Carol Oates

(b. 1938)

In her short stories, novels, poems, and plays, Joyce Carol Oates delves into the workings of the human mind. Her writtings often focuses on characters who are disturbed or who are searching anxiously for their identities. Oates grew up in a tiny town on the Erie Canal, and her earliest stories and first novel are accounts of life in Erie County. Oates's fictional Eden County is elaborately conceived and populated with inhabitants who turn up in various ways from story to story.

Connecting Literature Past and Present

1. Mystery plays an important role in the works of Poe, Hawthorne, and Melville. What is the role of mystery in Oates's story?
2. Compare Parson Hooper in "The Minister's Black Veil" with the stranger in "Where *Is* Here?" (a) In what sense are they the most powerful figures in their respective stories? (b) What role does imagination play in their power?

PART 3

The Human Spirit and the Natural World

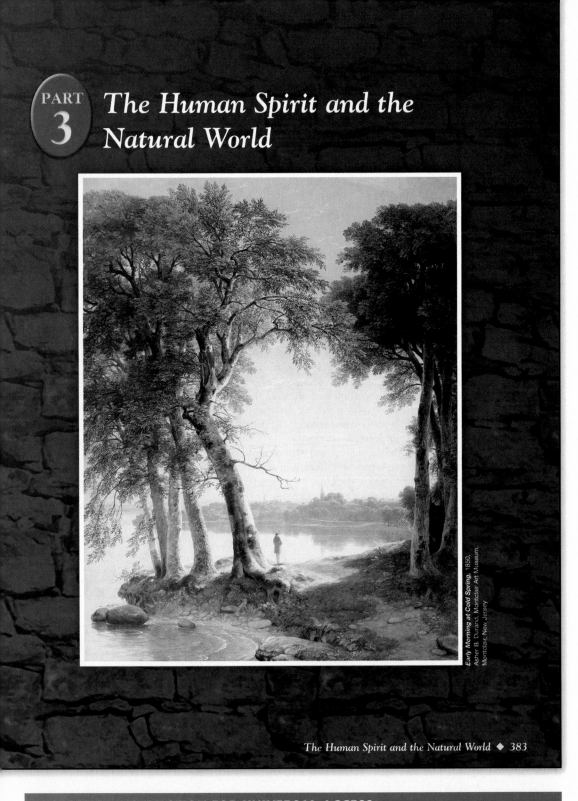

Early Morning at Cold Spring, 1850, Asher B. Durand, Montclair Art Museum, Montclair, New Jersey

The Human Spirit and the Natural World ◆ 383

CUSTOMIZE INSTRUCTION FOR UNIVERSAL ACCESS

When assigning the selections in this part, keep in mind these factors:

from *Nature*; from "Self-Reliance"; "The Snowstorm"; "Concord Hymn"

- Abstract concepts in the essays may present challenges to students.
- Personification and strong imagery bring "The Snowstorm" to life.

From *Walden*; from *Civil Disobedience*

- Most readers will be challenged by these essays.

- Lengthy sentences may add to the challenge.
- Many students may find Thoreau's ideas about government especially applicable to today's world.

Selection Planning Guide

The section introduces students to two of the most influential writers of the nineteenth century. Ralph Waldo Emerson and Henry David Thoreau helped define the American character by inspiring people to turn to nature in order to better understand both themselves and the universal truths. Students may be surprised to find that they share many of the views on nature and individuality Emerson expresses in *Nature* and "Self-Reliance." "Concord Hymn" and "The Snowstorm" reveal the poetic—and perhaps more accessible—side of Emerson's literary talent. Thoreau's views in *Walden* on how to live a productive life may intrigue students. Encourage them to assess the validity of his evaluation of government in *Civil Disobedience.*

Background

Art

Early Morning at Cold Spring, Asher B. Durand

One of the founders of the Hudson River school of painting, Asher B. Durand (1796–1886) began his career as an engraver, reproducing paintings by others and engraving banknotes; in fact, U.S. currency incorporates a number of the designs he developed. In his middle age, Durand turned to landscape painting and became one of the leaders of a group of northeastern artists who painted scenes from the Hudson River, Adirondack Mountains, and New England. Cold Spring is a city north of New York City along the Hudson River, a favorite haunt for Durand and his colleagues.

Use these questions for discussion:

1. Why might the artist have painted a solitary man, rather than a group of people, in such a setting?
   Possible response: He probably wanted to portray an individual quietly contemplating the beauty of the landscape.

2. What does the human figure add to this tranquil landscape painting?
   Possible responses: The figure adds a human dimension—it represents the human mind responding to or interacting with the beauty of nature.

383

A Closer Look

▶ Critical Viewing

Answer: Students should say that life must have been reduced to its simplest. They should note that there is nothing to distract Thoreau from enjoying the beauties of the forest in which the cabin is located. He must have lived free of most possessions at Walden.

A Closer Look

Transcendentalism: The Seekers

Ralph Waldo Emerson Searched for the Nature of Truth and Revolutionized American Literature

For the Transcendentalists, the loose-knit group of writers, artists, and reformers who flourished in the 1830s and 1840s, the individual was at the center of the universe. For them, no institution, whether political or religious, was as powerful as the individual. So it is fitting that the most influential literary and philosophical movement in American history began with the struggles of one man.

A Crisis of Confidence In the early 1830s, a young Boston pastor found himself wrestling with his faith. His wife of less than two years had died of tuberculosis, and the grieving pastor began questioning his beliefs. At the time, many religious and scholarly institutions downplayed the importance of the individual. The Industrial Revolution, which introduced mass production, had shown that machines could actually replace people. Individuals, it seemed, did not matter.

The pastor was troubled by this notion. He did not believe that individuals were insignificant. On the contrary, he felt that the human mind was the most important force in the universe. The pastor was so passionate about his search for a new way of thinking that he resigned his position and traveled to Europe to visit with some of the great philosophers of the day.

That pastor was Ralph Waldo Emerson, and what seemed like one man's crisis of confidence became a revolution in American thought. When Emerson returned to the United States in 1833, he helped forge the Transcendentalist movement.

The Individual Is the World In practical terms, the Transcendentalist movement was a ripple in history, lasting a mere ten years and producing only two major books—Emerson's *Nature* (1836) and Thoreau's *Walden* (1854). Nevertheless, the influence of the Transcendentalists on American life and letters continues to this day.

According to Emerson, the human mind is so powerful it can unlock any mystery, from the intricacies of nature to the wonder of God. To Emerson, "the individual is the world." This was a radical thought in an age that gave all authority to the organized institutions of government, religion, and education.

Emerson first proposed his ideas in 1833 in a speech at Harvard University. His audience responded with great enthusiasm. Then, he took his ideas further, proposing that every soul and all of nature was part of an "Over-Soul," a universal spirit to which all beings returned after death. In other words, every being was part of the mind of God. In an 1842 lecture, Emerson noted that,

▼ Critical Viewing Judging from this image of a replica of Thoreau's cabin, what do you think life was like on Walden Pond?

✦ ENRICHMENT: Literature Connection

Louisa May Alcott

The fame of Transcendentalist Amos Bronson Alcott was far eclipsed by his daughter Louisa May. Louisa's novel *Little Women*, and its sequels outsold the writing of Emerson, Hawthorne, Melville, and Thoreau combined, and have never gone out of print.

Popular though her children's stories were, Alcott preferred writing Gothic fiction. Because she was a woman, scandal would have resulted if she had published her thrilling tales of mesmerism, murder, adultery, and the supernatural under her own name. Her stories all appeared anonymously or under the pen name A.M. Barnard. Late in the 20th century, scholars identified her as the author of *A Modern Mephistopheles* and a number of Gothic tales by studying her journals and correspondence. Today these stories and novels are published as Alcott would have wished, under her own name.

"The Transcendentalist . . . believes in miracle, in the perpetual openness of the human mind to new influx of light and power; he believes in inspiration, and in ecstasy."

Meetings of Great Minds Many found Emerson's ideas blasphemous and denounced him as a heretic. Emerson's supporters, however, flocked to Concord, Massachusetts, to visit with him. During the height of Transcendentalist activities, Emerson's Concord house attracted so many great minds that it was dubbed the "Athens of America."

Amos Bronson Alcott Among Emerson's admirers was teacher and philosopher Amos Bronson Alcott, whose beliefs about education revolutionized American schools. Alcott insisted that students should not be taught through routine memorization, a practice common at that time. Instead, students should be challenged to think, to debate, and to discuss.

Margaret Fuller Feminist author and editor Margaret Fuller was another eminent Transcendentalist. Along with Emerson, Fuller was the driving force behind the Transcendentalist journal *The Dial.*

Henry David Thoreau Emerson's most famous protégé was Henry David Thoreau. As a twenty-year-old student, Thoreau heard Emerson speak at Harvard and was thrilled by his ideas. Not content to merely discuss Transcendentalist philosophy, Thoreau wanted to put it into action. In 1845, he built a rough cottage in the woods at Walden Pond and went there to live alone. He sought to experience life on a simpler level, in harmony with nature, untied to material things. Thoreau lived at Walden Pond for two years and wrote about his experiences. The result was his classic collection of essays, *Walden.*

A Lasting Legacy Like other Transcendentalists, Thoreau was a fierce abolitionist. In protest against slavery and the Mexican War, he refused to pay taxes and was imprisoned. Although Thoreau spent only a single night in jail, the experience gave him insights into the relationship of individuals to government. The theory of nonviolent civil disobedience that he developed as a result has had a profound effect on society, both in the United States and around the world. During India's struggle for independence in the 1940s, Mahatma Gandhi adopted Thoreau's ideas. Here in America, nonviolent civil protest served as the guiding principle for Dr. Martin Luther King, Jr., during the civil rights movement.

The influence of the Transcendentalists is so woven into the fabric of American culture that it is almost invisible, like the air—so bountiful we take it for granted. Yet, whenever writers celebrate the individual, whenever they look to the natural world as a mirror of human lives, whenever they state a belief in the power of intuition to grasp fundamental truths, they owe a debt to the great, brief meeting of minds in Concord.

▲ **Critical Viewing** What personality traits are conveyed in these images of Ralph Waldo Emerson and Margaret Fuller? Explain your responses. **[Interpret]**

Background

One of Margaret Fuller's closest friends was Elizabeth Palmer Peabody (1804–1894), the eldest of three remarkable sisters. A writer of an extraordinary collection of letters and a tireless correspondent with many of the foremost thinkers of her day, Elizabeth remained energetic until her death, teaching, running a literary bookshop, and eventually founding the first kindergartens in the United States. Mary Peabody Mann (1806–1887) worked with Elizabeth in the kindergarten movement. She also taught and wrote a book about the Paiute tribe based on interviews with Sarah Winnemucca, a Paiute leader and educator. Mary married a man who became famous: Horace Mann, the educator. Sophia Peabody (1809–1871) married Nathaniel Hawthorne after a long courtship. She wanted to become an artist, and later encouraged similar ambitions in her daughter Rose Hawthorne.

▶**Critical Viewing**

Answer: Students may say that Emerson looks kind, thoughtful, and good-humored, because of his smile. They may say that Fuller's cast-down eyes make her look thoughtful and introspective.

Critical Thinking

1. Why do you think the Transcendentalist movement appealed to people like Emerson and Alcott?
   Answer: They were concerned about the age of industrialization that threatened to reduce the individual to a mechanized state. Transcendentalism offered man the opportunity to make the most of mind and spirit.

2. What does the prominence of Margaret Fuller in the Transcendentalist movement suggest about it?
   Answer: Transcendentalists were willing to treat women as intellectual equals.

from Nature ✦ from Self-Reliance
The Snowstorm ✦ Concord Hymn

Lesson Objectives

1. **To analyze and respond to literary elements**
   - Literary Analysis: Transcendentalism
   - Comparing Literary Works

2. **To read, comprehend, analyze, and critique nonfiction and poetry**
   - Reading Strategy: Challenging the Text
   - Reading Check Questions
   - Review and Assess Questions
   - Assessment Practice (ATE)

3. **To develop word analysis skills, fluency, and systematic vocabulary**
   - Vocabulary Development Lesson: Latin Root: -radi-

4. **To understand and apply written and oral language conventions**
   - Spelling Strategy
   - Grammar and Style Lesson: Vary Sentence Length

5. **To understand and apply appropriate writing and research strategies**
   - Writing Lesson: Critical Evaluation of a Philosophical Essay
   - Extension Activity: Profile

6. **To understand and apply listening and speaking strategies**
   - Extension Activity: Public Service Announcement

STEP-BY-STEP TEACHING GUIDE	PACING GUIDE
PRETEACH	
Motivate Students and Provide Background	
Use the Motivation activity (ATE p. 386)	10 min.
Read and discuss the author and background information (SE/ATE pp. 386, 388)	10 min.
Introduce the Concepts	
Introduce the Literary Analysis and Reading Strategy (SE/ATE p. 387)	15 min.
Pronounce the vocabulary words and read their definitions (SE p. 387)	5 min.
TEACH	
Monitor Comprehension	
Informally monitor comprehension by circulating while students read independently or in groups	25 min.
Monitor students' comprehension with the Reading Check notes (SE/ATE pp. 389, 391, 393, 395)	as students read
Develop vocabulary with Vocabulary notes (SE pp. 388, 389, 391, 392, 395; ATE p. 395)	as students read
Develop Understanding	
Develop students' understanding of Transcendentalism with the Literary Analysis annotations (SE pp. 388, 391; ATE pp. 388, 391)	10 min.
Develop students' ability to challenge the text with the Reading Strategy annotations (SE p. 390; ATE p. 390)	10 min.
ASSESS	
Assess Mastery	
Assess students' mastery of the Reading Strategy and Literary Analysis by having them answer the Review and Assess questions (SE/ATE p. 397)	15 min.
Use one or more of the print and media Assessment Resources (ATE p. 399)	up to 45 min.
EXTEND	
Apply Understanding	
Have students complete the Vocabulary Development Lesson and the Grammar and Style Lesson (SE p. 398)	20 min.
Apply students' ability to support their writing with relevant examples by using the Writing Lesson (SE/ATE p. 399)	45 min.
Apply students' understanding using one or more of the Extension Activities (SE p. 399)	20–90 min.

A **ACCELERATED INSTRUCTION:**
Use the strategies and activities identified with an **A**.

UNIVERSAL ACCESS
● = Below Level Students
▲ = On-Level Students
■ = Above Level Students

Time and Resource Manager

Reading Level: Average, Average, Average, Average
Average Number of Instructional Days: 4

RESOURCES		
PRINT 📖	**TRANSPARENCIES**	**TECHNOLOGY** 💿 🎧 📼
• **Beyond Literature,** Community Connection: Local Landmarks, p. 20 ▲ ■		• **Interest Grabber Video,** Tape 3 ● ▲ ■
• **Selection Support Workbook:** ● ▲ ■ Literary Analysis, p. 94 Reading Strategy, p. 93 Build Vocabulary, p. 91	• **Literary Analysis and Reading Transparencies,** pp. 39 and 40 ● ▲ ■	
		• **Listening to Literature** ● ▲ ■ Audiocassettes, Side 13 Audio CDs, CD 9
• **Literatura en español** ● ▲ • **Literary Analysis for Enrichment** ■		
• **Formal Assessment:** Selection Test, pp. 99–101 ● ▲ ■ • **Open Book Test,** pp. 58–60 ● ▲ ■ • **Performance Assessment and Portfolio Management,** p. 23 ● ▲ ■ **PRENTICE HALL** **ASSESSMENT** *SYSTEM* ● ▲ ■	**PRENTICE HALL** **ASSESSMENT** *SYSTEM* ● ▲ ■ Skills Practice Answers and Explanations on Transparencies	• **Test Bank Software** ● ▲ ■ • **Got It! Assessment Videotapes,** Tape 2 ● ▲
• **Selection Support Workbook:** ● ▲ ■ Grammar and Style, p. 92 • **Writing and Grammar,** Ruby Level ● ▲ ■ • **Extension Activities,** p. 20 ● ▲ ■	• **Daily Language Practice Transparencies** ● ▲ • **Writing Models and Graphic Organizers on Transparencies,** p. 75 ● ▲ ■	• **Writing and Grammar iText CD-ROM** ● ▲ ■ 💻 *Take It to the Net* www.phschool.com

■ **BLOCK SCHEDULING:** Use one 90-minute class period to preteach the selection and have students read it. Use a second 90-minute class period to assess students' mastery of skills and have them complete one of the Extension Activities.

Step-by-Step Teaching Guide
for pp. 386–387

Motivation

In his writings, Emerson touches on an issue that is especially relevant to high-school students: conformity, that is, behaving according to societal rules and customs. Write the word *conformity* on the chalkboard. Create a two-column chart with the headings Advantages and Disadvantages. Then have the class brainstorm for a list of as many advantages and disadvantages of conformity as they can think of. Take a vote to see whether students think that the advantages of conformity outweigh the disadvantages, or vice versa. Let students know that the writer whose works they're about to read is one of history's greatest champions of nonconformity.

▶ Interest Grabber Video

As an alternative, play "Concord's Legacy" on Tape 3 to engage student interest.

❶ Background

More About the Author

Emerson published the ninety-five page book *Nature* anonymously in Boston. It predates *The Dial*—the journal of the Transcendentalist Club—by four years. Almost everything Emerson wrote after *Nature* amplified or extended the ideas that appeared in it.

Prepare to Read

❶ *from* Nature ◆ *from* Self-Reliance ◆ Concord Hymn ◆ The Snowstorm

Ralph Waldo Emerson
(1803–1882)

Individuality, independence, and an appreciation for the wonders of nature—these are just a few of the principles that Ralph Waldo Emerson helped to ingrain in our nation's identity. Although his ideas were sometimes considered controversial, he had a tremendous influence on the young people of his time, and his beliefs have continued to inspire people to this day.

Throughout his life, Emerson's mind was constantly in motion, generating new ideas and defining and redefining his view of the world. His natural eloquence in expressing these ideas—in essays, lectures, and poetry—makes him one of the most quoted writers in American literature.

A New England Childhood The son of a Unitarian minister, Emerson was born in Boston. When Emerson was seven, his father died. The boy turned to a brilliant and eccentric aunt, Mary Moody Emerson, who encouraged his independent thinking. At fourteen, Emerson entered Harvard, where he began the journal he was to keep all his life. After postgraduate studies at Harvard Divinity School, he became pastor of the Second Church of Boston.

Finding His Niche Emerson's career as a minister was short-lived. Grief-stricken at the death of his young wife, and dissatisfied with what he saw as the spiritual restrictions in Unitarianism, Emerson resigned after three years. He then went to Europe, where he met the English writers Thomas Carlyle, Samuel Taylor Coleridge, and William Wordsworth. On his return to the United States, Emerson settled in Concord, Massachusetts. He married again and began his lifelong career of writing.

Emerson's second wife, Lydia Jackson of Plymouth, provided a supportive and secure family life. Emerson was now receiving money from his first wife's legacy and, for the first time in his life, was not living in poverty. The Emerson household welcomed a slowly widening circle of friends and admirers that included many of the country's most important thinkers.

In time, Emerson became widely sought as a lecturer throughout the nation. In fact, many of his essays began as lectures. Emerson kept working on the ideas until he had honed them into essay form. His talks attracted people of many ages and social classes, but it was the young people of his time who were most receptive to the thoughts of this often controversial philosopher.

An Independent Thinker Emerson was a soft-spoken man, given to neither physical nor emotional excess. Beneath his calm, sober demeanor existed a restless, highly individualistic mind that resisted conformity. "Good men," he once wrote, "must not obey the laws too well."

Emerson first achieved national fame in 1841, when he published *Essays*, a collection based on material from his journals and lectures. He went on to publish several more volumes of nonfiction, including *Essays, Second Volume* (1844), *Representative Men* (1849), and *The Conduct of Life* (1860).

Though Emerson was known mostly for his essays and lectures, he considered himself primarily a poet. "I am born a poet," he once wrote, "of a low class without doubt, yet a poet. That is my nature and my vocation." He published two successful volumes of poetry, *Poems* (1847) and *May-Day and Other Pieces* (1867). Like his essays, Emerson's poems express his beliefs in individuality and in humanity's spiritual connection to nature.

386 ◆ *A Growing Nation (1800–1870)*

TEACHING RESOURCES

The following resources can be used to enrich or extend the instruction for pp. 386–387.

Motivation

▶ **Interest Grabber Video**, Tape 3 ▪

Background

📖 **Beyond Literature**, p. 20

💻 *Take It to the Net*
Visit www.phschool.com for background and hotlinks for the selections.

Literary Analysis

📖 **Literary Analysis and Reading Transparencies**, p. 40 ▪

📖 **Selection Support**: Literary Analysis, p. 94

Reading

📖 **Literary Analysis and Reading Transparencies**, Challenge the Text, p. 39

▪ **BLOCK SCHEDULING:** Resources marked with this symbol provide varied instruction during 90-minute blocks.

Preview

Connecting to the Literature

"Be true to yourself." "Follow your dream." Most of us have faced the choices these sentiments address: whether to conform to the expectations of others, or follow our own inner voice. Emerson's writings address such choices. He comes down squarely in favor of nonconformity.

❷ Literary Analysis

Transcendentalism

Transcendentalism was an intellectual movement founded by Emerson. These are the cornerstones of Transcendentalist beliefs:

- Human senses are limited; they convey knowledge of the physical world, but deeper truths can be grasped only through intuition.
- The observation of nature illuminates the nature of human beings.
- God, nature, and humanity are united in a shared universal soul, or Over-Soul.

These beliefs pervade all of Emerson's work.

Comparing Literary Works

The essays that appear here are concerned with the nature of the individual, but they explore two different arenas. In one, Emerson looks at the individual's relationship to nature, and in the other, he explores the individual's relationship to society. As you read, compare how Emerson depicts the individual in nature versus the way he describes the individual among his or her fellow human beings.

❸ Reading Strategy

Challenging the Text

When you read a work that presents an argument, do not simply accept the ideas—challenge them. To **challenge a text**, question the author's assertions and reasoning. Compare the evidence the author offers with your personal experience or other reading. Then, decide whether you agree. Use a chart like the one shown here to record your thinking.

Vocabulary Development

blithe (blīth) *adj.* carefree (p. 388)

connate (kän′ āt′) *adj.* existing naturally; innate (p. 389)

chaos (kā′ äs′) *n.* disorder of matter and space, supposed to have existed before the ordered universe (p. 391)

aversion (ə vʉr′ zhən) *n.* object arousing an intense dislike (p. 392)

suffrage (suf′ rij) *n.* vote or voting (p. 392)

divines (də vīnz′) *n.* clergy (p. 392)

radiant (rā′ dē ənt) *adj.* shining brightly (p. 395)

tumultuous (tōō mul′ chōō əs) *adj.* rough; stormy (p. 395)

bastions (bas′ chənz) *n.* fortifications (p. 396)

> **Emerson's Statement**
> Whoso would be a man must be a nonconformist.
>
> ↓
>
> **Evidence from the text**
>
> ↓
>
> **Your experiences**
>
> ↓
>
> **Your reaction**

from Nature / from Self-Reliance / Concord Hymn / The Snowstorm ◆ 387

---

❷ Literary Analysis

Transcendentalism

- Tell students that as they read Emerson's essays and poems, they will focus on Transcendentalism, an intellectual movement that guided the writer's work. Read aloud the instruction about Transcendentalism. Then tell students that Transcendentalism affected most of the writers of Emerson's day. Have volunteers read aloud the basic precepts of the movement.
- Discuss the instruction under Comparing Literary Works and stress the comparison between individual-nature and individual-society.
- Use the Transcendentalism transparency in **Literary Analysis and Reading Transparencies,** p. 40 to help students to highlight examples of Transcendentalist thinking in Emerson's work.

❸ Reading Strategy

Challenging the Text

- Remind students that challenging the text will make them more engaged and involved readers.
- Provide this example from "Self-Reliance": "Whoso would be a man must be a nonconformist." Model ways to challenge the statement, such as by examining Emerson's supporting evidence.
- Direct students to use charts such as the one on the student page to challenge Emerson's text as they read.

Vocabulary Development

- Pronounce each vocabulary word for students, and read the definitions as a class. Have students identify any words with which they are already familiar.

CUSTOMIZE FOR UNIVERSAL ACCESS

For Less Proficient Readers	For English Learners	For Advanced Readers
Provide students with detailed instruction on how to complete the graphic organizer on the student page. Discuss each entry in the transparency to help students grasp what information belongs in each cell. Monitor students' progress as they read.	Make sure students understand that the writer's *argument* means his main points, not a disagreement, and that to *challenge* the text means to question its views. Explain that readers need to decide whether they agree with a writer's idea. To do this, they must determine whether or not the writer has presented the idea convincingly.	Remind students that challenges must be constructed around evidence and ideas, not around personal preference. Encourage students to continue their exploration of Emerson by finding other essays in the library. Have them share what they learn from these essays—and how they have challenged each.

 E-Teach

Visit E-Teach at www.phschool.com for teacher's essays on how to teach, with questions and answers.

**CUSTOMIZE INSTRUCTION
For Kinesthetic Learners**

Tell students that they can respond more fully to Emerson's views about nature by reading the poems in a natural setting. Encourage students to find such a setting, whether in a park, backyard, or even on a city stoop. Challenge them to study their surroundings for elements of nature, such as clouds, sky, trees, squirrels, or weather.

❶ About the Selection

In this excerpt from his book *Nature*, Emerson expresses his belief that the meaning of existence can be found by exploring the natural world. He describes how, through his exploration of nature, he has discovered that he is spiritually connected with the universe, with God, and with every living thing.

❷ Literary Analysis

Transcendentalism

• Read the bracketed passage aloud. Ask students to identify the jarring image in the passage and to explain what Emerson means by it.
Possible response: "I become a transparent eyeball" is a jarring image. Emerson means that he sees everything; the metaphor suggests the poet is like a single, huge eye.

• Ask students the Literary Analysis question on p. 388: According to this passage, what is the relationship between Emerson and nature?
Possible response: Emerson feels spiritually a part of nature and every living thing, as well as God.

❶ *from* **Nature**

Ralph Waldo Emerson

❺

Background

During the 1830s and 1840s, Emerson and a small group of like-minded friends gathered regularly in his study to discuss philosophy, religion, and literature. Among them were Emerson's protégé, Henry David Thoreau, as well as educator Bronson Alcott, feminist writer Margaret Fuller, and ex-clergyman and author George Ripley. The intimate group, known as the Transcendental Club, developed a philosophical system that stressed intuition, individuality, and self-reliance. In 1836, Emerson published *Nature*, the lengthy essay (excerpted here) that became the Transcendental Club's unofficial statement of belief.

Nature is a setting that fits equally well a comic or a mourning piece. In good health, the air is a cordial of incredible virtue. Crossing a bare common,[1] in snow puddles, at twilight, under a clouded sky, without having in my thoughts any occurrence of special good fortune, I have enjoyed a perfect exhilaration. I am glad to the brink of fear. In the woods, too, a man casts off his years, as the snake his slough, and at what period soever of life is always a child. In the woods is perpetual youth. Within these plantations of God, a decorum and sanctity reign, a perennial festival is dressed, and the guest sees not how he should tire of them in a thousand years. In the woods, we return to reason and faith. There I feel that nothing can befall me in life—no disgrace, no calamity (leaving me my eyes), which nature cannot repair. Standing on the bare ground—my head bathed by the blithe air and uplifted into infinite space—all mean egotism

---

1. **common** *n.* piece of open public land.

❷ Literary Analysis
Transcendentalism
According to this passage, what is the relationship between Emerson and nature?

blithe (blīth) *adj.* carefree

TEACHING RESOURCES

The following resources can be used to enrich or extend the instruction for pp. 388–396.

Literary Analysis

📖 **Writing Models and Graphic Organizers on Transparencies**, p. 75

📖 **Literary Analysis and Reading Transparencies**, p. 40

Reading

📖 **Selection Support:** Reading Strategy, p. 93; Build Vocabulary, p. 91

🎧 **Listening to Literature Audiocassettes**, Side 13 ▪

💿 **Listening to Literature Audio CDs**, CD 9 ▪

▪ **BLOCK SCHEDULING:** Resources marked with this symbol provide varied instruction during 90-minute blocks.

vanishes. I become a transparent eyeball; I am nothing; I see all; the currents of the Universal Being circulate through me; I am part or parcel of God. The name of the nearest friend sounds then foreign and accidental: to be brothers, to be acquaintances, master or servant, is then a trifle and a disturbance. I am the lover of uncontained and immortal beauty. In the wilderness, I find something more dear and <u>connate</u> than in the streets or villages. In the tranquil landscape, and especially in the distant line of the horizon, man beholds somewhat as beautiful as his own nature.

The greatest delight which the fields and woods minister is the suggestion of an occult relation between man and the vegetable. I am not alone and unacknowledged. They nod to me, and I to them. The

connate (kän′ āt) *adj.* existing naturally; innate

❸ ☑Reading Check

Which emotions does Emerson experience when in the woods?

Sunset, Frederick E. Church, Munson-Williams-Proctor Institute Museum of Art, Utica, New York

❹ ▲ Critical Viewing Emerson says that nature often allows us to become transparent eyeballs, seeing all, but remaining detached from the business of the world. In what ways does this image reinforce his statement? **[Support]**

❺

from *Nature* ◆ 389

❸ ☑Reading Check

Answer: Emerson experiences delight.

❹ ▶Critical Viewing

Answer: Students may refer to the painting's serenity, its apparent meshing of land and heavens, the reflection of the landscape in the water, and the complete absence of any traces of humankind.

❺ Background

Art

Sunset, by Frederic E. Church

Frederic Church, a student of Hudson River School leader Thomas Cole, became a key member of that group. This painting reveals his deep love of nature and his belief that painting should depict the natural world in a grand way. The painting glows with the vibrancy of nature at the most colorful moment of the day—sunset. Use this question for discussion: Is this painting an appropriate illustration for Emerson's essay? Why or why not?

Answer: Some students may say that the painting is appropriate because it portrays the enduring grandeur of nature. Others may say that a painting portraying a person appreciating nature would be more appropriate.

CUSTOMIZE FOR UNIVERSAL ACCESS

For Less Proficient Readers

Given our fast-paced, technological society, students may have trouble understanding the basis of Transcendentalism. Explain that this philosophy centers on gaining spiritual knowledge through recognizing one's connection to the universe, God, and the surrounding world. One way to achieve this is to reduce the unnecessary clutter in one's life, striving for simplicity and a return to the basics. Create activities that encourage students to experience life in a more direct sense. For example, you could have them walk to a destination rather than ride in a car. They could also write their assignments out in longhand rather than type them. Encourage students to cook dinner or begin a craft. All these exercises will help them regain a transcendental connection to daily life. As they pursue such activities, students might consider whether they believe that all living things are connected, and if so, how.

❻ Reading Strategy

Challenging the Text

- According to Emerson, from where does the power to produce "this delight" come?
  Answer: The power comes from human beings, not nature, or from a combination of both.

- Then, ask students the Reading Strategy question on p. 390: Do you agree or disagree with this statement about a harmony between human beings and nature? Explain.
  Possible response: Students may say that the power to produce delight resides in nature, but the ability to experience it resides in us.

Review and Assess

1. Students' responses will vary.

2. (a) It vanishes in the woods. (b) Students should identify it as petty narcissism. (c) It's replaced with divinity and delight.

3. (a) He becomes this after he sheds "mean egotism" amidst nature. (b) He feels connected to nature and to God. (c) Emerson, like everyone and everything, is connected to the Universal Being.

4. (a) It comes from a harmony of man and nature. (b) Possible response: He means that it is forever linked and intertwined, but not necessarily that it is serene.

5. (a) No, sometimes nature is less welcoming. It depends, in part, on nature's mood and, in part, on the emotions we bring to the woods. (b) He means that nature reflects our emotions or mood.

6. (a) Possible response: Nature teaches us how we are connected to everyone and everything around us. (b) Students' responses should be well reasoned and supported by their evaluation of Emerson's ideas.

7. Students may respond that the growth of the environmental movement and the popularity of outdoor recreational activities prove that Americans still value nature.

---

waving of the boughs in the storm is new to me and old. It takes me by surprise, and yet is not unknown. Its effect is like that of a higher thought or a better emotion coming over me, when I deemed I was thinking justly or doing right.

❻ Yet it is certain that the power to produce this delight does not reside in nature, but in man, or in a harmony of both. It is necessary to use these pleasures with great temperance. For nature is not always tricked[2] in holiday attire, but the same scene which yesterday breathed perfume and glittered as for the frolic of the nymphs is over-spread with melancholy today. Nature always wears the colors of the spirit. To a man laboring under calamity, the heat of his own fire hath sadness in it. Then there is a kind of contempt of the landscape felt by him who has just lost by death a dear friend. The sky is less grand as it shuts down over less worth in the population.

---

2. **tricked** *v.* dressed.

Review and Assess

Thinking About the Selection

1. **Respond:** Which of your experiences have made you "glad to the brink of fear"? Explain.

2. (a) **Recall:** Under what circumstances, according to Emerson, does "mean egotism" vanish? (b) **Define:** How would you define Emerson's idea of "mean egotism"? (c) **Analyze Cause and Effect:** In nature, with what emotional state does Emerson suggest that "mean egotism" is replaced?

3. (a) **Recall:** When does Emerson become a "transparent eyeball"? (b) **Analyze:** What are the characteristics of this experience? (c) **Connect:** In what ways does this description reflect the Transcendentalist belief in an Over-Soul?

4. (a) **Recall:** Where does the power to produce delight come from? (b) **Define:** In stating that there is a harmony between human beings and nature, do you think Emerson means the relationship is always serene, or not? Explain.

5. (a) **Infer:** According to Emerson, is our experience with nature the same every time we go to the woods? Explain. (b) **Interpret:** What does Emerson mean when he says that "Nature always wears the colors of the spirit"?

6. (a) **Evaluate:** What is Emerson's main point in this essay? (b) **Assess:** Do you find Emerson's message convincing? Explain why you do or do not accept his ideas about nature.

7. **Take a Position:** Do you find any evidence of Emerson's reverence for nature in American culture today? Explain.

Reading Strategy
Challenging the Text Do you agree or disagree with this statement about a harmony between human beings and nature? Explain.

ENRICHMENT: Social Studies Connection

Emerson's Abolitionist Views

After the passage of the Fugitive Slave Act, which required people to return runaway slaves to the owners, Emerson became an active and vocal abolitionist. He remarked that anyone building a house should include space in it for fugitive slaves. Prompt students to discuss how Emerson's position on slavery relates to his statement in this essay that "Nothing is at last sacred but the integrity of your own mind."

Encourage interested students to find out more about the details of the Fugitive Slave Act and the Compromise of 1850 of which it was part. Have them research how abolitionists responded to the law. Invite students to share any incidents and anecdotes they encounter.

❼

from

Self-Reliance

Ralph Waldo Emerson

There is a time in every man's education when he arrives at the conviction that envy is ignorance; that imitation is suicide; that he must take himself for better, for worse, as his portion; that though the wide universe is full of good, no kernel of nourishing corn can come to him but through his toil bestowed on that plot of ground which is given to him to till. The power which resides in him is new in nature, and none but he knows what that is which he can do, nor does he know until he has tried. Not for nothing one face, one character, one fact makes much impression on him, and another none. This sculpture in the memory is not without preestablished harmony. The eye was placed where one ray should fall, that it might testify of that particular ray. We but half express ourselves, and are ashamed of that divine idea which each of us represents. It may be safely trusted as proportionate and of good issues, so it be faithfully imparted, but God will not have his work made manifest by cowards. A man is relieved and gay when he has put his heart into his work and done his best; but what he has said or done otherwise, shall give him no peace. It is a deliverance which does not deliver. In the attempt his genius deserts him; no muse befriends; no invention, no hope.

Trust thyself: every heart vibrates to that iron string. Accept the place the divine providence has found for you; the society of your contemporaries, the connection of events. Great men have always done so and confided themselves childlike to the genius of their age, betraying their perception that the absolutely trustworthy was stirring at their heart, working through their hands, predominating in all their being. And we are now men, and must accept in the highest mind the same transcendent destiny; and not minors and invalids in a protected corner, but guides, redeemers, and benefactors. Obeying the Almighty effort and advancing on <u>Chaos</u> and the Dark. . . .

Society everywhere is in conspiracy against the manhood of every one of its members. Society is a joint-stock company in which the members agree for the better securing of his bread to each shareholder, to surrender the liberty and culture of the eater. The virtue

❽

Literary Analysis
Transcendentalism
What does the passage beginning "Trust thyself" tell you about Emerson's belief in the importance of the individual?

chaos (kā′ äs′) *n.* disorder of matter and space, supposed to have existed before the ordered universe

✓ **Reading Check** ❾

What does Emerson believe about being true to oneself?

from Self-Reliance ◆ 391

CUSTOMIZE INSTRUCTION FOR UNIVERSAL ACCESS

For Less Proficient Readers	For Special Needs Students	For Gifted/Talented Students
Encourage students to look closely at the first sentence of each paragraph. These sentences essentially serve as an outline of the key points in the essay. By grasping the ideas in these sentences, students will be well on their way to identifying Emerson's main ideas. As they determine the meaning of each top-pic sentence, have students draft a list of the main points.	Have students read the essay in small groups, pausing at the end of each paragraph to identify the sentence that best sums up its meaning. Students should then try to restate the meaning of each topic sentence in their own words. Circulate to check on the progress of the groups and clarify any misinterpretations.	Provide students with time to research more information about Emerson at www.phschool.com. Then, challenge them to give a brief talk to the class in which they relate information about Emerson's personal experiences to the ideas he discusses in *Nature* and *Self-Reliance*.

---

❼ **About the Selections**

In his essay, "Self-Reliance," which echoes a theme common to many of his works, Emerson exhorts readers to avoid blindly conforming to the ideas and behavior dictated by society or peers. Instead, he urges people to think and act independently.

In the poems "Concord Hymn" (p. 393) and "The Snowstorm" (p.395), Emerson continues his celebration of country and nature. In "Concord Hymn," Emerson praises the bravery of the minutemen who fought at Lexington and Concord. The poem conveys the message that people who make great sacrifices for noble causes such as freedom will never be forgotten. In "The Snowstorm," Emerson develops an extended metaphor in which he compares nature's force during a snowstorm to an architect crafting a building. The poem conveys the message that nature is capable of creating works of amazing beauty that parallel or surpass those produced by human beings.

❽ **Literary Analysis**

Transcendentalism

• Read aloud the bracketed text to students, and then reread the opening two words: "Trust thyself." Urge students to find evidence in the paragraph for this opening exhortation.

• To help students, go around the classroom and have volunteers express the meaning of each sentence in their own words.

• Ask students the Literary Analysis question on p. 391: What does the passage beginning "Trust thyself" tell you about Emerson's belief in the importance of the individual? Possible response: He believes the individual's importance is from God and that people must therefore honor it and trust in it.

❾ ✓ **Reading Check**

Answer: Emerson believes it produces the best work and the most spiritual peace. He believes that unless one is true to oneself, one will never find inspiration.

Review and Assess

1. Students may cite our society's tendency to admire "self-made" people.

2. **(a)** He describes it as a joint-stock company.
   (b) Its purpose is to conspire against individual self-reliance.
   (c) People should not care how others perceive them.

3. **(a)** They were all misunderstood.
   (b) He points out that some of the greatest people who ever lived were misunderstood.

4. **(a)** It is important because it distinguishes between a rational consistency of thought and purpose and an unreasoning, compulsory conformity.
   (b) Possible response: Emerson clearly said that a *foolish* consistency was to be avoided. He would be unlikely to advocate inconsistency in scholarship, for example, or in friendships or family life.

5. **(a)** For Emerson, the divine is God's idea of what each of us might be if we had the courage to live up to our full creative potential. **(b)** Possible response: He would say that the reason for living is to seek out God's purpose for us and to pursue it without fear of society's pressures and opinions. Students' explanations should be supported with references from the text.

6. Students' responses should reflect a careful reading of the essay.

---

in most request is conformity. Self-reliance is its <u>aversion</u>. It loves not realities and creators, but names and customs.

Whoso would be a man must be a nonconformist. He who would gather immortal palms must not be hindered by the name of goodness, but must explore if it be goodness. Nothing is at last sacred but the integrity of your own mind. Absolve you to yourself, and you shall have the <u>suffrage</u> of the world. . . .

A foolish consistency is the hobgoblin of little minds, adored by little statesmen and philosophers and <u>divines</u>. With consistency a great soul has simply nothing to do. He may as well concern himself with his shadow on the wall. Speak what you think now in hard words and tomorrow speak what tomorrow thinks in hard words again, though it contradict everything you said today. "Ah, so you shall be sure to be misunderstood?"—is it so bad, then, to be misunderstood? Pythagoras was misunderstood, and Socrates, and Jesus, and Luther, and Copernicus, and Galileo, and Newton,[1] and every pure and wise spirit that ever took flesh. To be great is to be misunderstood. . . .

aversion (ə vur′ zhən) *n.* object arousing an intense or definite dislike

suffrage (suf′ rij) *n.* vote or voting

divines (də vīnz′) *n.* clergy

---

1. **Pythagoras . . . Newton** individuals who made major contributions to scientific, philosophical, or religious thinking.

Review and Assess

Thinking About the Selection

1. **Respond:** Which aspects, if any, of today's American culture reflect Emerson's belief in self-reliance?

2. **(a) Recall:** What terms does Emerson use to describe society? **(b) Interpret:** According to Emerson, what is society's main purpose? **(c) Draw Conclusions:** In what ways does Emerson believe people should be affected by the way others perceive them?

3. **(a) Recall:** According to Emerson, what do Pythagoras, Socrates, Jesus, Luther, Copernicus, Galileo, and Newton have in common? **(b) Support:** What evidence does Emerson use to support his claim that "to be great is to be misunderstood"?

4. **(a) Make a Judgment:** How important is Emerson's use of the adjective "foolish" in his discussion of consistency? **(b) Speculate:** Do you think there would be any circumstances in which Emerson would advocate the benefits of consistency? Explain.

5. **(a) Interpret:** According to Emerson, what role does the "divine" have in determining each person's circumstances? **(b) Generalize:** What would Emerson say is each person's reason for living? Explain.

6. **Apply:** Which of Emerson's statements, if any, would you choose as a guideline for personal conduct? Explain.

✹ ENRICHMENT: Social Studies Connection

Early Revolutionary Battles

In April 1775, a British military force marched to confiscate colonial arms they knew were stockpiled in Concord, Massachusetts. Along the way, they were confronted at dawn on April 19 by a small group of militia on the Lexington green. The British dispersed the Americans, killing ten, and then moved on to Concord, five miles away. There, they were met by a larger contingent of militia, who attacked them at the North Bridge. At this spot, the first British blood of the Revolution was spilled. The British retreated to Boston. On the way, they were repeatedly attacked by thousands of American militia. Many years later, sculptor Daniel Chester French created his commemorative statue with the support of a Concord resident who wished to memorialize the spot where Americans fell.

Concord Hymn

Sung at the Completion of the Battle Monument, April 19, 1836
Ralph Waldo Emerson

By the rude[1] bridge that arched the flood,
    Their flag to April's breeze unfurled,
Here once the embattled farmers stood,
    And fired the shot heard round the world.

5 The foe long since in silence slept;
    Alike the conqueror silent sleeps;
And Time the ruined bridge has swept
    Down the dark stream which seaward creeps.

On this green bank, by this soft stream,
10   We set today a votive[2] stone;
That memory may their deed redeem,
    When, like our sires, our sons are gone.

Spirit, that made those heroes dare
    To die, and leave their children free,
15 Bid Time and Nature gently spare
    The shaft we raise to them and thee.

1. **rude** (rood) *adj.* crude or rough in form or workmanship.
2. **votive** (vōt´ iv) *adj.* dedicated in fulfillment of a vow or pledge.

▲ Critical Viewing
"Concord Hymn" was written for the unveiling of this monument commemorating the minutemen, who fought the British at Lexington and Concord, Massachusetts, in April 1775. What aspect of the sculpture communicate the emotions of the poem? **[Connect]**

Review and Assess

Thinking About the Selection

1. **Respond:** What do you think of war monuments? Explain.

2. **(a) Recall:** What event took place by the "rude bridge"? **(b) Interpret:** What does the poet mean by the image of "the shot heard round the world"?

3. **(a) Recall:** What has happened to the bridge since the battle that took place there? **(b) Analyze:** How does the poem's organization reflect a sense of the passage of time?

4. **(a) Recall:** In the last stanza, whom does the poet address directly? **(b) Infer:** In what way does this direct address reflect Transcendentalist beliefs in an Over-Soul?

5. **Apply:** Which aspects of "Concord Hymn" would be appropriate for the dedication of other war monuments?

Concord Hymn ◆ 393

Background

Art

Minute Man, **1871–1875, by Daniel Chester French**

Daniel Chester French completed this commemorative statue for the centennial of the American Revolution. The project was funded by a Concorde resident who wished to mark the spot where Americans fell. *Minute Man* was cast using bronze from a decommissioned Civil War cannon. Emerson, a member of the committee that requested the work, praised the statue at its unveiling. Guide students to notice the position of the soldier's feet and the plow on which his hand rests. Then, use these questions for discussion:

1. What is the significance of the minuteman's firm grip on the plow?
   Answer: It symbolizes that he is a peaceful farmer who took up a rifle because his land and freedom were threatened.

2. Why do you think French placed the minuteman's foot in a raised position?
   Answer: It shows that the soldier is ready to fight.

▶ Critical Viewing

Answer: Students should note that, like the poem, the statue captures the courage and devotion of the minutemen.

Answers for p. 393

Review and Assess

1. Possible response: It is important to honor those who die defending their countries.

2. (a) Americans fell to British guns. (b) It heralded the founding of a new nation.

3. (a) It has fallen apart. (b) It acknowledges that the events are long past but that people today still revere them.

4. (a) He addresses a "Spirit." (b) It assumes that this spirit created the brave and nonconforming indivduals who fought at Concord and Lexington.

5. Possible response: The idea that we should honor those who have died for freedom could fit on any war memorial.

CUSTOMIZE FOR UNIVERSAL ACCESS

For Special Needs Students	For Less Proficient Readers	For English Learners
Work with students stanza by stanza to paraphrase the lines in the poem. Pause after each stanza to invite questions and suggestions about paraphrasing. Continue until all four stanzas have been paraphrased. Then, help students read the complete selection.	Have students read aloud the final stanza of the poem. Help them paraphrase the wish that Emerson expresses in this stanza. Point out that he asks the same Creator or Spirit who inspired the bravery of the minutemen to command time and nature to spare the monument from the ravages of time and the elements.	Direct students' attention to words such as *rude*. Remind students that words can have multiple meanings. In this case, Emerson has used an uncommon meaning for *rude*. Point out the definition in footnote #1: crude or rough in form or workmanship. Then help students paraphrase the first line. (By a simple bridge over a creek.)

Transcendentalism

- Read aloud the bracketed passage. Point out that Emerson describes nature's impact on the human experience.

- Ask students this Literary Analysis question: How does Emerson's description of the storm and the snowbound people reflect his Transcendentalist beliefs?

  Possible answer: It suggests that nature—which here keeps everyone inside—illuminates human experience by providing a moment of peace within the storm.

394 ◆ A Growing Nation (1800–1870)

☀ ENRICHMENT: Science Connection

New England Weather

Based on Emerson's description of this snowstorm, it probably qualified as a blizzard. Today, the National Weather Service defines a blizzard as any storm containing strong winds and large amounts of snow. Winds must be blowing steadily at more than thirty-five miles per hour while visibility must be reduced to one-quarter mile over a period of at least three hours.

While some may argue that New England's weather has changed in the years since Emerson wrote "The Snowstorm," the region still has plenty of snowy days and even a few blizzards. For example, the city of Boston has received an average of forty-two inches of snow each year since records have been kept. Other places in New England get significantly more snow, such as Caribou, Maine, which received more than one hundred inches of snow in 1998. About ten of those inches fell in one day during a late January storm.

⓬ **Build Vocabulary**

Latin Root –*radi*–

- Call students' attention to the word *radiant* and its definition. Tell students that the Latin word root –*radi*– means "spoke" or "ray."
- Challenge students to suggest other words containing this root. Possible answers: radial, radiate, radiator, radio, radiology
- Ask students how the word *radiant* contributes to the meaning of the stanza. Possible response: It evokes a cozy mood by suggesting that the fireplace's heat and security radiate through the room to shield occupants from the storm.

⓭ ✔**Reading Check**

Answer: He describes the arrival of the snow and wind, the wind's blowing of the snow, the snow's covering of buildings and landscape.

The Snowstorm

Ralph Waldo Emerson

Announced by all the trumpets of the sky,
Arrives the snow, and, driving o'er the fields,
Seems nowhere to alight: the whited air
Hides hills and woods, the river, and the heaven,
5 And veils the farmhouse at the garden's end.
The sled and traveler stopped, the courier's feet
Delayed, all friends shut out, the house mates sit
Around the <u>radiant</u> fireplace, enclosed
In a <u>tumultuous</u> privacy of storm.

radiant (rā′ dē ənt) *adj.* shining brightly

tumultuous (tŏŏ mul′ chŏŏ əs) *adj.* rough; stormy

⓭ ✔**Reading Check**

What action of the wind and snow does the poet describe?

The Snowstorm ◆ 395

CUSTOMIZE INSTRUCTION FOR UNIVERSAL ACCESS

For Less Proficient Readers	For English Learners	For Advanced Readers
As students read the poem, help them understand Emerson's extended metaphor. Direct students' attention to the final stanza. Guide students to understand that the snowstorm, by coating everything with snow, has created the illusion that it has formed from snow in a single night buildings that would take people years to build.	Review the definition of metaphor with students and explain that sometimes writers extend a metaphor throughout a work. In "The Snowstorm," Emerson compares nature to a human architect. Help students find examples of the metaphor, such as Emerson's description of the "north wind's masonry."	Draw students' attention to the extended metaphor Emerson uses to describe the effect of the snowstorm. Then, remind students of reading the excerpt from *Snowbound* (p. 274) and "The First Snowfall" (p. 272). Challenge students to compare and contrast the figurative language each poet uses to describe snow and snowstoms.

Answers for p. 396

Review and Assess

1. Possible response: I am similarly fascinated by the visual effects snow can create, although at times these cause me inconvenience.

2. **(a)** The sled and traveler must stop; the courier is delayed; the house mates remain inside together.
   (b) Possible response: He means that the storm's disturbance creates privacy by keeping visitors away and keeping residents from leaving.

3. **(a)** The following words relate to the design and construction of buildings: *masonry, quarry, furnished with tile, artificer, bastions, projected roof, work, number or proportion, coop or kennel, wall to wall.*
   (b) They suggest that he views the snowstorm as a gifted creator or artisan.

4. **(a)** It leaves human artists and architects to imitate, slowly and with difficulty, what the storm created overnight.
   (b) It reflects the idea that humans can find a parallel to their own creative force in nature and vice versa.

5. Possible response: Snowstorms can cause tremendous damage to buildings and to nature, as well as to business through transportation delays, stranded employees, and lack of commerce.

---

10 Come see the north wind's masonry.
    Out of an unseen quarry evermore
    Furnished with tile, the fierce artificer
    Curves his white <u>bastions</u> with projected roof
    Round every windward stake, or tree, or door.
15 Speeding, the myriad-handed, his wild work
    So fanciful, so savage, nought cares he
    For number or proportion. Mockingly,
    On coop or kennel he hangs Parian[1] wreaths;
    A swan-like form invests the hidden thorn;
20 Fills up the farmer's lane from wall to wall.

    Maugre[2] the farmer's sighs; and at the gate
    A tapering turret overtops the work.
    And when his hours are numbered, and the world
    Is all his own, retiring, as he were not,
25 Leaves, when the sun appears, astonished Art
    To mimic in slow structures, stone by stone,
    Built in an age, the mad wind's nightwork,
    The frolic architecture of the snow.

bastions (bas´ chənz) *n.* fortifications

---

1. **Parian** (per´ ē ən) *adj.* referring to a fine, white marble of the Greek city Paros.
2. **Maugre** (mô´ gər) *prep.* in spite of.

Review and Assess

Thinking About the Selection

1. **Respond:** How does your attitude toward snow compare with Emerson's?

2. **(a) Recall:** In the first stanza, what effect does the storm have on the "sled and traveler," the "courier," and the "house mates"? **(b) Analyze:** Explain what Emerson means when he refers to the "tumultuous privacy of the storm" in line 9.

3. **(a) Recall:** In the second stanza, which words relate to the design and construction of buildings? **(b) Analyze:** What do these words suggest about the comparison the poet is making between the storm and an architect or artist?

4. **(a) Recall:** According to lines 25–28, what has the storm left behind "when the sun appears"? **(b) Synthesize:** Which aspects of Emerson's Transcendentalist beliefs does this image reflect?

5. **Speculate:** Emerson expresses a favorable attitude toward the snowstorm. Why might some people living in northern climates not share Emerson's attitude?

ASSESSMENT PRACTICE: Reading Comprehension

Make Inferences and Generalizations   **(For more practice, see Test Preperation Workbook, p.22.)**

The reading sections of tests often require students to make inferences that are drawn from implied information in written texts. For example, students might be asked to recognize implied messages found in poetry.

According to the third stanza of "Concord Hymn," what is the purpose of the monument?

A to remember the sacrifices made by Revolutionary War soldiers

B to add support to the crumbling Lexington bridge

C to commemorate the British soldiers who died in the American Revolution

D to direct visitors to the towns of Lexington and Concord

The last three answers contain incorrect information. *A* is supported by the lines, "That memory may their deed redeem/When, like our sires, our sons are gone."

Review and Assess

Literary Analysis

Transcendentalism

1. What does "Nature" reveal about the **Transcendentalist** attitude toward nature? Support your answers with examples from the text.
2. Emerson writes: "Speak what you think now in hard words and tomorrow speak what tomorrow thinks in hard words, though it contradict everything you said today." In what ways does this statement reflect the Transcendentalist belief in intuition?
3. Does the image of a "transparent eyeball" effectively convey the Transcendentalist idea of a universal Over-Soul? Explain.

Comparing Literary Works

4. (a) Use a chart like the one shown to compare and contrast Emerson's descriptions of the bonds between people in society and those between people and nature. (b) Which bonds would Emerson say are more important? Explain.

People and Nature ·····> ( ) <····· People in Society

5. In "Nature," Emerson says the woods are the "plantations of God," and in "Self-Reliance," he portrays individuals as "that divine idea which each of us represents." Do these passages express similar ideas about the relationship of God to people and the world? Explain.

Reading Strategy

Challenging the Text

6. Consider this assertion from "Self-Reliance": "A foolish consistency is the hobgoblin of little minds." **Challenge the text** by answering these questions: (a) What evidence does Emerson provide to support his position? (b) Offer two arguments against this statement. (c) Do you agree with this statement? Support your answer.

Extend Understanding

7. **Cultural Connection:** Some cultures view children as innocents, and others view them as inherently bad. How do you think the Transcendentalists viewed childhood? Support your answer.

from Nature / from Self-Reliance / Concord Hymn / The Snowstorm ◆ *397*

Quick Review

The **Transcendentalist** philosophy asserts that knowledge of fundamental reality is beyond the reach of a person's limited senses and is derived through intuition rather than sensory experience.

To **challenge the text,** question the author's assertions and decide whether or not you agree with them.

 Take It to the Net
www.phschool.com

Take the interactive self-test online to check your understanding of these selections.

ENRICHMENT: Further Reading

Other Works by Ralph Waldo Emerson

The Complete Works of Ralph Waldo Emerson, Edward W. Emerson, ed.

The Letters of Ralph Waldo Emerson, Ralph L. Rusk, ed.

 Take It to the Net
Visit www.phschool.com for more information on Ralph Waldo Emerson.

Answers for p. 397

Review and Assess

1. The Transcendentalists had a deep love for nature and a deep interest in humanity's relationship to nature. Emerson says that nature has the power to fill him with great joy and to stimulate childlike wonder. He also expresses the belief that nature reflects our personal moods.

2. The Transcendentalists believed that since real truths cannot be found in physical reality, we must trust intuition, even if it changes from day to day.

3. The image suggests that the speaker sees all, but can also blend with everything around him, merging into the universal Over-Soul.

4. **(a)** Emerson suggests that our relationship to nature transcends our relationship to one another, since social ties are largely expedients for material survival, whereas our relationship to nature binds us to the spiritual foundation of all life. **(b)** Emerson seems to have regarded the relationship between people and nature as more essential than the relationships between people in society. For Emerson, society was mostly a constraining force on human individuality.

5. Both of these phrases suggest that Emerson believed in a God who had some role in creating both humans and nature.

6. **(a)** Emerson claims that only small-minded people are strictly consistent; people with great minds speak their opinions, even if they change with time. Inconsistency will cause you to be misunderstood, just as the greatest and wisest people in history have been misunderstood. **(b)** Possible response: People who are inconsistent don't take the time to think before they speak. Misunderstood people are not necessarily great; they may just have poorly organized their ideas. **(c)** Students should explain the reasoning behind their responses.

7. Possible response: They probably viewed childhood

continued

Answers continued

positively, seeing it as a time free of the constraints of social convention and abundant in the leisure to explore nature.

❶ Vocabulary Development

Word Analysis

Possible responses:

1. A radiator projects heat into a room.
2. To radiate is to send out rays of light, heat, or other energy.
3. A radio receives waves from a transmitter and converts them into sound that radiates from its speakers.
4. The radius of a circle is the measurement from the center to the periphery.
5. Radiation is the process by which energy in the form of rays of light, heat, etc. is emitted.
6. Matter is radioactive when it gives off radiation.

Spelling Strategy

1. breathe
2. clothe
3. lithe
4. writhe
5. seethe
6. lathe

Concept Development

1. antonyms
2. synonyms
3. synonyms
4. synonyms
5. antonyms
6. antonyms
7. synonyms
8. antonyms
9. synonyms

❷ Grammar and Style

Looking at Style

Students should identify passages in which sentence length varies by at least ten words and describe their effect on the reader.

Writing Application

Paragraphs should focus on a short journey and should contain at least three sentences that vary in length by more than ten words from the other sentences. Students should correctly highlight short and long sentences.

Integrate Language Skills

❶ Vocabulary Development Lesson

Word Analysis: Latin Root -radi-

The Latin root -radi- means "spoke" or "ray." This root contributes to the meaning of radiant— "shining brightly" or "giving off rays of light."

Knowing the meaning of the root -radi-, write a definition for each of these words.

1. radiator
2. radiate
3. radio
4. radius
5. radiation
6. radioactive

Spelling Strategy

A final silent e often helps create the sound of a long vowel followed by a voiced th—for example, as in blithe. Follow this principle to complete the spelling of each word.

1. brea__
2. clo__
3. li__
4. wri__
5. see__
6. la__

Concept Development: Antonyms or Synonyms?

Review the vocabulary list on page 387. Then, study each item below to identify which of the following word pairs are antonyms and which are synonyms.

1. chaos, order
2. aversion, repugnance
3. suffrage, vote
4. divines, ministers
5. blithe, anxious
6. connate, acquired
7. radiant, luminous
8. tumultuous, serene
9. bastions, bulwarks

❷ Grammar and Style Lesson

Varying Sentence Length

In "Nature" and "Self-Reliance," Emerson often follows a very long sentence with one or more short ones. **Varying sentence length** enables Emerson to sustain the reader's interest and to establish rhythm. In addition, he often uses a short sentence to clarify or emphasize ideas he has expressed in the longer sentence preceding it. Notice this pattern in the example from *Nature*:

> Crossing a bare common, in snow puddles, at twilight, under a clouded sky, without having in my thoughts any occurrence of special good fortune, I have enjoyed a perfect exhilaration. I am glad to the brink of fear.

Looking at Style Find three passages from Emerson's essays in which he varies the length of his sentences. Explain the effect of the sentence variations in each passage.

Writing Application Write one paragraph describing your walk home from school or some other short journey. Vary your sentence length to create rhythm and maintain reader interest.

After you draft, highlight your short sentences in one color and your long sentences in another color to see the pattern you have established. In what ways does varying your sentence length improve your writing?

W̶G̶ *Prentice Hall Writing and Grammar Connection: Chapter 20, Section 3*

TEACHING RESOURCES

The following resources can be used to enrich or extend the instruction for pp. 398–399.

Vocabulary

📖 **Selection Support:** Build Vocabulary, p. 91

📖 **Vocabulary and Spelling Practice Book** (Use this booklet for skills enrichment.) 📱

Grammar

📖 **Selection Support:** Grammar and Style, p. 92

W̶G̶ **Writing and Grammar,** Ruby Level, p. 487

📱 **Daily Language Practice Transparencies** 📱

Writing

W̶G̶ **Writing and Grammar,** Ruby Level, p. 309

💿 **Writing and Grammar iText CD-ROM**

📄 **Writing Models and Graphic Organizers on Transparencies,** p. 75

BLOCK SCHEDULING: Resources marked with this symbol provide varied instruction during 90-minute blocks.

3 Writing Lesson

Critical Evaluation of a Philosophical Essay

Ever since they were first published, Emerson's essays have incited argument, and inspired imitation. Now, it is your turn to add your voice. Write a critical evaluation of "Self-Reliance." Include a summary of Emerson's points, a statement of opinion, and an assessment of the ways in which the argument is made.

Prewriting Reread "Self-Reliance," noting key ideas from the beginning, middle, and end. Observe how Emerson leads the reader from one thought to the next. Then, write one sentence that summarizes Emerson's argument. Phrase his ideas in your own words.

Drafting In your introduction, state the goals of your essay. Then, write out your summary of Emerson's essay. Follow the summary with a statement of your opinion of his ideas and how he presents them. Support your ideas with citations from the text.

Model: Using Relevant Citations

Emerson pays tribute to the value of being true to oneself. While most of us would agree with him in theory, how many of us withstand the pressures to conform? Emerson notes, "The virtue in most request is conformity."

> Citations specific to the argument keep the writing focused.

Revising Highlight any citations that do not effectively support your point. Replace weak citations with more relevant support.

W͞G Prentice Hall Writing and Grammar Connection: Chapter 14, Section 3

Extension Activities

Listening and Speaking Create a **public service announcement** urging people to resist conformity. Strengthen your position with two types of reasoning:

- inductive reasoning (use details to draw a general conclusion)
- deductive reasoning (build on a generally accepted principle)

Begin your announcement with a catchy phrase that will stick in listeners' minds. Then, record your announcement and share it with the class.

Research and Technology According to Emerson, the misunderstood individual joins the ranks of Pythagoras, Socrates, Jesus, Joan of Arc, and others. With a group, research and write a **profile** of one of these "great souls" to learn how or why the person was misunderstood. Share your profile with other groups. **[Group Activity]**

 Take It to the Net www.phschool.com

Go online for an additional research activity using the Internet.

from Nature / from Self-Reliance / Concord Hymn / The Snowstorm ◆ 399

---

3 Writing Lesson

- Review the essay with students, confirming their understanding of its main ideas. Then remind them to use the Reading Strategy, Challenging the Text, to build arguments for their analysis.

- After discussing the steps in the Writing Lesson, emphasize the importance of building clear arguments that are solidly supported by evidence from the text.

- Have students use the Argument Organizer in **Writing Models and Graphic Organizers on Transparencies,** p. 75, to outline their reading of Emerson's ideas and their response to those ideas.

- Use the Response to Literature rubric in **Performance Assessment and Portfolio Management**, p. 23, to evaluate student essays.

4 Research and Technology

- Organize students into groups to research an individual from the provided list. You might also mention Martin Luther, Copernicus, Galileo, and Isaac Newton as possible topics.

- Encourage students to explore online and electronic resources, downloading original writings by or about their featured individual.

- Have the group organize a brief report and present it to the class.

CUSTOMIZE INSTRUCTION
For Universal Access

To address different learning styles, use the activities suggested in the **Extension Activities** booklet, p. 20.

For Intrapersonal Learners, use Activity 5.

For Visual/Spatial Learners, use Activity 6.

For Interpersonal Learners, use Activity 7.

ASSESSMENT RESOURCES

The following resources can be used to assess students' knowledge and skills.

Selection Assessment
- 📖 **Formal Assessment**, pp. 99–101
- 📖 **Open Book Test**, pp. 58–60
- 📼 **Got It! Assessment Videotapes**, Tape 2
- 💿 **Test Bank Software**
- 💻 **Take It to the Net**
  Visit www.phschool.com for self-tests and additional questions on the selections.

Writing Rubric
- 📖 **Performance Assess. and Portfolio Mgmt.**, p. 23

PRENTICE HALL
ASSESSMENT SYSTEM

- 📖 **Workbook**
- 📖 **Skill Book**
- 📄 **Transparencies**
- 💿 **CD-ROM**

from Walden ✦ *from* Civil Disobedience

Lesson Objectives

1. **To analyze and respond to literary elements**
   - Literary Analysis: Style
   - Comparing Literary Works
2. **To read, comprehend, analyze, and critique a [genre(s)]**
   - Reading Strategy: Evaluating the Writer's Statement of Philosophy
   - Reading Check Questions
   - Review and Assess Questions
   - Assessment Practice (ATE)
3. **To develop word analysis skills, fluency, and systematic vocabulary**
   - Vocabulary Development Lesson: Latin Root: *-flu-*
4. **To understand and apply written and oral language conventions**
   - Spelling Strategy
   - Grammar and Style Lesson: Infinitives and Infinitive Phrases
5. **To understand and apply appropriate writing and research strategies**
   - Writing Lesson: Editorial
   - Extension Activity: Oral Presentation
6. **To understand and apply listening and speaking strategies**
   - Extension Activity: Debate

STEP-BY-STEP TEACHING GUIDE	PACING GUIDE
PRETEACH	
Motivate Students and Provide Background	
Use the Motivation activity (ATE p. 400)	5 min.
Read and discuss the author and background information (SE pp. 400, 412/ATE p. 400) **A**	5 min.
Introduce the Concepts	
Introduce the Literary Analysis and Reading Strategy (SE/ATE p. 401) **A**	15 min.
Pronounce the vocabulary words and read their definitions (SE p. 401)	5 min.
TEACH	
Monitor Comprehension	
Informally monitor comprehension by circulating while students read independently or in groups **A**	30 min.
Monitor students' comprehension with the Reading Check notes (SE/ATE pp. 403, 405, 407, 409)	as students read
Develop vocabulary with Vocabulary notes (SE pp. 404, 406, 409, 412, 413; ATE p. 406)	as students read
Develop Understanding	
Develop students' understanding of style with the Literary Analysis annotations (SE pp. 404, 408; ATE pp. 404, 408, 410) **A**	5 min.
Develop students' ability to evaluate the writer's statement of philosophy with the Reading Strategy annotations (SE pp. 404, 405, 407, 409, 412; ATE pp. 404, 405, 407, 409, 412)	5 min.
ASSESS	
Assess Mastery	
Assess students' mastery of the Reading Strategy and Literary Analysis by having them answer the Review and Assess questions (SE/ATE p. 414)	15 min.
Use one or more of the print and media Assessment Resources (ATE p. 416) **A**	up to 45 min.
EXTEND	
Apply Understanding	
Have students complete the Vocabulary Development Lesson and the Grammar and Style Lesson (SE p. 415) **A**	20 min.
Apply students' ability to identify cause and effect by using the Writing Lesson (SE/ATE p. 416) **A**	45 min.
Apply students' understanding using one or more of the Extension Activities (SE p. 416)	20–90 min.

 ACCELERATED INSTRUCTION:
Use the strategies and activities identified with an **A**.

UNIVERSAL ACCESS
● = Below Level Students
▲ = On-Level Students
■ = Above Level Students

Time and Resource Manager

Reading Level: Challenging, Average
Average Number of Instructional Days: 3

RESOURCES		
PRINT 📖	**TRANSPARENCIES**	**TECHNOLOGY** 💿 🎧 📼
• **Beyond Literature,** Cross-Curricular Connection: Social Studies, p. 21 ▲ ■		• **Interest Grabber Video,** Tape 2 ● ▲ ■
• **Selection Support Workbook:** ● ▲ ■ Literary Analysis, p. 98 Reading Strategy, p. 97 Build Vocabulary, p. 95	• **Literary Analysis and Reading Transparencies,** pp. 41 and 42 ● ▲ ■	
• **Adapted Reader's Companion** ● • **Reader's Companion** ●		• **Listening to Literature** ● ▲ ■ Audiocassettes, Side 14 Audio CDs, CD 9
• **English Learner's Companion** ● ▲ • **Literatura en español** ● ▲ • **Literary Analysis for Enrichment** ■		
• **Formal Assessment:** Selection Test, pp. 102–104 ● ▲ ■ • **Open Book Test,** pp. 61–63 ● ▲ ■ • **PRENTICE HALL ASSESSMENT SYSTEM** ● ▲ ■	• **PRENTICE HALL ASSESSMENT SYSTEM** ● ▲ ■ Skills Practice Answers and Explanations on Transparencies	• **Test Bank Software** ● ▲ ■ • **Got It! Assessment Videotapes,** Tape 2 ● ▲
• **Selection Support Workbook:** ● ▲ ■ Grammar and Style, p. 96 • **Writing and Grammar,** Ruby Level ● ▲ ■ • **Extension Activities,** p. 21 ● ▲ ■	• **Daily Language Practice Transparencies** ● ▲ • **Writing Models and Graphic Organizers on Transparencies,** pp. 33–36, 91 ● ▲ ■	• **Writing and Grammar iText CD-ROM** ● ▲ ■ 💻 *Take It to the Net* www.phschool.com

BLOCK SCHEDULING: Use one 90-minute class period to preteach the selection and have students read it. Use a second 90-minute class period to assess students' mastery of skills and have them complete one of the Extension Activities.

Step-by-Step Teaching Guide for pp. 400–401

Motivation

Share with students the following quotation from Thoreau: "I went to the woods because I wished to live deliberately, to front only the essential facts of life." Have students imagine that they are about to spend some time alone in the wilderness. Ask them to tell what essentials they would bring with them other than the necessities associated with food and shelter. Prompt them to predict what the experience would be like, physically, emotionally, and spiritually. Invite students who have spent any time in wilderness areas to tell about it. Explain that the works they are about to read are drawn from the ideas and philosophies Thoreau developed while voluntarily living a life of rustic isolation.

▣ Interest Grabber Video

As an alternative, play "Thoreau's Thoughts on Walden" on Tape 2 to engage student interest.

❶ Background

More About the Author

In "Civil Disobedience," Thoreau questions the government's right to tell him what to do. In life, he also questioned its right to tax him, especially when those taxes supported policies with which he disagreed. In 1846, Thoreau—who opposed slavery—put his beliefs into practice by refusing to pay taxes that might in some way support slavery policies. For this passive resistance, Thoreau spent one night in jail.

Prepare to Read

❶ *from* Walden ◆ *from* Civil Disobedience

Henry David Thoreau (1817–1862)

From the time he was a child, Henry David Thoreau was known by his Concord, Massachusetts, neighbors as an eccentric. He rarely followed rules. He was independent and strong-willed but casual about his studies. It was his mother's drive and encouragement that convinced him to pursue an education. Thoreau attended Concord Academy, a college preparatory school. Five years later, he enrolled at Harvard, where he pursued his studies in his own unique style. Although Harvard University's code called for students to wear black coats, Thoreau wore a green one.

Questioning Authority Thoreau always questioned the rules that were presented to him. When his objection to corporal punishment forced him to quit his first teaching job, Thoreau and his older brother John opened their own school in Concord. The school was quite successful, but they had to close it when John became ill.

In 1841, Thoreau moved into the house of another famous Concord resident, Ralph Waldo Emerson. He lived there for two years, performing odd jobs to pay for his room and board. While there, Thoreau became fascinated by Emerson's Transcendentalist beliefs. Soon, Thoreau became Emerson's close friend and devoted disciple. Deciding not to go back to teaching and refusing to pursue another career, Thoreau dedicated himself to testing the Transcendentalist philosophy through personal experience. By simplifying his needs, Thoreau was able to devote the rest of his life to exploring and writing about the spiritual relationship between humanity and nature and supporting his political and social beliefs.

On Walden Pond From 1845 to 1847, Thoreau lived alone in a cabin he built himself at Walden Pond outside of Concord. Thoreau's experiences during this period provided him with the material for his masterwork, *Walden* (1854). Condensing his experiences at Walden Pond into a single year, Thoreau used the four seasons as a structural framework for the book. A unique blend of natural observation, social criticism, and philosophical insight, *Walden* is now generally regarded as the supreme work of Transcendentalist literature.

Thoreau wrote throughout his life, but only *A Week on the Concord and Merrimack Rivers* and some poems were published—at Thoreau's own expense—during his lifetime. *The Maine Woods, Cape Cod,* and *A Yankee in Canada* were published posthumously. Carefully and deliberately crafted, Thoreau's work reflects the economy for which he strove throughout his life and about which he wrote in *Walden*.

A Noble Soul When Henry David Thoreau died of tuberculosis at the age of forty-four, his work had received little recognition. Yet he had achieved an inner success that few others have experienced. Speaking at Thoreau's funeral, Ralph Waldo Emerson commented, "The country knows not yet, or in the least part, how great a son it has lost. . . . But he, at least, is content. His soul was made for the noblest society; he had in a short life exhausted the capabilities of this world; wherever there is knowledge, wherever there is virtue, wherever there is beauty, he will find a home."

Thoreau's reputation has steadily grown since his death. His work has inspired writers, environmentalists, and social and political leaders. It has made generations of readers aware of the possibilities of the human spirit and the limitations of society.

400 ◆ A Growing Nation (1800–1870)

TEACHING RESOURCES

The following resources can be used to enrich or extend the instruction for pp. 400–401.

Motivation

▣ **Interest Grabber Video**, Tape 2 ▣

Background

▣ **Beyond Literature**, p. 21

 Take It to the Net

Visit www.phschool.com for Background and hotlinks for the selections.

Literary Analysis

 Literary Analysis and Reading Transparencies, Style, p. 42 ▣

Reading

Literary Analysis and Reading Transparencies, Evaluating Writer's Statement of Philosophy, p. 41

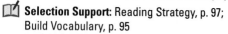 **Selection Support:** Reading Strategy, p. 97; Build Vocabulary, p. 95

▣ **BLOCK SCHEDULING:** Resources marked with this symbol provide varied instruction during 90-minute blocks.

Preview

Connecting to the Literature

In today's world, we use countless modern conveniences—cellular phones, computers, the Internet—often without stopping to think whether or not we truly need them. Thoreau took time to stop to think about what was truly essential in life.

❷ Literary Analysis

Style

Style refers to the manner in which a writer puts his or her thoughts into words. Thoreau constructs paragraphs so that the sentences build to a climax. Thoreau also repeats his main ideas to reinforce his message. As you read his essays, watch for these signposts of Thoreau's style.

Comparing Literary Works

While both of these selections reveal Thoreau's style, each is written for a different purpose. One selection is lyrical, presenting ideas at a leisurely pace. The other, in contrast, is logical, advancing a focused argument. In both cases, Thoreau uses **metaphor**—a figure of speech that implies a comparison between two unlike things—to achieve his aims.

Lyrical: Time is but the stream I go a-fishing in . . .

Logical: [Government] is a sort of a wooden gun to the people themselves . . .

As you read, compare the metaphors Thoreau employs and notice how their use reveals the author's distinct reasons for writing.

❸ Reading Strategy

Evaluating the Writer's Statement of Philosophy

As a reader, you are not bound to accept everything you see in print. In fact, when reading essays written about ideas, you should **evaluate the writer's philosophy**. To do this, pay special attention to the support the writer provides to back up his or her outlook. As you read Thoreau's works, compare his ideas and supporting details with your own experiences. Use a chart like the one shown here to organize your comparison.

Vocabulary Development

dilapidated (də lap´ə dāt´ id) *adj.* in disrepair (p. 404)

sublime (sə blīm´) *adj.* noble; majestic (p. 406)

superfluous (sə pʉr´floo əs) *adj.* excessive; not necessary (p. 406)

evitable (ev´i tə bəl) *adj.* avoidable (p. 406)

magnanimity (mag´nə nim´ə tē) *n.* generosity (p. 409)

expedient (ek spē´ dē ənt) *n.* resource (p. 412)

posterity (päs ter´ə tē) *n.* all succeeding generations (p. 412)

alacrity (ə lak´rə tē) *n.* speed (p. 413)

Thoreau's ideas

People should simplify their lives
• supporting detail:
• supporting detail:

Your experiences

Your reaction

from Walden / from Civil Disobedience ◆ 401

CUSTOMIZE FOR UNIVERSAL ACCESS

For Less Proficient Readers	For Less Proficient Readers	For English Learners
Have students read the adapted version of *Walden* in the **Adapted Reader's Companion.** This version provides basic-level instruction in an interactive format with questions and write-on lines. Completing the adapted version will prepare students to read the selection in the Student Edition.	Have students read Thoreaui's *Walden* in the **Reader's Companion.** This version provides basic-level instruction in an interactive format with questions and write-on lines. After students finish the selection in **Reader's Companion,** have them complete the questions and activities in the Student Edition.	Have students read the selection in the **English Learner's Companion.** This version provides basic-level instruction in an interactive format with questions and write-on lines. Completing the adapted version will prepare students to read the selection in the Student Edition.

---

❷ Literary Analysis

Style

- Tell students that as they read, they will focus on style, the manner in which a writer puts his or her ideas into words. Style can include sentence or paragraph structure, word choice, figurative language, rhythm, and imagery.

- After students read the Literary Analysis instruction, point out that Thoreau's style is intrinsic to his purpose, which is to encourage us to examine how we live and think.

- Review the stylistic device of metaphor with students as you introduce the instruction for **Comparing Literary Works.**

- Provide practice in recognizing stylistic elements by displaying and discussing the Style transparency in **Literary Analysis and Reading Transparencies,** p. 42.

❸ Reading Strategy

Evaluating the Writer's Statement of Philosophy

- Remind students that evaluating the writer's statement of philosophy can help them read critically and respond more effectively to essays.

- Draw students' attention to the graphic organizer in the minor column of their page. Clarify the information suited to each cell and direct students to complete their own organizer as they read.

- Explain that a philosophy is a system of beliefs and values that guide a person's life and actions. Emphasize that after evaluating a writer's philosophy—exploring the supporting evidence and considering their own experiences—students may still decide that they agree with it.

Vocabulary Development

- Pronounce each vocabulary word for students, and read the definitions as a class. Have students identify any words with which they are already familiar.

 E-Teach

Visit E-Teach at www.phschool.com for teacher's essays on how to teach, with questions and answers.

**Step-by-Step Teaching Guide
for pp. 402–413**

**CUSTOMIZE INSTRUCTION
For Kinesthetic Learners**

Tell students that Thoreau conducts a great deal of real estate business in *Walden*. He considers different properties, weighs their features, negotiates their purchase, but he does it all in his imagination. As they read, challenge students to think about how reviewing a process mentally differs from completing that process or task physically.

❶ About the Selection

Walden was published in 1854, seven years after Thoreau's two-year residence at Walden Pond. During the intervening years, Thoreau reflected upon and revised the journals he had kept at Walden. A celebration of life and nature, *Walden* presents Thoreau's views on society and his philosophy of life. In the sections that follow, Thoreau expresses the belief that society has become too complex and fast-paced and that people should do everything possible to simplify their lives. He also stresses the need to resist conformity and to follow our own inner voices, and he suggests that by doing so people can experience a spiritual awakening.

402 ◆ A Growing Nation (1800–1870)

TEACHING RESOURCES

The following resources can be used to enrich or extend the instruction for pp. 402–413.

Literary Analysis

- 📖 **Writing Models and Graphic Organizers on Transparencies,** pp. 33–36
- 📓 **Selection Support:** Literary Analysis p. 98

Reading

- 📓 **Reader's Companion**
- 📖 **English Learner's Companion**

- 🎧 **Listening to Literature Audiocassettes,** Side 14 ▪
- 💿 **Listening to Literature Audio CDs,** CD 9 ▪

▪ **BLOCK SCHEDULING:** Resources marked with this symbol provide varied instruction during 90-minute blocks.

from Walden

Henry David Thoreau

from Where I Lived, and What I Lived For

At a certain season of our life we are accustomed to consider every spot as the possible site of a house. I have thus surveyed the country on every side within a dozen miles of where I live. In imagination I have bought all the farms in succession, for all were to be bought, and I knew their price. I walked over each farmer's premises, tasted his wild apples, discoursed on husbandry[1] with him, took his farm at his price, at any price, mortgaging it to him in my mind; even put a higher price on it—took everything but a deed of it—took his word for his deed, for I dearly love to talk—cultivated it, and him too to some extent, I trust, and withdrew when I had enjoyed it long enough, leaving him to carry it on. This experience entitled me to be regarded as a sort of real-estate broker by my friends. Wherever I sat, there I might live, and the landscape radiated from me accordingly. What is a house but a sedes, a seat?—better if a country seat. I discovered many a site for a house not likely to be soon improved, which some might have thought too far from the village, but to my eyes the village was too far from it. Well, there might I live, I said; and there I did live, for an hour, a summer and a winter life; saw how I could let the years run off, buffet the winter through, and see the spring come in. The future inhabitants of this region, wherever they may place their houses, may be sure that they have been anticipated. An afternoon

---

1. **husbandry** (huz´ bən drē) *n.* farming.

From J. Lyndon Shanley, ed., Walden: The Writings of Henry D. Thoreau. Copyright © 1971 by Princeton University Press. Excerpts, pp. 81–98 and 320–333, reprinted with permission of Princeton University Press.

❷ ◄ Critical Viewing Based on this picture of Walden Pond, what do you think it would be like to live in such a place? **[Speculate]**

❸ ☑ Reading Check
Did Thoreau truly intend to purchase a farm?

---

❷ ▶ Critical Viewing
Answer: Students may respond that it must have been beautiful yet isolated. Others may say that it would be boring to live so far from society and modern conveniences.

❸ ☑ Reading Check
Answer: No, he was merely enjoying mental speculation about the land around him.

CUSTOMIZE INSTRUCTION FOR UNIVERSAL ACCESS

For Less Proficient Readers	For Special Needs Students	For Advanced Readers
Point out the sentence beginning "I walked over each farmer's premises . . . ." Note with students that it continues for seven lines of text. Help students work phrase by phrase, clause by clause, to build meaning from the sentence: I explored each farm, spoke with the farmer, negotiated for each farm but never actually completed the sale.	Thoreau uses dashes and semicolons to string many sentence parts into a single long sentence. Explain that readers can treat dashes as if they were commas while semicolons reflect more significant pauses in the writer's ideas. Have students reread long sentences as you help them recognize breaks and build meaning.	Challenge students to edit Thoreau's long sentences into more accessible text. Remind them, however, that an editor must avoid imprinting his or her own style on an author's work. Students should avoid the temptation to merely replace long sentences with shorter ones. Instead, they might reword or repunctuate for clarity.

- Read the bracketed passage with students and invite them to paraphrase it.
  Answer: The fewer encumbrances there are on one's life, the richer and freer that life will be.

- Ask students the Reading Strategy questions on p. 404: Do you think this philosophical statement about a man's wealth applies in today's world? Can Thoreau support it?
  Possible answer: Given today's emphasis on material possessions, students may have a different attitude from Thoreau's. If students express disagreement, encourage them to cite evidence to support their position. Thoreau supports his position by demonstrating in his own life that he feels richer and freer as he gives up material attachments.

❺ Literary Analysis

Style

- Have a volunteer read aloud the bracketed passage. Invite listeners to raise their hands each time Thoreau repeats his main point about the Hollowell farm.

- Have students discuss possible reasons for Thoreau's use of repetition in this passage.

- Then, ask students the Literary Analysis question on p. 404: What point does Thoreau make through his use of repetition in his description of the Hollowell farm?
  Possible answer: Repetition helps Thoreau make the point that he likes this farm because it is very isolated and private.

---

sufficed to lay out the land into orchard woodlot and pasture, and to decide what fine oaks or pines should be left to stand before the door, and whence each blasted tree could be seen to the best advantage; and then I let it lie, fallow[2] perchance, for a man is rich in proportion ❹ to the number of things which he can afford to let alone.

My imagination carried me so far that I even had the refusal of several farms—the refusal was all I wanted—but I never got my fingers burned by actual possession. The nearest that I came to actual possession was when I bought the Hollowell Place, and had begun to sort my seeds, and collected materials with which to make a wheelbarrow to carry it on or off with; but before the owner gave me a deed of it, his wife—every man has such a wife—changed her mind and wished to keep it, and he offered me ten dollars to release him. Now, to speak the truth, I had but ten cents in the world, and it surpassed my arithmetic to tell, if I was that man who had ten cents, or who had a farm, or ten dollars, or all together. However, I let him keep the ten dollars and the farm too, for I had carried it far enough; or rather, to be generous, I sold him the farm for just what I gave for it, and, as he was not a rich man, made him a present of ten dollars, and still had my ten cents, and seeds, and materials for a wheelbarrow left. I found thus that I had been a rich man without any damage to my poverty. But I retained the landscape, and I have since annually carried off what it yielded without a wheelbarrow. With respect to landscapes:

"I am monarch of all I *survey*,
My right there is none to dispute."[3]

I have frequently seen a poet withdraw, having enjoyed the most valuable part of a farm, while the crusty farmer supposed that he had got a few wild apples only. Why, the owner does not know it for many years when a poet has put his farm in rhyme, the most admirable kind of invisible fence, has fairly impounded it, milked it, skimmed it, and got all the cream, and left the farmer only the skimmed milk.

The real attractions of the Hollowell farm, to me, were: its complete retirement, being about two miles from the village, half a mile from the nearest neighbor, and separated from the highway by a broad field; its bounding on the river, which the owner said protected it by its fogs from frosts in the spring, though that was nothing to me; ❺ the gray color and ruinous state of the house and barn, and the dilapidated fences, which put such an interval between me and the last occupant; the hollow and lichen-covered apple trees, gnawed by rabbits, showing what kind of neighbors I should have; but above all, the recollection I had of it from my earliest voyages up the river, when the house was concealed behind a dense grove of red maples, through which I heard the house-dog bark. I was in haste to buy it, before the proprietor finished getting out some rocks, cutting down

---

2. **fallow** (fal´ ō) *adj.* left uncultivated or unplanted.
3. **"I . . . dispute"** from William Cowper's *Verses Supposed to Be Written by Alexander Selkirk.*

Reading Strategy
Evaluating the Writer's Statement of Philosophy
Do you think this philosophical statement about a man's wealth applies in today's world? Can Thoreau support it?

Literary Analysis
Style What point does Thoreau make through his use of repetition in his description of the Hollowell farm?

dilapidated (də lap´ ə dāt´ id) *adj.* in disrepair

 ENRICHMENT: Social Studies Connection

Touring Walden Pond

Today, tourists come from all over the world to visit Walden Pond. Some are drawn by the natural beauty of the place; others by its literary and historical significance. The pond and the surrounding forestland are now a public park preserve, the Walden Pond State Reservation. There are guided walks along the many pathways surrounding the pond, and visitors are welcome to swim, boat, picnic, and hike. During the summer months, large numbers of people from the area go to Walden Pond to sunbathe on the public beaches.

A re-creation of Thoreau's cabin stands a few dozen feet from the site of his original home. In a tradition begun decades ago, visitors still leave rocks and notes to Thoreau piled on the site. Above the house site, the stumps of some of the 400 white pines Thoreau planted can still be seen; they were wiped out by the great hurricane of 1938.

the hollow apple trees, and grubbing up some young birches which had sprung up in the pasture, or, in short, had made any more of his improvements. To enjoy these advantages I was ready to carry it on; like Atlas,[4] to take the world on my shoulders—I never heard what compensation he received for that—and do all those things which had no other motive or excuse but that I might pay for it and be unmolested in my possession of it; for I knew all the while that it would yield the most abundant crop of the kind I wanted if I could only afford to let it alone. But it turned out as I have said.

All that I could say, then, with respect to farming on a large scale (I have always cultivated a garden) was that I had had my seeds ready. Many think that seeds improve with age. I have no doubt that time discriminates between the good and the bad; and when at last I shall plant, I shall be less likely to be disappointed. But I would say to my fellows, once for all, As long as possible live free and uncommitted. It makes but little difference whether you are committed to a farm or the county jail.

Old Cato,[5] whose "De Re Rustica" is my "Cultivator," says, and the only translation I have seen makes sheer nonsense of the passage, "When you think of getting a farm, turn it thus in your mind, not to buy greedily; nor spare your pains to look at it, and do not think it enough to go round it once. The oftener you go there the more it will please you, if it is good." I think I shall not buy greedily, but go round and round it as long as I live, and be buried in it first, that it may please me the more at last. . . .

I do not propose to write an ode to dejection, but to brag as lustily as chanticleer[6] in the morning, standing on his roost, if only to wake my neighbors up.

When first I took up my abode in the woods, that is, began to spend my nights as well as days there, which, by accident, was on Independence Day, or the fourth of July, 1845, my house was not finished for winter, but was merely a defense against the rain, without plastering or chimney, the walls being of rough weatherstained boards, with wide chinks, which made it cool at night. The upright white hewn studs and freshly planed door and window casings gave it a clean and airy look, especially in the morning, when its timbers were saturated with dew, so that I fancied that by noon some sweet gum would exude from them. To my imagination it retained throughout the day more or less of this auroral[7] character, reminding me of a certain house on a mountain which I had visited the year before. This was an airy and unplastered cabin, fit to entertain a traveling god, and where a goddess might trail her garments. The winds which passed over my dwelling were such as sweep over the ridges of mountains, bearing the broken strains, or celestial parts only,

---

4. **Atlas** (at' ləs) from Greek mythology, a Titan who supported the heavens on his shoulders.
5. **Old Cato** Roman statesman (234–149 B.C.). "De Re Rustica" is Latin for "Of Things Rustic."
6. **chanticleer** (chan' tə klir') *n.* rooster.
7. **auroral** (ô rôr' əl) *adj.* resembling the dawn.

Reading Strategy
Evaluating the Writer's Statement of Philosophy
What difference do you see between a person's commitment to a farm and to a jail?

 Reading Check
What was the state of Thoreau's house in the woods when he first took up residence?

from *Walden* ◆ 405

Reading Strategy
Evaluating the Writer's Statement of Philosophy

- Direct students to read the bracketed text several times. Then, have them paraphrase the passage.
- Have students complete a graphic organizer like the one shown on p. 401 to explore their reactions to Thoreau's statement. Charts should look similar to the following:

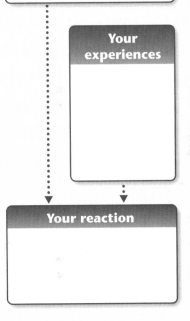

Thoreau's ideas

People should simplify their lives.
• supporting detail
• supporting detail

Your experiences

Your reaction

- Ask students to answer the Reading Strategy question on p. 405: What difference do you see between a person's commitment to a farm and to a jail?
  Possible Answer: While both curtail your freedom through commitment, you are free to leave the farm or to sell it while you are not free to leave jail.

Reading Check
Answer: It was unfinished, without the insulation or inside walls that provide winter protection.

CUSTOMIZE FOR UNIVERSAL ACCESS

For Less Proficient Readers	For English Learners	For Advanced Readers
Help students respond to Thoreau's ideas. For example, point out the lengthy paragraph about the Hallowell Farm. Lead students toward an understanding of the central point of this paragraph: Thoreau considers an ideal property one that is isolated and in a natural "unimproved condition."	Help these students understand and develop responses to Thoreau's comments about the Hallowell Farm. Use the Literary Analysis: Style question and the TE instruction on p. 404 to help students identify Thoreau's main point. Point out each incidence of repetition for those students who need this additional help.	Post these quotations on the chalkboard: "a man is rich in proportion to the number of things he can afford to let alone"; "time discriminates between the good and the bad [seeds]." Challenge students to deduce the implications of these comments and to decide whether they agree or disagree with Thoreau.

In the ancient Greek stories to which Thoreau refers, each Greek god was closely associated with a specific aspect of nature—such as the sun or the moon—or with specific emotions—such as love or anger.

The educated people of Thoreau's day would have been familiar with Greek language and lore, so a reference to Greek mythology in a discussion about nature would have been seen—then as now—as totally appropriate.

❾ Vocabulary Development

The Latin Root -flu-

- Draw students' attention to the word *superfluous*, which appears on page 406, and to its definition. Let students know that the word root *-flu-* derives from the Latin word *fluere*, which means "to flow."

- Invite students to volunteer words containing this word root, and list them on the chalkboard.

  Possibilities include: *fluid, influence, fluctuate,* and *fluency.*

- Next, have students look up the meanings of these words in a dictionary, and write a short paragraph for each word, describing how the word root contributes to the word's definition.

of terrestrial music. The morning wind forever blows, the poem of creation is uninterrupted; but few are the ears that hear it. Olympus* is but the outside of the earth everywhere. . . .

I went to the woods because I wished to live deliberately, to front only the essential facts of life, and see if I could not learn what it had to teach, and not, when I came to die, discover that I had not lived. I did not wish to live what was not life, living is so dear; nor did I wish to practice resignation, unless it was quite necessary. I wanted to live deep and suck out all the marrow of life, to live so sturdily and Spartanlike[8] as to put to rout all that was not life, to cut a broad swath and shave close, to drive life into a corner, and reduce it to its lowest terms, and, if it proved to be mean, why then to get the whole and genuine meanness of it, and publish its meanness to the world; or if it were sublime, to know it by experience, and be able to give a true account of it in my next excursion. For most men, it appears to me, are in a strange uncertainty about it, whether it is of the devil or of God, and have *somewhat hastily* concluded that it is the chief end of man here to "glorify God and enjoy him forever."[9]

Still we live meanly, like ants; though the fable tells us that we were long ago changed into men; like pygmies we fight with cranes:[10] it is error upon error, and clout upon clout, and our best virtue has for its occasion a superfluous and evitable wretchedness. Our life is frittered away by detail. An honest man has hardly need to count more than his ten fingers, or in extreme cases he may add his ten toes, and lump the rest. Simplicity, simplicity, simplicity! I say, let your affairs be as two or three, and not a hundred or a thousand; instead of a million count half a dozen, and keep your accounts on your thumbnail. In the midst of this chopping sea of civilized life, such are the clouds and storms and quicksands and thousand-and-one items to be allowed for, that a man has to live, if he would not founder and go to the bottom and not make his port at all, by dead reckoning,[11] and he must be a great calculator indeed who succeeds. Simplify, simplify. Instead of three meals a day, if it be necessary eat but one; instead of a hundred dishes, five; and reduce other things in proportion. Our life is like a German Confederacy,[12]

---

8. **Spartanlike** like the people of Sparta, an ancient Greek state whose citizens were known to be hardy, stoical, simple, and highly disciplined.
9. **"glorify . . . forever"** the answer to the question "What is the chief end of man?" in the Westminster catechism.
10. **like . . . cranes** In the *Iliad*, the Trojans are compared to cranes fighting against pygmies.
11. **dead reckoning** navigating without the assistance of stars.
12. **German Confederacy** At the time, Germany was a loose union of thirty-nine independent states, with no common government.

Literature
in context History Connection

❽ ◆ Olympus

When he describes his home in the woods, Thoreau rhapsodizes about another mountain cabin he had seen, an airy place where a "goddess might trail her garments." Thoreau goes on to say, "Olympus is but the outside of the earth everywhere."

Mount Olympus, to which Thoreau is referring, is both a real mountain in northern Greece and an important setting in ancient Greek mythology. Described as the home of the gods, Olympus was off-limits to mortals. From it, Zeus ruled the twelve gods who governed the world. Ancient Greeks pictured their gods in human form with human flaws, so Olympus was far from perfect. But as a place of relative beauty, harmony, and enlightenment, it was better than Earth.

sublime (sə blīm´) *adj.* noble; majestic

❾ superfluous (soo pur´ floo əs) *adj.* excessive; not necessary

evitable (ev´ i tə bəl) *adj.* avoidable

✹ ENRICHMENT: Science Connection

Geology

As the glacier that covered New England 12,000 years ago slowly melted, one huge block of ice remained behind on the site that is now Walden Pond. Streams of melted water—filled with once-embedded sand and gravel—ran off the main glacier. This gravelly sediment built up around the base of the detached ice-block; when the block melted, a steep-sided, water-filled basin, about 100 feet deep, remained.

Unlike other ponds, the water level of Walden Pond changes little. Walden's water also remains pure and clear. Science can explain Walden's mysteries. Because its permeable sandbanks quickly absorb water, draining rainwater does not rush down its banks, washing dirt and debris into the pond. The absence of any tributary streams or shoreline development protects Walden's water quality. The stable water level can also be explained: Walden Pond intersects a water table, so its levels are relatively unaffected by short-term wet and dry spells.

made up of petty states, with its boundary forever fluctuating, so that even a German cannot tell you how it is bounded at any moment. The nation itself, with all its so-called internal improvements, which, by the way, are all external and superficial, is just such an unwieldy and over-grown establishment, cluttered with furniture and tripped up by its own traps, ruined by luxury and heedless expense, by want of calcula-tion and a worthy aim, as the million households in the land; and the only cure for it as for them is in a rigid economy, a stern and more than Spartan simplicity of life and elevation of purpose. It lives too fast. Men think that it is essential that the *Nation* have commerce, and export ice, and talk through a telegraph, and ride thirty miles an hour, without a doubt, whether *they* do or not; but whether we should live like baboons or like men, is a little uncertain. If we do not get out sleepers,[13] and forge rails, and devote days and nights to the work, but go to tinkering upon our *lives* to improve *them*, who will build railroads? And if rail-roads are not built, how shall we get to heaven in season? But if we stay at home and mind our business, who will want railroads? We do not ride on the railroad; it rides upon us. . . .

Time is but the stream I go a-fishing in. I drink at it; but while I drink I see the sandy bottom and detect how shallow it is. Its thin current slides away, but eternity remains. I would drink deeper; fish in the sky, whose bottom is pebbly with stars. I cannot count one. I know not the first letter of the alphabet. I have always been regretting that I was not as wise as the day I was born. The intellect is a cleaver; it discerns and rifts its way into the secret of things. I do not wish to be any more busy with my hands than is necessary. My head is hands and feet. I feel all my best faculties concentrated in it. My instinct tells me that my head is an organ for burrowing, as some creatures use their snout and forepaws, and with it I would mine and burrow my way through these hills. I think that the richest vein is somewhere hereabouts; so by the divining rod[14] and thin rising vapors I judge; and here I will begin to mine. . . .

from The Conclusion

I left the woods for as good a reason as I went there. Perhaps it seemed to me that I had several more lives to live, and could not spare any more time for that one. It is remarkable how easily and insensibly we fall into a particular route, and make a beaten track for ourselves. I had not lived there a week before my feet wore a path from my door to the pondside; and though it is five or six years since I trod it, it is still quite distinct. It is true, I fear that others may have fallen into it, and so helped to keep it open. The surface of the earth is soft and impress-ible by the feet of men; and so with the paths which the mind travels. How worn and dusty, then, must be the highways of the world, how

---

13. **sleepers** (slē´ pərz) *n.* ties supporting railroad tracks.
14. **divining rod** a forked branch or stick alleged to reveal underground water or minerals.

from *Walden* ◆ 407

Reading Strategy
Evaluating the Writer's Statement of Philosophy
Evaluate this statement of philosophy about progress. Do you agree that railroads and other technology "ride upon us"?

⑪ ✓Reading Check
Why did Thoreau go to the woods?

⑩ Reading Strategy
Evaluating the Writer's Statement of Philosophy

- Have students read the bracketed text carefully. Direct them to the sentence, "It (the nation) lives too fast," and inform students that this is a good summary of Thoreau's belief about American life.
- Clarify the closing ideas in this paragraph: if people worked to simplify their lives, there would be much less demand for material goods and new technology.
- Direct students to respond to the Reading Strategy direction on p. 407: Evaluate this statement of philosophy about progress. Do you agree that railroads and other technology "ride upon us"? Lead a class discussion about students' ideas.
Possible responses: Technological progress enables people to expand their journeys—both physical and spiritual. I do not agree with Thoreau that progress is negative. However, I do agree that technology demands a lot of people. It can, if not carefully managed, "ride upon us" by requiring us to pay for it, care for it, constantly upgrade it, and speed up our lives to keep up with it.

⑪ ✓Reading Check

Answer: He went to the woods to live simply and deliberately, to try to understand the essential facts of life.

CUSTOMIZE FOR UNIVERSAL ACCESS

For Less Proficient Readers	For English Language Learners	For Gifted/Talented Students
Point out the first sentence of Thoreau's "Conclusion," and review the reasons Thoreau came to Walden Pond. If necessary, have them reread the paragraph on p. 406 in which Thoreau states his purpose for coming to Walden. Stress to students that it is helpful to reread for referenced information.	To help students identify Thoreau's purpose in living at Walden, suggest that students complete the sentence stem "I went to the woods because . . ." with phrases from the text. For example, "I went to the woods because I wished to live deep."	The beliefs that Thoreau expresses in these passages are echoed in the theme of the film *Dead Poets Society*. You may wish to show portions of this film or have students view it on their own. Be aware, however, that the film addresses some sensitive issues. Preview the film to determine its suitability for your students.

⑫ Literary Analysis

Style and Metaphor

- Direct students to read the bracketed passage. Ask students to define *metaphor*.
  Answer: A metaphor is a figure of speech in which one thing is described as being something else.

- Ask them the Literary Analysis question on p. 408: What metaphor does Thoreau use in the sentence beginning, "If a man does not keep pace with his companions"?
  Answer: He speaks of life as though it were a march in time with music—as though people were soldiers.

▶ **Monitor Progress** Have students explain Thoreau's metaphor. What two things is he comparing? Then, have students rephrase this metaphor as a simile.
  Answer: He is comparing life to a sea journey, with the ship's deck as full participation of life while a cabin passage would be a sheltered, hidden interaction with life.

▶ **Critical Viewing**

The aerial photograph reveals little modern development on Walden Pond. The photo suggests that inhabitants of the area have chosen to preserve the natural splendor of the landscape, perhaps in deference to Thoreau's ideas about honoring nature.

deep the ruts of tradition and conformity! I did not wish to take a cabin passage, but rather to go before the mast and on the deck of the world, for there I could best see the moonlight amid the mountains. I do not wish to go below now.

I learned this, at least, by my experiment; that if one advances confidently in the direction of his dreams, and endeavors to live the life which he has imagined, he will meet with a success unexpected in common hours. He will put some things behind, will pass an invisible boundary; new, universal, and more liberal laws will begin to establish themselves around and within him; or the old laws be expanded, and interpreted in his favor in a more liberal sense, and he will live with the license of a higher order of beings. In proportion as he simplifies his life, the laws of the universe will appear less complex, and solitude will not be solitude, nor poverty poverty, nor weakness weakness. If you have built castles in the air, your work need not be lost; that is where they should be. Now put the foundations under them. . . .

Why should we be in such desperate haste to succeed, and in such desperate enterprises? If a man does not keep pace with his companions, perhaps it is because he hears a different drummer. Let him step to the music which he hears, however measured or far away. It is not important that he should mature as soon as an apple tree or an oak. Shall he turn his spring into summer? If the condition of things which we were made for is not yet, what were any reality which we can substitute? We will not be shipwrecked on a vain reality. Shall we with pains erect a heaven of blue glass over ourselves, though when it is done we shall be sure to gaze still at the true ethereal heaven far above, as if the former were not? . . .

▲ **Critical Viewing**
What elements in this aerial photograph of Walden Pond reveal conventional notions of progress? What details suggest that the community has applied some of Thoreau's ideas? **[Analyze]**

Literary Analysis
Style and Metaphor
What metaphor does Thoreau use in the sentence beginning "If a man does not keep pace with his companions . . . "?

However mean your life is, meet it and live it; do not shun it and call it hard names. It is not so bad as you are. It looks poorest when you are richest. The faultfinder will find faults even in paradise. Love your life, poor as it is. You may perhaps have some pleasant, thrilling, glorious hours, even in a poorhouse. The setting sun is reflected from the windows of the almshouse[15] as brightly as from the rich man's abode; the snow melts before its door as early in the spring. I do not see but a quiet mind may live as contentedly there, and have as cheering thoughts, as in a palace. The town's poor seem to me often to live the most independent lives of any. Maybe they are simply great enough to receive without misgiving. Most think that they are above being supported by the town; but it oftener happens that they are not above supporting themselves by dishonest means, which should be more disreputable. Cultivate poverty like a garden herb, like sage. Do not trouble yourself much to get new things, whether clothes or friends. Turn the old; return to them. Things do not change; we change. Sell your clothes and keep your thoughts. God will see that you do not want society. If I were confined to a corner of a garret[16] all my days, like a spider, the world would be just as large to me while I had my thoughts about me. The philosopher said: "From an army of three divisions one can take away its general, and put it in disorder; from the man the most abject and vulgar one cannot take away his thought." Do not seek so anxiously to be developed, to subject yourself to many influences to be played on; it is all dissipation. Humility like darkness reveals the heavenly lights. The shadows of poverty and meanness gather around us, "and lo! creation widens to our view."[17] We are often reminded that if there were bestowed on us the wealth of Croesus,[18] our aims must still be the same, and our means essentially the same. Moreover, if you are restricted in your range by poverty, if you cannot buy books and newspapers, for instance, you are but confined to the most significant and vital experiences; you are compelled to deal with the material which yields the most sugar and the most starch. It is life near the bone where it is sweetest. You are defended from being a trifler. No man loses ever on a lower level by magnanimity on a higher. Superfluous wealth can buy superfluities only. Money is not required to buy one necessary of the soul. . . .

The life in us is like the water in the river. It may rise this year higher than man has ever known it, and flood the parched uplands; even this may be the eventful year, which will drown out all our muskrats. It was not always dry land where we dwell. I see far inland the banks which the stream anciently washed, before science began

---

15. **almshouse** *n.* home for people too poor to support themselves.
16. **garret** (gar' it) *n.* attic.
17. **"and . . . view"** from the sonnet "To Night" by British poet Joseph Blanco White (1775–1841).
18. **Croesus** (krē' səs) King of Lydia (d. 546 B.C.), believed to be the wealthiest person of his time.

Reading Strategy
Evaluating the Writer's Statement of Philosophy
Thoreau has strong opinions about how people should live, as shown in his advice to "cultivate poverty." Has he convinced you? Explain.

magnanimity (mag' nə nim' ə tē) *n.* generosity

 Reading Check
What does Thoreau feel about superfluous wealth?

from Walden ◆ 409

 Reading Strategy
Evaluating the Writer's Statement of Philosophy
- Ask a volunteer to read aloud the bracketed passage. Invite listening students to share their initial reactions to Thoreau's position.
- Encourage students to analyze Thoreau's support for his ideas and then compare it with their own experience in order to evaluate the writer's philosophy.
- Ask students the Reading Strategy question on p. 409: Thoreau has strong opinions about how people should live, as shown in his advice to "cultivate poverty." Has he convinced you?
  Possible response: Students may or may not be convinced that poverty is preferable to wealth.

⓮ ✓**Reading Check**

Answer: It is unimportant because it only buys unnecessary things. Money cannot buy the truly necessary items of the spirit.

CUSTOMIZE FOR UNIVERSAL ACCESS

For Less Proficient Readers	For English Language Learners	For Advanced Readers
Read students the text beginning "In proportion as he simplifies . . . ." Then focus on building an understanding of the metaphor "castles in the air." Guide students to understand that Thoreau is urging people to simplify their lives, to dream, and then to follow their dreams by building foundations for them.	Point out the sentence: "If a man does not keep pace with his companions, perhaps it is because he hears a different drummer." Tell students that the metaphor of hearing a different drummer has become common, signifying that someone approaches life differently than do most people.	Tell students that although not wealthy, Thoreau did have a Harvard education and a family business. Discuss with students how economic conditions today might lead Thoreau to change his advice about poverty. Ask students: How would living in a city affect one's ability to cope with poverty?

Style and Metaphor

- Read aloud the passage on pp. 410–411 in which Thoreau describes the egg deposited long ago in the wood later used for a table. Pause to emphasize the word *egg* when it appears.

- Ask students the question: To what does Thoreau compare the long-buried egg?
  Answer: He compares it to our human vitality, to our life energy, which can seem dead and buried but is still capable of emerging afresh.

▶Critical Viewing

The cabin is extremely humble—plain, small, and unadorned. Such a cabin would provide only the most basic shelter and require little attention, leaving its inhabitant to focus on matters of the mind and spirit.

to record its freshets. Everyone has heard the story which has gone the rounds of New England, of a strong and beautiful bug which came out of the dry leaf of an old table of apple-tree wood, which had stood in a farmer's kitchen for sixty years, first in Connecticut, and afterward in Massachusetts—from an egg deposited in the living tree many years earlier still, as appeared by counting the annual layers beyond it; which was heard gnawing out for several weeks, hatched

▼ Critical Viewing
In what ways does this replica of Thoreau's cabin reflect his desire to "front only the essential facts of life"? [Interpret]

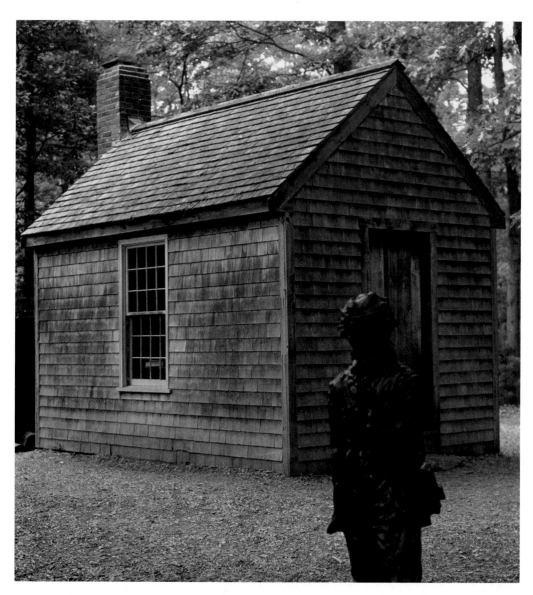

✹ ENRICHMENT: Culture Connection

Gandhi

Thoreau's beliefs have influenced people throughout the world in the decades since his death. For example, his concept of civil disobedience, which is vividly described in the selection that follows, greatly influenced Indian leader Mohandas Gandhi in his campaign against British rule in his homeland. Drawing on Thoreau's ideas, Gandhi formulated his philosophy of *Satyagraha* ("The Devotion to Truth" in Sanskrit, an ancient Indian language) in 1906. Guided by this philosophy, Gandhi called for massive boycotts of British

goods and British-run institutions in India that treated Indians unfairly. Thousands of Gandhi's supporters and Gandhi himself repeatedly went to prison without resistance. When India won its independence in 1947, it was largely due to Gandhi's nonviolent protests.

perchance by the heat of an urn. Who does not feel his faith in a resurrection and immortality strengthened by hearing of this? Who knows what beautiful and winged life, whose egg has been buried for ages under many concentric layers of woodenness in the dead dry life of society, deposited at first in the alburnum[19] of the green and living tree, which has been gradually converted into the semblance of its well-seasoned tomb—heard perchance gnawing out now for years by the astonished family of man, as they sat round the festive board—may unexpectedly come forth from amidst society's most trivial and handselled furniture, to enjoy its perfect summer life at last!

I do not say that John or Jonathan[20] will realize all this; but such is the character of that morrow which mere lapse of time can never make to dawn. The light which puts out our eyes is darkness to us. Only that day dawns to which we are awake. There is more day to dawn. The sun is but a morning star.

---

19. **alburnum** (al bur´ nəm) *n.* soft wood between the bark and the heartwood, where water is conducted.
20. **John or Jonathan** average person.

Review and Assess

Thinking About the Selection

1. **Respond:** From your point of view, what would be the advantages and disadvantages of spending two solitary years in a natural setting?

2. **(a) Recall:** What advice does Thoreau offer to his "fellows" about ownership of land or property? **(b) Interpret:** What does Thoreau mean by his comment, "It makes but little difference whether you are committed to a farm or the county jail"?

3. **(a) Recall:** What advice does Thoreau offer to those who live in poverty? **(b) Analyze:** What does this advice suggest about Thoreau's definition of true wealth?

4. **(a) Recall:** According to Thoreau, by what is our life "frittered away"? **(b) Interpret:** What does Thoreau mean by his advice to "Simplify, simplify."?

5. **(a) Deduce:** What did Thoreau hope to achieve by living at Walden Pond? **(b) Make a Judgment:** Do you believe Thoreau felt his time at Walden was well spent? Explain.

6. **(a) Apply:** How would you define those things that are necessary to the soul? **(b) Take a Position:** Do you agree with Thoreau that "Money is not required to buy one necessary of the soul"? Explain.

from Walden ◆ *411*

Answers for p. 411

Review and Assess

1. **Possible response:** Advantages include having a chance to get an intimate view of nature and develop one's inner resources. Disadvantages include being separated from family, friends, and modern conveniences.

2. **(a)** He tells them to avoid the commitments of ownership. **(b) Possible answer:** He means that all commitments create restrictions and demands.

3. **(a)** They should love life and find the best in it. **(b) Possible response:** He believes that true wealth is spiritual rather than financial.

4. **(a)** It is "frittered away" by detail. **(b) Possible response:** He means that people should reduce both their material possessions and the external demands of their lives.

5. **(a)** He hoped to identify and experience the very essence of life. **(b) Possible response:** Yes, he seems to feel that he's learned a great deal from his experience, for example, to "advance in the direction of his dreams" and "live the life which he has imagined."

6. **Possible response: (a)** Such things as truth, justice, beauty, and love are necessary to the soul. **(b)** Most students will agree that while the body must have its basic needs met, the soul needs nothing money can buy.

CUSTOMIZE FOR UNIVERSAL ACCESS

For Special Needs Students	For Less Proficient Readers	For Gifted/Talented Students
Take students for a walk to a natural setting. While outside, read aloud the final selection paragraph and work with students to build comprehension. Then, ask students to describe their reactions to nature. How do they feel when they are in natural settings? Does it give them hope, as it does Thoreau?	For students who find Thoreau's comparison of the hidden egg to life's energy difficult to comprehend, return to the paragraph's opening sentence. Highlight its subject "the life in us." Explain that this remains the subject of comparison throughout the paragraph.	Point out Thoreau's use of figurative language in "The Conclusion." For example, list or ask these students to list some of the metaphors that Thoreau uses for life. Discuss which of these—life is a road or path, a ship, a parade, a bone, a river, a day, and the seasons of the year—students find most effective.

16 About the Selection

This selection is excerpted from a long essay, about twenty pages in length, in which Thoreau advocates civil disobedience—the deliberate and public refusal to obey laws that violate one's personal principles. In the portions included here, Thoreau expresses his belief that government has been no more than an impediment to the productivity and achievements of the American people. Philosophically, he stands opposed to government. Practically, he urges readers to try to make a better government, one that commands respect.

17 Reading Strategy

Evaluating the Writer's Statement of Philosophy

• Have students read the bracketed passage. Explain that recognizing their initial personal response to a writer's philosophy can help readers respond to evidence.

• Encourage students to paraphrase Thoreau's statement of philosophy about government.
Possible response: He believes that there should be as little government as possible, because it generally creates more problems than it solves.

• Ask students the Reading Strategy question on p. 412: Before you read Thoreau's supporting arguments, do you think you will agree with his philosophy about government? Explain.
Possible answer: I disagree with Thoreau because in our modern, rapidly growing, fast-paced society, many tasks can be best accomplished by government.

16 from # CIVIL DISOBEDIENCE

Henry David Thoreau

Background

The Mexican War was a conflict between Mexico and the United States that took place from 1846 to 1848. The war was caused by a dispute over the boundary between Texas and Mexico, as well as by Mexico's refusal to discuss selling California and New Mexico to the United States. Believing that President Polk had intentionally provoked the conflict before gaining congressional approval, Thoreau and many other Americans strongly objected to the war. In protest, Thoreau refused to pay his taxes and was forced to spend a night in jail. After that experience, Thoreau wrote "Civil Disobedience," urging people to resist governmental policies with which they disagree.

I heartily accept the motto, "That government is best which governs least";[1] and I should like to see it acted up to more rapidly and systematically. Carried out, it finally amounts to this, which also I believe: "That government is best which governs not at all"; and when men are prepared for it, that will be the kind of government which they will have. Government is at best but an expedient; but most governments are usually, and all governments are sometimes, inexpedient. The objections which have been brought against a standing army, and they are many and weighty, and deserve to prevail, may also at last be brought against a standing government. The standing army is only an arm of the standing government. The government itself, which is only the mode which the people have chosen to execute their will, is equally liable to be abused and perverted before the people can act through it. Witness the present Mexican war, the work of comparatively a few individuals using the standing government as their tool; for in the outset, the people would not have consented to this measure.

This American government—what is it but a tradition, though a recent one, endeavoring to transmit itself unimpaired to posterity, but each instant losing some of its integrity? It has not the vitality and force of a single living man; for a single man can bend it to his will. It is a sort of wooden gun to the people themselves; and, if ever they should use it in earnest as a real one against each other, it will surely split.

---

1. **"That . . . least"** the motto of the *United States Magazine and Democratic Review*, a literary-political journal.

Reading Strategy
Evaluating the Writer's Statement of Philosophy
Before you read Thoreau's supporting arguments, do you think you will agree with his philosophy about government? Explain.

expedient (ik spē′ dē ənt) *n.* resource

posterity (päs ter′ e tē) *n.* all succeeding generations

☀ **ENRICHMENT: Social Studies**

Government

Discuss whether government is, as Thoreau contends, an impediment to our freedoms and progress or whether citizens can improve their local, state, and federal governments by exercising their right to participate. Explain that citizens have many opportunities to make their voices heard, particularly on the local level. Discuss the following ways groups and individuals can influence public policy. Ask students to add their own suggestions to this list:

• Write a letter to a civic leader

• Organize or sign a petition
• Submit a letter to the editor of a local paper
• Speak out at a town meeting
• Exercise the right to vote

Have students think about their own responses to governmental issues. Ask them whether they have ever signed a petition or written a letter voicing their feelings on a particular issue. Have students discuss their views on what roles and responsibilities individuals have as citizens in a democracy.

But it is not the less necessary for this; for the people must have some complicated machinery or other, and hear its din, to satisfy that idea of government which they have. Governments show thus how successfully men can be imposed on, even impose on themselves, for their own advantage. It is excellent, we must all allow; yet this government never of itself furthered any enterprise, but by the <u>alacrity</u> with which it got out of its way. *It* does not keep the country free. *It* does not settle the West. *It* does not educate. The character inherent in the American people has done all that has been accomplished; and it would have done somewhat more, if the government had not sometimes got in its way. For government is an expedient by which men would fain succeed in letting one another alone; and, as has been said, when it is most expedient, the governed are most let alone by it. Trade and commerce, if they were not made of India rubber,[2] would never manage to bounce over the obstacles which legislators are continually putting in their way; and, if one were to judge these men wholly by the effects of their actions, and not partly by their intentions, they would deserve to be classed and punished with those mischievous persons who put obstructions on the railroads.

But, to speak practically and as a citizen, unlike those who call themselves no government men, I ask for, not at once no government, but *at once* a better government. Let every man make known what kind of government would command his respect, and that will be one step toward obtaining it. . . .

alacrity (ə lak′ rə tē) *n.* speed

2. **India rubber** a form of crude rubber.

Review and Assess

Thinking About the Selection

1. **Respond:** What kind of government commands your respect? Why?

2. **(a) Recall:** What motto does Thoreau accept? **(b) Analyze:** How would he like to see that motto implemented?

3. **(a) Recall:** How does Thoreau define the best possible kind of government? **(b) Draw Conclusions:** According to Thoreau, when will Americans get the best possible kind of government?

4. **(a) Summarize:** What is Thoreau asking his readers to do? **(b) Evaluate:** Does Thoreau present a convincing argument for acting on one's principles?

5. **(a) Criticize:** What arguments might you use to counter Thoreau's objections to the idea of a standing government? **(b) Support:** What examples might you provide to support an argument that government benefits individuals?

from *Civil Disobedience* ◆ 413

ASSESS

Answers for p. 413

Review and Assess

1. Students should explain the reasoning behind their opinions.
2. **(a)** He accepts the motto "That government is best, which governs least." **(b)** He would like to see it implemented quickly and systematically.
3. **(a)** A government that governs least is the best possible kind of government. **(b)** Thoreau says that when people are ready, they will dispense with government altogether.
4. **(a)** He's asking them to step forward and state what they want from government. **(b)** Students should support their responses with an evaluation of Thoreau's arguments
5. **(a)** Possible response: Without a standing government, the nation cannot prepare itself for war, cannot make plans for future needs and cannot organize national elections. **(b)** Possible response: Governments provide schools, military and civil defense and transportation systems.

ASSESSMENT PRACTICE: Reading Comprehension

Make Inferences and Generalizations   (For more practice, see Test Preparation Workbook, p. 23.)

To help students practice making generalizations, have them complete this sample test item.

I heartily accept the motto, "That government is best which governs least"; and I should like to see it acted up to more rapidly and systematically.

Based on this statement, Thoreau probably believes that—

A governments should be more involved in the lives of the people.

B people could do more if governments did less.

C the American people need help from the government to improve their country.

D government should be abolished.

B is the most accurate generalization because it is based on details from the passage.

413

Review and Assess

1. Possible responses:
   (a) He begins with a simile about ants and proceeds to a statement about detail. Then he urges simplicity and gives examples about simplifying individual lives. He then makes another comparison and launches an attack on the complexities of progress.
   (b) The paragraph that begins "however mean your life" on p. 409 also builds to a single sentence that expresses the meaning of the entire paragraph.

2. **(a)** Suggested responses include the first paragraph from "The Conclusion" of *Walden*. **(b)** Yes, it is effective because it invites reader support with the details, so that the reader is convinced before even reaching the "larger truth."

3. Students' should accurately identify the meanings of Thoreau's metaphors.

4. Possible response: The government as "a wooden gun" metaphor is logical, while the "chopping sea of civilized life" is more artistic.

5. **(a)** He makes more elaborate use of metaphor in *Walden* than in *Civil Disobedience*.
   (b) Metaphor is more suited to *Walden*, which reflects a personal journey in which spiritual and physical journeys are intertwined. *Civil Disobedience* is a more specifically persuasive essay designed to express Thoreau's public views.

6. **(a)** He claims that we fritter away our lives in details that distract us from real living. As supporting evidence he offers his own experience of simplifying his life and experiencing greater freedom. **(b)** Possible response: The details of living add richness and variety to our lives. **(c)** Students should defend their responses.

7. **(a)** He contends that government is too easily perverted by a few individuals, and that government itself never did anything to further the country. **(b)** Students should explain the reasoning behind their reponses.

8. Students may feel that today, life is simply too complex for such an experiment.

Review and Assess

Literary Analysis

Style

1. (a) Explain how the paragraph on simplicity in *Walden* demonstrates Thoreau's tendency to make sentences build to a climax. (b) Find another example in *Walden* of Thoreau's climactic **style.**

2. Thoreau often starts a paragraph with specific examples. He then applies them to a larger truth. (a) Find one such paragraph. (b) Do you think this approach is effective? Explain.

Comparing Literary Works

3. Use a chart like the one shown here to examine the meanings of Thoreau's **metaphors.**

Metaphor	Things compared	Meaning
I wanted to live deep and suck out all the marrow of life		

4. In *Civil Disobedience*, Thoreau describes government as "a wooden gun." In *Walden*, he describes "this chopping sea of civilized life." Does each of these metaphors function primarily as a logical or an artistic tool? Explain.

5. (a) In which essay does Thoreau make more elaborate use of metaphor? (b) How does this choice reflect the purpose of the essay?

Reading Strategy

Evaluating the Writer's Statement of Philosophy

6. Thoreau writes that people should simplify their lives. (a) What support for this belief does he provide? (b) How could you argue against this idea? (c) Is his argument convincing? Explain.

7. (a) What evidence does Thoreau use to support his contention that "That government is best which governs not at all"? (b) Do you agree with Thoreau? Explain.

Extend Understanding

8. **World Events Connection:** Would it be possible for Thoreau to conduct his "experiment" of living at Walden Pond in today's society? Why or why not?

Quick Review

Style is the manner in which a writer puts his or her thoughts into words.

Metaphors compare two unlike things, without the use of *like* or *as*.

To **evaluate the writer's statement of philosophy**, weigh the writer's supporting evidence and your own experience. Decide whether you agree or disagree.

 Take It to the Net
www.phschool.com
Take the interactive self-test online to check your understanding of these selections.

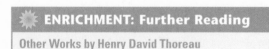

ENRICHMENT: Further Reading

Other Works by Henry David Thoreau

A Week on the Concord and Merrimack Rivers

The Maine Woods

"Slavery in Massachusetts"

 Take It to the Net
Visit www.phschool.com for more information on Henry David Thoreau.

Integrate Language Skills

❶ Vocabulary Development Lesson

Word Analysis: Latin Root -flu-

The Latin root -flu-, found in words like *fluid*, means "flow." The word *superfluous* means "overflowing" or "exceeding what is sufficient." Match each of the words with its definition. Check your answers in a dictionary.

    a. affluence   **b.** confluence   **c.** fluent

1. a flowing together, as in two streams
2. wealth; an abundant flow; prosperity
3. effortlessly smooth; flowing

Spelling Strategy

If a word ends in -*ent*, such as the word *expedient*, its parallel forms end in -*ence* (*expedience*) or -*ency* (*expediency*). For each of these words, correctly spell the parallel forms.

   1. resident   2. dependent   3. excellent

Concept Development: Synonyms

Select the word or phrase below whose meaning is closest to that of the first word.

1. dilapidated: (a) depressed, (b) in disrepair, (c) new
2. sublime: (a) tight, (b) filthy, (c) majestic
3. superfluous: (a) superb, (b) unnecessary, (c) wanted
4. evitable: (a) avoidable, (b) evident, (c) fair
5. magnanimity: (a) spontaneity, (b) horror, (c) kindness
6. expedient: (a) resource, (b) expense, (c) implosive
7. posterity: (a) future generations, (b) ancestors, (c) current generations
8. alacrity: (a) awareness, (b) readiness, (c) suspicion

❷ Grammar and Style Lesson

Infinitives and Infinitive Phrases

Thoreau makes frequent use of infinitives and infinitive phrases. **Infinitive phrases** combine an **infinitive** (the basic form of the verb preceded by the word *to*) and its complements and modifiers. Infinitive phrases function as nouns, adjectives, or adverbs. In the examples below, the infinitive phrases are underlined.

> **Noun:** I dearly love *to talk*. (object of the verb *love*)
>
> **Adjective:** I had several more lives *to live*. (modifies the noun *lives*)
>
> **Adverb:** This was an airy . . . cabin, fit *to entertain a traveling god*. (modifies the participle *fit*)

Practice Find at least six infinitives or infinitive phrases in the paragraph of *Walden* (page 406) that begins "I went to the woods . . ." Identify the grammatical function of the infinitive in each phrase.

Writing Application Write two paragraphs describing how you plan to achieve a difficult goal. Use infinitive phrases such as *to shine* in persuasive statements: "Give my plan an opportunity *to shine*."

After you draft, highlight the infinitives and infinitive phrases in your paragraphs. For each, identify the function it serves in the sentence.

 Prentice Hall Writing and Grammar Connection: Chapter 19, Section 2

from *Walden* / from *Civil Disobedience* ◆ 415

TEACHING RESOURCES

The following resources can be used to enrich or extend the instruction for pp. 415–416.

Vocabulary
- **Selection Support:** Build Vocabulary, p. 95
- **Vocabulary and Spelling Practice Book** (Use this booklet for skills enrichment.) 📖

Grammar
- **Selection Support:** Grammar and Style, p. 96
- **Writing and Grammar**, Ruby Level, p. 442

- 📄 **Daily Language Practice Transparencies** 📖

Writing
- 📖 **Writing and Grammar**, Ruby Level, p. 124
- 💿 **Writing and Grammar iText CD-ROM**
- 📄 **Writing Models and Graphic Organizers on Transparencies**, pp. 33–36, 91

EXTEND

Answers for p. 415

❶ Vocabulary Development

Word Analysis
1. b
2. a
3. c

Spelling Strategy
1. residence, residency
2. dependence, dependency
3. excellence, excellency

Concept Development: Synonyms
1. b
2. c
3. b
4. a
5. c
6. a
7. a
8. b

❷ Grammar and Style

Possible responses include: to live deliberately (noun); to front only the essential facts of life (noun); [to] see if I could not learn (noun); to teach (noun); to die (adverb); [to] discover that I had not lived (noun); to practice resignation (noun); to live deep (noun); [to] suck out all the marrow of life (noun); to live so sturdily and Spartanlike (noun); to put (adverb); to cut a broad swatch (noun); [to] shave close (noun); to drive life into a corner (noun); [to] reduce it to its lowest terms (noun); to be mean (adjective); to get the whole and genuine meanness of it (noun); [to] publish its meanness to the world (noun); to know it by experience (noun); to be able (noun); to give a true account of it (noun); to "glorify God (noun); [to] enjoy him forever" (noun)

Writing Application

Paragraphs should be free of major mechanical errors and should contain at least three infinitive phrases. Phrases should be accurately highlighted and labeled with correct grammatical function.

📄 **BLOCK SCHEDULING:** Resources marked with this symbol provide varied instruction during 90-minute blocks.

415

❸ Writing Lesson

- Discuss with students two possible organizations for their paper: begin with the cause and then discuss its effect OR begin with effects and then prove the cause.

- Provide students with the Cause-and-Effect Transparency, p. 91, in **Writing Models and Graphic Organizers on Transparencies** as an additional tool for organizing their prewriting notes.

- Read through the Writing Lesson steps with students and clarify any confusion.

- Use the Writing Process Model 6: Persuasive Essay, in **Writing Models and Graphic Organizers on Transparencies**, pp. 33–36, to model persuasive writing.

- Encourage students to work in pairs to try out their editorials on an audience.

❹ Listening and Speaking

- Consider assigning students to groups that require them to argue against their personal views. This can encourage more thorough investigation of persuasive arguments and force more rigorous logic.

- Encourage students to identify evidence that can support their arguments.

- Direct groups to sequence their arguments, with the strongest first or last, and to assign these elements to strong speakers.

- Conduct the debates as a class with yourself or a student as moderator. Remind students of courteous debate behavior.

CUSTOMIZE INSTRUCTION
For Universal Access

To address different learning styles, use the activities suggested in the **Extension Activities** booklet, p. 21.

For Visual/Spatial Learners, use Activity 5.

For Interpersonal and Verbal/Linguistic Learners, use Activity 6.

For Interpersonal and Bodily/Kinesthetic Learners, use Activity 7.

---

❸ Writing Lesson

Editorial

In the century-and-a-half-since Thoreau wrote *Walden*, life for most Americans has become increasingly complex rather than simpler. Write an editorial for a major newspaper either advocating or rejecting Thoreau's ideas of simplicity for today's world. Refer to the texts of *Walden* and *Civil Disobedience* to support your ideas.

Prewriting   Decide whether you think Thoreau was right or wrong, and brainstorm for a list of examples that support your point of view.

Drafting   Introduce Thoreau and outline his ideas. Use quotations from his work to illustrate your points. Make a strong statement either advocating or refuting his ideas, using your list of examples. Anticipate and answer the arguments of those who may disagree with you.

> **Model: Anticipating Opponents' Arguments**
>
> Today, Thoreau's ideas fall on deaf ears because everyone is glued to their cell phones. Instead of hearing his wisdom, people say, "But I can't live without my fax machine. It makes my life easier." Yet, people have less time with family, and less time for the simple pleasures of life than ever before.

Anticipating and answering opponents' arguments creates a more persuasive piece of writing.

Revising   Reread your editorial, adding examples, anecdotes, or quotations as necessary to sharpen your argument.

𝒲𝒢 *Prentice Hall Writing and Grammar Connection: Chapter 7, Section 2*

❹ Extension Activities

Listening and Speaking With a group, stage a **debate** to argue the pros and cons of civil disobedience as a form of protest. Keep the following strategies in mind as you work:

- Develop several key arguments supporting your position.
- Use analogies to familiar situations to help listeners appreciate your points.

Incorporate formal debate strategies, such as the use of syllogisms (arguments that link a major and minor premise) to strengthen your arguments. **[Group Activity]**

Research and Technology Conduct research to find out what Walden Pond is like today and what efforts have been made to preserve it. Share your findings with the class in an **oral presentation**. Follow with a discussion of the way Walden Pond has changed since Thoreau's day.

 Take It to the Net   www.phschool.com

Go online for an additional research activity using the Internet.

416 ◆ *A Growing Nation (1800–1870)*

ASSESSMENT RESOURCES

The following resources can be used to assess students' knowledge and skills.

Selection Assessment

📖 **Formal Assessment**, pp. 102–104

📖 **Open Book Test**, pp. 61–63

📼 **Got It! Assessment Videotapes**, Tape 2

💽 **Test Bank Software**

💻 ***Take It to the Net***
Visit www.phschool.com for self-tests and additional questions on the selections.

PRENTICE HALL **ASSESSMENT SYSTEM**

📖 **Workbook**   📰 **Transparencies**

📖 **Skill Book**   💿 **CD-ROM**

Looking at Literary Forms: Poetry

Walden Pond Revisited, 1942, N.C. Wyeth, Brandywine River Museum

A s the nation's boundaries pushed west in the nineteenth century, writers were pioneering new styles of poetry. Walt Whitman abandoned traditional poetic forms in favor of free verse. Emily Dickinson combined striking languages and a highly imaginative view of the world. Together, these two influential poets set the stage for a new American poetry.

Looking at Literary Forms: Poetry ◆ 417

STOMIZE INSTRUCTION FOR UNIVERSAL ACCESS

n assigning the selections in this part, keep in mind these factors:

Dickinson's Poetry

Vivid imagery may make these challenging poems more accessible.

Whitman's Poetry

"I Hear America Singing" is an accessible celebration of American workers.

Encourage readers to approach "Preface to the 1855 Edition of Leaves of Grass" and "Song of

Myself" in sections to increase understanding and enjoyment.

"I, Too"; "To Walt Whitman"

• Contemporary poets reflect on Whitman's legacy.

Selection Planning Guide

The selections in this section reveal the range of two of the nation's most famous poets. Emily Dickinson's poetry explores the vast inner landscape. "The Brain—is wider than the Sky—" asserts that the human soul can encompass all things in the natural world and an individual identity. In "Because I could not stop for Death—" and "I heard a Fly buzz when I died—," the poet describes the somber journey from life to death. Rich in imagery and symbolism and innovative in its form, Dickinson's poetry has been celebrated and emulated long after the poet's death. Similarly, Walt Whitman broke the poetic conventions of his time. Whitman's strong belief in the connection between humanity and nature as well as his unique catalog style are evident in the excerpt from "Song of Myself" and "I Hear America Singing."

Background

Art

Walden Pond Revisited,
N.C. Wyeth

Newell Convers Wyeth (1882–1945) was the premiere book illustrator of his day. Born in Needham, Massachusetts, Wyeth knew early on that he wanted to be an artist, and so he studied with the great American illustrator Howard Pyle, often visiting Pyle at his home in Chadds Ford, Pennsylvania. Wyeth eventually settled his family in this beautiful area.

This painting, a mixture of egg-based tempera and other media, is somewhat surrealistic in its style. Wyeth renders various natural elements in careful detail, but the unnaturally crowded composition and dramatic lighting of the painting suggest a kind of dreamscape. Painted nearly a century after Thoreau's historic sojourn at Walden Pond, this work reveres the writer as a kind of philosopher saint, setting him in an idealized landscape.

• Based on this painting, what would you say Wyeth felt about Thoreau, and what elements in the painting led you to this idea? Possible response: Wyeth seems to admire Thoreau, and this admiration is conveyed by the halo-like light that surrounds the writer.

417

Emily Dickinson's Poetry

Lesson Objectives

1. **To analyze and respond to literary elements**
   - Literary Analysis: Slant Rhyme
   - Comparing Literary Works

2. **To read, comprehend, analyze, and critique poems**
   - Reading Strategy: Analyzing Images
   - Review and Assess Questions
   - Assessment Practice (ATE)

3. **To develop word analysis skills, fluency, and systematic vocabulary**
   - Vocabulary Development Lesson: Latin Word Root: *-finis-*

4. **To understand and apply written and oral language conventions**
   - Spelling Strategy
   - Grammar and Style Lesson: Gerunds

5. **To understand and apply appropriate writing and research strategies**
   - Writing Lesson: Letter to an Author
   - Extension Activity: Report

6. **To understand and apply listening and speaking strategies**
   - Extension Activity: Poetry Reading

STEP-BY-STEP TEACHING GUIDE	PACING GUIDE
PRETEACH	
Motivate Students and Provide Background	
Use the Motivation activity (ATE p. 418)	5 min.
Read and discuss the author and background information (SE pp. 418, 420; ATE p. 418)	5 min.
Introduce the Concepts	
Introduce the Literary Analysis and Reading Strategy (SE/ATE p. 419) **A**	15 min.
Pronounce the vocabulary words and read their definitions (SE p. 419)	5 min.
TEACH	
Monitor Comprehension	
Informally monitor comprehension by circulating while students read independently or in groups **A**	30 min.
Develop vocabulary with Vocabulary notes (SE pp. 421, 424, 427; ATE p. 427)	as students read
Develop Understanding	
Develop students' understanding of slant rhyme with the Literary Analysis annotations (SE p. 423; ATE pp. 423, 424) **A**	5 min.
Develop students' ability to analyze images with the Reading Strategy annotations (SE p. 421; ATE pp. 421, 426)	5 min.
ASSESS	
Assess Mastery	
Assess students' mastery of the Reading Strategy and Literary Analysis by having them answer the Review and Assess questions (SE/ATE p. 429)	15 min.
Use one or more of the print and media Assessment Resources (ATE p. 431) **A**	up to 45 min.
EXTEND	
Apply Understanding	
Have students complete the Vocabulary Development Lesson and the Grammar and Style Lesson (SE p. 430) **A**	20 min.
Apply students' ability to use clear and logical organization by using the Writing Lesson (SE/ATE p. 431) **A**	45 min.
Apply students' understanding using one or more of the Extension Activities (SE p. 431)	20–90 min.

A **ACCELERATED INSTRUCTION:**
Use the strategies and activities identified with an **A**.

UNIVERSAL ACCESS
● = Below Level Students
▲ = On-Level Students
■ = Above Level Students

Time and Resource Manager

Reading Level: Challenging, Average, Challenging, Challenging, Challenging, Average
Average Number of Instructional Days: 4

RESOURCES		
PRINT 📝	**TRANSPARENCIES** 🔖	**TECHNOLOGY** 💿 🎧 📼
• **Beyond Literature,** Cross-Curricular Connection: Art, p. 22 ▲ ■		• **Interest Grabber Video,** Tape 3 ● ▲ ■
• **Selection Support Workbook:** ● ▲ ■ Literary Analysis, p. 102 Reading Strategy, p. 101 Build Vocabulary, p. 99	• **Literary Analysis and Reading Transparencies,** pp. 43 and 44 ● ▲ ■	
		• **Listening to Literature** ● ▲ ■ Audiocassettes, Sides 14, 15 Audio CDs, CDs 9, 10
• **Literatura en español** ● ▲ • **Literary Analysis for Enrichment** ■		
• **Formal Assessment:** Selection Test, pp. 108–110 ● ▲ ■ • **Open Book Test,** pp. 64–66 ● ▲ ■ • **Performance Assessment and Portfolio Management,** p. 12 ● ▲ ■ • **PRENTICE HALL ASSESSMENT** *SYSTEM* ● ▲ ■	• **PRENTICE HALL ASSESSMENT** *SYSTEM* ● ▲ ■ Skills Practice Answers and Explanations on Transparencies	• **Test Bank Software** ● ▲ ■ • **Got It! Assessment Videotapes,** Tape 2 ● ▲
• **Selection Support Workbook:** ● ▲ ■ Build Grammar Skills, p. 100 • **Writing and Grammar,** Ruby Level ● ▲ ■ • **Extension Activities,** p. 22 ● ▲ ■	• **Daily Language Practice Transparencies** ● ▲ • **Writing Models and Graphic Organizers on Transparencies** pp. 57, 95 ● ▲ ■	• **Writing and Grammar iText CD-ROM** ● ▲ ■ 💻 *Take It to the Net* www.phschool.com

▦ **BLOCK SCHEDULING:** Use one 90-minute class period to preteach the selection and have students read it. Use a second 90-minute class period to assess students' mastery of skills and have them complete one of the Extension Activities.

Prepare to Read

❶ Emily Dickinson's Poetry

**Step-by-Step Teaching Guide
for pp. 418–419**

Motivation

Many of Emily Dickinson's poems address the idea of solitude. Ask students to consider their personal response to the word *alone*. Each student should list the five words that first come to mind. Then elicit these words from each student. As you write responses on the chalk-board, ask the class to classify each response as positive or negative. When you have collected at least one response from every student, ask students to determine whether the word *alone* has a more positive or more negative connotation. Ask students to consider both aspects of solitude—independence and isolation—as they approach Emily Dickinson's poetry.

▭ Interest Grabber Video

As an alternative, play "A Visit With Emily Dickinson" on Tape 3 to engage student interest.

❶ Background

More About the Author

Although Emily Dickinson's reclusive lifestyle was most likely of emotional origin, it also may have been encouraged by the mores of the day. In the mid-nineteenth century, as an unmarried woman, Dickinson had little choice but to live with her family. Her decision to isolate herself may also have been the result of the inability of those around her to understand her. One eminent scholar and critic has said, "The poet Emily Dickinson complained that everybody said: 'What?' to her, until finally she practically gave up trying to talk altogether and con-fined herself to writing notes." Such an explanation is supported by Dickinson's poem on p. 425, "The soul selects her own society."

**Emily Dickinson
(1830–1886)**
Of the 1,775 poems Emily Dickinson wrote during her lifetime, only seven were pub-lished before her death—and these few appeared anonymously. Dickinson was a private person who was extremely reluctant to reveal herself or her work to the world. As a result, few people outside her family and a small circle of friends knew of her poetic genius until after her death. Today, however, she is widely regarded as one of the greatest American poets.

A Life Apart Dickinson was born in Amherst, Massachusetts, the daughter of a prominent lawyer. As a child, she was energetic and enjoyed the tasks of daily life—cooking, sewing, playing with friends, winter sports, even studying at a boarding school. Her childhood was normal in many respects. However, as an adult she became increasingly isolated. Though she traveled as a young woman to Boston, Washington, D.C., and Philadelphia to visit friends, she rarely left her hometown as she grew older. In fact, after her father's death in 1874, she seldom left the house, and during the last ten years of her life, she remained entirely within her house and garden. Dickinson's circle of friends grew smaller and smaller, and she communicated with the few that remained mainly through notes and fragments of poems. She dressed only in white and would not allow her neighbors or any strangers to see her. When her health failed, she allowed her doctor to examine her only by observing her from a dis-tance. Dickinson was fond of children, however, and sometimes lowered a basket of candy or fruit to them from her upstairs window.

Her Talent Is Recognized Though she chose to live most of her life in virtual isolation, Emily Dickinson was a deeply energetic, intense person. She possessed a clear sense of purpose—to write poetry—and devoted most of her time to doing so. Yet because she shared her work with few people, she sometimes doubted her abilities. In 1862, she sent four poems to Thomas Wentworth Higginson, an influential literary critic, and asked him to tell her whether her verse was "alive." Like the editors who first published her work after her death, Higginson sought to change her unconventional style—her eccentric use of punctuation and irregular meter and rhyme. He did not understand that she had crafted her poetry with great precision and that her unique style, marked by unconven-tional capitalization and the use of dashes, was an important element of her poetry. Still, he did recognize her talent and encouraged her to keep writing.

Dickinson's Legacy In 1886, after fighting illness for two years, Emily Dickinson died in the same house in which she had been born. After her death, her sister Lavinia discovered packets of poems in the drawers of Emily's dresser. Dickinson had given instructions that her poems were to be destroyed after her death. Nevertheless, the poems were organized and edited by various family members and were published in small installments. However, it was not until 1955, when *The Poems of Emily Dickinson* was published, that her work as a whole was revealed to the world and her genius fully recognized.

The Belle of Amherst In the years since the publication of her work, Dickinson has become the subject of numerous plays, novels, and poems that have romanticized her life and celebrated her genius with varying amounts of sentimentality and accuracy. But for the poets who came after her, Dickinson has no peer. She is a voice of intense delicacy and urgency, rising out of stillness.

TEACHING RESOURCES

The following resources can be used to enrich or extend the instruction for pp. 418–419.

Motivation
▭ **Interest Grabber Video**, Tape 3 ▮

Background
▭ **Beyond Literature**, p. 22 ▮

▭ *Take It to the Net*
Visit www.phschool.com for background and hotlinks for the selections.

Literary Analysis
▭ **Literary Analysis and Reading Transparencies**, Slant Rhyme, p. 44 ▮

▭ **Selection Support:** Literary Analysis, p. 102

Reading
▭ **Literary Analysis and Reading Transparencies**, Analyzing Images, p. 43

▭ **BLOCK SCHEDULING:** Resources marked with this symbol provide varied instruction during 90-minute blocks.

Preview

Connecting to the Literature

Although you may not often share your private thoughts about life's "big topics," you probably have many ideas about them. In her poems, Dickinson shines light on her shadowy "private" thoughts as well as on ideas about such vast subjects as death, solitude, consciousness, and the soul.

❷ Literary Analysis

Slant Rhyme

Poets use rhyme to create pleasant musical sounds and to unify groups of lines or stanzas. **Exact rhyme** occurs when two words have identical sounds in their final accented syllables. In **slant rhyme**, the final sounds are similar but not identical.

Exact rhyme: *glove-above*
Slant: *glove-prove*

Dickinson uses both exact and slant rhyme in her poetry. Her independence from strict rhyme is one of the reasons her poems are so surprising. As you read her poems, pay attention to her uses of both kinds of rhyme and consider the effects they create.

Comparing Literary Works

In all of her work, Emily Dickinson explored different aspects of human consciousness. In some poems, Dickinson saw human consciousness as an infinite universe. In others, she saw it as a small, isolated presence. In all of her poems, the conscious mind of the individual is "Where the meanings are." As you read these poems, compare the differing ways in which Dickinson defines human awareness.

❸ Reading Strategy

Analyzing Images

Poets often link abstract concepts such as love, life, and death to concrete images, or word pictures. In reading poetry, it is helpful to **analyze images** to clarify the abstract meaning the author is conveying. As you read Emily Dickinson's poems, use a chart like the one shown here to help you understand her images.

Image	Abstract Idea
Carriage, slow journey	Death
School-children, grain, sunset	Life

Vocabulary Development

cornice (kôr′ nis) *n.* projecting decorative molding along the top of a building (p. 421)

surmised (sər mīzd′) *v.* guessed (p. 421)

oppresses (ə pres′ əz) *v.* weighs heavily on the mind (p. 424)

finite (fī′ nīt) *adj.* having measurable or definable limits (p. 427)

infinity (in fin′ i tē) *n.* endless or unlimited space, time, or distance (p. 427)

Emily Dickinson's Poetry ◆ 419

❷ Literary Analysis

Slant Rhyme

- Tell students that as they read Emily Dickinson's poems, they will focus on slant rhyme, in which final ending sounds are related but not identical.

- Have volunteers read aloud the Literary Analysis instruction and excerpts. Help students hear the difference between exact and slant rhymes.

- Discuss the instruction under Comparing Literary Works and use it to help students connect Dickinson's poetic structure to her exploration of human consciousness.

❸ Reading Strategy

Analyzing Images

- Remind students that analyzing images can help them understand poetry's deeper, often symbolic, meanings.

- Explain to students that they can analyze images by questioning the emotions each image evokes. For example, a shiver in response to the image of the chill of nightfall might suggest the idea of a life ending.

- Direct students to use a chart like the one on the student page to analyze images as they read Dickinson's poetry.

Vocabulary Development

- Pronounce each vocabulary word for students, and read the definitions as a class. Have students identify any words with which they are already familiar.

CUSTOMIZE INSTRUCTION FOR UNIVERSAL ACCESS

For Less Proficient Readers	For English Learners	For Advanced Readers
The poems in this grouping are rich with imagery. To prepare students to recognize and analyze Dickinson's imagery, review examples of figurative language, such as simile, metaphor, and personification. For example, clarify for students that above Dickinson has depicted Death as a thoughtful neighbor who has picked her up for a ride in his carriage.	The words in these poems may be easy to decode, but the imagery and symbolism are less apparent. To help students analyze Dickinson's images, encourage them to sketch visual images. Studying their sketches will help students ascertain the symbolic meaning in images.	Emily Dickinson's words may seem straightforward, yet they conceal metaphors and hidden messages. Challenge students to read the poems on more then one level and analyze the meanings behind the simple words. Students might create reading keys for younger students detailing these meanings.

 E-Teach

Visit E-Teach at www.phschool.com for teacher's essays on how to teach, with questions and answers.

419

CUSTOMIZE INSTRUCTION
For Interpersonal Learners

Remind students that Dickinson spoke directly to fewer and fewer people as her life progressed. Have students compose imaginary dialogues in which Dickinson discusses her work and her ideas and students express in their turn what they might wish to tell the poet about the effect her poems have had on them.

❶ About the Selection

In this poem, Dickinson captures the inevitability of death and suggests a belief in an eternal afterlife through the personification of Death as a coach driver who carries people toward their final resting place.

❶ # Because I could not stop for Death—

Emily Dickinson

Waiting Outside No. 12, Anonymous, Crane Kalman Gallery

Background

The extent of Emily Dickinson's gift was not generally recognized until 1955, when a new edition of her poems was published under the guidance of Thomas H. Johnson. Previous editors had changed Dickinson's poems to reflect conventional ideas about poetry, but Johnson's edition restored the poet's original versions. For the first time, Dickinson's poetry was printed as she had meant it to be read, and the world experienced the power of her complex mind captured in concrete imagery and simple but forceful language. Dickinson's work is often compared with that of the modern poets, and she is now acknowledged as a visionary who was far ahead of her time.

Because I could not stop for Death—
He kindly stopped for me—
The Carriage held but just Ourselves—
And Immortality.

▲ **Critical Viewing** In what ways do the details of this painting mirror Dickinson's poem? **[Analyze]**

420 ◆ *A Growing Nation (1800–1870)*

TEACHING RESOURCES

The following resources can be used to enrich or extend the instruction for pp. 420–428.

Literary Analysis

📄 **Writing Models and Graphic Organizers on Transparencies,** p. 57, 95

📄 **Literary Analysis and Reading Transparencies,** p. 44

Reading

📖 **Selection Support:** Reading Strategy, p. 101; Build Vocabulary, p. 99

🎧 **Listening to Literature Audiocassettes,** Sides 14, 15 ▪

💿 **Listening to Literature Audio CDs,** CDs 9, 10 ▪

▪ **BLOCK SCHEDULING:** Resources marked with this symbol provide varied instruction during 90-minute blocks.

5   We slowly drove—He knew no haste
    And I had put away
    My labor and my leisure too,
    For his Civility—

    We passed the School, where Children strove
10 At Recess—in the Ring—
    We passed the Fields of Gazing Grain—
    We passed the Setting Sun—

    Or rather—He passed Us—
    The Dews drew quivering and chill—
15 For only Gossamer,[1] my Gown—
    My Tippet[2]—only Tulle[3]—

    We paused before a House that seemed
    A Swelling of the Ground—
    The Roof was scarcely visible—
20 The <u>Cornice</u>—in the Ground—

    Since then—'tis Centuries—and yet
    Feels shorter than the Day
    I first <u>surmised</u> the Horses Heads
    Were toward Eternity—

1. **Gossamer** *n.* very thin, soft, filmy cloth.
2. **Tippet** *n.* scarflike garment worn over the shoulders and hanging down in front.
3. **Tulle** (tool) *n.* thin, fine netting used for scarves.

Reading Strategy
Analyzing Images What idea do the images of Gossamer and Tulle suggest?

cornice (kôr′ nis) *n.* projecting decorative molding along the top of a building

surmised (sər mīzd′) *v.* guessed

Review and Assess

Thinking About the Selection

1. **Respond:** Which images in this poem were the most vivid for you? Why?
2. **(a) Recall:** In the first two lines, what adverb defines Death's actions? **(b) Analyze:** In what sense is this depiction ironic?
3. **(a) Recall:** What three scenes does the carriage pass in stanza three? **(b) Interpret:** What is the significance of these images?
4. **(a) Recall:** How much time passes for the speaker in this poem? **(b) Speculate:** Why do you think the speaker notes that the time "feels shorter than the Day"? **(c) Compare and Contrast:** What does the speaker seem to feel about the experience of death in contrast with life?
5. **(a) Draw Conclusions:** What is the message of this poem? **(b) Take a Position:** Do you agree with the message? Explain.

Because I could not stop for Death ◆ 421

❷ Reading Strategy
Analyzing Images

- Read the poem aloud for students. Then reread just the bracketed lines. Help students use the footnotes to define the words *gossamer*, *tippet*, and *tulle*.
- Ask students the Reading Strategy question on p. 421: What idea do the images of gossamer and tulle suggest?
  Possible answer: They suggest fragile fabrics such as those that were used in making shrouds.

Answers for p. 421

Review and Assess

1. Students should identify specific images and provide support for their responses.
2. **(a)** The adverb "kindly" describes Death's actions. **(b)** Possible response: Death is usually personified in negative terms.
3. **(a)** It passes "the School," "the Fields," and "the Setting Sun." **(b)** These details could represent the stages of life.
4. **(a)** It has been centuries since the speaker died. **(b)** The speaker depicts the timeless nature of eternity. **(c)** The speaker suggests that both life and death are journeys but that death's journey is free of the busy pace of life.
5. Possible responses:
   (a) The poem presents death as the coming of a friend who brings the dead to a new home. **(b)** Students should support their responses.

CUSTOMIZE FOR UNIVERSAL ACCESS

For Less Proficient Readers	For Special Needs Students	For Gifted/Talented Students
Students may find Dickinson's frequent use of dashes to be confusing. Explain that dashes may be treated as commas, to suggest a brief pause. Play the recording of the poem on **Listening to Literature Audiocassettes,** Side 14–15, or **Audio CDs**, CD 9–10. Direct students to follow along in their texts, listening for the pauses at each dash.	Point out Dickinson's unusual use of capitalization. Explain that the capitalized words serve either rhythmic purposes or provide emphasis on particular images and ideas. Encourage students to first read the poem as if the capitalization were not there. Then help them reread to understand the purpose of each incidence.	Have students prepare this poem as one of their choices for the Listening and Speaking Extension Activity on p. 431. Remind them to pay careful attention to both the dashes and capitalization that Dickinson uses to convey meaning and cadence.

❸ **About the Selection**

In this poem, Dickinson describes the final moments between life and death. A fly, an almost trivial symbol of life, is what the speaker is most aware of before death.

❹ **Background**

Art

Room With a Balcony, by Adolph von Menzel

Like von Menzel's other work, this painting is distinguished by its expressiveness, accurate details, and use of light and shade for subtle effects. It captures the contrasting ordinariness and extraordinariness of death. Use this question for discussion: How is the overall impression of the painting similar to that of the poem?

Answer: Both the image and the poem convey stillness. There appears to be no life in the painted room. The chairs and lamps are placed symmetrically around the mirror. The curtains do not move; this detail reinforces the "Stillness."

Use this question for discussion: What might the image of an open window mean in a room in which someone has died?

Possible answer: It suggests that something or someone may have just entered or left the room.

❺ ▶**Critical Viewing**

Answer: The mirrored image of a couch and painting, which are no longer in the room but are still suggested by shadows, reflect the poem's idea of death taking away life but leaving behind some mark of the departed.

❸ *I heard a Fly buzz — when I died*

Emily Dickinson

❹

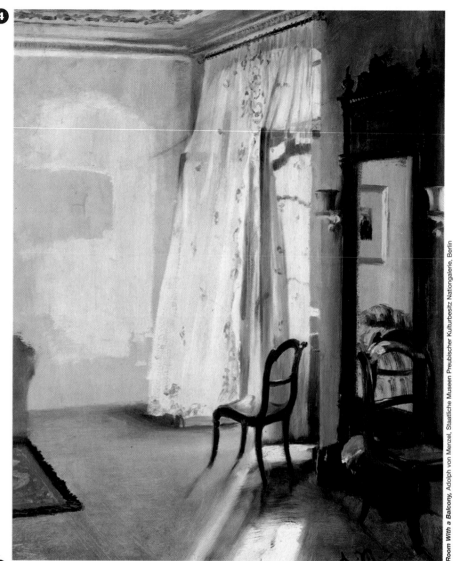

Room With a Balcony, Adolph von Menzel, Staatliche Museen Preubischer Kulturbesitz Nationalgalerie, Berlin

❺ ▲ **Critical Viewing** What details in this painting serve as an appropriate illustration for Dickinson's poem? **[Support]**

6

I heard a Fly buzz—when I died—
The Stillness in the Room
Was like the Stillness in the Air—
Between the Heaves of Storm—

5   The Eyes around—had wrung them dry—
And Breaths were gathering firm
For that last Onset—when the King
Be witnessed—in the Room—

I willed my Keepsakes—Signed away
10 What portion of me be
Assignable—and then it was
There interposed a Fly—

With Blue—uncertain stumbling Buzz—
Between the light—and me—
15 And then the Windows failed—and then
I could not see to see—

Literary Analysis
Slant Rhyme What two
words form a slant rhyme
in the third stanza?

Review and Assess

Thinking About the Selection

1. **Respond:** What was your first reaction to this poem? Explain.
2. **(a) Recall:** What do the speaker and those in attendance expect to experience when "the last Onset" occurs? **(b) Recall:** What happens instead? **(c) Analyze:** In what ways is this turn of events ironic?
3. **(a) Recall:** What actions has the speaker taken in preparation for death? **(b) Interpret:** Which "portion" of the speaker is "assignable," or able to be willed to others, and which is not?
4. **(a) Recall:** In the final stanza, what adjectives does the speaker use to describe the buzzing of the fly? **(b) Draw Conclusions:** What statement about dying is Dickinson making in this poem?
5. **Speculate:** If you were describing a deathbed scene from the perspective of the dying person, would you mention the buzzing of a fly? Why or why not?

I heard a fly buzz – when I died ◆ 423

---

❻ Literary Analysis

Slant Rhyme

- Have students read the bracketed passage.
- Ask them the Literary Analysis Question on p. 423: What two words form a slant rhyme in this stanza? **Answer:** *Be* and *fly* form a slant rhyme.

▶ Monitor Progress Post the Slant Rhyme transparency from **Literary Analysis and Reading Transparencies,** p. 44 and help students complete column 2 for the bracketed lines.

Answers for p. 423

Review and Assess

1. Students should support their responses with evidence from the text.
2. **(a)** They expect to witness the speaker's death. **(b)** A fly begins to buzz. **(c)** It suggests that death is highly ordinary, even pedestrian.
3. **(a)** The speaker wills away keepsakes and other worldly goods. **(b)** Possible response: The material aspects are "assignable," but the spirit is not.
4. **(a)** The speaker describes the fly with *Blue, uncertain, stumbling,* and *Buzz.* **(b)** Possible response: She shows that death is an everyday event; she points out that the experience does not match people's expectations.
5. Students should support their responses.

CUSTOMIZE FOR UNIVERSAL ACCESS

For Less Proficient Readers	For English Learners	For Advanced Readers
Explain that Emily Dickinson did not title her poems. Because an editorial decision was later made to use the first lines as titles, they do not reflect traditional capitalization for titles. Make sure that students follow the exact punctuation and capitalization shown in their book when writing about the poems.	Point out the word *heaves* in line 4 to students. In the poem's context, the word means "to rise and fall rhythmically." Explain that Dickinson refers to the calm between waves of rain or thunder in a storm.	Provide students with the factual background from For Less Proficient Readers. Then ask them to develop their own title for this poem. Suggest that they discuss the circumstances in which a person might become aware of the sound of a fly. Urge them to think about what a fly might represent as they search for an appropriate title.

❼ About the Selections

The first poem describes an unbearable hurt that fills the soul, and comes with winter, when the world is cold and still. The poet describes the hurt as a divine visitation, sent to teach the meaning of our own mortality. The second poem conveys the sense of pain that comes from parting with a loved one. The final poem is a meditation on the nature of the human soul. The poet depicts the soul as a feminine entity, separate from and indifferent to worldly claims on her attention. Dickinson portrays the soul as choosing, for unknowable reasons, a single person to share her society, and rejecting all others.

❽ Literary Analysis

Slant Rhyme

- After students read the entire poem "There's a certain Slant of light," direct them to reread the final bracketed stanza.

- Then, have students locate two words that form a slant rhyme in the stanza.
  Answer: The words *listens* and *Distance* form a slant rhyme.

❼ There's a certain Slant of light,

Emily Dickinson

There's a certain Slant of light,
Winter Afternoons—
That <u>oppresses</u>, like the Heft
Of Cathedral Tunes—

5 Heavenly Hurt, it gives us—
We can find no scar,
But internal difference,
Where the Meanings, are—

None may teach it—Any—
10 'Tis the Seal Despair—
An imperial affliction
Sent us of the Air—

❽ When it comes, the Landscape listens—
Shadows—hold their breath—
15 When it goes, 'tis like the Distance
On the look of Death—

oppresses (ə pres´ əz) v. weighs heavily on the mind

❼ My life closed twice before its close

Emily Dickinson

My life closed twice before its close—
It yet remains to see
If Immortality unveil
A third event to me.

5 So huge, so hopeless to conceive
As these that twice befell.
Parting is all we know of heaven,
And all we need of hell.

424 ◆ *A Growing Nation (1800–1870)*

✳ ENRICHMENT: Science Connection

Seasonal Affective Disorder

In "There's a certain Slant of light," Emily Dickinson describes an emotional response that resembles a medical condition unknown to her or to the doctors of her time. In the nineteenth century, a person who felt lethargic and depressed during winter months might be referred to as having "cabin fever." However, in the 1980s, doctors diagnosed this depression as a mood disorder that is triggered by a lack of sunlight. The major symptoms of this condition, called Seasonal Affective Disorder (SAD), are low energy and fatigue, difficulty concentrating, increased sensitivity to social rejection and avoidance of social situations, and change in appetite and weight gain. SAD usually occurs in late fall and lasts through early winter. One treatment for SAD is bright light therapy. Other treatments for depression, such as counselling and exercise, also can be effective for persons with SAD.

The Soul selects her own Society

Emily Dickinson

❼

The Soul selects her own Society—
Then—shuts the Door—
To her divine Majority—
Present no more—

5 Unmoved—she notes the Chariots—pausing—
At her low Gate—
Unmoved—an Emperor be kneeling
Upon her Mat—

I've known her—from an ample nation—
10 Choose One—
Then—close the Valves of her attention—
Like Stone—

Review and Assess

Thinking About the Selections

1. **Respond:** How does "My life closed twice before its close—" connect details of personal history to ideas about eternity?

2. **(a) Recall:** According to the speaker of "There's a certain Slant of light," in what ways does the winter light affect people? **(b) Analyze:** What does this light seem to represent to the speaker?

3. **(a) Interpret:** What is the third event to which the speaker of "My life closed before its close—" refers? **(b) Connect:** What is the relationship between the three events?

4. **(a) Recall:** In "The Soul selects her own Society—," what leaves the soul "unmoved"? **(b) Analyze:** How would you describe the soul's attitude toward the world's attractions?

5. **(a) Recall:** What happens after the soul makes her choice? **(b) Assess:** What adjectives would you use to characterize the speaker based on this choice?

6. **Relate:** Our culture places a premium on popularity for its own sake. What do Dickinson's poems suggest about other ways to view human relationships?

❾ **Critical Thinking**

Interpret

- Read the poem aloud for students at least twice.

- Discuss the central meaning of the poem and have students restate it in their own words.
  Possible response: The soul's role in our choice of friends is mysterious.

- Ask students to describe the kind of person the speaker is.
  Possible response: Students may say that the speaker, like the soul, is proud, defiant, solitary, and highly selective.

Answers for p. 425

Review and Assess

1. The speaker connects life experiences of loss to her expectations of heaven and hell.

2. **(a)** It oppresses them. **(b)** It seems to represent her own mortality.

3. **(a)** The third event is her death. **(b)** They are each kinds of endings.

4. **(a)** Chariots and emperors leave the soul unmoved. **(b)** The soul is indifferent to the world's attractions.

5. **(a)** The soul shuts the door. **(b)** Possible response: Sudents may suggest the adjectives *private, picky, detached,* or *divine.*

6. Possible response: The poems suggest that human relationships are complex, and that a single close friend may be more valuable than a whole group of less meaningful acquaintances.

CUSTOMIZE INSTRUCTION FOR UNIVERSAL ACCESS

For Special Needs Students	For Less Proficient Readers	For English Learners
Highlight Dickinson's use of a gerund, *parting,* in line 7 of "My life closed twice before its close." To help these students understand Dickinson's use of present participle verbs, both as gerunds and as verbs, present the Grammar and Style Lesson on Gerunds, p. 430.	Point out the gerund *parting* in line 7 of "My life closed twice before its close." Identify *parting* as the subject of the sentence. Then help students understand the lines: Death is all we know of heaven because we remain on Earth, yet it is all we need of hell because no hell could be as painful as losing someone deeply beloved.	With your students, review gerunds. Point out that the gerund *parting* in line 7 of "My life closed twice before its close" is the subject of the sentence. Emphasize that other -ing words in Dickinson's poems, such as *pausing* and *kneeling* in "The soul selects her own society" are not gerunds but present participles.

❿ About the Selections

The first poem contrasts the brain, as a metaphor for the soul, with the sky and the sea to arrive at the notion that the human soul is infinite, like God, and by implication it is of God. The second poem says that the strongest solitude is the solitude of inner loneliness.

⓫ Background

Art

Twilight in the Wilderness, **by Frederic E. Church**

This painting, like other early works by Church, is a panoramic composition with emphatic visual effects. Some critics call this Church's finest sunset painting. Use this question for discussion: How does the painting suit both "There is a solitude of space" and "The Brain—is wider than the Sky—"?

Possible answer: Church's expansive view echoes the widness of the sky Dickinson describes in the first poem and reflects the solitude central to the second poem.

⓬ Reading Strategy

Analyzing Images

• Have a volunteer read aloud the bracketed stanza.

• Ask students to identify Dickinson's comparison and suggest its effects on readers. Possible answer: Dickinson compares the human brain to the sky and sea. She suggests that the brain's capacity is unrelated to its size.

⓭ ▶ Critical Viewing

Answer: Students may cite general feelings of serenity, beauty, awe, or solemnity.

❿ The Brain— is wider than the Sky—

Emily Dickinson

Twilight in the Wilderness, Frederick E. Church, The Cleveland Museum of Art

⓬
The Brain—is wider than the Sky—
For—put them side by side—
The one the other will contain
With ease—and You—beside—

5 The Brain is deeper than the sea—
For—hold them—Blue to Blue—
The one the other will absorb—
As Sponges—Buckets—do—

The Brain is just the weight of God—
10 For—Heft them—Pound for Pound—
And they will differ—if they do—
As Syllable from Sound—

426 ◆ *A Growing Nation (1800–1870)*

⓭ ▲ Critical Viewing
What feelings do the sweep of sky, mountains, and water in this painting evoke in you? **[Respond]**

✹ ENRICHMENT: Science Connection

The Human Brain

In "The Brain—is wider than the Sky—," Dickinson compares the human brain's scope or size to the sky and the sea. In fact, the adult human brain weighs an average of about three pounds. The brain grows rapidly in a person's first six years, adding many nerve cells as well as a system of supporting and connecting cells. While representing just 2 percent of an adult's average total body weight, the brain requires 20 percent of the oxygen consumed by the body and can suffer serious damage in just three to five minutes without sufficient supply.

Many of the perceptions to which Dickinson refers arise from the cerebral cortex. The cortex receives and responds to sensory messages. It also controls motor functions and allows humans to think, speak, and remember. Recent brain research suggests some interesting physical differences between the brains of men and women. These differences may explain why, in general, men find spatial tasks easier and women excel at verbal tasks.

There is a solitude of space

⑩

Emily Dickinson

There is a solitude of space
A solitude of sea
A solitude of death, but these
Society shall be
5   Compared with that profounder site
That polar privacy
A soul admitted to itself—
Finite Infinity.

⑭ **finite** (fī´ nit´) *adj.* having measurable or definable limits

infinity (in fin´ i tē) *n.* endless or unlimited space, time, or distance

---

Review and Assess

Thinking About the Selections

1. **Respond:** Do you think it is a good idea for people to seek solitude? Why or why not?

2. **(a) Recall:** What comparisons does the speaker make in "The Brain is Wider Than the Sky"? **(b) Interpret:** What role does a surprising use of scale and size play in these comparisons?

3. **(a) Recall:** According to the poet, how is the brain wider than the sky? **(b) Recall:** How is the brain deeper than the sea? **(c) Interpret:** What do these images suggest about the power of the human mind and heart?

4. **(a) Compare and Contrast:** In what ways does the poet's comparison of the brain to God differ from the comparisons made in the earlier stanzas? **(b) Interpret:** What is the poet suggesting about the relationship between human consciousness and divinity?

5. **(a) Recall:** In "There is a solitude of space," what three things does the speaker compare to "polar privacy"? **(b) Contrast:** How does the solitude of "a soul admitted to itself" differ from the other solitudes described?

6. **Modify:** Dickinson did not give her poems titles, though her editors sometimes used a poem's first line. What titles would you give these two poems? Why?

CUSTOMIZE INSTRUCTION FOR UNIVERSAL ACCESS

For Less Proficient Readers

Use a concept map or web to show students how abstract concepts can be linked to concrete images in poetry and literature. Explain that by analyzing the images, a reader learns what the author is conveying.

Have students analyze the images in "There is a solitude of space" by Dickinson. Using a diagram like the one shown, help students link abstract words to concrete images and then tell what is being compared.

---

⑭ Vocabulary Development

The Latin Root -finis-

- Call students' attention to Dickinson's use of the related words *finite* and *infinity*, and their definitions.

- Let students know that the Latin root of each word is *finis*, which means "end."

- Invite students to volunteer other words containing this root. Possiblities include: *infinitude, final, finish, confine, refine*

- Make sure students recognize how prefixes act to change the meanings of words formed with the root *finis*. Have students look up etymologies for these words in the dictionary and record them in their journals.

Answers for p. 427

Review and Assess

1. Students should support their opinions.

2. **(a)** The speaker compares the brain to the sky, to the sea, and to God. **(b)** The speaker compares the brain to things that seem at first to be much larger.

3. **(a)** The brain can contain the sky with ease. **(b)** It can absorb the sea's blue. **(c)** The human mind and heart can hold images and experiences of limitless scope and size.

4. **(a)** The first two comparisons suggest that the brain is wider or deeper, while the third suggests a difference in substance rather than in size. **(b)** Possible response: Human consciousness has some similarity of scope to divinity, though it may be vastly different in substance.

5. **(a)** Privacy is compared to the solitude of space, sea, and death. **(b)** While the solitude of a "soul admitted to itself" cannot be shared, the other kinds of solitude can.

6. Students should be able to explain their title choices.

427

15 About the Selection

This poem suggests that comparison and contrast are useful ways to learn; we can only learn things by comparing them with very different things.

16 Critical Thinking

Analyze

• Direct students to read the bracketed text.

• Challenge students to explain the meaning of the last line.
Possible answer: Fallen snow is cold, still, and lifeless, while birds are vibrant, lovely, and contrast starkly with the snow.

Answers for p. 428

Review and Assess

1. Students' answers will vary.

2. **(a)** In each line, the speaker states that each line's first word is learned from the words that follow. **(b)** Possible responses: One knows a thing by its absence, by its opposite, or by need. Things have meaning only in context. **(c)** Students should be able to support their positions.

3. **(a)** Students may mention study skills they have learned only when these skills were necessary or people they recognized they cared about only when the people were absent **(b)** Students' additions should be consistent with the form and message of the poem.

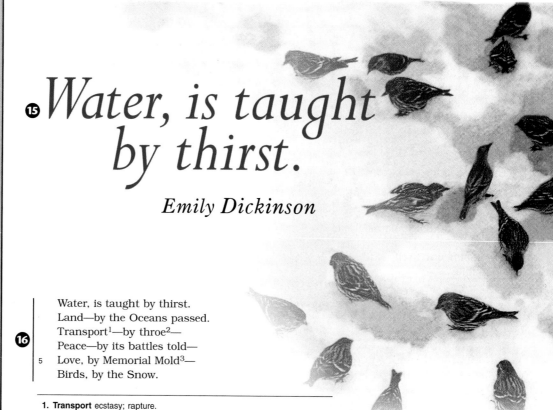

15 *Water, is taught by thirst.*

Emily Dickinson

Water, is taught by thirst.
Land—by the Oceans passed.
Transport[1]—by throe[2]—
Peace—by its battles told—
5   Love, by Memorial Mold[3]—
Birds, by the Snow.

---

1. **Transport** ecstasy; rapture.
2. **throe** spasm or pang of pain.
3. **Memorial Mold** memorial grounds or cemetery.

Review and Assess

Thinking About the Selection

1. **Respond:** How many lines did you read before you understood the title of this poem?

2. **(a) Recall:** What is the relationship between each line's first word and the following words? **(b) Interpret:** What is the theme or message of this poem? **(c) Take a Position:** Do you agree or disagree with this message? Explain.

3. **(a) Relate:** What situations or experiences in your daily life demonstrate the theme of this poem? **(b) Extend:** Based on these situations, add two lines to this poem that are in keeping with the theme.

428 ◆ *A Growing Nation (1800–1870)*

ASSESSMENT PRACTICE: Reading Comprehension

Make Inferences and Generalizations	**(For more practice, see Test Practice Workbook, p. 24)**

The reading sections of many tests require students to make inferences. Explain to students that making inferences will help them understand poetry because poets often leave much of their message unstated. Use the following example to help students make inferences about "There's a certain Slant of light," on p. 424:

Which of the following best describes the effect of the light?

A overwhelming
B uplifting
C encouraging
D energizing

The last three answers cannot be supported by details from the text. The light is oppressive and feels heavy, so *A* is the best choice.

Review and Assess

Literary Analysis

Slant Rhyme

1. In "Because I could not stop for Death—," what three words create **slant rhymes** for *immortality, civility,* and *eternity*?

2. (a) Using a chart like the one here and the abc system it models for notating rhyme scheme, examine the pattern of rhyme in "There's a certain slant of light." (b) What is the effect of Dickinson's patterned use of both slant and full rhyme?

	Stanza One	Two	Three	Four
Line 1	*light* (a)			
Line 2	*noons* (b)			
Line 3	*Heft* (a-slant)			
Line 4	*Tunes* (b-full)			

Comparing Literary Works

3. Does *soul* have the same meaning in both "The Soul selects her own Society," and "There is a solitude of space"? Explain.

4. (a) Which poems present human consciousness as something boundless? (b) Which present consciousness as something limited? (c) How would you define Dickinson's view of the individual self?

Reading Strategy

Analyzing Images

5. What image does Dickinson use to describe a gravesite in "Because I could not stop for Death—"?

6. (a) Identify two images in "Water, is taught by thirst." (b) Identify two images in "The Brain—is wider than the Sky—." (c) How do these images help the speaker communicate a specific abstract idea?

Extend Understanding

7. **Humanities Connection:** In real life, people select a wide variety of different "societies." (a) What are some of the "societies" people enjoy in your community? (b) What do you think this tendency indicates about human beings?

Emily Dickinson's Poetry ◆ 429

Quick Review

Slant rhyme occurs when two words have similar, but not identical, vowel sounds.

To **analyze images,** determine whether— and how—they relate to larger ideas.

 Take It to the Net
www.phschool.com
Take the interactive self-test online to check your understanding of these selections.

⬡ **ENRICHMENT: Further Reading**

Other Works by Emily Dickinson

"I never saw a Moor—"

"The Bustle in a House"

"Success is counted sweetest"

 Take It to the Net
Visit www.phschool.com for more information on Emily Dickinson.

Answers for p. 429

Review and Assess

1. *Me, away,* and *day* are slant rhymes for these words.

2. (a)

Stanza One	Stanza Two
light (a)	*us* (a)
noons (b)	*scar* (b)
Heft (a-slant)	*difference* (a-slant)
Tunes (b-full)	*are* (b-full)

Stanza Three	Stanza Four
any (a)	*listens* (a)
Despair (b)	*breath* (b)
affliction (c)	*Distance* (a-slant)
Air (b-full)	*Death* (b-full)

(b) The poem has a repetitive, musical quality.

3. Yes, both discuss the nature of the soul as the innermost core of our being.

4. (a) "There is a solitude of space," "The Soul selects her own Society" and "The Brain—is wider than the Sky—" present human consciousness as bound-less. (b) "There's a certain Slant of light," and "I heard a Fly buzz—when I died—" present human consciousness as limited by mortality. (c) Possible response: The self presented through these poems is engaged with the world but always aware of eternity and human mortality.

5. She uses the image of a house below ground.

6. (a) Each line of the poem presents an image. (b) Each stanza of the poem presents an image. (c) These images use concrete objects to illustrate abstract ideas.

7. Students may mention athletic groups, clubs, peer groups, or work colleagues. The choice of a variety of "societies" indicates that humans are diverse.

❶ Vocabulary Development

Word Analysis

1. *Finish* means "end."

2. *Confine* means "to limit or enclose."

3. *Final* means "of or coming at the end, last."

4. *Refinement* means "elegance of speech, manners, etc."

Spelling Strategy

1. confessor

2. processor

3. depressor

4. professor

Concept Development: Synonyms

1. a

2. b

3. b

4. c

5. c

❷ Grammar and Style

1. *Swelling* is a predicate nominative.

2. *Writing* is a subject.

3. *Parting* is a subject.

4. *Cooking* is a predicate nominative.

5. *Traveling* is a direct object.

Writing Application

Students should identify the gerunds in their paragraphs. Possible response: I am often found working on my *sewing*. *Choosing* a pattern and actually *creating* something to wear can be rewarding. I like *seeing* the smile on a friend's face when I give her a gift I've made.

Integrate Language Skills

❶ Vocabulary Development Lesson

Word Analysis: Latin Root -finis-

In "There is a solitude of space," Dickinson uses the words *finite* and *infinity*, both of which contain the Latin root -*finis*-, meaning "end" or "limit." A *finite* entity is limited in time or space; *infinity* is limitless. Explain the meaning of each of the following words, and then note how the root -*finis*- relates to the meaning of each one.

1. finish   3. final

2. confine   4. refinement

Spelling Strategy

When writing the noun forms of verbs ending in -*ess*, you will usually add the suffix -*or*, as in *oppress* + -*or* = *oppressor*. Write the noun form for each of the verbs listed below. Check your spelling in a dictionary.

1. confess   3. depress

2. process   4. profess

Concept Development: Synonyms

Review the vocabulary list on page 419. Then, identify the word or phrase whose meaning is most nearly the same as that of the first word in each item below.

1. cornice: (a) decorative ledge, (b) functional door, (c) elaborate spire

2. surmised: (a) explained, (b) inferred, (c) reduced

3. oppresses: (a) inhabits, (b) troubles, (c) judges

4. finite: (a) heavenly, (b) endless, (c) limited

5. infinity: (a) mystery, (b) multitude, (c) endlessness

❷ Grammar and Style Lesson

Gerunds

A **gerund** is a verb form that ends in -*ing* and is used as a noun. Like nouns, gerunds function in sentences as subjects, direct objects, predicate nominatives, and objects of prepositions. The gerunds are italicized in the following examples.

> **Subject:** *Writing* requires discipline.
>
> **Direct Object:** Dickinson left her *writing* in her dresser.
>
> **Object of Preposition:** She learned about *writing* by *practicing*.

Practice Identify each gerund below and tell how it is used in the sentence.

1. We paused before a House that seemed / A Swelling of the Ground—.

2. Writing was Dickinson's great passion.

3. Parting is all we know of heaven.

4. Her favorite activity was cooking.

5. Dickinson avoided traveling great distances.

Writing Application Write a paragraph of at least three sentences in which you describe a hobby—skiing or painting, for example. Include at least three gerunds.

W͞G *Prentice Hall Writing and Grammar Connection: Chapter 19, Section 2*

430 ◆ *A Growing Nation (1800–1870)*

TEACHING RESOURCES

The following resources can be used to enrich or extend the instruction for pp. 430–431.

Vocabulary

📖 **Selection Support:** Build Vocabulary, p. 99

📖 **Vocabulary and Spelling Practice Book** (Use this booklet for skills enrichment.) ▪

Grammar

📖 **Selection Support:** Grammar and Style, p. 100

W͞G **Writing and Grammar,** Ruby Level, p. 442

▪ **Daily Language Practice Transparencies** ▪

Writing

W͞G **Writing and Grammar,** Ruby Level, p. 309

💿 **Writing and Grammar iText CD-ROM**

📀 **Writing Models and Graphic Organizers on Transparencies,** pp. 57, 95

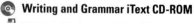 **BLOCK SCHEDULING:** Resources marked with this symbol provide varied instruction during 90-minute blocks.

❸ Writing Lesson

Letter to an Author

Dickinson's poetry may have stirred your emotions, challenged you to think about an idea or aspect of existence, or helped you to better understand yourself. Imagine that Dickinson is still alive. Write a letter to the poet in which you express your reactions to her verse. Be sure to use a clear organization in presenting your ideas.

Prewriting   Focus on one poem. Explore your thoughts and feelings about the poem and its effect on you. Edit your reactions down to three or four important points; then, consider how your notes support each idea.

Model: Creating Clear and Logical Organization

Salutation: Dear Emily Dickinson,

Intro: Explain that I admire her poetry.

First paragraph: Her poems explore complex ideas.

Second paragraph: Her imagery gives me new ways to think.

Conclusion: Thank her, and tell her to keep writing.

> An effective letter is organized clearly and logically.

Drafting   Open your letter with an explanation of why you are writing. Then, develop and support each important idea in a separate paragraph.

Revising   Check your tone and word choice. Confirm that you have conveyed your thoughts in a clear and logical way, with appropriate transitions from one paragraph to the next.

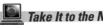 *Prentice Hall Writing and Grammar Connection: Chapter 14, Section 3*

❹ Extension Activities

Listening and Speaking   Choose three Dickinson poems to present in a **poetry reading.** Consider the meaning of each idea, image, and punctuation mark. Keep these tips in mind:

- Experiment with volume and tone until you achieve the desired effect.
- Speak clearly, letting the poem's meaning show in your emphasis.

Give a reading that you feel is as close as possible to the author's intention.

Research and Technology   Dickinson was close to her brother Austin. Using a variety of sources, research him and their relationship. Then, select two of Dickinson's poems that seem to speak to her relationship with her brother. Combine your research and the poems in a **report.**

 Take It to the Net   www.phschool.com

Go online for an additional research activity using the Internet.

Emily Dickinson's Poetry ◆ *431*

---

❸ Writing Lesson

- Organize students into groups. Have them exchange reactions to the poems as a way to choose a poem on which to focus.
- Suggest that students use the Outline transparency in **Writing Models and Graphic Organizers on Transparencies,** p. 95, to structure their ideas.
- Refer students to Writing Process Model 10: Cover Letter in **Writing Models and Graphic Organizers on Transparencies,** p. 57, for guidance with letter format.

❹ Research and Technology

- Suggest that students use the Internet as a research source.
- Encourage students to focus very specifically on historical evidence of the relationship between Emily and Austin, rather than on providing simple biographical information.
- Direct students to poem indices in your library or online that can help them identify pertinent Dickinson poems.
- If time allows, invite students to present oral versions of their reports to the class.
- Have students use the assessment rubric for Research: Historical Investigation in **Performance Assessment and Portfolio Management,** p. 12.

CUSTOMIZE INSTRUCTION
For Universal Access

To address different learning styles, use the activities suggested in the **Extension Activities** booklet, p. 22.

For Visual/Spatial Learners, use Activity 5.

For Musical/Rhythmic Learners, use Activity 6.

For Intrapersonal Learners, use Activity 7.

ASSESSMENT RESOURCES

The following resources can be used to assess students' knowledge and skills.

Selection Assessment
- Formal Assessment, pp. 108–110
- Open Book Test, pp. 64–66
- Got It! Assessment Videotapes, Tape 2
- Test Bank Software
- *Take It to the Net*
  Visit www.phschool.com for self-tests and additional questions on the selections.

Writing Rubric
- Performance Assess. and Portfolio Mgmt, p. 12

PRENTICE HALL ASSESSMENT SYSTEM
- Workbook
- Skill Book
- Transparencies
- CD-ROM

Walt Whitman's Poetry

Lesson Objectives

1. **To analyze and respond to literary elements**
   - Literary Analysis: Free Verse
   - Comparing Literary Works
2. **To read, comprehend, analyze, and critique a [genre(s)]**
   - Reading Strategy: Inferring the Poet's Attitude
   - Reading Check Questions
   - Review and Assess Questions
   - Assessment Practice (ATE)
3. **To develop word analysis skills, fluency, and systematic vocabulary**
   - Vocabulary Development Lesson: Latin Root: *-fus-*
4. **To understand and apply written and oral language conventions**
   - Spelling Strategy
   - Grammar and Style Lesson: Pronoun and Antecedent Agreement
5. **To understand and apply appropriate writing and research strategies**
   - Writing Lesson: Imitation of an Author's Style
   - Extension Activity: Research Poetry
6. **To understand and apply listening and speaking strategies**
   - Extension Activity: Collage

STEP-BY-STEP TEACHING GUIDE	PACING GUIDE
PRETEACH	
Motivate Students and Provide Background	
Use the Motivation activity (ATE p. 432)	5 min.
Read and discuss the author and background information (SE pp. 432, 434; ATE p. 432) [A]	5 min.
Introduce the Concepts	
Introduce the Literary Analysis and Reading Strategy (SE/ATE p. 433) [A]	15 min.
Pronounce the vocabulary words and read their definitions (SE p. 433)	5 min.
TEACH	
Monitor Comprehension	
Informally monitor comprehension by circulating while students read independently or in groups [A]	45 min.
Monitor students' comprehension with the Reading Check notes (SE/ATE p. 437)	as students read
Develop vocabulary with Vocabulary notes (SE pp. 436, 439; ATE p. 439)	as students read
Develop Understanding	
Develop students' understanding of free verse with the Literary Analysis annotations (SE pp. 434, 436, 438; ATE pp. 434, 436, 438) [A]	5 min.
Develop students' ability to infer the poet's attitude with the Reading Strategy annotations (SE pp. 435, 437; ATE pp. 435, 437)	5 min.
ASSESS	
Assess Mastery	
Assess students' mastery of the Reading Strategy and Literary Analysis by having them answer the Review and Assess questions (SE/ATE p. 445)	15 min.
Use one or more of the print and media Assessment Resources (ATE p. 447) [A]	up to 45 min.
EXTEND	
Apply Understanding	
Have students complete the Vocabulary Development Lesson and the Grammar and Style Lesson (SE p. 446) [A]	20 min.
Apply students' ability to use a consistent style by using the Writing Lesson (SE/ATE p. 447) [A]	45 min.
Apply students' understanding using one or more of the Extension Activities (SE p. 447)	20–90 min.

 ACCELERATED INSTRUCTION:
Use the strategies and activities identified with an [A].

UNIVERSAL ACCESS
- ● = Below Level Students
- ▲ = On-Level Students
- ■ = Above Level Students

Time and Resource Manager

Reading Level: Challenging, Average, Easy, Average, Average, Easy
Average Number of Instructional Days: 5

RESOURCES		
PRINT 📖	**TRANSPARENCIES** 🗂	**TECHNOLOGY** 💿 🎧 📼
• **Beyond Literature,** Cross-Curricular Connection: Science, p. 23 ▲ ■		• **Interest Grabber Video,** Tape 3 ● ▲ ■
• **Selection Support Workbook:** ● ▲ ■ Literary Analysis, p. 106 Reading Strategy, p. 105 Build Vocabulary, p. 103	• **Literary Analysis and Reading Transparencies,** pp. 45 and 46 ● ▲ ■	
• **Authors In Depth,** The American Experience ■		• **Listening to Literature** ● ▲ ■ Audiocassettes, Sides 15, 16 Audio CDs, CD 10
• **Literatura en español** ● ▲ • **Literary Analysis for Enrichment** ■	• **Fine Art Transparencies, Volume 1,** Art Transparencies 12 and 19 ● ▲ ■	
• **Formal Assessment:** Selection Test, pp. 111–113 ● ▲ ■ • **Open Book Test,** pp. 67–69 ● ▲ ■ • **Performance Assessment and Portfolio Management,** p. 30 ● ▲ ■ **PRENTICE HALL ASSESSMENT SYSTEM** ● ▲ ■	• **PRENTICE HALL ASSESSMENT SYSTEM** ● ▲ ■ Skills Practice Answers and Explanations on Transparencies	• **Test Bank Software** ● ▲ ■ • **Got It! Assessment Videotapes,** Tape 2 ● ▲
• **Selection Support Workbook:** ● ▲ ■ Grammar and Style, p. 104 • **Writing and Grammar,** Ruby Level ● ▲ ■ • **Extension Activities,** p. 23 ● ▲ ■	• **Daily Language Practice Transparencies** ● ▲	• **Writing and Grammar iText CD-ROM** ● ▲ ■ 💻 *Take It to the Net* www.phschool.com

BLOCK SCHEDULING: Use one 90-minute class period to preteach the selection and have students read it. Use a second 90-minute class period to assess students' mastery of skills and have them complete one of the Extension Activities.

Step-by-Step Teaching Guide
for pp. 432–433

Motivation

Walt Whitman's poetry celebrates his vision of the United States. Brainstorm with students for images or metaphors for a poem about America by completing this line:

America is _____.

Students may suggest ideas such as "America is energy," "America is a struggle for freedom," "America is another chance," and so forth. List the variety of responses on the board. Then examine them for both positive and negative images and examples of the dignity, intensity, diversity, and democracy that Whitman evokes in his poetry.

▣ Interest Grabber Video

As an alternative, play "Walt Whitman: Reading and Student Response" on Tape 3 to engage student interest.

❶ Background

More About the Author

In some of his poems, Whitman uses a form reflected in the poetry of the Hebrew Bible (sometimes known as the Old Testament). This form is also reminiscent of the *Bhagavad-Gita* (India's sacred books), which historians speculate Whitman read in translation. Given the lyrical and emotional nature of Whitman's poems, the undulating rhythm of this form fits well.

Prepare to Read

❶ Walt Whitman's Poetry

Walt Whitman
(1819–1892)

In the preface to his first volume of poetry, the 1855 edition of *Leaves of Grass*, Walt Whitman wrote: "The proof of a poet is that his country absorbs him as affectionately as he absorbed it." Whitman's hopes for such proof of his own merit as a poet were deferred: He was harshly denounced for his first volume of poetry, but in the following decades, his poems gained popularity, and he became famous as "the Good Gray Poet" and "the Bard of Democracy." In his later years, Whitman was admired by writers and intellectuals on both sides of the Atlantic. Today, he is widely recognized as one of the greatest and most influential poets the United States has ever produced.

The Poet at Work Whitman was born on Long Island and raised in Brooklyn, New York. His education was not formal, but he read widely, including the works of Sir Walter Scott, Shakespeare, Homer, and Dante. Trained to be a printer, Whitman spent his early years alternating between printing jobs and newspaper writing. When he was twenty-seven, he became the editor of the Brooklyn *Eagle*, a respected newspaper, but the paper fired him in 1848 because of his opposition to slavery. After accepting a position on a paper in New Orleans, Whitman traveled across the country for the first time, observing the diversity of America's landscapes and people.

Whitman soon returned to New York City, however, and in 1850 quit journalism to devote his energy to writing poetry. Impressed by Ralph Waldo Emerson's prophetic description of a new kind of American poet, Whitman had been jotting down ideas and fragments of verse in a notebook for years. His work broke every poetic tradition of rhyme and meter as it celebrated America and the common man. When the first edition of *Leaves of Grass* was published in 1855, critics attacked Whitman's subject matter and abandonment of traditional poetic devices and forms. Noted poet John Greenleaf Whittier hated Whitman's poems so much that he hurled his copy of *Leaves of Grass* into the fireplace. Emerson, on the other hand, responded with great enthusiasm, remarking that the collection was "the most extraordinary piece of wit and wisdom that America has yet contributed."

The Bard of Democracy Though Whitman did publish other works in the course of his career, his life's work proved to be *Leaves of Grass*, which he continually revised, reshaped, and expanded until his death in 1892. The poems in later editions became less confusing, repetitious, and raucous, and more symbolic, expressive, and universal. He viewed the volume as a single long poem that expressed his evolving vision of the world. Using his poetry to convey his passionate belief in democracy, equality, and the spiritual unity of all forms of life, he celebrated the potential of the human spirit. Though Whitman's philosophy grew out of the ideas of the Transcendentalists, his poetry was mainly shaped by his ability to absorb and comprehend everything he observed. From its first appearance as twelve unsigned and untitled poems, *Leaves of Grass* grew to include 383 poems in its final, "death-bed" edition (1892). The collection captures the diversity of the American people and conveys the energy and intensity of all forms of life. In the century since Whitman's death, *Leaves of Grass* has become one of the most highly regarded collections of poetry ever written. There is little doubt that, according to his own definition, Whitman has proven himself as a poet.

TEACHING RESOURCES

The following resources can be used to enrich or extend the instruction for pp. 432–433.

Motivation

▣ **Interest Grabber Video**, Tape 3

Background

▣ **Beyond Literature**, p. 23

▣ *Take It to the Net*

Visit www.phschool.com for Background and hotlinks for the selections.

Literary Analysis

▣ **Literary Analysis and Reading Transparencies,** Free Verse, p. 46 ▣

Reading

▣ **Literary Analysis and Reading Transparencies,** Inferring the Poet's Attitude, p. 45

▣ **Selection Support:** Reading Strategy, p. 105

▣ **BLOCK SCHEDULING:** Resources marked with this symbol provide varied instruction during 90-minute blocks.

Preview

Connecting to the Literature

You probably learn something new about yourself, your world, or life in general every day. As you will discover, Walt Whitman devoted his life and work to making new discoveries and reaching new understandings.

❷ Literary Analysis

Free Verse

In contrast to verse written with a fixed meter or line pattern, **free verse** is poetry that has irregular meter and line length. Free verse is designed to re-create the cadences of natural speech. Thus, Whitman uses whatever rhythms and line lengths are appropriate to his message:

> Do I contradict myself?
> Very well then I contradict myself...

Though free verse is as old as the Psalms in the Bible, Whitman was the first American poet to use it. It proved to be the perfect form for this individualist, allowing him to express himself without formal restraints.

Comparing Literary Works

Along with his use of free verse, Whitman's **diction**—word choice and arrangement—also plays a key role in his voice. Whitman's diction is characterized by the use of two main techniques:

- The use of catalogs, or long lists
- The use of parallel forms—the repetition of phrases or sentences with similar structures or meanings.

In his poems, Whitman addresses a wide range of subjects, modifying his diction to complement each one. In some poems, his diction emphasizes important ideas. In others, it builds crescendos of emotion. As you read, compare the ways in which the poet's diction varies from poem to poem in order to serve the purpose and meaning of each work.

❸ Reading Strategy

Inferring the Poet's Attitude

You can **infer a poet's attitude** toward a subject by examining his or her choice of words and details. Consider this passage from Whitman's "Song of Myself":

> I jump from the crossbeams and seize the clover and timothy,
> And roll head over heels . . .

Use a chart like the one shown to note key words and images in Whitman's poems and to clarify the attitudes each reveals.

Vocabulary Development

abeyance (ə bā′ əns) *n.* temporary suspension (p. 436)

effuse (e fyo͞oz′) *v.* pour out (p. 439)

CUSTOMIZE INSTRUCTION FOR UNIVERSAL ACCESS

For Less Proficient Readers	For English Learners	For Advanced Readers
To help students navigate the free verse, guide them to break down sentences to find the subject or main idea. Breaking down sentences will also help students to follow along in their text as they listen to the recorded selection on **Listening to Literature Audiocassettes**, Sides 15 and 16, or **Audio CDs**, CD 10.	Tell students that because free verse suggests natural speech, one way to recognize Whitman's rhythms is to hear the poems read aloud. Read the poems for students; then, encourage them to take turns reading passages aloud to a partner. With repeated readings, a sense of the poems' natural rhythm should appear.	Whitman rejected the restrictive poetic elements of meter, rhyme, and pattern to pioneer his style of free verse, but he did not resist all traditional poetic devices. Have students analyze his use of inverse word order, assonance, alliteration, personification, onomatopoeia, repetition, and other poetic devices.

---

❷ Literary Analysis

Free Verse

- Tell students that as they read Walt Whitman's poems, they will focus on free verse which uses irregular meter and line length.

- Share with students the More About the Author information from ATE p. 432. Explain that as with these other works, Whitman's poetry reflects the rise and fall of speech.

- Have volunteers read aloud the Literary Analysis instruction and excerpts. Help students hear the rhythm in the excerpt.

- Discuss the instruction under Comparing Literary Works and use it to help students understand how diction and free verse work together to create Whitman's unique poetic voice.

❸ Reading Strategy

Inferring the Poet's Attitude

- Remind students that inferring the poet's attitude can help them recognize a writer's unstated messages.

- Explain to students that they can infer a poet's attitude in much the same way as they make other inferences—by combining text clues and life experience for reasonable conclusions.

- Direct students to the excerpt on the student page. Point out, for example, that from words and phrases such as *jump, seize,* and *roll head over heels* readers can infer that Whitman is invigorated by rural life.

- Encourage students to highlight additional examples and clues in their own charts.

Vocabulary Development

- Pronounce each vocabulary word for students, and read the definitions as a class. Have students identify any words with which they are already familiar.

 E-Teach

Visit E-Teach at www.phschool.com for teacher's essays on how to teach, with questions and answers.

Step-by-Step Teaching Guide for pp. 434–444

CUSTOMIZE INSTRUCTION For Musical/Rhythmic Learners

Have students read the poems aloud to listen for poetic devices such as alliteration, assonance, consonance, and repetition.

Ask students what music they might choose to accompany a reading of the poem.

❶ About the Selection

In this preface to his historic 1855 Edition of *Leaves of Grass*, Whitman says that America has never been static. It is an ever-growing nation of people, ideas, and beliefs that evolve as the nation itself changes. Americans perceive that old ways are passing and strong new ways approaching. Whitman comments that the United States is a great poem, a nation characterized by activity, diversity, and the gifts of its rich natural bounties.

❷ Literary Analysis

Free Verse and Diction

- Invite volunteers to read each of the phrases in turn, then read all the phrases aloud yourself. Help students identify repeated words in the phrases.
  Answer: The words *that it* or *that its* are repeated.

- Ask students the Literary Analysis question on p. 434: How does Whitman's use of parallel phrases beginning with "perceives" help establish an uplifting tone?
  Possible answer: The parallel structure and repetition create a crescendo in which each phrase adds to those previous. This rhythmic crescendo creates an uplifting tone.

from Preface to the 1855 Edition of

❶ Leaves of Grass

Walt Whitman

Background

In his lifetime, Whitman's poetry, which broke traditional rules of rhythm and rhyme, provoked both glowing reviews and fiercely negative reactions. After receiving his complimentary copy of *Leaves of Grass,* Ralph Waldo Emerson had abundant praise for this poet. In a letter to Whitman, Emerson wrote:

. . . I give you joy of your free and brave thought, I have great joy in it. I find incomparable things said incomparably well, as they must be. I find the courage of treatment, which so delights me, and which large perception only can inspire. I greet you at the beginning of a great career. . . .

More than a century after his death, Whitman's poetry is still regarded as some of the bravest, most generous, and most stirring in American literature.

America does not repel the past or what it has produced under its forms or amid other politics or the idea of castes or the old religions. . . . accepts the lesson with calmness . . . is not so impatient as has been supposed that the slough still sticks to opinions and manners and literature while the life which served its requirements has passed into the new life of the new forms . . . perceives that the corpse is slowly borne from the eating and sleeping rooms of the house . . . perceives that it waits a little while in the door . . . that it was fittest for its days . . . that its action has descended to the stalwart and well-shaped heir who approaches . . . and that he shall be fittest for his days.

❷

Literary Analysis
Free Verse and Diction How does Whitman's use of parallel phrases beginning with "perceives" help establish an uplifting tone?

TEACHING RESOURCES

The following resources can be used to enrich or extend the instruction for pp. 434–444.

Literary Analysis

📖 **Literary Analysis and Reading Transparencies,** p. 46

📖 **Selection Support:** Literary Analysis, p. 106

Reading

🎧 **Listening to Literature Audiocassettes,** Sides 15, 16

💿 **Listening to Literature Audio CDs,** CD 10

Extension

📖 **Authors In Depth,** The American Experience (The collection includes five additional selections by Walt Whitman for extended reading.) ▪

📖 **Fine Art Transparencies, Volume 1,** Transparencies 12 and 19 (Encourage students to imagine what songs the figures in the artworks might compose.) ▪

▪ **BLOCK SCHEDULING:** Resources marked with this symbol provide varied instruction during 90-minute blocks.

The Americans of all nations at any time upon the earth have probably the fullest poetical nature. The United States themselves are essentially the greatest poem. In the history of the earth hitherto the largest and most stirring appear tame and orderly to their ampler largeness and stir. Here at last is something in the doings of man that corresponds with the broadcast doings of the day and night. Here is not merely a nation but a teeming nation of nations. Here is action untied from strings necessarily blind to particulars and details magnificently moving in vast masses. Here is the hospitality which forever indicates heroes. . . . Here are the roughs and beards and space and ruggedness and nonchalance that the soul loves. Here the performance disdaining the trivial unapproached in the tremendous audacity of its crowds and groupings and the push of its perspective spreads with crampless and flowing breadth and showers its prolific and splendid extravagance. One sees it must indeed own the riches of the summer and winter, and need never be bankrupt while corn grows from the ground or the orchards drop apples or the bays contain fish or men beget children upon women. . . .

Reading Strategy
Inferring the Poet's Attitude What can you infer about Whitman's attitude toward America from his use of the images of "roughs and beards and space and ruggedness"? Explain.

Review and Assess

Thinking About the Selection

1. **Respond:** Do you think that Whitman's characterization of the United States is still accurate? Why or why not?

2. **(a) Recall:** What subject does Whitman address in the first paragraph? **(b) Interpret:** What does Whitman mean when he says "the corpse is slowly borne from the eating and sleeping rooms of the house"?

3. **(a) Recall:** According to Whitman, what makes America different from all other nations? **(b) Interpret:** What is the meaning of Whitman's notion that the United States "is not merely a nation but a teeming nation of nations"?

4. **(a) Recall:** What riches do the seasons offer? **(b) Interpret:** What does the poet's mention of these riches suggest about his vision of America's promise?

5. **(a) Recall:** According to Whitman, what is the greatest of all poems? **(b) Analyze:** Based on this statement, how is Whitman redefining the idea of a poem?

6. **Extend:** What parallels can you draw between Whitman's ideas about the United States and those expressed by Michel-Guillaume Jean de Crèvecoeur in *Letters From an American Farmer* on p. 208?

7. **Compare and Contrast:** How does Whitman's idea of the United States compare with your idea? Explain.

from *Leaves of Grass* ◆ 435

---

❸ **Reading Strategy**
Inferring the Poet's Attitude

• Direct students to read the bracketed text alone and then in the context of the surrounding paragraph. Guide them to understand the literal meanings of Whitman's images.
Answer: *Roughs* and *beards* are Americans, living in rough conditions, probably off the land and on the move, and perhaps wearing beards as did Whitman.

• Ask students the Reading Strategy question on p. 435: What can you infer about Whitman's attitude toward America from his use of the images of "roughs and beards and space and ruggedness." Possible answer: He views America as rough but vital.

Answers for p. 435

Review and Assess

1. Students should support their responses with evidence.

2. **(a)** Possible response: The speaker addresses the subject of the past. **(b)** Possible response: He means that old habits die hard and that history is not quickly forgotten.

3. **(a)** It has the fullest poetical nature. **(b)** In this line, Whitman refers to the cultural diversity of the American people.

4. **(a)** The seasons offer food and the promise of new life. **(b)** He thinks America has the promise to grow and nurture its population.

5. **(a)** According to the speaker, "the United States themselves are essentially the greatest poem." **(b)** Usually a poem is a highly organized group of words on a page. Whitman's metaphor seems to replace lines with land and words with human beings.

6. Both writers view the United States as a country that welcomes people of different backgrounds, and both consider the land to be a rich source of food and opportunity.

7. Students should support their responses with examples.

CUSTOMIZE FOR UNIVERSAL ACCESS

For Less Proficient Readers	For English Learners	For Gifted/Talented Students
Help students access Whitman's ideas by providing support in understanding his style. For example, demonstrate how to interpret the ideas separated by ellipses by inserting a missing subject or verb to clarify meaning: "[America] accepts the lesson with calmness . . ." or "[perceives] that it was fittest for its days."	Point out to students that Whitman sometimes implies, rather than states, ideas. Words may be missing or simply suggested by the surrounding context. For example, when Whitman repeats *Here* in the second paragraph, he means here in the United States.	Give students the opportunity to read *Death of President Lincoln* in **Authors In Depth**, The American Experience, p. 85. Ask students to find additional examples of Whitman's inclination to leave out words or imply ideas. What effect does the use of such ellipses in the text have on the reader?

❹ About the Selection

In these sections from "Song of Myself," the poet gives his evolving vision of life through the perspective of a vast set of encounters and observations. Its tone is optimistic, exuberant, and energetic; its subject, the poet himself. Yet the poem reaches beyond individual experience to all humankind. Whitman conveys his belief in the limitless potential of the human spirit to embrace the world and to grow from everything it experiences.

❺ ▶ Critical Viewing

Answer: Students may respond that Whitman looks like a rugged free spirit who shuns the formal dress of his time for simple clothing that suits his wandering.

❻ Literary Analysis

Free Verse

- Call on a volunteer to read aloud Section 6. Point out the question and answer pattern in the text.
- Ask students the Literary Analysis question on p. 436: In Section 6, how does Whitman's rhythm reflect the natural cadences of speech?
  Answer: The question and answer pattern makes Section 6 sound like a conversation, in this case, between the poet and himself.

from Song of Myself
Walt Whitman

1

I celebrate myself, and sing myself,
And what I assume you shall assume,
For every atom belonging to me as good belongs to you.

I loaf and invite my soul,
5   I lean and loaf at my ease observing a spear of summer grass.

My tongue, every atom of my blood, formed from this soil, this air,
Born here of parents born here from parents the same, and their
    parents the same,
I, now thirty-seven years old in perfect health begin,
Hoping to cease not till death.

10 Creeds and schools in <u>abeyance</u>,
Retiring back a while sufficed at what they are, but never forgotten,
I harbor for good or bad, I permit to speak at every hazard,
Nature without check with original energy.

6

A child said *What is the grass?* fetching it to me with full hands,
How could I answer the child? I do not know what it is any
    more than he.

 I guess it must be the flag of my disposition, out of hopeful
    green stuff woven.

Or I guess it is the handkerchief of the Lord,
5 A scented gift and remembrancer[1] designedly dropped,

---

1. **remembrancer** reminder.

❺ ▲ Critical Viewing This illustration depicts Walt Whitman as a young man. What can you conclude about his attitudes and personality from this picture? How are they reflected in this poem? **[Infer; Support]**

abeyance (ə bā′ əns) *n.* temporary suspension

Literary Analysis
Free Verse In Section 6, how does the rhythm reflect the natural cadences of speech?

✹ **ENRICHMENT: Social Studies Connection**

Farming in Today's America

The largely agrarian society in which Walt Whitman lived for most of his life has almost disappeared from today's America. Although some Americans still live in rural areas, few still operate farms; those who do, work in vastly different ways from the way they did in the nineteenth century.

Farming—the sowing, tending, and harvesting of crops—is now largely mechanized. In 1992, one hundred years after Whitman's death, only 7 percent of rural residents lived on farms.

Have students research population trends in America over the past century. Students should consider such issues as changes in the percentage of people who live in urban, suburban, and rural areas; changes in the number of active family farms; variations in population density; and so forth. Students can share their findings orally, accompanied by graphs, tables, or charts.

Bearing the owner's name someway in the corners, that we
    may see and remark, and say *Whose?*

        . . .

What do you think has become of the young and old men?
And what do you think has become of the women and children?

  They are alive and well somewhere,
10 The smallest sprout shows there is really no death,
And if ever there was it led forward life, and does not wait at the
    end to arrest it,
And ceas'd the moment life appear'd.
All goes onward and outward, nothing collapses,
And to die is different from what anyone supposed, and luckier.

Reading Strategy
Inferring the Poet's Attitude What attitude toward the cycle of life is suggested by Whitman's use of the words "onward," "outward," and "luckier"? Explain.

9

The big doors of the country barn stand open and ready,
The dried grass of the harvest-time loads the slow-drawn wagon.
The clear light plays on the brown gray and green intertinged,
The armfuls are pack'd to the sagging mow.

5 I am there, I help, I came stretch'd atop of the load,
I felt its soft jolts, one leg reclined on the other,
I jump from the crossbeams and seize the clover and timothy,
And roll head over heels and tangle my hair full of wisps.

14

The wild gander leads his flock through the cool night,
Ya-honk he says, and sounds it down to me like an invitation,
The pert may suppose it meaningless, but I listening close,
Find its purpose and place up there toward the wintry sky.

5 The sharp-hoof'd moose of the north, the cat on the house-sill,
    the chickadee, the prairie dog,
The litter of the grunting sow as they tug at her teats,
The brood of the turkey hen and she with her half-spread wings,
I see in them and myself the same old law.

The press of my foot to the earth springs a hundred affections,
10 They scorn the best I can do to relate them.

I am enamor'd of growing outdoors,
Of men that live among cattle or taste of the ocean or woods,
Of the builders and steerers of ships and the wielders of axes and
    mauls, and the drivers of horses,
I can eat and sleep with them week in and week out.

Reading Check
What aspects of life does the poet celebrate in this poem?

from Song of Myself ◆ 437

---

⑦ Reading Strategy
Inferring the Poet's Attitude

- Have all students pause in their reading to study the bracketed passage.
- Elicit from students their ideas about the connotations of "onward," "outward," and "luckier."
- Then, ask students the Reading Strategy question on p. 437: What attitude toward the cycle of life is suggested by Whitman's use of the words "onward," "outward," and "luckier"?

   Answer: These words have positive, hopeful connotations. His attitude toward the life cycle is that it is natural and that it moves us ever forward.

▶ Monitor Progress Post the Inferring the Poet's Attitude transparency from **Literary Analysis and Reading Transparencies**, p. 45, and help students complete the organizer with details from lines 9–14 of Section 6.

⑧ Reading Check

Answer: He celebrates the natural aspects of life, those found in outdoor activities, in life's natural cycles, in animals, and in agriculture.

CUSTOMIZE FOR UNIVERSAL ACCESS

For Special Needs Students	For Less Proficient Readers	For Gifted/Talented Students
Point out to students how Whitman uses contractions such as *sharp-hoof'd* and *enamor'd*. Explain to students that the apostrophes represent missing letters, in these two cases the letter *e*. Encourage students to try inserting the letter *e* in Whitman's other contractions, reading out the resulting word to check for sense.	Tell students to note Whitman's use of italics to suggest the sounds of his poem and its speech. Point out the child's question in Section 6, line 1, and the gander's call of *Ya-honk* in Section 14, line 1. Explain that the italics invite readers to hear these lines as if they were spoken aloud by the indicated character.	Literary scholar James E. Miller, Jr., characterizes "Song of Myself" as a drama in which the poet is the main character. The complete work has fifty-two numbered sections that can be viewed as acts in the play. Challenge students to perform part or all of this excerpt from "Song of Myself."

❾ Literary Analysis

Free Verse and Diction

- Call on a volunteer to read aloud the bracketed passage. Have students identify the parallel structures in Section 17.

  Answer: Lines 1–4 contain the phrase "they are not." Lines 5–6 begin with "This is the."

▶ **Monitor Progress** Direct students to answer the Literary Analysis question on p. 438: In what way does Whitman's use of parallel structure in Section 17 emphasize the ideas he is expressing?

  Answer: It creates repetition that drives home Whitman's ideas.

❿ Literary Analysis

Free Verse

- Direct students to read the bracketed lines silently. Ask students what characterizes free verse.

  Answer: Free verse lacks regular meter or line length.

- Ask students to paraphrase lines 2–3 of Section 52.

  Answer: I won't be tamed or made to follow rules in expressing my ideas.

- Invite students' response to the Literary Analysis question on p. 438: In what ways does Whitman's use of free verse in lines 2–3 of section 52 emphasize the ideas he is expressing?

  Answer: Both reflect the same unwillingness to be tethered.

---

15 What is commonest, cheapest, nearest, easiest, is Me,
Me going in for my chances, spending for vast returns,
Adorning myself to bestow myself on the first that will take me,
Not asking the sky to come down to my good will,
Scattering it freely forever.

17

These are really the thoughts of all men in all ages and lands,
    they are not original with me,
If they are not yours as much as mine they are nothing, or next
    to nothing,
If they are not the riddle and the untying of the riddle they are
    nothing,
If they are not just as close as they are distant they are nothing.
5 This is the grass that grows wherever the land is and the water is,
This is the common air that bathes the globe.

51

The past and present wilt—I have fill'd them, emptied them,
And proceed to fill my next fold of the future.

Listener up there! what have you to confide to me?
Look in my face while I snuff the sidle of evening,[2]
5 (Talk honestly, no one else hears you, and I stay only a minute
    longer.)

Do I contradict myself?
Very well then I contradict myself,
(I am large, I contain multitudes.)
I concentrate toward them that are nigh,[3] I wait on the door-slab.

10 Who has done his day's work? who will soonest be through with
    his supper?
Who wishes to walk with me?

Will you speak before I am gone? will you prove already too late?

52

The spotted hawk swoops by and accuses me, he complains of
    my gab and my loitering.

I too am not a bit tamed, I too am untranslatable,
I sound my barbaric yawp over the roofs of the world.

---

2. **snuff . . . evening** put out the hesitant last light of day, which is moving sideways
   across the sky.
3. **nigh** near.

438 ◆ *A Growing Nation (1800–1870)*

Literary Analysis
Free Verse and Diction In what ways does Whitman's use of parallel structures in Section 17 emphasize the ideas he is expressing?

Literary Analysis
Free Verse In what ways does Whitman's use of free verse in lines 2–3 of section 52 emphasize the ideas he is expressing?

☀ ENRICHMENT: Culture Connection

Taoism

Walt Whitman found much inspiration in Asian philosophy and thought. Whitman believed in the sacredness of the self and in placing the individual above society, ideas that echo the beliefs of the Chinese philosophy of Taoism. Tao, or the Way, is the central force that makes each thing in the universe unique but also brings everything together in a whole that is reality. Taoist poetry, like Whitman's, shows a love of the beauty of nature and the importance of living one's life in harmony with it. Whitman also espoused the belief in a spiritual unity that connects all things. Such universal philosophy gives Whitman's poetry broad appeal.

Invite interested students to learn more about the principles of Taoism. They can use their research to create a report examining the similarities between Taoist philosophy and poetry and Whitman's ideas.

438

The last scud[4] of day holds back for me,
5   It flings my likeness after the rest and true as any on the
      shadow'd wilds,
It coaxes me to the vapor and the dusk.

I depart as air, I shake my white locks at the runaway sun,
I <u>effuse</u> my flesh in eddies, and drift it in lacy jags.

I bequeath myself to the dirt to grow from the grass I love,
10 If you want me again look for me under your boot soles.

You will hardly know who I am or what I mean,
But I shall be good health to you nevertheless,
And filter and fiber your blood.

Failing to fetch me at first keep encouraged,
15 Missing me one place search another,
I stop somewhere waiting for you.

---

4. **scud** low, dark, wind-driven clouds.

⑪ **effuse** (e fyōoz′) v. pour out

Review and Assess

Thinking About the Selection

1. **Respond:** Which of the ideas expressed in "Song of Myself" do you find most—and least—appealing?

2. (a) **Recall:** From what does Whitman say his tongue and blood are formed? (b) **Analyze:** How does he view his relationship with nature? (c) **Analyze:** How does he view his relationship with other people?

3. (a) **Recall:** In Section 17, what natural images does Whitman use to communicate the idea that his thoughts belong to everyone? (b) **Generalize:** Which elements of these images convey a belief in the spiritual unity of all natural forms?

4. (a) **Recall:** In the second stanza of Section 51, where does the speaker use apostrophe—a direct address to an absent person? (b) **Infer:** Whom do you think the speaker is addressing in this stanza? Explain.

5. (a) **Recall:** In Section 52, where does the speaker say readers can find him? (b) **Infer:** What does he suggest will happen to his spirit and message after he is gone?

6. **Evaluate:** In Section 52, Whitman proudly characterizes his poetry as "barbaric yawp." What terms would you use to describe and evaluate his work?

from Song of Myself ◆ 439

CUSTOMIZE INSTRUCTION FOR UNIVERSAL ACCESS

For Less Proficient Readers	For English Learners	For Special Needs Students
Clarify Whitman's use of pronouns by helping students to identify antecedents. Point out the words *These, they,* and *this is* in Section 17. Remind students of Whitman's personal connections to nature—his belief in its power. Explain that Whitman's pronouns refer to spiritual bonds that link humanity and nature.	In Section 51, Whitman uses the pronoun "I" to refer to both himself and the developing nation. Point out to students that Whitman believes both to be full of growing pains and contradictions. He also believes that for both, these contradictions lead to a treasured richness.	Students may be confused about who is who as they read Whitman's many pronouns. To help these students form a clear picture of the narrative, have them perform a choral reading of the poem. Each time a new pronoun appears, such as *I* or *you*, introduce a new reader. Help students understand to whom Whitman refers in each line.

---

⑪ **Vocabulary Development**

Latin Root -fus-

- Call students' attention to the word *effuse* on page 439. Let students know that the word root *-fus-* comes from a Latin word, *effusus,* which means "poured out."

- Ask students to volunteer words containing this word root. Possiblilities include: *infuse, diffuse,* or *profusion*

- Record students' suggestions on the chalkboard, and ask them to check the words' etymologies in a dictionary.

⑫ **Critical Thinking**

Synthesize

- Point out in the bracketed lines that the speaker bequeaths himself "to the dirt."

- Then, ask this critical thinking question: How does this statement take the grass and the speaker full cycle? Possible response: The speaker began the poem speculating about the meaning of the grass; by bequeathing himself to it, he echoes the biblical idea of "ashes to ashes, dust to dust"—in the eternal circle of life, he will become one with the earth.

Answers for p. 439

Review and Assess

1. Students' responses will reflect their attitudes toward life.

2. (a) He says they are formed from American soil and air. (b) He views himself as part of nature. (c) He views all people as being part of the same life cycle.

3. (a) He refers to the grass that grows everywhere and the air that everyone breathes. (b) Possible response: Whitman links these images to the "thoughts of all men in all ages and lands."

4. (a) In the second stanza of Section 51, he speaks directly to the "Listener up there!" (b) The "listener" may be God or Nature.

5. (a) He says they can find him under their boot soles in the earth. (b) He suggests that he will be "somewhere waiting."

6. Students should support their responses with a careful evaluation of Whitman's ideas.

439

⑬ About the Selections

In the first poem, the speaker reveals that he prefers imagining and experiencing the mystery of the stars to knowing the precise scientific facts an expert scientist can teach. "By the Bivouac's Fitful Flame" contrasts a sentry's physical surroundings in an army camp with the procession of "tender and wondrous thoughts" of life, love, home, family, and friends that carry him back to the life left behind.

⑭ Background

Art

The Lawrence Tree, by Georgia O'Keeffe

Georgia O'Keeffe discovered early that she could say things with color and shape that she could not say in any other way. The painting evokes O'Keeffe's memories of lying on a bench and looking up into this tree to the stars beyond. Like Whitman, O'Keeffe reveals her very personal experiences through her art. Use this question for discussion.

What is O'Keeffe saying about nature in this work? Do you think Whitman would agree?

Possible response: Nature is lofty. Its grandness and majesty dwarf people on Earth. Whitman would agree that nature is grand, but I think he feels more a part of nature and less dwarfed by it than does O'Keeffe.

⑮ ▶Critical Viewing

Answer: Both the artist and the poet view the stars with awe as they gaze upward at the canopy of the night sky. From such an angle, the viewer seems small and insignificant, while the stars appear very distant and mysterious.

The Lawrence Tree, 1929, Georgia O'Keeffe, Wadsworth Atheneum, Hartford

⑬ *When I Heard the Learn'd* Astronomer
Walt Whitman

When I heard the learn'd astronomer,
When the proofs, the figures, were ranged in columns before me,
When I was shown the charts and diagrams, to add, divide and
    measure them,
When I sitting heard the astronomer where he lectured with
    much applause in the lecture room,
5 How soon unaccountable I became tired and sick,
Till rising and gliding out I wander'd off by myself,
In the mystical moist night air, and from time to time,
Look'd up in perfect silence at the stars.

⑮ ▲ Critical Viewing
In what ways does the artist's viewpoint in this painting compare with Whitman's in "When I Heard the Learn'd Astronomer"? **[Connect]**

440 ◆ A Growing Nation (1800–1870)

By the Bivouac's Fitful Flame

Walt Whitman

By the bivouac's[1] fitful flame,
A procession winding around me, solemn and sweet and slow—
    but first I note,
The tents of the sleeping army, the fields' and woods' dim outline,
The darkness lit by spots of kindled fire, the silence,
5 Like a phantom far or near an occasional figure moving,
The shrubs and trees, (as I lift my eyes they seem to be stealthily
    watching me,)
While wind in procession thoughts, O tender and wondrous
    thoughts,
Of life and death, of home and the past and loved, and of those
    that are far away;
A solemn and slow procession there as I sit on the ground,
10 By the bivouac's fitful flame.

---

1. **bivouac** (biv′ wak′) *n.* night guard to prevent surprise attacks.

Review and Assess

Thinking About the Selections

1. **Respond:** To which of these poems do you relate most strongly? Why?

2. **(a) Recall:** In "When I Heard the Learn'd Astronomer," what does the speaker do in reaction to the lecture? **(b) Connect:** What do his actions reveal about his character?

3. **(a) Compare and Contrast:** In what ways does the "perfect silence" in the last line contrast with the lecture? **(b) Draw Conclusions:** What is the speaker saying about the value of science versus a personal experience with nature?

4. **(a) Recall:** In lines 3–4 of "By the Bivouac's Fitful Flame," what sights does the speaker look upon? **(b) Infer:** What is the procession to which he refers in line 2?

5. **(a) Recall:** Where does the speaker's mind go as he gazes upon the scene before him? **(b) Analyze:** Is the procession he refers to in line 9 the same one referred to earlier? Explain.

6. **Make a Judgment:** Whitman is known as a poet who celebrated life. Are these poems celebratory? If so, of what?

Answers for p. 441

Review and Assess

1. Students should explain their responses.

2. **(a)** He leaves the lecture hall to look at the stars himself. **(b)** It suggests that he wants to experience things personally.

3. **(a)** One is silent, while the other is filled with numbers and words. **(b)** He is saying that personal experience with nature is more important than science.

4. **(a)** He looks upon an army camp, the camp's fire, and the darkness around him. **(b)** The reader doesn't yet know.

5. **(a)** It goes to his friends and family at home. **(b)** Yes, it is revealed that the procession is one of the speaker's thoughts.

6. Possible response: Yes. "When I Heard the Learn'd Astronomer" celebrates nature's wonder, while "By the Bivouac's Fitful Flame" celebrates the human capacity for memory and for love.

CUSTOMIZE INSTRUCTION FOR UNIVERSAL ACCESS

For Advanced Readers

Suggest that students read additional works by Walt Whitman. Provide students with the titles listed in the Enrichment box, ATE p. 445. You may also wish to use **Authors In Depth**, The American Experience, which contains the following selections:

- "As I Ebb'd with the Ocean of Life" (poem, p. 79)
- "Broadway" (poem, p. 82)
- "Beat! Beat! Drums!" (poem, p. 83)
- "As Toilsome I Wander'd Virginia's Woods" (poem, p. 84)

- *Death of President Lincoln* (nonfiction, p. 85)

Before students read, have them choose particular issues or literary elements on which to focus. They might, for example, wish to study Whitman's use of free verse and diction, as well as his attitudes in the additional works they read. Lead a round-table discussion in which students can share their analysis of Whitman's other works.

This poem celebrates Whitman's joyous view of the indomitable American spirit. People distinguish themselves by their work, perform tasks that build the future, and demonstrate an exuberance of skill and purpose that makes each of them a vibrant contributor to the spirit of a proud nation.

Answers for p. 442

Review and Assess

1. Whitman's message might celebrate the same American spirit, but would probably mention new kinds of work.

2. **(a)** Whitman mentions mechanics, a carpenter, a mason, a boatman, a shoemaker, a woodcutter, a ploughboy, a mother, and a wife. **(b)** His list suggests that he views America as a vigorous and vast place to be tamed by great physical energy.

3. **(a)** He uses the word "singing." **(b)** Singing suggests a vibrant, hearty, and proud mood.

4. **(a)** At night, the workers share leisure time singing. **(b)** Whitman wants to emphasize his celebratory vision of America and its workers by leaving readers with an image of singing.

5. **Possible response:** Yes, he presents laborers as always happy and singing.

---

16 *I Hear America* Singing

Walt Whitman

I hear America singing, the varied carols I hear,
Those of mechanics, each one singing his as it should be blithe
    and strong,
The carpenter singing his as he measures his plank or beam,
The mason singing his as he makes ready for work, or leaves
    off work,
5 The boatman singing what belongs to him in his boat, the
    deckhand singing on the steamboat deck,
The shoemaker singing as he sits on his bench, the hatter[1]
    singing as he stands,
The wood-cutter's song, the ploughboy's on his way in the
    morning, or at noon intermission or at sundown,
The delicious singing of the mother, or of the young wife at work,
    or of the girl sewing or washing,
Each singing what belongs to him or her and to none else,
10 The day what belongs to the day—at night the party of young
    fellows, robust, friendly,
Singing with open mouths their strong melodious songs.

---

1. **hatter** person who makes, sells, or cleans hats.

Review and Assess

Thinking About the Selection

1. **Respond:** If Whitman were to write this poem today, do you think his message would be the same? Explain.

2. **(a) Recall:** What occupations does Whitman attribute to Americans? **(b) Draw Conclusions:** What does his catalog of occupations suggest about his vision of America?

3. **(a) Recall:** What word does Whitman use to describe all the workers' actions? **(b) Analyze:** In what ways does this word affect the poem's mood?

4. **(a) Recall:** What does Whitman describe the laborers doing at night? **(b) Analyze:** Why do you think the poem ends as it does?

5. **Evaluate:** Do you think Whitman romanticizes the life of a laborer? Explain your answer.

✹ ENRICHMENT: Social Studies Connection

A Man of the People

Clearly, Whitman loved and admired his nation. He believed in its peoples and relished the opportunity to mingle with them. Whitman attended countless events just for the pleasure of being with other Americans. According to one story, he even rode on stagecoaches and ferries just so that he could talk with ordinary people.

Whitman tried to imbue his poetry with the vibrant energy and diversity of American democracy. In an 1856 letter to Ralph Waldo Emerson, Whitman outlined this poetic goal. He wrote, "Every day I go among the people of Manhattan Island, Brooklyn, and other cities, and among the young men, to discover the spirit of them, and to refresh myself . . . In poems, the young men of The States shall be represented, for they outrival the best of the rest of the earth."

The Reaper, Louis C. Tiffany, National Academy of Design, New York City

◀ Critical Viewing 🔞
What might Whitman say
about the work of this
farmer? [Speculate]

🔞

I Hear America Singing ◆ 443

🔞 ▶ Critical Viewing

Answer: Whitman would probably
praise the merits of physical labor
done in the great outdoors.

🔞 Background

Art

The Reaper, by Louis C. Tiffany

Tiffany, though known best for his
work in decorative glass, was also an
accomplished painter. This oil-on-
canvas painting celebrates the harvest. The farmhand stands
surrounded by grain in the midst of
the field, sharpening his blade in
preparation for harvesting.

Use this question for discussion:

• What parallels can you draw
between the artist's and the poet's
attitudes toward their subjects?
Answer: Both men seem to have
admired and respected those who
earn their livings through manual
labor.

CUSTOMIZE INSTRUCTION FOR UNIVERSAL ACCESS

For English Learners	For Gifted/Talented Students	
Students may be unfamiliar with the words Whitman uses to label various workers. List some of these on the chalkboard: *mechanics, mason, deckhand, wood-cutter, ploughboy.* Use visual images, such as the painting on p. 443 and Fine Art Transparency 12, to convey information about the kind of work each laborer undertakes.	After students have read "I Hear America Singing," challenge them to list as many "singing" references in the poem as they can. Emphasize that Whitman referred to everyday people, pursuing everyday activities. Then display Art Transparency 12, pointing out the "everyday" look of the scene, the "slice of life" character of the	sculpture. Remind students that according to Whitman, everyone has "strong melodious songs" that belong "to him or her and to none else." Invite students to speculate about the "song" that the bowler in the transparency could be singing. Then ask them the same question about the farmer shown in the painting on p. 443.

19 About the Selection

Watching a spider spin its thread, the speaker in "A Noiseless Patient Spider" compares the insect to his soul. Like the spider, he stands in oceans of space, throwing out threads, seeking connections to the universe.

Answers for p. 444

Review and Assess

1. Some students may admire the spider's efforts, as Whitman does. Others may regard spiders as pests.

2. **(a)** A huge vast open space surrounds the spider. **(b)** They are the world around the soul, the world of people to whom the soul must forge a connection.

3. **(a)** It spins filament to explore its surroundings. **(b)** Both the speaker's soul and the spider are poised in isolation, and both seek to explore and connect themselves to the world.

4. **(a)** He uses *stood, mark'd, explore, launch'd forth, unreeling, speeding.* **(b)** He uses *stand, musing, venturing, throwing, seeking, connect, form'd hold, fling.* **(c)** The spider's exploration is purely physical, while the soul's journey is spiritual.

5. **(a)** The poet addresses his own soul. **(b)** The speaker wants the soul to succeed in forming a bridge.

6. The spider's physical efforts mirror the human soul's spiritual efforts to connect to the surrounding world.

7. Students should be able to support their responses with details from the poem and their own experiences.

19 A Noiseless Patient Spider

Walt Whitman

A noiseless patient spider,
I mark'd where on a little promontory it stood isolated,
Mark'd how to explore the vacant vast surrounding,
It launch'd forth filament, filament, filament, out of itself,
5 Ever unreeling them, ever tirelessly speeding them.

And you O my soul where you stand,
Surrounded, detached, in measureless oceans of space,
Ceaselessly musing, venturing, throwing, seeking the spheres
    to connect them,
Till the bridge you will need be form'd, till the ductile anchor hold,
10 Till the gossamer thread you fling catch somewhere, O my soul.

Review and Assess

Thinking About the Selection

1. **Respond:** Would your reaction to watching a spider spin a web be similar to Whitman's? Why or why not?

2. **(a) Recall:** In line three, what surrounds the spider? **(b) Interpret:** In line 6, what are the "measureless oceans of space" with which the speaker's soul is surrounded?

3. **(a) Recall:** Why does the spider "tirelessly" spin out filament? **(b) Connect:** How is the speaker's soul similar to the spider?

4. **(a) Recall:** What verbs does Whitman use to describe the spider's actions? **(b) Recall:** What verbs does he use to describe the activities of his soul? **(c) Compare and Contrast:** How are the two explorations the same, and how are they different?

5. **(a) Recall:** Who—or what—does the poet address directly? **(b) Interpret:** What is the speaker's attitude toward the recipient of this direct address?

6. **Synthesize:** Like the Transcendentalists, Whitman believed that the human spirit was mirrored in the world of nature. What aspects of "A Noiseless Patient Spider" reflect this belief?

7. **Evaluate:** Do you think the parallel Whitman draws between his soul and the spider is convincing? Explain.

ASSESSMENT PRACTICE: Reading Comprehension

Make Inferences and Generalizations   (For more practice, see Test Preparation Workbook, p. 25.)

Many tests require students to make inferences about a written passage. Explain that sometimes inferences need to be drawn concerning an author's point of view, opinions, or attitudes. Have students read "I Hear America Singing" on p. 442, then ask them the following question:

What is the poet's attitude toward the American workers about whom he writes?

A uncertain
B celebratory
C dismissive
D somber

The poet emphatically proclaims his admiration for the laborers. Thus *A, C,* and *D* cannot be correct. The best choice is *B.*

Review and Assess

Literary Analysis

Free Verse

1. In what ways does the use of **free verse** allow the poet to express his ideas more freely in "Song of Myself"?
2. How would the impact of "When I Heard the Learn'd Astronomer" be different if it had regular meter and line length?

Comparing Literary Works

3. Use a chart like the one shown to analyze Whitman's use of lists in both "By the Bivouac's Fitful Flame" and "When I Heard the Learn'd Astronomer."

Poem	Cataloging	What the Details Share	Effect

4. In what ways does the **diction** in "When I Heard the Learn'd Astronomer," especially the use of parallel structures in the first four lines, reinforce Whitman's description of the astronomer?
5. What effect does the catalog, or list, of workers in "I Hear America Singing" have on the poem's message?
6. In your opinion, which poem represents the best match between subject and diction? Explain.

Reading Strategy

Inferring the Poet's Attitude

7. **(a)** In Section 14, lines 11–14, of "Song of Myself," what can you **infer** about Whitman's **attitude** toward people who work outdoors? **(b)** What language helps you draw this inference?
8. Note at least five descriptive words or phrases in "When I Heard the Learn'd Astronomer" that help you infer Whitman's attitude toward the science of astronomy and his feelings about the stars.

Extend Understanding

9. **Literature Connection:** It has been said that Whitman's entire body of work was a spiritual autobiography. Do you think this assessment is accurate? Explain.

Quick Review

Free verse is poetry that has irregular meter and line length.

Diction involves the writer's choice and arrangement of words, and includes the use of such devices as catalogs and parallel structures.

You can **infer the poet's attitude** by noting his or her choice of subjects, details, and words.

 Take It to the Net
www.phschool.com
Take the interactive self-test online to check your understanding of these selections.

Answers for p. 445

Review and Assess

1. The use of free verse emphasizes Whitman's free, unconventional, and unconfined approach to the wonders of nature.

2. It would seem to support the scientist's approach to nature rather than the poet's unconventional point of view.

3. Possible response for "When I heard . . .": Cataloging: the proofs, the figures; the charts and diagrams; What the Details Have in Common: They all relate to organizing information; Effect: They support Whitman's attitude that science takes the mystery out of nature

4. Repeated use of the opening words *When I* set up the readers' expectation of the speaker's response to the astronomer's facts and figures.

5. It gives it a singsong, musical quality that reinforces Whitman's message about the poetry in everyday Americans.

6. Students' responses should be supported with examples from their chosen poem.

7. **(a)** Whitman values physical labor; he seems to exult in the work and the workers he observes. **(b)** The catalog of workers singing at their jobs helps one draw the inference.

8. Possible responses: *to add, divide, and measure them; sitting; tired and sick; rising and gliding; the mystical moist night air;* and *in perfect silence.*

9. Students should be able to support their responses with examples from the poems.

✸ ENRICHMENT: Further Reading

Other Works by Walt Whitman

Leaves of Grass

Drum Taps

Good-Bye, My Fancy

 Take It to the Net
Visit www.phschool.com for more information on Walt Whitman.

❶ Vocabulary Development

Word Analysis

1. a
2. d
3. c
4. b

Fluency: Denotations

1. No, because her ruling temporarily overturns the law.
2. Light that effuses spreads through the room.

Spelling Strategy

1. puny
2. feud
3. youth
4. value

❷ Grammar and Style Lesson

1. she, *mare*
2. their, *the woman and child*
3. its, *life*
4. his, *shoemaker*
5. they, *the laborers*

Writing Application

Students' sentences should be free of mechanical errors and should each contain a pronoun that correctly matches its antecedent.

Integrate Language Skills

❶ Vocabulary Development Lesson

Word Analysis: Latin Root *-fus-*

In "Song of Myself" Whitman writes, "I effuse my flesh in eddies, and drift it in lacy jags." The word *effuse* means "pour" or "spread." It is based on the Latin root *-fus-*, meaning "pour," combined with the prefix *e-*, which means "out" or "away."

Each of the words in the left column is based on the root *-fus-*. Match each word with its definition in the right column.

1. profusion   a. rich or lavish supply
2. infuse   b. dispersed
3. effusive   c. gushing
4. diffuse   d. fill

Fluency: Denotations

Answer the following questions. Then, explain your answers.

1. If a judge hands down a ruling in *abeyance* of a particular law, is she enforcing that law?
2. Does light that *effuses* from a lamp spread softly or shine in a sharply focused beam?

Spelling Strategy

The sound of *y* followed by long *u* is often created by the letter *u* alone, as in *effuse*. Other spellings include *ew*, *ue*, *eu*, and *ou*. Complete each word below with the correct spelling.

1. p__ny (small)
2. f__d (major argument)
3. y__th (a child)
4. val__ (worth)

❷ Grammar and Style Lesson

Pronoun and Antecedent Agreement

A **pronoun** must **agree** in number with its **antecedent**—the word to which it refers in the following ways:
- in number—singular or plural
- in gender—masculine or feminine

>   ANTECEDENT   PRONOUN
> **Singular:** The *shoemaker* singing as *he* sits on *his bench*. (masculine, singular)
>
>   ANTECEDENT
> **Plural:** . . . The *past* and *present* wilt—
>   PRONOUN
> I have fill'd *them* . . .

Two singular antecedents joined by *and* take a plural pronoun. Two singular antecedents joined by *or* take a singular pronoun.

Practice Choose the correct pronoun for each sentence below. Then, identify its antecedent.

1. The mare awoke, and then (she, it) stepped toward the door of the stall.
2. The woman and child opened (his, their) books and began to sing.
3. Life has (its, their) challenges and gratifications.
4. The shoemaker went on (their, his) lunch break.
5. All of the laborers received pay increases after (he, they) made requests.

Writing Application Write five sentences describing the work of various friends or family members. For each, use pronouns that correctly match their antecedents.

*W*G *Prentice Hall Writing and Grammar Connection: Chapter 23, Section 2*

446 ◆ *A Growing Nation (1800–1870)*

TEACHING RESOURCES

The following resources can be used to enrich or extend the instruction for pp. 446–447.

Vocabulary

📖 **Selection Support:** Build Vocabulary, p. 103

📖 **Vocabulary and Spelling Practice Book** (Use this booklet for skills enrichment.) ▪

Grammar

📖 **Selection Support:** Grammar and Style, p. 104

*W*G **Writing and Grammar,** Ruby Level, p. 596

🖫 **Daily Language Practice Transparencies**

Writing

*W*G **Writing and Grammar,** Ruby Level, p. 42

💿 **Writing and Grammar iText CD-ROM**

🖫 **Fine Art Transparencies,** Art Transparencies 12 and 19 ▪

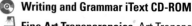
🖫 **BLOCK SCHEDULING:** Resources marked with this symbol provide varied instruction during 90-minute blocks.

❸ Writing Lesson

Imitation of an Author's Style

Write a poem in which you imitate Walt Whitman's unique style. Choose several elements of his style—word choice, tone, degree of formality, rhythm, use of lists, or organization—and use them throughout your poem.

Prewriting   Decide on a "Whitmanesque" topic, and review the characteristics of free verse. List or diagram sensory details and images related to your topic.

Model: Using a Cluster Diagram to Gather Details

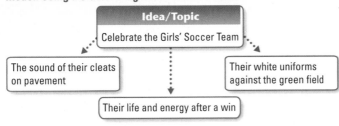

Drafting   Maintain a consistent style and tone, and let your meaning determine the lengths of lines and stanzas.

Revising   Read your poem aloud. Listen for natural rhythms of speech rather than formal rhythms or grammatical structures. Make any changes necessary to maintain the natural-sounding rhythms.

W̶G̶ Prentice Hall Writing and Grammar Connection: Chapter 3, Section 3

❹ Extension Activities

Listening and Speaking   Whitman's poems capture America at the dawn of the Industrial Age. With a group, look through magazines for images that capture America's essence today. Make a **collage.** Then, present your findings to the class. Let the following tips guide your presentation:

- Explain why you included each image.
- Discuss how the themes of the collage compare to Whitman's vision of the country.

Include passages from Whitman's poetry that speak to the images you present. **[Group Activity]**

Research and Technology   Compare the meter in Emily Dickinson's poetry with the free verse in Whitman's poetry. Use the Internet to locate and listen to oral readings of the two poets. Then, research the ways in which both poets have influenced American poetry. Deliver a **report** of your findings to the class.

 Take It to the Net   www.phschool.com

Go online for an additional research activity using the Internet.

ASSESSMENT RESOURCES

The following resources can be used to assess students' knowledge and skills.

Selection Assessment

- 📖 **Formal Assessment,** pp. 111–113
- 📖 **Open Book Test,** pp. 67–69
- 📼 **Got It! Assessment Videotapes,** Tape 2
- 💿 **Test Bank Software**
- 💻 *Take It to the Net*
  Visit www.phschool.com for self-tests and additional questions on the selections.

Writing Rubric

- 📖 **Performance Assess. and Portfolio Mgmt.,** p. 30

PRENTICE HALL ASSESSMENT SYSTEM

- 📖 **Workbook**
- 📖 **Skill Book**
- 📄 **Transparencies**
- 💿 **CD-ROM**

Lesson Support for p. 447

❸ Writing Lesson

- Have volunteers read aloud their favorite of the Whitman poems. Discuss with students the aspects of Whitman's style that they enjoy.
- Suggest exuberance, reflection, or wonder as possible tones to adopt in writing a Whitmanlike poem.
- Review the Writing Lesson to guide students in developing their poems. Offer students **Fine Art Transparencies, Volume1**, Transparency 19, *Builders in the City*, as an inspiration for their poems.

❹ Listening and Speaking

- Encourage groups to focus on a few areas of American life before they begin their image search.
- Provide students with a variety of magazines or suggest that they look at home or at rummage sales for old magazines.
- Remind students to refer frequently to their collages as they speak.
- Have students use the Self-Assessment: Delivering a Speech form, p. 30, in **Performance Assessment and Portfolio Management**.

CUSTOMIZE INSTRUCTION
For Universal Access

To address different learning styles, use the activities suggested in the **Extension Activities** booklet, p. 23.

For Intrapersonal and Visual/Spatial Learners, use Activity 5.

For Interpersonal Learners, use Activity 6.

For Verbal/Linguistic Learners, use Activity 7.

💻 *E-Teach*

Visit E-Teach at www.phschool.com for teachers' essays on how to teach, with questions and answers.

Lesson Objectives

1. To understand the connection between American poems of different centuries
2. To compare and contrast different definitions of the word "American"

Connections

Have students reread Walt Whitman's poems, pp. 432–447. Like Whitman, Hughes and de Hoyos write to express their uniquely American identity. Have students discuss what de Hoyos and Hughes think of Whitman's poetry and what Whitman might have thought of theirs.

The Emergence of an American Voice

• Ask students what they think of when they hear the word "American." What does it mean to them to be Americans? What did it mean to Walt Whitman? As students read these two poems, they should think about what it means to Hughes and de Hoyos.

Background

Art

Nobody Around Here Calls Me Citizen, by Robert Gwathmey

1. Ask what students think the number 2 in the painting symbolizes. Have them explain their answers.
   Answer: It may suggest that African Americans have two sides to them—the compliance they show to be safe and the rebellion they feel underneath.
2. Why did Gwathmey put the lion in the painting?
   Answer: He wanted to contrast the hopelessness in the man's face with the anger of the lion. The lion shows the anger that the man feels but does not show.

▶ Critical Viewing

Answer: The figure of the man more closely resembles the image of the speaker in the reader's mind. However, like the voice in the poem, the lion is bold.

The Emergence of an American Voice

Walt Whitman and Emily Dickinson were two of the poets most responsible for establishing a distinctly American poetic voice. The American poets who preceded them were all heavily influenced by the styles and themes of British poets of the time. Whitman and Dickinson, on the other hand, produced poetry that was fresh and original. Different in style and content from the work of any earlier poet, Whitman's poetry embodies the freedom that characterizes the American spirit and captures the immensity of the American landscape. Dickinson's poetry is filled with stylistic innovations and has a highly personal quality that parallels the American emphasis on individuality.

Whitman's Ideals, Today's World The America that Walt Whitman celebrates in his poetry has grown increasingly diverse. That increased diversity has once again expanded the boundaries of American literature, introducing readers to the traditions and issues of the many cultures represented in our population. Like Whitman and Dickinson, Langston Hughes helped establish a new American literature. He and a group of other African American poets associated with an artistic movement known as the Harlem Renaissance (see page 910) produced musical verse that captures the African American experience during the first half of the twentieth century. More recently, Angela de Hoyos and a growing number of Hispanic American poets brought the rhythms of the Spanish language to American literature, capturing the experiences of people descended from various Latin American cultures.

▲ **Critical Viewing** Which image in this painting better illustrates the sentiments of this poem—the man or the lion? Explain. **[Make a Decision]**

CUSTOMIZE INSTRUCTION FOR UNIVERSAL ACCESS

For Advanced Readers

Share the following excerpt from section 13 of *Song of Myself* with students:

> The negro holds firmly the reins of his four horses, the block swags underneath on its tied-over chain,
>
> The negro that drives the long dray of the stone-yard, steady and tall he stands pois'd on one leg on the string-piece . . . .
>
> His glance is calm and commanding, he tosses the slouch of his hat away from his forehead,
>
> The sun falls on his crispy hair and mustache, falls on the black of his polish'd and perfect limbs.

Have students re-evaluate "I, Too" in light of this excerpt. Did Whitman truly fail to recognize the great variety of the people who "sing America"?

Nobody Around Here Calls Me Citizen, 1943, Robert Gwathmey, University of Minnesota, © Estate Robert Gwathmey/Licensed by VAGA, New York, NY

I, Too

Langston Hughes

I, too, sing America.

I am the darker brother.
They send me to eat in the kitchen
When company comes,
5 But I laugh,
And eat well,
And grow strong.

Tomorrow,
I'll be at the table
10 When company comes.
Nobody'll dare
Say to me,
"Eat in the kitchen,"
Then.

15 Besides,
They'll see how beautiful I am
And be ashamed—

I, too, am America.

Langston Hughes

(1902–1967)

Langston Hughes emerged from the Harlem Renaissance as the most prolific and successful African American writer. Hughes published several volumes of poetry in which he experimented with a variety of forms and techniques and often tried to re-create the rhythms of contemporary jazz.

Connections: *I, Too* ◆ 449

The Emergence of an American Voice *(continued)*

- Point out that Hughes' opening line shows that his poem is a direct response to Whitman's poem "I Hear America Singing." Have students reread Whitman's poem and discuss their reactions to Hughes' response.
  Answer: Students may note that many of the people Whitman describes—the mechanics, carpenters, sewing girls—could well be African American. Nothing in Whitman's poem suggests that his American workers are all white. Suggest to students that Hughes' title asserts that he is also a singer of American songs—that his is as valuable a poetic voice as Walt Whitman's.

- Have students compare the tone of Hughes' poem to that of Whitman's.
  Answer: Whitman's poem is celebratory; Hughes' is celebratory and defiant.

CUSTOMIZE INSTRUCTION FOR UNIVERSAL ACCESS

For Less Proficient Readers	For English Learners	For Advanced Readers
Have students begin by paraphrasing Hughes' poem in prose. Then have them compare and contrast Hughes' message to the message of "I Hear American Singing." Do students think these are contradictory or related images of Americans?	Have students compare and contrast the vivid verbs used in Hughes' and Whitman's poems. Have them discuss which poem makes more effective use of verbs and why they think this.	Have students imagine what Walt Whitman would say if he could read Hughes' poem. Having read Whitman's work and something about his life, do students believe that Whitman deliberately neglected African Americans in his poetry? Why or why not?

▶Critical Viewing

Answer: The poem is somewhat angry and disappointed. The cast-down eyes of the girl in the painting make it reflective.

The Emergence of an American Voice

• Have students compare and contrast the speakers of the two poems in this grouping. Remind them that the speaker of Walt Whitman's poems was Walt Whitman. Do students feel they can safely assume that the speakers of "I, Too" and "To Walt Whitman" are the same as the poets? Why or why not?
Answer: Students should point out that the poets and speakers share an ethnic identity and that both are known for writings that focus on their identity. Therefore, it is reasonable to identify the speakers with the poets.

Mandolin, Rosa Ibarra

▲**Critical Viewing** Compare the mood of this painting with the mood of the poem. **[Compare]**

450 ◆ *A Growing Nation (1800–1870)*

✺ **ENRICHMENT: Literature Connection**

Leaves of Grass

The speaker of "To Walt Whitman" fails to find "my Native Amerindian race" in his poems. He or she has failed to read the poems carefully. Whitman repeatedly insists on the universality of the human race, never excluding anyone: in *Song of Myself,* section 20, he says, "In all people I see myself, none more and not one a barley-corn less." Moreover, Whitman's poems contain many specific references to Native Americans. The poem opposite, for example, appears in *Good-bye My Fancy,* the

final book of *Leaves of Grass.*

To Walt Whitman

Angela de Hoyos

hey man, my brother
world-poet
prophet democratic
here's a guitar
5   for you
—a chicana guitar—
so you can spill out a song
for the open road
big enough for my people
10   —my Native Amerindian race
that I can't seem to find
in your poems

Angela de Hoyos

(b. 1940)

Angela de Hoyos has emerged as a voice of her times, celebrating her heritage and knowledge of what it means to live in a world of diversity.

De Hoyos first published poetry in high school. By her early twenties, her poetry was published in literary journals. Between 1969 and 1975, de Hoyos studied, wrote, and established her reputation through readings at Mexican American gatherings in the Southwest. She has published five collections of poetry.

Connecting Literature Past and Present

1. (a) Compare and contrast the message of American identity in Hughes's and de Hoyos's poems to Whitman's "I Hear America Singing." (b) What message do you think Hughes and de Hoyos are trying to convey?
2. In what ways do "To Walt Whitman" and "I, Too" reflect changes in the American literary voice since the time of Dickinson and Whitman?

Connections: *To Walt Whitman* ◆ 451

The Emergence of an American Voice

- Share the Enrichment information on these pages with students. Identify other instances of Whitman's many poetic references to Native and African Americans (examples: section 10 of *Song of Myself* describes the wedding of an Indian girl and Whitman's own encounter with a runaway slave, and section 11 of *Salut au Monde!* refers to Africans as being "on equal terms with me."). Ask students what these references suggest to them about Whitman, especially given the time and place in which he wrote.
  Answer: Exposure to Whitman's poetry should show students that he lacked racial prejudice to a remarkable degree for a nineteenth-century white American.

- Ask students what they think being American means to Whitman, Hughes, and de Hoyos. Have them explain their answers.
  Answer: For Whitman, it means an energy and freedom that he celebrates. For Hughes, it means oppression that he is free to fight. For de Hoyos, it means a pride in her heritage.

Background

Point out the reference to "the open road" (line 8). Explain that Book VII of the epic *Leaves of Grass* is titled "Song of the Open Road."

Connecting Literature Past and Present

1. (a) Hughes' speaker threatens that one day he will rise up and take his proper place in America. Angela de Hoyos' speaker feels that she already has a place but others have failed to acknowledge it.
   (b) Both poets try to convey the importance of the races to which they belong.

2. Both poems suggest that the word "American" means all people who have played a part in shaping the country and its population.

OSCEOLA by Walt Whitman

When his hour for death had come,

He slowly rais'd himself from the bed on the floor,

Drew on his war-dress, shirt, leggings, and girdled the belt around his waist,

Call'd for vermilion paint (his looking-glass was held before him,)

Painted half his face and neck, his wrists, and back-hands,

Put the scalp-knife carefully in his belt—then lying down, resting a moment,

Rose again, half sitting, smiled, gave in silence his extended hand to each and all,

Sank faintly low to the floor (tightly grasping the tomahawk handle,)

Fix'd his look on wife and little children—the last:

(And here a line in memory of his name and death.)

Lesson Objectives

1. To write a comparison-contrast essay on literary trends

2. To use writing strategies to generate ideas and to plan, organize, evaluate, and revise writing

Prewriting

- Have a class discussion in which students compare and contrast the selections from the unit. Have students identify qualities they think several works have in common. This discussion should help students find ideas for topics.

- Suggest that students narrow their essays to focus on no more than three literary selections. Students can use these selections as examples of the trends they perceive in the historical period.

Writing About Literature

Compare and Contrast Literary Trends

In its formative years, American literature comprised a fairly random assortment of individual efforts. There were no literary movements, and there was no strong sense of a distinctly American literature. By the early to mid 1800s, this had changed, and American writers began to produce a distinctive body of work. The stories, poems, and essays published during these decades explored a range of themes and set their ideas within a uniquely American landscape.

Using the assignment outlined in the yellow box, write an essay to address this period in American literary history.

Prewriting

Identify trends. Review each selection in this unit to see how it fits into a larger trend. These questions may help frame your review:

- Are the setting and theme explicitly American, or could the selection just as easily have been written by an English author?

- Does the work reflect American values such as independence and optimism, or does it reflect a traditional, European outlook on life?

- Is the author's voice personal and strongly individualistic? If so, in what ways is this expressed?

- What other literary works in the unit does the selection resemble? In what ways?

Use your review of each selection and your knowledge of history and literature to classify the pieces in this unit according to the trends they exemplify.

Select trends to compare or contrast. After classifying the selections that appear in this unit, determine which ones you want to explore in your essay. Decide whether you are more interested in comparing points of similarity between two emerging trends or in contrasting extreme differences between the old and the new.

Focus on similarities and differences. Once you have identified the selections you intend to analyze, use a chart like the one shown to closely analyze specific features.

Unique to Emerson	Similarities	Unique to Poe
Emerson's belief in the power of the individual expresses a core American value.	Both writers believed that some aspects of the truth were beyond the realm of physical reality.	Allusions to European art, music, and architecture in "The Fall of the House of Usher" show Poe's kinship with European traditions.

452 ◆ *A Growing Nation (1800–1870)*

Assignment: Old vs. New in American Literature

Write an analytical essay that compares and contrasts one of the more distinctly American literary trends of this period with one of the more traditional schools of literature. Your essay will focus on two different trends and may require support from more than two authors.

Criteria:

- Include a thesis statement that identifies the trends and authors you will compare.

- Compare and contrast your subjects point by point, with references and quotations from the works.

- Approximate length: 1,500 words.

 Read to Write
Reread the texts carefully, looking for ways in which they reveal—or do not reveal—distinctly American sensibilities.

TEACHING RESOURCES

The following resources can be used to enrich or extend the instruction for pages 452–453

 Writing and Grammar, Ruby Level, Chapter 9, pp. 166–193

 Performance Assess. and Portfolio Mgmt., p. 19

 Writing Models and Graphic Organizers on Transparencies, p. 88

Writing and Grammar iText CD-ROM

Students can use the following tools as they complete their comparison-contrast essays:

- Topic Bank

- Self-Interview

- Comparatives

Drafting

Outline. Use the information from your chart to create a working outline. In the major headings of the outline, indicate the most important points of similarity or difference between the two trends under discussion. Beneath each heading, list the supporting details from the literature.

> **Model: Devising a Working Outline**
>
> I. Similarities between Poe and Emerson
> > A. belief in aspects of truth that are beyond physical reality
> > B. (other similarities)
>
> II. Differences between Poe and Emerson
> > A. Emerson exhibits new American value of self-determination.
> > B. Poe's stories reflect the European belief in fate.

Refer to historical context. Writers are individuals, but they also reflect the times and places in which they live. As you draft, analyze the extent to which each writer's work expresses ideas that were either shared by their contemporaries or that were innovative—even radical—at the time.

Revising and Editing

Review content: Check the accuracy of details. All the opinions in your essay must be supported with accurate details from the selections. Verify the accuracy of details by going back and checking the source.

Review style: Vary sentence length and structure. Review your draft to evaluate your sentences. If you find too many long sentences in a row, break some of them down into shorter sentences. If you find a string of short, choppy sentences, combine some of them.

> **Repetitive sentence length and structure:** American writing flourished during the 1800s. Poe wrote disturbing horror stories. Emerson produced striking essays.
>
> **Improved sentence variety:** During the 1800s, American writing flourished. Poe wrote disturbing horror stories, while Emerson produced original and striking essays.

Publishing and Presenting

Create a comparison and contrast poster. To share your analysis with others, take the major points from your essay and distill them into brief statements. Place the statements on a poster, with comparisons in one section and contrasting points in another section. Use graphic elements to draw visual attention to your main points.

W̶G *Prentice Hall Writing and Grammar Connection: Chapter 9*

✎ Write to Learn

If you have trouble finding details to support a conclusion, reconsider your ideas. Maybe you have jumped to a conclusion based on insufficient evidence. If so, rethink your argument.

✎ Write to Explain

The reader cannot follow your thought process; he or she can only follow the arguments you note on the page. Make sure that you explain your reasons for drawing conclusions, and do not omit any steps in your thought process.

Drafting

- Because this is a comparison-contrast essay, students may find it helpful to use Venn diagrams to organize their ideas.

Students might also make use of the Comparison and Contrast Blackline Master in **Writing Models and Graphic Organizers on Transparencies**, p. 88.

- Students may find it helpful to refer to the timeline at the beginning of the unit. This timeline shows the historical background against which Dickinson, Poe, and the other writers of the period lived and wrote. Students may want to do a little further research on some of these events for the purpose of this essay.

Revising and Editing

- Use Abraham Lincoln's "Gettysburg Address" (Unit 4) as a model for varied sentence length and structure. The speech contains only ten sentences, varying in length from ten to 82 words and varying from simple subject-verb structure to long complex-compound structure with multiple subordinate clauses. This variety keeps readers attentive by surprising them at every turn.

Use the rubric for Comparison and Contrast Essay in **Performance Assessment and Portfolio Management**, p. 19, to assess students' essays.

Publishing and Presenting

Students may want to collaborate on posters, with some doing the writing and others drawing the illustrations.

CUSTOMIZE INSTRUCTION FOR UNIVERSAL ACCESS

For Less Proficient Writers	For English Learners	For Advanced Writers
Students can use Venn diagrams to compare and contrast the two works they have chosen to write about. You may also wish to provide students with the Comparison and Contrast Blackline Master in **Writing Models and Graphic Organizers on Transparencies**, p. 88.	Encourage students to write about the works they found the easiest to comprehend and which they feel they understood the most thoroughly.	Encourage students to read one more short work or excerpt from a work by the writers they discuss in their essays. Students should analyze these additional works as well as those from the unit.

Lesson Objectives

1. To write a reflective composition

2. To use writing strategies to generate ideas and to plan, organize, evaluate, and revise the composition

Model from Literature

The poems of Emily Dickinson, pp. 418–431, are examples of reflective writing that explore the poet's thoughts and deepest emotions.

Prewriting

- Discuss the bulleted list of Assignment Criteria at the top of the page. Explain to students that they can focus an essay on a specific event or a series of events.

- Before students draft their essays, have them review the Rubric for Self-Assessment (p. 457) so they know what is expected.

A **reflective essay** is a work in which a writer explores a personal experience or event and reflects on its broader significance. In this workshop, you will write a reflective composition in which you describe a personal experience and examine its deeper meaning.

Assignment Criteria Your reflective composition should have the following characteristics:

- Writer as the main character
- The personal feelings, thoughts, or views of the writer
- Connections between specific incidents and broader themes
- An insight gained by the writer
- A balance between specific incidents and abstract ideas

To preview the criteria on which your reflective composition may be assessed, see the Rubric on page 457.

Prewriting

Choose a topic. To write a reflective essay, select a meaningful event from your life. To narrow down the possible subjects, **list and itemize**. First, list daily activities you engage in at home, at school, or in your community. Then, for each, itemize notable incidents that happened during these activities. Choose one event that has a wider meaning to explore in your reflective essay.

Draw comparisons. Once you have selected an experience to explore, use a diagram like the one shown to consider themes in the world at large that might compare to your own experience.

Exploring Backroads

In My Life	In the World
• Be like my brothers • Learn to navigate my world	• Connect to history • Create sense of family continuity between generations

Find an insight. The experience you describe in your reflective essay caused you to learn something new about yourself or to see the world in a different light. Review your notes and write a sentence that connects your discovery to an event removed from your own experience. Consider including this insight in your draft.

> **Example:** When I saw how far I could travel by car, I admired the pioneers who plodded west on horseback.

Gather evidence. To connect your personal event with an incident in the outside world, you may need to do some research. Consult friends, family, the library, or the Internet and incorporate any relevant information into your draft.

TEACHING RESOURCES

The following resources can be used to enrich or extend the instruction for pages 454–457

𝒲𝒢 Writing and Grammar,
Ruby Level, Chapter 4,
pp. 48–71

Ⓒ Writing and Grammar iText CD-ROM
Students can use the following tools as they complete their autobiographical narratives:

- Topic Bank
- Self-Interview
- Character Trait

Student Model

Before you begin writing, read this student model and review the characteristics of a successful reflective essay.

Graham Walker
Ruston, Louisiana

Backroads to Tomorrow

They are small country roads—the ones that change color and ride when you cross a simple parish line. They have four-ton limits assigned to small bridges that hop over waters like Bear Creek and Black Lake Bayou. Their ragged shoulders are missing chunks of pavement and rise three inches above the packed red clay that supports the asphalt. Bright ribbons of tape hang from the lower limbs of pine trees to escort log trucks to jobs. Now and again a color will halt at a worn path entering a clean-bottomed plot of trees, but the others remain loyal to the country road.

These are the roads I grew up on.

It was usually just my oldest brother, Judd, and me. In a blue and gray Ford truck, we would branch out from our home in Taylor, Louisiana, with the windows down. Whether we went and looked at natural gas wells or whether we shot big turtles sunning themselves on logs in a bayou, it never took too much to keep us rolling along on those old Bienville back roads.

But is was not the pure riding experience that I enjoyed so much. It was the infinite knowledge of the roads that I believed I gained from those trips. I was in Backroads 101: Knowing the Road. I made sure I asked my brother whether we would take a right here or keep straight at the intersections. I felt that I had to know three different ways to get to Minden, ten miles away, or which way the T below our house would take me in case I wanted to slip off for a spin in my pre-double digit years.

Looking back, I realize it was not my concern for my future driving years that led me to study those roads so intently and to map them in my memory. It was one of the lengths I went to so I could be like my three older brothers. All three of them knew the lay of the pavement throughout the Bienville Parish. They could tell me how to get wherever I wished by a backroad route—even to Shreveport, I am sure. And more than I wanted to get to Shreveport, I wanted to be like them.

So I soon knew most of the roads they knew. I could tell anyone three different ways to get to Minden, or which way the T would take me. But I was mapping more than Bienville Parish.

Now I am driving. Those old Bienville roads have acquired new meaning. I know that if I hang a right at the T, I can get to the cemetery that holds my relations from 150 years back, the same people that first helped settle North Louisiana. None of my brothers ever knew about the cemetery, but I do. I even know three ways to get to Minden that my brother Judd did not teach me. On the roads that my family has traveled for over a century, I am just starting to find my way of traveling. That journey, I now understand, is what all my rides with my brothers were really about.

> This descriptive language creates a strong sense of place and establishes a personal tone.

> Graham is the main character in his essay.

> Graham uses sensory details to convey a vivid picture of his experience.

> Graham begins to draw connections between the specific experience and a deeper meaning.

> Graham extends his personal experience into the abstract realm of family, identity, and history.

Student Model

- Explain that the Student Model is a sample. Students' own essays may be longer than this model.
- Have students read the model silently. Point out that Graham has based his narrative not on a specific event, but on an event repeated, with variations, many times—riding the roads in a pickup truck with his brother.
- Have students assess Graham's character. Have them identify details Graham uses to describe himself and to reveal his personality.
- Challenge students to summarize the theme of Graham's essay. What do his rides along the backroads mean to him? What symbolic value did these journeys come to have for him?

Real-World Connection

Professional writers often write reflective compositions. The majority of all poems are examples of reflective writing. Monologues spoken by characters in plays are often reflective in nature.

CUSTOMIZE INSTRUCTION FOR UNIVERSAL ACCESS

For Less Proficient Writers	For English Learners	For Advanced Writers
Have students choose partners to whom to tell the stories they will use as the basis for the essays. Telling their stories orally as a prewriting activity will help students organize their ideas, eliminate irrelevant details and events, and shape the plots of their narratives.	Encourage students to tackle subjects that will not pose difficulties of too many new and unfamiliar words. Students should be able to write effectively even in simple language.	Challenge students to think about and highlight the symbolic value of the people, places, and things in their essays. Students can look at the model to see the symbolic value that the backroads have for Graham.

Drafting

- Go over the organizational model in the textbook with students. This model may not work well for everyone's essay. Encourage students to use the model if it is a natural fit for their essay, and to develop another plan of organization if it is not.

Revising

- If time permits, give students 24 hours to let their drafts rest before they reread them with an eye to revision. A little time away from a piece of writing helps the writer see his or her work with fresh eyes and renewed attention and energy.

- Remind students that the more personal their writing is, the more interesting it will be to their readers. Urge them to look at places where they reveal their thoughts and to make sure that these thoughts are expressed as clearly as possible.

Writing WORKSHOP *continued*

Drafting

Organize your reflection.
Develop a draft that follows a logical organization and places the incident you are describing in a broader context. The organizational format shown at right is an effective way to build a reflective essay.

Begin with a compelling lead.
Reflective writing gives you the opportunity to interest someone in your life. Simple opening sentences can provide just the right amount of information to grab a reader's attention.

> **Organize your essay**
>
> Identify an experience from your life.
> ▼
> Describe thoughts or feelings from the event.
> ▼
> Compare your experiences with other related events.
> ▼
> End with a lesson learned from reflecting on the event.

Examples: Whenever I hear the song "Memory," I burst into laughter.

My sister refuses to wear the color yellow.

Elaborate to make your writing personal. As you draft, include details, such as the thoughts and feelings you remember experiencing during the event. Note sensory images that will make those details more vivid. Refer back to the notes you took during prewriting, and add these thoughts, feelings, and images to your draft.

Revising

Revise to achieve balance. Review your draft to find the connections between your experience and events in the world at large. Use this strategy to create a balance between ideas in your draft:

1. Place a blue star next to sentences that develop your own experiences.

2. Place a red check next to sentences that allude to related outside experiences. If you have too few checks, add more examples.

3. Check that your draft effectively balances reflections on your own experience with thoughts on larger themes.

Model: Revising for Balance

☆ Now I am driving. ☆ Those old Bienville roads have acquired new meaning. ✓ I know that if I hang a right at the T, I can get to the cemetery that holds my relations from 150 years back, the same people that first helped settle North Louisiana. ☆ None of my brothers ever knew about the cemetery, but I do. ☆ I even know three ways to get to Minden that my brother Judd did not teach me. ✓ *On the roads that my family has traveled for over a century, I am just starting to find my way of traveling. . . .*

Graham added information that enlarges upon the specific experiences he describes.

USING TECHNOLOGY IN WRITING

When they reach the revision stage, students working on word processors can use the Word Count command to find out whether their essays meet the required length. If they are about a hundred words over or under the limit, students have satisfied the requirement. If their essays are substantially longer or shorter than the requirement, students can go over the essays again, looking for points that can be eliminated or for arguments that can be discussed more fully.

Revise to vary sentences. Even though your reflective essay is about an event that happened to you, work to avoid beginning every sentence with *I*. Highlight the first word in every sentence in your draft, and vary sentence beginnings to make your writing more interesting.

Example: I remember the door. I remember it was locked. I remember being curious.

The door was locked, and I remember being curious.

Compare the model and nonmodel. What makes the model more effective?

Nonmodel	Model
They are small country roads. They change color and ride when you cross a parish line. They have four-ton limits. They have small bridges. The bridges hop over waters like Bear Creek and Black Lake Bayou.	They are small country roads—the ones that change color and ride when you cross a simple parish line. They have four-ton limits assigned to small bridges that hop over waters like Bear Creek and Black Lake Bayou.

Publishing and Presenting

Use the following technique to share your writing with a wider audience.

Deliver an oral presentation. Read your reflective composition aloud in front of your classmates. After you have finished reading, ask classmates to identify other outside events that would make good points of comparison with the personal event you explore in your composition.

WG Prentice Hall Writing and Grammar Connection: Chapter 4

Read to Write

To see an example of a reflective essay, read "Suspended" by Joy Harjo, page 1049.

Rubric for Self-Assessment

Evaluate your reflective essay using the following criteria and rating scale:

Criteria	Rating Scale				
	Not very				Very
How clearly drawn is the writer as the main character?	1	2	3	4	5
How well are the personal feelings, thoughts, or views of the writer conveyed?	1	2	3	4	5
How effectively are comparisons between specific incidents and broader themes made?	1	2	3	4	5
How well are the insights gained by the writer described?	1	2	3	4	5
How well is the balance between specific incidents and abstract ideas set out?	1	2	3	4	5

Writing Workshop: Reflective Essay ◆ 457

Publishing and Presenting

- Have students discuss how they might revise their essays if they planned to share them with an audience of people other than their classmates. What changes might they have to make?

- Have students try telling their stories from memory rather than reading their essays aloud. Since reflective narratives are autobiographical, students should easily be able to do this without having to memorize what they wrote. Have students discuss the differences between the written and oral versions of the stories. How are they different? Why are they different?

Assessment

- Go over the assessment criteria with the class before they begin the revision stage of the essay. The points in the chart are items students will want to consider and correct as they revise their drafts.

- You may want to have students exchange papers with partners and have partners score one another's essays. If students disagree strongly, partners should debate their reasons for disagreeing.

- Another rubric in an alternative format, can be found on page 11 of **Performance Assessment and Portfolio Management.**

TEST-TAKING TIP

Remind students not to spend too much time on any one stage of the writing process when they take an essay test. Students should not spend more than a few minutes deciding on a topic. They should leave about half the time for writing and the rest for rereading, revising, and proofreading.

Analyze Purpose

- Explain to students that the main purpose of all forms of media is to extend their audience. Makers of television shows want more people to watch; publishers of newspapers want more people to buy and read them; advertisers want to sell their products. All media are produced by companies whose main motivation is to stay in business and to make greater profits. Informing, entertaining, and persuading are secondary purposes.

Analyze Techniques

Discuss the examples of techniques listed in the textbook. Have students give examples of effective uses of each technique.

Listening and Speaking WORKSHOP

Analyzing Media

Every day, most of us are bombarded with media messages, from advertisements to radio talk shows to television news broadcasts. All of these different forms of media are created for specific purposes. The following strategies will help you to analyze the purposes and identify the techniques media makers use to advance their aims.

Analyze Purpose

Most forms of media seek to persuade, inform, or entertain. To identify media purposes, use the following guidelines:

- **Define media types.** Persuasive media seeks to convince you to think or act in a particular way. Informative media explains or describes a topic. Entertainment media creates enjoyment for the audience.

- **Identify uses of language.** Word choice can provide signals about the purpose of a media presentation. For example, persuasive media may contain evaluative terms, informative media may include technical language, and entertainment media may contain emotional language.

- **Consider strategies.** Look for the reasoning behind the media maker's choices. For example, even in news broadcasts, set design and lighting create a specific environment.

Analyze Techniques

As you observe media, evaluate the use of these techniques.

- **Interviews.** Real people help viewers identify with the message of a presentation. Informative media such as newscasts might use interviews with people who have played a role in the story and who can share their personal reactions.

- **Format.** Performers may choose media to heighten dramatic or comedic effect. For example, radio disc jockeys might focus on amusing word plays, while comedians in a theater might use sight gags.

- **Music and sound effects.** The music used in a presentation should help to reinforce the tone. For example, advertisements directed at children may use high-spirited music, while those conveying public safety messages might use somber music.

Activity:
View and Analyze Watch television for a week as an active viewer. For each show you see, note the intended audience, the show's purpose, and the techniques used, and their intended effects. Use an evaluation form like the one shown to aid your analysis.

Evaluation Form for Media Analysis

Name of Media _____
Media Type and Purpose _____
Intended Audience _____

Signal Characteristics:
Word/content choice _____
Tone _____

Reasoning:
Why do you think the media maker made specific choices about structure, content, and style? _____

Techniques:
Interviews _____
Format _____
Music/sound effects _____

Were the techniques used in this presentation effective? Did they advance the purpose you identified above?

CUSTOMIZE INSTRUCTION FOR UNIVERSAL ACCESS

For English Learners

Watching television is a good way to learn a new language. Most news shows include printed text of headlines and other messages. Students can use these printed titles and headlines to improve their vocabularies.

Assessment WORKSHOP

Inferences and Generalizations

The reading sections of some tests often require you to read a passage of fiction and draw inferences and generalizations about the plot, setting, characters, and mood. The following strategies will help you answer such test questions:

- As you read fiction, remember that to infer is to read between the lines, recognizing the implied message.
- Look in the passage for clues about the characters, setting, plot, and mood.
- Significant word choices, patterns of events, and other clues can help you understand the writer's implied message.

Test-Taking Strategies

- Before answering questions, review the passage and highlight the main points.
- Look for descriptive details to help you make inferences about character, setting, plot, and mood.

Sample Test Item

Directions: Read the passage, and then answer the question that follows.

A weak rain drizzled outside the cabin, and Dan sat at the kitchen table, trying to gather courage. The idea of quitting his new job filled him with fear. He thought returning home to Oregon would help. But as the thunder boomed outside, he tried in vain to overcome his worries. He was simply too afraid of failure to quit— even if he disliked his new boss and felt indifferent toward his co-workers.

1. In this passage, Dan's main conflict is with
   A the wilds of Oregon.
   B himself.
   C his new boss.
   D his co-workers.

Answer and Explanation

The correct answer is *B.* This answer describes Dan's internal struggle with fears of failure and future uncertainty if he quits his job. Answer *A* tells where Dan feels at home. *C* and *D* may be reasons to quit but are not his direct conflict.

▶ Practice

Directions: Read the passage, and then answer the questions that follow.

Ellen's plan to garden on the dusty plot of Oklahoma clay didn't surprise anyone. When the rain rotted her tomato sprouts, she simply planted more. When the deer nibbled her corn, she built a strong fence around the garden bed. When the summer skies withheld rain, she lugged bucketfuls of water from a nearby spring. And when the town amateur gardening contest gave out blue ribbons, Ellen won them all.

1. Which of the following most accurately describes Ellen?
   A talented
   B lucky
   C determined
   D strong

2. Which of the following inferences does the passage support?
   A Ellen lives with a large family.
   B Gardening is financially rewarding.
   C Oklahoma clay presents difficulties for gardening.
   D Tomatoes are easy to harvest.

Assessment Workshop ◆ 459

Lesson Objective
To infer and generalize in test situations

Applying Reading Strategies

When students are asked to make an inference, they should review the passage for hints and implications. When they are asked to generalize, they should review the passage to see what its statements have in common.

Test-Taking Skills

- Have students read the sample test item. Ask them to identify Dan's main conflict.
  Answer: Dan's main conflict is the fear that fills him.
- Have students vote for the correct answer.

Practice

Answers

1. The correct answer is *C.* All four qualities describe Ellen accurately, but the main point of each sentence in the passage shows her determination.

2. The correct answer is *C.* There is no mention of Ellen's family or of any financial reward, so *A* and *B* are clearly incorrect. The content of the passage directly contradicts *D.*

TEACHING RESOURCES

The following resources can be used to enrich or extend the instruction on page 459

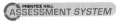 PRENTICE HALL
ASSESSMENT *SYSTEM*

📖 **Workbook**   📄 **Transparencies**

📖 **Skill Book**   💿 **CD-ROM**

Unit Objectives

1. To read selections from American literature written during the period (1850–1914)
2. To apply a variety of reading strategies, particularly interactive reading strategies, appropriate for reading these selections
3. To analyze literary elements
4. To use a variety of strategies to read unfamiliar words and to build vocabulary
5. To learn elements of grammar, usage, and style
6. To use recursive writing processes to write in a variety of forms
7. To develop listening and speaking skills
8. To express and support responses to various types of texts
9. To prepare, organize, and present literary interpretations

Meeting the Objectives

With each selection, you will find instructional materials and portfolio opportunities through which students can meet these objectives. Further, you will find additional practice pages for reading strategies, literary analysis, vocabulary, and grammar in the **Selection Support: Skills Development Workbook** in the **Teaching Resources** box.

Background

Art

Detail of Battle of Cedar Creek, by Julian Scott

The Battle of Cedar Creek (near Middletown, Virginia) was fought in October 1864. While its commander, General Phillip Sheridan, was at a meeting in Washington, the Union army was surprised by a Confederate attack.

• Based on what you see in the painting, speculate about the impression of war this painter intended to create.
  Possible response: The painter focuses on the confusion, panic, and destruction of war rather than on the heroism or fighting.

The Fall of Richmond, Currier & Ives

UNIT 4
Division, Reconciliation, and Expansion (1850–1914)

UNIT FEATURES

Connections

Every unit contains a feature that connects literature to a related topic, such as art, science, or history. In this unit:

Part 2: **Molly Moore: Gulf War Journal, from *A Woman at War*** on p. 553; Part 3: **Larry McMurtry: from *Lonesome Dove*** on p. 627; Part 4: **Anna Quindlen: Cats** on p. 689.

Use the information and questions on the Connections pages to help students enrich their understanding of the selections presented within the unit.

Reading Informational Materials

These selections will help students learn to analyze and evaluate informational texts, such as workplace documents, technical directions, and consumer materials. They will expose students to the organization and features unique to nonnarrative texts.

In this unit, the focus is on Public Documents. **THE EMANCIPATION PROCLAMATION** is on p. 531.

" *If we do not make common cause to save the good old ship of the Union on this voyage, nobody will have a chance to pilot her on another voyage.* "

—Abraham Lincoln, President of the
United States of America,
February 15, 1861

" *I worked night and day for twelve years to prevent the war, but I could not. The North was mad and blind, would not let us govern ourselves, and so the war came. Now it must go on until the last man of this generation falls in his tracks and his children seize his musket and fight our battles.* "

—Jefferson Davis, President of the
Confederate States of America,
July 17, 1864

Division, Reconciliation, and Expansion (1850–1914) ◆ 461

Assessing Student Progress

Listed below are the tools that are available to measure the degree to which students meet the unit objectives.

Informal Assessment

The questions in the Review and Assess sections are a first level of response to the concepts and skills presented within the selections. Students' responses are a brief, informal measure of their grasp of the material. These responses can indicate where further instruction and practice are needed. Then follow up with the practice pages in the **Selection Support: Skills Development Workbook.**

Formal Assessment

The **Formal Assessment** booklet contains Selection Tests and Unit Tests.

- Selection Tests measure comprehension and skills acquisition for each selection or group of selections.
- Each Unit Test provides students with thirty multiple-choice questions and five essay questions designed to assess students' knowledge of the literature and skills taught in the unit.

The **Open-Book Tests** ask students to demonstrate their ability to synthesize and communicate information from selections or groups of selections.

To assess student writing, you will find rubrics and scoring models in the **Performance Assessment and Portfolio Management** booklet. In this booklet you will also find scoring rubrics for listening and speaking activities.

Alternative Assessment

The **Extension Activities** booklet contains writing activities, listening and speaking activities, and research and technology activities that are appropriate for students with different ability levels. You may also use these activities as an alternative measurement of students' growth.

ASSESSMENT RESOURCES

Selection Assessment

📖 **Selection Support:** Skills Development Workbook

📖 **Formal Assessment,**

📖 **Open Book Tests**

📖 **Performance Assessment and Portfolio Management**

📖 **Extension Activities**

Using the Timeline

The Timeline can serve a number of instructional purposes, as follows:

Getting an Overview

Use the Timeline to help students get a quick overview of themes and events of the period. This approach will benefit all students but may be especially helpful for Visual/Spatial Learners, English Learners, and Less Proficient Readers. (For strategies in using the Timeline as an overview, see the bottom of this page.)

Thinking Critically

Questions are provided on the facing page. Use these questions to have students review the events, discuss their significance, and examine the *so what* behind the *what happened*.

Connecting to Selections

Have students refer back to the Timeline when they begin to read individual selections. By consulting the Timeline regularly, they will gain a better sense of the period's chronology. In addition, they will appreciate what was occurring in the world that gave rise to these works of literature.

Projects

Students can use the Timeline as a launching pad for projects like these:

- **Cause-and-Effect Connections** Have students scan the Timeline and speculate about cause-and-effect connections among events. They may want to diagram these links using the Cause-and-Effect Organizer, p. 91 in **Writing Models and Graphic Organizers on Transparencies**.

- **Additional Illustrations** Have students search for additional illustrations for items in the Timeline. They can find such illustrations in biographies of the figures mentioned in the Timeline, encyclopedias, books on American history, and books on the history of technology. Students should be prepared to justify each new illustration they suggest.

462

Timeline 1850–1914

1850   1860   1870

American Events

- **1855** Walt Whitman publishes first edition of *Leaves of Grass*.
- **1855** *My Bondage and My Freedom*, Frederick Douglass's second autobiography, makes its appearance. ▼
- **1858** Lincoln-Douglas debates help make Abraham Lincoln a national figure.
- **1859** John Brown, an abolitionist, leads a raid on federal arsenal at Harpers Ferry, Virginia; he is hanged for treason.

- **1860** Republican Abraham Lincoln is elected United States president.
- **1860** South Carolina secedes from the Union.
- **1861** Civil War begins in April with firing on Fort Sumter.
- **1863** Lincoln issues the Emancipation Proclamation.
- **1865** General Robert E. Lee surrenders to General Ulysses S. Grant at Appomattox. ▼

- **1876** Mark Twain publishes *The Adventures of Tom Sawyer*. ▲
- **1876** Baseball's National League founded.
- **1877** The Compromise of 1877 ends military occupation of the South.
- **1877** Thomas Edison patents the phonograph.

World Events

- **1857** France: Gustave Flaubert completes *Madame Bovary*, a classic novel of realism.
- **1859** England: Charles Dickens adds to his fame with *A Tale of Two Cities*.
- **1859** England: Charles Darwin introduces theory of evolution in *The Origin of Species*.

- **1862** France: Louis Pasteur proposes modern germ theory of disease.
- **1865** England: Lewis Carroll completes *Alice's Adventures in Wonderland*.
- **1865** Germany: Karl Benz builds first automobile powered by the internal-combustion engine.

- **1869** Russia: Leo Tolstoy publishes *War and Peace*.
- **1874** France: Claude Monet gathers Impressionist painters for first exhibition.
- **1877** England: First tennis championship held at Wimbledon.

462 ◆ *Division, Reconciliation, and Expansion (1850–1914)*

✸ ENRICHMENT: Getting an Overview of the Period

Introduction	Key Events
To give students an overview of the period, indicate the span of dates in the title of the Timeline. Next, point out that the Timeline is divided into American Events (on top) and World Events (on bottom). Have students scan the Timeline, looking both at the American Events and the World Events. Finally, point out that the events in the Timeline often represent beginnings, turning points, and endings.	Have students identify key events related to division, reconciliation, and expansion. **Possible responses:** division—South Carolina secedes from the Union (1860), Civil War begins (1861); reconciliation—Compromise of 1877 ends military occupation of the South (1877); expansion—last major battle between U.S. troops and Native Americans (1890), Henry Ford build his first Model T (1908).

American and World Events

- **1883** Railroads adopt standard time zones.
- **1883** The Brooklyn Bridge is opened.
- **1884** Mark Twain publishes *The Adventures of Huckleberry Finn.*

- **1886** Statue of Liberty dedicated in New York Harbor. ▲
- **1888** Great mid-March blizzard in eastern United States piles 30-foot drifts in New York's Herald Square.

- **1885** French scientist Louis Pasteur administers the first successful rabies vaccination. ▶
- **1886** Russia: Leo Tolstoy completes *The Death of Ivan Ilyich.*

- **1890** Last major battle between U.S. troops and Native Americans fought at Wounded Knee, South Dakota.
- **1895** Stephen Crane publishes *The Red Badge of Courage.*
- **1895** First professional football game played in Latrobe, Pennsylvania.
- **1896** *The Country of the Pointed Firs*, Sarah Orne Jewett's masterpiece, appears.

- **1891** England: Thomas Hardy publishes *Tess of the D'Urbervilles.*
- **1894** Sino-Japanese War breaks out; Japanese army easily defeats Chinese.
- **1895** Germany: Wilhelm Roentgen discovers X-rays.
- **1898** France: Pierre and Marie Curie discover radium and polonium.

- **1903** Jack London publishes *The Call of the Wild.*

- **1903** Wright Brothers stay aloft for 852 feet in their airplane at Kitty Hawk, North Carolina. ▲
- **1908** Henry Ford builds his first Model T. ▼

- **1901** Italy: First transatlantic radio telegraphic message is achieved by Marconi.
- **1903** Spain: Pablo Picasso paints *The Old Guitarist.*
- **1904** Russo-Japanese War begins.
- **1905** Germany: Albert Einstein proposes his relativity theory.

Introduction ◆ 463

Continued from right column

(b) Possible response: Because of these developments, America is a land of people on the move.

▶**Critical Viewing**

1. What does the portrait of Frederick Douglass suggest about the writer's character? Explain. **[Analyze]**
   Possible response: Douglass appears confident and proud in the portrait.

2. What details in the picture of the Statue of Liberty (1886) suggest that its dedication was a festive occasion? **[Analyze]**
   Answer: The sky seems to be filled with fireworks in honor of the occasion, and there are many ships in the harbor.

3. Which has more in common with its modern replacement, the first plane (1903) or the first mass-produced car (1908)? **[Compare and Contrast]**
   Possible response: The car, which has many recognizable features.

Analyzing the Timeline

1. **(a)** Name two American events during the decade 1850–1860 that relate to the conflict over slavery. **(b)** Explain how these events might have set the stage for the Civil War. **[Speculate]**
   Answer: **(a)** In 1855, Frederick Douglass's second autobiography appears; in 1859, John Brown led his raid on Harper's Ferry. **(b)** Possible response: Douglass's revelations about slavery may have encouraged abolitionists. John Brown's raid may have strengthened the resolve of the South to defend slavery.

2. **(a)** What key Civil War event occurred in 1863? **(b)** What does this event suggest about the course of the war? **[Infer]**
   Answer: **(a)** Lincoln issued the Emancipation Proclamation. **(b)** Possible response: It suggests that freeing the slaves had become a priority for the Union.

3. **(a)** Looking at both American and World Events, name two key sporting events that occurred during the decade 1870–1880. **(b)** What is the importance of these events for us today? **[Relate]**
   Answer: **(a)** In 1876, baseball's National League was founded, and in 1877, the first tennis championship was held at Wimbledon. **(b)** Baseball and the National League are still going strong, and tennis championships are still held at Wimbledon.

4. **(a)** What important battle was fought by in America in 1890? **(b)** In what way did this battle indicate that the frontier period was ending? **[Interpret]**
   Answer: **(a)** The last major battle between U.S. troops and Native Americans. **(b)** Native Americans were no longer in a position to oppose settlers, as they had during the period of the expanding frontier.

5. **(a)** Name two developments in transportation that occurred during the early 1900s. **(b)** What impact did these developments have? **[Connect]**
   Answer: **(a)** In 1903, first flight, brothers', and in 1908, first Model T.

continued

463

- In "An Episode of War" by Stephen Crane, p. 476, students will encounter a realistic view of the Civil War.

- The spirituals "Swing Low, Sweet Chariot," p. 488, and "Go Down, Moses," p. 490, will help students better understand the situation and aspirations of enslaved African Americans.

- In the excerpt from *My Bondage and My Freedom*, p. 497, students will learn about slavery from the first-person account of Frederick Douglass.

▶Critical Viewing

Possible response: A sixteen-year-old might become very homesick and might be shocked by the realities of wartime life.

Division, Reconciliation, and Expansion
(1850–1914)

The years between 1850 and 1914 witnessed a transformation of the United States. During those years, America changed from a decentralized, mostly agricultural nation to the modern industrial nation that we know today. This transformation began in the period leading up to the Civil War. In that war, Americans took up arms against one another to determine which should prevail: North or South? the federal Union or states' rights? freedom or slavery? The North won, the Union held, and slavery was abolished, but at a devastating cost to the nation.

Historical Background

Prelude to War By the mid-nineteenth century, it was evident that the North and the South had developed along very different lines. In the North, commerce, was king; in the South, cotton ruled. The Industrial Revolution and cheap transportation had helped turn northern towns and cities into centers of bustling activity. Education, banking, science, and reform movements—all were topics of interest and concern. Immigration, too, was changing the face of the North. A rising tide of Irish and German immigrants, among others, came seeking new lives in the United States. Most of these newcomers landed at seaports between Boston and Baltimore and settled in the northern states.

The South, in contrast, was a slower-paced region of plantations and small farms. There were cities, to be sure, but the area was defined by its cotton plantations, large and small. Sugar, rice, and tobacco were also important crops. The march of technological progress, with its hotly debated social issues and problems, had little impact on the prewar South. One issue, however, made an indelible impression: slavery. The South believed its lifeblood depended on the institution of slavery.

Disagreements between North and South over slavery were nothing new, but the controversy was rekindled in 1850 by the passage of the Fugitive Slave Act. It required all citizens—of free states as well as slave states—to help catch runaway slaves. Southerners saw the law as just; Northerners considered it an outrage.

The expansion of slavery into the West was hotly contested. In 1854, when the Kansas-Nebraska Act opened up a vast area of

▼ **Critical Viewing**
This picture shows a young Confederate soldier. Most of the soldiers in both armies were between the ages of 18 and 21. Some were even younger. What problems do you think a 16-year-old Union or Confederate soldier might have faced? **[Relate]**

☀ ENRICHMENT: Social Studies

The North and the South

The northern and southern United States had developed along different economic lines. In the North, commerce was king. The Industrial Revolution and cheap transportation had caused explosive urban growth. Immigration, too, was changing the face of the North. A rising tide of Irish and German immigrants, among others, were seeking new lives in northern cities.

The South was a slower-paced region of plantations and small farms. There were cities, but the area was most truly defined by its cotton plantations. Sugar, rice, and tobacco were also important crops. Technological progress, with its social issues and problems, had little impact on the prewar South.

Have students consider what these differences suggest about the outcome of a war between these regions. Guide students to recognize that the North, with its greater population and more developed industry, would have an advantage in a war.

previously free western land to slavery, the argument became a fight. "We will engage in competition for the virgin soil of Kansas," a senator from New York insisted. The "competition" turned Kansas into a bloody battleground.

Just as it dominated politics and preoccupied the nation, the controversy over slavery influenced the literature of the day, and in one classic case, literature fueled the controversy. Harriet Beecher Stowe's novel *Uncle Tom's Cabin*, published in 1852, vividly depicted the cruelty of slavery. The book became a powerful antislavery weapon, selling more than 300,000 copies within a year. Its impact was such that, within three years, no fewer than thirty southern novels came out attempting to counter its influence.

The deep national division intensified in 1859 when a group of antislavery extremists raided a federal arsenal at Harpers Ferry, West Virginia. Led by John Brown, the group had intended to provoke an armed slave revolt. The attempt failed and Brown was executed for treason, but his death only fed the controversy, which now threatened to escalate out of control.

The Union Is Dissolved The conflict between North and South came to a head when Abraham Lincoln was elected in 1860. Lincoln represented the newly formed Republican party, which had dedicated itself to halting the spread of slavery. South Carolina had threatened to secede if Lincoln was elected, and in December it did so. Five states followed South Carolina out of the Union. In February 1861, the secessionist states established the Confederate States of America.

Fighting began on April 12, 1861, when Confederate artillery fired on Union troops holding Fort Sumter, in Charleston Harbor. Many on both sides anticipated a short war ending in victory. No one could know what lay ahead: the carnage of Antietam, where more than 26,000 men fell in a single day; the deprivation of the siege of Vicksburg, where people survived by eating dogs and rats; the wholesale destruction of Georgia, when Union general William T. Sherman's troops marched to the sea. In fact, the devastating war would last four long years.

By the time Confederate general Robert E. Lee surrendered to Union general Ulysses S. Grant in the spring of 1865, nearly 620,000 soldiers on both sides had lost their lives. About 500,000 had been wounded. The South lay in ruins, its cities razed, its farms and plantations destroyed.

Lincoln guided the nation through the worst crisis in its history. He did not, however, have the chance to reconstruct the Union. Just days after Lee's surrender, Lincoln was assassinated. He died on April 15, 1865. The nation, war-torn and weary, would have to face the daunting tasks of reconciliation and reconstruction without him.

▲ **Critical Viewing** Robert E. Lee (left) and Ulysses S. Grant (right) were the leaders of the Confederate and Union armies, respectively. What can you infer about their different personalities and backgrounds by comparing and contrasting these photographs? Explain. **[Compare and Contrast]**

Background
Social Studies
The Civil War was the first American war in which black troops fought in large numbers. By the end of the war, there were some 180,000 black soldiers in more than a hundred Union regiments. On the Confederate side, both slaves and free blacks accompanied the army as cooks, teamsters, and laborers.

Background
Science
The South desperately needed a way to break the Union blockade of its ports. One method it tried was the ironclad ship. Confederates covered the *Merrimack*, an abandoned Union ship, with iron plates 4 inches thick and sent it into battle. On March 8, 1862, the *Merrimack* sank one Union ship, drove another aground, and forced a third to surrender. Cannonballs bounced harmlessly off the *Merrimack's* metal skin.

The Union countered with its own ironclads. One of these, the *Monitor*, struck back at the *Merrimack* in the waters off Hampton Roads, Virginia. In the end, neither ship seriously damaged the other, and both withdrew. Yet ironclad ships had changed naval warfare forever. Both sides rushed to build more of them. The South, however, never mounted a serious attack against the Union navy, and the Union blockade held.

▶**Critical Viewing**
Possible response: Lee's upright posture suggests that he is more formal than Grant, who leans informally against a tree. Also, Lee looks more aristocratic than Grant.

CUSTOMIZE INSTRUCTION FOR UNIVERSAL ACCESS

For Less Proficient Readers	For English Learners	For Advanced Readers
Have students preview the heads and subheads on pp. 464–471. Then, have them make connections between the "Historical Background" subheads and those under "Literature of the Period." For example, "The Union Is Dissolved" (p. 465) suggests the war that gave rise to "Wartime Voices" (p. 468).	Have students study the illustrations on pp. 464–471 to gain a better understanding of the themes of this period. Then, have them read the subheads under "Literature of the Period." Encourage them to draw connections between the illustrations and the literary themes.	Instruct these students to read pp. 464–471 independently, noting key ways in which national identity changed during those years. Then, have students discuss ways they might expect to find those changes expressed in the literature of the period.

Underscore that Abraham Lincoln was president during one of the most difficult periods of American history, and is widely regarded as one of the United States' greatest presidents. Then, ask the following questions.

1. In what way are these two view points different?
   Answer: Sandburg seems more enthusiastic about the genius and skill of Lincoln, while Oates seems more focused on Lincoln's problems.

2. In what way are these views similar?
   Answer: Both historians agree that Lincoln was a great and heroic man.

3. Can you imagine scholars having this argument about the legacy of a contemporary leader? Explain.
   Possible response: Most students will find it difficult to imagine any scholar arguing that a contemporary leader is as flawless and towering a figure as Sandburg's Lincoln. We know too much about the personal lives of our leaders today to see them in those terms.

Background

The Great Plains

People had to be strong to survive the hardships of life on the Great Plains. With few stores, women had to make clothing, quilts, soap, candles, and other goods by hand. They also had to cook and preserve all the food needed through the long winter.

Women had many other duties. They educated the children. With no doctors nearby, they treated the sick and injured. Women also helped with the planting and harvesting. When needed, they helped build sod houses.

Point /Counterpoint

Abraham Lincoln—Legendary Hero or "Flawed and Complex Man"

Was Abraham Lincoln a legendary hero, someone to be compared with such historic figures as Lao-tse or Caesar, or was he a flawed human being? Two biographers disagree on the answer to this question.

Legendary Hero "Perhaps no human clay pot has held more laughter and tears.

"The facts and myths of his life are to be an American possession, shared widely over the world, for thousands of years, as the tradition of Knute or Alfred, Lao-tse or Diogenes, Pericles or Caesar, are kept. This because he was not only a genius in the science of neighborly human relationships and an artist in the personal handling of life from day to day, but a strange friend and a friendly stranger to all forms of life that he met."

—Carl Sandburg,
A Lincoln Preface

Flawed and Complex Man "The historical Lincoln, as I have tried to approximate him, was a flawed and complex man who had the gift of vision that let him see things few others ever see. When I say that he was flawed, I am not profaning his memory, as many of my correspondents have accused me of doing. On the contrary, the historical Lincoln comes out more heroic than the immortal Man of the People, because we see him overcoming his deficiencies and self-doubts, often against tremendous odds."

—Stephen B. Oates,
Abraham Lincoln: The Man Behind the Myths

An Expanding America If conflict characterized the Civil War years, change—on an astonishing scale—characterized the period that followed. During the fifty-year period following the war, physical expansion and industrialization transformed the American landscape, economy, society, and identity.

The Homestead Act of 1862 promised 160 acres to anyone who would live on the land for a certain period and make minimal improvements to it. This shifted the westward movement into high gear. Half a million farmers, including tens of thousands of emancipated African Americans, staked claims on the Great Plains. Miners went west by the thousands, lured by the prospect of striking it rich in gold. Still others moved west to become cattle ranchers. Westward expansion was boosted by completion of the first transcontinental railroad in 1869. As the national railroad system grew, the covered wagon—symbol of the American pioneer—was replaced by the train as the principal means of transportation.

The Disappearing Frontier By 1890, the frontier as Americans had known it for centuries had ceased to exist. The steady influx of settlers, the burgeoning railroads, the growth of mining and cattle ranching—all had combined to transform the West. Gone were the great herds of buffalo. Gone was the expanse of open range. In its place was an enormous patchwork of

466 ◆ *Division, Reconciliation, and Expansion (1850–1914)*

✹ ENRICHMENT: Music Connection

Songs of the Civil War

Play for students renditions of the spirituals "Swing Low, Sweet Chariot" and "Go Down, Moses," from **Listening to Literature**: Audiocassette Side 16; CD 10.

Explain to students that spirituals were created among groups of enslaved African Americans, and that singers customarily embellish on the word and melody of spirituals. Consequently, each rendition of "Swing Low, Sweet Chariot" and "Go Down, Moses" is unique.

Ask students how all three songs throw new light on the Civil War.

Possible response: Students may respond that the spirituals reveal the deep feeling with which African Americans yearned for freedom, and that Foster's song discloses the personal sadness caused by wartime separations.

plowed fields and grazing lands, separated by miles of barbed wire fencing.

Gone, too, were the Indian nations, many of which had depended on the buffalo for survival. By 1890, virtually all the Native Americans in the West had been forced from their land. Decades of fierce and bloody resistance had ultimately proved futile. "I am tired of fighting," Chief Joseph of the Nez Percé reportedly said after being hunted down by the United States Army in 1877. Like others before them, Chief Joseph and his people were sent to live in Indian Territory, in what is now Oklahoma. However, even Indian Territory, which Congress had set aside in 1834, was not safe from white encroachment. In 1889, unassigned land in Indian Territory was opened up to settlers.

The frontier may have disappeared, but its legacy lived on in a rich western folk tradition. Larger-than-life folk heros like Pecos Bill were celebrated in tall tales and legends. The frontier survived, too, in the songs of sod busters, railroad workers, cowpokes, and miners.

A Changing American Society With the introduction of electricity in the 1880s, the second Industrial Revolution began in earnest. Electricity replaced steam power in many manufacturing industries. The now-familiar trappings of modern life began to make their appearance: electric lights, telephones, automobiles, motion pictures, and phonographs. The mass production of consumer goods sparked the rise of an important new medium: advertising. Skyscrapers, department stores, and mass transportation became part of city life—as did noise, traffic jams, air pollution, crime, and slums.

The country's industrial and urban growth was also fueled by immigration. In 1880, the population of the United States was just over 50 million. By the turn of the century, it was just under 76 million. A significant portion of this increase was due to the more than 9 million immigrants who came to the country during this twenty-year period. Most of the newcomers settled in cities. In the same period, millions of Americans left farms and small towns and moved to the cities to seek work. This influx swelled urban populations and provided an inexhaustible supply of cheap labor for industry.

The industrial boom of the late nineteenth century created new extremes of wealth and poverty. The wages of industrial workers were so low that a single worker, or even two, often could not support a family. Child labor became the norm among the poor working class. Immigrant families often lived in small, dark, unventilated apartments with no toilets. In these conditions, disease was rampant.

▲ **Critical Viewing**
Some African Americans traveled to the West. In this picture, the Shores family poses in front of their Nebraska sod house. What opportunities might the West have offered African Americans that the East did not? **[Analyze a Situation]**

Introduction ◆ 467

Background
Land Rush

As farmers spread across the Plains, fewer areas remained to be settled. The last major land rush took place in 1889, in Oklahoma. Late in April, as many as 100,000 land seekers waited at the Oklahoma border. The government had announced that farmers could claim free homesteads in Oklahoma starting at noon on April 22. As the "boomers" charged in, they found to their surprise that others were already there. "Sooners" had sneaked in and staked out much of the best land.

The 1890 census reported that the United States no longer had a frontier. For 100 years, the frontier had absorbed immigrants, adventurers, and city folks. Now the frontier was closed.

▶**Critical Viewing**

Possible response: As the picture suggests, the West offered African Americans the hope of owning their own house and land.

Literature of the Period

• Students will find alternative views of the expansion of the United States and the closing of the frontier in Miriam Davis Colt's "Heading West," p. 596, and Chief Joseph's "I Will Fight No More Forever," p. 602.

• Both "The Story of an Hour," by Kate Chopin, p. 632, and "A Wagner Matinée," by Willa Cather, p. 674, have themes related to the changes sweeping American society in this period.

Historical Background
Comprehension Check

1. What major transformation did America undergo in the years between 1850 and 1914?
Answer: It changed from a mostly agricultural nation to the urban, industrial nation that we know.

2. In what way did the Civil War surprise both sides?
Answer: It was longer and more costly than either side anticipated.

3. What three factors combined to transform the West in the years after the Civil War?
Answer: The influx of settlers, the burgeoning railroads, and the growth of mining and cattle ranching transformed the West.

continued

Historical Background continued

4. Why did Mark Twain call the late 1800s "The Gilded Age"?

Answer: A few powerful men displayed their wealth, but underneath this veneer, people were in need.

Critical Thinking

1. Why was literature such an important part of the conflict? **[Support]**
Possible response: Books such as Douglass's autobiography and Stowe's *Uncle Tom's Cabin* fueled antislavery sentiment and

widened national division.

2. If America had been a smaller country, without a frontier, how might its history have been different? **[Speculate]**
Possible response: It might have been urbanized more quickly, but it might not have attracted as many immigrants.

3. What were drawbacks to America's industrialization and expansion? **[Analyze]**
Possible response: Drawbacks included mistreatment of Native Americans and poverty among African Americans and immigrants.

Critical Viewing

Answer: **(a)** Among the most prosperous years were 1872, 1881, 1886, 1890, 1891, and 1900. **(b)** Severe depression struck in 1865, 1876–1878, 1884, 1893, and 1896.

Background

The Civil War

Perhaps surprisingly, Lincoln's two most able commanders—Ulysses S. Grant and William T. Sherman—produced memoirs that are still regarded as models of their kind. In fact, the quality of the writing done by high-ranking officers on both sides is remarkable.

A great many patriotic songs were written and sung during the war. Among the most popular ones in the North were "The Battle Cry of Freedom" and "Tenting Tonight on the Old Campground." The most famous Union song of all is probably Julia Ward Howe's stirring "The Battle Hymn of the Republic." Among southerners, "The Bonnie Blue Flag" and "The Yellow Rose of Texas" were favorites, as was the well-known "Dixie."

Meanwhile, a relative handful of men—the owners of big industrial corporations—made fortunes and lived like royalty. Their ostentatious displays of wealth led Mark Twain to dub this period "The Gilded Age," implying a thin veneer of glitter over something of poor quality.

Indeed, just below the surface of the nation's prosperity, discontentment grew. Women, African Americans, and workers agitated for changes in their social, economic, and political status: Women still did not have the vote; most African Americans, despite emancipation, were hardly better off in 1914 than they had been in 1850; labor reform was desperately needed. Bitter struggles erupted between emerging workers' unions and management.

Literature of the Period

Oh, Freedom! Of the blacks who remained in slavery in the 1850s, a significant number worked on cotton plantations. On these plantations and elsewhere, the slaves developed a unique style of music, the black spiritual. Spirituals fused traditional African music with such sources as the Bible, Protestant hymns, and popular music of the day. To enslaved African Americans, spirituals were—in addition to moving expressions of faith—work songs, war songs, laments, lullabies, and funeral dirges.

Not all of the black voices of the period surfaced in spirituals. One of the great black abolitionist leaders was Frederick Douglass. Born into slavery in Maryland, Douglass escaped as a young man and settled in the North, where he became a persuasive orator against slavery. In 1845, he published the first version of *Narrative of the Life of Frederick Douglass*, his eloquent autobiography that was also an indictment of slavery.

Wartime Voices Thousands of diaries, letters, journals, and speeches were produced during the war, providing a richly detailed and moving record of what Americans—from the lowliest private to General Lee himself—experienced. The lengthy diary of Mary Chesnut, the wife of a high-ranking Confederate officer, is a notable example of the extraordinary literary output of the Civil War years.

One of the greatest masters of the language at mid-century was President Lincoln. His speeches and letters are models of clarity and eloquence. His

▲ **Critical Viewing** The ups and downs of the economy, known as business cycles, were felt more sharply as the nation industrialized and more people worked for wages. **(a)** Which years were the most prosperous? **(b)** In which years did severe depression strike? **[Read a Graph]**

✸ ENRICHMENT: Literature Connection

Whitman in the Civil War

Walt Whitman was a northern poet who wrote movingly about the war. Whitman's younger brother George had enlisted in the Union army. When George was wounded at the Battle of Fredericksburg, Whitman went to Virginia to care for him. He remained in Washington, D.C., for the rest of the war, working as a volunteer in military hospitals. Out of this experience came such masterpieces as "Cavalry Crossing a Ford," "By the Bivouac's Fitful Flame," and "Beat! Beat! Drums!"

Upon the assassination of Lincoln, Whitman wrote "O Captain! My Captain" and the elegy "When Lilacs Last in the Dooryard Bloom'd."

Ask students how Whitman, a noncombatant, could have written so vividly about Civil War scenes. **Possible response:** The poet's contact with wounded soldiers may have given him a strong sense of what the war was like.

Gettysburg Address, a mere ten sentences in length, has become a classic expression of the meaning of American democracy.

Frontier Voices As America expanded westward, so, too, did America's literature. During this period, a number of writers represented the Midwest and the Far West for the first time. Some, like Bret Harte and Willa Cather, were born in the East or the South but later moved west. As a young man, Harte moved from New York to California. Cather moved from Virginia to Nebraska as a child. Mark Twain, one of the greatest writers in all of American literature, grew up in Hannibal, Missouri, but traveled widely, settling in a Nevada mining town during the Civil War. Twain drew on the colorful language and outsized sensibility of the West for his first short story, "The Notorious Jumping Frog of Calaveras County."

Not all the frontier voices were those of European settlers. Mexican Americans living in the Southwest had their own legends and tales. They also had songs, such as "The Legend of Gregorio Cortez," that can take their place beside such famous western ballads as "The Streets of Laredo." Also, few speeches in American history have been as eloquent as that given by Chief Joseph of the Nez Percé when accepting the terms of surrender from federal troops in 1877.

A Living Tradition

N. Scott Momaday and the Indian Oral Tradition

In an essay entitled "On Indian-White Relations: A Point of View," N. Scott Momaday, the Pulitzer Prize-winning author of Kiowa ancestry, responds to the beauty of the Indian oral tradition and of Indian oratory. The speech he cites was spoken by Satanta, a nineteenth-century Kiowa chief, but Momaday's observations might apply equally well to the famous speech by Chief Joseph on p. 602.

> The American Indian has a highly developed oral tradition. . . . One who has only an oral tradition thinks of language in this way: my words exist at the level of my voice. If I do not speak with care, my words are wasted. If I do not listen with care, my words are lost. If I do not remember carefully, the very purpose of words is frustrated. . . . [Momaday goes on to compare the elaborateness of a written executive order from the President, dated 1968, with the directness of the following speech by Satanta, who expresses his unwillingness to settle on a reservation.]

> I have heard that you intend to settle us on a reservation near the mountains. I don't want to settle. I love to roam over the prairies. There I feel free and happy, but when we settle down we grow pale and die. I have laid aside my lance, bow, and shield, and yet I feel safe in your presence. I have told the truth. I have no little lies hid about me, but I don't know how it is with the commissioners. Are they as clear as I am?

> [Satanta's speech] is in the plain style, a style that preserves, in its way, the power and beauty of language.

Background

Mexican *Cuentos*

On the southwestern frontier during this period, immigrants from Mexico developed a rich tradition of folklore. The tales and legends—or *cuentos*—of the Mexican-American Southwest include both stories with complex religious and social morals and fantasies filled with magic and the supernatural. This folk culture had its roots in the Old World, but the tales had developed their own flavor in the physical and social landscape of Mexico and the Southwest. Surviving texts, such as "The Legend of Gregorio Cortez," can be read today, but on the frontier they were spoken aloud and performed. Suggest that students try to imagine the frontier and the people who lived there as they read these selections.

Literature of the Period

Comprehension Check

1. What sources provide a detailed record of the Civil War from the perspective of those who experienced it?
   Answer: Thousands of diaries, letters, journals, and speeches provide such a record.

2. What are two qualities that make Lincoln's speeches and letters so memorable?
   Answer: They are models of clarity and eloquence.

3. Which region of the country most influenced Mark Twain's colorful language and use of humorous exaggeration?
   Answer: The West influenced Twain in this manner.

4. **(a)** In literature, what is Realism? **(b)** What event turned American writers toward Realism?
   Answer: **(a)** Writers in the Realist movement strove to describe the lives of ordinary people in an honest, objective way. **(b)** The Civil War turned writers toward Realism.

5. **(a)** Which literary movement was an offshoot of Realism? **(b)** What did writers in this new movement attempt to do?
   Answer: **(a)** Naturalism was an offshoot of Realism. **(b)** Writers in this new movement showed how forces such as nature, heredity, and fate shaped individuals.

Critical Viewing

Answer: **(a)** The Chisolm Trail ended in Abilene; the Goodnight-Loving Trail ended in Cheyenne. **(b)** Cattle trails tend to end at prominent railroad stations, so that cattle could be easily transported. Mining centers are often, but not always, close to railroad lines. This would make it easier to transport ore.

Realism and Naturalism The harsh reality of frontier life, coupled with artists' reactions to the Civil War—in fiction like Ambrose Bierce's "Incident at Owl Creek Bridge" and Stephen Crane's *The Red Badge of Courage*, for example—gave rise to a new movement in American literature called Realism. Realism in literature began after the Civil War. Although the outcome of the war had given the nation a hard-won sense of unity, the enormous cost in human life had shattered the nation's idealism. Young writers turned away from the Romanticism that was popular before the war. Instead, writers began to focus on portraying "real life" as ordinary people lived it and attempted to show characters and events in an honest, objective, almost factual way. Willa Cather, for example, was a Realist noted for her unflinching portrayal of the loneliness and cultural isolation of life on the prairie. In "A Wagner Matinée," she contrasts this isolation with the cultural richness of an eastern city.

Edith Wharton wrote fiction in the Realist vein, not about Western frontier life but about the Eastern high society into which she had been born. In *The House of Mirth* (1905), for example, she wrote about conflicts between the newly rich and the old aristocracy and about how social customs can prevent individuals from fulfilling themselves.

An important literary offshoot of Realism was Naturalism. Naturalist writers also depicted real people in real situations, but they believed that forces larger than the individual—nature, fate, heredity—shaped individual

Opening the West
+—+ Railroads ⚒ Mining centers
—— Cattle trails
0 ___ 250 ___ 500 Miles
0 __ 100 __ 500 Kilometers

◀ **Critical Viewing** Transportation by rail, mining, and cattle grazing helped open the Great Plains for settlement, as shown on this map. (a) Which cattle trail ended in Abilene? In Cheyenne? (b) What relationship do you see between railroads and cattle trails? Between railroads and mining centers? **[Read a Map]**

470 ◆ *Division, Reconciliation, and Expansion (1850–1914)*

✸ **ENRICHMENT: Literature Connection**

Naturalism Around the World

Naturalism flourished in Europe during the late nineteenth and early twentieth centuries. In fact, scholars point to France as the birthplace of the movement. The writer Emile Zola was its leading practitioner. His approach to literature, was similar to a scientist's approach to an experiment. Characters should be subjected to tests, Zola suggested, and the author should record their reactions objectively.

Overall, naturalism drew on advances in the world of science. Scientific principles were imported into literature, and writers created characters whose lives were shaped and actions dictated by powerful forces—heredity and nature, but also social and economic pressure—entirely beyond their control. Major American Naturalist authors included Jack London, Stephen Crane, Frank Norris, and Theodore Dreiser.

Art in the Historical Context

The Ashcan School and Realism in Painting

At the beginning of the twentieth century, a group of artists working in Philadelphia and New York developed a Realist vision in their work. These painters realized that America was becoming increasingly urban, and they wanted to depict this new urban reality. Some critics insultingly called them the Ashcan School (*ashcan* means "garbage can"). This name has endured, but it is no longer considered an insult.

One prominent member of this movement was John Sloan (1871–1951). Sloan said that he saw a city as a "vast stage set where all sorts of lively business was in progress." His painting *Six O'Clock* (c. 1912) shows the "lively business" of a New York City rush hour.

▶ **Make an Inference** What qualities of urban life does Sloan capture?

Six O' Clock, John Sloan, Phillips Collection, Washington, D.C.

destiny. Jack London, for example, set much of his fiction in Alaska, where the environment was cruel and unforgiving. The theme of human endurance in the face of overwhelming natural forces pervades his fiction, including the short story "To Build a Fire."

If the reality these writers depicted seemed always to be a harsh one, it was because hardship influenced their artistic vision. It was a vision rooted in war, in the frontier, and, increasingly, in America's growing cities.

Literature of Discontent The social ills that grew out of industrialization came under the sharp eye and pen of many talented writers of the day. Kate Chopin's writing, for example, explored women's desire for equality and independence. The Naturalists saw industrialization as a force against which individuals were powerless.

In 1897, one of the finest of all volumes of American poems appeared, Edwin Arlington Robinson's *The Children of the Night*. This volume contains unsparing and unforgettable psychological portraits of a variety of small-town characters. Eighteen years later, *Spoon River Anthology* by Edgar Lee Masters presented a disturbingly candid portrait of small-town life in the form of epitaphs spoken by the dead themselves.

By 1914, America had grown up, and in a sense, American literature had, too. The Civil War, the closing of the frontier, and industrialization had brought about a loss of innocence, a shift from idealism to pragmatism in the American character. In their rejection of Romanticism and their embrace of Realism, American writers reflected this change.

Critical Thinking continued

Possible response: The expanding frontier attracted people of adventurous spirit, no matter where they were born. Also, people drawn to the West from elsewhere may have had a special love for the region that inspired them to write about it.

3. In what ways did literary movements such as Realism and Naturalism suggest that the country was "growing up"? **[Analyze Causes and Effects]**
Possible response: These two literary movements were reactions to a national

crisis, the Civil War, and to the rapid urbanization and industrialization of the country. In the sense that these movements tried to take account of some problems and grim realities, they can be said to reflect a process of "growing up."

Background

Art

Six O'Clock, by John Sloan

Born in 1871, John Sloan began his artistic career at a Philadelphia newspaper as a commercial artist. However, he also studied with the artist Robert Henri. When Henri left Philadelphia for New York City, Sloan came with him. There, the artists were central to the Ashcan School.

The first two decades of the twentieth century proved to be Sloan's most important period. He became best known for his paintings of New York City and its daily routines. His paintings were realistic, and as warm and vital as the lives they captured. Sloan's art showed his sympathy for ordinary, working-class people, but on occasion his paintings would reflect a quiet sadness. He could also include a touch of satire in his work.

Ask students the following questions:

1. How would you describe the mood of this painting?
   Possible response: Students may answer that the painting's mood is claustrophobic or melancholy, suggesting that Sloan is ambivalent about the technology it portrays and its impact on people's lives. Students may support this by noting the painting's darkness.

2. What does the painting reveal about the social environment Sloan portrays? Explain.
   Possible response: Students may observe that the painting shows a new social development—rush hour commuting—made possible by the technology of the period.

Critical Thinking

1. How does the saying "Less is more" relate to Lincoln's Gettysburg Address? **[Connect]**
   Possible response: The speech supports the saying. It shows how a brief address, if eloquently written, can be more memorable than a long speech.

2. What accounts for the fact that the most famous Western writers were born in other regions? **[Speculate]**

continued

471

Critical Thinking

1. Why was it important that Twain "captured the everyday speech of characters"? **[Speculate]**
Possible response: If a writer hopes to capture a country's life, then his books ought to talk the way people do.

2. What did Twain mean by his observation about American English compared with British English? **[Interpret]**
Possible response: Twain meant that Americans would now influence the future development of the English language even more than the British would.

3. Why do you think Twain favored short words over long ones? **[Speculate]**
Possible response: He seems to have felt that long words were pretentious, flowery, and perhaps more European than American.

▶ **Critical Viewing**

Instruct students to look at the picture of Twain on this page. Ask: Does he look the way he sounds in the quotations? **[Connect]**
Possible response: Obviously, there is no "correct" answer, but students may say that Twain looks like a down-to-earth, no-nonsense person, and these are qualities reflected in the quotations.

Activities

1. Before students begin the discussion, be sure that they understand the quotation. Its gist is that dialects are ubiquitous. Define the word *dialect* for students, or help them to define it for themselves: the form or variety of a spoken language peculiar to a region, social group, or occupational group.

2. Be sure that students understand the quotations they choose. Essays should be focused on elaborating upon and supporting Twain's position.

3. Students should show how the passage exemplifies the down-to-earth directness of Twain's style—the way that his writing is, "like water," meant for everybody.

THE DEVELOPMENT OF AMERICAN ENGLISH

Mark Twain and the American Language

BY RICHARD LEDERER

AMERICAN LITERATURE COMES OF AGE

On February 18, 1885, thirty thousand copies of Mark Twain's *The Adventures of Huckleberry Finn* were released in the United States. The novel turned out to be Twain's masterpiece, and it changed the direction of American letters. Twain captured the everyday speech of characters, instead of the more formal, standard English that writers before him used. In *The Adventures of Huckleberry Finn*, Twain used seven distinct dialects to reflect the speech patterns of various characters, and he also became the first important author to show the freshness and vitality of the new American idiom in narrative as well as in dialogue. Just as Geoffrey Chaucer's *The Canterbury Tales* is the first significant work written in English, *Huckleberry Finn* is the first novel of world rank to be written entirely in American.

READIN', WRITIN', AND TWAIN

Twain held strong opinions about a passel of subjects, and he possessed the gift of being able to state these views in memorable ways: "It's better to keep your mouth shut and appear stupid than to open it and remove all doubt"; "Be careful about reading health books. You may die of a misprint."

Twain also had a lot to say about style, literature, and the American language that he, more than any other writer, helped to shape.

- *On American English, compared with British English:* The property has gone into the hands of a joint stock company, and we own the bulk of the shares.
- *On dialects:* I have traveled more than anyone else, and I have noticed that even the angels speak English with an accent.
- *On choosing words:* The difference between the almost right word and the right word is really a large matter—'tis the difference between the lightning-bug and the lightning.
- *On style* (in a letter to a twelve-year-old boy): I notice that you use plain, simple language, short words, and brief sentences. That is the way to write English—it is the modern way and the best way. Stick to it; and don't let fluff and flowers and verbosity creep in.
- *On being concise:* A successful book is not made of what is in it, but what is left out of it.
- *On using short words:* I never write metropolis for seven cents when I can get the same for city. I never write policeman because I can get the same for cop.
- *On reading:* The man who does not read good books has no advantage over the man who can't read them.

✳ ENRICHMENT: Literature Connection

More of Twain's Wit and Wisdom

Share these additional quotations from Mark Twain with students. Students interested in pursuing Activity 3 might choose one of these passages:

Soap and education are not as sudden as a massacre, but they are more deadly in the long run.

—*The Facts Concerning the Recent Resignation*

Work consists of whatever a body is obliged to do . . . Play consists of whatever a body is not obliged to do.

—*The Adventures of Tom Sawyer*

Hain't we got all the fools in town on our side? And ain't that a big enough majority in every town?

—*The Adventure of Huckleberry Finn*

War talk by men who have been in a war is always interesting; whereas moon talk by a poet who has not been in the moon is likely to be dull.

—*Life on the Mississippi*

ACTIVITIES

1. With a group, discuss Twain's statement on dialects, above. In your discussion, include some of the outstanding characteristics of the dialect that you speak.

2. Use one of Mark Twain's statements about writing or language, above, as the thesis for an essay or discussion on the subject.

3. In 1885, Twain wrote in his notebook, "My works are like water. The works of the great masters are like wine. But everyone drinks water." Choose a passage from one of Twain's stories or essays, and show how that passage exemplifies the author's philosophy of style.

A Nation Divided

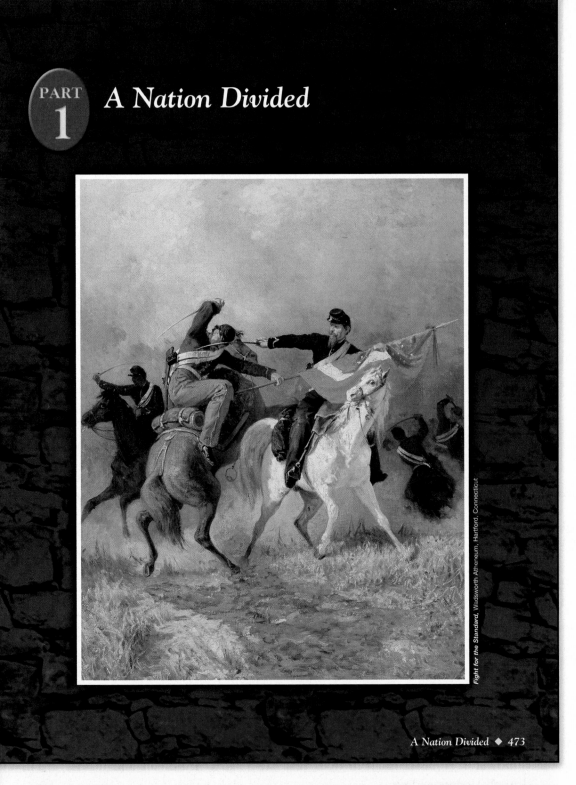

Fight for the Standard, Wadsworth Atheneum, Hartford, Connecticut

A Nation Divided ◆ 473

Selection Planning Guide

The selections in this section show the many faces of a nation divided. Stephen Crane's "An Episode of War" portrays the battlefront. The spirituals and Frederick Douglass excerpt provide a candid look at the divisive issue of slavery. "An Occurrence at Owl Creek Bridge" will have students debating whether all is really fair in love and war. Two of the war's greatest figures—Abraham Lincoln and Robert E. Lee—reveal in their own words the issues at the heart of the Civil War.

Background

Art

Fight for the Standard, by Daniel Wadsworth

In old-fashioned warfare, capturing the opponents' flag was meant to throw the other side into despair and confusion. Help students to see that this traditional painting seems posed for dramatic effect, with two cavalrymen emerging from a smoky background to fight. Point out that the Confederate soldier who grabs the Union flag is about to be mortally wounded by the Union soldier on the white horse.

Have students link the painting to the theme "A Nation Divided" by answering the following questions:

1. Do you think the painter favored one side over the other in this painting? What leads you to that impression?
   Possible response: Some students will say that the balance of the composition projects a balanced view of the fight. Others may point to details that favor the Northerner—he rides a white horse, his face and not the Southerner's is visible, and he is about to win.

2. Does this artist create a realistic or romanticized view of war? Explain.
   Possible response: Details like the excitement of hand-to-hand combat, the beautiful horses, and the almost knightly sabers support a romanticized view of warfare. The Southerner's imminent death reflects a realistic view.

CUSTOMIZE INSTRUCTION FOR UNIVERSAL ACCESS

When assigning the selections in this part, keep in mind the following factors:

"An Episode of War"
- A haunting short story

"Swing Low, Sweet Chariot"; "Go Down, Moses"
- Spirituals with accessible lyrics

from *My Bondage and My Freedom*
- Autobiographical excerpt
- Lengthy sentences may challenge less proficient readers.

"An Occurrence at Owl Creek Bridge"
- High interest story with surprising plot twist and shifting time frame

"The Gettysburg Address"; "Second Inaugural Address"; "Letter to His Son"
- Formal diction and abstract concepts may challenge less proficient readers.

473

An Episode of War ✦ Willie Has Gone to the War

Lesson Objectives

1. **To analyze and respond to literary elements**
   - Literary Analysis: Realism and Naturalism
   - Comparing Literary Works

2. **To read, comprehend, analyze, and critique a short story and song lyrics**
   - Reading Strategy: Recognizing Historical Details
   - Reading Check Questions
   - Review and Assess Questions
   - Assessment Practice (ATE)

3. **To develop word analysis skills, fluency, and systematic vocabulary**
   - Vocabulary Development Lesson: Latin Root: -greg-

4. **To understand and apply written and oral language conventions**
   - Spelling Strategy
   - Grammar and Style Lesson: Correct use of *Like* and *As*

5. **To understand and apply appropriate writing and research strategies**
   - Writing Lesson: Field Report on Hospital Conditions
   - Extension Activity: Definition Essay

6. **To understand and apply listening and speaking strategies**
   - Extension Activity: Musical Presentation

STEP-BY-STEP TEACHING GUIDE	PACING GUIDE
PRETEACH	
Motivate Students and Provide Background	
Use the Motivation activity (ATE p. 474)	5 min.
Read and discuss author and background features (SE/ATE p. 474) ▲	5 min.
Introduce the Concepts	
Introduce the Literary Analysis and Reading Strategy (SE/ATE p. 475) ▲	15 min.
Pronounce the vocabulary words and read their definitions (SE p. 475)	5 min.
TEACH	
Monitor Comprehension	
Informally monitor comprehension by circulating while students read independently or in groups ▲	20 min.
Monitor students' comprehension with the Reading Check notes (SE/ATE pp. 477, 479, 481)	as students read
Develop vocabulary with Vocabulary notes (SE pp. 478, 479, 480; ATE p. 478)	as students read
Develop Understanding	
Develop students' understanding of realism and naturalism with the Literary Analysis annotations (SE p. 480; ATE p. 480) ▲	5 min.
Develop students' ability to recognize historical details with the Reading Strategy annotations (SE pp. 477, 478; ATE pp. 477, 478)	5 min.
ASSESS	
Assess Mastery	
Assess students' mastery of the Reading Strategy and Literary Analysis by having them answer the Review and Assess questions (SE/ATE p. 483)	15 min.
Use one or more of the print and media Assessment Resources (ATE p. 485) ▲	up to 45 min.
EXTEND	
Apply Understanding	
Have students complete the Vocabulary Development Lesson and the Grammar and Style Lesson (SE p. 484) ▲	20 min.
Apply students' ability to use precise details by using the Writing Lesson (SE/ATE p. 485) ▲	45 min.
Apply students' understanding using one or more of the Extension Activities (SE p. 485)	20–90 min.

 ACCELERATED INSTRUCTION:
Use the strategies and activities identified with an Ⓐ.

UNIVERSAL ACCESS
● = Below Level Students
▲ = On-Level Students
■ = Above Level Students

Time and Resource Manager

Reading Level: Average, Easy
Average Number of Instructional Days: 3

RESOURCES

PRINT 📖	TRANSPARENCIES 🔒	TECHNOLOGY 💿 🎧 📼
• **Beyond Literature,** Humanities Connection: Photography, p. 24 ▲ ■		• **Interest Grabber Video,** Tape 4 ● ▲ ■
• **Selection Support Workbook:** ● ▲ ■ Literary Analysis, p. 111 Reading Strategy, p. 110 Build Vocabulary, p. 108	• **Literary Analysis and Reading Transparencies,** pp. 47 and 48 ● ▲ ■	
• **Adapted Reader's Companion** ● • **Reader's Companion** ●		• **Listening to Literature** ● ▲ ■ Audiocassettes, Side 16 Audio CDs, CD 10
• **English Learner's Companion** ● ▲ • **Literatura en español** ● ▲ • **Literary Analysis for Enrichment** ■		
• **Formal Assessment:** Selection Test, p. 119 ● ▲ ■ • **Open Book Test,** p. 70 ● ▲ ■ • **Performance Assessment and Portfolio Management,** p. 13 ● ▲ ■ • **PRENTICE HALL ASSESSMENT SYSTEM** ● ▲ ■	• **PRENTICE HALL ASSESSMENT SYSTEM** ● ▲ ■ Skills Practice Answers and Explanations on Transparencies	• **Test Bank Software** ● ▲ ■ • **Got It! Assessment Videotapes,** Tape 3 ● ▲
• **Selection Support Workbook:** ● ▲ ■ Build Grammar Skills, p. 109 • **Writing and Grammar,** Ruby Level ● ▲ ■ • **Extension Activities,** p. 24 ● ▲ ■	• **Daily Language Practice Transparencies** ● ▲ • **Writing Models and Graphic Organizers on Transparencies,** p. 61 ● ▲ ■	• **Writing and Grammar iText CD-ROM** ● ▲ ■ 🖥 **Take It to the Net** www.phschool.com

■ **BLOCK SCHEDULING:** Use one 90-minute class period to preteach the selection and have students read it. Use a second 90-minute class period to assess students' mastery of skills and have them complete one of the Extension Activities.

Step-by-Step Teaching Guide for pp. 474–475

Motivation

Play the scene from the 1993 film *Gettysburg* in which General Longstreet visits General Hood as the latter recovers from an amputation in a Confederate field hospital. Use this scene—which occurs at the beginning of Part 2—to help students gain an awareness of the conditions in a Civil War field hospital. Invite them to share their reactions to what they see and hear. Then, tell them that they are about to read a story in which an injured soldier makes a frightening journey to such a medical facility.

▨ Interest Grabber Video

As an alternative, you may wish to play "Life During the Civil War" on Tape 4 to engage student interest.

❶ Background

More About the Authors

Crane received firsthand experience fighting forces beyond his control when a boat on which he was traveling sank off the Florida coast. He and three other passengers spent nearly thirty hours afloat in a dinghy before landing safely at Daytona.

At one point, Stephen Foster's financial difficulties grew so extreme that he nearly starved to death while living on the streets of New York City. Although he worked with a collaborator on this Civil War ballad, he often wrote both lyrics and music for his songs.

Prepare to Read

❶ An Episode of War ◆ Willie Has Gone to the War

Stephen Crane (1871–1900)

Stephen Crane had not even been born when the last battle of the American Civil War was fought, yet he is best remembered for his compelling depiction of the conflict. During his brief life, Crane worked to establish himself as both a leader of the Naturalist movement and one of the greatest writers of his time.

Early in his career, Crane worked as a newspaper writer in New York City. His experiences there inspired his first novel, *Maggie: A Girl of the Streets* (1893). Its grimly realistic portrayal of life in the city's slums was so frank and shocking that Crane was unable to find a publisher, so he printed the book at his own expense.

The Red Badge of Courage Crane's second novel, published in 1895, was *The Red Badge of Courage: An Episode of the American Civil War*. A psychological exploration of a young soldier's mental and emotional reactions under enemy fire, the wildly successful novel earned international acclaim for the twenty-four-year-old writer. Although Crane had never experienced military combat, he interviewed Civil War veterans and studied photographs, battle plans, and biographical accounts before writing the realistic battle scenes.

Crane later viewed war firsthand when he served as a newspaper correspondent during the Greco-Turkish War in 1897 and the Spanish-American War in 1898. His war experiences provided material for a collection of poetry, *War Is Kind* (1899), but they took their toll on his health. He died of tuberculosis at the age of twenty-eight.

An Untimely Death Knowing he was going to die, Crane worked intensely in the last years of his life. His novels, short stories, poems, and other writings fill twelve volumes. He is considered a literary prodigy who wrote as quickly and passionately as he lived. Like other Naturalists, Crane depicts characters who are manipulated by forces that are beyond their understanding or control. His most common themes include the harsh reality of war, the degradation of humanity, social rebellion, betrayal, and guilt. Crane also wrote of the physical, emotional, and intellectual responses of people under extreme pressure. For so young a writer with so little time, Crane accomplished much.

Stephen Foster (1826–1864)

Stephen Foster was born in Pennsylvania on July 4, 1826—the fiftieth anniversary of American independence and the day that both Thomas Jefferson and John Adams died. As a young man, Foster worked as a bookkeeper but experienced little success. In fact, throughout his life he was plagued by financial failure. Music publishers took advantage of Foster, who never achieved monetary success to match his musical talent.

The popular minstrel songs and sentimental ballads that he wrote earned Foster an honored place in American music. Foster composed about 200 songs in his rather short lifetime, including such classics as "The Old Folks at Home" (popularly known as "Way Down Upon the Swanee River"), "Camptown Races," "Oh! Susanna," "My Old Kentucky Home," and "Jeanie With the Light Brown Hair." Foster collaborated with lyricist George Cooper on the Civil War ballad "Willie Has Gone to the War."

474 ◆ Division, Reconciliation, and Expansion (1850–1914)

TEACHING RESOURCES

The following resources can be used to enrich or extend the instruction for pp. 474–475.

Motivation

▨ **Interest Grabber Video**, Tape 4

Background

▨ **Beyond Literature**, p. 24 ▪

▨ *Take It to the Net*
Visit www.phschool.com for Background and hotlinks for the selections.

Literary Analysis

▨ **Literary Analysis and Reading Transparencies,** Realism and Naturalism, p. 48

▨ **Selection Support:** Literary Analysis, p. 111 ▪

Reading

▨ **Literary Analysis and Reading Transparencies,** Recognizing Historical Details, p. 47

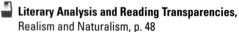 **BLOCK SCHEDULING:** Resources marked with this symbol provide varied instruction during 90-minute blocks.

Preview

Connecting to the Literature

Being in control of a situation and making responsible decisions helps you take command of your life. This luxury was not granted to the Civil War soldiers who had very little control over their own destinies in battle.

❷ Literary Analysis

Realism and Naturalism

In reaction to Romanticism—a movement which emphasized emotion, imagination, and nature—two literary movements emerged during the mid- to late-nineteenth century: **Realism and Naturalism.**

- Realism sought to portray life as faithfully and accurately as possible, focusing on ordinary people suffering the harsh realities of everyday life.
- Naturalism also sought to portray ordinary people's lives, but suggested that environment, heredity, and chance, or forces they could neither understand nor control, determined people's fate.

As you read, look for elements related to these two literary movements.

Comparing Literary Works

Both of these selections are set against a backdrop of the Civil War, but each presents a different perspective on the bloodiest conflict ever fought on American soil. As you read, determine which writer presents the more accurate description of events and which one presents a more idealized version of life during that bitter moment in history.

❸ Reading Strategy

Recognizing Historical Details

The social and political climate surrounding these Civil War snapshots form part of their setting and context. When you **recognize historical details,** you determine how the attitudes of both writers and characters reflect the ideas of their day. As you read, use a chart like the one shown to record events that suggest historical context.

Event	Historical Context
Battles	
Medical Practices	
Political Situations	
Social Attitudes	

Vocabulary Development

precipitate (prē sip′ ə tāt′) *v.* cause to happen before expected or desired (p. 478)

aggregation (ag′ rə gā′ shən) *n.* group of distinct objects or individuals (p. 478)

inscrutable (in skrōōt′ ə bəl) *adj.* impossible to see (p. 479)

disdainfully (dis dān′ fəl ē) *adv.* showing scorn or contempt (p. 480)

glade (glād) *n.* open space in a wood or forest (p. 482)

An Episode of War / Willie Has Gone to the War ◆ 475

---

❷ Literary Analysis

Realism and Naturalism

- Tell students that they will be exploring the literary movements of Realism and Naturalism as they read the two works in this grouping. Both Realists and Naturalists sought to portray real life as accurately as possible. Naturalists also believed that human lives are determined by chance, fate, or other forces beyond our control.

- As they read, encourage students to consider how accurately each selection portrays "real life."

- Invite students to think about a wide range of stories, novels, films, and television programs with which they are familiar. Might any of these works be deemed examples of Realism or Naturalism? Do any of them present real life accurately? Do any of them convey the idea that people's fates are determined by chance or by forces they cannot control?

❸ Reading Strategy

Recognizing Historical Details

- Point out to students that recognizing historical details will enrich their appreciation of a literary work, and will help them to better understand descriptions, characters, events, and themes.

- Remind students that the most obvious historical details are references to events, ideas, persons, or things. Less conspicuous (but equally important) are descriptions of social attitudes, political situations, and cultural practices.

- Invite students to look for details that indicate historical context in these works by Crane and Foster.

Vocabulary Development

- Pronounce each vocabulary word for students, and read the definitions as a class. Have students identify any words with which they are already familiar.

 E-Teach

Visit E-Teach at www.phschool.com for teachers' essays on how to teach, with questions and answers.

CUSTOMIZE INSTRUCTION FOR UNIVERSAL ACCESS

For Special Needs Students	For Less Proficient Readers	For English Learners
Have students read the adapted version of "An Episode of War" in the **Adapted Reader's Companion.** This version provides basic level instruction in an interactive format with questions and write-on lines. Completing the adapted version will prepare students to read the selection in the Student Edition.	Have students read "An Episode of War" in the **Reader's Companion.** This version provides basic level instruction in an interactive format with questions and write-on lines. After students finish the selection in **Reader's Companion,** have them complete the questions and activities in the Student Edition.	Have students read the adapted version of "An Episode of War" in the **English Learner's Companion.** This version provides basic level instruction in an interactive format with questions and write-on lines. Completing the adapted version will prepare students to read the selection in the Student Edition.

CUSTOMIZE INSTRUCTION
For Visual/Spatial Learners

Encourage students to use the photographs and fine art to help them picture the setting, characters, and events in the story. Make sure that they understand that the two photographs depict real soldiers who fought in the Civil War. Have students discuss how the photographs add to the details that Crane provides in his story. You may also wish to conduct a more general discussion about the differences between written and visual records of historical events.

❶ About the Selection

This stark account of how a Civil War lieutenant loses his arm to amputation is detached and impersonal, yet hauntingly moving. The lieutenant is rationing coffee when a stray bullet hits his arm and changes his life forever. So begins his dreamlike journey toward the field hospital. Although the nameless lieutenant appears numb, the reader can imagine his dread as he anticipates the medical attention he will receive. Despite his protests and the doctor's false assurances, the lieutenant loses his arm in just another "episode of war." Through his depiction of this gripping series of events, Crane conveys an important message about the tragedy of war and the helplessness of those caught up in the fighting.

❷ ▶ Critical Viewing

Answer: Students may say that the soldiers' facial expressions and the way the men recline in crowded and unsanitary conditions indicate that they are not receiving quality treatment.

---

❶ An EPISODE of War

Stephen Crane

Background

Both of these selections were inspired by the American Civil War, the bloodiest conflict in American history. The war claimed the lives of 600,000 soldiers—more American casualties than the combined total of all other wars in which the United States has fought. Hundreds of thousands more were left maimed by battle wounds and crude medical care.

When the war began, neither side was prepared to care for the wounded. The conditions were terrible, and twice as many Civil War soldiers died of infections as of combat wounds. As you read "An Episode of War," keep in mind that amputation was routine treatment for injured limbs. A wounded soldier knew that he faced the high probability of losing his arm or leg to a surgeon's saw.

476 ◆ *Division, Reconciliation, and Expansion (1850–1914)*

TEACHING RESOURCES

The following resources can be used to enrich or extend the instruction for pp. 476–482.

Reading Strategy

📘 **Selection Support:** Reading Strategy, p. 110; Build Vocabulary, p. 108

📘 **Adapted Reader's Companion**

📘 **Reader's Companion**

📘 **English Learner's Companion**

🎧 **Listening to Literature Audiocassettes,** Side 16 ▦

💿 **Listening to Literature CDs,** CD 10 ▦

▦ **BLOCK SCHEDULING:** Resources marked with this symbol provide varied instruction during 90-minute blocks.

The lieutenant's rubber blanket lay on the ground, and upon it he had poured the company's supply of coffee. Corporals and other representatives of the grimy and hot-throated men who lined the breast-work[1] had come for each squad's portion.

The lieutenant was frowning and serious at this task of division. His lips pursed as he drew with his sword various crevices in the heap, until brown squares of coffee, astoundingly equal in size, appeared on the blanket. He was on the verge of a great triumph in mathematics, and the corporals were thronging forward, each to reap a little square, when suddenly the lieutenant cried out and looked quickly at a man near him as if he suspected it was a case of personal assault. The others cried out also when they saw blood upon the lieutenant's sleeve.

He had winced like a man stung, swayed dangerously, and then straightened. The sound of his hoarse breathing was plainly audible. He looked sadly, mystically, over the breast-work at the green face of a wood, where now were many little puffs of white smoke. During this moment the men about him gazed statuelike and silent, astonished and awed by this catastrophe which happened when catastrophes were not expected—when they had leisure to observe it.

As the lieutenant stared at the wood, they too swung their heads, so that for another instant all hands, still silent, contemplated the distant forest as if their minds were fixed upon the mystery of a bullet's journey.

 The officer had, of course, been compelled to take his sword into his left hand. He did not hold it by the hilt. He gripped it at the middle of the blade, awkwardly. Turning his eyes from the hostile wood, he looked at the sword as he held it there, and seemed puzzled as to what to do with it, where to put it. In short, this weapon had of a sudden become a strange thing to him. He looked at it in a kind of stupefaction, as if he had been endowed with a trident, a sceptre,[2] or a spade.

Finally he tried to sheathe it. To sheathe a sword held by the left hand, at the middle of the blade, in a scabbard hung at the left hip, is a feat worthy of a sawdust ring.[3] This wounded officer engaged in a desperate struggle with the sword and the wobbling scabbard, and during the time of it breathed like a wrestler.

But at this instant the men, the spectators, awoke from their stonelike poses and crowded forward sympathetically. The orderly-sergeant

---

1. **breast-work** low wall put up quickly as a defense in battle.
2. **a trident, a sceptre** (trīd′ ənt; sep′ tər) three-pronged spear; decorated ornamental rod or staff symbolizing royal authority.
3. **sawdust ring** ring in which circus acts are performed.

◄ Critical Viewing This is an actual photograph of a temporary Civil War hospital. Do you think that soldiers received quality treatment in this setting? On what details do you base your answer? **[Assess]**

Reading Strategy
Recognizing Historical Details What details in this passage set the story at the time of the Civil War?

Reading Check
What has just happened to the lieutenant?

An Episode of War ◆ 477

---

❸ Reading Strategy
Recognizing Historical Details

- Have a student volunteer read the paragraph aloud slowly and clearly. Tell students to listen for details in the passage that establish the story's time and place.
- Then, ask students the Reading Strategy question on p. 477: What details in this passage set the story at the time of the Civil War? Answer: Students should mention the lieutenant's possessing a sword.
- If necessary, help students understand that the terms *trident* and *sceptre* do not relate to the Civil War setting. (The former was a weapon used in ancient Rome; the latter is an object used as a symbol of British royalty.) Crane includes these two images—as well as that of a humble digging tool, the spade—to emphasize the lieutenant's disorientation.

❹ ☑ Reading Check

Answer: The lieutenant has been shot in the arm.

CUSTOMIZE INSTRUCTION FOR UNIVERSAL ACCESS

For Special Needs Students	For Gifted/Talented Students
Inform students that a Civil War officer in uniform customarily carried a sword, and that when not in use, the sword rested in a scabbard slung at the officer's hip. Help students picture the lieutenant's maneuvers as he grasps and then attempts to sheathe his sword by having them act out his movements. After they perform these gestures, invite them to explain in their own words why the officer's wounded arm made him feel so awkward.	Stephen Crane opens this tale with a brief portrait of life in a military camp. The story begins during a lull just before shooting breaks out. Have students describe the activities in which the soldiers are engaged prior to the onset of gunfire. Then, encourage them to draw or create a tableau—based on Crane's description—that captures the ordinariness of camp life.

Inform students that Civil War officers, for the most part, were Victorian gentlemen who held romantic notions about war. To some, a wound was a sign of bravery and glory (hence, Crane's title *The Red Badge of Courage*). Tell students that as the bloody war raged on, this notion gradually began to lose its appeal.

⑥ Reading Strategy

Recognizing Historical Details

- Encourage students to review the story so far to try to find detailed references to the lieutenant's wound. If necessary, help students recognize that—other than a single allusion to "blood upon the lieutenant's sleeve" and references to his holding the arm gingerly—Crane provides no details about the wound.

▶ Monitor Progress Ask students the Reading Strategy question on p. 478: Using your knowledge of the historical context, what do you think is the potential outcome of the lieutenant's injury?

Answer: Students may mention amputation—or even death as a result of an infection.

⑦ Vocabulary Development

Latin Root -greg-

- Draw students' attention to Crane's use of the word *aggregation*, and read its definition. Then, tell students that the root -greg- derives from the Latin word meaning "herd," or "flock." The prefix ag- is equivalent to ad- and means "near," or "to," and the suffix -ion means a "state" or "condition."

- Invite students to brainstorm for a list of other words that share the root -greg- . Have them explain the ways in which all these words relate to the meaning of the root.

---

took the sword and tenderly placed it in the scabbard. At the time, he leaned nervously backward, and did not allow even his finger to brush the body of the lieutenant. A wound gives strange dignity to him who bears it. Well men shy from his new and terrible majesty. It is as if the wounded man's hand is upon the curtain which hangs before the revelations of all existence—the meaning of ants, potentates,[4] wars, cities, sunshine, snow, a feather dropped from a bird's wing; and the power of it sheds radiance upon a bloody form, and makes the other men understand sometimes that they are little. His comrades look at him with large eyes thoughtfully. Moreover, they fear vaguely that the weight of a finger upon him might send him headlong, <u>precipitate</u> the tragedy, hurl him at once into the dim, grey unknown. And so the orderly-sergeant, while sheathing the sword, leaned nervously backward.

There were others who proffered assistance. One timidly presented his shoulder and asked the lieutenant if he cared to lean upon it, but the latter waved him away mournfully. He wore the look of one who knows he is the victim of a terrible disease and understands his helplessness. He again stared over the breast-work at the forest, and then, turning, went slowly rearward. He held his right wrist tenderly in his left hand as if the wounded arm was made of very brittle glass.

And the men in silence stared at the wood, then at the departing lieutenant; then at the wood, then at the lieutenant.

As the wounded officer passed from the line of battle, he was enabled to see many things which as a participant in the fight were unknown to him. He saw a general on a black horse gazing over the lines of blue infantry at the green woods which veiled his problems. An aide galloped furiously, dragged his horse suddenly to a halt, saluted, and presented a paper. It was, for a wonder, precisely like a historical painting.

To the rear of the general and his staff a group, composed of a bugler, two or three orderlies, and the bearer of the corps standard,[5] all upon maniacal horses, were working like slaves to hold their ground, preserve their respectful interval, while the shells boomed in the air about them, and caused their chargers to make furious quivering leaps.

A battery, a tumultuous and shining mass, was swirling toward the right. The wild thud of hoofs, the cries of the riders shouting blame and praise, menace and encouragement, and, last, the roar of the wheels, the slant of the glistening guns, brought the lieutenant to an intent pause. The battery swept in curves that stirred the heart; it made halts as dramatic as the crash of a wave on the rocks, and when it fled onward this <u>aggregation</u> of wheels, levers, motors had a beautiful unity, as if it were a missile. The sound of it was a war-chorus that reached into the depths of man's emotion.

---

4. **potentates** (pōt´ ən tāts) *n.* rulers; powerful people.
5. **corps standard** (kôr) flag or banner representing a military unit.

precipitate (prē sip´ ə tāt´) *v.* cause to happen before expected or desired

Reading Strategy
Recognizing Historical Details Using your knowledge of the historical context, what do you think is the potential outcome of the lieutenant's injury?

aggregation (ag´ grə gā´ shən) *n.* group of distinct objects or individuals

---

✺ ENRICHMENT: Career Connection

Photojournalism

The work of photographers such as Mathew Brady (see pp. 476 and 479) and Alexander Gardner brought the horrors of the Civil War into parlors across the United States of America. Like their earlier counterparts, today's photojournalists capture news events or explore timely issues through images rather than words. Although some work as staff photographers for newspapers and magazines, most work as freelancers. These photojournalists may be hired for an assignment, or they may sell images to individual publications or to photo services that then distribute them to subscribers.

Invite students to discuss the idea of working as a photojournalist. Ask them to talk about the kinds of events they would most like to cover. Would they prefer to work as a staff or freelance photographer? Why? Suggest that they contact modern-day photojournalists to learn more about the nature and history of this career.

❽

The lieutenant, still holding his arm as if it were of glass, stood watching this battery until all detail of it was lost, save the figures of the riders, which rose and fell and waved lashes over the black mass.

Later, he turned his eyes toward the battle, where the shooting sometimes crackled like bush-fires, sometimes sputtered with exasperating irregularity, and sometimes reverberated like the thunder. He saw the smoke rolling upward and saw crowds of men who ran and cheered, or stood and blazed away at the <u>inscrutable</u> distance.

He came upon some stragglers, and they told him how to find the field hospital. They described its exact location. In fact, these men, no longer having part in the battle, knew more of it than others. They told the performance of every corps, every division, the opinion of every general. The lieutenant, carrying his wounded arm rearward, looked upon them with wonder.

At the roadside a brigade was making coffee and buzzing with talk like a girls' boarding school. Several officers came out to him and

❾ **▲ Critical Viewing**
What connections do you see between this photograph and Crane's description of the wounded lieutenant being helped by his men? **[Connect]**

inscrutable (in skrōōt′ ə bəl) *adj.* impossible to see

⓫ **☑ Reading Check**
Why does the lieutenant look upon the stragglers with wonder?

An Episode of War ◆ 479

CUSTOMIZE INSTRUCTION FOR UNIVERSAL ACCESS

For Less Proficient Readers

Students may need help determining the essential meaning of some of Crane's poetic passages. For instance, guide them through his description of the effect of the wound on p. 478—particularly the sentence beginning *It is as if the wounded man's hand.* Point out the phrase *as if* and explain that the author uses an imaginative word picture (a hand upon a curtain hanging in front of the answers to life's questions) to convey an important idea. Guide students through the list of nouns—*ants,*

wars, and so on—and invite them to suggest what the "meaning" of each might be.

Make sure students understand Crane's essential point that a wound carries with it a strange power: Other people believe that the wounded person stands closer to the essence of life itself. Moreover, Crane is suggesting that in the final analysis, human beings may not "mean" more than an insect or an inanimate object such as a feather.

---

❽ Background

Art

Photographs by Mathew Brady

The Civil War was the first war to be captured in photographs. Due to the limitations of the photographic process at that time, photographers rarely captured action or battle scenes. They took pictures of events behind the scenes or photographed the carnage that remained after battle. Have students contrast the photographs that accompany this story with photographs they have seen of later wars.

❾ ▶ Critical Viewing

Answer: Like the men in the story, this soldier expresses aloofness in his body language, as though proximity to the wounded man will cause his own doom. Nevertheless, he still attempts to help his fallen comrade by giving him water from a canteen, much as the soldiers in the story offer timid assistance to their lieutenant.

❿ Critical Thinking

Analyze Causes and Effects

• Have a student volunteer read the first three paragraphs on this page. Guide students to recognize that the lieutenant makes a variety of observations as he is walking.

• Then, ask students to explain why the stragglers might know more about the battle than the lieutenant does. Is their information reliable?
Answer: Students may say that the stragglers, removed as they are from the thick of battle, have seen more of the larger conflict than the lieutenant has. Others may suggest that these men may not have accurate information and know little of what the generals are thinking.

⓫ ☑ Reading Check

Possible answers: He looks upon them with wonder because of the breadth of their information and because he sees everything anew in light of his wound.

479

⓬ Literary Analysis
Realism and Naturalism

- Invite one or two student volunteers to explain the definitions of Realism and Naturalism. Ensure that students recognize the similarities as well as the fundamental difference between these two literary movements.

- You might wish to have students use a Venn diagram to clarify the similarities and differences between the two movements.

▶ **Monitor Progress** Ask students the Literary Analysis question on p. 480: What details of this description reflect the ideas of the Naturalists?
Answer: Details include the "deep mud" (environment) or the chance collision of two ambulances that could hasten the death of wounded soldiers.

⓭ ▶ Critical Viewing

Answer: This set of surgical instruments highlights the brutality and crudeness of Civil War medical practices. In particular, both the small hatchet and the saw suggest the frequency with which amputations were performed.

inquired concerning things of which he knew nothing. One, seeing his arm, began to scold. "Why, man, that's no way to do. You want to fix that thing." He appropriated the lieutenant and the lieutenant's wound. He cut the sleeve and laid bare the arm, every nerve of which softly fluttered under his touch. He bound his handkerchief over the wound, scolding away in the meantime. His tone allowed one to think that he was in the habit of being wounded every day. The lieutenant hung his head, feeling, in this presence, that he did not know how to be correctly wounded.

The low white tents of the hospital were grouped around an old schoolhouse. There was here a singular commotion. In the foreground two ambulances interlocked wheels in the deep mud. The drivers were tossing the blame of it back and forth, gesticulating and berating, while from the ambulances, both crammed with wounded, there came an occasional groan. An interminable crowd of bandaged men were coming and going. Great numbers sat under the trees nursing heads or arms or legs. There was a dispute of some kind raging on the steps of the schoolhouse. Sitting with his back against a tree a man with a face as grey as a new army blanket was serenely smoking a corncob pipe. The lieutenant wished to rush forward and inform him that he was dying.

A busy surgeon was passing near the lieutenant. "Good-morning," he said, with a friendly smile. Then he caught sight of the lieutenant's arm, and his face at once changed. "Well, let's have a look at it." He seemed possessed suddenly of a great contempt for the lieutenant. This wound evidently placed the latter on a very low social plane. The doctor cried out impatiently, "What mutton-head had tied it up that way anyhow?" The lieutenant answered, "Oh, a man."

When the wound was disclosed the doctor fingered it <u>disdainfully</u>. "Humph," he said. "You come along with me and I'll 'tend to you." His voice contained the same scorn as if he were saying: "You will have to go to jail."

The lieutenant had been very meek, but now his face flushed, and he looked into the doctor's eyes. "I guess I won't have it amputated," he said.

"Nonsense, man! Nonsense! Nonsense!" cried the doctor. "Come along, now. I won't amputate it. Come along. Don't be a baby."

"Let go of me," said the lieutenant, holding back wrathfully, his glance fixed upon the door of the old schoolhouse, as sinister to him as the portals of death.

And this is the story of how the lieutenant lost his arm. When he reached home, his sisters, his mother, his wife, sobbed for a long time at the sight of the flat sleeve. "Oh, well," he said, standing shamefaced amid these tears, "I don't suppose it matters so much as all that."

© Museum of the Confederacy, Richmond, Virginia

⓬ Literary Analysis
Realism and Naturalism
What details of this description reflect the ideas of the Naturalists?

disdainfully (dis dān′ fəl ē) *adv.* showing scorn or contempt

⓭ ▼ Critical Viewing
What do these Civil War surgical instruments suggest about the nature of the medical treatment the lieutenant faces? **[Interpret]**

✺ ENRICHMENT: Music Connection

Stephen Foster

Stephen Foster is widely regarded as the first great American songwriter. In the wealth of songs that Foster composed, one can hear the beginnings of popular music, jazz melodies based on folk tunes, even the first hints of American musical theater. Foster was influenced strongly by the Anglo-Irish folk tradition as well as by the music and speech of African Americans. He drew on these influences to create distinctly American music.

In turn, Foster influenced nearly every other great American songwriter who followed, from Irving Berlin, the composer of such favorites as "White Christmas" and "Easter Parade," to Broadway composer Jerome Kern to 1960s folk-rock icon Bob Dylan.

Obtain a copy of *American Dreamer: Songs of Stephen Foster*. Invite students to listen to these songs and to note the rich melodies and the variety of emotions they evoke.

Willie Has Gone to the War

14

Words by George Cooper
Music by Stephen Foster

Young Soldier: Separate Study of a Soldier Giving Water to a Wounded Companion, 1861, Winslow Homer, Cooper-Hewitt, National Museum of Design, Smithsonian Institution

The blue bird is singing his lay,[1]
To all the sweet flow'rs of the dale,
The wild bee is roaming at play,
And soft is the sigh of the gale;
5   I stray by the brookside alone,
Where oft we have wander'd before,
And weep for my lov'd one, my own,
My Willie has gone to the war!

Willie has gone to the war, Willie,
10 Willie my lov'd one, my own;
Willie has gone to the war, Willie,
Willie my lov'd one is gone!

'Twas here, where the lily bells grow,
I last saw his noble young face,
15 And now while he's gone to the foe,
Oh! dearly I love the old place;
The whispering waters repeat
The name that I love o'er and o'er,
And daisies that nod at my feet,
20 Say Willie has gone to the war!

---

1. **lay** n. song or melody.

▲ **Critical Viewing** This teenaged Union soldier may have enlisted in the army hoping to find glory on the battlefield. In what way does "Willie Has Gone to the War" show another side to the experience of war? **[Contrast]**

☑ **Reading Check**
Where does the speaker wait for Willie?

An Episode of War ◆ 481

CUSTOMIZE INSTRUCTION FOR UNIVERSAL ACCESS

For Special Needs Students	For Advanced Readers
Students may need help clarifying and articulating the essential difference between the story's and the song's portrayal of the Civil War. If necessary, guide them to see that Crane reflects the harsh realities experienced by the soldiers who fought the war, whereas Foster reflects a romanticized vision of war cherished by those at home. Ask students to speculate why those at home might prefer the version of war Foster expresses.	Encourage students to write song lyrics or a poem that Willie might send back to the person who misses him. Suggest that they review Crane's story for details of battle, soldiers' behaviors, important incidents, and the setting of both encampment and battlefield that Willie could mention in his lyrics or poem. Have students think about the variety of ways in which a young soldier might convey his experiences to someone back home who worries for his life and safety. Invite interested students to share their work with the class.

---

14 ▶ **About the Selection**
Using a stanza and chorus format, lyricist George Cooper and composer Stephen Foster created this Civil War ballad that romanticizes the idea of waiting for a loved one to return from war.

15 ▶ **Background**
Art

Young Soldier, by Winslow Homer
Considered one of the greatest painters of the nineteenth century, Homer (1836–1910) is best known for his watercolors. His first claim to fame, however, came as an illustrator. After an apprenticeship to a lithographer, he worked as a freelance illustrator for such publications as *Harper's Weekly*. During the Civil War, he abandoned this lucrative career to serve as an artist for the Army of the Potomac. His work, mostly drawings and oil sketches done at or near the front lines and in the encampments, was superior to the lifeless depictions of other wartime illustrators. Homer's renderings featured unsentimental images of the fear and despair that permeated the life of the Civil War soldier.

Use these questions for discussion:

1. What emotions does the artist capture in this image?
   Possible answer: Homer captures the shyness and exhaustion of the young Union soldier.

2. The lightest area on this canvas is the soldier's face. Why might the artist have wished to lead the viewer's eye to the soldier's face?
   Answer: The soldier's face not only shows his tender age but also suggests his feelings.

16 ▶ **Critical Viewing**
Answer: Students may say that the eager young volunteers soon came to understand all too well that "glory on the battlefield" was not to be. By contrast, the song suggests a romantic, but still painful experience, of waiting for a soldier's return.

17 ☑ **Reading Check**
Answer: The speaker waits for Willie "by the brookside" where they "have wander'd before."

Review and Assess

1. Students may be disturbed by the soldiers' and the doctor's attitude toward the wounded lieutenant or by the amputation itself.

2. **(a)** A bullet hits his arm as he apportions coffee to various squads of soldiers.
(b) Because the lieutenant is wounded while working at a humble task, his wound seems especially unjust.

3. **(a)** The lieutenant waves him off "mournfully."
(b) Possible answer: He is already dreading the amputation of his arm.

4. **(a)** Possible answer: He sees the battle as though it were a painting, and he looks at others "with wonder"; the doctor treats the lieutenant with contempt once he realizes that he is injured; the lieutenant tries to downplay the importance of his injury; his empty sleeve is a lifelong reminder of how he is different from other people. **(b)** These examples suggest that the lieutenant is seen not only as separate from other people, but also as less human than they are.

5. The song is idealized and sentimental; it doesn't portray the hardships that face those left at home.

6. Possible answer: The nameless lieutenant symbolizes an unfortunate Everyman, helpless to prevent his injury, to sheathe his own sword, or to avoid amputation. He is wounded by chance and swept toward a fate he is powerless to escape.

7. Students should support their responses with specific reasons and with references to the text.

Willie has gone to the war, Willie,
Willie my lov'd one, my own;
Willie has gone to the war, Willie,
Willie my lov'd one is gone!

25 The leaves of the forest will fade,
The roses will wither and die,
But spring to our home in the glade,
On fairy like pinions[2] will fly;
And still I will hopefully wait
30 The day when these battles are o'er,
And pine like a bird for its mate,
Till Willie comes home from the war!

Willie has gone to the war, Willie,
Willie my lov'd one, my own;
35 Willie has gone to the war, Willie,
Willie my lov'd one is gone!

glade (glād) *n.* open space in a wood or forest

---

2. **pinions** (pin' yenz) *n.* antiquated term meaning "wings."

Review and Assess

Thinking About the Selections

1. **Respond:** Which aspects of "An Episode of War" did you find particularly tragic or unsettling? Explain.

2. **(a) Recall:** What happens to cause the lieutenant's injury? **(b) Analyze:** How does the manner in which the lieutenant is wounded make him a sympathetic character?

3. **(a) Recall:** Describe the lieutenant's reaction when a soldier offers him a helpful shoulder. **(b) Infer:** What accounts for his mournful detachment?

4. **(a) Recall:** Note three examples of the lieutenant's distance from the uninjured people around him. **(b) Interpret:** What do these examples suggest about the way that he is seen by others, and the way in which he sees himself?

5. **Analyze:** In what ways does "Willie Has Gone to the War" romanticize the monotony and anguish of waiting for a soldier to return from war?

6. **Apply:** According to the Naturalists, humans are weak and ineffectual beings at the mercy of mysterious forces. In what way might this statement apply to "An Episode of War"?

7. **Take a Position:** In your view, is the story—in which no battle is described—more or less frightening than contemporary war movies? Explain.

✎ ASSESSMENT PRACTICE: Reading Comprehension

Context   **(For more practice, see Test Preparation Workbook, p. 26.)**

The reading sections of some tests require students to use context to determine the meaning of figurative language. Remind students that the words surrounding the targeted expression can provide clues to its meaning. Use the following sample test item to demonstrate.

But at this instant the men, the spectators,
<u>awoke from their stone-like poses</u> and crowded forward sympathetically.

In this passage, "awoke from their stone-like poses" most nearly means

  A got off their stone beds.

  B moved suddenly after being still.

  C got up to look at statues.

  D posed for a sculpture.

The men, referred to as impassive "spectators," were like "stone" until they "awoke" and roused themselves from their stupor. Context clues support *B*.

Review and Assess

Literary Analysis

Realism and Naturalism

1. Explain how the lieutenant's rationing coffee at the time of his injury contributes to the quality of **Realism** in "An Episode of War."

2. In what way can the same situation be used to support the assertion that this story is distinctly **Naturalistic**?

3. Give two examples that show how the lieutenant exhibits the quiet, courageous endurance typical of characters in Naturalistic works.

4. Use a chart like the one shown to note two examples each of Realistic and Naturalistic characterization from the story.

Realism	Naturalism

5. Citing examples from the lyrics to support your argument, refute the statement that "Willie Has Gone to the War" reflects Realism.

Comparing Literary Works

6. (a) What details in the selections suggest that they were written about the same period of time? (b) What details make it seem as if the writers describe different historical events?

7. In your opinion, which selection would be more useful to historians? Explain.

Reading Strategy

Recognizing Historical Details

8. Using your knowledge of Civil War medical practices, why do you think the doctor promises the lieutenant that he will not amputate?

9. What does the lieutenant's struggle to resheath his sword tell you about battle practices of the Civil War?

10. How does the orderly-sergeant's sympathetic attitude to the lieutenant reflect the romantic notions Civil War officers had of their role in the war?

Extend Understanding

11. **Science Connection:** In what ways might a doctor describe the task of caring for the Civil War wounded?

An Episode of War / Willie Has Gone to the War ◆ 483

Quick Review

Realism depicts ordinary people coping with everyday realities.

Naturalism focuses on people's helplessness in the face of chance.

To **recognize historical details,** look for elements that indicate the time period, and determine how the attitudes of both writers and characters reflect the ideas of their day.

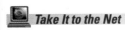 **Take It to the Net**
www.phschool.com
Take the interactive self-test online to check your understanding of these selections.

Answers for p. 483

Review and Assess

1. Soldiers did not spend all their time in glorious battle. Instead, they were often occupied with ordinary tasks.

2. It is a random bullet—the type of chance event characteristic of Naturalistic literature—that causes the lieutenant's injury.

3. He submits to the doctor, even when he suspects his worst fear is about to be made real. Later, he downplays the trauma so that his family won't be unduly upset.

4. Possible responses:

Realism	Naturalism
Injured soldier smoking a corncob pipe	The men's fearful reaction to the wound

5. The ballad is a sentimental depiction of a woman whose longing for her loved one is reflected in idealized nature ("all the sweet flow'rs of the dale"). There is no mention of true hardship.

6. Possible answers: **(a)** The story clearly documents The Civil War in the mid-1800s. The romantic language of the song, with words like "lay" and "pinions," suggests a work from that time period. **(b)** Details from the song include *blue bird, wild bee is roaming at play,* and so on, and from the story include *winced like a man stung, victim of a terrible disease,* and so on.

7. The Crane story would be more useful because it presents a realistic, detailed portrait of a few hours in the life of a Union soldier.

8. It was probably the only way for the doctor to get the lieutenant to agree to be treated.

9. Possible answer: His struggle indicates that there was a certain formality to one's behavior in battle. It seems that a certain level of decorum was expected of officers.

10. The orderly-sergeant behaves as if the lieutenant's wound is a sign of bravery.

11. A physician might focus on the difficulties caused by the risk of infection, the sheer volume of injuries, and the difficulty of providing care in makeshift facilities.

ENRICHMENT: Further Reading

Other Works by the Authors

Works by Stephen Crane

Maggie: A Girl of the Streets

The Red Badge of Courage

The Little Regiment

"The Open Boat"

Works by Stephen Foster

"Camptown Races"

"Jeanie with the Light Brown Hair"

 Take It to the Net
Visit www.phschool.com for more information on Stephen Crane and Stephen Foster.

❶ Vocabulary Development

Word Analysis

congregated; gregarious; aggregate

Concept Development:

1. disdainfully
2. inscrutable
3. glade
4. precipitate
5. aggregation

Spelling Strategy

1. precipitate
2. staid
3. aggregate

❷ Grammar and Style

1. The lieutenant divided the coffee evenly, just as he promised he would.
2. *Correct*
3. The men stood like stones, frightened as though they had never seen a man wounded in battle.
4. The lieutenant stumbled toward the field hospital like a man in a trance.
5. *Correct*

Writing Application

Students' descriptions should describe a chance event and should use *like, as, as if,* or *as though* correctly at least three times.

Integrate Language Skills

❶ Vocabulary Development Lesson

Word Analysis: Latin Root -greg-

The word *aggregation* contains the root -greg-, meaning "herd" or "flock." An *aggregation* is a group of people or things considered as a whole, while a *congregation* is a group and a *gregarious* person enjoys being part of a crowd.

Copy the paragraph below, filling in each blank with the appropriate -greg- word from the following list.

aggregate	gregarious	congregated

The wounded soldiers ___?___ on the steps, waiting to see the doctor. They were silent, except for one ___?___ private who described his injury to everyone. In the ___?___, a nearby orderly reflected, wounded men are a quiet bunch, though there is always an exception.

Concept Development: Analogies

Copy the following analogies, completing each one with the appropriate vocabulary word.

1. *Quickly* is to *rapidly* as ___?___ is to *scornfully*.
2. *Hidden* is to *revealed* as ___?___ is to *obvious*.
3. *Brook* is to *stream* as ___?___ is to *meadow*.
4. *Laugh* is to *cry* as ___?___ is to *delay*.
5. *Sum* is to *parts* as ___?___ is to *individual*.

Spelling Strategy

The long *a* sound can be spelled *a*-consonant-*e*, as in *glade*, or it can be spelled *ai*, as in *disdain*. In your notebook, complete the spelling of these words.

1. precipit__   2. st__d   3. aggreg__

❷ Grammar and Style Lesson

Usage: *Like* and *As*

Like and *as, as if,* and *as though* are often used interchangeably, but they actually serve different purposes. **Like** is a preposition; it takes a noun or pronoun as its object and introduces a prepositional phrase. **As, as if,** and **as though** are subordinating conjunctions that introduce subordinating—or less important—ideas.

> **Like:** He had winced *like a man stung.* . . . (preposition)
>
> **As if:** [The lieutenant] looked quickly at a man near him *as if he suspected it was a case of personal assault.* (introduces a clause)
>
> **As though:** The men regarded him *as though their hearts would break.* (introduces a clause)

Practice Rewrite the following sentences, correcting any errors in the use of *like, as, as if,* or *as though*. Write "correct" for sentences without errors.

1. The lieutenant divided the coffee evenly, just like he promised he would.
2. He staggered as though weak with fatigue.
3. The men stood as stones, frightened like they had never seen a man wounded.
4. The lieutenant stumbled toward the field hospital as if a man in a trance.
5. Like any wounded man, he dwelled on the possibility of amputation.

Writing Application Use *like, as, as if,* or *as though* at least three times in a description of a chance event you experienced.

W̶G̶ Prentice Hall Writing and Grammar Connection: Chapter 25, Section 2

484 ◆ *Division, Reconciliation, and Expansion (1850–1914)*

TEACHING RESOURCES

The following resources can be used to enrich or extend the instruction for pp. 484–485.

Vocabulary

📓 **Selection Support:** Build Vocabulary, p. 108

📓 **Vocabulary and Spelling Practice Book** (Use this booklet for skills enrichment.) ▪

Grammar

📓 **Selection Support:** Build Grammar Skills, p. 109

W̶G̶ **Writing and Grammar,** Ruby Level, p. 648

▪ **Daily Language Practice Transparencies** ▪

Writing

W̶G̶ **Writing and Grammar,** Ruby Level, p. 104

📓 **Extension Activities**

🖼 **Writing Models and Graphic Organizers on Transparencies,** p. 61

💿 **Writing and Grammar iText CD-ROM**

▪ **BLOCK SCHEDULING:** Resources marked with this symbol provide varied instruction during 90-minute blocks.

③ Writing Lesson

Field Report on Hospital Conditions

Imagine that a Civil War colonel wants to know why so many of his soldiers are dying from minor wounds. As the lieutenant, report to the colonel on the treatment you received and the problems you observed at the army hospital.

Prewriting Review the Background on page 476 and the photographs in the selection to develop a list of issues for your report. Jot down the precise details from the story you will use to support each issue. If necessary, consult a Civil War reference book for more facts.

Drafting State your report's purpose in an introduction. Then, present each issue and supporting details in a separate paragraph. Use precise details. Summarize your main points in the conclusion.

Model: Using Precise Details

We must have better conditions immediately or more men will die. The wounded are often neglected and forced to lie on filthy beds, or even the floor, for hours and even days at a time without being fed, bathed, or treated.

> Rather than simply stating that wounded soldiers are neglected, precise details like the ones highlighted provide a complete picture.

Revising Reread your report, checking for logical order and sufficiently precise supporting details. Take steps to improve your organization and strengthen or clarify your writing.

Prentice Hall Writing and Grammar Connection: Chapter 6, Section 3

④ Extension Activities

Listening and Speaking Among the most famous Civil War songs are "Battle Hymn of the Republic" and "Dixie." In a **musical presentation,** provide historic context and a discussion of a Civil War song of your choice.

- Evaluate several songs before choosing one.
- Consider the musical qualities of the song, such as the tempo and the mood.
- Provide background on the song's origins.

Play a recording of the song as part of your presentation.

Research and Technology In the library or on the Internet, research the definition of Naturalism and its presence in literature. Then, write a **definition essay,** defining Naturalism and giving examples of it from "An Episode of War." Be sure to include events in the story that reflect the belief that humankind is helpless in the face of events it cannot control.

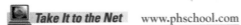 **Take It to the Net** www.phschool.com

Go online for an additional research activity using the Internet.

An Episode of War / Willie Has Gone to the War ◆ 485

ASSESSMENT RESOURCES

The following resources can be used to assess students' knowledge and skills.

Selection Assessment
- **Formal Assessment,** p. 119
- **Open Book Test,** p. 70
- **Got It! Assessment Videotapes,** Tape 3
- **Test Bank Software**

 Take It to the Net
Visit www.phschool.com for self-tests and additional questions on the selections.

Listening and Speaking Rubric
- **Performance Assessment and Portfolio Management,** p. 13

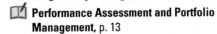 PRENTICE HALL ASSESSMENT SYSTEM

- **Workbook**
- **Skill Book**
- **Transparencies**
- **CD-ROM**

---

③ Writing Lesson

- Students' field reports should convey a sense of the overall situation facing army hospitals on Civil War battlefields, as well as appropriate details that support each point.

- Remind students to put themselves in the position of the lieutenant, a proper Civil War officer. They must see the relevant medical issues through his eyes and express views about the situation as he might have done.

- Use the Writing Lesson as well as Writing Process Model 10 in **Writing Models and Graphic Organizers on Transparencies,** p. 61, into guide students in developing their field reports.

④ Listening and Speaking

- Point out that the Civil War produced a wealth of songs. Many have been recorded. Two albums that attempt to re-create the music of the Civil War period are the *Original Soundtrack Recording: The Civil War,* produced by Ken Burns and John Colby, and *The Blue and the Gray in Black and White,* by Sparky and Rhonda Rucker.

- Once students have selected and researched their songs, allow time for presentations. Ask students to introduce their songs and then to play or sing them for the class. If they have found more than one version of a song, invite them to play both and to discuss which seems most authentic.

- Adapt the Multimedia Presentation rubric in **Performance Assessment and Portfolio Management,** p. 13, to evaluate students' presentations.

CUSTOMIZE INSTRUCTION
For Universal Access

To address different learning styles, use the following activities suggested in the **Extension Activities** booklet, p. 24.

For Verbal/Linguistic Learners, use Activities 5 and 6.

For Bodily/Kinesthetic Learners, use Activity 7.

BLOCK SCHEDULING: Resources marked with this symbol provide varied instruction during 90-minute blocks.

Swing Low, Sweet Chariot ✦ Go Down, Moses

Lesson Objectives

1. **To analyze and respond to literary elements**
   - Literary Analysis: Refrain
   - Comparing Literary Works

2. **To read, comprehend, analyze, and critique song lyrics**
   - Reading Strategy: Listening
   - Review and Assess Questions
   - Assessment Practice (ATE)

3. **To develop word analysis skills, fluency, and systematic vocabulary**
   - Vocabulary Development Lesson: Latin Root: -press-

4. **To understand and apply written and oral language conventions**
   - Spelling Strategy
   - Grammar and Style Lesson: Direct Address

5. **To understand and apply appropriate writing and research strategies**
   - Writing Lesson: Reflective Essay
   - Extension Activity: Anthology

6. **To understand and apply listening and speaking strategies**
   - Extension Activity: Choral Reading

STEP-BY-STEP TEACHING GUIDE	PACING GUIDE
PRETEACH	
Motivate Students and Provide Background	
Use the Motivation activity (ATE p. 486)	5 min.
Read and discuss More About the Literature and Background features (SE/ATE p. 486) **A**	5 min.
Introduce the Concepts	
Introduce the Literary Analysis and Reading Strategy (SE/ATE p. 487) **A**	15 min.
Pronounce the vocabulary words and read their definitions (SE p. 487)	5 min.
TEACH	
Monitor Comprehension	
Informally monitor comprehension by circulating while students read independently or in groups **A**	10 min.
Develop vocabulary with Vocabulary notes (SE p. 490; ATE p. 490)	
	as students read
Develop Understanding	
Develop students' understanding of refrains with the Literary Analysis annotations (SE p. 489; ATE p. 489) **A**	5 min.
ASSESS	
Assess Mastery	
Assess students' mastery of the Reading Strategy and Literary Analysis by having them answer the Review and Assess questions (SE/ATE p. 491)	15 min.
Use one or more of the print and media Assessment Resources (ATE p. 493) **A**	up to 45 min.
EXTEND	
Apply Understanding	
Have students complete the Vocabulary Development Lesson and the Grammar and Style Lesson (SE p. 492) **A**	20 min.
Apply students' ability to freewrite to tap personal experiences by using the Writing Lesson (SE/ATE p. 493) **A**	45 min.
Apply students' understanding using one or more of the Extension Activities (SE p. 493)	20–90 min.

 ACCELERATED INSTRUCTION:
Use the strategies and activities identified with an **A**.

UNIVERSAL ACCESS
- ● = Below Level Students
- ▲ = On-Level Students
- ■ = Above Level Students

Time and Resource Manager

Reading Level: Easy, Average
Average Number of Instructional Days: 2

RESOURCES		
PRINT 📓	**TRANSPARENCIES** 📄	**TECHNOLOGY** 💿 🎧 📼
• **Beyond Literature,** Cross-Curricular Connection: Social Studies, p. 25 ▲ ■		• **Interest Grabber Video,** Tape 4 ● ▲ ■
• **Selection Support Workbook:** ● ▲ ■ Literary Analysis, p. 115 Reading Strategy, p. 114 Build Vocabulary, p. 112	• **Literary Analysis and Reading Transparencies,** pp. 49 and 50 ● ▲ ■	
		• **Listening to Literature** ● ▲ ■ Audiocassettes, Side 16 Audio CDs, CD 10
• **Literatura en español** ● ▲ • **Literary Analysis for Enrichment** ■		
• **Formal Assessment:** Selection Test, p. 122 ● ▲ ■ • **Open Book Test,** p. 73 ● ▲ ■ • **Performance Assessment and Portfolio Management,** p. 11 ● ▲ ■ • **PRENTICE HALL ASSESSMENT SYSTEM** ● ▲ ■	• **PRENTICE HALL ASSESSMENT SYSTEM** ● ▲ ■ Skills Practice Answers and Explanations on Transparencies	• **Test Bank Software** ● ▲ ■ • **Got It! Assessment Videotapes,** Tape 3 ● ▲
• **Selection Support Workbook:** ● ▲ ■ Grammar and Style, p. 113 • **Writing and Grammar,** Ruby Level ● ▲ ■ • **Extension Activities,** p. 25 ● ▲ ■	• **Daily Language Practice Transparencies** ● ▲ • **Writing Models and Graphic Organizers on Transparencies,** p. 5 ● ▲ ■	• **Writing and Grammar iText CD-ROM** ● ▲ ■ 💻 *Take It to the Net* www.phschool.com

BLOCK SCHEDULING: Use one 90-minute class period to preteach the selection and have students read it. Use a second 90-minute class period to assess students' mastery of skills and have them complete one of the Extension Activities.

Step-by-Step Teaching Guide for pp. 486–487

Motivation

The best way to engage students' interest in the spirituals is by having them listen to the songs. Play the recordings of "Go Down, Moses" and "Swing Low, Sweet Chariot" on the *Listening to Literature Audiocassettes* or *Listening to Literature CDs.* As students listen, have them focus more on the sound of the spirituals than on the meanings of the lyrics. Follow with a discussion in which you help students explore why spirituals have remained popular for so long. With whom are they most likely to be popular? Why? Why have spirituals been so strong an influence on other types of music? After you've completed the discussion, have students read the texts of the spirituals.

▨ Interest Grabber Video

As an alternative, you may wish to play "African-American Spirituals" on Tape 4 to engage student interest.

❶ Background

More About the Literature

Cultural historian Bernice Johnson Reagon writes, "Spirituals were songs created as leverage, as salve, as voice, as a bridge over troubles one could not endure without the flight of song and singing. . . . [They] record the struggle of a people to survive, but like no other histories, have the power to touch the soul and stir the emotions of the people who sing and hear them."

Comparing Literary Works

Prepare to Read

❶ Swing Low, Sweet Chariot ◆ Go Down, Moses

Spirituals

Spirituals are folk songs that originated among enslaved and oppressed African Americans. They are one of the earliest and most widely known forms of American folk song to have survived to the twenty-first century. Spirituals took on the forms of anthems, ballads, shouts, and jubilees to reflect different moods and circumstances. Containing both social and religious content, spirituals helped to shape the conscious identity of an enslaved people; they also helped slaves persevere under the physical and psychological pressures of their daily life. These songs conveyed the singers' pain, their yearning for freedom, and their rage against slavery. In doing so, they brought to life the emotional impact of slavery, which divided our nation for decades and played a key role in causing the Civil War. Frederick Douglass, a slave who became one of the most important writers of his time, said of the spirituals, "Every tone was a testimony against slavery and a prayer to God for deliverance from chains." At the same time, the songs helped to replace lost African religious traditions and allowed men and women to maintain a connection to their musical heritage.

Song of the Fields Plantation owners, fearing discontent among their slaves, encouraged field hands to sing while they picked cotton or sugar, reasoning that people who were busy singing could not plot escape or rebellion. They generally accepted spirituals because the songs had religious content. The slaves, however, found ways to benefit from singing. Their songs provided an outlet for the grief and frustration they often kept bottled up inside. Spirituals also fostered a sense of personal self-worth by portraying slaves as innocents of a mighty God, deserving of a heavenly reward for their earthly labors. By grafting their memories of traditional African music and rhythms onto religious hymns of early nineteenth-century Christian revivalists, enslaved Africans managed to hold on to part of their heritage. In addition, the language in some songs provided a means to communicate forbidden thoughts and feelings.

A Double Message Many spirituals had a double meaning. Most included references to people, places, or events in the Bible. They frequently referred to Moses, who in the Old Testament led the Jews out of slavery in Egypt. Slaves identified with the ancient Israelites, who had once been the slaves of the Egyptians. Singing about the Israelites was a safe way to voice their own yearning for liberty. For example, in spirituals such as "Swing Low, Sweet Chariot" and "Go Down, Moses," slaves expressed their hope that they would someday escape to their own "promised land," just as the Israelites escaped to ancient Israel. References to figures and events in the Bible thus became a kind of code for the slaves' own experience. One work song did more than just express discontent; it gave directions for escape: In "Follow the Drinking Gourd," fugitive slaves were advised to follow the Big Dipper north to freedom.

Path to Popularity Spirituals were almost unknown outside the South until after the Civil War. In 1867, a collection of African American music called *Slave Songs of the United States* was published. In 1871, a black choral group, the Jubilee Singers from Fisk University, traveled throughout the United States and to England and Germany singing spirituals to raise money for their school. The Jubilee Singers were extremely gifted, and became highly successful, even singing for Queen Victoria in England. Students from other schools followed their example and helped popularize the spiritual. Today, spirituals are performed by gospel singers, and their influence is apparent in contemporary music forms such as blues and jazz.

486 ◆ *Division, Reconciliation, and Expansion (1850–1914)*

TEACHING RESOURCES

The following resources can be used to enrich or extend the instruction for pp. 486–487

Motivation

▨ **Interest Grabber Video,** Tape 4 ▨

Background

▨ **Beyond Literature,** p. 25

▨ *Take It to the Net*
Visit www.phschool.com for Background and hotlinks for the selections.

Literary Analysis

▨ **Literary Analysis and Reading Transparencies,** Refrain, p. 50

▨ **Selection Support:** Literary Analysis, p. 115

Reading

▨ **Literary Analysis and Reading Transparencies,** Listening, p. 49 ▨

▨ **BLOCK SCHEDULING:** Resources marked with this symbol provide varied instruction during 90-minute blocks.

Preview

Connecting to the Literature

Songs have an amazing power to sway our emotions. They can soothe us when we are feeling sad or bring back special memories. As these two spirituals demonstrate, songs can even help people endure great hardships. As you read, think about a song that had a strong emotional impact on you.

❷ Literary Analysis

Refrain

If you are searching for the meaning of a song or poem, you will often find it in the **refrain**—a word, phrase, line, or group of lines repeated at regular intervals throughout the work. Refrains serve these key functions:

- They emphasize the most important ideas.
- They help establish the rhythm of the song.

Most spirituals contain at least one refrain. For example, the line "Coming for to carry me home" is repeated throughout "Swing Low, Sweet Chariot." As you read these songs, think about the message each refrain conveys.

Comparing Literary Works

Most spirituals were not meant to be sung alone. Instead, the refrain facilitated a call-and-response format in which a leader sang the verses and the rest of the group acted like a chorus and sang the refrain. Each song produced a different mood or feeling within the group: some songs focused more on the pain or rage caused by the conditions of slavery, while other songs looked hopefully toward the future. Compare the mood of these two songs and imagine how you might feel as you sang or heard them.

❸ Reading Strategy

Listening

Since songs are created for the ear and not the eye, **listening** is an especially important skill for appreciating lyrics.

- Read each spiritual aloud, listening to its rhythm.
- Pay attention to rhymes and other repeated sounds. For example, the opening line in "Go Down, Moses" contains three stressed syllables in a row.

Often, the rhythms and sounds of a song suggest a specific mood. As you read these spirituals, think about the different moods and effects that the sounds of the songs create. Record some of these effects in a chart like the one shown.

Vocabulary Development

oppressed (ə prest´) v. kept down by cruel or unjust power (p. 490)

smite (smīt) v. to kill by a powerful blow (p. 490)

❷ Literary Analysis

Refrain

- Explain that students will focus on refrains as they study the two songs in this grouping.
- Invite students to draw on their prior knowledge of music to explain what they know about refrains. Many students may be familiar with the refrain's primary defining characteristic: the repetition of words, phrases, or lines at regular intervals.
- Encourage students to think of examples of songs they know that contain memorable refrains. Have students review the lyrics of the songs to see how the refrain emphasizes or complements each song's most important ideas.

❸ Reading Strategy

Listening

- Point out to students that all language contains rhythm. Good songwriters link a song's melody with the inherent rhythms of the lyrics.
- Thus, students should understand that rhythm in songs is not limited to the melody or instrumental passages. Students can hear rhythm in the language of the lyrics, as well.
- Explain that listening is a skill that is often taken for granted. Encourage students to reflect on how their own experiences prove the profound difference between close and distracted listening.

Vocabulary Development

- Pronounce each vocabulary word for students, and read the definitions as a class. Have students identify any words with which they are already familiar.

CUSTOMIZE INSTRUCTION FOR UNIVERSAL ACCESS

For Less Proficient Readers	For English Learners	For Advanced Readers
Guide students to understand the underlying meanings of important lines and details in the spirituals. For example, help them see that the line "Coming for to carry me home" refers not only to the hope of freedom in heaven, but also to the chance for escape to worldly freedom on the Underground Railroad.	To help students grasp the underlying meaning of the spirituals, make sure that they have at least a basic understanding of the historical context in which the spirituals were composed. Provide them with brief explanations of both American slavery and the Underground Railroad.	Ask students to consider connections between their own lives and today's popular music. Encourage students to compare and contrast the political, economic, and social conditions of the people who composed and sang the spirituals with those who compose and perform popular music today.

 E-Teach

Visit E-Teach at www.phschool.com for teachers' essays on how to teach, with questions and answers.

**CUSTOMIZE INSTRUCTION
For Musical/Rhythmic Learners**

Invite students to look for ways in which today's rhythm and blues, gospel, jazz, or hip-hop music reflects the influence of spirituals. Challenge them to identify specific musical elements that are common to all these styles.

❶ About the Selection

This spiritual, constructed around the refrain "Coming for to carry me home," expresses both a desire for eternal salvation in heaven and a longing for freedom from slavery. The "sweet chariot" and the "band of angels" are symbols for the Underground Railroad. This song is based on an Old Testament story in which the prophet Elijah is taken to heaven in a fiery chariot.

❷ ▶ Critical Viewing

Answer: The clothing appears to be homemade, tattered, and dirty. One can infer that fugitive slaves had difficult lives and few material possessions.

❸ Background

Spirituals

In his autobiography, former slave Frederick Douglass discusses why enslaved Africans sang spirituals as they worked: "Slaves are generally expected to sing as well as to work. A silent slave is not liked by masters or overseers. . . . The remark is not unfrequently made, that slaves are the most contented and happy laborers in the world. They dance and sing, and make all manner of joyful noise—so they do; but it is a great mistake to suppose them happy because they sing. The songs of the slave represent the sorrows rather than the joys, of his heart; and he is relieved by them, only as an aching heart is relieved by its tears."

SWING LOW, SWEET CHARIOT ❶
SPIRITUAL

❷ ▲ Critical Viewing
Looking at the clothing of the escaped slaves in this photograph, what can you infer about their lives as fugitives? **[Infer]**

Background

Africans first came to this country as slaves in 1619. Although the slave trade was banned in 1808, slavery remained legal. In response to slave rebellions of the 1820s and 1830s, many southern states enacted tough new laws that deprived slaves of nearly all their rights. In the years before the Civil War, many enslaved Africans fled captivity. They were hidden and transported by the Underground Railroad, a secret network of activists dedicated to helping fugitives reach freedom in the North and in Canada. ❸

One of those activists was Harriet Tubman, who was born a slave around 1820. Tubman was called the Moses of her people. In the Bible, Moses led the Israelites out of captivity in Egypt. Following Moses' example, Tubman escaped along the Underground Railroad and then risked her life to return for her family. Driven by the desire to help others still oppressed, she returned to the South again and again to rescue other enslaved Africans, eventually leading more than 300 people to freedom.

488 ◆ *Division, Reconciliation, and Expansion (1850–1914)*

TEACHING RESOURCES

The following resources can be used to enrich or extend the instruction for pp. 488–490.

Reading Strategy

📖 **Selection Support:** Reading Strategy, p. 114; Build Vocabulary, p. 112

🎧 **Listening to Literature Audiocassettes,** Side 16 ▪

💿 **Listening to Literature CDs,** CD 10 ▪

▪ **BLOCK SCHEDULING:** Resources marked with this symbol provide varied instruction during 90-minute blocks.

Swing low, sweet chariot,
Coming for to carry me home,
Swing low, sweet chariot,
Coming for to carry me home.

5   I looked over Jordan[1] and what did I see
Coming for to carry me home,
A band of angels coming after me,
Coming for to carry me home.

If you get there before I do,
10   Coming for to carry me home,
Tell all my friends I'm coming too,
Coming for to carry me home.

Swing low, sweet chariot,
Coming for to carry me home,
15   Swing low, sweet chariot,
Coming for to carry me home.

---

1. **Jordan** river of the Near East that flows from the Lebanon Mountains through the Sea of Galilee to the Dead Sea. Many spirituals use the phrase "crossing over Jordan" as a metaphor for crossing the Ohio River to freedom or going to heaven.

Literary Analysis
Refrain In what ways does the song's refrain emphasize the speaker's yearning?

Review and Assess

Thinking About the Selection

1. **Respond:** What mood did this spiritual evoke in you? Explain.
2. **(a) Recall:** Where does the speaker want to go?
   (b) Infer: What do you think this place represents?
3. **(a) Recall:** In what vehicle will the speaker travel "home"?
   (b) Interpret: What do you think this vehicle represents?
4. **(a) Recall:** Who is coming over Jordan to carry the speaker home? **(b) Interpret:** If the song is an expression of the slaves' desire for escape, what do these figures represent?
5. **Interpret:** Knowing that spirituals were often "code" songs for escape, do you think there are any hidden messages in this song? Explain.
6. **Apply:** In what ways do you think such a song could offer comfort to the slaves?

Swing Low, Sweet Chariot ◆ 489

❹ Literary Analysis
Refrain
- Have students participate in a choral reading of "Swing Low, Sweet Chariot."

▶ **Monitor Progress** Ask students the Literary Analysis question on p. 489: How does the song's refrain emphasize the speaker's yearning?
Answer: The repetition emphasizes the steady hope or belief that release will come—either through literal freedom or through death and an afterlife in heaven.

Answers for p. 489

Review and Assess

1. Students should be specific about the mood the song evoked in them.
2. **(a)** The speaker wants to go "home." **(b)** *Home* represents either heaven or a place where African Americans are no longer enslaved.
3. **(a)** The speaker will be carried in a chariot. **(b)** This vehicle may represent death or the Underground Railroad.
4. **(a)** "A band of angels" is coming across the Jordan River to carry the speaker home. **(b)** The angels might be abolitionists or those helping fugitives on the Underground Railroad.
5. This song seems to contain secret messages about the Underground Railroad's helping slaves escape to freedom.
6. The song offers the hope of freedom and reunion with friends.

CUSTOMIZE INSTRUCTION FOR UNIVERSAL ACCESS

For Special Needs Students	For Gifted/Talented Students
You may wish to clarify for students a few examples of vocabulary and usage in the spirituals. For instance, students may be confused by the antiquated phrase *coming for*; explain that the phrase means simply "coming." You might point out that—in this context—a *band* is "a group of people joined together for a common purpose" and that the archaic verb *saith* means "says."	Moses does not just "tell old Pharaoh" to let his people go; he threatens that the Lord will "smite" Pharaoh's first-born child. Can nonviolent methods be used to end oppression, or is violence an inevitable result? What are the moral choices inherent in a struggle against oppression? Challenge students to debate these issues, using their knowledge of oppression in any historical period.

489

❺ About the Selection

These lyrics refer to the biblical account of Moses leading the Hebrews out of bondage. In this song, the Pharaoh is a metaphor for any slaveholder; the Israelites are the slaves; Moses is a redeemer or savior; and Egypt represents the American South.

❻ Literary Analysis

Refrain

- Have students listen to the spiritual as it is read aloud.

> Monitor Progress Ask students to identify the refrain and to explain how they can recognize it. Answer: The refrain is found in the first four lines, and again in lines 8–12 and 16–20. This is the refrain because it is the part that repeats.

❼ Vocabulary Development

Latin Root -press-

- Draw students' attention to the use of the word *oppressed*, and read its definition. Then, tell students that the root -press- derives from the Latin word *premere* meaning "to press."

- In small groups, have students brainstorm for a list of other words that share the root -press-. As each group reports its list, write the words on the chalkboard. Possible responses: *pressure, suppress, repress, impress*

Answers for p. 490

Review and Assess

1. Students should support their answers with details.

2. (a) The people of Israel are oppressed. (b) The two groups share the experience of slavery.

3. (a) He will destroy their "first-born." (b) enslaved African Americans

4. (a) Moses issues his demand to Pharaoh. (b) Pharaoh represents slave owners.

5. The song uses both informal language, such as *Way down in Egypt land*, and formal language, such as *smite*. Students may find this an effective way to differentiate between the voice of the speaker and that of Moses.

490

---

❺ # GO DOWN, MOSES

SPIRITUAL

Go down, Moses,
Way down in Egypt land
Tell old Pharaoh
To let my people go.

5 When Israel was in Egypt land
Let my people go
<u>Oppressed</u> so hard they could not stand   ❼
Let my people go.

❻ Go down, Moses,
10 Way down in Egypt land
Tell old Pharaoh
"Let my people go."

"Thus saith the Lord," bold Moses said,
"Let my people go;
15 If not I'll <u>smite</u> your first-born dead
Let my people go."

Go down, Moses,
Way down in Egypt land,
Tell old Pharaoh,
20 "Let my people go!"

oppressed (ə prest') *v.* kept down by cruel or unjust power

smite (smīt) *v.* to kill by a powerful blow

Review and Assess

Thinking About the Selection

1. **Respond:** What emotions does this song most strongly convey to you? Explain.

2. **(a) Recall:** Who is oppressed in this song? **(b) Connect:** What connection might these oppressed people have with the slaves?

3. **(a) Recall:** With what punishment does the Lord threaten the Egyptians if they refuse to free the Israelites? **(b) Interpret:** Whom do the Israelites represent?

4. **(a) Recall:** Whom does Moses tell to "let my people go"? **(b) Interpret:** If this song is related to the slaves, whom might this figure represent?

5. **Evaluate:** Explain the effectiveness of the mix of formal and informal language in "Go Down, Moses."

✎ ASSESSMENT PRACTICE: Reading Comprehension

Context Clues   **(For more practice, see Test Preparation Workbook, p. 27.)**

Many tests require students to use context clues to determine the meaning of unfamiliar words. Use the following sample test item to give students practice in this skill.

> . . . bold Moses said,
>
> "Let my people go;
>
> If not I'll <u>smite</u> your first-born dead
>
> Let my people go."

In this passage, <u>smite</u> most nearly means—

A build   **C** cure

B strike   **D** affect

From the context of this passage, students should be able to determine that *smite* means a violent, destructive action. Even if they are not certain of the meaning of *strike*, students should recognize that none of the other choices fits this definition. Guide students to recognize that *B* is the correct answer.

Review and Assess

Literary Analysis

Refrain

1. What **refrains,** both lines and entire stanzas, are used in "Swing Low, Sweet Chariot"?
2. List the refrains, both lines and entire stanzas, used in "Go Down, Moses."
3. What idea or message is emphasized through the single-line refrain in "Go Down, Moses"?

Comparing Literary Works

4. In each **spiritual,** which lines might have been sung by a soloist and which by the chorus? Explain.
5. (a) What symbolic words do you note in each of the spirituals?
   (b) What do you think the symbols represent?
6. How might these spirituals soothe the feelings of longing, sadness, and injustice they express?
7. Compare the moods of these two spirituals.

Reading Strategy

Listening

8. Explain how each of the songs uses rhythm, rhyme, and repetition to reinforce meaning.
9. Using the sound elements you identified in both songs, compare the musical qualities of "Go Down, Moses" with those of "Swing Low, Sweet Chariot." Record your ideas in a chart like the one shown.

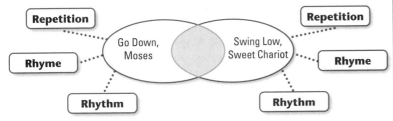

Repetition — Go Down, Moses — Swing Low, Sweet Chariot — Repetition
Rhyme — Rhyme
Rhythm — Rhythm

Extend Understanding

10. **Social Studies Connection:** Harriet Tubman once said, "We got to be free or die. And freedom's not bought with dust." What other American heroes would agree with her words? Explain your choices.

Quick Review

The **refrain** is a word, phrase, line, or group of lines repeated at regular intervals in a poem or song.

Spirituals are folk songs developed by enslaved Africans that often feature Biblical references and a call-and-response format.

Listening to a song's rhyme, rhythm, and repetition helps you appreciate its message and mood.

 Take It to the Net
www.phschool.com
Take the interactive self-test online to check your understanding of these selections.

ENRICHMENT: Further Reading

Works About Spirituals

Walk Together Children, Ashley Bryan

Black Song: The Forge and The Flame: The Story of How the Afro-American Spiritual Was Hammered Out, Hohm Lovell

Take It to the Net
Visit www.phschool.com for more information on spirituals.

Answers for page 491

Review and Assess

1. The entire first stanza is a refrain that appears twice in "Swing Low, Sweet Chariot." The line "Coming for to carry me home" is also used as a refrain.

2. The entire first stanza is a refrain that appears three times in the song. The line "let my people go" is also a refrain.

3. The refrain "let my people go" expresses the slaves' desire for freedom. This is the main idea of the song.

4. The soloist would probably sing the verses, which tell the story. The refrains would be sung by a chorus to reinforce the theme of the song.

5. **(a)** Students may mention words such as *chariot, home, Jordan, band of angels*, and all of the proper nouns in "Go Down, Moses."
   (b) The chariot represents the Underground Railroad; home represents freedom; Jordan represents the Ohio River; the band of angels represents conductors on the Underground Railroad; the Pharaoh and Egyptians represent slave owners; Egypt represents the United States of America; the Israelites represent enslaved African Americans.

6. The songs offer the hope of freedom.

7. "Go Down, Moses" is dignified and determined in mood, while "Swing Low" is calmer and more melancholy.

8. Possible response: In both songs, the refrain, which is repeated many times, clearly states the theme. Rhyme is used to frame the refrains and to reinforce the meaning of the other lines. The rhythms support the messages by drawing readers into the songs.

9. Both spirituals repeat single lines and entire stanzas; both use end rhymes extensively; both feature strong, regular rhythms. The rhythm of "Swing Low" is smoother and gentler.

10. Students might mention Martin Luther King Jr., or Abraham Lincoln, because both held strong beliefs in freedom and equality.

EXTEND

Answers for p. 492

❶ Vocabulary Development

Word Analysis

1. impress
2. compress
3. depress
4. repress

Concept Development

1. b
2. c

Spelling Strategy

1. c, *installed*
2. b, *bossed*
3. a, *possessed*

❷ Grammar and Style

1. <u>Selena</u>, sing slowly and with great feeling.
2. The choir performed well, <u>Ms. Dodd</u>.
3. <u>Choir members</u>, please stand straight.
4. Everyone agrees, <u>Joe</u>, that you have a great voice.
5. Still, <u>Mr. Jones</u>, I'd rather play the guitar.

Writing Application

Students' sentences should discuss a particular musical genre, and each one should contain a correctly punctuated example of direct address.

Integrate Language Skills

❶ Vocabulary Development Lesson

Word Analysis: Latin Root *-press-*

The root *-press-* means "push." People who are *oppressed* are pushed or kept down. Copy each sentence, completing each blank with an appropriate word formed with the root *-press-* and one of the prefixes defined below.

com- (together)   re- (back)
de- (down)   im- (into)

1. _____?_____ the metal seal on the hot wax to make your mark.
2. Watch as I _____?_____ the paper into a tight ball.
3. When you _____?_____ the button, a buzzer sounds.
4. The enthusiastic fans weren't able to _____?_____ their squeals.

Concept Development: Antonyms

Select the word that is the closest antonym, or opposite, of the first word.

1. oppressed: (a) crushed, (b) assisted, (c) punished
2. smite: (a) hit, (b) question, (c) caress

Spelling Strategy

When adding *-ed* to a word ending in a double consonant, keep both consonants, as in *oppress* + *ed* = *oppressed*. Match the correct word for each definition given below, adding *-ed* to each word to form a new word.

1. fixed in position   **a.** possess
2. ordered   **b.** boss
3. owned   **c.** install

❷ Grammar and Style Lesson

Direct Address

In both these spirituals, the speaker uses **direct address** by speaking directly to someone or something by name.

When you use direct address, put a comma after the name if it comes first in the sentence, before the name if it comes last in the sentence, and on both sides of the name if it comes in the middle of the sentence.

> **Examples:** Swing low, *sweet chariot*,
> Coming for to carry me home.
>
> Go down, *Moses*,
> Way down in Egypt land.
> *Lord*, hear our prayer.

Practice Copy these sentences in your notebook. Underline the words of direct address and add punctuation where necessary.

1. Selena sing slowly and with great feeling.
2. The choir performed well Ms. Dodd.
3. Choir members please stand straight.
4. Everyone agrees Joe that you have a great voice.
5. Still Mr. Jones I'd rather play the guitar.

Writing Application Write three sentences or questions related to your interest in music. Include direct address, with correct punctuation, in each sentence.

𝒲𝒢 *Prentice Hall Writing and Grammar Connection: Chapter 27, Section 2*

TEACHING RESOURCES

The following resources can be used to enrich or extend the instruction for pp. 492–493.

Vocabulary

📖 **Selection Support:** Build Vocabulary, p. 112

📖 **Vocabulary and Spelling Practice Book** (Use this booklet for skills enrichment.)

Grammar

📖 **Selection Support:** Grammar and Style, p. 113 ▪

𝒲𝒢 **Writing and Grammar,** Ruby Level, p. 696

📖 **Daily Language Practice Transparencies** ▪

Writing

𝒲𝒢 **Writing and Grammar,** Ruby Level, p. 58 ▪

📖 **Writing Models and Graphic Organizers on Transparencies,** p. 5

💿 **Writing and Grammar iText CD-ROM**

▪ **BLOCK SCHEDULING:** Resources marked with this symbol provide varied instruction during 90-minute blocks.

❸ Writing Lesson

Reflective Essay

Imagine that you are a free person living in the South before the Civil War. You hear these spirituals, and for the first time, truly pay attention to the lyrics. In a reflective essay, analyze what the songs have taught you about the realities of slavery.

Prewriting   Freewrite about the songs by writing quickly and continuously for five minutes. Review your notes to choose a few ideas to explore.

> **Model: Freewriting to Tap Personal Experiences**
>
> I think "Go Down, Moses" expresses several emotions—pride, anger, sorrow, yearning. . . . That refrain, "Let my people go," really sums it up. Someone else is keeping me and my people from freedom. Let my people go. I can hardly imagine having to live my life like that . . .
>
> To capture ideas, freewriting relaxes the rules of grammar. Errors can be edited later.

Drafting   In your introduction, summarize the songs. Then, in the body of your essay, discuss the insights the songs have revealed to you.

Revising   A reflective essay should indicate the significance of an experience. Review your draft. If necessary, add more information to show what the songs mean to you, or how they might change your life.

W̸G Prentice Hall Writing and Grammar Connection: Chapter 4, Section 2

❹ Extension Activities

Listening and Speaking With a small group, conduct a **choral reading** of a spiritual. Use a call-and-response format, with one student calling out the verses and the rest answering with the refrains. Each "soloist" should improvise to create at least one new verse. Use these tips to prepare:

- Determine who will say which lines.
- Learn your lines from memory.
- Emphasize the call-and-response format.

After you have practiced, perform the spiritual for your class. **[Group Activity]**

Research and Technology Using the Internet or other library resources, find several other spirituals to present in an **anthology.** For each song you include, write a brief introduction that provides background information or necessary context for readers.

 Take It to the Net   www.phschool.com

Go online for an additional research activity using the Internet.

Swing Low, Sweet Chariot / Go Down, Moses ◆ 493

---

❸ Writing Lesson

- Students' reflective essays should express the personal significance of their listening to the spirituals. They should also include details about the experience of slavery that helped students come to a new understanding of the topic.

- Suggest that students do their freewriting as they listen to the recordings of the spirituals on the **Listening to Literature Audiocassettes** or **CDs.**

- Use the Writing Lesson as well as Writing Process Model 1 in **Writing Models and Graphic Organizers on Transparancies,** p. 5, to guide students in developing their reflective essays.

- Use the Reflective Essay rubric in **Performance Assessment and Protfolio Management,** p. 11, to evaluate students' reflective essays.

❹ Research and Technology

- Students might find examples of spirituals in a variety of forms, including audio recordings, sheet music, poetry anthologies, and nonfiction and reference books.

- Remind students to review each of the spirituals they select for words, idioms and other unusual syntax, and historical allusions. Any such elements will need to be illuminated in students' introductory passages.

CUSTOMIZE INSTRUCTION
For Universal Access

To address different learning styles, use the following activities suggested in the **Extension Activities** booklet, p. 25.

For Musical/Rhythmic Learners, use Activity 5.

For Interpersonal Learners, use Activity 6.

For Verbal/Linguistic Learners, use Activity 7.

ASSESSMENT RESOURCES

The following resources can be used to assess students' knowledge and skills.

Selection Assessment

📖 **Formal Assessment,** p. 122

📖 **Open Book Test,** p. 73

📼 **Got It! Assessment Videotapes,** Tape 3

💿 **Test Bank Software**

🖥 *Take It to the Net*
   Visit www.phschool.com for self-tests and additional questions on the selections.

Writing Rubric

📖 **Performance Assessment and Portfolio Management,** p. 11

PRENTICE HALL ASSESSMENT SYSTEM

📖 **Workbook**   📖 **Transparencies**

📖 **Skill Book**   💿 **CD-ROM**

■ **BLOCK SCHEDULING:** Resources marked with this symbol provide varied instruction during 90-minute blocks.

from My Bondage and My Freedom

Lesson Objectives

1. **To analyze and respond to literary elements**
   - Literary Analysis: Autobiography
   - Connecting Literary Elements: Tone

2. **To read, comprehend, analyze, and critique nonfiction**
   - Reading Strategy: Establishing a Purpose
   - Reading Check Questions
   - Review and Assess Questions
   - Assessment Practice (ATE)

3. **To develop word analysis skills, fluency, and systematic vocabulary**
   - Vocabulary Development Lesson: Latin Root: *-bene-*

4. **To understand and apply written and oral language conventions**
   - Spelling Strategy
   - Grammar and Style Lesson: Correlative Conjunctions

5. **To understand and apply appropriate writing and research strategies**
   - Writing Lesson: College Admission Essay
   - Extension Activity: Multimedia Presentation

6. **To understand and apply listening and speaking strategies**
   - Extension Activity: Oral Presentation

STEP-BY-STEP TEACHING GUIDE	PACING GUIDE
PRETEACH	
Motivate Students and Provide Background	
Use the Motivation activity (ATE p. 494)	5 min.
Read and discuss author and background features (SE/ATE p. 494)	5 min.
Introduce the Concepts	
Introduce the Literary Analysis and Reading Strategy (SE/ATE p. 495)	15 min.
Pronounce the vocabulary words and read their definitions (SE p. 495)	5 min.
TEACH	
Monitor Comprehension	
Informally monitor comprehension by circulating while students read independently or in groups	25 min.
Monitor students' comprehension with the Reading Check notes (SE/ATE pp. 497, 499, 501)	as students read
Develop vocabulary with Vocabulary notes (SE pp. 497, 499, 501; ATE p. 497)	as students read
Develop Understanding	
Develop students' understanding of autobiography with the Literary Analysis annotations (SE pp. 499, 501; ATE pp. 499, 501)	5 min. 5 min.
ASSESS	
Assess Mastery	
Assess students' mastery of the Reading Strategy and Literary Analysis by having them answer the Review and Assess questions (SE/ATE p. 503)	15 min.
Use one or more of the print and media Assessment Resources (ATE p. 505)	up to 45 min.
EXTEND	
Apply Understanding	
Have students complete the Vocabulary Development Lesson and the Grammar and Style Lesson (SE p. 504)	20 min.
Apply students' ability to plan clear and logical organization by using the Writing Lesson (SE/ATE p. 505)	45 min.
Apply students' understanding using one or more of the Extension Activities (SE p. 505)	20–90 min.

A **ACCELERATED INSTRUCTION:**
Use the strategies and activities identified with an **A**.

UNIVERSAL ACCESS
- ● = Below Level Students
- ▲ = On-Level Students
- ■ = Above Level Students

Time and Resource Manager

Reading Level: Challenging
Average Number of Instructional Days: 4

RESOURCES		
PRINT 📖	**TRANSPARENCIES**	**TECHNOLOGY** 💿 🎧 📼
• **Beyond Literature,** Career Connection: Teaching, p. 26 ▲ ■		• **Interest Grabber Video,** Tape 4 ● ▲ ■
• **Selection Support Workbook:** ● ▲ ■ Literary Analysis, p. 115 Reading Strategy, p. 114 Build Vocabulary, p. 112	• **Literary Analysis and Reading Transparencies,** pp. 51 and 52 ● ▲ ■	
• **Adapted Reader's Companion** ● • **Reader's Companion** ●		• **Listening to Literature** ● ▲ ■ Audiocassettes, Side 17 Audio CDs, CD 11
• **English Learner's Companion** ● ▲ • **Literatura en español** ● ▲ • **Literary Analysis for Enrichment** ■	• **Fine Art Transparencies, Volume 1,** Transparency 5 ● ▲ ■	
• **Formal Assessment:** Selection Test, p. 125 ● ▲ ■ • **Open Book Test,** p. 76 ● ▲ ■ • **Performance Assessment and Portfolio Management,** p. 13 ● ▲ ■ • **PRENTICE HALL ASSESSMENT SYSTEM** ● ▲ ■	• **PRENTICE HALL ASSESSMENT SYSTEM** ● ▲ ■ Skills Practice Answers and Explanations on Transparencies	• **Test Bank Software** ● ▲ ■ • **Got It! Assessment Videotapes,** Tape 3 ● ▲
• **Selection Support Workbook:** ● ▲ ■ Grammar and Style, p. 117 • **Writing and Grammar,** Ruby Level ● ▲ ■ • **Extension Activities,** p. 26 ● ▲ ■	• **Daily Language Practice Transparencies** ● ▲ • **Writing Models and Graphic Organizers on Transparencies,** p. 5 ● ▲ ■	• **Writing and Grammar iText CD-ROM** ● ▲ ■ 💻 *Take It to the Net* www.phschool.com

BLOCK SCHEDULING: Use one 90-minute class period to preteach the selection and have students read it. Use a second 90-minute class period to assess students' mastery of skills and have them complete one of the Extension Activities.

Step-by-Step Teaching Guide
for pp. 494–495

Motivation

Engage students' interest by sharing an idea of Douglass's that is seemingly paradoxical: both slaves and slaveholders were victims of slavery. Have students react to this idea and consider questions such as, how can slaveholders be perceived as victims of a system from which they benefit? Invite students to speculate about what evidence Douglass might offer to support his point. Then, have them read the selection to find out. When they've finished reading, conduct a follow-up discussion in which students explain whether their views have been changed in any way by Douglass's argument.

▣ Interest Grabber Video

As an alternative, you may wish to play "Frederick Douglass Speaks" on Tape 4 to engage student interest.

❶ Background

More About the Author

Frederick Bailey was born on the Eastern Shore of Maryland, on land facing west toward Chesapeake Bay. His first owner was Aaron Anthony, who worked for the wealthy planter Edward Lloyd. Before his years with Sophie and Hugh Auld in Baltimore, Frederick lived on Lloyd's plantation. At fifteen, Douglass was sent to St. Michaels on the Eastern Shore to work for Thomas Auld. There, he was hired out as a laborer to a number of farmers, and there, he attempted to escape his bondage for the first time. At twenty, Frederick Bailey took the name Frederick Douglass.

Prepare to Read

❶ *from* My Bondage and My Freedom

Frederick Douglass (1818–1895)

Frederick Douglass rose out of slavery to become one of the most gifted writers and orators of his time. Using these talents, he dedicated his life to fighting for the abolition of slavery and for civil rights. Douglass's life served as an inspiration and example for both blacks and whites throughout the country.

Early Years Douglass was born on a Maryland plantation. Historians believe that his name at birth was Frederick Augustus Bailey. At the age of eight, he was sent as a slave to the Baltimore home of the Auld family. While there, Douglass learned to read and write, at first with the strong encouragement of Mrs. Auld and later despite her objections. Learning soon became an unquenchable thirst for Douglass. He often traded biscuits for reading lessons from his playmates.

His reading fueled a quest for freedom. At age twenty, he escaped to Massachusetts, a free state, and took the surname Douglass to avoid arrest as a fugitive.

A Public Life Although he had never spoken in public before, Douglass delivered a tremendously powerful and moving debut speech at the 1841 convention of an abolitionist organization. Despite the constant fear of being arrested as a fugitive slave, he spent the next four years lecturing against slavery and arguing for the need for civil rights for all people.

Rumors spread that a man of such eloquence could not possibly have been a slave. In response, Douglass published his first autobiography, *Narrative of the Life of Frederick Douglass, an American Slave,*

Written By Himself (1845). Fearing that the book would lead to his re-enslavement, Douglass then fled to England, where he spent years trying to gain British support for the abolitionist movement in the United States.

Freedom at Last After English friends raised money to buy his freedom, Douglass returned to the United States, established a newspaper for African Americans, and resumed lecturing. In 1855, he published *My Bondage and My Freedom,* an updated version of his autobiography.

During the Civil War, Douglass helped recruit African American soldiers for the Union army. After slavery was abolished, he fought vigorously for civil rights for African Americans. He became a consultant to President Lincoln and held several government positions, including United States minister to Haiti.

A Vision for the Future As an abolitionist, orator, and journalist, Douglass favored political methods for emancipating the slaves and bringing them into the mainstream of American life—a goal he was determined they should reach. In 1883, speaking as a vigorous fighter for civil rights, Douglass commented that the American people "must learn, or neglect to do so at their own peril. . . .The American people must stand each for all and all for each, without respect to color or race. . . . I expect to see the colored people of this country enjoying the same freedom, voting at the same ballot-box, using the same cartridge-box, going to the same schools, attending the same churches, . . . proud of the same country, fighting the same foe, and enjoying the same peace and all its advantages. . . ."

Douglass did not limit himself to fighting for the civil rights of African Americans. He also helped women in their battle to win the vote. Because he did not segregate his causes, Douglass is a model for all who struggle against injustice.

494 ◆ *Division, Reconciliation, and Expansion (1850–1914)*

TEACHING RESOURCES

The following resources can be used to enrich or extend the instruction for pp. 494–495.

Motivation

▣ **Interest Grabber Video,** Tape 4 ▣

Background

▣ **Beyond Literature,** p. 26

 Take It to the Net

Visit www.phschool.com for Background and hotlinks for *My Bondage and My Freedom.*

Literary Analysis

▣ **Literary Analysis and Reading Transparencies,** Autobiography, p. 52 ▣

▣ **Selection Support:** Literary Analysis, p. 119

Reading

▣ **Literary Analysis and Reading Transparencies,** Using Background Knowledge, p. 51

 BLOCK SCHEDULING: Resources marked with this symbol provide varied instruction during 90-minute blocks.

Preview

Connecting to the Literature

Imagine another person denying your right to read just as you were discovering the power of le▓▓▓g. If you were enslaved like Frederick Douglass, you w▓▓▓▓▓▓▓ice but to submit (or at least appear to submit)

❷ Liter▓▓▓

Autobiography

An **autobiography** is a person's written account of his or her own life, focusing on the events the author considers most significant. Because the writer's life is presented as he or she views it, the portrayal of people and events is colored by the author's feelings and beliefs. Usually, writers of autobiographies believe that their lives are interesting or important and can in some way help others. Frederick Douglass wrote his autobiography because he believed that his life proved that blacks were no less perceptive, intelligent, or capable than whites, as he states directly in these lines:

> I could talk and sing; I could laugh and weep; I could reason
> and remember . . .

As you read about the experiences that shaped Douglass's life, notice how they might serve as examples for others.

Connecting Literary Elements

When reading autobiographies, you can usually detect a clear **tone**—the writer's attitude toward the subject, characters, or audience. Tone is created through a choice of words and details. It may be formal or informal, friendly or distant. As you read, listen for Douglass's tone just as you would if he were speaking to you aloud.

❸ Reading Strategy

Establishing a Purpose

Establishing a purpose for reading gives you an idea or concept on which to focus. For example, as you read from Douglass's autobiography, establish the purpose of learning about his special qualities and expanding your understanding of what it was like to be a slave. Record details that reflect this purpose in a chart like the one shown.

Vocabulary Development

congenial (kən jēn′ yəl) *adj.* agreeable (p. 497)

benevolent (bə nev′ ə lənt) *adj.* kindly; charitable (p. 497)

stringency (strin′ jən sē) *n.* strictness; severity (p. 497)

depravity (dē prav′ ə tē) *n.* corruption; wickedness (p. 497)

consternation (kän′ stər nā′ shən) *n.* great fear or shock that makes one feel helpless or bewildered (p. 499)

redolent (red′ əl ənt) *adj.* suggestive (p. 501)

---

❷ Literary Analysis

Autobiography

- Tell students that they will focus on autobiography—a person's written account of his or her own life—as they read this excerpt from Frederick Douglass's *My Bondage and My Freedom*.

- Read the instruction about autobiography aloud. Point out the sentences concerning the subjective nature of autobiographical writing. Encourage students to discuss the range of choices a writer must make in the process of planning and drafting an autobiography. Speculate about the process a writer might use to select specific life experiences on which to focus.

- As they read Douglass's narrative, encourage students to take note of the episodes, ideas, people, and emotions on which Douglass has placed his emphasis.

❸ Reading Strategy

Establishing a Purpose

- Ask student volunteers to suggest examples of texts—such as a technical manual for using software, a lyric poem, or the autobiography of a former slave—that require readers to set a variety of purposes. As discussion ensues, list and categorize these purposes on the chalkboard.

- Remind students that setting purposes for reading is a way for them to exert control over their literary experiences. If they realize early in a text that their chosen purpose is inappropriate, they are free to set another purpose for reading.

Vocabulary Development

- Pronounce each vocabulary word for students, and read the definitions as a class. Have students identify any words with which they are already familiar.

 E-Teach

Visit E-Teach at www.phschool.com for teachers' essays on how to teach, with questions and answers.

CUSTOMIZE INSTRUCTION FOR UNIVERSAL ACCESS

For Special Needs Students	For Less Proficient Readers	For English Learners
Have students read the adapted version of *My Bondage and My Freedom* in the **Adapted Reader's Companion.** This version provides basic-level instruction in an interactive format with questions and write-on lines. Completing the adapted version will prepare students to read the selection in the Student Edition.	Have students read *My Bondage and My Freedom* in the **Reader's Companion**. This version provides basic-level instruction in an interactive format with questions and write-on lines. After students finish the selection in **Reader's Companion**, have them complete the questions and activities in the Student Edition.	Have students read the adapted version of *My Bondage and My Freedom* in the **English Learner's Companion.** This version provides basic-level instruction in an interactive format with questions and write-on lines. Completing the adapted version will prepare students to read the selection in the Student Edition.

Step-by-Step Teaching Guide for pp. 496–502

CUSTOMIZE INSTRUCTION
For Interpersonal Learners

Douglass wrote that his mistress was a "most kind and tenderhearted woman. . . ." Have students discuss whether it is possible for a slave owner to be a "good" person or, more broadly, whether it is possible for a good person to do bad things.

❶ Background

Art

The Chimney Corner, by Eastman Johnson

Eastman Johnson (1824–1906) was the son of a wealthy Maine politician. He studied art in Germany, Holland, and France, and he returned to the United States well-trained in genre painting. Johnson painted portraits of some of the most notable Americans of his time, including John Quincy Adams and Henry Wadsworth Longfellow. During the Civil War, he used his talents to record topical scenes and events.

Use these questions for discussion:

1. Do you think this man is a slave? Explain.
Possible answer: Students may say that because the painting dates from 1863, the man may be a slave who, by the look of his clothing, works in a house. Perhaps he has found a moment of privacy to indulge a love of reading. If he is not a slave, he may be a house servant who was not discouraged from reading.

2. How would you describe the mood of the painting?
Possible answer: Students may say that the dark, uncomfortable corner provides a sense of privacy and calm. The man is quietly engrossed in his book, despite the meanness of his surroundings.

❷ ▶Critical Viewing

Answer: Students might say that the light shining on this man reading in a dark chamber symbolizes the beacon of knowledge, an awakening of understanding, or a glimmer of hope.

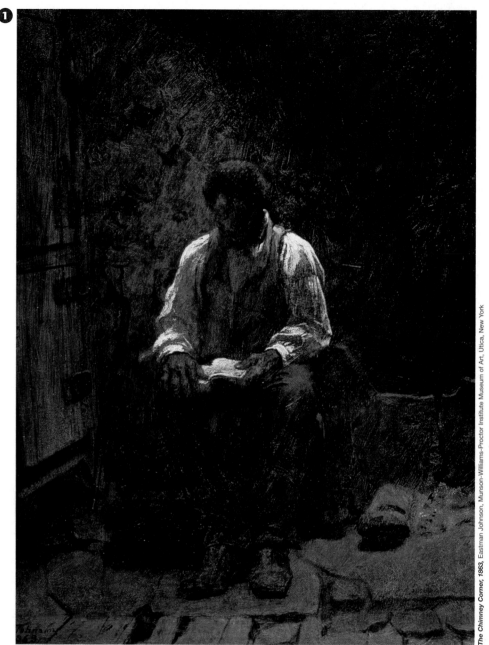

❶

The Chimney Corner, 1863, Eastman Johnson, Munson-Williams-Proctor Institute Museum of Art, Utica, New York

❷ ▲ **Critical Viewing** What might the light shining on the reader symbolize for Douglass? **[Interpret]**

496 ◆ *Division, Reconciliation, and Expansion (1850–1914)*

TEACHING RESOURCES

The following resources can be used to enrich or extend the instruction for pp. 496–502.

Reading Strategy

📖 **Selection Support:** Reading Strategy, p. 118; Build Vocabulary, p. 116

📖 **Adapted Reader's Companion**

📖 **Reader's Companion**

📖 **English Learner's Companion**

🎧 **Listening to Literature Audiocassettes,** Side 17 ■

💿 **Listening to Literature CDs,** CD 11 ■

Extension

🖼 **Fine Art Transparencies,** Volume 1, Art Transparency 5 ■

■ **BLOCK SCHEDULING:** Resources marked with this symbol provide varied instruction during 90-minute blocks.

from My Bondage and My Freedom

Frederick Douglass

Background

Frederick Douglass was perhaps the most prominent African American leader of the nineteenth century, and his influence is still felt. As a crusader for human rights, Douglass served as a role model for African American leaders such as Booker T. Washington and W.E.B. DuBois. In our own era, the civil rights movement has drawn inspiration from Douglass, who opposed segregation decades before other voices were raised. As a young man, Douglass protested segregated seating on trains by sitting in cars reserved for whites until the authorities forcibly removed him. Later, he fought job discrimination against African Americans, protested segregation in school, and fought for civil rights for all Americans.

I lived in the family of Master Hugh, at Baltimore, seven years, during which time—as the almanac makers say of the weather—my condition was variable. The most interesting feature of my history here, was my learning to read and write, under somewhat marked disadvantages. In attaining this knowledge, I was compelled to resort to indirections by no means congenial to my nature, and which were really humiliating to me. My mistress—who had begun to teach me—was suddenly checked in her benevolent design, by the strong advice of her husband. In faithful compliance with this advice, the good lady had not only ceased to instruct me, herself, but had set her face as a flint against my learning to read by any means. It is due, however, to my mistress to say, that she did not adopt this course in all its stringency at the first. She either thought it unnecessary, or she lacked the depravity indispensable to shutting me up in mental darkness. It was, at least, necessary for her to have some training, and some hardening, in the exercise of the slaveholder's prerogative, to make her equal to forgetting my human nature and character, and to treating me as a thing destitute of a moral or an intellectual nature.

congenial (kən jēn´ yəl) *adj.* agreeable

❹ **benevolent** (bə nev´ ə lənt) *adj.* kindly; charitable

stringency (strin´ jən sē) *n.* strictness; severity

depravity (di prav´ ə tē) *n.* corruption; wickedness

❺ ✔**Reading Check**
Why did Douglass's mistress stop teaching him to read and write?

from My Bondage and My Freedom ◆ 497

---

❸ **About the Selection**

In this excerpt from his second autobiography, Douglass tries to show that slavery corrupted, dehumanized, and victimized everyone—including slaveholders. The passage describes how his master's kind wife, Mrs. Auld, feels compelled to abandon her efforts to educate young Frederick. Convinced by her husband that slavery and education are incompatible, she attempts to block any learning opportunities for the young boy, even though such hard-heartedness goes against her nature. Douglass continues to learn from his white playmates, trading biscuits for lessons. Influenced by the ideas he discovers through his reading, Douglass becomes consumed by a constant yearning for freedom and thoughts about the evils of slavery. He grows to hate the institution of slavery, which has made enemies of him and his mistress, who might otherwise have been friends.

❹ Vocabulary Development

Latin Root -bene-

- Draw students' attention to Douglass's use of the word *benevolent*, and read its definition. Then, tell students that the root *-bene-* derives from the Latin word meaning "well," or "good."

- Invite students to suggest other words that Douglass might have used to convey his meaning, and list these words on the chalkboard. Possibilities include *kind*, *good-hearted*, and *generous*.

- Guide students to see that the word *benevolent* encompasses the ideas of both kindness and generosity. Douglass uses it to emphasize his mistress's natural greatness of heart.

❺ ✔Reading Check

Answer: The mistress's husband insisted that she stop.

CUSTOMIZE INSTRUCTION FOR UNIVERSAL ACCESS

For English Learners	For Advanced Readers
Help students use context clues and a dictionary to decode the meanings of unfamiliar words such as *marked*, *checked*, and *waxed*, used here by Douglass in less familiar ways. Then, have them brainstorm for other words that Douglass might have used to convey similar meanings. For example, for the word *marked*, students might provide the synonyms *noticeable*, *striking*, or *distinct*. For the word *checked*, students might suggest words such as *prevented*, *stopped*, or *prohibited*.	Encourage students to look closely at Douglass's opening paragraph, examining it for the ways in which he begins to convey his essential message about the unnaturalness of slavery. Ask students to answer this question: What does Douglass say his mistress must undergo in order to become an effective slaveholder? Then, invite students to speculate about what might be involved in such "training." Why is it essential that a slaveholder "forget" the "human nature and character" of a slave?

❻ Background

Racist Views

Help students put this remarkable statement into historical perspective. In 1825, many whites in the United States of America, in their ignorance, did not believe that people with dark skin were truly human. Through her experience with Frederick, Mrs. Auld learned the truth.

❼ ▶ Critical Viewing

Possible response: The painting suggests that plantation owners lived lives of luxury that contrasted sharply with the experiences of the slaves.

❽ Background

Art

A Home on the Mississippi, 1871, by Currier and Ives

Nathaniel Currier (1813–1888) and James Ives (1824–1895) started the firm of Currier and Ives in 1857 to produce commercially countless lithographic chronicles of nineteenth-century American life. Hand-colored scenes like this one were immensely popular with the American public. People obtained them by mail order, from traveling salespeople, and from the partners' shop in New York City. A favorite Currier and Ives theme was the home. *A Home on the Mississippi* was reproduced more than 3.5 billion times on the label of a popular beverage. The scene is filled with typical Southern atmosphere accentuated by the gracious verandah on the house and the Spanish moss hanging from the trees.

Use these questions for discussion:

1. What impression of southern living does this print convey? Possible answer: Students may say that it suggests a calm, genteel, leisurely lifestyle.

2. Do you think this view of the South matches Frederick Douglass's? Why or why not? Answer: Students may say that it does in that it shows the southern gentry riding in elegant carriages while the slaves walk along the side of the road or stand outside the fences.

498

Mrs. Auld—my mistress—was, as I have said, a most kind and tender-hearted woman; and, in the humanity of her heart, and the simplicity of her mind, she set out, when I first went to live with her, to treat me as she supposed one human being ought to treat another.

It is easy to see, that, in entering upon the duties of a slaveholder, some little experience is needed. Nature has done almost nothing to prepare men and women to be either slaves or slaveholders. Nothing but rigid training, long persisted in, can perfect the character of the one or the other. One cannot easily forget to love freedom; and it is as hard to cease to respect that natural love in our fellow creatures. On entering upon the career of a slaveholding mistress, Mrs. Auld was singularly deficient; nature, which fits nobody for such an office, had done less for her than any lady I had known. It was no easy matter to induce her to think and to feel that the curly-headed boy, who stood by her side, and even leaned on her lap; who was loved by little Tommy, and who loved little Tommy in turn; sustained to her only the relation of a chattel. I was *more* than that, and she felt me to be more than that. I could talk and sing; I could laugh and weep; I could reason and remember; I could love and hate. I was human, and she, dear lady, knew and felt me to be so. How could she, then, treat me as a brute, without a mighty struggle with all the noble powers of her own soul. That struggle came, and the will and power of the husband

❼ ▼ **Critical Viewing**
How does this idealized picture of plantation life contrast with Douglass's experiences as an enslaved African American? **[Contrast]**

A Home on the Mississippi, Currier & Ives, The Museum of the City of New York

---

✹ ENRICHMENT: Cultural Connection

Slavery

Slavery neither began nor ended with southern plantation owners. A common practice since ancient times, slavery originated with conquest; it was the fate that awaited the conquered. Slave markets existed by the time of the first Babylonian Empire, more than three thousand years ago. Sadly, slavery continues to exist in parts of the world even today.

Students have read about one slave's reaction to his circumstances. Invite them to find out how other slaves have responded to their bondage. They might, for instance, obtain a copy of a Haggadah (the narrative of the Exodus from Egypt that is read every year at the Jewish festival of Passover) to read about what the slave Nachshon did to obtain his freedom. Or they can research one of the several slave revolts in America; in particular, they can find out about the only sustained slave revolt in American history, the 1831 rebellion led by Nat Turner.

was victorious. Her noble soul was overthrown; but, he that over-threw it did not, himself, escape the consequences. He, not less than the other parties, was injured in his domestic peace by the fall.

When I went into their family, it was the abode of happiness and contentment. The mistress of the house was a model of affection and tenderness. Her fervent piety and watchful uprightness made it impossible to see her without thinking and feeling—"that woman is a Christian." There was no sorrow nor suffering for which she had not a tear, and there was no innocent joy for which she did not [have] a smile. She had bread for the hungry, clothes for the naked, and comfort for every mourner that came within her reach. Slavery soon proved its ability to divest her of these excellent qualities, and her home of its early happiness. Conscience cannot stand much violence. Once thoroughly broken down, *who* is he that can repair the damage? It may be broken toward the slave, on Sunday, and toward the master on Monday. It cannot endure such shocks. It must stand entire, or it does not stand at all. If my condition waxed bad, that of the family waxed not better. The first step, in the wrong direction, was the violence done to nature and to conscience, in arresting the benevolence that would have enlightened my young mind. In ceasing to instruct me, she must begin to justify herself *to* herself; and, once consenting to take sides in such a debate, she was riveted to her position. One needs very little knowledge of moral philosophy, to see *where* my mistress now landed. She finally became even more violent in her opposition to my learning to read, than was her husband him-self. She was not satisfied with simply doing as *well* as her husband had commanded her, but seemed resolved to better his instruction. Nothing appeared to make my poor mistress—after her turning toward the downward path—more angry, than seeing me, seated in some nook or corner, quietly reading a book or a newspaper. I have had her rush at me, with the utmost fury, and snatch from my hand such newspaper or book, with something of the wrath and <u>consternation</u> which a traitor might be supposed to feel on being discovered in a plot by some dangerous spy.

Mrs. Auld was an apt woman, and the advice of her husband, and her own experience, soon demonstrated, to her entire satisfaction, that education and slavery are incompatible with each other. When this conviction was thoroughly established, I was most narrowly watched in all my movements. If I remained in a separate room from the family for any considerable length of time, I was sure to be suspected of having a book, and was at once called upon to give an account of myself. All this, however, was entirely *too late*. The first, and never to be retraced, step had been taken. In teaching me the alphabet, in the days of her simplicity and kindness, my mistress had given me the "inch," and now, no ordinary precaution could prevent me from taking the "ell."[1]

---

1. **ell** *n.* former English measure of length, equal to forty-five inches.

Literary Analysis
Autobiography Douglass blames the institution of slavery, rather than Mrs. Auld for the changes in the household. What does this tell you about him?

consternation (kän′ stər nā′ shən) *n.* great fear or shock that makes one feel helpless or bewildered

❿ ☑ Reading Check
What extreme measure does Mrs. Auld take?

from My Bondage and My Freedom ◆ 499

❾ Literary Analysis
Autobiography
- Have a student volunteer read this passage aloud, and invite students to listen for the distinctive tone of civility, intelligence, compassion, and determination in the narrative voice of Frederick Douglass.
- Ask students the Literary Analysis question on p. 499: Douglass blames the institution of slavery, rather than Mrs. Auld, for the changes in the household. What does this tell you about him? Answer: Students may respond that Douglass has a positive view of human nature despite his experiences as a slave.

❿ ☑ Reading Check
Answer: Mrs. Auld becomes "even more violent [than Mr. Auld] in her opposition" to Douglass's reading.

CUSTOMIZE INSTRUCTION FOR UNIVERSAL ACCESS

For Special Needs Students	For Gifted/Talented Students
Frederick Douglass makes frequent use of long sentences that may pose a challenge for students. Help them break down the long sentences by identifying the core of each one—its subject and verb—and stating the main action described. Then, have students look at how the other groups of words in the sentence relate to the subject and the verb.	Guide students to appreciate Douglass's views on the intrinsic right of an individual to acquire knowledge and on the negative effects of denying a person that right. Invite students to discuss why the Aulds' decision regarding Douglass's education places them in a "condition" Douglass views as worse than his own. Encourage students to create a drawing or other visual image that captures the power of knowledge and the opposing relationships of the Aulds and Douglass.

11 Background

Slave Narratives

The first known slave narrative—*A Narrative of the Uncommon Sufferings and Surprising Deliverance of Briton Hammon, a Negro Man*—appeared in 1760 in Boston. Other notable examples of this sub-genre of autobiography include *A Narrative of the Lord's Wonderful Dealings with J. Murrant, a Black, Taken Down from His Own Relation* (1784), *Incidents in the Life of a Slave Girl, Written by Herself* (1861) by Harriet Jacobs, and *Scenes in the Life of Harriet Tubman* (1869).

12 Critical Thinking

Interpret/Support

- Invite students to explain the meaning of the expression "Give [him] an inch and [he'll] take a mile" and to support their definitions with examples.

- Then, point out that this saying summarizes Mr. Auld's fears regarding the potential results of Douglass's education. Auld once said that if Frederick learned to read "there would be no keeping him. . . . If you learn him how to read, he'll want to know how to write; and this accomplished, he'll be running away with himself."

13 Background

Maryland

Remind students that Maryland was *not* one of the states that seceded from the United States of America to join the Confederacy. Point out that although slavery was present in Maryland, it was not as prevalent as it was in states of the Deep South.

12 Seized with a determination to learn to read, at any cost, I hit upon many expedients to accomplish the desired end. The plea which I mainly adopted, and the one by which I was most successful, was that of using my young white playmates, with whom I met in the street, as teachers. I used to carry, almost constantly, a copy of Webster's spelling book in my pocket; and, when sent on errands, or when play time was allowed me, I would step, with my young friends, aside, and take a lesson in spelling. I generally paid my *tuition fee* to the boys, with bread, which I also carried in my pocket. For a single biscuit, any of my hungry little comrades would give me a lesson more valuable to me than bread. Not everyone, however, demanded this consideration, for there were those who took pleasure in teaching me, whenever I had a chance to be taught by them. I am strongly tempted to give the names of two or three of those little boys, as a slight testimonial of the gratitude and affection I bear them, but prudence forbids; not that it would injure me, but it might, possibly, embarrass them; for it is almost an unpardonable offense to do anything, directly or indirectly, to promote a slave's freedom, in a slave state. It is enough to say, of my warm-hearted little play fellows, that they lived on Philpot Street, very near Durgin & Bailey's shipyard.

Although slavery was a delicate subject, and very cautiously talked about among grownup people in Maryland, I frequently talked about it—and that very freely—with the white boys. I would, sometimes, say to them, while seated on a curbstone or a cellar door, "I wish I could be free, as you will be when you get to be men." "You will be free, you know, as soon as you are twenty-one, and can go where you like, but I am a slave for life. Have I not as good a right to be free as you have?" Words like these, I observed, always troubled them; and I had no small satisfaction in wringing from the boys, occasionally, that fresh and bitter condemnation of slavery, that springs from nature, unseared **13** and unperverted.[2] Of all consciences let me have those to deal with which have not been bewildered by the cares of life. I do not remember ever to have met with a *boy*, while I was in slavery, who defended the slave system; but I have often had boys to console me, with the hope that something would yet occur, by which I might be made free. Over and over again, they have told me, that "they believed *I* had as good a right to be free as *they* had"; and that "they did not believe God ever made anyone to be a slave." The reader will easily see, that such little conversations with my play fellows, had no tendency to weaken my love of liberty, nor to render me contented with my condition as a slave.

---

2. **unperverted** (un′ pər vʉrt′ id) *adj.* uncorrupted; pure.

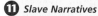

The American Experience

11 *Slave Narratives*

From 1760 to the end of the Civil War, when slavery was officially abolished, the testimonies of hundreds of fugitive and former slaves appeared in the form of slave narratives. Like the precedent-setting *Interesting Narrative of the Life of Olaudah Equiano* (p. 44), these slave narratives exposed the inhumanities of the slave system. Former slaves recorded the oppressive conditions they suffered under their owners, not only to document their experiences but also to ensure that the reunified nation would not soon forget. These personal testimonies appeared in the form of narratives, reports, and interviews. The Federal Writers Project of the 1920s and 1930s gathered the narratives and documented them, creating an archive attesting to the terrible experience of American slavery.

When I was about thirteen years old, and had succeeded in learning to read, every increase of knowledge, especially respecting the free states, added something to the almost intolerable burden of the thought—"I am a slave for life." To my bondage I saw no end. It was a terrible reality, and I shall never be able to tell how sadly that thought chafed my young spirit. Fortunately, or unfortunately, about this time in my life, I had made enough money to buy what was then a very popular schoolbook, the *Columbian Orator.* I bought this addition to my library, of Mr. Knight, on Thames street, Fell's Point, Baltimore, and paid him fifty cents for it. I was first led to buy this book, by hearing some little boys say they were going to learn some little pieces out of it for the exhibition. This volume was, indeed, a rich treasure, and every opportunity afforded me, for a time, was spent in diligently perusing it . . . The dialogue and the speeches were all <u>redolent</u> of the principles of liberty, and poured floods of light on the nature and character of slavery. As I read, behold! the very discontent so graphically predicted by Master Hugh, had already come upon me. I was no longer the light-hearted, gleesome boy, full of mirth and play, as when I landed first at Baltimore. Knowledge had come . . . This knowledge opened my eyes to the horrible pit, and revealed the teeth of the frightful dragon that was ready to pounce upon me, but it opened no way for my escape. I have often wished myself a beast, or a bird—anything, rather than a slave. I was wretched and gloomy, beyond my ability to describe. I was too thoughtful to be happy. It was this everlasting thinking which distressed and tormented me; and yet there was no getting rid of the subject of my thoughts. All nature was redolent of it. Once awakened by the silver trump[3] of knowledge, my spirit was roused to eternal wakefulness. Liberty! the inestimable birthright of every man, had, for me, converted every object into an asserter of this great right. It was heard in every sound, and beheld in every object. It was ever present, to torment me with a sense of my wretched condition. The more beautiful and charming were the smiles of nature, the more horrible and desolate was my condition. I saw nothing without seeing it, and I heard nothing without hearing it. I do not exaggerate, when I say, that it looked from every star, smiled in every calm, breathed in every wind, and moved in every storm.

I have no doubt that my state of mind had something to do with the change in the treatment adopted, by my once kind mistress toward me. I can easily believe, that my leaden, downcast, and discontented look, was very offensive to her. Poor lady! She did not know my trouble, and I dared not tell her. Could I have freely made her acquainted with the real state of my mind, and given her the reasons therefor, it might have been well for both of us. Her abuse of me fell upon me like the blows of the false prophet upon his ass;

---

3. **trump** trumpet.

redolent (red′ əl ənt) *adj.* suggestive

Literary Analysis
Autobiography and Tone
What does Douglass's tone here reveal about the importance of reading this book?

 Reading Check
What significant changes take place in Douglass after reading *Columbian Orator?*

from My Bondage and My Freedom ◆ 501

⑭ **Literary Analysis**
Autobiography and Tone
• Ask a strong reader to read aloud this powerful, impassioned passage from Douglass's autobiography. Invite students to describe Douglass's tone using details in the passage to support their ideas.

▶ Monitor Progress Then, ask students the Literary Analysis question on p. 501: What does Douglass's tone here reveal about the importance of reading this book?
Answer: For Douglass, reading the book was crucial: it validated his private thoughts and feelings and fueled his determination to break the bonds of slavery.

⑮ ☑ **Reading Check**
Answer: He grows "wretched and gloomy" and "too thoughtful to be happy."

CUSTOMIZE INSTRUCTION FOR UNIVERSAL ACCESS

For Special Needs Students	For Less Proficient Readers
Clarify the meaning of the term *nature* for students by pointing out that Douglass is not using it in the strict sense as a reference to the natural world. Instead, he uses *nature* to mean all of creation—the natural world as well as the human. On page 502, when he states that "Nature had made us friends," he is referring to "human nature"—the qualities all human beings share.	In the long paragraph that begins at the top of p. 501, Douglass presents one of the key ideas of this selection: reading the *Columbian Orator* caused him to develop an overpowering desire for freedom. This point is made toward the middle of the paragraph, and it is restated and reinforced in the sentences that follow. Assist students in identifying the main idea and noting the ways in which Douglass develops and supports it.

Review and Assess

1. Students should offer clear, solid reasons to back up their points of view.

2. **(a)** He is first taught by Mrs. Auld and later, by young white playmates. **(b)** At first, she approves of it and actively supports it. **(c)** In order to compensate for her initial, natural reaction of support, Mrs. Auld adopts an attitude even more extreme than her husband's. In this way she may hope to fool herself into thinking that she is comfortable with suppressing the intellectual curiosity of a boy.

3. **(a)** They believe slavery is wrong and that black and white children are inherently equal. **(b)** Students may point out that a human being's "natural" or "pure" impulse is to treat other people as equals. Children may be closer to this state of purity.

4. **(a)** He reads a book about liberty and realizes he can no longer tolerate his bondage. **(b)** Knowledge opens his eyes to the pain and evil of slavery, but gives him few tools—at least initially—with which to escape it.

5. **(a)** He is consumed by his desire for freedom. **(b)** The ability to read gives Douglass access to voices and ideas that challenge and condemn the institution of slavery. Without education, he would have remained ignorant of these ideas and received no validation for his innate desire to be free.

6. Some students may observe that, in one sense, Douglass was free because he realized his self-worth and saw slavery as an invalid system. This awareness led him to seek actual freedom. Many other students will respond that Douglass was not free while still in bondage.

---

she did not know that an *angel* stood in the way;[4] and—such is the relation of master and slave—I could not tell her. Nature had made us *friends*; slavery made us *enemies*. My interests were in a direction opposite to hers, and we both had our private thoughts and plans. She aimed to keep me ignorant; and I resolved to know, although knowledge only increased my discontent. My feelings were not the result of any marked cruelty in the treatment I received; they sprung from the consideration of my being a slave at all. It was *slavery*—not its mere *incidents*—that I hated. I had been cheated. I saw through the attempt to keep me in ignorance . . . The feeding and clothing me well, could not atone for taking my liberty from me. The smiles of my mistress could not remove the deep sorrow that dwelt in my young bosom. Indeed, these, in time, came only to deepen my sorrow. She had changed; and the reader will see that I had changed, too. We were both victims to the same overshadowing evil—*she*, as mistress, *I*, as slave. I will not censure her harshly; she cannot censure me, for she knows I speak but the truth, and have acted in my opposition to slavery, just as she herself would have acted, in a reverse of circumstances.

---

4. **blows . . . the way** allusion to a biblical tale (Numbers 22:21–35) about an ass that cannot move, though she is beaten by her master, because her path is blocked by an angel.

Review and Assess

Thinking About the Selection

1. **Respond:** Do you think it is possible to be a benevolent slaveholder? Why or why not?

2. **(a) Recall:** How does Douglass learn to read? **(b) Recall:** What does Mrs. Auld initially think about Douglass's reading? **(c) Draw Conclusions:** Why do you think she was later "violent in her opposition" to Douglass's reading?

3. **(a) Recall:** What is the attitude toward slavery of the white boys who help Douglass learn to read? **(b) Analyze:** Why do you think they have that attitude toward the slaves?

4. **(a) Recall:** What circumstance transforms Douglass from "light-hearted" to "wretched and gloomy"? **(b) Connect:** What does knowledge do for him?

5. **(a) Recall:** What consumed Douglass once he obtained knowledge? **(b) Support:** How does his experience prove his mistress's belief that education and slavery are incompatible?

6. **Apply:** Mahatma Gandhi wrote, "The moment the slave resolves that he will no longer be a slave, his fetters fall." Explain whether or not you feel Douglass was free even while in bondage.

⬗ ASSESSMENT PRACTICE: Reading Comprehension

Context   **(For more practice, see Test Preparation Workbook, p. 28.)**

Many tests require students to use context to determine the appropriate meaning of a multiple-meaning word. Use the following sample test item to give students practice in this skill.

> I was compelled to resort to indirections by no means congenial to my nature, and which were really humiliating to me.

In this passage, <u>congenial</u> most nearly means—

  A friendly   **C** kindred
  B sympathetic   **D** suited

The word *humiliating* provides a context clue that the indirections are not suited to the speaker's nature or temperament. Although the other choices are also definitions of *congenial*, *D* is the appropriate meaning in the context of this passage.

Review and Assess

Literary Analysis

Autobiography

1. Douglass is relatively well cared for as a slave. In what way does he use his **autobiography** to make his case against slavery?
2. Find a passage in which Douglass conveys his opposition to slavery through his description of events.
3. In what ways would this account be different if it had been written by Mrs. Auld?

Connecting Literary Elements

4. (a) Describe Douglass's attitude toward Mrs. Auld. (b) Why do you think he feels as he does?
5. (a) What is the **tone** of the end of the selection? (b) Which specific words and phrases reveal Douglass's attitude toward slavery?
6. How does the tone—including word choice—of this selection support Douglass's desire to serve as a model?

Reading Strategy

Establishing a Purpose

7. Which of Douglass's special qualities are conveyed through this section of his autobiography? Explain.
8. Using a chart like the one shown, identify what you learned about the effects of slavery from Douglass's account.

Douglass's Account	Effects of Slavery

....▶

9. In what ways did reading this selection add to your understanding of the effects of slavery? Expain.

Extend Understanding

10. **Social Studies Connection:** Many writers have paid tribute to Douglass's ideas. (a) Why do you think his messsage strikes such a chord with Americans? (b) In what ways does it reflect the core values on which America was founded?

from *My Bondage and My Freedom* ◆ 503

Quick Review

An **autobiography** is the account of a person's life written in his or her own words.

The **tone** of a work reflects the author's attitude toward the subject, characters, or audience.

Establish a purpose for reading by choosing an idea or concept on which to focus.

 Take It to the Net
www.phschool.com
Take the interactive self-test online to check your understanding of the selection.

✹ ENRICHMENT: Further Reading

Other Works by or About Frederick Douglass

Narrative of the Life of Frederick Douglass, an American Slave, Written by Himself, 1845

"Speech at the Civil Rights Mass Meeting," 1833, Washington, D. C.

Frederick Douglass, William S. McFeely

Frederick Douglass, A Biography, Philip S. Foner

 Take It to the Net
Visit www.phschool.com for more information on Frederick Douglass.

Answers for page 503

Review and Assess

1. He uses his relationship with his mistress as an example of the many ways in which slavery forces people to betray their natural tendencies—hers toward kindness and his toward liberty.

2. The paragraph that begins "When I went into their family" is one example of this approach.

3. Possible response: She may have denied any change in her personality and would have seen her actions as proper.

4. (a) He does not blame her for becoming an oppressor. Instead, he sees her as another victim of the institution of slavery. (b) Possible answer: He feels this way because he has witnessed her earlier, natural response.

5. (a) To describe Douglass's tone, students might use words such as *determined, steadfast,* and *intense.* (b) Words and phrases include *like the blows of the false prophet upon his ass; it was* slavery—*not its mere incidents—that I hated.*

6. Douglass's eloquent telling of his life's story reflects his intelligence and his ability to understand human nature. It illustrates that African Americans of Douglass's time were capable of achieving great things despite great obstacles.

7. Possible answer: It reveals his intelligence, persistence, and ingenuity.

8. Possible answer: Douglass's Account: *I was compelled to resort to indirections by no means congenial to my nature;* Effects: Sometimes slavery caused African Americans to act in ways that they considered to be morally offensive.

9. Students should support their answers with details from the text.

10. (a) Students may mention Douglass's evenhandedness and clarity, as well as his compassion and sympathy. (b) Douglass's central ideas concern the fundamental humanity of African Americans and the basic impulse of human beings to regard each other as equals.

❶ Vocabulary Development

Word Analysis

1. "a positive effect"
2. "someone who does good things for someone or something"
3. "a blessing"

Spelling Strategy

1. stringency
2. leniency
3. insistence
4. reverence

Fluency: Sentence Completion

consternation; redolent; benevolent; depravity; stringency

❷ Grammar and Style

1. Neither ... nor
2. Not only ... but also
3. Whether ... or
4. Just as ... so
5. Either ... or

Writing Application

Check to see that students have used correlative conjunctions in proper pairs.

Integrate Language Skills

❶ Vocabulary Development Lesson

Word Analysis: Latin Root -bene-

The Latin root -bene- means "well" or "good." The word *benevolent* literally means "with good wishes" or "kindly."

Define each of the following words, incorporating the meaning of the root -bene- into your definition.

   1. benefit   **2.** benefactor   **3.** benediction

Spelling Strategy

When creating the noun form of an adjective that ends in *-ent*, replace the *t* with *-ce* or *-cy*: *benevolent* becomes *benevolence*. Add the *-ce* or *-cy* ending to each adjective below.

   1. stringent   **3.** insistent
   2. lenient   **4.** reverent

Fluency: Sentence Completion

Copy the following passage and fill in the blanks with the appropriate vocabulary words from the list on page 495.

I could see my neighbor scowling with a look of   __?__ , so I knew something was wrong. She spent hours in her well-manicured garden. It was usually __?__ with the fragrance of roses, which she was __?__ enough to share with me. The previously robust bushes were cut to the ground! I was stunned and silenced by the __?__ of the deed. I could understand the __?__ of her message as she sadly tacked up a KEEP OUT sign.

❷ Grammar and Style Lesson

Correlative Conjunctions

Correlative conjunctions—pairs of connecting words—link similar kinds of words and word groups and connect ideas. In this example, the italicized words show the relationship between the two actions in the sentence.

> **Example:** . . . the good lady had *not only* ceased to instruct me, herself, *but* had set her face as a flint against my learning to read by any means.

Correlative conjunctions are usually used in these combinations:

- *either . . . or*
- *not only . . . but (also)*
- *whether . . . or*
- *neither . . . nor*
- *just as . . . so*

Practice For each item, create a logical sentence by adding a pair of correlative conjunctions from the italicized list.

1. __?__ slave __?__ mistress was truly free.
2. __?__ Maryland __?__ Mississippi and Tennessee were slave states.
3. __?__ a slave __?__ a slaveholder, all people are harmed by slavery.
4. __?__ Douglass worked to abolish slavery, __?__ did Sojourner Truth.
5. __?__ Mrs. Auld __?__ Mr. Auld would win the moral struggle.

Writing Application Write an original paragraph about slavery, using each of the five pairs of correlative conjunctions listed.

WG *Prentice Hall Writing and Grammar Connection: Chapter 17, Section 4*

TEACHING RESOURCES

The following resources can be used to enrich or extend the instruction for pp. 504–505.

Vocabulary

📖 **Selection Support:** Build Vocabulary, p. 116

📖 **Vocabulary and Spelling Practice Book** (Use this booklet for skills enrichment.)

Grammar

📖 **Selection Support:** Grammar and Style, p. 117 ▪

WG **Writing and Grammar,** Ruby Level, p. 388

▪ **Daily Language Practice Transparencies** ▪

Writing

WG **Writing and Grammar,** Ruby Level, p. 56 ▪

▪ **Writing Models and Graphic Organizers on Transparencies,** p. 5

💿 **Writing and Grammar iText CD-ROM**

▪ **BLOCK SCHEDULING:** Resources marked with this symbol provide varied instruction during 90-minute blocks.

❸ Writing Lesson

College Admission Essay

A college application often requires you to write about an experience that helped shape you as a person. Just as Douglass described how knowledge freed him, you, too, can identify a key event or shaping force in your life, and write an essay explaining it.

Prewriting   Outline the details of the event, and describe its effect on you. List the details in chronological order to establish organization.

> ### Model: Planning a Clear and Logical Organization
>
> A. Worked in local campaign office
>   1. Met the candidate; was inspired
>   2. Distributed flyers; polled voters
>   3. Phoned residents to encourage voting
> B. Learned team work and the power of democracy

> Chronological order makes it easy for readers to follow an essay.

Drafting   Introduce the experience and explain why you are writing about it. Then, write the body paragraphs to follow your outline. Conclude with a paragraph that insightfully sums up the impact of the experience on your life.

Revising   Add time transition words like *first*, *next*, and *finally* to show chronological order and cause-effect words like *since* and *therefore* to reinforce the way this event helped shape you.

W͞G   *Prentice Hall Writing and Grammar Connection: Chapter 4, Section 3*

❹ Extension Activities

Listening and Speaking   Select a passage from this selection to read to an audience of abolitionist sympathizers. Add statements of your own for emphasis that you believe would represent Douglass's intent and purpose. Consider the following:

- Add strong emotion to convey Douglass's tone.
- Use persuasive language to compel your audience.

Deliver the **oral presentation** to the class.

Research and Technology   Using words, pictures, and sounds, work with a group to create a **multimedia presentation** that expresses the importance of literacy. Draw your materials from printed sources such as magazines, newspapers, and photographs. Consider recordings of speeches that will add vitality to your presentation. [**Group Activity**]

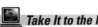 **Take It to the Net**   www.phschool.com

Go online for an additional research activity using the Internet.

from My Bondage and My Freedom ◆ *505*

ASSESSMENT RESOURCES

The following resources can be used to assess students' knowledge and skills.

Selection Assessment
- 📖 **Formal Assessment**, p. 125
- 📖 **Open Book Test**, p. 76
- 💿 **Test Bank Software**
- 📼 **Got It! Assessment Videotapes**, Tape 3

📖 **Take It to the Net**
Visit www.phschool.com for self-tests and additional questions on the selection.

- 📖 **Performance Assessment and Portfolio Management**, p. 13

PRENTICE HALL
ASSESSMENT SYSTEM
- 📖 **Workbook**
- 📖 **Skill Book**
- 📼 **Transparencies**
- 💿 **CD-ROM**

---

❸ Writing Lesson

- Students' college admission essays should describe an event that had great significance for them and should explain in detail the impact of the event on their lives.

- Remind students that their audience knows nothing about the context in which this key event occurred. Therefore, early in their essays, students must describe what their lives and viewpoints were like *before* the event. Readers will then understand both the nature of the event and its significance in their lives.

- Use the Writing Lesson, as well as Writing Process Model 1 in **Writing Models and Graphic Organizers on Transparencies,** p. 5, to guide students in developing their college admission essays.

❹ Research and Technology

- Encourage students to review the passages in this selection that deal specifically with the power of reading. Have students make a list of words and phrases that Douglass uses to convey his ideas about the topic.

- Then, have students gather in small groups in order to generate lists of their own thoughts and feelings about all aspects of literacy.

- Finally, invite groups to brainstorm for a variety of ways to express both Douglass's and their own ideas, using visual images or sound.

- Use the Multimedia Presentation rubric in **Performance Assessment and Portfolio Management,** p. 13, to evaluate students' multimedia presentations.

CUSTOMIZE INSTRUCTION
For Universal Access

To address different learning styles, use the following activities suggested in the **Extension Activities** booklet, p. 26.

For Verbal/Linguistic Learners, use activities 5 and 6.

For Interpersonal and Musical/Rhythmic Learners, use Activity 7.

An Occurrence at Owl Creek Bridge

Lesson Objectives

1. **To analyze and respond to literary elements**
   - Literary Analysis: Point of View
   - Connecting Literary Elements: Stream of Consciousness

2. **To read, comprehend, analyze, and critique a short story**
   - Reading Strategy: Identifying Chronological order
   - Reading Check Questions
   - Review and Assess Questions
   - Assessment Practice (ATE)

3. **To develop word analysis skills, fluency, and systematic vocabulary**
   - Vocabulary Development Lesson: Latin Root: *-summa-*

4. **To understand and apply written and oral language conventions**
   - Spelling Strategy
   - Grammar and Style Lesson: Semicolons in Compound Sentences

5. **To understand and apply appropriate writing and research strategies**
   - Writing Lesson: Critical Essay
   - Extension Activity: Visual Model

6. **To understand and apply listening and speaking strategies**
   - Extension Activity: Summary

STEP-BY-STEP TEACHING GUIDE	PACING GUIDE
PRETEACH	
Motivate Students and Provide Background	
Use the Motivation activity (ATE p. 506)	5 min.
Read and discuss author and background features (SE/ATE p. 506) **A**	5 min.
Introduce the Concepts	
Introduce the Literary Analysis and Reading Strategy (SE/ATE p. 507) **A**	15 min.
Pronounce the vocabulary words and read their definitions (SE p. 507)	5 min.
TEACH	
Monitor Comprehension	
Informally monitor comprehension by circulating while students read independently or in groups **A**	30 min.
Monitor students' comprehension with the Reading Check notes (SE/ATE pp. 509, 511, 513, 515)	as students read
Develop vocabulary with Vocabulary notes (SE pp. 509, 510, 511, 512, 515; ATE p. 511)	as students read
Develop Understanding	
Develop students' understanding of point of view with the Literary Analysis annotations (SE p. 510; ATE p. 510) **A**	5 min.
Develop students' understanding of chronological order with the Reading Strategy annotations (SE pp. 512, 514; ATE pp. 512, 514)	5 min.
ASSESS	
Assess Mastery	
Assess students' mastery of the Reading Strategy and Literary Analysis by having them answer the Review and Assess questions (SE/ATE p. 517)	15 min.
Use one or more of the print and media Assessment Resources (ATE p. 519) **A**	up to 45 min.
EXTEND	
Apply Understanding	
Have students complete the Vocabulary Development Lesson and the Grammar and Style Lesson (SE p. 518) **A**	20 min.
Apply students' ability to incorporate quotations from the story by using the Writing Lesson (SE/ATE p. 519) **A**	45 min.
Apply students' understanding using one or more of the Extension Activities (SE p. 519)	20–90 min.

 ACCELERATED INSTRUCTION:
Use the strategies and activities identified with an **A**.

UNIVERSAL ACCESS
● = Below Level Students
▲ = On-Level Students
■ = Above Level Students

Time and Resource Manager

RESOURCES		
PRINT 📖	**TRANSPARENCIES**	**TECHNOLOGY** 💿 🎧 📼
• **Beyond Literature,** Community Connection: The Legal System, p. 27 ▲ ■		• **Interest Grabber Video,** Tape 4 ● ▲ ■
• **Selection Support Workbook:** ● ▲ ■ Literary Analysis, p. 123 Reading Strategy, p. 122 Build Vocabulary, p. 120	• **Literary Analysis and Reading Transparencies,** pp. 53 and 54 ● ▲ ■	
		• **Listening to Literature** ● ▲ ■ Audiocassettes, Side 17 Audio CDs, CD 11
• **Literatura en español** ● ▲ • **Literary Analysis for Enrichment** ■		
• **Formal Assessment:** Selection Test, p. 128 ● ▲ ■ • **Open Book Test,** p. 79 ● ▲ ■ • **Performance Assessment and Portfolio Management,** p. 23 • (PRENTICE HALL ASSESSMENT *SYSTEM*) ● ▲ ■	• (PRENTICE HALL ASSESSMENT *SYSTEM*) ● ▲ ■ Skills Practice Answers and Explanations on Transparencies	• **Test Bank Software** ● ▲ ■ • **Got It! Assessment Videotapes,** Tape 3 ● ▲
• **Selection Support Workbook:** ● ▲ ■ Build Grammar Skills, p. 121 • **Writing and Grammar,** Ruby Level ● ▲ ■ • **Extension Activities,** p. 27 ● ▲ ■	• **Daily Language Practice Transparencies** ● ▲ • **Writing Models and Graphic Organizers on Transparencies,** p. 37 ● ▲ ■	• **Writing and Grammar iText CD-ROM** ● ▲ ■ 💻 *Take It to the Net* www.phschool.com

■ **BLOCK SCHEDULING:** Use one 90-minute class period to preteach the selection and have students read it. Use a second 90-minute class period to assess students' mastery of skills and have them complete one of the Extension Activities.

Motivation

Play the opening scene of the video *An Occurrence at Owl Creek Bridge.* Pause the video after the noose is placed around the civilian's neck. Have students discuss possible reasons the man is in this situation. Then, tell students to read the story to discover the man's fate.

▣ Interest Grabber Video

As an alternative, play "The Oscar-Winning Film" on Tape 4 to engage student interest.

❶ Background

More About the Author

Ernest Hopkins, an editor and author who has specialized in the work of Ambrose Bierce, claims that Bierce's general philosophy was a "realistic, pessimistic, hard-boiled attitude toward life. This first-handed approach made him rather difficult to work with, no doubt, but it did make his writings refreshingly original and does so today—to read Bierce is to enter a different world."

Prepare to Read

❶ An Occurrence at Owl Creek Bridge

Ambrose Bierce (1842–1914?)

Ambrose Bierce's writing and philosophy were shaped by his career as a Union officer in the Civil War. The extreme poverty in which he was raised helped to foster Bierce's unsentimental, pessimistic view of the world; the brutality he saw during the war only cemented his cynicism. Bierce explored themes of cruelty and death in his writing, earning himself the nickname "Bitter Bierce."

A Civil War Soldier Bierce was born in Ohio and raised on a farm in Indiana. Having educated himself by reading his father's books, he left the farm while in his teens to attend a military academy in Kentucky. When the Civil War broke out, he enlisted in the Union army. Bierce fought in several important battles, rose from private to lieutenant, and won many awards for bravery. Toward the end of the war he was seriously wounded, but he returned to battle a few months later.

Poisoned Pen After the war, Bierce settled in San Francisco as a journalist. His "Prattler" column, which appeared in *The Argonaut* (1877–1879), the *Wasp* (1881–1886), and the San Francisco *Sunday Examiner* (1887–1896), mixed political and social satire, literary reviews, and gossip. The broodingly handsome writer was dubbed "the wickedest man in San Francisco" for his cynical and often malicious commentary. Though his journalistic barbs angered many key political and business figures, Bierce's dark reputation only added to his personal popularity. He was a magnetic figure who charmed those around him despite the malice of his words.

Establishing His Legacy Although Bierce published many of his finest short stories in his column, he decided in the early 1890s to publish his collected short stories in two volumes entitled *Tales of Soldiers and Civilians* (1891) and *Can Such Things Be?* (1893). The concise, carefully plotted stories in these collections, set for the most part during the Civil War, capture the cruelty and futility of war and the indifference of death. Bierce's pessimism is also reflected in *The Devil's Dictionary* (1906), a book of humorous and cynical definitions, and in a book of quotations published after his death. Challenging, spiteful, or merely macabre, these comments more than justify Bierce's reputation as a hard-nosed, hard-boiled critic of nearly everything.

The Perfect Cynic Writer George Sterling wrote of Bierce, his longtime friend, that he "never troubled to conceal his justifiable contempt of humanity. . . . Bierce was a 'perfectionist,' a quality that in his case led to an intolerance involving merciless cruelty. He demanded in all others, men or women, the same ethical virtues that he found essential to his own manner of life. . . . To deviate from his point of view, indeed, to disagree with him even in slight particulars, was the unpardonable sin."

While he was successful professionally, Bierce found little happiness in a world where so few people met his expectations. His marriage ended in divorce, and both of his sons died at an early age. In 1913, at age 71, the lonely writer traveled to Mexico, a country in the midst of a bloody civil war. To this day, his fate is unknown, although a reasonable speculation is that he was killed during the siege of Ojinaga in 1914. "An Occurrence at Owl Creek Bridge" may foreshadow that death during wartime.

506 ◆ *Division, Reconciliation, and Expansion (1850–1914)*

TEACHING RESOURCES

The following resources can be used to enrich or extend the instruction for pp. 506–507.

Motivation

▣ **Interest Grabber Video**, Tape 4 ▣

Background

📖 **Beyond Literature**, p. 27

💻 *Take It to the Net*

Visit www.phschool.com for Background and hotlinks for the selection.

Literary Analysis

📄 **Literary Analysis and Reading Transparencies,** Point of View, p. 54

📖 **Selection Support:** Literary Analysis, p. 123

Reading

📄 **Literary Analysis and Reading Transparencies,** Identifying Chronological Order, p. 53 ▣

▣ **BLOCK SCHEDULING:** Resources marked with this symbol provide varied instruction during 90-minute blocks.

Preview

Connecting to the Literature

"All's fair in love and war." This phrase has been used to excuse everything from trivial lies to wide-scale atrocities. Do you think there are times when the rules of the game involve no rules at all?

❷ Literary Analysis

Point of View

In this story, Bierce uses his main character's warped perception of time to distort the reader's sense of reality. The way that you perceive time in a story may depend on the **point of view** from which it is told.

- In stories told from an *objective point of view,* you follow the action without understanding any character's thoughts about the events.
- In stories told from a *third-person limited point of view,* the narrator relates the inner thoughts and feelings of a single character.

As the point of view in this story shifts from objective to third-person limited, the emotional tone and sense of time change as well.

Connecting Literary Elements

In order to convey the strange and stressful events of this story, Bierce uses a literary technique known as **stream-of-consciousness.** Using this style, Bierce reports thoughts and ideas the way the human mind experiences them—in short bursts, without full sentences, and often without clear or logical connections. As you read, try to fill in the missing pieces by considering which events spark the thoughts or feelings the narrator describes.

❸ Reading Strategy

Identifying Chronological Order

In Bierce's story, the action jumps backward and forward in time. To see the true **chronological order,** reorder events to represent the sequence in which they occurred. To understand the order of events in this story, create a timeline like the one shown.

Vocabulary Development

etiquette (et´ i kit) *n.* appropriate behavior and ceremonies (p. 509)

deference (def´ ər əns) *n.* respect; courtesy; regard (p. 509)

imperious (im pir´ ē əs) *adj.* urgent; imperative (p. 510)

dictum (dik´ təm) *n.* formal statement of fact or opinion (p. 511)

summarily (sə mer´ ə lē) *adv.* promptly and without formality (p. 511)

effaced (ə fāsd´) *adj.* erased; wiped out (p. 512)

oscillation (äs´ ə lā´ shən) *n.* act of swinging back and forth (p. 512)

apprised (ə prīzd´) *v.* informed; notified (p. 512)

malign (mə līn´) *adj.* malicious; very harmful (p. 515)

ineffable (in ef´ ə bəl) *adj.* too overwhelming to be spoken (p. 516)

Event

[box]
↓
[box]
↓
[box]

An Occurrence at Owl Creek Bridge ◆ 507

❷ Literary Analysis

Point of View

- Tell students that as they read this story, they will focus on the author's artful use of point of view to convey the main character's unique experience.
- Read the instruction about point of view together as a class. Draw students' attention to the distinctions between the objective and the third-person limited points of view. Ensure that students understand that an author might choose to shift between two points of view in a single story to create a particular effect.
- As they read the story, invite students to look for words that indicate distortions in the main character's perceptions of time and space.

❸ Reading Strategy

Identifying Chronological Order

- Inform students that an author may choose to present the events of a narrative in an order that is significantly different from the sequence in which they occurred in real time.
- Encourage students to understand that authors alter chronological order to create dramatic effects of one kind or another.
- Point out that alert readers take note whenever the action of a story jumps either forward or backward in time. Remind them of the usefulness of graphic organizers (or a simple list) in keeping track of chronological order.

Vocabulary Development

- Pronounce each vocabulary word for students, and read the definitions as a class. Have students identify any words with which they are already familiar.

 E-Teach

Visit E-Teach at www.phschool.com for teachers' essays on how to teach, with questions and answers.

CUSTOMIZE INSTRUCTION FOR UNIVERSAL ACCESS

For Less Proficient Readers	For English Learners	For Advanced Readers
The shifts in time in Bierce's story may prove to be a challenge for students. To help them understand the story's structure, have them pause at the end of each section, and list the actions it describes. Then, have them note the time relationships between each set of actions.	Students may be unfamiliar with the terms used to identify the officers on the bridge and the military hiearchy that defines their relationships. Inform students that a *sergeant* would take orders from a *lieutenant,* who, in turn, takes his orders from a *captain.* The sentinels were most likely *privates.*	Guide students to look for contradictory descriptions Bierce carefully inserts to introduce a sense of uncertainty in the reader. For instance, students may note the different ways in which Bierce describes the passage of time, the soldiers' movements, and the sounds Peyton Farquhar hears.

CUSTOMIZE INSTRUCTION
For Bodily/Kinesthetic Learners

Students may be better able to imagine the events that occur on the bridge if they clearly identify the positions, stances, and actions of the soldiers standing near the condemned man. Instruct a small group of students to use textual clues to "block" the scene, much as a director blocks a play.

❶ About the Selection

Ambrose Bierce creates a compelling depiction of the Civil War hanging of a Southern planter who has attempted (and failed at) an act of sabotage. Bierce explores the rapid movement of people's thoughts in the moments before death and the way in which the perception of time can become distorted in traumatic situations. As the character, Peyton Farquhar, falls toward his death by hanging, he imagines that the rope breaks and sets him free. In his fantasy, Farquhar plunges into the stream below, swims to safety, and returns home. Unaware that the events are taking place in the condemned man's imagination, the reader is surprised by the story's abrupt ending, when Farquhar's thoughts suddenly stop. Bierce describes Farquhar's dead body swinging "gently from side to side beneath the timbers of the Owl Creek bridge."

❶ An Occurrence at
OWL CREEK BRIDGE
Ambrose Bierce

Background

The senseless violence, death, and destruction Ambrose Bierce witnessed during the American Civil War (1861–1865) convinced him that war was terrible and futile. He set much of his best fiction, including this story, against the backdrop of this divisive war in which the agricultural South, whose economy was based on slavery, battled the more industrialized North. Fought mostly in the South, the war caused hundreds of thousands of casualties on both sides.

I

A man stood upon a railroad bridge in northern Alabama, looking down into the swift water twenty feet below. The man's hands were behind his back, the wrists bound with a cord. A rope closely encircled his neck. It was attached to a stout cross timber above his head and the slack fell to the level of his knees. Some loose boards laid upon the sleepers supporting the metals of the railway supplied a footing for him and his executioners—two private soldiers of the Federal army, directed by a sergeant who in civil life may have been a deputy sheriff. At a short remove upon the same temporary platform was an officer in the uniform of his rank, armed. He was a captain. A sentinel at each end of the bridge stood with his rifle in the position known as "support," that is to say, vertical in front of the left shoulder, the hammer resting on the forearm thrown straight across the chest—a formal and unnatural position, enforcing an erect carriage of the body. It did not appear to be the duty of these two men to know what was occurring at the center of the bridge; they merely blockaded the two ends of the foot planking that traversed it.

Beyond one of the sentinels nobody was in sight; the railroad ran straight away into a forest for a hundred yards, then, curving, was lost to view. Doubtless there was an outpost farther along. The other bank of the stream was open ground—a gentle acclivity[1] topped with a stockade of vertical

---

1. **acclivity** (ə kliv′ ə tē) *n.* upward slope.

TEACHING RESOURCES

The following resources can be used to enrich or extend the instruction for pp. 508–516.

Reading

📖 **Selection Support:** Reading Strategy, p. 122; Build Vocabulary, p. 120

🎧 **Listening to Literature Audiocassettes,** Side 17 ▪

💿 **Listening to Literature CDs,** CD 11 ▪

▪ **BLOCK SCHEDULING:** Resources marked with this symbol provide varied instruction during 90-minute blocks.

tree trunks, loopholed for rifles, with a single embrasure through which protruded the muzzle of a brass cannon commanding the bridge. Midway of the slope between bridge and fort were the spectators—a single company of infantry in line, at "parade rest," the butts of the rifles on the ground, the barrels inclining slightly backward against the right shoulder, the hands crossed upon the stock. A lieutenant stood at the right of the line, the point of his sword upon the ground, his left hand resting upon his right. Excepting the group of four at the center of the bridge, not a man moved. The company faced the bridge, staring stonily, motionless. The sentinels, facing the banks of the stream, might have been statues to adorn the bridge. The captain stood with folded arms, silent, observing the work of his subordinates, but making no sign. Death is a dignitary who when he comes announced is to be received with formal manifestations of respect, even by those most familiar with him. In the code of military etiquette silence and fixity are forms of deference.

The man who was engaged in being hanged was apparently about thirty-five years of age. He was a civilian, if one might judge from his habit, which was that of a planter. His features were good—a straight nose, firm mouth, broad forehead, from which his long, dark hair was combed straight back, falling behind his ears to the collar of his well-fitting frock coat. He wore a mustache and pointed beard, but no whiskers; his eyes were large and dark gray, and had a kindly expression which one would hardly have expected in one whose neck was in the hemp. Evidently this was no vulgar assassin. The liberal military code makes provision for hanging many kinds of persons, and gentlemen are not excluded.

The preparations being complete, the two private soldiers stepped aside and each drew away the plank upon which he had been standing. The sergeant turned to the captain, saluted and placed himself immediately behind that officer, who in turn moved apart one pace. These movements left the condemned man and the sergeant standing on the two ends of the same plank, which spanned three of the

etiquette (et´ i kit) *n.* appropriate behavior and ceremonies

deference (def´ ər əns) *n.* respect; courtesy; regard

❸ ▼ Critical Viewing
Which of the men in this photo seem to show an attitude of military etiquette? Explain. **[Interpret]**

❹ ✔Reading Check
What event is about to take place on the bridge?

❷ Background
Civil War Executions
During the Civil War, executions were always carried out according to strict military code. In that war, as in most others, civilian attempts at sabotage were treated harshly; the culprits were immediately hanged or shot. Saboteurs knew the extreme penalty for their deeds.

❸ ▶Critical Viewing
Answer: The posture and bearing of the figure at far right suggests a formal military etiquette. The other men, engaged in preparing their weapons, reveal less formal postures and attitudes.

❹ ✔Reading Check
Answer: A civilian is about to be hanged by members of the Federal army.

An Occurrence at Owl Creek Bridge ◆ 509

CUSTOMIZE INSTRUCTION FOR UNIVERSAL ACCESS

For Less Proficient Readers	For Advanced Readers
Suggest that as they read independently, students use self-sticking notes to mark any passages that present them with confusing ideas or vocabulary but do not stop reading. Sustained reading like this may clarify many ambiguous points. If students remain confused about certain passages, they can use the self-sticking notes to return to these pages and to ask questions during a class discussion.	Invite students to analyze the second paragraph in which Bierce carefully describes the preparations for the man's hanging. Have them consider both Bierce's style and the content of the passage by addressing these questions: In what ways does Bierce's precise language echo the actions he describes? What does Bierce mean by the idea of "Death" being a "dignitary"? Is such a sentiment particular to the military—especially in wartime—or does it find application in ordinary life?

Point of View

- Ask a student volunteer to explain the difference between the objective and the third-person limited points of view. Then, ask students which point of view Bierce has employed in the story so far (objective).

▶ Monitor Progress Ask students the Literary Analysis question on p. 510: What phrase indicates that the point of view has shifted from objective to third-person limited? Explain.

Answer: Students may point to the phrase *fix his last thoughts upon his wife and children* as a clear indication that the point of view has shifted. This shift allows Bierce to introduce the man's thoughts and emotions.

6 Critical Thinking

Make Connections

- Guide students to notice the man's over-acute senses: A watch's ticking sounds to him like *the stroke of a blacksmith's hammer upon the anvil.* Invite students to explain what this description indicates about Farquhar.
Answer: Students may say that Farquhar's perceptions are compromised by the trauma he is experiencing.

- Ask students to compare the man's heightened senses with those of other characters depicted in this textbook.
Answer: Students may recall Roderick's ability to hear his sister in Poe's "Fall of the House of Usher."

7 Reading Strategy

Identifying Chronological Order

- Read these two sentences for the class. Then, help students clarify the action described.

- Point out that the first sentence contains information about the first "action" (the condemned man's thinking) and the second action (the captain's nod). The third action occurs when the sergeant steps off the plank.

- If necessary, help students visualize the effect of this third action: with the sergeant's weight removed, the plank will tilt and send the man tumbling to his death by hanging.

510

---

crossties of the bridge. The end upon which the civilian stood almost, but not quite, reached a fourth. This plank had been held in place by the weight of the captain; it was now held by that of the sergeant. At a signal from the former the latter would step aside, the plank would tilt and the condemned man go down between two ties. The arrangement commended itself to his judgment as simple and effective. His face had not been covered nor his eyes bandaged. He looked a moment at his "unsteadfast footing," then let his gaze wander to the swirling water of the stream racing madly beneath his feet. A piece of dancing driftwood caught his attention and his eyes followed it down the current. How slowly it appeared to move! What a sluggish stream!

5 He closed his eyes in order to fix his last thoughts upon his wife and children. The water, touched to gold by the early sun, the brooding mists under the banks at some distance down the stream, the fort, the soldiers, the piece of drift—all had distracted him. And now he became conscious of a new disturbance. Striking through the thought of his dear ones was a sound which he could neither ignore nor understand, a sharp, distinct, metallic percussion like the stroke of a blacksmith's hammer upon the anvil; it had the same ringing quality. He wondered what it was, and whether immeasurably distant or near by—it seemed both. Its recurrence was regular, but as slow as the tolling of a death knell. He awaited each stroke with impatience **6** and—he knew not why—apprehension. The intervals of silence grew progressively longer; the delays became maddening. With their greater infrequency the sounds increased in strength and sharpness. They hurt his ear like the thrust of a knife; he feared he would shriek. What he heard was the ticking of his watch.

He unclosed his eyes and saw again the water below him. "If I could free my hands," he thought, "I might throw off the noose and spring into the stream. By diving I could evade the bullets and, swimming vigorously, reach the bank, take to the woods and get away home. My home, thank God, is as yet outside their lines; my wife and little ones are still beyond the invader's farthest advance."

7 As these thoughts, which have here to be set down in words, were flashed into the doomed man's brain rather than evolved from it the captain nodded to the sergeant. The sergeant stepped aside.

II

Peyton Farquhar was a well-to-do planter, of an old and highly respected Alabama family. Being a slave owner and like other slave owners a politician he was naturally an original secessionist and ardently devoted to the Southern cause. Circumstances of an <u>imperious</u> nature, which it is unnecessary to relate here, had prevented him from taking service with the gallant army that had fought the disastrous campaigns ending with the fall of Corinth,[2] and he

---

2. **Corinth** Mississippi town that was the site of an 1862 Civil War battle.

Literary Analysis
Point of View What phrase indicates that the point of view has shifted from objective to third-person limited? Explain.

imperious (im pir′ ē əs) *adj.* urgent; imperative

✹ ENRICHMENT: Cultural Connection

Civil War Geography

The Civil War was fought in thousands of places all over the United States of America. Have students find out about ways in which the war affected the area in which you live. Guide their exploration with the following questions:

- Were any battles fought in your community, region, or state?
- What roads or railroads were built at the time?
- What historical structures were destroyed?

- Which factories were built to respond to the demands of the war, or were quickly retooled to make ammunition or uniforms?
- Which buildings became temporary hospitals?
- After which leaders and generals were streets or schools named?

Have students share their findings with the class.

chafed under the inglorious restraint, longing for the release of his energies, the larger life of the soldier, the opportunity for distinction. That opportunity, he felt, would come, as it comes to all in war time. Meanwhile he did what he could. No service was too humble for him to perform in aid of the South, no adventure too perilous for him to undertake if consistent with the character of a civilian who was at heart a soldier, and who in good faith and without too much qualification assented to at least a part of the frankly villainous <u>dictum</u> that all is fair in love and war.

One evening while Farquhar and his wife were sitting on a rustic bench near the entrance to his grounds, a gray-clad soldier rode up to the gate and asked for a drink of water. Mrs. Farquhar was only too happy to serve him with her own white hands. While she was fetching the water her husband approached the dusty horseman and inquired eagerly for news from the front.

"The Yanks are repairing the railroads," said the man, "and are getting ready for another advance. They have reached the Owl Creek bridge, put it in order and built a stockade on the north bank. The commandant has issued an order, which is posted everywhere, declaring that any civilian caught interfering with the railroad, its bridges, tunnels or trains will be <u>summarily</u> hanged. I saw the order."

"How far is it to the Owl Creek bridge?" Farquhar asked.

"About thirty miles."

"Is there no force on this side the creek?"

"Only a picket post[3] half a mile out, on the railroad, and a single sentinel at this end of the bridge."

"Suppose a man—a civilian and student of hanging—should elude the picket post and perhaps get the better of the sentinel," said Farquhar, smiling, "what could he accomplish?"

The soldier reflected. "I was there a month ago," he replied. "I observed that the flood of last winter had lodged a great quantity of driftwood against the wooden pier at this end of the bridge. It is now dry and would burn like tow."[4]

The lady had now brought the water, which the soldier drank. He thanked her ceremoniously, bowed to her husband and rode away. An hour later, after nightfall, he repassed the plantation, going northward in the direction from which he had come. He was a Federal scout.

III

As Peyton Farquhar fell straight downward through the bridge he lost consciousness and was as one already dead. From this state he

---

3. **picket post** troops sent ahead with news of a surprise attack.
4. **tow** (tō) *n.* coarse, broken fibers of hemp or flax before spinning.

An Occurrence at Owl Creek Bridge ◆ 511

Literature in context History Connection

❽ The Battle of Shiloh

Owl Creek is the stream that runs through Tennessee at the sight of the Battle of Shiloh, one of the bloodiest battles of the Civil War where more than 20,000 soldiers died.

Railroad bridges like the Owl Creek Bridge were important during Civil War times because they enabled the armies access over bodies of water. It is the same Owl Creek which serves as the setting for Peyton Farquhar's "escape" into the torrent waters.

Key

| ⟵ Union troops | ⟵ Confederate troops | ★ Union victories |

---

dictum (dik´ təm) *n.* formal statement of fact or opinion

summarily (sə mer´ ə lē) *adv.* promptly and without formality

❿ Reading Check

In the war that divides his nation, which side does Farquhar support?

---

❽ Background

The Battle of Shiloh

In early April 1862, Union troops were headed toward Corinth—an Alabama town that was strategically important because two key railroads crossed at that point. On their journey, the Union soldiers collided with Confederate troops at Shiloh. Soon after the Battle of Shiloh, a Federal army occupied and then defended Corinth. They held the town until it was no longer strategically important.

❾ Vocabulary Development

Latin Word Root *-summa-*

• Draw students' attention to the word *summarily*, and read its definition. Then, tell students that the root *-summa-* comes from the Latin word *summa*, meaning "sum," or "whole."

• Remind students that the suffix *-ily* indicates that the word is an adverb, modifying the manner in which an action takes place.

• Guide students to see that Bierce's use of the word indicates the swiftness—or wholeness—with which punishment will be meted out to civilian saboteurs.

• Inform students that the root *-summa-* appears in many familiar words, including *summarize*.

❿ Reading Strategy

Identifying Chronological Order

• Discuss with students how the first paragraph of the story's second section differs from the paragraphs that precede it.

• If necessary, explain that here, for the first time, Bierce provides background information on Peyton Farquhar. Then, ask two or three student volunteers to read the remainder of the section.

▶ **Monitor Progress** Ask students this question: Does the encounter with the "gray-clad soldier" take place before or after the opening scene on the bridge?

Answer: This scene occurs before the story's opening events. Here, the reader learns what generated Farquhar's interest in the bridge and can infer the reason for his execution.

⓫ Reading Check

Answer: Farquhar supports the Confederacy

CUSTOMIZE INSTRUCTION FOR UNIVERSAL ACCESS

For Less Proficient Readers	For Special Needs Students	For Gifted/Talented Students
Students may need to reread (or to act out) the paragraph that begins on p. 509 with the words *The preparations being complete* in order to understand the procedure for hanging the man. Make sure students understand that when the sergeant steps off the plank, the condemned man will fall to his death.	Help students understand that the Federal scout plants an idea in Farquhar's mind. The reader is expected to infer that Farquhar then set about to burn the bridge and that the scout reported this possibility to Union officers. Guide students to understand that Farquhar's capture is the result of the scout's trickery.	Students should note that Bierce describes the waters of Owl Creek as *swirling* and *racing* and then as *sluggish*. This contradiction hints that things may not be what they seem and that the man's perceptions of his environment and the events taking place may not be altogether reliable.

- Ask a student volunteer to summarize the information Bierce conveys in section II of the story.

- Then, have students respond to the Reading Strategy question on p. 512: Describe the shift in time that occurs between sections II and III.

  Answer: Students may respond that the scene shifts back abruptly to the "present," in which Farquhar stands with a noose around his neck in the middle of Owl Creek Bridge and is about to be hanged.

⑫ was awakened—ages later, it seemed to him—by the pain of a sharp pressure upon his throat, followed by a sense of suffocation. Keen, poignant agonies seemed to shoot from his neck downward through every fiber of his body and limbs. These pains appeared to flash along well-defined lines of ramification[5] and to beat with an inconceivably rapid periodicity. They seemed like streams of pulsating fire heating him to an intolerable temperature. As to his head, he was conscious of nothing but a feeling of fullness—of congestion. These sensations were unaccompanied by thought. The intellectual part of his nature was already <u>effaced</u>: he had power only to feel, and feeling was torment. He was conscious of motion. Encompassed in a luminous cloud, of which he was now merely the fiery heart, without material substance, he swung through unthinkable arcs of <u>oscillation</u>, like a vast pendulum. Then all at once, with terrible suddenness, the light about him shot upward with the noise of a loud plash; a frightful roaring was in his ears, and all was cold and dark. The power of thought was restored; he knew that the rope had broken and he had fallen into the stream. There was no additional strangulation; the noose about his neck was already suffocating him and kept the water from his lungs. To die of hanging at the bottom of a river!—the idea seemed to him ludicrous. He opened his eyes in the darkness and saw above him a gleam of light, but how distant, how inaccessible! He was still sinking, for the light became fainter and fainter until it was a mere glimmer. Then it began to grow and brighten, and he knew that he was rising toward the surface—knew it with reluctance, for he was now very comfortable. "To be hanged and drowned," he thought, "that is not so bad; but I do not wish to be shot. No; I will not be shot; that is not fair."

He was not conscious of an effort, but a sharp pain in his wrist <u>apprised</u> him that he was trying to free his hands. He gave the struggle his attention, as an idler might observe the feat of a juggler, without interest in the outcome. What splendid effort!—what magnificent, what superhuman strength! Ah, that was a fine endeavor! Bravo! The cord fell away; his arms parted and floated upward, the hands dimly seen on each side in the growing light. He watched them with a new interest as first one and then the other pounced upon the noose at his neck. They tore it away and thrust it fiercely aside, its undulations resembling those of a watersnake. "Put it back, put it back!" He thought he shouted these words to his hands, for the undoing of the noose had been succeeded by the direst pang that he had yet experienced. His neck ached horribly; his brain was on fire; his heart, which had been fluttering faintly, gave a great leap, trying to force itself out at his mouth. His whole body was racked and wrenched with an insupportable anguish! But his disobedient hands gave no heed to the command. They beat the water vigorously with quick, downward

---

5. **flash along well-defined lines of ramification** spread out quickly along branches from a central point.

Reading Strategy

Identifying Chronological Order Describe the shift in time that occurs between sections II and III.

effaced (ə fāsd′) *adj.* erased; wiped out

oscillation (äs′ ə lā′ shən) *n.* act of swinging back and forth

apprised (ə prīzd′) *v.* informed; notified

strokes, forcing him to the surface. He felt his head emerge; his eyes were blinded by the sunlight; his chest expanded convulsively, and with a supreme and crowning agony his lungs engulfed a great draft of air, which instantly he expelled in a shriek!

He was now in full possession of his physical senses. They were, indeed, preternaturally[6] keen and alert. Something in the awful disturbance of his organic system had so exalted and refined them that they made record of things never before perceived. He felt the ripples upon his face and heard their separate sounds as they struck. He looked at the forest on the bank of the stream, saw the individual trees, the leaves and the veining of each leaf—saw the very insects upon them: the locusts, the brilliant-bodied flies, the gray spiders stretching their webs from twig to twig. He noted the prismatic colors in all the dew-drops upon a million blades of grass. The humming of the gnats that danced above the eddies of the stream, the beating of the dragonflies' wings, the strokes of the water spiders' legs, like oars which had lifted their boat—all these made audible music. A fish slid along beneath his eyes and he heard the rush of its body parting the water.

He had come to the surface facing down the stream; in a moment the visible world seemed to wheel slowly round, himself the pivotal point, and he saw the bridge, the fort, the soldiers upon the bridge, the captain, the sergeant, the two privates, his executioners. They were in silhouette against the blue sky. They shouted and gesticulated, pointing at him. The captain had drawn his pistol, but did not fire; the others were unarmed. Their movements were grotesque and horrible, their forms gigantic.

Suddenly he heard a sharp report and something struck the water smartly within a few inches of his head, spattering his face with spray. He heard a second report, and saw one of the sentinels with his rifle at his shoulder, a light cloud of blue smoke rising from the muzzle. The man in the water saw the eye of the man on the bridge gazing into his own through the sights of the rifle. He observed that it was a gray eye and remembered having read that gray eyes were keenest, and that all famous marksmen had them. Nevertheless, this one had missed.

A counterswirl had caught Farquhar and turned him half round; he was again looking into the forest on the bank opposite the fort. The sound of a clear, high voice in a monotonous singsong now rang out behind him and came across the water with a distinctness that pierced and subdued all other sounds, even the beating of the ripples in his ears. Although no soldier, he had frequented camps enough to know the dread significance of that deliberate, drawling, aspirated

---

6. **preternaturally** (prēt′ ər nach′ ər əl ē) *adv.* abnormally; extraordinarily

13 ▲ **Critical Viewing**
Based on this map, why is the bridge so important to the Union army? **[Interpret]**

14 ✔ **Reading Check**
What unusual event happens upon Farquhar's hanging?

An Occurrence at Owl Creek Bridge ◆ 513

13 ▶ **Critical Viewing**
Answer: Students should note that this bridge supports railroad tracks. Since trains were critical to the movement of troops and supplies, both Federal and Confederate forces would have wanted control of this bridge. However, the Union would be especially concerned about maintaining access, because one of their stockades lay within a few miles of the river.

14 ✔ **Reading Check**
Answer: Apparently, the rope breaks, and he falls into the water below.

CUSTOMIZE INSTRUCTION FOR UNIVERSAL ACCESS

For English Learners	For Advanced Readers
The term *report* is one of several examples in this story of a familiar word used in an unfamiliar way. *Habit*, *smartly*, *sleepers*, and *bank* are others. Guide students to use context clues or to consult a dictionary to ascertain the meanings of these words as Bierce uses them.	Students may enjoy reading Edgar Allan Poe's short story "The Tell-Tale Heart" to appreciate another striking example of a character who is "preternaturally keen and alert." As his mental condition deteriorates, the narrator of Poe's famous story hears "all things in heaven and hell." Likewise, students may draw comparisons to Usher's ability to hear his sister in Poe's "Fall of the House of Usher." Invite students to compare and contrast the reasons for these heightened senses in all three characters.

- Ask one or more students to review the story so far to find passages that describe the locations and weaponry of the Union soldiers. For example, students might identify this passage from the story's first paragraph: *A sentinel stood at each end of the bridge . . . with his rifle in the position known as "support."* . . .

- Ask students the Reading Strategy question on p. 514: What event might these words announce? **Answer:** These words probably announce the commencement of gunfire aimed at Farquhar by the company of Federal soldiers.

⓰ Background

Civil War Weapons

In 1862, soldiers fired muzzle-loading rifles, so a capable marksman could get off just two shots per minute. Thus, after the men on the bridge fire once, Farquhar has about thirty seconds of safety before the next round of shots.

⓱ Literary Analysis

Point of View and Stream of Consciousness

- Read aloud this paragraph, in which Bierce describes Farquhar's perceptions of and reactions to various physical phenomena. Have students evaluate the reliability of the narrator as you read.

 Monitor Progress Ask students the Literary Analysis question on p. 514: What clues does Bierce give you to suggest that the speaker may not be totally reliable as a witness? **Answer:** Students may note details such as the narrator's use of exclamation points and his presentation of patently absurd information (*heard the deflected shot humming through the air ahead, and in an instant it was cracking and smashing . . . in the forest beyond*).

---

chant; the lieutenant on shore was taking a part in the morning's work. How coldly and pitilessly—with what an even, calm intonation, presaging,[7] and enforcing tranquillity in the men—with what accurately measured intervals fell those cruel words:

⓯ "Attention, company! . . . Shoulder arms! . . . Ready! . . . Aim! . . . Fire!"

Farquhar dived—dived as deeply as he could. The water roared in his ears like the voice of Niagara, yet he heard the dulled thunder of the volley and, rising again toward the surface, met shining bits of metal, singularly flattened, oscillating slowly downward. Some of them touched him on the face and hands, then fell away, continuing their descent. One lodged between his collar and neck; it was uncomfortably warm and he snatched it out.

As he rose to the surface, gasping for breath, he saw that he had been a long time under water; he was perceptibly farther down stream—nearer to safety. The soldiers had almost finished reloading; **⓰** the metal ramrods flashed all at once in the sunshine as they were drawn from the barrels, turned in the air, and thrust into their sockets. The two sentinels fired again, independently and ineffectually.

The hunted man saw all this over his shoulder; he was now swimming vigorously with the current. His brain was as energetic as his arms and legs; he thought with the rapidity of lightning.

"The officer," he reasoned, "will not make that martinet's[8] error a second time. It is as easy to dodge a volley as a single shot. He has probably already given the command to fire at will. God help me, I cannot dodge them all!"

An appalling plash within two yards of him was followed by a loud, rushing sound, *diminuendo*,[9] which seemed to travel back through the air to the fort and died in an explosion which stirred the very river to its deeps! A rising sheet of water curved over him, fell down **⓱** upon him, blinded him, strangled him! The cannon had taken a hand in the game. As he shook his head free from the commotion of the smitten water he heard the deflected shot humming through the air ahead, and in an instant it was cracking and smashing the branches in the forest beyond.

"They will not do that again," he thought; "the next time they will use a charge of grape.[10] I must keep my eye upon the gun; the smoke will apprise me—the report arrives too late; it lags behind the missile. That is a good gun."

Suddenly he felt himself whirled round and round—spinning like a top. The water, the banks, the forests, the now distant bridge, fort and men—all were commingled and blurred. Objects were represented

---

7. **presaging** (prē sāj´ in) predicting; warning.
8. **martinet** (märt´ 'n et´) strict military disciplinarian.
9. ***diminuendo*** (də min´ yōō en´ dō) musical term used to describe a gradual reduction in volume.
10. **charge of grape** cluster of small iron balls—"grape shot"—that disperse once fired from a cannon.

514 ◆ *Division, Reconciliation, and Expansion (1850–1914)*

✸ **ENRICHMENT: Career Connection**

Civil Engineers

During the Civil War, armies regularly blew up bridges and destroyed tracks to set back the pursuing armies. Civil engineers rapidly put these structures together again. Today, people with advanced mathematics skills can find work in several different engineering fields.

Share these distinctions with students:

- ***Civil engineers*** plan and implement municipal projects such as highways and airport runways.

- ***Mechanical engineers*** plan the design of engines and machinery such as elevators and water-sprinkler and irrigation systems.

- ***Electrical engineers*** design power systems and lighting for bridges and stadiums.

- ***Aeronautical engineers*** design aircraft, helicopters, and spacecraft.

Have interested students find out more about the work of engineers today.

by their colors only; circular horizontal streaks of color—that was all he saw. He had been caught in a vortex and was being whirled on with a velocity of advance and gyration that made him giddy and sick. In a few moments he was flung upon the gravel at the foot of the left bank of the stream—the southern bank—and behind a projecting point which concealed him from his enemies. The sudden arrest of his motion, the abrasion of one of his hands on the gravel, restored him, and he wept with delight. He dug his fingers into the sand, threw it over himself in handfuls and audibly blessed it. It looked like diamonds, rubies, emeralds; he could think of nothing beautiful which it did not resemble. The trees upon the bank were giant garden plants; he noted a definite order in their arrangement, inhaled the fragrance of their blooms. A strange, roseate[11] light shone through the spaces among their trunks and the wind made in their branches the music of aeolian harps.[12] He had no wish to perfect his escape—was content to remain in that enchanting spot until retaken.

A whiz and rattle of grapeshot among the branches high above his head roused him from his dream. The baffled cannoneer had fired him a random farewell. He sprang to his feet, rushed up the sloping bank, and plunged into the forest.

All that day he traveled, laying his course by the rounding sun. The forest seemed interminable; nowhere did he discover a break in it, not even a woodman's road. He had not known that he lived in so wild a region. There was something uncanny in the revelation.

By night fall he was fatigued, footsore, famishing. The thought of his wife and children urged him on. At last he found a road which led him in what he knew to be the right direction. It was as wide and straight as a city street, yet it seemed untraveled. No fields bordered it, no dwelling anywhere. Not so much as the barking of a dog suggested human habitation. The black bodies of the trees formed a straight wall on both sides, terminating on the horizon in a point, like a diagram in a lesson in perspective. Overhead, as he looked up through this rift in the wood, shone great golden stars looking unfamiliar and grouped in strange constellations. He was sure they were arranged in some order which had a secret and <u>malign</u> significance. The wood on either side was full of singular noises, among which—once, twice, and again, he distinctly heard whispers in an unknown tongue.

His neck was in pain and lifting his hand to it he found it horribly swollen. He knew that it had a circle of black where the rope had bruised it. His eyes felt congested: he could no longer close them. His tongue was swollen with thirst; he relieved its fever by thrusting it forward from between his teeth into the cold air. How softly the turf

malign (mə līn′) *adj.* malicious; very harmful

---

11. **roseate** (rō′ zē it) *adj.* rose-colored.
12. **aeolian** (ē ō′ lē ən) **harps** stringed instruments that produce music when played by the wind. In Greek mythology, Aeolus is the god of the winds.

19 ☑ **Reading Check**

What is Farquhar's state of mind after his dive?

An Occurrence at Owl Creek Bridge ◆ 515

---

18 **Critical Thinking**

Interpret

- Draw students' attention to language that indicates the foreignness of Farquhar's surroundings. Invite students to speculate about why everything seems so unfamiliar to Farquhar, even though he is not far from home.

- Have students identify a handful of examples of sensory details that convey the idea that the man's flight is marked by strangeness and wonder. Encourage students to use a chart like the one shown to record these sensory details.

Sense	Detail
Touch	
Sight	great golden stars
Taste	
Smell	
Sound	

Possible answer: The details students select should be well-observed and clearly related to each of the five senses.

- Ask students to explain what these details may indicate (or have them refer back to this passage after they have finished reading). **Answer:** Students may say that Farquhar's journey is more dreamlike than real. This sense of unreality is suggested by the fact that the surroundings seem unfamiliar, the journey seems endless, and the path seems untraveled.

19 ☑ **Reading Check**

Answer: He seems exhausted and perhaps delirious.

CUSTOMIZE INSTRUCTION FOR UNIVERSAL ACCESS

For Special Needs Students	For Advanced Readers
Once students know how the story ends, they can go back and read it a second time. During this second reading, encourage them to look for clues that indicate which elements are real and which exist only in Farquhar's imagination. Make sure students understand that nearly all of Farquhar's actions, observations, and thoughts described in Section III occur solely in his mind.	After completing a first reading, suggest that students go back through the story and look for clues that show what was actually happening to Farquhar as he was imagining his escape. For example, in the passage in which he gasps for breath after rising to the surface of the water, Farquhar in reality may have been gasping because of the tightened noose. Later in the story, his swollen neck, congested eyes, and swollen tongue are all symptoms of death by hanging.

515

Review and Assess

1. Most students will probably say that they were shocked by the story's ending.

2. **(a)** The reader learns only that a man who is about to be hanged is a 35-year-old civilian with a wife and children, as well as various details of his appearance. **(b)** They make the reader want to read on to learn more about the man and what is happening to him.

3. **(a)** Possible answer: He mistakes the ticking of his watch for "a sharp, distinct, metallic percussion like the stroke of a blacksmith's hammer upon the anvil." **(b)** Possible answer: His perceptions are distorted by his fear.

4. **(a)** He visualizes freeing his hands, releasing the noose, and fleeing. **(b)** His journey is an extended, detailed version of this brief visualization.

5. **(a)** He sees light shoot "upward" and hears "the noise of a loud plash" and "a frightful roaring" in his ears before everything goes "cold and dark." **(b)** Possible answers: The narrator says that he "was one already dead" and that he experienced a "sense of suffocation."

6. Many students will respond that this portrayal seems realistic because it suggests that someone who knows he is about to die could lapse into a dreamlike state.

7. **(a)** The story suggests that someone facing imminent death may escape the trauma and express the longing to live by lapsing into a dreamlike state. **(b)** These insights are especially apt for extreme circumstances, but also suggest the power of the imagination to create an alternate reality—one that is preferable to ordinary life.

---

had carpeted the untraveled avenue—he could no longer feel the roadway beneath his feet!

Doubtless, despite his suffering, he had fallen asleep while walking, for now he sees another scene—perhaps he has merely recovered from a delirium. He stands at the gate of his own home. All is as he left it, and all bright and beautiful in the morning sunshine. He must have traveled the entire night. As he pushes open the gate and passes up the wide white walk, he sees a flutter of female garments: his wife, looking fresh and cool and sweet, steps down from the veranda to meet him. At the bottom of the steps she stands waiting, with a smile of <u>ineffable</u> joy, an attitude of matchless grace and dignity. Ah, how beautiful she is! He springs forward with extended arms. As he is about to clasp her he feels a stunning blow upon the back of the neck; a blinding white light blazes all about him with a sound like the shock of a cannon—then all is darkness and silence!

Peyton Farquhar was dead; his body, with a broken neck, swung gently from side to side beneath the timbers of the Owl Creek bridge.

ineffable (in ef′ ə bel) *adj.* too overwhelming to be spoken

Review and Assess

Thinking About the Selection

1. **Respond:** With what emotions did you respond to the story's ending? Explain your answer.

2. **(a) Recall:** In Part I, what do you learn about the condemned man? **(b) Analyze:** Bierce makes deliberate decisions about what information to reveal and when to reveal it. How do his choices create suspense?

3. **(a) Recall:** Identify one example of Farquhar's distorted perceptions. **(b) Interpret:** What causes this distortion?

4. **(a) Recall:** What does Farquhar visualize moments before he is hanged? **(b) Connect:** In what way is his journey connected with this earlier vision?

5. **(a) Recall:** What sensation does Farquhar experience "with terrible suddenness" after he has been hanged? **(b) Distinguish:** What details suggest that Farquhar's escape occurs in his mind?

6. **Evaluate:** Do you think the portrayal of Farquhar's final thoughts is realistic? Why or why not?

7. **(a) Extend:** What does this story suggest about the psychology of a person facing a life or death situation? **(b) Speculate:** Are such insights applicable in daily life, or merely in extreme circumstances, like those of war? Explain.

ASSESSMENT PRACTICE: Reading Comprehension

Context (For more practice, see Test Preparation Workbook, p. 29)

Use the following sample item to teach students how to use context clues to determine the meanings of specialized terms.

The two private soldiers stepped aside and each drew away the plank upon which he had been standing. The sergeant turned to the captain, saluted and placed himself immediately behind that officer.

Which answer lists the soldiers in order from lowest to highest in rank?

A captain, sergeant, private

B sergeant, private, captain

C private, sergeant, captain

D private, captain, sergeant

The privates perform duties, the sergeant salutes the captain, and the captain is an officer. The correct answer is *C*.

Review and Assess

Literary Analysis

Point of View

1. Analyze the story to find examples of the two different points of view Bierce uses. Complete the chart below to identify the effects of these choices.

Objective Point of View		Effect
	·····►	

Limited Point of View		Effect
	·····►	

2. What is the effect of the shift in point of view in the last paragraph of the story?

Connecting Literary Elements

3. (a) What details in the second paragraph of section III are revealed through the use of **stream of consciousness**? (b) What "sharp pain" sparks Farquhar's thoughts? (c) In what ways does this passage mimic the natural, jumbled flow of thoughts?

4. Why is stream-of-consciousness technique particularly appropriate for this story?

Reading Strategy

Identifying Chronological Order

5. Which takes place first: Farquhar's encounter with the Federal scout or his preoccupation with the ticking of his watch?

6. How much real time do you estimate elapses from the opening to the closing scene of the story? Explain.

7. How did the story's ending change your initial perception of the sequence and duration of the events it describes?

Extend Understanding

8. **Social Studies Connection:** Farquhar was a civilian in the war—not a soldier. Do you think his death was justified? Why or why not?

An Occurrence at Owl Creek Bridge ◆ 517

Quick Review

Point of view is the vantage point from which a story is told.

In **objective point of view**, events are described without information about the thoughts or feelings of the characters.

Narration from a **third-person limited point of view** uses the pronouns *he, she,* or *it* and reveals the thoughts of a single character.

The **stream-of-consciousness** technique of narration captures the chaotic nature of the human thought process by jumping from one idea to another without transition.

To **identify chronological order,** reorder events into the proper time sequence.

 Take It to the Net
www.phschool.com
Take the interactive self-test online to check your understanding of the selection.

Answers for page 517

Review and Assess

1. Possible responses: Objective—*A man stood upon a railroad bridge . . . twenty feet below;* Effect: conveys a sense of straightforward reporting, as well as a dry emotional tone; Limited—*A piece of dancing driftwood . . . What a sluggish stream!;* Effect: conveys a sense of wonder, as well as an emotionally engaging personal tone.

2. The abrupt shift surprises the reader and emphasizes the finality of Farquhar's death.

3. **(a)** Examples include *gave the struggle his attention, as an idler might observe the feat of a juggler* and *Bravo! The cord fell away.* **(b)** The sharp pain is caused by the rope tightening around his neck. **(c)** The passage moves from straightforward description of a physical sensation to the thoughts, and admonishments it triggers. There is a feeling of informality and exuberant disorder in the connections between sentences.

4. Stream of consciousness is appropriate for this story because Bierce's protagonist suffers a warped sense of time and reality. That distorted sense of reality is effectively conveyed through the stream-of-consciousness technique.

5. The encounter comes first.

6. A few minutes elapse.

7. The ending makes it clear that the events have taken place in a matter of seconds, rather than hours.

8. Students should support their answers with clear reasons.

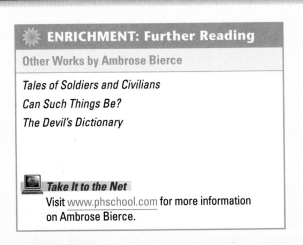

ENRICHMENT: Further Reading

Other Works by Ambrose Bierce

Tales of Soldiers and Civilians

Can Such Things Be?

The Devil's Dictionary

Take It to the Net
Visit www.phschool.com for more information on Ambrose Bierce.

517

Answers for p. 518

❶ Vocabulary Development

Word Analysis

1. false
2. false
3. false

Spelling Strategy

1. malign
2. align
3. resign

Fluency: Words in Context

1. etiquette, deference, summarily, dictum
2. malign, ineffable
3. apprised, imperious, effaced
4. oscillation

❷ Grammar and Style

Peyton Farquhar desperately surveyed the landscape; plans of escape rushed through his mind.

Peyton Farquhar dropped from the bridge to the stream below; the shock of the cold water jolted him.

The silent interminable moment ended; a thunderous roar shattered the calm.

Writing Application

Students' paragraphs should use vivid descriptive language, including numerous compound sentences joined by semicolons.

Integrate Language Skills

❶ Vocabulary Development Lesson

Word Analysis: Latin Root -summa-

Summary suggests a brief, general idea. Likewise, *summarily* describes an action taken hastily or promptly. These words derive from the Latin word *summa*, meaning "sum, whole." Use your understanding of this root to decide whether each of the following statements is true or false.

1. *Consummate* professionals do poor work.
2. When you *summarize*, you elaborate.
3. A court *summation* covers every legal detail.

Spelling Strategy

When *gn* follows the vowel *i* at the end of a word, as in *sign*, you do not need a final *e* to make the vowel long. Complete the words below.

1. to speak evil of: mal__
2. to bring into line: al__
3. to give up one's position: res__

❷ Grammar and Style Lesson

Semicolons in Compound Sentences

Compound sentences are formed by linking independent clauses—clauses that can stand alone as sentences—with a **semicolon** rather than a conjunction. This style is used to connect two closely related ideas.

> **Example:** They hurt his ear like the thrust of a knife; he feared he would shriek.

Practice Choose from among the independent clauses below to create compound sentences. Use semicolons to join clauses that will form powerful sentences.

1. Plans of escape rushed through his mind.

Fluency: Words in Context

Review the vocabulary words on page 507. Then, use them to answer these questions. Use each word from the list only once, and explain your answers.

1. Which four words best relate to a book entitled *Lady Windmere's Authoritative Guide to Manners for Servants*?
2. Which two words best relate to an unspeakably vicious comment?
3. Which three words best relate to a court clerk who hastily interrupts a judge to inform her that audiotaped evidence had been accidentally erased?
4. Which word relates to a table fan that revolves to cool an entire room?

2. Peyton Farquhar dropped from the bridge to the stream below.
3. The silent, interminable moment ended.
4. The shock of the cold water jolted him.
5. A thunderous roar shattered the calm.
6. Peyton Farquhar surveyed the landscape.

Writing Application Write a paragraph describing a scary experience. Mimic Bierce's style by using compound sentences joined by semicolons.

Looking at Style Bierce makes effective use of compound sentences in the objective parts of the story, where the pattern of short, linked clauses creates a rhythm like that of gunfire.

WG Prentice Hall Writing and Grammar Connection: Chapter 27, Section 3

TEACHING RESOURCES

The following resources can be used to enrich or extend the instruction for pp. 518–519.

Vocabulary

📖 **Selection Support:** Build Vocabulary, p. 120

📖 **Vocabulary and Spelling Practice Book** (Use this booklet for skills enrichment.)

Grammar

📖 **Selection Support:** Grammar and Style, p. 121 ■

WG **Writing and Grammar,** Ruby Level, p. 716

📖 **Daily Language Practice Transparencies**

Writing

WG **Writing and Grammar,** Ruby Level, p. 309 ■

📖 **Extension Activities,** p. 27

📄 **Writing Models and Graphic Organizers on Transparencies,** p. 37

💿 **Writing and Grammar iText CD-ROM**

■ **BLOCK SCHEDULING:** Resources marked with this symbol provide varied instruction during 90-minute blocks.

❸ Writing Lesson

Critical Essay

Bierce was one of the first writers to use stream of consciousness—a style that imitates the natural flow of thoughts, images, and feelings. In an essay, explain how this style makes the story more dramatic. Use details from the story to support your ideas.

Prewriting Reread the story and generate a list of passages where the use of stream of consciousness helps you to understand the speaker's thoughts. Then, select two or three passages to discuss.

Drafting Focus on one passage at a time. Explain why the use of stream of consciousness reveals the character's thoughts with heightened realism and drama.

Revising As you review your draft, note points where quotations from the story will help support your opinions and analysis. Make strong connections between your opinions and the passage you are quoting.

Model: Incorporating Quotations From the Story

In his own words, Farquhar thinks he "must have traveled the entire night."

Through stream of consciousness, Bierce enables readers to empathize with Farquhar as he desperately imagines a struggle to save his life. The moment of full peace when he reunites with his wife is especially powerful.

Appropriate quotations from the story create strong connections between the writer's opinions and the text.

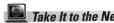 *Prentice Hall Writing and Grammar Connection: Chapter 14, Section 3*

❹ Extension Activities

Listening and Speaking Locate scientific reports about the ways in which perceptions of time change when people are under duress. Write a **summary** of your findings and their connections to this story.

- Summarize the reports you have reviewed.
- Summarize the distortions of time that Farquhar experiences.
- Note the ways in which Bierce's use of time supports or contradicts the research.

Share your summary with the class.

Research and Technology Use the map on page 513 to estimate how long it would have taken Farquhar to reach the bridge, destroy it, and return. Include key information, such as Farquhar's mode of travel (on horse or foot) and rate of speed. Then, use slide show software or manual art materials to create a **visual model** of Farquhar's journey.

 Take It to the Net   www.phschool.com

Go online for an additional research activity using the Internet.

An Occurrence at Owl Creek Bridge ◆ 519

ASSESSMENT RESOURCES

The following resources can be used to assess students' knowledge and skills.

Selection Assessment
- 📖 **Formal Assessment**, p. 128
- 📖 **Open Book Test**, p. 79
- ▭ **Got It! Assessment Videotapes**, Tape 3
- 💿 **Test Bank Software**
- ***Take It to the Net***
  Visit www.phschool.com for self-tests and additional questions on the selection.

Writing Rubric
- 📖 **Performance Assessment and Portfolio Management**, p.23 ▪
- PRENTICE HALL **ASSESSMENT SYSTEM**
- 📖 **Workbook**
- 📖 **Skill Book**
- ▪ **Transparencies**
- 💿 **CD-ROM**

Lesson Support for p. 519

❸ Writing Lesson

- Students' critical essays should analyze various passages from the story to explain the dramatic effect of Bierce's use of stream of consciousness.

- Encourage students to scour Bierce's story for passages that show how the use of stream of consciousness captures Peyton Farquhar's experience better than a conventional narrative approach would do.

- Use the Writing Lesson, as well as Writing Process Model 7 in **Writing Models and Graphic Organizers on Transparencies,** p. 37, to guide students in developing their critical essays.

- Use the Response to Literature rubric in **Performance Assessment and Portfolio Management**, p. 23, to evaluate student's critical essays.

❹ Research and Technology

- Urge students to study the map closely and to start by calculating the distance between Farquhar's plantation and the Owl Creek bridge according to one or more routes.

- Encourage pairs or small groups of students to put themselves in Farquhar's position and reflect on the best possible route and means of travel to accomplish the destruction of the bridge.

CUSTOMIZE INSTRUCTION
For Universal Access

To address different learning styles, use the following activities suggested in the **Extension Activities** booklet, p. 27.

For Intrapersonal Learners, use Activity 5.

For Visual/Spatial Learners, use Activity 6.

For Interpersonal Learners, use Activity 7.

519

The Gettysburg Address ✦ Second Inaugural Address ✦ Letter to His Son

Lesson Objectives

1. **To analyze and respond to literary elements**
   - Literary Analysis: Diction
   - Comparing Literary Works
2. **To read, comprehend, analyze, and critique speeches and a letter**
   - Reading Strategy: Using Background Knowledge
   - Reading Check Questions
   - Review and Assess Questions
   - Assessment Practice (ATE)
3. **To develop word analysis skills, fluency, and systematic vocabulary**
   - Vocabulary Development Lesson: Greek Word Part: -archy-
4. **To understand and apply written and oral language conventions**
   - Spelling Strategy
   - Grammar and Style Lesson: Parallel Structure
5. **To understand and apply appropriate writing and research strategies**
   - Writing Lesson: Diary Entry
   - Extension Activity: Web Site
6. **To understand and apply listening and speaking strategies**
   - Extension Activity: Mock Court

STEP-BY-STEP TEACHING GUIDE	PACING GUIDE
PRETEACH	
Motivate Students and Provide Background	
Use the Motivation activity (ATE p. 520)	5 min.
Read and discuss author and background features (SE/ATE p. 520) [A]	5 min.
Introduce the Concepts	
Introduce the Literary Analysis and Reading Strategy (SE/ATE p. 521) [A]	15 min.
Pronounce the vocabulary words and read their definitions (SE p. 521)	5 min.
TEACH	
Monitor Comprehension	
Informally monitor comprehension by circulating while students read independently or in groups [A]	30 min.
Monitor students' comprehension with the Reading Check notes (SE/ATE pp. 523, 525)	as students read
Develop vocabulary with Vocabulary notes (SE pp. 522, 524, 525; ATE p. 525)	as students read
Develop Understanding	
Develop students' understanding of diction with the Literary Analysis annotations (SE pp. 522, 524; ATE pp. 522, 524) [A]	5 min.
Develop students' ability to use background knowledge with the Reading Strategy annotations (SE p. 526; ATE p. 525)	5 min.
ASSESS	
Assess Mastery	
Assess students' mastery of the Reading Strategy and Literary Analysis by having them answer the Review and Assess questions (SE/ATE p. 527)	15 min.
Use one or more of the print and media Assessment Resources (ATE p. 529) [A]	up to 45 min.
EXTEND	
Apply Understanding	
Have students complete the Vocabulary Development Lesson and the Grammar and Style Lesson (SE p. 528) [A]	20 min.
Apply students' ability to use persuasive language by using the Writing Lesson (SE/ATE p. 529) [A]	45 min.
Apply students' understanding using one or more of the Extension Activities (SE p. 529)	20–90 min.

 ACCELERATED INSTRUCTION:
Use the strategies and activities identified with an [A].

UNIVERSAL ACCESS
- ● = Below Level Students
- ▲ = On-Level Students
- ■ = Above Level Students

Time and Resource Manager

Reading Level: Average, Challenging, Challenging
Average Number of Instructional Days: 5

RESOURCES

PRINT 📖	TRANSPARENCIES 🗂	TECHNOLOGY 💿 🎧 📼
• **Beyond Literature,** Cross-Curricular Connection: Music, p. 28 ▲ ■		• **Interest Grabber Video,** Tape 4 ● ▲ ■
• **Selection Support Workbook:** ● ▲ ■ Literary Analysis, p. 127 Reading Strategy, p. 126 Build Vocabulary, p. 124	• **Literary Analysis and Reading Transparencies,** pp. 55 and 56 ● ▲ ■	
		• **Listening to Literature** ● ▲ ■ Audiocassettes, Side 17–18 Audio CDs, CD 11
• **Literatura en español** ● ▲ • **Literary Analysis for Enrichment** ■		
• **Formal Assessment:** Selection Test, p. 131 ● ▲ ■ • **Open Book Test,** p. 82 ● ▲ ■ • **Performance Assessment and Portfolio Management,** p. 13 ● ▲ ■ • **PRENTICE HALL ASSESSMENT** *SYSTEM* ● ▲ ■	• **PRENTICE HALL ASSESSMENT** *SYSTEM* ● ▲ ■ Skills Practice Answers and Explanations on Transparencies	• **Test Bank Software** ● ▲ ■ • **Got It! Assessment Videotapes,** Tape 3 ● ▲
• **Selection Support Workbook:** ● ▲ ■ Build Grammar Skills, p. 125 • **Writing and Grammar,** Ruby Level ● ▲ ■ • **Extension Activities,** p. 28 ● ▲ ■	• **Daily Language Practice Transparencies** ● ▲ • **Writing Models and Graphic Organizers on Transparencies,** p. 37 ● ▲ ■	• **Writing and Grammar iText CD-ROM** ● ▲ ■ 💻 *Take It to the Net* www.phschool.com

BLOCK SCHEDULING: Use one 90-minute class period to preteach the selection and have students read it. Use a second 90-minute class period to assess students' mastery of skills and have them complete one of the Extension Activities.

Motivation

If you can obtain a taped version of Ward and Burns's documentary *The Civil War,* you might wish to use it to give students some sense of the carnage and destruction that the war created. Tell students that the selections presented here address the turmoil caused by a war between two opposed groups of states. Ask students to discuss the ways in which a civil war might be considered more devastating than a war with an "external" enemy.

▭ Interest Grabber Video

As an alternative, you may wish to play "Lincoln: A Gift for Oratory" on Tape 4 to engage student interest.

❶ Background

More About the Authors

Stories abound regarding Lincoln's drafting of the Gettysburg Address: He wrote it the week before; he wrote it the night before; he wrote it on the train; he wrote it on a piece of scrap paper. Certainly, we know that he was still revising it even as he spoke, adding the phrase "under God" to describe the nation. An experienced orator, Lincoln probably anticipated the positive effect this suggestion of divine approval of the United States and its goals of freedom would have on the audience.

It has been computed that Lincoln's printed speeches and writings contain 1,078,365 words. This figure is even more impressive when one considers that his writing style is admired especially for its precision and conciseness.

Robert E. Lee may have been the most respected and admired Southerner of his time. Even Ulysses S. Grant remarked, "There was not a man in the Confederacy whose influence with the whole people was as great as his."

Prepare to Read

❶ **The Gettysburg Address ◆ Second Inaugural Address ◆ Letter to His Son**

Abraham Lincoln (1809–1865)

Serving as president during one of the most tragic periods in American history, Abraham Lincoln fought to reunite a nation torn apart by war. His courage, strength, and dedication in the face of an overwhelming national crisis have made him one of the most admired and respected American presidents.

A man of humble origins, Lincoln developed an early interest in politics. He served in the Illinois state legislature and the United States Congress, where he earned a reputation as a champion of emancipation. In 1858, he ran for the United States Senate against Stephen Douglas. Lincoln lost the election, but his heated debates with Douglas brought him national recognition and helped him win the presidency in 1860.

Troubled Times Shortly after his election, the Civil War erupted. Throughout the war, Lincoln showed great strength and courage. He also demonstrated his gift for oratory. He was invited to make "a few appropriate remarks" in November 1863 for a dedication of the Gettysburg battlefield as a national cemetery. The world has long remembered what he said there.

Lincoln's great care as a writer shows in the Gettysburg Address, as it does in many of his other speeches. He worked diligently and thoughtfully to prepare messages that would have the effect he desired. Two important aspects of the Gettysburg speech are its brevity—just 272 words—and its reaffirmation of the democratic principles at the heart of American government. Lincoln was killed by an assassin's bullet in 1865 while attending the theater with his wife.

Robert E. Lee (1807–1870)

Robert E. Lee was born into a respected Virginia family and graduated with high honors from the United States Military Academy at West Point. During the Mexican War, Lee established a reputation as one of the finest military leaders in the United States Army.

Divided Loyalties Despite his military traditions, the job of commanding the Confederate army during the Civil War was not one that Robert E. Lee wanted. As the dispute over slavery grew, Lee was torn. A descendant of a number of distinguished patriots and statesmen, he believed in the Union and opposed both slavery and secession. Still, when President Lincoln offered him command of the Union forces, Lee refused to lead an army against his native state and resigned from the army, vowing to fight only in defense of Virginia.

A Difficult Task Unlike many Confederate leaders, Lee had no illusions about the South's power. Serving initially as commander of the army of northern Virginia and later of all the Confederate armies, he expected the widespread bloodshed and destruction caused by the war. He was an extraordinary military leader whose accomplishments and personal integrity in the face of overwhelming odds inspired great loyalty in both soldiers and civilians.

An avid letter writer, Lee wrote frequently to family members explaining his actions and expressing his feelings. On the eve of resigning his U.S. Army commission, Lee explored his divided loyalties in "Letter to His Son." After the war, Lee served as president of Washington College (now Washington and Lee) until his death.

520 ◆ *Division, Reconciliation, and Expansion (1850–1914)*

TEACHING RESOURCES

The following resources can be used to enrich or extend the instruction for pp. 520–521.

Motivation

▭ **Interest Grabber Videotapes,** Tape 4

Background

📖 **Beyond Literature,** p. 28 ▪

 Take It to the Net

Visit www.phschool.com for Background and hotlinks for the selection.

Literary Analysis

▭ **Literary Analysis and Reading Transparencies,** Diction, p. 56 ▪

📖 **Selection Support:** Literary Analysis, p. 127

Reading

▭ **Literary Analysis and Reading Transparencies,** Using Background Knowledge, p. 55

 BLOCK SCHEDULING: Resources marked with this symbol provide varied instruction during 90-minute blocks.

Preview

Connecting to the Literature

Imagine being swept up in a conflict like the Civil War that pits friends and family members against each other. Divided loyalties, like those expressed by Robert E. Lee, were painfully common.

❷ Literary Analysis

Diction

Diction, a writer's choice and arrangement of words, gives a piece of writing its unique quality. Whether formal or informal, concrete or abstract, the words a writer chooses help to convey feelings beyond the ideas presented. Look at these examples from the selections:

- **Lincoln:** To . . . extend this interest was the object for which the insurgents would rend the Union . . .
- **Lee:** I see that four states have declared themselves out of the Union . . .

As you read, contrast the ways in which Lincoln's and Lee's diction reflect the different audiences, purposes, and occasions of their writing.

Comparing Literary Works

Lee's diction in writing to his son was more informal than the public speech drafted by President Lincoln. Despite this contrast, both documents provide a window into the private and public conflicts of the Civil War. Compare and contrast the information and insights these selections provide about the nation's great war.

❸ Reading Strategy

Using Background Knowledge

If you read a historical document without understanding the situations that inspired it, you may miss most of its underlying value and meaning. **Use prior background knowledge** of the Civil War to analyze ideas, actions, and decisions in historical context. Complete a chart like the one shown to organize your ideas.

Vocabulary Development

consecrate (kän′ si krāt′) *v.* cause to be revered or honored (p. 522)

hallow (hal′ ō) *v.* honor as sacred (p. 522)

deprecated (dep′ rə kāt′ id) *v.* expressed disapproval of; (p. 524)

insurgents (in sur′ jənts) *n.* rebels; those who revolt against authority (p. 524)

discern (di surn′) *v.* receive or recognize; make out clearly (p. 524)

scourge (skurj) *n.* cause of serious trouble or affliction (p. 524)

malice (mal′ is) *n.* ill will; spite (p. 524)

anarchy (an′ ər kē) *n.* absence of government (p. 525)

redress (ri dres′) *n.* atonement; rectification (p. 525)

> **Concept in the Text**
>
> ↓
>
> **Prior Knowledge**
>
> | History | Concept |
> |---------|---------|
> | | |
>
> ↓
>
> **What Text Means**

The Gettysburg Address / Second Inaugural Address / Letter to His Son ◆ 521

CUSTOMIZE INSTRUCTION FOR UNIVERSAL ACCESS

For Less Proficient Readers	For English Learners	For Advanced Readers
Although the selections are brief, they contain difficult vocabulary and long sentences. To help readers meet these challenges, preview the vocabulary words and make a list of familiar synonyms, Then, clarify the meaning of the challenging sentences by reading them aloud and replacing the difficult words with the familiar ones.	To help them grasp the meaning of Lincoln's and Lee's sentences, have students listen to recordings of the selections as they follow along in their books. You can use the **Listening to Literature Audiocassettes** or the **Listening to Literature CDs.**	Lincoln's diction in the Gettysburg Address was greatly influenced by Greek funeral oratory. Invite interested students to research the style and rhetoric of these ancient speeches and to look for passages in the Gettysburg Address that reflect this influence.

---

❷ Literary Analysis

Diction

- Tell students that as they read the two speeches and the personal letter in this grouping, they will focus on the diction of Lincoln and Lee.

- Read the instruction about diction aloud. Draw students' attention to the ways in which word choice and arrangement relate to a writer's audience and to his or her purpose in writing. Inform students that it is inaccurate to say that formal, abstract words create better diction than do informal, concrete ones (or vice versa). Instead, a writer's diction can be judged based on its appropriateness to the purpose and audience.

- As they read, suggest that students note and draw conclusions about each writer's word choices and style.

❸ Reading Strategy

Using Background Knowledge

- Help students recognize that they already possess knowledge about the Civil War. To do so, lead the class in a brainstorming session about the war. As discussion ensues, list and organize information on the chalkboard.

- Encourage students to offer not only factual information about the war but also any associations, impressions, thoughts, and feelings they have about the nation's geographical and ideological split during the middle of the nineteenth century.

- You might wish to have students examine photographs of various Civil War subjects to spur their ideas.

Vocabulary Development

- Pronounce each vocabulary word for students, and read the definitions as a class. Have students identify any words with which they are already familiar.

 E-Teach

Visit E-Teach at www.phschool.com for teachers' essays on how to teach, with questions and answers.

Step-by-Step Teaching Guide for pp. 522–526

CUSTOMIZE INSTRUCTION
For Musical/Rhythmic Learners

Like Lincoln's moving speeches, the lyrics of popular songs can carry the cry for peace to large audiences. Ask students to discuss why popular music can be a powerful tool for political ends. You might wish to follow up with the Cross-Curricular Connection: Music page in **Beyond Literature** (p. 28).

❶ About the Selection

Lincoln's short but powerful Gettysburg Address places the Civil War into the historical context of the American fight for freedom. Lincoln asserts that the war is a test of the ideals for which colonials fought in 1776—in a sense, it is a continuation of the American Revolution. In an attempt to give direction to his divided country, Lincoln urges Americans to devote themselves to the task begun but not completed— to preserve freedom for *all* Americans.

❷ Literary Analysis

Diction

• Explain that "four score and seven years" is eighty-seven years. (A score equals twenty years.) Eighty-seven years before 1863 was the year 1776, the year the Declaration of Independence was signed.

• Ask students the Literary Analysis question on p. 522: What impression do you get of the speaker from the level of diction in "four score and seven years ago"? Answer: Students should note that these formal words add to the eloquence of the speech.

The ❶ Gettysburg Address

Abraham Lincoln November 19, 1863

Background

The battle of Gettysburg, Pennsylvania, fought in July 1863, was an important Union victory and marked a turning point in the war. More than 51,000 soldiers were injured in the battle. On November 19, 1863, while the war still raged, a military cemetery on the battlefield was dedicated. Unsure of President Lincoln's availability, the dedication organizers slated him as a secondary speaker, asking him to make only "a few appropriate remarks." In drafting that brief address, Lincoln wanted to lead the 15,000 American citizens attending the dedication through an emotional, final rite of passage. He also needed to gain continuing support for a bloody conflict that was far from over.

---

❷ Four score and seven years ago our fathers brought forth on this continent a new nation, conceived in Liberty, and dedicated to the proposition that all men are created equal.

Now we are engaged in a great civil war, testing whether that nation, or any nation so conceived and so dedicated, can long endure. We are met on a great battle-field of that war. We have come to dedicate a portion of that field, as a final resting place for those who here gave their lives that that nation might live. It is altogether fitting and proper that we should do this.

But, in a larger sense, we can not dedicate—we can not consecrate— we can not hallow—this ground. The brave men, living and dead, who struggled here, have consecrated it, far above our poor power to add or detract. The world will little note, nor long remember what we say here, but it can never forget what they did here. It is for us the living, rather, to be dedicated here to the unfinished work which they who fought here have thus far so nobly advanced. It is rather for us to be here dedicated to the great task remaining before us—that from these honored dead we take increased devotion to that cause for which they gave the last full measure of devotion—that we here highly resolve that these dead shall not have died in vain—that this nation, under God, shall have a new birth of freedom—and that government of the people, by the people, for the people, shall not perish from the earth.

Literary Analysis
Diction What impression do you get of the speaker from the level of diction in "four score and seven years ago"?

consecrate (kän′ si krāt′) *v.* cause to be revered or honored

hallow (hal′ ō) *v.* honor as sacred

522 ◆ Division, Reconciliation, and Expansion (1850–1914)

TEACHING RESOURCES

The following resources can be used to enrich or extend the instruction for pp. 522–526.

Reading Strategy

📖 **Selection Support:** Reading Strategy, p. 126; Build Vocabulary, p. 124

🎧 **Listening to Literature Audiocassettes,** Sides 17 and 18 ▪

💿 **Listening to Literature CDs,** CD 11 ▪

▪ **BLOCK SCHEDULING:** Resources marked with this symbol provide varied instruction during 90-minute blocks.

❸ Second Inaugural Address

Abraham Lincoln
March 4, 1865

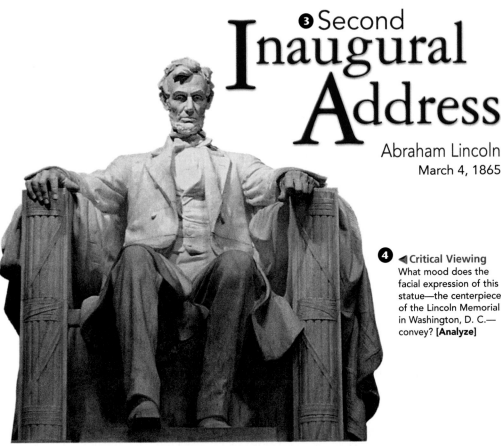

❹ ◀ Critical Viewing
What mood does the facial expression of this statue—the centerpiece of the Lincoln Memorial in Washington, D. C.—convey? **[Analyze]**

❸ About the Selection

In his Second Inaugural Address, delivered a month before his death, Lincoln recalls the issues that challenged the country four years earlier, acknowledges slavery as the real cause of the ongoing war, and laments the suffering caused by the war. He expresses hope for the end of the conflict and urges Americans to strive for a lasting peace.

❹ ▶ Critical Viewing

Answer: Students might describe Lincoln's facial expression with words such as *grave, serious, resolute, concerned,* and *solemn.*

❺ ✔ Reading Check

Answer: In the intervening four years, he has made numerous public declarations about the course he believes the nation must take.

At this second appearing to take the oath of the presidential office, there is less occasion for an extended address than there was at the first. Then a statement, somewhat in detail, of a course to be pursued, seemed fitting and proper. Now, at the expiration of four years, during which public declarations have been constantly called forth on every point and phase of the great contest which still absorbs the attention, and engrosses the energies of the nation, little that is new could be presented. The progress of our arms, upon which all else chiefly depends, is as well known to the public as to myself; and it is, I trust, reasonably satisfactory and encouraging to all. With high hope for the future, no prediction in regard to it is ventured.

On the occasion corresponding to this four years ago, all thoughts were anxiously directed to an impending civil war. All dreaded it—all sought to avert it. While the inaugural address was being delivered from this place, devoted altogether to *saving* the Union without war,

❺ ✔ Reading Check
Why does Lincoln say there is less call for an extended address than there was at his first inauguration?

Second Inaugural Address ◆ 523

CUSTOMIZE INSTRUCTION FOR UNIVERSAL ACCESS

For Special Needs Students	For Gifted/Talented Students
Invite students to reflect on what they may already know about how personal and political freedom is protected by law in the United States of America. Point out Lincoln's reference to the Declaration of Independence ("Four score . . ."), which demands freedom for all. Lincoln implies that Americans should seek to promote the views of that document rather than those of the Constitution, which does not recognize the rights of all people.	Encourage students to share with the class any background knowledge they may have about inaugurations. For instance, students may know that the President and Vice-President are sworn into office in an inauguration ceremony and that this ceremony is the occasion of the President's inaugural address. Some may know, also, that the Twentieth Amendment to the Constitution, ratified in 1933, set the terms of President and Vice President to begin on January 20.

Inform students that when Lincoln was elected, the country boasted a population of about thirty-one million, of which nine million lived in southern states. Of that nine million, four million were slaves. By the time of Lincoln's first inauguration, seven states had already seceded and others were on the verge of joining those in the newly formed Confederacy.

7 Literary Analysis

Diction

- Have a strong reader deliver this section of Lincoln's speech clearly and slowly to the rest of the class.

- Point out that Lincoln not only alludes to God and to the Bible, but also uses a Biblical quote to support his point about the Civil War.

▶ Monitor Progress Ask students the Literary Analysis question on p. 524: What can you infer about Lincoln from his diction in the passage beginning "It may seem Strange"?

Answer: Lincoln's diction shows that he is intelligent, well-educated, and knowledgeable about (as well as respectful toward) Biblical scripture.

---

insurgent agents were in the city seeking to *destroy* it without war—seeking to dissolve the Union, and divide effects, by negotiation. Both parties deprecated war; but one of them would *make* war rather than let the nation survive; and the other would *accept* war rather than let it perish. And the war came.

6 One eighth of the whole population were colored slaves, not distributed generally over the Union, but localized in the Southern part of it. These slaves constituted a peculiar and powerful interest. All knew that this interest was, somehow, the cause of the war. To strengthen, perpetuate, and extend this interest was the object for which the insurgents would rend the Union, even by war; while the government claimed no right to do more than to restrict the territorial enlargement of it. Neither party expected for the war, the magnitude, or the duration, which it has already attained. Neither anticipated that the *cause* of the conflict might cease with, or even before, the conflict itself should cease. Each looked for an easier triumph, and a result less fundamental and astounding. Both read the same Bible, and pray to the same God; and each invokes His aid against the other. It may seem strange that any men should dare to ask a just God's assistance in wringing their bread from the sweat of other men's faces; but let us judge not that we be not judged. The prayers of both could not be answered; that of neither has been answered fully. The Almighty has his own purposes. "Woe unto the world because of offences! for it must needs be that offences come; but woe to that man by whom the offence cometh!"[1] If we shall suppose that American Slavery is one of those offences which, in the providence of God,[2] must needs come, but which, having continued through His appointed time, He now wills to remove, and that He gives to both

7 North and South, this terrible war, as the woe due to those by whom the offence came, shall we discern therein any departure from those divine attributes which the believers in a Living God always ascribe to Him? Fondly do we hope—fervently do we pray—that this mighty scourge of war may speedily pass away. Yet, if God wills that it continue, until all the wealth piled by the bond-man's two hundred and fifty years of unrequited toil shall be sunk, and until every drop of blood drawn with the lash, shall be paid by another drawn with the sword, as was said three thousand years ago, so still it must be said "the judgments of the Lord, are true and righteous altogether."[3]

With malice toward none; with charity for all; with firmness in the right, as God gives us to see the right, let us strive on to finish the work we are in; to bind up the nation's wounds; to care for him who shall have borne the battle, and for his widow, and his orphan—to do all which may achieve and cherish a just and lasting peace, among ourselves, and with all nations.

---

1. **"Woe unto the world . . . offence cometh"** from Matthew 18:7 of the King James Version of the Bible.
2. **providence of God** benevolent care or wise guidance of God.
3. **"The judgments . . . altogether"** from Psalm 19:9.

deprecated (dep´ rə kāt´ id) *v.* expressed disapproval of

insurgents (in sur´ jənts) *n.* rebels; those who revolt against authority

Literary Analysis
Diction What can you infer about Lincoln from his diction in the passage beginning "It may seem strange"?

discern (di surn´) *v.* receive or recognize; make out clearly

scourge (skurj) *n.* cause of serious trouble or affliction

malice (mal´ is) *n.* ill will; spite

☀ **ENRICHMENT: Music Connection**

Aaron Copland

At the outbreak of World War II, American composer Aaron Copland (1900–1990) was commissioned to write a musical portrait of a great American. In response, Copland chose Abraham Lincoln as his subject. "A Lincoln Portrait" blends original music with familiar American folk tunes to accompany a script based on Lincoln's own words. In his notes about the work, Copland explained the structure he attempted to create: "In the opening section I wanted to suggest something of the mysterious sense of fatality that surrounds Lincoln's personality. . . . The quick middle section briefly sketches in the background of the times he lived in. This merges into the concluding section where my sole purpose was to draw a simple but impressive frame about the words of Lincoln himself."

Invite students to listen to a recording of the piece and determine whether or not Copland succeeded in creating the effects he intended.

Letter to His Son

Robert E. Lee   January 23, 1861

I received Everett's[1] *Life of Washington* which you sent me, and enjoyed its perusal. How his spirit would be grieved could he see the wreck of his mighty labors! I will not, however, permit myself to believe, until all ground of hope is gone, that the fruit of his noble deeds will be destroyed, and that his precious advice and virtuous example will so soon be forgotten by his countrymen. As far as I can judge by the papers, we are between a state of <u>anarchy</u> and civil war. May God avert both of these evils from us! I fear that mankind will not for years be sufficiently Christianized to bear the absence of restraint and force. I see that four states[2] have declared themselves out of the Union; four more will apparently follow their example. Then, if the border states are brought into the gulf of revolution, one half of the country will be arrayed against the other. I must try and be patient and await the end, for I can do nothing to hasten or retard it.

The South, in my opinion, has been aggrieved by the acts of the North, as you say. I feel the aggression and am willing to take every proper step for <u>redress</u>. It is the principle I contend for, not individual or private benefit. As an American citizen, I take great pride in my

---

1. **Everett's** referring to Edward Everett (1794–1865), an American scholar and orator who made a long speech at Gettysburg before Lincoln delivered his famous address.
2. **four states** South Carolina, Mississippi, Florida, and Alabama.

⑩ ▲ Critical Viewing
Why is this posture, on horseback, appropriate for a statue memorializing Robert E. Lee? **[Defend]**

anarchy (an´ ər kē) *n.* absence of government

redress (ri dres´) *n.* atonement; rectification

⑫ ☑ Reading Check
According to Lee, what is the political state of the country?

Letter to His Son ◆ 525

CUSTOMIZE INSTRUCTION FOR UNIVERSAL ACCESS

For Less Proficient Readers	For Advanced Readers
Read Lee's letter aloud, working paragraph by paragraph or even sentence by sentence, so that students can recognize Lee's formal tone, his sense of regret, and his deep respect for his state and its rights. You may wish to clarify that as a trained military leader, Lee would not actually "draw [his] sword," but rather would lead an army into battle from a position on horseback. Lee is, thus, speaking figuratively.	Have students identify textual examples that reflect Lincoln's solid understanding of his audience's thoughts and emotions. Students may note that Lincoln recognizes the suffering people have endured and the losses they have experienced. In keeping with the times, he also invokes religious sentiments and appeals for divine inspiration. Encourage students to infer the issues, values, and goals Lincoln's audience held dear.

---

⑧ About the Selection

In this letter Robert E. Lee addresses the difficult decision he faces as the country approaches a war that will pit the states against each other. The most respected officer in the United States Army, Lee explains that despite his strong belief in the Constitution and in preserving the Union, his strongest loyalty is to his home state of Virginia. He expresses his willingness to take up arms to defend his state. The letter illustrates Lee's dignity, loyalty, and bravery.

⑨ Vocabulary Development

Greek Root -archy-

• Draw students' attention to Lee's use of the word *anarchy*, and read its definition. Then, tell students that the root -archy- derives from the Greek word meaning "rule" or "government."

• Write these words that share the root -archy- on the chalkboard: *patriarchy*, *oligarchy*, and *matriarchy*.

• Have students research each word's prefix and determine the meaning it adds to the root. Then, instruct them to write their own definitions of each word.

Answer: *Pater* is Latin for "father"; a patriarchy is a government led by a strong male figure. *Oligos*, from the Greek, means "few"; an oligarchy is government ruled by a small faction. *Mater* is Latin for "mother"; a matriarchy is a government led by women.

⑩ ▶ Critical Viewing

Answer: Students may note that this posture accentuates the bravery, power, and heroism of the man.

⑪ Background

Georgia Secedes

Just four days before Lee wrote this letter, Georgia seceded from the United States, joining South Carolina, Mississippi, Florida, and Alabama. Virginia seceded in April, 1861.

⑫ ☑ Reading Check

Answer: He states that it is "between a state of anarchy and civil war."

⓭ Reading Strategy

Using Background Knowledge

- Help students proceed through this dense paragraph in order to clarify the two warring impulses within Lee—his loyalty to both his nation and to his home state.

▶ **Monitor Progress** Ask students the Reading Strategy question on p. 526: Given what you know about Lee, why was he so committed to the Union and to Virginia?

Answer: Lee was trained for the military in the North and served the Union Army as an officer in Mexico. Many of his ancestors were statesmen and American patriots. Yet, Lee was a proud native of Virginia, and this "simple" fact led him to defend the Confederacy rather than the Union.

Answers for p. 526

Review and Assess

1. Students should support their responses with clear reasons.

2. **(a)** The first was delivered after the Battle of Gettysburg; the second was delivered toward the end of the war, after he had been reelected.
   (b) His purpose was to rally the American public around the cause of winning the war.
   (c) His purpose was to lead people to recognize the need to heal the nation's wounds.

3. **(a)** He describes a vision of the nation as healthy, peaceful, and free. **(b)** This expression of hope and optimism effectively ends both speeches because it emphasizes the idea of regaining national unity.

4. **(a)** "Secession is nothing but revolution." **(b)** He argues that secession conflicts with the goals of the Constitution.

5. **(a)** He has given him a biography of Washington.
   (b) Lee asserts that Washington would be upset if he knew that the Union, that Washington worked so hard to create, might soon be destroyed.

6. **Possible answer:** Today's addresses are longer and usually far less eloquent.

---

country, her prosperity and institutions, and would defend any state if her rights were invaded. But I can anticipate no greater calamity for the country than a dissolution of the Union. It would be an accumulation of all the evils we complain of, and I am willing to sacrifice everything but honor for its preservation. I hope, therefore, that all constitutional means will be exhausted before there is a resort to force. Secession is nothing but revolution. The framers of our Constitution never exhausted so much labor, wisdom, and forbearance in its formation, and surrounded it with so many guards and securities, if it was intended to be broken by every member of the Confederacy at will. It was intended for "perpetual union," so expressed in the preamble, and for the establishment of a government, not a compact, which can only be dissolved by revolution or the consent of all the people in convention assembled. It is idle to talk **⓭** of secession. Anarchy would have been established, and not a government, by Washington, Hamilton, Jefferson, Madison, and the other patriots of the Revolution. . . . Still, a Union that can only be maintained by swords and bayonets, and in which strife and civil war are to take the place of brotherly love and kindness, has no charm for me. I shall mourn for my country and for the welfare and progress of mankind. If the Union is dissolved, and the government disrupted, I shall return to my native state and share the miseries of my people; and, save in defense, will draw my sword on none.

Reading Strategy
Using Background Knowledge Given what you know about Lee, why was he so committed to the Union and to Virginia?

Review and Assess

Thinking About the Selections

1. **Respond:** Which phrases in Lincoln's speeches do you find the most memorable? Explain your response.

2. **(a) Recall:** Briefly describe the occasion for each of Lincoln's speeches. **(b) Infer:** Beyond the stated reasons, what was Lincoln's underlying purpose in "The Gettysburg Address"? **(c) Infer:** What was his main purpose in the "Second Inaugural Address"?

3. **(a) Recall:** What vision of the nation does Lincoln describe at the close of both speeches? **(b) Connect:** In what way does an expression of this vision further his purpose?

4. **(a) Recall:** How does Lee define secession? **(b) Summarize:** In your own words, explain Lee's argument against secession.

5. **(a) Recall:** What gift has Lee's son given him? **(b) Connect:** Explain the line of reasoning that links Lee's acknowledgment of his son's gift to an argument against secession.

6. **Apply:** In what ways, if any, are Lincoln's speeches different from modern presidential addresses? Explain.

✎ ASSESSMENT PRACTICE: Reading Comprehension

Context (For more practice, see Test Preparation Workbook, p. 30.)

Many tests require students to use context clues such as synonyms and antonyms to determine the meanings of unfamiliar words. Write the following passage from p. 524 on the chalkboard. Then, ask students the question that follows.

> Both parties deprecated war; but one of them would *make* war rather than let the nation survive; and the other would *accept* war rather than let it perish .

In this passage, the word <u>perish</u> means—

A flourish **C** expand
B compromise **D** die

The parallel construction of the sentence—"let the nation *survive*/rather than let it *perish*"—combined with the use of "rather," which means *to the contrary*, or *instead*, suggests that <u>perish</u> means the opposite of *survive*. D is the correct answer.

Review and Assess

Literary Analysis

Diction

1. Using a chart like the one shown here, analyze the **diction** of each writer.

	Examples of Diction	Audience	Purpose
Lincoln			
Lee			

2. In what ways does each writer's diction reflect and suit his audience and purpose?

Comparing Literary Works

3. (a) What words does Lincoln use to describe the war? (b) What words does Lee use to describe it?

4. (a) Based on the ideas and insights revealed in these selections, what personal qualities do you think Lee and Lincoln share? (b) In what ways do they differ?

5. Which voice do you find more engaging, Lincoln's or Lee's? Why?

Reading Strategy

Using Background Knowledge

6. Using **background knowledge,** explain why President Lincoln wrote such a short speech for his address at Gettysburg.

7. Why did Lincoln connect the honoring of the Gettysburg dead with the goal of continuing the war toward a Union victory?

8. In the "Second Inaugural Address," why did Lincoln suggest that both the war and an end to slavery were part of God's plan?

9. Why was Lee so opposed to secession?

Extend Understanding

10. **Social Studies Connection:** Lee describes the relationship between the states and the Union as "a government, not a compact." What are some of the ways in which people, organizations, and governments make compacts with one another?

The Gettysburg Address / Second Inaugural Address / Letter to His Son ◆ 527

Quick Review

Diction is a writer's choice and arrangement of words.

To **use background knowledge,** refer to information you already know about a subject to help you create meaning for current reading.

 Take It to the Net
www.phschool.com
Take the interactive self-test online to check your understanding of these selections.

✹ ENRICHMENT: Further Reading

Other Works by or About the Authors

Works by or About Lincoln

The Collected Works of Abraham Lincoln (nine volumes), Basler, Pratt, and Dunlap, eds.

With Malice Toward None, Stephen B. Oates

Lincoln, David Herbert Donald

Works by or About Lee

R. E. Lee, Douglass Southall Freeman (four volumes)

Lee's Dispatches, Douglass Southall Freeman, ed.

 Take It to the Net
Visit www.phschool.com for more information on Abraham Lincoln and Robert E. Lee.

Answers for p. 527

Review and Assess

1. Possible answers: Lincoln—Diction: we cannot consecrate—we cannot hallow this ground; we here highly resolve that these dead shall not have died in vain; Audience: several thousand Union supporters; Purpose: to help further the mourning process for the slain soldiers, and to gain support for the war. Lee—Diction: It is the principle I contend for, not individual or private benefit; Audience: his son; Purpose: to explain his support of the Confederacy.

2. Lincoln's address is intended for a general audience; Lee's writing is intended only for his son.

3. **(a)** Lincoln describes the war as *a great civil war, the great task remaining before us, the great contest,* and *this mighty scourge of war.* **(b)** Lee describes the war with the word *evils.*

4. **(a)** Possible answer: Both are dignified, thoughtful, and courageous.
(b) Possible answer: Perhaps because of his extensive military background, Lee seems to revile war more deeply and personally than does Lincoln; never does Lee describe a military effort in glorified terms. By contrast, Lincoln does so on several occasions.

5. Students should support their answers with clear reasons and with details from the texts.

6. He was asked only to "make a few appropriate remarks."

7. As president, he wanted to see the nation survive. He did not want the enormous loss of life to have been in vain.

8. Possible answer: He did so because both sides shared the same religious beliefs.

9. Having served in the United States military and having descended from generations of loyal Americans, Lee felt strong ties to the Union.

10. Students might mention such "compacts" as marriage, mergers of companies, and international treaties.

527

❶ Vocabulary Development

Word Analysis

1. government with one ruler
2. a family or culture in which the father possesses ultimate authority
3. a government in which a select few hold all power

Spelling Strategy

1. confess
2. distress
3. stress
4. compress

Concept Development:

1. b 2. a 3. a 4. c 5. b 6. a
7. c 8. c 9. a

❷ Grammar and Style

Practice

1. Fondly do we hope/fervently do we pray
2. we cannot dedicate/we cannot consecrate/we cannot hallow
3. until all the wealth/until every drop
4. all dreaded/all sought
5. of the people/by the people/for the people

Writing Application

Check student responses for faulty parallelism.

Looking at Style

Make sure students have chosen a clear example of parallelism, explained why it is parallel, and how it is effective.

Integrate Language Skills

❶ Vocabulary Development Lesson

Word Analysis: Greek Word Part -archy-

The word *anarchy* derives from the Greek word *archein*, meaning "to rule" or "to govern." With the prefix *an-*, meaning "without," *anarchy* means "without government." Use your knowledge of the root and the supplied information to write a definition for each word below.

1. monarchy (*mono* = single; one)
2. patriarchy (*patri* = father)
3. oligarchy (*olig* = few)

Spelling Strategy

Except when forming plurals, use *ss* to spell the s sound at the end of a word, as in *redress*. In your notebook, complete the spelling of the words below.

1. confe__
2. distre__
3. stre__
4. compre__

❷ Grammar and Style Lesson

Parallel Structure

Parallel structure is the repeated expression of similar ideas in a similar grammatical form. Parallelism can involve the repeated use of similar words, phrases, clauses, or sentences. In the example, each phrase begins with the word *with*.

> *With* malice toward none; *with* charity for all; *with* firmness in the right . . .

Practice Identify the parallel structures in each of the following items.

1. Fondly do we hope—fervently do we pray—that this mighty scourge . . .

Concept Development: Synonyms

Review the vocabulary list on p. 521. Then, choose the word that is the best synonym, or word with similar meaning, for each first word.

1. consecrate: (a) destroy, (b) bless, (c) join
2. hallow: (a) honor, (b) greet, (c) enlarge
3. deprecated: (a) condemned, (b) proved, (c) enlarged
4. insurgents: (a) patriots, (b) loyalists, (c) rebels
5. discern: (a) hear, (b) understand, (c) ask
6. scourge: (a) punishment, (b) reward, (c) desire
7. malice: (a) grace, (b) scent, (c) spite
8. anarchy: (a) honor, (b) order, (c) chaos
9. redress: (a) atonement, (b) fear, (c) disturbance

2. . . . we cannot dedicate—we cannot consecrate—we cannot hallow—this ground . . .
3. . . . until all the wealth piled by the bondman's . . . and until every drop of blood . . .
4. All dreaded it—all sought to avert it.
5. . . . that government of the people, by the people, for the people . . .

Writing Application Rewrite a sentence from "Letter to His Son," using parallel structure to emphasize Lee's ideas.

Looking at Style Review Lincoln's speeches to find a particularly strong example of parallel structure. Explain your choice, noting the effect of the example you have chosen.

𝒲𝒢 *Prentice Hall Writing and Grammar Connection: Chapter 8, Section 4*

528 ◆ *Division, Reconciliation, and Expansion (1850–1914)*

TEACHING RESOURCES

The following resources can be used to enrich or extend the instruction for pp. 528–529.

Vocabulary

📖 **Selection Support:** Build Vocabulary, 124

📖 **Vocabulary and Spelling Practice Book** (Use this booklet for skills enrichment.)

Grammar

📖 **Selection Support:** Grammar and Style, p. 125

𝒲𝒢 **Writing and Grammar,** Ruby Level, p. 154

📖 **Daily Language Practice Transparencies** 📖

Writing

𝒲𝒢 **Writing and Grammar,** Ruby Level, p. 129

📖 **Extension Activities,** p. 28

📖 **Writing Models and Graphic Organizers on Transparencies,** p. 37

💿 **Writing and Grammar iText CD-ROM**

■ **BLOCK SCHEDULING:** Resources marked with this symbol provide varied instruction during 90-minute blocks.

❸ Writing Lesson

Diary Entry

It is the eve of the dedication of the cemetery at Gettysburg. As Lincoln, write a diary entry describing the message you will strive to deliver. Using the Gettysburg Address as your model, imagine Lincoln's feelings and note the main points he wanted to stress.

Prewriting Take notes on what you consider the three or four main points of the Gettysburg Address. Rank them in order of importance and summarize them in plain language. Spend a few minutes freewriting about each point. Use this as the basis of your draft.

Drafting From your notes, begin writing the diary entry. Use personal reflections and opinions as Lincoln would have in drafting the address. Emphasize your main points with persuasive language.

Revising Reread your draft to make sure it captures Lincoln's feelings with persuasive language. Add details to strengthen your argument.

Model: Revising to Add Persuasive Language

I know our country was born on the principle of

freedom because our forefathers believed all men to be

we must fight to   *Slavery is wrong.*

equal. Now ~~I want to stop a terrible evil. We can't have~~

~~slavery.~~ We must ensure freedom and equality for all.

> Statements such as *we must fight* and *slavery is wrong* make the writing powerful and persuasive.

W̶G Prentice Hall Writing and Grammar Connection: Chapter 7, Section 3

❹ Extension Activities

Speaking and Listening With a group, stage a **mock Supreme Court hearing** and argue for or against a state's rights to secede from the Union. After hearing arguments from "lawyers," each "judge" should render an opinion. As you plan, consider the following tips.

- Lawyers should present their strongest arguments.
- Judges should identify and rank the arguments before rendering a decision.

Stage the hearing in class. **[Group Activity]**

Research and Technology Develop a plan for an **Internet Web site** that provides information and images related to the Civil War. Create a flow chart that illustrates the links you plan to include in your site. If possible, use HTML software to develop an offline version of your site.

 Take It to the Net www.phschool.com

Go online for an additional research activity using the Internet.

---

❸ Writing Lesson

- Students' diary entries should include all the main points in Lincoln's Gettysburg Address, reflect a strong organization, and employ slightly less formal diction than does the finished speech.

- Encourage students to reread the speech several times in order to identify Lincoln's main points and several crucial details that might be mentioned in the diary entry.

- Remind students to include interesting ideas or images in the diary entry that Lincoln might later have omitted.

- Use the Reflective Essay rubric in **Performance Assessment and Portfolio Management,** p. 11, to evaluate students' diary entries.

❹ Listening and Speaking

- Encourage groups to spend more time preparing their arguments than they will delivering them. You might suggest a ratio such as 3:1 or 4:1 as a guideline.

- As they prepare, students should develop arguments for both sides of the issue in order to anticipate and answer opponents' arguments.

- Have students use the Peer Assessment form for Persuasive Speech, p. 17 in **Performance Assessment and Portfolio Management.**

CUSTOMIZE INSTRUCTION
For Universal Access

To address different learning styles, use the following activities suggested in the **Extension Activities** booklet, p. 28.

For Interpersonal and Visual/Spatial Learners, use Activity 5.

For Musical/Rhythmic Learners, use Activity 6.

ASSESSMENT RESOURCES

The following resources can be used to assess students' knowledge and skills.

Selection Assessment

- **Formal Assessment** p. 131
- **Open Book Test,** p. 82
- **Got It! Assessment Videotapes,** Tape 3
- **Test Bank Software**
- **Take It to the Net**
  Visit www.phschool.com for self-tests and additional questions on the selections.

Writing Rubric

- **Perf. Assess. and Portfolio Mgmt.,** p. 11

Listening and Speaking Rubric

- **Perf. Assess. and Portfolio Mgmt.,** p. 17

PRENTICE HALL ASSESSMENT *SYSTEM*

- **Workbook**
- **Skill Book**
- **Transparencies**
- **CD-ROM**

Lesson Objectives

1. To analyze the beliefs of the authors of public documents
2. To read the legal and formal language of public documents
3. To understand the importance of the information in public documents such as the Emancipation Proclamation

About Public Documents

- Have students read "About Public Documents." Ask students to identify and describe any such documents that they have encountered.

  Possible response: Students may mention such documents as statements of liability in hotels and other establishments, automobile insurance policies, and even the United States Constitution.

- Have students consider how public documents affect people's lives. Offer laws as an example. Help students recognize that laws are documents that affect their everyday behavior. Students should understand that public documents can be very important.

- Have students discuss the value of being able to read public documents. Ask students to name reasons that people should read such documents, and write the reasons on the chalkboard.

Reading Strategy

Analyzing an Author's Beliefs

- Have students read the information about the Reading Strategy.

- Call students' attention to the Identifying an Author's Beliefs chart on p. 530. Review the chart with the class, emphasizing that explicit statements usually reflect implicit beliefs. Ask students to apply this concept to the selection.

- Explain to students that public documents often contain highly formal and legal language that must be read and decoded carefully.

Public Documents

About Public Documents

What do the text of a law, the deed to a house, and minutes from a legislative meeting have in common? They are examples of public documents, official government papers that affect everyone living in a given part of a state or nation. These documents are referred to as public because they concern laws and issues that all citizens have a stake in. For this reason, these documents are made available for average citizens to read, analyze, and discuss.

The public document that you are about to read is one of the most important in United States history. It is the text of a formal announcement that President Abraham Lincoln signed on January 1, 1863, calling for the freeing of "all persons held as slaves" within the rebellious southern states. Many historians believe that this public document altered the nature of the Civil War.

Reading Strategy

Analyzing an Author's Beliefs

Some public documents, such as census reports, are almost completely objective; they merely record information without seeking to support a particular point of view. Sometimes, however, public documents contain opinions.

- Opinions may be hinted at through choice of words or the decision to emphasize certain details.

- In contrast, beliefs may be stated outright, making them explicit.

- Beliefs and opinions about a specific issue depend on assumptions—claims that must be true if the opinion or belief is true. Writers may state their assumptions, making them explicit. Often, though, writers' assumptions are simply implied in the argument they make. You can tell they are making these implicit assumptions by noting what general ideas must be true for their arguments to be true.

To identify an author's beliefs, follow the steps outlined in the chart shown.

As you read the Emancipation Proclamation, consider the implicit and explicit beliefs it represents.

Identifying an Author's Beliefs

Step one

Look for opinion words such as *I think, I believe,* or *in my opinion,* which signal explicit beliefs.

Step two

Look for other words that suggest opinion. These may be adjectives that have clear opposites. For example, a writer might say that a course of action is *just;* another might say it is *unfair.*

Step three

Look for details that suggest a specific point of view. Read the document sentence by sentence. Consider whether each detail is factual or whether someone could make an argument against it.

By the President of the United States of America:

A Proclamation.

The source and type of public document should always be clear.

Whereas, on the twenty-second day of September, in the year of our Lord one thousand eight hundred and sixty-two, a proclamation was issued by the President of the United States, containing, among other things, the following, to wit:

"That on the first day of January, in the year of our Lord one thousand eight hundred and sixty-three, all persons held as slaves within any State or designated part of a State, the people whereof shall then be in rebellion against the United States, shall be then, thenceforward, and forever free; and the Executive Government of the United States, including the military and naval authority thereof, will recognize and maintain the freedom of such persons, and will do no act or acts to repress such persons, or any of them, in any efforts they may make for their actual freedom"

Many public documents go into a great amount of detail. The details may slow down your reading of the document, but they are very important.

"That the Executive will, on the first day of January aforesaid, by proclamation, designate the States and parts of States, if any, in which the people thereof, respectively, shall then be in rebellion against the United States; and the fact that any State, or the people thereof, shall on that day be, in good faith, represented in the Congress of the United States by members chosen thereto at elections wherein a majority of the qualified voters of such State shall have participated, shall, in the absence of strong countervailing testimony, be deemed conclusive evidence that such State, and the people thereof, are not then in rebellion against the United States."

Now, therefore I, Abraham Lincoln, President of the United States, by virtue of the power in me vested as Commander-in-Chief, of the Army and Navy of the United States in time of actual armed rebellion against the authority and government of the United States, and as a fit and necessary war measure for suppressing said rebellion, do, on this first day of January, in the year of our Lord one thousand eight hundred and sixty-three, and in accordance with my purpose so to do publicly proclaimed for the full period of one hundred days, from the day first above mentioned, order and designate as the States and parts of States wherein the people thereof respectively, are this day in rebellion against the United States, the following, to wit:

Arkansas, Texas, Louisiana, (except the Parishes of St. Bernard, Plaquemines, Jefferson, St. John, St. Charles, St. James Ascension, Assumption, Terrebonne, Lafourche, St. Mary, St. Martin, and Orleans, including the City of New Orleans) Mississippi, Alabama, Florida, Georgia, South Carolina, North Carolina, and Virginia, (except the forty-eight counties designated as West Virginia, and also the counties of Berkley, Accomac, Northampton, Elizabeth City, York, Princess Ann, and Norfolk, including the cities of Norfolk and Portsmouth[)], and which excepted parts, are for the present, left precisely as if this proclamation were not issued.

And by virtue of the power, and for the purpose aforesaid, I do order and declare that all persons held as slaves within said designated States, and parts of States, are, and henceforward shall be free; and that the Executive government of the United States, including the military and naval authorities thereof, will recognize and maintain the freedom of said persons.

Legal and formal language *(for the purpose aforesaid; within said designated States)* is common in proclamations.

Emancipation Proclamation

- Ask students to share their background knowledge about the Emancipation Proclamation. Remind them that they probably studied it in history class.

- Point out that this document signs into law a proclamation first made public 100 days earlier. It frees slaves in the rebellious Confederate States—territories in Union control are excluded.

- Have students read the Proclamation and the notes that identify the elements of this document.

- Call students' attention to the first note. Ask them to identify the source and type of this document. **Answer:** This is a proclamation made by the President of the United States.

- Call students' attention to the second note before they read the second paragraph. As students read, ask them to record in their notebooks the main points and the details that support the main points.

- If students are confused by the legal and formal language in the Proclamation, call their attention to the third note. Ask students why they think such language is used. **Possible response:** Students may say that the language makes the document very specific; and ensures that the law is clear.

CUSTOMIZE INSTRUCTION FOR UNIVERSAL ACCESS

For Less Proficient Readers	For English Learners	For Advanced Readers
These students will be challenged by the long sentences and detailed, highly formal language of the Proclamation. Have them identify and write down the main point of each sentence in their notes. Then, have them synthesize these points to determine the document's meaning.	These students may also find the language of the Proclamation to be difficult. Help them to identify the main points of each paragraph. Then, have them read the paragraphs through once for an overview of meaning. Students should use this context to determine the meanings of unfamiliar words.	While these students may not find the Proclamation's language difficult, they may find the document to be less than clear. Encourage students to rewrite the document in a simple, clear style to make sure they understand all of the main points.

Check Your Comprehension

1. Lincoln has the authority to make this proclamation because he is the Commander-in-Chief of the Army and Navy, and because it is a "fit and necessary measure" for ending the rebellion against the United States government.

2. The northern states and various parts of Louisiana and Virginia are not included in the proclamation.

Applying the Reading Strategy

3. **(a)** Implicitly, Lincoln believes in the power that the Constitution vests in the president. Explicitly, Lincoln says that the emancipation of slaves is warranted by the Constitution. **(b)** Lincoln states explicitly that emancipation is Constitutional and that it is "an act of justice." His decisive words suggest that he also believes implicitly that emancipation is necessary and just. **(c)** Lincoln asks explicitly for "the favor of Almighty God"; Lincoln clearly believes implicitly in God's existence.

Activity

Remind students to use language and a tone that are appropriate for a public document. When they finish, have students present their proclamations orally to the class.

Comparing Informational Materials

Encourage students to use the Internet and the library to find copies of recent government proclamations. They might also contact the offices of their local or state representatives.

532

And I hereby enjoin upon the people so declared to be free to abstain from all violence, unless in necessary self-defence; and I recommend to them that, in all cases when allowed, they labor faithfully for reasonable wages.

And I further declare and make known, that such persons of suitable condition, will be received into the armed service of the United States to garrison forts, positions, stations, and other places, and to man vessels of all sorts in said service.

And upon this act, sincerely believed to be an act of justice, warranted by the Constitution, upon military necessity, I invoke the considerate judgment of mankind, and the gracious favor of Almighty God.

In witness whereof, I have hereunto set my hand and caused the seal of the United States to be affixed.

Done at the City of Washington, this first day of January, in the year of our Lord one thousand eight hundred and sixty three, and of the Independence of the United States of America the eighty-seventh.

By the President: Abraham Lincoln

Secretary of State. William H. Seward

> Considering their legal and, at times, historic effects, place and date are key elements of public documents.

Check Your Comprehension

1. According to Lincoln, why does he have the authority to make this proclamation?
2. Which parts of the United States that practiced slavery are not included in the proclamation?

Applying the Reading Strategy

Analyzing an Author's Beliefs

3. Identify Lincoln's explicit and implicit beliefs in the Emancipation Proclamation. Note beliefs about (a) the Constitution's authority, (b) the necessity of emancipation, (c) God's existence.

Activity

Writing a Proclamation

Consider creating a new national holiday or selecting a new national anthem. Then, write a proclamation of your own.

Comparing Informational Materials

Modern Proclamations

Find a contemporary government proclamation. Compare it to the Emancipation Proclamation in purpose and language.

PART 2
Focus on Literary Forms:
Diaries, Journals, and Letters

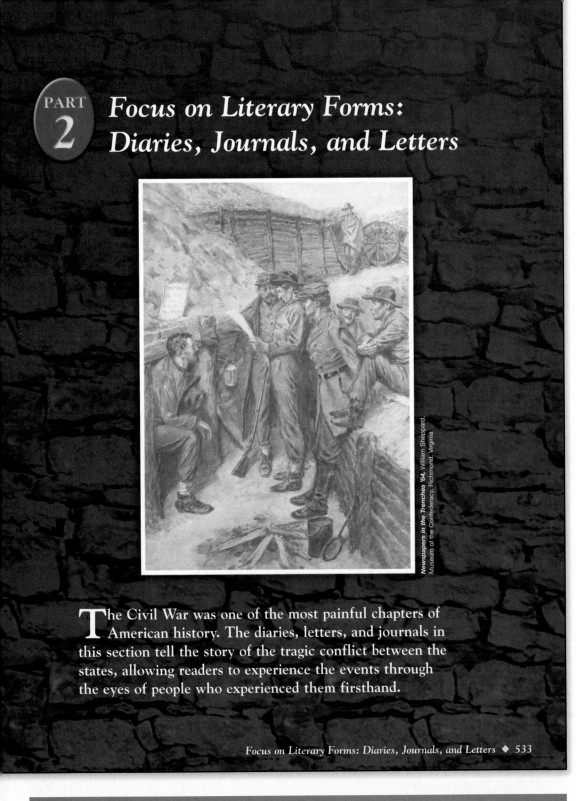

Newspapers in the Trenches '64, William Sheppard.
Museum of the Confederacy, Richmond, Virginia

The Civil War was one of the most painful chapters of American history. The diaries, letters, and journals in this section tell the story of the tragic conflict between the states, allowing readers to experience the events through the eyes of people who experienced them firsthand.

Focus on Literary Forms: Diaries, Journals, and Letters ◆ 533

Selection Planning Guide

The firsthand accounts in Part 2 tell the story of the Civil War and its aftermath in the words of those who experienced it, both on and off the battlefield. In her journal, southern gentlewoman Mary Chesnut describes the attack on Fort Sumter. The accounts of Warren Lee Goss, Randolph McKim, and Stonewall Jackson provide three perspectives on the war from the soldiers who fought it. "Reaction to the Emancipation Proclamation" shows how the African American community responded to Lincoln's momentous proclamation, while Sojourner Truth's account demonstrates how much was still to be done in the fight for equality. Journalist Molly Moore's account of the 1991 Gulf War takes a behind-the-scenes look at the media's role in reporting—and shaping our perceptions of—modern warfare.

Background
Art

Newspapers in the Trenches '64,
William Ludwell Sheppard

This work shows another side of the war—the human faces of the men who, between battles, turned from soldiers into letter writers, journal keepers, and sharers of news.

Use these questions for discussion:

1. How does the artist communicate the fact that reading a newspaper is a special event for the soldiers?
   Possible response: They are gathered attentively around the single soldier who is holding a newspaper and they appear eager to hear the latest news.

2. Why might letters, journals, diaries, and newspapers have been so important to Civil War soldiers?
   Possible response: Besides being a diversion, reading and writing were a means of contact with the world outside the trenches; writing also helped them preserve a sense of their own individuality and humanity and gave them some hope of living on in some form, even if they died in battle.

CUSTOMIZE INSTRUCTION FOR UNIVERSAL ACCESS

When assigning the selections in this part, keep in mind these factors:

from *Mary Chesnut's Civil War*	**"A Confederate Account of the Battle of Gettysburg" and "An Account of the Battle of Bull Run"**	**"Reaction to the Emancipation Proclamation" and "An Account of an Experience With Discrimination"**
• Southern woman's reaction to attack on Fort Sumter	• Brief, personal accounts of battles	• African American perspective
"Recollections of a Private"		**"Gulf War Journal"**
• Brief, accessible account		• Journalist's firsthand account of Gulf War
• Contrasts soldier's expectation with reality of military life		

Civil War Diaries, Journals, and Letters

Lesson Objectives

1. **To analyze and respond to literary elements**
   - Literary Analysis: Diaries, Journals, and Letters
   - Comparing Literary Works
2. **To read, comprehend, analyze, and critique nonfiction**
   - Reading Strategy: Distinguishing Fact From Opinion
   - Reading Check Questions
   - Review and Assess Questions
   - Assessment Practice (ATE)
3. **To develop word analysis skills, fluency, and systematic vocabulary**
   - Vocabulary Development Lesson: Latin Prefix: *ob-*
4. **To understand and apply written and oral language conventions**
   - Spelling Strategy
   - Grammar and Style Lesson: Capitalization of Proper Nouns
5. **To understand and apply appropriate writing and research strategies**
   - Writing Lesson: Problem-and-Solution Essay
   - Extension Activity: Model/Map
6. **To understand and apply listening and speaking strategies**
   - Extension Activity: Dramatic Reading

STEP-BY-STEP TEACHING GUIDE	PACING GUIDE
PRETEACH	
Motivate Students and Provide Background	
Use the Motivation activity (ATE p. 534)	5 min.
Read and discuss author and background features (SE/ATE p. 534)	5 min.
Introduce the Concepts	
Introduce the Literary Analysis and Reading Strategy (SE/ATE p. 535) A	15 min.
Pronounce the vocabulary words and read their definitions (SE p. 535)	5 min.
TEACH	
Monitor Comprehension	
Informally monitor comprehension by circulating while students read independently or in groups A	30 min.
Monitor students' comprehension with the Reading Check notes (SE/ATE pp. 537, 539, 543, 545, 547)	as students read
Develop vocabulary with Vocabulary notes (SE pp. 537, 538, 539; ATE p. 541)	as students read
Develop Understanding	
Develop students' understanding of diaries, letters, and journals with the Literary Analysis annotations (SE pp. 536, 538, 540, 545; ATE pp. 536, 538, 540, 545) A	5 min.
Develop students' ability to distinguish fact from opinion with the Reading Strategy annotations (SE pp. 541, 543, 544; ATE pp. 541, 543, 544)	5 min.
ASSESS	
Assess Mastery	
Assess students' mastery of the Reading Strategy and Literary Analysis by having them answer the Review and Assess questions (SE/ATE p. 549)	15 min.
Use one or more of the print and media Assessment Resources (ATE p. 551) A	up to 45 min.
EXTEND	
Apply Understanding	
Have students complete the Vocabulary Development Lesson and the Grammar Lesson (SE p. 550) A	20 min.
Apply students' ability to gather details by using the Writing Lesson (SE/ATE p. 551) A	45 min.
Apply students' understanding using one or more of the Extension Activities (SE p. 551)	20–90 min.

A **ACCELERATED INSTRUCTION:**
Use the strategies and activities identified with an **A**.

UNIVERSAL ACCESS
● = Below Level Students
▲ = On-Level Students
■ = Above Level Students

Time and Resource Manager

RESOURCES

PRINT 📖	TRANSPARENCIES	TECHNOLOGY 💿 🎧 📼
• **Beyond Literature,** Humanities Connection: Journals, p. 29 ▲ ■		• **Interest Grabber Video,** Tape 4 ● ▲ ■
• **Selection Support Workbook:** ● ▲ ■ Literary Analysis, p. 131 Reading Strategy, p. 130 Build Vocabulary, p. 128	• **Literary Analysis and Reading Transparencies,** pp. 57 and 58 ● ▲ ■	
		• **Listening to Literature** ● ▲ ■ Audiocassettes, Side 18 Audio CDs, CD 11
• **Literatura en español** ● ▲ • **Literary Analysis for Enrichment** ■		
• **Formal Assessment:** Selection Test, p. 138 ● ▲ ■ • **Open Book Test,** p. 85 ● ▲ ■ • **Performance Assessment and Portfolio Management,** p. 31 ● ▲ ■ • **PRENTICE HALL ASSESSMENT SYSTEM** ● ▲ ■	• **PRENTICE HALL ASSESSMENT SYSTEM** ● ▲ ■ Skills Practice Answers and Explanations on Transparencies	• **Test Bank Software** ● ▲ ■ • **Got It! Assessment Videotapes,** Tape 3 ● ▲
• **Selection Support Workbook:** ● ▲ ■ Grammar and Style, p. 129 • **Writing and Grammar,** Ruby Level ● ▲ ■ • **Extension Activities,** p. 29 ● ▲ ■	• **Daily Language Practice Transparencies** ● ▲ • **Writing Models and Graphic Organizers on Transparencies,** p. 33 ● ▲ ■	• **Writing and Grammar iText CD-ROM** ● ▲ ■ 🖥 *Take It to the Net* www.phschool.com

▦ **BLOCK SCHEDULING:** Use one 90-minute class period to preteach the selection and have students read it. Use a second 90-minute class period to assess students' mastery of skills and have them complete one of the Extension Activities.

Step-by-Step Teaching Guide for pp. 534–535

Motivation

The words of actual witnesses to history are often more powerful than those of any secondhand account. Ask students to bring to class any firsthand accounts of historic events that may be in their family's possession, such as a letter from a grandfather who fought in World War II, or a diary entry recounting President Kennedy's assassination. To help students better appreciate the power of firsthand accounts, show an excerpt from *The Civil War* series, or display the companion book. Then, explain that the diaries, journals, and letters they are about to read were written by people from different walks of life, each of whom offers a unique perspective on the events surrounding the Civil War.

▭ Interest Grabber Video

As an alternative, play "Ain't I a Woman?" on Tape 4 to engage student interest.

❶ Background

More About the Authors

Mary Chesnut's circle of friends included Jefferson Davis and others in the highest ranks of the Confederacy.

Along with several generals and other officers, Warren Lee Goss was one of 230 contributors to *Battles and Leaders of the Civil War*, a four-volume compilation of essays published in the 1880s.

During the war, Randolph McKim became the chaplain for a Virginia cavalry regiment.

Thomas J. Jackson left his teaching position at the Virginia Military Institute to join the Confederate Army. He was killed at Chancellorsville just a few months before the Battle of Gettysburg.

Henry M. Turner was one the leaders of the post-war African American community.

Sojourner Truth was born Isabella Baumfree. According to Frederick Douglass, she had a "strange compound of wit and wisdom, of wild enthusiasm, and flint-like common sense..."

534

Prepare to Read

❶ Civil War Diaries, Journals, and Letters

Civil War Voices

The Civil War was one of the most painful chapters in American history, tearing families apart and scarring the lives of millions of soldiers and civilians. The following diaries, journals, and letters tell the story of the war through the eyes of just a few of those whose lives were affected by it.

A Daughter of the South No one was hurt when the opening shots of the war were fired on Fort Sumter on April 12, 1860, but **Mary Boykin Chesnut** (1823–1886) seems to have sensed the carnage to come. The daughter of a cotton plantation owner and United States senator, Mary Boykin was raised in an aristocratic family in Charleston, South Carolina. At the age of seventeen, she married James Chesnut, Jr., a wealthy lawyer and future senator. Her journal entries convey the Southern aristocracy's mingled optimism and dread that marked the opening days of the Civil War.

On the Front Lines Men hurried to enlist in what most believed would be a swift and glorious conflict. Some young men saw the military as an opportunity for respect and advancement as we learn from the account of Union soldier **Warren Lee Goss**. The harsh realities of the training camp and battlefield soon taught soldiers on both sides that lives and limbs were the price of glory. The cost was especially high at the Battle of Gettysburg—a stunning defeat for Confederate general Robert E. Lee. In his diary, Confederate soldier **Randolph McKim** recounts the bravery of his companions, many of whom were among the 51,000 killed or wounded at Gettysburg after Confederate troops advanced on Culp's Hill, led by McKim.

A Master Strategist Confederate general and military strategist **Thomas Jonathan "Stonewall" Jackson** (1824–1863) earned his nickname early in the war for his steadiness and determination during the Battle of Bull Run in 1861. Jackson, who recounted the battle in a letter to his wife, died two years after his great victory; he was accidentally shot by his own troops and died of complications.

Freedom's Cry The war raged on, but the Emancipation Proclamation, issued by President Lincoln on September 22, 1862, changed the purpose of the war. By declaring that all slaves would be freed on January 1, 1863, the Proclamation transformed the conflict into a war to end slavery, as well as a war to restore the Union. **Reverend Henry M. Turner,** a free-born African American who lived in Washington, D.C., recounts his community's joyous reaction to the news of Lincoln's proclamation.

The Enduring Battle When the war ended in 1865, abolitionist **Sojourner Truth** (1797–1883) had only begun to battle discrimination. A preacher and former slave, Truth also earned fame as an advocate of women's rights, temperance, and workplace and prison reform.

Born into slavery in Ulster County, New York, Truth was freed when the state emancipated slaves in 1827. In 1843, she began preaching along the east coast. During the Civil War, Truth gathered contributions of food and clothing for the African American regiments. She met with President Abraham Lincoln in the White House in 1864. Truth was a powerful speaker whose passion and charisma often drew large crowds to her informal lectures.

534 ◆ Division, Reconciliation, and Expansion (1850–1914)

TEACHING RESOURCES

The following resources can be used to enrich or extend the instruction for pp. 534–535.

Motivation

▭ **Interest Grabber Video,** Tape 4 ▪

Background

📖 **Beyond Literature,** p. 29 ▪

Take It to the Net

Visit www.phschool.com for Background and hotlinks for the selections.

Literary Analysis

▬ **Literary Analysis and Reading Transparencies,** Diaries, Journals, and Letters, p. 58

📖 **Selection Support:** Literary Analysis, p. 131

Reading

▬ **Literary Analysis and Reading Transparencies,** Distinguishing Fact from Opinion, p. 57 ▪

Preview

Connecting to the Literature

Today, you can learn about events almost immediately through instant access news sources. The Civil War took place before news networks were invented, however, so the best way to learn about the war and share the experiences of those involved is through their letters, journals, diaries, and photographs.

❷ Literary Analysis

Diaries, Journals, and Letters

Diaries, journals, and letters are personal records of events, thoughts, feelings, and observations written on a day-to-day basis. These literary forms allow people to record immediate responses to their experiences.

- Diaries and journals are generally for personal use. Usually written in an informal style, they capture the writers' ideas and emotions.
- Personal letters are not written for general publication, but because they are addressed to another person, the writing is not entirely private.

As you read these selections, use a chart like the one shown to analyze the information each selection provides and to determine what those details reveal about the writer.

Comparing Literary Works

The selections presented here reflect a wide spectrum of opinions and experiences related to the Civil War. As first-hand accounts of the period, these are valuable examples of **historical narratives.** In this kind of writing, people living through historic events describe their personal experiences and reactions, providing historians an intimate perspective on history. As you read, compare the different perspectives these selections offer of the Civil War.

❸ Reading Strategy

Distinguishing Fact From Opinion

A *fact* is a statement that can be proved true; an *opinion* is a judgment that cannot be proved, though it can be supported by arguments. As you read, **distinguish facts from opinions** by determining whether a statement can be proved or whether it simply reflects the writer's opinions.

Vocabulary Development

capitulate (kə pich′ ə lāt′) *v.* surrender conditionally (p. 537)

audaciously (ô dā′ shəs lē) *adv.* boldly or daringly (p. 537)

foreboding (fôr bōd′ iŋ) *n.* presentiment (p. 537)

obstinate (äb′ stə nit) *adj.* stubborn (p. 538)

imprecations (im′ pri kā′ shənz) *n.* curses (p. 538)

serenity (sə ren′ ə tē) *n.* calmness (p. 539)

---

❷ Literary Analysis

Diaries, Journals, and Letters

- Explain that students will focus on diaries, journals, and letters as they read the six selections in this lesson.
- Read the instruction about diaries, journals, and letters aloud as students read silently. Draw students' attention to the description of how these literary forms allow people to record their immediate responses to people, events, and other experiences.
- As they read each selection, have students look for elements of informality that indicate the private nature of the writing. Point out that letters—and especially diaries and journals—are likely to contain passages that reveal the writer's true emotions and ideas.

❸ Reading Strategy

Distinguishing Fact from Opinion

- Invite a student volunteer to suggest an example of a provable fact. Have the student share the fact and identify the sources one could use to verify it. Then, encourage other students to state whether or not they agree that the statement is a fact rather than an opinion.
- You might wish to engage students in a discussion of the "gray areas" between fact and opinion, such as human emotions. For example, if a person says, "I feel sad," is that a fact or is it an opinion? How might one verify such a statement?
- As they read the selections in this grouping, urge students to remain aware of the differences between facts and opinions.

Vocabulary Development

- Pronounce each vocabulary word for students, and read the definitions as a class. Have students identify any words with which they are already familiar.

 E-Teach

Visit E-Teach at www.phschool.com for teachers' essays on how to teach, with questions and answers.

CUSTOMIZE INSTRUCTION FOR UNIVERSAL ACCESS

For Less Proficient Readers	For English Learners	For Advanced Readers
To help students through these diary and journal entries and letters, suggest that partners paraphrase complex passages. Have them focus in particular on passages filled with terminology peculiar to the Civil War era or on passages that contain military terms that might present difficulties.	Help students understand that the informality of diaries, journals, and letters is often evident in a writer's use of sentence fragments. For practice, have students write a fragment and then revise it as a complete sentence. Then, have them write a complete sentence and reduce it to a fragment. Discuss the different effects produced by fragments and complete sentences.	As they read the selections in this grouping, guide students to "read between the lines" by looking for evidence of each writer's emotions, such as fear, passion, and anger. Encourage students to examine the relationship between these various emotions and each writer's personal circumstances and biases.

535

**CUSTOMIZE INSTRUCTION
For Intrapersonal Learners**

To help these students appreciate the value of journals, use the Humanities Connection: Journals page in *Beyond Literature* (p. 29).

❶ About the Selection

Mary Chesnut, who was both on the scene and privy to the actions and reactions of higher-ups in the Confederacy, started keeping a diary as the tension mounted in Charleston. In these entries, she provides readers with a vivid picture of the chaos and excitement accompanying the dizzying events during the days leading up to the bombardment of Fort Sumter.

❷ Literary Analysis

Diaries, Journals, and Letters

• Read aloud for students the first four paragraphs of Chesnut's account.

• Ask students the Literary Analysis question on p. 536: What details of style and context tell you that you are reading a diary or journal entry?

Answer: The inclusion of the date and the reflective recounting of daily events indicate that this is a diary or journal entry.

❶ *from* Mary Chesnut's
Civil War
Mary Chesnut

Background

In the early days of April 1861, the nation held its collective breath as the tension between North and South mounted. On April 12, the opening shots of the Civil War were fired on Fort Sumter, a Union military post in Charleston, South Carolina, as the city's citizens watched from their rooftops.

Filmmaker and historian Ken Burns, who produced the 1990 television documentary *The Civil War*, noted that during the war "Soldiers at the front and civilians at home left an astonishingly rich and moving record of what they saw and felt . . . hundreds of voices from across the spectrum of American experience, men and women whose lives were touched or destroyed or permanently changed by the war." Here, Mary Chesnut's journal is a memorable chapter in that record.

❷ **April 7, 1861.** Today things seem to have settled down a little.

One can but hope still. Lincoln or Seward[1] have made such silly advances and then far sillier drawings back. There may be a chance for peace, after all.

Things are happening so fast.

My husband has been made an aide-de-camp[2] of General Beauregard.

Three hours ago we were quietly packing to go home. The convention has adjourned.

Now he tells me the attack upon Fort Sumter[3] may begin tonight. Depends upon Anderson and the fleet outside. The *Herald* says that this show of war outside of the bar is intended for Texas.

John Manning came in with his sword and red sash. Pleased as a boy to be on Beauregard's staff while the row goes on. He has gone with Wigfall to Captain Hartstene with instructions.

Mr. Chesnut is finishing a report he had to make to the convention.

Mrs. Hayne called. She had, she said, "but one feeling, pity for those who are not here."

---

1. **Seward** William Henry Seward (1801–1872), U.S. Secretary of State from 1861 through 1869.
2. **aide-de-camp** (ād′ də kamp′) *n.* officer serving as assistant and confidential secretary to a superior.
3. **Fort Sumter** fort in Charleston Harbor, South Carolina. At the time, the fort was occupied by Union troops commanded by Major Robert Anderson.

Literary Analysis

Diaries, Journals, and Letters What details of style and context tell you that you are reading a diary or journal entry?

TEACHING RESOURCES

The following resources can be used to enrich or extend the instruction for pp. 536–548.

Reading Strategy

📖 **Selection Support:** Reading Strategy, p. 130; Build Vocabulary, p. 128

🎧 **Listening to Literature Audiocassettes,** Side 18 ▪

💿 **Listening to Literature Audio CDs,** CD 11 ▪

▪ **BLOCK SCHEDULING:** Resources marked with this symbol provide varied instruction during 90-minute blocks.

Jack Preston, Willie Alston—"the take-life-easys," as they are called—with John Green, "the big brave," have gone down to the island—volunteered as privates.

Seven hundred men were sent over. Ammunition wagons rumbling along the streets all night. Anderson burning blue lights—signs and signals for the fleet outside, I suppose.

Today at dinner there was no allusion to things as they stand in Charleston Harbor. There was an undercurrent of intense excitement. There could not have been a more brilliant circle. In addition to our usual quartet (Judge Withers, Langdon Cheves, and Trescot) our two governors dined with us, Means and Manning.

These men all talked so delightfully. For once in my life I listened.

That over, business began. In earnest, Governor Means rummaged a sword and red sash from somewhere and brought it for Colonel Chesnut, who has gone to demand the surrender of Fort Sumter.

And now, patience—we must wait.

Why did that green goose Anderson go into Fort Sumter? Then everything began to go wrong.

Now they have intercepted a letter from him, urging them to let him surrender. He paints the horrors likely to ensue if they will not.

He ought to have thought of all that before he put his head in the hole.

April 12, 1861. Anderson will not capitulate.

Yesterday was the merriest, maddest dinner we have had yet. Men were more audaciously wise and witty. We had an unspoken foreboding it was to be our last pleasant meeting. Mr. Miles dined with us today. Mrs. Henry King rushed in: "The news, I come for the latest news—all of the men of the King family are on the island"—of which fact she seemed proud.

While she was here, our peace negotiator—or envoy—came in. That is, Mr. Chesnut returned—his interview with Colonel Anderson had been deeply interesting—but was not inclined to be communicative, wanted his dinner. Felt for Anderson. Had telegraphed to President Davis[4] for instructions.

What answer to give Anderson, etc., etc. He has gone back to Fort Sumter with additional instructions.

---

4. **President Davis** Jefferson Davis (1808–1889), president of the Confederacy (1861–1865).

Bombardment of Sumter, Harper's Weekly, 1861

❸

❹ ▲ **Critical Viewing**
Describe the people's reaction to the bombing of Fort Sumter as depicted in this illustration.
[Analyze]

capitulate (kə pich′ ə lāt′) v. surrender conditionally

audaciously (ô dā′ shəs lē) adv. boldly or daringly

foreboding (fôr bōd′ iŋ) n. presentiment

❺ ☑ **Reading Check**
What does Colonel Chesnut demand?

❸ ▶ **Background**
Art

Bombardment of Fort Sumter, 1861

This wood engraving was done by an unknown artist for the May 4, 1861 edition of *Harper's Weekly,* one of two major illustrated Northern newspapers that provided on-the-spot coverage of the Civil War. Correspondents and artists were dispatched by the paper to war zones in order to provide a steady flow of written and pictorial information for publication. Although photography had recently been invented, there was as yet no method for reproducing photographs in a newspaper. On-the-scene drawings were the means by which events of the war were visually recorded for the public. These drawings were sent to the newspaper, where a skilled artisan engraved the image into a block of wood that was then inked and pressed onto paper.

Use these questions for discussion:

1. What details correspond to those in Chesnut's account? **Possible response:** Chesnut describes the women as being "wild" as they watched from the rooftops.

2. Do you think a photograph of the same scene would have been more or less effective than the drawing? Why? **Answer:** Students might note that a photograph captures only a single moment, whereas an artist is free to document two or more events that may have happened over a period of time.

❹ ▶ **Critical Viewing**
Answer: Most of the women seem to be quite upset by the shelling and are trying to console one another. A number of them appear to be in a state of collapse.

❺ ☑ **Reading Check**
Answer: He demands "the surrender of Fort Sumter."

CUSTOMIZE INSTRUCTION FOR UNIVERSAL ACCESS

For Gifted/Talented Students

Encourage these students to study the details of the artwork, which is closely related to Chesnut's text. Have them consider these questions:

- What does the artwork reveal about the battle for Fort Sumter?
- What does it reveal about the city of Charleston at the time of the battle?
- What does it reveal about the attitude of those living in Charleston toward the events that were

taking place?

The fact that Fort Sumter is burning suggests that the Southerners are in the process of winning a decisive victory. The buildings in the illustration and the clothing worn by the people suggest that Charleston is a thriving, cosmopolitan city. The number of people on the rooftops and their body language indicate that the people of Charleston are engrossed by the conflict and are concerned about where the fighting might lead.

❻ Literary Analysis

Diaries, Journals, and Letters

- Invite students to read this passage silently. Then, read the passage aloud to them once again. Encourage students to discuss briefly why Chesnut is so distracted and anxious.
- Ask students the first Literary Analysis question on p. 538: What characteristics of a diary or journal do these sentences have?
  Answer: These sentences feature a first-person narrator, use informal language, and express fragmented thoughts and feelings.

❼ Literary Analysis

Diaries, Journals, and Letters

- Have students scan earlier sections of Chesnut's journal and locate descriptions of her dinner guests. Then, have a student volunteer read the bracketed passage aloud for the class.
- Ask students the second Literary Analysis question on p. 538: What do you learn about Mary Chesnut's life based on her dinner guests?
  Answer: She is one of Charleston's elite citizens.

When they were about to leave the wharf, A. H. Boykin sprang into the boat, in great excitement; thought himself ill-used. A likelihood of fighting—and he to be left behind!

I do not pretend to go to sleep. How can I? If Anderson does not accept terms—at four—the orders are—he shall be fired upon.

❻ I count four—St. Michael chimes. I begin to hope. At half-past four, the heavy booming of a cannon.

I sprang out of bed. And on my knees—prostrate—I prayed as I never prayed before.

There was a sound of stir all over the house—pattering of feet in the corridor—all seemed hurrying one way. I put on my double gown and a shawl and went, too. It was to the housetop.

The shells were bursting. In the dark I heard a man say "waste of ammunition."

I knew my husband was rowing about in a boat somewhere in that dark bay. And that the shells were roofing it over—bursting toward the fort. If Anderson was <u>obstinate</u>—he was to order the forts on our side to open fire. Certainly fire had begun. The regular roar of the cannon—there it was. And who could tell what each volley accomplished of death and destruction.

The women were wild, there on the housetop. Prayers from the women and <u>imprecations</u> from the men, and then a shell would light up the scene. Tonight, they say, the forces are to attempt to land.

The *Harriet Lane*[5] had her wheelhouse[6] smashed and put back to sea.

We watched up there—everybody wondered. Fort Sumter did not fire a shot.

❼ Today Miles and Manning, colonels now—aides to Beauregard— dined with us. The latter hoped I would keep the peace. I give him only good words, for he was to be under fire all day and night, in the bay carrying orders, etc.

Last night—or this morning truly—up on the housetop I was so weak and weary I sat down on something that looked like a black stool.

"Get up, you foolish woman—your dress is on fire," cried a man. And he put me out.

It was a chimney, and the sparks caught my clothes. Susan Preston and Mr. Venable then came up. But my fire had been extinguished before it broke out into a regular blaze.

Do you know, after all that noise and our tears and prayers, nobody has been hurt. Sound and fury, signifying nothing.[7] A delusion and a snare. . . .

5. The *Harriet Lane* federal steamer that had brought provisions to Fort Sumter.
6. **wheelhouse** *n.* enclosed place on the upper deck of a ship, in which the helmsman stands while steering.
7. **Sound . . . nothing** from Shakespeare's *Macbeth,* Act V, Scene v, lines 27–28. Macbeth is contemplating the significance of life and death after learning of his wife's death.

Literary Analysis

Diaries, Journals, and Letters What characteristics of a diary or journal do these sentences have?

obstinate (äb′ stə nət) *adj.* stubborn

imprecations (im′ pri kā′ shənz) *n.* curses

Literary Analysis

Diaries, Journals, and Letters What do you learn about Mary Chesnut's life based on her dinner guests?

✳ ENRICHMENT: History Connection

Fort Sumter

South Carolina had seceded from the Union on December 20, 1860, and demanded all the Federal property within the state. Federal Major Robert Anderson refused to surrender Fort Sumter, a fortification on an island in Charleston Harbor. On April 6, President Lincoln notified the governor of South Carolina that a ship would be bringing provisions to the fort. In response, the Confederacy decided to attack before relief arrived. After 34 hours of fighting, the Union surrendered the fort to the Confederates. Although there were no casualties during the actual bombardment, one Union soldier was killed and three were wounded during the evacuation. The fort became a national monument in 1948.

Coincidentally, while an artillery instructor at West Point, Major Anderson taught Pierre Gustave Toutant Beauregard, the Confederate brigadier general in charge of the batteries that fired on Fort Sumter.

Somebody came in just now and reported Colonel Chesnut asleep on the sofa in General Beauregard's room. After two such nights he must be so tired as to be able to sleep anywhere. . . .

April 13, 1861. Nobody hurt, after all. How gay we were last night.

Reaction after the dread of all the slaughter we thought those dreadful cannons were making such a noise in doing.

Not even a battery[8] the worse for wear.

Fort Sumter has been on fire. He has not yet silenced any of our guns. So the aides—still with swords and red sashes by way of uniform—tell us.

But the sound of those guns makes regular meals impossible. None of us go to table. But tea trays pervade the corridors, going everywhere.

Some of the anxious hearts lie on their beds and moan in solitary misery. Mrs. Wigfall and I solace ourselves with tea in my room.

These women have all a satisfying faith.

April 15, 1861. I did not know that one could live such days of excitement.

They called, "Come out—there is a crowd coming."

A mob indeed, but it was headed by Colonels Chesnut and Manning.

The crowd was shouting and showing these two as messengers of good news. They were escorted to Beauregard's headquarters. Fort Sumter had surrendered.

Those up on the housetop shouted to us, "The fort is on fire." That had been the story once or twice before.

When we had calmed down, Colonel Chesnut, who had taken it all quietly enough—if anything, more unruffled than usual in his serenity—told us how the surrender came about.

Wigfall was with them on Morris Island when he saw the fire in the fort, jumped in a little boat and, with his handkerchief as a white flag, rowed over to Fort Sumter. Wigfall went in through a porthole.

When Colonel Chesnut arrived shortly after and was received by the regular entrance, Colonel Anderson told him he had need to pick his way warily, for it was all mined.

As far as I can make out, the fort surrendered to Wigfall.

But it is all confusion. Our flag is flying there. Fire engines have been sent to put out the fire.

Everybody tells you half of something and then rushes off to tell something else or to hear the last news. . . .

---

8. **battery** *n.* artillery unit.

from *Mary Chesnut's Civil War* ◆ 539

The American Experience

❽ ***The Angel of the Battlefield***
Like Mary Chesnut, many women were on the scene and also in action during the Civil War. Clara Barton is known for her brave assistance to wounded soldiers. Barton spent two years, from 1862–1864, at the front, delivering bandages, socks, and other goods to wounded soldiers. In so doing, she earned the name "Angel of the Battlefield." In 1864, Barton was given the position of superintendent of Union nurses. After the Civil War, she engaged in a search for missing soldiers and lectured about her war experiences.

In 1881, the American Red Cross organization was formed and Barton served as its first president. This organization still exists today and provides relief around the world during wartime and in times of disaster.

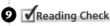

serenity (sə ren´ ə tē) *n.* calmness

❾ ✔**Reading Check**
What news do Colonels Chesnut and Manning bring back to camp?

❽ Background
Clara Barton
Several years after the American Red Cross was established, Clara Barton amended the organization's mission statement to clarify that the group would offer assistance during peacetime as well as during wartime. While Barton served the American Red Cross, she directed the relief work that followed countless famines, floods, pestilence outbreaks, and earthquakes.

❾ ✔**Reading Check**
Answer: They bring news that Fort Sumter has surrendered to the Confederate forces.

CUSTOMIZE INSTRUCTION FOR UNIVERSAL ACCESS

For Gifted/Talented Students

Explain to students that, in past eras, it was not uncommon for women's skirts to catch fire. Long, flowing skirts and open hearths were a deadly combination that left thousands of women badly—even fatally—injured. Encourage students to conduct research on the clothes worn by women during the Civil War period in the United States. Interested students may also research the dress reform movement, led by such figures as Amelia Bloomer, that emerged in the United States shortly after the Civil War.

Recollections of a Private

Warren Lee Goss

In the weeks that followed the attack on Fort Sumter, thousands of men on both sides volunteered to fight. Among the early enlistees was Warren Lee Goss of Massachusetts.

"Cold chills" ran up and down my back as I got out of bed after the sleepless night, and shaved preparatory to other desperate deeds of valor. I was twenty years of age, and when anything unusual was to be done, like fighting or courting, I shaved.

With a nervous tremor convulsing my system, and my heart thumping like muffled drumbeats, I stood before the door of the recruiting office, and before turning the knob to enter read and reread the advertisement for recruits posted thereon, until I knew all its peculiarities. The promised chances for "travel and promotion" seemed good, and I thought I might have made a mistake in con-sidering war so serious after all. "Chances for travel!" I must confess now, after four years of soldiering, that the "chances for travel" were no myth; but "promotion" was a little uncertain and slow.

I was in no hurry to open the door. Though determined to enlist, I was half inclined to put it off awhile; I had a fluctuation of desires; I was fainthearted and brave; I wanted to enlist, and yet—Here I turned the knob, and was relieved. . . .

My first uniform was a bad fit: My trousers were too long by three or four inches; the flannel shirt was coarse and unpleasant, too large at the neck and too short elsewhere. The forage cap[1] was an ungainly bag with pasteboard top and leather visor; the blouse was the only part

---

1. **forage cap** cap worn by infantry soldiers.

Sidebar (left margin)

❿ About the Selection

In this journal entry, a recent Union recruit describes the reality of the drudgery of camp life for enlisted men—mud, drill, and more drill. His observations contrast sharply with the expectations that he and many other recruits had prior to enlisting.

⓫ Literary Analysis

Diaries, Journals, and Letters

• Have students listen to an oral reading of the passage before they reread it silently.

▶ **Monitor Progress**

Then, ask students the Literary Analysis question on p. 540: What details of Goss's writing style indicate that this is part of a diary or journal entry?

Answer: Goss's use of first-person pronouns, his stringing together a series of clauses with semicolons, and his inclusion of incomplete thoughts indicates that this is a diary or journal entry.

Sidebar (right margin)

Literary Analysis

Diaries, Journals, and Letters What details of Goss's writing style indicate that this is part of a diary or journal entry?

✷ ENRICHMENT: Social Studies Connection

Women in the Civil War

While men fought the Civil War on the battlefield, women participated at home in several crucial ways. Many women single-handedly ran family businesses, farms, and plantations while their husbands and sons were away. Women from both the North and South worked in factories, hospitals, and in relief efforts. Some sewed uniforms at home; others functioned as spies. Hundreds even disguised themselves as men and joined the ranks.

Invite students to find out more about the role of women during the war. For instance, they can research the work of Dorothea Dix and of Clara Barton. They can find out about Sally Tompkins and the hospital she ran in Richmond, Virginia, and of organizations such as the Women's Central Association of Relief. Some students might find it interesting to look into the espionage work of Belle Boyd, Elizabeth Van Lew, or Rose Greenhow. Encourage students to share their findings with the class.

which seemed decent; while the overcoat made me feel like a little nubbin of corn in a large preponderance of husk. Nothing except "Virginia mud" ever took down my ideas of military pomp quite so low.

After enlisting I did not seem of so much consequence as I had expected. There was not so much excitement on account of my military appearance as I deemed justly my due. I was taught my facings, and at the time I thought the drillmaster needlessly fussy about shouldering, ordering, and presenting arms. At this time men were often drilled in company and regimental evolutions long before they learned the manual of arms, because of the difficulty of obtaining muskets. These we obtained at an early day, but we would willingly have resigned them after carrying them a few hours. The musket, after an hour's drill, seemed heavier and less ornamental than it had looked to be.

The first day I went out to drill, getting tired of doing the same things over and over, I said to the drill sergeant: "Let's stop this fooling and go over to the grocery." His only reply was addressed to a corporal: "Corporal, take this man out and drill him"; and the corporal did! I found that suggestions were not so well appreciated in the army as in private life, and that no wisdom was equal to a drillmaster's "Right face," "Left wheel," and "Right, oblique, march." It takes a raw recruit some time to learn that he is not to think or suggest, but obey. Some never do learn. I acquired it at last, in humility and mud, but it was tough. Yet I doubt if my patriotism, during my first three weeks' drill, was quite knee high. Drilling looks easy to a spectator, but it isn't. After a time I had cut down my uniform so that I could see out of it, and had conquered the drill sufficiently to see through it. Then the word came: on to Washington! . . .

Reading Strategy
Distinguishing Fact from Opinion Identify one opinion in this description of enlisting.

Review and Assess

Thinking About the Selections

1. **Respond:** Would you have volunteered to fight during the early days of the Civil War? Why or why not?

2. **(a) Recall:** What events does Mary Chesnut describe in her diary entries? **(b) Interpret:** What does her diary reveal about her attitude toward the war?

3. **(a) Summarize:** Describe Warren Lee Goss's feelings on the day he was to enlist in the army. **(b) Analyze:** How did Private Goss's attitudes and expectations change after he enlisted?

4. **(a) Recall:** According to Goss, what takes a long time for a recruit to learn? **(b) Infer:** What do you think happened to cause him to say, "I acquired it at last, in humility and mud, but it was tough"?

5. **Apply:** How might Chesnut's diary have been different if she had been from the North?

Recollections of a Private ◆ 541

Answers continued

3. **(a)** He is nervous and excited and feels "a fluctuation of desires." **(b)** Before enlisting, he imagines himself looking impressive and exciting in uniform; after enlisting, he develops a more realistic and humble image of himself.

4. **(a)** It takes a long time for a recruit to learn to obey without thinking or making suggestions. **(b)** Students may say that Goss was "drilled," or vigorously trained, until he responded instinctively with obedience.

5. **Suggested response:** She probably would have dreaded the shelling even more, and would have seen the Union soldiers who defended Fort Sumter as heroes.

⑫ Reading Strategy
Distinguishing Fact from Opinion

- Have two student volunteers read the passage aloud—the first using a flat, impersonal tone, the second using an animated tone.

- Then, ask students the Reading Strategy question on p. 541: Identify one opinion in this description of enlisting. Answer: Students might mention the passage's first, second, third, and final sentences.

⑬ Vocabulary Development
Latin Prefix: *ob-*

- Read the passage aloud and ask students to listen for any words that contains the Latin prefix *ob-*.

- If necessary, point out that the word *obtaining* contains the Latin prefix *ob-*. What word in the next paragraph also contains the prefix? Answer: The word *oblique* contains the prefix *ob-*.

- Tell students that the prefix *ob-* has a variety of meanings, including *to* or *toward*, *against*, *over*, and *completely*.

- Gives students the definitions of the words *oblique* and *obtain*, and an explanation of the meanings of their roots. (The root of the word *oblique*, which means "slanted," derives from the Latin *liqu*, meaning "bent." The root of the word *obtain*, which means "to gain a hold of," derives from the Latin *tenere*, meaning "to hold").

- Then, ask students to explain which meaning of the prefix *ob-* is at work in each word. Possible answers: In the word *oblique*, the prefix means "to" or "toward." In the word *obtain*, the prefix means *completely*.

Answers for p. 541

Review and Assess

1. Students should explain the reasoning behind their responses.

2. **(a)** She describes the events surrounding the firing on Fort Sumter by Confederate troops. **(b)** She thinks the South has no choice but to fight, but she is afraid of the war's consequences.

continued

541

14 About the Selection

In this diary entry, Confederate soldier Randolph McKim describes the futile and bloody attempts of his and others' regiments to capture Culp's Hill, the extreme right of the Federal position.

14 A Confederate Account of the Battle of Gettysburg

Randolph McKim

⟨✦⟩

From July 1 to July 3, 1863, Union and Confederate troops fought near the small town of Gettysburg, Pennsylvania. After Union troops gained control of the hills surrounding the town, the Confederate troops commanded by Robert E. Lee launched a risky attack on the strongest Union position. When the attack failed, the Confederate troops were forced to retreat at a great cost of lives. The battle, the first in which troops commanded by Lee were defeated, marked a turning point in the war. In a diary entry, Confederate soldier Randolph McKim described the final day of the battle.

⟨✦⟩

542   *Division, Reconciliation, and Expansion (1850–1914)*

☀ ENRICHMENT: Music Connection

Civil War Music

In 1862, abolitionist and suffragist Julia Ward Howe wrote "The Battle Hymn of the Republic" and sold it to the *Atlantic Monthly*. Reportedly, Union soldiers sang this song over and over. In fact, music was ever-present during the American Civil War. Robert E. Lee said that he didn't believe there could be an army without music. Drumbeats spurred soldiers into battle, and regimental bands raised the spirits of marching soldiers and entertained at reviews and parades. During the lengthy and lonely encampments, soldiers sang both patriotic and sentimental songs.

Today one can identify a wide selection of music that was composed around the time of (or became associated with) the Civil War. Have students research the songs the Federal and Confederate armies sang and listened to, and have students listen to the music themselves. Invite them to learn more about the origins of some songs and to present their findings to the class.

Then came General Ewell's order to assume the offensive and assail the crest of Culp's Hill, on our right. . . . The works to be stormed ran almost at right angles to those we occupied. Moreover, there was a double line of entrenchments, one above the other, and each filled with troops. In moving to the attack we were exposed to enfilading fire[1] from the woods on our left flank, besides the double line of fire which we had to face in front, and a battery of artillery posted on a hill to our left rear opened upon us at short range. . . .

On swept the gallant little brigade, the Third North Carolina on the right of the line, next the Second Maryland, then the three Virginia regiments (10th, 23d, and 37th), with the First North Carolina on the extreme left. Its ranks had been sadly thinned, and its energies greatly depleted by those six fearful hours of battle that morning; but its nerve and spirit were undiminished. Soon, however, the left and center were checked and then repulsed, probably by the severe flank fire from the woods; and the small remnant of the Third North Carolina, with the stronger Second Maryland (I do not recall the banners of any other regiment), were far in advance of the rest of the line. On they pressed to within about twenty or thirty paces of the works—a small but gallant band of heroes daring to attempt what could not be done by flesh and blood.

The end soon came. We were beaten back to the line from which we had advanced with terrible loss, and in much confusion, but the enemy did not make a countercharge. By the strenuous efforts of the officers of the line and of the staff, order was restored, and we re-formed in the breastworks[2] from which we had emerged, there to be again exposed to an artillery fire exceeding in violence that of the early morning. It remains only to say that, like Pickett's men[3] later in the day, this single brigade was hurled unsupported against the enemy's works. Daniel's brigade remained in the breastworks during and after the charge, and neither from that command nor from any other had we any support. Of course it is to be presumed that General Daniel acted in obedience to orders. We remained in this breastwork after the charge about an hour before we finally abandoned the Federal entrenchments and retired to the foot of the hill.

1. **enfilading** (en´ fə lād´ iŋ) **fire** gunfire directed along the length of a column or line of troops.
2. **breastworks** low walls put up quickly as a defense in battle.
3. **Pickett's men** General George Pickett was a Confederate officer who led the unsuccessful attack on the Union position.

Reading Strategy
Distinguishing Fact From Opinion What is Randolph McKim describing in the sentence beginning "On they pressed"? Is he stating the facts or giving his opinion?

◀ **Critical Viewing**
The battlefield of Gettysburg, shown here, draws visitors to this day. Which details of this picture memorialize the war?

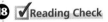

✔ **Reading Check**
What happens at the end of the battle?

A Confederate Account of the Battle of Gettysburg ◆ 543

⓯ **Reading Strategy**
Distinguishing Fact from Opinion

- Have one or two student volunteers provide concise, one-sentence definitions that clarify the essential difference between a fact and an opinion.
- Then, read aloud the bracketed passage slowly for the class. Ask students the Reading Strategy question on p. 543: What is Randolph McKim describing in the sentence beginning "On they pressed."? Is he stating the facts or giving his opinion?
Answer: He is describing the Confederate soldiers engaged in battle at Culp's Hill. The first half of the sentence is factual, while the second half states an opinion gained from firsthand experience.

⓰ **Background**
McKim correctly observes that, like Pickett's disastrous charge, the attack in which he participated was not sufficiently supported by artillery—nor were its flanks, or sides, protected from enfilading fire.

⓱ ▶ **Critical Viewing**
Answer: Numerous stone markers memorialize the war's fallen soldiers.

⓲ ✔ **Reading Check**
Answer: At the end of the battle, the Confederate troops retreat to the foot of Culp's Hill.

⑲ About the Selection

Stonewall Jackson writes to his wife to inform her that he has been in a great battle. He credits God with providing for his own safety and the achievements of his troops. The letter reveals Jackson's bravery, modesty, and religious devotion.

⑳ Background

Art

Stonewall Jackson at Bull Run, c. 1900, by H. A. Ogden

Henry Alexander Ogden was an illustrator who specialized in military subjects. This image was created approximately forty years after the Battle of Bull Run actually took place.

Use the following questions for discussion:

1. Based on both this illustration and his letter, what can you infer about Jackson's personality?
   Answer: He seems calm and controlled, even in battle.

2. Reread Jackson's description of the battle, and explain how it differs from the illustration.
   Answer: Students should note that Jackson mentions his horse, suggesting that he commanded from horseback. He also speaks of having led troops into battle, though he appears to be removed from the fighting in the illustration.

㉑ ▶ Critical Viewing

Answer: Jackson's confident, composed posture, his full officer's dress, and his flamboyant hat mark him as the officer in charge.

㉒ Reading Strategy

Distinguishing Fact from Opinion

• Have a student volunteer read the passage aloud. Draw students' attention to phrases—such as *hardest that I have ever been in*—that show that Jackson participated in the events he describes.

• Ask students the Reading Strategy question on p. 544: Is the general being factual or stating his opinion in describing the nature of the victory and indicating to whom the glory belongs?
   Answer: He is offering his opinion about the nature and cause of the victory.

⑲ An Account of the Battle of Bull Run

Stonewall Jackson

Stonewall Jackson at Bull Run

⑳

In this letter to his wife, Confederate General Thomas "Stonewall" Jackson recounts the first southern victory of the war: a battle fought in July 1861, outside Washington, D.C., near a small stream named Bull Run.

My precious pet,

Yesterday we fought a great battle and gained a great victory, for which all the glory is due to God alone. Although under a heavy fire for several continuous hours, I received only one wound, the breaking of the longest finger of my left hand; but the doctor says the finger can be saved. It was broken about midway between the hand and knuckle, the ball passing on the side next [to] the forefinger. Had it struck the center, I should have lost the finger.

My horse was wounded, but not killed. Your coat got an ugly wound near the hip, but my servant, who is very handy, has so far repaired it that it doesn't show very much. My preservation was entirely due, as was the glorious victory, to our God, to whom be all the honor, praise and glory. The battle was the hardest that I have ever been in, but not near so hot in its fire. I commanded the center more particularly, though one of my regiments extended to the right for some distance. There were other commanders on my right and left. Whilst great credit is due to other parts of our gallant army, God made my brigade more instrumental than any other in repulsing the main attack. This is for your information only—say nothing about it. Let others speak praise, not myself.

544 ◆ *Division, Reconciliation, and Expansion (1850–1914)*

㉑ ▲ Critical Viewing How does this depiction of Jackson enable the viewer to distinguish the general from his officers and soldiers? **[Analyze]**

Reading Strategy
Distinguishing Fact From Opinion Is the general being factual or stating his opinion in describing the nature of the victory and indicating to whom the glory belongs? Explain.

✺ ENRICHMENT: History Connection

Stonewall Jackson

Jackson's stand at Bull Run is the reason for his nickname, Stonewall. He held his line against overwhelming odds, bringing about an unexpected Confederate victory. His repeated references to God's hand in the victory reflect his religious fervor, which his detractors mocked with another nickname, Deacon Jackson.

Ironically, Jackson, a master tactician, died as an indirect result of a careless error. Returning at dusk after a daring and successful maneuver, he was shot accidentally by his own men. His arm was amputated, complications resulted, and he died two weeks later on May 10, 1863.

From August 1851 until the beginning of the Civil War in April 1861, Jackson had served on the faculty of the Virginia Military Institute (VMI) as professor of natural and experimental philosophy and instructor of artillery. After Jackson's death, the school honored his memory with gun salutes every half-hour from sunrise to sunset and draped his lecture hall in mourning black for six months.

Reaction to the Emancipation Proclamation

Reverend Henry M. Turner

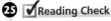

On September 22, 1862, President Lincoln issued the Emancipation Proclamation, declaring that all slaves in states still in rebellion would be free as of January 1, 1863. Because those states were not under Union control at the time, no slaves were actually set free that day. The Proclamation, however, was a powerful symbol of hope for those still in slavery and inspired a wave of Union support from free African Americans. In this account, Reverend Henry M. Turner, a free-born African American living in Washington, D.C., describes his people's reaction to the news of the Proclamation.

Seeing such a multitude of people in and around my church, I hurriedly sent up to the office of the first paper in which the proclamation of freedom could be printed, known as the *Evening Star*, and squeezed myself through the dense crowd that was waiting for the paper. The first sheet run off with the proclamation in it was grabbed for by three of us, but some active young man got possession of it and fled. The next sheet was grabbed for by several, and was torn into tatters. The third sheet from the press was grabbed for by several, but I succeeded in procuring so much of it as contained the proclamation, and off I went for life and death. Down Pennsylvania Avenue I ran as for my life, and when the people saw me coming with the paper in my hand they raised a shouting cheer that was almost deafening. As many as could get around me lifted me to a great platform, and I started to read the proclamation. I had run the best end of a mile,

Literary Analysis
Diaries, Journals, and Letters How would you describe the tone of Reverend Turner's description?

✔ Reading Check
What do people do when they see the reverend running down the street?

Reaction to the Emancipation Proclamation ◆ 545

CUSTOMIZE INSTRUCTION FOR UNIVERSAL ACCESS

For Special Needs Students	For Less Proficient Readers
Help students summarize what they learn about Confederate General Thomas "Stonewall" Jackson from this letter to his wife. Through discussion and oral rereading of the text, guide students to perceive Jackson's pride and confidence, which he conveys without boastfulness, as well as his strong religious beliefs.	You might wish to discuss some of the ways in which the distinctions between fact and opinion can be blurred. For instance, a firsthand observer of an event sometimes expresses an opinion so fervently and eloquently that a reader or listener believes these observations are factual. For this reason, students may need help recognizing that Reverend Turner's euphoric conclusion, however forceful, is pure opinion.

㉓ About the Selection
Reverend Henry M. Turner uses an effusive tone to describe the exciting experience of being among the exhilarated crowd clamoring to read the Emancipation Proclamation when it is still hot off the presses.

㉔ Literary Analysis
Diaries, Journals, and Letters

• As you read the bracketed passage aloud, encourage students to listen for words and phrases, such as *hurriedly*, *squeezed*, *grabbed for*, *went for life and death*, *a shouting cheer*, *a great platform*, *great force and clearness*, that indicate Reverend Turner's attitude toward his subject.

▶ **Monitor Progress**
Ask students the Literary Analysis question on p. 545: How would you describe the tone of Reverend Turner's description?
Answer: Students might describe Turner's tone as excited, anxious, joyous, or wondrous.

㉕ ✔ Reading Check
Answer: They cheer.

26 **Background**

Point out that during this period in American history, African Americans were commonly referred to as "colored people."

27 **Background**

Art

Reading the Emancipation Proclamation, 1865, Anonymous

This lithograph is a dramatization of an event that must have occurred countless times in the South in 1863, the year the Emancipation Proclamation was issued. Created by an artist whose name is lost to history, the lithograph shows a Union soldier reading the proclamation to African Americans living in a cabin in the South. Although the artist may have been overly sentimental in this depiction, the proclamation must have inspired an intense emotional reaction.

Use these questions for discussion:

1. How does the artist create a sense of drama?
   Answer: Students may note how a burning torch is held over the soldier, lighting both the proclamation and the dramatic figure of the kneeling woman, who is dressed in white.

2. What emotions do the people in the picture exhibit?
   Answer: The soldier has the undivided attention of the listeners. Their faces, gestures, and body language appear to express relief, amazement, awe, and excitement.

28 ▶ **Critical Viewing**

Answer: Students may respond that the rapt attention the readers and listeners display bears similarities to the scene described by Reverend Turner.

26 I was out of breath, and could not read. Mr. Hinton, to whom I handed the paper, read it with great force and clearness. While he was reading every kind of demonstration and gesticulation was going on. Men squealed, women fainted, dogs barked, white and colored people shook hands, songs were sung, and by this time cannons began to fire at the navy yard, and follow in the wake of the roar that had for some time been going on behind the White House. . . . Great processions of colored and white men marched to and fro and passed in front of the White House and congratulated President Lincoln on his proclamation. The President came to the window and made responsive bows, and thousands told him, if he would come out of that palace, they would hug him to death. . . . It was indeed a time of times, and nothing like it will ever be seen again in this life.

27

Reading the Emancipation Proclamation, Artist unknown

28 ▲ **Critical Viewing** In what way does this illustration relate to Reverend Turner's account? **[Connect]**

546 ◆ *Division, Reconciliation, and Expansion (1850–1914)*

An Account of an Experience with Discrimination

Sojourner Truth

29 **About the Selection**

Sojourner Truth describes her proactive responses to acts of racial discrimination on a streetcar.

30 ▶ **Critical Viewing**

Answer: Students should support their responses with clear reasoning and with detailed references to the image and to the text.

31 ✔ **Reading Check**

Answer: Griffing stopped the streetcar that was dragging Truth, reported the conductor to the city railway, and advised Truth to take the number of the streetcar whenever she was mistreated by a conductor or driver.

Although the Civil War brought an end to slavery, the struggle against racial discrimination was just beginning. Before the war, Sojourner Truth worked tirelessly to free slaves. After the war, she fought for a number of causes, including the woman's suffrage movement and the desegregation of public transportation. Once, when a driver of a street car refused her passage, she brought a local street to a standstill. With the support of a crowd behind her, the driver was forced to allow her on board. In the following letter, written on October 1, 1865, Sojourner Truth describes other encounters with racism.

30 ▲ **Critical Viewing**
In what ways does this image compare with your impression of Sojourner Truth based on her account? Explain.
[Compare and Contrast]

A few weeks ago I was in company with my friend Josephine S. Griffing, when the conductor of a streetcar refused to stop his car for me, although [I was] closely following Josephine and holding on to the iron rail. They dragged me a number of yards before she succeeded in stopping them. She reported the conductor to the president of the City Railway, who dismissed him at once, and told me to take the number of the car whenever I was mistreated by a conductor or driver.

31 ✔ **Reading Check**
What does Josephine S. Griffing do to help her friend?

An Account of an Experience With Discrimination ◆ 547

CUSTOMIZE INSTRUCTION FOR UNIVERSAL ACCESS

For English Learners	For Advanced Readers
When reading Reverend Turner's account, students may need your help understanding the reasons for capitalization of the word *president*. Tell them that the word *President* is capitalized in the first instance because it is a title, and in the second instance because it refers to a particular chief executive of the United States, Abraham Lincoln.	To gain a richer appreciation of the common soldier's experience in the Civil War, historians rely heavily on regimental histories and individual memoirs. Students interested in pursuing further reading of such firsthand accounts may enjoy the published histories of the First Minnesota or of the Iron Brigade. Or they may enjoy *All for the Union: The Civil War Diary* and *Letters of Elisha Hunt Rhodes*.

Answers for p. 548

Review and Assess

1. Students' responses should reflect a new awareness of the impact of the war on the lives of individuals.

2. **(a)** McKim describes how Confederate forces retreated from Union forces at Culp's Hill; Jackson describes a Confederate victory at Bull Run. **(b)** The accounts are similar in that both provide detailed descriptions of specific battles and were written by actual participants. **(c)** McKim's account contains more details, and is written from the perspective of an enlisted soldier. Jackson's account provides an overview of the battle, as seen by a strategist and leader. In addition, Jackson's account is marked by repeated references to his subservience to God's power.

3. **(a)** The proclamation is received with jubilation, relief, and gratitude. **(b)** Possible response: It represented an official recognition of the rights of African Americans to live in freedom and symbolized the beginning of a new era in United States history.

4. **(a)** He says, "Does she belong to you?" **(b)** It reveals that the slaveholding spirit is still alive in the streetcar conductor.

5. **(a)** He is dismissed from his job, arrested, and tried for assault and battery. **(b)** Both demonstrate the struggles involved in ending segregation in stores, public places, schools, on public transportation, and in other areas of American society.

6. **(a)** Reverend Turner's tone is one of excitement and hope, whereas Sojourner Truth's tone reflects the pain of discrimination. **(b)** Students may note that Turner's attitude reflects the newness of emancipation, while Truth's feelings reflect her bitterness and disappointment that the struggle must continue.

7. Students should support their responses with clear reasoning.

On the 13th I had occasion to go for necessities for the patients in the Freedmen's Hospital where I have been doing and advising for a number of months. I thought now I would get a ride without trouble as I was in company with another friend, Laura S. Haviland of Michigan. As I ascended the platform of the car, the conductor pushed me, saying "Go back—get off here." I told him I was not going off, then "I'll put you off" said he furiously, clenching my right arm with both hands, using such violence that he seemed about to succeed, when Mrs. Haviland told him he was not going to put me off. "Does she belong to you?" said he in a hurried angry tone. She replied, "She does not belong to me, but she belongs to humanity." The number of the car was noted, and conductor dismissed at once upon the report to the president, who advised his arrest for assault and battery as my shoulder was sprained by his effort to put me off. Accordingly I had him arrested and the case tried before Justice Thompson. My shoulder was very lame and swollen, but is better. It is hard for the old slaveholding spirit to die. But die it must. . . .

Review and Assess

Thinking About the Selections

1. **Respond:** In what ways have these accounts added to your understanding of the Civil War? Explain.

2. **(a) Recall:** Explain the events described in the accounts of Randolph McKim and Stonewall Jackson. **(b) Compare:** How are they similar? **(c) Contrast:** How do they differ?

3. **(a) Recall:** What is the reaction to the Emancipation Proclamation among the members of Reverend Turner's audience? **(b) Speculate:** Why do you think the Emancipation Proclamation had such an emotional effect?

4. **(a) Recall:** What does the streetcar conductor say to Laura Haviland about Sojourner Truth? **(b) Infer:** What does his question reveal about the "old slaveholding spirit"?

5. **(a) Recall:** What happens to the conductor who wanted to refuse service to Truth? **(b) Connect:** What do details of these events of 1865 have in common with the Civil Rights Movement of the 1960s?

6. **(a) Compare and Contrast:** In what ways do the tones or attitudes of Sojourner Truth and Henry Turner differ? **(b) Speculate:** Why do you think their feelings are different?

7. **Take a Position:** If you were alive during the Civil War, which position might you have taken—the North's or South's? Explain.

548 ◆ *Division, Reconciliation, and Expansion (1850–1914)*

ASSESSMENT PRACTICE: Reading Comprehension

Context (For more practice, see the Test Preparation Workbook, p. 31.)

Many tests require students to use context clues to determine the meaning of unfamiliar words. Use this sample test item to give students practice in this skill.

With a nervous tremor <u>convulsing</u> my system, and my heart thumping like <u>muffled</u> drumbeats, I stood before the door of the recruiting office.

In this passage, the word <u>convulsing</u> most nearly means—

A shaking **C** straightening
B settling **D** deadening

There is no contextual support for the last three answers. A "tremor" is a trembling motion. The overall context—the nervousness, the thumping heart—suggests agitation. *A* is correct.

Review and Assess

Literary Analysis

Diaries, Journals, and Letters

1. Note at least two examples from Mary Chesnut's **diaries** that indicate her dislike for the war.
2. Find three details or ideas that Jackson probably would have omitted from his **letter** if it were intended for publication.
3. What does Sojourner Truth's letter reveal about her personality?

Comparing Literary Works

4. What details about the Civil War can you learn from Mary Chesnut's diary that you might not learn from a history book?
5. What facts or details can you learn from two of the other selections?
6. (a) What makes these **historical narratives** valuable to students of the Civil War? (b) What might make them unreliable?
7. Which selection would you say is most valuable to historians? Why?

Reading Strategy

Distinguishing Fact From Opinion

8. **Distinguish the facts and opinions** in the following passage from Goss's account:

   > The forage cap was an ungainly bag with pasteboard top and leather visor; the blouse was the only part which seemed decent; while the overcoat made me feel like a little nubbin of corn in a large preponderance of husk.

9. Identify two facts and two opinions from Jackson's account. Record them in a chart like the one shown.

Statement	Fact or Opinion	Why?

10. In the accounts by Reverend Turner and Sojourner Truth, which contains more facts and which contains more opinions? Explain your answer.

Extend Understanding

11. **Social Studies Connection:** More than a century later, the Civil War continues to engage the interest of Americans. Why do you think this is so?

Quick Review

Diaries and journals are personal records of daily events, usually written in prose. A **personal letter** is one that is written without the intention of publication.

Historical narratives are personal accounts of significant historical events.

To **distinguish fact from opinion**, determine whether or not a statement can be proved conclusively true.

 Take It to the Net
www.phschool.com
Take the interactive self-test online to check your understanding of these selections.

Answers for p. 549

Review and Assess

1. **Possible answers include:** She writes, "I begin to hope [that there will be no fighting]." She is so distracted by the prospect of war that she accidentally sets herself on fire.

2. **Possible answer:** He would have omitted the salutation to his wife, the details about the wound to his finger, and the information about his brigade being central to the Confederate victory.

3. It reveals that she is a strong, determined woman who will not allow herself to be intimidated.

4. One can learn about the ways in which ordinary citizens responded to the war, details about the social atmosphere of the South, and even details about the makeshift uniforms worn by Confederate leaders.

5. **Possible answer:** Private Goss—details about how it felt for an ordinary citizen to enlist; McKim—details about Confederate maneuvers.

6. **(a)** These narratives provide intimate, firsthand looks at historic events. **(b)** They may be unreliable because each presents the potentially biased view of an individual.

7. Students may point to Jackson's letter, which provides insights into the thoughts of a Confederate general, McKim's diary, which offers a soldier's view of battle, or Chesnut's journal, which gives a "backstage" view of Confederate leaders in action.

8. **Facts:** The forage cap had a pasteboard top and leather visor. **Opinions:** The cap was an "ungainly bag"; the blouse was "decent"; and the coat made him feel like a small ear of corn lost in its husk.

9. **Sample answer—Facts:** Jackson's coat was damaged; his servant repaired it. **Opinions:** The word *ugly* and the statement that the repair "doesn't show very much."

10. Both accounts are composed of presumably factual observations; at the conclusion of each account, the writer offers an opinion.
continued

※ **ENRICHMENT: Further Reading**

Other Firsthand Accounts of the Civil War

For Cause & Comrades: Why Men Fought in the Civil War, James M. McPherson

The Life of Johnny Reb, Bell I. Wiley

The Life of Billy Yank, Bell I. Wiley

Take It to the Net
Visit www.phschool.com for more information on the authors.

Answers continued

11. Responses should reflect a new awareness of the impact of the war on the nation.

❶ Vocabulary Development

Word Analysis

1. c
2. a
3. b

Spelling Strategy

1. celebration
2. litigation
3. speculation

Fluency: Sentence Completion

1. imprecations
2. serenity
3. foreboding
4. capitulate
5. obstinate
6. audaciously

❷ Grammar and Style

1. *Herald*; Texas
2. Third North Carolina; Second Maryland; Virginia
3. Avenue; people
4. Culp's
5. President; proclamation

Writing Application

Students' paragraphs should reflect correct capitalization.

Integrate Language Skills

❶ Vocabulary Development Lesson

Word Analysis: Latin Prefix *ob-*

The word *obstinate* comes from a combination of the Latin prefix *ob-*, meaning "against," and a form of the Latin root *-stare-*, meaning "stand." Use your understanding of the meaning of *ob-* to match each word to the numbered item that most closely relates to it.

a. obstruction   **b.** obscure   **c.** object

1. voice opposition in the courtroom
2. a fallen tree blocking the road
3. cloud an issue with confusing arguments

Spelling Strategy

Verbs that end in *-ate* have noun forms ending in *-ion*. Drop the final *e* before adding the suffix, as in *imprecate/imprecation* and *capitulate/capitulation*. Spell the noun forms of the following words:

1. celebrate   2. litigate   3. speculate

❷ Grammar and Style Lesson

Capitalization of Proper Nouns

The name of a person, street, road, town, city, county, or state is considered a **proper noun** and should begin with a **capital letter.** Directional words (*east*, *west*, and so on) that are part of the name of a place should also begin with a capital, as in *West Virginia*.

> **Proper Nouns:** Why did that green goose *Anderson* go into *Fort Sumter*?

Practice Rewrite each of the following sentences in your notebook, correcting any errors in capitalization.

1. The *herald* says that this show of war outside of the bar is intended for texas.

✍ *Prentice Hall Writing and Grammar Connection: Chapter 26*

550 ◆ *Division, Reconciliation, and Expansion (1850–1914)*

Fluency: Sentence Completion

Complete these sentences with the correct word from the vocabulary list on page 535.

1. When the rifle jammed, the soldier muttered ____?____ at his bad luck.
2. There was no ____?____ to be found in the troubled hearts and minds of soldiers and civilians.
3. As enemy shells exploded in the distance, a sense of ____?____ hung over the camp like fog.
4. Despite the overwhelming odds facing his brigade, the general refused to ____?____.
5. What one person would call ____?____, another might call courageous.
6. After midnight, the spies crept ____?____ close to the enemy's encampment.

2. On swept the gallant little brigade, the third north Carolina on the right of the line, next the second maryland, and then the three virginia regiments.
3. Down Pennsylvania avenue I ran as for my life, and when the People saw me coming . . . they raised a shouting cheer.
4. Then came General Ewell's order to assume the offensive and assail the crest of culp's Hill.
5. They passed the White House and congratulated president Lincoln on his Proclamation.

Writing Application Write a paragraph about a recent trip you took. Be sure to name places and use capital letters when necessary.

TEACHING RESOURCES

The following resources can be used to enrich or extend the instruction for pp. 550–551.

Vocabulary

📖 **Selection Support:** Build Vocabulary, p. 128

📖 **Vocabulary and Spelling Practice Book** (Use this booklet for skills enrichment.)

Grammar

📖 **Selection Support:** Grammar and Style, p. 129 ▪

✍ **Writing and Grammar,** Ruby Level, p. 364

📖 **Daily Language Practice Transparencies**

Writing

✍ **Writing and Grammar,** Ruby Level, p. 52 ▪

📖 **Extension Activities,** p. 29

📖 **Writing Models and Graphic Organizers on Transparencies,** p. 33

💿 **Writing and Grammar iText CD-ROM**

▪ **BLOCK SCHEDULING:** Resources marked with this symbol provide varied instruction during 90-minute blocks.

❸ Writing Lesson

Problem-and-Solution Essay

Today, few take the time to write letters or keep a journal. In what way might this be a loss? In an essay, explore the personal benefits and historical value of engaging in this type of private writing. Use examples and insights from these selections to illustrate your point.

Prewriting Brainstorm for a list of the benefits of journal writing and the disadvantages that could occur when historical events are not documented in this way. Use a chart like the one shown to gather your ideas.

Model: Gathering Details

Personal Benefits	Historical Value	Loss From No Journal
Journals can be passed down through family.	History is documented for society at large.	Valuable information could be lost forever.

Drafting Begin with an introduction of the topic. Then, write one paragraph on three of your ideas, connecting them with personal experiences to provide insight. Tie your thoughts together in the conclusion.

Revising Compare your draft with your list to be sure you have included the essential points you want to make. Make sure that your personal reflections clearly connect with your main ideas.

WG Prentice Hall Writing and Grammar Connection: Chapter 4, Section 2

❹ Extension Activities

Listening and Speaking Rev. Turner recounts the emotional impact of the Emancipation Proclamation. Deliver a **dramatic reading** of the document, accompanied by music that conveys the tone of your interpretation. Consider the following:

- Read main points with emotion for emphasis.
- Make eye contact or use hand gestures that convey power or determination.

After practicing, present the reading to your class.

Research and Technology Research the Battle of Gettysburg, one of the turning points of the Civil War. Create a **model or map** of the battlefield, identify the locations of key events, and provide explanatory captions. Integrate Internet graphics and word-processed text. **[Group Activity]**

 Take It to the Net   www.phschool.com

Go online for an additional research activity using the Internet.

Civil War Diaries, Journals, and Letters ◆ 551

ASSESSMENT RESOURCES

The following resources can be used to assess students' knowledge and skills.

Selection Assessment

- 📓 **Formal Assessment**, p. 138
- 📓 **Open Book Test**, p. 85
- 📼 **Got It! Assessment Videotapes**, Tape 3
- 💿 **Test Bank Software**
- 💻 **Take It to the Net**
  Visit www.phschool.com for self-tests and additional questions on the selections.

Writing Rubric

- 📓 **Perf. Assess. and Portfolio Mgmt**, p. 10

Listening and Speaking Rubric

- 📓 **Perf. Assess. and Portfolio Mgmt**, p. 31

PRENTICE HALL *ASSESSMENT SYSTEM*

- 📓 **Workbook**
- 📓 **Skill Book**
- 📖 **Transparencies**
- 💿 **CD-ROM**

❸ Writing Lesson

- Students' problem-and-solution essays should clearly articulate the ways in which a modern inattention to journal writing might present a loss, both to individuals and to society. They should also suggest some solutions to this loss.
- Students might benefit from brainstorming for two lists—one noting the value of documenting their own daily lives in the 21st century, and another noting the value of documenting more obviously dramatic or historic events.
- Use the Writing Lesson, as well as Writing Process Model 6 in **Writing Models and Graphic Organizers on Transparencies**, to guide students in developing their reflective essays.
- Use the Problem-Solution Essay rubric in **Performance Assessment and Portfolio Management**, p. 10, to evaluate students' problem-and-solution essays.

❹ Listening and Speaking

- Encourage students to reread Lincoln's text many times and "score" it by noting passages requiring emphasis, shifts in tone, and emotional intensity.
- Students should rehearse the speech in front of one or more trusted peers or family members. Some students may find it helpful to record themselves on videotape or audiotape, in order to learn where adjustments might be made to strengthen their presentations.
- Have students use the Listening and Speaking Progress Chart, p. 31, in **Performance Assessment and Portfolio Management**.

CUSTOMIZE INSTRUCTION
For Universal Access

To address different learning styles, use the following activities suggested in the **Extension Activities** booklet, p. 29.

For Interpersonal and Visual/Spatial Learners, use Activity 5.

For Musical/Rhythmic Learners, use Activity 6.

For Visual/Spatial Learners, use Activity 7.

1. To understand the connection between firsthand accounts of the Civil War and firsthand accounts of modern wars, such as the Persian Gulf War

2. To understand how such factors as technology have changed the way journalists and others report on war

Connections

The Civil War lasted for four years, and reports from the front took days, even weeks, to reach the public. The Persian Gulf War was much shorter, and news reports were filed almost instantaneously. Have students reread the firsthand accounts of the Civil War after they have read "Gulf War Journal." What differences and similarities can they discover?

War Diaries, Journals, and Letters

• Using the head note on p. 553, explain to students that the Persian Gulf War was fought by United Nations forces against Iraq in 1991. The war was fought with technologically advanced weaponry, and reported to the public by teams of journalists in the Gulf.

• Explain that technology has also changed the way journalists report on wars. Even with modern news reporting, however, non-partici-pants cannot really know the chaos and fear of war. Only firsthand accounts can convey these true faces of war.

• Suggest that Molly Moore's firsthand account of the Gulf War allows readers a close-up look at the nature of war, as do such accounts of the Civil War as Mary Chesnut's and Warren Lee Goss's.

• As students read, instruct them to make comparisons between the Civil War and the Persian Gulf War: For example, what are some similarities and differences in how the wars were fought, in how the public received information, and in the emotions experienced by those involved?

CONNECTIONS
Literature Past and Present
War Diaries, Journals, and Letters

The letters and diary and journal entries in Part 2 tell the story of the Civil War as seen through the eyes of people who experienced it firsthand. Each of these intimate literary forms presents personal views of the events of the time from eyewitnesses—none of whom was a professional writer. In her book *A Woman at War*, journalist Molly Moore records her impressions of a modern con-flict, the Persian Gulf War between Iraq and a coalition of forces led by the Unit-ed States. Although Moore, as a newspaper reporter, usually writes objective news stories, this personal account of her experiences as a witness to history makes excit-ing reading. In this excerpt, she relates her story behind the news story—what it was like to cover the Persian Gulf War from the military zone. Like the personal accounts you have already read, Moore's narrative reveals a human side to war.

Revealing the Hidden Faces of War The Civil War was a long, bloody conflict that tore the nation apart. Those living outside the war zone, however, never fully comprehended the horror and devastation wrought by the war. Communication was limited and slow. Newspapers, where available, were a key source of informa-tion, but the news they contained was often days old. The only way to really understand the impact of the war was to live through it.

In the late 1960s, Americans experienced their first "living-room war" as vio-lent, disturbing footage of the Vietnam War flashed across television screens every evening. In 1991, the Persian Gulf War was a full-scale media event that unfolded in real time before the eyes of millions worldwide who watched round-the-clock cover-age on satellite and cable news stations. Though viewers were able to "experience" war as never before, there is still something unique and compelling about a personal account by an eyewitness near the action. Molly Moore provides this account.

552 ◆ *Division, Reconciliation, and Expansion (1850–1914)*

Gulf War Journal from A Woman at War

Molly Moore

In August 1990, Iraqi troops under the command of dictator Saddam Hussein invaded neighboring Kuwait, a tiny oil-rich nation on the Persian Gulf. Despite economic sanctions and repeated demands by the United Nations Security Council, Iraq refused to withdraw from Kuwait. In late November 1990, the council presented the invaders with an ultimatum: leave Kuwait by January 15, 1991, or a coalition of nations, including the United States, would use "all necessary means" to remove Iraqi troops from Kuwait. Iraq ignored the threat. Early on the morning of January 17, 1991, coalition forces began bombing Iraqi targets, marking the official launch of the Persian Gulf War, also known as Operation Desert Storm. Hundreds of reporters, Molly Moore among them, were gathered at the Dhahran International Hotel in Dhahran, Saudi Arabia, when the airstrike began.

A thunderous roar jarred me out of a light sleep. The hotel windows rattled and the entire building shook. I recognized the sound almost instantly: The U.S. Air Force's 1st Tactical Fighter Wing was taking off outside my window. The fighter jets normally took off in pairs, seldom more than six at a time. But this was a massive, continuous wave of noise as a dozen or more of the F-15 Eagle fighters fired their afterburners and sped into the night sky. It could mean only one thing: The war had started. I glanced at my watch. It was 1:45 a.m.

Almost simultaneously I heard dozens of footsteps pounding down the hallways outside my door. The telephone rang. It was my *Washington Post* colleague in the room across the hall.

◀ **Critical Viewing** In what ways did computer-guided missiles such as the one in this photograph change the nature of combat? **[Speculate]**

☑ **Reading Check**
What specific event awakens Moore from sleep?

from A Woman at War ◆ 553

Background

"Gulf War Journal"

This piece blends the objective reporting style of a seasoned military correspondent at the brink of war with the human reactions of a person suddenly put in a life-threatening situation. The author provides a glimpse into the chaotic life of a war reporter racing to do her job in the face of fear, confusion, technical problems, and ethical questions.

▶ **Critical Viewing**

Possible response: Due to the sophistication of today's computer-guided weaponry, the military can launch attacks from great distances. Today's soldiers may fight an entire war without ever confronting enemy troops.

☑ **Reading Check**

Answer: The launching of the U.S. Air Force's 1st Tactical Fighter Wings—countless F-15 Eagle fighter jets roaring into the sky—awakens Moore, signalling the start of the Persian Gulf War.

CUSTOMIZE INSTRUCTION FOR UNIVERSAL ACCESS

For Less Proficient Readers	For English Learners	For Advanced Readers
These students may find "Gulf War Journal" particularly challenging. Explain to them that Molly Moore recounts the events of the early hours of the morning of January 17, 1991. Encourage them to create a timeline of events as they read and to note any military or journalistic jargon they do not recognize.	Help these students comprehend journalistic jargon, such as *pool, zones,* and *squeezed . . . for details.* Also, explain political and military terms English learners may not know, such as *coalition of nations* or *collateral damage.*	Ask these students to pay attention to Molly Moore's fast-paced writing and use of jargon. Encourage them to discuss the effect her style has on the story she tells. Does it help her communicate the experience of war to her readers?

War Diaries, Journals, and Letters

- Be sure students understand that Molly Moore's job is to report on the Gulf War for an American newspaper, the *Washington Post*. Encourage them to discuss news reports they have read in newspapers or seen on television.

- Have students read the paragraph beginning "I joined the mob . . ." and the paragraph that follows it. Then, ask them to compare the polished news reports they typically see or read with the chaotic moments the journalist experiences behind the scenes.
  Possible response: Students should note that most news reports are delivered with a sense of calm and authority that contrasts with the chaos described here.

- Ask students: Why do you think "the enormity of the moment and the uncertainty of its consequences" felt so overwhelming to the author?
  Possible response: Students may say that when a long-awaited event finally happens, the fears of the unknown outcome become very real.

▶**Critical Viewing**

Possible response: This location adds a sense of immediacy and drama to the report—falsely creating a sense that the reporter is on the front lines in the middle of the action.

"It's started," said Guy Gugliotta, a seasoned foreign correspondant who'd been sent to Saudi Arabia to relieve me when I'd returned to Washington in December.

"I just heard the planes take off," I replied, collecting notebooks and a pen from the small desk in my room.

"We just got the first pool report[1] from another air base up north," Gugliotta said. "I'm calling the foreign desk now."

"I'll be upstairs," I told him. "See you there."

I joined the mob surging up the steps to the military's Joint Information Bureau on the third floor of the hotel. Despite the months of waiting and speculation and the more than one hundred stories I'd written dissecting Operation Desert Shield, the enormity of the moment and the uncertainty of its consequences were almost overwhelming.

So much for "military disinformation." More than three hundred reporters now jammed the Dhahran International's opulent third-floor ballroom, which had been converted into large pressrooms. Reporters squeezed the public affairs officers for details and snatched copies of the media pool reports as soon as they were dictated by the pool of reporters assigned to an air base northwest of Dhahran.

Gugliotta joined me after giving the *Post* the meager information he had from the first pool report. "There's nothing coming out of Washington," he said. "Nobody has announced anything. Cheney[2] is supposed to make a statement later tonight."

An ABC *Nightline* reporter thrust a microphone into my face. "How do you feel about the information the military is providing about the war?"

I was tempted to say, "What information?" It's always a sure sign that there isn't any real information when reporters start interviewing each other.

"The only information we've gotten so far has been from the reporters on one of the pools," I replied. "At least that worked pretty well. Reporters were at the base where some of the first planes took off and they managed to get to a telephone to dictate a story before Washington even admitted the war had started."

Suddenly an ear-piercing siren wailed through the building.

"What is that?" I shouted to Gugliotta.

"Bomb shelter, get down to the bomb shelter," he yelled.

I followed the herd. As I sprinted down the stairs I noticed the signs that had been added since I'd left six weeks earlier: "To the shelters," with arrows pointing the way.

---

1. **pool report** During the Persian Gulf War, firsthand information was compiled, or pooled, in reports that then were released to all of the media organizations covering the war.
2. **Cheney** (chā′ nē) U.S. Secretary of Defense Richard Cheney. Cheney would become Vice President in 2001.

554 ◆ *Division, Reconciliation, and Expansion (1850–1914)*

▼**Critical Viewing** These journalists are presenting their report from atop a tank. Why might the journalists have chosen this location for filming? **[Hypothesize]**

✹ **ENRICHMENT: Social Studies Connection**

News Journalism

The field of news journalism offers professional writers the opportunity to report on newsworthy events on the local, national, and international levels. From parades and town meetings to politics, finance, and war, the news media deliver information on a broad range of topics each day. Journalists may write for newspapers, news magazines, or news services, or they may broadcast their reports via radio, television, or cable news programming.

Within the field of news journalism, the training requirements are as varied as the career options. While many journalists enter the job market with a liberal arts degree, others pursue specialized degrees at universities with schools of journalism. Internships with local newspapers and radio and television stations provide potential news journalists with valuable, hands-on experience.

Almost six hundred hotel guests and staff spilled down the stairwells in near panic. Had the Iraqis launched a counterattack? Were they roaring down the coastal highway toward Dhahran? Had Saddam Hussein fired Scud missiles at us? We'd known since August that the hotel was in a prime target zone. It sat beside the most active military airfield in Saudi Arabia.

In the basement, frantic hotel employees tried to guide the frenzied crowd into half a dozen rooms, including the kitchen. Above the din, Philip Congdon, a former officer of the British special forces, who had been hired as the hotel's defense consultant, threatened, "Sit down or you will be tried!"

I was in a group that was shoved into the kitchen and ordered to lie on the floor. We were surrounded by large plate-glass windows. An explosion would send shards ripping through the air. I crawled beneath a large steel table, thinking it might protect me from flying glass.

"Everyone please sit down and put on your gas masks," directed Congdon, a wiry man who looked to be in his early fifties. Even when

✔**Reading Check**

From where did the reporters receive their information?

from *A Woman at War* ◆ 555

War Diaries, Journals, and Letters

- Explain to students that during the Civil War, journalists usually traveled with the commander's staff, well behind the firing lines. Photographers and artists did their work before or after battles.

- Ask students to compare the situation faced by Gulf War journalists to that faced by journalists during the Civil War. **Possible response:** Journalists during the Civil War were usually not in immediate danger. During the Gulf War, however, some journalists were within the range of technologically advanced weapons.

✔**Reading Check**

Answer: The reporters at the hotel were getting their information from "one of the pools"— other reporters at one of the air bases.

CUSTOMIZE INSTRUCTION FOR UNIVERSAL ACCESS

For Special Needs Students	For Less Proficient Readers
These students may have difficulty following the events in Moore's account. Have them read the selection once to form a first impression. Then, encourage them to discuss what happens in the text. Students may say the selection was exciting, but may require guidance to understand that Moore is describing the efforts of journalists to cover the beginning of a war. Instruct students to reread, this time pausing to note what is happening.	These students might be confused by the description of the Joint Information Bureau (JIB) on p. 554. Explain to them that the JIB is an office established by the United Nations military forces during the Gulf War for disseminating information to journalists. At this point—the very beginning of the war—almost no information has been provided, so "reporters start interviewing each other."

▶Critical Viewing

Possible response: Students may say that he was filming something he was not allowed to film. They may suggest that the men in the background could have been Saudi dignitaries.

giving frightening directives, Congdon had one of those self-assured voices that could calm a hysterical mob.

The people around me were pulling gas masks over their faces. I panicked. I had no mask. *The Washington Post's* chemical protection suits had not yet arrived from British Aerospace in London even though we'd ordered them almost two months earlier.

"I don't have a mask," I called in a strained voice to Congdon. He looked at me with exasperation. "Just sit down, I'll get you something," he said impatiently.

Moments later he returned with a crude, spongy contraption that looked somewhat like a surgical mask and covered only my nose and mouth. I slipped it on, knowing it would merely postpone death a microsecond. I sat on the gritty kitchen floor, surrounded by slimy, rotting tomato halves and colleagues in full-face masks. If I could smell the stench of the tomatoes on the floor and the spoiled chicken parts on

▲ Critical Viewing
Speculate about the events leading up to this photograph taken outside the Dhahran International Hotel. What might the camera operator have been doing that caused the Saudi Arabian security guard to intervene? **[Speculate]**

556 ◆ Division, Reconciliation, and Expansion (1850–1914)

✳ ENRICHMENT: Social Studies/Science Connection

Technology and the News

Major newspapers cover stories that break all over the world. How do they accomplish this? Advances in technology have transformed the way news is gathered, reported, and delivered to our nation's newspapers and news magazines. Digital phones, satellite links, computer modems, the Internet, and even e-mail now make it possible for reporters to file stories in seconds from virtually anywhere in the world. Photographs, which once took hours, even days, to develop, print, and ship, are now digitized and transmitted electronically.

Computer desktop publishing programs give publications the speed and flexibility to make last-minute changes and additions that were once difficult, if not impossible, to make.

Have each interested student research one of the many ways in which newspapers report, photograph, and transmit news from all corners of the globe so that articles are accurate, prompt, and compelling. Students can combine their findings in a group presentation.

the counter above me, I figured chemical particles would have no trouble penetrating my pathetic mask.

The information vacuum was almost unbearable. We knew nothing about what was going on at the air base outside our windows or the world outside Saudi Arabia. The siren continued its annoying wail.

Someone pulled out a shortwave radio.

". . . In the event of an attack, there is likely to be a reprisal," the crackly voice said. "There is no reaction from the Iraqi side yet."

I breathed a little easier.

At 3:50 a.m., about thirty minutes after the siren sounded, the hotel security chief called an all clear, the signal that we could remove our gas masks and leave the basement shelter. The civil defense alert had been called because of uncertainty about how the Iraqi military would react to the first bombs dropped on Baghdad. As we pushed our way into the crowded corridors, Congdon warned, "You should be aware that the early stage of an offensive is the most likely time for an attack on Dhahran."

As soon as we were released from our temporary captivity, the JIB began activating emergency media pools in an effort to get reporters across the street to the air base, where pilots would soon be returning with tales of the first bombing runs. The reporters who would serve on these quick-reaction pools had been selected days earlier after acrimonious debates among feuding news organizations. Now, the public affairs officers couldn't find the *New York Times* reporter assigned to the pool. Guy Gugliotta volunteered to take his place. As he collected his sleeping bag and rucksack, Gugliotta rattled off the instructions for operating the satellite telephone the *Post* had leased for our war coverage. For a $53,000 leasing fee, we could have instant communications to Washington from anywhere on the battlefield, including the roof of the Dhahran International Hotel, where the high-tech contraption now sat.

Within the last hour, a convoy of humvees[3] with machine guns mounted on their roofs had formed a tight ring around the front of the hotel.

I began piecing together the details. At 1:30 a.m., the guided-missile cruiser USS *San Jacinto*, stationed in the Red Sea, had fired the opening shot of the war: a 1.6 ton, twenty-foot-long Tomahawk cruise missile aimed at downtown Baghdad. Minutes later fighter planes based across the street from our hotel, as well as warplanes from bases across the Arabian Peninsula, roared into the sky toward Iraq.

---

3. **humvees** large, rugged military vehicles known as High Mobility Multi-Purpose Wheeled Vehicles. The term *humvee* is derived from the acronym HMMWV.

Thematic Connection
Compare the description of this scene with the descriptions of fear and chaos expressed by Mary Chesnut and Randolph McKim.

✔**Reading Check**
In the early morning hours, what causes the reporters to put on gas masks and huddle on the kitchen floor?

from *A Woman at War* ◆ 557

Thematic Connection
Possible response: Students should note that Chesnut's vivid, emotional description of the chaotic impact of war on civilians is closer in tone to Moore's description than McKim's objective descriptions of military maneuvers.

✔**Reading Check**
Answer: An air raid siren sounds as the war begins, in anticipation of an Iraqi counterattack. The hotel security staff moves the reporters to the kitchen, ordering them to crouch and put on gas masks.

CUSTOMIZE INSTRUCTION FOR UNIVERSAL ACCESS

For English Learners	For Gifted/Talented Students	For Advanced Readers
Your class may include immigrants from the Persian Gulf whose relatives fought in the Gulf War or whose families were affected by it. Speak to these students privately and ask whether there are any family stories about the war they would like to share with the class.	Have these students gather images of the Gulf War—including photographs, illustrations, and editorial cartoons. Instruct them to create collages representing the war as Molly Moore might have seen it. If students are interested, they may incorporate images of the Civil War to make a more universal statement.	Challenge these students to read more news articles of the time. Then, instruct them to compare the early coverage of Operation Desert Storm with Molly Moore's account. Can they find the confusion she describes in the news reports?

1. Mary Chesnut gets her information from personal observation, her husband, the newspaper, and various acquaintances. Molly Moore gets her information from personal observation, her colleagues, and official announcements.

2. Molly Moore's situation in the Dhahran International hotel more closely resembles the situation of Randolph McKim. Both are on—or perilously near—a battlefield or military target. Mary Chesnut writes from the relative safety of her own home, far from Charleston Harbor.

Pool reports from reporters interviewing pilots began trickling into the JIB.

"Baghdad lit up like a Christmas tree," Air Force colonel George Walton told reporters as he climbed out of his F-4G Wild Weasel electronic warfare jet.

"It was the scariest thing I've ever done," Lieutenant Ian Long, a British Tornado pilot, recounted. "Some tracers came off the target[4] down our left-hand side. We tried to avoid that by going right. On our right-hand side was a mass of white explosions, and yellow explosions that looked like flak.[5] You're frightened of failure, you're frightened of dying. You're flying as low as you dare, but high enough to get the weapons off. As the bombs come off, you just run . . . "

I tried to telephone the new details to the *Post*. I dialed and redialed and redialed. The hotel's switchboard was jammed. I raced to the roof of the hotel. Since I had last been there six weeks earlier, it had become a jungle of satellite dishes, talk-show sets, and camera tripods. The hotel employees called it "Little Hollywood." Wires and electrical cords were coiled and stretched in every direction like a giant plate of spaghetti. It was dark and starting to mist.

I found the *Post* satellite telephone, a midget beside the monster network dishes. Its collapsible dish was about the size of a large umbrella. I pulled out my scribbled instructions and read them in the beam of my flashlight.

"Turn the generator on. The choke is on the back. Give pull one jerk. Adjust the choke." It operated like a lawn mower. Unlike a lawn mower, it started on the first try.

I switched on the telephone, encased in a metal box that looked like a large suitcase, and punched numbers on a keypad until "Indian"—as in Indian Ocean—appeared on a digital readout. I pressed the keypad again to find the designated satellite shore station at Perth, Australia. I dialed a code and *The Washington Post* foreign desk number. I heard three rings. "Foreign desk," said the perfectly clear voice on the other end of the telephone.

---

4. **"Some tracers . . . target** The Iraqi military bases targeted for bombing responded by firing tracers, ammunition that traces its own course with a visible trail of smoke or fire.
5. **flak** (flak) anti-aircraft gunfire.

Connecting Literature Past and Present

1. Compare and contrast the way Mary Chesnut and Molly Moore get information about the wars.
2. Does Molly Moore's situation in the Dhahran International Hotel more closely resemble the situation of Mary Chesnut or of Randolph McKim? Explain your answer.

Molly Moore

(b. 1956)

Molly Moore has worked for *The Washington Post* since 1981, covering local and state government; and the Pentagon for five years, including the Gulf War. She also served as a foreign correspondent in South Asia, covering India, Pakistan, Afghanistan, Bangladesh, Nepal, Bhutan and Sri Lanka. Moore says she wrote *A Woman at War* because she came away from the Gulf War believing that most of the world had seen only the television version that was portrayed as a quick and effortless victory by the American armed forces.

Forging New Frontiers

The Old Stage Coach of the Plains, Frederic Remington,
Amon Carter Museum, Fort Worth, Texas

INSTRUCTION FOR UNIVERSAL ACCESS

the selections in this part, keep in mind these factors:

**Jumping Frog of
ty"**

aging tall tale can
rners with dialect

f Poker Flat"

of western justice

"Heading West"

• Juxtaposition of pioneers'
  expectations and reality

"I Will Fight No More Forever"

• Poignant and brief surrender
  speech

• Challenge advanced students to
  contrast with contemporary

portrayal of Native Americans

"To Build a Fire"

• High-interest story of a battle for
  survival against nature

Selection Planning Guide

The selections in this section capture the flavor of frontier life in the Old West, a unique time and place in American history. The hilarious narrative of "The Notorious Jumping Frog of Calaveras County" takes students deep into the American frontier. "The Outcasts of Poker Flat" presents an entirely different aspect of frontier life— its singular system of justice. "Heading West" is an excerpt from a diary of a woman who, along with her husband, leaves the comfortable East to move to a community in the Kansas frontier. "I Will Fight No More Forever" is Native American Chief Joseph's poignant surrender speech in which he relates the tragic plight of his people, who are scattered, dead, or starving because of battles with the United States Army. The classic story "To Build a Fire" pits the brutal cold of the Yukon against a foolish traveler. Part 3 ends with an excerpt from *Lonesome Dove*, a contemporary work that presents an idealized picture of the Old West.

Background

Art

The Old Stage Coach of the Plains,
Frederic Remington

Remington was a New Yorker who fell in love with the West after a trip to Montana; he continued to live in the East but traveled extensively throughout the West and became known for lively paintings that captured the spirit of the American frontier. Remington's earlier paintings are full of precise detail, but his later work focused on communicating emotion.

1. What ideas does Remington convey by focusing more on the horses than on the coach and its passengers?
   Possible response: Remington suggests the power and physical effort needed to transport people and settle the West.

2. How does the twilight help to convey a mood?
   Possible response: Since the travelers are moving at night, the painting suggests that life on the frontier is one of endlessness or exhaustion.

Background

Many people have described *Huckleberry Finn* as the quintessential American novel. Its appeal to adult readers is surprising, given that it is nominally the sequel to a children's classic, *The Adventures of Tom Sawyer*. Twain picks up Huck's story where he left it at the end of the previous book; the orphaned Huck has been adopted by a rich widow who plans to "civilize" her new son. Civilization does not suit Huck, however, and soon he is running away across country with Jim, the widow's African slave. At first, Huck condescends to Jim because he is black and a slave, but he eventually learns to appreciate and respect him. Huck narrates his own story in the colorful dialect Twain excelled at reproducing in print.

▶ **Critical Viewing**

Answer: Students should say it must have been exciting and challenging.

A Closer Look

Mark Twain: The American Bard

His humor captivated readers and created a new style of American writing.

In the late 1800s, readers might have known him as Thomas Jefferson Snodgrass, W. Epaminandos Adrastus Blab, or simply Josh. Today, we know Samuel Langhorne Clemens as Mark Twain, his most famous literary pseudonym. Whichever name he used, Twain pulled off a rare literary feat—he created stories, novels, and essays that were both wildly popular in his own day and models of wit and skill more than a century later. Twain was so influential that, fifty years after his death, Ernest Hemingway said "all American literature begins" with Twain's novel *The Adventures of Huckleberry Finn.*

Life on the River Born in 1835, Samuel Clemens grew up in the small town of Hannibal, Missouri. Hannibal was a river town, a stop on the Mississippi. Steamboat men, religious revivalists, circus performers, minstrel companies, showboat actors, and every other kind of traveler imaginable made appearances in Hannibal. As a boy, Clemens met many of the characters that he would later write about.

After his father's death in 1847, Clemens was forced to leave school and take a job as a printer's apprentice. During the 1850s, he wrote a few stories, some of which were published under the pseudonyms of Snodgrass, Blab, and Josh. Twain also traveled the country from St. Louis to New York to Iowa. When he returned home, he took a boat trip down the Mississippi. He had planned to go to South America to seek his fortune, but during the trip he recalled childhood memories of river life and decided to become a

▼ **Critical Viewing** What do you think it would have been like to captain a Mississippi riverboat like the one shown in this photograph? **[Speculate]**

MISSISSIPPI QUEEN

560 ◆ *Division, Reconciliation, and Expansion (1850–1914)*

✹ ENRICHMENT: Literature Connection

"Mark Twain!"

Twain borrowed his pen name from his days as a riverboat pilot. "Mark twain" is a call indicating that the boat is sailing on water two fathoms deep. In his book *Life on the Mississippi,* Twain recounts his days as an apprentice or "cub" pilot on the Mississippi, including a hard lesson he learned the first time he was allowed to pilot the boat without supervision. As a joke, the crew told the young pilot that he was in shallow water; panicking, Twain begged the engineer to reverse the great paddlewheels. As the crew began laughing at him, the pilot, Mr. Bixby, appeared and warned him never to be tricked again. "Didn't you *know* there was no bottom in that crossing? . . . Then you shouldn't have allowed me or anyone else to shake your confidence in that knowledge." Twain never forgot this lesson.

riverboat pilot. He served as a riverboat captain until 1861, when the Civil War closed the Mississippi River to boat traffic.

Mark Twain Is Born In 1862, Clemens took a job as a reporter on the Virginia City *Territorial Enterprise*. Working on the newspaper, he found his calling as a humorist. It was also the first time he used the name Mark Twain for his byline.

The new name, which is actually a signal yelled out by riverboat pilots, not only connected the writer to his youth, but also freed him to develop a new style. Before becoming "Twain," his work was typical of the low humor of the time, filled with bad puns and intentional misspellings. But in 1865, Twain published a short story entitled "The Notorious Jumping Frog of Calaveras County" (page 569). The story won the author fame and financial success, and it marked the first appearance of his distinctive comic style.

Ordinary American Speech The targets of Twain's jokes were not new. He distrusted technology and disliked machines. He railed against political figures, calling them swindlers and con men. What was new was Twain's feel for ordinary American people and their language. He wrote using the American English that people actually spoke. In that unlikely source, he found rich and comic poetry.

Twain's novels, like *Tom Sawyer* (1876) and *Huckleberry Finn* (1884), were unlike any other books the world had ever seen. At a time when most American writers were copying European novelists, Twain wrote about American themes. His heroes were dirt-poor and plain-spoken. In Twain's hands, the moral choices of his characters had as much drama and gravity as those of any tormented member of the nobility in a European novel.

Not everyone appreciated Twain's humor. The author fled Virginia City when a rival journalist, offended by a story, challenged him to a pistol duel. He was chased out of San Francisco by policemen angered by critical articles. Even as his fame grew, some critics dismissed him as little more than a jokester.

Despite the occasional disapproval of his work, the American public adopted Twain as one of their own. He made a fortune from his writings, settling with his wife and family into a Hartford, Connecticut, mansion that was elaborately decorated to look like the inside of a river steamboat. Though he squandered much of his money on bad investments, he remained comfortable throughout his life, garnering huge paychecks as a professional speaker.

The Old Man in a White Suit At the end of the 1800s, the deaths of Twain's wife and daughters left the writer bitter and cynical. Near the end of his life, Twain became so reclusive that a newspaper reported he was dead. Twain immediately wired the editors: "Reports of my death have been greatly exaggerated."

History has not exaggerated Twain's legacy. He was the first, and possibly the greatest, authentically American writer.

▲ **Critical Viewing**
In what ways does this illustration for an early edition of *The Adventures of Tom Sawyer* convey the wit that marks Twain's writing? **[Connect]**

▶**Critical Viewing**
Answer: The viewer can clearly see how Tom Sawyer's feigned interest in his chore will fool his friend into doing the work for him.

Critical Thinking

1. What does the popularity of Twain's stories suggest about the American reading public?
   Answer: Since Twain wrote about ordinary working people, his popularity suggests that similar people bought and enjoyed his books. This in turn suggests that America was a highly literate country in which people of all social classes and income levels liked to read for entertainment.

2. How do you think Twain's travels and varied experiences helped him in his writing?
   Answer: Wherever he traveled, he could find new people and things to write about. His many different job experiences meant that he could write knowledgeably about others who had those jobs. He saw a great deal of life by traveling and working. He was able to write about actual experiences rather than about things he had only read or heard about.

The Boy's Ambition *from* Life on the Mississippi ✦ The Notorious Jumping Frog of Calaveras County

Lesson Objectives

1. **To analyze and respond to literary elements**
   - Literary Analysis: Humor
   - Comparing Literary Works
2. **To read, comprehend, analyze, and critique nonfiction and a short story**
   - Reading Strategy: Understanding Regional Dialect
   - Reading Check questions
   - Review and Assess questions
   - Assessment Practice (ATE)
3. **To develop word analysis skills, fluency, and systematic vocabulary**
   - Vocabulary Development Lesson: Greek Prefix: *mono-*
4. **To understand and apply written and oral language conventions**
   - Spelling Strategy
   - Grammar and Style Lesson: Double Negatives
5. **To understand and apply appropriate writing and research strategies**
   - Writing Lesson: Analytic Essay
   - Extension Activity: Multimedia Report
6. **To understand and apply listening and speaking strategies**
   - Extension Activity: Interview

STEP-BY-STEP TEACHING GUIDE	PACING GUIDE
PRETEACH	
Motivate Students and Provide Background	
Use the Motivation activity (ATE p. 562)	5 min.
Read and discuss author and background features (SE/ATE pp. 562, 565) **A**	5 min.
Introduce the Concepts	
Introduce the Literary Analysis and Reading Strategy (SE/ATE p. 563) **A**	15 min.
Pronounce the vocabulary words and read their definitions (SE p. 563)	5 min.
TEACH	
Monitor Comprehension	
Informally monitor comprehension by circulating while students read independently or in groups **A**	35 min.
Monitor students' comprehension with the Reading Check notes (SE/ATE pp. 565, 567, 569, 571, 573)	as students read
Develop vocabulary with Vocabulary notes (SE pp. 565, 566, 567, 569, 571; ATE p. 569)	as students read
Develop Understanding	
Develop students' understanding of humor with the Literary Analysis annotations (SE pp. 565, 570, 572; ATE pp. 565, 570, 572) **A**	5 min.
Develop students' ability to understand regional dialect with the Reading Strategy annotations (SE pp. 567, 570, 571; ATE pp. 567, 570, 571)	5 min.
ASSESS	
Assess Mastery	
Assess students' mastery of the Reading Strategy and Literary Analysis by having them answer the Review and Assess questions (SE/ATE p. 575)	15 min.
Use one or more of the print and media Assessment Resources (ATE p. 577) **A**	up to 45 min.
EXTEND	
Apply Understanding	
Have students complete the Vocabulary Development Lesson and the Grammar and Style Lesson (SE p. 576) **A**	20 min.
Apply students' ability to organize to show comparison by using the Writing Lesson (SE/ATE p. 577) **A**	45 min.
Apply students' understanding using one or more of the Extension Activities (SE p. 577)	20–90 min.

 ACCELERATED INSTRUCTION:
Use the strategies and activities identified with an **A**.

UNIVERSAL ACCESS
● = Below Level Students
▲ = On-Level Students
■ = Above Level Students

Time and Resource Manager

Average, Challenging
Average Number of Instructional Days: 4

RESOURCES		
PRINT	**TRANSPARENCIES**	**TECHNOLOGY**
• **Beyond Literature,** Workplace Skills: Jargon, p. 30 ▲ ■		• **Interest Grabber Video,** Tape 4 ● ▲ ■
• **Selection Support Workbook:** ● ▲ ■ Literary Analysis, p. 137 Reading Strategy, p. 136 Build Vocabulary, p. 134	• **Literary Analysis and Reading Transparencies,** pp. 59 and 60 ● ▲ ■	
• **Adapted Reader's Companion** ● • **Reader's Companion** ● • **Authors In Depth,** The American Experience, p. 91 ■		• **Listening to Literature** ● ▲ ■ Audiocassettes, Side 19 Audio CDs, CD 12
• **English Learner's Companion** ● ▲ • **Literatura en español** ● ▲ • **Literary Analysis for Enrichment** ■	• **Fine Art Transparencies, Volume 1,** Art Transparency 3 ● ▲ ■	
• **Formal Assessment:** Selection Test, pp. 146–148 ● ▲ ■ • **Open Book Test,** pp. 88–90 ● ▲ ■ • **Performance Assessment and Portfolio Management,** p. 23 ● ▲ ■ • PRENTICE HALL ASSESSMENT *SYSTEM* ● ▲ ■	• PRENTICE HALL ASSESSMENT *SYSTEM* ● ▲ ■ Skills Practice Answers and Explanations on Transparencies	• **Test Bank Software** ● ▲ ■ • **Got It! Assessment Videotapes,** Tape 3 ● ▲
• **Selection Support Workbook:** ● ▲ ■ Grammar and Style, p. 135 • **Writing and Grammar,** Ruby Level ● ▲ ■ • **Extension Activities,** p. 30 ● ▲ ■	• **Daily Language Practice Transparencies** ● ▲ • **Writing Models and Graphic Organizers on Transparencies,** pp. 37–40 ● ▲ ■	• **Writing and Grammar iText CD-ROM** ● ▲ ■ *Take It to the Net* www.phschool.com

BLOCK SCHEDULING: Use one 90-minute class period to preteach the selection and have students read it. Use a second 90-minute class period to assess students' mastery of skills and have them complete one of the Extension Activities.

Motivation

Tell students that Mark Twain was a writer who used exaggeration, embellishment, regional dialect, and boyhood recollections to make his stories humorous. Then ask students to brainstorm for a list of different kinds of humor that they enjoy— such as humorous stories, jokes, or riddles—and invite students to name examples for each category. Ask them to distinguish between spoken humor and humor meant to be read, and have them describe what it is about written humor that makes them laugh. Then invite them to enjoy two selections by an eminent American writer and humorist, Mark Twain.

▭ Interest Grabber Video

As an alternative, play "Twain's Life on the Mississippi" on Tape 4 to engage student interest.

❶ Background

More About the Author

The critic Maurice LeBreton said of Mark Twain's accomplishments: "[His] work is a panorama of the West in all its vitality. He has observed everything: landscapes, environments, ways of life, customs, beliefs, superstitions. Through him we know the little Missouri town . . . He has described for us the Mississippi . . . We follow him into the isolated Arkansas farm . . . The entire West files past us in a succession of precise, faithful images."

Poet T. S. Eliot wrote that Twain had "discovered a new way of writing . . . a literary language based on American colloquial speech."

Prepare to Read

❶ The Boys' Ambition *from* Life on the Mississippi ◆ The Notorious Jumping Frog of Calaveras County

Mark Twain (1835–1910)

Although Mark Twain is widely regarded as one of the greatest American writers, the world-renowned author once indicated that he would have preferred to spend his life as a Mississippi riverboat pilot. The comment was probably not entirely serious, but Twain so loved life on the river that as a young man, he did in fact work as a riverboat pilot for several years. His childhood on the banks of the Mississippi fostered more than a love of riverboats—it also became the basis for many of his most famous works, including *The Adventures of Tom Sawyer* (1876) and *The Adventures of Huckleberry Finn* (1884).

Life on the River Twain, whose given name was Samuel Langhorne Clemens, felt so closely tied to the Mississippi River that he even took his pen name, Mark Twain, from a river man's call meaning "two fathoms deep," indicating that the river is deep enough for a boat to pass safely. He grew up in the Mississippi River town of Hannibal, Missouri. His father died when he was eleven, and he left school to become a printer's apprentice. He worked as a printer in a number of different cities before deciding at age twenty-one to pursue a career as a riverboat pilot.

A Traveling Man When the Civil War closed traffic on the Mississippi, Twain went west to Nevada. There, he supported himself as a journalist and lecturer, developing the entertaining writing

style that made him famous. In 1865, Twain published "The Notorious Jumping Frog of Calaveras County," his version of a tall tale he had heard in a mining camp in California while he was working as a gold prospector. The story made him an international celebrity.

Following the publication of *The Innocents Abroad* (1869), a successful book of humorous travel letters, Twain moved to Hartford, Connecticut, where he was to make his home for the rest of his life. There, Twain began using his past experiences as raw material for his books. He drew on his travels in the western mining region for *Roughing It* (1872). He turned to his childhood experiences on the Mississippi for *The Adventures of Tom Sawyer*, *Life on the Mississippi*, and his masterpiece, *The Adventures of Huckleberry Finn*.

A Restless Soul Twain traveled widely throughout his life, including residential stints in such major American cities as St. Louis, New York, Philadelphia, Cincinnati, and San Francisco. He made extended visits to England, Germany, Switzerland, Italy, and Palestine. His adventures, both at home and abroad, were fuel for a number of books. After living in Europe for several years, he returned home with his family. Following the death of his wife and three of their four children, Twain was unable to reproduce the balance between pessimism and humor that he had captured so brilliantly in *Huckleberry Finn*. In his later works, such as *A Connecticut Yankee in King Arthur's Court* (1889), *Pudd'nhead Wilson* (1894), and *The Man That Corrupted Hadleyburg* (1900), Twain's writing depicted an increasingly pessimistic view of society and human nature. However, he continued to display the same masterful command of language that had already established him as one of America's finest fiction writers.

TEACHING RESOURCES

The following resources can be used to enrich or extend the instruction for pp. 562–563.

Motivation

▭ **Interest Grabber Video**, Tape 4 ▪

Background

▭ **Beyond Literature**, p. 30

▭ *Take It to the Net*
Visit www.phschool.com for Background and hotlinks for the selection.

Literary Analysis

▭ **Literary Analysis and Reading Transparencies,** Humor, p. 60

▭ **Selection Support:** Literary Analysis, p. 137

Reading

▭ **Literary Analysis and Reading Transparencies,** Understanding Regional Dialect, p. 59 ▪

 BLOCK SCHEDULING: Resources marked with this symbol provide varied instruction during 90-minute blocks.

Preview

Connecting to the Literature

Today's world is being transformed through almost daily advances in technology. During Twain's day, America was also changing quickly as new forms of transportation helped settlers venture across the expanding frontier.

❷ Literary Analysis

Humor

Humor is writing intended to evoke laughter. Humorists use a variety of techniques to make their work amusing. Many western humorists of the 1800s perfected these comic techniques:

- Exaggerating and embellishing incidents to build comedy
- Using a narrator or story teller who takes a serious tone, adding humor by suggesting that the teller of the tale is unaware of its ridiculous qualities

As you read, take note of the details in these selections that make the stories humorous.

Comparing Literary Works

As these two selections demonstrate, Twain could find humor in any subject. However, instead of always writing just to get a laugh, he used humor for a variety of purposes. One of these stories is set in a California gold rush town and the story is deliberately funny. In the other, set on the Mississippi River, humor is secondary to the writer's goal of describing a place and a way of life. As you read, determine whether the ideas each story conveys are serious or not. Then consider the ways in which humor provides a vehicle for those ideas.

❸ Reading Strategy

Understanding Regional Dialect

Much of the humor in Twain's writing comes from his colorful uses of language. Twain was a master at re-creating **regional dialect**—language specific to a particular area of the country. If you read unfamiliar words aloud, you will find that they are regional pronunciations of words you already know. Use a chart like the one shown to translate dialect into modern Standard English.

Regional Dialect

. . . there couldn't be no solit'ry thing mentioned but that feller'd offer to bet on it, and take ary side you please. . . .

Standard English

Not one thing could be mentioned without him offering to bet on it, taking any side.

Vocabulary Development

transient (tran´ zē ənt) *adj.* not permanent (p. 565)

prodigious (prə dij´ əs) *adj.* of great power or size (p. 566)

eminence (em´ ə nəns) *n.* greatness; celebrity (p. 567)

garrulous (gar´ ə ləs) *adj.* talking too much (p. 569)

conjectured (kən jek´ chərd) *v.* guessed (p. 569)

monotonous (mə nät´ ən əs) *adj.* tiresome because unvarying (p. 569)

interminable (in tur´ mi nə bəl) *adj.* seeming to last forever (p. 569)

ornery (ôr´ nər ē) *adj.* having a mean disposition (p. 571)

The Boys' Ambition from *Life on the Mississippi* / *The Notorious Jumping Frog of Calaveras County* ◆ 563

❷ Literary Analysis

Humor

- Explain to students that as they read the two selections in this grouping, they will focus on humor in writing.
- Read the instruction together as a class and discuss students' associations with humorous writing. Encourage them to think about how literary forms of humor compare and contrast with other forms, such as physical comedy or visual caricatures.
- Invite students as they read to look for—and to *enjoy*—examples of exaggerations and embellishments and the comments of wry narrators.

❸ Reading Strategy

Understanding Regional Dialect

- Point out to students that regional dialect can convey the "flavor" and atmosphere of a place vividly. It can be used to create either comic or dramatic effect.
- Explain that readers can detect regional dialect in an author's word choice, the spelling of those words, and unusual sentence structures and grammatical constructions.
- As they read the following two tales, encourage students to read aloud certain sentences in order to clarify the meaning and the tone of the regional dialect.

Vocabulary Development

- Pronounce each vocabulary word for students, and read the definitions as a class. Have students identify any words with which they are already familiar.

CUSTOMIZE INSTRUCTION FOR UNIVERSAL ACCESS

For Special Needs Students	For Less Proficient Readers	For English Learners
Have students read the adapted version of "The Notorious Jumping Frog of Calaveras County" in the **Adapted Reader's Companion**. This version provides basic-level instruction in an interactive format with questions and write-on lines. Completing the adapted version will prepare students to read the selection in the Student Edition.	Have students read this selection in the **Reader's Companion**. This version provides basic-level instruction in an interactive format with questions and write-on lines. After students finish the selection in **Reader's Companion**, have them complete the questions and activities in the Student Edition.	Have students read the adapted version of "The Notorious Jumping Frog of Calaveras County" in the **English Learner's Companion**. This version provides basic-level instruction in an interactive format with questions and write-on lines. Completing the adapted version will prepare students to read the selection in the Student Edition.

 E-Teach

Visit E-Teach at www.phschool.com for teachers' essays on how to teach, with questions and answers.

Step-by-Step Teaching Guide for pp. 564–574

CUSTOMIZE INSTRUCTION
For Musical/Rhythmic and Verbal/Linguistic Learners
Invite students to listen to the recordings of these stories on the **Listening to Literature** audiocassettes or CDs to hear and appreciate the cadences, colloquial expressions and pronunciations, ironic understatements, and exaggerations that contribute to Twain's humorous effects.

❶ About the Selection

With charm and wit, Mark Twain draws an insightful picture of the hopes and ambitions of a boy growing up in a town along the Mississippi River. The boy dreams of becoming a steamboatman working on one of the great riverboats on the majestic river. His desire for the opportunities and prestige the job affords, his envy of a boy who already has such a job, and the contrast he sees between the dullness of his small town and the adventures the river promises provide a rich bounty of humorous situations and descriptions.

❷ Background

Art

***Paddle Steamboat* Mississippi**

This painting provides a visual record of a steamboat plying the Mississippi and of what the river banks looked like when Mark Twain was writing. The size of the boats (in contrast to the houses on land) suggests the vessel's grandeur.

Use this question for discussion:

> What was it about steamboats that excited people such as the young Mark Twain and the boys in the painting?
> Answer: Students may say that the steamboats offered a way out of small-town life and promised travel, adventure, and a sophisticated, modern life.

❸ ▶ Critical Viewing

Answer: Students may say that the majestic portrayal of the steamboat and the boys waving energetically conveys the excitement of the steamboat's arrival.

564

---

❶ *from* Life on the
MISSISSIPPI
Mark Twain

❸ ▲ **Critical Viewing** How does the painting convey the excitement generated by the arrival of a steamboat? **[Analyze]**

564 ◆ *Division, Reconciliation, and Expansion (1850–1914)*

TEACHING RESOURCES

The following resources can be used to enrich or extend the instruction for pp. 564–574.

Reading Strategy

📖 **Selection Support:** Reading Strategy, p. 136; Build Vocabulary, p. 134

📖 **Adapted Reader's Companion**

📖 **English Learner's Companion**

🎧 **Listening to Literature Audiocassettes,** Side 19 ■

💿 **Listening to Literature Audio CDs,** CD 12 ■

Extension

📖 **Authors In Depth, The American Experience** This collection includes five additional selections by Mark Twain for extended reading.

■ **BLOCK SCHEDULING:** Resources marked with this symbol provide varied instruction during 90-minute blocks.

Background

Mark Twain was an eyewitness to the nineteenth-century expansion of the western frontier. He was a young man when wagon trains left his home state of Missouri to cross the prairies, and he later saw the transcontinental railroad built. He traveled throughout the growing nation, working first on the Mississippi and then in the West, before settling in Connecticut. The rich variety of people and places he observed is reflected in the setting, characters, and dialogue of his uniquely American literature.

The Boys' Ambition

When I was a boy, there was but one permanent ambition among my comrades in our village[1] on the west bank of the Mississippi River. That was, to be a steamboatman. We had transient ambitions of other sorts, but they were only transient.

When a circus came and went, it left us all burning to become clowns; the first Negro minstrel show that came to our section left us all suffering to try that kind of life; now and then we had a hope that if we lived and were good, God would permit us to be pirates. These ambitions faded out, each in its turn; but the ambition to be a steamboatman always remained.

Once a day a cheap, gaudy packet[2] arrived upward from St. Louis, and another downward from Keokuk.[3] Before these events, the day was glorious with expectancy; after them, the day was a dead and empty thing. Not only the boys, but the whole village, felt this. After all these years I can picture that old time to myself now, just as it was then: the white town drowsing in the sunshine of a summer's morning; the streets empty, or pretty nearly so; one or two clerks sitting in front of the Water Street stores, with their splint-bottomed chairs tilted back against the wall, chins on breasts, hats slouched over their faces, asleep—with shingle shavings enough around to show what broke them down; a sow and a litter of pigs loafing along the sidewalk, doing a good business in watermelon rinds and seeds; two or three lonely little freight piles scattered about the levee;[4] a pile of skids[5] on the slope of the stone-paved wharf, and the fragrant town drunkard asleep in the shadow of them; two or three wood flats[6] at the head of the wharf, but nobody to listen to the peaceful lapping of the wavelets against them; the great Mississippi, the majestic, the magnificent Mississippi, rolling its mile-wide tide along, shining in

---

1. **our village** Hannibal, Missouri.
2. **packet** *n.* boat that travels a regular route, carrying passengers, freight, and mail.
3. **Keokuk** (kē´ ə kuk´) town in southeastern Iowa.
4. **levee** (lev´ ē) *n.* landing place along the bank of a river.
5. **skids** *n.* low, movable wooden platforms.
6. **flats** *n.* small, flat-bottomed boats.

---

transient (tran´ zē ənt) *adj.*
not permanent

Reading Check ⑤
In what way did the boys' ambitions change with each new visitor to their town?

---

from *Life on the Mississippi* ◆ 565

---

④ Background
Emphasize to students the importance of riverboat trade to the economy around the river. In an age without television or radio, the boats were also an important link between river communities and the rest of the world.

⑤ ✓ Reading Check
Answer: The boys want (for a short while) to try the kind of life lived by each glamorous visitor to their town.

CUSTOMIZE INSTRUCTION FOR UNIVERSAL ACCESS

For Special Needs Students	For Gifted/Talented Students
Encourage students to obtain and examine a map showing the Mississippi River and the states of Missouri, Indiana, Nebraska, and Iowa. You might need to help students get more specific bearings by locating Hannibal, Keokuk, and St. Louis for them. Have students use the Internet to identify which of these towns have museums or festivals that celebrate the days of riverboats.	Have students jot notes and create storyboards or sketches to demonstrate how they would capture the mood of Twain's opening lines in the opening scene of a video. Encourage students to suggest sound effects and camera effects as well as the actual images to be filmed. Have students research the role of river traffic in the lives of river dwellers of the 19th century to support their storyboards or sketches.

❻ Critical Thinking

Draw Conclusions

• Point out that "husbanded grandeur" refers to a deliberately created effect. Tell students that pitch pine is wood from the heart of a pine tree, and that it is heavily saturated with pitch, burns quickly, and emits large amounts of black smoke.

• Then ask students this question: Why would the crew want to create a special effect with black smoke?
Answer: Clouds of smoke made the boat's entrance very dramatic. It suggested that the crew was performing extremely difficult, dangerous or important work.

❼ ▶ Critical Viewing

Answer: Students may suggest that the Mississippi River served as a highway, a wide thoroughfare for shipping goods, such as tobacco and cotton, that the plantations produced. Products shipped downriver to the port of New Orleans could go from there to the East Coast and to Europe, as could the goods shipped to the river (and railroad) cities of Memphis, Vicksburg, and St. Louis. Land near the Mississippi riverbank was extremely fertile.

the sun; the dense forest away on the other side; the point above the town, and the point below, bounding the river-glimpse and turning it into a sort of sea, and withal a very still and brilliant and lonely one. Presently a film of dark smoke appears above one of those remote points; instantly a Negro drayman,[7] famous for his quick eye and <u>prodigious</u> voice, lifts up the cry, "S-t-e-a-m-boat a-comin'!" and the scene changes! The town drunkard stirs, the clerks wake up, a furious clatter of drays follows, every house and store pours out a human contribution, and all in a twinkling the dead town is alive and moving. Drays, carts, men, boys, all go hurrying from many quarters to a common center, the wharf. Assembled there, the people fasten their eyes upon the coming boat as upon a wonder they are seeing for the first time. And the boat is rather a handsome sight, too. She is long and sharp and trim and pretty; she has two tall, fancy-topped chimneys, with a gilded device of some kind swung between them; a fanciful pilothouse, all glass and gingerbread, perched on top of the texas deck[8] behind them; the paddleboxes are gorgeous with a picture or with gilded rays above the boat's name; the boiler deck, the hurricane deck, and the texas deck are fenced and ornamented with clean white railings; there is a flag gallantly flying from the jackstaff;[9] the furnace doors are open and the fires glaring bravely; the upper decks are black with passengers; the captain stands by the big bell, calm, imposing, the envy of all; great volumes of the blackest smoke are rolling and tumbling out of the chimneys—a husbanded grandeur created with a bit of pitch pine just before arriving at a town; the crew are grouped on the forecastle;[10] the broad stage is run far out over the port bow, and an envied deckhand stands picturesquely on the end of it with a coil of rope in his hand; the pent steam is screaming through the gauge cocks; the captain lifts his hand, a bell rings, the wheels stop; then they turn back, churning the water to foam, and the steamer is at rest. Then such a scramble as there is to get aboard, and to get ashore, and to take in freight and to discharge freight, all at one and the same time; and such a yelling and cursing as the mates facilitate it all with! Ten minutes later the steamer is under way again, with no flag on the jackstaff and no black smoke issuing from the chimneys. After ten more minutes the town is dead again, and the town drunkard asleep by the skids once more.

prodigious (prə dij´ əs) *adj.* of great power or size

❼ ▲ **Critical Viewing** This map shows the location of plantation lands on the banks of the Mississippi. Why might the river have been a desirable location for plantations, as well as for towns? **[Infer]**

---

7. **drayman** (drā´ mən) *n.* driver of a dray, a low cart with detachable sides.
8. **texas deck** deck adjoining the officers' cabins, the largest cabins on the ship.
9. **jackstaff** (jak´ staf) *n.* small staff at the bow of a ship for flying flags.
10. **forecastle** (fōk´ səl) *n.* front part of the upper deck.

566 ◆ *Division, Reconciliation, and Expansion (1850–1914)*

✦ ENRICHMENT: Literary Connection

Life on the Mississippi

Life on the Mississippi was published in 1883. Loved and admired second only to *Huckleberry Finn* (1884), the book grew out of a series of articles about Mississippi River piloting that Twain wrote for the *Atlantic Monthly* in 1875. The first half of the book tells how Twain became a pilot and relates his experiences learning about the river. The second half tells about the author's 1882 trip down the river and his visit to his home in Hannibal, Missouri.

Life on the Mississippi offers an outstanding depiction of the profession of steamboat piloting. The steamboat and the job of pilot are seen through the eyes of a boy who romanticizes and glamorizes whatever is foreign to his limited experience. At the same time, however, the reader gets a second point of view: the older narrator looks back on his boyhood, and gently mocks his own innocence.

My father was a justice of the peace, and I supposed he possessed the power of life and death over all men and could hang anybody that offended him. This was distinction enough for me as a general thing; but the desire to be a steamboatman kept intruding, nevertheless. I first wanted to be a cabin boy, so that I could come out with a white apron on and shake a tablecloth over the side, where all my old comrades could see me; later I thought I would rather be the deckhand who stood on the end of the stage plank with the coil of rope in his hand, because he was particularly conspicuous. But these were only daydreams—they were too heavenly to be contemplated as real possibilities. By and by one of our boys went away. He was not heard of for a long time. At last he turned up as apprentice engineer or striker on a steamboat. This thing shook the bottom out of all my Sunday-school teachings. That boy had been notoriously worldly, and I just the reverse; yet he was exalted to this <u>eminence</u>, and I left in obscurity and misery. There was nothing generous about this fellow in his greatness. He would always manage to have a rusty bolt to scrub while his boat tarried at our town, and he would sit on the inside guard and scrub it, where we could all see him and envy him and loathe him. And whenever his boat was laid up he would come home and swell around the town in his blackest and greasiest clothes, so that nobody could help remembering that he was a steamboatman; and he used all sorts of steamboat technicalities in his talk, as if he were so used to them that he forgot common people could not understand them. He would speak of the labboard[11] side of a horse in an easy, natural way that would make one wish he was dead. And he was always talking about "St. Looey" like an old citizen; he would refer casually to occasions when he "was coming down Fourth Street," or when he was "passing by the Planter's House," or when there was a fire and he took a turn on the brakes of "the old Big Missouri"; and then he would go on and lie about how many towns the size of ours were burned down there that day. Two or three of the boys had long been persons of consideration among us because they had been to St. Louis once and had a vague general knowledge of its wonders, but the day of their glory was over now. They lapsed into a humble silence, and learned to disappear when the ruthless cub engineer approached. This fellow had money, too, and hair oil. Also an ignorant silver watch and a showy brass watch chain. He wore a leather belt and used no suspenders. If ever a youth was cordially admired and hated by his comrades, this one was. No girl could withstand his charms. He cut out every boy in the village. When his boat blew up at last, it diffused a tranquil contentment among us such as we had not known for months. But when he came home the next week, alive, renowned, and appeared in church all battered up and bandaged, a shining hero, stared at and wondered over by everybody, it seemed to us that the partiality of Providence for an undeserving reptile had reached a point where it was open to criticism.

___

11. **labboard** (lab´ ərd) larboard, the left-hand side of a ship.

eminence (em´ i nəns) *n.* greatness; celebrity

Reading Strategy
Understanding Regional Dialect What does the apprentice engineer's use of riverboat jargon reveal about him?

✔**Reading Check** ❾
What activities and actions of the boy who worked on a steamship inspired envy?

from *Life on the Mississippi* ◆ 567

---

❽ **Reading Strategy**
Understanding Regional Dialect
- Read the passage aloud for students and urge them to note any examples of jargon or other terms that indicate a familiarity with the world of riverboats. If necessary, draw students' attention to terms such as *labboard, St. Looey, Fourth Street, Planter's House,* and *the old Big Missouri.*
- Ask students the Reading Strategy question on p. 567: What does the apprentice engineer's use of riverboat jargon reveal about him? Answer: Some students may say that the apprentice uses jargon to enhance the celebrity of his position before his envious former peers. Others might say that it reveals that he is little different from young Twain and his friends—they plan to do the same if they get the chance.

❾ ✔**Reading Check**
Answer: The boy inspires envy merely by scrubbing a rusty bolt, walking around town in his dirty work clothes, or by using riverboat jargon.

CUSTOMIZE INSTRUCTION FOR UNIVERSAL ACCESS

For Special Needs Students	For Advanced Readers
To extend these students' understanding of specialized vocabulary, use the Workplace Skills: Jargon page in ***Beyond Literature*** (p. 30). Encourage students to identify other pursuits that require the use of specialized terms, or jargon. Examples might include medicine, law, or their own science or social studies classes. Help students see that such terms help people communicate effectively about specialized topics.	Inform students that Twain actually did become a riverboat pilot. Suggest that they read and compare other excerpts from *Life on the Mississippi* with this one in order to learn more about that phase of the writer's life. Ask students to speculate about what Twain as a young pilot might have thought about his younger, envious self.

Review and Assess

1. Students' responses should be supported by details from the selection.

2. **(a)** All want to be steamboat men. **(b)** Twain's ambition to travel to different places as captain of a steamboat reflects the American desire for expansion and adventure.

3. **(a)** They hurry to greet the boat as it arrives, and watch the boat's operations with fascination. **(b)** Twain's description of the town suggests that it is a sleepy place where not much happens: the arrival of the steamboat causes great excitement.

4. **(a)** His boat blows up. **(b)** The other boys are at once resentful and envious of him.

5. **(a)** Most students will probably say that Twain's firsthand experience as a pilot was crucial to his writing so convincingly about riverboat life. **(b)** Possible response: Twain's love for the Mississippi River led him to describe the river, its towns, and its people eloquently. His love for the river also led him to use regional dialect that brings the people of the area vividly to life.

6. Students should support their responses with clear reasoning.

This creature's career could produce but one result, and it speedily followed. Boy after boy managed to get on the river. The minister's son became an engineer. The doctor's and the postmaster's sons became mud clerks; the wholesale liquor dealer's son became a barkeeper on a boat; four sons of the chief merchant, and two sons of the county judge, became pilots. Pilot was the grandest position of all. The pilot, even in those days of trivial wages, had a princely salary—from a hundred and fifty to two hundred and fifty dollars a month, and no board to pay. Two months of his wages would pay a preacher's salary for a year. Now some of us were left disconsolate. We could not get on the river—at least our parents would not let us.

So by and by I ran away. I said I never would come home again till I was a pilot and could come in glory. But somehow I could not manage it. I went meekly aboard a few of the boats that lay packed together like sardines at the long St. Louis wharf, and very humbly inquired for the pilots, but got only a cold shoulder and short words from mates and clerks. I had to make the best of this sort of treatment for the time being, but I had comforting daydreams of a future when I should be a great and honored pilot, with plenty of money, and could kill some of these mates and clerks and pay for them.

Review and Assess

Thinking About the Selection

1. **Respond:** Would working on a riverboat appeal to you? Explain why or why not.

2. **(a) Recall:** What is the one permanent ambition of the narrator and his boyhood friends? **(b) Connect:** How does this childhood ambition reflect the American spirit that gave rise to the settlement of new frontiers?

3. **(a) Recall:** How do the people of Hannibal respond to the arrival of the steamboat? **(b) Interpret:** What impression does Twain convey of this town by this response?

4. **(a) Recall:** What happens to the young apprentice engineer? **(b) Infer:** How would you describe the attitude of the other boys toward the apprentice engineer?

5. **(a) Hypothesize:** Do you think Twain could have written so well about riverboat life had he not become a pilot himself? Explain. **(b) Apply:** In what ways do you think Twain's love for the Mississippi River contributed to his success as a writer?

6. **Evaluate:** The last paragraph suggests that the narrator was driven by a desire for glory. Is a desire for glory a reasonable motivation in life? Explain.

✹ ENRICHMENT: Social Studies Connection

Steamboats

By the early nineteenth century, steamboats were regularly carrying cargo upstream on the Mississippi and Ohio rivers. The boats were essential to the economy of towns along these rivers, linking them to each other and to the rest of the world. Until the 1850s, when railroad development grew rapidly in the West, steamboats carried more freight than trains did.

Have students do research to find out about life on the great riverboats. Among other things, they can research routes, available jobs, and on-board entertainment. Have them look into how large the boats were, how fast they traveled, and what cargo they carried. Students can also learn about tours and trips, such as Civil War excursions, that can be enjoyed today in modern riverboats.

The Notorious Jumping Frog of Calaveras County

Mark Twain

Mark Twain (Samuel L. Clemens) Riding the Celebrated Jumping Frog—an English caricature, 1872, Frederic Waddy

In compliance with the request of a friend of mine, who wrote me from the East, I called on good-natured, <u>garrulous</u> old Simon Wheeler, and inquired after my friend's friend, Leonidas W. Smiley, as requested to do, and I hereunto append the result. I have a lurking suspicion that *Leonidas W.* Smiley is a myth; that my friend never knew such a personage: and that he only <u>conjectured</u> that if I asked old Wheeler about him, it would remind him of his infamous *Jim* Smiley, and he would go to work and bore me to death with some exasperating reminiscence of him as long and as tedious as it should be useless to me. If that was the design, it succeeded.

I found Simon Wheeler dozing comfortably by the barroom stove of the dilapidated tavern in the decayed mining camp of Angel's, and I noticed that he was fat and baldheaded, and had an expression of winning gentleness and simplicity upon his tranquil countenance. He roused up, and gave me good day. I told him a friend of mine had commissioned me to make some inquiries about a cherished companion of his boyhood named *Leonidas W.* Smiley—*Rev. Leonidas W.* Smiley, a young minister of the Gospel, who he had heard was at one time a resident of Angel's Camp. I added that if Mr. Wheeler could tell me anything about this Rev. Leonidas W. Smiley, I would feel under many obligations to him.

Simon Wheeler backed me into a corner and blockaded me there with his chair, and then sat down and reeled off the <u>monotonous</u> narrative which follows this paragraph. He never smiled, he never frowned, he never changed his voice from the gentle-flowing key to which he tuned his initial sentence, he never betrayed the slightest suspicion of enthusiasm; but all through the <u>interminable</u> narrative there ran a vein of impressive earnestness and sincerity, which showed me plainly that, so far from his imagining that there was anything ridiculous or funny about his story, he regarded it as a really

The Notorious Jumping Frog of Calaveras County ◆ 569

▲ Critical Viewing

Would Twain have been amused or offended by this caricature of himself? Explain. **[Make a Judgment]**

garrulous (gar´ ə ləs) *adj.* talking too much

conjectured (kən jek´ chərd) *v.* guessed

monotonous (mə nät´ ən əs) *adj.* tiresome because unvarying

interminable (in tur´ mi nə bəl) *adj.* seeming to last forever

✔ Reading Check

What does the narrator suspect about Leonidas W. Smiley?

---

❿ About the Selection

According to one of Mark Twain's biographers, Twain first heard the story that was the inspiration for this one while in the bar of a rundown tavern in Angel's Camp, California. Like the storyteller in that bar, Twain's narrator, Simon Wheeler, spins a funny, improbable yarn about the exploits of a betting man.

⓫ Background

Art

Mark Twain Riding the Celebrated Jumping Frog, [1872] by Frederick Waddy

A caricature is a drawing made to satirize or poke fun at someone by exaggerating certain features so that the person looks ridiculous, yet recognizable. Waddy was an English caricaturist, whose drawings were reproduced as wood engravings in the *Illustrated London News.*

Use this question for discussion:

- At what aspects of Twain does Waddy poke fun in this drawing? Possible response: Students may say that the artist lampoons the idea that Twain's fame could ride on something as silly as a jumping frog.

⓬ ▶ Critical Viewing

Answer: Students may say that Twain, as a writer who knew the effectiveness of exaggeration, would have enjoyed the humor in this caricature— particularly the deadpan expression on his face.

⓭ Vocabulary Development

The Greek Prefix *mono-*

- Explain that one of the meanings of the prefix *mono-* is "single." Invite students to look for context clues (such as *reeled off* and *never changed his voice*) that will help them determine the meaning of *monotonous.*

- Have students brainstorm a list of other English words containing *mono-.* Answer: Students might mention words such as *monogamy, monopoly,* or *monorail.*

⓮ ✔ Reading Check

Answer: The narrator suspects that he does not exist.

CUSTOMIZE INSTRUCTION FOR UNIVERSAL ACCESS

For Less Proficient Readers

Help students understand the premise of the story as set forth in the opening paragraph. Point out that Twain knows that he might be the target of his friend's prank. As needed, have students refer back to this opening passage when they have finished reading the story. As they read, have students locate moments in the story when the reader is given clues that indicate that Simon Wheeler's garrulousness is intended to make the reader laugh and appreciate the narrator's plight all the more. Such moments include the extended description of Smiley's mare, or the careful pause in which Wheeler makes sure the narrator knows the bull pup's name—Andrew Jackson—even though the information is completely irrelevant. Have students record these junctures in a chart.

569

Understanding Regional Dialect

- Invite a student volunteer to read aloud the first several sentences of Wheeler's narrative. Then have students go back and read the same sentences silently once more.

- Ask students the Reading Strategy question on p. 570: What examples of dialect can you find as Wheeler's tale begins?
  Answer: Examples include *feller, by the name of, recollect, warn't, when he first come, curiousest, you ever see, he'd,* and *so's.*

16 Literary Analysis

Humor

- Review with students some of the techniques writers use to create humor, such as exaggerating and embellishing incidents and personal characteristics.

- Then, read aloud the last paragraph on p. 570 as students listen for examples of Twain's use of these techniques.

- Ask students the Literary Analysis question on p. 570: What is humorous about this description of the mare?
  Answer: Students might mention the nickname "the fifteen-minute nag," the idea of betting on such a slow horse, or the host of medical conditions from which the mare is said to suffer.

---

important matter, and admired its two heroes as men of transcendent genius in *finesse.* I let him go on in his own way, and never interrupted him once.

"Rev. Leonidas W. H'm, Reverend Le—well, there was a feller here once by the name of *Jim* Smiley, in the winter of '49—or maybe it was the spring of '50—I don't recollect exactly, somehow, though what makes me think it was one or the other is because I remember the big flume[1] warn't finished when he first come to the camp; but anyway, he was the curiousest man about always betting on anything that turned up you ever see, if he could get anybody to bet on the other side; and if he couldn't he'd change sides. Any way that suited the other man would suit *him*—any way just so's he got a bet, *he* was satisfied. But still he was lucky, uncommon lucky; he most always come out winner. He was always ready and laying for a chance; there couldn't be no solit'ry thing mentioned but that feller'd offer to bet on it, and take ary side you please, as I was just telling you. If there was a horse race, you'd find him flush or you'd find him busted at the end of it; if there was a dogfight, he'd bet on it; if there was a cat fight, he'd bet on it; if there was a chicken fight, he'd bet on it; why, if there was two birds setting on a fence, he would bet you which one would fly first; or if there was a camp meeting,[2] he would be there reg'lar to bet on Parson Walker, which he judged to be the best exhorter about here and so he was too, and a good man. If he even see a straddle bug[3] start to go anywheres, he would bet you how long it would take him to get to—to wherever he was going to, and if you took him up, he would foller that straddle bug to Mexico but what he would find out where he was bound for and how long he was on the road. Lots of the boys here has seen that Smiley, and can tell you about him. Why, it never made no difference to *him*—he'd bet on *any* thing—the dangdest feller. Parson Walker's wife laid very sick once, for a good while, and it seemed as if they warn't going to save her; but one morning he come in, and Smiley up and asked him how she was, and he said she was considable better—thank the Lord for his inf'nite mercy—and coming on so smart that with the blessing of Prov'dence she'd get well yet; and Smiley, before he thought, says, 'Well, I'll resk two-and-a-half she don't anyway.'

Thish-yer Smiley had a mare—the boys called her the fifteen-minute nag, but that was only in fun, you know, because of course she was faster than that—and he used to win money on that horse, for all she was so slow and always had the asthma, or the distemper, or the consumption, or something of that kind. They used to give her two or three hundred yards start, and then pass her under way; but always at the fag end[4] of the race she'd get excited and desperate like,

---

1. **flume** (floom) *n.* artificial channel for carrying water to provide power and transport objects.
2. **camp meeting** religious gathering at the mining camp.
3. **straddle bug** insect with long legs.
4. **fag end** last part.

Reading Stategy
Understanding Regional Dialect What examples of dialect do you notice as Wheeler's tale begins?

Literary Analysis
Humor What is humorous about this description of the mare?

✹ ENRICHMENT: Community Connection

Calaveras County

Inform students that Calaveras County is a real place located in central California, southeast of Sacramento and northeast of Modesto. It borders Tuolomne County to the east, home of Yosemite National Park. Every spring, on the Calaveras Fairgrounds in Angel's Camp, California, there is a fair and a re-enactment of Twain's celebrated contest. The contest annually attracts people from all over the world who bring more than 3,000 frogs.

Invite students to find out more about the history of—and records associated with—this "Olympics" of frog jumping. Students can find out how to enter the contest and what kind of jump it would take to win. They can get information by writing to the 39th District Agricultural Association, Box 489, S. Highway 49, Angels Camp, CA 95222, or by visiting the Internet website www.visitcalaveras.org.

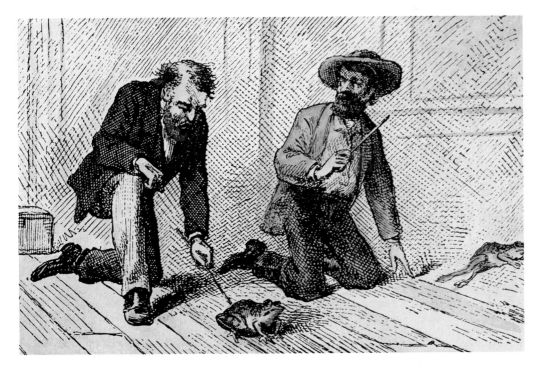

and come cavorting and straddling up, and scattering her legs around limber, sometimes in the air, and sometimes out to one side among the fences, and kicking up m-o-r-e dust and raising m-o-r-e racket with her coughing and sneezing and blowing her nose—and *always* fetch up at the stand just about a neck ahead, as near as you could cipher it down.

18 And he had a little small bull-pup, that to look at him you'd think he warn't worth a cent but to set around and look <u>ornery</u> and lay for a chance to steal something. But as soon as money was up on him he was a different dog; his under-jaw'd begin to stick out like the fo' castle[5] of a steamboat, and his teeth would uncover and shine like the furnaces. And a dog might tackle him and bullyrag him, and bite him, and throw him over his shoulder two or three times, and Andrew Jackson—which was the name of the pup—Andrew Jackson would never let on but what *he* was satisfied, and hadn't expected nothing else—and the bets being doubled and doubled on the other side all the time, till the money was all up; and then all of a sudden he would grab that other dog jest by the j'int of his hind leg and freeze to it—not chaw, you understand, but only just grip and hang on till they throwed up the sponge, if it was a year. Smiley always come out winner on that pup, till

---

5. **fo'castle** (fōk′ səl) *n.* forecastle; the forward part of the upper deck.

17 ▲ **Critical Viewing**
Which moment of the story is depicted in this illustration? **[Connect]**

Reading Strategy
Understanding Regional Dialect How would you rephrase the sentence beginning "And he had . . . " in Standard English?

ornery (ôr′ nər ē) *adj.* having a mean disposition

19 ☑ **Reading Check**
What was most unusual about Smiley and his betting habits?

The Notorious Jumping Frog of Calaveras County ◆ 571

17 ▶ **Critical Viewing**
Answer: Students may say that the illustration shows the defeat of Dan'l by the stranger's frog.

18 ⓑ **Reading Strategy**
Understanding Regional Dialect
• Have two or three student volunteers read this sentence aloud slowly for their classmates. Point out potentially challenging examples of dialect, such as *warn't* ("wasn't").
• Ask students the Reading Strategy question on p. 571: How would you rephrase the sentence beginning "And he had . . ." in Standard English?
Answer: Smiley's bulldog puppy looked as though it did nothing but look bad-tempered and try to sneak food.

19 ☑ **Reading Check**
Possible response: He would wager on anything, but often won unlikely bets, such as the ones on the mare and the dog named Andrew Jackson.

CUSTOMIZE INSTRUCTION FOR UNIVERSAL ACCESS

For Less Proficient Readers

Humor can be the driving force of a story. It can also be subtle and coy, teasing the reader just enough to lighten the mood of the story or to break up a long narrative paragraph. Either way, humor provides added enjoyment when reading. Help students recognize the humorous elements in Twain's writing, from his creation of unique characters to his deadpan delivery of absurd statements. Reading to be entertained is a valid purpose for reading, and many books are written primarily for entertainment.

Encourage students to read to be entertained, looking for the humorous elements in Twain's writing. Suggest that students try their hands at writing or telling their own "shaggydog" stories. Do they know of any comical events that would lend themselves to such humorous exaggeration?

• Invite a student volunteer to read the passage aloud as other students jot down Twain's humorous embellishments.

• Ask students the Literary Analysis question on p. 572: What embellishments in this passage make the description humorous? **Answer:** Students might mention details such as *nothing for three months, give him a little punch behind, whirling in the air like a doughnut, turn one summerset, come down flatfooted, nail a fly,* and *all a frog wanted was education.*

he harnessed a dog once that didn't have no hind legs, because they'd been sawed off in a circular saw, and when the thing had gone along far enough, and the money was all up, and he come to make a snatch for his pet holt,[6] he see in a minute how he'd been imposed on, and how the other dog had him in the door, so to speak, and he 'peared surprised, and then he looked sorter discouraged-like, and didn't try no more to win the fight, and so he got shucked out bad. He give Smiley a look, as much as to say his heart was broke, and it was his fault, for putting up a dog that hadn't no hind legs for him to take holt of, which was his main dependence in a fight, and then he limped off a piece and laid down and died. It was a good pup, was that Andrew Jackson, and would have made a name for hisself if he'd lived, for the stuff was in him and he had genius—I know it, because he hadn't no opportunities to speak of, and it don't stand to reason that a dog could make such a fight as he could under them circumstances if he hadn't no talent. It always makes me feel sorry when I think of that last fight of his'n, and the way it turned out.

Well, thish-yer Smiley had rat terriers,[7] and chicken cocks,[8] and tomcats and all them kind of things, till you couldn't rest, and you couldn't fetch nothing for him to bet on but he'd match you. He ketched a frog one day, and took him home, and said he cal'lated to educate him; and so he never done nothing for three months but set in his back yard and learn that frog to jump. And you bet you he *did* learn him, too. He'd give him a little punch behind, and the next minute you'd see that frog whirling in the air like a doughnut—see him turn one summerset, or maybe a couple, if he got a good start, and come down flatfooted and all right, like a cat. He got him up so in the matter of ketching flies, and kep' him in practice so constant, that he'd nail a fly every time as fur as he could see him. Smiley said all a frog wanted was education, and he could do 'most anything—and I believe him. Why, I've seen him set Dan'l Webster down here on this floor—Dan'l Webster was the name of the frog—and sing out, "Flies, Dan'l, flies!" and quicker'n you could wink he'd spring straight up and snake a fly off'n the counter there, and flop down on the floor ag'in as solid as a gob of mud, and fall to scratching the side of his head with his hind foot as indifferent as if he hadn't no idea he'd been doin' any more'n any frog might do. You never see a frog so modest and straightfor'ard as he was, for all he was so gifted. And when it come to fair and square jumping on a dead level, he could get over more ground at one straddle than any animal of his breed you ever see. Jumping on a dead level was his strong suit, you understand; and when it come to that, Smiley would ante up money on him as long as he had a red.[9] Smiley was monstrous proud of his frog, and well he

---

6. **holt** hold.
7. **rat terriers** dogs skilled in catching rats.
8. **chicken cocks** roosters trained to fight.
9. **a red** red cent; colloquial expression for "any money at all."

Literary Analysis

Humor What embellishments in this passage make the description humorous?

CUSTOMIZE INSTRUCTION FOR UNIVERSAL ACCESS

For Advanced Readers

Suggest that students read additional works by Mark Twain. Provide students with the titles listed in the enrichment box, ATE p. 575. You may also wish to use **Authors In Depth, The American Experience,** which contains the following selections:

• "Perplexing Lessons" from *Life on the Mississippi* (nonfiction p. 91)

• "An Encounter With an Interviewer" (fiction, p. 97)

• "A General Reply" (nonfiction, p. 101)

• "The Boss" and "The Yankee Fights With the Knights" from *A Connecticut Yankee in King Arthur's Court*

After students have read these or other works by Twain, have them form discussion groups in which they compare and contrast the selections they have read. Suggest criteria for comparison, such as author's perspective or implied readership. To extend the activity, have volunteers present brief reports on Twain's status as a celebrity during his lifetime.

might be, for fellers that had traveled and been everywheres all said he laid over any frog that ever *they* see.

Well, Smiley kep' the beast in a little lattice box, and he used to fetch him downtown sometimes and lay for a bet. One day a feller—a stranger in the camp, he was—come acrost him with his box, and says:

'What might it be that you've got in the box?'

And Smiley says, sorter indifferent-like, 'It might be a parrot, or it might be a canary, maybe, but it ain't—it's only just a frog.'

And the feller took it, and looked at it careful, and turned it round this way and that, and says, 'H'm—so 'tis. Well, what's *he* good for?'

'Well,' Smiley says, easy and careless, 'he's good enough for *one* thing, I should judge—he can outjump any frog in Calaveras county.'

The feller took the box again, and took another long, particular look, and give it back to Smiley, and says, very deliberate, 'Well,' he says, 'I don't see no p'ints about that frog that's any better'n any other frog.'

'Maybe you don't,' Smiley says. 'Maybe you understand frogs and maybe you don't understand 'em; maybe you've had experience, and maybe you ain't only a amature, as it were. Anyways, I've got *my* opinion, and I'll resk forty dollars that he can outjump any frog in Calaveras county.'

And the feller studied a minute, and then says, kinder sad like, 'Well, I'm only a stranger here, and I ain't got no frog; but if I had a frog, I'd bet you.'

And then Smiley says, 'That's all right—that's all right—if you'll hold my box a minute, I'll go and get you a frog.' And so the feller took the box, and put up his forty dollars along with Smiley's, and set down to wait.

So he set there a good while thinking and thinking to hisself, and then he got the frog out and prized his mouth open and took a teaspoon and filled him full of quailshot[10]—filled him pretty near up to his chin—and set him on the floor. Smiley he went to the swamp and slopped around in the mud for a long time, and finally he ketched a frog, and fetched him in, and give him to this feller, and says:

'Now, if you're ready, set him alongside of Dan'l, with his forepaws just even with Dan'l's, and I'll give the word.' Then he says, 'One—two—three—*git!*' and him and the feller touched up the frogs from behind, and the new frog hopped off lively, but Dan'l give a heave, and hysted up his shoulders—so—like a Frenchman, but it warn't no use—he couldn't budge; he was planted as solid as a church, and he couldn't no more stir than if he was anchored out. Smiley was a good deal surprised, and he was disgusted too, but he didn't have no idea what the matter was, of course.

The feller took the money and started away; and when he was going out at the door, he sorter jerked his thumb over his shoulder—so—at Dan'l, and says again, very deliberate, 'Well,' he says, 'I don't see no p'ints about that frog that's any better'n any other frog.'

---

10. **quailshot** small lead pellets used for shooting quail.

Literary Analysis

Humor How does the use of dialect add to the humor of this passage?

Reading Check ㉒

What bet does Smiley make concerning Dan'l Webster?

The Notorious Jumping Frog of Calaveras County ◆ 573

㉑ Literary Analysis

Humor

- As you read this passage aloud, have students identify examples of Twain's use of dialect. If students need help focusing on the dialect, point out examples such as *git*, *hopped off lively*, *give a heave*, *hysted up his shoulders*, *warn't no use*, or *couldn't no more stir*.

- Ask students the Literary Analysis question on p. 573: How does the use of dialect add to the humor of this passage?
  Answer: It both grounds the characters—the stranger, the frog, and especially Smiley—in time and place, as well as exaggerating certain aspects of their personalities or behaviors.

㉒ ✔Reading Check

Answer: He bets a stranger that the frog, Dan'l Webster, can out-jump any other frog in Calaveras County.

CUSTOMIZE INSTRUCTION FOR UNIVERSAL ACCESS

For Special Needs Students	For Gifted/Talented Students
Have students recall favorite funny stories, involving exaggeration and embellishment, that are retold by family members. Invite these students to explain the accounts and to compare and contrast their knowledge of what actually happened with how it is rendered in those amusing tales.	Explain to students that forty dollars was a great deal of money—perhaps equal to a month's wages—at the time of this story. Have these students do research to learn what basic necessities cost in 1865, as well as how much people were paid for various jobs, in this country around the middle of the nineteenth century.

Answers for p. 574

Review and Assess

1. You may wish to have students listen to Hal Holbrook's *Mark Twain Tonight* to appreciate the kind of verbal humor that was characteristic of Twain.

2. (a) The narrator's friend suggests that he ask about a friend with the same last name. **(b)** The narrator now suspects that his friend knew that Wheeler would tell the story of Jim Smiley.

3. (a) He would bet on anything and everything. **(b)** Sample response: He is a comic, exaggerated character.

4. (a) He was proud because he had taught the frog to be a champion jumper. **(b)** Students may say that it is important because he expects the frog to earn him a lot of money.

5. (a) Suggested response: The story does succeed in conveying the character of Simon Wheeler. Twain's depiction of Wheeler's mannerisms and dialect gives us a portrait of Wheeler as a garrulous bore greatly given to hyperbole. **(b)** Twain probably chose to have Wheeler (instead of the narrator) tell the tale because it allowed him to relate the story in regional dialect, thereby making it more humorous.

6. The tale suggests that entertainment was hard to come by and people were often eccentric on the frontier.

Smiley he stood scratching his head and looking down at Dan'l a long time, and at last he says, 'I do wonder what in the nation that frog throw'd off for—I wonder if there ain't something the matter with him—he 'pears to look mighty baggy, somehow.' And he ketched Dan'l by the nap of the neck, and hefted him, and says, 'Why blame my cats if he don't weigh five pound!' and turned him upside down and he belched out a double handful of shot. And then he see how it was, and he was the maddest man—he set the frog down and took out after that feller, but he never ketched him. And—"

Here Simon Wheeler heard his name called from the front yard, and got up to see what was wanted. And turning to me as he moved away, he said: "Just set where you are, stranger, and rest easy—I ain't going to be gone a second."

But, by your leave, I did not think that a continuation of the history of the enterprising vagabond *Jim* Smiley would be likely to afford me much information concerning the Rev. *Leonidas W.* Smiley, and so I started away.

At the door I met the sociable Wheeler returning, and he button-holed me and recommenced:

"Well, thish-yer Smiley had a yaller one-eyed cow that didn't have no tail, only just a short stump like a bannanner, and—"

However, lacking both time and inclination, I did not wait to hear about the afflicted cow, but took my leave.

Review and Assess

Thinking About the Selection

1. **Respond:** If Mark Twain were a stand-up comic today, would you want to see him perform? Explain why or why not.

2. **(a) Recall:** What prompts Simon Wheeler to tell the story of Jim Smiley? **(b) Infer:** Why had the narrator's friend suggested that he ask Wheeler about Leonidas Smiley?

3. **(a) Recall:** What was Jim Smiley's response to any event? **(b) Infer:** Based on this behavior, what can you infer about his character?

4. **(a) Recall:** Why was Smiley so proud of his frog? **(b) Draw Conclusions:** Why is the frog important to Smiley?

5. **(a) Evaluate:** Does this story convey the character of Simon Wheeler as effectively as it does the character of Jim Smiley, the subject of the tale? **(b) Hypothesize:** Why might Twain have chosen to develop the story this way?

6. **Apply:** Telling tall tales like this one was a common form of entertainment on the western frontier. What does such a tale suggest about the characters of the developing West?

✎ ASSESSMENT PRACTICE: Reading Comprehension

Context   **(For more practice, see Test Preparation Workbook, p. 32.)**

Many tests require students to use contextual analysis to determine the meaning of figurative expressions. Use the following sample test item to demonstrate.

I went meekly aboard a few of the boats that lay <u>packed together like sardines</u> at the long St. Louis wharf, and very humbly inquired for the pilots, but got only a cold shoulder and short words from mates and clerks.

In this passage, the expression <u>packed together</u> like sardines means—

A The boats were docked close together.

B The boats had been fishing for sardines.

C The boats were made of metal like tins for sardines.

D The boats were packed with passengers.

A is the correct answer.

Review and Assess

Literary Analysis

Humor

1. In "The Boys' Ambition," what does Twain's use of the word "heavenly" to describe ordinary steamboat activities, such as shaking out a tablecloth or holding a rope, add to the **humor** of his narrative?

2. Find two examples of exaggeration in "The Notorious Jumping Frog of Calaveras County," and explain why each is amusing.

3. (a) How does the use of **dialect** in "The Notorious Jumping Frog" add to the story's humor? (b) Why would the story be less effective if Wheeler spoke in Standard English?

Comparing Literary Works

4. (a) What is Twain's main purpose in "The Boys' Ambition"? (b) In what ways does humor help him achieve this purpose?

5. (a) What is Twain's main purpose in telling the story of the notorious jumping frog? (b) How does humor help him achieve this purpose?

6. In which selection does Twain seem to view the characters with more respect? Explain your choice.

Reading Strategy

Understanding Regional Dialect

7. Interpret the following passage in your own words:

   . . . he 'peared surprised, and then he looked sorter discouraged-like, and didn't try no more to win the fight, and so he got shucked out bad.

8. Interpret the given examples of dialect in Standard English by completing a chart like the one shown.

Regional Dialect	St. Looey	chaw	yaller	bannanner	thish-yer
Standard English					

Extend Understanding

9. **Career Connection:** Why do you think young people dream of romantic or adventurous careers, like Twain's riverboat pilot or its modern equivalent, the astronaut?

The Boys' Ambition from Life on the Mississippi / The Notorious Jumping Frog of Calaveras County ◆ 575

Quick Review

Humor is writing meant to evoke laughter.

To **understand regional dialect**, sound out words so that you may recognize their Standard English counterparts.

 Take It to the Net
www.phschool.com
Take the interactive self-test online to check your understanding of these selections.

Answers for p. 575

Review and Assess

1. Twain's description adds humor by showing through contrast how foolish some of his childhood ambitions were.

2. One example of exaggeration is the frog whirling in the air, doing one or two somersaults, and landing like a cat. Another example is the frog leaping upward on command to catch flies. Each example is amusing because it attributes abilities to the frog like those of dogs or cats.

3. (a) The use of dialect underscores the exaggerated qualities Twain gives to characters and situations. (b) The story would be less effective because the dialect adds humor, particularly to those moments when Wheeler is trying to be serious and straightforward.

4. (a) His main purpose is to portray life in a small river town—with special attention to the hopes and dreams of young males there. (b) Humor helps Twain avoid sentimentality as he shows the sleepy town and the eager, impressionable boys.

5. (a) His main purpose is to entertain the reader. (b) Humor makes the story immediately entertaining.

6. Students may say that Twain views the characters with more respect in "The Boys' Ambition," since that story involves people involved in honest, interesting work, such as piloting riverboats, whereas the latter story involves primarily loafers and rascals.

7. He appeared surprised and discouraged. He gave up the fight and was badly fooled.

8. *St Louis; chew; yellow; banana; this here*

9. Students should support their responses with clear reasoning.

ENRICHMENT: Further Reading

Other Works by Mark Twain

The Adventures of Tom Sawyer

The Adventures of Huckleberry Finn

A Connecticut Yankee in King Arthur's Court

The Innocents Abroad

The Mysterious Stranger

Roughing It

Pudd'nhead Wilson

The Man That Corrupted Hadleyburg

 Take It to the Net
Visit www.phschool.com for more information on Mark Twain.

❶ Vocabulary Development

Word Analysis

1. monotheism = belief in one god
2. monologue = speech given by one person
3. monolith = a single giant stone
4. monochrome = something of one color

Spelling Strategy

a. hard
b. soft
c. hard

Concept Development:

1. d
2. b
3. g
4. c
5. f
6. a
7. h
8. e

❷ Grammar and Style

Practice

1. Why, it <u>never made any</u> difference to him. . . .
2. . . . you <u>couldn't fetch anything</u> for him to bet on but he'd match you.
3. . . . maybe you've had experience and maybe <u>you are only</u> an amateur.
4. . . . it <u>wasn't any use</u>—he couldn't budge.
5. a yellow, one-eyed cow that had no tail . . .

Looking at Style

Wheeler's use of double negatives shows him to be a rugged frontiersman, and it adds to the humor by adding extra flair to the story.

Integrate Language Skills

❶ Vocabulary Development Lesson

Word Analysis: Greek Prefix *mono-*

The Greek prefix *mono-* means "alone," "one," or "single." A monotonous storyteller uses a single tone, without varying voice quality or pace.

Use your understanding of the prefix *mono-* and the definition of the roots given below to tell the meaning of the new word formed by adding the prefix *mono-*.

1. *theism* = belief in god
2. *logue* = speaking
3. *lith* = stone
4. *chrome* = color

Spelling Strategy

The vowels *a*, *o*, and *u* after the letter *g* indicate the "hard" sound of *g*, as in *garrulous*, *gob*, and *guide*. The vowels *i* and *e* after *g* often indicate the "soft" *g* sound, as in *prodigious* and *generous*. Identify whether the *g* sound in each of these words is hard or soft:

1. vagabond   2. managed   3. obligation

Concept Development: Antonyms

Antonyms are words with opposite meanings. Review the words in the vocabulary list on page 563. Then, select the letter of the word in the right column that is the best antonym for each vocabulary word in the left column.

1. transient   a. varied
2. prodigious   b. meager
3. eminence   c. quiet
4. garrulous   d. permanent
5. conjectured   e. kind
6. monotonous   f. verified
7. interminable   g. obscurity
8. ornery   h. brief

❷ Grammar and Style Lesson

Double Negatives

Double negatives are created by using two negative words in a sentence where only one is needed. In effect, two negatives cancel each other out, thereby changing the intended meaning of a sentence. Double negatives are not accepted in Standard English, but they do appear in some regional dialects. Here, Simon Wheeler speaks with a double negative:

> **Examples:** ". . . he hadn't *no* opportunities to speak of . . ."
> "there couldn't be *no* solit'ry thing mentioned but that feller'd offer to bet on it . . ."

Practice Rewrite the following sentences from the story, revising them to eliminate double negatives.

1. Why, it never made no difference to him. . . .
2. . . . you couldn't fetch nothing for him to bet on but he'd match you.
3. . . . maybe you've had experience and maybe you ain't only a amature.
4. . . . it warn't no use—he couldn't budge.
5. . . . a yaller one-eyed cow that didn't have no tail . . .

Looking at Style Explain how Simon Wheeler's frequent use of double negatives fits his character and contributes to the story's humor.

WG Prentice Hall Writing and Grammar Connection: Chapter 25, Section 1

TEACHING RESOURCES

The following resources can be used to enrich or extend the instruction for pp. 576–577.

Vocabulary
- 📖 **Selection Support:** Build Vocabulary, 134
- 📖 **Vocabulary and Spelling Practice Book** (Use this booklet for skills enrichment.)

Grammar
- 📖 **Selection Support Workbook:** Grammar and Style, p. 135 ■
- *WG* **Writing and Grammar,** Ruby Level, p. 642

- 📖 **Daily Language Practice Transparencies**

Writing
- *WG* **Writing and Grammar,** Ruby Level, p. 309 ■
- 📖 **Extension Activities**
- 📖 **Writing Models and Graphic Organizers on Transparencies,** pp. 37–40
- 💿 **Writing and Grammar iText CD-ROM**

■ **BLOCK SCHEDULING:** Resources marked with this symbol provide varied instruction during 90-minute blocks.

Writing Lesson

Analytic Essay

Mark Twain wrote, "The humorous story may be spun out to great length, and may wander around as much as it pleases, and arrive nowhere in particular . . . [It] is told gravely; the teller does his best to conceal the fact that he even dimly suspects there is anything funny about it." Write an essay discussing Twain's use of these techniques in "Jumping Frog."

Prewriting Select several humorous passages to assess according to the main ideas in Twain's comment. Create a chart like the one shown to organize your thoughts.

Model: Organizing to Show Comparison

spins out at length	arrives nowhere	is told gravely	conceals humor

Drafting Organize your essay point by point, connecting Twain's comment to passages from the story. Make sure you clearly explain the connection in each case.

Revising Review your essay to find places where you could elaborate by providing examples, details, or quotations to support your ideas. Return to your notes or to the story to find needed support.

WG Prentice Hall Writing and Grammar Connection: Chapter 14, Section 3

Extension Activities

Listening and Speaking In "The Boy's Ambition," Twain wrote about one of his career dreams. Prepare a list of questions about a career that interests you. Then, conduct an **interview** with someone in that field. Be sure to include the following questions:

- Why did you choose this career?
- How did you prepare for it?
- What are its responsibilities and rewards?
- What advice would you give about this career?

Share your findings with the class.

Research and Technology With a group, create a **multimedia report** on Mississippi riverboats. Draw information from a variety of sources, such as audio and video clips, newspapers, magazines, CD-ROMs, and the Internet to convey the sights and sounds of nineteenth-century riverboat life. [Group Activity]

 Take It to the Net www.phschool.com

Go online for an additional research activity using the Internet.

The Boys' Ambition from Life on the Mississippi / The Notorious Jumping Frog of Calaveras County ◆ 577

ASSESSMENT RESOURCES

The following resources can be used to assess students' knowledge and skills.

Selection Assessment

- 📖 **Formal Assessment**, pp. 146–148
- 📖 **Open Book Test**, pp. 88–90
- 📼 **Got It! Assessment Videotapes**, Tape 4
- 💿 **Test Bank Software**

🖥️ **Take It to the Net**
Visit www.phschool.com for self-tests and additional questions on the selections.

Writing Rubric

- 📖 **Performance Assess. and Portfolio Mgmt.**, p. 23

PRENTICE HALL **ASSESSMENT SYSTEM**

- 📖 **Workbook**
- 📖 **Skill Book**
- 📁 **Transparencies**
- 💿 **CD-ROM**

---

❸ Writing Lesson

- You might suggest that students begin by writing down their impressions of Twain's humor in the story after a single reading. Then have students reread the story at least once, taking notes about Twain's humor and his use of the techniques mentioned in his quoted comment.

- Remind students to consider why Twain frames the comic tale involving Jim Smiley with brief scenes between an unnamed narrator and Simon Wheeler.

- Use the Writing Lesson, as well as Writing Process Model 7, pp. 37–40, in **Writing Models and Graphic Organizers on Transparencies**, to guide students in developing their analytic essays.

- Use the Response to Literature rubric in **Performance Assessment and Portfolio Management**, p. 23, to evaluate students' essays.

❹ Research and Technology

- Group members might divide research tasks according to types of sources. One person might be responsible for researching printed reference and history books, another for newspaper and periodicals, a third for Internet sites, and a fourth for CD-ROMs, for instance.

- Students might consider including a map of the Mississippi River as a part of their report. The river could be annotated and illustrated to show the various features and "faces" mentioned by Twain.

CUSTOMIZE INSTRUCTION
For Universal Access

To address different learning styles, use the following activities suggested in the **Extension Activities** booklet, p. 30.

For Visual/Spatial Learners, use Activity 5.

For Verbal/Linguistic Learners, use Activity 6.

For Musical/Rhythmic Learners, use Activity 7.

The Outcasts of Poker Flat

Lesson Objectives

1. **To analyze and respond to literary elements**
   - Literary Analysis: Regionalism
   - Connecting Literary Elements: Local Color

2. **To read, comprehend, analyze, and critique a short story**
   - Reading Strategy: Questioning the Text
   - Reading Check Questions
   - Review and Assess Questions
   - Assessment Practice (ATE)

3. **To develop word analysis skills, fluency, and systematic vocabulary**
   - Vocabulary Development Lesson: Latin Word Part: *-bel-*

4. **To understand and apply written and oral language conventions**
   - Spelling Strategy
   - Grammar and Style Lesson: Coordinating Conjunctions in Compound Sentences

5. **To understand and apply appropriate writing and research strategies**
   - Writing Lesson: Critical Review
   - Extension Activity: Mining Report

6. **To understand and apply listening and speaking strategies**
   - Extension Activity: Eulogy

STEP-BY-STEP TEACHING GUIDE	PACING GUIDE
PRETEACH	
Motivate Students and Provide Background	
Use the Motivation activity (ATE p. 578)	5 min.
Read and discuss More About the Author and Background features (SE/ATE p. 578) **A**	5 min.
Introduce the Concepts	
Introduce the Literary Analysis and Reading Strategy (SE/ATE p. 579) **A**	15 min.
Pronounce the vocabulary words and read their definitions (SE p. 579)	5 min.
TEACH	
Monitor Comprehension	
Informally monitor comprehension by circulating while students read independently or in groups **A**	35 min.
Monitor students' comprehension with the Reading Check notes (SE/ATE pp. 581, 583, 585, 587, 589)	as students read
Develop vocabulary with Vocabulary notes (SE pp. 582, 583, 587, 588; ATE p. 583)	as students read
Develop Understanding	
Develop students' understanding of regionalism with the Literary Analysis annotations (SE pp. 581, 587; ATE pp. 581, 582, 587) **A**	5 min.
Develop students' ability to question the text with the Reading Strategy annotations (SE pp. 585, 589; ATE pp. 585, 588, 589)	5 min.
ASSESS	
Assess Mastery	
Assess students' mastery of the Reading Strategy and Literary Analysis by having them answer the Review and Assess questions (SE/ATE p. 591)	15 min.
Use one or more of the print and media Assessment Resources (ATE p. 593) **A**	up to 45 min.
EXTEND	
Apply Understanding	
Have students complete the Vocabulary Development Lesson and the Grammar and Style Lesson (SE p. 592) **A**	20 min.
Apply students' ability to use evaluative modifiers by using the Writing Lesson (SE/ATE p. 593) **A**	45 min.
Apply students' understanding using one or more of the Extension Activities (SE p. 593)	20–90 min.

 ACCELERATED INSTRUCTION:
Use the strategies and activities identified with an **A**.

UNIVERSAL ACCESS
● = Below Level Students
▲ = On-Level Students
■ = Above Level Students

Time and Resource Manager

RESOURCES		
PRINT	**TRANSPARENCIES**	**TECHNOLOGY**
• **Beyond Literature,** Cross-Curricular Connection: Social Studies, p. 31 ▲ ■		• **Interest Grabber Video,** Tape 4 ● ▲ ■
• **Selection Support Workbook:** ● ▲ ■ Literary Analysis, p. 141 Reading Strategy, p. 140 Build Vocabulary, p. 138	• **Literary Analysis and Reading Transparencies,** pp. 61 and 62 ● ▲ ■	
		• **Listening to Literature** ● ▲ ■ Audiocassettes, Side 20 Audio CDs, CD 12
• **Literatura en español** ● ▲ • **Literary Analysis for Enrichment** ■		
• **Formal Assessment:** Selection Test, p. 149 ● ▲ ■ • **Open Book Test,** p. 91 ● ▲ ■ • **Performance Assessment and Portfolio Management,** p. 30 ● ▲ ■ • **PRENTICE HALL ASSESSMENT** *SYSTEM* ● ▲ ■	• **PRENTICE HALL ASSESSMENT** *SYSTEM* ● ▲ ■ Skills Practice Answers and Explanations on Transparencies	• **Test Bank Software** ● ▲ ■ • **Got It! Assessment Videotapes,** Tape 3 ● ▲
• **Selection Support Workbook:** ● ▲ ■ Grammar and Style, p. 139 • **Writing and Grammar,** Ruby Level ● ▲ ■ • **Extension Activities,** p. 31 ● ▲ ■	• **Daily Language Practice Transparencies** ● ▲ • **Writing Models and Graphic Organizers on Transparencies,** p. 37 ● ▲ ■	• **Writing and Grammar iText CD-ROM** ● ▲ ■ *Take It to the Net* www.phschool.com

■ **BLOCK SCHEDULING:** Use one 90-minute class period to preteach the selection and have students read it. Use a second 90-minute class period to assess students' mastery of skills and have them complete one of the Extension Activities.

Motivation

Discuss the idea that in both life and literature, people may not be as they appear at first impression. Point out, for example, that students may know seemingly tough characters who inevitably reveal a heart of gold—or weak ones who show an unexpected inner strength during a crisis. Have students think about and suggest a list of fictional characters from short stories, books, movies, and television who turn out to be different than their initial impressions suggest. Guide students to notice how their views of the different characters in this story change as they read.

📼 Interest Grabber Video

As an alternative, play "Bret Harte: An American Writer" on Tape 4 to engage student interest.

❶ Background

More About the Author

When he was eleven years old, Bret Harte published his first poem, "Autumn Musings," in the *Sunday Morning Atlas*. His family members criticized the poem for being too emotional. Harte later said, "I sometimes wonder that I ever wrote another line of verse." But he did, and eventually won the respect of many writers.

Prepare to Read

❶ The Outcasts of Poker Flat

Bret Harte
(1836–1902)

A literary pioneer, Bret Harte played a key role in creating a vivid, lasting portrait of the Old West. His stories, filled with picturesque, intriguing characters and colorful dialogue, provided much of post-Civil War America with its first glimpse of western life and established the Old West as a popular literary setting. In their locations, plots, characters, and uses of both humor and violence, the roots of the Hollywood western can be traced back to Harte's tales.

Heading West Harte was born and raised in Albany, New York. In 1854, when he was eighteen, he traveled across the country to California, a land undergoing a turbulent period of rapid growth due to the discovery of gold in 1848. During his first few years in California, Harte worked as a schoolteacher, tutor, messenger, clerk, and prospector. While Harte's life seemed to have little direction at the time, his observations of the rugged, often violent, life in the mining camps and the towns and cities of the new frontier provided him with the inspiration for his most successful short stories.

A Career of Ups and Downs After working as a typesetter and writer for two California periodicals and publishing two books of verse, *Outcroppings* (1865) and *The Lost Galleon* (1867), Harte became the editor in 1868 of the *Overland Monthly*, a new literary magazine. At that time, the country's population and geographical area were both expanding at a rapid pace. Yet, there were few ways for people to learn about life in regions other than their own.

The American public was eager to learn about life in the new frontier. Harte's writing addressed this need. When he published his story "The Luck of Roaring Camp," in *Overland Monthly's* second issue, he immediately became famous. Over the next two years, he published "The Outcasts of Poker Flat" and several other stories for the magazine about life on the frontier. His popularity continued to climb.

Following the publication of *The Luck of Roaring Camp and Other Sketches* in 1870, Harte's popularity reached its peak. In 1871, *The Atlantic Monthly*, a distinguished literary magazine, contracted to pay Harte the large sum of $10,000 for any twelve sketches or stories he contributed over the next year. Harte returned to the East to fulfill his contract, but the stories he wrote were flat and disappointing compared with his earlier work. His celebrity waned almost as quickly as it had grown.

A Political Appointment Harte continued to publish stories, short novels, and plays during the next twenty years, but most of his later work was unsuccessful. Some friends helped him land a diplomatic post, however, and from 1878 to 1885 Harte served as a United States consul in Germany and Scotland. He retired to London for the remainder of his life.

Recognition by His Peers Richard O'Conner, a biographer of Harte, summarized Harte's legacy this way:

> "Kipling said he owed 'many things' to the storyteller's art he learned from reading Harte . . . [and] H. L. Mencken believed he was entitled to a 'sort of immortality' . . . and the even tougher critic Ambrose Bierce granted Harte a place 'very close to the head' of all American writers."

578 ◆ Division, Reconciliation, and Expansion (1850–1914)

TEACHING RESOURCES

The following resources can be used to enrich or extend the instruction for pp. 578–579.

Motivation

📼 **Interest Grabber Video**, Tape 4 ■

Background

📖 **Beyond Literature**, p. 31

💻 ***Take It to the Net***
Visit www.phschool.com for Background and hotlinks for the selection.

Literary Analysis

🎞 **Literary Analysis and Reading Transparencies**, Regionalism, p. 62

📑 **Selection Support**: Literary Analysis, p. 141

Reading

🎞 **Literary Analysis and Reading Transparencies**, Questioning the Text, p. 61 ■

 BLOCK SCHEDULING: Resources marked with this symbol provide varied instruction during 90-minute blocks.

Preview

Connecting to the Literature

The "outcasts" in Bret Harte's story are tested by circumstances. Think about a situation in which you, or someone that you know, described an event as, "a real test of character." What qualities did the situation bring out in the people involved?

❷ Literary Analysis

Regionalism

Regionalism is a literary movement in which writers attempt to depict and analyze the distinctive and unique qualities of a geographical area and its people. Stories like "The Outcasts of Poker Flat" paint vivid and engaging portraits of what life was like in the far reaches of the country. As you read, notice how Harte captures the characteristics of the region and its inhabitants.

Connecting Literary Elements

The unique characters in this story are an essential part of the **local color** of a rough mining town in the Sierras. An aspect of regionalism, local color highlights characteristics and details unique to a specific area. Local color captures the physical environment, as well as the mood of a time and a place, and includes the ways in which people talk and how they think. Use a chart like the one shown to record the elements of local color in the story.

❸ Reading Strategy

Questioning the Text

When you read any literature, **question the text** to improve your involvement and understanding. Ask yourself questions like these:

- What is happening?
- What is the author's purpose?
- What are the motives for the characters' actions?

Look for answers to questions like these as you read.

Vocabulary Development

expatriated (eks pā′ trē āt id) *adj.* deported; driven from one's native land (p. 582)

anathema (ə nath′ ə mə) *n.* curse (p. 582)

bellicose (bel ə kōs) *adj.* quarrelsome (p. 583)

recumbent (ri kum′ bənt) *adj.* resting (p. 583)

equanimity (ek′ wə nim ə tē) *n.* composure (p. 583)

vociferation (vō sif ər ā shən) *n.* loud or vehement shouting (p. 587)

vituperative (vī t′ōō′ pər ə tiv) *adj.* spoken abusively (p. 588)

querulous (kwer′ ə ləs) *adj.* inclined to find fault (p. 588)

The Outcasts of Poker Flat ◆ 579

---

❷ Literary Analysis

Regionalism

- Explain to students that as they read this story they will focus on the literary movement known as regionalism.

- Read the instruction about regionalism aloud. Point out that writers of regional literature are especially interested in conveying what is unique about a particular place and its people.

- Explain that regionalism was especially popular in the United States during the mid- to late-1800s, when the nation's population and geographical area were expanding at a rapid pace. At that time, there were few ways for people to learn about life in regions other than their own.

- Invite students to look for descriptions, dialogue, and attitudes in this story that are characteristic of the Old West.

❸ Reading Strategy

Questioning the Text

- Point out to students that, with practice, their ability to question the text will become almost second nature. Encourage them to see the important link between reading a text and writing notes about it. In short, encourage students to cultivate the habit of reading with a pencil in hand.

- Remind students that questioning the text can involve clarifying seemingly irrelevant details that might also create confusion. It can also involve clarifying a literary work's central ideas.

Vocabulary Development

- Pronounce each vocabulary word for students, and read the definitions as a class. Have students identify any words with which they are already familiar.

 E-Teach

Visit E-Teach at www.phschool.com for teachers' essays on how to teach, with questions and answers.

CUSTOMIZE INSTRUCTION FOR UNIVERSAL ACCESS

For Less Proficient Readers	For English Learners	For Advanced Readers
Encourage students to pause frequently to reflect on questions that arise during their reading of the story. You might wish to have pairs of students take turns reading aloud to one another and jotting down questions about confusing passages of text.	Students will probably have numerous questions about Harte's rendering of the local dialect. Encourage students to keep a list of terms and phrases—such as *reckon, agin, yer,* and *shift for myself*—that are specific to the story's setting. Work with students to clarify the meanings of these words.	Students are likely to make observations and inferences as they read, and also to formulate questions as they try to grasp characters' motivations and plot twists. Suggest that students keep a reader's response journal to note inferences, record answers to questions, and identify which questions remain unanswered.

Step-by-Step Teaching Guide for pp. 580–590

For Interpersonal Learners

Guide students to notice the composition of characters in the group of outcasts, and how each contributes to the group's dynamics. Compare this combination of individuals with those depicted in typical contemporary disaster movies. Explain how these groups routinely include an intrepid male leader, a young innocent, a corrupt old man, a tough, worldly woman, and an untrustworthy young drifter.

❶ About the Selection

In a regenerative effort, the mining town of Poker Flat has been ridding itself of unsavory characters. The gambler John Oakhurst and three other outcasts attempt to make their way to the more hospitable camp of Sandy Bar. A snowstorm stops their travel and links them with two "innocents" heading in the opposite direction. As the story of survival unfolds, readers come to understand each of the characters in a new light.

❷ Background

Art

Edge of Town, by Charles Burchfield

Charles Burchfield (1893–1967) studied at the Cleveland Art Institute, where he developed his poetic and introspective painting style. This work, the last of Burchfield's "main street" paintings, provides a view of a small-town street on a bleak winter day.

Use these questions for discussion.

1. How does the artist create a scene filled with mystery?
   Answer: The buildings glow with a dull light that is in eerie contrast to the stormy sky. The static figures are more like elements of the landscape than people.

2. Why is this painting an appropriate image for this story?
   Answer: The painting is appropriate because it depicts a small western town with an ominous undercurrent.

580

---

❶ # THE OUTCASTS OF POKER FLAT

BRET HARTE

Edge of Town, Charles Burchfield. The Nelson-Atkins Museum of Art, Kansas City, Missouri

❸ ▲ **Critical Viewing** Does the mood of this painting echo the mood of the story's opening paragraphs? Explain. **[Compare]**

580 ◆ *Division, Reconciliation, and Expansion (1850–1914)*

TEACHING RESOURCES

The following resources can be used to enrich or extend the instruction for pp. 580–590.

Reading Strategy

📖 **Selection Support:** Reading Strategy, p. 140; Build Vocabulary, p. 138

🎧 **Listening to Literature Audiocassettes,** Side 20 ▪

💿 **Listening to Literature Audio CDs,** CD 12 ▪

Background

Mr. Oakhurst, a gambler and the main character of "The Outcasts of Poker Flat," is a generous, genial man who is seemingly nonchalant in the face of danger. As you read the story, you may find yourself wondering how true-to-life Mr. Oakhurst is. Harte's biographer, Henry Childs Merwin, described a real-life character named Lucky Bill, a gambler who demonstrated traits similar to Mr. Oakhurst's. According to Merwin, Lucky Bill was known for his generosity, and, although he was hanged by a vigilance committee, he was also known to have advised his own son to avoid bad company, keep out of saloons, and lead an industrious and honest life.

A s Mr. John Oakhurst, gambler, stepped into the main street of Poker Flat on the morning of the twenty-third of November, 1850, he was conscious of a change in its moral atmosphere since the preceding night. Two or three men, conversing earnestly together, ceased as he approached, and exchanged significant glances. There was a Sabbath lull in the air which, in a settlement unused to Sabbath influences, looked ominous.

Mr. Oakhurst's calm, handsome face betrayed small concern in these indications. Whether he was conscious of any predisposing cause was another question. "I reckon they're after somebody," he reflected; "likely it's me." He returned to his pocket the handkerchief with which he had been whipping away the red dust of Poker Flat from his neat boots, and quietly discharged his mind of any further conjecture.

In point of fact, Poker Flat was "after somebody." It had lately suffered the loss of several thousand dollars, two valuable horses, and a prominent citizen. It was experiencing a spasm of virtuous reaction, quite as lawless and ungovernable as any of the acts that had provoked it. A secret committee had determined to rid the town of all improper persons. This was done permanently in regard of two men who were then hanging from the boughs of a sycamore in the gulch, and temporarily in the banishment of certain other objectionable characters. I regret to say that some of these were ladies. It is but due to the sex, however, to state that their impropriety was professional, and it was only in such easily established standards of evil that Poker Flat ventured to sit in judgment.

Mr. Oakhurst was right in supposing that he was included in this category. A few of the committee had urged hanging him as a possible example, and a sure method of reimbursing themselves from his pockets of the sums he had won from them. "It's agin justice," said Jim Wheeler, "to let this yer young man from Roaring Camp—an entire stranger—carry away our money." But a crude sentiment of equity residing in the breasts of those who had been fortunate enough to win from Mr. Oakhurst overruled this narrower local prejudice.

Mr. Oakhurst received his sentence with philosophic calmness, none the less coolly that he was aware of the hesitation of his judges. He was

Literary Analysis
Regionalism What does this passage reveal about some of the inhabitants of Poker Flat?

5 ☑ **Reading Check**
Why are the residents of Poker Flat "after somebody"?

The Outcasts of Poker Flat ◆ 581

CUSTOMIZE INSTRUCTION FOR UNIVERSAL ACCESS

For Special Needs Students

To launch students into their reading of "The Outcasts of Poker Flat," pick a strong reader to read aloud the first several paragraphs while students follow in their texts. Afterward, answer any questions that students might have. Then, have students read the rest of the selection aloud in pairs or small groups. Suggest that they note any difficult lines or passages for later discussion.

For Less Proficient Readers

This story contains an abundance of lengthy and potentially confusing compound sentences. To help students better understand these sentences, suggest that they break them down into discrete sections as they read. Have students identify the core of each sentence—its main subject and verb—and state the action each sentence describes. Guide students to use coordinating conjunctions to clarify the connections between pairs of ideas.

3 ▶ **Critical Viewing**
Answer: The mood of the painting accurately echoes the mood of the opening paragraphs. The painting shows a small western town that is quite still except for the few people milling about in the street. The daylight upon the buildings is eerie, and the dark clouds are ominous. The scene evokes not only a calm similar to the "Sabbath lull" Harte describes, but also a sense of foreboding.

4 **Literary Analysis**
Regionalism

- Have a student volunteer read the third and fourth paragraphs of the story aloud, and encourage listeners to distinguish two groups of Poker Flat "committee members."

- Ask students the Literary Analysis question on p. 581: What does this passage reveal about some of the inhabitants of Poker Flat?
  Answer: Students may say that some of the inhabitants are hypocritical, and motivated by revenge and greed—if they have lost money, they would hang a gambler; if they have won money, they would not.

▶ Monitor Progress Have students use a graphic organizer to track the regional qualities reflected in the story. To do so, create two charts on the chalkboard and ask students to copy them in their notebooks. Label the first chart *Physical Environment*, then list the following categories: *weather, climate, vegetation*, and *landscape*. Label the second chart *Cultural Environment*, then list the following categories: *political attitudes, religious beliefs, social attitudes, language/dialect, art*, and *traditions*. Have students fill in both charts as they read the story.

5 ☑ **Reading Check**
Answer: The town had lately "suffered the loss of several thousand dollars, two valuable horses, and a prominent citizen."

581

⑥ Background

Sierra Nevada

It was in the Sierra Nevadas that a group of some eighty immigrants led by George and Jacob Donner became trapped by snowstorms during the winter of 1846–47. More than half of "the Donner Party" eventually died in what came to be known as the Donner Pass on the route between Reno and San Francisco.

too much of a gambler not to accept Fate. With him life was at best an uncertain game, and he recognized the usual percentage in favor of the dealer.

A body of armed men accompanied the deported wickedness of Poker Flat to the outskirts of the settlement. Besides Mr. Oakhurst, who was known to be a coolly desperate man, and for whose intimidation the armed escort was intended, the <u>expatriated</u> party consisted of a young woman familiarly known as the "Duchess"; another, who had won the title of "Mother Shipton";[1] and "Uncle Billy," a suspected sluice robber[2] and confirmed drunkard. The cavalcade provoked no comments from the spectators, nor was any word uttered by the escort. Only, when the gulch which marked the uttermost limit of Poker Flat was reached, the leader spoke briefly and to the point. The exiles were forbidden to return at the peril of their lives.

As the escort disappeared, their pent-up feelings found vent in a few hysterical tears from the Duchess, some bad language from Mother Shipton, and a Parthian volley of expletives[3] from Uncle Billy. The philosophic Oakhurst alone remained silent. He listened calmly to Mother Shipton's desire to cut somebody's heart out, to the repeated statements of the Duchess that she would die in the road, and to the alarming oaths that seemed to be bumped out of Uncle Billy as he rode forward. With the easy good humor characteristic of his class, he insisted upon exchanging his own riding horse, "Five Spot," for the sorry mule which the Duchess rode. But even this act did not draw the party into any closer sympathy. The young woman readjusted her somewhat draggled plumes with a feeble, faded coquetry; Mother Shipton eyed the possessor of "Five Spot" with malevolence, and Uncle Billy included the whole party in one sweeping <u>anathema</u>.

The road to Sandy Bar—a camp that, not having as yet experienced the regenerating influences of Poker Flat, consequently seemed to offer some invitation to the emigrants—lay over a steep mountain range. It was distant a day's severe travel. In that advanced season, the party soon passed out of the moist, temperate regions of the foothills into the dry, cold, bracing air of the Sierras.[*] The trail was narrow and difficult. At noon the Duchess, rolling out of her saddle upon the ground, declared her intention of going no farther, and the party halted.

---

1. **"Mother Shipton"** English woman who lived in the sixteenth century and was suspected of being a witch.
2. **sluice robber** person who steals gold from sluices—long troughs used for sifting gold.
3. **Parthian . . . expletives** hostile remarks made while leaving. The Parthians were an ancient society whose cavalrymen usually shot at the enemy while retreating or pretending to retreat.

ℒiterature in context — Geography Connection

⑥ ♦ Sierra Nevada

The outcasts find shelter in the Sierra Nevadas, a majestic mountain range in Northern California. The Sierra Nevada range is about 450 miles long and 60 to 80 miles wide. The craggy granite peaks include the national parks of Yosemite, Sequoia, and Kings Canyon, as well as the giant sequoia forests. Five hundred peaks in the Sierras exceed 12,000 feet; Mount Whitney, at 14,494 feet, is the tallest mountain in the continental United States, excluding Alaska. Despite its beauty, this mountain range presents challenges to the characters in Harte's story.

expatriated (eks pā´ trē āt´ id) *adj.* deported; driven from one's native land

anathema (ə nath´ ə mə) *n.* curse

❋ ENRICHMENT: Social Studies Connection

Mining Towns

Visitors to any of several western states can see vestiges of what was once for a brief time a booming mining industry. Not only the discovery of gold, but silver and copper strikes brought fortune seekers by the thousands to sites in the mountains of Nevada, Arizona, Colorado, and other states and territories. Today, some of these towns are gone completely, while others are "ghost towns" whose remains might include a dilapidated building or two and an abandoned mine shaft. Still others have transformed themselves into artist communities or tourist destinations.

Have students choose a specific mining town and research its boom and bust. One such town is Virginia City, Nevada. Students can gather information about life there in its heyday and learn about its current status. Invite students to share any interesting findings about the place or the people who lived there.

The spot was singularly wild and impressive. A wooded amphitheater, surrounded on three sides by precipitous cliffs of naked granite, sloped gently toward the crest of another precipice that overlooked the valley. It was, undoubtedly, the most suitable spot for a camp, had camping been advisable. But Mr. Oakhurst knew that scarcely half the journey to Sandy Bar was accomplished, and the party were not equipped or provisioned for delay. This fact he pointed out to his companions curtly, with a philosophic commentary on the folly of "throwing up their hand before the game was played out." But they were furnished with liquor, which in this emergency stood them in place of food, fuel, rest, and prescience. In spite of his remonstrances, it was not long before they were more or less under its influence. Uncle Billy passed rapidly from a <u>bellicose</u> state into one of stupor, the Duchess became maudlin, and Mother Shipton snored. Mr. Oakhurst alone remained erect, leaning against a rock calmly surveying them.

Mr. Oakhurst did not drink. It interfered with a profession which required coolness, impassiveness, and presence of mind, and, in his own language, he "couldn't afford it." As he gazed at his <u>recumbent</u> fellow exiles, the loneliness begotten of his pariah trade, his habits of life, his very vices, for the first time seriously oppressed him. He bestirred himself in dusting his black clothes, washing his hands and face, and other acts characteristic of his studiously neat habits, and for a moment forgot his annoyance. The thought of deserting his weaker and more pitiable companions never perhaps occurred to him. Yet he could not help feeling the want of that excitement which singularly enough, was most conducive to that calm <u>equanimity</u> for which he was notorious. He looked at the gloomy walls that rose a thousand feet sheer above the circling pines around him; at the sky, ominously clouded; at the valley below, already deepening into shadow. And, doing so, suddenly he heard his own name called.

A horseman slowly ascended the trail. In the fresh, open face of the newcomer Mr. Oakhurst recognized Tom Simson, otherwise known as the "Innocent" of Sandy Bar. He had met him some months before over a "little game," and had, with perfect equanimity, won the entire fortune—amounting to some forty dollars—of that guileless youth. After the game was finished, Mr. Oakhurst drew the youthful speculator behind the door and thus addressed him: "Tommy, you're a good little man, but you can't gamble worth a cent. Don't try it over again." He then handed him his money back, pushed him gently from the room, and so made a devoted slave of Tom Simson.

There was a remembrance of this in his boyish and enthusiastic greeting of Mr. Oakhurst. He had started, he said, to go to Poker Flat to seek his fortune. "Alone?" No, not exactly alone; in fact (a giggle), he had run away with Piney Woods. Didn't Mr. Oakhurst remember Piney? She that used to wait on the table at the Temperance House? They had been engaged a long time, but old Jake Woods had objected, and so they had run away, and were going to Poker Flat to be married, and here they were. And they were tired out, and how lucky it

bellicose (bel′ ə kōs) *adj.* quarrelsome

recumbent (ri kum′ bənt) *adj.* resting

equanimity (ek′ wə nim ə tē) *n.* composure

Reading Check
What occurred between Oakhurst and Simson the last time they met?

The Outcasts of Poker Flat ◆ 583

CUSTOMIZE INSTRUCTION FOR UNIVERSAL ACCESS	
For Special Needs Students	**For Gifted/Talented Students**
Students may be confused by the reference to "the usual percentage in favor of the dealer" at the end of the first paragraph on p. 582. Explain the principle that in games of chance, the gambling institution, known as the "house," usually has the mathematical advantage, and therefore the greater probability of winning. Although the odds usually favor the house the degree to which they do so may differ from game to game. A professional gambler like Oakhurst must know the precise advantage held by the dealer.	Ask students to describe Oakhurst's view of life. Students may say that he believes that luck determines the direction one's life will take. They may guess that, as a gambler, Oakhurst plays the odds, calculates the probability of events, and responds in a way that will give him the best chance of success. Students may note that when Oakhurst says that he "recognized the usual percentage . . . ," he means that he knows when to accept defeat. Students might also note that the "dealer" Oakhurst refers to is God, or fate.

---

❼ Vocabulary Development

Latin Word Part -bel-

- Point out the word *bellicose* and read its definition.
- Tell students that the word derives its meaning from the Latin word *bellum*, which means war.
- Then, give students the meaning of the prefix *ante-*, which means "before," and ask them what the word *antebellum* might mean. **Answer:** *Antebellum* means "before the war."
- After they have correctly answered the question, inform students that references to the antebellum period in the United States usually indicate the years before the Civil War.

❽ Critical Thinking

Analyze

- Have students read the two bracketed paragraphs and think about their assessment of Mr. Oakhurst.
- In particular, encourage students to identify any paradoxes Mr. Oakhurst's personality and to speculate on why he became a gambler in the first place. **Answer:** Students may say that although he thrives on the excitement he finds in card games, Oakhurst has the bearing of someone who relies on cool, dispassionate reason, and who likes to be in control. They may say that his composure and calm personality, combined with his belief in the significance of luck and the inevitability of fate, ideally suit him to his chosen profession.

❾ ☑Reading Check

Answer: Oakhurst won forty dollars from Simson and subsequently returned it to him along with the advice not to gamble again.

583

America's Love for the Western

Even before the makers of motion pictures and radio and television programs took advantage of Americans' thirst for stories about white settlement of the Old West, authors such as James Fenimore Cooper (*The Prairie*, 1827), Stephen Crane ("The Bride Comes to Yellow Sky," 1898), Owen Wister (*The Virginian*, 1902), and Zane Grey (*Riders of the Purple Sage*, 1912) had great success with westerns. The ancestor of Hollywood westerns is Edwin S. Porter's *The Great Train Robbery* (1903). During the 1930s Americans went to local cinemas to see *Cimarron* and *Stagecoach* (starring John Wayne). In the next decade, films such as *Red River*, *The Ox-Bow Incident*, and *Duel in the Sun* were released. The 1950s saw such classics as *High Noon*, *Shane*, *The Big Country*, and *Rio Bravo*.

11 Literary Analysis

Regionalism and Local Color

• Read the bracketed passage aloud, inviting students to jot down notes about details suggesting local color. Make sure students listen for details describing both the physical place and time and the cultural norms.

• Invite volunteers to share their notes with the class as you write their responses on the chalkboard.

▶ **Monitor Progress** Ask the Literary Analysis question on p. 584: In what ways does this description of both the physical environment and the characters reflect qualities unique to the region?

Answer: Elements suggesting distinctive qualities of local color in the physical environment include Uncle Billy's retiring "up the canyon" to laugh among the "tall pine trees"; the strange chill in the air and the tethered animals. Local color in the characters is revealed by Uncle Billy's finding comedy in the idea of the Duchess being "Mrs. Oakhurst"; Uncle Billy's use of dialect, his body language—leg slapping and facial contortions—and his use of profanity.

---

was they had found a place to camp and company. All this the Innocent delivered rapidly, while Piney, a stout, comely damsel of fifteen, emerged from behind the pine tree, where she had been blushing unseen, and rode to the side of her lover.

Mr. Oakhurst seldom troubled himself with sentiment, still less with propriety; but he had a vague idea that the situation was not fortunate. He retained, however, his presence of mind sufficiently to kick Uncle Billy, who was about to say something, and Uncle Billy was sober enough to recognize in Mr. Oakhurst's kick a superior power that would not bear trifling. He then endeavored to dissuade Tom Simson from delaying further, but in vain. He even pointed out the fact that there was no provision, nor means of making a camp. But, unluckily, the Innocent met this objection by assuring the party that he was provided with an extra mule loaded with provisions and by the discovery of a rude attempt at a log house near the trail. "Piney can stay with Mrs. Oakhurst," said the Innocent, pointing to the Duchess, "and I can shift for myself."

11 Nothing but Mr. Oakhurst's admonishing foot saved Uncle Billy from bursting into a roar of laughter. As it was, he felt compelled to retire up the canyon until he could recover his gravity. There he confided the joke to the tall pine trees, with many slaps of his leg, contortions of his face, and the usual profanity. But when he returned to the party, he found them seated by a fire—for the air had grown strangely chill and the sky overcast—in apparently amicable conversation. Piney was actually talking in an impulsive, girlish fashion to the Duchess, who was listening with an interest and animation she had not shown for many days. The Innocent was holding forth, apparently with equal effect, to Mr. Oakhurst and Mother Shipton, who was actually relaxing into amiability. "Is this yer a d——d picnic?" said Uncle Billy with inward scorn as he surveyed the sylvan[4] group, the glancing firelight, and the tethered animals in the foreground. Suddenly an idea mingled with the alcoholic fumes that disturbed his brain. It was apparently of a jocular nature, for he felt impelled to slap his leg again and cram his fist into his mouth.

As the shadows crept slowly up the mountain, a slight breeze rocked the tops of the pine trees, and moaned through their long and gloomy aisles. The ruined cabin, patched and covered with pine boughs, was set apart for the ladies. As the lovers parted, they unaffectedly exchanged a kiss, so honest and sincere that it might have been heard above the swaying pines. The frail Duchess and the malevolent Mother Shipton were probably too stunned to remark upon this last evidence of simplicity, and so turned without a word to the hut. The fire was replenished, the men lay down before the door, and in a few minutes were asleep.

---

4. **sylvan** (sil' vən) *adj.* characteristic of the forest.

The American Experience

10 *America's Love for the Western*

The American West was settled from the middle to late 1800s. As settlers moved west on the Santa Fe and Oregon trails, they developed thriving businesses in livestock. Cow towns grew up around railroad stations, and immense cattle drives moved across the plains. This period in American life provided the material for the American western—a literary and film genre that has been a staple of popular culture ever since.

Both legendary and real-life characters, such as Jesse James, Wild Bill Hickok, Kit Carson, and Buffalo Bill Cody, were featured in stagecoach dramas and books. Soon, filmmakers produced minute-long "Cowboys and Indians" flicks. By 1939, the film industry was booming and Hollywood churned out westerns. The biggest box office returns went to villains such as Jesse James and Billy the Kid—outlaws whose brawling and gun fighting, often aboard burning or runaway trains, provided hours of diversion for American filmgoers.

Literary Analysis
Regionalism and Local Color In what ways does this description of both the physical environment and the characters reflect qualities unique to the region?

⚜ ENRICHMENT: Cultural Connection

Outcasts

Ever since the beginning of civilization, individuals have been rejected from societies for a wide range of reasons. Outcasts may have been seen as antisocial, or their religious beliefs may have challenged popularly accepted views. About five hundred years ago, Jews were forced to leave Spain unless they converted to Catholicism. Until the American Revolution, Great Britain shipped criminals to America, and continued to send them to Australia well into the nineteenth century. Until 1950, India's rigid caste system forced an entire class of people, called Untouchables, to live a life of poverty.

Have students research a group of people who have been considered outcasts of society. Students' research should attempt to uncover the reasons the people were viewed as outcasts, descriptions of their daily lives, and —in the cases in which the outcasts were not criminals —explanations of why the exclusion was allowed to occur. Invite students to report their findings to the class.

Mr. Oakhurst was a light sleeper. Toward morning he awoke benumbed and cold. As he stirred the dying fire, the wind, which was now blowing strongly, brought to his cheek that which caused the blood to leave it—snow!

 He started to his feet with the intention of awakening the sleepers, for there was no time to lose. But turning to where Uncle Billy had been lying, he found him gone. A suspicion leaped to his brain and a curse to his lips. He ran to the spot where the mules had been tethered; they were no longer there. The tracks were already rapidly disappearing in the snow.

The momentary excitement brought Mr. Oakhurst back to the fire with his usual calm. He did not waken the sleepers. The Innocent slumbered peacefully, with a smile on his good-humored, freckled face; the virgin Piney slept beside her frailer sisters as sweetly as though attended by celestial guardians; and Mr. Oakhurst, drawing his blanket over his shoulders, stroked his mustaches and waited for the dawn. It came slowly in a whirling mist of snowflakes that dazzled and confused the eye. What could be seen of the landscape appeared magically changed. He looked over the valley, and summed up the present and future in two words—"snowed in!"

A careful inventory of the provisions, which, fortunately for the party, had been stored within the hut and so escaped the felonious fingers of Uncle Billy, disclosed the fact that with care and prudence they might last ten days longer. "That is," said Mr. Oakhurst, sotto voce[5] to the Innocent, "if you're willing to board us. If you ain't—and perhaps you'd better not—you can wait till Uncle Billy gets back with provisions." For some occult reason, Mr. Oakhurst could not bring himself to disclose Uncle Billy's rascality, and so offered the hypothesis that he had wandered from the camp and had accidentally stampeded the animals. He dropped a warning to the Duchess and Mother Shipton, who of course knew the facts of their associate's defection. "They'll find out the truth about us *all* when they find out anything," he added, significantly, "and there's no good frightening them now."

Tom Simson not only put all his worldly store at the disposal of Mr. Oakhurst, but seemed to enjoy the prospect of their enforced seclusion. "We'll have a good camp for a week, and then the snow'll melt, and we'll all go back together." The cheerful gaiety of the young man, and Mr. Oakhurst's calm, infected the others. The Innocent with the aid of pine boughs extemporized a thatch for the roofless cabin, and the Duchess directed Piney in the rearrangement of the interior with a taste and tact that opened the blue eyes of that provincial maiden to their fullest extent. "I reckon now you're used to fine things at Poker Flat," said Piney. The Duchess turned away sharply to conceal something that reddened her cheek through its professional tint, and Mother Shipton requested Piney not to "chatter." But when Mr. Oakhurst returned from a weary search for the trail, he heard

_____

5. **sotto voce** (sät´ ō vō´ chē) in an undertone.

Reading Strategy
Questioning the Text
What question can you ask about Oakhurst's discovery that Uncle Billy is missing?

⓭ ✓**Reading Check**
What explanation does Oakhurst give for Uncle Billy's disappearance?

The Outcasts of Poker Flat ◆ 585

⓬ **Reading Strategy**

Questioning the Text

- Invite students to listen as you read the bracketed passage aloud. Ask students to think about what they have just heard and to identify the discovery that Mr. Oakhurst has just made.

- Then, ask students the Reading Strategy question on p. 585: What question can you ask about Oakhurst's discovery that Uncle Billy is missing?
  Possible response: "What is the meaning behind Uncle Billy's disappearance?"

⓭ ✓**Reading Check**

Answer: He says that Uncle Billy wandered from the camp in search of more provisions.

CUSTOMIZE INSTRUCTION FOR UNIVERSAL ACCESS

For Advanced Readers

This story was made into a movie in the late 1930s. Here is a review of the film from *Time* magazine.

"Though skimpily produced, it invokes with a fidelity unusual in a double-biller the wild land and rugged times in which its scene is laid, and the nostalgic charm of the Harte stories. Its worst fault is the failure of explicitness in the last sequence, leaving the audience completely fuddled."

Use these questions for discussion:

1. Do you agree with the reviewer that there is a nostalgic charm to Harte's story? Why or why not?
Answer: Students may say yes because of regional descriptions of an earlier era in the West.

2. The reviewer considers the last scenes to be confusing. Do you think that the end of the original story is believable and logical? Why or why not?
Answer: Students might say that the ending of the story is a believable resolution of the conflict.

⓮ ▶ Critical Viewing

Answer: The photograph illustrates enormous mountains like those that surround the group of outcasts. The snow in the photograph also indicates a wintry scene. However, the image does not illustrate snow of considerable depth, and it does not present the hopelessly snowbound condition that has stranded the group in Harte's tale.

the sound of happy laughter echoed from the rocks. He stopped in some alarm, and his thoughts first naturally reverted to the whisky, which he had prudently cached.[6] "And yet it don't somehow sound like whisky," said the gambler. It was not until he caught sight of the blazing fire through the still-blinding storm and the group around it that he settled to the conviction that it was "square fun."

Whether Mr. Oakhurst had cached his cards with the whisky as something debarred the free access of the community, I cannot say.

---

6. **cached** (kasht) *v.* hidden.

⓮ ▼ Critical Viewing
Compare and contrast this photograph of the Sierras with the group's wintry surroundings.
[Compare and Contrast]

586 ◆ *Division, Reconciliation, and Expansion (1850–1914)*

✳ ENRICHMENT: Science Connection

Personal Space

In "The Outcasts of Poker Flat," several strangers or near-strangers are forced to camp together for a while. The challenges people face in living with others in cramped conditions for long periods of time is an issue that NASA and astronauts must address when planning and executing space missions. Scientists designing vehicles for space travel usually place technical and research needs above human comfort. Ask students to imagine, for example, what it would be like to live in a spaceship on a mission to Mars. The

trip would take many months and would require that a group of people live and work together in very tight quarters.

Ask students to discuss what they think would be easy, difficult, or impossible about that experience or one like it. Have them talk about what kind of person might survive best in tight quarters. Ask them if they would be willing to try such an adventure themselves.

It was certain that, in Mother Shipton's words, he "didn't say cards once" during that evening. Haply the time was beguiled by an accordion, produced somewhat ostentatiously by Tom Simson from his pack. Notwithstanding some difficulties attending the manipulation of this instrument, Piney Woods managed to pluck several reluctant melodies from its keys, to an accompaniment by the Innocent on a pair of bone castanets. But the crowning festivity of the evening was reached in a rude camp-meeting hymn, which the lovers, joining hands, sang with great earnestness and <u>vociferation</u>. I fear that a certain defiant tone and Covenanter's[7] swing to its chorus, rather than any devotional quality, caused it speedily to infect the others, who at last joined in the refrain:

> "I'm proud to live in the service of the Lord,
> And I'm bound to die in His army."[8]

The pines rocked, the storm eddied and whirled above the miserable group, and the flames of their altar leaped heavenward as if in token of the vow.

At midnight the storm abated, the rolling clouds parted, and the stars glittered keenly above the sleeping camp. Mr. Oakhurst, whose professional habits had enabled him to live on the smallest possible amount of sleep, in dividing the watch with Tom Simson somehow managed to take upon himself the greater part of that duty. He excused himself to the Innocent by saying that he had "often been a week without sleep." "Doing what?" asked Tom. "Poker!" replied Oakhurst, sententiously; "when a man gets a streak of luck, he don't get tired. The luck gives in first. Luck," continued the gambler, reflectively, "is a mighty queer thing. All you know about it for certain is that it's bound to change. And it's finding out when it's going to change that makes you. We've had a streak of bad luck since we left Poker Flat—you come along, and slap you get into it, too. If you can hold your cards right along you're all right. For," added the gambler, with cheerful irrelevance,

> " 'I'm proud to live in the service of the Lord,
> And I'm bound to die in His army.' "

The third day came, and the sun, looking through the white-curtained valley, saw the outcasts divide their slowly decreasing store of provisions for the morning meal. It was one of the peculiarities of that mountain climate that its rays diffused a kindly warmth over the wintry landscape, as if in regretful commiseration of the past. But it revealed drift on drift of snow piled high around the hut—a hopeless,

---

7. **Covenanter's** (kuv´ ə nan´ tərz) seventeenth-century Scottish Presbyterians who resisted the rule of the Church of England.
8. **"I'm . . . army"** lines from the early American spiritual "Service of the Lord."

Literary Analysis
Regionalism and Local Color What aspects of local color does this description of the evening's music convey?

vociferation (vō sif´ ər ā´ shən) *n.* loud or vehement shouting

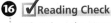

Reading Check
What does the group do in the evening before going to sleep?

The Outcasts of Poker Flat ◆ 587

⑮ Literary Analysis
Regionalism and Local Color
- Review with students the definition of local color on p. 579. Encourage students to think about how authors use details and descriptive language to convey information about a particular place and time.
- Then, read the passage aloud and ask students the Literary Analysis question on p. 587: What aspects of local color does this description of the evening's music convey? Answer: Students may say that the outcasts unite in singing hymns. Students may know that in the nineteenth century many Americans had strong religious beliefs, and that even for people living in the wildest parts of the country, religion was often a unifying force.

⑯ ✓ Reading Check
Answer: They play music and sing together.

CUSTOMIZE INSTRUCTION FOR UNIVERSAL ACCESS

For Less Proficient Readers	For English Learners
Students may benefit from pausing occasionally during their reading of the story in order to predict what will happen next. One likely place for students to ask themselves such questions is after the outcasts become snowbound. Invite students to offer their predictions about how the plot will unfold. Have them identify the outcasts' major challenges, and predict ways in which the characters will — or will not — successfully meet those challenges.	Help students understand difficult passages by paraphrasing them using simpler language. For instance, the sentence on p. 586 that begins "Whether Mr. Oakhurst had cached . . ." can be paraphrased as *I don't know whether he hid his cards with the whiskey so that the others couldn't get at them.*

- Ask students to describe in their own words what Mother Shipton has done. Ask them to explain why she did it and what this action reveals about her.
  Answer: Mrs. Shipton has been starving herself while stockpiling her food for Piney to eat later. She has sacrificed herself so that the younger woman might survive. Students may surmise that underneath her coarse, hard-hearted exterior, the old woman has a loving heart—and that she has been taken by Piney's purity and innocence.

- Have students discuss why Harte included this event in the story.
  Answer: Mother Shipton's death underscores the severity of the group's situation.

uncharted, trackless sea of white lying below the rocky shores to which the castaways still clung. Through the marvelously clear air the smoke of the pastoral village of Poker Flat rose miles away. Mother Shipton saw it, and from a remote pinnacle of her rocky fastness hurled in that direction a final malediction. It was her last <u>vituperative</u> attempt, and perhaps for that reason was invested with a certain degree of sublimity. It did her good, she privately informed the Duchess. "Just you go out there and cuss, and see." She then set herself to the task of amusing "the child," as she and the Duchess were pleased to call Piney. Piney was no chicken, but it was a soothing and original theory of the pair thus to account for the fact that she didn't swear and wasn't improper.

When night crept up again through the gorges, the reedy notes of the accordion rose and fell in fitful spasms and long-drawn gasps by the flickering campfire. But music failed to fill entirely the aching void left by insufficient food, and a new diversion was proposed by Piney— storytelling. Neither Mr. Oakhurst nor his female companions caring to relate their personal experiences, this plan would have failed too but for the Innocent. Some months before he had chanced upon a stray copy of Mr. Pope's[9] ingenious translation of the *Iliad*.[10] He now proposed to narrate the principal incidents of that poem—having thoroughly mastered the argument and fairly forgotten the words—in the current vernacular of Sandy Bar. And so for the rest of that night the Homeric demigods again walked the earth. Trojan bully and wily Greek wrestled in the winds, and the great pines in the canyon seemed to bow to the wrath of the son of Peleus.[11] Mr. Oakhurst listened with quiet satisfaction. Most especially was he interested in the fate of "Ash-heels," as the Innocent persisted in denominating the "swift-footed Achilles."

So with small food and much of Homer and the accordion, a week passed over the heads of the outcasts. The sun again forsook them, and again from leaden skies the snowflakes were sifted over the land. Day by day closer around them drew the snowy circle, until at last they looked from their prison over drifted walls of dazzling white that towered twenty feet above their heads. It became more and more difficult to replenish their fires, even from the fallen trees beside them, now half-hidden in the drifts. And yet no one complained. The lovers turned from the dreary prospect and looked into each other's eyes, and were happy. Mr. Oakhurst settled himself coolly to the losing game before him. The Duchess, more cheerful than she had been, assumed the care of Piney. Only Mother Shipton—once the strongest of the party—seemed to sicken and fade. At midnight on the tenth day she called Oakhurst to her side. "I'm going," she said, in a voice of <u>querulous</u> weakness, "but don't say anything about it. Don't waken the kids. Take the bundle from under my head and open it."

vituperative (vĭ to͞o′ pər ə tiv) *adj.* spoken abusively

querulous (kwer′ ə ləs) *adj.* inclined to find fault

---

9. **Mr. Pope** English poet Alexander Pope (1688–1744).
10. *Iliad* (il′ ē əd) Greek epic poem written by Homer that tells the story of the Trojan War.
11. **son of Peleus** (pē′ lē əs) Achilles (ə kil′ ēz), the Greek warrior hero in the *Iliad*.

Mr. Oakhurst did so. It contained Mother Shipton's rations for the last week, untouched. "Give 'em to the child," she said, pointing to the sleeping Piney. "You've starved yourself," said the gambler. "That's what they call it," said the woman, querulously, as she lay down again and, turning her face to the wall, passed quietly away.

The accordion and the bones were put aside that day, and Homer was forgotten. When the body of Mother Shipton had been committed to the snow, Mr. Oakhurst took the Innocent aside, and showed him a pair of snowshoes, which he had fashioned from the old pack saddle. "There's one chance in a hundred to save her yet," he said, pointing to Piney; "but it's there," he added, pointing toward Poker Flat. "If you can reach there in two days she's safe." "And you?" asked Tom Simson. "I'll stay here," was the curt reply.

The lovers parted with a long embrace. "You are not going, too?" said the Duchess as she saw Mr. Oakhurst apparently waiting to accompany him. "As far as the canyon," he replied. He turned suddenly, and kissed the Duchess, leaving her pallid face aflame and her trembling limbs rigid with amazement.

Night came, but not Mr. Oakhurst. It brought the storm again and the whirling snow. Then the Duchess, feeding the fire, found that someone had quietly piled beside the hut enough fuel to last a few days longer. The tears rose to her eyes, but she hid them from Piney.

The women slept but little. In the morning, looking into each other's faces, they read their fate. Neither spoke; but Piney, accepting the position of the stronger, drew near and placed her arm around the Duchess's waist. They kept this attitude for the rest of the day. That night the storm reached its greatest fury, and, rending asunder the protecting pines, invaded the very hut.

Toward morning they found themselves unable to feed the fire, which gradually died away. As the embers slowly blackened, the Duchess crept closer to Piney, and broke the silence of many hours: "Piney, can you pray?" "No, dear," said Piney, simply. The Duchess, without knowing exactly why, felt relieved, and, putting her head upon Piney's shoulder, spoke no more. And so reclining, the younger and purer pillowing the head of her soiled sister upon her virgin breast, they fell asleep.

The wind lulled as if it feared to waken them. Feathery drifts of snow, shaken from the long pine boughs, flew like white-winged birds, and settled about them as they slept. The moon through the rifted clouds looked down upon what had been the camp. But all human stain, all trace of earthly travail, was hidden beneath the spotless mantle mercifully flung from above.

They slept all that day and the next, nor did they waken when voices and footsteps broke the silence of the camp. And when pitying fingers brushed the snow from their wan faces, you could scarcely have told from the equal peace that dwelt upon them which was she that had sinned. Even the law of Poker Flat recognized this, and turned away, leaving them still locked in each other's arms.

Reading Strategy

Questioning the Text
Why did the gambler make only one pair of shoes?

Reading Strategy

Questioning the Text
What question might you ask about Mr. Oakhurst's decision to stay?

20 ✓ **Reading Check**
What happens to Mother Shipton?

18 Reading Strategy

Questioning the Text

- Reread the passage aloud, and ask students if they have noticed anything odd about the description of the snowshoes. Make sure they understand the significance of the snowshoes as a way to increase the possibility of survival.

- Then, ask students the first Reading Strategy question on p. 589: Why did the gambler make only one pair of shoes?
  Answer: Students might say that Oakhurst had enough material for only a single pair.

19 Reading Strategy

Questioning the Text

- Read the passage aloud for students. Ask them to explain what Mr. Oakhurst has done for Tom.
  Answer: Mr. Oakhurst has fashioned a single pair of snowshoes, which he gives to Tom instead of keeping them for himself. This allows Tom to escape the camp, and will maximize his chances of reaching Poker Flat.

▶ **Monitor Progress** Ask the second Reading Strategy question on p. 589: What question might you ask about Mr. Oakhurst's decision to stay?
  Possible answer: Does Mr. Oakhurst really intend to remain?

20 ✓ **Reading Check**

Answer: After starving herself and giving her accumulated rations to Piney, Mother Shipton dies.

CUSTOMIZE INSTRUCTION FOR UNIVERSAL ACCESS

For Special Needs Students	For Advanced Readers
Help these students make sense of the language Harte uses to describe the fate of the two woman left at the camp (. . . *all human stain, all trace of earthly travail, was hidden beneath the spotless mantle mercifully flung from above*). Discuss the symbolism of the "spotless mantle" that covers the outcasts. Guide students to understand that beneath that layer of snow, both the innocent and the sinner reach the same peaceful state.	Invite students to compare and contrast the views of fate and death expressed in this story with those expressed in other selections they may have read, such as stories and poems by Irving, Hawthorne, Melville, Dickinson, Bierce, and Poe. Which characters are stoic and accepting in the face of death? Which characters find new strength in dire circumstances? Which sink to new lows? Which complain or become bitter? Which become heroic?

Answers for p. 590

Review and Assess

1. Many students are likely to name Mr. Oakhurst, because he proves to be coolheaded and compassionate. Some might name Mother Shipton, because she sacrifices her own life to save Piney's.

2. **(a)** They have decided to rid the town of unwanted people by hanging two and banishing several others. **(b)** Some of the secret committee's members are angry that they lost money while gambling against Mr. Oakhurst.

3. **(a)** Tom Simson and Piney Woods, who are running away in order to get married, join the outcasts. **(b)** They evoke the outcasts' feelings of protectiveness, and they also lift everyone's spirits. Tom and Piney are young, open-hearted, and naïve; these qualities bring out tenderness in the others.

4. **(a)** He discovers that Uncle Billy has disappeared, along with the mules. **(b)** Students' responses will vary. Accept all logical answers.

5. **(a)** She stops eating and stores her rations for Piney's later use. **(b)** She may believe that only a few of those snowbound will survive—and that a young woman's life is more valuable than her own.

6. **(a)** He indicates that his "professional habits" as a gambler have trained him to function on little sleep. **(b)** Students may say that Oakhurst clearly knows their chances for survival are low at best, and so he leaves the camp and takes his own life.

7. **(a)** They find the frozen bodies of Piney and the Duchess, the farewell note, and the body of Mr. Oakhurst. **(b)** Sample response: Regardless of one's "good" or "bad" deeds during life, in the end death spares no person.

8. Students may cite natural disasters, such as hurricanes and floods, and situations in which people unite in the name of a social, political, or environmental cause.

But at the head of the gulch, on one of the largest pine trees, they found the deuce of clubs pinned to the bark with a bowie knife. It bore the following, written in pencil, in a firm hand:

> BENEATH THIS TREE
> LIES THE BODY
> OF
> JOHN OAKHURST,
> WHO STRUCK A STREAK OF BAD LUCK
> ON THE 23D OF NOVEMBER, 1850
> AND
> HANDED IN HIS CHECKS
> ON THE 7TH DECEMBER, 1850.

And pulseless and cold, with a Derringer[12] by his side and a bullet in his heart, though still calm as in life, beneath the snow lay he who was at once the strongest and yet the weakest of the outcasts of Poker Flat.

---

12. **Derringer** small pistol.

Review and Assess

Thinking About the Selection

1. **Respond:** Which character did you admire the most? Why?

2. **(a) Recall:** At the opening of the story, what has the secret committee of Poker Flat decided? **(b) Infer:** What motivates the committee to take action against Mr. Oakhurst?

3. **(a) Recall:** Who joins the outcasts at their camp? **(b) Analyze:** What effect do the newcomers have on the outcasts?

4. **(a) Recall:** What does Mr. Oakhurst discover when he awakens after his first night at the camp? **(b) Draw Conclusions:** What do you think happened to Uncle Billy?

5. **(a) Recall:** What does Mother Shipton do with her rations? **(b) Analyze:** Why do you think she does this?

6. **(a) Recall:** What explanation does Oakhurst give for his ability to go without sleep? **(b) Infer:** Do you think Oakhurst knew their "luck" was about to run out? Explain.

7. **(a) Recall:** What does the rescue party discover? **(b) Interpret:** What theme or message might their discovery—and this story—convey?

8. **Apply:** Although the characters in the story have little in common, they band together. For what reasons do people tend to draw together in life? Explain.

✎ ASSESSMENT PRACTICE: Reading Comprehension

Context   (For more practice, see Test Preparation Workbook, p. 33.)

Many tests require students to use context to determine the meaning of unfamiliar words. Use the following sample test item to give students practice in this skill.

> But even this act did not draw the group into any closer sympathy. . . . Mother Shipton eyed the possessor of "Five Spot" with <u>malevolence</u>, and Uncle Billy included the whole party in one sweeping anathema.

In this passage, <u>malevolence</u> means--

A sympathy   **C** hatred

B contentment   **D** mellowness

The *but* at the beginning of the passage indicates that sympathy is in contrast to malevolence. The *and* before Uncle Billy's reaction indicates that *anathema* is similar to *malevolence*. These context clues should lead students to discover that the correct response is *C*.

Review and Assess

Literary Analysis

Regionalism

1. Find three details that establish the **regionalism** of the story.
2. (a) Find a passage in which Harte describes the physical environment. (b) What details help you picture the California landscape?
3. What point about the culture of the West does Harte convey? Explain.

Connecting Literary Elements

4. What inferences about the **local color** of Poker Flat can you make from the following passage?

   > A few of the committee had urged hanging him as a possible example, and a sure method of reimbursing themselves from his pocket of the sums he had won from them.

5. Explain why the story would not be as effective if the setting were changed—for example—to New England.

Reading Strategy

Questioning the Text

6. What is meant by the following passage?

   > There was a Sabbath lull in the air which, in a settlement unused to Sabbath influences, looked ominous.

7. What does Harte mean when he writes that Oakhurst "was at once the strongest and yet the weakest of the outcasts of Poker Flat"?
8. Find three complex passages in the text. Use a chart like the one shown to record your questions and answers.

Passage From Text	Question	Answer

Extend Understanding

9. **Social Studies Connection:** What conclusions can you draw about law in the settlements that emerged during the Gold Rush?

Quick Review

Regionalism is a literary movement that depicts and analyzes the unique qualities of a geographical area and its people.

Details of **local color** capture the attitudes or customs of a geographical area.

To **question the text,** analyze important ideas, plot development, and the author's purpose.

 Take It to the Net

www.phschool.com

Take the interactive self-test online to check your understanding of the selection.

The Outcasts of Poker Flat ◆ 591

✹ ENRICHMENT: Further Reading

Other Works by Bret Harte

"The Luck of Roaring Camp"

Outcroppings

The Lost Galleon

Take It to the Net

Visit www.phschool.com for more information on Bret Harte.

Answers for p. 591

Review and Assess

1. Examples that appear early in the story include: *the main street of Poker Flat, a settlement unused to Sabbath influences,* "I reckon . . .", *red dust, neat boots, hanging from the boughs of a sycamore in the gulch,* "agin justice to let this yer young man from Roaring Camp," and so on.

2. **(a)** Students might cite the paragraph on p. 582 beginning "The road to Sandy Bar . . ." **(b)** Details include "steep mountain range," "day's severe travel," "moist, temperate regions," "cold, bracing air," and "narrow and difficult."

3. Harte notes that the challenging terrain shapes people's attitudes, perhaps making them tougher, and less sympathetic.

4. The inhabitants of Poker Flat have a distorted conception of justice and try to use this idea to serve their own needs.

5. The story's effectiveness depends on the frigid and changeable mountain landscape of the Sierra Nevadas, as well as on the sense of "law and order" and "justice" at work in the newly established communities of the Old West.

6. Given that people in Poker Flat did not observe the Sabbath in any significant way, a sober and serene atmosphere, such as one might find on Sunday in a town of churchgoers, seemed unnatural and of ill omen.

7. He is the strongest in that he squarely faces the hopelessness of the group's situation; he is also the only one who actively takes measures to secure their survival. He is the weakest in that he "hand[s] in his checks" rather than see the "losing game" through to the end.

8. Students' responses should contain entries for each section of the chart. Their questions should concern important matters of the story.

9. Justice was not blind. Law was a convenience of those in the majority, and could be bent to suit their personal wills or to enact vendettas.

Answers for p. 592

❶ Vocabulary Development

Word Analysis

1. b
2. a

Spelling Strategy

1. quarreled
2. queasy
3. quest

Concept Development:

1. c	5. c
2. a	6. b
3. b	7. a
4. b	8. c

❷ Grammar and Style

Practice

1. He wasn't joking, yet she continued.
2. He raced to the gate, for the plane was about to depart.
3. Vitamins can be good supplements, but they are no substitute for a healthy diet.
4. The cat jumped up onto the table, and spilled the milk.
5. I am very tired, so I will take a nap.

Writing Application

Students' editorials should contain at least two compound sentences.

Integrate Language Skills

❶ Vocabulary Development Lesson

Word Analysis: Latin Word Part -bel-

The word *bellicose*, like *belligerent*, uses the Latin word part *-bel-* from the word *bellum*, meaning "war." Both *bellicose* and *belligerent* mean "warlike" or "ready to fight or quarrel."

Choose the letter of the item that best defines the italicized word in each sentence.

   a. quarrelsome   **b.** act of resistance

1. The *rebellion* was the result of opposition to the government.
2. He must control his rage and not be so *bellicose*.

Spelling Strategy

In English words, the letter *q* is almost always followed by the letter *u*, as in *querulous*. Find a synonym that begins with *qu* for each of the following words.

   1. argued   2. nauseated   3. mission

❷ Grammar and Style Lesson

Coordinating Conjunctions in Compound Sentences

Coordinating conjunctions connect words or groups of words. These conjunctions include *and*, *but*, *for*, *nor*, *or*, *so*, and *yet*. Place a comma before a coordinating conjunction that joins the independent clauses in a compound sentence.

> They slept all day, *and* they did not awaken . . .

Practice Use the coordinating conjunction provided to form compound sentences.

1. He wasn't joking. She continued. (*yet*)

Concept Development: Synonyms

Select the letter of the word that is closest in meaning to the first word.

1. expatriated: (a) honored, (b) ignored, (c) expelled
2. anathema: (a) curse, (b) riddle, (c) chant
3. bellicose: (a) strong, (b) quarrelsome, (c) beautiful
4. recumbent: (a) full, (b) reclining, (c) unnecessary
5. equanimity: (a) fairness, (b) precision, (c) serenity
6. vociferation: (a) uncertainty, (b) loudness, (c) cleverness
7. vituperative: (a) scolding, (b) healthful, (c) complex
8. querulous: (a) trustworthy, (b) mysterious, (c) disagreeable

2. He raced to the gate. The plane was about to depart. (for)
3. Vitamins can be good supplements. They are no substitute for a healthy diet. (*but*)
4. The cat jumped up onto the table. It spilled the milk. (*and*)
5. I am very tired. I will take a nap. (*so*)

Writing Application As a newspaper editor serving mining towns, write a brief editorial about the outcasts and their fate. Use at least two compound sentences.

WG *Prentice Hall Writing and Grammar Connection: Chapter 17, Section 4*

TEACHING RESOURCES

The following resources can be used to enrich or extend the instruction for pp. 592–593.

Vocabulary

📖 **Selection Support:** Build Vocabulary, 138

📖 **Vocabulary and Spelling Practice Book,** (Use this booklet for skills enrichment.)

Grammar

📖 **Selection Support:** Grammar and Style, p. 139 ▪

WG **Writing and Grammar,** Ruby Level, p. 388

▪ **Daily Language Practice Transparencies**

Writing

WG **Writing and Grammar,** Ruby Level, p. 31 ▪

📖 **Extension Activities,** p. 31

▪ **Writing Models and Graphic Organizers on Transparencies,** p. 37

💿 **Writing and Grammar iText CD-ROM**

▪ **BLOCK SCHEDULING:** Resources marked with this symbol provide varied instruction during 90-minute blocks.

❸ Writing Lesson

Critical Review

Write a critical review of "The Outcasts of Poker Flat" to appear in a magazine targeted at fans of westerns. Support your opinion of the story while analyzing its plot, main ideas, and effect on the reader.

Prewriting   Select passages describing the characters, conflicts, main ideas, or setting that move you to respond. Jot down your thoughts on each of these passages.

Drafting   Begin with an introduction that summarizes your opinions about the story. Then, analyze each passage you have selected, and explain what it reveals about the story.

Revising   The evaluative words you use to convey praise or judgment about the story should be precise. Review your conclusion to be sure it incorporates language that conveys a strong evaluation.

Model: Revising to Include Evaluative Modifiers

These examples reinforce my belief that this story is

well-crafted and entertaining

~~interesting and good.~~ People who like westerns will find

engaging and

Harte's setting and the characters realistic.

> Specific modifiers such as *well-crafted, entertaining,* and *engaging* convey the writer's attitude toward the work.

 Prentice Hall Writing and Grammar Connection: Chapter 14, Section 4

❹ Extension Activities

Listening and Speaking As Tom Simson, the only survivor of the stranded group, prepare and deliver a **eulogy**—a speech in honor of someone who has died—for Mr. Oakhurst. Speaking candidly but respectfully, be sure to include these details:

- Colorful, informal "western" language
- Personal experiences you have had with Mr. Oakhurst.

After rehearsing, deliver the eulogy to classmates.

Research and Technology Use library databases or the Internet to learn about the activities at the center of the gold rush. Then, develop a **prospecting and mining report,** identifying the main steps in each of these processes. Include photographs, flow-charts, or other visuals to communicate your findings.

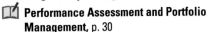 **Take It to the Net**   www.phschool.com

Go online for an additional research activity using the Internet.

The Outcasts of Poker Flat ◆ 593

ASSESSMENT RESOURCES

The following resources can be used to assess students' knowledge and skills.

Selection Assessment

 Formal Assessment, p. 149

📖 **Open Book Test**, p. 91

📼 **Got It! Assessment Videotapes**, Tape 3

💿 **Test Bank Software**

📱 *Take It to the Net*

Visit www.phschool.com for self-tests and additional questions on the selections.

Listening and Speaking Rubric

📖 **Performance Assessment and Portfolio Management**, p. 30

 PRENTICE HALL ASSESSMENT *SYSTEM*

 Workbook   **Transparencies**

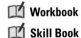 **Skill Book**   💿 **CD-ROM**

❸ Writing Lesson

- Students' critical reviews should contain clear opinions about the story as well as careful, insightful analysis of the story's content, themes, and effect on the reader.

- Remind students that the springboard for each of their critical reviews is his or her own authentic response to the story. In other words, there is no single "correct" response. Each reader must find the best possible ways to support his or her own view of Harte's work.

- Use the Writing Lesson, as well as Writing Process Model 7 in **Writing Models and Graphic Organizers on Transparencies**, p. 37, to guide students in developing their critical reviews.

❹ Listening and Speaking

- Encourage students to reread all passages from "The Outcasts of Poker Flat" that contain information about Simson. After they have reviewed Harte's descriptions of the "innocent" and his relationship with Oakhurst, encourage students to write a few sentences that concisely summarize the younger man.

- Point out that eulogies usually contain remarks about the deceased person's positive qualities, as well as anecdotes that illustrate the personality of the individual.

- As they work, remind students to view Mr. Oakhurst through Simson's eyes.

- Have students use the Peer Assessment form for Delivering a Speech, p. 30 in **Performance Assessment and Portfolio Management**.

CUSTOMIZE INSTRUCTION
For Universal Access

To address different learning styles, use the following activities suggested in the **Extension Activities** booklet, p. 31.

For Visual/Spatial Learners, use Activity 5.

For Interpersonal Learners, use Activity 6.

For Intrapersonal Learners, use Activity 7.

Heading West ✦ I Will Fight No More Forever

Lesson Objectives

1. **To analyze and respond to literary elements**
   - Literary Analysis: Tone
   - Comparing Literary Works
2. **To read, comprehend, analyze, and critique nonfiction and a speech**
   - Reading Strategy: Responding
   - Reading Check questions
   - Review and Assess questions
   - Assessment Practice (ATE)
3. **To develop word analysis skills, fluency, and systematic vocabulary**
   - Vocabulary Development Lesson: Latin Term: *terra firma*
4. **To understand and apply written and oral language conventions**
   - Spelling Strategy
   - Grammar and Style Lesson: Sentence Fragments
5. **To understand and apply appropriate writing and research strategies**
   - Writing Lesson: Position Paper on Development
   - Extension Activity: Marketing Brochure
6. **To understand and apply listening and speaking strategies**
   - Extension Activity: Oral Interpretation

STEP-BY-STEP TEACHING GUIDE	PACING GUIDE
PRETEACH	
Motivate Students and Provide Background	
Use the Motivation activity (ATE p. 594)	5 min.
Read and discuss the author and background features (SE/ATE pp. 594, 596)	5 min.
Introduce the Concepts	
Introduce the Literary Analysis and Reading Strategy (SE/ATE p. 595) Ⓐ	15 min.
Pronounce the vocabulary words and read their definitions (SE p. 595)	5 min.
TEACH	
Monitor Comprehension	
Informally monitor comprehension by circulating while students read independently or in groups Ⓐ	20 min.
Monitor students' comprehension with the Reading Check notes (SE/ATE pp. 597, 599, 601)	as students read
Develop vocabulary with Vocabulary notes (SE pp. 597, 598, 599, 600; ATE p. 597)	as students read
Develop Understanding	
Develop students' understanding of tone with the Literary Analysis annotations (SE pp. 596, 598, 600; ATE pp. 596, 598, 600) Ⓐ	5 min.
Develop students' ability to respond to reading with the Reading Strategy annotations (SE pp. 597, 601; ATE pp. 597, 599, 601)	5 min.
ASSESS	
Assess Mastery	
Assess students' mastery of the Reading Strategy and Literary Analysis by having them answer the Review and Assess questions (SE/ATE p. 603)	15 min.
Use one or more of the print and media Assessment Resources (ATE p. 605) Ⓐ	up to 45 min.
EXTEND	
Apply Understanding	
Have students complete the Vocabulary Development Lesson and the Grammar and Style Lesson (SE p. 604) Ⓐ	20 min.
Apply students' understanding of coherence in writing by using the Writing Lesson (SE/ATE p. 605) Ⓐ	45 min.
Apply students' understanding using one or more of the Extension Activities (SE p. 605)	20–90 min.

Ⓐ ACCELERATED INSTRUCTION:
Use the strategies and activities identified with an Ⓐ.

UNIVERSAL ACCESS
● = Below Level Students
▲ = On-Level Students
■ = Above Level Students

Time and Resource Manager

RESOURCES		
PRINT 📖	**TRANSPARENCIES** 🔒	**TECHNOLOGY** 💿 🎧 📼
• **Beyond Literature,** Cross-Curricular Connection: Social Studies, p. 32 ▲ ■		• **Interest Grabber Video,** Tape 4 ● ▲ ■
• **Selection Support Workbook:** ● ▲ ■ Literary Analysis, p. 145 Reading Strategy, p. 144 Build Vocabulary, p. 142	• **Literary Analysis and Reading Transparencies,** pp. 63 and 64 ● ▲ ■	
		• **Listening to Literature** ● ▲ ■ Audiocassettes, Side 20 Audio CDs, CD 12
• **Literatura en español** ● ▲ • **Literary Analysis for Enrichment** ■		
• **Formal Assessment:** Selection Test, pp. 152–154 ● ▲ ■ • **Open Book Test,** pp. 94–96 ● ▲ ■ • **Performance Assessment and Portfolio Management,** p. 30 ● ▲ ■ • **PRENTICE HALL ASSESSMENT SYSTEM** ● ▲ ■	• **PRENTICE HALL ASSESSMENT SYSTEM** ● ▲ ■ Skills Practice Answers and Explanations on Transparencies	• **Test Bank Software** ● ▲ ■ • **Got It! Assessment Videotapes,** Tape 3 ● ▲
• **Selection Support Workbook:** ● ▲ ■ Grammar and Style, p. 143 • **Writing and Grammar,** Ruby Level ● ▲ ■ • **Extension Activities,** p. 32 ● ▲ ■	• **Daily Language Practice Transparencies** ● ▲ • **Writing Models and Graphic Organizers on Transparencies,** p. 75 ● ▲ ■	• **Writing and Grammar iText CD-ROM** ● ▲ ■ **Take It to the Net** www.phschool.com

BLOCK SCHEDULING: Use one 90-minute class period to preteach the selection and have students read it. Use a second 90-minute class period to assess students' mastery of skills and have them complete one of the Extension Activities.

Step-by-Step Teaching Guide for pp. 594–595

Motivation

Ask students to imagine that they must leave America to relocate elsewhere. Have them form groups to discuss how they will respond. Where will they go? How and with whom will they travel? How will they bid goodbye to friends and family? Then tell students they will read about two people who left home for very different reasons: Miriam Davis Colt's family left their upstate New York home by choice to live in a prairie settlement, while Chief Joseph and his people were forced off their land.

▣ Interest Grabber Video

As an alternative, play "The Long Journey West" on Tape 4 to engage student interest.

❶ Background

More About the Authors

"The earth is the mother of all people, and all people should have equal rights upon it." Chief Joseph's words express the point of view of Native Americans, who saw themselves as using land but never owning it. Because they were a culture of hunters, the Nez Percé ranged over a vast territory. Settlers like Miriam Davis Colt, however, were farmers, and they had a very different view of the land. They wanted individual plots to cultivate, and they considered the land they settled as their own. These opposing viewpoints were a source of ongoing strife in frontier America.

Prepare to Read

❶ Heading West ◆ I Will Fight No More Forever

Miriam Davis Colt (1815–c.1900)

Miriam Davis Colt was one of a quarter of a million Americans who traveled across the United States in the mid-1800s to forge a new frontier. These pioneers knew they were making history, and hundreds of them kept diaries to send to relatives back east or to pass down to their children.

The Women's Perspective Usually, the pioneer men, filled with a sense of destiny and excitement, made the decision to sell their homes and move their families west. The women's diaries, however, reveal a different point of view. Many women describe their anguish at leaving home, their struggle to maintain some domestic comforts in harsh conditions, and their fear of the dangers ahead.

A Vision of the Future The women, nevertheless, did share their husbands' belief that they were building a better future for their children. The path to that future might be hard, but it was also filled with moments of sudden beauty, like the "crab-apple trees . . . blooming in sheets of whiteness" that Colt saw by the side of a Kansas road as she and her family traveled to a new life in a "city" established by a group of vegetarians. Her family was one of many that invested money to create this new settlement, where they hoped to live with people "whose tastes and habits" would coincide with their own.

The Extending Frontier In 1856, when Colt and her family set out on their journey, they were heading for Kansas. At the time, Kansas was considered to be in the far "West," the destination for many emigrants from the country's Eastern regions. It was not until later in the 19th century that settlers sought the even further reaches of California and Oregon, journeys which required the treacherous crossings of the plains and mountains, and presented even more spectacular hardships than those suffered by the Colts.

Chief Joseph (1840–1904)

Chief Joseph was born in the Wallowa Valley in what is now Oregon. In 1871, he succeeded his father as leader of the Nez Percé (nez′ pʉrs′ or pər sā′) tribe. At that time, the United States government was trying to force the tribe to relocate to Idaho. The Nez Percé had signed a treaty in 1863 giving the government control of the tribe's land, but Chief Joseph felt that the treaty was illegal and refused to recognize it.

A Reluctant Warrior In 1877, the dispute between the Nez Percé and the United States government erupted into war. Chief Joseph, hoping to join forces with the Sioux, led his people on a long march through Idaho and Montana, during which the outnumbered Nez Percé frequently clashed with federal troops. Under Chief Joseph's astute and able military leadership, they won several battles.

The Bitter End By the fall, however, the Nez Percé were cold, starving, and scattered. On October 5, after defeat in a battle in the Bear Paw Mountains of Montana, Chief Joseph finally surrendered. The Nez Percé were sent to live in a barren Oklahoma territory. There, many of them became ill and died.

The speech in which Chief Joseph finally accepted defeat contains some of the most achingly sad and beautiful words ever spoken. Because of the attention his words received, Chief Joseph became for many a symbol of the Nez Percé and their tragic plight.

594 ◆ *Division, Reconciliation, and Expansion (1850–1914)*

TEACHING RESOURCES

The following resources can be used to enrich or extend the instruction for pp. 594–595.

Motivation
▣ **Interest Grabber Video**, Tape 4 ▣

Background
📖 **Beyond Literature**, p. 32

 Take It to the Net
Visit www.phschool.com for Background and hotlinks for the selections.

Literary Analysis
📑 **Literary Analysis and Reading Transparencies,** Tone, p. 64 ▣

📖 **Selection Support:** Literary Analysis, p. 154

Reading
📑 **Literary Analysis and Reading Transparencies,** Responding, p. 63

 BLOCK SCHEDULING: Resources marked with this symbol provide varied instruction during 90-minute blocks.

Preview

Connecting to the Literature

Both Chief Joseph and Miriam Davis Colt had to say goodbye to the places they called home. Think about how you would feel if you suddenly had to leave everything that you loved, with no possibility of ever returning.

❷ Literary Analysis

Tone

Tone is a quality of language you encounter every day in speech. Two people might say the exact same words, but differences in tone reveal their distinct emotions. In much the same way, a writer's attitude emerges in his or her tone. Consider the optimistic tone in this passage from Colt's diary:

> Full of hope, as we leave the smoking embers of our camp-fire this morning. Expect tonight to arrive at our new home.

The tone of a literary work is established by the writer's choice of descriptions and details. Use a chart like the one shown to interpret the tone of these selections.

Comparing Literary Works

These selections put a human face on two different aspects of the western expansion of the United States. Fueled by hope, Colt journeyed in search of a new life. In contrast, Chief Joseph lost the battle to save his people and their ancient way of life. These opposing circumstances are reflected in each piece's **mood**—the feeling created in the reader. As you read, compare the conflicts that motivated each writer. Note the circumstances and emotions each experienced, and identify the mood that each evokes.

Excerpt

No escort is seen! No salute is heard! We move slowly and drippingly into town . . . .

Tone

Angry, even sarcastic

❸ Reading Strategy

Responding

The selections you are about to read describe life-changing events, the kind that are sure to evoke responses that will affect your appreciation of the works. As you read, take time to **respond** to the literature. Note the emotions you feel, and the images each work prompts in your imagination.

Vocabulary Development

genial (jēn′ yəl) *adj.* promoting life and growth (p. 597)

pervading (pər vād′ iŋ) *adj.* spreading throughout (p. 597)

terra firma (ter′ ə fur′ mə) (Latin) *n.* firm earth; solid ground (p. 597)

emigrants (em′ i grənts) *n.* people who leave one area to move to another (p. 598)

profusion (prō fyōō′ zhən) *n.* abundance; rich supply (p. 598)

depredations (dep′ rə dā′ shənz) *n.* acts of robbing (p. 598)

nonplused (nän′ plüsd′) *adj.* bewildered; perplexed (p. 600)

Heading West / I Will Fight No More Forever ◆ 595

❷ Literary Analysis

Tone

- Explain that an author's choice of details reveals how he or she feels about a subject. As they read "Heading West" and "I Will Fight No More Forever," have students pay special attention to tone.

- Tell students they can determine tone from the way an author describes events and details. A text's historical context can also affect tone.

- Use the instruction for Comparing Literary Works to point out that Miriam Davis Colt and Chief Joseph had very different relationships with land. Have students consider how this might affect the tone of their writings.

- Use the Tone transparency in **Literary Analysis and Reading Transparencies,** p. 64, to model for students how to determine tone by carefully reading passages of text.

❸ Reading Strategy

Responding

- Explain that responding to a text involves carefully considering the emotions you feel as you read.

- To help students appreciate their responses to texts, suggest that they pause after reading powerful passages and write down their responses.

- Using the Responding transparency in **Literary Analysis and Reading Transparencies,** p. 63, model responses to "Heading West." Have students write their own responses to the excerpt from "I Will Fight No More Forever."

Vocabulary Development

- Pronounce each vocabulary word for students, and read the definitions as a class. Have students identify any words with which they are already familiar.

 E-Teach

Visit E-Teach at www.phschool.com for teachers' essays on how to teach, with questions and answers.

CUSTOMIZE INSTRUCTION FOR UNIVERSAL ACCESS

For Less Proficient Readers	For English Learners	For Advanced Readers
Model responding using the Responding transparency in **Literary Analysis and Reading Transparencies,** p. 63. Encourage students to pause regularly as they read the selection and write down their responses and any questions they might have about the texts.	Students may find responding difficult, due to the challenge of interpreting emotionally powerful passages. Have students write down any words they find confusing and find definitions. Then, students should use their new knowledge of word meanings to respond to the texts.	Encourage students to consider the historical context of the selection as they read. Have students respond to the texts in their notes, connecting their responses to the impact of historical forces on the authors. Students may use their notes to help them complete the Writing Lesson at the end of the selection.

Step-by-Step Teaching Guide
for pp. 596–602

CUSTOMIZE INSTRUCTION
For Visual/Spatial Learners
Have students locate Potsdam and Antwerp on a map of New York State. Suggest that they follow the Colt family's route west by locating the other places the author mentions, such as Kansas City, Westport, and the Little Osage River.

❶ About the Selection
Miriam Davis Colt and her family are among a group of families making the trip to join a commune of vegetarians in the Kansas territory. Her journal entries describe what she saw, felt, and experienced en route and upon arrival.

❷ ▶Critical Viewing
Possible response: Students may say that it is surprising that despite being in the wilderness, the family still eats lunch graciously on a white tablecloth.

❸ Literary Analysis
Tone
• Have students read the entry for January 5th. Ask them to pay special attention to the details of the plans that Colt describes.
• Ask students the Literary Analysis question on p. 596: What is the tone of this description of Colt's experiences on January 5th?
Possible response: Students should recognize the hopeful, optimistic tone of this passage. They may guess that the author is trying to convince herself of the strengths of her family's plans.

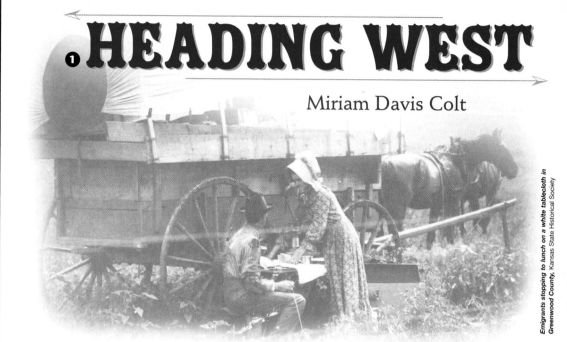

❶ HEADING WEST
Miriam Davis Colt

Emigrants stopping to lunch on a white tablecloth in Greenwood County, Kansas State Historical Society

Background
Most of the settlers of the American West, like Miriam Davis Colt and her family, were farmers who sought a better life for themselves and their children. A better life meant fertile land that they could own, cultivate, and pass on to their children. For Native Americans, however, the land was a gift that belonged to no one individual. "The earth is the mother of all people, and all people should have equal rights upon it," Chief Joseph once said. These opposing views were a source of ongoing strife in frontier America.

❸ **JANUARY 5TH, 1856.** We are going to Kansas. The Vegetarian Company that has been forming for many months, has finally organized, formed its constitution, elected its directors, and is making all necessary preparations for the spring settlement . . . . We can have, I think, good faith to believe, that our directors will fulfill on their part; and we, as settlers of a new country, by going in a company will escape the hardships attendant on families going in singly, and at once find ourselves surrounded by improving society in a young and flourishing city. It will be better for ourselves pecuniarily,[1] and better in the future for our children.

---

1. **pecuniarily** (pi kyōō′ nē er′ i lē) *adv.* financially.

596 ◆ *Division, Reconciliation, and Expansion (1850–1914)*

❷ ▲ **Critical Viewing**
Which details of this photograph of pioneers stopping for lunch seem surprising or out of place? **[Analyze]**

Literary Analysis
Tone What is the tone of this description of Colt's experiences on January 5?

TEACHING RESOURCES

The following resources can be used to enrich or extend the instruction for pp. 596–602.

Literary Analysis
📖 **Literary Analysis and Reading Transparencies,** p. 64

💿 **Listening to Literature Audio CDs,** CD 12 ■

Reading
📖 **Selection Support:** Reading Strategy, p. 144; Build Vocabulary, p. 142

🎧 **Listening to Literature Audiocassettes,** Side 20 ■

■ **BLOCK SCHEDULING:** Resources marked with this symbol provide varied instruction during 90-minute blocks.

My husband has long been a practical vegetarian, and we expect much from living in such a genial clime, where fruit is so quickly grown, and with people whose tastes and habits will coincide with our own.

JANUARY 15TH. We are making every necessary preparation for our journey, and our home in Kansas. My husband has sold his farm, purchased shares in the company, sent his money as directed by H.S. Clubb . . . . I am very busy in repairing all of our clothing, looking over bags of pieces, tearing off and reducing down, bringing everything into as small a compass as possible, so that we shall have no unnecessary baggage.

APRIL 15TH. Have been here in West Stockholm, at my brother's, since Friday last. Have visited Mother very hard, for, in all probability, it is the last visit we shall have until we meet where parting never comes—believe we have said everything we can think of to say.

APRIL 16TH. Antwerp, N.Y. Bade our friends good bye, in Potsdam, this morning, at the early hour of two o'clock.

APRIL 22ND. Have been on the cars[2] again since yesterday morning. Last night was a lovely moonlit night, a night of thought, as we sped almost with lightning speed, along in the moonlight, past the rail fences.

Found ourselves in this miserable hotel before we knew it. Miserable fare—herring boiled with cabbage—miserable, dirty beds, and an odor pervading the house that is not at all agreeable. Mistress gone.

APRIL 23RD. On board steamer "Cataract," bound for Kansas City.

APRIL 24TH. A hot summer day. The men in our company are out in the city, purchasing wagons and farming implements, to take along on the steamer up to Kansas City.

APRIL 28TH. The steamer struck a "snag" last night; gave us a terrible jar; tore off a part of the kitchen; ladies much frightened. Willie is not very well; the water is bad; it affects all strangers.

APRIL 30TH. Here we are, at Kansas City, all safely again on terra firma. Hasten to the hotel—find it very much crowded. Go up, up, up, and upstairs to our lodging rooms.

MAY 1ST. Take a walk out onto the levee—view the city, and see that it takes but a few buildings in this western world to make a city. The houses and shops stand along on the levee, extending back into the hillsides. The narrow street is literally filled with huge merchandise wagons bound for Santa Fe. The power attached to these wagons

---

2. **cars** train cars.

genial (jēn´ yəl) *adj.* promoting life and growth

Reading Strategy
Responding How would you feel if you were allowed to keep only a few items out of all the things you own?

pervading (pər vād iŋ) *adj.* spreading throughout

terra firma (ter´ ə fur´ mə) *n.* firm earth; solid ground (Latin)

☑ **Reading Check**
Why do the Colts decide to travel to Kansas?

Heading West ◆ 597

---

❹ **Reading Strategy**
Responding

- Have students read the entry for January 15th. Ask students what possessions they think the Colt family might have brought with them.
  Possible response: Students may think the Colts brought only necessities—clothing, tools, supplies—and left behind anything unnecessary.

- Then, ask students the Reading Strategy question on p. 597: How would they feel if they were allowed to keep only a few of the things they own?
  Possible response: Students may feel strong attachments to their possessions and be daunted by the prospect of choosing only a few items to keep.

- Encourage students to apply their responses by imagining how Colt felt about leaving behind most of the things her family owned.

❺ **Vocabulary Development**
The Latin Term *terra firma*

- Call students' attention to the phrase *terra firma* and its definition: "firm earth" or "solid ground."

- Explain to students that Latin phrases such as *terra firma* are often used in literature. They can often find the definitions of such Latin phrases in the dictionary.

- Ask students what tone Miriam Davis Colt creates by using the phrase *terra firma*.
  Possible response: The phrase creates a relieved tone; Colt was very happy to be off of the steamboat.

❻ ☑ **Reading Check**
Answer: The Colts have decided to move to Kansas in order to live in a commune organized by the Vegetarian Company, where they expect to improve their lives and their children's futures.

CUSTOMIZE INSTRUCTION FOR UNIVERSAL ACCESS

For Less Proficient Readers	For English Learners	For Advanced Readers
Have these students list the events of Colt's trip thus far and construct a chain-of-events chart. This strategy can help students comprehend the events related in "Heading West." Have students use the Chain of Events Organizer in the **Reader's Companion**.	The many sentence fragments in "Heading West" may confuse students. Help them to identify the missing subjects or verbs. You may guide them to restate the fragments as complete sentences. The description of the hotel in the April 22nd entry, on p. 597, is an example of sentence fragments.	Encourage students to compare and contrast Miriam Davis Colt's journal entries with any others they have read. Also, guide them to look for the ways in which the entries written by women are different from and similar to those written by men.

❼ Literary Analysis

Tone

- Distribute copies of the *Tone* graphic organizer on p. 64 of **Literary Analysis and Reading Transparencies.**

- Have students copy the bracketed passage in the *Passage* circle. Ask them to explain what Colt is writing about.
  Answer: On her eleventh wedding anniversary, Colt is looking back on her past and worrying about her future.

- Ask students the Literary Analysis question on p. 598: What is Colt's tone as she looks back on her life? Have them write their answers in the chart shown on p. 595.
  Possible Response: Colt writes fondly of the years of her marriage. But as she thinks of the future her tone becomes anxious and uncertain.

❽ Critical Thinking

Compare and Contrast

- Ask students to consider what it would be like to travel long distances in a wagon drawn by oxen.

- Read aloud the bracketed passage. Ask students: What are some of the difficulties nineteenth-century pioneer travelers faced that made traveling more difficult than today?
  Possible Response: The pioneers had to depend upon oxen and other animals for power. Such animals had to be fed and cared for. Wagons traveled slowly and often needed repairs. Roads in some areas were little more than dirt trails.

---

is seven or eight and sometimes nine pair of long-eared mules, or as many pair of oxen, with a Mexican driver who wields a whip long enough to reach the foremost pair, and who does not hesitate to use it with severity, and a noise, too.

Large droves of cattle are driven into town to be sold to <u>emigrants</u>, who like us, are going into the Territory. Our husbands are all out today buying oxen, provisions and cooking utensils for our ox-wagon journey into the Territory.

❼ This is the anniversary of my wedding-day, and as I review the past pleasant years as they have passed, one after another, until they now number eleven, a shadow comes over me, as I try to look away into the future and ask, "What is my destiny?"

Ah! away with all these shadowings. We shall be very busy this year in making our home comfortable, so that no time can be spared for that dreaded disease, "home-sickness," to take hold of us, and we mean to obey physical laws,[3] thereby securing to ourselves strength of body and vigor of mind.

MAY 2ND. A lovely day. Our husbands are loading the ox-wagons. . . . Women and children walk along up the hill out of this "Great City," wait under a tree—what a beautiful country is spread out before us! Will our Kansas scenery equal this . . . ?

❽ One mile from the city, and Dr. Thorn has broke his wagon tongue;[4] it must be sent back to Kansas City to be mended. Fires kindled—women cooking—supper eaten sitting round on logs, stones and wagon tongues. This I am sure is a "pic-nic." We expect "pic-nic" now all the time. We are shaded by the horse-chestnut, sweet walnut, and spreading oak; flowers blooming at our feet, and grasshoppers in <u>profusion</u> hopping in every direction. This is summer time.

MAY 3RD. The women and children, who slept in their wagons last night, got a good drenching from the heavy shower. It was fortunate for mother, sister, myself and children, that lodgings were found for us in a house. My husband said not a rain drop found him; he had the whole wagon to himself, besides all of our Indian blankets. Father, it seems, fell back a little and found a place to camp in a tavern (not a hotel), where he fell in with the scores of Georgians who loaded a steamer and came up the river the same time that we did. He said he had to be very shrewd indeed not to have them find out that he was a "Free States"[5] man. These Bandits have been sent in here, and will commit all sorts of <u>depredations</u> on the Free State settlers, and no doubt commit many a bloody murder.

Have passed Westport, the foothold for Border-Ruffianism. The town looks new, but the hue is dingy. Our drivers used their goads

---

3. **physical laws** community's by-laws that dictated members abstain from alcohol and meat.
4. **wagon tongue** harnessing pole attached to the front axle of a horse-drawn vehicle.
5. **"Free States"** Free Soil movement; a group whose goal was to keep slavery out of the western territories.

598 ◆ *Division, Reconciliation, and Expansion (1850–1914)*

---

emigrants (em´ i grəntz) *n.* people who leave one area to move to another

Literary Analysis
Tone What is Colt's tone as she looks back on her life?

profusion (prō fyo͞o´ zhən) *n.* abundance; rich supply

depredations (dep´ rə dā´ shənz) *n.* acts of robbing

❂ ENRICHMENT: Social Studies Connection

Troubles on the Western Frontier

When students think of a pioneer excursion westward, they may imagine a long and treacherous one across the heartland, the plains, and the mountains to reach California or Oregon. Remind students that in 1856, Kansas was the western frontier. The then territories of Kansas, Nebraska, and the Dakotas often were final destinations for intrepid settlers in search of the frontier.

According to the Kansas-Nebraska Act of 1854, settlers in these two territories were to determine for themselves whether the territories would be slave or free territories. Hostilities between bands of pro-slavery and anti-slavery settlers erupted. Pro-slavery southerners known as "border ruffians" sacked the anti-slavery town of Lawrence, Kansas. In response, John Brown and his sons slaughtered five pro-slavery settlers along Pottawatomie Creek. The violence in "bleeding Kansas" continued into 1861. Miriam Davis Colt's family entered Kansas during this time of bloodshed and chaos.

to hurry up the oxen's heavy tread, for we felt somewhat afraid, for we learned the Georgians had centered here. Here, too, came in the Santa Fe and Indian trade—so here may be seen the huge Mexican wagon, stubborn mule, swarthy driver with his goad-like whip, and the red man of the prairie on his fleet Indian pony, laden with dried meat, furs, and buffalo robes.

"What! fast in the mud, and with our wagon tongue broke?" "Why yes, to be sure." So a long time is spent before my husband and Dr. House can put our vehicle in moving order again. Meanwhile, we women folks and children must sit quietly in the wagon to keep out of the rain—lunch on soda biscuit, look at the deep, black mud in which our wagon is set, and inhale the sweet odor that comes from the blossoms of the crab-apple trees that are blooming in sheets of whiteness along the roadside. . . .

MAY 6TH. Dined on the prairie, and gathered flowers, while our tired beasts filled themselves with the fresh, green grass. . . . Have driven 18 miles to-day . . . so here we are, all huddled into this little house 12 by 16—cook supper over the fire . . . fill the one bed lengthwise and crosswise; the family of the house take to the trundle-bed,[6] while the floor is covered . . . with men, women and children, rolled in Indian blankets like silk worms in cocoons.

MAY 11TH. "Made" but a few miles yesterday. Forded the Little Osage; the last river, they say, we have to ford . . . our "noble lords" complained of the great weight of the wagons. . . . That our wagon is heavily loaded, have only to make a minute of what we have stowed away in it—eight trunks, one valise, three carpet bags, a box of soda crackers, 200 lbs. flour, 100 lbs. corn meal, a few lbs. of sugar, rice, dried apple, one washtub of little trees, utensils for cooking, and two provision boxes—say nothing of mother, a good fat sister, self, and two children, who ride through the rivers. . . .

At nightfall came to a log-cabin at the edge of the wood, and inquired of the "Lord of the Castle" if some of the women and children could take shelter under his roof for the night; the masculine number and whichever of the women that chose, couching in the wagons and under them. He said we could. His lady, who was away, presently came, with bare feet, and a white sack twisted up and thrown over her shoulder, with a few quarts of corn meal in the end that hung down her back. I said to myself—"Is that what I have got to come to?" She seemed pleased to have company—allowed us the first chance of the broad, Dutch-backed fireplace with its earthy hearth, and without pot hooks or trammels,[7] to make ready our simple evening repast. . . .

---

6. **trundle-bed** low, portable bed that can be stored beneath a larger bed.
7. **trammels** (tram´ elz) *n.* devices for hanging several pothooks in a fireplace.

The American Experience

⑩ *Moving West*

The search for "greener pastures" has been a constant factor in our nation's history. The phrase "The Great Migration" describes a steady westward shift of the American population. It includes the westward movement of the Puritans from Europe to the New World in the 1630s, of the coastal colonists to inland farms and towns, and of pioneer families headed west over the plains and prairies throughout the nineteenth century. Transience was fundamental to pioneer life, as "movers" continually searched for the next open space. Of course, some pioneers—the "stickers"— had strong urges to put down roots and develop communities. The Great American Migration blends tales of how both the movers and the stickers endured physical, financial, political, and spiritual challenges in hopes of establishing better lives for themselves and for their families.

⑪ ✓ Reading Check

What methods of travel do the Colts use in their journey?

Responding

- Have students read the bracketed passage. Ask them how Miriam Davis Colt tries to put a positive spin on this latest disaster. **Answer:** She focuses on the sweetness of the crabapple blossoms.

- Ask students how they think they themselves would cope under such trying circumstances. **Possible Response:** Students may hope that they would have Miriam Davis Colt's patience, but many will admit that they would be angry and frustrated.

▶ Monitor Progress Ask students to write descriptive paragraphs about what traveling in Colt's day would have been like. **Answer:** Student paragraphs should respond on a personal level to the details in Colt's diary.

⑩ Background

The American Experience: Manifest Destiny

Manifest Destiny was a phrase used by politicians and leaders to explain territorial expansion of U.S. boundaries westward to the Pacific Ocean. The idea of Manifest Destiny encompassed the belief that it was the mission of the United States not only to extend its borders territorially, but to spread the democratic ideals upon which the nation was built.

Practically, Manifest Destiny allowed for individuals and families to seek new opportunities on the frontier. Land was cheap and natural resources were plentiful. Politically, it allowed the government the necessary justification needed to claim new territories, sometimes through war, and often at the expense of Native American populations.

⑪ ✓ Reading Check

Answer: The Colts travel by train, by steamboat, and by ox-wagon.

CUSTOMIZE INSTRUCTION FOR UNIVERSAL ACCESS

For Special Needs Students	For Advanced Readers
These students may have difficulty reading Miriam Davis Colt's diary entries because of their relatively informal nature. To help them, have them read the selection along with **Listening to Literature,** Audiocassette, Side 20 or Audio CD, CD 12. Make sure students pay equal attention to the text and to the recorded selection.	Discuss the style that Miriam Colt uses in her diary. This is a first-person narrative, arranged chronologically, and it contains sentence fragments as well as complete sentences. Students should also notice that Colt's writing style changes, from providing facts to describing her surroundings to personal reflections. Have students identify these elements in Colt's writings and in other journals they have read.

⑫ Literary Analysis

Tone and Mood

- Have students read the bracketed passage. Ask them to pay special attention to the details of the Colts' final approach to their new home.

▶ **Monitor Progress** Ask students the Literary Analysis question on p. 598: What contrasting moods does Colt seem to feel as the settlers near their new home? **Possible Response:** Students should notice that the heavy rain creates a somber mood. Despite the rain, the ordeals of the journey, and the many disappointments, Colt's mood is optimistic—she still has great hopes for her new home.

⑬ ▶ Critical Viewing

Possible Response: Students may conclude that in these frontier towns, travelers such as the Colts might get to sleep under a roof, or join groups heading back east. They could get supplies and medical help, get their wagons fixed, and learn what they would face in the miles ahead.

Are now [May 11th] crossing the 20 mile prairie, no roads—Think Mrs. Voorhees will get walking enough crossing this prairie. She is quite a pedestrian, surely, for she has walked every bit of the way in, so far, from Kansas City, almost 100 miles.

Arrive at Elm Creek—no house to lodge in tonight—campfire kindled—supper cooked, and partaken of with a keen relish, sitting in family groups around the "great big" fire. Some will sleep in wagons, others under the canopy of the blue vault of Heaven. The young men have built some shady little bowers of the green boughs; they are looking very cosily under them, wrapped in their white Indian blankets.

We ladies, or rather, "emigrant women," are having a chat around the camp-fire—the bright stars are looking down upon us—we wonder if we shall be neighbors to each other in the great "Octagon City. . . ."

MAY 12TH. Full of hope, as we leave the smoking embers of our camp-fire this morning. Expect tonight to arrive at our new home.

⑫ It begins to rain, rain, rain, like a shower; we move slowly on, from high prairie, around the deep ravine—are in sight of the timber that skirts the Neosho river. Have sent three men in advance to announce our coming; are looking for our Secretary, (Henry S. Clubb) with an escort to welcome us into the embryo city. If the booming of cannon is not heard at our approach, shall expect a salute from the firing of Sharp's rifles, certainly.

No escort is seen! no salute is heard! We move slowly and drippingly into town just at nightfall—feeling not a little <u>nonplused</u> on learning that our worthy, or unworthy Secretary was out walking in the rain with his *dear* wife. We leave our wagons and make our way to the large camp-fire. It is surrounded by men and women cooking their suppers—while others are busy close by, grinding their hominy[8] in hand mills.

---

8. **hominy** (häm′ ə nē) *n.* dry corn, usually ground and boiled for food.

Literary Analysis

Tone and Mood What contrasting moods does Colt seem to feel as the settlers near their new home?

nonplused (nän′ plüsd′) *adj.* bewildered; perplexed

---

⑬ ▼ Critical Viewing

This 1866 photograph shows covered wagons on Main Street in Ottawa, Kansas. What does Colt's diary suggest about the importance of towns like this one to the wagon trains of settlers traveling westward? [**Draw Conclusions**]

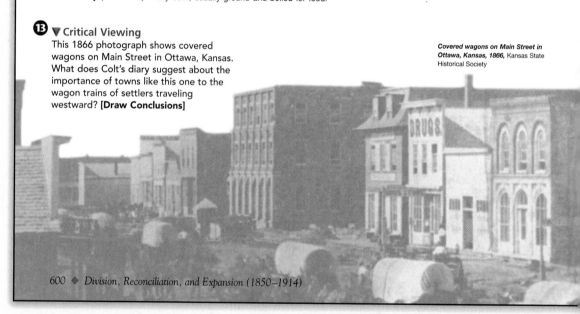

Covered wagons on Main Street in Ottawa, Kansas, 1866, Kansas State Historical Society

600 ◆ *Division, Reconciliation, and Expansion (1850–1914)*

CUSTOMIZE INSTRUCTION FOR UNIVERSAL ACCESS

For Less Proficient Readers	For Gifted/Talented Students
If students are having difficulty understanding what is happening to the Colt family towards the end of Miriam Davis Colt's journal, have them pair up with more advanced readers to help them draw conclusions based on the tone in the selection.	Ask students to consider what might happen to Miriam Davis Colt and her family after May 13, 1856. Would the family remain at the settlement, despite their disappointment? Would they begin to build a home? Would they move on to parts further west? Have students write a new final entry for Miriam Colt's journal. They can present their entries to the class.

14 Look around, and see the grounds all around the camp-fire are covered with tents, in which the families are staying. Not a house is to be seen. In the large tent here is a cook stove—they have supper prepared for us; it consists of hominy, soft Johnny cake (or corn bread, as it is called here), stewed apple, and tea. We eat what is set before us, "asking no questions for conscience' sake."

The ladies tell us they are sorry to see us come to this place; which shows us that all is not right. Are too weary to question, but with hope depressed go to our lodgings, which we find around in the tents, and in our wagons.

MAY 13TH. Can anyone imagine our disappointment this morning, on learning from this and that member, that no mills have been built; that the directors, after receiving our money to build mills, have not fulfilled the trust reposed in them, and that in consequence, some families have already left the settlement . . . ?

As it is, we find the families, some living in tents of cloth, some of cloth and green bark just peeled from the trees, and some wholly of green barn, stuck up on the damp ground, without floors or fires. Only two stoves in the company. . . .

We see that the city grounds, which have been surveyed . . . contain only one log cabin, 16 by 16, muddled between the logs on the inside, instead of on the outside; neither door nor window; the roof covered with "shakes" (western shingles), split out of oak I should think, 3½ feet in length, and about as wide as a sheet of fools cap paper.[9]

---

9. **fools cap paper** writing paper usually measuring 13 by 16 inches.

Reading Strategy
Responding Do you share the surprise and disappointment Colt describes when she arrives at her new home? Explain.

Review and Assess

Thinking About the Selection

1. **Respond:** Would you have had the courage and determination to leave your home and family to become a pioneer? Explain.

2. **(a) Recall:** What financial arrangements did the Colts make as part of their preparations for heading west? **(b) Evaluate:** Do you think they were too naive and trusting? Explain.

3. **(a) Recall:** What is the appearance of the settler woman whom Colt describes meeting in her entry of May 11? **(b) Analyze:** What does this settler woman suggest to Colt about her own future?

4. **Compare and Contrast:** How do Colt's expectations about life at Octagon City compare with reality?

5. **Synthesize:** Based on Colt's experiences, explain which character traits you feel were necessary to being a successful pioneer.

14 Reading Strategy

Responding

- Have students read the bracketed passage. Then, tell them to pause and consider Colt's reaction to what she sees.

- Ask students to describe Colt's reaction to the settlement. Possible Response: Students should recognize that Colt is very disappointed by the lack of buildings and the poor quality of the food.

- Ask students the Reading Strategy question on p. 601: Do you share the surprise and disappointment Colt describes when she arrives at her new home? Explain. Possible Response: Students may note that the dismal conditions are consistent with the conditions of the journey; therefore, however disappointing, they should have come as no surprise.

Answers for p. 601

Review and Assess

1. Possible Response: Students should discuss the requirements of pioneer life.

2. **(a)** Colt's husband sold their farm, invested in the Vegetarian Company, and sent money for the settlement at a company director's direction. **(b)** Possible Response: Being aware that the directors failed to fill their obligations, most students will think that the Colts were too naïve and trusting.

3. **(a)** The woman has bare feet and carries a white sack of corn meal slung over her shoulder. **(b)** Colt fears that she will become just as unkempt.

4. Colt expected a better life for herself and her family; the reality is very disappointing.

5. Possible Response: Successful pioneers had to be courageous, flexible, adaptable, and dedicated, even in the face of enormous disappointment.

⑮ **About the Selection**

In this speech, a weary and demoralized Chief Joseph, speaking for a people in desperate straits, decides to stop his losing fight with the pursuing United States Army.

Answers for p. 602

Review and Assess

1. Possible Response: Students should describe in terms of their own experience the difference between knowing something intellectually and knowing something emotionally or intuitively.

2. **(a)** The other chiefs have been killed. **(b)** The young men have been left to carry on the fight. **(c)** Possible Response: He directs part of his speech to the chiefs because he needs to explain his surrender to them.

3. **(a)** He is tired of fighting, the chiefs have been killed, and his people are cold and hungry. **(b)** Possible Response: Many students will feel that the stark and spare details of the speech are deeply moving and thus effective.

4. **(a)** He wants to find his children, some of whom may be dead. **(b)** He is like a father to his people; he cannot bear to see them suffering and dying.

5. His purpose was to build awareness of his people's plight.

6. Possible response: Some students may say that surrendering was the only choice Chief Joseph had because it was winter, his people were starving and defeat was certain.

⑮ I Will Fight No More Forever
Chief Joseph

Tell General Howard I know his heart. What he told me before, I have in my heart. I am tired of fighting. Our chiefs are killed. Looking Glass is dead. Toohoolhoolzote is dead. The old men are all dead. It is the young men who say yes and no. He who led on the young men is dead. It is cold and we have no blankets. The little children are freezing to death. My people, some of them, have run away to the hills and have no blankets, no food; no one knows where they are—perhaps freezing to death. I want to have time to look for my children and see how many I can find. Maybe I shall find them among the dead. Hear me, my chiefs. I am tired; my heart is sick and sad. From where the sun now stands I will fight no more forever.

Review and Assess

Thinking About the Selection

1. **Respond:** Chief Joseph says that he knows his enemy's heart. Have you ever felt that you knew something with your heart rather than with your head? What is the difference?

2. **(a) Recall:** What has happened to the other Nez Percé chiefs? **(b) Infer:** Who has been left to carry on the fight? **(c) Speculate:** Why do you think Chief Joseph directs part of his speech to his chiefs?

3. **(a) Recall:** What reasons does Chief Joseph give for his surrender? **(b) Evaluate:** Would Chief Joseph's speech have been more or less effective had it contained more detailed explanations of his reasons for surrender? Explain.

4. **(a) Recall:** What does Chief Joseph want to do now that the battle is lost? **(b) Infer:** Based on this speech, how would you describe Chief Joseph's relationship to his people? Explain.

5. **Synthesize:** Although Chief Joseph delivered his speech to confirm his tribe's surrender, the speech had another, equally important purpose. What was that purpose?

6. **Take a Position:** Do you think surrender was the right choice? Why or why not?

602 ◆ *Division, Reconciliation, and Expansion (1850–1914)*

✎ ASSESSMENT PRACTICE: Reading Comprehension

Context   **(For more practice, see Test Preparation Workbook, p. 34.)**

The reading sections of many tests require students to use context clues such as definitions and explanations to determine the meanings of unfamiliar words and phrases. Write the following passage from p. 601 on the chalkboard. Then use the following exercise to help them use context clues to identify the correct definition.

In the large tent here is a cook stove—they have supper prepared for us; it consists of hominy, soft Johnny cake (or corn bread, as it is called here), stewed apple, and tea.

According to information found in this passage, what is "Johnny cake"?

A apple cake   **C** hominy
B corn bread   **D** tea cake

B is the correct answer, because it contains the explanation found in the parenthetical phrase: "Johnny cake (or corn bread, as it is called here)."

Review and Assess

Literary Analysis

Tone

1. Find two examples of an upbeat, positive **tone** in Miriam Davis Colt's diary.

2. Find two examples of a negative, downcast tone in Colt's diary.

3. A military leader might adopt many tones when admitting defeat. (a) What is the overall tone of Chief Joseph's surrender? (b) What details contribute to this tone?

Comparing Literary Works

4. Chief Joseph's speech generates a single **mood,** while Colt's journal entries inspire varying moods. Identify a passage in Colt's work that most closely echoes the mood of Chief Joseph's speech.

5. Both Colt and Chief Joseph face struggles and disappointments as they work for what they feel is right, yet their conflicts differ greatly. Identify the conflict each writer faces. Then, compare and contrast these conflicts.

6. Using a Venn diagram like the one shown, compare the future Chief Joseph faces with the one Colt faces. (a) How are their hopes for the future different? (b) How are their hopes similar?

Reading Strategy

Responding

7. (a) Cite a passage from Colt's journal that affected you strongly, and describe your response. (b) Cite a passage from Chief's Joseph's speech that affected you deeply, and describe your response.

8. Did the way in which you responded to each of these selections affect your appreciation of it? Explain.

Extend Understanding

9. **Social Studies Connection:** Moving west was a risky and difficult endeavor for pioneers. Why were so many of them willing to emigrate west despite the dangers?

Heading West / I Will Fight No More Forever ◆ 603

Quick Review

Tone is a writer's attitude toward his or her subject.

Mood, or atmosphere, is the feeling created in the reader by a literary work or passage.

To **respond** to literature, regonize your personal reactions to the work and notice how the writing affected you.

 Take It to the Net

www.phschool.com

Take the interactive self-test online to check your understanding of these selections.

✹ ENRICHMENT: Further Reading

Other Works About the West

Pioneer Women: Voices from the Frontier, Joanna L. Stratton

Women and Their Families on the Overland Trail 1846–1867, J.M. Faragher and C. Stansell

Bury My Heart at Wounded Knee: An Indian History of the American West, Dee Brown

 Take It to the Net

Visit www.phschool.com for other information on the West.

Answers for p. 603

Review and Assess

1. **Possible response:** Examples include Colt's first entry, describing her family's goals; the beginning of the April 22 entry, describing the lovely moonlit journey by train; and the May 2 description of the "pic-nic."

2. **Possible response:** Examples include her April 22 description of the "miserable hotel," and her subdued reaction when she actually arrives in "Octagon City."

3. **(a)** The overall tone of Chief Joseph's surrender is one of weary resignation to his fate. **(b)** He describes his own exhaustion and his people's desperate plight, and conveys his understanding of the enemy's position.

4. **Possible response:** The dark and disappointed mood of Colt's descriptions of the "Octagon City" settlement closely echoes the mood of Chief Joseph's speech.

5. **Possible response:** Both Colt and Chief Joseph face overwhelming disappointment with their circumstances. Colt's struggles are undertaken voluntarily in the hopes of a better life, however, while Chief Joseph has lost his final struggle and is resigned to his fate.

6. **Possible response:**

Chief Joseph   **Colt**

Hopes to save his people; hopes to find his children | Hope for a better future for themselves and their children. | Hopes to reach Octagon City; hopes that Octagon City lives up to its promise

7. **(a) Possible response:** Students may cite Colt's May 11 description of an encounter with a settler woman, which could make students wonder about their own futures.

   (b) Possible response: Students may cite a personal response to his description of his people and their children freezing without blankets.

continued

Answers continued

8. **Possible response:** Students' appreciation of the selections may have increased when they were able to form personal responses and connect to the authors.

9. **Possible response:** People moved west in search of free land, opportunities, and a better life.

Answers for p. 604

❶ Vocabulary Development

Word Analysis

1. Possible response: After their voyage, the Pilgrims were glad to be on *terra firma*.

2. Possible response: The balloon's basket jolted violently as it struck *terra firma*.

Spelling Strategy

1. bragged
2. stopped
3. flitted

Fluency: Word Choice

1. emigrants
2. depredations
3. genial
4. pervading
5. profusion
6. nonplused
7. Ah, *terra firma*!

❷ Grammar and Style

1. fragment; sample sentence: It was a hot summer day.

2. fragment; sample sentence: I have been here in West Stockholm, at my brother's, since Friday last.

3. fragment; sample sentence: We hasten to the hotel and find it very much crowded.

4. complete sentence

5. fragment; sample sentence: That evening, we dined on the prairie and gathered flowers.

Looking at Style

Students should recognize that Colt's short, choppy style evokes her demanding journey.

Integrate Language Skills

❶ Vocabulary Development Lesson

Word Analysis: Latin Term *terra firma*

Miriam Davis Colt uses the Latin term *terra firma*, which means "firm earth" or "solid ground." If you encounter an unfamiliar Latin word or phrase when reading, you can often find its meaning in a dictionary.

Follow the directions for each item below by writing sentences including the term *terra firma*.

1. Describe the Pilgrims landing on Plymouth Rock after months at sea in a tiny boat.

2. Describe a hot-air balloon safely touching down after a rough flight.

Spelling Strategy

When adding *-ed* to a one-syllable word that ends in a single consonant preceded by a vowel, double the final consonant. For example, *rub* becomes *rubbed*. Add *-ed* to each of the following words.

1. brag   2. stop   3. flit

Fluency: Word Choice

Select the word from the vocabulary list on page 595 that best describes or relates to each description below.

1. People who left America to live in another country

2. Acts committed by hostile invading troops against civilians

3. The personality of a pleasant host

4. The scents in a perfume shop

5. A buffet of more than fifty sumptuous and inviting desserts

6. An auto mechanic perplexed by a car he cannot fix despite six days of problem solving

7. A phrase said when stepping off a roller coaster

❷ Grammar and Style Lesson

Sentence Fragments

Sentence fragments are incomplete sentences that may lack either a subject or a verb.

Although they may lend a sense of urgency to a piece of writing, sentence fragments are not acceptable in formal English.

> **Fragment:** Expect tonight to arrive at our new home. *(no subject)*

> **Fragment:** Even if we traveled for five more days. *(not a complete thought)*

Practice Identify which of the following sentences is incomplete. Then, rewrite each sentence fragment as a complete sentence.

1. A hot summer day.

2. Have been here in West Stockholm, at my brother's, since Friday last.

3. Hasten to the hotel—find it very much crowded.

4. We are going to Kansas.

5. Dined on the prairie and gathered flowers.

Looking at Style Write an evaluation in which you explain how Colt's use of sentence fragments affects your understanding of her experiences.

WG *Prentice Hall Writing and Grammar Connection: Chapter 20, Section 4*

604 ◆ *Division, Reconciliation, and Expansion (1850–1914)*

TEACHING RESOURCES

The following resources can be used to enrich or extend the instruction for pp. 604–605.

Vocabulary

📖 **Selection Support:** Build Vocabulary, p. 142

📖 **Vocabulary and Spelling Practice Book**
(Use this booklet for skills enrichment.)

Grammar

📖 **Selection Support:** Grammar and Style, p. 143

WG **Writing and Grammar,** Ruby Level, p. 492 ▪

📖 **Daily Language Practice Transparencies** ▪

Writing

WG **Writing and Grammar,** Ruby Level, p. 132. ▪

🔘 **Writing and Grammar iText CD-ROM**

📖 **Writing Models and Graphic Organizers on Transparencies,** p. 75

 BLOCK SCHEDULING: Resources marked with this symbol provide varied instruction during 90-minute blocks.

❸ Writing Lesson

Position Paper on Development

The vast stretches of land where both Chief Joseph and Miriam Davis Colt lived have almost disappeared. Imagine that you live in a town where the last open piece of land is about to be turned into a mall. Support or oppose the development in a position paper—a formal piece of writing that argues one side of a controversial issue.

Prewriting	List the reasons you support or oppose the project, along with facts to back up your reasons.
Drafting	Start with a clear statement of your position. Provide reasons and specific details to support your case. End with a persuasive conclusion.
Revising	Make sure your argument flows smoothly from one paragraph to the next. Check this coherence by highlighting and evaluating the transitions you have used.

Model: Revising for Coherence

The mall will not create jobs, as some believe. Instead of new

In addition,

jobs, we will get traffic and pollution. ⌃The mall will steal

business from locally owned shops.

> Using transition words and phrases builds coherence in a piece of writing.

Prentice Hall Writing and Grammar Connection: Chapter 7, Section 4

❹ Extension Activities

Listening and Speaking Chief Joseph's speech so moved the officers who heard it that they were unable to speak. Recite the speech for the class in an **oral interpretation**. Use these tips to prepare:

- Identify the tone of Chief Joseph's voice as he gave his speech.
- Think about his bearing—how he held his body.

Picture Chief Joseph in your imagination as you re-create his speech. Then, ask classmates to evaluate your presentation.

Research and Technology The history of the West is full of stories like that of the Colts, who sought an ideal—or utopian—way of life. Using a variety of research tools, research these communities and their effect on the development of the American frontier. Identify how these communities attracted new members. Then, produce a **marketing brochure** to draw new settlers to such a community.

 Take It to the Net   www.phschool.com

Go online for an additional research activity using the Internet.

Heading West / I Will Fight No More Forever ◆ 605

ASSESSMENT RESOURCES

The following resources can be used to assess students' knowledge and skills.

Selection Assessment

- **Formal Assessment,** pp. 152–154
- **Open Book Test,** pp. 94–96
- **Got It! Assessment Videotapes,** Tape 3
- **Test Bank Software**

 Take It to the Net
Visit www.phschool.com for self-tests and additional questions on the selections.

Listening and Speaking Rubric

- **Performance Assessment and Portfolio Management,** p. 30

 PRENTICE HALL
ASSESSMENT *SYSTEM*

- **Workbook**
- **Skill Book**
- **Transparencies**
- 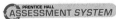 **CD-ROM**

Lesson Support for p. 605

❸ Writing Lesson

- Remind students that a position paper must persuade readers by stating its position as clearly as possible and supporting that position with compelling details.

- To aid in prewriting, have students use the Argument Organizer in **Writing Models and Graphic Organizers on Transparencies,** p. 75, to organize their arguments.

- Urge students to write coherently by choosing an organizational method (for example, chronological order, comparison and contrast, or cause and effect) and using it consistently; using specific rather than vague terminology; and by repeating words to emphasize important points.

❹ Listening and Speaking

- Remind students that to recite a speech is not just to say the words aloud but to say them with feeling and with regard for the audience.

- Have groups of students find out more about the tragic experience of the Nez Percé. Groups can discuss how to best capture Chief Joseph's passion and resignation, and select a member to deliver the speech.

- Have one member of a group introduce the speech by providing background information on the Nez Percé. Then, have the speaker give the dramatic presentation of Chief Joseph's words.

- Have students use the Peer Assessment form for Delivering a Speech, p. 30 in **Performance Assessment and Portfolio Management.**

CUSTOMIZE INSTRUCTION
For Universal Access

To address different learning styles, use the activities suggested in the **Extension Activities** booklet, p. 32.

For Visual/Spatial Learners, use Activity 5.

For Visual/Spatial and Bodily/Kinesthetic Learners, use Activity 6.

For Verbal/Linguistic Learners, use Activity 7.

To Build a Fire

Lesson Objectives

1. **To analyze and respond to literary elements**
   - Literary Analysis: Conflict
   - Connecting Literary Elements: Irony
2. **To read, comprehend, analyze, and critique a short story**
   - Reading Strategy: Predicting
   - Reading Check questions
   - Review and Assess questions
   - Assessment Practice (ATE)
3. **To develop word analysis skills, fluency, and systematic vocabulary**
   - Vocabulary Development Lesson: Latin Word Root: *-ject-*
4. **To understand and apply written and oral language conventions**
   - Spelling Strategy
   - Grammar and Style Lesson: Adverb Clauses
5. **To understand and apply appropriate writing and research strategies**
   - Writing Lesson: Literary Analysis
   - Extension Activity: Booklet
6. **To understand and apply listening and speaking strategies**
   - Extension Activity: Enactment

STEP-BY-STEP TEACHING GUIDE	PACING GUIDE
PRETEACH	
Motivate Students and Provide Background	
Use the Motivation activity (ATE p. 606)	5 min.
Read and discuss author and background features (SE/ATE pp. 604, 606)	5 min.
Introduce the Concepts	
Introduce the Literary Analysis and Reading Strategy (SE/ATE p. 605)	15 min.
Pronounce the vocabulary words and read their definitions (SE p. 605)	5 min.
TEACH	
Monitor Comprehension	
Informally monitor comprehension by circulating while students read independently or in groups	65 min.
Monitor students' comprehension with the Reading Check notes (SE/ATE pp. 609, 611, 613, 615, 617, 619, 621)	as students read
Develop vocabulary with Vocabulary notes (SE pp. 609, 610, 616, 620; ATE p. 609)	as students read
Develop Understanding	
Develop students' understanding of conflict with the Literary Analysis annotations (SE pp. 610, 612, 613, 614, 615, 616, 618, 619, 621; ATE pp. 610, 612, 613, 614, 615, 616, 617, 618, 619, 621)	5 min.
Develop students' ability to predict events in the reading with the Reading Strategy annotations (SE pp. 609, 612, 615, 618, 620; ATE pp. 609, 611, 612, 615, 616, 618, 620)	5 min.
ASSESS	
Assess Mastery	
Assess students' mastery of the Reading Strategy and Literary Analysis by having them answer the Review and Assess questions (SE/ATE p. 623)	15 min.
Use one or more of the print and media Assessment Resources (ATE p. 625)	up to 45 min.
EXTEND	
Apply Understanding	
Have students complete the Vocabulary Development Lesson and the Grammar and Style Lesson (SE p. 624)	20 min.
Apply students' ability to elaborate to support an argument by using the Writing Lesson (SE/ATE p. 625)	45 min.
Apply students' understanding using one or more of the Extension Activities (SE p. 625)	20–90 min.

 ACCELERATED INSTRUCTION:
Use the strategies and activities identified with an .

UNIVERSAL ACCESS
- ● = Below Level Students
- ▲ = On-Level Students
- ■ = Above Level Students

Time and Resource Manager

Reading Level: Average
Average Number of Instructional Days: 6

RESOURCES		
PRINT 📖	**TRANSPARENCIES** 📑	**TECHNOLOGY** 💿 🎧 📼
• **Beyond Literature,** Media Connection: Films About Survival, p. 33 ▲ ■		• **Interest Grabber Video,** Tape 4 ● ▲ ■
• **Selection Support Workbook:** ● ▲ ■ Literary Analysis, p. 149 Reading Strategy, p. 148 Build Vocabulary, p. 146	• **Literary Analysis and Reading Transparencies,** pp. 65 and 66 ● ▲ ■	
		• **Listening to Literature** ● ▲ ■ Audiocassettes, Side 21, 22 Audio CDs, CD 13
• **Literatura en español** ● ▲ • **Literary Analysis for Enrichment** ■		
• **Formal Assessment:** Selection Test, pp. 155–157 ● ▲ ■ • **Open Book Test,** pp. 97–99 ● ▲ ■ • **Performance Assessment and Portfolio Management,** p. 23 ● ▲ ■ • PRENTICE HALL **ASSESSMENT SYSTEM** ● ▲ ■	PRENTICE HALL **ASSESSMENT SYSTEM** ● ▲ ■ Skills Practice Answers and Explanations on Transparencies	• **Test Bank Software** ● ▲ ■ • **Got It! Assessment Videotapes,** Tape 3 ● ▲
• **Selection Support Workbook:** ● ▲ ■ Grammar and Style, p. 147 • **Writing and Grammar,** Ruby Level ● ▲ ■ • **Extension Activities,** p. 33 ● ▲ ■	• **Daily Language Practice Transparencies** ● ▲ • **Writing Models and Graphic Organizers on Transparencies** pp. 91–93 ● ▲ ■	• **Writing and Grammar iText CD-ROM** ● ▲ ■ 💻 *Take It to the Net* www.phschool.com

■ **BLOCK SCHEDULING:** Use one 90-minute class period to preteach the selection and have students read it. Use a second 90-minute class period to assess students' mastery of skills and have them complete one of the Extension Activities.

Step-by-Step Teaching Guide
for pp. 606–607

Motivation

Draw students into the story by using the following description:

"Day had broken, cold and gray. . . There was no sun nor hint of sun. . . The Yukon lay a mile wide and hidden under three feet of ice. On top of this ice was as many feet of snow. North and South, as far as he could see, it was unbroken white. . . Undoubtedly it was colder than fifty degrees below zero. . . ."

Encourage students to speculate about what might happen to a person who sets out on a day-long journey on foot in such conditions.

▣ Interest Grabber Video

As an alternative, you may wish to play "The Origin of Fire in Myth" on Tape 4 to engage student interest.

❶ Background

Arthur Calder-Marshall, in his introduction to a collection of Jack London's works, commented: "Jack London's stories still compel the reader to read on. He learned to tell a tale, he says, when he was bumming across the United States . . . He tells his stories like a tramp. At the end you are left with no distillation of truth, no new vision of life. But you have experienced something vicariously. . . ."

Prepare to Read

❶ To Build a Fire

Jack London (1876–1916)

Jack London had endured more hardships by the age of twenty-one than most people experience in a lifetime. His struggles gave him a sympathy for the working class and a lasting dislike of drudgery. They also provided inspiration for novels and short stories, and became the foundation of his success as a writer.

Difficult Beginnings London grew up in San Francisco in extreme poverty. At the age of eleven, he left school and supported himself through a succession of unskilled jobs—working as a paper boy, in bowling alleys, on ice wagons, and in canneries and mills. Despite the long hours spent toiling at these jobs, London was able to read constantly, borrowing travel and adventure books from the library.

The books London read inspired him to travel, and his job experiences led him to become active in fighting for the rights of workers. He sailed to Japan on a sealing expedition and joined a cross-country protest march with a group of unemployed workers. After being arrested for vagrancy near Buffalo, New York, London decided to educate himself and reshape his life. He completed high school in a single year and then enrolled at the University of California.

After only one semester, however, the lure of fortune and adventure proved irresistible. In 1897, London abandoned his studies and traveled to the Alaskan Yukon in search of gold. Although he was unsuccessful as a miner, London's experiences in Alaska taught him about the human desire for wealth and power and about humankind's inability to control the forces of nature. While in Alaska, London also absorbed memories and stories that would make him a household name.

A Writing Life Once back in California, London became determined to earn a living as a writer. He rented a typewriter and worked up to fifteen hours a day, spinning his Alaskan adventures into short stories and novels.

According to legend, London's stack of rejection slips from publishers grew to five feet in height. Even so, London persevered. He wrote diligently every morning, setting himself a 1,000-word minimum.

In 1903, he earned national fame when he published the popular novel *The Call of the Wild*. He soon became the highest-paid and most-industrious writer in the country. During his career, London produced more than fifty books, including both fiction and nonfiction, and earned more than a million dollars—the first American writer to earn such a staggering sum. Several of his novels, including *The Call of the Wild* (1903), *The Sea-Wolf* (1904), and *White Fang* (1906), have become American classics. His best works depict an individual's struggle for survival against the powerful forces of nature. "To Build a Fire," for example, tells the story of an unnamed man's fight to survive the bitter cold of the Alaskan wilderness.

Recognition by His Peers The well-known writer Upton Sinclair wrote that Jack London "was the true king of our storytellers." London's friend Oliver Madox Hueffer agreed. He recalled that London "was the ideal yarnster—his spoken stories were even better than his written—and one reason why I think him likely to be numbered as among the writers of real mark was that he was perfectly unconscious of it. Like Peter Pan, he never grew up, and he lived in his own stories with such intensity that he ended by believing them himself."

TEACHING RESOURCES

The following resources can be used to enrich or extend the instruction for pp. 606–607.

Motivation

▣ **Interest Grabber Video**, Tape 4

Background

▣ **Beyond Literature**, p. 33 ▣

 Take It to the Net
Visit www.phschool.com for Background and hotlinks for "To Build a Fire."

Literary Analysis

▣ **Literary Analysis and Reading Transparencies**, Conflict, p. 66

▣ **Selection Support**: Literary Analysis, p. 149 ▣

Reading

▣ **Literary Analysis and Reading Transparencies**, Predict, p. 65

▣ **BLOCK SCHEDULING:** Resources marked with this symbol provide varied instruction during 90-minute blocks.

Preview

Connecting to the Literature

Some people enjoy pushing themselves to their limits through sports such as rock climbing and sky diving. In some cases, as in this story, people push themselves to such extremes that they place their lives in jeopardy.

❷ Literary Analysis

Conflict

Conflict, the struggle between two opposing forces, can take two forms:

- **internal,** occurring within the mind of a character
- **external,** occurring between a character and society, nature, another person, God, or fate.

A character's efforts to resolve conflict form the basis for the plot of a literary work. In "To Build a Fire," a man is in the throes of a deadly external conflict, struggling to survive in the bitter cold of the Alaskan wilderness.

Connecting Literary Elements

Irony involves a contrast between what is stated and what is meant, or between what is expected to happen and what actually happens. In **dramatic irony,** there is a contradiction between what a character thinks and what the reader knows to be true. Dramatic irony often serves to heighten the sense of conflict. For example, in "To Build a Fire," the reader knows that the temperature is far lower than the man realizes:

> He pulled the mitten on hurriedly and stood up. He was a bit frightened. He stamped up and down until the stinging returned into the feet. It certainly was cold, was his thought.

As you read, notice those passages where it is clear that the reader understands more than the man does.

❸ Reading Strategy

Predicting

The main character in this story fails to recognize the depth of the conflict he faces until it is too late. A more alert person might have interpreted the signs of danger, anticipated their outcome, and taken action. As a reader, you too can anticipate, or **predict,** what will happen by noting clues that hint at later events. Use a chart like the one shown to identify clues and record your predictions.

Clues
repeated references to the cold

Prediction

Vocabulary Development

conjectural (kən jek′ chər əl) *adj.* based on guesswork (p. 609)

unwonted (un wän′ tid) *adj.* unusual; unfamiliar (p. 610)

conflagration (kän′ flə grā′ shən) *n.* big, destructive fire (p. 615)

peremptorily (pər emp′ tə rə lē) *adj.* decisively; commandingly (p. 619)

To Build a Fire ◆ 607

---

❷ Literary Analysis

Conflict

- Tell students that *conflict* drives literary works. Works of literature are about characters struggling to resolve the conflicts that they face.

- Use the Conflict transparency in **Literary Analysis and Reading Transparencies,** p. 68, to model external conflict. In "To Build a Fire," the external conflict is between the main character and the forces of nature.

- Explain that conflicts may also be internal—that is, a character may face a conflict within him- or herself.

- Use the Conflict transparency to illustrate that the main character in "To Build a Fire" also faces an internal conflict. Encourage students to consider what that internal conflict might be as they read.

❸ Reading Strategy

Predicting

- Explain to students that they can often predict what will happen in a literary work by paying close attention to the details in the text.

- Have students read the passage in the instruction for Connecting Literary Elements. Then, direct them to the graphic organizer on the student page. Point out that "Repeated references to the cold" is written in the box labeled "Clues."

- Ask students to consider what predictions they might make based on this clue. Encourage them to use similar charts as they read the selection.

Vocabulary Development

- Pronounce each vocabulary word for students, and read the definitions as a class. Have students identify any words with which they are already familiar.

 E-Teach

Visit E-Teach at www.phschool.com for teachers' essays on how to teach, with questions and answers.

CUSTOMIZE INSTRUCTION FOR UNIVERSAL ACCESS

For Less Proficient Readers	For English Learners	For Advanced Readers
Students may have difficulty with the concept of external and internal conflict. Use the Conflict transparency in **Literary Analysis and Reading Transparencies,** p. 68, to model external conflict. Point out that conflict with nature is external, while a character's conflicts with his or her own weaknesses would be internal.	These students may find recognizing external conflicts challenging because of this selection's specialized vocabulary. Help them with language specific to the Arctic weather and landscape, such as *cold snap, husky, timber jam, ice muzzle, freeze-up,* and so on.	After reviewing external conflict using the Conflict transparency in **Literary Analysis and Reading Transparencies,** p. 68, ask these students to write down the internal conflicts the main character might face. After reading the selection, have them discuss the accuracy of their answers.

Step-by-Step Teaching Guide for pp. 608–622

CUSTOMIZE INSTRUCTION
For Visual/Spatial Learners

It would be helpful to provide these students with a map of Alaska and of the Yukon Territory so that they can orient themselves as to the main character's locations. They can see how far north the man was and note the remoteness of the region.

❶ About the Selection

Along the Yukon River in the frozen northern wilderness, an inexperienced but confident prospector and his work dog make a long and dangerous journey on foot toward a camp. The temperature is far colder than the man thinks, too cold for a solitary journey. That is his first mistake. His second mistake—building a fire in the wrong spot—proves fatal. Though nature is the antagonist of this tale, the man's own overconfidence contributes to his downfall. The dog, sensing the danger of their predicament from the start, still stays with the man until the very end. Then its instincts direct it on toward the camp, where other food and fire providers are to be found.

❷ ▶Critical Viewing

Possible response: When students have read the story, they may choose several descriptive words or passages from the story to describe the scenes, including "intangible pall over the face of things," "subtle gloom," "gentle undulations," "spruce-covered island," "silent creek," and "arctic winter."

❶ To Build a Fire
Jack London

❷ ▲ **Critical Viewing**
Which words or passages from the story could be used to describe this scene? **[Analyze]**

Background

The United States Secretary of State William Seward purchased Alaska from Russia in 1867 for two cents an acre. Many Americans, believing it to be nothing but a frozen, barren wasteland, called the purchase "Seward's Folly." In 1896, the discovery of a rich lode of gold in the Yukon, part of the Arctic wilderness, led to the Klondike stampede of 1897–1898. Thousands of prospectors headed for the frozen north, lured by the promise of quick riches. Jack London was among the first of these prospectors. He may have searched for more than gold, however. London once commented, "True, the new territory was mostly barren; but its several hundred thousand square miles of frigidity at least gave breathing space to those who else would have suffocated at home."

608 ◆ *Division, Reconciliation, and Expansion (1850–1914)*

TEACHING RESOURCES

The following resources can be used to enrich or extend the instruction for pp. 608–622.

Literary Analysis

📖 **Literary Analysis and Reading Transparencies,** p. 66

Reading

📖 **Selection Support:** Reading Strategy, p. 148; Build Vocabulary, p. 146

🎧 **Listening to Literature Audiocassettes,** Sides 21, 22 ▪

🔊 **Listening to Literature Audio CDs,** CD 13 ▪

▪ **BLOCK SCHEDULING:** Resources marked with this symbol provide varied instruction during 90-minute blocks.

Day had broken cold and gray, exceedingly cold and gray, when the man turned aside from the main Yukon[1] trail and climbed the high earth-bank, where a dim and little-traveled trail led eastward through the fat spruce timberland. It was a steep bank, and he paused for breath at the top, excusing the act to himself by looking at his watch. It was nine o'clock. There was no sun nor hint of sun, though there was not a cloud in the sky. It was a clear day, and yet there seemed an intangible pall over the face of things, a subtle gloom that made the day dark, and that was due to the absence of sun. This fact did not worry the man. He was used to the lack of sun. It had been days since he had seen the sun, and he knew that a few more days must pass before that cheerful orb, due south, would just peep above the skyline and dip immediately from view.

The man flung a look back along the way he had come. The Yukon lay a mile wide and hidden under three feet of ice. On top of this ice were as many feet of snow. It was all pure white, rolling in gentle undulations where the ice jams of the freeze-up had formed. North and south, as far as his eye could see, it was unbroken white, save for a dark hairline that curved and twisted from around the spruce-covered island to the south, and that curved and twisted away into the north, where it disappeared behind another spruce-covered island. This dark hairline was the trail—the main trail—that led south five hundred miles to the Chilcoot Pass, Dyea,[2] and salt water; and that led north seventy miles to Dawson, and still on to the north a thousand miles to Nulato,[3] and finally to St. Michael on Bering Sea, a thousand miles and half a thousand more.

But all this—the mysterious, far-reaching hairline trail, the absence of sun from the sky, the tremendous cold, and the strangeness and weirdness of it all—no impression on the man. It was not because he was long used to it. He was a newcomer in the land, a *chechaquo*,[4] and this was his first winter. The trouble with him was that he was without imagination. He was quick and alert in the things of life, but only in the things, and not in the significances. Fifty degrees below zero meant eighty-odd degrees of frost. Such fact impressed him as being cold and uncomfortable, and that was all. It did not lead him to meditate upon his frailty as a creature of temperature, and upon man's frailty in general, able only to live within certain narrow limits of heat and cold; and from there on it did not lead him to the conjectural field of immortality and man's place in the universe. Fifty degrees below zero stood for a bite of frost that hurt and that must be guarded against by the use of mittens, earflaps, warm moccasins, and thick socks. Fifty degrees below zero was to him just precisely fifty degrees below zero. That there should be anything more to it than that was a thought that never entered his head.

---

1. **Yukon** (yoo′ kän) territory in northwestern Canada, east of Alaska; also, a river.
2. **Dyea** (dī′ ā) former town in Alaska at the start of the Yukon trail.
3. **Dawson . . . Nulato** former gold-mining villages in the Yukon.
4. *chechaquo* (chē chä′ kwō) slang for newcomer.

Reading Strategy
Predicting What do you predict will happen to the "newcomer" in the "tremendous cold and the strangeness and weirdness"? Why?

conjectural (kən jek′ chər əl) *adj.* based on guesswork

✓ **Reading Check**
Where is the man, and what weather conditions is he experiencing?

To Build a Fire ◆ 609

CUSTOMIZE INSTRUCTION FOR UNIVERSAL ACCESS

For Less Proficient Readers	For English Learners	For Advanced Readers
These students will be challenged by the fact that London's story contains no dialogue and consists mostly of long passages filled with detailed descriptions. To help students overcome these obstacles, encourage them to pause at the end of each paragraph to jot down the key descriptive details that it contains.	This story's long and detailed descriptive passages often contain language specific to the time and place in which it is set and may be especially challenging. Encourage students to pause at the end of each setting and jot down key descriptive terms. Then, have them define difficult words and paraphrase descriptive passages.	Challenge these students to place this selection in an appropriate historical and literary context by identifying how it illustrates the key characteristics of Naturalism—a late nineteenth century literary movement that stressed the idea that people's lives are shaped by forces of society and nature beyond their control.

❸ **Reading Strategy**
Predicting

- Have students read the bracketed passage. Ask them to identify any details that might hint at events to come.
  Possible response: Students may notice that the passage refers to the mysteriousness of the trail, the extreme cold, the strange landscape, and the man's failure to respond to any of this.

- Point out that London presents a picture of the man and his limitations, and also of a dangerous environment.

- Ask students the Reading Strategy question on p. 609: What do you predict will happen to the "newcomer" in the "tremendous cold and the strangeness and weirdness"? Why?
  Possible response: Students may predict that the unimaginative man will be challenged by the cold in ways that he does not foresee. His lack of foresight is due to his newness to the land and to his lack of imagination—his inability to perceive the meaning in his experiences and observations.

❹ **Vocabulary Development**
The Latin Root -ject-

- Call students' attention to the word *conjectural* and its definition. Explain that the Latin word root *-ject-* means "to throw."

- Have students suggest words and phrases that contain this root, and list them on the chalkboard.
  Possibilities include: *abject, reject, project, interject, inject,* and *object.*

- Next, have students look up the meanings of these words in a dictionary.

❺ ✓ **Reading Check**

Answer: The man is in the frozen wilderness along the Yukon River, far from any settlement, and he is experiencing the extreme cold of the Arctic winter.

❻ Literary Analysis
Conflict

- Instruct students to create a chart identifying conflicts the man faces. Have them begin by drawing a box and writing "The Man" in its center.

- Have them read the bracketed passage. Point out that London elaborates extensively on the cold.

- Suggest that these details point out the story's central conflict. Then, ask students the Literary Analysis question on p. 610: With what or whom is the man in conflict?

  Possible response: The man is in conflict with the forces of extreme weather conditions. Students may say that he is also in conflict with the limits of his own perceptions.

- Have students place their answers in a circle drawn on to their charts and connect the circles to "The Man."

❼ Literary Analysis
Conflict and Irony

- Remind students that dramatic irony is created when what the reader knows about a character's circumstances contradicts what a character believes to be true.

- Have students read the bracketed passage. Encourage them to pay special attention to the dog's instincts.

- Point out to students that the dog's basic instincts tell it what the man has yet to conclude: that it is too dangerously cold to be traveling.

- Ask students the Literary Analysis question on p. 610: In what ways does the description of the dog's instinct create a sense of dramatic irony?

  Possible response: The dog's instincts let the reader know just how dangerous the situation is, which ironically emphasizes how poorly the man understands his environment.

---

❻ As he turned to go on, he spat speculatively. There was a sharp, explosive crackle that startled him. He spat again. And again, in the air, before it could fall to the snow, the spittle crackled. He knew that at fifty below spittle crackled on the snow, but this spittle had crackled in the air. Undoubtedly it was colder than fifty below—how much colder he did not know. But the temperature did not matter. He was bound for the old claim on the left fork of Henderson Creek, where the boys were already. They had come over across the divide from the Indian Creek country, while he had come the roundabout way to take a look at the possibilities of getting out logs in the spring from the islands in the Yukon. He would be in to camp by six o'clock; a bit after dark, it was true, but the boys would be there, a fire would be going, and a hot supper would be ready. As for lunch, he pressed his hand against the protruding bundle under his jacket. It was also under his shirt, wrapped up in a handkerchief and lying against the naked skin. It was the only way to keep the biscuits from freezing. He smiled agreeably to himself as he thought of those biscuits, each cut open and sopped in bacon grease, and each enclosing a generous slice of fried bacon.

He plunged in among the big spruce trees. The trail was faint. A foot of snow had fallen since the last sled had passed over, and he was glad he was without a sled, traveling light. In fact, he carried nothing but the lunch wrapped in the handkerchief. He was surprised, however, at the cold. It certainly was cold, he concluded, as he rubbed his numb nose and cheekbones with his mittened hand. He was a warm-whiskered man, but the hair on his face did not protect the high cheekbones and the eager nose that thrust itself aggressively into the frosty air.

At the man's heels trotted a dog, a big native husky, the proper wolf dog, gray-coated and without any visible or temperamental difference from its brother, the wild wolf. The animal was depressed by the tremendous cold. It knew that it was no time for traveling. Its instinct told it a truer tale than was told to the man by the man's judgment. In reality, it was not merely colder than fifty below zero; it was colder than sixty below, than seventy below. It was seventy-five below zero. Since the freezing point is thirty-two above zero, it meant that one hundred and seven degrees of frost obtained. The dog did ❼ not know anything about thermometers. Possibly in its brain there was no sharp consciousness of a condition of very cold such as was in the man's brain. But the brute had its instinct. It experienced a vague but menacing apprehension that subdued it and made it slink along at the man's heels, and that made it question eagerly every unwonted movement of the man as if expecting him to go into camp or to seek shelter somewhere and build a fire. The dog had learned fire, and it wanted fire, or else to burrow under the snow and cuddle its warmth away from the air.

The frozen moisture of its breathing had settled on its fur in a fine powder of frost, and especially were its jowls, muzzle, and eyelashes

610 ◆ Division, Reconciliation, and Expansion (1850–1914)

Literary Analysis
Conflict The great elaboration on the cold in this description points out the central conflict in this story. With what or whom is the man in conflict?

Literary Analysis
Conflict and Irony In what ways does the description of the dog's instinct create a sense of dramatic irony?

unwonted (un wän´ tid) *adj.* unusual; unfamiliar

✺ ENRICHMENT: Science Connection

Dangers of Cold Weather

Discuss with students how the rising popularity of winter outdoor activities has led to a rise in cold-weather accidents. Frostbite is one result of prolonged exposure to extremely cold temperatures, and so is hypothermia, or sub-normal body temperature. The most obvious signs of frostbite are progressive, painful loss of feeling (usually beginning in vulnerable areas, such as the hands, feet, and face) leading to numbness, skin discoloration, and then loss of function. Students can find out about the effects of hypothermia by following what happens to the man in this story. They can notice his difficulty moving, his confusion, his drowsiness, and his eventual death.

Interested students can research the precautions that people who plan to spend time in sub-freezing temperatures can take to prevent these severe problems, and what first-aid steps to follow if frostbite or hypothermia occurs.

whitened by its crystalled breath. The man's red beard and mustache were likewise frosted, but more solidly, the deposit taking the form of ice and increasing with every warm, moist breath he exhaled. Also, the man was chewing tobacco, and the muzzle of ice held his lips so rigidly that he was unable to clear his chin when he expelled the juice. The result was that a crystal beard of the color and solidity of amber was increasing its length on his chin. If he fell down it would shatter itself, like glass, into brittle fragments. But he did not mind the appendage. It was the penalty all tobacco-chewers paid in that country, and he had been out before in two cold snaps. They had not been so cold as this, he knew, but by the spirit thermometer[5] at Sixty Mile he knew they had been registered at fifty below and at fifty-five.

He held on through the level stretch of woods for several miles, crossed a wide flat, and dropped down a bank to the frozen bed of a small stream. This was Henderson Creek, and he knew he was ten miles from the forks. He looked at his watch. It was ten o'clock. He was making four miles an hour, and he calculated that he would arrive at the forks at half past twelve. He decided to celebrate that event by eating his lunch there.

The dog dropped in again at his heels, with a tail drooping discouragement, as the man swung along the creek bed. The furrow of the old sled trail was plainly visible, but a dozen inches of snow covered the marks of the last runners. In a month no man had come up or down that silent creek. The man held steadily on. He was not much given to thinking, and just then particularly he had nothing to think about save that he would eat lunch at the forks and that at six o'clock he would be in camp with the boys. There was nobody to talk to; and, had there been, speech would have been impossible because of the ice-muzzle on his mouth. So he continued monotonously to chew tobacco and to increase the length of his amber beard.

Once in a while the thought reiterated itself that it was very cold and that he had never experienced such cold. As he walked along he rubbed his cheekbones and nose with the back of his mittened hand. He did this automatically, now and again changing hands. But rub as he would, the instant he stopped his cheekbones went numb, and the following instant the end of his nose went numb. He was sure to frost his cheeks; he knew that, and experienced a pang of regret that he had not devised a nose strap of the sort Bud wore in cold snaps. Such a strap passed across the cheeks, as well, and saved them. But it didn't

---

5. **spirit thermometer** thermometer containing alcohol; used in extreme cold.

Literature in context — History Connection

❿ *Dogs and the Yukon*

Dogs, like the one that accompanies the man in London's "To Build a Fire," have long played a key role in the life of the Alaskan Yukon. For centuries, native people in Alaska have bred dogs to serve a variety of purposes, including transportation. When the Yukon gold rush that began in the 1890s brought thousands of miners to the northern wilderness, the problem of transportation became acute. In 1910, the federal government constructed a trail more than 1,000 miles long for use by dog sled teams. That trail became known as the Iditarod.

Sled dogs were—and are—some of the most powerful draft animals on Earth. A team of twenty dogs is capable of pulling a ton or more. Though the man in London's story does not treat his dog with affection, for many dog sled drivers these valiant dogs provided warmth and companionship on the long, cold trail.

⓫ ✔Reading Check

Is the man aware of how cold it truly is? How do you know?

To Build a Fire ◆ 611

---

❽ Critical Thinking

Evaluate

• Have students read the bracketed passage. Ask them to pay close attention to the plan that the man makes here.

• Ask students: Does the man's plan make sense? Why or why not? Possible response: Students may point out that four miles an hour is a very quick walking pace, and one that he is unlikely to be able to keep up for very long in the snow.

❾ Reading Strategy

Predicting

• Have students read the bracketed passage. Point out that the path the man is traveling on has not been used for a long time, as the snow indicates.

• Ask students to tell whether they believe the man will reach camp as he plans, now that he is traveling on an unused trail. Possible response: Unlike the man, students may recognize that the trail has been unused for a reason; perhaps it is too dangerous to travel on now. They may predict he won't arrive as planned.

▶ **Monitor Progress** Ask students to support their predictions with details from the story. Possible response: Students may cite such details as the dog's discouragement and the fact that the man "was not given much to thinking."

❿ Background

Literature in Context: Alaskan Huskies

The exact blood line of the Alaskan husky is often debated. Some experts believe the Alaskan husky to be a cross-breed between wolves, Siberian huskies—the genetic source of the blue eyes found in many Alaskan huskies—Irish setters, or any other breed known for speed and endurance.

⓫ ✔Reading Check

Answer: The man is not aware of how cold it truly is; we know because the dog does understand.

CUSTOMIZE INSTRUCTION FOR UNIVERSAL ACCESS

For Special Needs Students	For Advanced Readers
Students may have difficulty understanding the narrator's detailed explanation of the temperature in the bracketed passage 7. Guide them through this passage. Then, ask them why London points out that the freezing point is thirty-two above zero—even though they almost certainly know this. Explain that London uses the freezing point to provide the reader with perspective to understand the true severity of the cold.	After students read the bracketed passage 7 on p. 610, ask them to ponder Jack London's attitude toward animal instinct. Encourage them to discuss what the dog represents in this story. Help students recognize that London places high value on natural instinct as a survival mechanism and model for humans. London clearly shows that the man fails to learn from the cues in his environment, such as the dog's behavior.

⑫ Reading Strategy
Predicting

- Instruct students to construct a chart with two columns. Have them write "Clues in Passage" on the left and "You Can Predict" on the right. You can model the chart using the Predicting transparency in **Literary Analysis and Reading Transparencies**, p. 67.

- Have students read the bracketed passage. Ask them to write clues they find in the left columns of their charts.
  Possible response: Students may include such details as "the changes in the creek," the springs that never freeze, the word "traps," and the fact that a person could "wet himself to the waist."

- Ask students the Reading Strategy question on p. 612: Based on the passage describing the hidden creek, what do you predict might happen? Have them write their answers on the right side of their charts.
  Possible response: Students will probably predict that the man might step into a spring and get soaking wet.

⑬ Literary Analysis
Conflict

- Remind students that the major external conflict the man has faced up to this point has been the cold.

- Have students read the bracketed passage. Encourage them to look for new dangers the man faces in the world around him.

- Ask students the Literary Analysis question on p. 612: What other element of conflict is introduced in the passages describing the creek?
  Answer: Students can recognize that now the man faces the danger of hidden traps in the landscape, such as hidden pockets of water. These hidden traps place him at an even greater disadvantage in his struggle against the harsh environment.

matter much, after all. What were frosted cheeks? A bit painful, that was all: they were never serious.

Empty as the man's mind was of thoughts, he was keenly observant, and he noticed the changes in the creek, the curves and bends and timber jams, and always he sharply noted where he placed his feet. Once, coming around a bend, he shied abruptly, like a startled horse, curved away from the place where he had been walking, and retreated several paces back along the trail. The creek he knew was frozen clear to the bottom—no creek could contain water in that arctic winter—but he knew also that there were springs that bubbled out from the hillsides and ran along under the snow and on top the ice of the creek. He knew that the coldest snaps never froze these springs, and he knew likewise their danger. They were traps. They hid pools of water under the snow that might be three inches deep, or three feet. Sometimes a skin of ice half an inch thick covered them, and in turn was covered by the snow. Sometimes there were alternate layers of water and ice skin, so that when one broke through he kept on breaking through for a while, sometimes wetting himself to the waist.

That was why he had shied in such panic. He had felt the give under his feet and heard the crackle of a snow-hidden ice skin. And to get his feet wet in such a temperature meant trouble and danger. At the very least it meant delay, for he would be forced to stop and build a fire, and under its protection to bare his feet while he dried his socks and moccasins. He stood and studied the creek bed and its banks, and decided that the flow of water came from the right. He reflected awhile, rubbing his nose and cheeks, then skirted to the left, stepping gingerly and testing the footing for each step. Once clear of the danger, he took a fresh chew of tobacco and swung along at his four-mile gait.

In the course of the next two hours he came upon several similar traps. Usually the snow above the hidden pools had a sunken, candied appearance that advertised the danger. Once again, however, he had a close call; and once, suspecting danger, he compelled the dog to go on in front. The dog did not want to go. It hung back until the man shoved it forward, and then it went quickly across the white, unbroken surface. Suddenly it broke through, floundered to one side, and got away to firmer footing. It had wet its forefeet and legs, and almost immediately the water that clung to it turned to ice. It made quick efforts to lick the ice off its legs, then dropped down in the snow and began to bite out the ice that had formed between the toes. This was a matter of instinct. To permit the ice to remain would mean sore feet. It did not know this. It merely obeyed the mysterious prompting that arose from the deep crypts of its being. But the man knew, having achieved a judgment on the subject, and he removed the mitten from his right hand and helped tear out the ice particles. He did not expose his fingers more than a minute, and was astonished at the swift numbness that smote them. It certainly was cold. He pulled on the mitten hastily, and beat the hand savagely across his chest.

Reading Strategy
Predicting Based on this passage describing the hidden creek, what do you predict might happen?

Literary Analysis
Conflict Until now, the man has struggled with the cold. What other element of conflict is introduced in the passages describing the creek?

✷ ENRICHMENT: Social Studies Connection

The Race to the South Pole

Inform students that the deadly situation presented in "To Build a Fire" has many parallels in real-life explorations of the Arctic regions. Relate the story of the race to the South Pole, in which British explorer Robert Falcon Scott and Norwegian explorer Roald Amundsen competed to see who would be the first to lead an exploration party to the newly-charted pole. Their goal: to reach the South Pole in 1910. When Amundsen and his party finally arrived in December 1911, they were the first to set foot on the fabled South Pole. Traveling by sled, Scott and four others reached the spot in January 1912, only to find that Amundsen's party had beaten them to their goal. By March, Scott and his party were dead, victims of illness, extreme weather conditions, and a shortage of supplies.

Encourage interested students to research the details of the race and to share their findings with the class.

At twelve o'clock the day was at its brightest. Yet the sun was too far south on its winter journey to clear the horizon. The bulge of the earth intervened between it and Henderson Creek, where the man walked under a clear sky at noon and cast no shadow. At half-past twelve, to the minute, he arrived at the forks of the creek. He was pleased at the speed he had made. If he kept it up, he would certainly be with the boys by six. He unbuttoned his jacket and shirt and drew forth his lunch. The action consumed no more than a quarter of a minute, yet in that brief moment the numbness laid hold of the exposed fingers. He did not put the mitten on, but, instead, struck the fingers a dozen sharp smashes against his leg. Then he sat down on a snow-covered log to eat. The sting that followed upon the striking of his fingers against his leg ceased so quickly that he was startled. He had had no chance to take a bite of biscuit. He struck the fingers repeatedly and returned them to the mitten, baring the other hand for the purpose of eating. He tried to take a mouthful, but the ice muzzle prevented. He had forgotten to build a fire and thaw out. He chuckled at his foolishness, and as he chuckled he noted the numbness creeping into the exposed fingers. Also, he noted that the stinging which had first come to his toes when he sat down was already passing away. He wondered whether the toes were warm or numb. He moved them inside the moccasins and decided that they were numb.

He pulled the mitten on hurriedly and stood up. He was a bit frightened. He stamped up and down until the stinging returned into the feet. It certainly was cold, was his thought. That man from Sulphur Creek had spoken the truth when telling how cold it sometimes got in the country. And he had laughed at him at the time! That showed one must not be too sure of things. There was no mistake about it, it was cold. He strode up and down, stamping his feet and threshing his arms, until reassured by the returning warmth. Then he got out matches and proceeded to make a fire. From the undergrowth, where high water of the previous spring had lodged a supply of seasoned twigs, he got his firewood. Working carefully from a small beginning, he soon had a roaring fire, over which he thawed the ice from his face and in the protection of which he ate his biscuits. For the moment the cold of space was outwitted. The dog took satisfaction in the fire, stretching out close enough for warmth and far enough away to escape being singed.

When the man had finished, he filled his pipe and took his comfortable time over a smoke. Then he pulled on his mittens, settled the earflaps of his cap firmly about his ears, and took the creek trail up the left fork. The dog was disappointed and yearned back toward the fire. This man did not know cold. Possibly all the generations of his ancestry had been ignorant of cold, of real cold, of cold one hundred and seven degrees below freezing point. But the dog knew; all its ancestry knew, and it had inherited the knowledge. And it knew that it was not good to walk abroad in such fearful cold. It was the time to lie snug in a hole in the snow and wait for a curtain of cloud to be

Literary Analysis
Conflict and Irony In what ways is the man's thought that "one must not be too sure of things" ironic?

16 ☑**Reading Check**
Why do the hidden creeks present such peril?

To Build a Fire ◆ 613

● **14** Critical Thinking
Analyze

- Explain to students that in literary works, a seemingly trivial detail can symbolize or represent an important truth.
- Have students read the bracketed passage. Call their attention to the point that at noon, the man casts no shadow.
- Ask students what the idea that the man casts no shadow might symbolize.
  Possible response: Students may understand it to suggest that he has no presence there and shouldn't be there at all, or that he is marked for death and, like one already dead, no longer exists in the physical world.

● **15** Literary Analysis
Conflict and Irony

- Remind students that irony involves a contrast between what a character expects to happen and what actually happens.
- Have students read the bracketed passage. Encourage them to reflect on what the man has done to arrive here.
- Ask students the Literary Analysis question on p. 613: In what ways is the man's thought that "one must not be too sure of things" ironic?
  Possible response: His thought is ironic because he has gotten himself into this very dangerous and frightening situation by being too sure that he knew what he was doing.

● **16** ☑**Reading Check**
Answer: The creek is so perilous because it hides springs, pockets of water that can soak the man's clothing and freeze solid in a matter of seconds.

CUSTOMIZE INSTRUCTION FOR UNIVERSAL ACCESS

For Special Needs Students	For English Learners	For Gifted/Talented Students
These students may have difficulty with London's dense text. You can have them read along with the recording of this selection on **Listening to Literature Audiocassettes,** Sides 21 and 22 and **Listening to Literature Audio CDs,** CD 13. Encourage students to keep pace with the recording.	Students might be confused by London's dispassionate description of the dog in the bracketed passage 12. Guide students through the passage. Emphasize that dogs are not regarded as pets in this environment. Help students recognize the boundaries between the man and the dog; it is his worker and he uses it as a tool.	Encourage these students to create an illustration of the forks of Henderson Creek, where the man stops to have lunch and builds a fire. Students may use any materials they choose, but should try to capture both the comfort of the fire and the danger of the landscape.

Analyze

- Before students read the bracketed passage, have them pause and consider the man's situation. Remind them that the man is traveling on an unused trail that conceals dangerous pools of unfrozen water.

- Have students read the bracketed passage. Then, ask them: How has the narrator prepared us for this possibility and what it might mean?

  Possible response: Students should respond that the narrator has already detailed the great danger presented by water in such an environment. He has also explained that stepping in water would require a traveler to stop and build a fire, or risk freezing to death.

⑱ Literary Analysis

Conflict and Irony

- Have students read the bracketed passage. Then ask them this question: What are the man's biggest concerns when he falls into the creek?

  Answer: He is angry because making a fire and drying his footgear will delay his return to the camp by an hour.

- Ask students this follow-up question: Given his situation, how are his concerns ironic?

  Answer: His concerns are ironic because London has made it very clear that the man is in very grave danger and may not make it back to the camp at all.

▶**Critical Viewing**

The landscape is spare and severe; there seems to be no sources of food or warmth for miles. Nevertheless, the dog appears to be moving with great speed and energy.

drawn across the face of outer space whence this cold came. On the other hand, there was no keen intimacy between the dog and the man. The one was the toil slave of the other, and the only caresses it had ever received were the caresses of the whiplash and of harsh and menacing throat sounds that threatened the whiplash. So the dog made no effort to communicate its apprehension to the man. It was not concerned in the welfare of the man; it was for its own sake that it yearned back toward the fire. But the man whistled, and spoke to it with the sound of whiplashes, and the dog swung in at the man's heels and followed after.

The man took a chew of tobacco and proceeded to start a new amber beard. Also, his moist breath quickly powdered with white his mustache, eyebrows, and lashes. There did not seem to be so many springs on the left fork of the Henderson, and for half an hour the man saw no signs of any. And then it happened. ⑰ At a place where there were no signs, where the soft, unbroken snow seemed to advertise solidity beneath, the man broke through. It was not deep. He wet himself halfway to the knees before he floundered out to the firm crust.

⑱ He was angry, and cursed his luck aloud. He had hoped to get into camp with the boys at six o'clock, and this would delay him an hour, for he would have to build a fire and dry out his footgear. This was imperative at that low temperature—he knew that much; and he turned aside to the bank, which he climbed. On top, tangled in the underbrush about the trunks of several small spruce trees, was a high-water deposit of dry firewood—sticks and twigs, principally, but also larger portions of seasoned branches and fine, dry, last year's grasses. He threw down several large pieces on top of the snow. This served for a foundation and prevented the young flame from drowning itself in the snow it otherwise would melt. The flame he got by touching a match to a small shred of birch bark that he took from his pocket. This burned even more readily than paper. Placing it on the foundation, he fed the young flame with wisps of dry grass and with the tiniest dry twigs.

He worked slowly and carefully, keenly aware of his danger. Gradually, as the flame grew stronger, he increased the size of the twigs with which he fed it. He squatted in the snow, pulling the twigs out from their entanglement in the brush and feeding directly to the flame. He knew there must be no failure. When it is seventy-five below zero, a man must not fail in his first attempt to build a fire—that is, if his ⑲ feet are wet. If his feet are dry, and he fails, he can run along the trail for half a mile and restore his circulation. But the circulation of wet and freezing feet cannot be restored by running when it is seventy-five below. No matter how fast he runs, the wet feet will freeze the harder.

▲ **Critical Viewing**
In what ways does this image convey both the starkness of the Yukon wilderness and the dog's comfort in that landscape? **[Assess]**

Reading Strategy
Predicting Now that he is wet, what do you predict will happen to the man?

All this the man knew. The old-timer on Sulphur Creek had told him about it the previous fall, and now he was appreciating the advice. Already all sensation had gone out of his feet. To build the fire he had been forced to remove his mittens, and the fingers had quickly gone numb. His pace of four miles an hour had kept his heart pumping blood to the surface of his body and to all the extremities. But the instant he stopped, the action of the pump eased down. The cold of space smote the unprotected tip of the planet, and he, being on that unprotected tip, received the full force of the blow. The blood of his body recoiled before it. The blood was alive, like the dog, and like the dog it wanted to hide away and cover itself up from the fearful cold. So long as he walked four miles an hour, he pumped that blood, willy-nilly, to the surface; but now it ebbed away and sank down into the recesses of his body. The extremities were the first to feel its absence. His wet feet froze the faster, and his exposed fingers numbed the faster, though they had not yet begun to freeze. Nose and cheeks were already freezing, while the skin of all his body chilled as it lost its blood.

But he was safe. Toes and nose and cheeks would be only touched by the frost, for the fire was beginning to burn with strength. He was feeding it with twigs the size of his finger. In another minute he would be able to feed it with branches the size of his wrist, and then he could remove his wet foot-gear, and, while it dried, he could keep his naked feet warm by the fire, rubbing them at first, of course, with snow. The fire was a success. He was safe. He remembered the advice of the old-timer on Sulphur Creek, and smiled. The old-timer had been very serious in laying down the law that no man must travel alone in the Klondike after fifty below. Well, here he was; he had had the accident; he was alone; and he had saved himself. Those old-timers were rather womanish, some of them, he thought. All a man had to do was to keep his head, and he was all right. Any man who was a man could travel alone. But it was surprising, the rapidity with which his cheeks and nose were freezing. And he had not thought his fingers could go lifeless in so short a time. Lifeless they were, for he could scarcely make them move together to grip a twig, and they seemed remote from his body and from him. When he touched a twig, he had to look and see whether or not he had hold of it. The wires were pretty well down between him and his finger ends.

All of which counted for little. There was the fire, snapping and crackling and promising life with every dancing flame. He started to untie his moccasins. They were coated with ice; the thick German socks were like sheaths of iron halfway to the knees; and the moccasin strings were like rods of steel all twisted and knotted as by some conflagration. For a moment he tugged with his numb fingers, then, realizing the folly of it, he drew his sheath-knife.

But before he could cut the strings, it happened. It was his own fault or, rather, his mistake. He should not have built the fire under the spruce tree. He should have built it in the open. But it had been

Literary Analysis

Conflict and Irony Has the man saved himself, as he believes? What does the reader understand about the old-timer's advice that the man does not?

conflagration (kän′ flə grā′ shən) *n.* big, destructive fire

21 ☑ Reading Check

What does the man do after he falls into the creek?

To Build a Fire ◆ 615

CUSTOMIZE INSTRUCTION FOR UNIVERSAL ACCESS

For Less Proficient Readers	For Advanced Readers
If students are excessively surprised by the bracketed passage 17 or have difficulty with the Step-by-Step activity 17, they may need to review the story up to this point. Guide students to understand how the narrator has prepared readers for this crisis; then, have them reread the passage.	Encourage students to discuss the man's reaction to having saved himself at the end of p. 615. Then, ask them to analyze the man's thoughts and actions. Some may respond that he is being cocky, but others might suggest that he is a man who is all alone, deep in a harsh wilderness, and simply talks to himself to keep his spirits up, as anyone might do in similar circumstances.

19 Reading Strategy

Conflict

- Have students read the bracketed passage. Ask them to identify clues in the text that suggest what will happen.

  Answer: Students should answer that "a man must not fail in his first attempt to build a fire—that is, if his feet are wet," because his feet will freeze.

- Ask students the Reading Strategy question on p. 614: Now that he is wet, what do you predict will happen to the man?

  Possible response: Students will probably predict that he will fail to build a fire, and his feet will freeze.

20 Literary Analysis

Conflict and Irony

- Have students read the bracketed passage. Then, ask them the first part of the Literary Analysis question on p. 615: Has the man saved himself, as he believes?

  Possible response: Students will suspect that he has not saved himself, because his hands are too frozen to build the fire.

- Point out to students that the man still faces a major conflict—he is still struggling against nature, and he is still at a great disadvantage.

- Ask students the second part of the Literary Analysis question on p. 615: What does the reader understand about the old-timer's advice that the man does not?

  Possible response: The reader understands that it is much colder than fifty below zero, weather that is more than anyone can face alone. The man still does not understand this, and his ignorance creates dramatic irony.

21 ☑ Reading Check

Answer: He struggles to build a fire to dry out his footgear before his feet freeze.

- Before they read the bracketed passage, ask students to pause and consider the man's progress up to this point. Have his efforts been successful?

  Possible response: Students may observe that he remains calm after falling into the water and successfully builds a fire. Others may feel that getting wet in the first place indicates that the man is failing in his effort to get to the camp.

- Have students read the bracketed passage. Then, ask them to tell whether they were able to predict this accident. Have them provide details to back up their predictions.

  Possible response: Most students will have been caught by surprise, but they are likely to have expected some type of disaster to occur. Details are likely to include the man's dismissive memory of the old-timer's warning, which suggests that the man is much too confident.

23 Literary Analysis

Conflict

- Remind students that the main conflict in this story comes from the man's struggle against natural forces. Ask them to consider what the man has done so far to resolve this conflict.

- Have students read the bracketed passage. Then, ask them the Literary Analysis question on p. 616: In what ways does the conflict intensify as the man begins to build another fire?

  Possible response: The situation becomes far more dangerous; the man feels as if "he had just heard his own sentence of death," and realizes that if he survives, he will at least lose some toes.

  ▶ Monitor Progress Encourage students to discuss the ways in which the story has built conflict. To what climax do they think the conflict will build?

  Possible response: At this point, students may have concluded that the man is going to freeze to death.

22 easier to pull the twigs from the brush and drop them directly on the fire. Now the tree under which he had done this carried a weight of snow on its boughs. No wind had blown for weeks, and each bough was fully freighted. Each time he had pulled a twig he had communicated a slight agitation to the tree—an imperceptible agitation, so far as he was concerned, but an agitation sufficient to bring about the disaster. High up in the tree one bough capsized its load of snow. This fell on the boughs beneath, capsizing them. This process continued, spreading out and involving the whole tree. It grew like an avalanche, and it descended without warning upon the man and the fire, and the fire was blotted out! Where it had burned was a mantle of fresh and disordered snow.

The man was shocked. It was as though he had just heard his own sentence of death. For a moment he sat and stared at the spot where the fire had been. Then he grew very calm. Perhaps the old-timer on Sulphur Creek was right. If he had only had a trail mate he would **23** have been in no danger now. The trail mate could have built the fire. Well, it was up to him to build the fire over again, and this second time there must be no failure. Even if he succeeded, he would most likely lose some toes. His feet must be badly frozen by now, and there would be some time before the second fire was ready.

Such were his thoughts, but he did not sit and think them. He was busy all the time they were passing through his mind. He made a new foundation for a fire, this time in the open, where no treacherous tree could blot it out. Next, he gathered dry grasses and tiny twigs from the high-water flotsam. He could not bring his fingers together to pull them out, but he was able to gather them by the handful. In this way he got many rotten twigs and bits of green moss that were undesirable, but it was the best he could do. He worked methodically, even collecting an armful of the larger branches to be used later when the fire gathered strength. And all the while the dog sat and watched him, a certain yearning wistfulness in its eyes, for it looked upon him as the fire provider, and the fire was slow in coming.

When all was ready, the man reached in his pocket for a second piece of birch bark. He knew the bark was there, and, though he could not feel it with his fingers, he could hear its crisp rustling as he fumbled for it. Try as he would, he could not clutch hold of it. And all the time, in his consciousness, was the knowledge that each instant his feet were freezing. This thought tended to put him in a panic, but he fought against it and kept calm. He pulled on his mittens with his teeth, and threshed his arms back and forth, beating his hands with all his might against his sides. He did this sitting down, and he stood up to do it; and all the while the dog sat in the snow, its wolf brush of a tail curled around warmly over its forefeet, its sharp wolf ears pricked forward intently as it watched the man. And the man, as he beat and threshed with his arms and hands, felt a great surge of envy as he regarded the creature that was warm and secure in its natural covering.

Literary Analysis
Conflict In what ways does the conflict intensify as the man begins to build another fire?

of the tenseness of the effort, his shivering got away with him, and the twigs were hopelessly scattered. Each twig gushed a puff of smoke and went out. The fire provider had failed. As he looked apathetically about him, his eyes chanced on the dog, sitting across the ruins of the fire from him, in the snow, making restless, hunching movements, slightly lifting one forefoot and then the other, shifting its weight back and forth on them with wistful eagerness.

The sight of the dog put a wild idea into his head. He remembered the tale of the man, caught in a blizzard, who killed a steer and crawled inside the carcass, and so was saved. He would kill the dog and bury his hands in the warm body until the numbness went out of them. Then he could build another fire. He spoke to the dog, calling it to him; but in his voice was a strange note of fear that frightened the animal, who had never known the man to speak in such way before. Something was the matter, and its suspicious nature sensed danger—it knew not what danger, but somewhere, somehow, in its brain arose an apprehension of the man. It flattened its ears down at the sound of the man's voice, and its restless, hunching movements and the liftings and shiftings of its forefeet became more pronounced; but it would not come to the man. He got on his hands and knees and crawled toward the dog. This unusual posture again excited suspicion, and the animal sidled mincingly away.

The man sat up in the snow for a moment and struggled for calmness. Then he pulled on his mittens, by means of his teeth, and got upon his feet. He glanced down at first in order to assure himself that he was really standing up, for the absence of sensation in his feet left him unrelated to the earth. His erect position in itself started to drive the webs of suspicion from the dog's mind; and when he spoke <u>peremptorily</u>, with the sound of whiplashes in his voice, the dog rendered its customary allegiance and came to him. As it came within reaching distance, the man lost his control. His arms flashed out to the dog, and he experienced genuine surprise when he discovered that his hands could not clutch, that there was neither bend nor feeling in the fingers. He had forgotten for the moment that they were

Literary Analysis
Conflict What conflict is intensified in the passage beginning "the sight of the dog . . ."?

peremptorily (pər emp´ tər ə lē) *adj.* decisively; commandingly

30 ✔**Reading Check**
What happens to the man's second attempt to build a fire?

To Build a Fire ❯ 619

CUSTOMIZE INSTRUCTION FOR UNIVERSAL ACCESS	
For Less Proficient Readers	**For English Learners**
Have students summarize what is happening between the man and the dog. Guide them to understand that the man is making an awkward, desperate attempt to capture the dog, kill it, and use its body warmth to undo his numbness, and that his movements and sounds make the dog apprehensive. Encourage students to reread if necessary.	These students may have difficulty decoding the passage describing the man's second attempt to start a fire. Ask students to write down and look up words they do not understand. Guide them to recognize that the man drops his first match, burns his hands with the rest but lights his kindling, and finally puts out the fire himself with his frozen and useless hands.

29 Literary Analysis
Conflict

- Ask students to consider how the man's conflict with nature has developed up to this point in the story. Point out that his struggles with his environment have become steadily more difficult.
- Have students read the bracketed passage. If any students find this passage upsetting, encourage them to consider how their discomfort builds their sense of the story's conflict.
- Ask students the Literary Analysis question on p. 619: What conflict is intensified in this passage? **Possible response:** The conflict between the man and the extreme cold is intensified when killing the dog becomes his last chance to escape the cold.
  ▶**Monitor Progress** Ask students what details add to the intensity of the conflict. **Possible response:** Students may cite such details as "put a wild idea into his head," the "strange note of fear" in the man's voice, the dog's building suspicions of the man, and the dog's "restless, hunching movements."

30 ✔**Reading Check**
Answer: Shivering uncontrollably, he drops a large piece of moss on the fire; when he tries to poke the moss out, he extinguishes the fire.

31 Reading Strategy

Predicting

• Before they read the bracketed passage, ask students to compare the man's survival skills with the dog's. Remind them that the narrator indicates that the dog's instincts give it a better grasp of the cold than the man has.

• Have students read the bracketed passage. Then, ask them to predict whether the man will survive and whether the dog will survive. Students should support their answers with details.
Possible response: Based on the fact that the man has no means by which to start a fire, it is unlikely he will survive. The dog, on the other hand, is likely to survive because of its protective coat and strong instincts for survival.

32 Reading Strategy

Predicting

• Instruct students to construct or add to previously constructed Predicting charts, with two columns. You can model the chart using the Predicting transparency in **Literary Analysis and Reading Transparencies**, p. 67.

• Have students read the bracketed passage. Ask them to write clues from the passage in the left-hand column of their charts.
Possible response: Students may note the man's growing "fear of death" and panic, as well as his new hope that he might run all the way to the camp.

• Ask students the Reading Strategy question on p. 620: Does the man still have a chance for survival? Explain why or why not.
Possible response: Students might say that the man will die because his hypothermia is too severe and the camp is too far away. Others might feel there's still a hope that someone will catch up to him on the trail and save him.

• Have students write their responses in the right-hand columns on their charts.

frozen and that they were freezing more and more. All this happened quickly, and before the animal could get away, he encircled its body with his arms. He sat down in the snow, and in this fashion held the dog, while it snarled and whined and struggled.

But it was all he could do, hold its body encircled in his arms and sit there. He realized that he could not kill the dog. There was no way to do it. With his helpless hands he could neither draw nor hold his sheath-knife nor throttle the animal. He released it, and it plunged wildly away, with tail between its legs, and still snarling. It halted forty feet away and surveyed him curiously, with ears sharply pricked forward. The man looked down at his hands in order to locate them, and found them hanging on the ends of his arms. It struck him as curious that one should have to use his eyes in order to find out where his hands were. He began threshing his arms back and forth, beating the mittened hands against his sides. He did this for five minutes, violently, and his heart pumped enough blood up to the surface to put a stop to his shivering. But no sensation was aroused in the hands. He had an impression that they hung like weights on the ends of his arms, but when he tried to run the impression down, he could not find it.

A certain fear of death, dull and oppressive, came to him. This fear quickly became poignant as he realized that it was no longer a mere matter of freezing his fingers and toes, or of losing his hands and feet, but that it was a matter of life and death with the chances against him. This threw him into a panic, and he turned and ran up the creek-bed along the old, dim trail. The dog joined in behind and kept up with him. He ran blindly, without intention, in fear such as he had never known in his life. Slowly, as he plowed and floundered through the snow, he began to see things again—the banks of the creek, the old timber jams, the leafless aspens, and the sky. The running made him feel better. He did not shiver. Maybe, if he ran on, his feet would thaw out; and, anyway, if he ran far enough, he would reach camp and the boys. Without doubt he would lose some fingers and toes and some of his face; but the boys would take care of him, and save the rest of him when he got there. And at the same time there was another thought in his mind that said he would never get to the camp and the boys; that it was too many miles away, that the freezing had too great a start on him, and that he would soon be stiff and dead. This thought he kept in the background and refused to consider. Sometimes it pushed itself forward and demanded to be heard, but he thrust it back and strove to think of other things.

It struck him as curious that he could run at all on feet so frozen that he could not feel them when they struck the earth and took the weight of his body. He seemed to himself to skim along above the surface, and to have no connection with the earth. Somewhere he had once seen a winged Mercury,[6] and he wondered if Mercury felt as he felt when skimming over the earth.

---

6. **Mercury** from Roman mythology, the wing-footed messenger of the gods.

Reading Strategy
Predicting Does the man still have a chance for survival? Explain why or why not.

His theory of running until he reached camp and the boys had one flaw in it: he lacked the endurance. Several times he stumbled, and finally he tottered, crumpled up, and fell. When he tried to rise, he failed. He must sit and rest, he decided, and next time he would merely walk and keep on going. As he sat and regained his breath, he noted that he was feeling quite warm and comfortable. He was not shivering, and it even seemed that a warm glow had come to his chest and trunk. And yet, when he touched his nose or cheeks, there was no sensation. Running would not thaw them out. Nor would it thaw out his hands and feet. Then the thought came to him that the frozen portions of his body must be extending. He tried to keep this thought down, to forget it, to think of something else; he was aware of the panicky feeling that it caused, and he was afraid of the panic. But the thought asserted itself, and persisted, until it produced a vision of his body totally frozen. This was too much, and he made another wild run along the trail. Once he slowed down to a walk, but the thought of the freezing extending itself made him run again.

And all the time the dog ran with him, at his heels. When he fell down a second time, it curled its tail over its forefeet and sat in front of him, facing him, curiously eager and intent. The warmth and security of the animal angered him, and he cursed it till it flattened down its ears appeasingly. This time the shivering came more quickly upon the man. He was losing in his battle with the frost. It was creeping into his body from all sides. The thought of it drove him on, but he ran no more than a hundred feet, when he staggered and pitched headlong. It was his last panic. When he had recovered his breath and control, he sat up and entertained in his mind the conception of meeting death with dignity. However, the conception did not come to him in such terms. His idea of it was that he had been making a fool of himself, running around like a chicken with its head cut off—such was the simile that occurred to him. Well, he was bound to freeze anyway, and he might as well take it decently. With this new-found peace of mind came the first glimmerings of drowsiness. A good idea, he thought, to sleep off to death. It was like taking an anaesthetic. Freezing was not so bad as people thought. There were lots worse ways to die.

He pictured the boys finding his body next day. Suddenly he found himself with them, coming along the trail and looking for himself. And, still with them, he came around a turn in the trail and found himself lying in the snow. He did not belong with himself any more, for even then he was out of himself; standing with the boys and looking at himself in the snow. It certainly was cold, was his thought. When he got back to the States he could tell the folks what real cold was. He drifted on from this to a vision of the old-timer on Sulphur Creek. He could see him quite clearly, warm and comfortable, and smoking a pipe.

"You were right, old hoss; you were right," the man mumbled to the old-timer of Sulphur Creek.

Literary Analysis

Conflict and Irony As the man begins to feel "quite warm and comfortable" what does the reader know that the man does not?

✔ **Reading Check**

What does the man try to do when he realizes he is freezing to death?

CUSTOMIZE INSTRUCTION FOR UNIVERSAL ACCESS

For Less Proficient Readers

If students need help understanding the concept of conflict in this story, have them use the following graphic organizer. Remind them that conflict is a common ingredient in fictional plots, and that it follows a pattern. Show students the organizer and suggest that they copy it. On the left side, have them list the events that lead up to the turning point, or climax, of the main character's conflict. On the right side, have them list the events that follow this turning point.

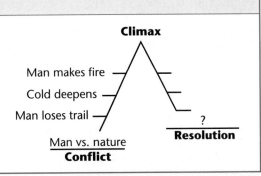

③③ Literary Analysis

Conflict and Irony

- Use the Enrichment: Science Connection note at the bottom of p. 610 in this Teacher's Edition to inform students about the symptoms of hypothermia.

- Ask students the Literary Analysis question on p. 621: As the man begins to feel "quite warm and comfortable," what does the reader know that the man does not?
  Answer: The reader knows that the feeling of comfortable warmth is a sign that the man is dying of hypothermia.

- Point out to students that this situation is ironic because the man believes he is now all right while the reader knows that he is about to die.

③④ Literary Analysis

Conflict

- Remind students that in literary works, conflict builds up to a *climax*—a crisis or turning point in the story's plot. From the climax, the story moves to a resolution, where the conflict comes to an end.

- Have students read the bracketed passage. Point out that the man undergoes an important change here; for the first time, he accepts the inevitability of his death.

- Ask students: How does this passage suggest the story's conflict—man versus nature—will be resolved?
  Possible response: Students should recognize that the man is dying and answer that he has lost in his struggle with the extreme weather conditions, and thus will lose his life.

③⑤ ✔ Reading Check

Answer: He tries to meet his death with dignity—to "take it decently."

Answers for p. 622

Review and Assess

1. **Possible response:** Students may respond that they would never have set out alone or chosen to travel in such harsh weather.

2. **(a)** No one should travel alone in the Klondike if the temperature is colder than fifty below zero. **(b) Possible response:** It suggests that he is thoughtless and overly self-confident.

3. **Possible responses: (a)** The dog's instincts tell it not to travel, but to stay where there is fire. **(b)** The man does not have the imagination to understand the significance of the cold or the possible consequences of traveling in such weather. **(c)** The dog is better equipped to survive.

4. **(a)** The man tries to avoid the hidden pools of water. **(b)** His feet get wet, requiring him to build a fire; he builds his fire by a tree, which dumps snow on it; his hands are too frozen to build a second fire; he freezes to death.

5. **(a)** He curses his luck. **(b) Possible response:** Students may respond that the man's own character flaws—lack of imagination and overconfidence—contribute to his downfall.

6. **Possible responses: (a)** Perhaps because the man serves as a symbol for the human desire to control or disregard the power of nature. **(b)** Students may recognize that they would have greater sympathy with the man, despite his flaws.

7. **Possible responses: (a)** It suggests that human strength cannot control nature. Nature is a much more powerful force than humanity, and must be respected. **(b)** Students may agree with London's message because today ecological problems persist despite our efforts to solve them.

Then the man drowsed off into what seemed to him the most comfortable and satisfying sleep he had ever known. The dog sat facing him and waiting. The brief day drew to a close in a long, slow twilight. There were no signs of a fire to be made, and, besides, never in the dog's experience had it known a man to sit like that in the snow and make no fire. As the twilight drew on, its eager yearning for the fire mastered it, and with a great lifting and shifting of forefeet, it whined softly, then flattened its ears down in anticipation of being chidden[7] by the man. But the man remained silent. Later, the dog whined loudly. And still later it crept close to the man and caught the scent of death. This made the animal bristle and back away. A little longer it delayed, howling under the stars that leaped and danced and shone brightly in the cold sky. Then it turned and trotted up the trail in the direction of the camp it knew, where were the other food providers and fire providers.

---

7. chidden scolded.

Review and Assess

Thinking About the Selection

1. **Respond:** Could you imagine yourself falling into the same circumstances as the man? How could you avoid them?

2. **(a) Recall:** What advice from an old-timer does the man choose to ignore? **(b) Infer:** What does this decision suggest about the man's character?

3. **(a) Recall:** What do the dog's instincts tell it about the cold? **(b) Compare and Contrast:** By contrast, why does the extreme cold "make no impression" on the man? **(c) Make a Judgment:** Which is better equipped to survive in the cold, the dog or the man? Explain.

4. **(a) Recall:** What trap does the man try—unsuccessfully—to avoid? **(b) Analyze Cause and Effect:** What deadly chain of events is started by his inability to avoid the trap?

5. **(a) Recall:** When the man breaks through the snow into the icy water, he becomes angry and curses. What is it that he curses? **(b) Evaluate:** Is the outcome of the story due to fate, to the man's character, or to some other cause? Explain.

6. **(a) Assess:** Why do you think London did not give the man a name? **(b) Speculate:** How might the effect of this story be different if the man had a name?

7. **(a) Draw Conclusions:** What does the story suggest about human strength in the face of nature's power? **(b) Take a Position:** Is London's message true? Explain.

622 ◆ *Division, Reconciliation, and Expansion (1850–1914)*

✎ ASSESSMENT PRACTICE: Reading Comprehension

Context	(For more practice, see Test Preparation Workbook, p. 35)

Many tests require students to use contextual analysis to determine the meanings of words and phrases. Use the following to demonstrate.

Fifty degrees below zero meant eighty-odd degrees of frost. Such fact. . . did not lead him to meditate upon his *frailty as a creature of temperature*, and upon man's frailty in general, able only to live within certain narrow limits of heat and cold.

In this passage, the phrase *frailty as a creature of*

temperature means—

A Humans can be killed by heat and cold.
B Humans are frail when they have a temperature.
C Humans can survive in the cold.
D Even frail humans can withstand extreme temperatures.

The last part of the sentence gives context clues that show *A* is the correct answer.

Review and Assess

Literary Analysis

Conflict

1. (a) What external **conflict** is central to the plot of "To Build a Fire"? (b) Use a chart like the one shown to examine the details London uses to portray the central conflict.

The Man versus ?	Details
	1. _____
	2. _____
	3. _____

2. Does the man's awareness of the conflict intensify as the story unfolds? Explain.
3. What events finally resolve the conflict?
4. What is the **internal conflict** that develops as the story progresses?

Connecting Literary Elements

5. What is ironic about the fact that the man breaks through the snow and steps in the spring?
6. What is ironic about the location in which he builds his fire?
7. In what way do London's descriptions of the dog's feelings and its instincts about survival increase the story's dramatic **irony**?

Reading Strategy

Predicting

8. (a) What information do the man's recollections of his conversation with the old-timer provide? (b) In what ways does this information help you **predict** the end of the story?
9. (a) At what point did you first predict that the man would not survive his journey? (b) On what clues did you base your prediction?

Extend Understanding

10. **Social Studies Connection:** Suppose that you were the editor of a newspaper in Alaska during the time of the Klondike Gold Rush. If you learned of this man's sad tale, what might you have written in an editorial about the event?

Quick Review

A **conflict** is a struggle between two opposing forces. Conflicts can be internal or external.

Irony involves a discrepancy between what is stated and what is meant. **Dramatic irony** occurs when the reader knows more than the character does about the character's circumstances.

To **predict** what will happen in a story, look for clues that hint at later events.

 Take It to the Net
www.phschool.com
Take the interactive self-test online to check your understanding of the selection.

ENRICHMENT: Further Reading

Other works by Jack London

The Call of the Wild

The Sea Wolf

White Fang

Martin Eden

 Take It to the Net
Visit www.phschool.com for more information on Jack London.

Answers for p. 621

Review and Assess

1. **(a)** The conflict is between man and nature. **(b)** Possible response: The central conflict is man vs. nature. Students' charts should list appropriate details from the story.

2. Possible response: The forces of nature affect the man more and more as the story progresses; gradually, the man becomes aware of how dangerous his situation has become.

3. Falling snow puts out the man's fire; he is unable to start a second fire. He freezes to death.

4. The man's lack of judgment and overconfidence conflict with his genuine fear for his own safety as he battles to stay calm in the face of rising panic.

5. It is ironic because he has been keeping a careful eye out for exactly the trap he falls into.

6. It is ironic because in his overconfidence, he builds it beneath a snow-laden tree.

7. By describing the dog's feelings and instincts, London lets the reader know what the man does not: that he is walking into deadly danger.

8. **(a)** One should never travel alone in the Klondike when the temperature is less than fifty degrees below zero. **(b)** Possible response: Each time the man remembers the advice and laughs, it is a reminder of the fatal danger he faces.

9. Possible responses: **(a)** and **(b)** Student answers will vary, but should be supported with details from the text.

10. Possible response: Student responses should accurately summarize the basic information in the story and perhaps use the man's death as a warning to others.

623

❶ Vocabulary Development

Word Analysis

1. b
2. a
3. d
4. c

Fluency: Sentence Completions

conflagration; unwonted; peremptorily; conjectural

Spelling Strategy

1. accompanied
2. happily

❷ Grammar and Style

1. as far as the eye could see; modifies *was*

2. since the last sled had passed over; modifies *had fallen*

3. where no treacherous tree could blot it out; modifies *made*

4. If he kept it up; modifies *would be*

5. When he could endure no more; modifies *jerked*

Writing Application

Each of the four sentences should contain an adverb clause—always a dependent clause that functions as an adverb. All four sentences should relate to a frightening encounter with nature.

Integrate Language Skills

❶ Vocabulary Development Lesson

Word Analysis: Latin Root -ject-

The Latin root *-ject-* means "to throw." If you *reject* an idea, you throw it back. Each word below contains the root *-ject-*. Use the clues to match each word with the situation to which it applies.

1. object
   (*ob* = toward; over; against)
2. conjecture
   (*con* = with; *ure* = noun of action)
3. abject
   (*ab* = away from)
4. eject
   (*e* = out; away)

a. you throw your thoughts in with others
b. you speak out against something
c. you remove someone from the premises
d. you feel this way when your friends shun you

Fluency: Sentence Completions

Fill in the blanks with the appropriate words from the vocabulary list on page 607.

A lightning storm in the parched woodland sparked a ___?___. The shy fire chief acted with ___?___ authority, ___?___ ordering all firefighters to work round the clock, though his estimates of how long it would take to overcome the fire were ___?___ at best.

Spelling Strategy

To add a suffix to a word ending in a *y* preceded by a consonant, change the *y* to *i* (*peremptory* + *ly* = *peremptorily*). For each of the following sentences, write the correct form of the word in italics.

1. Last year, my parents *accompany* me on my trip to Alaska.
2. We *happy* watched as the winning run scored.

❷ Grammar and Style Lesson

Adverb Clauses

An **adverb clause** is a group of words with a subject and a verb that cannot stand by itself as a sentence. Adverb clauses modify verbs, adjectives, or other adverbs, explaining *how*, *where*, *when*, *why*, *to what extent*, or *under what circumstances*.

> Day had broken cold and gray, exceedingly cold and gray, *when the man turned aside from the main Yukon trail* . . . . (tells *when*)

Practice Identify the adverb clause and the word it modifies in each item below.

1. North and south, as far as the eye could see, it was unbroken white . . . .

2. A foot of snow had fallen since the last sled had passed over.

3. He made a new foundation for a fire, where no treacherous tree could blot it out.

4. If he kept it up, he would certainly be with the boys by six.

5. At last, when he could endure no more, he jerked his hands apart.

Writing Application Write four sentences describing a frightening encounter with nature. Use at least one adverb clause in each sentence. Identify the function of each adverb clause in your draft.

W/G Prentice Hall Writing and Grammar Connection: Chapter 19, Section 3

TEACHING RESOURCES

The following resources can be used to enrich or extend the instruction for pp. 624–625.

Vocabulary

📖 **Selection Support:** Build Vocabulary, p. 146
📖 **Vocabulary and Spelling Practice Book**
(Use this booklet for skills enrichment.)

Grammar

📖 **Selection Support:** Grammar and Style, p. 147
W/G **Writing and Grammar**, Ruby Level, p. 458
▣ **Daily Language Practice Transparencies** ▣

Writing

W/G **Writing and Grammar**, Ruby Level, p. 311
W/G **Writing and Grammar iText CD-ROM** ▣
▣ **Writing Models and Graphic Organizers on Transparencies**, pp. 91–93 ▣

▣ **BLOCK SCHEDULING:** Resources marked with this symbol provide varied instruction during 90-minute blocks.

③ Writing Lesson

Literary Analysis

A literary analysis explores how the elements of a piece of literature, such as plot, setting, characters, and point of view, work together to convey a message. Write a literary analysis in which you explain the message of "To Build a Fire," and discuss how the various elements of the story contribute to its meaning.

Prewriting   Review the story to identify London's message about the relationship between humanity and nature. Gather details that support your interpretation.

Drafting   In your introduction, state your thesis and outline your main points. Focus each body paragraph on one main point. Cite supporting details from the story.

Model: Elaborating to Support an Argument

The dog, equipped by centuries of evolution for life in the bitter cold, serves as a symbolic foil to the man. Unlike the man, who disregards plain evidence, ". . . the dog knew; all its ancestry knew, and it had inherited the knowledge. And it knew that it was not good to walk abroad in such fearful cold."

> Providing details from the work helps to elaborate on the main point, underlined here.

Revising   Review your draft, making sure your thesis is clear and your support is convincing. Look for opportunities to elaborate on your key points.

 Prentice Hall Writing and Grammar Connection: Chapter 14, Section 4

④ Extension Activities

Listening and Speaking If the dog could voice its thoughts about the man, what would it say? Write and present an **enactment** of the dog's thoughts and feelings as a scene of this story unfolds. Keep these tips in mind as you work:

- Refer to the text of the story for accuracy.
- Include details that reflect the dog's highly developed senses of smell and hearing.

Work to create a specific sense of character, so that your dog has an individual voice.

Research and Technology The man in the story dies of hypothermia, or subnormal body temperature. Research this condition using a variety of sources, including the Internet. Then, create a word-processed **booklet** of guidelines for avoiding hypothermia.

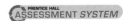 *Take It to the Net*   www.phschool.com

Go online for an additional research activity using the Internet.

ASSESSMENT RESOURCES

The following resources can be used to assess students' knowledge and skills.

Selection Assessment

- 📖 **Formal Assessment**, pp. 155–157
- 📖 **Open Book Test**, pp. 97–99
- 📼 **Got It! Assessment Video**, Tape 3
- 💿 **Test Bank Software**

📓 *Take It to the Net*
Visit www.phschool.com for self-tests and additional questions on "To Build a Fire."

Writing Rubric

- 📖 **Performance Assessment and Portfolio Management**, p. 23

PRENTICE HALL ASSESSMENT SYSTEM

- 📖 **Workbook**
- 📖 **Skill Book**
- 🖨 **Transparencies**
- 💿 **CD-ROM**

---

③ Writing Lesson

- Explain to students that unlike a book report that simply restates the story, a literary analysis digs beneath the surface to present an interpretation of the work. This interpretation forms the thesis, or main point, of the analysis.

- Using the Writing Lesson, guide students to begin prewriting. Emphasize that each point in the essay will need to be supported with details from the story.

- Literary Analyses should present convincing interpretations supported by appropriate details from the story.

- Use the Response to Literature rubric in **Performance Assessment and Portfolio Management**, p. 23, to evaluate students' essays.

④ Research and Technology

- Explain that booklets will present general information. Because they offer condensed information, booklets should give readers only the most important or useful facts, guidelines, or details.

- Have students work in pairs to research the causes, symptoms, and recommended treatment for hypothermia. Have students use the Cause and Effect organizer in **Writing Models and Graphic Organizers on Transparencies**, pp. 91–93.

- Partners can combine the most important points, guidelines, and tips for avoiding, detecting, and treating hypothermia. Help students to print and assemble their booklets.

- Assess students' booklets based on the completeness and effective presentation of the information.

CUSTOMIZE INSTRUCTION
For Universal Access

To address different learning styles, use the activities suggested in the Extension Activities booklet, p. 33.

For Verbal/Linguistic and Bodily/Kinesthetic Learners, use Activity 5.

For Visual/Spatial Learners, use Activity 6.

For Verbal/Linguistic Learners, use Activity 7.

Lesson Objectives

1. To understand the connection between literature of the western frontier and contemporary historical fiction about the West

2. To understand the difference between romanticized and realistic literary visions of the American West

Connections

This excerpt from Larry McMurtry's *Lonesome Dove* has all the elements of the classic tale of the American West: cowboys, horses, cattle, and the challenges of the untamed wilderness. As students read, prompt them to look for connections to the plots and themes of the folk literature and the works of Bret Harte, Miriam Davis Colt, and Jack London in Part 3. How has the passing time changed the western? In what ways has the genre stayed the same?

Forging New Frontiers

- Explain to students that Americans have been heading west from the beginning of their history. Settlers left the settled East, pushing gradually to the Mississippi River and beyond. By the mid-1800s, Americans thronged the 2,000-mile trail to Oregon.

- Point out to students that this westward movement gave rise to the western genre, first in literature and later in film. If possible, show students examples of early western films.

- Be sure students understand that the cowboy is a central figure of the western genre. Other important elements include long cattle drives and the dangers of the untamed frontier.

- Explain to students that *Lonesome Dove* tells a story about the cowboys of the last days of the frontier. The novel was published in 1985, however, perhaps giving it a different perspective on its subject.

Forging New Frontiers

Among the greatest legends of the American West were the cowboys, who drove longhorn cattle from the open ranges of Texas up to the railroad yards in Kansas. As they made the journey, cowboys faced loneliness and danger—yet they seemed glamourous to those who lived more settled lives. The cowboy came to symbolize a side of the American dream that was being lost to development. Toward the end of the nineteenth century, the spread of the railroads and the fencing of the once open range spelled the end for most working cowboys. However, the national obsession with the cowboy myth refused to die.

The Western For most of the twentieth century, fictional cowboys pursued their lonely quests in thousands of books and movies. The first western movie, *The Great Train Robbery*, was made in 1903, and hundreds more were filmed in the decades that followed. In all of them, the cowboy was a solitary hero forced to prove himself in the wilderness. Beginning in 1903, an Ohio dentist named Zane Grey published more than eighty westerns, many of which are still popular today.

Contemporary writers like Larry McMurtry and Cormac McCarthy have tapped into this American passion. Their novels set in the West have captured the public's imagination and enjoy both popular and critical success.

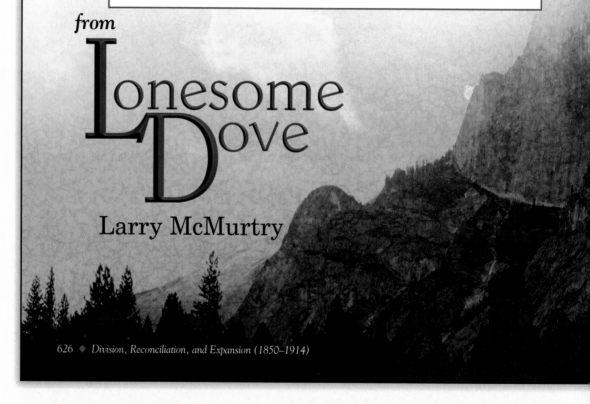

from

Lonesome Dove

Larry McMurtry

626 ◆ *Division, Reconciliation, and Expansion (1850–1914)*

✹ ENRICHMENT: Media Connection

McMurtry on the Screen

Several of Larry McMurtry's novels have been adapted for film and television, including *Lonesome Dove*. Discuss with students the difficulties involved in adapting a novel for another medium. Guide them to consider how writers for the big or small screen must make decisions about issues like these:

- whether to cut back the plot by deleting characters or story lines

- how to convey information provided by the narrator in the novel

- how to develop characterization, conflict, and drama on the screen

Students may be interested in reading *Lonesome Dove* and then in seeing the video adaptation to compare and contrast the two versions. You might also encourage them to read other western novels and then view their film or television adaptations.

Captain Woodrow Call and Augustus McCrae are two former Texas Rangers who helped bring peace to the Texas frontier. Call now feels a yearning for adventure. With his friend Augustus, he gathers together a ragtag bunch of cowboys and embarks on a cattle drive from Lonesome Dove, Texas, on the Rio Grande, to the wilderness of Montana.

In the late afternoon they strung a rope corral around the remuda,[1] so each hand could pick himself a set of mounts, each being allowed four picks. It was slow work, for Jasper Fant and Needle Nelson could not make up their minds. The Irishmen and the boys had to take what was left after the more experienced hands had chosen.

Augustus did not deign to make a choice at all. "I intend to ride old Malaria all the way," he said, "or if not I'll ride Greasy."

Once the horses were assigned, the positions had to be assigned as well.

"Dish, you take the right point," Call said. "Soupy can take the left and Bert and Needle will back you up."

Dish had assumed that, as a top hand, he would have a point, and no one disputed his right, but both Bert and Needle were unhappy that Soupy had the other point. They had been with the outfit longer, and felt <u>aggrieved</u>.

The Spettle boys were told to help Lippy with the horse herd, and Newt, the Raineys and the Irishmen were left with the drags. Call saw that each of them had bandanas, for the dust at the rear of the herd would be bad.

They spent an hour patching on the wagon, a vehicle Augustus regarded with scorn. "That dern wagon won't get us to the Brazos,"[2] he said.

"Well, it's the only wagon we got," Call said.

"You didn't assign me no duties, nor yourself either," Augustus pointed out.

"That simple," Call said. "I'll scare off bandits and you can talk to Indian chiefs."

"You boys let these cattle string out," he said to the men. "We ain't in no big hurry."

Augustus had ridden through the cattle and had come back with a count of slightly over twenty-six hundred.

"Make it twenty-six hundred cattle and two pigs," he said. "I guess we've seen the last of the dern Rio Grande. One of us ought to make a speech, Call. Think of how long we've rode this river."

Call was not willing to indulge him in any dramatics. He mounted the mare and went over to help the boys get the cattle started. It was

---

1. **remuda** (rə mōō′ də) *n.* group of extra saddle horses kept as a supply of remounts.
2. **the Brazos** (brä′ zəs) river in central and southeastern Texas.

aggrieved (ə grēvd′) *v.* offended; wronged

Thematic Connection
What does this group have in common with the characters in "The Outcasts of Poker Flat"?

✓**Reading Check**
Why are Bert and Needle unhappy?

Connections: from Lonesome Dove ◆ 627

Background
Lonesome Dove

Old friends Woodrow Call and Augustus McCrae begin a 2,500-mile cattle drive from Lonesome Dove, their Texas ranch, to the unfamiliar wilds of Montana. Call, a hard, silent man, initiates the plan and runs the crew; easygoing Augustus, who has gotten used to a lazy life of drinking and stargazing, regrets leaving Lonesome Dove. This excerpt recounts the first day of the long journey toward Montana.

Thematic Connection

Possible response: Students may find the characters' dialects similar; also, both Call and Mr. Oakhurst are taciturn.

✓**Reading Check**

Answer: They are unhappy because Soupy, who has not been with the outfit as long as they have, is given a better position.

CUSTOMIZE INSTRUCTION FOR UNIVERSAL ACCESS

For Less Proficient Readers	For English Learners	For Advanced Readers
This selection contains many "cowboy" terms and colorful Western verbs that may be unfamiliar to students. Examples include *hand, point, drags, spooked,* and *reckon.* Help students use context clues to determine the meanings of these words, or substitute more familiar words as needed.	Students may be unfamiliar with the concept of a cattle drive. Explain that the point was to raise cattle on a ranch. When the animals were ready to be sold, cowboys would travel with the herd to a major railroad junction, such as Kansas City. From there the cattle could be transported to other parts of the country.	Encourage students to research the history of the cattle trade and the cattle drive. Be sure that they recognize that the history of transportation, especially of the railroad, has shaped the history of the cattle drive. Students can present their findings to the class.

Background

Art

Open Range, by Maynard Dixon

Dixon (1875–1946), who was born in Fresno, California, was essentially a self-taught artist. Most of his work portrays the West, through which he traveled extensively. He even worked as a cowboy to support himself before launching a career as an illustrator at the age of twenty. His works appeared in top magazines, including *Harper's* and *Collier's.* After seventeen successful years, Dixon gave up illustration to devote himself to painting in the West.

This painting, which displays Dixon's characteristically bold approach to composition, captures a scene of the Old West: a cattle drive across the wide-open western landscape. Use these questions for discussion:

1. What does this painting suggest about the role or importance of the cowboy?
   Possible response: The fact that the figures of the cowboys are relatively small and faceless suggests they are of small importance in the landscape. Yet, in keeping with the romantic myth of the American cowboy, the artist shows them tall in the saddle, nearly alone.

2. Like parts of the Southwest, Montana is called "Big Sky Country." How does Dixon evoke this image?
   Possible response: The sky fills more than half the painting; despite the dramatic land forms, the eye goes first to the big sky.

►Critical Viewing

Possible response: Students may say that McMurtry's descriptions of the drive emphasize the thick dust, hard work, and fatigue. By contrast, Dixon's work idealizes the cowboys. They are clean and tall in their saddles; bright, sunny colors illuminate the background. The forms may be realistic, but the sense is entirely romantic.

628

---

not a hard task. Most of the cattle were still wild as antelope and instinctively moved away from the horsemen. In a few minutes they were on the trail, strung out for more than a mile. The point riders soon disappeared in the low brush.

Lippy and the Spettle boys were with the wagon. With the dust so bad, they intended to keep the horses a fair distance behind.

Bolivar sat on the wagon seat, his ten-gauge across his lap. In his experience trouble usually came quick, when it came, and he meant to keep the ten-gauge handy to discourage it.

Newt had heard much talk of dust, but had paid little attention to it until they actually started the cattle. Then he couldn't help noticing it, for there was nothing else to notice. The grass was sparse, and every hoof sent up its little spurt of dust. Before they had gone a mile he himself was white with it, and for moments actually felt lost, it was so thick. He had to tie the bandana around his nose to get a good breath. He understood why Dish and the other boys were so anxious to draw assignments near the front of the herd. If the dust was going to be that bad all the way, he might as well be riding to Montana with his eyes shut. He would see nothing but his own horse and the few cattle that happened to be within ten yards of him. A grizzly bear could walk in and eat him and his horse both, and they wouldn't be missed until breakfast the next day.

But he had no intention of complaining. They were on their way, and he was part of the outfit. After waiting for the moment so long, what was a little dust?

Once in a while, though, he dropped back a little. His bandana got sweaty, and the dust caked on it so that he felt he was inhaling mud. He had to take it off and beat it against his leg once in a while. He was riding Mouse, who looked like he could use a bandana of his own. The dust seemed to make the heat worse, or else the heat made the dust worse.

The second time he stopped to beat his bandana, he happened to notice Sean leaning off his horse as if he were trying to vomit. The horse and Sean were both white, as if they had been rolled in powder, though the horse Sean rode was a dark bay.

"Are you hurt?" he asked anxiously.

"No, I was trying to spit," Sean said. "I've got some mud in my mouth. I didn't know it would be like this."

"I didn't either," Newt said.

"Well, we better keep up," he added nervously—he didn't want to neglect his responsibilities. Then to his dismay, he looked back and saw twenty or thirty cattle standing behind them. He had ridden right past

▲ **Critical Viewing**
Based on the descriptions in the selection, would you characterize this image of a cattle drive as realistic or romanticized? Explain. **[Distinguish]**

✷ ENRICHMENT: Social Studies Connection

The Diversity of the American West

The American West was a magnet that drew settlers from all backgrounds. Each culture lent things of its own to establish a rich multicultural tradition that continues to this day. Freed blacks came from the southeast after the Civil War to start new lives in western territories; Mexicans arrived from south of the border; and immigrants from all parts of Europe sought their fortunes.

Different languages left their marks on the region.

Travel west and you will see and hear many English words borrowed from Spanish, such as *chaparral, mesa,* and *arroyo.* Place names, such as Wichita, Muskogee, and Ogallala, come from Native American languages. Invite students to examine aspects of Western culture to find more evidence of its multicultural roots.

Open Range, 1942, Maynard Dixon, Museum of Western Art, Denver, Colorado

them in the dust. He immediately loped back to get them, hoping the Captain hadn't noticed. When he turned back, two of the wild heifers spooked. Mouse, a good cow horse, twisted and jumped a medium-sized chaparral[3] bush in an effort to gain a step on the cows. Newt had not expected the jump and lost both stirrups, but fortunately diverted the heifers so that they turned back into the main herd. He found his heart was beating fast, partly because he had almost been thrown and partly because he had nearly left thirty cattle behind. With such a start, it seemed to him he would be lucky to get to Montana without disgracing himself.

Call and Augustus rode along together, some distance from the herd. They were moving through fairly open country, flats of chaparral with only here and there a strand of mesquite.[4] That would soon change: the first challenge would be the brush country, an almost impenetrable band of thick mesquite between them and San Antonio. Only a few of the hands were experienced in the brush, and a bad run of some kind might cost them hundreds of cattle.

"What do you think, Gus?" Call asked. "Think we can get through the brush, or had we better go around?"

Augustus looked amused. "Why, these cattle are like deer, only faster." he said. "They'll get through the brush fine. The problem will be with the hands. Half of them will probably get their eyes poked out."

"I still don't know what you think," Call said.

"The problem is, I ain't used to being consulted," Augustus said. "I'm usually sitting on the porch drinking whiskey at this hour. As for the brush, my choice would be to go through. It's that or go down to the coast and get et by the mosquitoes."

"Where do you reckon Jake will end up?" Call asked.

"In a hole in the ground, like you and me," Augustus said.

"I don't know why I ever ask you a question," Call said.

"Well, last time I seen Jake he had a thorn in his hand," Augustus said. "He was wishing he'd stayed in Arkansas and taken to his hanging."

They rode up on a little knobby hill and stopped for a moment to watch the cattle. The late sun shone through the dust cloud, making the white dust rosy. The riders to each side of the herd were spread wide, giving the cattle lots of room. Most of them were horned stock, thin and light, their hides a mixture of colors. The riders at the rear were all but hidden in the rosy dust.

"Them boys on the drags won't even be able to get down from their horses unless we take a spade and spade 'em off a little," Augustus said.

"It won't hurt 'em," Call said. "They're young."

---

3. **chaparral** (chap´ ə ral´) *n.* thicket of shrubs or thorny bushes.
4. **mesquite** (mes kēt´) *n.* type of small, thorny tree.

Thematic Connection
Which other selections in Part 3 make use of the exaggeration and dry wit that fill this exchange between Call and McCrae? Explain.

✔**Reading Check**
Why is Call concerned about the stretch of trail that the cowboys are about to go through?

Connections: from Lonesome Dove ◆ 629

Thematic Connection

Possible response: Students will probably respond that the Mark Twain selections, especially "The Notorious Jumping Frog of Calaveras County," use laconic exaggeration and dry dialogue to humorous effect. Students may also mention the situational exaggeration of the tall tale "Pecos Bill Becomes a Coyote."

✔**Reading Check**

Answer: Call is concerned because the trail leads through a band of thick mesquite brush that is difficult to traverse.

CUSTOMIZE INSTRUCTION FOR UNIVERSAL ACCESS

For Special Needs Students	For Less Proficient Readers	For Gifted/Talented Students
These students may be confused by the main characters, Call and Augustus. Help them to recognize that Call is a driven man in need of a mission or purpose, while Augustus does not relish the rigors of the drive and wonders whether he should have stayed in Lonesome Dove.	These students may find tracking the many characters introduced in this excerpt to be challenging. Encourage them to make a chart of the characters. Students should enter each character's name, and list all the information McMurtry provides about each character below his name.	Call these students' attention to the art on pp. 628–629. Encourage them to gather other representations of the West of the cattle drive. Have them sort the images into "romantic" and "realistic" categories. Students can then make a visual presentation to the class, illustrating each view of the West.

Forging New Frontiers

- Encourage students to pause and consider what they have learned so far about Augustus McCrae and Woodrow Call. Then, have them read the story text on page 630.

- Instruct students to compare and contrast the characters of Augustus and Call. In what ways are they different?
  Possible response: Call is strict, orderly, and works too hard; Augustus is funny and easy-going, even lazy. Call is tough on the young cowhands, while Augustus is more lenient. Call is driven, but Augustus tries to be conciliatory.

- Ask students: Why are these men still friends when they seem to have so little in common?
  Possible response: Students may say that Augustus and Call seem like an old married couple who have shared so much that they can't imagine not staying together. Their different personalities balance one another.

Connecting Literature Past and Present

1. Possible response: Most students will answer that the cattle drive fails to live up to Call's expectations. He still lacks a sense of purpose—the cattle drive feels "less imperative" than the war did.

2. Answer: Students will note the more realistic portrayal of a western trek in Colt's account.

3. Possible response: Students may cite the elements of danger, excitement, and wide-open spaces that characterize most stories about the American West.

In the clear late afternoon light they could see all the way back to Lonesome Dove and the river and Mexico. Augustus regretted not tying a jug to his saddle—he would have liked to sit on the little hill and drink for an hour. Although Lonesome Dove had not been much of a town, he felt sure that a little whiskey would have made him feel sentimental about it. Call merely sat on the hill, studying the cattle. It was clear to Augustus that he was not troubled in any way by leaving the border or the town.

"It's odd I partnered with a man like you, Call," Augustus said. "If we was to meet now instead of when we did, I doubt we'd have two words to say to one another."

"I wish it could happen, then, if it would hold you to two words," Call said. Though everything seemed peaceful, he had an odd, confused feeling at the thought of what they had undertaken. He had quickly convinced himself it was necessary, this drive. Fighting the Indians had been necessary, if Texas was to be settled. Protecting the border was necessary, else the Mexicans would have taken south Texas back.

A cattle drive, for all its difficulty, wasn't so imperative. He didn't feel the old sense of adventure, though perhaps it would come once they got beyond the settled country. Augustus, who could almost read his mind, almost read it as they were stopped on the little knob of a hill.

"I hope this is hard enough for you, Call," he said. "I hope it makes you happy. If it don't, I give up. Driving all these skinny cattle all that way is a funny way to maintain an interest in life, if you ask me."

"Well, I didn't," Call said.

"No, but then you seldom ask," Augustus said. "You should have died in the line of duty, Woodrow. You'd know how to do that fine. The problem is you don't know how to live."

"Whereas you do?" Call asked.

"Most certainly," Augustus said. "I've lived about a hundred to your one. I'll be a little riled if I end up being the one to die in the line of duty, because this ain't my duty and it ain't yours, either. This is just fortune hunting."

"Well, we wasn't finding one in Lonesome Dove," Call said. He saw Deets returning from the northwest, ready to lead them to the bedground. Call was glad to see him—he was tired of Gus and his talk. He spurred the mare on off the hill. It was only when he met Deets that he realized Augustus hadn't followed. He was still sitting on old Malaria, back on the little hill, watching the sunset and the cattle herd.

Connecting Literature Past and Present

1. Do you think the cattle drive on which Woodrow Call embarks fails to live up to his romantic expectations?

2. How does this fictional story compare with Miriam Davis Colt's account, "Heading West"?

3. Not all historical periods capture the modern imagination. Why do you think stories about the American West are still popular today?

Larry McMurtry

(b. 1936)

Larry McMurtry, a descendant of Texas cattle ranchers, published his first western when he was only twenty-six. In his many novels, McMurtry has trained a humorous, critical eye on the culture of the American West. Labeled by some critics as the creator of the "urban western," McMurtry first attracted attention as a new kind of writer of western novels who mixed the traditional elements of the genre with sharp social observation and a strong dose of dark humor.

PART 4

Living in a Changing World

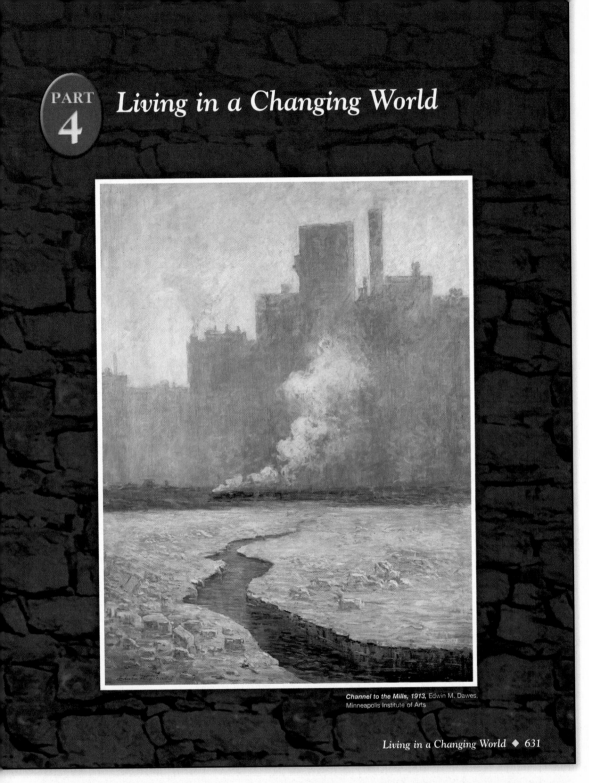

Channel to the Mills, 1913, Edwin M. Dawes.
Minneapolis Institute of Arts

Living in a Changing World ◆ 631

Selection Planning Guide

These works examine the effects of the societal changes taking place at the turn of the twentieth century. Students will be interested to learn that Kate Chopin's dark tale, "The Story of an Hour," was considered scandalous because it suggested that a woman might be happier without her husband. African Americans' struggle for acceptance and equality is reflected in the poems of Paul Laurence Dunbar. Edwin Arlington Robinson and Edgar Lee Masters paint memorable verbal portraits of four uniquely American characters who reflect the changing values of their day. Willa Cather contrasts the rigors of American frontier life with the cultural centers of the East in "A Wagner Matinée." The recurring theme of social alienation takes on a contemporary setting in Anna Quindlen's "Cats."

Background

Art

Channel to the Mills, 1913,
Edwin M. Dawes

Encourage students to contrast this artwork with pieces like *Early Morning at Cold Spring* (page 383). Help them see that the natural landscape had dominated earlier paintings. In contrast, Dawes chooses a group of mills to dominate the landscape of this painting.

1. What changes in the American environment does this artwork suggest?
   Possible response: The artwork focuses on the change from a rural to an industrial society.

2. What attitude toward these changes does the artist communicate, and how?
   Possible responses: The soft, shimmering colors of the artwork suggest that the artist's attitude is positive. A negative attitude is suggested by the title, which draws attention to the water that the mills are polluting, and by the way the buildings loom so large and blot out the horizon.

CUSTOMIZE INSTRUCTION FOR UNIVERSAL ACCESS

When assigning the selections in this part, keep in mind these factors:

"The Story of an Hour"
• Very short story
• Darkly ironic surprise ending

"Douglass" and "We Wear the Mask"
• Brief, emotionally charged poems
• Formal, antiquated language may challenge some readers

"Luke Havergal"; "Richard Cory"; "Lucinda Matlock"; "Richard Bone"
• Four portraits in verse
• Vivid character profiles

"A Wager Matinee"
• Accessible short story
• Concert setting will intrigue most students

631

The Story of an Hour

Lesson Objectives

1. **To analyze and respond to literary elements**
   - Literary Analysis: Irony
   - Connecting Literary Elements: Climax

2. **To read, comprehend, analyze, and critique a short story**
   - Reading Strategy: Recognizing Ironic Details
   - Reading Check Questions
   - Review and Assess Questions
   - Assessment Practice (ATE)

3. **To develop word analysis skills, fluency, and systematic vocabulary**
   - Vocabulary Development Lesson: Word Analysis: Anglo-Saxon Prefix: *fore-*

4. **To understand and apply written and oral language conventions**
   - Spelling Strategy
   - Grammar and Style Lesson: Appositives and Appositive Phrases

5. **To understand and apply appropriate writing and research strategies**
   - Writing Lesson: Reflective Essay
   - Extension Activity: Oral Report

6. **To understand and apply listening and speaking strategies**
   - Extension Activity: Soliloguy

STEP-BY-STEP TEACHING GUIDE	PACING GUIDE
PRETEACH	
Motivate Students and Provide Background	
Use the Motivation activity (ATE p. 632)	5 min.
Read and discuss author and background features (SE/ATE pp. 632, 634)	5 min.
Introduce the Concepts	
Introduce the Literary Analysis and Reading Strategy (SE/ATE p. 633)	15 min.
Pronounce the vocabulary words and read their definitions (SE p. 633)	5 min.
TEACH	
Monitor Comprehension	
Informally monitor comprehension by circulating while students read independently or in groups	20 min.
Monitor students' comprehension with the Reading Check notes (SE/ATE p. 637)	as students read
Develop vocabulary with Vocabulary notes (SE pp. 636, 637, 638; ATE p. 636)	as students read
Develop Understanding	
Develop students' understanding of irony with the Literary Analysis annotations (ATE p. 637)	5 min.
Develop students' ability to recognize ironic details with the Reading Strategy annotations (SE pp. 636, 637; ATE pp. 636, 637)	5 min.
ASSESS	
Assess Mastery	
Assess students' mastery of the Reading Strategy and Literary Analysis by having them answer the Review and Assess questions (SE/ATE p. 639)	15 min.
Use one or more of the print and media Assessment Resources (ATE p. 641)	up to 45 min.
EXTEND	
Apply Understanding	
Have students complete the Vocabulary Development Lesson and the Grammar and Style Lesson (SE p. 640)	20 min.
Apply students' ability to gather details by using the Writing Lesson (SE/ATE p. 641)	45 min.
Apply students' understanding using one or more of the Extension Activities (SE p. 641)	20–90 min.

A ACCELERATED INSTRUCTION:
Use the strategies and activities identified with an **A**.

UNIVERSAL ACCESS
- ● = Below Level Students
- ▲ = On-Level Students
- ■ = Above Level Students

RESOURCES		
PRINT 📖	**TRANSPARENCIES**	**TECHNOLOGY** 💿 🎧 📼
• **Beyond Literature,** Cross-Curricular Connection: Social Studies, p. 34 ▲ ■		• **Interest Grabber Video,** Tape 4 ● ▲ ■
• **Selection Support Workbook:** ● ▲ ■ Literary Analysis, p. 155 Reading Strategy, p. 154 Build Vocabulary, p. 152	• **Literary Analysis and Reading Transparencies,** pp. 67 and 68 ● ▲ ■	
• **Adapted Reader's Companion** ● • **Reader's Companion** ●		• **Listening to Literature** ● ▲ ■ Audiocassettes, Side 23 Audio CDs, CD 13
• **English Learner's Companion** ● ▲ • **Literatura en español** ● ▲ • **Literary Analysis for Enrichment** ■	• **Fine Art Transparencies, Volume 1,** Art Transparency 6 ● ▲ ■	
• **Formal Assessment:** Selection Test, pp. 164–166 ● ▲ ■ • **Open Book Test,** pp. 100–102 ● ▲ ■ • **Performance Assessment and Portfolio Management,** p. 11 ● ▲ ■ • **PRENTICE HALL ASSESSMENT SYSTEM** ● ▲ ■	• **PRENTICE HALL ASSESSMENT SYSTEM** ● ▲ ■ Skills Practice Answers and Explanations on Transparencies	• **Test Bank Software** ● ▲ ■ • **Got It! Assessment Videotapes,** Tape 3 ● ▲
• **Selection Support Workbook:** ● ▲ ■ Grammar and Style, p. 153 • **Writing and Grammar,** Ruby Level ● ▲ ■ • **Extension Activities,** p. 34 ● ▲ ■	• **Daily Language Practice Transparencies** ● ▲ • **Writing Models and Graphic Organizers on Transparencies,** p. 5 ● ▲ ■	• **Writing and Grammar iText CD-ROM** ● ▲ ■ 💻 **Take It to the Net** www.phschool.com

BLOCK SCHEDULING: Use one 90-minute class period to preteach the selection and have students read it. Use a second 90-minute class period to assess students' mastery of skills and have them complete one of the Extension Activities.

Motivation

To get started, have students generate a list of "news flashes" that would change their lives. For example, you might suggest winning the lottery, the death of a loved one, or early admission to college.

Then, tell students that in the story they are about to read, a character has unexpected reactions to unanticipated news. Discuss the idea that in life, things are not always as they appear, that there's often more than one way to look at them.

▣ Interest Grabber Video

As an alternative, play "Women's Rights" on Tape 4 to engage student interest.

❶ Background

Chopin's story addresses issues of women's liberation in a time when these issues were not frequently raised. Activists were just beginning to stir the national conscience. Women and minorities were seeking to expand their civil rights. In addition, psychologists such as William James were debating free will, the ability of individuals to control their own destiny. These developments began a social revolution whose effects are still being felt today.

Prepare to Read

❶ The Story of an Hour

Kate Chopin (1850–1904)

Despite her conservative, aristocratic upbringing, Kate O'Flaherty Chopin (shō´ pan) became one of the most powerful and controversial writers of her time. In her stories, sketches, and novels, she not only captured the local color of Louisiana but also boldly explored the role of women in society.

Family Life Kate O'Flaherty was born in St. Louis, Missouri, the daughter of a wealthy businessman. When Kate was five years old, her father died in a railroad accident. The young Kate was taken out of school and educated at home for the next two years by her mother, grandmother, and great-grandmother. When she was twenty, Kate married Oscar Chopin, a Louisiana cotton trader. The couple settled in New Orleans, where they lived for ten years before moving to a plantation in rural northwestern Louisiana.

Tragedy Strikes In 1882, Chopin's husband died, leaving her to raise their six children on her own. Chopin carried on the work of the plantation alone for more than a year, using her knowledge of finance and developing skills as a business-woman. However, in 1884 she yielded to her mother's urgings, sold most of her holdings, and returned to St. Louis with her children. Her mother's sudden death in 1885 left Chopin in deep sorrow. It was at the suggestion of her family doctor, who was concerned about her emotional health, that she began to write fiction. Chopin kept St. Louis as her home for the rest of her life and devoted much of her energy to writing.

Chopin the Writer and Rebel Influenced by American Regionalists such as Sarah Orne Jewett, and fascinated by the mixture of cultures in Louisiana, Chopin focused on capturing the essence of life in Louisiana in her writing. Like most of her other works, Chopin's first novel, *At Fault* (1890), was set in a small Louisiana town inhabited by Creoles, descendants of the original French and Spanish settlers, and Cajuns, descendants of French Canadian settlers who arrived later. Through her vivid descriptions and use of dialect, Chopin captured the local color of the region. In her stories, published in *Bayou Folk* (1894) and *A Night In Acadie* (1897), she exhibited her deep understanding of the different attitudes and concerns of the Louisiana natives.

Her charming portraits of Louisiana life often obscured the fact that she explored themes considered radical at the time: the nature of marriage, racial prejudice, and women's desire for social, economic, and political equality. Chopin understood the risk she took in challenging social boundaries, but felt that true art required bravery. She once wrote, "The artist must possess the courageous soul that dares and defies."

The Awakening Chopin's finest novel, *The Awakening* (1899), is a psychological account of a woman's search for independence and fulfillment. Because the novel explored the issue of infidelity, it aroused a storm of protest. The book was severely attacked by critics and eventually banned. As a result, Chopin's reputation was badly damaged. Then, in the 1950s, *The Awakening* was resurrected. Today, the book is among the five most-read American novels in colleges and universities. Chopin is now considered an early practitioner of American Realism—a literary style that seeks to avoid sentimental depictions of life. She is widely respected for her portrayal of the psychology of women and her ability to capture local color.

632 ◆ *Division, Reconciliation, and Expansion (1850–1914)*

TEACHING RESOURCES

The following resources can be used to enrich or extend the instruction for pp. 632–633.

Motivation

▣ **Interest Grabber Video**, Tape 4 ▪

Background

▤ **Beyond Literature**, p. 34 ▪

▣ **Take It to the Net**
Visit www.phschool.com for background and hotlinks for "The Story of an Hour."

Literary Analysis

▨ **Literary Analysis and Reading Transparencies,** Irony, p. 68

Reading

▤ **Selection Support:** Reading Strategy, p. 154; Build Vocabulary, p. 152 ▪

▨ **Literary Analysis and Reading Transparencies,** Recognizing Ironic Details, p. 67

▪ **BLOCK SCHEDULING:** Resources marked with this symbol provide varied instruction during 90-minute blocks.

Preview

Connecting to the Literature

Often, life-changing events—a chance encounter with someone who becomes important in our lives, the loss of a loved one, a sudden move to a new place—sneak up on us unexpectedly. The story you are about to read focuses on a woman's surprising reaction to a shocking piece of news.

❷ Literary Analysis

Irony

Irony involves a contrast between what is stated and what is meant, or between what is expected and what actually happens. In literature, readers frequently encounter three types of irony:

- **Verbal irony** is the use of words to suggest the opposite of their usual meaning.
- **Dramatic irony** occurs when readers are aware of something that a character in a literary work does not know.
- **Situational irony** occurs when the outcome of an action or situation is very different from what one expects.

As you read, decide which type of irony best describes the events in this story.

Connecting Literary Elements

The **climax** is the high point of interest or suspense in a story. It also marks the moment at which the conflict is resolved. As in many other works of fiction or drama, the climax of "The Story of an Hour" involves a keen sense of irony.

❸ Reading Strategy

Recognizing Ironic Details

The details of a story often lead readers to have certain expectations. When events are not resolved as details have led us to expect, we recognize a sense of irony. While reading "The Story of an Hour," use a chart like the one shown to note how specific details imply certain feelings, circumstances, or events that may not, in fact, be what they appear. After reading the story, note whether or not your expectations were met.

Vocabulary Development

forestall (fôr stôl′) *v.* prevent by acting ahead of time (p. 636)

repression (ri presh′ ən) *n.* restraint (p. 637)

elusive (ē lōō′ siv) *adj.* hard to grasp (p. 637)

tumultuously (tōō mul′ chōō wəs lē) *adv.* in an agitated way (p. 637)

importunities (im′ pôr tōōn′ ə tēz) *n.* persistent requests or demands (p. 638)

Detail

Care is taken to reveal bad news to Mrs. Mallard.

Expected outcome

She would be upset.

Actual outcome

The Story of an Hour ◆ 633

Irony

- Tell students that as they read "The Story of an Hour," they will notice that Mrs. Mallard's reactions to the news she receives are the opposite of what everyone around her expects. Explain that this contrast is *irony*.

- Review the instruction for Irony on p. 633. Make sure students understand that there are three major categories of irony: *verbal irony*, *dramatic irony*, and *situational irony*.

- Suggest that students keep notes on the story's ironic events, identifying each type of irony as it occurs.

- When students have finished the story, review its use of irony using the Irony transparency in **Literary Analysis and Reading Transparencies,** p. 68.

❸ Reading Strategy

Recognizing Ironic Details

- Remind students that the details of a story can create *irony*. If the details suggest one outcome but the actual outcome is different, irony can result.

- Use the graphic organizer that appears on p. 633 to model the Reading Strategy, Recognizing Ironic Details. Encourage students to keep a chart like this one as they read the selection.

- After they have completed the selection, use the Recognizing Ironic Details transparency in **Literary Analysis and Reading Transparencies,** p. 67, to review and discuss the ironic details in the story.

Vocabulary Development

- Pronounce each vocabulary word for students, and read the definitions as a class. Have students identify any words with which they are already familiar.

E-Teach

Visit E-Teach at www.phschool.com for teachers' essays on how to teach, with questions and answers.

CUSTOMIZE INSTRUCTION FOR UNIVERSAL ACCESS

For Special Needs Students	For Less Proficient Readers	For English Learners
Have students read the adapted version of "The Story of an Hour" in the **Adapted Reader's Companion.** This version provides basic-level instruction in an interactive format with questions and write-on lines. Completing the adapted version will prepare students to read the selection in the Student Edition.	Have students read "The Story of an Hour" in the **Reader's Companion.** This version provides basic-level instruction in an interactive format with questions and write-on lines. After students finish the selection in **Reader's Companion,** have them complete the questions and activities in the Student Edition.	Have students read the adapted version of "The Story of an Hour" in the **English Learner's Companion.** This version provides basic-level instruction in an interactive format with questions and write-on lines. Completing the adapted version will prepare students to read the selection in the Student Edition.

Step-by-Step Teaching Guide
for pp. 634–638

CUSTOMIZE INSTRUCTION
For Visual/Spatial Learners

After they have read "The Story of an Hour," show students Art Transparency 6 in **Fine Art Transparencies, Volume 1**. Encourage students to draw connections between the woman in Cassatt's painting and Mrs. Mallard. Have students create their own art projects, using whatever materials they'd like, to represent the contrast between Mrs. Mallard's domestic life and the deep unhappiness and desire for escape that she actually felt. Students should explain how their projects represent the story's themes.

❶ About the Selection

Chopin's story presents its heroine with one unexpected shock and its readers with another.

Mrs. Mallard gets the unexpected news that her husband has been killed in an accident. She quickly recovers from the shock to discover that what she really feels is relief. Though she mourns his passing, she delights in the freedom that is now hers. She shuts herself in her room and relishes the opportunities ahead of her. When Mr. Mallard returns as unexpectedly as he supposedly died, Mrs. Mallard suffers a fatal heart attack caused by the sudden loss of independence. The doctors, mistakenly assuming that she had been grieving, attribute the death to "joy that kills."

The Story of an Hour ❶

Kate Chopin

Afternoon in Piedmont, Xavier Martinez, Courtesy of the Oakland Museum ❷

Background

"The Story of an Hour" was considered daring in the nineteenth century. The editors of at least two magazines refused the story because they thought it was immoral. They wanted Chopin to soften her female character, to make her less independent and unhappy in her marriage. Undaunted, Chopin continued to deal with issues of women's growth and emancipation in her writing, advancing ideas that are widely accepted today.

❸ ▶ Critical Viewing This story presents a "subtle and elusive" revelation. What connection do you see between the light shining through the uncovered portion of the window and such a discovery? **[Connect]**

TEACHING RESOURCES

The following resources can be used to enrich or extend the instruction for pp. 634–638.

Literary Analysis
📖 **Selection Support:** Literary Analysis, p. 155

Reading
📖 **Adapted Reader's Companion**
📖 **English Learner's Companion**
📖 **Reader's Companion**
🎧 **Listening to Literature Audiocassettes,** Side 23 ■

💿 **Listening to Literature Audio CDs,** CD 13 ■

Extension
📖 **Fine Art Transparencies, Volume 1,** Art Transparency 6 ■ (After students have read the selection, display Art Transparency 6 and have students find details in the story that might describe the woman in the painting.)

■ **BLOCK SCHEDULING:** Resources marked with this symbol provide varied instruction during 90-minute blocks.

❷ Background

Art

Afternoon in Piedmont,
by Xavier Martinez

Xavier Martinez was born in Guadalajara, Mexico, in 1869. He eventually moved to San Francisco, where he later taught at the California School of Fine Arts. Martinez's work has been described as poetic. His *Afternoon at Piedmont* used as its inspiration James Whistler's famous painting of his mother. In his work, Martinez moved the scene to his house and used his wife as the model.

After students have read the selection, return to this painting and use these questions for discussion:

1. How would you describe the mood of this painting?
   Possible response: Students may see the yellow light entering the dark interior as the coming of dawn, bringing with it a comforting awakening.

2. What scene in the story does the painting best represent?
   Possible response: Students may say that it describes the scene in which Mrs. Mallard is looking out at the signs of early spring and is herself awakening to her true feelings and a new approach to life.

❸ Critical Viewing

Possible response: Students may say that the light shows Mrs. Mallard's calm contentment upon recognizing the first stages of her newly found freedom. They may suggest that the light is symbolic of the new beginning of her life.

CUSTOMIZE INSTRUCTION FOR UNIVERSAL ACCESS

For Less Proficient Readers	For English Learners	For Advanced Readers
To help students get the most from this story, have them read it twice, once to follow the plot and once more to notice the ironic details. You may use the **Reader's Companion** to provide further guidance for these students.	Students may come from cultures in which gender roles are strictly defined. Discuss the role of women and marriage in late nineteenth century America, making clear the contrast between life then and now. Help students recognize the radical ideas Chopin presents.	Point out that the idea of an emancipated woman was a radical notion in the 1890s. Then, guide students to look for further examples of ideas in this story that were ahead of their time.

- Call students' attention to the word *forestall* and its definition. Tell students that the Anglo-Saxon prefix *fore-* means "before"—in time, place, or condition.

- Have students suggest words and phrases that begin with this prefix, and list them on the chalkboard. Possibilities include *foretell*, *forethought*, *foreman*, *foremost*, and *forefathers*.

- Next, have students look up the meanings of these words in a dictionary.

- Finally, direct students to reread the story, looking for places where they can replace an existing word or phrase with a word beginning with the Anglo-Saxon prefix *fore-*. Call on volunteers to read their new sentences aloud.

❺ **Reading Strategy**

Recognizing Ironic Details

- Remind students that a story's details can create irony by failing to meet a reader's expectations or by encouraging false expectations.

- Have students read the bracketed passage. Encourage them to note its details in a chart such as the one on p. 633.

- Ask students the Reading Strategy question on p. 636: Considering the news she has just received, what is ironic about the details Mrs. Mallard notices through her window?
  Answer: It is ironic that Mrs. Mallard, newly widowed, should see signs of the new life of spring and breaks in the clouds, and hear the sounds and songs of life.

- Encourage students to add their responses to their charts.

Monitor Progress Make sure students can explain why each detail on their charts is ironic.

---

*K*nowing that Mrs. Mallard was afflicted with a heart trouble, great care was taken to break to her as gently as possible the news of her husband's death.

It was her sister Josephine who told her, in broken sentences; veiled hints that revealed in half concealing. Her husband's friend Richards was there, too, near her. It was he who had been in the newspaper office when intelligence of the railroad disaster was received, with Brently Mallard's name leading the list of "killed." He had only taken the time to assure himself of its truth by a second telegram, and had hastened ❹ to forestall any less careful, less tender friend in bearing the sad message.

She did not hear the story as many women have heard the same, with a paralyzed inability to accept its significance. She wept at once, with sudden, wild abandonment, in her sister's arms. When the storm of grief had spent itself she went away to her room alone. She would have no one follow her.

There stood, facing the open window, a comfortable, roomy armchair. Into this she sank, pressed down by a physical exhaustion that haunted her body and seemed to reach into her soul.

She could see in the open square before her house the tops of trees that were all aquiver with the new spring life. The delicious breath of rain was in the air. In the street below a peddler was crying his wares. The ❺ notes of a distant song which someone was singing reached her faintly, and countless sparrows were twittering in the eaves.

There were patches of blue sky showing here and there through the clouds that had met and piled one above the other in the west facing her window.

She sat with her head thrown back upon the cushion of the chair, quite motionless, except when a sob came up into her throat and shook her, as a child who has cried itself to sleep continues to sob in its dreams.

forestall (fôr stôl´) *v.* prevent by acting ahead of time

Reading Strategy
Recognizing Ironic Details Considering the news she has just received, what is ironic about the details Mrs. Mallard notices through her window?

✹ **ENRICHMENT: Workplace Skills Connection**

Communication Technology

Point out that the failure of long-distance communication in this story leads to a fatal misunderstanding. While the telegram was a major method of long-distance communication in Chopin's time, newer, faster modes have since made the telegram obsolete.

By 1887, the telephone was becoming widely available and U.S. telephone companies served more than 150,000 customers. One hundred years later, fax machines became a popular mode of communication, allowing people to send reproductions of documents through telephone lines. In the early 1990s, the Internet was introduced to the general public with the highly designed World Wide Web. Personal Internet access allowed people to send and receive e-mail from the comfort of their homes.

She was young, with a fair, calm face, whose lines bespoke <u>repression</u> and even a certain strength. But now there was a dull stare in her eyes, whose gaze was fixed away off yonder on one of those patches of blue sky. It was not a glance of reflection, but rather indicated a suspension of intelligent thought.

There was something coming to her and she was waiting for it, fearfully. What was it? She did not know; it was too subtle and <u>elusive</u> to name. But she felt it, creeping out of the sky, reaching toward her through the sounds, the scents, the color that filled the air.

Now her bosom rose and fell <u>tumultuously</u>. She was beginning to recognize this thing that was approaching to possess her, and she was striving to beat it back with her will—as powerless as her two white slender hands would have been.

When she abandoned herself, a little whispered word escaped her slightly parted lips. She said it over and over under her breath: "free, free, free!" The vacant stare and the look of terror that had followed it went from her eyes. They stayed keen and bright. Her pulses beat fast, and the coursing blood warmed and relaxed every inch of her body.

She did not stop to ask if it were or were not a monstrous joy that held her. A clear and exalted perception enabled her to dismiss the suggestion as trivial.

❻ She knew that she would weep again when she saw the kind, tender hands folded in death; the face that had never looked save with love upon her, fixed and gray and dead. But she saw beyond that bitter moment a long procession of years to come that would belong to her absolutely. And she opened and spread her arms out to them in welcome.

There would be no one to live for her during those coming years; she would live for herself. There would be no powerful will bending hers in that blind persistence with which men and women believe they have a right to impose a private will upon a fellow creature. A kind intention or a cruel intention made the act seem no less a crime as she looked upon it in that brief moment of illumination.

And yet she had loved him—sometimes. Often she had not. What did it matter! What could love, the unsolved mystery, count for in face of this possession of self-assertion which she suddenly recognized as the strongest impulse of her being!

"Free! Body and soul free!" she kept whispering.

❼ Josephine was kneeling before the closed door with her lips to the keyhole, imploring for admission. "Louise, open the door! I beg; open the door—you will make yourself ill. What are you doing, Louise? For heaven's sake open the door."

"Go away. I am not making myself ill." No; she was drinking in a very elixir of life[1] through that open window.

---

1. **elixir of life** (i liks´ ər) imaginary substance believed in medieval times to prolong life indefinitely.

---

repression (ri presh´ ən) *n.* restraint

elusive (ē lōō´ siv) *adj.* hard to grasp

tumultuously (tōō mul´ chōō əs lē) *adv.* in an agitated way

Reading Strategy
Recognizing Ironic Details What does the passage describing "a long procession of years" lead you to expect?

❽ ☑ **Reading Check**
What is the general state of Mrs. Mallard's health?

The Story of an Hour ◆ 637

---

❻ Reading Strategy
Recognizing Ironic Details

- Remind students that the story includes ironic details. Point out that ironic details can lead readers to expect an outcome very different from the one the author has planned.

- Have students read the bracketed passage. Encourage them to write the details in charts such as the one on p. 633.

- Ask students the Reading Strategy question on p. 637: What does the passage describing "a long procession of years" lead you to expect?
  Possible response: Mrs. Mallard will begin a long and fulfilling life as an independent woman.

- Discuss with students what outcomes could render this detail ironic. Encourage them to complete their charts when they learn the outcome.

❼ Literary Analysis

Irony

- Remind students that there are three major kinds of irony: *verbal irony*, *dramatic irony*, and *situational irony*. Explain that dramatic irony occurs when readers have information that a character in a story does not have.

- Have students read the bracketed passage. Then, ask why Josephine's reaction is an example of dramatic irony.
  Answer: Josephine is very worried that her sister is suffering from intense grief, but the reader knows that Louise feels a sense of relief.

  ▶ Have students discuss how Chopin has built the story's irony to this point, and speculate on how the story will be resolved.

❽ ☑ Reading Check

Answer: Mrs. Mallard has a weak heart.

CUSTOMIZE INSTRUCTION FOR UNIVERSAL ACCESS

For Special Needs Students

This story is filled with irony. To help students recognize and appreciate the irony, have them use a chart like the one shown. Begin by pointing out some examples, and then have students continue reading to record the different examples they find.

Detail	"There was something coming to her and she was waiting for it, fearfully."
Expected Outcome	grief, even death
Actual Outcome	signs of spring coming through the window
Type of Irony	situational

BLOCK SCHEDULING: Resources marked with this symbol provide varied instruction during 90-minute blocks.

637

Review and Assess

1. Possible response: Students may respond that they were surprised; they should support their opinions with details from the story. Invite students who disagree to defend their positions.

2. (a) The author writes that Mrs. Mallard was afflicted with "a heart trouble." (b) Possible response: It might refer to her lack of love for her husband and her unenthusiastic outlook on life.

3. (a) She sees green trees, sparrows, and patches of blue sky—all signs of the new life of spring. (b) The spring scene conveys a sense of rebirth.

4. (a) She whispers "free, free, free!" (b) Possible response: Mrs. Mallard resented the limits placed upon her freedom.

5. (a) They say she died "of heart disease—of joy that kills." (b) Possible response: Her death is caused by the feelings of shock and disappointment that result from the return of her husband.

6. (a) Possible response: Chopin does not elaborate more about Mrs. Mallard's death because she wants to focus on the irony of it, not on the physical details. (b) Students will probably say that the lack of details draws their attention to the irony of the situation as a whole.

7. Possible responses: Many students will feel it would not be believable because women's roles in marriage have changed a great deal since Chopin's time. Students should support their responses.

638

Her fancy was running riot along those days ahead of her. Spring days, and summer days, and all sorts of days that would be her own. She breathed a quick prayer that life might be long. It was only yesterday she had thought with a shudder that life might be long.

She arose at length and opened the door to her sister's importunities. There was a feverish triumph in her eyes, and she carried herself unwittingly like a goddess of Victory. She clasped her sister's waist, and together they descended the stairs. Richards stood waiting for them at the bottom.

Someone was opening the front door with a latchkey. It was Brently Mallard who entered, a little travel-stained, composedly carrying his gripsack[2] and umbrella. He had been far from the scene of accident, and did not know there had been one. He stood amazed at Josephine's piercing cry; at Richards's quick motion to screen him from the view of his wife.

But Richards was too late.

When the doctors came they said she had died of heart disease—of joy that kills.

importunities (im´ pôr tōōn´ i tēz) n. persistent requests or demands

---

2. **gripsack** (grip´ sak) n. small bag for holding clothes.

Review and Assess
Thinking About the Selection

1. **Respond:** Were you surprised by the end of the story? Explain why or why not.

2. **(a) Recall:** At the beginning of the story, what does the narrator call the ailment that afflicts Mrs. Mallard? **(b) Interpret:** What, in addition to a medical condition, might the narrator mean by this phrase?

3. **(a) Recall:** What does Mrs. Mallard see as she gazes out the window of her room? **(b) Connect:** In what ways does the scene outside Mrs. Mallard's window foreshadow the feelings that sweep over her as she sits in her chair?

4. **(a) Recall:** What word does Mrs. Mallard whisper to herself repeatedly? **(b) Infer:** What has Mrs. Mallard apparently resented about her marriage?

5. **(a) Recall:** According to the doctors, what is the cause of Mrs. Mallard's sudden death? **(b) Draw Conclusions:** What do you believe is the actual reason for Mrs. Mallard's death?

6. **(a) Speculate:** Why do you think Chopin does not elaborate more about Mrs. Mallard's death? **(b) Evaluate:** Is this choice effective? Explain.

7. **Evaluate:** Would "The Story of an Hour" seem believable as a modern tale? Explain.

ASSESSMENT PRACTICE: Reading Comprehension

Context	(For more practice, see Test Preparation Workbook, p. 37)

The reading sections of many tests specify that students use the context of a targeted word or phrase to determine its meaning. Because figurative expressions are not literally true, students must try to infer the meaning of the expression from the surrounding context. Use the following sample test item to demonstrate.

Her fancy was running riot along those days ahead of her. Spring days, and summer days, and all sorts of days that would be her own.

In this passage, the words running riot most nearly mean—

A quietly contemplating

B causing a public disturbance

C becoming overactive

D going numb

The excitement communicated in the second sentence should lead students to recognize that *C* is correct.

Review and Assess

Literary Analysis

Irony

1. (a) In what ways is Mrs. Mallard's reaction to her husband's death an example of **situational irony?** (b) Do you think Mrs. Mallard is as surprised by her reaction as the reader is? Explain.

2. (a) In what ways is Mrs. Mallard's death an example of situational irony? (b) Note two details from earlier in the story that add to the poignancy of this ironic ending.

3. In what way is the diagnosis of Mrs. Mallard's cause of death an example of **dramatic irony?**

4. Use a chart like the one shown to examine elements of irony evident in the story's descriptive passages.

Passage

...the tops of trees were all aquiver with new spring life.

Ironic Elements

Connecting Literary Elements

5. Review the story to identify the moment of **climax**.

6. What is ironic about the story's climax?

Reading Strategy

Recognizing Ironic Details

7. What **ironic details** lead you to believe that Mrs. Mallard will be truly grieved by her husband's death?

8. Which detail in the second paragraph makes Mr. Mallard's arrival at the end all the more ironic?

Extend Understanding

9. **Sociology Connection:** With her husband dead, Mrs. Mallard notes:

> "There would be no powerful will bending hers in that blind persistence with which men and women believe they have a right to impose a private will upon a fellow creature."

Do you think this statement accurately reflects interactions between people in close relationships? Explain.

Quick Review

Irony is a contrast between what is stated and what is meant, or between what is expected and what happens. **Verbal irony** is the use of words to suggest the opposite of their usual meaning. **Dramatic irony** occurs when a reader knows something a character does not. **Situational irony** occurs when a reader is surprised by an unexpected turn of events.

The **climax** is the point in the plot at which the conflict reaches its highest point of interest or suspense.

To **recognize ironic details,** look for elements that imply specific feelings or circumstances.

Take It to the Net

www.phschool.com

Take the interactive self-test online to check your understanding of the selection.

The Story of an Hour ◆ 639

Answers for p. 639

Review and Assess

1. Possible responses: **(a)** Neither the reader nor Mrs. Mallard knows that Mr. Mallard is actually alive. **(b)** Most students will believe she is as surprised as they are by her response, because she expects only to grieve.

2. **(a)** Mrs. Mallard has just begun to look forward to leading a long life. **(b)** Possible response: Details include the beauty of the spring world outside Mrs. Mallard's window and her prayer for a long life.

3. It is dramatic irony because the reader knows that the diagnosis is wrong.

4. Possible response:
   Passage:
   ... the tops of trees were all aquiver with new spring life.
   Ironic Elements:
   We expect her thoughts to be of death.
   Passage:
   ... she was drinking the very elixir of life through that open window.
   Ironic Elements:
   Within minutes, her heart fails and she dies.

5. The climax comes when Mr. Mallard returns home and Mrs. Mallard dies.

6. It is ironic because Mrs. Mallard was relieved that her husband was dead, and dies, in part, of her disappointment.

7. Possible response: Her family is careful to break the news gently; her husband's friend is in attendance.

8. Two sources confirm Mr. Mallard's death.

9. Possible response: Many students will see Mrs. Mallard's thought as a very negative view of close relationships; students may believe that people in such relationships make compromises for each other.

✹ ENRICHMENT: Further Reading

Other Works by Kate Chopin

The Awakening

Bayou Folk

Take It to the Net

Visit www.phschool.com for more information on Kate Chopin

➊ Vocabulary Development

Word Analysis

1. *Fortell* means to tell or announce beforehand.
2. A *foreman* is a person in charge of a group of workers.
3. To *forestall* means to prevent ahead of time.
4. *Forefathers* are ancestors.

Spelling Strategy

1. agencies
2. attorneys
3. penalties

Fluency: Word Choice

1. importunities
2. forestall
3. repression
4. tumultuously
5. elusive

➋ Grammar and Style

1. Mrs. Mallard, *an unconventional woman*, was not grieved by her husband's death.
2. She sank gratefully into the chair, *a comfortable, roomy armchair*.
3. She felt like a new woman, *the goddess of Victory*, as she left her room.
4. Her friend *Richards* tried to shield the visitor from Mrs. Mallard's sight.
5. Though "travel-stained," the person at the door, *Brently Mallard*, was very much alive.

Writing Application

Students' paragraphs should use appositives and appositive phrases correctly. They should contain both *nonessential* (set off by commas) and *essential* (without commas) appositives.

Integrate Language Skills

➊ Vocabulary Development Lesson

Word Analysis: Anglo-Saxon Prefix *fore-*

The Anglo-Saxon prefix *fore-* means "before," in the sense of time, place, or condition. Using this knowledge, write a definition for each of the following words.

1. foretell
2. foreman
3. forestall
4. forefathers

Spelling Strategy

To form the plural of a word that ends in a consonant plus *y*, change the *y* to *i* and add *es*—for example, *importunity* becomes *importunities*. For words that end in a vowel plus *y*, add *s* to form the plural, as in *days* or *monkeys*. Write the plurals of the following words.

1. agency
2. attorney
3. penalty

Fluency: Word Choice

Replace the italicized words or phrases in the following sentences with the appropriate vocabulary word from the list on page 633.

1. Chopin gave in to her mother's *insistent pleas* and returned to St. Louis.
2. A doctor thought that writing would *head off* a slide into depression.
3. Chopin exposed the conventions of her time that kept women in a state of near constant *restraint*.
4. Her characters often lived *in a state of agitation*.
5. Outrage over one of her novels taught Chopin that acclaim can be *difficult to hold on to*.

➋ Grammar and Style Lesson

Appositives and Appositive Phrases

An **appositive** is a noun or pronoun placed near another noun or pronoun to provide more information about it. When an appositive is accompanied by its own modifiers, it forms an **appositive phrase.**

If an appositive can be omitted from a sentence without altering its basic meaning, it must be set off by commas. If the appositive is essential to the sentence's meaning, commas are not used. Appositive phrases are always set off by commas or dashes.

> **Nonessential:** Richards, the attorney, was also present.
>
> **Essential:** The long novel *Moby-Dick* has a tragic ending.

Practice Rewrite each sentence below, incorporating the information given as an appositive.

1. Mrs. Mallard was not grieved by her husband's death. (*unconventional woman*)
2. She sank gratefully into the chair. (*comfortable, roomy armchair*)
3. She felt like a new woman as she left her room. (*the goddess of Victory*)
4. Her friend tried to shield the visitor from Mrs. Mallard's sight. (Richards)
5. Though "travel-stained," the person at the door was very much alive. (*Brently Mallard*)

Writing Application Write a paragraph in which you use at least three appositives or appositive phrases to describe three people.

W̶G *Prentice Hall Writing and Grammar Connection: Chapter 19, Section 1*

TEACHING RESOURCES

The following resources can be used to enrich or extend the instruction for pp. 640–641.

Vocabulary

📖 **Selection Support:** Build Vocabulary, p. 152

📖 **Vocabulary and Spelling Practice Book** (Use this booklet for skills enrichment.) ▪

Grammar

📖 **Selection Support:** Grammar and Style, p. 153

W̶G **Writing and Grammar,** Ruby Level, p. 437 ▪

📖 **Daily Language Practice Transparencies**

Writing

W̶G **Writing and Grammar,** Ruby Level, p. 52 ▪

W̶G **Writing and Grammar, iText CD-ROM** ▪

📖 **Writing Models and Graphic Organizers on Transparencies,** p. 5

▪ **BLOCK SCHEDULING:** Resources marked with this symbol provide varied instruction during 90-minute blocks.

❸ Writing Lesson

Reflective Essay

In a reflective essay, a writer describes personal experiences and conveys his or her feelings about them. Draw upon your memory and observations to write your own "Story of an Hour" about a moment when your life dramatically changed. As you write your essay, strive for a personal tone.

Prewriting   To gather details for your essay, use a diagram like the one shown. Write your topic in the center circle and then write your observations and feelings about the topic on spokes radiating from the circle.

Model: Gathering Details

The new house was raw and unfurnished

I watch my old home disappear through the rear window of the car

Moving away

Drafting   Organize the details in either chronological order or order of importance. Use words and phrases that come naturally, and write honestly about your subject.

Revising   Read your essay, focusing on sections that could be made clearer. Add or eliminate details to strengthen the overall impression.

 Prentice Hall Writing and Grammar Connection: Chapter 4, Section 2

❹ Extension Activities

Listening and Speaking   What might Mrs. Mallard have made of her life if her husband had not returned? Present a **soliloquy** in which she reflects on her life ten years later. As you work, address these questions:

- Has Mrs. Mallard's heart trouble improved, or not?
- What has it meant to "live for herself"?

Create an authentic voice for Mrs. Mallard, so that she is a believable extension of Chopin's character.

Research and Technology   Research the status of women in another culture, and present an **oral report** comparing women's lives in the United States with those in the culture you have researched. Use a variety of research tools, including the Internet. After your report, lead your class in a discussion of the issues you have raised.

Take It to the Net   www.phschool.com

Go online for an additional research activity using the Internet.

The Story of an Hour ◆ 641

ASSESSMENT RESOURCES

The following resources can be used to assess students' knowledge and skills.

Selection Assessment

- **Formal Assessment,** pp. 164–166
- **Open Book Test,** pp. 100–102
- **Got It! Assessment Videotapes,** Tape 3
- **Test Bank Software**
- **Take It to the Net**
  Visit www.phschool.com for self-tests and additional questions on "The Story of an Hour."

Writing Rubric

- **Performance Assess. and Portfolio Mgmt.,** p. 11

Listening and Speaking Rubric

- **Performance Assess. and Portfolio Mgmt.,** p. 30

 PRENTICE HALL *ASSESSMENT SYSTEM*

- **Workbook**
- **Skill Book**
- **Transparencies**
- **CD-ROM**

---

❸ Writing Lesson

- Be sure students understand that a reflective essay describes a personal experience and explains how the author feels about it. Reflective essays also explain the experience's significance.

- When they have selected subjects for their essays, direct students to use in their prewriting the Gathering Details organizer modeled on p. 641.

- Encourage students to use a personal tone in their essays by writing in the first person, using an informal conversational style, and including personal opinions and feelings.

- Use the Reflective Composition rubric in **Performance Assessment and Portfolio Management,** p. 11, to evaluate students' essays.

❹ Listening and Speaking

- Divide the class into pairs to work on developing and writing soliloquies. Make sure students understand that their soliloquies should present an authentic voice for Mrs. Mallard, based on her character in the story.

- Pairs should begin by answering the bulleted questions on p. 641. Then, instruct students to imagine Mrs. Mallard's first ten years as a widow.

- When soliloquies are ready, pairs should decide who will make the speech. Have partners introduce each soliloquy.

- Use the rubric for Delivering a Speech, p. 30 in **Performance Assessment and Portfolio Management,** to assess students' work.

CUSTOMIZE INSTRUCTION
For Universal Access

To address different learning styles, use the activities suggested in the **Extension Activities** booklet, 34.

- For Verbal/Linguistic Learners, use Activities 5 and 7.

- For Verbal/Linguistic and Interpersonal Learners, use Activity 6.

641

April Showers

Lesson Objectives

1. **To analyze and respond to literary elements**
   - Literary Analysis: Elements of Plot
   - Connecting Literary Elements: Single Effect

2. **To read, comprehend, analyze, and critique a short story**
   - Reading Strategy: Anticipating Events
   - Reading Check questions
   - Review and Assess questions
   - Assessment Practice (ATE)

3. **To develop word analysis skills, fluency, and systematic vocabulary**
   - Vocabulary Development Lesson: Latin Roots: *-man-*, *-manu-*

4. **To understand and apply written and oral language conventions**
   - Spelling Strategy
   - Grammar and Style Lesson: Gerund Phrases

5. **To understand and apply appropriate writing and research strategies**
   - Writing Lesson: Personal Narrative
   - Extension Activity: Flowchart

6. **To understand and apply listening and speaking strategies**
   - Extension Activity: Brief Speech

STEP-BY-STEP TEACHING GUIDE	PACING GUIDE
PRETEACH	
Motivate Students and Provide Background	
Use the Motivation activity (ATE p. 642)	5 min.
Read and discuss author and background features (SE/ATE pp. 642, 645)	5 min.
Introduce the Concepts	
Introduce the Literary Analysis and Reading Strategy (SE/ATE p. 643)	15 min.
Pronounce the vocabulary words and read their definitions (SE p. 643)	5 min.
TEACH	
Monitor Comprehension	
Informally monitor comprehension by circulating while students read independently or in groups	325 min.
Monitor students' comprehension with the Reading Check notes (SE/ATE pp. 647, 649, 651)	as students read
Develop vocabulary with Vocabulary notes (SE pp. 645, 646, 647, 648, 652; ATE p. 646, 648)	as students read
Develop Understanding	
Develop students' understanding elements of plot with the Literary Analysis annotations (SE pp. 646, 647, 651; ATE pp. 646, 647, 651)	5 min.
Develop students' ability to anticipate events in reading by using the Reading Strategy annotations (SE pp. 649, 651, 652; ATE pp. 649, 651, 652)	5 min.
ASSESS	
Assess Mastery	
Assess students' mastery of the Reading Strategy and Literary Analysis by having them answer the Review and Assess questions (SE/ATE p. 653)	15 min.
Use one or more of the print and media Assessment Resources (ATE p. 655)	up to 45 min.
EXTEND	
Apply Understanding	
Have students complete the Vocabulary Development Lesson and the Grammar and Style Lesson (SE p. 654)	20 min.
Apply students' ability to create a mood in their writing by using the Writing Lesson (SE/ATE p. 655)	45 min.
Apply students' understanding using one or more of the Extension Activities (SE p. 655)	20–90 min.

A **ACCELERATED INSTRUCTION:**
Use the strategies and activities identified with an **A**.

UNIVERSAL ACCESS
- ● = Below Level Students
- ▲ = On-Level Students
- ■ = Above Level Students

Time and Resource Manager

Reading Level: Average
Average Number of Instructional Days: 5

RESOURCES		
PRINT 📖	**TRANSPARENCIES** 📓	**TECHNOLOGY** 💿 🎧 📼
• **Beyond Literature,** Career Connection: Publishing, p. 35 ▲ ■		• **Interest Grabber Video,** Tape 4 ● ▲ ■
• **Selection Support Workbook:** ● ▲ ■ Literary Analysis, p. 159 Reading Strategy, p. 158 Build Vocabulary, p. 156	• **Literary Analysis and Reading Transparencies,** pp. 69 and 70 ● ▲ ■	
		• **Listening to Literature** ● ▲ ■ Audiocassettes, Side 29 Audio CDs, CD 16
• **Literatura en español** ● ▲ • **Literary Analysis for Enrichment** ■		
• **Formal Assessment:** Selection Test, pp. 167–169 ● ▲ ■ • **Open Book Test,** pp. 103–105 ● ▲ ■ • **Performance Assessment and Portfolio Management,** pp. 11, 30 ● ▲ ■ • ⬤ PRENTICE HALL ASSESSMENT *SYSTEM* ● ▲ ■	• ⬤ PRENTICE HALL ASSESSMENT *SYSTEM* ● ▲ ■ Skills Practice Answers and Explanations on Transparencies	• **Test Bank Software** ● ▲ ■ • **Got It! Assessment Videotapes,** Tape 3 ● ▲
• **Selection Support Workbook:** ● ▲ ■ Grammar and Style, p. 157 • **Writing and Grammar,** Ruby Level ● ▲ ■ • **Extension Activities,** p. 35 ● ▲ ■	• **Daily Language Practice Transparencies** ● ▲ • **Writing Models and Graphic Organizers on Transparencies,** pp. 13–16 ● ▲ ■	• **Writing and Grammar iText CD-ROM** ● ▲ ■ 🖥 *Take It to the Net* www.phschool.com

BLOCK SCHEDULING: Use one 90-minute class period to preteach the selection and have students read it. Use a second 90-minute class period to assess students' mastery of skills and have them complete one of the Extension Activities.

Step-by-Step Teaching Guide for pp. 642–643

Motivation

Hold up four envelopes. Tell students to imagine that you have in your hand awards for *Student Most Likely to Become President, Student Most Likely to Become a Writer, Student Most Likely to Win a Nobel Prize,* and *Student Most Likely to Become a Celebrity.* Ask students to jot down their feelings and ideas about their chances to win one or more of those awards, and to describe how they would feel if their expectations were or were not met. Tell them that in the story they are about to read, expectations play a key part; as a young woman eagerly waits to learn the fate of a novel she has submitted for publication.

▥ Interest Grabber Video

As an alternative, play "Edith Wharton" on Tape 4 to engage student interest.

❶ Background

More About the Author

In 1913, Edith Wharton settled permanently in Paris. During World War I, she was active in relief work in France. In 1915 she was decorated with the Cross of the Legion of Honor for her service. In addition to her novels and stories, Wharton wrote books on travel that reflect her interest in landscape gardening and architecture. She also wrote a manual, *The Writing of Fiction.*

Prepare to Read

❶ April Showers

Edith Wharton (1862–1937)

Colorful Old New York, the high society of London and Paris, the French Riviera—these settings, from the late nineteenth century through the 1930s, were all part of Edith Wharton's world. They also played an important role in the creation of her remarkable literary career and the more than fifty volumes she published.

A Daughter of Privilege Born Edith Newbold Jones, Wharton was the daughter of a socially prominent New York City family and was educated privately by tutors and governesses in New York and Europe. In 1885, she married Edward Wharton, a Boston banker and part of a social class much like her own. The couple spent the next few years immersing themselves in the social life of the high society in Newport, Rhode Island; Lenox, Massachusetts; and Europe.

Surprisingly, it was on the advice of a doctor that Wharton began to write fiction. Wharton was caring for her husband, known as Teddy, who had become chronically ill, and the doctor advised Wharton to take up writing as a way to relieve stress. Her first stories appeared in *Scribner's* magazine. Several volumes of her fiction were published around the turn of the century. However, it was her best-selling novel *The House of Mirth* (1905)—a devastating portrait of a young woman who tries and fails to survive in New York high society—that established her as an important writer. It was well received by critics and reached a wide audience.

Watching the Shift in Power Wharton was a master at re-creating the staid, rule-bound atmosphere of the upper-class society of her time. As a member of that elite, Wharton witnessed the transfer of wealth and power from the families of her friends to the new masters of the Industrial Revolution. She observed the lack of energy and purpose among the members of her own class. Even though her group maintained a strict code of honor and morality, it was not enough to stop the rise of what she considered the amoral and vulgar robber barons. This disruption of the older class system is the background for much of her fiction.

An Expatriate Writer In 1913, Wharton moved to Paris. She began a friendship with the novelist Henry James, who became her literary mentor, as well as with other writers who helped her refine her work. As World War I loomed, she produced some of her finest novels: *Ethan Frome* (1911), *The Reef* (1912), and *The Custom of the Country* (1913). During the war, Wharton remained in France and wrote little. Instead, she organized aid for Belgian refugees. Wharton also collected American money for the cause well before America entered the war. She received honors from the French government for her efforts.

Age of Innocence In 1920, her novel *The Age of Innocence*, which more than seventy years later was made into a popular movie, won the Pulitzer Prize. Wharton also published *Old New York* (1924), *The Mother's Recompense* (1925), and 85 short stories. In addition, she published an autobiography, *A Backward Glance*, in 1934. In her fiction, which continues to attract readers and earn critical acclaim, Wharton explores the conflict between money and morality and exposes the cruelty of the social "game," with its rivalries, rules, and punishments.

Wharton continued to write until her death in 1937. She is buried in the American cemetery at Versailles in France.

642 ◆ *Division, Reconciliation, and Expansion (1850–1914)*

TEACHING RESOURCES

The following resources can be used to enrich or extend the instruction for pp. 642–643.

Motivation
▥ **Interest Grabber Video,** Tape 4 ▨

Background
📖 **Beyond Literature,** p. 35

🖥 *Take It to the Net*
Visit www.phschool.com for Background and hotlinks for the selection.

Literary Analysis
📑 **Literary Analysis and Reading Transparencies,** Elements of Plot, p. 70

📖 **Selection Support:** Literary Analysis, p. 159

Reading
📑 **Literary Analysis and Reading Transparencies,** Anticipating Events, p. 69 ▨

▨ **BLOCK SCHEDULING:** Resources marked with this symbol provide varied instruction during 90-minute blocks.

Preview

Connecting to the Literature

It takes courage to risk having your work criticized or rejected. In this story, a young writer braves the world of publishing—and gets not one surprise, but two.

❷ Literary Analysis

Elements of Plot

Like most short story writers, Wharton brings together the **elements of plot** to lead readers through the events of a story.

- The **exposition** introduces characters, setting, and situation.
- An event sets up the **conflict,** or struggle.
- During the **rising action,** the conflict is developed.
- The conflict increases until it reaches a **climax,** or high point of suspense.
- The events that follow the climax are the **falling action.**
- The story ends with the **resolution** of the central conflict.

As you read, use a chart like the one shown to record the events as they develop in Wharton's story.

Connecting Literary Elements

In his literary criticism, Edgar Allan Poe, the great horror writer, wrote that a short story should create "a certain unique or **single effect.**" His ideas, which have influenced writers ever since, state that each character, incident, and detail in a story should contribute to the single effect. As you read "April Showers," note the details Wharton includes and consider what single effect the story creates.

❸ Reading Strategy

Anticipating Events

As you read this story, you will probably find yourself **anticipating events**—looking forward to what happens next. Anticipating events is more emotional than the logical process of predicting. When you anticipate events, you connect to characters as you watch their lives unfold.

Vocabulary Development

admonitory (ad män´ i tôr´ ē) *adj.* warning (p. 645)

manuscript (man´ yōō skript´) *n.* document submitted to a publisher (p. 645)

retrospective (re´ trə spek´ tiv) *adj.* looking back on or directed to the past (p. 646)

antagonism (an tag´ ə niz´ əm) *n.* hostility (p. 647)

contrition (kən trish´ ən) *n.* remorse for having done wrong (p. 647)

commiseration (kə miz´ ər ā´ shən) *n.* sympathy (p. 652)

April Showers ◆ 643

---

❷ Literary Analysis

Elements of Plot

- Tell students that as they read the short story in this lesson, they will focus on the elements of plot—exposition, conflict, rising action, climax, falling action, and resolution.

- Read the instruction about the elements of plot together as a class. Draw students' attention to the chart that gives a visual representation of how plot elements interrelate. Point out that the introduction of the conflict causes the rising action to begin; similarly, the arrival of the climax signals the shift from rising action to falling action.

- As they read, invite students to be aware of the conflict or conflicts facing the main character and to note when the text reaches its highest level of tension.

❸ Reading Strategy

Anticipating Events

- Help students recognize that anticipating events is a skill that becomes more developed when a reader is engaged with a text. Explain that this story will offer students an opportunity to strengthen their control of a skill with which they already have some experience.

- Explain that readers faced with a challenging text can deepen their involvement with the characters and themes by reminding themselves to anticipate events in the narrative.

Vocabulary Development

- Pronounce each vocabulary word for students, and read the definitions as a class. Have students identify any words with which they are already familiar.

CUSTOMIZE INSTRUCTION FOR UNIVERSAL ACCESS

For Less Proficient Readers	For English Learners	For Advanced Readers
Encourage students to spend time familiarizing themselves with the chart showing how plot functions. Discuss with students how plots can be understood as a chain of causes and effects. You may wish to use the Cause and Effect transparency in **Writing Models and Graphic Organizers on Transparency,** p. 91, to help students track plot elements.	Spend time helping students get comfortable with specific plot terms. Students may be familiar already with the terms *action*, *rising*, and *falling*, so they will need only to understand the concept of action unfolding in contrasting directions.	Help students to distinquish between *story* and *plot*. Story is a term for a series of events that occur in order; it is the "what happened next" followed by "what happened after that." On the other hand, plotting involves flashbacks, foreshadowings, leaps in time, omissions, and additions of scenes, characters, and so on.

E-Teach

Visit E-Teach at www.phschool.com for teachers' essays on how to teach, with questions and answers.

CUSTOMIZE INSTRUCTION
For Interpersonal Learners

Ask students whether they agree with Theodora's opinion, mentioned on pages 644–645, of the strategy of writers' "dumbing down" their early work in order to get published. Invite students (perhaps in pairs) to argue for or against her notions about how a writer should achieve success and recognition.

❶ About the Selection

A romantic, suggestible young woman distracts herself from the responsibilities of running the family household by writing a florid novel and submitting it to a magazine. After much anxious anticipation, she is surprised and thrilled to learn that her work has been accepted for publication. To her dismay, she soon learns that it was another story with the same name that the publisher really wanted. Though she fears her father's derision, she is surprised and comforted when he exhibits compassion for her disappointment; he, too, once harbored dreams of becoming a writer.

❷ Background

Art

Memories, 1885–86, by William Merritt Chase

William Merritt Chase (1849–1916) studied in New York with artist Joseph O. Eaton and then took classes at the National Academy of Design. After his painting *Keying Up—The Court Jester* established his credibility, he enjoyed a successful career as an artist and teacher for the rest of his life.

Use this question for discussion:

In what ways does this painting capture Theodora's attitude toward her writing?
Possible response: Her dreamy, faraway expression shows her romantic view of the craft of writing; moreover, the manuscript lights up the table, her heart, and her face: it is the only thing in the picture that seems to generate light.

❶ April Showers

Edith Wharton

Memories, 1885–86, William Merritt Chase, Munson-Williams-Proctor Institute Museum of Art, Utica, New York

❷

644 ◆ *Division, Reconciliation, and Expansion (1850–1914)*

TEACHING RESOURCES

The following resources can be used to enrich or extend the instruction for pp. 644–652.

Reading Strategy

📖 **Selection Support:** Reading Strategy, p. 158; Build Vocabulary, p. 156

🎧 **Listening to Literature Audiocassettes,** Side 25 ▪

💿 **Listening to Literature Audio CDs,** CD 15 ▪ here is a write on rule _____

▪ **BLOCK SCHEDULING:** Resources marked with this symbol provide varied instruction during 90-minute blocks.

Background

The publishing world of the late nineteenth and early twentieth centuries was far different from today's book world. If Wharton's novels were published today, they would stand on bookstore shelves crowded with many other novels. Wharton's publisher would probably send her on a whirlwind book tour; you might even hear her books read on audiotape by a famous actor. Around the turn of the century, however, things were different. Novels were customarily serialized in magazines and newspapers. *The House of Mirth*, one of Wharton's most famous novels, appeared in *Scribner's* magazine before it was published as a book in 1905. Readers of the time would eagerly await the next monthly installment of the latest novel by their favorite author. Some great writers, including England's Charles Dickens earlier in the century, established their reputations this way.

❸ ▶ Critical Viewing

Answer: Students may say that this portrait presents a dreamy, romanticized look at the writing process—one that accurately captures how Theodora sees herself.

❹ ✔ Reading Check

Answer: She is working to finish writing her novel.

"But Guy's heart slept under the violets on Muriel's grave."

It was a beautiful ending; Theodora had seen girls cry over last chapters that weren't half as pathetic. She laid her pen aside and read the words over, letting her voice linger on the fall of the sentence; then, drawing a deep breath, she wrote across the foot of the page the name by which she had decided to become known in literature—Gladys Glyn.

Downstairs the library clock struck two. Its muffled thump sounded like an <u>admonitory</u> knock against her bedroom floor. Two o'clock! and she had promised her mother to be up early enough to see that the buttons were sewn on Johnny's reefer, and that Kate had her cod-liver oil before starting for school!

Lingeringly, tenderly she gathered up the pages of her novel—there were five hundred of them—and tied them with the blue satin ribbon that her Aunt Julia had given her. She had meant to wear the ribbon with her new dotted muslin on Sundays, but this was putting it to a nobler use. She bound it round her <u>manuscript</u>, tying the ends in a pretty bow. Theodora was clever at making bows, and could have trimmed hats beautifully, had not all her spare moments been given to literature. Then, with a last look at the precious pages, she sealed and addressed the package. She meant to send it off next morning to the Home Circle. She knew it would be hard to obtain access to a paper which numbered so many popular authors among its contributors, but she had been encouraged to make the venture by something her Uncle James had said the last time he had come down from Boston.

He had been telling his brother, Doctor Dace, about his new house out at Brookline. Uncle James was prosperous, and was always moving into new houses with more "modern improvements." Hygiene was his passion, and he migrated in the wake of sanitary plumbing.

admonitory (ad män′ i tôr′ ē) *adj.* warning

manuscript (man′ yōō skript) *n.* document submitted to a publisher

❸ ◀ **Critical Viewing** What emotions does this portrait evoke? In what ways do they relate to Theodora's literary hopes and dreams? [Connect]

❹ ✔ **Reading Check**
What prevents Theodora from helping her mother?

April Showers ◆ 645

CUSTOMIZE INSTRUCTION FOR UNIVERSAL ACCESS

For Special Needs Students	For English Learners
Point out to these students that historically many writers have chosen to publish their work under a pseudonym. For example, Mark Twain was the pen name of Samuel Clemens, and best-selling author Stephen King has published five novels using the name Richard Bachman. Invite students to speculate about why writers choose to use pen names.	The passage about Uncle James's new house contains a number of terms that may prove challenging. As you guide them to understand words such as *prosperous, hygiene, migrated, wake*, and *sanitary plumbing*, make sure that they understand that Uncle James is excited about a new upgrade in home construction—that is, indoor plumbing. Explain that in turn-of-the-century America, few homes contained this "luxury."

❺ Literary Analysis

Elements of Plot

- Encourage students to pause for a moment to think about how Edith Wharton begins her story. Ask students to recall the name of the plot element in which an author introduces characters, setting, and a situation. If necessary, remind them that this plot element is called exposition.

- Ask students the Literary Analysis question on p. 646: What details have you learned so far about Theodora and her family? **Answer:** The reader learns that bookish, romantic Theodora Dace is a seventeen-year-old girl who lives with her mother, and seems to have at least two younger siblings—Johnny and Kate—and a father who is a physician. She has an Aunt Julia, as well as a "prosperous" Uncle James who lives in Brookline near Boston.

❻ Vocabulary Development

Prefixes

- Direct students to the word *retrospective* near the bottom of p. 646. Tell students that the word contains the Latin prefix *retro-*, which means "backward," "back," or "behind." Students who know that the Latin root *-spect-* means "look" will be able to deduce that *retrospective* means "looking back on things in the past."

- Invite students to find the meaning of other words that use the prefix *retro-*, such as *retroactive, retrogression,* and others.

"The bathrooms alone are worth the money," he was saying, cheerfully, "although it is a big rent. But then, when a man's got no no children to save up for—" he glanced compassionately round Doctor Dace's crowded table "—and it is something to be in a neighborhood where the drainage is A-one. That's what I was telling our neighbor. Who do you suppose she is, by the way?" He smiled at Theodora. "I rather think that young lady knows all about her. Ever heard of Kathleen Kyd?"

Kathleen Kyd! The famous "society novelist," the creator of more "favorite heroines" than all her predecessors put together had ever turned out, the author of *Fashion and Passion, An American Duchess, Rhona's Revolt.* Was there any intelligent girl from Maine to California whose heart would not have beat faster at the mention of that name?

"Why, yes," Uncle James was saying, "Kathleen Kyd lives next door. Frances G. Wollop is her real name, and her husband's a dentist. She's a very pleasant, sociable kind of woman; you'd never think she was a writer. Ever hear how she began to write? She told me the whole story. It seems she was a saleswoman in a store, working on starvation wages, with a mother and a consumptive sister to support. Well, she wrote a story one day, just for fun, and sent it to the *Home Circle.* They'd never heard of her, of course, and she never expected to hear from them. She did, though. They took the story and passed their plate for more. She became a regular contributor and eventually was known all over the country. Now she tells me her books bring her in about ten thousand a year. Rather more than you and I can boast of, eh, John? Well, I hope *this* household doesn't contribute to her support." He glanced sharply at Theodora. "I don't believe in feeding youngsters on sentimental trash; it's like sewer gas—doesn't smell bad, and infects the system without your knowing it."

Theodora listened breathlessly. Kathleen Kyd's first story had been accepted by the *Home Circle,* and they had asked for more! Why should Gladys Glyn be less fortunate? Theodora had done a great deal of novel reading—far more than her parents were aware of—and felt herself competent to pronounce upon the quality of her own work. She was almost sure that "April Showers" was a remarkable book. If it lacked Kathleen Kyd's lightness of touch, it had an emotional intensity never achieved by that brilliant writer. Theodora did not care to amuse her readers; she left that to more frivolous talents. Her aim was to stir the depths of human nature, and she felt she had succeeded. It was a great thing for a girl to be able to feel that about her first novel. Theodora was only seventeen; and she remembered, with a touch of <u>retrospective</u> compassion, that George Eliot[1] had not become famous till she was nearly forty.

No, there was no doubt about the merit of "April Showers." But would not an inferior work have had a better chance of success? Theodora recalled the early struggles of famous authors, the notorious

---

1. **George Eliot** pseudonym of Mary Ann Evans (1819–1880), a celebrated English novelist.

Literary Analysis
Elements of Plot What details have you learned so far about Theodora and her family?

retrospective (re′ trə spek′ tiv) *adj.* looking back on or directed to the past

---

❋ ENRICHMENT: Culture Connection

Censorship

For the editors at *Home Circle,* the decision not to publish Theodora's novel was a matter of taste and economics. In certain parts of the world, however, some writers have to contend not only with the realities of editors' tastes and budgets, but also with censorship. In Nigeria, for example, the government banned the writings of contemporary poet and playwright Wole Soyinka. The first black African to receive the Nobel Prize for Literature, Soyinka had spoken out against the dictatorship in Nigeria and called for human rights. In 1998, after several years of exile, Soyinka was finally allowed to return to Nigeria, where he continues to write.

<u>antagonism</u> of publishers and editors to any new writer of exceptional promise. Would it not be wiser to write the book down to the average reader's level, reserving for some later work the great "effects" into which she had thrown all the fever of her imagination? The thought was sacrilege! Never would she lay hands on the sacred structure she had reared; never would she resort to the inartistic expedient of modifying her work to suit the popular taste. Better obscure failure than a vulgar triumph. The great authors never stooped to such concessions, and Theodora felt herself included in their ranks by the firmness with which she rejected all thought of conciliating an unappreciative public. The manuscript should be sent as it was.

She woke with a start and a heavy sense of apprehension. The *Home Circle* had refused "April Showers!" No, that couldn't be it; there lay the precious manuscript, waiting to be posted. What was it, then? Ah, that ominous thump below stairs—nine o'clock striking! It was Johnny's buttons!

She sprang out of bed in dismay. She had been so determined not to disappoint her mother about Johnny's buttons! Mrs. Dace, helpless from chronic rheumatism, had to entrust the care of the household to her eldest daughter; and Theodora honestly meant to see that Johnny had his full complement of buttons, and that Kate and Bertha went to school tidy. Unfortunately, the writing of a great novel leaves little time or memory for the lesser obligations of life, and Theodora usually found that her good intentions matured too late for practical results.

Her <u>contrition</u> was softened by the thought that literary success would enable her to make up for all the little negligences of which she was guilty. She meant to spend all her money on her family; and already she had visions of a wheeled chair for her mother, a fresh wallpaper for the doctor's shabby office, bicycles for the girls, and Johnny's establishment at a boarding school where sewing on his buttons would be included in the curriculum. If her parents could have guessed her intentions, they would not have found fault with her as they did; and Doctor Dace, on this particular morning, would not have looked up to say, with his fagged, ironical air:

"I suppose you didn't get home from the ball till morning?"

Theodora's sense of being in the right enabled her to take the thrust with a dignity that would have awed the unfeeling parent of fiction.

"I'm sorry to be late, father," she said.

Doctor Dace, who could never be counted on to behave like a father in a book, shrugged his shoulders impatiently.

"Your sentiments do you credit, but they haven't kept your mother's breakfast warm."

"Hasn't mother's tray gone up yet?"

"Who was to take it, I should like to know? The girls came down so late that I had to hustle them off before they'd finished breakfast, and Johnny's hands were so dirty that I sent him back to his room to make himself decent. It's a pretty thing for the doctor's children to be the dirtiest little savages in Norton!"

---

antagonism (an tag′ ə niz′ əm) *n.* hostility

Literary Analysis
Elements of Plot Where does the exposition end and the rising action begin?

contrition (kən trish′ ən) *n.* remorse for having done wrong

Literary Analysis
Elements of Plot and Single Effect What single effect has the story developed up to this point? Which details help you decide?

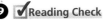 **Reading Check**

What are some of Theodora's family responsibilities?

April Showers ◆ 647

CUSTOMIZE INSTRUCTION FOR UNIVERSAL ACCESS

For Less Proficient Readers	For Gifted/Talented Students
Help students recognize the conflicts that exist within Theodora—the struggle between her desire to be a novelist and the very real need for her to tend to her domestic obligations. You might also point out some of Wharton's elaborate or archaic usages, for example, the sentences on pp. 646 and 647 that begin "Would it not be wiser. . ." and "Never would she. . . ." Let students know that Wharton uses these to reflect Theodora's own overly-dramatic diction.	Theodora is a young woman who is about the same age as your students. Ask them whether they believe her actions (and reactions) are typical of someone their age. After students have finished reading the work, ask them to speculate about how the story might have turned out differently if Wharton had made Theodora an older, more experienced person.

---

❼ Literary Analysis

Elements of Plot

- Have a student explain what plot elements always precede a story's rising action (exposition and conflict). Discuss with students why a story's conflict must be established before the rising action can begin.

- Ask one or more student volunteers to read aloud the paragraphs on the bottom of p. 646 and the top of p. 647. Encourage listeners to think about the exact place in the story where the rising action begins.

- Ask students the first Literary Analysis question on p. 647: Where does the exposition end and the rising action begin? **Answer:** Students may say that the exposition of the story ends and the rising action begins when Theodora awakens after working late to complete her book and realizes she has failed to take care of her household responsibilities.

❽ Literary Analysis

Elements of Plot and the Single Effect

- Have one or more students summarize Edgar Allan Poe's theory about the creation of a single effect in a short story.

- Ask students the Literary Analysis questions on p. 647: What single effect has the story developed up to this point? What details help you decide? **Answer:** Students may say that Wharton has animated Theodora's imaginative life to the extent that the reader sees the setting and other characters as she does—through the eyes of a teenager who perceives herself as a brilliant writer approaching fame and fortune. Students might cite details such as *the lesser obligations of life, the little negligences of which she was guilty,* and *visions of a wheeled chair.*

❾ Reading Check

Answer: She is responsible for making breakfast for the family (including delivering a breakfast tray to her mother in an upstairs bedroom) and readying her siblings for school.

647

⑩ Vocabulary Development

Latin Word Roots -manu-, -man-

- Call students' attention to the word *manuscript* and its definition. Let students know that the Latin word *manus* means hand.

- Lead students to recognize that this prefix, together with the word "script" signifies a document written by hand.

- Let students know that although Theodora's manuscript was indeed written by hand using pen and ink, the word is used today to describe writing that is typed or created in word-processing software. Any text before it is typeset is considered manuscript.

- Ask students to volunteer words that contain this prefix, and to explain their meaning.
Possibilities include: manual, manufacture, mandate, manipulate, emancipate

Theodora had hastily prepared her mother's tray, leaving her own breakfast untouched. As she entered the room upstairs, Mrs. Dace's patient face turned to her with a smile much harder to bear than her father's reproaches.

"Mother, I'm so sorry—"

"No matter, dear. I suppose Johnny's buttons kept you. I can't think what that boy does to his clothes!"

Theodora sat the tray down without speaking. It was impossible to own to having forgotten Johnny's buttons without revealing the cause of her forgetfulness. For a few weeks longer she must bear to be misunderstood; then—ah, then if her novel were accepted, how gladly would she forget and forgive! But what if it were refused? She turned aside to hide the dismay that flushed her face. Well, then she would admit the truth—she would ask her parents' pardon, and settle down without a murmur to an obscure existence of mending and combing.

⑩ She had said to herself that after the manuscript had been sent, she would have time to look after the children and catch up with the mending; but she had reckoned without the postman. He came three times a day; for an hour before each ring she was too excited to do anything but wonder if he would bring an answer this time, and for an hour afterward she moved about in a leaden stupor of disappointment. The children had never been so trying. They seemed to be always coming to pieces, like cheap furniture; one would have supposed they had been put together with bad glue. Mrs. Dace worried herself ill over Johnny's tatters, Bertha's bad marks at school, and Kate's open abstention from cod-liver oil; and Doctor Dace, coming back late from a long round of visits to a fireless office with a smoky lamp, called out furiously to know if Theodora would kindly come down and remove the "East, West, home's best" that hung above the empty grate.

In the midst of it all, Miss Sophy Brill called. It was very kind of her to come, for she was the busiest woman in Norton. She made it her duty to look after other people's affairs, and there was not a house in town but had the benefit of her personal supervision. She generally came when things were going wrong, and the sight of her bonnet on the doorstep was a surer sign of calamity than a crepe bow on the bell. After she left, Mrs. Dace looked very sad, and the doctor punished Johnny for warbling down the entry:

"Miss Sophy Brill
Is a bitter pill!"

while Theodora, locking herself in her room, resolved with tears that she would never write another novel.

The week was a long nightmare. Theodora could neither eat nor sleep. She was up early enough, but instead of looking after the children and seeing that breakfast was ready, she wandered down the road to meet the postman, and came back wan and empty-handed, oblivious of her morning duties. She had no idea how long the

---

✸ ENRICHMENT: Career Connection

Editors

Theodora sees the editors at *Home Circle* as heartless animals. However, editors perform a vital function in the publishing process. Guide students to appreciate that the success and quality of the final version of any kind of book is often due in large part to the efforts of the book's editor. Essential to the many technical, managerial, financial, and interpersonal skills required of a successful editor is an ability to focus on details.

Guide students to think about and discuss the variety of details they need to consider when they edit their own essays and stories. Then tell students that editing is one kind of job in which attention to detail is critical to success. Ask students to brainstorm for a list of other jobs that require attention to detail. Invite them to elaborate on their choices.

suspense would last; but she didn't see how authors could live if they were kept waiting more than a week.

Then, suddenly, one afternoon—she never quite knew how or when it happened—she found herself with a *Home Circle* envelope in her hands, and her dazzled eyes flashing over a wild dance of words that wouldn't settle down and make sense.

11 "Dear Madam:" [They called her *Madam!* And then; yes, the words were beginning to fall into line now.] "Your novel, 'April Showers,' has been received, and we are glad to accept it on the usual terms. A serial on which we were counting for immediate publication has been delayed by the author's illness, and the first chapters of 'April Showers' will therefore appear in our midsummer number. Thanking you for favoring us with your manuscript, we remain," and so forth.

Theodora found herself in the wood beyond the schoolhouse. She was kneeling on the ground, brushing aside the dead leaves and pressing her lips to the little bursting green things that pushed up eager tips through last year's decay. It was spring—spring! Everything was crowding toward the light and in her own heart hundreds of germinating hopes had burst into sudden leaf. She wondered if the thrust of those little green fingers hurt the surface of the earth as her springing raptures hurt—yes, actually hurt!—her hot, constricted breast! She looked up through interlacing boughs at a tender, opaque blue sky full of the coming of a milky moon. She seemed enveloped in an atmosphere of loving comprehension. The brown earth throbbed with her joy, the treetops trembled with it, and a sudden star broke through the branches with an audible "I know!"

Theodora, on the whole, behaved very well. Her mother cried, her father whistled and said he supposed he must put up with grounds in his coffee now, and be thankful if he ever got a hot meal again; while the children took the most deafening and harassing advantage of what seemed a sudden suspension of the laws of nature.

Within a week everybody in Norton knew that Theodora had written a novel, and that it was coming out in the *Home Circle.* On Sundays, when she walked up the aisle, her friends dropped their prayer books and the soprano sang false in her excitement. Girls with more pin money than Theodora had ever dreamed of copied her hats and imitated her way of speaking. The local paper asked her for a poem; her old school teachers stopped to shake hands and grew shy over their congratulations; and Miss Sophy Brill came to call. She had put on her Sunday bonnet and her manner was almost abject. She ventured, very timidly, to ask her young friend how she wrote, whether it "just came to her," and if she had found that the kind of pen she used made any difference; and wound up by begging Theodora to write a sentiment in her album.

Even Uncle James came down from Boston to talk the wonder over. He called Theodora a "sly baggage," and proposed that she should give him her earnings to invest in a new patent grease-trap company. From what Kathleen Kyd had told him, he thought Theodora would

12 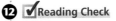 Reading Check
What exciting news does Theodora receive?

April Showers ◆ 649

---

11 Reading Strategy
Anticipating Events

- Read aloud to students the bracketed paragraphs. Ask students to describe their emotions as Theodora opens the envelope.

- Then ask students the Reading Strategy question on p. 649: What event do you and Theodora anticipate as she opens the envelope?
  Answer: Students will probably say that they anticipate a rejection of her manuscript.

12 ☑ Reading Check
Answer: She receives the news that "April Showers" will be published in *Home Circle.*

CUSTOMIZE INSTRUCTION FOR UNIVERSAL ACCESS

For Less Proficient Readers	For Advanced Readers
Point out the bracketed passage in the paragraph beginning "Dear Madam." Help students understand that Wharton uses brackets here to show that these are Theodora's thoughts as she reads the letter. Guide them to see that, as a 17-year-old girl, she is excited to be called *Madam*, which she interprets as an address of maturity and respect.	Invite students to read aloud the paragraph beginning "Theodora found herself" in order to appreciate how Edith Wharton herself utilizes the florid style of the sentimental romance potboiler to express Theodora's emotions and romantic fantasies. Encourage students to seek out and discuss other examples of this technique in the story.

Today there are even fewer American general-interest magazines that publish fiction of high literary quality than there were in Wharton's day. Some of these American magazines, however, have had a surprisingly long life. For instance, *The New Yorker* was established in 1925, *The Atlantic Monthly* in 1857, and *Harper's* in 1850. Many of today's leading "women's magazines"—*Good Housekeeping* (established in 1885), *Better Homes and Gardens*, *Woman's Day*, *Family Circle*, *McCall's* (1897), and *Ladies' Home Journal* (1883)—have a similarly long history of publishing fiction. The *Ladies' Home Journal* alone has published writing by Booth Tarkington; Zane Grey, Dorothy Parker, Ogden Nash, James M. Cain, Kurt Vonnegut, Peter Beagle, and Amy Tan.

probably get a thousand dollars for her story. He concluded by suggesting that she should base her next romance on the subject of sanitation, making the heroine nearly die of sewer gas poisoning because her parents won't listen to the handsome young doctor next door, when he warns them that their plumbing is out of order. That was a subject that would interest everybody, and do a lot more good than the sentimental trash most women wrote.

At last the great day came. Theodora had left an order with the bookseller for the midsummer number of the *Home Circle* and before the shop was open she was waiting on the sidewalk. She clutched the precious paper and ran home without opening it. Her excitement was almost more than she could bear. Not heeding her father's call to breakfast, she rushed upstairs and locked herself in her room. Her hands trembled so that she could hardly turn the pages. At last—yes, there it was: "April Showers."

The paper dropped from her hands. What name had she read beneath the title? Had her emotion blinded her?

"April Showers, by Kathleen Kyd."

Kathleen Kyd! Oh, cruel misprint! Oh, dastardly typographer! Through tears of rage and disappointment Theodora looked again; yes, there was no mistaking the hateful name. Her glance ran on. She found herself reading a first paragraph that she had never seen before. She read farther. All was strange. The horrible truth burst upon her: *It was not her story!*

She never knew how she got back to the station. She struggled through the crowd on the platform, and a gold-banded arm pushed her into the train just starting for Norton. It would be dark when she reached home; but that didn't matter—nothing mattered now. She sank into her seat, closing her eyes in the vain attempt to shut out the vision of the last few hours; but minute by minute memory forced her to relive it; she felt like a rebellious school child dragged forth to repeat the same detested "piece."

Although she did not know Boston well, she had made her way easily enough to the *Home Circle* building; at least, she supposed she had, since she remembered nothing till she found herself ascending the editorial stairs as easily as one does incredible things in dreams. She must have walked very fast, for her heart was beating furiously, and she had barely breath to whisper the editor's name to a young man who looked out at her from a glass case, like a zoological specimen. The young man led her past other glass cases containing similar specimens to an inner enclosure which seemed filled by an enormous presence. Theodora felt herself enveloped in the presence, submerged by it, gasping for air as she sank under its rising surges.

*L*iterature
in context History Connection

Women and Publishing

Theodora had dreams of seeing her name and her work in print. However, there was little opportunity for women in the 1800s who harbored such dreams—they were merely expected to tend to the home.

Magazines such as *Women's Home Companion*, *The Ladies World*, and *Ladies' Home Journal* emerged in the 1800s as prospective forums for women's literary works. Although these publications were popular, they focused largely on housekeeping issues, fashion, and etiquette instead of literature. For example, a March 1894 article in *Ladies' Home Journal* gave instruction on "Wedding Etiquette" and "The Art of Dressing the Bride."

✺ ENRICHMENT: Math Connection

Bestsellers

Copy and distribute to students a recent list of the best-selling books in the nation, as published by the *New York Times Book Review*. Discuss how the list divides the books into fiction and nonfiction and into hardcover and paperback editions. Review the information provided about each book, including its price, position on the current list, and number of weeks spent on the list.

Invite pairs or small groups of students to analyze

the data presented. Interested students might compare the makeup of this bestseller list with one or more lists from the past—say, one year ago, ten years ago, and/or fifty years ago. Invite students to prepare a report of their findings, and encourage a class discussion about the results.

Gradually fragments of speech floated to the surface. "'April Showers?' Mrs. Kyd's new serial? Your manuscript, you say? You have a letter from me? The name, please? Evidently some unfortunate misunderstanding. One moment." And then a bell ringing, a zoological specimen ordered to unlock a safe, her name asked for again, the manuscript, her own precious manuscript, tied with Aunt Julia's ribbon, laid on the table before her, and her outcries, her protests, her interrogations, drowned in a flood of bland apology: "An unfortunate accident—Mrs. Kyd's manuscript received the same day—extraordinary coincidence in the choice of a title—duplicate answers sent by mistake—Miss Dace's novel hardly suited to their purpose—should of course have been returned—regrettable oversight—accidents would happen—sure she understood."

The voice went on, like the steady pressure of a surgeon's hand on a shrieking nerve. When it stopped she was in the street. A cab nearly ran her down, and a car bell jangled furiously in her ears. She clutched her manuscript, carrying it tenderly through the crowd, like a live thing that had been hurt. She could not bear to look at its soiled edges and the ink stain on Aunt Julia's ribbon.

14 The train stopped with a jerk and she opened her eyes. It was dark, and by the windy flare of gas on the platform she saw the Norton passengers getting out. She stood up stiffly and followed them. A warm wind blew into her face the fragrance of the summer woods, and she remembered how, two months earlier, she had knelt among the dead leaves, pressing her lips to the first shoots of green. Then for the first time she thought of home. She had fled away in the morning without a word, and her heart sank at the thought of her mother's fears. And her father—how angry he would be! She bent her head under the coming storm of his derision.

The night was cloudy, and as she stepped into the darkness beyond the station a hand was slipped in hers. She stood still, too weary to feel frightened, and a voice said, quietly:

"Don't walk so fast, child. You look tired."

"Father!" Her hand dropped from his, but he recaptured it and drew it through his arm. When she found voice, it was to whisper, "You were at the station?"

15 "It's such a good night I thought I'd stroll down and meet you."

Her arm trembled against his. She could not see his face in the dimness, but the light of his cigar looked down on her like a friendly eye, and she took courage to falter out: "Then you knew—"

"That you'd gone to Boston? Well, I rather thought you had."

They walked on slowly, and presently he added, "You see, you left the *Home Circle* lying in your room."

How she blessed the darkness and the muffled sky! She could not have borne the scrutiny of the tiniest star.

"Then mother wasn't very much frightened?"

"Why, no, she didn't appear to be. She's been busy all day over some toggery of Bertha's."

Literary Analysis
Elements of Plot
What details indicate that Theodora's mood is different when she returns from Boston?

Reading Strategy
Anticipating Events What event are you anticipating during Theodora's conversation with her father?

16 ☑ **Reading Check**
What happens in Boston?

April Showers ◆ 651

CUSTOMIZE INSTRUCTION FOR UNIVERSAL ACCESS

For Special Needs Students

Draw students' attention to the paragraph beginning "Kathleen Kyd! Oh, cruel misprint!" Encourage students to speculate freely about what might have happened here, as you help them address questions such as these:

- Has there been a typographer's error?
- Has her story been changed by someone whose name now appears above it?
- Was the title to her story placed above another story by mistake?
- Is the truth immediately clear—that another writer wrote a story with the same title and that the other writer's story, not Theodora's, was accepted?
- If so, why has Theodora received an acceptance letter?

14 **Literary Analysis**
Elements of Plot

- After students have digested the events of the story's climax (the explanation that two stories with the same title were submitted and that the editors sent Theodora an acceptance letter by mistake), have them read the two paragraphs that portray the girl's reactions to this event.

- Ask students the Literary Analysis question on p. 651: What details indicate that Theodora's mood is very different when she returns from Boston?
  Answer: Students might mention details such as *steady pressure of a surgeon's hand on a shrieking nerve, cab nearly ran her down, carrying it tenderly . . . like a live thing that had been hurt, could not bear to look, stood up stiffly, her heart sank,* and *bent her head under the coming storm.*

15 **Reading Strategy**
Anticipating Events

- Remind students that engaged readers continually look forward with eagerness to what will happen next in a story—and that this anticipation derives from their emotional connection to one or more characters.

- Ask students the Reading Strategy question on p. 651: What event are you anticipating during Theodora's conversation with her father?
  Answer: Students may say that they anticipate that Theodora will be chastised for fleeing the house and her responsibilities.

16 ☑ **Reading Check**

Answer: Theodora learns from an editor at *Home Circle* that the acceptance letter was mistakenly sent to her, as well as the fact that the magazine is uninterested in publishing her novel.

⓱ Reading Strategy

Anticipating Events

- Read aloud the bracketed passage. Encourage students to think about how they would characterize the father's behavior in this scene.

- Then ask students the Reading Strategy question on p. 652: Do you find Dr. Dace's reaction surprising in any way? Explain. Answer: Few students are likely to expect the father's empathetic reaction.

Answers for p. 652

Review and Assess

1. Students may express surprise at Dr. Dace's compassion.

2. **(a)** She is responsible for running the household. **(b)** She fails to do her job well because she is distracted by her need to write fiction and her fantasies about her success as an author.

3. **(a)** She is planning to submit her manuscript to *Home Circle* magazine for possible publication. **(b)** Students should cite textual passages that show that Theodora is all too confident about her ability and destiny as a writer.

4. **(a)** Her family becomes more tolerant, and the townspeople view her with awe. **(b)** Sample response: Wharton dryly observes, "Theodora, on the whole, behaved very well."

5. **(a)** She takes the train into Boston to ask the editor or publisher what happened. **(b)** Students should support their responses with clear reasoning.

6. **(a)** He is sympathetic and consoling. **(b)** Though Dr. Dace is a secondary character, his experience enables Theodora to put her failure into perspective.

7. Possible response: Given that it was the publisher that made the mistake, the editors should have taken much more care to treat her with gentleness and respect.

652

Theodora choked. "Father, I'll—" She groped for words, but they eluded her. "I'll do things—differently; I haven't meant—" Suddenly she heard herself bursting out: "It was all a mistake, you know—about my story. They didn't want it; they won't have it!" and she shrank back involuntarily from his impending mirth.

She felt the pressure of his arm, but he didn't speak, and she figured his mute hilarity. They moved on in silence. Presently he said:

"It hurts a bit just at first, doesn't it?"

"O father!"

He stood still, and the gleam of his cigar showed a face of unexpected participation.

"You see I've been through it myself."

"You, father? You?"

⓱ "Why, yes. Didn't I ever tell you? I wrote a novel once. I was just out of college, and didn't want to be a doctor. No; I wanted to be a genius, so I wrote a novel."

The doctor paused, and Theodora clung to him in a mute passion of <u>commiseration</u>. It was as if a drowning creature caught a live hand through the murderous fury of the waves.

"Father—O father!"

"It took me a year—a whole year's hard work; and when I'd finished it the public wouldn't have it, either; not at any price and that's why I came down to meet you, because I remembered my walk home."

Review and Assess

Thinking About the Selection

1. **Respond:** Did this story surprise you? Explain.

2. **(a) Recall:** What is Theodora's job in the family? **(b) Evaluate:** Does she do her job well? Why or why not?

3. **(a) Recall:** As the story begins, what does Theodora hope to accomplish? **(b) Analyze:** Does Theodora feel confident about her ability and her hopes? Support your answer.

4. **(a) Recall:** In what way does the acceptance of Theodora's story change the way others behave toward her? **(b) Interpret:** Do you think it changes Theodora? Explain.

5. **(a) Recall:** What does Theodora do when she sees that the story in the magazine is not her story? **(b) Relate:** Would you have acted differently? Explain.

6. **(a) Recall:** What is Theodora's father's reaction to her experience? **(b) Assess:** What do you think is the importance of Doctor Dace in the story?

7. **Take a Position:** Do you think Theodora was treated fairly by the publishing company? Explain.

Reading Strategy
Anticipating Events
Do you find Dr. Dace's reaction surprising in any way? Explain.

commiseration (kə miz′ ər ā′ shən) *n.* sympathy

✎ ASSESSMENT PRACTICE: Reading Comprehension

Anticipate Missing Words	**(For more practice, see Test Preparation Workbook, p. 49.)**

Many tests ask students to correctly answer sentence-completion questions. Use the following example to show students how to use context and their own knowledge to guess the word that completes the following passage.

> On the advice of a doctor, Edith Wharton began to write fiction to relieve the _____ of caring for her chronically ill husband.

A relaxation
B stress
C amusement
D annoyance

After reading the passage, students might think the word *pressure* completes the sentence. Looking at the choices, they would find that *B, stress,* comes closest to the meaning of their guess.

Review and Assess

Literary Analysis

Elements of Plot

1. Describe the central **conflict** of this story.
2. What incident introduces the conflict?
3. What is the **climax** of the story? Explain.
4. What events make up the story's **falling action**?

Connecting Literary Elements

5. (a) Review the following details to state the single effect the story creates.
   - Theodora has a blue satin ribbon around her novel.
   - Kathleen Kyd's first story is accepted by *Home Circle*.
   - Theodora does not do her chores.
   - *Home Circle's* offices are in Boston, a sophisticated city.

   (b) Explain the ways in which each detail contributes to the effect you have identified.

Reading Strategy

Anticipating Events

6. What was your emotional response to the letter Theodora received from *Home Circle* magazine? Explain.
7. What did you think would happen next?
8. How did the news that *Home Circle* had published the wrong story affect your sense of anticipation?
9. Using a chart like the one shown, find three passages in the story in which you **anticipated** what would happen based on what you had previously read.

Event	What You Thought Would Happen
1.	
2.	
3.	

Extend Understanding

10. **Career Connection:** If Theodora were trying to get published today, what options besides magazines might she explore?

Quick Review

The **elements of plot** follow these stages: The **exposition** introduces a story's characters, setting, and situation. The **conflict** is the internal or external struggle in a story. The events of the **rising action** lead to a **climax,** or high point, in a story. The events that occur after the climax are called the **falling action.** The **resolution** is the end of the central conflict.

In writing constructed to achieve a **single effect,** every character, event, and detail contributes to an overall mood or idea.

When you **anticipate events,** you connect to characters' lives and look forward to what might happen next.

 Take It to the Net
www.phschool.com
Take the interactive self-test online to check your understanding of the selection.

Review and Assess

1. The central conflict is Theodora's inner struggle between fulfilling her dream of becoming a novelist and fulfilling her responsibilities.

2. The conflict is introduced when Theodora fails to awaken in time to complete her household duties because she stayed up late completing her novel.

3. The climax occurs when Theodora learns that the magazine has no interest in her manuscript.

4. Everything that happens after Theodora learns that her work will not be published can be considered the falling action.

5. (a) Possible response: Wharton crystallizes an adolescent girl's passion and myopia concerning her ability as a writer.
   (b) The use of the blue ribbon shows her consuming interest in literature (exposition); Kyd's story's acceptance introduces the possibility that Theodora's story could also be accepted, (exposition); Theodora's failure to do chores underscores her immaturity and distraction (conflict, rising action); the location of the magazine's offices accentuates the sense of glamour and fame that Theodora believes is her destiny (rising action, climax); Dr. Dace's admission conveys the notion of a natural if poignant tendency of teenagers to have unrealistic perceptions about their own powers (resolution).

6. Students may have been excited for Theodora, but Wharton's earlier ironic tone was a clue that things were not going to turn out well.

7. Students should be prepared to support their answers with elements from the story.

8. Students' sense of anticipation was probably heightened by the discovery. They may have wondered what caused the mistake, what Theodora would do next, and how her family would react.

9. Students should specify three passages from the story and explain what they thought would happen.

continued

Answers continued

10. Students should support their answers.

 ENRICHMENT: Further Reading

Other Works by Edith Wharton

Ethan Frome

The House of Mirth

The Age of Innocence

The Buccaneers

A Backward Glance

Take It to the Net
Visit www.phschool.com for more information on Edith Wharton.

❶ Vocabulary Development

Word Analysis

1. manufacture—"the making of goods by hand"
2. manual—"made, done, or worked with the hands"
3. manipulate—"to work, operate, or treat with the hands"
4. emancipate—"to free from restraint or the control of another"

Spelling Strategy

1. anticipatory
2. manipulatory
3. contributory
4. reformatory

Concept Development: Synonyms

1. b
2. c
3. a
4. a
5. a
6. b

❷ Grammar and Style

Practice

1. writing of a great novel; subject
2. looking after the children and seeing that breakfast was ready; objects of preposition
3. being in the right; object of preposition
4. mistaking the hateful name; subject
5. forgetting the terrible thing; subject complement

Writing Application

Students' paragraphs should use at least three gerund phrases in explaining how a favorite sport is played.

Integrate Language Skills

❶ Vocabulary Development Lesson

Word Analysis: Latin Root -man-/-manu-

The Latin root -man-/-manu- means "hand," so *manuscript* literally means "a handwritten document." Using your knowledge of this root, define the following words.

1. manufacture   3. manipulate
2. manual   4. emancipate

Spelling Strategy

The suffix *-ory* is preceded by the letter *t* in many adjectives formed from verbs: *admonish* becomes *admonitory* and *accuse* becomes *accusatory*. Write the adjective that is formed from each verb:

1. anticipate   3. contribute
2. manipulate   4. reform

Concept Development: Synonyms

Write the letter of the word closest in meaning to each of the following words from the vocabulary list on page 643.

1. admonitory: (a) sorry (b) warning (c) financial
2. retrospective: (a) futuristic (b) under (c) back
3. antagonism: (a) hostility (b) fright (c) arrogance
4. contrition: (a) regret (b) jocularity (c) passivity
5. manuscript: (a) draft (b) map (c) autograph
6. commiseration: (a) wrath (b) sympathy (c) angst

❷ Grammar and Style Lesson

Gerund Phrases

A **gerund phrase** is a group of words serving as a noun and consisting of a gerund (the *-ing* verb form) and its modifiers or complements. Like nouns, gerund phrases function as subjects, direct objects, subject complements, and objects of prepositions.

> **Subject:** *Writing short stories* is my hobby.
>
> **Direct Object:** They exchanged their *writing about characters*.
>
> **Indirect Object:** She gives her *writing about challenges* full attention.
>
> **Object of Preposition:** She'd do anything for better *writing about themes*.

Practice In each numbered item below, underline at least one gerund phrase and identify its function in the sentence.

1. Unfortunately, the writing of a great novel leaves little time or memory for the lesser obligations of life . . .
2. . . . instead of looking after the children and seeing that breakfast was ready . . .
3. Theodora's sense of being in the right enabled her . . .
4. . . . there was no mistaking the hateful name.
5. . . . there is no forgetting the terrible thing that was done.

Writing Application Write a paragraph about a favorite sport, using at least three gerund phrases to explain how it is played.

*W*G *Prentice Hall Writing and Grammar Connection: Chapter 19, Section 2*

TEACHING RESOURCES

The following resources can be used to enrich or extend the instruction for pp. 654–655.

Vocabulary

📖 **Selection Support:** Build Vocabulary, p. 156

📖 **Vocabulary and Spelling Practice Book** (Use this booklet for skills enrichment.) ▪

Grammar

📖 **Selection Support Workbook:** Grammar and Style, p. 157 ▪

*W*G **Writing and Grammar**, Ruby Level, p. 442

📄 **Daily Language Practice Transparencies**

Writing

*W*G **Writing and Grammar**, Ruby Level, p. 56 ▪

📖 **Extension Activities**

📄 **Writing Models and Graphic Organizers on Transparencies**, pp. 13–16

*W*G **Writing and Grammar**, iText CD-ROM

▪ **BLOCK SCHEDULING:** Resources marked with this symbol provide varied instruction during 90-minute blocks.

❸ Writing Lesson

Personal Narrative

Most writers experience rejection many times before publishing. Dr. Dace is sympathetic to Theodora because he had faced such rejection himself. As Dr. Dace, write a personal narrative explaining your experience as a struggling writer, and applying it to your relationship with your daughter.

Prewriting   Reread the last three lines of the story. Then, as Dr. Dace, list details of the events that led to the rejection of your manuscript. Jot down some of the feelings associated with that rejection.

Drafting   Writing in the first-person, refer to your notes and describe the experience and its effect on you. Use carefully chosen language to describe the feelings associated with it.

Revising   Reread your narrative, making sure you have included sensory descriptions to make your experience more vivid. End on a positive note, with pointers about working toward a dream.

Model: Elaborating to Add Emotional Depth

I know well the heartache of seeing your hard work treated as if it were worthless. I will never forget the day my own manuscript was rejected. I thought my whole world had ended. I could hardly speak for days.

> Sensory descriptions such as *heartache* and *I could hardly speak* add emotional depth.

 Prentice Hall Writing and Grammar Connection: Chapter 5, Section 2

❹ Extension Activities

Speaking and Listening Imagine that Theodora's neighbors throw a surprise party to celebrate her story. As Theodora, write a brief **speech** explaining to your neighbors what happened in Boston. Be sure to include the following details:

- The reason for going to Boston
- Your discussion with the publisher
- The lessons you learned from your ordeal

After rehearsing, deliver the speech to your class.

Research and Technology Research the ways in which publishing has expanded since Wharton's time. Modern publishing encompasses print media, such as newspapers, books, and magazines, as well as multimedia produced for CD-ROM and the Internet. Create a **flowchart** to highlight the new facets of publishing.

 Take It to the Net   www.phschool.com

Go online for an additional research activity using the Internet.

Lesson Support for p. 655

❸ Writing Lesson

- Students' personal narratives should convey in Dr. Dace's voice some of the thoughts and feelings he experienced at having had his own manuscript rejected for publication years ago.

- Use the Writing Lesson, as well as Writing Process Model 3, pp. 13–16, in **Writing Models and Graphic Organizers on Transparencies**, to guide students in developing their personal narratives.

- Use the rubric for Reflective Composition in **Performance Assessment and Portfolio Management**, p. 11, to evaluate students' personal narratives.

❹ Listening and Speaking

- Encourage students to reread for an explanation of why Theodora travels to Boston, precisely what is said in the publisher's offices, and what thoughts and feelings she has on the train and at the station in her father's company.

- Urge students to draft the speech so that it sounds "off the cuff." Explain that students may wish to use some fragments and other informal constructions to reflect the ad-libbed quality of the speech.

- Have students use the Peer Assessment form for Delivering a Speech, p. 30 in **Performance Assessment and Portfolio Management**.

CUSTOMIZE INSTRUCTION
For Universal Access

To address different learning styles, use the following activities suggested in the **Extension Activities** booklet, p. 35.

For Verbal/Linguistic Learners, use Activity 5.

For Bodily/Kinesthetic Learners, use Activity 6.

For Visual/Spatial Learners, use Activity 7.

ASSESSMENT RESOURCES

The following resources can be used to assess students' knowledge and skills.

Selection Assessment
- 📖 **Formal Assessment,** pp. 167–169
- 📖 **Open Book Test,** pp. 103–105
- 💽 **Got It! Assessment Videotapes,** Tape 3
- 💿 **Test Bank Software**

📟 *Take It to the Net*
Visit www.phschool.com for self-tests and additional questions on the selection.

Writing Rubric
- 📖 **Performance Assess. and Portfolio Mgmt.,** p. 11

Listening and Speaking Rubric
- 📖 **Performance Assess. and Portfolio Mgmt.,** p. 30

PRENTICE HALL
ASSESSMENT *SYSTEM*

- 📖 **Workbook**
- 📖 **Skill Book**
- ■ **Transparencies**
- 💿 **CD-ROM**

Douglass ✦ We Wear the Mask

Lesson Objectives

1. **To analyze and respond to literary elements**
   - Literary Analysis: Rhyme
   - Comparing Literary Works

2. **To read, comprehend, analyze, and critique poetry**
   - Reading Strategy: Interpreting
   - Reading Check questions
   - Review and Assess questions
   - Assessment Practice (ATE)

3. **To develop word analysis skills, fluency, and systematic vocabulary**
   - Vocabulary Development Lesson: Related Words: Forms of *guile*

4. **To understand and apply written and oral language conventions**
   - Spelling Strategy
   - Grammar and Style Lesson: Punctuation of Interjections

5. **To understand and apply appropriate writing and research strategies**
   - Writing Lesson: Poem to Honor a Hero
   - Extension Activity: Research Report

6. **To understand and apply listening and speaking strategies**
   - Extension Activity: Oral Interpretation

STEP-BY-STEP TEACHING GUIDE	PACING GUIDE
PRETEACH	
Motivate Students and Provide Background	
Use the Motivation activity (ATE p. 656)	5 min.
Read and discuss author and background features (SE/ATE pp. 656–657)	5 min.
Introduce the Concepts	
Introduce the Literary Analysis and Reading Strategy (SE/ATE p. 657)	15 min.
Pronounce the vocabulary words and read their definitions (SE p. 657)	5 min.
TEACH	
Monitor Comprehension	
Informally monitor comprehension by circulating while students read independently or in groups	20 min.
Monitor students' comprehension with the Reading Check notes (SE/ATE p. 657)	as students read
Develop vocabulary with Vocabulary notes (SE pp. 659, 660)	as students read
Develop Understanding	
Develop students' understanding of rhyme with the Literary Analysis annotations (SE p. 660; ATE p. 660)	5 min.
	5 min.
ASSESS	
Assess Mastery	
Assess students' mastery of the Reading Strategy and Literary Analysis by having them answer the Review and Assess questions (SE/ATE p. 661)	15 min.
Use one or more of the print and media Assessment Resources (ATE p. 663)	up to 45 min.
EXTEND	
Apply Understanding	
Have students complete the Vocabulary Development Lesson and the Grammar Lesson (SE p. 662)	20 min.
Apply students' ability to create a main impression by using the Writing Lesson (SE/ATE p. 663)	45 min.
Apply students' understanding using one or more of the Extension Activities (SE p. 663)	20–90 min.

 ACCELERATED INSTRUCTION:
Use the strategies and activities identified with an .

UNIVERSAL ACCESS
● = Below Level Students
▲ = On-Level Students
■ = Above Level Students

Time and Resource Manager

Reading Level: Average, Average
Average Number of Instructional Days: 3

RESOURCES		
PRINT 📖	**TRANSPARENCIES**	**TECHNOLOGY** 💿 🎧 📼
• **Beyond Literature,** Humanities Connection: Art, p. 36 ▲ ■		• **Interest Grabber Video,** Tape 4 ● ▲ ■
• **Selection Support Workbook:** ● ▲ ■ Literary Analysis, p. 163 Reading Strategy, p. 162 Build Vocabulary, p. 160	• **Literary Analysis and Reading Transparencies,** pp. 71 and 72 ● ▲ ■	
		• **Listening to Literature** ● ▲ ■ Audiocassettes, Side 23 Audio CDs, CD 13
• **Literatura en español** ● ▲ • **Literary Analysis for Enrichment** ■	• **Fine Art Transparencies, Volume 1,** Art Transparency 6 ● ▲ ■	
• **Formal Assessment:** Selection Test, pp. 170–172 ● ▲ ■ • **Open Book Test,** pp. 106–108 ● ▲ ■ • **Performance Assessment and Portfolio Management,** p. 23 ● ▲ ■ • **PRENTICE HALL ASSESSMENT SYSTEM** ● ▲ ■	• **PRENTICE HALL ASSESSMENT SYSTEM** ● ▲ ■ Skills Practice Answers and Explanations on Transparencies	• **Test Bank Software** ● ▲ ■ • **Got It! Assessment Videotapes,** Tape 3 ● ▲
• **Selection Support Workbook:** ● ▲ ■ Grammar and Style, p. 161 • **Writing and Grammar,** Ruby Level ● ▲ ■ • **Extension Activities,** p. 36 ● ▲ ■	• **Daily Language Practice Transparencies** ● ▲ • **Writing Models and Graphic Organizers on Transparencies,** pp. 67–69 ● ▲ ■	• **Writing and Grammar iText CD-ROM** ● ▲ ■ 💻 ***Take It to the Net*** www.phschool.com

BLOCK SCHEDULING: Use one 90-minute class period to preteach the selection and have students read it. Use a second 90-minute class period to assess students' mastery of skills and have them complete one of the Extension Activities.

PRETEACH

Step-by-Step Teaching Guide
for pp. 656–657

Motivation

Prepare students for reading and interpreting these poems by asking them to wear a mask to class. Students' masks might range from simple eye coverings to surgical face masks to homemade masks of paper or fabric. Have groups discuss what it is like for two or more people to communicate when wearing a mask. Guide students to notice that masks can fool, hide, frighten, or amuse, but seldom do they encourage honesty or frankness. Then have students remove the physical masks but assume mask-like facial expressions—joy, fear, boredom, and so on. How convincing can they be in maintaining the mask of an emotion when talking with friends? With strangers?

▣ Interest Grabber Video

As an alternative, play "Frederick Douglass" on Tape 4 to engage student interest.

❶ Background

More About the Author

Dunbar long idolized Frederick Douglass, and on one occasion the two men met. The young poet appeared with Douglass in Chicago at the 1893 World's Columbian Exposition, where he recited the poem "Colored Americans," which he had written for the occasion.

Writing at a time when prejudice against African Americans was mounting in both the northern and southern regions of the United States, Dunbar created poetry that disputed the unflattering image of his people found in magazines and newspapers. He gained national prominence as a poet by the turn of the century.

Prepare to Read

❶ Douglass ◆ We Wear the Mask

Paul Laurence Dunbar
(1872–1906)

Paul Laurence Dunbar was the first African American to attain national recognition and support himself entirely with his writing. Throughout his short career, he displayed great versatility in his literary work. Dunbar wrote poems in both a formal, elegant style and in regional dialect. He also wrote four novels and four volumes of short stories.

A Literary Child Dunbar was born in Dayton, Ohio, the son of former slaves. Encouraged by his mother, he began writing poetry at an early age. During high school, Dunbar, who was the only African American student in his class, frequently recited his poetry during school assemblies. He also served as president of the literary society, class poet, and editor of the school newspaper.

Dunbar Attains Recognition Following his graduation, Dunbar sought work in a legal office or a newspaper, but he found it difficult because of his race. He finally took a job as an elevator operator, earning four dollars a week and supporting himself while continuing to write. He first earned recognition among writers and critics in 1892, when he gave a poetry reading during a meeting of the Western Association of Writers. A year later, he took out a loan and published his first collection of poetry, *Oak and Ivy*. In 1895, he published a second collection, *Majors and Minors*, which was received with great enthusiasm by critics. In fact, William Dean Howells, the leading critic of the

day, was so impressed with the book that he wrote an introduction for Dunbar's next collection, *Lyrics of a Lowly Life* (1896). That book sold over twelve thousand copies and established Dunbar's reputation and audience.

Characters, Themes, and Forms Dunbar's fiction often focuses on daily life in the vanished world of the southern plantation. Sometimes, however, his writing revolves around social problems facing African Americans in Midwestern towns and urban ghettoes at the turn of the century. His characters include farmers, politicians, preachers, traders, entertainers, and professional people.

Popularity at a Price Dunbar composed poems in two styles—one formal and elegant, the other informal, using a rural dialect, which he called "jingles in a broken tongue." His gift for re-creating dialect and using it to create believable characters was profound. However, it also drew criticism. Called the "Poet Laureate of the Negro Race" by Booker T. Washington, Dunbar was criticized by other African Americans who believed that his dialect poems pandered to white readers' desire for sentimental stereotypes of prewar African Americans. In poems such as "Douglass" and "We Wear the Mask," however, Dunbar demonstrates a command of the English language that was often overlooked, capturing the struggles of African Americans in a dignified, graceful manner.

Despite his success as a poet, Dunbar was disillusioned by the critics' tendency to focus on the poetry he wrote in dialect, while virtually ignoring the poetry he wrote in more formal verse.

An Untimely Death By his late twenties, Dunbar was a nationally prominent poet. Unfortunately, his life was cut short by tuberculosis in 1906. By the end of his life, his poetry was so popular that he was able to write from Florida, "Down here one finds my poems recited everywhere."

656 ◆ *Division, Reconciliation, and Expansion (1850–1914)*

TEACHING RESOURCES

The following resources can be used to enrich or extend the instruction for pp. 656–657.

Motivation

▣ **Interest Grabber Video**, Tape 4 ▪

Background

📖 **Beyond Literature**, p. 36 ▪

💻 *Take It to the Net*
Visit www.phschool.com for Background and hotlinks for the selection.

Literary Analysis

📃 **Literary Analysis and Reading Transparencies**, Rhyme, p. 72

📖 **Selection Support**: Literary Analysis, p. 163

Reading

📃 **Literary Analysis and Reading Transparencies**, Interpreting, p. 71 ▪

▪ **BLOCK SCHEDULING:** Resources marked with this symbol provide varied instruction during 90-minute blocks.

Preview

Connecting to the Literature

The rules of courtesy often dictate that people smile even when they feel sad or disappointed. Paul Laurence Dunbar describes such a reaction in his poems as he explores the struggle for identity and truth.

❷ Literary Analysis

Rhyme

Rhyme, which along with rhythm gives poetry its musical quality, is the repetition of sounds in the accented syllables of two or more words appearing close together. Poets use rhyme in different ways:

- **True rhyme** occurs when the vowel sounds and any consonants appearing after them are exactly the same, as in *days* and *ways*.
- **Slant rhymes** link two similar (but not exact) vowel sounds, as in *prove* and *love*.
- **End rhymes** occur at the ends of two or more poetic lines.
- **Internal rhymes** appear within a single line.

As you read the following poems, take note of Dunbar's use of rhyme.

Comparing Literary Works

Each of the following poems addresses African American struggles for racial identity, but they express different emotions. While "Douglass" expresses indignation for the injustices suffered by African Americans, "We Wear the Mask" conveys a profound sorrow. As you read these two poems, compare Dunbar's varying attitudes and identify the emotions each one evokes in you.

❸ Reading Strategy

Interpreting

Poets often mean much more than the surface of their poems might initially convey. For example, to **interpret** "We Wear the Mask," consider who "we" refers to and the time and historical context in which the poem was written. Then, consider what the image of a mask suggests—what it reveals and what it hides. Use a chart like the one shown to help interpret and understand these poems.

Vocabulary Development

salient (sāl′ yənt) *adj.* standing out from the rest (p. 659)

tempest (tem′ pist) *n.* violent storm (p. 659)

stark (stärk) *adj.* stiff; rigid (p. 659)

guile (gīl) *n.* craftiness (p. 660)

myriad (mir′ ē əd) *adj.* countless (p. 660)

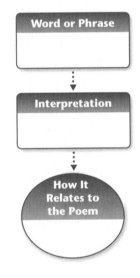

Word or Phrase

Interpretation

How It Relates to the Poem

Douglass / We Wear the Mask ◆ 657

---

❷ Literary Analysis

Rhyme

- Tell students that as they read the two poems in this grouping, they will focus on several variations of the sound device called rhyme.

- Read the instruction about rhyme aloud with students. Draw their attention to the four different ways in which poets use rhyme—two of which relate to the actual sounds of a rhyme, and two of which relate to where rhymes fall in a poetic line.

- Invite students as they read not only to enjoy the musical quality of rhyming words, but also to note how Dunbar uses sound repetitions differently in the two poems.

❸ Reading Strategy

Interpreting

- Point out that interpreting is the process of finding meaning in a literary work. Especially as it relates to poetry, interpreting usually involves reading between and beyond the lines to discover what the poet really means.

- As they read the following two poems, urge students to read each work once aloud before returning to the first line and starting to interpret Dunbar's meanings.

Vocabulary Development

- Pronounce each vocabulary word for students, and read the definitions as a class. Have students identify any words with which they are already familiar.

CUSTOMIZE INSTRUCTION FOR UNIVERSAL ACCESS

For Less Proficient Readers	For English Learners	For Advanced Readers
Have students follow along in their texts as they listen to the recordings of the poems on *Listening to Literature Audiocassettes* or *CDs*. Students will benefit from seeing—perhaps on the chalkboard—various obsolete word forms paired with their contemporary counterparts. For instance, *thou = you*, and *didst = did*.	In order to interpret Dunbar's work, students will need help understanding that the poet adjusts inflections ("heard thee with amaze"), reverses typical word order ("to thee from tortured souls arise"), and uses unfamiliar word forms ("dispraise"). Help students identify and understand usages like these in the poems.	In small groups, have students explain their interpretations of each poem and discuss how the two relate to one another. Students should address matters of form as well as content as they compare and contrast the poems.

 E-Teach

Visit E-Teach at www.phschool.com for teachers' essays on how to teach, with questions and answers.

Step-by-Step Teaching Guide
for pp. 658–660

CUSTOMIZE INSTRUCTION
For Interpersonal Learners

Invite students to imagine that they are the speaker of "We Wear the Mask." Have them write diary entries describing a day in the life of the speaker. Encourage students to focus on imaginary encounters in which they are required to "wear the mask."

❶ Background

Art

Frederick Douglass, artist unknown

This portrait of the abolitionist Frederick Douglass (1817–1895) appeared in the November 24, 1883, issue of *Harper's Weekly*.

Use this question for discussion:

> What qualities of Douglass does the artist capture in this portrait?
> **Answer:** Students might cite the powerful face, intense stare, and expression of determination.

❷ Critical Viewing

Answer: Douglass was an abolitionist who helped to bring about great change in the lives of African Americans.

❶

❷ ▲ **Critical Viewing** Why is a civil rights activist like Frederick Douglass an appropriate inspiration for Dunbar? **[Speculate]**

658 ◆ *Division, Reconciliation, and Expansion (1850–1914)*

TEACHING RESOURCES

The following resources can be used to enrich or extend the instruction for pp. 658–660

Reading Strategy

📖 **Selection Support:** Reading Strategy, p. 162; Build Vocabulary, p. 160

🎧 **Listening to Literature Audiocassettes,** Side 23 ▪

💿 **Listening to Literature Audio CDs,** CD 13 ▪

▪ **BLOCK SCHEDULING:** Resources marked with this symbol provide varied instruction during 90-minute blocks.

Douglass ❸

Paul Laurence Dunbar

❸ **About the Selections**
In both of the poems in this lesson, the writer addresses the struggles of African Americans. In "Douglass," the speaker cries out to a hero of an earlier age. In "We Wear the Mask," the speaker describes how African Americans hide their despair from the eyes of white America.

❹ ☑️**Reading Check**
Answer: The speaker says that the current time is harsher even than Douglass's time was.

Background

Paul Laurence Dunbar was among the last generation to have an ongoing contact with former African American slaves. As a child, Dunbar heard many stories from his father, who had escaped captivity and joined the Civil War cause. In these poems, Dunbar speaks of the social issues faced by those struggling to rebuild the country after the Civil War. He expresses the pain of racial injustice and conveys the ongoing struggles of African Americans to achieve equality.

Ah, Douglass,[1] we have fall'n on evil days,
    Such days as thou, not even thou didst know,
    When thee, the eyes of that harsh long ago
Saw, <u>salient</u>, at the cross of devious ways,
5 And all the country heard thee with amaze.
    Not ended then, the passionate ebb and flow.
    The awful tide that battled to and fro;
We ride amid a <u>tempest</u> of dispraise.

Now, when the waves of swift dissension swarm,
10   And Honor, the strong pilot, lieth[2] <u>stark</u>,
Oh, for thy voice high-sounding o'er the storm,
    For thy strong arm to guide the shivering bark,[3]
The blast-defying power of thy form,
    To give us comfort through the lonely dark.

---

1. **Douglass** Frederick Douglass, an American abolitionist (1818–1895).
2. **lieth** (lī′ eth) *v.* lies.
3. **bark** boat.

salient (sāl′ yənt) *adj.* standing out from the rest

tempest (tem′ pist) *n.* violent storm

stark (stärk) *adj.* stiff; rigid

☑️**Reading Check** ❹
What does the speaker say is the difference between the current time and the time in which Douglass lived?

Douglass ◆ 659

CUSTOMIZE INSTRUCTION FOR UNIVERSAL ACCESS

For Special Needs Students

Give students who are having difficulty interpreting "We Wear the Mask" some strategies for reading between the lines to determine the poet's meaning. Point out the words *we* and *mask* in the title.

    Tell students to ask themselves three questions as they read: What's the purpose of the mask? What is the mask hiding? Who is the "we" the speaker mentions? Draw the following chart on the chalkboard to get students started. Have students fill in more information as they read the poem.

We	Mask's Purpose	What Mask Hides
African Americans wearing masks	lies hides	torn hearts tears and sighs tortured souls

❺ Literary Analysis

Rhyme

- Have students identify the rhyme scheme in this poem, in which most lines are either true or slant rhymes. If necessary, help students see that the rhyme scheme is *aabba, aabc, aabbac.*

- Ask students the Literary Analysis question on p. 660: What is the effect of the lack of rhyme in lines 9 and 15, where the poet repeats the title?

  Answer: Students may observe that these lines stand out. Perhaps Dunbar isolated the lines to reflect the speaker's feelings of isolation from his surroundings.

Answers for p. 660

Review and Assess

1. Students may say that they feel awkward or angry.

2. **(a)** Dunbar refers to the abolitionist Frederick Douglass. **(b)** He thinks that Douglass could help African Americans out of their current difficulties.

3. **(a)** It was heard "long ago" in a harsher time. **(b)** According to the speaker, the present day needs Douglass's singleness of purpose to counter criticism and dissent.

4. **(a)** Dunbar speaks for African Americans. **(b)** They struggle against prejudice and injustice. **(c)** Students might say that "the lonely dark" refers to a time of injustice and unenlightenment about racial issues.

5. **(a)** The mask hides pain and torment. **(b)** The speaker implies that showing the world their "tears and sighs" would weaken African Americans' position in society.

6. **(a)** Students might say that Dunbar would like to see greater honesty and equality in the world. **(b)** Sample response: Students may differ over whether relations between African Americans and other races have improved greatly.

660

---

❸ We Wear the Mask

Paul Laurence Dunbar

We wear the mask that grins and lies,
It hides our cheeks and shades our eyes—
This debt we pay to human <u>guile</u>;
With torn and bleeding hearts we smile,
5   And mouth with <u>myriad</u> subtleties.

Why should the world be overwise,
In counting all our tears and sighs?
Nay, let them only see us, while
    We wear the mask.

10   We smile, but, O great Christ, our cries
To thee from tortured souls arise.
We sing, but oh the clay is vile
Beneath our feet, and long the mile;
But let the world dream otherwise,
15   We wear the mask!

guile (gīl) *n.* craftiness

myriad (mir′ ē əd) *adj.* countless

Literary Analysis
Rhyme What is the effect of the lack of rhyme in lines 9 and 15, where the poet repeats the title?

Review and Assess

Thinking About the Selections

1. **Respond:** How do you feel when you must appear or behave as others expect?

2. **(a) Recall:** Who is the Douglass to whom Dunbar refers? **(b) Draw Conclusions:** Why do you think the speaker addresses Douglass?

3. **(a) Infer:** When was Douglass's voice heard by the nation? **(b) Compare:** How does Douglass's message relate to what the speaker of "Douglass" describes?

4. **(a) Infer:** Who is the "we" in this poem? **(b) Analyze:** What struggles do they face? **(c) Interpret:** What is the "lonely dark"?

5. **(a) Recall:** In "We Wear the Mask," what emotions does the mask hide? **(b) Draw Conclusions:** Why do you think they wear the mask?

6. **(a) Extend:** How might Dunbar like to see the world change? **(b) Apply:** If Dunbar were alive today, do you think he would still have the views he expresses in this poem? Why or why not?

ASSESSMENT PRACTICE: Reading Comprehension

Context
(For more practice, see Test Preparation Workbook, p. 38.)

Some tests require students to use context to determine the meanings of unfamiliar words. Write the following passage from p. 659 on the chalkboard. Then have students answer the question that follows.

> We ride amid a <u>tempest</u> of dispraise,/Now, when the waves of swift dissension swarm,/And Honor, the strong pilot, lieth stark,/Oh, for thy voice high-sounding o'er the storm

In this passage, <u>tempest</u> means—

A storm
B sinking boat
C discussion
D voice

The first part of the passage says the speaker rides amid a tempest. *Amid*, in combination with the references to waves and a storm, should provide the context that helps students choose *A* as the correct answer.

Review and Assess

Literary Analysis

Rhyme

1. List all the words in "We Wear the Mask" that are **true rhymes** with the word *lies*.
2. What **slant rhyme** does Dunbar use in this poem?
3. The **rhyme scheme,** or pattern, in the first stanza of "Douglass" can be expressed as *abbaabba*. (The letter *a* stands for words rhyming with *days* and the letter *b* stands for words rhyming with *know*.) What is the rhyme scheme for the second stanza?
4. In your opinion, what is the effect of rhyme in these poems?

Comparing Literary Works

5. (a) Note three emotions Dunbar addresses in "Douglass."
   (b) Note three emotions he expresses in "We Wear the Mask."
   (c) In what ways is the emotional content of these poems similar?
   (d) In what ways is it different?
6. (a) In what ways are the tones or attitudes of these poems similar?
   (b) In what ways do they differ?
7. Which poem do you think is more personal—related most directly to Dunbar's daily experience? Explain.

Reading Strategy

Interpreting

8. What situation might Dunbar's speaker be describing for African Americans in general in "We Wear the Mask"?
9. Poets use symbolic language—words and images that represent larger ideas. In a chart like the one shown, list and **interpret** the symbolic language you find in both poems.

	Symbolic Language	Interpretation
"Douglass"		
"We Wear the Mask"		

Extend Understanding

10. **Social Studies Connection:** How might Dunbar have characterized the situation of African Americans in the past decade? Explain.

Douglass / We Wear the Mask ◆ 661

⁂ ENRICHMENT: Further Reading

Other Works by Paul Laurence Dunbar

Oak and Ivy

Majors and Minors

Lyrics of Lowly Life

🖥 Take It to the Net
Visit www.phschool.com for more information on Paul Laurence Dunbar.

Quick Review

Rhyme occurs when two or more words have similar or identical vowel and final consonant sounds in their accented syllables.

To **interpret** a poem, consider the poet's word choice, symbolism, and historical context to discover the poet's deeper meaning.

 Take It to the Net
www.phschool.com
Take the interactive self-test online to check your understanding of these selections.

Answers

Review and Assess

1. *eyes, overwise, sighs, cries, arise, otherwise*
2. *lies/subtleties*
3. The rhyme scheme is *cdcdcd*.
4. Students may say that rhyme makes the poems more musical, coherent, and engaging.
5. **(a)** Students may mention emotions such as amazement and loneliness, as well as characteristics such as leadership, honor, strength, and power. **(b)** Students might use words such as desperate, miserable, valiant, sad, and angry in their responses.
   (c) In both poems, the speakers convey an attitude of determination and inner strength in the face of terrible conflict.
   (d) The speaker of "We Wear the Mask" is resolute and defiant, whereas the speaker of "Douglass" seems more vulnerable.
6. **(a)** Both poems address the pain and frustration of living in a bigoted society. **(b)** "We Wear the Mask" conveys anger, while "Douglass" addresses the situation in more measured tones.
7. Students should support their answers.
8. Sample response: He might be describing the situation of emancipated African Americans who are trying to overcome the crippling effects of their former slavery.
9. "Douglass"—*that harsh long ago* and *the cross of devious ways* (the era of slavery), *passionate ebb and flow, awful tide, tempest of dispraise, waves of swift dissension, storm, lonely dark* (stormy race relations), *pilot* (Douglass, a leader of the African American cause), *shivering bark* (the effort to gain true freedom for African Americans); "Mask" —*mask* (behavior that conceals true feelings), *debt* (the consequence for hiding truth), *torn and bleeding hearts* (hopelessness, despair), *tears and sighs* (sorrow, exhaustion), *clay* (living conditions for African Americans), *mile* (the effort to gain true freedom for African Americans)

continued

Answers continued

10. Possible response: He would see great improvements but also see the continuing need for true equality.

❶ Vocabulary Development

Word Analysis

1. guileful (*adj.*)
2. guilefully (*adv.*)
3. guilefulness (*n.*)
4. guileless (*adj.*)
5. guilelessly (*adv.*)
6. guilelessness (*n.*)

Concept Development:

1. e
2. a
3. d
4. c
5. b

Spelling Strategy

1. pyre
2. type
3. myriad

❷ Grammar and Style

1. Hey! We need you to guide us!
2. Ah, we long to be comforted by your wisdom!
3. No, I'm afraid I can't reveal my authentic feelings.
4. Oh! Is that what you think?
5. Yes, one must remain as strong as possible in the face of a great challenge.

Writing Application

Students' paragraphs should focus on a topic with special meaning for them and should contain three correctly-used interjections.

---

❶ Integrate Language Skills

Vocabulary Development Lesson

Word Analysis: Forms of *guile*

The word *guile* is a noun meaning "craftiness." By adding prefixes or suffixes to *guile*, you can form related words such as the adjective *guileless* ("innocent" or "naïve") and the verb *beguile* ("mislead" or "trick").

Combine *guile* with the suffixes below to create six words. Label each word's part of speech.

1. *-ful*
2. *-fully*
3. *-fulness*
4. *-less*
5. *-lessly*
6. *-lessness*

❷ Grammar and Style Lesson

Punctuation of Interjections

An **interjection,** a word used to express emotion, has no grammatical relation to other words in a sentence. An interjection can express a variety of sentiments, such as happiness, fear, anger, pain, surprise, sorrow, exhaustion, or hesitation. Use a comma to punctuate an interjection that expresses mild emotion. Use an exclamation point to punctuate an interjection that expresses strong emotion. Consider the following examples:

Mild Emotion: *Ah,* Douglass, we have fall'n on evil days, . . .

Strong Emotion: *Oh!* If you could only help!

Concept Development: Antonyms

An antonym is a word meaning the opposite of another. Match each word in the left column with its antonym in the right column.

1. guile   a. tranquility; stillness
2. tempest   b. not many
3. salient   c. elastic; flexible
4. stark   d. inconspicuous
5. myriad   e. honesty

Spelling Strategy

There is no spelling rule governing the use of y as a vowel; you will need to memorize the spelling of such words. For each of these pairs of words, choose the correct spelling.

1. pyre/pire   2. tipe/type   3. myriad/miriad

Practice Add a comma or an exclamation point to correct the punctuation of the interjections in each of the following sentences. Capitalize the resulting sentences as necessary.

1. Hey we need you to guide us!
2. Ah we long to be comforted by your wisdom!
3. No I'm afraid I can't reveal my authentic feelings.
4. Oh is that what you think?
5. Yes one must remain as strong as possible in the face of a great challenge.

Writing Application Write a paragraph on a topic that has special meaning for you. Use at least three examples of interjections.

WG *Prentice Hall Writing and Grammar Connection: Chapter 17, Section 4*

662 ◆ *Division, Reconciliation, and Expansion (1850–1914)*

TEACHING RESOURCES

The following resources can be used to enrich or extend the instruction for pp. 662–663.

Vocabulary

📖 **Selection Support:** Build Vocabulary, p. 160

📖 **Vocabulary and Spelling Practice Book** (Use this booklet for skills enrichment) ■

Grammar

📖 **Selection Support: Workbook** Grammar and Style, p. 161 ■

WG **Writing and Grammar,** Ruby Level, p. 394 ■

📖 **Daily Language Practice Transparencies**

Writing

WG **Writing and Grammar,** Ruby Level, p. 129 ■

📖 **Extension Activities**

📖 **Writing Models and Graphic Organizers on Transparencies,** pp. 67–69

WG **Writing and Grammar, iText CD-ROM** ■

■ **BLOCK SCHEDULING:** Resources marked with this symbol provide varied instruction during 90-minute blocks.

❸ Writing Lesson

Poem to Honor a Hero

Think of another historical figure who, if alive today, might help inspire people to solve some of society's problems. Compose a poem in which you address this hero as Dunbar addresses Douglass.

Prewriting   First, list the accomplishments and character traits that contribute to your subject's heroism. Then, brainstorm for sensory details and descriptions of behavior that illustrate this person's ability to tackle challenging aspects of today's world.

Drafting   Choose a form for your poem, such as a regular rhythm and rhyme scheme or free verse. Use images and sound devices that convey a vivid main impression of your subject.

Model: Creating a Main Impression

Oh, Martin Luther King, like an oak in a storm,

Your life was not in vain.

Through all the blustering wind and rain,

Your strength was our gain.

> The images comparing the subject to an oak convey the sense of the subject as a powerful figure.

Revising   Reread your poem. Consider adding or eliminating details to sharpen the main impression of your subject. If necessary, use images and descriptive language to convey your ideas more effectively.

W̧G Prentice Hall Writing and Grammar Connection: Chapter 7, Section 3

Extension Activities

Listening and Speaking Prepare an **oral interpretation** of one of the two Dunbar poems. Begin by analyzing the meaning and form of each line. The following tips will help you:

- Look for interjections and imagery that emphasize tone and cadence.
- Read the poem aloud several times to evoke emotion.

Present your oral interpretation to the class, inviting classmates to comment.

Research and Technology Dunbar's work received mixed reviews from critics. Using library and Internet resources, conduct research to find examples of both positive and negative responses. In a **report,** summarize your findings and then take a position about Dunbar's legacy as a poet.

 Take It to the Net   www.phschool.com

Go online for an additional research activity using the Internet.

ASSESSMENT RESOURCES

The following resources can be used to assess students' knowledge and skills

Selection Assessment

- 📝 **Formal Assessment,** pp. 170–172
- 📝 **Open Book Test,** pp. 106–108
- 📼 **Got It! Assessment Videotapes,** Tape 4
- 💿 **Test Bank Software**

🖥 **Take It to the Net**

Visit www.phschool.com for self-tests and additional questions on the selection.

Listening and Speaking Rubric

- 📖 **Performance Assess. and Portfolio Mgmt.,** p. 23

PRENTICE HALL ASSESSMENT SYSTEM

- 📖 **Workbook**
- 📖 **Skill Book**
- 🖨 **Transparencies**
- 💿 **CD-ROM**

Lesson Support for p. 663

❸ Writing Lesson

- Students' poems to honor a hero should convey a vivid main impression of their subjects, as well as containing effective imagery and sound devices.

- Point out to students that the choice of subject matter is crucial to their poems' success. Moreover, they must make every effort to link particular hereos with specific societal problems in a way that makes sense.

- Encourage them to spend time in groups brainstorming for lists of accomplishments and character traits of their chosen heroes.

- Use the Branching Organizer in **Writing Models and Graphic Organizers on Transparencies,** pp. 67–69, to help students in listing details for their poems.

❹ Listening and Speaking

- Encourage students to paraphrase every line (in its entirety) for a listener as part of the preparation process. Any line that they cannot paraphrase—or that the listener fails to comprehend—indicates a passage that needs further study.

- Point out the effectiveness of a natural speaking style and urge students to avoid a stagy, presentational delivery. You might suggest that students choose a single (unnamed, and not necessarily present) person to whom they will imagine they are addressing their poems. This device can help foster true, specific expressions of ideas.

- Have students use the Peer Assessment form for Response to Literature, p. 23 in **Performance Assessment and Portfolio Management**.

CUSTOMIZE INSTRUCTION
For Universal Access

To address different learning styles, use the following activities suggested in the **Extension Activities** booklet, p. 36.

For Visual/Spatial Learners, use Activity 5.

For Verbal/Linguistic Learners, use Activity 6.

For Bodily/Kinesthetic Learners, use Activity 7.

Luke Havergal ✦ Richard Cory ✦ Lucinda Matlock ✦ Richard Bone

Lesson Objectives

1. **To analyze and respond to literary elements**
   - Literary Analysis: Speaker
   - Comparing Literary Works
2. **To read, comprehend, analyze, and critique poetry**
   - Reading Strategy: Recognizing Attitudes
   - Reading Check questions
   - Review and Assess questions
   - Assessment Practice (ATE)
3. **To develop word analysis skills, fluency, and systematic vocabulary**
   - Vocabulary Development Lesson: Words Analysis: Latin Root: *-pose-*
4. **To understand and apply written and oral language conventions**
   - Spelling Strategy
   - Grammar and Style Lesson: Noun Clauses
5. **To understand and apply appropriate writing and research strategies**
   - Writing Lesson: Firsthand Biography
   - Extension Activity: Illustrated Booklet
6. **To understand and apply listening and speaking strategies**
   - Extension Activity: Class Discussion

STEP-BY-STEP TEACHING GUIDE	PACING GUIDE
PRETEACH	
Motivate Students and Provide Background	
Use the Motivation activity (ATE p. 664)	5 min.
Read and discuss author and background features (SE/ATE pp. 664, 667) **A**	5 min.
Introduce the Concepts	
Introduce the Literary Analysis and Reading Strategy (SE/ATE p. 665) **A**	15 min.
Pronounce the vocabulary words and read their definitions (SE p. 665)	5 min.
TEACH	
Monitor Comprehension	
Informally monitor comprehension by circulating while students read independently or in groups **A**	25 min.
Monitor students' comprehension with the Reading Check notes (SE/ATE p. 667)	as students read
Develop vocabulary with Vocabulary notes (SE pp. 668, 669, 670)	as students read
Develop Understanding	
Develop students' understanding of the poem's speaker with the Literary Analysis annotations (SE p. 667; ATE pp. 667) **A**	5 min.
Develop students' ability to recognize attitudes with the Reading Strategy annotations	5 min.
ASSESS	
Assess Mastery	
Assess students' mastery of the Reading Strategy and Literary Analysis by having them answer the Review and Assess questions (SE/ATE p. 671)	15 min.
Use one or more of the print and media Assessment Resources (ATE p. 673) **A**	up to 45 min.
EXTEND	
Apply Understanding	
Have students complete the Vocabulary Development Lesson and the Grammar and Style Lesson (SE p. 672) **A**	20 min.
Apply students' ability to use transitions to show order of importance by using the Writing Lesson (SE/ATE p. 673) **A**	45 min.
Apply students' understanding using one or more of the Extension Activities (SE p. 673)	20–90 min.

 ACCELERATED INSTRUCTION:
Use the strategies and activities identified with an **A**.

UNIVERSAL ACCESS
- ● = Below Level Students
- ▲ = On-Level Students
- ■ = Above Level Students

Time and Resource Manager

Reading Level: Average, Average, Average, Average
Average Number of Instructional Days: 4

RESOURCES		
PRINT 📖	**TRANSPARENCIES** 🗋	**TECHNOLOGY** 💿 🎧 📼
• **Beyond Literature,** Humanities Connection: Dance, p. 37 ▲ ■		• **Interest Grabber Video,** Tape 4 ● ▲ ■
• **Selection Support Workbook:** ● ▲ ■ Literary Analysis, p. 167 Reading Strategy, p. 166 Build Vocabulary, p. 167	• **Literary Analysis and Reading Transparencies,** pp. 73 and 74 ● ▲ ■	
		• **Listening to Literature** ● ▲ ■ Audiocassettes, Side 23 Audio CDs, CD 13
• **Literatura en español** ● ▲ • **Literary Analysis for Enrichment** ■		
• **Formal Assessment:** Selection Test, pp. 173–175 ● ▲ ■ • **Open Book Test,** pp. 109–111 ● ▲ ■ • **Performance Assessment and Portfolio Management,** p. 16 ● ▲ ■ • **PRENTICE HALL ASSESSMENT SYSTEM** ● ▲ ■	• **PRENTICE HALL ASSESSMENT SYSTEM** ● ▲ ■ Skills Practice Answers and Explanations on Transparencies	• **Test Bank Software** ● ▲ ■ • **Got It! Assessment Videotapes,** Tape 3 ● ▲
• **Selection Support Workbook:** ● ▲ ■ Grammar and Style, p. 165 • **Writing and Grammar,** Ruby Level ● ▲ ■ • **Extension Activities,** p. 37 ● ▲ ■	• **Daily Language Practice Transparencies** ● ▲ • **Writing Models and Graphic Organizers on Transparencies,** pp. 9–12 ● ▲ ■	• **Writing and Grammar iText CD-ROM** ● ▲ ■ 💻 **Take It to the Net** www.phschool.com

BLOCK SCHEDULING: Use one 90-minute class period to preteach the selection and have students read it. Use a second 90-minute class period to assess students' mastery of skills and have them complete one of the Extension Activities.

Step-by-Step Teaching Guide for pp. 664–665

Motivation

Bring in several obituary notices from newspapers or news magazines. (You might duplicate them for students, or you might prefer to read them aloud.) Alternately, have students visit a local cemetery to see the kinds of messages inscribed on gravestones there. Then, challenge students to write their own obituary notice or gravestone epitaph in the style of the ones they have read or seen. Allow ten to fifteen minutes for this task, and then invite volunteers to share the obituaries or epitaphs. Finally, tell students that all four poems in this grouping concern people who have died, though the texts are neither typical obituaries nor epitaphs.

▦ Interest Grabber Video

As an alternative, play "Reading and Student Response" on Tape 4 to engage student interest.

❶ Background

More About the Authors

Among the later works of Edwin Arlington Robinson are several long, blank-verse narrative poems—such as *Merlin* (1917), *Lancelot* (1920), and *Tristram* (1927)—based on the King Arthur legends.

In commenting on Edgar Lee Masters's *Spoon River Anthology*, poet May Swenson wrote that Masters gave "outlet to all his grudges, beliefs, indignations, insights, prophesies, discoveries of glaring injustice, revelations of life's mysteries and paradoxes—and his own eccentric philosophy. Miraculously he also created . . . a world in microcosm, new in form, timeless in space."

Prepare to Read

❶ Luke Havergal ◆ Richard Cory ◆ Lucinda Matlock ◆ Richard Bone

Edwin Arlington Robinson (1869–1935)

In his mid-thirties, Edwin Arlington Robinson earned twenty cents per hour as a New York City subway inspector. Yet, friends helped him arrange the private printing of three books of his poetry during these lean times, allowing Robinson to become the most successful American poet of the 1920s.

Robinson grew up in Gardiner, Maine, a small town that was the model for Tilbury Town, the fictional setting of many of his poems. He attended college for two years, but he was forced to return to Gardiner after his father's death. Upon his return, Robinson began writing poetry, depending on friends and patrons for financial support. Four years later, he returned to New York City, hoping to improve his financial situation. When President Theodore Roosevelt appointed him to a post at the New York Customhouse, Robinson was set free from his financial worries.

The Inner Struggle Robinson continued to write poems and established his poetic voice. His best poems focus on people's inner struggles. They paint portraits of desperate characters who view their lives as trivial and meaningless or who long to live in another place or time. Despite his characters' pessimistic outlook, Robinson's poems possess a certain dignity that results from his traditional style, command of language, and imagination and wit.

Robinson found success when his fourth volume of verse, *The Town Down the River* (1910), sold well and received much critical acclaim. He went on to publish many acclaimed books and receive three Pulitzer Prizes.

Edgar Lee Masters (1868–1950)

For years, Edgar Lee Masters practiced criminal law by day in a successful Chicago firm and wrote poems, plays, and essays by night. In 1914, however, Masters' direction as a writer changed dramatically when a friend gave him a copy of *Selected Epitaphs from the Greek Anthology*. This collection included many concise, interconnected epitaphs that captured the essence of people's personal lives.

Spoon River Anthology Using the structure suggested by that anthology, and abandoning conventional rhyme and meter, Masters wrote a series of poems about the lives of people in rural southern Illinois. Published as *Spoon River Anthology* in 1915, the book provoked strong reactions among critics and became a bestseller. The volume was so successful that Masters quit his law career and moved to New York to earn a living as a writer.

The anthology consists of 244 epitaphs for characters buried in the mythical Spoon River cemetery. The dead themselves serve as the speakers of the poems, often revealing secrets they kept hidden during their lifetimes. Many types of people are represented, including storekeepers, housewives, and murderers. Some had happy lives, but many more had lives filled with frustration and despair. Presented together, the epitaphs paint a vivid portrait of the loneliness and isolation confronting people in small Midwestern towns around the turn of the century.

Masters went on to produce other volumes of poetry, novels, biographies, and his autobiography, *Across Spoon River*. However, he is still remembered almost exclusively for *Spoon River Anthology*.

TEACHING RESOURCES

The following resources can be used to enrich or extend the instruction for pp. 664–665.

Motivation

▦ **Interest Grabber Video**, Tape 4 ▪

Background

📖 **Beyond Literature**, p. 37

💻 *Take It to the Net*
Visit www.phschool.com for Background and hotlinks for the selections.

Literary Analysis

◪ **Literary Analysis and Reading Transparencies**, Speaker, p. 74

📖 **Selection Support**: Literary Analysis, p. 167

Reading

◪ **Literary Analysis and Reading Transparencies**, Recognizing Attitudes, p. 73 ▪

▪ **BLOCK SCHEDULING:** Resources marked with this symbol provide varied instruction during 90-minute blocks.

Preview

Connecting to the Literature

Have you ever wondered how you will be remembered a century from now? The following poems create a memorable impression of four characters from small-town America one hundred years ago. Compare them with the impression you would like to leave behind.

❷ Literary Analysis

Speaker

The **speaker** is the voice of a poem. Although the speaker is often the poet, it can also be a fictional character or a non-human entity. For example, the speakers of the poems in Masters' *Spoon River Anthology* are characters buried in a cemetery in the fictional town of Spoon River, as these lines from "Lucinda Matlock" demonstrate:

> At ninety-six I had lived enough, that is all,
> And passed to a sweet repose.

Instead of using a neutral speaker, Masters allows characters to speak candidly for themselves. In this way, the poet can delve deeply into the minds and hearts of Spoon River's former citizens.

Comparing Literary Works

All of these poems share the common themes of life and death. The speakers—some of whose voices come from the grave—examine the quality of the lives they have lived. Lucinda Matlock, whose life was long and satisfying, says "It takes life to love Life." By contrast, Richard Cory appears to have lived with terrible secrets. As you read these poems, compare the speakers and the message each expresses about how we spend our days.

❸ Reading Strategy

Recognizing Attitudes

The **attitudes** and beliefs of a poem's speaker color the depiction of the characters, settings, and events. As you read a poem, determine who the speaker is, and look for clues to the speaker's attitudes or outlook on life. For example, in "Lucinda Matlock," the speaker believes that the younger generation is not as tough and hard-working as her generation was. Use a chart like the one shown to help you recognize the speaker's attitudes in these poems.

Speaker's Attitude	Evidence

Vocabulary Development

imperially (im pir´ ē əl ē) *adv.* majestically (p. 668)

repose (ri pōz´) *n.* state of being at rest (p. 669)

degenerate (dē jen´ ər it) *adj.* morally corrupt (p. 669)

epitaph (ep´ ə taf´) *n.* inscription on a tombstone or grave marker (p. 670)

Luke Havergal / Richard Cory / Lucinda Matlock / Richard Bone ◆ 665

---

❷ Literary Analysis

Speaker

- Tell students that as they read the four poems in this grouping, they will focus on each poem's speaker.

- Read the instruction about speaker together as a class. Explain that the speaker can take the form of a character, or it can take a more "neutral" form as the poet him- or herself.

- Invite students as they read to think about the identity of the speaker, and to reflect on how the speaker's sensibility affects the poem's look, sound, and meaning.

❸ Reading Strategy

Recognizing Attitudes

- Point out that identifying a poem's speaker and recognizing how his or her attitudes and beliefs affect the details of the poem is akin to analyzing the point of view of a prose story.

- Explain to students that recognizing a speaker's attitudes involves analyzing how the poet uses language to express the thoughts, feelings, and behavior of the speaker. Of course, sometimes readers may need to look *between* the lines to recognize attitudes that are implied but not stated directly.

Vocabulary Development

- Pronounce each vocabulary word for students, and read the definitions as a class. Have students identify any words with which they are already familiar.

CUSTOMIZE INSTRUCTION FOR UNIVERSAL ACCESS

For Less Proficient Readers	For English Learners	For Advanced Readers
Students may have difficulty understanding the distinction between a poet and a speaker. Focus on the concept of "poet"—a person whose literary expression takes the form of verse. Then, explain that sometimes a poet creates a character to tell the "story" of a poem; this character is called the speaker.	Draw students' attention to the four names that comprise the titles of the poems in this lesson. Explain that Havergal and Cory are characters in (but not the speakers of) those poems. On the other hand, Matlock and Bone are the speakers of their poems.	Masters wrote all of the poems in *Spoon River Anthology* in free verse. Encourage these students to read additional poems from that volume and to think about how Masters's choice of speakers for these poems might have influenced his decision to write in free verse.

 E-Teach

Visit E-Teach at www.phschool.com for teachers' essays on how to teach, with questions and answers.

Step-by-Step Teaching Guide for pp. 666–670

CUSTOMIZE INSTRUCTION
For Verbal/Linguistic Learners

Students may notice repetition in the last two lines of each stanza of "Luke Havergal"—as well as in the western gate image that is introduced in the first stanza and echoed in the last. Have students discuss the soothing and hypnotic effects of repetition in this poem.

❶ About the Selections

These two poems by Robinson address the pain of loss. Luke Havergal grieves for his beloved and questions whether he can go on living. The speaker seems to suggest that Havergal can commune with her spirit until it is his rightful time to die and his beloved meet again in the next life. In contrast, "Richard Cory" reveals a whole town in shock and grief. Because ordinary townsfolk idealized the life of a wealthy, elegant man, they are unprepared for his sudden suicide.

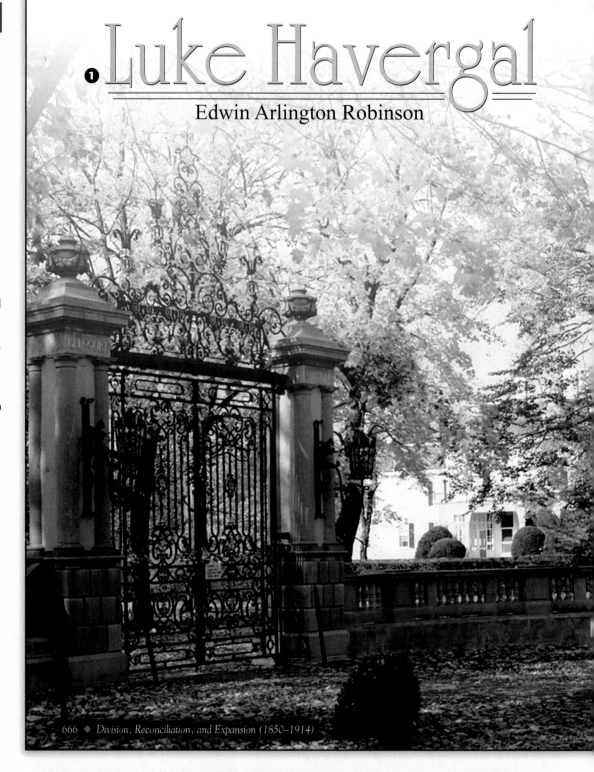

❶ Luke Havergal
Edwin Arlington Robinson

666 ◆ Division, Reconciliation, and Expansion (1850–1914)

TEACHING RESOURCES

The following resources can be used to enrich or extend the instruction for pp. 666–670.

Reading Strategy

📖 **Selection Support:** Reading Strategy, p. 166; Build Vocabulary, p. 164

🎧 **Listening to Literature Audiocassettes,** Side 23 ■

💿 **Listening to Literature Audio CDs,** CD 13 ■

■ **BLOCK SCHEDULING:** Resources marked with this symbol provide varied instruction during 90-minute blocks.

Background

Two years into Edwin Arlington Robinson's college career at Harvard, he was forced to leave school to support his family, which had suffered devastating financial losses. Both of Robinson's brothers died young after lives marred by failure. Robinson himself endured years of poverty. When success finally arrived it was abundant, but the years of struggle had shaped Robinson's worldview. He filled his poems with the voices of the lost and the sorrowful, exploring the themes of personal defeat and unfulfilled longing. Luke Havergal, who suffers the loss of a loved one, and Richard Cory, who suffers with hidden pain, are typical of his work.

Go to the western gate, Luke Havergal,
There where the vines cling crimson on the wall,
And in the twilight wait for what will come.
The leaves will whisper there of her, and some,
5 Like flying words, will strike you as they fall;
But go, and if you listen she will call.
Go to the western gate, Luke Havergal—
Luke Havergal.

No, there is not a dawn in eastern skies
10 To rift the fiery night that's in your eyes;
But there, where western glooms are gathering,
The dark will end the dark, if anything:
God slays Himself with every leaf that flies,
And hell is more than half of paradise.
15 No, there is not a dawn in eastern skies—
In eastern skies.

❷ Out of a grave I come to tell you this,
Out of a grave I come to quench the kiss
That flames upon your forehead with a glow
20 That blinds you to the way that you must go.
Yes, there is yet one way to where she is,
Bitter, but one that faith may never miss.
Out of a grave I come to tell you this—
To tell you this.

25 There is the western gate, Luke Havergal,
There are the crimson leaves upon the wall.
Go, for the winds are tearing them away,—
Nor think to riddle the dead words they say,
Nor any more to feel them as they fall;
30 But go, and if you trust her she will call.
There is the western gate, Luke Havergal—
Luke Havergal.

Literary Analysis
Speaker Who is the "I" who speaks in this poem?

❸ **Reading Check**
What will happen at the Western gate if Luke Havergal goes there?

Luke Havergal ◆ 667

---

❷ Literary Analysis
Speaker

- Have a student volunteer read the poem aloud clearly and slowly. Ask students to offer comments about their overall impressions of the setting, characters, and sound devices of the poem.
- Then, ask students the Literary Analysis question on p. 667: Who is the speaker in this poem? **Answer:** Students might suggest that the speaker is a supreme being, the spirit of Havergal's lost love, or part of Havergal's inner self.

❸ ✓ Reading Check
Answer: Luke Havergal will hear his love calling.

CUSTOMIZE INSTRUCTION FOR UNIVERSAL ACCESS

For Special Needs Students	For Less Proficient Readers
Help these students recognize and interpret key symbols in these poems. For instance, in "Luke Havergal," the western gate can represent not only an actual cemetery gate, but also (because it is where the sun descends) death itself.	It may help students to paraphrase some lines to uncover Robinson's meaning. For instance, students might paraphrase lines 9 and 10 as "This is not just a bad dream that you can wake up from."

❹

❹ Background

Art

***The Thinker* (Portrait of Louis N. Kenton),** 1900, by Thomas Eakins

Thomas Eakins (1844–1916) was an American portrait and genre painter from Philadelphia. He studied art in Paris and at the Pennsylvania Academy of Fine Arts, where he later became the director. He also studied anatomy. Eakins grew interested in using photography to record human and animal locomotion. Some of his photographic studies served as a basis for paintings that show a penetrating knowledge of the structure and motion of the human body. His later work reveals deep psychological insights, especially in representing contemplative moods. *The Thinker* is a fine example of Eakins's presentation of a state of mind. The intense and haunting image of a man embodies sadness, frustration, and resignation.

Use the following questions for discussion:

1. What might the man in the portrait be thinking?
Answer: Responses should reflect the serious and somber expression on the man's face.

2. How does the artist's use of color affect the message of the portrait?
Answer: Students may say that the black suit and the brown walls suggest depression, dark thoughts, and a lack of hope.

❺ ▶ Critical Viewing

Answer: Students may say that the demeanor of the man, his fine clothes, and the quiet, sober expression on his face suggest Richard Cory more than they do the envious speaker.

Answers for p. 668

Review and Assess

1. Students should support their responses with clear reasons and examples.

2. (a) He should go there if he wishes to hear his beloved calling. (b) The gate symbolizes death.

3. (a) He has come from "out of a grave." (b) Possible response: The message urges Luke Havergal to visit the cemetery to

---

❶ RICHARD CORY
Edwin Arlington Robinson

Whenever Richard Cory went down town,
We people on the pavement looked at him:
He was a gentleman from sole to crown,
Clean favored, and <u>imperially</u> slim.

5 And he was always quietly arrayed,
And he was always human when he talked;
But still he fluttered pulses when he said,
"Good-morning," and he glittered when he walked.

And he was rich—yes, richer than a king—
10 And admirably schooled in every grace:
In fine, we thought that he was everything
To make us wish that we were in his place.

So on we worked, and waited for the light,
And went without the meat, and cursed the bread;
15 And Richard Cory, one calm summer night,
Went home and put a bullet through his head.

Review and Assess

Thinking About the Selections

1. **Respond:** Were you surprised by the last line of "Richard Cory"? Explain.

2. **(a) Recall:** Why should Luke Havergal go to the gate? **(b) Speculate:** What might the gate symbolize?

3. **(a) Recall:** In "Luke Havergal," from where has the speaker come? **(b) Interpret:** What is the speaker's message?

4. **(a) Recall:** Why was Richard Cory envied? **(b) Contrast:** In what ways does Richard Cory differ from the other townspeople?

5. **(a) Recall:** What does Cory do one night? **(b) Infer:** Do you think the town was surprised by his action? Explain.

6. **(a) Apply:** Why might Richard Cory have been miserable? **(b) Relate:** What do you think are the keys to individual happiness?

The Thinker (Portrait of Louis N. Kenton, 1900), Thomas Eakins, The Metropolitan Museum of Art

❺ ▲ Critical Viewing
Do you think this painting more accurately suggests Richard Cory or the poem's speaker? Explain. **[Connect]**

imperially (im pir′ ē əl ē) *adv.* majestically

Answers continued

commune with the spirit of his beloved until it is his rightful time to die.

4. **(a)** He was envied for his wealth, grace, and social position. **(b)** In contrast to Cory's fine qualities, the townspeople are ordinary working people who struggle to make ends meet.

5. **(a)** He shoots himself. **(b)** Since they imagined Cory had everything, they probably wouldn't expect him to take his own life.

6. **(a)** Possible response: Cory might not have had close, gratifying personal relationships; he may have achieved material success and still have felt empty. **(b)** Students should support their responses with clear reasoning.

Lucinda Matlock

Edgar Lee Masters

I went to the dances at Chandlerville,
And played snap-out[1] at Winchester.
One time we changed partners,
Driving home in the moonlight of middle June,
5   And then I found Davis.
We were married and lived together for seventy years,
Enjoying, working, raising the twelve children,
Eight of whom we lost
Ere I had reached the age of sixty.
10 I spun, I wove, I kept the house, I nursed the sick,
I made the garden, and for holiday
Rambled over the fields where sang the larks,
And by Spoon River gathering many a shell,
And many a flower and medicinal weed—
15 Shouting to the wooded hills, singing to the green valleys.
At ninety-six I had lived enough, that is all,
And passed to a sweet repose.
What is this I hear of sorrow and weariness,
Anger, discontent and drooping hopes?
20 Degenerate sons and daughters,
Life is too strong for you—
It takes life to love Life.

repose (ri pōz´) *n.* state of being at rest

degenerate (dē jen´ ər it) *adj.* morally corrupt

---

1. **snap-out** game in which a long line of players who are holding hands spin around in a circle, causing the players on the ends to be flung off by centrifugal force.

Review and Assess

Thinking About the Selection

1. **Respond:** What is your opinion of Lucinda Matlock? Is she someone you would strive to emulate? Why or why not?
2. **(a) Recall:** Summarize Lucinda Matlock's domestic life. **(b) Analyze:** What is her attitude about her life?
3. **(a) Recall:** How old was Lucinda Matlock when she died? **(b) Infer:** Why might she have thought she "lived enough"?
4. **(a) Recall:** Whom does she address at the end of the poem? **(b) Interpret:** What is the meaning of Matlock's message to those she addresses?
5. **(a) Apply:** How might Matlock respond to the complaint that life today is too complex? **(b) Connect:** Do you agree? Explain.

Lucinda Matlock ◆ 669

CUSTOMIZE INSTRUCTION FOR UNIVERSAL ACCESS

For Gifted/Talented Students

Have students complete a graphic organizer like the one shown to analyze the personality of the speakers in "Lucinda Matlock" and "Richard Bone." Then, have students compare and contrast the speakers. Suggest that students explore the fact that, even though both poems are written in the first person, the voices of the speakers are distinct.

Emotional Words — Personal Words — Speaker — Opinion Words — Attitude Words

❻ About the Selections

The two poems by Masters demonstrate two characters' abilities to face life in a changing world. From the detached distance of the grave, both characters speak frankly about their lives. Matlock died when she was ninety-six after a hard but fulfilling life. She dismisses the complaints she hears from the younger generation, whom she feels never developed the power to embrace life and survive its many troubles.

As a carver of tombstones, Bone came to know the people in Spoon River and to learn how closeness and affection caused relatives to ask him to carve "false chronicles" into the stone.

Answers for p. 669

Review and Assess

1. Whether students like or dislike Matlock, they should support their opinions with evidence from the poem.
2. **(a)** She had a marriage that produced twelve children (although eight had died before she turned sixty), and she was charitable and hard-working. **(b)** She seems to think that she lived well.
3. **(a)** She died at ninety-six. **(b)** Being a pragmatic woman, she may have felt that she had accomplished everything she wanted or needed to do.
4. **(a)** She addresses younger generations, who complain of hopelessness. **(b)** They must live and experience the joys and stand up to the sorrows.
5. **(a)** Matlock would probably disagree and point out that her life was equally complex. **(b)** Students should support their responses with clear reasoning and examples from the text.

1. Students should support their responses with clear reasoning and examples from the text.

2. **(a)** He is a tombstone carver. **(b)** He becomes familiar with the townspeople and can determine whether their epitaphs are true. **(c)** He continues to make his living carving gravestones, though the work implicates him in the hypocrisy of the epitaphs.

3. **(a)** He is familiar with the true natures of the deceased persons. **(b)** Possible responses: The townspeople believe them; they want to show their love for the deceased.

4. Both provide a written record of lives in the past.

5. Possible answers: Yes, Bone played an important role because he gave the townspeople a way to honor their loved ones.

❻ Richard Bone

Edgar Lee Masters

When I first came to Spoon River
I did not know whether what they told me
Was true or false.
They would bring me the <u>epitaph</u>
5   And stand around the shop while I worked
And say "He was so kind," "He was wonderful,"
"She was the sweetest woman," "He was a consistent Christian."
And I chiseled for them whatever they wished,
All in ignorance of its truth.
10 But later, as I lived among the people here,
I knew how near to the life
Were the epitaphs that were ordered for them as they died.

But still I chiseled whatever they paid me to chisel
and made myself party to the false chronicles
15 Of the stones,
Even as the historian does who writes
Without knowing the truth,
Or because he is influenced to hide it.

epitaph (ep´ ə taf) *n.* inscription on a tombstone or grave marker

Review and Assess

Thinking About the Selection

1. **Respond:** What is your opinion of Richard Bone after reading this poem? Explain.

2. **(a) Recall:** What is Richard Bone's occupation?
   (b) Infer: What does he learn after years in Spoon River?
   (c) Speculate: Does his attitude change? If so, how?

3. **(a) Interpret:** Why does Bone think the epitaphs are "false chronicles"? **(b) Speculate:** Why do you think the townspeople compose such epitaphs for their loved ones?

4. **Analyze:** Explain why Bone might compare a tombstone carver to a historian.

5. **Apply:** Do you think Bone played an important role in Spoon River? Support your answer.

ASSESSMENT PRACTICE: Reading Comprehension

Context	(For more practice, see Test Preparation Workbook, p. 39.)

The reading sections of many tests require students to use context clues to identify the appropriate meaning of a multiple-meaning word in a given passage. Use the following sample test item to demonstrate.

   Whenever Richard Cory went to town,

   We people on the pavement looked at him:

   He was a gentleman from sole to <u>crown</u>.

   Clean favored, and imperially slim.

In this passage, the word <u>crown</u> most nearly means—

   A symbol of royalty
   B hit on the head
   C top of head
   D royal government

The juxtaposition of *sole* and *crown,* and the general context of describing a gentleman's appearance should lead students to recognize that *C* is the most appropriate choice.

Review and Assess

Literary Analysis

Speaker

1. What details suggest that the **speaker** of "Richard Cory" is speaking for the entire town?
2. In what ways does the speaker's admiration for Richard Cory add to the power of the poem?
3. (a) In what ways might "Lucinda Matlock" be different if Masters had used a different speaker? (b) If "Richard Cory" spoke for himself, how might the poem be different?
4. The speakers in Master's *Spoon River Anthology* are dead. Why might this allow them to discuss their lives more openly?

Comparing Literary Works

5. In both "Luke Havergal" and "Lucinda Matlock," voices speak from the grave. Compare and contrast the messages they deliver.
6. If Richard Bone were asked to carve epitaphs for Luke Havergal, Richard Cory, and Lucinda Matlock, what would he write? Explain each response.

Reading Strategy

Recognizing Attitudes

7. In what way does the speaker's **attitude** toward Richard Cory differ from Cory's attitude toward himself? Support your answer.
8. Identify and explain the attitude of the speaker in "Richard Bone."
9. Use a chart like this to describe Lucinda Matlock's outlook on life.

Extend Understanding

10. **Psychology Connection:** Consider the ways in which these characters deal with change and explain other, healthier options.

Luke Havergal / Richard Cory / Lucinda Matlock / Richard Bone ◆ 671

Quick Review

The **speaker** is the voice of a poem.

To **recognize the attitudes** of a poem's speaker, look for details that suggest how a speaker feels about a subject.

 Take It to the Net
www.phschool.com

Take the interactive self-test online to check your understanding of these selections.

Answers for p. 671

Review and Assess

1. The speaker uses the words *We people* in line 2.
2. The speaker's admiration prepares the reader to believe that Cory is destined for a great, long life.
3. **(a)** Another speaker might convey different attitudes about the details—and overall significance—of Matlock's life. **(b)** Cory might have explained his true feelings and why he committed suicide.
4. Speakers who are "dead" are detached from the world and thus have nothing to gain or lose from their honesty.
5. In "Luke Havergal," an anguished man is drawn toward death by the promise of reunion with his lost love. In "Lucinda Matlock," the speaker celebrates a life well lived and a peaceful, contented death.
6. The epitaphs might aim to idealize the lives of the dead.
7. Cory does not believe that he has everything to live for; the speaker thinks Cory does.
8. The speaker seems disdainful of the people he serves.
9. Tragedies such as outliving eight children, pleasures such as singing and gathering shells, and opinions such as disapproving of the younger generation's moral weakness contribute to her belief that one must live with gusto and strength.
10. Matlock seems almost to ignore change as she proceeds vigorously through life; Bone grows more bitter and cynical as his relationships with the townspeople develop. Students might describe ways in which people can deal with change without isolating themselves from others.

✳ ENRICHMENT: Further Reading

Other Works by the Authors

Works by Edwin Arlington Robinson

The Man Against the Sky

Collected Poems

The Man Who Died Twice

Works by Edgar Lee Masters

Vachel Lindsay: A Poet in America

Across Spoon River

Mitch Miller

 Take It to the Net
Visit www.phschool.com for more information on Edwin Arlington Robinson and Edgar Lee Masters.

671

EXTEND

Answers for p. 672

❶ Vocabulary Development

Word Analysis

1. b
2. c
3. a

Concept Development: Synonyms

1. a
2. c
3. a
4. a

Spelling Strategy

1. symphonic
2. sinful
3. decipher
4. catastrophe

❷ Grammar and Style

1. *where she is*: object of a preposition
2. *whatever they wished*: direct object
3. *whether what they told me was true or false*: direct object
4. *the epitaphs that were ordered*: predicate noun
5. *whatever they paid me to chisel*: direct object

Writing Application

Each student's sentences should include at least three noun clauses and should describe various aspects of a familiar person or place.

Integrate Language Skills

❶ Vocabulary Development Lesson

Word Analysis: Latin Root -*pose*-

The word *repose* combines the Latin root -*pose*- ("place" or "rest") with the prefix *re*- ("back"). Using this word analysis, *repose* can be defined as "the state of being at rest."

Use each of the words below to complete the sentences.

a. depose   **b.** impose   **c.** interpose

1. He hated to ___?___ on his friends, but he was unable to find a hotel room.
2. Each time audience members ___?___ comments, the speaker loses his train of thought.
3. When we ___?___ the prime minister, we will set this nation on a course toward true freedom.

Concept Development: Synonyms

Write the letter of the best synonym for the first word.

1. imperially: (a) grandly, (b) scornfully, (c) strongly
2. repose: (a) model, (b) silence, (c) ease
3. degenerate: (a) evil, (b) degraded, (c) slow
4. epitaph: (a) inscription, (b) homily, (c) graph

Spelling Strategy

In many English words of Greek origin, *ph* is used to spell the *f* sound, as in *epitaph*, *trophy*, and *physique*. For each of the following pairs, choose the correct spelling.

1. symfonic/symphonic   3. decifer/decipher
2. sinful/sinphul   4. catastrofe/catastrophe

❷ Grammar and Style Lesson

Noun Clauses

A **noun clause** is a subordinate clause used as a noun. It can be used as a subject, a predicate nominative, a direct object, an indirect object, or the object of a preposition. Noun clauses are commonly introduced by words such as *that*, *which*, *where*, *what*, *who*, *whatever*, *whoever*, and *why*.

> **Subject:** *Whoever knows about life* will tell you.
>
> **Direct Object:** We thought *that he was everything*.
>
> **Predicate Nominative:** He is *whatever we admire*.
>
> **Object of a Preposition:** He tells his story to *whomever will listen*.

Practice Copy the following sentences and underline the noun clause in each. Explain the function of each noun clause.

1. There is yet one way to where she is.
2. I chiseled for them whatever they wished.
3. I did not know whether what they told me was true or false.
4. I knew how near to the life were the epitaphs that were ordered.
5. I chiseled whatever they paid me to chisel.

Writing Application Write three or four sentences to describe different aspects of a familiar person or place. In your writing, include at least three noun clauses.

W̶G̶ *Prentice Hall Writing and Grammar Connection: Chapter 19, Section 3*

672 ◆ *Division, Reconciliation, and Expansion (1850–1914)*

TEACHING RESOURCES

The following resources can be used to enrich or extend the instruction for pp. 672–673.

Vocabulary

📖 **Selection Support:** Build Vocabulary, p. 164

📖 **Vocabulary and Spelling Practice Book**
(Use this booklet for skills enrichment)

Grammar

📖 **Selection Support Workbook:** Grammar and Style, p. 165 ▪

W̶G̶ **Writing and Grammar**, Ruby Level, p. 454 ▪

🎞 **Daily Language Practice Transparencies**

Writing

W̶G̶ **Writing and Grammar**, Ruby Level, p. 67 ▪

🎞 **Writing Models and Graphic Organizers on Transparencies**, pp. 9–12

W̶G̶ **Writing and Grammar**, iText CD-ROM

▪ **BLOCK SCHEDULING:** Resources marked with this symbol provide varied instruction during 90-minute blocks.

③ Writing Lesson

Firsthand Biography

Poems like Robinson's and Masters's are one way to create vivid portraits of people. Another way to present a portrait of a person is through a firsthand biography—a story about events in the life of a person with whom the writer has a personal relationship. Write a firsthand biography in which you share your impressions of a person.

Prewriting   After you have selected your subject, list his or her key personality traits and the events that reveal them. Then, arrange these details in their order of importance.

Drafting   Focus your draft on a single event or a series of events that illustrate the person's most important personality traits. Use transitional words like the ones shown.

Model: Choosing Transitions

Sequence	Superiority	Inferiority
first	good	few
second	better	last
primarily	best	less importantly
last	above all	least effective
finally	more importantly	worst of all

Revising   Review your biography and add more details to make sure that it conveys the impression of your subject that you intended.

W̶G *Prentice Hall Writing and Grammar Connection: Chapter 4, Connected Assignment*

④ Extension Activities

Speaking and Listening Find a copy of folk duo Simon and Garfunkel's adaptation of "Richard Cory" and compare it with the poem, addressing the following issues:

- Is the song effective?
- Does it capture the message of the poem?
- In what ways, if any, does the song alter Robinson's meaning?

Lead a **class discussion** in which you compare the poem to the song. [**Group Activity**]

Research and Technology Review *Spoon River Anthology* to find several poems that convey a similar theme, such as jealousy, honesty, or love. Prepare an **illustrated booklet** of these poems. In addition to providing images that enhance the meaning of the poems, write an introduction explaining the connection among the poems.

 Take It to the Net   www.phschool.com

Go online for an additional research activity using the Internet.

Luke Havergal / Richard Cory / Lucinda Matlock / Richard Bone ◆ 673

ASSESSMENT RESOURCES

The following resources can be used to assess students' knowledge and skills.

Selection Assessment

📖 **Formal Assessment,** pp. 173–175

📖 **Open Book Test,** pp. 109–111

📼 **Got It! Assessment Videotapes,** Tape 3

💿 **Test Bank Software**

💻 *Take It to the Net*

Visit www.phschool.com for self-tests and additional questions on the selections.

Writing Rubric

📖 **Performance Assess. and Portfolio Mgmt.,** p. 16

PRENTICE HALL ASSESSMENT SYSTEM

📖 **Workbook**   🖥 **Transparencies**

📖 **Skill Book**   💿 **CD-ROM**

Lesson Support for p. 673

③ Writing Lesson

- Students' firsthand biographies should use detailed descriptions of events and character traits to convey a clear impression of a person they know well.

- Encourage students to be specific about the aspects of the subject's personality they wish to evoke. They might focus on an experience or an occasion that conveys the subject's personality.

- Use the Writing Lesson, as well as Writing Process Model 2 on pp. 9–12 of **Writing Models and Graphic Organizers on Transparencies**, to guide students in developing their firsthand biographies.

- Use the Description rubric, p. 16 in **Performance Assessment and Portfolio Management,** to assess students' work.

④ Listening and Speaking

- Encourage students to listen to Simon's song (and to reread Robinson's poem) several times before the class discussion. Students might benefit from taking the time to transcribe the song's lyrics for close comparison with the poem.

- Invite students to explore questions on p. 673 in writing or with partners to prepare for leading the class discussion.

CUSTOMIZE INSTRUCTION
For Universal Access

To address different learning styles, use the following activities suggested in the **Extension Activities** booklet, p. 37.

For Interpersonal Learners, use Activity 5.

For Musical/Rhythmic Learners, use Activity 6.

For Verbal/Linguistic Learners, use Activity 7.

A Wagner Matinée

Lesson Objectives

1. **To analyze and respond to literary elements**
   - Literary Analysis: Characterization
   - Connecting Literary Elements: First-person Narrator
2. **To read, comprehend, analyze, and critique a short story**
   - Reading Strategy: Clarifying
   - Reading Check questions
   - Review and Assess questions
   - Assessment Practice (ATE)
3. **To develop word analysis skills, fluency, and systematic vocabulary**
   - Vocabulary Development Lesson: Using Words From Music
4. **To understand and apply written and oral language conventions**
   - Spelling Strategy
   - Grammar and Style Lesson: Reflexive and Intensive Pronouns
5. **To understand and apply appropriate writing and research strategies**
   - Writing Lesson: Editorial
   - Extension Activity: Musical Presentation
6. **To understand and apply listening and speaking strategies**
   - Extension Activity: Monologues

STEP-BY-STEP TEACHING GUIDE	PACING GUIDE
PRETEACH	
Motivate Students and Provide Background	
Use the Motivation activity (ATE p. 674)	5 min.
Read and discuss author and background features (SE/ATE pp. 674, 677)	5 min.
Introduce the Concepts	
Introduce the Literary Analysis and Reading Strategy (SE/ATE p. 675)	15 min.
Pronounce the vocabulary words and read their definitions (SE p. 675)	5 min.
TEACH	
Monitor Comprehension	
Informally monitor comprehension by circulating while students read independently or in groups	30 min.
Monitor students' comprehension with the Reading Check notes (SE/ATE pp. 677, 679, 681, 683)	as students read
Develop vocabulary with Vocabulary notes (SE pp. 679, 681, 682, 683; ATE p. 680)	as students read
Develop Understanding	
Develop students' understanding of characterization with the Literary Analysis annotations (SE pp. 678, 679, 681; ATE pp. 678, 679, 681)	5 min.
Develop students' ability to clarify points in the reading with the Reading Strategy annotations (ATE pp. 682)	5 min.
ASSESS	
Assess Mastery	
Assess students' mastery of the Reading Strategy and Literary Analysis by having them answer the Review and Assess questions (SE/ATE p. 685)	15 min.
Use one or more of the print and media Assessment Resources (ATE p. 687)	up to 45 min.
EXTEND	
Apply Understanding	
Have students complete the Vocabulary Development Lesson and the Grammar and Style Lesson (SE p. 686)	20 min.
Apply students' ability to use specific language in writing by using the Writing Lesson (SE/ATE p. 687)	45 min.
Apply students' understanding using one or more of the Extension Activities (SE p. 687)	20–90 min.

 ACCELERATED INSTRUCTION:
Use the strategies and activities identified with an .

UNIVERSAL ACCESS
● = Below Level Students
▲ = On-Level Students
■ = Above Level Students

Time and Resource Manager

PRINT 📖	TRANSPARENCIES 📄	TECHNOLOGY 💿 🎧 📼
RESOURCES		
• **Beyond Literature,** Cross-Curricular Connection: Music, p. 38 ▲ ■		• **Interest Grabber Video,** Tape 4 ● ▲ ■
• **Selection Support Workbook:** ● ▲ ■ Literary Analysis, p. 171 Reading Strategy, p. 170 Build Vocabulary, p. 168	• **Literary Analysis and Reading Transparencies,** pp. 75 and 76 ● ▲ ■	
• **Authors In Depth,** The American Experience, p. 123 ■		• **Listening to Literature** ● ▲ ■ Audiocassettes, Side 24 Audio CDs, CD 14
• **Literatura en español** ● ▲ • **Literary Analysis for Enrichment** ■	• **Fine Art Transparencies, Volume 1,** Art Transparency 3 ● ▲ ■	
• **Formal Assessment:** Selection Test, pp. 176–178 ● ▲ ■ • **Open Book Test,** pp. 112–114 ● ▲ ■ • **Performance Assessment and Portfolio Management,** p. 30 ● ▲ ■ • **PRENTICE HALL ASSESSMENT** *SYSTEM* ● ▲ ■	• **PRENTICE HALL ASSESSMENT** *SYSTEM* ● ▲ ■ Skills Practice Answers and Explanations on Transparencies	• **Test Bank Software** ● ▲ ■ • **Got It! Assessment Videotapes,** Tape 3 ● ▲
• **Selection Support Workbook:** ● ▲ ■ Grammar and Style, p. 169 • **Writing and Grammar,** Ruby Level ● ▲ ■ • **Extension Activities,** p. 38 ● ▲ ■	• **Daily Language Practice Transparencies** ● ▲ • **Writing Models and Graphic Organizers on Transparencies,** pp. 33–36 ● ▲ ■	• **Writing and Grammar iText CD-ROM** ● ▲ ■ *Take It to the Net* www.phschool.com

BLOCK SCHEDULING: Use one 90-minute class period to preteach the selection and have students read it. Use a second 90-minute class period to assess students' mastery of skills and have them complete one of the Extension Activities.

Motivation

Before class, write "Wagner Matinée" on the chalkboard, as if to announce a concert, and give the composer's full name and dates (1813–1883). Prepare a list of the pieces mentioned in the story: Overture from *Tannhäuser*, Prelude to *Tristan and Isolde*, selections from *The Flying Dutchman*, *The Ring* (*The Rheingold*, *The Valkyrie*, *Siegfried*, and *Dusk of the Gods*), Forest Music from *Siegfried*, and Siegfried's funeral march. As students enter the room, pass out the "program" and dim the lights, as if in a concert hall. Play one or more excerpts from these pieces, all of which are readily available. Invite students to respond to the emotion of the music. Then let students know that an afternoon concert featuring the composer whose work they have just heard is a key event in the story they are about to read.

Interest Grabber Video

As an alternative, play "Willa Cather: Reflections and Memory" on Tape 4 to engage student interest.

❶ Background

More About the Author

In 1944, Willa Cather received the Gold Medal of the National Institute of the American Academy of Arts and Letters in recognition of the entire body of her work. Cather wrote fiction with a contemporary setting, as well as stories and novels that explored the traditional values of the pioneer era. Although she continued to live in New York after leaving *McClure's Magazine*, Cather visited her home town of Red Cloud, Nebraska, twice a year and maintained close ties with her family.

Prepare to Read

❶ A Wagner Matinée

Willa Cather (1873–1947)

Although Willa Cather lived more than half her life in New York City, she turned again and again to the Nebraska prairie of her youth— at the time, a recently settled area of the American frontier—for inspiration and material for her writing. Cather captured with unflinching honesty the difficulties of life on the expanding frontier.

A Prairie Childhood Born in a small town in western Virginia, Cather moved to the Nebraska frontier when she was nine. Many of her new neighbors were immigrants struggling to build new lives while preserving their native cultures. Commenting on the diversity that surrounded her during her childhood, Cather once wrote, "On Sundays we could drive to a Norwegian church and listen to a sermon in that language, or to a Danish or Swedish church. We could go to a French Catholic settlement or into a Bohemian township and hear one in Czech, or we could go to the church with the German Lutherans."

In addition to all that she learned from observing the diverse group of people who surrounded her, Cather received a rich formal education, studying foreign languages, history, classical music, and opera. In 1891, Cather left home to study at the University of Nebraska, becoming one of the first women to receive a college education.

The Making of a Literary Giant After graduating from the University of Nebraska in 1895, Cather worked as an editor at a Pittsburgh newspaper while she wrote poems and short stories in her spare time. Her first collection of stories, *The Troll Garden*, was published in 1905. In 1906, she moved to New York and joined the editorial staff of *McClure's Magazine*. After her first novel, *Alexander's Bridge*, was published in 1912, Cather left *McClure's* to devote herself to writing. She remained in New York for the rest of her life, but her memories of the prairie inspired her greatest work.

Over the next 35 years, Cather produced ten novels, two short-story collections, and two collections of essays. Among her outstanding works are *O Pioneers!* (1913), *My Ántonia* (1918), and *One of Ours* (1922), all of which capture the flavor of life on the Midwestern prairie. *One of Ours* won Cather the Pulitzer Prize in 1923. Cather then shifted her attention from the Midwest to New Mexico in *Death Comes for the Archbishop* (1927) and to seventeenth-century Canada in *Shadows on the Rock* (1931).

Portraits of Prairie Life Although Cather's fiction was by no means limited to "prairie stories"—her fictional settings ranged from contemporary New York City to the American Southwest to Quebec—it was her stories about Nebraskan immigrants that most appealed to readers and critics. In these stories, she displayed her admiration for the courage and spirit of the immigrants and other settlers of the frontier. At the same time, she conveyed an intense awareness of the loss felt by the pioneers and the loneliness and isolation from which they suffered. In "A Wagner Matinée," for example, Cather captures this sense of loneliness and isolation by contrasting the stark realities of frontier life with the possibilities of life in a more cultured world.

TEACHING RESOURCES

The following resources can be used to enrich or extend the instruction for pp. 674–675.

Motivation

  Interest Grabber Video, Tape 4 ■

Background

  Beyond Literature, p. 38

  Take It to the Net
  Visit www.phschool.com for Background and hotlinks for the selection.

Literary Analysis

  Literary Analysis and Reading Transparencies, Characterization, p. 76

  Selection Support: Literary Analysis, p. 171

Reading

  Literary Analysis and Reading Transparencies, Clarifying, p. 75 ■

■ **BLOCK SCHEDULING:** Resources marked with this symbol provide varied instruction during 90-minute blocks.

Preview

Connecting to the Literature

Music can exert a powerful tug on our feelings, memories, and fantasies. In this story, a woman experiences a flood of long-buried emotions when she attends a special concert.

❷ Literary Analysis

Characterization

A writer uses **characterization** to reveal a character's personality. Characterization is generally developed through one of the following methods:

- Direct statements about the character
- Physical descriptions
- The character's actions, thoughts, or comments
- Comments about the character made by other characters.

As you read, note how these methods of characterization are used to develop the personality of Aunt Georgiana.

Connecting Literary Elements

When a story is told by a character involved in the action, the writer is using **first-person point of view**. In such a story, all impressions of events, places, and characters are filtered through the narrator. In "A Wagner Matinée," Aunt Georgiana is presented to the reader exactly as she is perceived by the narrator—her nephew, Clark.

❸ Reading Strategy

Clarifying

Cather's story is packed with details about its main character. To fully understand the character's actions, **clarify** the details that are provided. This may involve reading a footnote or looking up a word in a dictionary. You may also need to reread a passage to refresh your memory about previous details or even read ahead to find details that clarify meaning. Use a chart like the one shown to clarify difficult passages from the text.

Vocabulary Development

reverential (rev´ə ren´ shəl) *adj.* caused by a feeling of deep respect and love (p. 679)

tremulously (trem´ yoo ləs lē) *adv.* fearfully; timidly (p. 679)

semi-somnambulant (sem´ i säm nam´ byoo lənt) *adj.* half-sleepwalking (p. 679)

inert (in urt´) *adj.* motionless (p. 680)

prelude (prel´ yood´) *n.* introductory section or movement of a work of music (p. 682)

jocularity (jäk´ yoo lar´ ə tē) *n.* joking good humor (p. 683)

Detail	Clarifying Strategy
"Howard followed her."	*Reread to find out who Howard is.*
inexplicable	*Look the word up in the dictionary.*
"took a homestead in Red Willow County"	*Find out where Red Willow County is.*

❷ Literary Analysis

Characterization

- Read the instruction about characterization as a class. Encourage student volunteers to create an example to illustrate each of the four bulleted methods of characterization.

- Discuss how point of view relates to characterization. Point out that a third-person omniscient narrator can provide detailed information about the actions, feelings, and thoughts of every character in a story, whereas a first-person narrator can only speculate about the feelings and thoughts of other characters.

❸ Reading Strategy

Clarifying

- Point out that even the most experienced and skillful readers must clarify details as they read by rereading a text or previewing later passages.

- Guide students to see the importance of monitoring their own understanding as they read. Most readers know the sensation of suddenly realizing that they have been reading for several seconds with no awareness of what they are reading. Tell students that it is vital at such times to go back and pick up where they stopped making sense of the text.

- Encourage students to see how leaving the narrative momentarily to clarify details is a sign of respect for oneself as a learner. It is a skill that students can use over and over as they encounter various types of texts.

Vocabulary Development

- Pronounce each vocabulary word for students, and read the definitions as a class. Have students identify any words with which they are already familiar.

 E-Teach

Visit E-Teach at www.phschool.com for teachers' essays on how to teach, with questions and answers.

CUSTOMIZE INSTRUCTION FOR UNIVERSAL ACCESS

For Less Proficient Readers	For English Learners	For Advanced Readers
Cather's story includes many long sentences that may prove challenging. To help students clarify meanings, show them how to get to decipher a challenging sentence by finding its subject and predicate—and then by recognizing how the other sentence parts relate to the subject and predicate.	This selection contains many musical terms, such as *scale*, *score*, *strain*, *motif*, *melody*, *chorus*, and *tenor*, as well as the names of various instruments. To help students clarify the meanings of these terms, use sheet music, recordings, and photographs to illustrate the meanings of the words for students.	In Aunt Georgiana, Cather has created a character with layers of meaning. Invite students to analyze those layers. Encourage students as they read to keep a list of details that help them clarify the various ways in which her character is revealed—ranging from how she appears outwardly on to what she is like inside.

Step-by-Step Teaching Guide for pp. 676–684

CUSTOMIZE INSTRUCTION
For Musical/Rhythmic Learners

Have these students listen to the musical pieces mentioned in the story and comment on their emotional impact. Also have them identify terms, used here and elsewhere, that have general meanings as well as specific definitions as musical terms. Examples include *motif*, *crescendo*, *development*, and *counterpoint*.

❶ About the Selection

The story explores the contrast between cultured city life and the rugged life that nineteenth-century settlers led after moving to the frontier. The narrator's Aunt Georgiana returns to Boston for a visit years after moving to Nebraska with her husband. A former music teacher, Georgiana has been outwardly toughened by frontier life. Yet when her nephew takes her to the opera, she has a deep emotional response: she cries with joy at the music and with grief at the cultural opportunities she has forfeited to live with her husband. Through his aunt's pain, the narrator learns that the soul never really dies, but "withers to the outward eye only" as it waits to be reawakened.

From Arkansas, George Schreiber, Sheldon Swope Art Museum, Terre Haute, Indiana

❸ ▲ **Critical Viewing** In what ways does the woman in the painting seem like Aunt Georgiana? **[Connect; Interpret]**

676 ◆ *Division, Reconciliation, and Expansion (1850–1914)*

TEACHING RESOURCES

The following resources can be used to enrich or extend the instruction for pp. 676–684.

Reading Strategy

📖 **Selection Support:** Reading Strategy, p. 170; Build Vocabulary, p. 168

🎧 **Listening to Literature Audiocassettes,** Side 24 ■

💿 **Listening to Literature Audio CDs,** CD 14 ■

Extension

📖 **Authors In Depth, The American Experience:** This collection includes one poem and two additional prose selections by Willa Cather for extended reading.

■ **BLOCK SCHEDULING:** Resources marked with this symbol provide varied instruction during 90-minute blocks.

A Wagner Matinée

Willa Cather

Background

When "A Wagner Matinée" first appeared in 1904, Cather's readers would have been as familiar with Richard Wagner (Väg nər) as people are today with the Beatles. Wagner, who was German, was one of the nineteenth century's greatest composers. His operas are characterized by their adventurous harmonic language and their innovative intermarriage of music and drama. Although many critics judged Wagner's music unfavorably during his lifetime, his operas became enormously popular after his death in 1883.

I received one morning a letter written in pale ink, on glassy, blue-lined notepaper, and bearing the postmark of a little Nebraska village. This communication, worn and rubbed, looking as though it had been carried for some days in a coat pocket that was none too clean, was from my Uncle Howard. It informed me that his wife had been left a small legacy by a bachelor relative who had recently died, and that it had become necessary for her to come to Boston to attend to the settling of the estate. He requested me to meet her at the station, and render her whatever services might prove necessary. On examining the date indicated as that of her arrival, I found it no later than tomorrow. He had characteristically delayed writing until, had I been away from home for a day, I must have missed the good woman altogether.

The name of my Aunt Georgiana called up not alone her own figure, at once pathetic and grotesque, but opened before my feet a gulf of recollections so wide and deep that, as the letter dropped from my hand, I felt suddenly a stranger to all the present conditions of my existence, wholly ill at ease and out of place amid the surroundings

❹ ☑ Reading Check
Why is Aunt Georgiana going to Boston?

A Wagner Matinée ◆ 677

❷ Background

Art

From Arkansas, 1939, by George Schreiber

Belgian-born George Schreiber came to the United States in the 1920s. Like many artists during the Great Depression, Schreiber turned his focus to the great Midwestern farmlands. Although Schreiber was not a major figure in the Regionalist art movement, this painting demonstrates his talent and interest in recording the spirit of rural America during one of its most trying times. He portrays the woman with stark realism: her face, ragged apron, and stance reflect the hardships she has endured and the strength with which she has met them.

Use these questions for discussion:

1. What can you infer about the woman's feelings from the way she holds her arms?
   Answer: Students may say that she is weary, resigned to a difficult life, or frustrated.

2. What details of the setting reflect the description of Aunt Georgiana's homestead?
   Answer: The flat, barren land, bare tree branches, and dilapidated building are similar to those described in the story.

❸ ▶ Critical Viewing

Answer: Students may say that both women look bent, weary, and worn from suffering and hard work.

❹ ☑ Reading Check

Answer: She needs to be present for the settling of the estate of one of her recently deceased relatives.

CUSTOMIZE INSTRUCTION FOR UNIVERSAL ACCESS

For Special Needs Students	For Gifted/Talented Students
Students may benefit from spending time rereading and discussing the first two paragraphs of the story. Help them identify and understand Clark's reaction to thinking about his aunt. He is shocked at how quickly her name transports him to his modest past as "the gangling farmer boy" his aunt had once known, yet he recalls with affection the influence she had upon him when he was young.	One of Cather's long-held, deeply-felt concerns was the conflict between the artist and the workaday world. "A Wagner Matinée" explores the conflict between a woman's love for music and the withering effects of the harsh farming life that leaves neither time nor energy for the pursuit of fine arts. Invite students to read one or more additional stories from *The Troll Garden,* the collection from which this story comes, and discuss how each story explores the theme of the artist in—or against—society.

❺ Literary Analysis

Characterization

- Read this paragraph aloud for students and ask them to listen for details about Georgiana's early life in Boston and about her subsequent life in Nebraska. Encourage them to be alert, also, for indications of how much time has elapsed since she left Boston.

- Ask students the Literary Analysis question on p. 678: What do the contrasting details of Aunt Georgiana's life in Boston and Nebraska reveal about her character?

  Answer: They reveal that she was once a refined and cultured woman who, for the sake of romantic passion, exchanged life in Boston for a life that transformed her into a figure "at once pathetic and grotesque."

of my study. I became, in short, the gangling farmer boy my aunt had known, scourged with chilblains and bashfulness, my hands cracked and raw from the corn husking. I felt the knuckles of my thumb tentatively, as though they were raw again. I sat again before her parlor organ, thumbing the scales with my stiff, red hands, while she beside me made canvas mittens for the huskers.

The next morning, after preparing my landlady somewhat, I set out for the station. When the train arrived I had some difficulty in finding my aunt. She was the last of the passengers to alight, and when I got her into the carriage she looked not unlike one of those charred, smoked bodies that firemen lift from the *débris* of a burned building. She had come all the way in a day coach; her linen duster[1] had become black with soot and her black bonnet gray with dust during the journey. When we arrived at my boardinghouse the landlady put her to bed at once, and I did not see her again until the next morning.

Whatever shock Mrs. Springer experienced at my aunt's appearance she considerably concealed. Myself, I saw my aunt's misshapen figure with that feeling of awe and respect with which we behold explorers who have left their ears and fingers north of Franz Josef Land,[2] or their health somewhere along the upper Congo.[3] My Aunt Georgiana had been a music teacher at the Boston Conservatory, somewhere back in the latter sixties. One summer, which she had spent in the little village in the Green Mountains[4] where her ancestors had dwelt for generations, she had kindled the callow[5] fancy of the most idle and shiftless of all the village lads, and had conceived for this Howard Carpenter one of those absurd and extravagant passions which a handsome country boy of twenty-one sometimes inspires in a plain, angular, spectacled woman of thirty. When she returned to her duties in Boston, Howard followed her; and the upshot of this inexplicable infatuation was that she eloped with him, eluding the reproaches of her family and the criticism of her friends by going with him to the Nebraska frontier. Carpenter, who of course had no money, took a homestead in Red Willow County,[6] fifty miles from the railroad. There they measured off their eighty acres by driving across the prairie in a wagon, to the wheel of which they had tied a red cotton handkerchief, and counting its revolutions. They built a dugout in the red hillside, one of those cave dwellings whose inmates usually reverted to the conditions of primitive savagery. Their water they got from the lagoons where the buffalo drank, and their slender stock of provisions was always at the mercy of bands of roving Indians. For thirty years my aunt had not been farther than fifty miles from the homestead.

---

1. **duster** *n.* short, loose smock worn to protect clothing from dust.
2. **Franz Josef Land** group of islands in the Arctic Ocean.
3. **Congo** river in central Africa.
4. **Green Mountains** mountains in Vermont.
5. **callow** (kal´ ō) *adj.* immature; inexperienced.
6. **Red Willow County** county in southwestern Nebraska that borders on Kansas.

Literary Analysis
Characterization What do the contrasting details of Aunt Georgiana's life in Boston and Nebraska reveal about her character?

✺ ENRICHMENT: Literary Connection

Reaction to Cather's Story

When this story appeared, it created a hue and cry among some of Willa Cather's fellow-Nebraskans, who claimed it was unfair to the state in which she had been raised. The story also offended Cather's family, because her uncle and aunt were obviously the models for the fictional Uncle Howard and Aunt Georgiana. (Cather's Aunt Franc, who had attended Smith College and Mount Holyoke College, later married George Cather and went to live in a sod house in Nebraska.) Cather defended her story, saying that it paid tribute to the brave women who endured the desolation and loneliness of life on the frontier.

But Mrs. Springer knew nothing of all this, and must have been considerably shocked at what was left of my kinswoman. Beneath the soiled linen duster, which on her arrival was the most conspicuous feature of her costume, she wore a black stuff dress whose ornamentation showed that she had surrendered herself unquestioningly into the hands of a country dressmaker. My poor aunt's figure, however, would have presented astonishing difficulties to any dressmaker. Her skin was yellow from constant exposure to a pitiless wind, and to the alkaline water which transforms the most transparent cuticle into a sort of flexible leather. She wore ill-fitting false teeth. The most striking thing about her physiognomy, however, was an incessant twitching of the mouth and eyebrows, a form of nervous disorder resulting from isolation and monotony, and from frequent physical suffering.

In my boyhood this affliction had possessed a sort of horrible fascination for me, of which I was secretly very much ashamed, for in those days I owed to this woman most of the good that ever came my way, and had a <u>reverential</u> affection for her. During the three winters when I was riding herd for my uncle, my aunt, after cooking three meals for half a dozen farmhands, and putting the six children to bed, would often stand until midnight at her ironing board, hearing me at the kitchen table beside her recite Latin declensions and conjugations, and gently shaking me when my drowsy head sank down over a page of irregular verbs. It was to her, at her ironing or mending, that I read my first Shakespeare; and her old textbook of mythology was the first that ever came into my empty hands. She taught me my scales and exercises, too, on the little parlor organ which her husband had bought her after fifteen years, during which she had not so much as seen any instrument except an accordion, that belonged to one of the Norwegian farmhands. She would sit beside me by the hour, darning and counting, while I struggled with the "Harmonious Blacksmith"; but she seldom talked to me about music, and I understood why. She was a pious woman; she had the consolation of religion; and to her at least her martyrdom was not wholly sordid. Once when I had been doggedly beating out some passages from an old score of "Euryanthe" I had found among her music books, she came up to me and, putting her hands over my eyes, gently drew my head back upon her shoulder, saying <u>tremulously</u>, "Don't love it so well, Clark, or it may be taken from you. Oh! dear boy, pray that whatever your sacrifice be it is not that."

When my aunt appeared on the morning after her arrival, she was still in a <u>semi-somnambulant</u> state. She seemed not to realize that she was in the city where she had spent her youth, the place longed for hungrily for half a lifetime. She had been so wretchedly trainsick throughout the journey that she had no recollection of anything but her discomfort, and, to all intents and purposes, there were but a few hours of nightmare between the farm in Red Willow County and my study on Newbury Street. I had planned a little pleasure for her that afternoon, to repay her for some of the glorious moments she had given me when

Literary Analysis
Characterization and First-Person Narrator
Which details of this paragraph show who is narrating this story?

reverential (rev´ ə ren´ shəl) *adj.* caused by a feeling of deep respect and love

tremulously (trem´ yōō ləs lē) *adv.* fearfully; timidly

semi-somnambulant (sem´ i säm nam´ byōō lənt) *adj.* half-sleepwalking

8 ✓**Reading Check**
When Clark was a boy, what subjects did he learn from his aunt?

---

6 **Literary Analysis**
Characterization and First-Person Narrator

- Ask a student volunteer to summarize the characteristics of first-person narration. Then invite students to identify the narrator of this story and to state the relationship between him and the main characters.

- Ask students the Literary Analysis question on p. 679: Which details of this paragraph show who is narrating the story?
  Answer: Students might mention details such as *my kinswoman* and *My poor aunt's figure.*

7 **Critical Thinking**
Connect; Analyze

- Explain to students that in *Euryanthe*, the opera by Carl Maria von Weber (1786–1826), Euryanthe is falsely accused and then led by the man she loves into the desert to die. If necessary, point out how Euryanthe's story echoes the theme of martyrdom in the wilderness to which Cather alludes in this passage.

- Invite students to discuss Aunt Georgiana's martyrdom, and its relation to the strong feelings she has for music. Ask students how these things influence her warning to Clark.
  Possible response: Students may say that Aunt Georgiana is a martyr because she left something she loved deeply in order to be with her husband. Recognizing the pain of her decision, she advises Clark to moderate his love for music, lest he lose it and feel pain, as she did.

8 ✓**Reading Check**
Answer: He studied Latin, Shakespeare, mythology, and music.

CUSTOMIZE INSTRUCTION FOR UNIVERSAL ACCESS

For Less Proficient Readers	For Advanced Readers
Slowly read aloud—and then have students reread— the first paragraph on p. 679. Then, guide students to notice how this passage presents physical descriptions of Georgiana that provide further insight into her character. What can students infer about Georgiana's temperament from this description of the effects of life on the prairie? What does the narrator's description tell the reader about *his* character?	Encourage students to do research in order to report on the effect of the Homestead Act, which allowed Georgiana's husband to get land without paying for it. In 1862, Congress passed the Homestead Act to advance settlement of the prairie lands of the American West. The Act offered 160 acres of free land to anyone over twenty-one years of age who was an American citizen. Permanent ownership of the land came after five years of residence or after six months and payment of $1.25 an acre.

Wagner's tragic opera *Tristan and Isolde* (the prelude of which Clark and his aunt hear toward the end of the story) is an example of a tragic ending brought on by love. Isolde has been promised to the King, and Tristan must deliver her to him. As Tristan and Isolde declare their love for one another, one of the King's knights surprises them in the King's garden. Tristan is mortally wounded and Isolde breathes her last breath over his body.

❿ **Vocabulary Development**

Word Origins

• Read aloud this passage for students and draw their attention to the capitalized word *Conservatory*. Invite a student volunteer to explain why the word is capitalized here. (It refers to a particular institution, the Boston Conservatory, first mentioned on p. 678.)

• Have students look up the origins of the word *conservatory* as a strategy for understanding its meaning. Ask them to trace the changes in the word's usage.

• Invite some students to explain to the rest of the class how the origins of *conservatory* relate to its use in the story.

Answer: The word derives from the Latin word *servare* ("to keep, preserve"), which in turn comes from the Indo-European stem *ser* ("to watch over"). A conservatory is a school devoted to the preservation and teaching of an art form such as music, as well as to the nurture of developing artists.

---

we used to milk together in the straw-thatched cowshed, and she, because I was more than usually tired, or because her husband had spoken sharply to me, would tell me of the splendid performance of Meyerbeer's *Les Huguenots*[7] she had seen in Paris in her youth. At two o'clock the Boston Symphony Orchestra was to give a Wagner* program, and I intended to take my aunt, though as I conversed with her I grew doubtful about her enjoyment of it. Indeed, for her own sake, I could only wish her taste for such things quite dead, and the long struggle mercifully ended at last. I suggested our visiting the Conservatory and the Common[8] before lunch, but she seemed altogether too timid to wish to venture out. She questioned me absently about various changes in the city, but she was chiefly concerned that she had forgotten to leave instructions about feeding half-skimmed milk to a certain weakling calf, "Old Maggie's calf, you know, Clark," she explained, evidently having forgotten how long I had been away. She was further troubled because she had neglected to tell her daughter about the freshly opened kit of mackerel in the cellar, that would spoil if it were not used directly.

I asked her whether she had ever heard any of the Wagnerian operas, and found that she had not, though she was perfectly familiar with their respective situations and had once possessed the piano score of *The Flying Dutchman*. I began to think it would have been best to get her back to Red Willow County without waking her, and regretted having suggested the concert.

From the time we entered the concert hall, however, she was a trifle less passive and <u>inert</u>, and seemed to begin to perceive her surroundings. I had felt some trepidation[9] lest one might become aware of the absurdities of her attire, or might experience some painful embarrassment at stepping suddenly into the world to which she had been dead for a quarter of a century. But again I found how superficially I had judged her. She sat looking about her with eyes as impersonal, almost as stony, as those with which the granite Ramses[10] in a museum watches the froth and fret that ebbs and flows about his pedestal, separated from it by the lonely stretch of centuries. I have seen this same aloofness in old miners who drift into the Brown Hotel at Denver, their pockets full of bullion, their linen soiled, their haggard faces unshorn, and who

---

7. **Les Huguenots** (läz hyōō′ gə nät′) opera written in 1836 by Giacomo Meyerbeer (1791–1864).
8. **Common** Boston Common, a small park in Boston.
9. **trepidation** (trep′ ə dā′ shən) *n.* fearful anxiety; apprehension.
10. **Ramses** (ram′ sēz) one of the eleven Egyptian kings by that name who ruled from c. 1292 to c. 1075 B.C.

---

*L*iterature
in context Music Connection

❾ ◆ *Wagner Operas*

Aunt Georgiana has a strong reaction to the music of Richard Wagner, the composer of *The Flying Dutchman* (1843). Wagner rejected some of the traditions of opera. To that end, he usually avoided lengthy musical speeches and instead originated the *leitmotif*, a dominant recurring musical theme used to symbolize an important emotion or event. Wagner also wrote what he called "music dramas." An entire series of these works, which would later be called *The Ring of the Nibelung*, consumed twenty-six years of his life. In "A Wagner Matinée," the audience hears excerpts from the *Ring* and from *Siegfried*, an opera based on the adventures of a legendary hero in medieval German literature.

inert (in urt′) *adj.* motionless

❋ **ENRICHMENT: Cultural Connection**

Opera

Opera is as rich culturally as it is musically. Richard Wagner's opera brought German mythology to life with stirring music and drama. Earlier opera composers, such as Claudio Monteverdi and Christoph Gluck, relied on classical stories of ancient Greece and Rome for their subjects. Nationalism burst onto the musical scene in Czechoslovakia and Russia in the operas of Antonin Dvorák and Modest Mussorgsky, who incorporated their cultures' rich folk music into their operas. English composer Gustav Holst's opera *Savitri* is based on an episode from the Hindu epic *Mahabharata*, and George Gershwin dramatized African American life in *Porgy and Bess*. Today, opera is truly an international art form: singers perform in many languages in opera houses around the world. Have students listen to some or all of an opera or watch a video of an operatic performance. Ask them to analyze how the music conveys the characters' feelings and thoughts, and reaches audiences in ways that differ from non-musical theatrical productions.

stand in the thronged corridors as solitary as though they were still in a frozen camp on the Yukon, or in the yellow blaze of the Arizona desert, conscious that certain experiences have isolated them from their fellows by a gulf no haberdasher could conceal.

The audience was made up chiefly of women. One lost the contour of faces and figures, indeed any effect of line whatever, and there was only the color contrast of bodices past counting, the shimmer and shading of fabrics soft and firm, silky and sheer, resisting and yielding: red, mauve, pink, blue, lilac, purple, ecru, rose, yellow, cream, and white, all the colors that an impressionist finds in a sunlit landscape, with here and there the dead black shadow of a frock coat. My Aunt Georgiana regarded them as though they had been so many daubs of tube paint on a palette.

When the musicians came out and took their places, she gave a little stir of anticipation, and looked with quickening interest down over the rail at that invariable grouping; perhaps the first wholly familiar thing that had greeted her eye since she had left old Maggie and her weakling calf. I could feel how all those details sank into her soul, for I had not forgotten how they had sunk into mine when I came fresh from plowing forever and forever between green aisles of corn, where, as in a treadmill, one might walk from daybreak to dusk without perceiving a shadow of change in one's environment. I reminded myself of the impression made on me by the clean profiles of the musicians, the gloss of their linen; the dull black of their coats, the beloved shapes of the instruments, the patches of yellow light thrown by the green-shaded stand-lamps on the smooth, varnished bellies of the cellos and the bass viols in the rear, the restless, wind-tossed forest of fiddle necks and bows; I recalled how, in the first orchestra I had ever heard, those long bow strokes seemed to draw the soul out of me, as a conjuror's stick reels out paper ribbon from a hat.

The first number was the Tannhäuser overture. When the violins drew out the first strain of the Pilgrims' chorus, my Aunt Georgiana clutched my coat sleeve. Then it was that I first realized that for her this singing of basses and stinging frenzy of lighter strings broke a silence of thirty years, the inconceivable silence of the plains. With the battle between the two motifs, with the bitter frenzy of the Venusberg[11] theme and its ripping of strings, came to me an overwhelming sense of the waste and wear we are so powerless to combat. I saw again the tall, naked house on the prairie, black and grim as a wooden fortress; the black pond where I had learned to swim, the rain-gullied clay about the naked house; the four dwarf ash seedlings on which the dishcloths were always hung to dry before the kitchen door. The world there is the flat world of the ancients; to the east, a cornfield that stretched to daybreak; to the west, a corral that stretched to sunset; between, the sordid conquests of peace, more merciless than those of war.

---

11. **Venusberg** (vē′ nəs bûrg′) legendary mountain in Germany where Venus, the Roman goddess of love, held court.

Literary Analysis

Characterization What does Aunt Georgiana's excitement about the upcoming performance reveal about her?

 Reading Check

What is Clark's initial feeling about being in public with Aunt Georgiana? How does that attitude change?

A Wagner Matinée ◆ 681

⓫ Literary Analysis
Characterization

- Encourage students to summarize how Aunt Georgiana has behaved up until this point in the story.

- Then ask students the Literary Analysis question on p. 681: What does Aunt Georgiana's excitement about the upcoming performance reveal about her?
  Answer: It reveals that her love for music is reawakening; her suffering has not numbed her soul completely.

⓬ ✓ Reading Check

Answer: At first he feels anxious and embarrassed about how out of place and ill at ease his aunt seems. When he sees that she is absorbing details of the musicians' appearances, however, his mind wanders to memories of his own first passionate responses to the sights and sounds of an orchestra in a concert hall.

CUSTOMIZE INSTRUCTION FOR UNIVERSAL ACCESS

For Less Proficient Readers	For Advanced Readers
Encourage students to reread the two paragraphs beginning at the bottom of p. 680 to appreciate them. Help them notice that Clark was at first embarrassed by being seen with Aunt Georgiana because she looked so out of place, yet it was his idea to bring her to the concert in the first place. Clark still thinks of her as a haggard pioneer, a confused stranger in her own land. His appreciation for her grows as he realizes how much her isolation has provided her with an austere dignity.	Explain that students can dig deeper into Cather's meaning by understanding more about her references to Wagner and his operas. For example, *The Flying Dutchman*, a milestone in Wagner's career, is about a Dutch sea captain who is doomed forever to roam the seas until a curse he rashly uttered can be broken by the love of a faithful woman. Discuss how Aunt Georgiana's rash decision to marry and live out her life on the prairie has doomed her to live without her greatest joy.

- Have a student volunteer read this passage aloud. Encourage students to listen for a word that today has a meaning relating to the visual arts—but which here has a different meaning.

- Ask students: What does the author mean by "films"?

- To help students clarify, remind them to consider when Willa Cather wrote this short story.
  Answer: Students should realize that, in this context, films are probably thin layers of grime or thin membranes that grow over aging eyes, separating Aunt Georgiana from the sights of the concert hall and the world she once knew. When this story was written, the word *film* did not mean "moving picture," as it does today.

The overture closed. My aunt released my coat sleeve, but she said nothing. She sat staring at the orchestra through a dullness of thirty years, through the films made, little by little, by each of the three hundred and sixty-five days in every one of them. What, I wondered, did she get from it? She had been a good pianist in her day, I knew, and her musical education had been broader than that of most music teachers of a quarter of a century ago. She had often told me of Mozart's operas and Meyerbeer's, and I could remember hearing her sing, years ago, certain melodies of Verdi. When I had fallen ill with a fever she used to sit by my cot in the evening, while the cool night wind blew in through the faded mosquito netting tacked over the window, and I lay watching a bright star that burned red above the cornfield, and sing "Home to our mountains, oh, let us return!" in a way fit to break the heart of a Vermont boy near dead of homesickness already.

I watched her closely through the prelude to *Tristan and Isolde,* trying vainly to conjecture what that warfare of motifs, that seething turmoil of strings and winds, might mean to her. Had this music any message for her? Did or did not a new planet swim into her ken? Wagner had been a sealed book to Americans before the sixties. Had she anything left with which to comprehend this glory that had flashed around the world since she had gone from it? I was in a fever of curiosity, but Aunt Georgiana sat silent upon her peak in Darien.[12] She preserved this utter immobility throughout the numbers from the *Flying Dutchman,* though her fingers worked mechanically upon her black dress, as though of themselves they were recalling the piano score they had once played. Poor old hands! They were stretched and pulled and twisted into

prelude (prel´ yōōd) *n.* introductory section of a work of music

---

12. **peak in Darien** (der´ ē ən´) mountain on the Isthmus of Panama; from "On First Looking at Chapman's Homer" by English poet John Keats (1795–1821).

CUSTOMIZE INSTRUCTION FOR UNIVERSAL ACCESS

For Advanced Readers

Suggest that students read additional works by Willa Cather. Provide students with the titles listed in the enrichment box, ATE p. 685. You may also wish to use **Authors In Depth: The American Experience,** which contains the following selections:

- From *My Ántonia* (fiction, p. 123)
- "Prairie Spring" (poem, p. 131)
- "The Sentimentality of William Taverner" (fiction, p. 133)

After students have read these or other works by Cather, have them form discussion groups in which they compare and contrast the selections they have read. Suggest criteria for comparison, such as historical context or sense of place. To extend the activity, have volunteers present brief reports on Cather's influence on later writers, such as Truman Capote.

mere tentacles to hold, and lift, and knead with; the palms unduly swollen, the fingers bent and knotted, on one of them a thin worn band that had once been a wedding ring. As I pressed and gently quieted one of those groping hands, I remembered, with quivering eyelids, their services for me in other days.

Soon after the tenor began the "Prize Song," I heard a quick-drawn breath, and turned to my aunt. Her eyes were closed, but the tears were glistening on her cheeks, and I think in a moment more they were in my eyes as well. It never really dies, then, the soul? It withers to the outward eye only, like that strange moss which can lie on a dusty shelf half a century and yet, if placed in water, grows green again. My aunt wept gently throughout the development and elaboration of the melody.

During the intermission before the second half of the concert, I questioned my aunt and found that the "Prize Song" was not new to her. Some years before there had drifted to the farm in Red Willow County a young German, a tramp cow puncher who had sung in the chorus at Bayreuth,[13] when he was a boy, along with the other peasant boys and girls. Of a Sunday morning he used to sit on his blue gingham-sheeted bed in the hands' bedroom, which opened off the kitchen, cleaning the leather of his boots and saddle, and singing the "Prize Song," while my aunt went about her work in the kitchen. She had hovered about him until she had prevailed upon him to join the country church, though his sole fitness for this step, so far as I could gather, lay in his boyish face and his possession of this divine melody. Shortly afterward he had gone to town on the Fourth of July, lost his money at a faro[14] table, ridden a saddled Texas steer on a bet, and disappeared with a fractured collarbone.

"Well, we have come to better things than the old *Trovatore* at any rate, Aunt Georgie?" I queried, with well-meant jocularity.

jocularity (jäk´ yoo lar´ ə tē) *n.* joking good humor

Her lip quivered and she hastily put her handkerchief up to her mouth. From behind it she murmured, "And you've been hearing this ever since you left me, Clark?" Her question was the gentlest and saddest of reproaches.

"But do you get it, Aunt Georgiana, the astonishing structure of it all?" I persisted.

"Who could?" she said, absently; "why should one?"

The second half of the program consisted of four numbers from the *Ring*. This was followed by the forest music from *Siegfried*[15] and the program closed with Siegfried's funeral march. My aunt wept quietly, but almost continuously. I was perplexed as to what measure of musical comprehension was left to her, to her who had heard nothing for so many years but the singing of gospel hymns in Methodist

---

13. **Bayreuth** (bī roit´) city in Germany known for its annual Wagnerian music festivals.
14. **faro** (fer´ ō) gambling game in which players bet on the cards to be turned up from the top of the dealer's deck.
15. **Siegfried** (sēg´ frēd) opera based on the adventures of Siegfried, a legendary hero in medieval German literature.

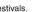 **✓ Reading Check**

Describe Aunt Georgiana's reaction during the "Prize Song."

 ✓ Reading Check

Answer: After a quickly-drawn breath, she begins to weep as she listens to the melody played by the musicians.

CUSTOMIZE INSTRUCTION FOR UNIVERSAL ACCESS

For Less Proficient Readers	For Gifted/Talented Students
Help students understand the meaning of the end of this story. For instance, help students clarify that the phrase *just outside the door* at the beginning of the story's last paragraph is intended to be taken both literally and symbolically. The concert hall represents an oasis in Aunt Georgiana's life; once she leaves it, she must return to a life of deprivation on the prairie. Clark recognizes that Georgiana might as well step directly from the hall into her bleak yard in Nebraska.	The passage beginning at the bottom of p. 681 contains many technical words from music, including *overture, violins, strain, chorus, basses,* and *motifs,* as well as descriptions of the way the violin passages sound: *singing, lighter strings, ripping of strings.* Invite students to use a musical dictionary or other resource to explore the meaning of all of these terms.

Review and Assess

1. Students should be prepared to explain their answers.

2. **(a)** She taught music at the Boston Conservatory. **(b)** Life in Red Willow County is physically and psychologically brutal: the climate is harsh; the work never-ending and back-breaking; there are few people with whom to socialize; and there is no music or sophisticated culture. By contrast, life amid Boston's cultural opportunities, people, and society seems stimulating and enjoyable.

3. **(a)** He practiced musical scales, exercises, the "Harmonious Blacksmith," and some passages from "Euryanthe." **(b)** She means that when one loves something deeply, that person can become vulnerable to a profound sense of loss if that thing disappears. **(c)** Her own deep engagement with music was lost when she moved to the Nebraska prairie.

4. **(a)** She stirs in her seat, breathes quickly, and weeps. **(b)** She hasn't heard such music in decades, and it awakens her long-dormant passion for music.

5. **(a)** It evokes memories of "a young German, a tramp cow puncher" who sang the song while she worked in the kitchen. **(b)** She doesn't get up, and she cries out that she doesn't want to leave.

6. Some may agree that it would be better if she had not come, because her visit is a cruel reminder of all that she lost when she moved to Nebraska.

---

services at the square frame schoolhouse on Section Thirteen. I was unable to gauge how much of it had been dissolved in soapsuds, or worked into bread, or milked into the bottom of a pail.

The deluge of sound poured on and on; I never knew what she found in the shining current of it; I never knew how far it bore her, or past what happy islands, or under what skies. From the trembling of her face I could well believe that the *Siegfried* march, at least, carried her out where the myriad graves are, out into the gray, burying grounds of the sea; or into some world of death vaster yet, where, from the beginning of the world, hope has lain down with hope, and dream with dream and, renouncing, slept.

The concert was over; the people filed out of the hall chattering and laughing, glad to relax and find the living level again, but my kinswoman made no effort to rise. I spoke gently to her. She burst into tears and sobbed pleadingly, "I don't want to go, Clark, I don't want to go!"

I understood. For her, just outside the door of the concert hall, lay the black pond with the cattle-tracked bluffs, the tall, unpainted house, naked as a tower, with weather-curled boards; the crook-backed ash seedlings where the dishcloths hung to dry, the gaunt, moulting turkeys picking up refuse about the kitchen door.

Review and Assess

Thinking About the Selection

1. **Respond:** Do you feel sorry for Aunt Georgiana? Why or why not?

2. **(a) Recall:** What part did Boston play in Aunt Georgiana's earlier life? **(b) Compare and Contrast:** In what ways would you compare and contrast life in Boston and life in Red Willow County?

3. **(a) Recall:** As a boy, what did the narrator practice on the "parlor organ" in the Nebraska farmhouse? **(b) Interpret:** What does Aunt Georgiana mean when she says, "Don't love it so well, Clark, or it may be taken from you"? **(c) Connect:** Do the events of the story reinforce her statement? Explain.

4. **(a) Recall:** What physical reactions indicate that Aunt Georgiana is affected powerfully by the concert? **(b) Analyze:** Why does the music have this effect on her?

5. **(a) Recall:** What memories does the "Prize Song" evoke in Aunt Georgiana? **(b) Connect:** How does Aunt Georgiana react at the end of the concert?

6. **Take a Position:** Would it have been better for Aunt Georgiana if she had not come to Boston? Explain.

ASSESSMENT PRACTICE: Reading Comprehension

Context	(For more practice, see Test Preparation Workbook, p. 40.)

Many tests require students to use context clues to choose the appropriate definition of multiple-meaning words. Use the following sample test item:

> When the train arrived I had some difficulty in finding my aunt. She was the last of the passengers to <u>alight</u>, and when I got her into the carriage she looked not unlike one of those charred, smoked bodies that firemen lift from the débris of a burned building.

In this passage, the word <u>alight</u> means—

A light a fire on the platform

C descend from the train

B turn on the light

D enter her compartment

The narrator is waiting for his aunt and has trouble finding her because she is the last passenger to get off the train. *B* is the correct answer.

Review and Assess

Literary Analysis

Characterization

1. What is revealed about Aunt Georgiana's character through descriptions of her appearance or comments by her and other characters? Record your findings in a chart like the one shown.

Aunt Georgiana

Physical Description | Direct Statements Made by Clark | Her Own Actions and Words

2. What does Aunt Georgiana's reaction to the opera reveal about her personality?

3. What do his thoughts and feelings about his aunt reveal about Clark's personality?

Connecting Literary Elements

4. What effect does Clark's **first-person point of view** have on your perception of Aunt Georgiana?

5. (a) Find two examples of events Clark recalls from living with Aunt Georgiana. (b) How do these events help to shape your impression of her?

6. (a) How do Clark's feelings toward his aunt change during the course of the story? (b) How do his feelings affect your response to her?

7. If the story were told by Aunt Georgiana, how would it change?

Reading Strategy

Clarifying

8. Which details about the harshness of life in Nebraska help to **clarify** your understanding of Aunt Georgiana's background?

9. Which details about Aunt Georgiana's life in Nebraska help you understand her timid behavior upon arriving in Boston?

10. Explain the significance of the fact that Aunt Georgiana's husband bought her "a little parlor organ" after fifteen years in Nebraska.

Extend Understanding

11. **Cultural Connection:** How are people's personalities shaped by the environment in which they live? Support your answer.

☀ ENRICHMENT: Further Reading

Other Works by Willa Cather

O Pioneers!

My Ántonia

Death Comes for the Archbishop

 Take It to the Net

Visit www.phschool.com for more information on Willa Cather.

Quick Review

Characterization is the variety of techniques a writer uses to reveal a character's personality.

When a story is told in the **first-person point-of-view**, a character involved in the action relates the events.

To **clarify meaning** about something you do not understand, reread a passage, read a footnote, look up a word, or read ahead.

 Take It to the Net
www.phschool.com
Take the interactive self-test online to check your understanding of the selection.

Answers continued

10. **Possible response:** The well-meaning gesture merely accentuates the enormity of her sacrifice.

11. Students' responses should reflect their understanding of how Georgiana was changed by her years on the farm.

Answers for p. 685

Review and Assess

1. Physical description—roughened and aged, twitches nervously Clark's statements—"with that feeling of awe and respect with which we behold explorers . . .", "She was a pious woman. . . ."; Her actions/words "Don't love it so well, Clark, or it may be taken from you."

2. Her passionate love for music is still alive; her harsh life has not deadened her spirit.

3. He is grateful and affectionate toward his aunt for all she has done for him. Yet, as a cultured Bostonian, he is embarrassed by his aunt's appearance.

4. Because we learn from him about the type of person she once was and all that she has done for Clark, we come to view Aunt Georgiana with respect and sympathy.

5. **(a)** Students might mention events such as her listening to him practice Latin and musical scales, or exhorting him not to love music too much. **(b)** Despite the harshness of her life and her physical oddities, Georgiana feels a deep, constant passion for music and for a cultured life.

6. **(a)** At the beginning of the story he feels embarrassed about her, since he sees her as a pathetic figure; by the story's end, he recognizes that her soul, as revealed in her love of music, is intact. **(b)** His feelings encourage the reader to see her first as merely a victim, but later as a fascinating, deeply conflicted person of great imagination and feeling.

7. **Possible response:** The reader would see Clark's role in in her past and present life more clearly.

8. Students might mention details such as the dugout likened to a "cave dwelling," "cooking three meals a day for half a dozen farmhands . . .", or her concern about the weak calf and about the uneaten mackerel.

9. After decades of isolation from the elegance and culture of Boston, Georgiana feels and acts as though she is walking through a dream world.

continued

Answers for p. 686

❶ Vocabulary Development

Concept Development

1. b
2. b

Spelling Strategy

1. potential
2. exponential

Fluency: Word Meanings

1. They respect her. They feel reverent towards her.

2. a child—A child is more likely to speak fearfully or timidly. Students may also respond that Georgiana is a musician, and speaks tremulously.

3. dazed—A half-sleep walking person is dazed.

4. motionless—Students may point out that an inert substance does not react with other elements, while an inert object does not move.

5. seriousness—An introduction to bad news is most often serious.

6. a talk-show host—Talk-show hosts often display joking good humor.

❷ Grammar and Style

1. *herself*, reflexive
2. *herself*, reflexive
3. *itself*, intensive
4. *themselves*, reflexive
5. *herself*, intensive

Writing Application

Students' descriptions of conversations among three or more people should contain at least one reflexive and one intensive pronoun.

Integrate Language Skills

❶ Vocabulary Development Lesson

Concept Development: Words From Music

Musical vocabulary can have two meanings. A *prelude* is a musical introduction, but it also refers to preparation for any important matter. Select the best definition for each sentence.

overture: (a) an introductory movement to an extended musical work, (b) any first movement

concert: (a) a performance of several short compositions, (b) working together

1. We put a *concerted* effort into the game.
2. He made an *overture* to pay my bill.

Spelling Strategy

When adding the suffix *-ial* to words ending in two consonants, keep the spelling of the base word. For example, *reverent* becomes *reverential*. Fill in the blanks with *-ial* words.

1. A talented person has great p__ial.
2. Our speed grew at an ex__ial rate.

❷ Grammar and Style Lesson

Reflexive and Intensive Pronouns

Both reflexive and intensive pronouns end in *-self* or *-selves*, but they function differently. **Reflexive pronouns** refer to the subject and are necessary to the meaning of a sentence. **Intensive pronouns** emphasize a word in a sentence, but can be omitted without changing the meaning of a sentence. Consider the following examples:

Reflexive: He took *himself* to the box office.

Intensive: *Myself*, I saw her approaching.

WG *Prentice Hall Writing and Grammar Connection: Chapter 17, Section 1*

686 ◆ *Division, Reconciliation, and Expansion (1850–1914)*

Fluency: Word Meanings

Review the words in the vocabulary list on p. 675. Then, answer the following questions. Explain your responses.

1. If students are *reverential* toward a teacher, do they ignore or respect her?
2. Who is most likely to speak *tremulously*—a musician, a truck driver, or a child?
3. Does *semi-somnambulant* describe some-one who is angry, dazed, or busy?
4. Is an *inert* substance motionless or weightless?
5. As a *prelude* to bad news, would you expect sarcasm or seriousness?
6. Is *jocularity* likely to be the trademark of a funeral director or a talk-show host?

Practice Identify the reflexive and intensive pronouns in these sentences.

1. Cather devoted herself to writing.
2. She quit her job to give herself time.
3. For Cather, writing itself was a full-time job.
4. Books don't write themselves.
5. Cather herself said writing was challenging.

Writing Application Write a description of a conversation among three or more people. Use reflexive and intensive pronouns.

TEACHING RESOURCES

The following resources can be used to enrich or extend the instruction for pp. 686–687.

Vocabulary

📖 **Selection Support:** Build Vocabulary, 168

📖 **Vocabulary and Spelling Practice Book**
(Use this booklet for skills enrichment.)

Grammar

📖 **Selection Support Workbook:** Grammar and Style, p. 169 ■

WG **Writing and Grammar,** Ruby Level, p. 367

📑 **Daily Language Practice Transparencies**

Writing

WG **Writing and Grammar,** Ruby Level, p. 330 ■

📖 **Extension Activities**

📑 **Writing Models and Graphic Organizers on Transparencies,** pp. 33–36

💿 **Writing and Grammar iText CD-ROM**

■ **BLOCK SCHEDULING:** Resources marked with this symbol provide varied instruction during 90-minute blocks.

❸ Writing Lesson

Editorial

"A Wagner Matinée" provoked an outcry among Nebraskans who felt Cather had portrayed the state unfairly. Cather responded that the story was a tribute to pioneer strength and endurance. As the editor of a Nebraska newspaper, take a position and write an editorial stating and defending your view.

Prewriting	Reread the story. Analyze the details Cather gives to portray both Nebraska and Boston, and decide whether or not you agree with her views. Jot down your thoughts that support or rebut Cather.
Drafting	Arrange your views in order of priority. Provide both factual evidence and emotional appeals to support your statements.
Revising	Reread your editorial to make sure that your language is specific and persuasive and that you have defended your views. Replace vague words to make your writing stronger and add more support as needed.

Model: Using Specific Language

Cather implies that Boston offers more than Nebraska.

While it may be true that Boston is a center for art,

cultural resources   *pollution and congestion*

Nebraska offers many ~~things~~ without the ~~trouble~~ of a

major city.

> Specific references such as *cultural resources* and *pollution and congestion* make the editorial clear and persuasive.

 Prentice Hall Writing and Grammar Connection: Chapter 15, Section 2

❹ Extension Activities

Listening and Speaking With a classmate, take on the roles of Aunt Georgiana and Clark. Create **monologues** that give contrasting interpretations of the effect of the opera on Aunt Georgiana. Consider the following details:

- What memories were drawn out?
- What were the physical reactions?

Present both monologues to the class.
[Group Activity]

Research and Technology Listen to a recording of one of Wagner's operas, and research the opera's story. Give a **musical presentation** of one of the passages from the opera to your classmates, explaining the piece's significance in the opera.

 Take It to the Net   www.phschool.com

Go online for an additional research activity using the Internet

---

ASSESSMENT RESOURCES

The following resources can be used to assess students' knowledge and skills.

Selection Assessment

- **Formal Assessment**, pp. 176–178
- **Open Book Test**, pp. 112–114
- **Got It! Assessment Videotapes**, Tape 3
- **Test Bank Software**

Take It to the Net
Visit www.phschool.com for self-tests and additional questions on the selection.

Listening and Speaking Rubric

- **Performance Assess. and Portfolio Mgmt.**, p. 30

 PRENTICE HALL **ASSESSMENT SYSTEM**

- **Workbook**
- **Skill Book**
- **Transparencies**
- **CD-ROM**

---

❸ Writing Lesson

- Students' editorials should clearly express and support an opinion about Cather's portrayal of Nebraska in "A Wagner Matinée."

- If students have trouble identifying with Cather's fellow-Nebraskans, as a prewriting activity you might wish to have students reflect on how an author such as Willa Cather might portray the area in which you live. Encourage students to identify and discuss any aspects of your community or region that might be portrayed in what some might consider an "unfavorable light."

- Use the Writing Lesson, as well as Writing Process Model 6 in **Writing Models and Graphic Organizers on Transparencies**, pp. 33–36, to guide students in developing their editorials.

❹ Listening and Speaking

- Encourage students to reread several times the paragraphs concerning Clark's and Georgiana's time in the concert hall.

- You might have each group divide itself into Aunt Georgianas and Clarks and urge them to discuss their contrasting interpretations while they are "in character." One student might write down especially convincing details to be used in each character's monologue.

- Have students use the Peer Assessment form for Delivering a Speech, p. 30 in **Performance Assessment and Portfolio Management**.

CUSTOMIZE INSTRUCTION
For Universal Access

To address different learning styles, use the following activities suggested in the **Extension Activities** booklet, p. 38.

For Visual/Spatial Learners, use Activity 5.

For Musical/Rhythmic Learners, use Activity 6.

For Verbal/Linguistic Learners, use Activity 7.

Lesson Objectives

1. To understand the connection between the isolation described by such contemporary authors as Anna Quindlen and that described by writers during the period 1850–1914, such as Willa Cather

2. To understand how universal themes appear in various forms in literature from different historical periods

Connections

The themes of alienation, isolation, and loneliness emerged strongly at the turn of the twentieth century, a time of tremendous change that separated people from one another, leaving many alone. As students read this contemporary essay about an elderly woman's alienation from society, instruct them to look for emotions and themes that echo the work of the authors featured in Part 4, especially Willa Cather.

Living in a Changing World

- Be sure that students understand that in a time of great change—social, economic, technological—people can become alienated from their world and left isolated and alone.

- Remind students that this aspect of life in the changing America of the turn of the twentieth century was a major theme linking the works in Part 4. You can point to Willa Cather's Aunt Georgiana in "A Wagner Matinee."

- Explain to students that they, too, live in a time of great change. Encourage them to discuss these changes. You can suggest: cellular phones, the Internet, and digital television and music.

- Point out to students that these changes, like those of Cather's time, could leave people alienated and lonely. Instruct them to look for these themes as they read Anna Quindlen's "Cats."

Writer Joyce Carol Oates once described Willa Cather as "a passionate chronicler of her time and place." The same can be said of Anna Quindlen. Although separated by nearly a century, both writers explore similar emotional terrain, charting the inner struggles and conflicts of the individual in a changing society.

A New Literary Sensibility The America of Willa Cather's youth was a nation in the midst of rapid and massive change. Industry and technology were booming. Confronted by these changes in society and its values, many writers struggled to find meaning in lives that were isolated from others. Out of this struggle, a new literary movement emerged. Known as Realism, this body of literature was often colored by loneliness and alienation.

A Loss of Community With the dawning of the Information Age, America is again undergoing a transformation. While some find the changes exciting, for others the loneliness and alienation of a century ago are still a reality. The symptoms are not hard to spot. People log anonymously onto chat rooms or spend hours watching television instead of chatting with flesh-and-blood neighbors. They move every few years in pursuit of better jobs, often losing family and community ties.

In her column "Life in the '30s," Anna Quindlen took the school, the neighborhood, and the office as her territory. In her work, Quindlen reveals a profound underside of loneliness and isolation.

688   *Division, Reconciliation, and Expansion (1850–1914)*

Cats

Anna Quindlen

The cats came with the house. They lived in the backyards, tiger gray, orange marmalade, calico, black. They slithered through the evergreens at the back perimeter, and during mating season their screams were terrible. Sometimes I shook black pepper along the property line, and for a night or two all was still. Then the rain came and they were back.

The cats came because of the woman next door. She and her husband, said to be bedridden, had lived on the third floor for many years. Every evening after dinner she went into the alley with a foil pie plate heaped with cat food and scraps: cabbage, rice, the noodles from chicken noodle soup, whatever they had had for dinner. Before she would even get to the bottom of the stairs the cats would begin to assemble, narrowing their eyes. She would talk to them roughly in a voice like sandpaper, coarse from years of cigarette smoke. ". . . Cats," she grumbled as she bent to put the food down.

She had only two interests besides the cats: my son and her own. She and her husband had one grown child. I never heard her say a bad word about him. He had reportedly walked and talked early, been as beautiful as a child star, never given a bit of trouble. He always

☑ **Reading Check**

What are the neighbor's main interests?

Background
Anna Quindlen

Anna Quindlen writes of an elderly neighbor, a woman who felt a certain connection to Quindlen's small son because of his resemblance to her own son, whom she rarely sees. Quindlen muses about what her boy may remember about the woman, who has since died, and describes the inexorable end of her modest influence on the animals of the neighborhood. By extension, she examines the impact of life and death in any contemporary family or community, all far less closely knit than families and communities once were.

☑ **Reading Check**

Answer: The neighbor woman's main interests are the cats living in the alley, her son, and the narrator's son, who reminds her of her own.

CUSTOMIZE INSTRUCTION FOR UNIVERSAL ACCESS

For Less Proficient Readers	For English Learners	For Advanced Readers
Help students read this story on several levels. Most simply, it is a narrative observation with facts and details. On a deeper level, it is a personal essay that explores how an interaction between the author and a lonely neighbor made her examine the value of connections in the world.	Help these students to recognize the irony in this story by assisting them with the passage describing the neighbor's son's gifts and visit. Students may need help understanding the potential for sadness in such American traditions as Mother's Day cards and Christmas poinsettias.	When they have finished the essay, ask students to reread the last two paragraphs. Encourage them to consider the effect the woman's death had on the neighborhood and on Quindlen and her son. Have these students discuss what Quindlen might be saying here about alienation and isolation.

Living in a Changing World

- Remind students that Quindlen's neighbor reports that her son was a lovely child, and is now a dutiful adult. Then, have students read the first paragraph on this page.

- Ask students to explain whether they think the young man is as devoted to his parents as his mother says he is. On what do they base their responses? **Possible response:** Students should realize that the son may be estranged from his parents; he visits only rarely.

▶**Critical Viewing**

Answer: They are of several colors, and live in a group like Quindlan's cats. Unlike them, they are clean, well fed, and well cared for.

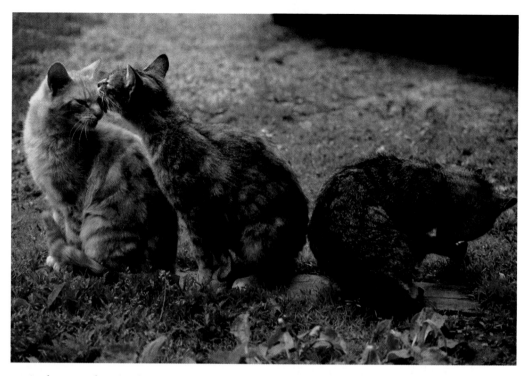

sent a large card on Mother's Day, and each Christmas a poinsettia came, wrapped in green foil with a red bow. He was in the military, stationed here and there. During the time we lived next door to her, he came home once. She said it broke his heart not to see his father more. She said they had always been close when he lived at home, that he played baseball for the high school team and that his father never missed a game. He was a crack shortstop, she said, and a superior hitter.

She called my son "Bop Bop" because of the way he bounced in my arms. It was one of the first things he learned to say, and when he was in the backyard on summer evenings he would call "Bop Bop" plaintively until she came to her apartment window. As she raised the screen the cats would begin to mass in a great Pavlovian[1] gesture at the head of the alley. "Are you being a good boy?" she would call down. Bop Bop would smile up, his eyes shining. "Cat," he said, pointing, and the cats looked, too. Some summer nights she and my little boy would sit together companionably on the front stoop, watching the cars go by. She did not talk to him very much, and she wasn't tender, but when he was very good and not terribly dirty she sometimes

▲**Critical Viewing**
In what ways are these cats like the ones Quindlen describes? How are they different? **[Compare and Contrast]**

---

1. **Pavlovian** (pav lō′ vē ən) *adj.* referring to Russian physiologist Ivan Pavlov (1849–1936), who showed that acquired habits depend on chains of conditioned reflexes.

☀ ENRICHMENT: Science Connection

Domestic Cats

The cats in Quindlen's essay are strays that lived in the alley by the author's house. Cats are also, of course, very popular pets. They appear to have been domesticated as long ago as 1500 B.C., in ancient Egypt. From the start, domestic cats were valued for their natural instincts as hunters—they were used to get rid of rodents and other pests. Cats have figured in many cultures throughout the history of their domestication, and have even played roles in some of the world's religions.

As pets today, cats are generally clean and graceful, independent in personality and yet subtly affectionate. Unlike dogs, who were pack animals before they were domesticated by humans, cats are not especially sociable and tend to be loners. This characteristic makes cats less than ideal pets for owners who expect unswerving devotion. It also indicates why household pets can turn into the alley cats of Quindlen's essay. Even pampered house cats can become completely self-reliant if necessary—or almost completely, if a stranger is willing to put out food where the cats can find it.

said he looked just like her own little boy, only his hair wasn't quite as thick.

Last year she fell on the street and broke her hip, but while she was in the hospital, they found that she had fallen because she had had a stroke, and she had had a stroke because of brain cancer. I went to see her in the hospital, and brought a picture of my son. She propped it against the water pitcher. She asked me to take care of her parakeet until she came home, to look in on her husband and to feed the cats. At night, when I came back from work, they would be prowling the yards, crying pitifully. My dogs lunged at the back windows.

When the ambulance brought her home, she looked like a scarecrow, her arms broomsticks in the armholes of her housecoat, her white hair wild. A home health-care aide came and cared for her and her husband. The woman across the street told me she was not well enough to take the bird back. The cats climbed the fire escape and banged against the screens with their bullet heads, but the aide shooed them away. My son would stand in the backyard and call "Bop Bop" at the window. One evening she threw it open and leaned out, a death's head, and shouted at him, and he cried. "Bop Bop is very sick," I said, and gave him a Popsicle.

She died this winter, a month after her husband. Her son came home for the funerals with his wife, and together they cleaned out the apartment. We sent roses to the funeral home, and the son's wife sent a nice thank-you note. The bird died the next month. Slowly the cats began to disperse. The two biggest, a tom and a female, seem to have stayed. I don't really feed them, but sometimes my son will eat lunch out back; if he doesn't finish his food, I will leave it on the table. When I look out again it is gone, and the dogs are a little wild.

My son likes to look through photo albums. In one there is a picture of her leaning out the window, and a picture of him looking up with a self-conscious smile. He calls them both "Bop Bop." I wonder for how long he will remember, and what it will mean to him, years from now, when he looks at the picture and sees her at her window, what reverberations will begin, what lasting lessons will she have subliminally taught him, what lasting lessons will she not so subliminally have taught me.

Thematic Connection
Setting Compare and contrast the alienated and disconnected life of Quindlen's neighbor with that of Aunt Georgiana in "A Wagner Matinée."

Anna Quindlen

(b. 1953)

Anna Quindlen was a *New York Times* reporter and editor and an aspiring novelist when the *Times* asked her to write a weekly column. She accepted the offer, never dreaming of where it might lead. Quindlen's column, "Life in the '30s," was a well-loved *Times* feature for more than two years, beginning in 1986. Quindlen's approach to the column—honest, personal, empathetic, astute—helps explain its immense popularity. She won a Pulitzer Prize for a commentary in 1992.

Connecting Literature Past and Present

1. With which characters from the selections in this section does Quindlen's neighbor have the most in common?
2. In what ways do Quindlen's neighbor and the character from another selection try to give meaning to their lonely lives?
3. Could "Cats" have been written one hundred years ago? Why or why not?

Connections: Cats ◆ 691

Thematic Connection

Possible response: Both women lead isolated lives, separated from what they love most dearly. Georgiana left her world behind voluntarily, out of love; however, we do not know what brought the neighbor to her disconnected state.

Answers for p. 691
Connecting Literature Past and Present

1. **Possible response:** She has the most in common with Aunt Georgiana in "A Wagner Matinée." Students may say she has something in common with Edgar Lee Masters's "Lucinda Matlock." Students should be able to explain the connection between the neighbor and the character they cite.

2. **Possible response:** The neighbor "adopts" cats and Quindlen's small son. For example, Georgiana also "adopts" her nephew, Cather's narrator.

3. **Possible response:** Students may say that absent contemporary details, the premise of an emotionally isolated old woman who loses ties to her beloved son could have been explored by any of the writers in Part 4. Its themes and emotions are timeless and universal. Others may disagree, saying Quindlen centers on today's impersonal world, one increasingly devoid of communal ties.

Objectives

1. To write an analytical essay comparing and contrasting literary themes
2. To analyze three or more selections from Unit 4 and determine the writers' views toward their enemies
3. To construct a thesis statement summing up the similarities and differences and support it with examples
4. To use writing strategies to generate ideas, plan, organize, evaluate, and revise writing

Prewriting

- Explain to students that they should begin prewriting by carefully considering their impressions of the works in Unit 4. Review the questions on p. 692 with the class.

- Instruct students to reread any selections from Unit 4 that made strong impressions on them. As they read, students should ask themselves the Review the Material questions on p. 692 and write the answers in their notes.

- Have students review their notes and choose several works that offer the most striking similarities and contrasts. Then, ask them to create charts like the one on p. 692 to analyze the similarities and differences among the works. **Possible responses: The Gettysburg Address:** enemy is not mentioned explicitly; enemy is fighting *against* a just and noble cause; **An Account of the Battle of Bull Run:** enemy is not mentioned explicitly; no mention of either side's cause for fighting

- As students make their final selections, remind them that they can either work in depth on three works or address more works in less depth.

Writing About Literature
Compare and Contrast Literary Themes

Many of the selections in this unit address the American experience in the years just before and during the Civil War. Unlike other wars, in which the enemy was a separate and distant power, the Civil War pitted neighbor against neighbor, friend against friend, son against father. The enemy, as both an idea and a reality, had never before posed so painful or complex a problem.

Explore this issue in greater depth by completing the assignment given in the yellow box at right.

Prewriting

Review the material. After reading the selections in this unit, make notes exploring your impressions about each writer's attitude toward the enemy. Use the following questions to organize your thinking:

- Did each writer seem sure of the rightness of his or her cause?
- Did each writer seem eager for armed conflict?
- Did any writer express fear that the enemy might be victorious?
- Did any writer express sympathy for or understanding of the enemy?
- Did any writer seem to lack strong feeling toward the enemy?

As you address these and other questions, write brief statements identifying the selections that show the strongest connections or present the starkest contrasts.

Select works to compare and contrast. To create an engaging essay, the writers whose work you select should present marked differences or surprising similarities. Use a chart like the one shown to develop your analysis of the selections.

Model: Charting to Analyze Similarities and Differences

"Go Down, Moses"	My Bondage and My Freedom
Enemy is seen as evil and oppressive.	Enemy is seen as trapped and pathetic.
Attitude toward enemy is one of eagerness for revenge.	Attitude toward enemy is one of criticism but also sympathy.

After completing your analysis, identify the points of comparison and contrast that you find most interesting and important. Determine an initial approach to organizing your essay. You may either compare three selections in depth, or discuss a larger number of selections more briefly.

692 ◆ *Division, Reconciliation, and Expansion (1850–1914)*

Assignment: Attitudes Toward the Enemy

Write an analytical essay that compares and contrasts the way three or more writers viewed the enemy during or directly preceding the American Civil War.

Criteria:

- Include a clear thesis statement that sums up the similarities or differences among the writers' attitudes toward the enemy.
- Support your thesis with details from at least three selections.
- Approximate length: 1,500 words

Read to Write
Reread the selections, paying careful attention to the attitudes behind the words.

TEACHING RESOURCES

The following resources can be used to enrich or extend the instruction for pp. 692–693.

Writing and Grammar, Ruby Level, Chapter 9, pp. 166–186

Writing Models and Graphic Organizers on Transparencies, pp. 37–40

Writing and Grammar iText CD-ROM
Students can use the following tools as they complete their compare and contrast essays:

- Venn Diagram Organizer
- Character Trait Word Bin
- Comparatives Revising Tool

Drafting

Organize examples. Make some organizational decisions before you begin to write. For example, consider using either one of the following strategies:

- **Grouping Ideas:** With this type of organization you discuss all the similarities between selections, and then discuss all of the differences.
- **Grouping Selections:** With this type of organization, you break your discussion down selection by selection, analyzing both similarities and differences for each one.

Draw conclusions. As you draft, draw conclusions about writers' attitudes toward the enemy based on the specific selections you have chosen to analyze. Make sure that you offer clear supporting evidence for every point you make.

Revising and Editing

Review content: Check for completeness and accuracy. Once you have decided to discuss a particular selection, you have a responsibility to analyze it thoroughly and accurately. You may not merely skim it for the details that support your thesis. Instead, you must account for each aspect of the selection that is relevant to your subject.

> **Model: Revising for Thoroughness**
>
> In "Go Down, Moses," the attitude of the slave toward the slaveowner is one of moral condemnation and rage. In *My Bondage and My Freedom*, however, Frederick Douglass ~~expresses sympathy for his master's wife.~~ ∧ *condemns his owner's wife, arguing that she is morally corrupt because she is a slaveowner. Surprisingly, he also expresses some sympathy for her position.*

Review style: Correctly punctuate and capitalize titles. Make sure you have correctly formatted and capitalized titles. The titles of full-length books are generally capitalized and italicized or underlined, while those of shorter works usually appear capitalized in quotation marks.

Publishing and Presenting

Generate a poster. Use the ideas developed in your essay to create a poster about attitudes toward the enemy during the Civil War. Emphasize main ideas with headlines. Then, note your primary supporting evidence.

W̶G Prentice Hall Writing and Grammar Connection: Chapter 9

✎ Write to Learn
The writers whose works you are exploring cared deeply about their subjects. By writing about them, you, too, can develop your own ideas about moral and political conflict.

✎ Write to Explain
Because you will be making subtle distinctions about attitudes and emotions, make sure that your language is especially precise. Your reader must always know exactly what you are talking about.

Drafting

- Be sure students understand the two major strategies for organizing compare and contrast essays: organizing by points of similarity or difference, and organizing by literary works.
- Encourage students to choose an organizing strategy carefully. Instruct students to consider which will be more important in their essays: the literary works themselves, or the patterns of similarity and difference among them.
- You may wish to use Writing Process Model 7, Interpreting a Work of Literature, pp. 37–40 in **Writing Models and Graphic Organizers on Transparencies.**
- Remind students that they must draw conclusions about the writers' views of their enemies, and then clearly state and support those conclusions.

Revising and Editing

- Remind students to read their writing closely and be sure they have treated literary works completely and accurately. If they find their treatment of a work to be incomplete or inaccurate, instruct them to reread the work, making new notes to use in revising.
- After they have revised their essays for content and organization, have students go through their essays, checking the titles of works for correct punctuation and capitalization.

Presenting

- Be sure students understand that the major focus of their posters should be their analysis of the literary works they are comparing and of the similarities and differences among them. Each poster should clearly state—in writing—its thesis and major points.
- Tell students that posters may also include illustrations, and encourage them to gather images of the Civil War that highlight their major points.

CUSTOMIZE INSTRUCTION FOR UNIVERSAL ACCESS

For Less Proficient Writers	For English Learners	For Advanced Writers
To help these students with prewriting, instruct them to copy the Review the Material questions on p. 692 into their notes. For each work, have these students write a clear answer to each question. Answers should be in full sentences. Then, students can sort their answers to look for patterns.	Answering the Review the Material questions on p. 692 may prove challenging for students. For each selection, ask students to find sentences that they feel support their answers to these questions. Then, have them look up any unfamiliar words in the sentences they cite. Do the sentences still support students' interpretations?	It is not likely that these students will have difficulty reviewing the selections. You can place them into small groups with less proficient writers and English learners to review key works. Students can help guide their classmates through the Review the Material questions.

Objectives

1. To write a research paper

2. To use writing strategies to generate ideas, plan, organize, evaluate, and revise writing

Model From Literature

Although Stephen Crane does not document his sources for "An Episode of War," he relied on research —interviews with veterans —for his detailed and accurate descriptions of the Civil War.

Prewriting

• Point out to students that the examples of topics on p. 694—presidents American, or wars—are all of general interest. Explain that their topics, like these, should be ones that most people would find interesting enough to read about.

• Emphasize that research questions should be the right scale for the assignment. Students should avoid questions that are too broad ("Why was the Civil War fought?") or too narrow ("When did Lincoln issue the Emancipation Proclamation?").

• As they begin to conduct research, remind students to write the information they find on index cards—along with the author, title, and publication information of the source.

• Review the Analyze Audience chart on p. 694 with students. Guide them to recognize that the appropriate audience level for this assignment is "General Audiences."

• Before students draft their essays, have them review the Rubric for Self-Assessment (p. 699), so they know what is expected.

Writing WORKSHOP

Research: Research Paper

A **research paper** is a formal, written presentation of research on a single topic, based on information gathered from a variety of sources. In this workshop, you will write a research paper that presents your findings on a subject of interest to you.

Assignment Criteria Your research paper should demonstrate the following characteristics of research writing:

• A clear thesis statement

• Factual support from a variety of sources

• An explanation of how sources vary in their representation of events

• Consideration of the reliability of sources

• A clear organizational strategy

• A complete bibliography or works-cited list

To preview the criteria on which your research paper may be assessed, see the Rubric on page 699.

Prewriting

Choose a topic. Identify an area of interest, and brainstorm for a list of focused categories. For example, you might choose the categories of American presidents or wars. Within these categories, narrow your list further. Review your final list for a topic you would like to research.

Identify your purpose. Consider a question you would like to answer. Make sure the question is general enough to allow you to find sufficient material but narrow enough to be meaningful and manageable.

Sample Question: Is Phillis Wheatley a significant American poet?

Gather information. As you do research, create an index card recording each relevant fact or scholarly opinion that you find. Record the author, title, publisher, city, and date of publication of each source you consult.

Determine your audience. Use a chart like the one shown to determine the appropriate level of information to include in your paper.

Model: Charting to Analyze Audience

Audience	Specialized References Requiring Definition
Novices	Neoclassical, Milton, Pope, heroic couplet, panegyric, Homer, Virgil, Ovid, Aeschylus, Sophocles
General Audiences	Neoclassical, Milton, Pope, heroic couplet, panegyric
Experts	panegyric

TEACHING RESOURCES

The following resources can be used to enrich or extend the instruction for pp. 694–699.

Writing and Grammar, Ruby Level, Chapter 13, pp. 266–288

Performance Assess. and Portfolio Mgmt., p. 22

Writing Models and Graphic Organizers on Transparencies, p. 95

Writing and Grammar iText CD-ROM

Students can use the following tools as they complete their research papers:

• Research Topic Bank

• Customizable Outliner

• Transition Word Bin

• Sticky Notes Revising Tool

Student Model

Before you begin writing, review this student model and note the characteristics of an effective research paper.

Lauren Shepherd
Tupelo, Mississippi

The Writing Style of Phillis Wheatley

In an era when African Americans were struggling to carve an identity for themselves, Phillis Wheatley emerged as the first truly significant black poet in American literature. Although many do not consider her to be an important writer judged by today's values of originality, she persevered through the challenges of her social status to become not only a celebrated poet but the starting point for the study of African-American literature. In this paper, I will discuss her work as a whole, and present a detailed analysis of one of her most famous poems, "To His Excellency General Washington."

> Lauren clearly states her thesis in the opening paragraph.

Religious Message Wheatley was highly educated for her time, and had read the classics as well as the best English poets (Miller, de Dwyer, Wood 48). She was deeply influenced by the work of the great English poet John Milton (1608–1674), who saw himself as a writer in the service of God. Like Milton, Wheatley expressed a constant awareness of "God, His Son, His beneficence and His power." Almost every one of Wheatley's poems develops around a central theme of religious morality, and sometimes has an "air of message from the pulpit" (Mason 15–17). One theme, Christian salvation, underlies nearly everything she wrote (Redding 10).

> Lauren provides thorough support for all the opinions expressed in this passage.

Wheatley's religious messages are often conveyed through embellished Bible stories. In fact, a tradition within African American literature of augmenting biblical accounts with creative license and poetic flair can be traced directly to Wheatley. Both her poems "Goliath and Gath" and "Isaiah LXIII" add creative information to a foundation of biblical narrative.

African Influences In addition to the key role of Christian religious messages in Wheatley's work, many of her writings also exhibit a subtle presence of African traditions. For example, Wheatley uses solar imagery throughout her body of poems. Her frequent use of sun imagery in such poems as "A Hymn to the Morning," and "A Hymn to Evening," suggest that her early religious training in Africa may have consisted of some kind of hierophantic—or sun—worship (Smith, Baechler, Litz 474). Wheatley usually uses such sun imagery as a metaphor for Christian revelation, thus connecting the two essential elements of her religious life.

> Subheads add to the orderliness of her essay.

> Lauren provides factual support for an interesting literary analysis.

Also reminiscent of Wheatley's childhood in Africa is her constant interest in panegyric—or praise—poetry. In many of the cultures of Africa, poets were instructed that political praise constituted the very core of their responsibility as writers (Smith, Baechler, Litz 476). In keeping with that tradition, the majority of Wheatley's works are directed toward politically and socially prominent individuals, such as George Whitehead, a famous English clergyman, and George Washington (Johnson 29).

Student Model

- Explain that the Student Model is a sample, and that their own essays may be longer.
- After students read the first paragraph, ask them to identify the essay's topic and its thesis statement.
  Answer: The topic is the significance of Phillis Wheatley's poetry. Lauren's thesis is: "Although many do not consider her to be an important writer judged by today's values of originality, she persevered through the challenges of her social status to become not only a celebrated poet but the starting point for the study of African-American literature."
- Call students' attention to Lauren's second paragraph and the note attached to it. Ask students to identify the sources Lauren uses to support the opinions she expresses.
  Answer: She cites Miller, de Dwyer, Wood, Mason, and Redding.
- Explain to students that Lauren uses subheads to introduce the areas she addresses, making her essay more orderly and organized.
- Point out that in her fourth paragraph, Lauren combines factual evidence from sources with interpretation of Wheatley's poetry, giving her opinions strong support.

CUSTOMIZE INSTRUCTION FOR UNIVERSAL ACCESS

For Less Proficient Writers	For English Learners	For Advanced Writers
Students may need help with their research questions. Ask them what they, as "general" readers, would like to know about their topics. Help them scale their questions for the assignment by asking them: Is there more than one answer to this question? Are there more than three answers? Can you choose one answer and support it?	Encourage students to work carefully on the wording of their research questions. Explain that the point of the thesis is to provide a question that the writer can answer with supporting information. Questions should be written so that an answer must be more than a simple "yes" or "no."	Point out to these students that preliminary research can lead to a more effective thesis statement. Encourage students to learn more about their topics by reading encyclopedia entries and general reference sources. Then, have them write research questions that acknowledge previous scholarship on a topic.

- Point out that Lauren offers a variety of interpretations of Wheatley's poetry. For example, the essay discusses the issue of racial consciousness—a subhead on p. 696—in several poems. This makes the essay richer and more complete.

- Call students' attention to Lauren's explanation of Neoclassicism in paragraph 7. Tell students that the audience of general readers needs this background information to understand this interpretation. Would they have understood the reference without this information?
  Possible response: Most students will not be familiar with neoclassicism.

- Be sure students recognize that in her eighth paragraph, Lauren refers to the point of view of a scholar —Julian Mason, Jr.—in order to support her own argument about the influence of neoclassicism on Wheatley's poetry.

- Tell students that historical documents and other primary sources provide especially valuable evidence. As an example, point to Lauren's use of Thomas Paine's publication of Wheatley's poem. Ask students: How does this reference enhance the essay?
  Possible response: It provides very strong evidence that Wheatley's poetry was important even during her lifetime, despite her social status.

Racial Consciousness Although many have ventured to say that Wheatley's "unquestioning embrace of New England and white cultures" prompted her to neglect the issue of slavery (Smith, Baechler, Litz 476), a closer examination of her poetry reveals that she was quite "race conscious" (Davis 192). She refers to herself on several occasions as "Africa's muse," and even uses her skin color and presumed low social status as a reference point for her religious message of salvation (Davis 192–193).

Neoclassical Style The majority of Wheatley's poems adhere to the established patterns of the neoclassical style. Neoclassicism was a widespread movement in the visual and literary arts that began in the 1760s and lasted until the 1840s and 1850s. Classical history and mythology provided much of the subject matter of Neoclassical works. The poetry of Homer, Virgil, and Ovid, and the plays of Aeschylus, Sophocles, and Euripides provided the bulk of classical sources. Neoclassical writers, such as Alexander Pope (1688–1744) stressed order, harmony, and restraint.

Like the Neoclassicists she admired, Wheatley's work was noted for an unfaltering preoccupation with regular rhyme and rhythm (Mason 14). Breaking out of her usual form on only six occasions Wheatley most frequently wrote using the heroic couplet—two-line stanzas written in iambic pentameter—that Alexander Pope made so effective (Mason 20). Considering that she is labeled as a spontaneous poet who would write during bouts of inspiration, the general regularity of her meter is remarkable. The influence of the Neoclassical writers also shows in Wheatley's use of elevated language (Mason 16), and in her numerous classical and mythological allusions.

"To His Excellency General Washington" The poem "To His Excellency General Washington" serves as a good example of Wheatley's style. Troubled by poor health since her arrival in America in 1761, when she was only eight years old (Perkins et al. 272), Wheatley traveled from Boston to London in 1773 in hope that the sea air would improve her well-being. Upon her return to the rebellious colonies in 1774, she found the fighting in the Boston vicinity had escalated. Wheatley composed her poem to George Washington and crossed the battle lines to deliver it in person. Two years later, Wheatley received a letter from the General himself thanking her for her adulation but insisting that she had placed him on too high a pedestal. In April 1776, Thomas Paine published her poem, its accompanying note, and Washington's reply in *Pennsylvania Magazine or American Monthly Museum* (Sheeler 8–10).

Although Washington's response to Wheatley's poem was modest, Wheatley gives the reader clear insight as to her opinions of the man. The entire poem is devoted to the veneration of the Continental Army and the leadership of General Washington. Wheatley adheres to her favorite poetic form of heroic couplets. She does not merely revere Washington, she portrays him as a royal figure, referring to him as "Your Excellency," and ascribing to him "a crown, a mansion and a throne that shine."

The essay provides a variety of interpretations of the material.

Necessary background information is essential to the readers' understanding.

Lauren refers to other points of view regarding Wheatley's work.

The essay makes use of a variety of historical documents, including this primary source.

Wheatley resorts to a striking use of personification in the poem. In the opening lines, she mentions the sorrow of "mother earth" at the bloodshed ravaging the land. In line 15, she personifies heaven as a maiden with a "fair face." Her use of alliteration in that image adds to its effect. Wheatley also gives life to the "nations" in line 33, and describes Brittania as a defeated being who "droops the pensive head" (line 35).

Perhaps Wheatley's most notable use of personification lies in her image of the American colonies as the Goddess Columbia (line 9) who is a "native of the skies" (line 11). Wheatley created this new goddess in honor of Christopher Columbus. Later popularized by Revolutionary War poets such as Philip Freneau, the image of Columbia had its first appearance in Wheatley's poem (Jensen).

Wheatley also weaves various allusions into her poem, For example, the European countries in conflict with America are said to be "Gallic powers" (line 30). This allusion refers to the Gallic Wars at the time of Julius Caesar when France was called Gaul. Further evidence of her classical knowledge appears in the reference to "Aeolus," the God of the wind (line 15). Aeolus appeared in Homer's *Odyssey* (Tripp 24), which Wheatley read in Alexander Pope's famous translation. Wheatley scholars generally agree that Pope's translation of Homer greatly affected her poetry (Mason 16).

Although Phillis Wheatley never achieved a truly original poetic style, she is undoubtedly an important figure in American literature. She transcended racial and language barriers to occupy a significant position in the social and intellectual scene of both Boston and London. If one judges her work based on the impact of her poetry on her contemporaries, she is an important pioneer in the development of American literature.

> Lauren concludes by reiterating her thesis.

Works Cited

Davis, Arthur P. "Personal Elements in the Poetry of Phillis Wheatley." Phylon: The Atlanta University Review of Race and Culture. 13 vols. June 1953, pp. 191–198.

Johnson, James Weldon., ed. The Book of American Negro Poetry. New York: Harcourt Bruce Jovanovich Inc., 1922.

Mason, Julian D., Jr., ed. The Poems of Phillis Wheatley. North Carolina: The University of North Carolina Press, 1989.

Miller, James E., Jr., Carlota Cárdenas de Dwyer, and Kerry M. Wood. The United States in Literature. Illinois: Scott, Foresman, and Company, 1985.

Perkins, George, et al., eds. The American Tradition in Literature. 1 vol. New York: McGraw-Hill Publishing Company, 1990.

Redding, J. Saunders. To Make a Poet Black. New York: Cornell University Press, 1988.

Sheeler, Karissa L. Phillis Wheatley. 11 February 2000. http://www.kutztown.edu/faculty/reagan/wheat1.html.

Smith, Valerie., Lea Baechler, and A. Walton Litz., eds. African American Writers. New York: Charles Scribner's Sons, 1991.

Tripp, Edward. Cromwell's Handbook of Classical Mythology. New York: Thomas Y. Cromwell Company, 1970.

> A complete Works-Cited list provides information on the sources Lauren references in the essay.

Student Model

- Before students read Lauren's final paragraph, ask them to pay special attention to its first sentence. Then, point out that this sentence reiterates Lauren's thesis, in simpler terms; the paragraph goes on to explain her argument.

- Call students' attention to Lauren's "Works Cited" list. Point out that each entry provides information about one of Lauren's sources, including: the author's name, the title of the source, and where and when the book was published. Ask students: Why is a complete, accurate Works Cited list important for a research paper? Possible response: Students may say that the information emphasizes the legitimacy of the sources. The list allows readers to confirm what Lauren says about Wheatley. Also, the list can serve as a starting point for readers who want to learn more about the topic.

Real-World Connections

Tell students that research writing is not limited to school. Many useful and important real-world documents are based on the same types of research. Government reports, medical findings, scientific discoveries—all involve research papers, with every source properly identified and cited. Much journalism can also be considered research writing; journalists research an issue and, whenever possible, identify their sources. Editorial writers do not always credit their sources, but if they do not support their arguments with evidence, they do not convince their readers.

CUSTOMIZE INSTRUCTION FOR UNIVERSAL ACCESS

For Special Needs Students	For Gifted/Talented Students
Students may find the independent reading involved in research to be especially challenging. Instruct students to write notes on index cards for each source they find. Then, review students' cards with them. Make sure that students have correctly identified the major points of each source. To check comprehension, have students explain the points in their own words.	Explain that in some cases, visual materials can be used as sources. For example, paintings of Phillis Wheatley and George Washington could have been useful sources for Lauren. Encourage students to choose topics and ask research questions that will allow them to find, interpret, and use visual sources as a supplement to written ones.

Drafting

- Explain to students that their thesis statements should be the conclusions they reach based on their research. The thesis should not be taken directly from a source—it should be the student's own—but it must be supported by the sources.

- Review the Selecting an Organizational Approach chart. Point out that Lauren's essay uses the Parts to Whole approach. For each of the other approaches, ask students to identify an appropriate research paper topic. Possible response: *Chronological*: A paper arguing that Lincoln's youth made him a great president; *Order of Importance*: A paper discussing the most important impact of railroads; *Comparison and Contrast*: A paper examining similarities and differences between Miriam Davis Colt's and Bret Harte's views of the west.

- Model formal outlines for students using the Outline transparency in **Writing Models and Graphic Organizers on Transparencies,** p. 95.

- Be sure that students understand the importance of crediting sources properly. Tell them that if they fail to credit sources, they will appear to be stealing another writer's hard work.

Revising

- Supply students with flags to mark their drafts. Then, instruct them to read their drafts and mark each passage where material is presented as fact.

- Have students review marked passages and ask of each: Is this fact documented? If not, is it essential to my thesis? If the answer to the second question is "yes," the fact needs a source; if "no," the fact should be cut.

continued on page 699

continued on page 699

Writing WORKSHOP *continued*

Drafting

Propose a thesis statement. An effective thesis statement expresses a position that can be supported by research. Review your notes and develop a statement that reflects a general tendency in the data you collected. Incorporate this statement into your draft.

Choose a type of organization. There are numerous effective methods for organizing your information and ideas. Depending on the main purpose of your paper, you may want to present events in the order in which they occurred, in order of importance, by comparing and contrasting events or trends, or by relating elements of a single event or topic to the whole. Use a chart like the one shown to select an organizational strategy that is best suited to your topic, audience, and purpose.

Write a formal outline. After you have selected an organizational strategy, prepare a formal outline.

Prepare to credit sources. When you include a direct quotation, present an original idea that is not your own, or report a fact that is available in only one source, you must include documentation. As you draft, circle ideas or words that are not your own. Use parentheses to note the author's last name and the page numbers of the materials used. Later, you can use this record to create formal citations.

Organizational Approaches

Purpose of Paper: Examine Wheatley's style and argue her importance in American literature	
Approach	**Benefit/Drawback**
Chronological	Does not establish her significance
Order of importance	Possible
Comparison and contrast	Not as useful
Parts to whole	Since I am exploring elements of her life and work, this makes best sense.

Revising

Revise to confirm your facts. When presenting material as fact, confirm that the information is accurate.

- Review your draft and mark points at which you state facts without providing documentation.
- If the fact is essential to your thesis, you must provide a reliable source.
- If the fact is not essential, or cannot be supported with data, remove it from your draft.

Model: Revising for Accuracy

~~Wheatley was~~ troubled by poor health since her arrival in America,

in 1761, when she was only eight years old, Wheatley traveled from Boston to London in 1773 in hope that the sea air would improve her well-being (Perkins et al. 272).

> Lauren added additional information with reliable citation to clearly document the validity of her claim.

---

698 ◆ *Division, Reconciliation, and Expansion (1850–1914)*

USING TECHNOLOGY IN WRITING

If students have access to word processors to use in writing their research papers, encourage them to use the Insert mode rather than Type-over. By using the Insert mode in revising, students will be able to insert proper citations and any additional information or words as needed. In addition, many word processing programs have features for constructing and managing Works Cited pages. Students can also use the organizing tools and revision checkers on **Writing and Grammar iText.**

Revise for variety. Avoid using the same word repeatedly. Add variety with pronouns, synonyms, and proper nouns. In the following example, note how proper nouns spice up the language.

> **General names and places:** The poetry of Latin and Greek writers provided the bulk of classical sources.

> **Specific names and places:** The poetry of Homer, Virgil, and Ovid and the plays of Aeschylus, Sophocles, and Euripides provided the bulk of classical sources.

Publishing and Presenting

Create a reference list. Your research paper should document all your sources of information. A works-cited page provides readers with full bibliographic information on each source you cite. Standards for documentation are set by several organizations.

Identify the format your teacher prefers. Following that format, check that each entry is complete and properly punctuated. (For more information, see Writing Criticism and Citing sources, page R30.)

Deliver an oral presentation. Present the findings of your research paper in an oral report. Provide classmates with a handout outlining key points and indicating the sources you used in your research.

Submit your paper to an appropriate journal. Research the scholarly journals and magazines that publish essays in the field covered by your paper. Select a journal, and submit your essay for possible publication.

W̶G *Prentice Hall Writing and Grammar Connection: Chapter 13*

Rubric for Self-Assessment

Evaluate your research paper using the following criteria and rating scale:

Criteria	Rating Scale				
	Not very				Very
How clearly worded is the thesis statement?	1	2	3	4	5
Is the thesis supported with a variety of sources?	1	2	3	4	5
Are differences between sources clearly explained?	1	2	3	4	5
Is the reliability of sources adequately addressed?	1	2	3	4	5
How effective is the organizational strategy?	1	2	3	4	5
How complete is the bibliography or works-cited list?	1	2	3	4	5

TEST-TAKING TIP

Some writing tests include prompts that direct students to read articles and synthesize information from them. Students can approach these tests as research paper assignments for which a topic has already been chosen and sources have already been gathered. The prompt asks a research question; students should note how the articles address that question. A student's thesis statement should answer the prompt directly, and the essay should support the thesis with evidence from the articles.

Revising (continued)

- Direct students' attention to the examples of general and specific language on p. 699. Ask them to identify the specific words in the second sentence and describe their impact.
  Answer: The specific words are the proper nouns *Homer, Virgil, Ovid, Aeschylus, Sophocles,* and *Euripides.* Together, they make the sentence more interesting, informative, and persuasive.

Publishing and Presenting

- Ask students to think about the audience they had in mind when they planned, drafted, and revised their essays.

- Remind students that you are a part of their audience—they must follow your requirements regarding reference lists. Instruct them to prepare second, less formal reference list to distribute to classmates along with presentations.

- Encourage students to organize and outline their presentation with their audience—their classmates—in mind.

Assessment

- Review the self-assessment criteria with the class.

- When students are familiar with the criteria, ask them to consider how well the student model meets them. Encourage students to discuss their evaluations.
  Possible response: Students are likely to agree that the model has a clearly worded thesis, is well supported with historical documents, is effectively organized, and has a very complete Works Cited list. They are less likely to agree on the explanation of differences between sources and the essay's addressing of reliability of sources.

- Another rubric in an alternative format,can be found on p. 22 of **Performance Assessment and Portfolio Management.**

Objectives

1. To critically evaluate and respond to persuasive arguments

2. To recognize logical fallacies and avoid being persuaded by them

3. To critique the reasoning in an argument, identifying faulty reasoning

4. To critique the reliability of the information used to support an argument

Critique Reasoning

- Explain to students that faulty reasoning makes an argument less persuasive. Suggest that they maintain a Feedback Form for logical fallacies, based on the model on p. 700.

- Review the major fallacies of reasoning with students. Be sure that students understand and can identify each fallacy; they should recognize "But my friends get to stay out late!" as an example of *bandwagon effect*. Have students discuss how these fallacies undermine the persuasiveness of an argument.

Critique Information

- Explain that logical fallacies can undermine the information a speaker uses to support an argument, as well as the speaker's reasoning.

- Review the informational fallacies with the class. Be sure students understand and can identify the fallacies; for example, they should recognize "Something at the arena makes people sick because I went there and afterwards I got sick" as an example of *false causality*.

- Once again, encourage students to fill out Feedback Forms to help them spot logical fallacies when they evaluate persuasive arguments.

700

Listening and Speaking WORKSHOP

Critique Persuasive Arguments

Speakers employ many kinds of arguments to convince listeners of the soundness of their positions. These arguments sometimes contain logical fallacies that can influence listeners' responses. The listening strategies outlined below will help you critically review persuasive speeches and recognize logical fallacies. Use the form on this page to record your reactions.

Critique Reasoning

In order to be persuasive, arguments must be logical and rational. Consider the following in critiquing persuasive arguments.

- **Challenge generalizations.** Make sure the speaker supports general claims with facts or verifiable experiences. Listen for generalizations drawn from samples that may be too small to represent broad truths.

- **Identify circular reasoning.** Listen for arguments in which the support merely restates the claim—for example, "Teenagers should not be hired because they lack experience." To check for circular reasoning, study the proof and make sure it offers new information.

- **Spot bandwagon effect.** Speakers may urge listeners' agreement by appealing to the desire for acceptance in a group. Likewise, a speaker may cite a celebrity's support. Analyze arguments on their merits, and avoid accepting a bandwagon appeal.

Critique Information

Speakers may also build arguments on faulty or misleading information. Listen for the following kinds of misleading structures.

- **Attack *ad hominem*** In this type of argument, named for the Latin phrase meaning "to the man," a speaker attacks an opponent personally, rather than responding to his or her arguments.

- **Red Herring** Named for the odorous fish once used to distract hunting dogs, the red herring argument presents dramatic but irrelevant information designed to confuse and distract listeners.

- **False Causality** When speakers suggest that events or facts have a cause-and-effect relationship, determine whether the events are actually causally linked or merely sequential or coincidental.

Activity:

Oral Address and Feedback

Choose a topic about which you feel strongly and deliver a persuasive oral address stating your position and urging listeners' agreement. Take turns with classmates delivering addresses and critiquing arguments.

700 ◆ Division, Reconciliation, and Expansion (1850–1914)

Feedback Form for Persuasive Arguments

Rating System: Logical Fallacies
+ = Not Present
✔ = Sometimes Present
– = Present Often

Reasoning
Weak generalizations _____
Circular reasoning _____
Bandwagon effect _____

Information
Attack *ad hominum* _____
Red herring _____
False causality _____

Answer the following questions:
Was the speaker's argument built on any faulty reasoning or information?

Without that faulty reasoning or information, does the speaker's argument remain convincing?

CUSTOMIZE INSTRUCTION FOR UNIVERSAL ACCESS

For Special Needs Students	For Less Proficient Readers	For English Learners
Students may find identifying logical fallacies in persuasive presentations challenging. Encourage them to practice in pairs or small groups with written texts. Have them use the Feedback Form on p. 700. Review their responses before students begin to evaluate spoken arguments.	Be sure students understand how logical fallacies undermine arguments. Explain that to be persuasive, arguments must be supported by evidence, rather than logical fallacies. Students should notice how speakers support arguments and determine whether credible evidence or logical fallacies have been used.	Spotting logical fallacies in an argument may be challenging for English learners. Encourage them to note the main points that a speaker makes. Under each point, these students should sum up the support the speaker provides. If evidence does not support a point, students should look for a logical fallacy.

Assessment WORKSHOP

Context Clues

Lesson Objective

To use context in order to determine the meanings of unfamiliar words in a test situation

The reading sections of some tests often require you to use context to determine the meaning of unfamiliar or uncommon words and figurative expressions. The following strategies will help you answer such test questions:

- Remember that context is defined as the words and phrases that surround a word or figurative expression and provide clues to its meaning.
- Try to determine the meaning of certain words and figurative expressions by restating the passage in your own words.
- Read the passage, leaving out the unfamiliar word, and then substitute your possible meaning to see if it makes sense.

Test-Taking Strategies

- Restate the passage in your own words to clarify the author's message.
- Familiar words sometimes have unfamiliar meanings. Use phrases and sentences surrounding the word to help determine its meaning in the passage.

Applying Reading Strategies

Explain to students that they can use prior background knowledge—especially knowledge they already have about context—to help determine the meanings of unfamiliar words. Students should apply any relevant prior knowledge to the context before answering these questions.

Test-Taking Skills

- Have students read the sample test item. Then, ask them to identify and explain what the passage describes.
  Answer: The passage describes the first Thanksgiving, celebrated by Pilgrims and Native Americans in Massachusetts.

- Next, ask students to describe any prior knowledge they can apply to this passage.
  Possible response: Most students will say that Thanksgiving is a celebration of plentiful food.

- Point out to students that this prior knowledge, applied to the context, could help them identify C as the correct answer.

Answer

1. The correct answer is B, because the context of ominous includes a description of "dangerous weather conditions" and Amy and Jane's disappointment. Answer A is opposite of the mood established in the context. Answers C and D have no connection to the context at all.

2. The correct answer is C, because the context indicates that Amy and Jane's mood is a negative one. A, B, and C describe mental states that do not match the mood produced by such bad news.

Sample Test Item

Directions: Read the passage, and then answer the question that follows.

The practice of celebrating Thanksgiving dates back to the year 1621, when the Pilgrims of Plymouth, Massachusetts, joined with local Wampanoag Indians to give thanks for the bountiful harvest. The feast included ducks, geese, corn, potatoes, lobsters, bass, clams, and dried fruit. For the Pilgrims, the food was like manna to the Israelites.

1. Judging from the context of the passage, what might you determine the meaning of the word *bountiful* to be?

A lacking

B spoiled

C abundant

D tasty

Answer and Explanation

The correct answer is **C,** because the context of *bountiful* includes a lengthy list of food and "giving thanks." Answers A and B describe a harvest that would not be worth celebrating. D could be correct, but no information in the text supports the idea that the food tasted good.

▶ Practice

Directions: Read the passage, and then answer the questions that follow.

Amy and Jane listened closely to the weather forecast as they packed their bags. For nearly a year, they had eagerly anticipated taking a ski trip to Colorado. As they listened to the ominous predictions of freezing rain, sleet, and snow, their hearts sank like lead. Such dangerous weather conditions would surely ground their plane and force them to cancel their plans.

1. Judging from the context of the passage in which it is used, which of these words best defines the word *ominous*?

A optimistic

B troubling

C incorrect

D long-range

2. Judging from context, which of these phrases best defines the idiom *their hearts sank like lead*?

A their spirits rose

B they changed their minds

C they experienced sudden despair

D they felt balanced

Assessment Workshop ◆ *701*

TEACHING RESOURCES

The following resources can be used to enrich or extend the instruction for pp. 700–701.

📖 **Assessment Practice Workbook,** p. 31
Provides additional practice on Context Clues

PRENTICE HALL
ASSESSMENT SYSTEM

📖 **Workbook**   📷 **Transparencies**

📖 **Skill Book**   💿 **CD-ROM**

Index of Authors and Titles   Page numbers in *italics* refer to biographical information.

Index of Skills

Literary Analysis

Alienation, 1097, 1105, 1106
Allegory, R12
Alliteration, R12
Allusion, 717, 719, 723, 1266, 1269, 1276, 1280, 1285, 1288, R12
Ambiguity, R12
Analogy, R12
Analytical essay, 1111, 1123, R14
Anapest, R16
Anecdote, 1041, 1044, 1051, R12
Antagonist, R12
Anticlimax, 785, 787, 788, 789, 791
Aphorism, 139, 149, 163, R12
Apostrophe, 99, 837, 841, R12
Approximate rhyme, R19
Archetypal literary elements, R12
Assonance, R12
Atmosphere, 1001, 1002, 1004, 1005, 1006, 1009. *See also* Mood
Audience, 155, 163
Author's point of view, 61, 65
Author's style, 31, 36, 39
Autobiography, 139, 141, 143, 145, 149, 495, 499, 501, 503, R12
   social context in, 913, 915, 916, 921
Ballad, R12, R17
Biography, R13
Blank verse, 881, 883, 885, 886, 888, 889, 892, 893, R13, R17
Character
   defined, R13
   dynamic, 1201, 1205, 1209, 1211, 1213, 1215, R13
   flat, R13
   grotesque, 971, 974, 976, 978, 979, 980, 983, R15
   main, R13
   major, R13
   minor, R13
   motivation of, 743, 747, 751, 753, 761, 763, 1055, 1057, 1058, 1059, 1060, 1065, R17
   static, 1201, 1205, 1209, 1211, 1213, 1215, R13
Characterization, 241, 675, 678, 679, 681, 685, 743, 746, 747, 750, 751, 752, 755, 759, 761, 763, 971, 974, 976, 979, 983, R13
   direct, 241, 253, 743, 763, 971, 983, R13
   indirect, 241, 253, 743, 763, 971, 983, R13
Cinquain, 257, R21
Classicism, R13
Climax, 633, 639, 653, 785, 787, 788, 789, 791, R13
   as plot element, 643, 653, 1081, R13, R18
Compare and contrast styles, 31
Compare and contrast themes, 692
Comparing literary works, 85, 483, 739
Conceit, 103
Concept and perception, 103
Conflict, 607, 610, 612, 613, 615, 616, 618, 619, 621, 623, 643, 653, 987, 989, 990, 991, 993, 994, 996, 997, R13
   external, 607, 623, 987, 997
   internal, 607, 623, 987, 997
   as plot element, 643, 653, 1081
Connotation, R13
Consonance, R13
Conventional symbol, R21
Couplet, 177, 257, R21

Crisis, R13
Cultural context, 1201, 1205, 1209, 1215
Cultural details, 27
Dactyl, R16
Dead metaphor, R16
Denotation, R13
Denouement, 1081, R18. *See also* Plot
Description, 285, 293, R14
Descriptive essay, R14
Development, 1081, R18. *See also* Plot
Dialect, 575, 859, 861, 863, 865, 866, 867, 877, R14
Dialogue, 913, 921, 1232, 1234, 1235, 1239, 1243, 1245, 1246, 1247, 1250, 1251, 1252, 1256, 1257, 1258, 1261, 1264, R14
Diaries, journals, and letters, 534, 535, 536, 538, 540, 545, 549
Diction, 185, 187, 193, 433, 434, 438, 445, 521, 522, 524, 527, 1013, 1014, 1017, 1018, 1021, 1023, R14
Dimeter, R16
Direct address, 99
Direct characterization, 241, 253, 743, 763, 971, 983, R13
Drama, R14
Dramatic exposition, 1232, 1235, 1245, 1252, 1257, 1264
Dramatic irony, 607, 623, 633, 639, 1290, 1293, 1296, 1297, 1298, 1301, 1303, 1306, 1307, 1310, 1311, 1313, 1314, 1316, R16
Dramatic monologue, 717, 719, 720, 723, R14
Dramatic poem, R14
Dynamic character, R13
Elegy, R16
Elements of plot, 643, 646, 647, 651, 653
   climax, 643, 653. *See also* Climax
   conflict, 643, 653. *See also* Conflict
   exposition, 643, 653, 1081, R14
   falling action, 643, 653, R18
   resolution, 643, 653, 1081, R18
   rising action, 643, 653, 785, 787, 791, R18
Emotional appeals, 43, 49
End rhyme, 657, R19
English sonnet, R20
Epic, R17
Epigram, R14
Epiphany, 987, 989, 990, 991, 993, 994, 995, 996, 997, R14
Epistle, 203, 206, 209, 211, R16
Essay, 1111, 1112, 1116, 1120, 1122, 1123, R14
   analytical, 1111, 1123, R14
   descriptive, R14
   expository, 1111, 1123, R14
   formal or informal, R14
   narrative, R14
   personal or impersonal, R14
   persuasive, R14
   reflective, 1127, 1128, 1130, 1131, 1134, 1136, 1137, 1138, 1140, 1142, R14
   satirical, 1111, 1123, R14
Exact rhyme, 419
Exploration narrative, 31, 33, 35, 36, 37, 39, R17
Exposition, 643, 653, 1081, R14
Expository essay, 1111, 1123, R14
Expressing emotions, 103
Extended metaphor, 935, 939, 1318, 1324, 1331, 1335
External conflict, 607, 623, 987, 997
Eyewitness perspective, 65

Falling action, 643, 653, R18
Fiction, R14
Figurative language, R14
Figures of speech, 99, R15
Firsthand accounts, 71
First-person narrator, 679, 1219, 1220, 1222, 1225
First-person point of view, 675, 685, 808, 829, 1055, 1058, 1065, R19
Flashback, 845, 850, 852, 855, 1081, 1084, 1093, 1191, 1197, R15
Flat character, R13
Foil, R15
Folk literature, R15
Foreshadowing, 1027, 1029, 1030, 1032, 1033, 1034, 1037, R15
Form, 1219, 1225
Formal essay, R14
Free verse, 433, 434, 436, 438, 445, R15, R17
Genre, R15
Gothic style, 307, 314, 320, 324, 329, 331, R15
Grotesque characters, 971, 974, 976, 978, 979, 980, 983, R15
Harlem Renaissance, R15
Heptastich, R21
Historical context, 1266, 1276, 1288
Historical influences, 76
Historical narrative, 535, 549, R17
Humor, 563, 570, 572, 573, 575, 897, 899, 907
Hyperbole, R15
Iamb, R16
Iambic pentameter, R15, R17
Identity, 1127, 1131, 1134, 1137, 1140, 1142
Idyll, R15
Image, R15
Imagery, 795, 802, 935, 939, R15. *See also* Imagism; Imagist poetry
Imagism, 727, R15. *See also* Imagery; Imagist poetry
Imagist poetry, 728, 730, 732, 733, 739, R15. *See also* Imagism; Imagery
Impersonal essay, R14
Implied theme, 1161, 1165, 1167, 1168, 1171, 1175, R21
Inciting incident, 1081, R18
Indirect characterization, 241, 253, 743, 763, 971, 983, R13
Informal essay, 897, 898, 899, 901, 905, 907, R14
Internal conflict, 607, 623, 987, 997
Internal rhyme, 657
Irony, 607, 610, 613, 615, 621, 623, 633, 639, R16
   dramatic, 633, 639, 1290, 1293, 1296, 1297, 1298, 1301, 1303, 1306, 1307, 1310, 1311, 1313, 1314, 1316, R16
   situational, 633, 639, R16
   verbal, 633, 639, 1290, 1293, 1296, 1297, 1298, 1301, 1303, 1306, 1307, 1310, 1311, 1313, 1314, 1316, R16
Italian sonnet, R20
Journal, 61, 63, 65, R16. *See also* Diaries, journals, and letters
Legend, R16
Letter, R16
   business, R46
   personal, 549
   public and private, 203, 206, 209, 211, R16
   See also Diaries, journals, and letters
Limited narrator, R17

Reading Strategies

Grammar and Style

Writing
Writing Applications

Writing Strategies

Index of Features

Estate of Gwendolyn Brooks "The Explorer" from *Blacks by Gwendolyn Brooks,* published by The David Company, Chicago, IL. Copyright © 1987, renewed by Third World Press, Chicago, IL, 1991. Used by permission of The Estate of Gwendolyn Brooks.

Diana Chang "Most Satisfied by Snow" from *Most Satisfied by Snow* by Diana Chang. Copyright by Diana Chang. Used by permission of the author.

Sandra Dijkstra Literary Agency for Amy Tan "Mother Tongue" by Amy Tan. Copyright © 1990 by Amy Tan. First appeared in *Threepenny Review.* Reprinted by permission of the author and Sandra Dijkstra Literary Agency.

Doubleday, A division of Random House, Inc. "The Adamant" and "The Light Comes Brighter," copyright 1938 by Theodore Roethke, from *The Collected Poems of Theodore Roethke* by Theodore Roethke. From *Roots* by Alex Haley, copyright © 1976 by Alex Haley. Used by permission of Doubleday, a division of Random House, Inc.

Rita Dove Rita Dove, "For the Love of Books," first published as part of the *Introduction to Selected Poems,* Pantheon Books/Vintage Books, © 1993 by Rita Dove.

Farrar, Straus & Giroux, Inc. "Coyote v. Acme" from *Coyote V. Acme* by Ian Frazier. Copyright © 1996 by Ian Frazier. "The Death of the Ball Turret Gunner" and "Losses" from *The Complete Poems* by Randall Jarrell. Copyright © 1969 by Mrs. Randall Jarrell. "Hawthorne" from *The Union Dead* by Robert Lowell. Copyright © 1959 by Robert Lowell. Copyright renewed © 1987 by Harriot Lowell, Caroline Lowell, and Sheridan Lowell. "The First Seven Years" from *The Magic Barrel* by Bernard Malamud. Copyright © 1950, 1958 and copyright renewed © 1977, 1986 by Bernard Malamud. Excerpt from *The Right Stuff* by Tom Wolfe. Copyright © 1979 by Tom Wolfe. From "Homage to Mistress Bradstreet" by John Berryman from *Homage to Mistress Bradstreet and Other Poems.* Copyright © 1948, 1956, 1958, 1959, 1967, 1968 by John Berryman.

Fulcrum Publishing "The Earth on Turtle's Back" from *Keepers of the Earth: Native American Stories and Environmental Activities for Children,* by Michael J. Caduto and Joseph Bruchac (© 1988) Fulcrum Publishing, 350 Indiana St., #350, Golden, CO 80401, 800-992-2908. Used by permission.

Graywolf Press "Traveling through the Dark" copyright 1962, 1998 by the Estate of William Stafford. Reprinted from *The Way It Is: New and Selected Poems* with the permission of Graywolf Press, Saint Paul, Minnesota.

Harcourt Brace & Company "A Worn Path" from A *Curtain of Green and Other Stories,* copyright 1941 and renewed 1969 by Eudora Welty. "The Jilting of Granny Weatherall" from *Flowering Judas And Other Stories,* copyright 1930 and renewed 1958 by Katherine Anne Porter. "Chicago" and "Grass" from *Chicago Poems* by Carl Sandburg, copyright 1916 by Holt, Rinehart and Winston, Inc.; renewed 1944 by Carl Sandburg. "The Life You Save May Be Your Own" from *A Good Man Is Hard To Find And Other Stories,* copyright © 1953 by Flannery O'Connor and renewed 1981 by Regina O'Connor. This material may not be reproduced in any form or by

any means without the prior written permission of the publisher. "Everyday Use" from *In Love & Trouble: Stories of Black Women,* copyright © 1973 by Alice Walker. Reprinted by permission of Harcourt Brace & Company.

Joy Harjo "Suspended" by Joy Harjo from *In Short: A Collection of Brief Creative Nonfiction,* edited by Judith Kitchen and Mary Paumier Jones. Copyright © 1996. Reprinted by permission of the author.

HarperCollins Publishers, Inc. "Bidwell Ghost" from *Baptism of Desire* by Louise Erdrich. Copyright © 1990 by Louise Erdrich. "Seeing" from *Pilgrim at Tinker Creek* by Annie Dillard. Copyright © 1974 by Annie Dillard. Used by permission of HarperCollins Publishers, Inc. "Where Is Here" taken from *Where Is Here?* by Joyce Carol Oates. Copyright © 1992 by The Ontario Review, Inc. First published by The Ecco Press in 1992. From *Dust Tracks On a Road* by Zora Neale Hurston. Copyright 1942 by Zora Neale Hurston. Copyright renewed 1970 by John C. Hurston. Used by permission.

HarperCollins Publishers, Inc. and Faber & Faber Ltd. "Mirror" from *Crossing the Water* by Sylvia Plath. Copyright © 1963 by Ted Hughes. Originally appeared in *The New Yorker.* Used by permission of HarperCollins Publishers, Inc.

HarperTorch, An imprint of HarperCollins Publishers, Inc. "Old-Time Cowboys in the Modern World" by John Graves from *A JOHN GRAVES READER.*

John Bret-Harte "The Outcasts of Poker Flat" by Bret Harte from *SELECTED STORIES OF BRET HARTE.*

Harvard University Press "There's a certain Slant of light" (#258), "Because I could not stop for Death" (#712), "There is a solitude of space" (#1695), "My life closed twice before its close—" (#1732), "I heard a Fly buzz—when I died" (#465), and "The Soul selects her own Society" (#303) by Emily Dickinson from *The Poems of Emily Dickinson,* Thomas H. Johnson, ed., Cambridge, Mass.: The Belknap Press of Harvard University Press, Copyright (c) 1951, 1955, 1979 by the Presidents and Fellows of Harvard College. Reprinted by permission of the publishers and the Trustees of Amherst College.

Henry Holt and Company, Inc. "Acquainted with the Night" and "The Gift Outright" from *The Poetry of Robert Frost* edited by Edward Connery Latham, Copyright 1928, © 1969 by Henry Holt and Co., © 1970 by Lesley Frost Ballantine, © 1942, 1956 by Robert Frost. Reprinted by permission of Henry Holt and Company, LLC. "Out, Out—" and "Mending Wall" from *The Poetry of Robert Frost* edited by Edward Connery Lathem. Copyright 1944, © 1958 by Robert Frost, © 1967 by Lesley Frost Ballantine, Copyright 1916, 1930, 1939, © 1969 by Henry Holt and Company, Inc.

Houghton Mifflin Company "Ars Poetica" by Archibald MacLeish from *NEW AND COLLECTED POEMS,* 1917–1982. Copyright © 1985 by the Estate of Archibald MacLeish. Reprinted by permission of Houghton Mifflin Company. All rights reserved.

Houghton Mifflin Company and The Estate of Carson McCullers From *The Mortgaged Heart* by Carson McCullers. Copyright 1940, 1941, 1942, 1945, 1948, 1949, 1953, © 1956, 1959, 1963, 1971 by Floria V. Lasky, Executrix of The Estate of Carson McCullers. Used by permission of Houghton Mifflin Company and The Estate of Carson McCullers.

National Council of Teachers of English (NCTE) "NCTE/IRA (National Council of Teachers of English/International Reading Association) Standards" is reproduced with kind permission of NCTE, 1111 W. Kenyon Road, Urbana, IL 61801. www.ncte.org

International Creative Management, Inc. "Ambush" by Tim O'Brien from THE THINGS THEY CARRIED.

The Estate of Martin Luther King, Jr., c/o Writer's House Inc. "Letter from Birmingham City Jail " ("Why We Can't Wait") by Martin Luther King, Jr. Reprinted by arrangement with The Heirs to the Estate of Martin Luther King, Jr. c/o Writers House as agent for the proprietor. Copyright 1963 Martin Luther King, Jr., renewed 1991 by Coretta Scott King.

Alfred A. Knopf, Inc., a division of Random House, Inc. "The Brown Chest" from *The Afterlife: and Other Stories* by John Updike, copyright © 1994 by John Updike. "I, Too," "Refugee in America," "Dream Variations," "The Negro Speaks of Rivers," and "Ardella" from *The Collected Poems of Langston Hughes* by Langston Hughes, copyright © 1994 by The Estate of Langston Hughes. "A Noiseless Flash" from *Hiroshima* by John Hersey, copyright 1946 and renewed 1974 by John Hersey. "Ancedote of the Jar" from *The Collected Poems of Wallace Stevens* by Wallace Stevens, copyright 1954 by Wallace Stevens. From *The Woman Warrior* by Maxine Hong Kingston, copyright © 1975, 1976 by Maxine Hong Kingston. From *Of Plymouth Plantation 1620–1647* by William Bradford, edited by Samuel Eliot Morison. Copyright 1952 by Samuel Eliot Morison and renewed 1980 by Emily M. Beck. Used by permission of Alfred A. Knopf, a division of Random House, Inc.

Latin American Literary Review Press, "Freeway 280" by Lorna Dee Cervantes from *Freeway 280*. Copyright by Latin American Literary Review, Volume V, Number 10. Used by permission.

Liveright Publishing Corporation, a subsidiary of W. W. Norton & Company, Inc. "Frederick Douglass." Copyright © 1966 by Robert Hayden, from *Collected Poems of Robert Hayden* by Robert Hayden, edited by Frederick Glaysher. "Storm Ending," from *Cane* by Jean Toomer. Copyright 1923 by Boni & Liveright, renewed 1951 by Jean Toomer. "Runagate Runagate." Copyright © 1966 by Robert Hayden, from *Collected Poems of Robert Hayden* by Robert Hayden, edited by Frederick Glaysher. "anyone lived in a pretty how town." Copyright 1940, © 1968, 1991 by the Trustees for the E.E. Cummings Trust, "old age sticks." Copyright © 1958, 1986, 1991 by the Trustees for the E.E. Cummings Trust, from *COMPLETE POEMS: 1904–1962* by E.E. Cummings, edited by Fumage. Used by permission of Liveright Publishing Corporation.

Louisiana State University Press, "Dunbar" by Anne Spencer from *Time's Unfading Garden: Anne Spencer's Life and Poetry*, edited by J. Lee Greene. Copyright © 1977 by Lousiana State University Press. Reprinted by permission of Louisiana State University Press.

Archives of Claude McKay "The Tropics in New York" from *The Poems of Claude McKay* by Claude McKay, Harcourt Brace, publisher, copyright © 1981.

Elaine Markson Literary Agency, Inc. "Anxiety" from *Later the Same Day* by Grace Paley (Farrar, Straus and Giroux, 1985). Copyright © 1985 by Grace Paley. All rights reserved.

Ellen C. Masters, c/o Hillary Masters, POA "Richard Bone" and "Lucinda Matlock" from *Spoon River Anthology* by Edgar Lee Masters, published by Macmillan Co. Used by permission.

N. Scott Momaday From *The Names: A Memoir by N. Scott Momaday* published by Harper & Row Publishers, Inc. Copyright © 1976 by N. Scott Momaday. Reprinted by permission of the author.

William Morris Agency, Inc. "Gold Glade" by Robert Penn Warren from *New and Selected Poems*. Copyright © 1985 by Robert Penn Warren. Reprinted by permission of William Morris Agency, Inc., on behalf of the author.

New Directions Publishing Corporation "Heat" and "Pear Tree" by H. Doolittle, *Collected Poems, 1912–1944*. Copyright © 1982 by the Estate of Hilda Doolittle. "In a Station of the Metro" and "The River-Merchant's Wife: A Letter" by Ezra Pound, from *Personae*. Copyright © 1926 by Ezra Pound. "The Great Figure," "The Red Wheelbarrow," and "This is Just to Say" by William Carlos Williams, from *Collected Poems Volume 1: 1909-1939*. Copyright 1938 by New Directions Publishing Corporation. Used by permission of New Directions Publishing Corporation. Excerpts form "The Imagist Manifesto" from *Literary Essays of Ezra Pound*, edited with an introduction by T.S. Eliot. Copyright 1918, 1920, 1935 by Ezra Pound.

The New York Times "Onomatopoeia" by William Safire from *You Could Look It Up*. Copyright © 1988 by The Cobbett Corporation. Originally appeared in *The New York Times*. Reprinted by permission.

W. W. Norton & Company, Inc. "Garbage" by Ammons A.R. from *Garbage*. Copyright © 1993 by A.R. Ammons. From "Civil Disobedience" reprinted from *Walden and Civil Disobedience, A Norton Critical Edition*, by Henry David Thoreau, edited by Owen Thomas. Copyright ©1966 by W. W. Norton & Company, Inc. "Who Burns for the Perfection of Paper" from *City of Coughing and Dead Radiators* by Martin Espada. Copyright © 1993 by Martin Espada. Used by permission of W. W. Norton & Company, Inc.

W. W. Norton & Company, Inc. and Adrienne Rich "In a Classroom" from *Time's Power: Poems 1985–1988* by Adrienne Rich. Copyright © 1989 by Adrienne Rich. All rights reserved. Used by permission.

Harold Ober Associates, Inc. "The Corn Planting" from *Sherwood Anderson Short Stories*, edited by Maxwell Geismar. © 1962 by Eleanor Anderson. "A Black Man Talks of Reaping" by Arna Bontemps. Copyright © 1963 by Arna Bontemps. Reprinted by permission of Harold Ober Associates Incorporated.

Simon J. Ortiz "Hunger in New York City" from *Woven Stone* by Simon J. Ortiz. Published by University of Arizona Press, 1992 © 1976 by Simon J. Ortiz. Used by permission of Simon J. Ortiz.

Penguin Books Ltd. "Melting Snow" by Kobayashi Issa (18 lines) from THE PENGUIN BOOK OF JAPANESE VERSE translated by Geoffrey Bownas and Anthony Thwaite (Penguin Books, 1964) Translation copyright © Geoffrey Bownas and Anthony Thwaite, 1964.

Plimoth Plantation Excerpt from Plimoth Plantation Web site (www.plimoth.org).

Princeton University Press From *Walden* by Henry David Thoreau. Copyright © 1971 by Princeton University Press. Used by permission of Princeton University Press.

Random House, Inc. "The Unknown Citizen," copyright 1940 & renewed 1968 by W.H. Auden, from *W.H. Auden: Collected Poems.*

"The Writer in the Family" from *Lives of the Poets* by E. L. Doctorow, copyright © 1984 by E. L. Doctorow. "Cats" from *Living Out Loud* by Anna Quindlen, copyright © 1987 by Anna Quindlen. "Race at Morning" from *Big Woods* by William Faulkner, copyright © 1955 by The Curtis Publishing Company. Used by permission of Random House, Inc.

Russell & Volkening, Inc. "Average Waves in Unprotected Waters" by Anne Tyler. Copyright © 1977 by Anne Tyler. This story originally appeared in *The New Yorker*, February 28th, 1977. Reproduced by permission of Russell & Volkening as agents for the author.

Estate of Ricardo Sanchez "i yearn" by Ricardo Sanchez. Copyright © 1975 by Ricardo Sanchez. Reprinted by permission of the Estate of Ricardo Sanchez.

Scribner, a division of Simon & Schuster, Inc. "The Far and the Near" from *Death to Morning* by Thomas Wolfe. Copyright © 1935 by Charles Scribner's Sons; copyright renewed © 1963 by Paul Gitlin. "In Another Country" from *Men Without Women* by Ernest Hemingway. Copyright 1927 by Charles Scribner's Sons. Copyright renewed 1955 by Ernest Hemingway. Reprinted with the permission of Scribner, a division of Simon & Schuster.

Scribner, a division of Simon & Schuster and The Literary Estate of Marianne Moore "Poetry" from *The Collected Poems of Marianne Moore* by Marianne Moore. Copyright © 1935 by Marianne Moore, copyright renewed © 1963 by Marianne Moore and T.S. Eliot. Used by permission of Scribner, a division of Simon & Schuster, Inc., and The Literary Estate of Marianne Moore.

Scribner, a division of Simon & Schuster and Melanie Jackson Agency, LLC "Gulf War Journal from a Woman at War" from *A Woman at War* by Molly Moore. Copyright © 1993 by Molly Moore. Used by permission of Scribner, a division of Simon & Schuster and Melanie Jackson Agency, LLC.

Simon & Schuster, Inc. from *Lonesome Dove* by Larry McMurtry. Copyright © 1985 by Larry McMurtry. Used by permission of Simon & Schuster.

Sterling Lord Literistic, Inc. "The Crisis, Number 1" by Thomas Paine from CITIZEN TOM PAINE. Copyright by Howard Fast. Used by permission of Sterling Lord Literistic, Inc.

Estate of William Stafford "Traveling Through the Dark" from *Stories That Could Be True: New and Collected Poems* by William Stafford. Copyright © 1960 by William Stafford. Used by permission.

Charles Scribner's Sons, a division of Simon & Schuster, Inc. "Winter Dreams" by F. Scott Fitzgerald, from *All The Sad Young Men*. Copyright 1922 by Frances Scott Fitzgerald Lanahan; copyright renewed 1950. "Richard Cory" from *The Children of the Night* by Edwin Arlington Robinson, published by Charles Scribner's Sons.

Syracuse University Press "The Iroquois Constitution" from *Parker on the Iroquois: Iroquois Uses of Maize and Other Food Plants; The Code of Handsome Lake; The Seneca Prophet; The Constitution of the Five Nations* by Arthur C. Parker, edited by William N. Fenton (Syracuse University Press, Syracuse, NY, 1981). Used by permission.

Rosemary Thurber and the Barbara Hogenson Agency, Inc. "The Night the Ghost Got In" copyright 1933, © 1961 by James Thurber. From *My Life and Hard Times*, published by Harper & Row. Reprinted by arrangement with Rosemary Thurber and the Barbara Hogenson Agency. All rights reserved.

University of Nebraska Press, Reprinted from the *Journals of the Lewis and Clark Expedition, volume 5,* edited by Gary E. Moulton by permission of the University of Nebraska Press. Copyright © 1988 by the University of Nebraska Press. Used by permission.

The University of North Carolina Press "To His Excellency, General Washington" and lines from "An Hymn to the Evening" from *The Poems of Phillis Wheatley* edited and with an introduction by Julian D. Mason, Jr. Copyright © 1966 by The University of North Carolina Press, renewed 1989. Used by permission of the publisher.

University of Texas Press and the author "El Corrido de Gregorio Cortez" from *With His Pistol In His Hand: A Border Ballad And Its Hero* by Americo Paredes, Copyright © 1958, renewed 1986. By permission of the author and the University of Texas Press.

USA Today and Robert N. Wiener Pro bono work headlined "Lawyers leave poor behind" by Robert N. Wiener, from *USA Today* (September 25, 2000). Copyright © 2000 by *USA Today*. Used by permission.

Viking Penguin, Inc., a division of Penguin Putnam, Inc. From "On Social Plays," copyright © 1955, 1978 by Arthur Miller, from *The Theater Essays of Arthur Miller* by Arthur Miller, edited by Robert A. Martin. From *The Crucible* by Arthur Miller, copyright 1952, 1953, 1954, renewed © 1980, 1981, 1982 by Arthur Miller. "The Turtle (Chapter 3)" from *The Grapes of Wrath* by John Steinbeck, copyright 1939, renewed © 1967 by John Steinbeck. Used by permission of Viking Penguin, a division of Penguin Putnam Inc.

Wesleyan University Press "For My Children" by Colleen McElroy from *What Madness Brought Me Here*. "Camouflaging the Chimera" by Yusef Komunyakaa from *Neon Vernacular*. "What For" by Garrett Kaoru Hongo from *Yellow Light*. Used by permission of Wesleyan University Press.

Joel White, for the Estate of E.B. White From "Here Is New York" by E.B. White from *Essays of E.B. White*.

Darryl Babe Wilson "Diamond Island: Alcatraz" by Darryl Babe Wilson. Copyright © 1991 by Darryl Babe Wilson. Reprinted by permission of the author.

Yale University Press From *Mary Chesnut's Civil War*, edited by C. Vann Woodward. Copyright © 1981 by C. Vann Woodward, Sally Bland Metts, Barbara G. Carpenter, Sally Bland Johnson, and Katherine W. Herbert. All rights reserved. Reproduced by permission of the publisher, Yale University Press.

Note: Every effort has been made to locate the copyright owner of material reprinted in this book. Omissions brought to our attention will be corrected in subsequent editions.

CREDITS

Cover and Title Page: *Travel by Ox-Drawn Covered Wagons,* Artist unknown, Courtesy of the Bancroft Library, University of California, Berkeley; **xxiii** Mark Lewis/Tony Stone Images; **vi** Nicole Galeazzi/Omni-Photo Communications, Inc.; **vii** *Red Jacket,* George Catlin, From the Collection of Gilcrease Museum, Tulsa, Oklahoma; **ix** *The Declaration of Independence,* John Trumbull, Yale University Art Gallery; **x** Stock Newport, Inc.; **xii** *Young Soldier: Separate Study of a Soldier Giving Water to a Wounded Companion* (detail), 1861, Winslow Homer, Oil, gouache, black crayon on canvas, 36 x 17.5 cm., United States, 1836–1910, Cooper-Hewitt, National Museum of Design, Smithsonian Institution, Gift of Charles Savage Homer, Jr., 1912-12-110, Photo by Ken Pelka, Courtesy of Art Resource, New York; **xiv** Digital Imagery ©Copyright 2001 PhotoDisc, Inc.; **xv** *School Bell Time,* 1978. From the Profile/Part I: The Twenties series (Mecklenburg County), Romare Bearden, 29 1/4 x 41" Collection: Kingsborough Community College, The City University of New York; ©Romare Bearden Foundation/ Licensed by VAGA, New York, NY; **xvi** Corel Professional Photos CD-ROM™; **xviii** Pocumtuck Valley Memorial Association, Memorial Hall Museum, Deerfield, Massachusetts; **1** *World Map,* 1630, Jan Jansson, The Huntington Library, Art Collections and Botanical Gardens, San Marino, CA; **2** (1492) CORBIS-Bettmann, (1558) Victoria & Albert Museum, London/Art Resource, NY, (1608) *John Smith* (detail), The National Portrait Gallery, Smithsonian Institution, Washington, D.C./Art Resource, NY, (1620) The Granger Collection, New York, **3** (1675) North Wind Picture Archives, (1727) Corel Professional Photos CD-ROM™, (1741) The Granger Collection, New York; **5** North Wind Picture Archives; **6** (t.) North Wind Picture Archives, (b.) Colonial Williamsburg Foundation; **9** The Bettmann Archive; **11** North Wind Picture Archives; **13** *Oneida Chieftain Shikellamy,* Unknown American, c.1820, 45 1/2" x 32", oil on canvas, Philadelphia Museum of Art. The Collection of Edgar William and Bernice Chrysler Garbisch; **14** Silver Burdett Ginn; **16** Nicole Galeazzi/Omni-Photo Communications, Inc.; **20** *Dreamwalker,* Nancy Wood Taber, colored pencil, courtesy of the artist; **25** *Red Jacket,* George Catlin, From the Collection of Gilcrease Museum, Tulsa, Oklahoma; **32–33** Corel Professional Photos CD-ROM™; **34** *Painting of Cabeza de Vaca, Esteban, and their companions among various Texas Indian tribes,* Tom Mirrat, The Institute of Texan Cultures, San Antonio, Texas; **37** Jeff Greenberg/Photo Researchers, Inc.; **42** *Olaudah Equiano* (detail), National Portrait Gallery, Smithsonian Institution, Washington, D.C./Art Resource, NY; **44** National Maritime Museum, London; **46** Courtesy of the Library of Congress; **52** *Native American male* (Wailaki tribe), Edward S. Curtis, Courtesy of the Southwest Museum, Los Angeles, Photo #N.40042; **56–57** *San Francisco,* 1849, Attributed to Joshua Pierce, Oil on canvas, Photo by John Lei/Omni-Photo Communications, Inc.; **58** Courtesy of the author; **59** *Building the Fort,* ca. 1960, Julien Binford, oil on canvas, 86" x 101", The Jamestown Yorktown Educational Trust; **60** Erich Lessing/Art Resource, NY; **62** Astrolabe, Museum fur Kunst und Gewerbe, Hamburg; **63** CORBIS-Bettmann; **68** Peabody Museum of Archaeology and Ethnology, Harvard University; **69** The Rosenbach Museum & Library; **70** (l.) *John Smith* (detail), National Portrait Gallery, Smithsonian Institution, Washington, D.C./Art Resource, NY, (r.) CORBIS-Bettmann; **72** *The First Day at Jamestown,* 14th May 1607, from "The Romance and Tragedy of Pioneer Life" by Augustus L. Mason, 1883, William Ludlow Sheppard/Bridgeman Art Library, London/New York; **74** Print Collection, Miriam and Ira D. Wallach Division of Art, Prints and Photographs, The New York Public Library, Astor, Lenox and Tilden Foundations; **76** Architect of the Capitol; **79** *The Coming of the Mayflower,* N.C. Wyeth, from the Collection of Metropolitan Life Insurance Company, New York City, photograph by Malcolm Varon; **80** *The Mayflower in Plymouth Harbor,* William Halsall, Burstein Collection/ CORBIS; **83** Cary Wolinsky/Stock, Boston; **92** NASA; **95** Audio Visual Archives at the John F. Kennedy Library; **96** AP/Wide World Photos; **97** *Pilgrims Going to Church,* George Henry Boughton, Collection of The New York Historical Society; **98** *The Puritan,* Augustus Saint-Gaudens, The Metropolitan Museum of Art, Bequest of Jacob Ruppart, 1939 (39.65.53) All Rights Reserved; **100** Crewel Work Chair Seat Cover, Gift of Samuel Bradstreet, Courtesy, Museum of Fine Arts, Boston; **106** CORBIS-Bettmann; **109** *The Puritan,* c. 1898, Frank E. Schoonover, Oil on canvas, Collection of The Brandywine River Museum, Gift of Mr. and Mrs. Jacob J. Foster; **118** David Young-Wolff/PhotoEdit; **124–125** *Washington Crossing the Delaware,* Emanuel Gottlieb Leutze, oil on canvas, H.149 in., W.255 in. (378.5 x 647.7cm.) The Metropolitan Museum of Art, Gift of John S. Kennedy, 1897. (97.34), Copyright © 1992 By the Metropolitan Museum of Art; **126** (1748) The Granger Collection, New York, (1776) Courtesy, Independence National Historical Park Collection; **127** (all) The Granger Collection, New York; **129** Courtesy, American Antiquarian Society; **131** ©Archive Photos; **135** *George Washington* (Vaughan portrait), Gilbert Stuart, Photograph ©Board of Trustees, National Gallery of Art, Washington, Andrew Mellon Collection; **136** ©Archive Photos; **137** *Miss Liberty,* Abby Aldrich Rockefeller Folk Art Center, Williamsburg, VA; **138** *Benjamin Franklin* (detail), c.1790, Pierre Michel Alix, National Portrait Gallery, Smithsonian Institution, Washington, D.C./Art Resource, New York; **140** *Quaker Meeting,* Courtesy, Museum of Fine Arts, Boston. Reproduced with permission. ©2000 Museum of Fine Arts, Boston. All Rights Reserved; **142** ©British Museum; **144, 146** The Granger Collection, New York; **152** ©Bettmann/CORBIS; **153** (t.) CORBIS, (b.) Smithsonian Institution, Photo no. 86-4091; **154** (r.), (l.) The Granger Collection, New York; **156** Corel Professional Photos CD-ROM™; **157** Yale University Art Gallery; **158** Ron Watts/ CORBIS; **160** Munson-Williams-Proctor Institute Museum of Art, Utica, New York; **170** *Phillis Wheatley* (detail), Unidentified artist after Scipio Moorhead, National Portrait Gallery, Smithsonian Institution, Washington, D.C./Art Resource, New York; **172–173** Corel Professional Photos CD-ROM™; **174** New York State Historical Association, Cooperstown; **181, 182** UPI/ CORBIS-Bettmann; **183** *George Washington standing on the platform,* Penn State Capitol, Harrisburg, Photo: Brian K. Foster. Courtesy Senate Communications; **184** (l.) *Patrick Henry* (detail), c.1835, James Barton Longacre after Lawrence Sully, The National Portrait Gallery, Smithsonian Institution, Washington, D.C./Art Resource, New York, (r.) The Granger Collection, New York; **186** *Patrick Henry Before the Virginia House of Burgesses 1851,* Peter F. Rothermel, Red Hill, The Patrick Henry National Memorial, Brookneal, Virginia; **189** Courtesy of the Library of Congress; **191** The American Philosophical Society; **196** Bettmann/CORBIS; **199** *Retroactive I,* Robert Rauschenberg, 1964, Wadsworth Atheneum, Hartford, Connecticut, Gift of Susan Morse Hilles, ©Robert Rauschenberg/Licensed by VAGA, New York, NY; **200** AP/ Wide World Photos; **201** 18th c. New England needlework, Colonial Williamsburg Foundation; **202** (l.) The Granger Collection, New York, (r.) CORBIS-Bettmann; **204** *Building the First White House,* 1930, N.C. Wyeth, Copyrighted © by the White House Historical Association, photo by the National Geographical Society; **208** *Independence (Squire Jack Porter),* 1858, Frank Blackwell Mayer, National Museum of American Art, Smithsonian Institution, Bequest of Harriet Lane Johnson, Art Resource, New York; **214** Owen Franken/Stock, Boston; **216** *Dance Africa,* 1996, Synthia Saint James, Courtesy of the artist; **217** AP/Wide World Photos; **220** ©The Stock Market /Michal Heron; **226–227** *Niagara Falls, about 1832–1840,* Thomas Chamber, © Wadsworth Atheneum, Hartford, Ella Gallup Sumner and Mary Catlin Sumner Collection; **228** (1804) Seltzer, *Lewis' First Glimpse of the Rockies,* The Thomas Gilcrease Institute of Art Tulsa, Oklahoma, (1804 France) Giraudon/Art Resource, NY, (1814) The Granger Collection, New York, (1825) Samuel S. Spaulding Collection, Buffalo and Erie County Historical Society, (1829) Adam Woolfit/CORBIS; **229** (1831 France) Christie's Images/SuperStock, (1831) Image Select/Art Resource, NY, (1838) The Granger Collection, New York; **232** The Granger Collection, New York; **234** The National Portrait Gallery, Smithsonian Institution/Art Resource, NY; **237** American Steel Foundries; **238** Copyrighted by the White House Historical Association, Photograph by the National Geographic Society; **239** *Fredericksburg Refugee Family at Campfire,* D.E. Henderson, Gettysburg National Military Park Museum; **240** *Washington Irving* (detail), Daniel Huntington, National Portrait Gallery, Smithsonian Institution, Washington, D.C./Art Resource, New York; **245** *The Devil and Tom Walker,* 1856, John Quidor, oil on canvas, 68.8 x 86.6 cm. © The Cleveland Museum of Art, Mr. and Mrs. William H. Marlatt Fund, 1967.18; **246** Walking stick, King Georges County, Virginia, 1846, carved wood with ink decoration, 37 x 2 inches in diameter, Abby Aldrich Rockefeller Folk Art Center, Williamsburg, VA; **247** Yale University Art Gallery, New Haven. The Mabel Brady Garvan Collection; **248** Leonard Lee Rue III/Stock, Boston; **250** Index Stock Photography, Inc.; **251** Ron Watts/CORBIS; **256** *Henry Wadsworth Longfellow* (detail), Thomas B. Read, The National Portrait Gallery, Smithsonian Institution, Washington, D.C./Art Resource, New York; **258** Stephanie Maze/Woodfin Camp & Associates; **264** (b.) The Granger Collection, New York, (t.) *William Cullen Bryant* (detail), Unidentified photographer, The National Portrait Gallery, Smithsonian Institution, Washington, D.C./Art Resource, New York, (m.) CORBIS-Bettmann; **265** (t.) *John Greenleaf Whittier* (detail), 1881, William Notman, The National Portrait Gallery, Smithsonian Institution, Washington, D.C./Art Resource, New York, (b.) The Granger Collection, New York; **267** *Kindred Spirits,* Asher B. Durand, New York Public Library, Astor, Lenox and Tilden Foundations; **270** Charles Krups/AP/Wide World Photos; **272** ©Ulrike Welsch; **274** *Old Holley House, Cos Cob,* John Henry Twachtman, Cincinnati Art Museum, John J. Emery Endowment; **276–277** Digital Imagery ©Copyright 2001 PhotoDisc, Inc.; **284** (r.) *John Wesley Powell* (detail), Edmund Clarence Messer, The National Portrait Gallery, Smithsonian Institution, Washington, D.C./Art Resource, NY, (l.) The Granger Collection, New York; **286** (r.) *Draught of the Falls and Portage of the Missouri River* (Clark's map of the Missouri River), Missouri Historical Society, Clark Papers, Voorhis #1, 2 July 1805, ink on paper, L/A 464b., (l.) *Lewis and Clark with Sacajawea at the Great Falls of the Missouri,* Olaf Seltzer, #0137.871. The Thomas Gilcrease Institute of Art, Tulsa, Oklahoma; **287** *White Salmon Trout,* ink on paper (Clark's drawing of salmon from his journal), Missouri Historical Society MHS Archives, entry before 17 March 1806. L/A #407b; **289** Corel Professional Photos CD-ROM™; **291** *Grand Canyon with Rainbow,* 1912, Thomas Moran, oil on canvas, 25" x 30" (63.5 x 76.3cm) Collection of the Fine Arts Museums of San Francisco, Gift of

Mr. and Mrs. Robert Gill through the Patrons of Art and Music (1981.89); **300** Tammy Rice/The Learning Source; **302** ©Visuals Unlimited; **304** Thomas Victor; **305** *Mysterious Night*, ca. 1895, watercolor on board, 30-1/2 x 21-1/2 inches, Morris Museum of Art, Augusta, GA; **306** CORBIS-Bettmann; **309** "I at length . . .," Edgar Allen Poe's Tales of Mystery and Imagination (London: George G. Harrap, 1935), Arthur Rackham, Print Collection, Miriam and Ira D. Wallach Division of Art, Prints and Photographs, The New York Public Library; Astor, Lenox and Tilden Foundations; **312** Ron Watts/CORBIS; **316** Steve Mohlenkamp/Index Stock Photography, Inc.; **323** ©2000 The Munch Museum/The Munch-Ellingsen Group/ Artists Rights Society (ARS), New York; **328** *The Raven*, 1845, Edmund Dulac, The Granger Collection, New York; **334** *Nathaniel Hawthorne* (detail), 1862, Emanuel Gottlieb Leutze, The National Portrait Gallery, Smithsonian Institution, Washington, D.C./Art Resource, New York; **337** New York State Historical Association, Cooperstown, New York; **340** Ron Watts/CORBIS; **344** *Cemetery*, Peter McIntyre, Courtesy of the artist; **352** The Granger Collection, New York; **356** *Captain Ahab on the deck of the Pequod*, 1930, pen and ink drawing, The Granger Collection, New York; **357** Stock Newport, Inc.; **359** CORBIS; **361** *Moby-Dick*, 1930, pen and ink drawing, The Granger Collection, New York; **362** The Whaling Museum; **364** *Moby-Dick*, 1930, pen and ink drawing, The Granger Collection, New York; **369** Culver Pictures, Inc.; **375** Phil Schermeister/CORBIS; **377, 380** Digital Imagery ©Copyright 2001 PhotoDisc, Inc.; **382** Alex Oliveira/Globe Photos; **383** *Early Morning at Cold Spring*, 1850, oil on canvas, 60 x 48" Asher B. Durand, Collection of the Montclair Art Museum, Montclair, New Jersey; **384** ©Lee Snider; Lee Snider/CORBIS; **385** (b.) Courtesy of the Library of Congress, (t.) Hulton-Deutsch Collection/CORBIS; **386** *Ralph Waldo Emerson* (detail), Frederick Gutekunst/The National Portrait Gallery, Smithsonian Institution, Washington, D.C./Art Resource, NY; **389** *Sunset*, Frederick Edwin Church, Munson-Williams-Proctor Institute Museum of Art, Utica, New York; **393** Leonard Harris/Stock, Boston; **394** Frank Whitney/The Image Bank; **400** The Granger Collection, New York; **402** Owen Franken/PNI; **406** Burstein Collection/ CORBIS; **408** ©The Stock Market/Dan McCoy; **410** ©Lee Snider; Lee Snider/CORBIS; **417** *Walden Pond Revisited*, 1942, N.C. Wyeth, tempera, possibly mixed with other media on panel, 42 x 48" Collection of the Brandywine River Museum, Bequest of Miss Carolyn Wyeth; **418** The Granger Collection, New York; **420** *Waiting Outside No. 12*, Anonymous, Crane Kalman Gallery; **422** *Room With a Balcony*, Adolph von Menzel, Staatliche Museen Preubischer Kulturbesitz, Nationgalerie, Berlin; **426** Frederic Edwin Church, American, 1826–1900. *Twilight in the Wilderness*, 1860s. Oil on canvas, 101.6 x 162.6 cm. © The Cleveland Museum of Art, 1997, Mr. and Mrs. William H. Marlett Fund, 1965.233; **432** The Granger Collection, New York; **440** *The Lawrence Tree*, 1929, Georgia O'Keeffe, Wadsworth Atheneum, Hartford, The Ella Gallup Sumner and Mary Catlin Sumner Collection, ©1998 The Georgia O'Keeffe Foundation/Artists Rights Society (ARS), New York; **443** *The Reaper*, c.1881, Louis C. Tiffany, oil on canvas, National Academy of Design, New York City; **448–449** *Nobody Around Here Calls Me Citizen*, 1943, Robert Gwathmey, oil on canvas, H. 14-1/4" x W. 17" Collection Frederick R. Weisman Art Museum at the University of Minnesota, Minneapolis, Bequest of Hudson Walker from the Ione and Hudson Walker Collection. ©Estate of Robert Gwathmey/Licensed by VAGA, New York, NY; **449** *Langston Hughes* (detail), c.1925, Winold Reiss, The National Portrait Gallery, Smithsonian Institution, Washington, D.C./Art Resource, New York; **450** *Mandolin*, Rosa Ibarra, Courtesy of the artist; **451** Photo by M&A Productions; **454** Digital Imagery ©Copyright 2001 PhotoDisc, Inc.; **460–461** *The Fall of Richmond*, Currier & Ives, SuperStock; **461** (t.) *Portrait of Abraham Lincoln* (detail), William Willard, The National Portrait Gallery, Smithsonian Institution, Washington, D.C./Art Resource, New York, (b.) The Granger Collection, New York; **462** (all) The Granger Collection, New York; **463** (1886), (1903), (1908) The Granger Collection, New York, (1881) CORBIS-Bettmann; **464** CORBIS-Bettmann; **465** (both) Courtesy of the Library of Congress; **467** Nebraska State Historical Society; **471** *Six O'Clock, Winter*, 1912, John Sloan, The Phillips Collection; **472** *Samuel Longhorne Clemens (Mark Twain)* (detail), 1935, Frank Edwin Larson, The National Portrait Gallery, Smithsonian Institution, Washington, D.C./Art Resource, New York; **473** *Fight for the Standard*, oil on canvas, H 26 3/4 inches, W 21 1/2 inches, Wadsworth Atheneum, Hartford. The Ella Gallup Sumner and Mary Catlin Sumner Collection Fund; **474** (l.) CORBIS-Bettmann, (r.) The Granger Collection, New York; **476** Courtesy of the Library of Congress; **479** Courtesy National Archives; **480** Museum of the Confederacy, Richmond, Virginia; **481** *Young Soldier: Separate Study of a Soldier Giving Water to a Wounded Companion* (detail), 1861, Winslow Homer, Oil, gouache, black crayon on canvas, 36 x 17.5 cm., United States, 1836–1910, Cooper-Hewitt, National Museum of Design, Smithsonian Institution, Gift of Charles Savage Homer, Jr., 1912-12-110, Photo by Ken Pelka, Courtesy of Art Resource, New York; **488** Courtesy of the Library of Congress; **494** *Frederick Douglass* (detail), c. 1844, Attributed to Elisha Hammond, The National Portrait Gallery, Smithsonian Institution, Washington, D.C./Art Resource, New York; **496** *The Chimney Corner*, 1863, Eastman Johnson, oil on cardboard, 15 1/2 x 13 in., Munson-Williams-Proctor Institute Museum of Art, Utica, New York; Gift of Edmund G. Munson, Jr.; **498** *A Home on the Mississippi*, 1871, Currier & Ives, The Museum of the City of New York, Harry T. Peters Collection; **500** Ron Watts/CORBIS; **506** CORBIS-Bettmann; **508** Superstock; **509** The Kobal Collection; **520** (l.) *Portrait of Abraham Lincoln* (detail), William Willard, The National Portrait Gallery, Smithsonian Institution, Washington, D.C./Art Resource, New York, (r.) *Robert E. Lee* (detail), 1864–1865, Edward Caledon Bruce, The National Portrait Gallery, Smithsonian Institution, Washington, D.C./Art Resource, New York; **523** CORBIS; **525** Buddy Mays/ CORBIS; **532** Courtesy of the Library of Congress; **533** *Newspapers in the Trenches '64*, William Ludwell Sheppard, Museum of the Confederacy, Richmond, Virginia, Photography by Katherine Wetzel; **534** Courtesy of the Library of Congress; **537** Courtesy of the Library of Congress; **539** Ron Watts/CORBIS; **542** Andre Jenny/Focus Group/PictureQuest; **544, 546** The Granger Collection, New York; **547** Bettmann/CORBIS; **552** Sygma; **555** Chip Hires/Liaison International; **556** D. Hudson/ Sygma; **558** The Washington Post; **559** *The Old Stage Coach of the Plains*, 1901, Frederic Remington, oil on canvas, Amon Carter Museum, Forth Worth; **560** (b.) Corel Professional Photos CD-ROM™, (t.) Courtesy National Archives; **561** ©Bettmann/ CORBIS; **562** *Samuel Longhorne Clemens (Mark Twain)* (detail), 1935, Frank Edwin Larson, The National Portrait Gallery, Smithsonian Institution, Washington, D.C./Art Resource, New York; **564** *Paddle Steamboat* Mississippi, Shelburne Museum, Shelburne, Vermont, Photo by Ken Burris; **566** The Historic New Orleans Collection, Museum/Research Center; **569** *Mark Twain (Samuel L. Clemens) Riding the Celebrated Jumping Frog*—an English caricature, 1872, Frederic Waddy, The Granger Collection, New York; **571** The Granger Collection, New York; **572** ©Craig K. Lorenz/Photo Researchers, Inc.; **578** The Granger Collection, New York; **580** *Edge of Town*, Charles Ephraim Burchfield, The Nelson-Atkins Museum of Art, Kansas City, Missouri; **582** Corel Professional Photos CD-ROM™; **584** Ron Watts/CORBIS; **586** Esbin/Anderson/Omni-Photo Communications, Inc.; **594** *Chief Joseph* (detail), 1878, Cyrenius Hall, National Portrait Gallery, Smithsonian Institution, Washington, D.C./Art Resource, New York; **596** Kansas State Historical Society; **599** Ron Watts/ CORBIS; **600** Kansas State Historical Society; **602** National Museum of American History, Smithsonian Institution; **606** CORBIS-Bettmann; **608** Wayne Lynch/DRK Photo; **611, 614** Corel Professional Photos CD-ROM™; **617** Annie Griffiths/DRK Photo; **618–619** CORBIS; **626** Corel Professional Photos CD-ROM™; **628** *Open Range*, 1942, Maynard Dixon, oil on canvas, 34 1/2 x 39" Museum of Western Art, Denver. #36.79. Bernard O. Milmoe, Photographer.; **630** AP/Wide World Photos; **631** *Channel to the Mills*, 1913, Edwin M. Dawes, oil on canvas, 51 x 39 1/2 in. Minneapolis Institute of Arts, anonymous gift; **632** The Granger Collection, New York; **635** *Afternoon in Piedmont* (Elsie at the Window), c. 1911, Xavier Martínez, Collection of The Oakland Museum of California, Gift of Dr. William S. Porter; **636** Corel Professional Photos CD-ROM™; **642** ©Archive Photos; **644** *Memories*, 1885–86, William Merritt Chase, oil on canvas, Munson-Williams-Proctor Institute Museum of Art, Utica, New York; **648** Digital Imagery ©Copyright 2001 PhotoDisc, Inc.; **650** Bettmann/CORBIS; **656** The Granger Collection, New York; **658** Stock Montage, Inc.; **664** (l.) *Edwin Arlington Robinson* (detail), 1933, Thomas Richard Hood, The National Portrait Gallery, Smithsonian Institution, Washington, D.C./Art Resource, New York, (r.) *Edgar Lee Masters* (detail), 1946, Francis J. Quirk, The National Portrait Gallery, Smithsonian Institution, Washington, D.C./Art Resource, New York; **666** Horst Oesterwinter/International Stock Photography, Ltd.; **668** *The Thinker (Portrait of Louis N. Kenton, 1900)*, Thomas Eakins, The Metropolitan Museum of Art, Kennedy Fund, 1917, Copyright © 1967, 1984 by The Metropolitan Museum of Art; **670** Joel Greenstein/Omni-Photo Communications, Inc.; **674** CORBIS-Bettmann; **676** George Schreiber (1904–1977), *From Arkansas*, 1939, oil on canvas, Sheldon Swope Art Museum, Terre Haute, Indiana; **680** Robbie Jack/CORBIS; **682** The Granger Collection, New York; **688** Tim Davis/Photo Researchers, Inc.; **690** ©Julie Habel/CORBIS; **691** John Barrett/Globe Photos; **694** ©The Stock Market/José L. Peláez; **702–703** Edward Hopper, American, 1882–1967, *Nighthawks*, oil on canvas, 1942, 84.1 x 152.4 cm, Friends of American Art Collection, 1942.51, ©2000 The Art Institute of Chicago. All Rights Reserved; **704** (1915) CORBIS-Bettmann, (1919) National Archives, (1920) Bettmann/CORBIS, (1929) The Granger Collection, New York; **705** (1931) *The Persistence of Memory*, 1931, Salvador Dali, The Museum of Modern Art, New York. Given anonymously. Photograph © 2000 The Museum of Modern Art, New York, (1939) SuperStock, (1941) The Granger Collection, New York, (1945) Alfred Eisenstaedt, Life Magazine © Time Warner; **706** Culver Pictures, Inc.; **707** Museum of Connecticut History; **708** Culver Pictures, Inc.; **710** Courtesy of the Library of Congress; **712** Photographs and Prints Division, Schomburg Center for Research in Black Culture, The New York Public Library, Astor, Lenox and Tilden Foundations; **714** Historical Pictures Collection/Stock Montage, Inc.; **715** *No Place to Go*, 1935, Maynard Dixon, Oil on canvas, 25 x 30 inches. The Herald Clark Memorial Collection, Courtesy of Brigham Young University Museum of Fine Arts. All

Rights Reserved. Photo by David W. Hawkinson; **716** *T. S. Eliot* (detail), 1888–1965, Sir Gerald Kelly, The National Portrait Gallery, Smithsonian Institution, Art Resource, New York; **720** Corel Professional Photos CD-ROM™; **726** (l.) The Granger Collection, New York, (r.) *William Carlos Williams* (detail), The National Portrait Gallery, Smithsonian Institution, Washington, D.C./Art Resource, NY; **727** CORBIS-Bettmann; **730** The Granger Collection, New York; **733** Zha Shibiao, Chinese, 1615–1698, Qing dynasty. Shibiao, *Waiting for the Moon* from *Landscape Album in Various Styles,* 1684. Album of twelve leaves, ink or ink and color on paper; each 29.9 x 39.4 cm. © The Cleveland Museum of Art, 1998, Gift of Mr. and Mrs. Severance A. Millikin, 1955.37; **735** *The Figure 5 in Gold,* 1928, Charles Demuth, oil on composition board. H. 36 in. W. 29-3/4 in. (91.4 x 75.6 cm) Signed (lower left): C.D. Inscribed (bottom center): W.C.W. (William Carlos Williams), The Metropolitan Museum of Art, Alfred Stieglitz Collection, 1949. (49.59.1). Photograph Copyright © 1996 By the Metropolitan Museum of Art; **737** Adam Jones/Photo Researchers, Inc.; **738** *Overhanging Cloud in July,* Charles Burchfield, Collection of Whitney Museum of American Art. Purchase, with funds from the Friends of the Whitney Museum of American Art (60.23). Photography Copyright © 2000: Whitney Museum of American Art; **742** *F. Scott Fitzgerald* (detail), David Silvette, The National Portrait Gallery, Smithsonian Institution, Washington, D.C./Art Resource, New York; **744** Corel Professional Photos CD-ROM™; **748–749** *Golf Course—California,* 1917, George Wesley Bellows, Oil on canvas, 30 x 38 inches, Collection Cincinnati Art Museum, The Edwin and Virginia Irwin Memorial, 1966.6; **750** Digital Imagery ©Copyright 2001 PhotoDisc, Inc.; **754** *The Morning Sun,* c. 1920, o/c, 50 x 40 ins., Pauline Palmer, Collection Rockford Art Museum, Gift of the Friends of American Art, 1922; **756** Bettmann/ CORBIS; **758** Digital Imagery ©Copyright 2001 PhotoDisc, Inc.; **760** Ron Watts/CORBIS; **766** UPI/CORBIS-Bettmann; **768** ©The Stock Market/Milt/Patti Putnam; **774** (l.) *E. E. Cummings* (detail), 1958, Self-Portrait, The National Portrait Gallery, Smithsonian Institution, Washington, D.C./Art Resource, New York, (r.) CORBIS-Bettmann; **776** *Remember Now the Days of Thy Youth,* 1950, Paul Starrett Sample, Oil on canvas, 34 x 48 inches, Hood Museum of Art, Dartmouth College, Hanover, NH; Gift of Frank L. Harrington, class of 1954; **779** *The Turret Lathe Operator,* 1925, Grant Wood, oil on canvas, 18" x 24", Cedar Rapids Museum of Art, Cedar Rapids, Iowa, Cherry Burrell Charitable Foundation Collection. Courtesy Associated American Artists, ©Estate of Grant Wood/Licensed by VAGA, New York, NY; **784** *Thomas Wolfe,* 1938, Soss Melik, The National Portrait Gallery, Smithsonian Institution, Washington, D.C./Art Resource, New York; **786** *Stone City, Iowa,* 1930, Grant Wood, Joslyn Art Museum, Omaha, Nebraska, ©Estate of Grant Wood/Licensed by VAGA, New York, NY; **789** Ron Watts/CORBIS **794** (t.l.) The Granger Collection, New York, (t.r.) CORBIS-Bettman, (b.) AP/ Wide World Photos; **797** Silver Burdett Ginn; **798, 799** Index Stock Photography, Inc.; **800** *Untitled,* 1964, Alexander Calder (one of seven lithographs in series), 19 1/2 x 25 1/2", Solomon R. Guggenheim Museum, New York, Gift of the artist, 1965, Photo by David Heald, © The Solomon R. Guggenheim Foundation, New York, ©1998 Estate of Alexander Calder/Artists Rights Society (ARS), New York; **805** *Do It Yourself Landscape,* 1962, Andy Warhol, Museum Ludwig, Cologne, photo courtesy of Rheinisches Bildarchiv Köln. ©1998 Andy Warhol Foundation for the Visual Arts/ARS, New York; **806** (l.) Larry Burrows/Life Magazine © Time Warner Inc., (r.) CORBIS-Bettmann; **807** Thomas Victor; **809** American Red Cross; **811** Verlag Suddeutscher-Bilderdienst; **812** ©FPG International LLC; **813** American Red Cross; **815** Digital Imagery ©Copyright 2001 PhotoDisc, Inc.; **816** © Ryan Beyer/Stone; **820** *Miz Emily,* Joseph Holston, 24" x 16", Holston Reproductions; **824** *Georgia Red Clay,* 1946, Nell Choate Jones, oil on canvas, 25 x 30 inches, 1989.01.094, Morris Museum of Art, Augusta, Georgia; **833** Jay Dorin/Omni-Photo Communications, Inc.; **834** Thomas Victor; **835** *The Tower,* 1920, Charles Demuth, Tempera on pasteboard, 23 1/4 x 19 1/2 in. (58.4 x 49.4 cm) Initialed and inscribed in pencil on reverse: After Christopher Wren (?) Provincetown, Mass./1BO (?)—CD, Columbus Museum of Art, Ohio; Gift of Ferdinand Howald, 31.146; **836** *Carl Sandburg,* Miriam Svet, The National Portrait Gallery, Smithsonian Institution, Washington, D.C./Art Resource, New York; **838** Stock Montage, Inc.; **840** Corel Professional Photos CD-ROM™; **844** Thomas Victor; **847** *Garden of Memories,* 1917, Charles Burchfield, The Museum of Modern Art, New York. Gift of Abby Aldrich Rockefeller (by exchange). Photograph ©2000The Museum of Modern Art, New York; **848** ©Bettmann/CORBIS; **852** ©1993 J. Fishkin. All Rights Reserved; **858** *William Faulkner* (detail), Soss Melik, The National Portrait Gallery, Smithsonian Institution, Washington, D.C./Art Resource, New York; **860** Superstock; **863** Digital Imagery ©Copyright 2001 PhotoDisc, Inc.; **864** *Winter in Southern Louisiana,* 1911, Ellsworth Woodward, oil on canvas, Collection of Mississippi Museum of Art, Jackson, Purchase by Mississippi Art Association and Art Study Club, 1912.005; **869** *Old Man and The Boy,* John Head, Russell A. Fink Gallery; **871** Digital Imagery ©Copyright 2001 PhotoDisc, Inc.; **872** Ron Watts/CORBIS; **873** Corel Professional Photos CD-ROM™; **880** Dimitri Kessel/Life Magazine; **882–883, 885** Corel Professional Photos CD-ROM™; **886** Dewitt Jones/Woodfin Camp & Associates; **888** Corel Professional Photos CD-ROM™; **890** UPI/CORBIS-Bettmann; **892** Ellis Herwig/ PNI; **896** (l.) CORBIS-Bettmann, (r.) AP/Wide World Photos; **898, 900, 901** *My Life and Hard Times,* Copyright ©1933 by James Thurber. Copyright © renewed 1961 by James Thurber. Reprinted by arrangement with Rosemary A. Thurber and The Barbara Hogenson Agency; **903** Culver Pictures, Inc.; **910** Bettmann/ CORBIS; **911** *Zora and Langston,* Phoebe Beasley, Bettmann/CORBIS; **912** Courtesy of the Estate of Carl Van Vechten, Joseph Solomon, EXECUTOR, The National Portrait Gallery, Smithsonian Institution, Washington, D.C./Art Resource, New York; **914** ©Hulton Getty/Archive Photos; **917** *School Bell Time,* 1978 From the Profile/Part I: The Twenties series (Mecklenburg County), Romare Bearden, 29 1/4 x 41" Collection: Kingsborough Community College, The City University of New York; ©Romare Bearden Foundation/ Licensed by VAGA, New York, NY; **919** Ron Watts/CORBIS; **924** (l.) *Langston Hughes* (detail), c. 1925, Winold Reiss, The National Portrait Gallery, Smithsonian Institution, Washington, D.C./Art Resource, New York, (r.) The Granger Collection, New York; **926** Corel Professional Photos CD-ROM™; **928** *Girls Skipping,* 1949, Hale Woodruff, oil on canvas, 24" x 32", Private Collection. Courtesy of Michael Rosenfeld Gallery, New York; **930** Michael Skott/The Image Bank; **934** (b.) UPI/CORBIS-Bettmann, (t.) *Countee Cullen* (detail), c. 1925, Winold Reiss, The National Portrait Gallery, Smithsonian Institution, Washington, D.C./Art Resource, New York, (m.) *Jean Toomer* (detail), c. 1925, Winold Reiss, Gift of Laurence A. Fleischman and Howard Garfinkle with a matching grant from the National Endowment of the Arts, The National Portrait Gallery, Smithsonian Institution, Washington, D.C./Art Resource, New York; **937** *Hoeing,* Robert Gwathmey, Oil on canvas, 40" by 60 1/4" (101.6 cm by 153 cm) Carnegie Institute Museum of Art, Pittsburgh, Pennsylvania, Patrons Art Fund, 44.3. Photograph by Richard Stoner, ©Estate of Robert Gwathmey /Licensed by VAGA, New York, NY; **938** Corel Professional Photos CD-ROM™; **946** Huipil (blouse) from the Tarascans of Michoacan. Embroidered cotton. Museo de Indumentaria Mexicana, Mexico City, D.F. Mexico. Schalkwijk/Art Resource, NY; **947** Rikard Sergei Sanchez/Arte Público Press; **950** © Ian Shaw/Stone; **956–957** *Telephones* (detail), 1954, Colleen Browning, oil on plywood, 14 x 32.5" (33.56 x 82.55 cm) Signed, lower right. Butler Institute of American Art. Museum purchase, 1955; **958** (1952) Nancy Crampton, (1955) Leviton/Black Star, (1969) The Granger Collection, New York, (1972) Peter Garfield/Folio, Inc., (1972 China) UPI/CORBIS-Bettmann; **959** (1982) ©1985 Peter Marlow/Magnum Photos, Inc., (1987) ©Larry Downing/ Woodfin Camp & Associates, (1990) ©The Stock Market/Wes Thompson, (1997) ©Dan Groshong/CORBIS Sygma; **960** The Granger Collection, New York; **965** *Down 18th Street,* 1980, Wayne Thiebaud, Hirshorn Museum and Sculpture Garden, Smithsonian Institution, Museum Purchase with Funds Donated by Edward R. Downe, Jr., 1980. Photography by Ricardo Blanc; **967** ©Mark Bolster/International Stock Photography, Ltd.; **968** Digital Imagery ©Copyright 2001 PhotoDisc, Inc.; **969** *Television Moon,* 1978–79, Alfred Leslie, oil on canvas, Wichita Art Museum, gift of Virginia and George Ablah; **970** Flannery O'Connor Collection, Ina Dillard Russel Library, Georgia College; **972** *Deep Fork Overlook,* Joan Marron-LaRue, Courtesy of the artist; **977** *Black Walnuts,* Joseph Pollet, Collection of Whitney Museum of American Art. Purchase and gift of Gertrude Vanderbilt Whitney, by exchange (52.30). Photograph Copyright © 2000: Whitney Museum of American Art; **981** Ron Watts/CORBIS; **986** Nancy Crampton; **988** Culver Pictures, Inc.; **992** Ron Watts/CORBIS; **994** ©The Stock Market/ Shiki; **1000** Thomas Victor; **1003** Corel Professional Photos CD-ROM™; **1004** Ron Watts/CORBIS; **1007** ©The Stock Market/Dick Frank Studios 1996; **1012** (b.r.) Kit Stafford, (t.l.) Rollie McKenna, (b.l.) *Robert Penn Warren* (detail), 1935, Conrad A. Albrizio, The National Portrait Gallery, Smithsonian Institution, Washington, D.C./Art Resource, New York, (t.r.) AP/Wide World Photos; **1014–1015** *Crowninshield's Wharf, Around the Wharf are the Vessels America, Fame, Prudent, and Belisaurius,* George Ropes, Peabody Museum of Salem, Photo by Mark Sexton; **1017** Corel Professional Photos CD-ROM™; **1019** Tim Lynch/Stock, Boston; **1021** Corel Professional Photos CD-ROM™; **1026** Diana Walker; **1028** © Fred Charles/Stone; **1035** *Girl Looking at Landscape,* 1957, Richard Diebenkorn, oil on canvas, 59 x 60 3/8 inches (149.9 x 153.4 cm), Gift of Mr. and Mrs. Alan H. Temple, 61.49, Collection of Whitney Museum of American Art, photograph by Geoffrey Clements, N.Y., Photograph copyright (c) 1997: Whitney Museum of American Art; **1040** (b.) Photo by Michael Nye, (m.) Photo by Paul Abdoo, (t.) Thomas Victor; **1043** *Passion of Paints,* ©1997 Bob Peters, Exclusively represented by Applejack Licensing International; **1045** Museo de Santa Cruz/Bridgeman Art Library, London/ New York; **1047** Culver Pictures, Inc.; **1049** *Getting Down,* Joseph Holston, 14" x 14", Holston Originals; **1054** Thomas Victor; **1056** Jeff Greenberg/Omni-Photo Communications, Inc.; **1061** Museum of English Rural Life/© Dorling Kindersley; **1062** Lee Russell/CORBIS; **1063** Jeff Greenberg/Omni-Photo Communications, Inc.; **1068** ©Anthony Barboza/Life Magazine; **1070** AP/Wide World Photos; **1073** Ron Watts/CORBIS; **1074–1075** © Matt Lambert/Stone; **1080** Prentice Hall; **1082** *Fruit Vendor,* 1951, Olga Costa, Museo de Arte Moderno,

Mexico. © Olga Costa—SOMAAP, Mexico, 1999; **1087** Richard Bickel/ CORBIS; **1090** Andre Jenny/Focus Group/PictureQuest; **1096** (m.l.) Shelley Rotner/Omni-Photo Communications, Inc., (t.) Georgia McInnis/Courtesy of Arte Público Press, (m.r.) Marlene Fostor, (b.) Rollie McKenna; **1098** *Untitled*, Peter Malone, Chen/Art Resource, NY; **1100** Collins/ Monkmeyer; **1101** Corel Professional Photos CD-ROM™; **1102** Mitchell Funk/The Image Bank; **1103** ©John Lemker/Animals Animals; **1109** *My Mother's Book of Life*, 1987, Lee Lawson, acrylic on panel, 34 x 30 in., Photo courtesy of Pomegranate Artbooks; **1110** (t.) The Granger Collection, New York, (m.) © 1996 Sigrid Estrada, (b.) AP/Wide World Photos; **1112** © Paul Edmondson/Stone; **1115** *Blam*, 1962, ©Roy Lichtenstein, oil on canvas, 68 x 80 in.; **1116** © Annabelle Breakey/Stone; **1119, 1120, 1121** Warner Bros./ Photofest; **1126** (m.) Robert Foothorap, (t.) AP/Wide World Photos, (b.) Robert Severi/Liaison International; **1129** *Biography*, 1988, Marina Gutierrez, Courtesy of the artist; **1133** Digital Imagery ©Copyright 2001 PhotoDisc, Inc.; **1136** Jim McHugh; **1139** Gary Gay/The Image Bank; **1145** *Choke*, 1964, Robert Rauschenberg, Oil and screenprint on canvas, 60" x 48", Washington University Gallery of Art, St. Louis, Gift of Mr. and Mrs. Richard K. Weil, 1972, ©Robert Rauschenberg/Licensed by VAGA, New York, NY; **1146** Thomas Victor; **1148** *Push to Walk*, collage 48" x 48" Phoebe Beasley; **1153** ©Telegraph Colour Library 1998/FPG International LLC; **1160** (t.) AP/Wide World Photos, (b.) Rollie McKenna; **1162** FPG International Corp.; **1164** ©CORBIS; **1166** FPG International Corp.; **1168–1169** Courtesy National Archives; **1170** Ron Watts/CORBIS; **1173, 1174** Stock Montage, Inc.; **1178** (b.r.) Pach/CORBIS-Bettmann, (t.l.) AP/Wide World Photos, (b.l.) Thomas Victor, (t.r.) CORBIS-Bettmann; **1180** *Mirror II*, George Tooker (1920–1938), Egg tempera on gesso panel, 20 x 20 in., 1968.4, Gift of R. H. Donnelley Erdman (PA 1956), Addison Gallery of American Art, Phillips Academy, Andover, Massachusetts. All Rights Reserved; **1183** *Part II, The Free Man, No. 30*, The Frederick Douglass Series, Jacob Lawrence, Hampton University Museum, Hampton,

Virginia; **1185** © Pekka Parviainen/Science Photo Library/Photo Researchers, Inc.; **1190** (r.) Thomas Victor, (l.) Nihad Becirovic; **1192** *The Madonna and Child*, 1990, Momodou Ceesay, Dialogue Systems, Inc.; **1195** *Winter*, Ozz Franca, Oil, 24 x 18", Edition of 1999 s/n, Courtesy of The Hadley Companies; **1200** Andrea Renault/Globe Photos; **1203** *Laurence Typing*, 1952, Fairfield Porter, oil on canvas, 40 x 30 1/8 inches, The Parrish Art Museum, Southampton, New York, Gift of the Estate of Fairfield Porter; **1205** Digital Imagery ©Copyright 2001 PhotoDisc, Inc.; **1206** Courtesy of Rebecca Graziano; **1208** Letters and Postcards, Reid Christman, 24" x 18" (61cm x 45.7cm) Fredrix linen canvas; **1212–1213** Courtesy of General Motors; **1218** (r.) AP/ Wide World Photos, (l.) Photo by Mandy Sayer; **1220** Brian Parker/Tom Stack & Associates; **1222–1223** P.J. Griffiths/Magnum Photos, Inc.; **1228** ©Bettmann/CORBIS; **1229** (t.) Courtesy of the Library of Congress, (b.) Oscar White/CORBIS; **1230** AP/ Wide World Photos; **1231** *The Trial of Two "Witches" at Salem, Massachusetts, in 1662*, Howard Pyle, The Granger Collection, New York; **1234** © James Cotier/Stone; **1236** *The Execution of the Reverend Stephen Burroughs for Witchcraft at Salem Massachusetts*, in 1692, 19th century engraving, The Granger Collection, New York; **1240** AP/Wide World Photos; **1242, 1244, 1248** Photofest; **1253** Musée Condé, Chantilly, France/Bridgeman Art Library, London/New York; **1254** Digital Imagery ©Copyright 2001 PhotoDisc, Inc.; **1259** Photofest; **1267** © James Cotier/Stone; **1270** Photofest; **1272** Ron Watts/CORBIS; **1280** Pocumtuck Valley Memorial Association, Memorial Hall Museum, Deerfield, Massachusetts; **1284** Photofest; **1291** © James Cotier/Stone; **1295** © Joe Sohm/ Stone; **1302, 1306, 1308** Photofest; **1310** Richard Stoddard; **1312** Penguin USA; **1319** © James Cotier/Stone; **1323, 1326** Photofest; **1328** ©Reuters/Brad Rickerby/Archive Photos; **1333** Photofest; **1339** Digital Imagery ©Copyright 2001 PhotoDisc, Inc.; **1344** Brent Jones/Stock, Boston

Staff Credits

The people who made up the *Prentice Hall Literature: Timeless Voices, Timeless Themes* team—representing design services, editorial, editorial services, market research, marketing services, media resources, online services & multimedia development, production services, project office, and publishing processes—are listed below. Bold type denotes the core team members.

Susan Andariese, Rosalyn Arcilla, Laura Jane Bird, Betsy Bostwick, **Anne M. Bray,** Evonne Burgess, **Louise B. Capuano, Pam Cardiff,** Megan Chill, Ed Cordero. Laura Dershewitz, Phillip Fried, **Elaine Goldman,** Barbara Goodchild, Barbara Grant, **Rebecca Z. Graziano, Doreen Graizzaro,** Dennis Higbee, **Leanne Korszoloski,** Ellen Lees, David Liston, **Mary Luthi, George Lychock,** Gregory Lynch, Sue Lyons, **William McAllister,** Frances Medico, Gail Meyer, Jessica S. Paladini, Wendy Perri, Carolyn Carty Sapontzis, **Melissa Shustyk, Annette Simmons, Alicia Solis,** Robin Sullivan, Cynthia Sosland Summers, Lois Teesdale, **Elizabeth Torjussen, Doug Utigard,** Bernadette Walsh, Helen Young

Additional Credits

Gregory Abrom, Robert Aleman, Diane Alimena, Michele Angelucci, Gabriella Apolito, Penny Baker, Sharyn Banks, Anthony Barone, Barbara Blecher, Helen Byers, Rui Camarinha, Lorelee J. Campbell, John Carle, Cynthia Clampitt, Jaime L. Cohen, Martha Conway, Dina Curro, Nancy Dredge, Johanna Ehrmann, Josie K. Fixler, Steve Frankel, Kathy Gavilanes, Allen Gold, Michael E. Goodman, Diana Hahn, Kerry L. Harrigan, Jacki Hasko, Evan Holstrom, Beth Hyslip, Helen Issackedes, Cathy Johnson, Susan Karpin, Raegan Keida, Stephanie Kota, Mary Sue Langan, Elizabeth Letizia, Christine Mann, Vickie Menanteaux, Kathleen Mercandetti, Art Mkrtchyan, Karyl Murray, Kenneth Myett, Stefano Nese, Kim Ortell, Lissette Quinones, Erin Rehill-Seker, Patricia Rodriguez, Mildred Schulte, Adam Sherman, Mary Siener, Jan K. Singh, Diane Smith, Barbara Stufflebeem, Louis Suffredini, Lois Tatarian, Tom Thompkins, Lisa Valente, Ryan Vaarsi, Linda Westerhoff, Jeff Zoda

Prentice Hall gratefully acknowledges the following teachers who provided student models for consideration in the program.

Kate Anders, Suzanne Arkfeld, Elizabeth Bailey, Bill Brown, Diane Cappillo, Mary Chapman, Deedee Chumley, Terry Day, Cheryl Devoe, Dan Diercks, Ellen Eberly, Nancy Fahner, Terri Fields, Patty Foster, Joanne Giardino, Julie Gold, Christopher Guarraia, Dianne Hammond, Jo Higgins, Pauline Hodges, Gaye Ingram, Charlotte Jefferies, Bill Jones, Ken Kaiser, Linda Kramer, Karen Lopez, Catherine Lynn, Ashley MacDonald, Kathleen Marshall, LouAnn McCarty, Peggy Moore, Ann Okamura, Will Parker, Maureen Rippee, Tucky Roger, Terrie Saunders, Marilyn Shaw, Ken Spurlock, Mary Stevens, Sandra Sullivan, Wanda Thomas, Jennifer Watson, Amanda Wolf